The
Maya World

THE ROUGH GUIDE

There are more than one hundred Rough Guide titles
covering destinations from Amsterdam to Zimbabwe

Forthcoming titles include
Chile • Indonesia • New Orleans • Toronto

Rough Guide Reference Series
Classical Music • European Football • The Internet • Jazz
Opera • Reggae • Rock Music • World Music

Rough Guide Phrasebooks
Czech • French • German • Greek • Hindi & Urdu • Hungarian • Indonesian
Italian • Japanese • Mandarin Chinese • Mexican Spanish • Polish
Portuguese • Russian • Spanish • Thai • Turkish • Vietnamese

Rough Guides on the Internet
http://www.roughguides.com

ROUGH GUIDE CREDITS

Text editor: Sophie Martin
Series editor: Mark Ellingham
Editorial: Martin Dunford, Jonathan Buckley, Jo Mead, Kate Berens, Amanda Tomlin, Ann-Marie Shaw, Paul Gray, Chris Schüler, Helena Smith, Judith Bamber, Kieran Falconer, Orla Duane, Olivia Eccleshall, Ruth Blackmore, Jennifer Dempsey, Sue Jackson, Geoff Howard, Claire Saunders, Anna Sutton, Gavin Thomas, Alexander Mark Rogers (UK); Andrew Rosenberg, Andrew Taber (US)
Production: Susanne Hillen, Andy Hilliard, Link Hall, Helen Ostick, James Morris, Julia Bovis, Michelle Draycott, Cathy Edwards

Cartography: Melissa Flack, Maxine Burke, Nichola Goodliffe
Picture research: Eleanor Hill, Louise Boulton
Online editors: Alan Spicer, Kate Hands (UK); Geronimo Madrid (US)
Finance: John Fisher, Celia Crowley, Neeta Mistry, Katy Miesiaczek
Marketing & Publicity: Richard Trillo, Simon Carloss, Niki Smith (UK); Jean-Marie Kelly, SoRelle Braun (US)
Administration: Tania Hummel, Charlotte Marriott

....

ACKNOWLEDGEMENTS

Peter: Thanks to Matt and Marga at Monkey Bay, Jean Shaw MBE in Belize City, Lori Reed in San Pedro, Doris and Terry Creasey in Caye Caulker, Martha and John August in San Ignacio, Derek and Debbie Jones in Dangriga, Wende Bryan in Placencia, Charles Wright in Punta Gorda, and the Toledo Maya Cultural Council, Toledo Alcaldes Association and North Atlantic Books for the Southern Toledo map.

Iain: Thanks to Mike Shawcross, Geovanny Mendoza, all at the Iguana Perdida in Santa Cruz, Tony Oswald, Phillipa at the Rainbow, Tammy Ridenour and Maya Expeditions, all at the Mango Inn and UDC in Utila, Susan Aubs for support and encouragement, Susanna Nicol for news

support, Jamie and Krystyna at the Guatemalan Indian Centre, the Guatemala Embassy in London, Oliver Morgan of CIAO, Neil and Donald Stewart, Mark Whatmore for the superb foundations, and Fiona Stewart, with whom I first explored the Maya World.

Alex: Thanks to Gardenia D'Almeida Franca de Robinson.

At **Rough Guides**, the authors would like to thank Sophie Martin for her good-natured professionalism, Maxine Burke and Stratigraphics for cartography, Jennifer Speake for proofreading, Eleanor Hill for picture research and Link Hall for typesetting.

....

PUBLISHING INFORMATION

This first edition published February 1999 by
   Rough Guides Ltd, 62–70 Shorts Gardens,
   London, WC2H 9AB.
Distributed by the Penguin Group:
Penguin Books Ltd, 27 Wrights Lane, London W8 5TZ
Penguin Books USA Inc., 375 Hudson Street, New York
   10014, USA
Penguin Books Australia Ltd, 487 Maroondah Highway,
   PO Box 257, Ringwood, Victoria 3134, Australia
Penguin Books Canada Ltd, 10 Alcorn Avenue, Toronto,
   Ontario, Canada M4V 1E4
Penguin Books (NZ) Ltd, 182–190 Wairau Road,
   Auckland 10, New Zealand
Typeset in Linotron Univers and Century Old Style to an
   original design by Andrew Oliver.
Printed in the United States of America by R.R.
   Donnelley & Sons Company

Illustrations in Part One and Part Three by Edward Briant.
Illustrations on p.1 & p.479 by Henry Iles
© Peter Eltringham, John Fisher and Iain Stewart 1999

560pp – Includes index
A catalogue record for this book is available from the
   British Library
ISBN 1-85828-406-6

....

The Maya World

THE ROUGH GUIDE

written and researched by

Peter Eltringham, John Fisher and Iain Stewart

with additional research by

Alex Robinson, Dominique Young and Natasha Ward

THE ROUGH GUIDES

THE ROUGH GUIDES

TRAVEL GUIDES • PHRASEBOOKS • MUSIC AND REFERENCE GUIDES

 We set out to do something different when the first Rough Guide was published in 1982. Mark Ellingham, just out of university, was travelling in Greece. He brought along the popular guides of the day, but found they were all lacking in some way. They were either strong on ruins and museums but went on for pages without mentioning a beach or taverna. Or they were so conscious of the need to save money that they lost sight of Greece's cultural and historical significance. Also, none of the books told him anything about Greece's contemporary life – its politics, its culture, its people, and how they lived.

So with no job in prospect, Mark decided to write his own guidebook, one which aimed to provide practical information that was second to none, detailing the best beaches and the hottest clubs and restaurants, while also giving hard-hitting accounts of every sight, both famous and obscure, and providing up-to-the-minute information on contemporary culture. It was a guide that encouraged independent travellers to find the best of Greece, and was a great success, getting shortlisted for the Thomas Cook travel guide award,

and encouraging Mark, along with three friends, to expand the series.

The Rough Guide list grew rapidly and the letters flooded in, indicating a much broader readership than had been anticipated, but one which uniformly appreciated the Rough Guide mix of practical detail and humour, irreverence and enthusiasm. Things haven't changed. The same four friends who began the series are still the caretakers of the Rough Guide mission today: to provide the most reliable, up-to-date and entertaining information to independent-minded travellers of all ages, on all budgets.

We now publish more than 100 titles and have offices in London and New York. The travel guides are written and researched by a dedicated team of more than 100 authors, based in Britain, Europe, the USA and Australia. We have also created a unique series of phrasebooks to accompany the travel series, along with an acclaimed series of music guides, and a best-selling pocket guide to the Internet and World Wide Web. We also publish comprehensive travel information on our web site:

http://www.roughguides.com

HELP US UPDATE

A lot of effort has gone in to ensure that *Rough Guide to The Maya World* is up-to-date and accurate. However, things change — places get "discovered", opening hours are notoriously fickle, restaurants and rooms raise prices or lower standards, extra buses are laid on or off. If you feel we've got it wrong or left something out, we'd like to know, and if you can remember the address, the price, the time, the phone number, so much the better.

We'll credit all contributions, and send a copy of the next edition (or any other Rough Guide if you prefer) for the best letters. Please mark letters: "Rough Guide The Maya World Update" and send to:
Rough Guides, 62–70 Shorts Gardens, London WC2H 9AB, or Rough Guides, 375 Hudson St, 9th floor, New York NY 10014. Or send email to: mail@roughguides.co.uk
Online updates about this book can be found on Rough Guides' Web site at http://www.roughguides.com

THE AUTHORS

Peter Eltringham's first visit to Belize was when he volunteered to do a tour of duty in what was considered a "hardship posting" by the Royal Air Force. After returning briefly to the UK, he set off again for Central America to co-write the first edition of *The Rough Guide to Guatemala and Belize*. Since then he has co-authored Rough Guides to Mexico, Belize and Central America, spending several months each year in the region. This year he promises to return to Portsmouth University to complete his Latin American Studies degree.

On graduating, **Iain Stewart** spent a couple of years as an oriental carpet dealer before leaving the UK to travel round the world for two years. It was on this trip that he first visited all five countries of the Maya World. Now a London-based journalist, he is also co-author of the Rough Guides to Guatemala and Central America.

John Fisher was one of the authors of the first ever Rough Guide – in 1981 – and has been inextricably involved with the series ever since. These days, John can normally be found chained to a desk at Rough Guide HQ in London, where work takes up far too much time that could be spent in a hammock. He lives in South London with his wife and two young sons.

CONTENTS

Introduction xii

PART ONE — BASICS — 3

Getting there from North America 3
Getting there from the UK and Ireland 8
Getting there from Australasia 12
Visas and entry requirements 14
Insurance 17
Health 19
Costs and money 23
Information and maps 25
Getting around 28

Accommodation 31
Eating and drinking 33
Mail, phones and the Internet 39
The media 40
Opening hours and holidays 42
Music and dance 43
Crime and personal safety 44
Work and study 46

PART TWO — SOUTHERN MEXICO — 49

Introduction 50
Chapter One: Yucatán and Campeche 57
Chapter Two: Quintana Roo 97
Chapter Three: Chiapas and Tabasco 127

PART THREE — BELIZE — 181

Introduction 182
Chapter Four: Northern Belize and the Northern Cayes 187
Chapter Five: Cayo and the West 232
Chapter Six: The South 254

PART FOUR — GUATEMALA — 283

Introduction 284
Chapter Seven: Guatemala City and Antigua 291
Chapter Eight: The Western Highlands and Pacific Coast 321
Chapter Nine: The North and East 374

PART FIVE   HONDURAS & EL SALVADOR   425

Introduction 426
Chapter Ten: Honduras 433
Chapter Eleven: El Salvador 464

PART SIX   CONTEXTS   479

Chronology of the Maya 481
The Maya Achievement 484
The Maya Today 488
Landscape and wildlife 498

Index 524

Conservation and ecotourism 505
Books 510
Languages 518
Glossary 521

HURRICANE MITCH

Just as this book was due to go to press, in late October 1998, **Hurricane Mitch** hit Central America. At least nine thousand people were killed outright and two million left homeless, while millions more were reported missing. In Honduras, three-quarters of the banana and coffee crop was wiped out, bridges and other infra-structure destroyed, and whole villages washed away. In the space of just three days, Hurricane Mitch obliterated all hopes of recovery for a region only just emerging from years of conflict.

Reconstruction is likely to take decades and, given the affected countries' crip-pling debt and the cost involved – estimated at at least US$4 billion – the region is almost totally dependent on the efforts of the international community. Roads, villages and bridges have to be rebuilt, coffee bushes and banana plantations to be replanted, and the increasingly important tourism sector will take years to recover.

As far as **this guide** goes, the very worst devastation occurred just outside the Maya region. In Honduras, San Pedro Sula suffered extensive damage and the Bay Islands of Utila and Guanaja were also badly hit. Elsewhere in the Maya World, how-ever, all the major transport routes reopened within days of the hurricane and trav-el in the region has not been seriously affected.

If you have access to the Internet, you can check out the **latest information** on the UK's Foreign and Commonwealth Office Web site at *www.fco.gov.uk*, or the US State Department site at *travel.state.gov*. Updates will also be posted on the Rough Guides Web site.

LIST OF MAPS

The Maya World x–xi
**Southern Mexico
  chapter divisions** 49
Southern Mexico 52–53
Yucatán and Campeche 58–59
Central Mérida 61
Uxmal 73
Chichén Itzá 79
Quintana Roo 98
Downtown Cancún 100
Playa del Carmen 110
Tulum 116
Chetumal 123
Chiapas and Tabasco 127
Palenque Town 130
Palenque Ruins 133
San Cristóbal de las Casas 145
The San Cristóbal area 152
Central Tuxtla Gutiérrez 157
Central Tapachula 166
Central Villahermosa 170

Belize chapter divisions 181
Belize 184

Northern Belize and the
  Northern Cayes 188–189
Belize City 192–193
Altun Ha 204
Corozal 213
San Pedro 218
Cayo and the West 232
Belmopan 236
San Ignacio 241
Xunantunich 252
The South 255
Dangriga 259
Punta Gorda 274
Southern Toledo 278

**Guatemala
  chapter divisions** 283
Guatemala 286–287
Guatemala City, Antigua
  and around 291
Central Guatemala City 294–295
Guatemala City:
  Zona 1 299
Antigua 309

The Western Highlands and
  Pacific Coast 322–323
Chichicastenango 329
Lago de Atitlán 340
Panajachel 342
Quetzaltenango 351
Central Quetzaltenango 352
Huehuetenango 359
Zaculeu 361
The North and East 376–377
Quiriguá 378
Lago de Izabal & Río Dulce
  area 385
Cobán 393
Flores and Santa Elena 404
Tikal 412–413

**Honduras and El Salvador
  chapter divisions** 425
Honduras and El Salvador 428
Copán 434
San Pedro Sula 441
Bay Islands 450

Maya languages 489

MAP SYMBOLS

CA 1 Carretera Interamericana	◆ Site of interest	ⓟ Gas station
Other major highways and roads	⬟ Ruin	🛉 Lighthouse
Minor highways and roads (paved)	◓ Cave	ⓘ Information centre
Unpaved highways	⌁ Mountain range	Ⓒ Telephone
Footpath	▲ Mountain peak	⊠ Post office
Train line	⫽ Volcano	★ Bus stop
Ferry route	⋙ Escarpment	■ Building
International boundary	⋙ Reef	✚ Church (town maps)
Chapter division boundary	⫿ Waterfall	⌗ Cemetery
District boundary	⫪ Immigration post	▒ Park
River	◉ Hotel	▓ National park
Wall	■ Restaurant	░ Beach
✈ Airport		

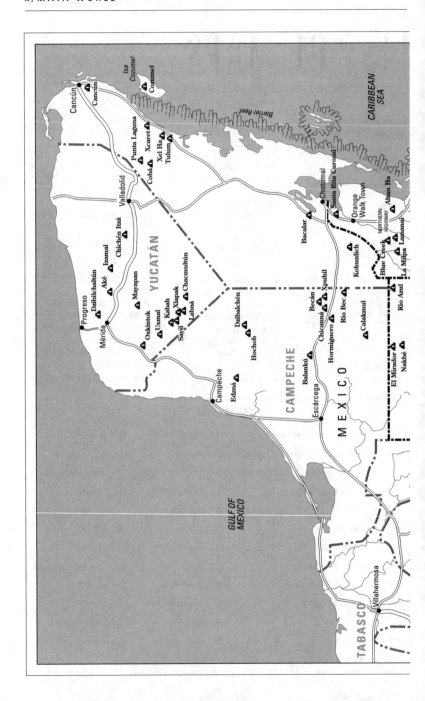

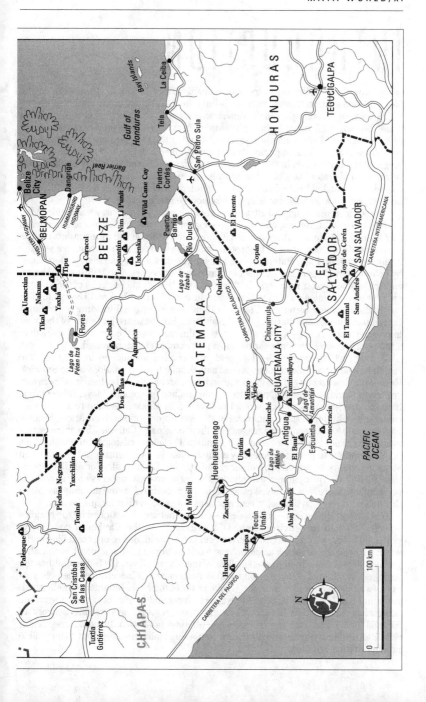

INTRODUCTION

Some three thousand years ago, nomadic tribes began to settle deep in the Mesoamerican rainforests, establishing the foundations of the most sophisticated ancient civilization on the American continent. The land they chose, the **Maya World**, today extends through southern Mexico, Guatemala, Belize and a sliver of El Salvador and Honduras. It's an astonishingly diverse environment, with the flat, arid plateau of the Yucatán peninsula in the north blending gradually into the lowland jungle of the centre, and in the south a spectacular mountainous region, studded with volcanoes and crater lakes and draped with pine and cloudforests. While the southern coastline is pounded by the Pacific Ocean, gentler Caribbean waters lap the white-sand beaches and coral islands that fringe the region's eastern shores.

This is a land whose natural attractions would draw visitors anyway – and indeed the Caribbean coast of Mexico, and to a lesser extent the cayes of Belize and Honduras's Bay Islands, are big resort areas – but it's the chance to visit the **monumental ruins** of ancient Maya cities, some of them stranded in dense, tropical rainforest, that sets the region apart. **Tikal** and **Palenque** are among the most atmospheric sites, dominated by colossal temple pyramids and set in jungle that screeches with toucans, parakeets, and spider and howler monkeys. To the north, the less humid environs of the Yucatán are home to the equally magnificent architecture of **Chichén Itzá** and **Uxmal**; further south, the turbulent history of **Copán** in Honduras is recorded in some of the finest carved monuments and stelae in the Maya World. But these are just a few of the most impressive Maya ruins – scattered throughout the region are the remains of more than a thousand other settlements, for the most part completely unexcavated.

Although all the major cities had been mysteriously abandoned by 1200 AD, the region was never completely depopulated and, despite the depredations of the **Spanish Conquest**, descendants of the great astronomers, architects and calendar-keepers survive in the region today. Of approximately nine million indigenous Maya, Guatemala is home to over six million, with around two million in Mexico, and the rest in smaller communities in Belize and Honduras. For the vast majority of **modern Maya**, Spanish has always been a second language, and their nominally Catholic (but increasingly evangelical) faith is still tempered with traditional religious customs. Inimitable Maya textiles continue to be worn, especially in the highlands of Guatemala and Chiapas, and some isolated communities still observe the 260-day Tzolkin calendar of their ancestors. Having survived almost five hundred years of colonial oppression and political persecution, there are unmistakeable signs of a **cultural reawakening**, as Maya throughout the region develop a renewed sense of pride in their unique identity.

This staggering ancient – and modern – cultural heritage is matched by the region's equally rich **natural environment**. Offshore, much of the Caribbean coastline is protected by the second longest **barrier reef** in the world: diving and snorkelling in the warm waters here, amidst a kaleidoscopic world of tropical fish and coral, is an unforgettable experience. Though the smallest of the Maya nations, it's Belize that has the strongest tradition of state environmental protection, which has ensured the preservation of a landscape ranging from the granite peaks of the Maya Mountains, riddled with caves holding Maya artefacts, to the western rivers and jungle, best visited from the ecotourism base of San Ignacio. Throughout the region, however, the network of national parks and reserves is growing, offering protection to some spectacular **wildlife**, including jaguars and other cats, lumbering tapirs, monkeys and an incredible number of **bird species**.

Travelling around the Maya World is an adventure in itself. There's an excellent network of roads – of varying quality – almost constantly traversed by buses. This is how most people travel and, though not always comfortable, taking the bus is a quintessential Central American experience – you may find yourself sharing a seat with a Maya woman and her three kids, or even a chicken or two. The countless Caribbean islands of the Yucatán, Belize and Honduras are served by regular boats and ferries; while internal flights can save days of travel and won't necessarily break the bank.

Now that the civil wars in El Salvador and Guatemala are over, the only ongoing **conflict** in the region is in the Chiapas highlands, where a Zapatista-led rebellion has been smouldering since 1994; this has little effect on travellers to the area, though. **Safety** is a real issue, however, and, though it's the usual pickpocketing and bag-snatching that most travellers need to worry about, where risks are more significant we've outlined them in the text.

Where to go

In **Mexico**'s Yucatán peninsula, the entire Caribbean coastline of Quintana Roo state is blessed with stunning white-sand beaches. The arrival point for most visitors is the manufactured mega-resort of **Cancún**, the region's twentieth-century temple of the sun; further down the coast, Cozumel and Playa del Carmen have also been heavily developed. If you're in search of somewhere quieter, head for relaxed **Tulum**, with its cliff-perched Maya ruin – many travellers' favourite spot on this coast – or for complete undisturbed peace, there are any number of tiny beaches dotted between the resorts. Further south, **Laguna Bacalar** and the **Sian Ka'an** biosphere reserve offer spectacular scenery and wildlife-spotting possibilities.

Mérida, the capital of Yucatán state and the largest city in the region, is a likeable place with a maze-like market and a stately collection of well-preserved colonial buildings. It's an excellent base for visiting most of the well-known sites. **Chichén Itzá**, probably the most visited of them all, is in easy reach, as is **Uxmal** with its vertiginous pyramid temple. A series of lesser sites lie nearby in the Puuc hills. Moving into the neighbouring state, the colonial capital city of **Campeche** makes an enjoyable excursion. From here you can visit the decorative Chenes ruins, of which Edzná is the most accessible. To the south, stretching down towards the Guatemalan border, the immense **Calakmul** biosphere reserve is surrounded by ruins in the distinctive Río Bec style.

In Chiapas, modern Maya culture is more in evidence, especially around the delightful highland city of **San Cristóbal del las Casas**, a focal point for the local Tzeltal and Tzotzil Maya. Chiapas also has some first-class ruins. **Palenque** is perhaps the finest, but along the Río Usumacinta lie a number of smaller sites, none with a more splendid location than **Yaxchilán**, situated in a great loop in the river. The exquisite pools and waterfalls of **Agua Azul** are another major attraction, while the unspoilt scenery around the fifty **Lagos de Montebello** offers endless hiking and camping opportunities. The state of Tabasco has rather less to offer the visitor aside from some fascinating archeological sites, including **La Venta**, Comalcalco and Malpasito.

It's in **Guatemala**, where over half the country's population is indigenous, that Maya traditions and customs are most obvious. The mesmerizing beauty of the **Western Highlands** is the first place to head for, where the strength of traditional culture is most apparent in the markets and fiestas. **Lago de Atitlán** is postcard picturesque – a vast lake dwarfed by three giant volcanoes, its shores ringed by some of the most traditional villages in the country. The scenery around **Quetzaltenango** is also breathtaking, with more volcanoes and alpine peaks dotted with indigenous villages; it's an easy trip from here to the weekly market at **San Francisco el Alto**, the largest and finest in the Maya World. **Chichicastenango** has another fantastic market: this is the one everyone goes to for textiles, masks and souvenirs.

Guatemala City, with poverty and pollution to match most Latin American capitals, is probably not worth spending too long in, especially as the old colonial capital of **Antigua** is just an hour away. Antigua could hardly be more different – a supremely relaxing historic city, with an endless supply of cafés, restaurants and bars to revitalize the jaded traveller.

The sparsely populated north and east region of Guatemala is home to the country's finest Maya ruins, most buried in the dense rainforest of the Maya biosphere reserve, giving you a chance to see some of Petén's **wildlife** too. If you only see one ruin in Guatemala, make it **Tikal**, a vast complex of gigantic temples, acropolises, palaces and plazas. Further south, the mist-soaked hills, caves and rivers around sleepy **Cobán** and the jungle-coated gorge of the **Río Dulce** are also worth exploring. The one notable ruin in these parts is **Quiriguá**, whose spectacular stelae are the largest in the Maya World.

Belize also harbours a rich number of Maya sites. Caracol, Xunantunich, Lamanai and Lubaantun are the main ones, though only Caracol compares in scale to the great ruins of Mexico or Guatemala. It's the natural environment that's Belize's main draw, from the abundant flora and fauna of the lagoons at Sarteneja and Crooked Tree in the north of the country to the **Cockscomb Basin**, a reserve designed to protect the jaguar, in the south. Offshore are scattered hundreds of tiny islands known as "cayes", the main targets being upmarket **Ambergris Caye**, and **Caye Caulker**, the choice spot for young independent travellers. Other, mostly uninhabited cayes offer dramatic scuba-diving and snorkelling, with the coral atolls of **Lighthouse Reef** and **Glover's Reef** perhaps offering the ultimate underwater scenery.

Belize City is the only sizeable town in the country, but it's no beauty and you won't need to spend much time there – nor in the sleepy capital, Belmopan. Make your way, instead, to **San Ignacio** in the west, surrounded by forested hills and rivers, or **Dangriga**, a centre of Garífuna culture and a good stepping-stone to the Maya Mountains and central cayes. In the far south, **Punta Gorda** is a centre for the Maya who make up over half the population of Toledo district.

In **Honduras**'s western highlands, the magnificent ruins of **Copán** offer exquisitely carved stelae and a hieroglyphic stairway that represents the longest known glyphic text. North of here, the cities of San Pedro Sula and La Ceiba serve as stopping-off points en route to the idyllic **Bay Islands**. Each of the three main islands has its aficionados, but **Utila** is the cheapest and most popular with backpackers, while **Guanaja** and **Roatán** are geared up more for scuba-divers on package holidays.

The Maya slice of **El Salvador** holds some of the most fantastic scenery in the country. One of the biggest attractions is **Lago de Coatepeque**, a pristine crater lake bordered by Cerro Verde and the Izalco volcano. The Maya ruins here are less imposing than further north, though **Tazumal**, and **Joya de Cerén**, where an entire community was buried in volcanic ash, are well worth a look.

When to go

Seasons in the Maya World are less marked than in Europe or North America, and though there is a rainy period between May and October, travel is rarely affected except on the dirt roads of mountainous regions. Even in the rainy season, days are often sunny and the rain confined to a brief – if torrential – late-afternoon downpour. The hottest time of year is in April and early May, before the first of the rains.

The most important factor determining climate is **altitude**. Much of Guatemala and Chiapas is above 1500m, and these parts enjoy a benign climate with warm days and mild or cool evenings. In the lowlands, temperatures are higher and the increased humidity can be quite uncomfortable – especially if you're exploring the forests of Belize, lowland Chiapas and Petén. The climate of Yucatán is a little different to the rest of the region, and in December and January night-time temperatures here can be unexpectedly cool. The most serious weather threat is from **hurricanes,** which occasionally sweep through the region from August to November, normally affecting only the Caribbean coast.

Everywhere, the main **tourist season** is from mid-December to March, and this is when you can expect the luxury hotels to push up their prices, though rates at budget places tend to fluctuate less. The popular resorts are always packed out at Christmas, New Year and Easter – if you're planning a visit then, you'll need to plan and book rooms ahead. There's another surge in visitor numbers from mid-July to early September, during the European and North American holidays.

AVERAGE TEMPERATURES AND MONTHLY RAINFALL

	Jan	Feb	Mar	Apr	May	Jun	Jul	Aug	Sept	Oct	Nov	Dec
Mérida, Mexico												
Max °C	28	29	37	41	40	33	33	33	32	31	29	28
Min °C	17	17	19	21	22	23	23	23	23	22	19	18
Rainfall (mm)	25	18	28	28	79	173	122	135	155	102	33	31
Belize City												
Max °C	27	28	29	30	31	31	31	31	31	30	28	27
Min °C	19	21	22	23	24	24	24	24	23	22	20	20
Rainfall (mm)	137	61	38	56	109	196	163	170	244	305	226	185
Guatemala City												
Max °C	23	25	27	28	29	27	26	26	26	24	23	22
Min °C	12	12	14	14	16	16	16	16	16	16	14	13
Rainfall (mm)	8	3	13	31	152	274	203	198	231	173	23	8
Santa Ana, El Salvador												
Max °C	32	33	34	34	33	31	32	32	31	31	31	32
Min °C	16	16	17	18	19	19	18	19	19	18	17	16
Rainfall (mm)	8	5	10	43	196	328	292	297	307	241	41	10
San Pedro Sula, Honduras												
Max °C	25	27	29	30	30	28	27	28	28	27	26	25
Min °C	14	14	15	17	18	18	18	17	17	17	16	15
Rainfall (mm)	12	2	1	26	180	177	70	74	151	87	38	14

GETTING THERE FROM NORTH AMERICA

Getting to the Maya region from the US and Canada is simplest and usually cheapest by air. The main US, Mexican and Central American airlines all have regular flights to the region's main airports: Guatemala City, Belize City, Mérida and Cancún in Mexico and San Pedro Sula in Honduras. A vast number of possible destinations, routes and prices make any comprehensive listing virtually impossible, but most non-stop flights leave from Miami, Houston, Los Angeles, Atlanta and New Orleans. Airlines serving these hubs have excellent connections throughout the US and Canada (whose gateways are Toronto, Montréal and Vancouver).

AIRLINES IN NORTH AMERICA

In addition to the destinations listed below, many airlines have frequent departures for Mexico City and other capitals just outside the Maya region, including San Salvador and Tegucigalpa, the Honduran capital. Detailed below are all the major airlines serving the region; for **fares** and information on direct routes and possible connections see "Routes and fares" on p.4. For details of **air passes**, see p.29.

Aeroméxico (☎1-800/237-6639 or 713/939-7535; *www.wotw.com/aeromexico*). Direct flights from many US gateways to Mexico City. Tickets can be linked to the Mex-AmeriPass for connections throughout Mexico, including Cancún and Mérida, and via Mexicana Airlines to Guatemala.

American (☎1-800/624-6262; *www.americanair. com*). Daily non-stops from Miami, and some from Dallas/Ft Worth, to Belize City, Guatemala City, San Pedro Sula and Cancún. Non-stop from Toronto to Miami and Vancouver to Dallas for connections.

Aviateca (☎1-800/327-9832). Non-stop flights to Guatemala from Houston, Miami and LA.

Canada 3000 (☎416/674-2661). Inexpensive charter flights (Nov–April) from Toronto to Belize City.

Continental (☎1-800/231-0856; *www.flycontinental. com*). Daily non-stops from Houston, and some from Newark, to all the region's main airports. Route-sharing with Air Canada ensures good connections from Canada.

Delta (☎1-800/241-4141; *www.delta-air.com*). Non-stop daily flights from Atlanta to Guatemala City and San Salvador.

Iberia (☎1-800/772-4642). Daily non-stop flights from Miami to Guatemala City.

Lacsa (☎1-800/225-2272). The Costa Rican national airline flies from New Orleans to Cancún and Mérida and also connects numerous US cities with Mexico City.

Mexicana (☎1-800/531-7921; *www.mexicana. com*). Frequent flights from Chicago, Denver, LA, New York, San Francisco, Montréal and Toronto to Mexico City, with connections to Guatemala City, Cancún and Cozumel. Tickets can be linked to the Mex-AmeriPass and flights on the subsidiary airline, Aerocaribe, from airports in Yucatán to Flores in Guatemala and Belize City.

Taca (☎1-800/535-8780). Regular non-stop flights from Houston, Miami and New York to Belize City and Guatemala City, and a frequent service from Chicago, New Orleans, LA and San Francisco via San Salvador. Tickets can be linked to the Visit Central America Airpass. Also provides information and reservations for Aviateca, Nica and Lacsa.

Taesa (☎1-800/328-2372; *www.wotw.com/wow/ mexico/city/taesa.html*). Chicago and Oakland to Mexico City.

United (☎1-800/622-1015; *www.usairways.com*). Daily non-stop flights from Chicago, Washington and LA to Guatemala City, as well as services to Mexico City and San Salvador.

US Airways (☎1-800/428-4322). New York, Newark and Pittsburgh to Cancún.

Utilizing one of the **air passes** that link the Maya region to North America is an extremely cost-effective way of getting to the region; the Central America Airpass operated by the Taca group and the two passes run by Aeroméxico and Mexicana are good value. For full details and price examples, see the box p.29.

If you live close to the US/Mexican border, a cheap option for getting to southern Mexico is to cross into Mexico and take an **internal flight** (which you can arrange through your local travel agent) to Cancún or another Mexican airport. This can represent very good value for money: for example, the Tijuana–Mexico City flight costs little more than a first-class bus. In southern Mexico, the main airports are at Cozumel, Tuxtla Gutiérrez, Mérida and Villahermosa, and there are smaller airports at Palenque and Chetumal.

You can also travel overland inexpensively **by bus** from the US/Mexico border to Mexico. Some buses are quite luxurious, but the journey can take between two and four days, so most travellers choose to break the journey in Mexico City. **Trains** offer a final option, though most of the services from the border towns are in decline and almost everyone takes luxury buses, which are quicker and cheaper. More comprehensive information on travelling through Mexico is provided in *The Rough Guide to Mexico*.

SHOPPING FOR TICKETS

In general, **fares** depend more on how and when you book your flight and how long you plan to stay than on a particular season. However, prices to most destinations do go up in the **high seasons** of July–August, Easter and Christmas, when seat availability can become a problem. It certainly pays to book ahead.

The cheapest of the airlines' published fares is usually an **Apex** ticket, which needs to be booked and paid for at least fourteen days before departure and gives you a maximum stay of three months. There are some discounts for students and under-26s, though you may be subject to eccentric booking conditions.

You can cut costs further by going through a **specialist flight agent** – either a consolidator, who buys up blocks of tickets from the airlines and sells them at a discount, or a discount agent, who in addition to dealing with discounted flights may also offer special student and youth fares and a range of other travel-related services. Bear

in mind, though, that the penalties for changing your plans can be stiff. Also, these companies make their money by dealing in bulk, so don't expect them to entertain lots of questions.

Some agents specialize in **charter flights**, which may be cheaper than scheduled flights, but again departure dates are fixed and withdrawal penalties are high. **Open-jaw tickets**, where you fly into one city and out of another, are readily available, and, depending on which airline you use, often cost little more than a return to one city, particularly if combined with an air pass (for more on which, see p.29).

The companies listed on p.5 are a good place to begin your search, and if you've got access to the Internet, then the **eXito Web site** (see p.5) is very useful.

ROUTES AND FARES

Though correct at the time of going to press, the following **fares**, quoted by the airlines, should be taken as an indication only. At peak times they may well be higher, while if you hunt around, the specialist agents will almost certainly offer better deals.

Flying to **Belize**, American's non-stop flight from Miami costs US$450 year round. Though American could connect you to Miami from any major American city, fares from New York and Chicago are US$600 and around US$50 more from LA. Taca has three non-stop flights to Belize, all of which leave four times a week: from Houston they cost US$480, from Miami US$500, and from New Orleans US$455. Continental's non-stop flight from Houston costs US$500.

To **Guatemala City**, Iberia has the best non-stop from Miami at US$392, with American and Aviateca both charging around US$500 return. Aviateca's fare from Houston is especially good, at US$245. From LA, Aviateca's fare is US$620, as is Taca's, which costs the same as from San Francisco. United's is slightly higher at US$670 – the same as from Chicago. Taca's direct flight from Washington DC is US$700, with a stop in San Salvador. Delta non-stop from Atlanta costs US$535.

If you have a problem booking a flight direct to the region, consider flying to **San Salvador**, which is just five hours' bus journey away from Guatemala City. American's non-stop from Miami to San Salvador is the cheapest fare to El Salvador, at US$535. Taca's non-stop flight from

DISCOUNT TRAVEL COMPANIES IN THE US AND CANADA

Air-tech (☎1-800/575-TECH or 212/219-7000; *fly@aerotech.com*); *www.airtech.com*. Standby seat broker; also deals in consolidator fares and courier flights.

Air Courier Association (☎1-800/282-1202 or ☎303/215-9000; *www.aircourier.org*). Courier flight broker. Annual fee US$28, plus US$30 initiation. Only accepts 150 new members per month.

Council Travel (☎1-800/226-8624, fax 212/822-2699; *www.ciee.org*). Student/budget travel agency with branches in many US cities.

eXito (☎1-800/655-4053 or 510/655-2154; *exito@wonderlink.com; www.wonderlink.com/exito*). Latin American independent travel specialists. Their Web page has a particularly useful air-fare finder and much other invaluable information.

International Association of Air Travel Couriers (☎561/582-8320, fax 561/582-1581; *www.courier.org*). Courier flight broker. Membership US$45 per year.

Last Minute Club (☎1-800-563-CLUB; *www.lastminuteclub.com*). Travel club specializing in standby flights and packages.

Now Voyager (☎212/431-1616, fax 212/219-1753; *www.nowvoyagertravel.com*). Courier flight broker and consolidator.

STA Travel (☎1-800/781-4040 or ☎212/627-3111; *www.sta-travel.com*). Worldwide discount travel firm specializing in student/youth fares, with branches in the New York, LA, San Francisco and Boston areas; also arranges student IDs, travel insurance, car rental and rail passes.

Travel Avenue (☎1-800/333-3335 or ☎312/876-6866; *www.travelavenue.com*). Full service travel agent that offers discounts in the form of rebates.

Travel CUTS (☎1-800/667-2887 (Canada only) or ☎416/979-2406 or ☎1-888/838-CUTS; *www.travelcuts.com*). Specializes in student fares, IDs and other travel services, with branches all over Canada.

Travelocity (*www.travelocity.com*). Online consolidator.

LA costs US$660, while Continental's non-stop from Houston costs US$620 and Delta's from Atlanta costs US$625. United's non-stop from LA costs anywhere between US$396 and US$610.

American and Taca do the best deals to **Honduras**, flying non-stop from Miami to San Pedro Sula for US$539; Iberia's non-stop from Miami costs around US$20 more. Taca also has four direct flights from New York costing US$700, and stopping in Cancún. Continental flies non-stop from Houston to San Pedro Sula for around US$563.

There are no non-stop **flights from Canada** to Mexico, Belize, Guatemala, Honduras or El Salvador. Your best bet is to fly to Miami or Houston on either American or Continental and change there. Non-stop flights from Toronto to Miami with American cost as little as CAN$236, while Continental can fly you from Vancouver to Houston for CAN$538; continuing on to Miami from there costs CAN$604. Toronto to Miami on Continental, stopping in Cleveland, costs CAN$540. There are also charter flights with Canada 3000.

PACKAGES AND ORGANIZED TOURS

The range of **package tours** to the Maya region increases every year. Specialist companies take escorted groups on tours to Maya ruins, colonial towns, markets and beaches, often crossing several borders, and with options including biking, diving, rafting and bird-watching. If time is short, these can be very good value, especially for first-time visitors to the region, and the tour companies often have special arrangements with airlines for seat prices.

Budget tour groups usually travel by van, staying at comfortable, family-run hotels or camping, and calling at the main tourist attractions as well as some lesser-known places. More **expensive tours** can offer caving, rafting and sea-kayaking, or take you on expeditions with archeologists and scientists to remote sites and nature reserves.

Though in many cases you could organize the same or very similar itineraries yourself for less money, you'd probably need more time and some knowledge of Spanish. However, sea-kayaking trips and expeditions to remote jungle ruins and rivers are more difficult (or even impossible) to organize on your own, and are best done in an organized group, with expert leaders and emergency back-up.

ROUTES THROUGH MEXICO

It's a long haul **overland** to the Maya region from the US, with numerous possible routes through

SPECIALIST TOURS OPERATORS IN THE US

Bahia Tours, 105 S Federal Hwy, Dania, FL 33004 (☎1-800/443-0717). Diving specialists who organize horse-riding, diving and canoeing trips in the Honduras Bay Islands. Seven-day trips start at US$825, excluding air fare.

Ceiba Adventures PO Box 2274, Flagstaff, AZ 86003 (☎520/527-0171, fax 520/527-8127; *ceiba@primenet.com*). Rafting, kayaking and caving trips throughout the Maya region, including the Lacandón forest in Chiapas.

Elderhostel, 75 Federal St, Boston, MA 02110 (☎617/426-8056). Maya-related tours in Honduras, Guatemala and Belize. Over-55s only (companions may be younger).

Far Horizons, PO Box 91900, Albuquerque, NM 87199-1900 (☎1-800/552-4575; *journey@farhorizon.com*; *www.farhorizon.com*). Superb archeological trips to remote Maya sites in Guatemala, Belize, Mexico and Honduras, led by archeologists or renowned experts in the field. Around US$3200 for a nine-day expedition to Belize, including air fare. Highly recommended.

Green Tortoise Adventure Travel, 494 Broadway, San Francisco, CA 94133 (☎1-800/867-8647 or 415/956-7500; *info@greentortoise.com*; *www.greentortoise.com*). Tours to "cool places off the beaten-path" on converted buses with sleeping space (Nov–April). The "Southern Migration" is a very popular 23-day journey from San Francisco to Antigua in Guatemala via Baja California and Chiapas. Leaves in December and costs US$900 including food. Links with their "Central American Experience" trip, which continues on to Costa Rica.

Guatemala Unlimited, PO Box 786, Berkeley, CA 94701 (☎1-800/733-3350, fax 415/661-5364; *Guatemala@aol.com*). Offers an extensive array of set and custom-arranged tours to obscure and better-known Maya ruins, as well as jungle trekking, river-rafting, mountain-biking and volcano tours.

Imagine Travel Alternatives, PO Box 13219, Burton, WA 98103 (☎1-800/777-3975). Arrangements for independent travellers and escorted small-group tours in Belize.

International Expeditions Inc, 1 Environs Park, Helena, AL 35080 (☎1-800/633-4734). Top-notch

group tours or all-inclusive independent ones in Belize and Honduras. The "Natural Quest" eleven-day tour of Belize includes guided natural walks, horse-riding, canoeing and snorkelling (US$2598 including air fare from Miami). The "Maya heartland" tour concentrates on archeological ruins in all three countries.

Journeys, 4011 Jackson Rd, Ann Arbor, MI 48103–1825 (☎1-800/255-8735 or 734/655-4407, fax 655-2945; *info@journeys-intl.com*; *www.journeys-intl.com*). Superb nature- and culture-oriented tours to Belize and Guatemala; some for women only. Around US$1500 for a week in Guatemala. Highly recommended.

Nature Expeditions International, 474 Willamette St, PO Box 11496, Eugene, OR 97440 (☎1-800/869-0639). Excellent small-group adventure expeditions in Belize and Honduras, led by anthropology, biology and natural history specialists.

REI Adventures, PO Box 1938, Sumner, WA 98390-0800 (☎1-800/622-2236). Excellent adventure tours for small groups. Nine-day trips to Belize staying in jungle camps and including visits to ruins, snorkelling, kayaking and white-water rafting (US$1950 excluding air fare). Eight-day trips to Honduras exploring the undeveloped coast and islands with an emphasis on outdoor activities (US$1750 excluding air fare).

Slickrock Adventures, PO Box 1400, Moab, UT 84532 (☎1-800/390-5715, fax 801/259-6996; *slickrock@slickrock.com*). One of the best tour companies, offering sea-kayaking, caving and jungle and river (some white-water) expeditions in Belize, Guatemala and Honduras. US$1800 for a nine-day adventure "week" in Belize.

Toucan Adventure Tours, PO Box 1073, Cambria, CA 93428 (☎805/927-5885, fax 927-0929; *www.toucanadventures.com*). Inexpensive camping tours through the Maya region. The three-week "Ruta Maya" trip through Mexico, Guatemala, Belize and Honduras focuses on the ruins and the rainforest (US$1245 excluding air fare), and there are two-week tours visiting all the major Maya ruins in the Yucatán peninsula and Chiapas (US$1100 excluding air fare).

Mexico, combining bus and train travel. All these routes and the attractions on the way are fully covered in *The Rough Guide to Mexico*. For those needing a **visa** to visit any of the Central American countries, there are Guatemalan con-

sulates in Tapachula and Comitán and a Belize consulate in Chetumal; for more on entry requirements, see p.14.

Greyhound (☎1-800/231-2222; *www.greyhound.com*) runs to all the major border crossings

Travel Loves Company, 430 1st Ave North, Suite 216, Minneapolis, MN 55401 (☎612/824-4313). Group tours and individual itineraries to all countries in the region. Tours are escorted by one of six female experts.

Tread Lightly Limited, PO Box 329, 37 Juniper Meadow Rd, Washington Depot, CT 06794 (☎1-800/643-0060 or 860/868-1710, fax 868-1718; *info@treadlightly.com*; *www.treadlightly.com*). Wide selection of top-notch "low impact" natural history and cultural trips to Belize, Guatemala, the Yucatán and Honduras, often including kayaking, rafting and hiking. The eight-day Honduras-based "Searching for the Maya" trip is US$1150 excluding air fare.

Tropical Adventures Travel, 111 Second Ave North, Seattle, WA 98109 (☎1-800/247-3483, fax 206/441-5431; *www.divetropical.com*). Well-

organized three- to seven-day diving vacations on the Caribbean coast of Mexico.

Tropical Travel, 5 Grogans Park, Suite 102, Woodlands, TX 77380-2190 (☎1-800/451-8017 or 713/688-1985). Tailor-made trips to Belize, Costa Rica, Guatemala and Honduras, taking in ruins and rainforests. Diving packages also available.

Victor Emanuel Nature Tours, PO Box 33008, Atin, TX 78764 (☎1-800/328 VENT or 512/3285221, fax 512/328-2919; *VENTBIRD @aol.com*; *www.VENTBIRD.com*). Specialist bird-watching tour operator, with expert-led trips to Belize and Tikal, the Yucatán and Cozumel.

White Magic Unlimited, PO Box 5506, Mill Valley, CA 94942 (☎1-800/869-9874 or 415/381-8889). Excellent trips to Guatemala (white-water rafting and Maya sites) and Belize (the reef).

SPECIALIST TOUR OPERATORS IN CANADA

Adventures Abroad, 1037 W Broadway, Suite 202, Vancouver, BC, V6H 1E3 (☎1-800/321-2121). Excellent small-group tours, focusing on archeology, culture, nature and relaxation throughout the Maya region. Tours last from one to four weeks. A two-and-a-half-week Belize/Tikal tour costs CAN$2251 excluding air fare.

Eco-Summer Expeditions, 1516 Duranleau St, Vancouver, BC, V6H 3S4 (☎1-800/465-8884 or 604/669-7741, fax 465-3244; *trips@ ecosummer.com*; *www.ecosummer.com*). Wildlife tours, whale-watching and sea-kayaking in Mexico and Belize; around US$1300 a week.

Fun Sun Adventures, 10316-124 St, #201, Edmonton, Alberta, T5N 1R2 (☎403/482-2030). Hotel-based holidays in Belize and Guatemala. Around CAN$1100–1600 for two weeks.

Gap Adventures, 266 Dupont St, Toronto, Ontario, M5R IV7 (☎1-800/465-5600 or 416/922-8899, fax 922-0822; *adventure@gap.org*; *www.gap.ca*). Good group trips (some camping) to Guatemala, Belize and Honduras including diving and kayaking. Individual trips to El Salvador are

also available. The "Hummingbird Highway" tour (CAN$1595) and "Kayak Belize" tour (CAN$1195) focus on bird-watching, canoeing, exploring jungles and ruins, and island-hopping. All trips can be mixed and matched, with transport by public bus and private van.

Island Expeditions, 368–916 W Broadway, Vancouver, BC, V5Z 1K7 (☎1-800/667-1630 or 604/452-3212; fax 452-3433; *info@islandexpeditions.com*; *www.islandexpeditions.com*). Expertly led sea- and river-kayaking expeditions: CAN$1200 for a week on a Belize atoll, CAN$1300 for a week exploring rainforest rivers in southern Belize.

Pacific Sun Spots Tours, 201–196 W Third Ave, Vancouver, BC, V5Y 1E9 (☎1-800/663-0755 or 604/606-1750; *res@pacsun.com*). Hotel-based holidays mainly in Belize, but some hotels in Guatemala and Honduras too. CAN$520–1000 for a week in Belize.

Quest Nature Tours, 36 Finch Ave W, Toronto, Ontario, M2N 2G9 (☎416/221-3000). Wildlife tours to Belize given by naturalists. CAN$1700 for the reefs and rainforests tour.

on a regular basis. Some of their buses even take you over the frontier and into the Mexican bus station, and in many cases you can reserve tickets with their Mexican counterparts. Mexican buses similarly cross the border into US bus stations.

Green Tortoise (see p.6) run cheap and cheerful long-haul trips through Mexico to Guatemala.

There are constant buses to Mexico City from every Mexican border crossing (roughly 18–24hr), and beyond Mexico City there are good **bus con-**

nections to all the main Guatemala and Belize border crossings. Probably the best route **into Guatemala** takes you along the Carretera Interamericana through Oaxaca and San Cristóbal de las Casas (see p.160), and then on to Huehuetenango. The other main routes are along Mexico's Pacific coast to Tapachula, where you can take an international bus to Guatemala City, and along the Caribbean coast, to Chetumal and then into **Belize**. An interesting option is to travel from the Maya sites of Palenque and Yaxchilán in Chiapas, by boat along the Río Usumacinta to a border crossing in the department of Petén in Guatemala, about five hours by bus from Flores; for details of this journey see p.138.

Driving south may give you a lot of freedom, but it does entail a great deal of bureaucracy. You need a separate **insurance** policy for Central America (sold at the border). Sanborn's (☎1-800/222-0158) arranges insurance for Mexico and Central America, and also offers legal assistance, road maps and guides, and a 24-hour emergency hotline. The car will also require an **entry permit**, for which you'll need to show the registration and licence. There are strict controls everywhere to

make sure you're not importing the vehicle to sell it – if you attempt to leave without it (even if it's been destroyed in a crash) you'll face a massive duty bill. US, Canadian, EU, Australian and New Zealand **driving licences** are valid in Mexico and throughout Central America, but it's a good idea to arm yourself with an International Driving Licence – available for a nominal fee from the American Automobile Association (☎1-800/222-4357). If you run into problems with a traffic cop for any reason, show your international licence first, and if they abscond with it, you at least still have your own, more difficult to replace, licence.

Obviously, the simplest way to get to the Maya region from Mexico City is by air. There are daily **flights** to a number of destinations in southern Mexico, Yucatán and all the Central American capitals. A popular option is to fly to Palenque or Cancún, and from there to Flores or Belize City on Aerocaribe. If you're thinking of doing several journeys by air, it may be worth contacting Aeroméxico, Mexicana or Taca in advance about their **air passes**, which must be bought outside the country. For more on this, see "Getting Around", p.29.

GETTING THERE FROM THE UK AND IRELAND

There is just one direct scheduled flight from the UK to Central America (twice-weekly from Gatwick to Cancún on British Airways), and flying there involves changing aircraft (and sometimes airline), usually in the US. That said, it's possible to reach

Guatemala City, Cancún, Mérida or San Pedro Sula in one day from London (the best connections are on Continental, Iberia, KLM and American); it'll take an extra day to reach Belize City. While no airport in Britain offers the same degree of choice as London, most of the main carriers to Latin America and the US have two or three options available, often for the same fares as you would pay from the capital.

Another option for same-day arrival is to fly on one of the main **European carriers**: KLM (via Amsterdam) has good connections from throughout the UK and Ireland with KLM-UK, with flights to Mexico City and Guatemala City (arriving early next morning) at least three or four times a week. On Iberia from London or Manchester (via Madrid and Miami) you can reach Cancún, Guatemala City and San Salvador in a day. Iberia flights from Manchester require an overnight stop in Madrid.

If time is a less pressing concern, you could consider flying to **Mexico City** first (around £450 in high season, with special deals often available off-peak) and then travelling overland into the Maya region. This nearly always works out a little cheaper than flying to Guatemala City or Belize City, though prices to Cancún are often comparable. Several European airlines fly to Mexico City, although the only non-stop flights from London are on British Airways, which has three flights a week. For a complete list of carriers, see the box below. It's also worth checking if your transatlantic carrier has an air pass which links flights in the US and Mexico (usually only Mexico City) – most major US airlines do. For details of the Mex-AmeriPass from Aeroméxico and the Visit Central America pass from Taca, see p.29.

SHOPPING FOR TICKETS

Flights to Central America fill up early, so **book ahead** as far as you can. Official fares, quoted by the airlines, are generally more expensive than those booked through a travel agent; wherever you book, peak season rates apply in July, August, December and at Easter. If you simply want a plain return ticket, the best deal you'll get is usually an **Apex**, which means booking at least two weeks ahead and committing yourself to flight dates that you cannot change without paying a hefty penalty. Tickets are usually valid for between three and six months; you'll pay more for one that allows you to stay for up to a year. There's always some deal available for young people or students, though don't expect massive reductions.

If you want to travel through several countries in Central America, or continue into South America, then it's worth considering an **open-jaw** ticket (which lets you fly into one city and out of another). The low-season price for an open-jaw flying London–Cancún and returning Guatemala City–London is around £512/US$860. Don't forget the **air pass** options either (see p.29).

Web sites in the UK are not as geared to Mexican and Central American destinations as their US counterparts, but a check through *www.cheapflights.co.uk* will allow you to make

AIRLINES IN THE UK

Aeroflot ☎0171/355-2233
Aeroméxico ☎0171/823-5231
American Airlines ☎0345/789-789
British Airways ☎0345/222-111
Continental ☎0800/776-464
Delta ☎0800/414-767
Iberia ☎0171/830-0011

KLM ☎0990/750-900
Mexicana ☎0171/267-3787
Taca Group ☎01293-23330: representatives for Aviateca (the Guatemala airline) and three other Central American airlines.
United ☎0845/844-4777
Virgin Atlantic ☎01293/747-747

SPECIALIST FLIGHT AGENTS

Usit Campus, 52 Grosvenor Gdns, London SW1W 0AG (☎0171/730-2101; *www.campustravel.co.uk*); 53 Forest Rd, Edinburgh EH1 2QP (☎0131/668-3303); 166 Deansgate, Manchester M3 3FE (☎0161/833-2046). Student/youth travel specialists. Branches in YHA shops, in cities and on university campuses all over Britain.

Journey Latin America, 12–13 Heathfield Terrace, London W4 (☎0181/747-3108); Barton Arcade, 51–63 Deansgate, Manchester M3 2BH (☎0161/832-1441; *sales@journeylatinamerica.co.uk*). The leaders in the field on air fares and tours to Latin America; some of the best prices on high-season flights, plus good open-jaw options.

STA Travel, 86 Old Brompton Rd, London SW7 3LH; 117 Euston Rd, London NW1 2SX (☎0171/361-6262; *enquiries@sta.travel.co.uk*; *www.statravel.co.uk*). Student/youth travel specialists with an international help desk if you have problems while abroad. Dozens of branches throughout the UK, and many more worldwide.

Trailfinders, 42–50 Earls Court Rd, London W8 6FT (☎0171/938-3366). Air fare specialists; also tailor-made packages for independent travellers. Offices throughout the UK and in Dublin.

Travel Cuts, 295a Regent St, London W1R 7YA (☎0171/255-2082; *sales@travelcuts.co.uk*; *www.travelcuts.co.uk*). Air fare and independent travel specialists.

some comparisons on fares from various UK airports to North America and Mexico, and there are good links to travel agents and other sources of information. Usit Campus's Web page also has a reasonable fare-finder.

PACKAGES AND INCLUSIVE TOURS

Many companies offer **package tours** to the Maya region, which save hassle and can be good value. They are generally relaxed and friendly, usually led by someone from the UK or North America who knows the area well; in many cases there may also be a local guide. Transport varies from local buses and comfortable air-conditioned minibuses to fast launches or light aircraft. The list below covers the best and most experienced UK operators. Prices quoted are a guide only; some tours also require a local payment for

meals. Most operate through the UK winter only, but several run year-round.

GETTING THERE FROM IRELAND

No airline offers direct **flights from Ireland** to the Maya region, but there is a direct flight to Mexico City – once weekly with Aeroflot from Shannon. You can, however, take a direct flight to the US or Europe and connect easily with flights to Mexico and Central America. Delta has the widest range of direct flights from Dublin (and several from Shannon) to JFK and Atlanta, with daily connections to Mexico City and Guatemala. Aer Lingus from Dublin (and some from Shannon) has same-day connections to Mexico City and Cancún, for example, by flying to New York (JFK); and you can also fly with them from Dublin to Amsterdam and pick up KLM's flights to Mexico

---

SPECIALIST TOUR OPERATORS

Cathy Matos Mexican Tours, 215 Chalk Farm Rd, London NW1 8AF (☎0171/284 2550, fax 267 2004; *sales@mextours.demon.co.uk*). Wide variety of tailor-made tours, including sightseeing and archeology, and trips to colonial cities and beaches.

Dragoman, Camp Green, Kenton Rd, Debenham, Suffolk IP14 6LA (☎01728/861133; *100344.1342 @compuserve.com*; *www.dragoman.co.uk*). Eight-week overland camping expeditions through Central America; around £1400, plus food kitty.

Encounter Overland, 267 Old Brompton Rd, London, SW5 9JA (☎0171/370-6845; *adventure @encounter-overland.co.uk*). Three- to six-week overland camping and hotel trips through Mexico to Panamá. From Mexico City via Yucatán to Guatemala (42 days) costs £1800 excluding air fare.

Exodus, 9 Weir Rd, London, SW12 0LT (☎0181/673-0859; *sales@exodustravels.co.uk*, *www.exodustravels.co.uk*). Fifteen-day escorted tours staying at hotels throughout the Maya region; around £1400, including air fare.

Explore Worldwide, 1 Frederick St, Aldershot GU11 1LQ (☎01252/344161; *info@explore.co.uk*; *www.explore.co.uk*). Wide range of two- to three-week hotel-based tours to the Maya region. Some tours run year-round. About £1100 for fifteen days in Mexico, Guatemala and Belize, including air fare.

Global Travel Club, 1 Kiln Shaw, Langdon Hills, Basildon, Essex SS16 6LE (☎01268/541732, fax

542275; *info@global-travel.co.uk*; *www.global-travel.co.uk*). Small company specializing in individually arranged diving tours to Mexico and Belize.

Journey Latin America, 14–16 Devonshire Rd, London W4 2HD (☎0181/747-8315, fax 747-8315; *tours@journeylatinamerica.co.uk*). Wide range of high-standard tours and individual itineraries from the acknowledged experts.

Reef and Rainforest Tours, Prospect House, Jubilee Rd, Totnes, Devon TQ9 5BP (☎01803/866965, fax 865916; *reefrain@btinternet.com*). Individual itineraries from a very experienced company, focusing on nature reserves, research projects and diving in Belize and Honduras.

Travelbag Adventures, 15 Turk St, Alton, Hants GU34 1AG (☎01420/541007, fax 541022; *mail@travelbag-adventures.co.uk*; *www.travelbag-adventures.co.uk*). Small group hotel-based tours through the region. "Realm of the Maya", an eighteen-day trip from Cancún through Guatemala and Belize, costs around £950 excluding air fare.

Trips, 9 Byron Place, Clifton, Bristol BS8 1JT (☎0117/987-2626, fax 987-2627; *trips@trips. demon.co.uk*). Friendly, experienced company with an inspired range of tailor-made itineraries throughout the region. Two-week Guatemala and Belize tour starts from £1975, including flights. Also offers some excellent scuba-diving packages in the Honduran Bay Islands.

and Central America there. BA also flies from Dublin to meet its connections in London to Mexico City and Cancún. KLM's flights from Belfast connect with their services from Amsterdam to Mexico City and Central America.

Discount fares from Dublin or Belfast to Cancún or Guatemala City Mexico range from IR£480 to IR£580 return (Mexico City is IR£440–500); from Dublin to Guatemala from around IR£572.

USEFUL CONTACTS IN IRELAND

AIRLINES

Aer Lingus ☎01/705-3333
British Airways Belfast ☎0345/222111; Dublin ☎01-800/626747
British Midland Belfast ☎0345/240-530; Dublin ☎01/283-8833

Delta Dublin ☎01-800/768-080
KLM Belfast ☎0990/750-900
Ryanair in Ireland ☎01/609-7800; in the UK ☎0541/569-569

FLIGHT AND TOUR AGENTS

Maxwell's Travel, D'Olier Chambers, 1 Hawkins St, Dublin 2 (☎01/677-9479, fax 679-3948). Very experienced agent to Latin America, and Ireland's representatives for many of the British specialist tour operators (see box opposite).
Trailfinders, 4–5 Dawson St, Dublin 2 (☎01/677-7888). Irish branch of the air fare and independent travel experts.

USIT, 19–21 Aston Quay, O'Connell Bridge, Dublin 2 (☎01/602-1700); Fountain Centre, College St, Belfast BT1 6ET (☎01232/324073; *www.usit.ie*). All-Ireland student travel agents, with seventeen offices (mainly on campuses) in the Republic and the North.

GETTING THERE FROM AUSTRALASIA

There are no direct flights from Australasia to Mexico, Belize, Guatemala, Honduras or El Salvador, so consequently you've little choice but to fly via the US or Mexico. For most airlines, low season is from mid-January to the end of February and October to the end of November; high season mid-May to the end of August and December to mid-January. Seat availability on international flights out of Australia and New Zealand is often limited, so it's best to book several weeks ahead.

The **best deals** are with Air New Zealand-Continental and United Airlines, who have daily scheduled fares via LA, at around A$2299/NZ$2499 during their low seasons. At other times the cheapest fare is JAL's at A$1550–1850/NZ$1850–2250 to either LA or Mexico City via Tokyo, plus an add-on to the country's gateway city. Qantas-Continental also have daily scheduled fares to Central America, but are a little more expensive, starting at A$2399 low season.

If you want to stop off in North America before travelling on, then you may want to look into some of the **air passes** that can be booked before you leave (see p.29). United Airlines, Taca and Aviateca all offer flight coupons for single flights to Central America.

Few **round-the-world** tickets include Central American countries, but it is possible to visit them on a side trip (at extra cost) with Cathay Pacific-UA's "Globetrotter" and Air New Zealand–KLM–Northwest's "World Navigator"; prices range from A$2699–3299/ NZ$3189–3699.

Note that tickets bought direct from the airlines are usually at published rates. The **discount agents** listed in the box opposite offer better deals on fares and have the latest information on limited special offers.

AUSTRALASIAN AIRLINES

Air New Zealand (Australia ☎13 2476; New Zealand ☎09/357-3000). Daily from Sydney, Brisbane, Melbourne and Adelaide to LA, either direct or via Honolulu/Tonga/Fiji/Papeete; onward connections with Continental.

Continental Airlines (Australia ☎02/9321-9242). No NZ office. Offers a through service to Mexico City and the Maya region from LA.

Garuda (Australia ☎02/9334-9944 or 1-800/800-873; New Zealand ☎09/366-1855). Several flights a week to LA from major Australasian cities, with a stopover in Denpasar or Jakarta.

JAL (Australia ☎02/9272-1111; New Zealand ☎09/379-9906). Several flights a week from Sydney, Brisbane, Cairns and Auckland to LA and Mexico City with a stopover in Tokyo or Osaka.

Philippine Airlines (Australia ☎02/9262-3333). No NZ office. Several flights a week to LA from Sydney, Melbourne or Brisbane, with a transfer or overnight stop in Manila.

Qantas (Australia ☎13 1211; New Zealand: ☎09/357-8900 or 0800/808-767). Daily flights to LA from major cities with onward connections using Continental.

Taca and **Aviateca** (Australia ☎03/9329-5211). No NZ office. Air passes from LA to Guatemala City.

Singapore Airlines (Australia ☎13 1011; New Zealand ☎09/379-3209). Twice a week to LA from major Australian cities and once a week from Auckland via Singapore.

United Airlines (Australia ☎13 1777; New Zealand ☎09/379-3800). Daily flights direct to LA from Sydney, Melbourne and Auckland with onward connections to Mexico and all Central American capitals; also air passes.

AUSTRALASIAN DISCOUNT AGENTS

Anywhere Travel, 345 Anzac Parade, Kingsford, Sydney (☎02/9663-0411).

Brisbane Discount Travel, 260 Queen St, Brisbane (☎07/3229-9211).

Budget Travel, 16 Fort St, Auckland, plus branches around the city (☎09/366-0061 or 0800/808-040).

Destinations Unlimited, 3 Milford Rd, Auckland (☎09/373-4033).

Flight Centres Australia: 82 Elizabeth St, Sydney (☎13 1600), plus branches nationwide; New Zealand: 205 Queen St, Auckland (☎09/309-6171), plus branches nationwide.

Northern Gateway, 22 Cavenagh St, Darwin (☎08/8941 1394).

STA Travel, Australia: 702 Harris St, Ultimo, Sydney; 256 Flinders St, Melbourne; other offices in state capitals and major universities (nearest branch ☎13 1776; fastfare telesales ☎1300/360-960); New Zealand: 10 High St, Auckland (☎09/309-0458; fastfare telesales ☎09/366-6673), plus branches in Wellington, Christchurch, Dunedin, Palmerston North, Hamilton and at major universities; *traveller@statravelA.com.au; www.statravelA.com.au*

Thomas Cook, Australia: 175 Pitt St, Sydney; 257 Collins St, Melbourne; plus branches in other state capitals (local branch ☎13 1771; telesales ☎1800/063- 913); New Zealand: 96 Anzac Ave, Auckland (☎09/379- 3920).

Tymtro Travel, Level 8, 130 Pitt St, Sydney (☎02/9223-2211 or 1300/652-969).

FLIGHTS AND FARES

The cheapest way to get to **LA** or **Mexico City** is via Asia. Currently JAL flies from Sydney, Brisbane and Cairns to both cities, with an overnight stop in Tokyo (included in the fare) from A$1550/NZ$1850 low season. Garuda flies to LA, via either Jakarta or Denpasar, and Philippine Airlines flies to LA via Manila; both start at around A$1750 low season. United Airlines flies direct to LA, while Qantas and Air New Zealand fly either direct or via stopovers in the Pacific (from A$1850 low season). Air Pacific costs around the same and includes a stopover in Fiji. From New Zealand, Singapore Airlines offers a good connecting service to LA via Singapore for NZ$2099 low season. For the same price you can take the faster Air New Zealand flight (non-stop, or via Honolulu, Fiji, Tonga or Papeete), or United Airlines non-stop. All the above fares are from

SPECIALIST AGENTS

Adventure Associates, 197 Oxford St, Bondi Junction (☎02/389-7466). Two- to twelve-day jungle, archeological and cultural tours in Guatemala and Belize.

Adventure Specialists, 69 Liverpool St, Sydney 2000 (☎02/261-2927 or 1800/634-465). Variety of adventure-travel options to Central America, specializing in Guatemala and Belize.

Adventure World, Australia: 73 Walker St, North Sydney (☎02/956-7766 or 1800/221-931), plus branches in Melbourne, Brisbane, Adelaide and Perth; New Zealand: 101 Great South Rd, Remuera, Auckland (☎09/524-5118). Variety of tours, including trips to Tikal and Chichicastenango from Guatemala City and reef-river cruises in Belize.

Contours, 466 Victoria St, North Melbourne 3051 (☎03/9329-5211). Specialists in tailored city stopover packages to Central America.

Exodus, Top Deck Adventure, 350 Kent St, Sydney (☎02/9299-8844 or 1800/800-724); in New Zealand contact Adventure World. Eight-week overland tours trucking between Mexico City and Panamá City, through the heart of the Maya World.

Padi Travel Network, 4/372 Eastern Valley Way, Chatswood, NSW (☎1800/678-100), with agents throughout Australasia. Dive packages to the prime sites of the Belize coast.

Peregrine Adventures, 258 Lonsdale St, Melbourne (☎03/9663-8611), plus offices in Brisbane, Sydney, Adelaide and Perth. Extended overland-sea adventures from southern Mexico through Guatemala and Belize.

Auckland — expect to pay an extra NZ$150 for Christchurch and Wellington departures.

Continental and United Airlines have daily scheduled through fares to all the **Central American capitals** via LA, at around A$2140/NZ$2499 low season. Qantas–Continental's fares are a little more expensive, starting at A$2365 to Guatemala and A$2420 to Belize, El Salvador and Honduras.

If you're flying **via Asia** the cheapest add-ons are from Mexico City, with year-round flat rates of US$349 to San Salvador or San Pedro Sula in Honduras, US$440 to Belize and US$425 to Guatemala. From LA expect to pay anything between US$429 and US$660 (year-round flat rates).

If you prefer to have all the arrangements made for you before you leave, then the **specialist agents** on p.13 can help you plan your trip. Most can do anything from booking a few nights' accommodation to arranging fully escorted archeological-cultural tours. Some of the "adventure" specialists can also help organize activities such as diving and jungle treks.

Note that few of the tour prices include air fares, but the same agents can usually assist with flight arrangements. Many of the tours we have listed can also be arranged through your local travel agent.

VISAS AND ENTRY REQUIREMENTS

Information on the entry requirements of the five countries covered in this book, while correct at the time of going to press, is liable to change. For citizens of most Western countries, visas are generally not necessary in any of the countries in the region (except for El Salvador), but before travelling, it's crucial to contact a consulate to check what's required of you.

The length of time visitors are permitted to stay in the various countries varies considerably – Mexico often grants six-month visas (unless you enter the country in Chiapas; see p.15), whereas Belize, Honduras, Guatemala and El Salvador usually give out thirty-day stamps, though these can be extended. Once you get your stamp (and

visa/tourist card if required), you should keep your **passport** with you at all times, or at the very least carry a photocopy, as you may be asked to show it.

If travelling overland through **Mexico**, you won't need to get a visa in advance as there are consulates for every country in the capital. There's also a Guatemalan consulate in Comitán, Guatemalan and El Salvadorean consulates in Tapachula, and a Belize consulate in Chetumal.

MEXICO

Citizens of the US, Canada, EU countries, Australia and New Zealand don't need a visa to enter Mexico as tourists if staying for less than 180 days. Non-US citizens travelling via the US, however, may need a US visa.

What every visitor does need is a **valid passport** and a **tourist card** (or FMT – *folleto de migración turística*). Tourist cards are free: if you're flying you should get given one on the plane, or on arrival at the airport; if you're travelling overland into Mexico, you should be able to get one at the border crossing. If you want to be especially safe you can apply to any Mexican consulate in advance.

A tourist card is valid for a single entry only and it's a good idea to apply for a longer length of time than you think you'll need – getting an extension is a time-consuming business and travel plans can change quickly. If you're arriving in Mexico from

Belize or Guatemala, insist on as long a time as possible as you may only be offered thirty days. In 1998 many travellers (including a *Rough Guide* author) **entering the state of Chiapas** bordering Guatemala were only receiving fifteen-day cards and extensions were extremely difficult to obtain. If the tense political situation in Chiapas persists, it may well be worth crossing into a neighbouring state (Campeche, Tabasco, Yucatán or Oaxaca) and applying for an extension there, or crossing the Guatemalan or Belizean border and getting a new tourist card on re-entry.

You should keep the blue copy of your tourist card, which you are legally required to carry at all times, and it must be handed in when you depart the country. Should you lose it, you can get a replacement at your nearest immigration office (*migracíon*).

Visas, valid for between thirty and ninety days, are obtainable only through a consulate (in person or by mail) and are required by South Africans and most non-industrialized countries, as well as by anyone entering Mexico to work or to study for more than 180 days. Business visitors need a Business Authorization Card, available from consulates, and usually a visa, too. Anyone under eighteen travelling without both parents needs their written consent.

GUATEMALA

Citizens of the EU, the US, Canada, Japan, Switzerland, Norway, Mexico, Israel, Brazil, Australia, New Zealand and all Central American countries do not need a visa, only a valid passport to enter Guatemala. When you arrive at immigration you may be asked by the official how long you plan to stay, and offered thirty, sixty or ninety days. If you want ninety days make sure you get it. There is no charge to enter Guatemala, though it's common for border officials at land crossings to ask for a fee (typically Q10 = US$1.80), which is destined straight for his back pocket.

Passport-holders from some countries – including the Czech Republic, Poland, South Africa and most Gulf States – need a **tourist card**. These are available at the point of entry and cost US$5. They are also valid for up to ninety days. Finally, citizens from a number of countries including most of Africa and Asia need **visas** (US$10), which must be bought in advance and may take up to a month to process from a Guatemalan consulate.

If you want to extend your visit by up to ninety days, go to the immigration department (**migración**) in Guatemala City at 41 C and 17 Av, Zona 8. The process can take a full day, so get there in the morning. Most people simply cross a border and re-enter.

Before you enter Guatemala it's always worth phoning an embassy or consulate to check up on the latest entry requirements; there are embassies in all the region's capitals.

BELIZE

Citizens of the US, Canada, the EU, Australia and New Zealand do not need visas to enter Belize. Swiss citizens, however, do need one: it costs US$25 and is not officially obtainable at the border. There is no charge to enter the country and Belizean immigration personnel don't ask for the mysterious payments often demanded in other countries in the region. You'll generally be allowed a stay of **thirty days**, which can be renewed for Bz$25 each month, for a maximum of six months, after which you may have to leave the country for 24 hours.

EL SALVADOR

Citizens of the EU (except Greece and Portugal) and citizens of Switzerland, Norway, Israel and Japan do not need a visa or tourist card to enter El Salvador and are issued with a ninety-day stamp on arrival. Citizens of the US, Canada, Australia, South Africa, New Zealand, Greece and Portugal can get a tourist card at the point of entry ($10 and valid 15–90 days). If you need ninety days, make sure you ask for it.

Mexicans and citizens from all other Central American countries do not need a visa or tourist card to enter El Salvador. Most nationalities that are not mentioned above need a visa in advance from an embassy, which takes a month to process.

HONDURAS

Citizens of the US, EU, Canada, Japan, Switzerland, Norway, Australia and New Zealand with a valid passport get a thirty-day stamp on arrival, which can be extended to a maximum of ninety days at immigration offices throughout the country.

South Africans and citizens from most developing countries need a visa in advance from a

Honduran embassy or consulate. These cost $10–20 depending on where they are issued and can be extended within Honduras for up to ninety days.

When you enter Honduras there is officially no charge, but as in Guatemala, border officials usually demand a "fee" to enter the country, typically L20 (US$1.50).

EMBASSIES AND CONSULATES

IN THE US

Belize 2535 Massachusetts Ave NW, Washington DC 20009 (☎202/332-9636).

El Salvador 2308 California St NW, Washington DC 20008 (☎202/265-9671).

Guatemala 2220 R St NW, Washington DC 20008 (☎202/745-4952). There are also consulates in Chicago, Houston, LA, Miami, New York and San Diego.

Honduras 3007 Tilden St NW, Washington DC 20008 (☎202/966-7702).

Mexico USA: 2827 16th St NW, Washington, DC 20036 (☎202/736-1000); and consulates in fifty other US towns and cities; phone the main number for your nearest office.

IN CANADA

Belize Honorary Consuls, Suite 3800, South Tower, Royal Bank Plaza, Toronto M5J 2JP (☎416/865-7000, fax 864-70480; in Quebec ☎514/871-4741).

El Salvador 209 Kent St, Ottawa ON K2P 1Z8 (☎613/238 2939).

Honduras 151 Slater St, Suite 908a, Ottawa, ON K1P 5H3 (☎613/233 8900).

Guatemala 130 Albert St, Suite 1010, Ottawa ON K1P 5G4 (☎613/2337188).

Mexico 45 O'Connor St, Suite 1500, Ottawa, ON K1P 1A4 (☎613/233-8988), plus consulates in Toronto, Montréal and Vancouver.

IN THE UK AND IRELAND

Belize 22 Harcourt House, 19 Cavendish Square, London W1M 9AD (☎0171/499-9728, fax 491-4139). No Ireland office.

El Salvador Tennyson House, 159 Great Portland St, London W1N 5FD (☎0171/436-8282, fax 436-8181). No Ireland office.

Guatemala 13 Fawcett St, London SW10 9HN (☎0171/351-3042, fax 376-5708). No Ireland office.

Honduras 115 Gloucester Place, London W1H 3PJ (☎0171/486-4880, fax 486-4550). No Ireland office.

Mexico 8 Halkin St, London SW1X 8QR (☎0171/235-6393); 43 Ailesbury Rd, Ballsbridge, Dublin 4 (☎01/260-0699).

IN SOUTH AFRICA

Mexico Southern Life Plaza, 1st floor, Hatfield, Pretoria 0083 (☎012/342-5190).

IN AUSTRALASIA

Belize Australia: British High Commission, Commonwealth Ave, Yarralumla, Canberra (☎06/257-1982); New Zealand: British High Commission, 44 Hill St, Wellington (☎04/495-0889).

El Salvador Australia: Honorary Consulate, 3 Donnington St, Carindale, Brisbane, Qld 4152 (☎07/3398-8658). New Zealand: contact consulate in Australia.

Guatemala The nearest representative is in LA (☎213 /365- 9251).

Honduras Australia: Consulate-General, Level 7, 19–31 Pitt St, Sydney, NSW 2000 (☎02/9350-8121). New Zealand: contact consulate in Australia.

Mexico Australia: 14 Perth Ave, Yarralumla, Canberra, ACT 2600 (☎02/6273-3963); 135 New South Head Rd, Edgecliff, Sydney, NSW 2027 (☎02/9326-1292). New Zealand: 111–115 Customhouse Quay, 8th floor, Wellington (☎04/472-5555).

INSURANCE

Wherever you go in Central America, medical insurance is essential. Make sure your policy offers coverage of at least US$2,000,000, which should include provision for repatriation by air ambulance. Some specialist travel policies also offer cover for loss or theft of personal possessions and travel delay, though on most this is optional. Whether you take this part depends on how valuable your belongings are, but be warned that theft is rife in some areas and expensive-looking luggage attracts attention.

Before **buying a policy**, check to see if you're already covered for certain eventualities. **Credit and charge cards** often have certain levels of medical or other insurance included, especially if you use them to pay for your trip. This can be quite comprehensive, anticipating anything from lost or stolen baggage and missed connections to charter companies going bankrupt. That said, however, the medical cover offered is usually insufficient for Central American destinations, so check the small print carefully, as you should for any policy.

If you plan to participate in **water-sports**, including scuba-diving, you'll probably have to pay an extra premium. Note also that very few insurers will arrange on-the-spot payments in the event of a major expense or loss; you will usually be reimbursed only after going home. In all cases of loss or theft of goods, you will have to contact the local police to have a report made out so that your insurer can process the claim.

NORTH AMERICAN COVER

Canadian provincial health plans typically provide some overseas medical coverage, although they are unlikely to pick up the full tab in the event of a mishap. Holders of official **student/teacher/youth cards** are entitled to accident coverage and hospital in-patient benefits – the annual membership is far less than the cost of comparable insurance. Students may also find that their student health coverage extends during the vacations and for one term beyond the date of last enrolment. **Homeowners' or renters' insurance** often covers theft or loss of documents, money and valuables while overseas.

TRAVEL INSURANCE COMPANIES

AUSTRALASIA

Cover More Australia ☎02/9202-8000 or 1800/251-881

Ready Plan Australia ☎03/9791-5077 or 1800/337-462; New Zealand ☎09/379-3208

NORTH AMERICA

Access America ☎1-800/284-8300

Carefree Travel Insurance ☎1-800/323-3149

International Student Insurance Service (ISIS) – sold by STA Travel ☎1-800/777-0112

Travel Assistance International ☎1-800/821-2828

Travel Guard ☎1-800/826-1300

Travel Insurance Services ☎1-800/937-1387

UK

Colossus Direct ☎0990/775-885

Columbus Travel Insurance ☎0171/375-0011

Endsleigh Insurance ☎0171/436-4451

Frizzell Insurance ☎01202/292-333

Marcus Hearn ☎0171/739-3444

After exhausting the possibilities above, you might want to contact a **specialist travel insurance company**; your travel agent can usually recommend one, or see the box on p.17. Policies vary: some are comprehensive while others cover only certain risks (accidents, illnesses, delayed or lost luggage, cancelled flights, etc). In particular, ask whether the policy pays medical costs up-front or reimburses you later, and whether it provides for medical evacuation home. For policies that include lost or stolen luggage, check exactly what is and isn't covered, and make sure the per-article limit will cover your most valuable possessions.

The best premiums are usually to be had through **student/youth travel agencies** – ISIS policies, for example, cost US$60 for fifteen days, US$110 for a month, US$165 for two months and US$665 for a year for any of the Central American countries, but they do not include coverage for adventure sports or underwater activities.

Most North American travel policies apply only to items lost, stolen or damaged while in the custody of an identifiable, responsible third party. Even in these cases you will have to contact the local police within a certain time limit.

BRITISH COVER

If you have a good "all risks" home insurance policy, it may well cover your possessions against loss or theft even when overseas, and many private medical schemes also cover you when abroad – make sure you know the procedure and the helpline number. Otherwise, comprehensive travel insurance is sold by almost every travel agent (many will offer insurance when you book your flight or holiday), but you'll almost certainly be better off arranging your own from a specialist company. The growing number of travel insurance companies, especially those offering multi-trip or year-round cover, makes shopping for a policy ever more time-consuming, but competition means that prices are keen. Colossus Direct offers some of the cheapest prices, at £25 for one month's cover and £199 for a year.

When phoning for a quote, apart from asking about the level of cover, check if it includes insurance premium tax – now seventeen percent.

AUSTRALASIAN COVER

Travel insurance is available from most travel agents and some banks, or direct from insurance companies, for periods ranging from a few days to a year or even longer. All are fairly similar in premium and coverage, which includes medical expenses, loss of personal property and travellers' cheques, cancellations and delays, as well as most adventure sports. If you plan to indulge in high-risk activities, such as scuba-diving, check the policy carefully to make sure you'll be covered – it may be necessary to tailor a policy to suit your requirements. A normal policy for Mexico and Central America costs around A$100/NZ$120 for two weeks, A$170/NZ$200 for one month, A$250/NZ$300 for two months.

HEALTH

It's always easier to become ill in a country with a different climate, different food and different germs – still more so in a poor country with lower standards of sanitation than you might be used to. Most visitors, however, get home again without catching anything more serious than a dose of "traveller's diarrhoea". The most important precaution is to be aware of health risks posed by poor hygiene, untreated water, insect bites, undressed open cuts and unprotected sex.

Above all, it's vital to get the best **health advice** you can before you set off; pay a visit to your doctor or a travel clinic (see p.21) as far in advance of travel as possible. Many clinics also sell travel-related accessories, malaria tablets, mosquito nets, water filters and the like. Regardless of how well prepared you are medically, you will still want the security of **health insurance** (see "Insurance" on p.17).

VACCINATIONS, INOCULATIONS AND MALARIA PRECAUTIONS

If possible, all **inoculations** should be sorted out at least ten weeks before departure. The only obligatory jab for the region is a **yellow fever** vaccination if you're arriving from a "high-risk" area – northern South America and much of central Africa – in which case you need to carry your vaccination certificate.

Diphtheria vaccinations are considered essential, and long-term travellers should look at the combined **hepatitis A and B** and the **rabies** vaccines (though see p.22 for a caveat on that). All travellers should also check that they are up to date with **polio**, **tetanus**, **typhoid** and hepatitis A jabs.

North Americans can get inoculations at any immunization centre or at most local clinics, and will have to pay a fee. Most GPs in the **UK** have a travel surgery where you can get advice and certain vaccines on prescription, though they may not administer some of the less common immunizations. Note too that though some jabs (diphtheria, typhoid) are free, others will incur quite a hefty charge; it can be worth checking out a travel clinic where you can receive vaccinations almost immediately, some of them (hepatitis, rabies) at lower prices than at the doctor's. In

Australasia, vaccination centres are always less expensive than doctors' surgeries.

Malaria is a danger in some parts of the region (particularly in the rural lowlands). It's not a problem at anywhere over 1500m (which includes most of the Chiapas and Guatemalan highlands) and the touristy areas of Quintana Roo including Cozumel and Cancún. It's also extremely rare in the big cities. If you plan to visit these areas you may decide not to take a course of tablets, but if you plan to visit any lowland areas at all (including the sites of Palenque and Tikal), tablets are strongly advisable.

The recommended prophylactic is Chloroquine, or alternatively Mefloquine. However, as Mefloquine (also known as Larium) can have upsetting side-effects, it's worth discussing its suitability with a medical practitioner. You need to begin taking the tablets one week before arrival and for four weeks after leaving the area. You should still take precautions to avoid getting bitten by insects: sleep in screened rooms or under nets, burn mosquito coils containing permethrin (available everywhere), cover up arms and legs, especially around dawn and dusk when the mosquitoes are most active, and use insect repellent containing over 35 percent Deet.

Also prevalent in some parts (usually occurring in epidemic outbreaks), **dengue fever** is a viral infection transmitted by mosquitoes which are active during the day. There is no vaccine or specific treatment, so you need to pay great attention to avoiding bites.

OTHER SIMPLE PRECAUTIONS

What you **eat or drink** while you're travelling is crucial: a poor diet lowers your resistance. Be sure to drink clean water and eat a good balanced diet. Eating plenty of peeled fresh fruit helps keep up your vitamin and mineral intake, but it might be worth taking daily multi-vitamin and mineral tablets with you. It is also important to eat enough and get enough **rest**, as it's easy to become run-down if you're on the move a lot, especially in a hot climate; don't try anything too exotic in the first few days before your body has had a chance to adjust to local microbes. You should avoid food that has been on display for a while and is not freshly cooked or is obviously dirty and also steer clear of raw shellfish and salads. In addition to the hazards mentioned under "Intestinal Troubles" below, contaminated food and water can also transmit the hepatitis A virus, which can lay a victim low for several months with exhaustion, fever, and diarrhoea, and can even cause liver damage. For advice on **water**, see box below. Even more serious are **hepatitis B**, and **HIV** and **AIDS**, all transmitted through blood or sexual contact; you should take all the usual, well-publicized precautions to avoid them.

Two other common causes of illnesses are **altitude** and the **sun**. The best advice in both cases is to take it easy; allow yourself time to acclimatize before you race up a volcano, and build up exposure to the sun gradually. Use a strong sunscreen and, if you're walking during the day, wear a hat and try to keep in the shade. Avoid dehydration by drinking plenty of water or fruit juice. The most serious result of overheating is heatstroke, which can be potentially fatal. Lowering the body temperature (by taking a tepid shower, for example) is the first step in treatment.

Finally you might want to consider carrying a **travel medical kit**. These range from a box of Band-aids to a full compact sterilized kit, complete with syringes and sutures; you can buy them from pharmacies and the specialist suppliers listed in the box on p.21.

INTESTINAL TROUBLES

Despite all the dire warnings given here, a bout of **diarrhoea** is the medical problem you're most likely to encounter. No one, however cautious, seems to avoid it altogether. Its main cause is simply the change of diet: the food in the region contains a whole new set of bacteria, as well as perhaps rather more of them than you're used to. The best cure is the simplest one: take it easy for a day or two, drink lots of bottled water and eat only the blandest of foods – papaya is good for soothing the stomach and also crammed with vitamins. Only if the symptoms last more than four or five days do you need to worry.

Cholera is an acute bacterial infection, recognizable by watery diarrhoea and vomiting. However, risk of infection is considered low, particularly if you're following the health advice above, and symptoms are rapidly relieved by prompt medical attention and clean water. If you're spending any time in rural areas you also run the risk of picking up various **parasitic infections**: protozoa – amoeba and giardia – and intestinal worms. These sound (and can be) hideous, but they're easily treated once detected. If you suspect you may have an infestation, take a stool sample to a good **pathology lab** and go to a doctor or pharmacist with the test results (see "Getting Medical Help" on p.22).

WHAT ABOUT THE WATER?

Contaminated water is a major cause of sickness in Central America, and even if it looks clean, all drinking water should be regarded with caution. That said, however, it is also essential to increase fluid intake to prevent dehydration. Bottled water is widely available, but stick with known brands and always check that the seal is intact since refilling empties with tap water for resale is not unknown (carbonated water is generally a safer bet in that respect). Many restaurants use purified water (*agua purificada*), but always check; hotels frequently have a supply and will often provide bottles in your room.

There are various methods of treating water while you are travelling, whether your source is a tap or a river: **boiling** for a minimum of five minutes is the most effective method of sterilization, but it is not always practical, and will not remove unpleasant tastes. **Water filters** remove visible impurities

and larger pathogenic organisms (most bacteria and cysts). The Swiss-made Katadyn filter is expensive but extremely useful (various sizes available from outdoor equipment stores). To be really sure your filtered water is also purified, however, **chemical sterilization** is advisable, using either chlorine or iodine tablets, or a tincture of iodine liquid. Both chlorine and iodine leave a nasty aftertaste (though it can be masked with lemon or lime juice). Iodine is more effective in destroying amoebic cysts, but pregnant women or people with thyroid problems should consult their doctor before using iodine sterilizing tablets or iodine-based purifiers. Inexpensive iodine removal filters are recommended if treated water is being used continuously for more than a month or is being given to babies. Any good outdoor equipment shop will stock a range of water treatment products and their experts will give you the best advice for your particular needs.

More serious is **amoebic dysentery**, which is endemic in many parts of the region. The symptoms are similar to a bad dose of diarrhoea but include bleeding too. On the whole, a course of flagyl (metronidazole or tinidozole) will cure it. If you plan to visit far-flung corners then it's worth getting hold of this before you go, and some advice from a doctor on its use.

BITES AND STINGS

Taking steps to avoid getting bitten by **insects**, particularly mosquitoes, is always good practice. **Sandflies**, often present on beaches, are tiny, but their bites, usually on feet and ankles, itch like hell and last for days. Head or body **lice** can be picked up from people or bedding, and are best

MEDICAL RESOURCES FOR TRAVELLERS

IN NORTH AMERICA

Center for Disease Control, 1600 Clifton Rd NE, Atlanta, GA 30333 (☎404/639-3311; *netinfo@cdc. gov; www.cdc.gov/travel/cameri-ca*). Current information on health risks and precautions and clear and comprehensive Web pages covering Mexico and Central America.

International Association for Medical Assistance to Travellers (IAMAT), 417 Center St, Lewiston, NY 14092 (☎716/754-4883); 40 Regal Rd, Guelph, ON N1K 1B5 (☎519/836-0102). Non-profit organization supported by donations. Can provide climate charts and leaflets on various diseases and inoculations.

Medic Alert, 2323 Colorado Ave, Turlock, CA 95381 (☎1-800/432-5378; in Canada ☎1-800/668-1507). Sells bracelets engraved with the traveller's medical requirements in case of emergency.

Travel Medicine, 351 Pleasant St, Northampton, MA 01060 (☎1-800/872-8633). Sells first-aid kits, mosquito netting, water filters and other health-related travel products.

Travellers Medical Center, 31 Washington Square, New York, NY 10011 (☎212/982-1600). Consultation service on immunizations and treatment.

IN THE UK AND IRELAND

British travellers should pick up a copy of the free booklet *Health Advice for Travellers*, published by the Department of Health; it's available from GPs' surgeries, many chemists and most of the agencies listed here.

British Airways Travel Clinic, 156 Regent St, London W1R 5TA (Mon–Fri 9am–4.15pm, Sat 10am–4pm; ☎0171/439-9584); and over thirty other clinics throughout the UK; call ☎01276/685-040 or check *www.british-airways.com* to find your nearest branch. Excellent medical advice, vaccinations and a comprehensive range of travel health items – and you even get air miles. No appointments necessary at Regent Street; call ahead at other clinics.

Hospital for Tropical Diseases Travel Clinic, Mortimer Market Centre, Capper St, London WC1 (Mon–Fri 9am–5pm; ☎0171/530-3454). Phone for area-specific health information or call the recorded message service on ☎0839/337722 for hints on hygiene, illness prevention and appropriate immunizations.

MASTA (Medical Advisory Service for Travellers Abroad), London School of Hygiene and Tropical Medicine, Keppel St, London WC1E 7HT (☎0171/631-4408; *http://dspace.dial.pipex.com/masta/index/html*). Calling the phone number automatically refers you to the premium rate Travellers' Health Line (☎0891/224-100), which operates round the clock, giving written information tailored to your journey by return of post.

Trailfinders Travel Clinic, 194 Kensington High St, London W8 6BD (☎0171/338-3999); 254–284 Sauchiehall St, Glasgow G2 3EH (☎0141/353-0066). Expert medical advice and a full range of travel vaccines and medical supplies. No appointments necessary in London. Discounts on vaccinations for anyone travelling with Trailfinders.

Travel Medicine Services, PO Box 254, 16 College St, Belfast 1 (☎01232/315220). Operates a travel clinic (Mon 9–11am & Weds 2–4pm), primarily administering yellow fever vaccine, but can also give inoculations after referral from a GP.

Tropical Medical Bureau, Grafton St Medical Centre, Dublin 2 (☎01/671 9200; *tmb@iol.ie www.tmb.ie*).

IN AUSTRALASIA

Travellers' Medical and Vaccination Centre, 7/428 George St, Sydney (☎02/9221-7133); 3/393 Little Bourke St, Melbourne (☎03/9602-5788); 6/29 Gilbert Place, Adelaide (☎08/8212-7522); 6/247 Adelaide St, Brisbane (☎07/3221-9066); 1 Mill St, Perth (☎08/9321-1977); Level 1, Canterbury Arcade, 170 Queen St, Auckland 1 (☎09/373-3531); *www.tmvc.com.au*

treated with medicated soap or shampoo; very occasionally, they may spread typhus, characterized by fever, muscle aches, headaches and eventually a measles-like rash. If you think you have it, seek treatment.

Scorpions are common; mostly nocturnal, they hide during the heat of the day under rocks and in crevices. If you're camping, or sleeping in a village cabaña, shake your shoes out before putting them on and try not to wander round barefoot. Their sting is painful (occasionally fatal) and can become infected, so you should seek medical treatment. You're less likely to be bitten by a **spider**, but the advice is the same as for scorpions and venomous insects: seek medical treatment if the pain persists or increases.

You're unlikely to see a **snake**, and most are harmless in any case. Wearing boots and long pants will go a long way towards preventing a bite – walk heavily and they will usually slither away. Exceptions are the fer-de-lance (which, thankfully, lives on dense, mountainous territory, and rarely emerges during the day) and the bushmaster (which can be found in places with heavy rainfall, or near streams and rivers), both of which can be aggressive, and whose venom can be fatal. If you do get bitten, remember what the snake looked like (kill it if you can), immobilize the bitten limb as far as possible and seek medical help immediately: antivenins are available in most hospitals.

Swimming and snorkelling might bring you into contact with potentially dangerous or venomous **sea creatures**. You're extremely unlikely to be a victim of a shark attack (though the dubious practice of shark-feeding as a tourist attraction is growing, and could lead to an accidental bite), but jellyfish are common and all corals will sting. Some jellyfish, like the Portuguese man-o'-war, with its distinctive purple, bag-like sail, have very long tentacles with stinging cells, and an encounter will result in raw, red weals. Equally painful is a brush against fire coral. In each case, clean the wound with vinegar or iodine and seek medical help if the pain persists or infection develops. The spines of sting rays, scorpion fish and stonefish are all extremely poisonous, so be careful where you put your feet.

Finally, **rabies** is present in the region. The best advice is to give dogs a wide berth and not to play with animals at all, no matter how cuddly they may look. Treat any bite as suspect: wash any wound immediately with soap or detergent and apply alcohol or iodine if possible. Act immediately to get treatment – rabies is fatal once symptoms appear. There is a **vaccine**, but it is expensive, serves only to shorten the course of treatment you need anyway and is effective for no more than three months.

GETTING MEDICAL HELP

For minor medical problems, head for a **farmacia** – look for the green cross. Pharmacists are knowledgeable and helpful, and many speak some English. They can also sell drugs over the counter (if necessary) which are only available on prescription at home. Every capital city has **doctors** and dentists, many trained in the US, who are experienced in treating visitors and speak good English. Your embassy will always have a list of recommended doctors, and we've included some in our "Listings" for the main towns. Health insurance (see p.17) is essential and for anything serious you should to go to the best **private hospital** you can reach; again, these are located mainly in the capital cities. If you suspect something is amiss with your insides, it might be worth heading straight for the local **pathology lab** (all the main towns have them), before seeing a doctor, as the doctor will probably send you there anyway. Many rural communities have a **health centre** (*centro de salud* or *puesto de salud*), where health care is free, although there may only be a nurse or health-worker available and you can't rely on finding anyone who speaks English. Should you need an injection or transfusion, make sure that the equipment is sterile (it might be worth bringing a sterile kit from home) and ensure any blood you receive is screened.

COSTS AND MONEY

By European or North American standards, the cost of living in the Maya World is low, and, with most currencies gradually dropping in value against the dollar and pound sterling, it's possible to live quite cheaply here. Belize is the most expensive country, while the others are all roughly comparable. Of course in some areas (Cancún, Guanaja and Roatán especially), where the local economy is tourism-driven, things can be much more expensive.

The **US dollar** is by far the most widely accepted foreign currency. **Credit cards** are very useful for withdrawing currency from bank ATMs, but don't count on paying with them except in upmarket hotels and restaurants.

It's always a good idea to have some **travellers' cheques**, which you can cash in most towns, and some US dollar bills, in case you run short of local currency a long way from the nearest bank. You'll get the best rate for your dollars if you change them in the country you're in. All the international airports have a bank for **currency exchange**, while at the main land border crossings there might be a bank, or more likely a swarm of moneychangers, who will often give fair rates for cash and sometimes travellers' cheques. Even at the most remote border crossings, such as the "jungle route" between Honduras and Guatemala, you'll usually find a moneychanger loitering.

All the local currencies (with the exception of Belize, which has fixed exchange rates of Bz$2 to US$1) float against the US dollar. Prices throughout the guide are quoted in US dollars.

CREDIT CARDS, TRAVELLERS' CHEQUES AND WIRING MONEY

Credit cards are becoming increasingly widely accepted in the region, though you shouldn't expect to be able to use them as you would in North America or Europe. They are usually accepted in upmarket shops, hotels and restaurants, but you won't be able to pay for your comedor meal or pensión bill with plastic.

Visa is the most useful brand, followed by Mastercard. You can use your card to get cash over the counter at banks and from ATMs, everywhere except in Belize. Although most ATMs are in service 24 hours, it's wiser to use them when the bank is open: firstly you can see a bank employee if something goes wrong and the machine keeps your card (though this is very rare), and secondly you benefit from the security of daylight. Using your **debit card** means you don't have to buy and countersign travellers' cheques and, though you pay a handling charge each time you use it, the amount may be less than the commission on cheques and you may benefit from a better exchange rate.

Travellers' cheques are a safe way to bring money, as they offer the security of a refund if they're stolen. To facilitate this you want to make sure that you have cheques issued by one of the big names (such as American Express, Visa, Thomas Cook or Citibank), which are also more readily accepted. You should also always carry your proof of purchase when trying to change travellers' cheques, as some places will refuse to deal with you otherwise. Note that in El Salvador, travellers' cheques are difficult to cash outside the capital.

Having money **wired from home** is never convenient or cheap, and should be considered a last resort. Funds can be sent via **Western Union** or **American Express MoneyGram**. Both companies' fees depend on the destination and the amount being transferred. The funds should be available for collection at the local branch within minutes of being sent.

It's also possible – for a fee – to have money wired directly from a bank in your home country to a bank in Central America, although this is somewhat less reliable as it involves two separate institutions, and can take between a couple of days and several months. If you use this route, the person wiring the funds to you will need to know the routing number of the bank the funds are being wired to.

COSTS

In most circumstances, the cost of living in the region is much **cheaper** than in North America and Europe (though in Belize and Cancún prices are not that different from the US). As a general rule, locally produced goods are cheap and anything imported is overpriced.

To an extent, what you spend will obviously depend on where, when and how you choose to travel. **Peak tourist seasons**, such as Christmas and Easter, tend to push up hotel prices, and certain tourist centres are notably more expensive at these times. **Public transport**, geared to locals, is invariably a bargain – though bear in mind that in some places (such as Lago de Atitlán in Guatemala) there's a quasi-institutionalized two-tier price system. Travelling by car is expensive, and the cost of renting a car is higher in the Maya region than it is in the US, as is the cost of fuel – although this is still cheaper than in Europe.

It may be worth carrying a **student card** if you have one, as it sometimes opens the way for a reduction, but it won't save you a great deal and, unless you need one to clinch a deal on air fares, it's not worth buying one for the trip.

Mexico is especially good value presently thanks to the chronically weak peso, and because of its range of hotels at all levels of the price scale, the great food and comfortable transport, it represents superb value for money. Guatemala is another cheap country, with probably the very cheapest budget hotel rooms, though the midrange hotels are sometimes only fair value for money. Restaurant meals are inexpensive, but the transport system, though cheap, is crowded, slow and rudimentary. Honduras and El Salvador are also very cheap for eating and travel, but you may find yourself paying a little more for your hotel.

The careful **budget traveller** can reckon on getting by on a minimum of **US$15 a day in Mexico, Guatemala, Honduras or El Salvador**. Accommodation is typically US$3–5 a night (based on sharing a double room), with food costing perhaps US$5 a day, and another US$5 accounted for by travel costs, entry charges to the sites and museums. Add on a dollar for every beer.

Moving into the **mid-range market**, a couple travelling together sharing hotel rooms and meals might expect to spend US$75 a day. This is based on two people sharing a comfortable double hotel room (usually with air-conditioning, cable TV and private bathroom) costing US$12–25 each a night, eating three good meals a day including some wine or a couple of beers each, costing around US$15-20 each a day, and including first-class bus travel and entry charges, which might add another US$7–10 a day each. Single travellers should reckon on perhaps US$45–50 a day for the same standards.

At the **luxury** end of the market it's possible to really blow out by taking specialized tour excursions, internal flights, scuba-diving and renting a car, but you'll still get excellent value for money compared to the US and Europe.

Belize is the most expensive country in the region with prices about forty percent higher than in any other country. The budget hotel that costs US$12 a night in Belize is probably half that price in Guatemala or Mexico. The budget traveller should reckon on a minimum of US$25 a day in Belize, while a couple requiring a little more comfort should expect to pay more like US$100 a day. Travel by public bus is a relative bargain in Belize, probably just a shade more expensive than in the other countries.

INFORMATION AND MAPS

Information about the Maya World is available from a number of sources, though much of the promotional puff provided by the official tourist offices is pretty to look at, but of little practical use. However, the quality of such information is improving, and if you have specific questions you could try contacting some of the official organizations listed here.

When digging out information on the Maya region, don't forget the **specialist travel agents** (see pp.6-7,10,13) and the **embassies** (see p.16). Best of all for practical details, are the **Internet sites** in the box below.

Current political analysis and an interesting and informative overview of the society, economy and environment of each country is provided by

two **specialist publishers**: the Resource Center in the US who produce the *Inside* series covering each country, and the Latin America Bureau in the UK, an independent, non-profit research organization, whose *In Focus* series so far covers Belize, Guatemala and Mexico as well as much of South America. Though detailed, the books are not large, around 100–200 pages, and if you're going to spend any length of time in the region it's well worth having a look at these before you go.

The **Latin American Travel Advisor** is a quarterly newsletter with a comprehensive report on each country in the region, covering safety, health, politics and the economy, along with a special feature on a relevant topic. One issue costs US$15, or you can pay US$39 for a year's subscription. Send a cheque to Latin American Travel Consultants, PO Box 17-17-908, Quito, Ecuador (fax 593/2-562-566). Headlines and excerpts are published on their Web site: *www.amerispan.com/latc/*

While you're in the region you'll find **government tourism offices** in each capital city, the international airports and in the main tourist centres. The information they're able to give is variable, but they can usually provide at the very least a city map, a bus timetable and perhaps a list of hotels (and they may even call them for you). SECTUR (the Mexican tourism department) are probably the best organized, but again the information they dispense varies from office to office. Addresses (and an idea of how useful a particular office will be) are given throughout the guide. In addition, there are some locally run initiatives, often set up by an association of tourism businesses. Many of the tour or travel agents mentioned in the guide should also be reliable sources of information.

TOURIST OFFICES: WEB SITES AND EMAIL ADDRESSES

Belize *www.belizenet.com*

El Salvador no tourist Web site: *www.elsalvador.nv* is a government page with some information.

Guatemala *www.travel-guatemala.org.gt; inguat@guate.net*

Honduras *www.hondunet.net/turis.html*

Mexico *www.mexico-travel.com; www.wotw.com/mundomaya*

See also the list of useful Internet sites on p.27.

UK RESOURCES

In London you can visit **Canning House Library**, 2 Belgrave Square, SW1X 8PJ (☎0171/235-2303), which has the UK's largest publicly accessible collection of books and periodicals on Latin America. It's free to use, though you have to be a member to take books out and receive the twice-yearly *Bulletin*, a review of recently published books on Latin America. An excellent resource centre also in London is **Maya – The Guatemalan Indian**

TOURIST INFORMATION

IN AUSTRALASIA

It's difficult to find official tourist information about the Maya region in **Australia** or **New Zealand**; your best bet is to contact the Web sites, Bushbooks (see box below), the consulate (listed on p.16) or specialist travel agents (p.13).

IN NORTH AMERICA

Mexico has numerous tourist offices scattered around North America; the other countries less so. The information lines listed below will be able to send you tourist information or direct you to your nearest office.

Belize US ☎212/563-6011 or
1-800/624-0686

El Salvador US ☎212/889-3608;
Canada: ☎613/238-2939

Guatemala US ☎212/689-1014 or

1-800/742-4529, fax 305/442-1013;
Canada ☎613/233-2339

Honduras US ☎1-800/410-9608
Mexico US & Canada ☎1-800/44-MEXICO

IN THE UK

The Mexico and Guatemala offices and the consular representatives of the other countries (addresses are listed on p.16) will send you information on their respective countries if you send a SAE with a 39p stamp; give them a call first to check what they have.

Guatemala ☎0171/349-0346
Mexico ☎0171/734-1058
Belize ☎0171/499-9728
El Salvador ☎0171/436-8282
Honduras ☎0171/486-4880

Centre, 94A Wandsworth Bridge Rd, London SW6 2TF (☎ & fax 0171/371-5291 for opening times; closed Jan, Easter and August; *http://web.ukonline/jamie.marshall/index.html*). Membership (£5 annually) gives you access to the library (reference only) and video collection, and you receive information of the monthly events and film shows held at the centre. There is a particularly fine textile collection here and the centre's director, Krystyna Deuss, is the acknowledged English authority on historic and contemporary Maya dress and ritual.

For general information on **independent travel**, pick up a copy of the excellent *Everything You*

Need to Know Before You Go (Abroadsheet Publications, from specialist bookshops); author Mark Ashton has managed to compile an enormous amount of essential advice and tips into one amazingly well-organized (large) glossy sheet. Finally, if you're planning an expedition from the UK, you should avail yourself of the services of the **Expedition Advisory Centre** at the Royal Geographic Society, 1 Kensington Gore, London SW7 2AR (☎0171/581-2057; *eac@rgs.org*). As well as expedition planning seminars, the EAC also publishes a range of specialist books.

THE INTERNET

The number of pages on the **Internet** devoted to Mexico and Central America is growing daily. The first place to check out is the comprehensive and logically laid-out homepage of the **Latin American Information Center** (LANIC; *www.lanic.utexas.edu*), which has a seemingly never-ending series of superb links for each country. You can reach almost anywhere and anything in the region connected to the Net from here. **Green Arrow**'s pages (*www.greenarrow.com*) are a good source of travel and environmental information and volunteering opportunities throughout Mexico and Central America. It's also worth checking the Web page of the **Latin American Travel Advisor** (see p.25). The

---

RESOURCE CENTRE OUTLETS

UK Latin America Bureau ☎0171/278-2829;
lab@gn.apc.org; www.lab.org.uk

IRELAND Trocaire Resource Centre ☎01/874-3875

USA Interlink Publishing Group ☎413/582-7054; *interpg@aol.com*

Monthly Review Press ☎212/691-2555; *mreview@igc.apc.org*

CANADA Fernwood Books ☎902/422-3302;
fernwood@istar.ca

AUSTRALIA Bushbooks ☎02/4323-3274;
bushbooks@ozmail.com.au

USEFUL WEB SITES

BELIZE

www.turq.com/belizefirst/
www.belizereport.com
www.belizenet.com
www.belize.com
www.belizeit.com

GUATEMALA

www.pronet.net.gt/gweekly/
www.sigloxxi.com

HONDURAS

www.globalnet.hn/hondutip.htm
www.marrder.com/htw/
www.bayislands.com

MEXICO

mexico-travel.com
www.wotw.com/mexico
www.planeta.com/madea/ecotravel/mexico/
mexinterior.html

Central Index of Appointments Overseas (CIAO; *www.ciao-directory.org*) has links with dozens of organizations accepting volunteers with specialist skills in Guatemala. Finally, the ever-helpful members of the **newsgroup** *rec.travel.latin-america* have a huge (and generally accurate) information base and will answer any query about travel in the region.

MAPS

The best **maps** of the region are produced by International Travel Map Productions (736A Granville St, Vancouver, BC, V62 1G3, Canada). Their range includes individual maps of Southeast Mexico, the Yucatán, Guatemala and El Salvador, Honduras and Belize; there's also a small-scale Central America map. You should be able to find them in specialist map shops and they are sometimes available in Central American cities, though it's wise to try to get what you need before you go.

If you need a good **road atlas** of Mexico, the Nelles 1:2,500,000 is one of the clearest, though the International Travel Map 1:300,300,000 also shows relief and has many mileage and driving times. In Mexico, the best maps are those published by Patria, which cover each state individually, and by Guía Roji, who also publish a Mexican Road Atlas and a Mexico City street guide. Both makes of map are easy to locate – try branches of Sanborn's or large Pemex stations.

Detailed **hiking and climbing maps** are more difficult to come by. In Mexico, INEGI, the governmental cartographers, produce very good topographic maps on various scales; they have an office in every state capital. In Guatemala the

MAP OUTLETS

US

Rand McNally, 444 N Michigan Ave, Chicago, IL 60611 (☎312/321-1751); 150 E 52nd St, New York, NY 10022 (☎212/758-7488); 595 Market St, San Francisco, CA 94105 (☎415/777-3131); 1201 Connecticut Ave NW, Washington DC 20003 (☎202/223-6751).
For other locations, or for maps by mail order, call ☎1-800/333-0136 (ext 2111).

CANADA

Ulysses Travel Bookshop, 4176 St-Denis, Montréal PQ, H2W 2M5 (☎514/843-9447).
Open Air Books and Maps, 25 Toronto St, Toronto, ON, M5R 2C1 (☎416/363-0719).

World Wide Books and Maps, 552 Seymour St, Vancouver, BC, V6B 3J5.

UK

Stanfords, 12–14 Long Acre, London WC2 (☎0171/836-1321); 52 Grosvenor Gdns, London SW1W 0AG; 156 Regent St, London W1R 5TA.
For mail order maps call the Long Acre branch.

AUSTRALASIA

Specialty Maps, 58 Albert St, Auckland (☎09/307-2217).
Travel Bookshop, Shop 3, 175 Liverpool St, Sydney, NSW (☎02/926- 8200).

large-scale maps (1:50,000) produced by the Instituto Geográfico Militar (see p.295) are out of date but are at least accurately contoured. Topographic maps produced by Ordnance Survey in the UK are available for Belize: two sheets at 1:250,000 cover the whole country, with 44 sheets at 1:50,000 scale providing greater detail, though many are out of date and not all are readily available. The available sheets are sold in the UK by Stanfords and in Belize by the Ministry of Natural Resources in Belmopan (see p.237) and Belize City.

In Honduras, topographical maps are available in the capital Tegucigalpa from the Instituto Geográfico, Edifico Secopt, Barrio La Bolsa, Comayagüela (☎337 166). In San Pedro Sula there are good detailed maps of all the national parks at Fundación Ecologista, 7 Av and 1 C. Topographic maps seem to be impossible to find in El Salvador, but you could try the tourist office.

GETTING AROUND

Most travellers in the region (and most locals) get around by public bus – with perhaps an occasional flight or boat trip. Only the privileged few are able to afford a car, so the public bus network is generally extremely comprehensive and very cheap. Except in Mexico, local buses tend to be extremely full. If you're travelling independently without your own vehicle you'll have to get used to spending a lot of time in (and waiting for) them.

Each country has at least one domestic airline, and taking an occasional, inexpensive **flight** can save hours of road travel over difficult terrain. If you're heading for the Tikal ruins from Guatemala City, for example, the hour-long flight (from US$60) will save you a twelve-hour bus journey from hell. Air passes can also be very good value; see p.29.

BY BUS

Public **buses** are cheap, crowded, convenient and sometimes wildly entertaining. There is a huge network, with daily services connecting most towns with the regional and state capitals. Generally, buses will stop anywhere (the concept of bus stops has yet to really catch on) regardless of how many people are already on board.

There are, loosely, two classes of bus, first (*primera*) and second (*segunda*). On a **first-class bus** (also sometimes called a pullman) you can book your seat in advance. Generally, first-class buses ply the main highways, leaving the minor roads to the second-class services. They vary tremendously from country to country, but the best of them, especially on international routes, are air-conditioned and complete with videos and reclining seats. In Mexico, buses are extremely comfortable, punctual and speedy, and seats are usually allocated by computer. Travel in Mexico on luxury buses works out around US$1.60 an hour. In Guatemala and Honduras, on the other hand, a first-class bus can be a very old Greyhound with cracked windows, ripped seats and bald tyres; travel normally works out around US$1.30 an hour.

On **second-class buses** (known as *camionetas* in Chiapas and Guatemala) travel works out at around US$1 an hour in all the countries. The buses are invariably ramshackle, third-hand, recycled US school buses, easily recognized by their trademark clouds of thick black noxious fumes and rasping exhausts. They're often garishly painted and serve mainly to carry villagers, their shopping and their animals to and from market – the original and ubiquitous "chicken bus". Snack vendors tout for business, and merengue and Mexican ranchero assaults your eardrums from decrepit speakers. The general onboard "etiquette" is three to a bench seat (with no exceptions for gringos), the aisles crammed with another twenty or thirty standing sufferers, and the roof loaded with mountainous baskets of vegetables and fruit from the marketplace. Except in Belize, the driver always seems to be a moustachioed ladino with an eye for the ladies and his helper (*ayudante*) always overworked and underage. It's the *ayudante*'s job alone to scramble up to the roof to retrieve your rucksack, collect the fares and bellow out the destination to all and sundry.

In remote villages and places where buses cannot or do not reach, **pickup** trucks transport passengers. Unless it's raining, or the road is really atrocious, a bumpy pickup ride is often vastly preferable to a crowded bus as you get a chance to see the countryside and breathe fresh air. Expect to pay the driver the same rate as you would for a second-class bus fare – around US$1 an hour.

At **land borders**, some buses cross over to the adjacent country's terminal to drop off and pick up passengers. This simplifies transport and immigration, especially if the immigration posts and terminals are some distance apart. Heading further south in Central America, the best **international bus service** is the Ticabus, running from Guatemala City to Panamá City, calling at San Salvador, Managua and San José. The whole

journey takes two and a half days, including overnights (at your own expense) at San Salvador and Managua.

BY PLANE

With the exception of the Yucatán peninsula, most of the areas covered in this book are very mountainous, and though distances between the major sites may not look too lengthy on a map, rudimentary roads and difficult terrain mean that the going can be slow. So if time is tight, or you just can't face another bus journey, it's worth considering a flight – prices are generally very reasonable. Each country has an internal air network, and there are also numerous international flights within the region.

Within **Guatemala** the only flight that is really worth considering is from Guatemala City to Flores (for Tikal). Four airlines fly this route and prices start from a bargain US$60 return (though this fare reflects a ongoing price war and rates may well return to previous levels, still reasonable at US$90 return). A new domestic airline, Inter, offers numerous other destinations within Guatemala, but it has quickly developed a poor reputation for cancelling flights at short notice and changing schedules frequently. There also daily international connections from Guatemala

---

AIR PASSES

The best way to find out how (or if) an air pass will benefit you is to call JLA in the UK (☎0181/747-3018; *sales@journeylatinamerica.co.uk*); or contact eXito in the US (☎1-800/655-4053 or 510/655-2154; *exito@ wonderlink.com*; *www.wonderlink.com/exito*).

The Visit Central America Airpass

If want to visit the whole region in a fairly short time, this can cut costs considerably. For example, a routing Miami–Belize City–Guatemala City–Roatán–Miami will cost US$633 low season/US$697 high season (plus taxes) – at least one-third less than flying the same route on a normal ticket. The pass links North American gateways with all the capitals and some other cities in Central America, as well as some destinations in South America and the Caribbean – the possible routes are mind-boggling. You have to buy the pass (in the form of coupons for each flight) before leaving home, book your route in advance and

enter the region on one of the participating airlines (Aviateca, Copa, Lacsa, Nica and Taca). Free date changes are allowed if space is available (within the sixty-day validity of the pass), but a change of route will cost US$50.

The Mexipass International

This combines the extensive networks of Aeroméxico and Mexicana, linking North American gateways with Mexico and onto several Central and South American cities. Houston–Cancún–Guatemala City–Houston is US$695 (plus taxes).

The Mexipass Domestic

This is a final option if you want to travel extensively within Mexico. It's valid for travel with Aeroméxico, Mexicana, Aerocaribe and Aerocozumel airlines and there's a minimum purchase of three flights. Mexico City–Oaxaca–Tuxtla Gutierrez–overland to Mérida–Cancún is US$190.

to Cancún, Belize City and San Pedro Sula, and numerous flights south to Costa Rica (around US$150 return) and South America.

In **Belize** there are two scheduled domestic carriers and a number of charter airlines. The main routes are between Belize City and San Pedro (US$24 one way), Caye Caulker (US$24), Dangriga (US$28), Placencia (US$53) and Punta Gorda (US$68). Popular international destinations include Flores (for Tikal), Guatemala City, Chetumal and Cancún in Mexico, San Pedro Sula, La Ceiba and Roatán in Honduras and San Salvador.

In **Honduras** many people fly from San Pedro Sula (around US$40 one way) or La Ceiba (from US$15 one way) to the Bay Islands. From San Pedro Sula there are numerous international flights within the Maya region (Cancún US$140, Guatemala City and Belize City from US$90 one way) and also plenty of international departures to other Central American destinations, plus North and South America.

BY BOAT

Boats are the main form of transport in many parts of the Maya region. On the Caribbean coast (Isla Mujeres, Cozumel, the Belize cayes and the Honduran Bay Islands), boats, ferries and skiffs are an essential link between the islands and the mainland. There are also daily **sea connections** between Punta Gorda (Belize) and Puerto Barrios (Guatemala), and less regular boats connecting Puerto Cortés (Honduras) with Dangriga (Belize) and Puerto Barrios (Guatemala).

The isolated Garifúna village of Lívingston in Guatemala is only accessible by boat, either from Puerto Barrios or Río Dulce town, or by occasional speedboats from Omoa in Honduras and Punta Gorda in Belize. Within Guatemala, boats will get you around the three large **lakes** of Atitlán, Izabal and Petén Itzá, as well as the Río Dulce area. Finally, between the jungles of Chiapas in Mexico and Petén in Guatemala, the Río Usumacinta that divides the two nations has numerous **river connections** (see pp.136, 138, 139).

If you're a **canoe** enthusiast, an ideal base to explore Belize's river network is the town of San Ignacio where canoes are readily available to rent, whether for an hour or a week. **Sea kayaks** can be rented in Caye Caulker, Placencia and at a number of resorts in the Belize cayes and Guanaja and Roatán in the Bay Islands.

BY TAXI

Taxis are readily available at every international airport and from virtually every domestic terminal; prices to the city centre are usually fixed. In the main towns, drivers often loiter around the main plazas and transport terminals, but **meters** are a rarity – always fix a price before you set off. Taxis can also be a good substitute for a rental car; you have the advantage of your own transport without the responsibility of driving it, and it often works out cheaper for half-day excursions.

BY CAR

Prices vary a little for **car rental** throughout the region but are generally on the expensive side considering the relatively low cost of hotels and restaurants. In Mexico and Guatemala rates start from around US$250 a week for a standard car, but in Belize, where companies only offer sport/utility vehicles, the cheapest rate for a week is around US$400. In Honduras you can expect to pay from US$270 a week, while El Salvador has the cheapest rates – from US$200 a week.

If you plan to rent a car make sure you get a good map (see p.27) and bear in mind the high **accident rates**, and that as a foreigner any collision is likely to be construed as your fault. Always take full-cover insurance and beware that many companies will make you sign a "waiver" document so you are responsible for the first US$1000 of damage in the event of an accident or damage.

If you've succeeded in getting your own car here (see "Getting There" p.8), any further problems you face are likely to seem fairly minor. If you belong to a **motoring organization** at home, it's worth calling to see if they'll offer advice, maps and even help from reciprocal organizations in Mexico and Central America. **Security** is a major headache – always park in a safe place and never leave your car in the street overnight. Traffic is generally light outside the main cities and major routes are paved. **Fuel** is marginally more expensive than in the US but cheaper than in Europe, though filling stations are scarce outside the main cities. Unleaded fuel is now widely available in all countries.

BY BICYCLE AND MOTORBIKE

Motorbikes are not that common in the Maya region, and rental outlets few and far between. Expect to pay around US$25 a day for an old

200cc machine, including insurance and unlimited mileage. In Guatemala there are rental outlets in Panajachel and Antigua and in Mexico at the main resorts including Cancún and Cozumel.

Bicycles are everywhere in Central America, and increasing numbers of visitors bring their own. If you do, you'll find a repair shop in every town, though it will inevitably be difficult to find spare parts for high-tech models. Some buses can carry bikes on the roof, giving greater flexibility. Unfortunately, renting a bike is not usually good value, with prices from US$1 an hour or around US$7–10 a day (which is more than the average daily wage). Consequently few travellers choose to rent bikes here. For real two-wheeled enthusiasts, an excellent contact in Guatemala is Beat at Maya Mountain Bike Tours in Antigua .

Membership of the UK's Cyclists' Touring Club (69 Meadrow, Godalming, Surrey GU7 3HS ☎01483/417217; *cycling@ctc.org.uk*; *www.ctc. org.uk*) means you can access trip reports from cyclists who have taken bikes to Central America, as well as other information.

ACCOMMODATION

Accommodation comes in all shapes and sizes and it's usually not hard to find somewhere reasonable. Places go by a bewildering range of names; hotel, obviously, but you'll frequently see pensión, casa de huéspedes, hospedaje, posada and even parador. The different names don't always mean a great deal: in theory a casa de huéspedes is less formal than a hotel but in reality the main difference will be the price. Rancho and campamento usually refer to some form of camping. In English-speaking Belize and the Honduran Bay Islands you're more likely to find the words hotel, inn, guest house, lodge and resort used.

Most countries have some form of price (and in theory, quality) regulation and there's sometimes also a **hotel tax** to pay: always check if this included in the rate you're quoted. It's highly advisable to have a look at the room before you take it: make sure the light and fan work, and if you've been told there's hot water, find out what that means.

BUDGET ROOMS

Even if you're travelling through Central America on a tight budget you can expect reasonable levels of comfort and cleanliness in most **budget hotels**. In any town in the region (except in Belize) you should be able to find a clean double room for under US$10 a night, and in many places you'll pay half that. Inevitably, the better deals are

ACCOMMODATION PRICE CODES

All the accommodation listed in this book has been categorized into one of nine price bands, as set out below. The prices quoted are in US dollars and refer to the cheapest room available for two people sharing in high season.

① under US$5	④ US$15–25	⑦ US$60–80
② US$5–10	⑤ US$25–40	⑧ US$80–100
③ US$10–15	⑥ US$40–60	⑨ over S$100

often where young travellers congregate in large numbers: there are superb, cheap places around Lago de Atitlán and in San Cristóbal de las Casas and some good options in El Salvador.

A basic room in a **lowland** town will have a light and a fan (*ventilador*) in addition to the bed, though don't expect a reading light or anywhere to put clothes; many places also supply a towel, soap and toilet paper. In the **highlands** of Guatemala and Chiapas, a fan is rarely standard. It's much more important to check that there are sufficient blankets to keep out the cold and that there's hot water. Plenty of budget places also give you the option of a private bathroom (ie, a toilet and basic shower), which will typically add US$3–4 to the price of the room. It always works out much cheaper to **share a room** with other travellers; many hotels have rooms with three or four beds that are popular with local families. **Single travellers** will have to get used to paying at least seventy percent of the cost of a double room; we have indicated in the guide the places that offer good deals.

If the **price** seems a little high for the type of establishment, it's worth asking if there's a less expensive room (¿*Tiene un cuarto más barato, por favor?*) – you'll often get the same room at a lower price. It's always better to get a room at the back, away from the noise of the street, and upstairs you're more likely to benefit from a breeze. Most small hotels will be family run, and the owners usually take pride in the cleanliness of the rooms. There will usually be a place to hand-wash clothes (a *pila*); ask first before you use it. The very best cheap hotels in the smaller towns also have beautifully tended garden courtyards – perfect for sitting in the sun and reading.

As a rule, budget hotels in the **big cities** tend to be less attractive and more expensive than those in smaller towns and the tourist areas, though we've listed the exceptions in the relevant chapters. In the bigger cities it's worth paying a little more or even moving to one grade of hotel higher than you might otherwise be, to stay in a more secure place – particularly for your first night. Cheap hotels are often crowded around bus stations and markets; some of these can be very dismal, being used by prostitutes and their clients. However, in every capital there are at least one or two hotels where other travellers congregate (as well as plenty where they don't) to offer company and perhaps security.

Budget hotels in **rural areas** or **coastal locations** not geared to the tourist market are usually quite basic: a ramshackle building or perhaps a stick-and-thatch cabaña. These can be delightful – you'll be less of a guest and more like an extra member of the family – but they can also be very uncomfortable, with lumpy mattresses and poor ventilation. This is where serviceable insect proofing can make the difference between misery and a good night's sleep.

Booking ahead for a budget room is not usually necessary (and often not possible as most don't have phones), though it might be worth trying at busy times like Christmas and Easter. Otherwise, arriving early at your destination will give you a better selection.

HOTELS, RESORTS AND LODGES

If you spend around US$20–25 for a double room, you can expect a fairly plain but clean room with a private bathroom – often with hot water in the highlands, and with a fan or air conditioning in the lowlands. There are plenty of excellent deals in the **mid-range** price bracket and you'll find the better places make an effort to decorate the room attractively, sometimes with wall-hangings or textiles. You can also expect better-quality mattresses and perhaps a reading light or a writing desk. Generally, the differences between a hotel in the **upper mid-range** (US$40–80) and the luxury price bracket come down to facilities: you'll rarely find a swimming pool or gym, the in-house restaurant (if there is one) will be less ambitious, and there may be no service after 10pm. Nevertheless, you'll find there are some very attractive, enjoyable places to stay in the mid-range bracket, many with real colonial character and lovely gardens, and lacking the "corporate" feel of many of the luxury places.

Moving into the **luxury hotel** end of the market (above US$80), certain features become virtually standard. Hotels will usually have a swimming pool and health facilities, a restaurant or two, landscaped gardens, manicured lawns and sometimes a tennis court, and often all sorts of shops offering overpriced touristy trinkets. Many have in-house tourism desks from where you'll be able to organize excursions. Rooms will nearly always have air conditioning (*aire acondicionado*), tea- and coffee-making facilities and often a couple of double beds. Service levels should also be good. The major disadvantage with many of the large hotels at this level is that they can be frighteningly impersonal places where all sense of the region is lost once you're behind the security gates. For this reason we prefer to recommend the smaller-scale luxury options, of which there are many. Service facilities may not be able to match the larger hotels, but the pay-off is that they are often located in wonderfully atmospheric colonial buildings, with individually decorated rooms, delightful mature gardens full of flowering shrubs and shady trees. They are also often locally or foreign (rather than corporation) owned.

Some of the most spectacular accommodation is found in the network of upmarket **jungle lodges**, mainly in Belize, which are often in beautiful, remote locations in or near national parks. Here you'll often have a private thatched cabaña, with a balcony overlooking the forest, lake or other natural attraction. Many of these places charge upwards of US$150 a night, though the experience of a rainforest dawn chorus and the chance of getting close to wildlife can make the cost worthwhile. They are often used by adventure and nature tour operators (see pp.6, 10, 13), and occupancy varies with the season; if the lodge is open out of season, ask about possible discounts.

There are also an increasing number of luxury **beach resorts** being developed in the Honduran Bay Islands and the Belizean cayes. Many of these are geared to scuba-divers on all-in packages

booked in North America or Europe and are often prohibitively expensive for the independent traveller. The best of these places in Guanaja, Roatán, Ambergris Caye and Placencia offer wonderful environments for divers, where almost everything is organized around the reef, tanks, fins and compressed air – though non-divers will probably feel alienated by the one topic of conversation.

YOUTH HOSTELS, CAMPING AND HAMMOCKS

The region is so full of inexpensive hotels that you'll rarely need to consider staying in a **youth hostel**, which is just as well as they are extremely rare. There are five hostels in southern Mexico (including Campeche and Cancún), but you'll probably pay the same as in a budget hotel and have to sleep in a single-sex dorm and conform to silly curfew rules. There are also woefully few **campsites**, primarily because camping has yet to catch on with the locals. You'll only need a tent and a sleeping bag if you're hiking right off the beaten track, climbing a volcano or jungle trekking. A **hammock** can be useful, especially by the beach in Quintana Roo or Belize; some of the finest in the world are manufactured in Mérida, and they make great souvenirs too.

EATING AND DRINKING

Corn and beans, the key essentials of the Maya diet, have been grown in the region for thousands of years. Though there are numer-ous methods of preparation, most meals are still incomplete without a portion of these twin staples, often seasoned with chilli. The food in the south of the region is uniformly Central American, with corn tortillas, beans and eggs on almost every menu. Cuisine is not a particular highlight of Belize either, though there are some excellent seafood dishes. Southern Mexico offers the most varied menus, including some superb Yucatecan specialities.

The monotony of the Central American diet can get to travellers after a while. Fortunately, however, there is a tremendous variety of food available in the big cities and main tourist centres, as enterprising locals and foreigners have opened restaurants to cater for the more adventurous gringo tastebuds. In places like San Cristóbal de las Casas, Panajachel, Antigua and Utila, there is ethnic food from all over the world on offer: Thai and Indian curries, vegetarian wholefood, Mediterranean specialities, all-American favourites and even Middle Eastern and Japanese dishes. Much of this culinary smorgasbord may not be very authentic, but if you've spent any time in the wilds subsisting on a diet of eggs, beans and tortillas, this cosmopolitan eating scene will come as quite a relief.

WHERE TO EAT

Except for the very rich, the people of the Maya world cannot regularly afford to eat out. Most **basic restaurants** reflect this and serve simple, filling food at low prices. The very cheapest place to eat is always the **comedor**, which is a basic eatery with a very simple line-up of dishes costing US$1–2. Often there's no menu (*carta*), so you'll have to ask what's on offer or look inside the bubbling pots. You'll almost always be able to get something to suit **vegetarians**, as any comedor will have eggs, beans and tortillas or tacos. There will also be fried chicken (*pollo frito*), steak (*bistek*) and soups (*caldos*). Many places do a set lunch menu (*comida corrida* or *menú del día*) which is usually an excellent deal, comprising three courses for around US$2, sometimes less. In Belize, you can count on getting rice and beans and fried chicken, but you'll have pay more: reckon on at least US$3 a meal.

Upmarket restaurants only exist in the big cities or the main tourist centres. They tend to be more formal and expensive, but except in the tourist places, the menu will be pretty familiar, dominated by meat dishes. There are also thousands of **fast-food** joints, all modelled on the American originals. Prices are high compared to comedor nosh (around US$3 a meal) and for many locals a trip to *McDonald's* or *Pollo Campero* is a big treat.

Finally, there is some excellent **street food** available, some of the most common offerings being pupusas, tacos and tamales (see p.35), and you'll find *papas fritas* (fried potato chips) almost everywhere. You should exercise a little caution with street food, however, as hygiene standards are somewhat variable.

WHAT TO EAT

Corn (*maíz*) is the single most important ingredient in the Maya diet – the ancient Maya even believed that they originated from it – and it's most commonly consumed as a **tortilla**, a thin, flat pancake made from cornflour that accompanies almost every meal in the region (except in Belize). The maize is traditionally ground by hand and shaped by clapping it between two hands – though in Mexico, tortilla presses are now widespread. It is cooked on a **comal**, a hot plate made of metal or clay, and usually brought to the table wrapped in cloth. Tortillas should be eaten while warm as they don't stay fresh for very long. The very best tortillas have a delicate taste and a pliable texture; if you're served hard, leathery tortillas, you should send them back. The slightly burnt, smoky taste of tortillas will become very much a part of your trip.

Tortillas can be adapted in a multitude of different ways, especially in Mexico where **tacos** (fried, rolled tortillas stuffed with almost anything), **enchiladas** (baked stuffed tortillas) and **quesadillas** (toasted tortillas wrapped around a cheese filing) are ubiquitous. In El Salvador and Guatemala the **pupusa** (a thick, toasted tortilla topped with ingredients including avocado, refried beans and cheese, and served with crunchy cabbage and carrot) is more common, while in Honduras the most popular snack is a **baleada** (tortilla stuffed with beans and cheese). **Tamales** (maize dough, steamed in a banana leaf and stuffed with a little meat or something sweet) are popular throughout the region.

Beans (*frijoles*) are the second essential item in the Maya diet. The beans themselves are either of the black or pinto variety and they are usually served in two ways: *volteados* (or *refritos*), where the beans are boiled, mashed, and then refried in a great dollop; or *parados*, which are whole boiled beans, often prepared with a few slices of onion and served in their own black juice. For breakfast, beans are usually served refried with eggs and cream, and at other times of the day they're often offered up on a separate plate to the main dish. Almost all truly Maya meals include a portion of beans, and for many of the region's indigenous people, beans are the only regular source of protein.

Chillies (*chiles*) are the final essential ingredient of Maya cuisine, sometimes placed raw or pickled in the middle of the table in a jar, but also served as a sauce – *salsa picante*. With over a hundred different varieties, the strength can vary tremendously, so treat them with caution until you know what you're dealing with. In Mexico the

A GLOSSARY OF FOOD AND DRINK TERMS

Basics

arroz	rice	*leche*	milk	*sal*	salt
azúcar	sugar	*mantequilla*	butter	*salsa*	sauce
carne	meat	*pan*	bread	*verduras/*	vegetables
crema	cream	*pescado*	fish	*legumbres*	
ensalada	salad	*pimienta*	pepper		
huevos	eggs	*queso*	cheese		

Soups (*sopas*) and starters

caldo	broth (with bits in)	*entremeses*	hors d'oeuvres
		sopa	soup
ceviche	raw fish salad, marinated in lime juice	*de arroz*	with rice
		de fideos	with noodles
		de lentejas	lentil
consome	consommé	*de verduras*	vegetable

Eggs (*huevos*)

con jamón	with ham	*rancheros*	fried and smothered in a hot chilli sauce
a la Mexicana	scrambled with tomato, onion and mild chilli sauce	*revueltos*	scrambled
motuleños	fried, served on a tortilla with ham, cheese and salsa	*tibios*	lightly boiled
		con tocino	with bacon

Snacks (*antojitos*)

baleada	tortilla stuffed with cheese and refried beans	*pan de coco*	coconut bread
burritos	wheatflour tortillas, rolled and filled	*pupusa*	toasted tortilla served with assorted toppings and raw vegetables
chilaquiles	torn-up tortillas cooked with meat and sauce	*quesadillas*	toasted or fried tortillas with cheese
chiles rellenos	stuffed peppers	*queso fundido*	melted cheese, served with tortillas and salsa
chuchito	stuffed maize dumpling		
enchiladas	rolled-up tacos, covered in chilli sauce and baked	*sopes*	smaller bite-size versions of tostadas
enchiladas suizas	as above, in sour cream	*tacos*	fried tortillas with filling
flautas	small rolled tortillas filled with meat or chicken and then fried	*tacos al pastor*	tacos filled with pork
gorditas	small, fat, stuffed corn tortillas	*tamales*	cornmeal pudding, usually stuffed and steamed in banana leaves
machaca	shredded dried meat scrambled with eggs	*tlacoyo*	fat tortilla stuffed with beans
molletes	split torta covered in beans and melted cheese, often with ham and avocado too	*torta*	filled bread roll
		tostadas	flat crispy tortillas piled with meat and salad

Fish and seafood (*pescados y mariscos*)

anchoas	anchovies	*filete entero*	whole, filleted fish	*ostión*	oyster
atún	tuna			*pez espada*	swordfish
cabrilla	sea Bass	*huachinango*	red Snapper	*pulpo*	octopus
calamares	squid	*jurel*	yellowtail	*robalo*	bass
camarones	prawns	*langosta*	crawfish (rock lobster)	*sardinas*	sardines
cangrejo	crab			*tiburón*	shark
corvina Blanca	white sea bass	*langostinos*	king prawns	*trucha*	trout
dorado	dolphin (mahi mahi)	*lenguado*	sole		
		merluza	hake		*continued overleaf*

A GLOSSARY OF FOOD AND DRINK TERMS contd

Meat (*carne*) and Poultry (*aves*)

alambre	kebab	chorizo	spicy sausage	milanesa	breaded
albóndigas	meatballs	chuleta	chop		escalope
barbacoa	barbecued meat	codorniz	quail	pata	feet
bistec	steak (not	conejo	rabbit	pato	duck
	always beef)	cordero	lamb	pavo/guajolote	turkey
cabeza	head	costilla	rib	pechuga	breast
cabrito	kid	filete	tenderloin/fillet	pierna	leg
carne (de res)	beef	guisado	stew	pollo	chicken
carne adobado	barbecued/	hígado	liver	salchicha	hot dog or
	spicily stewed	lengua	tongue		salami
	meat	longaniza	cooked spicy	ternera	veal
carnitas	spicy pork		sausage	tocino	bacon
cerdo	pork	lomo	loin (of pork)	tripa/callos	tripe
chivo	goat	machaca	shredded meat	venado	venison

Vegetables (*legumbres, verduras*)

aceitunas	olives	ejotes	green beans	papas	potatoes
aguacate	avocado	elote	corn on the cob	pepino	cucumber
betabel	beetroot (often	espáragos	asparagus	plátano	plantain
	as a juice)	frijoles	beans	rajas	strips of green
calabacita	zucchini	hongos	mushrooms		pepper
	(courgette)	jitomate	red tomato	tomate	green tomato
calabaza	squash	lechuga	lettuce	zanahoria	carrot
cebolla	onion	lentejas	lentils		
champiñones	mushrooms	nopales	prickly pear		
chícharos	peas		leaves,		
col	cabbage		something		
coliflor	cauliflower		like squash		

Fruits (*fruta*) and juices (*jugos*)

chabacano	apricot	mamey	like a large zapote, with
cherimoya	custard apple (sweetsop)		sweet pink flesh and a big pip
ciruelas	tiny yellow plums	mango	mango
coco	coconut	manzana	apple
durazno	peach	melón	melon
frambuesas	raspberries	naranja	orange
fresas	strawberries	papaya	papaya
granada	yellow passion fruit	piña	pineapple
guanabana	soursop, like a large custard	plátano	banana
	apple	sandía	watermelon
guayaba	guava	toronja	grapefruit
higos	figs	tuna	prickly pear (cactus fruit)
limón	lime	uvas	grapes
		zapote	sapodilla (*chicu*), fruit of the
			chicle tree

Sweets (*dulces, postres*)

ate	quince paste	crepas	pancakes	helado	ice cream
cajeta	caramel confection	ensalada de	fruit salad	nieve	sorbet
	often served	frutas		pastel	cake
	with...	flan	crème caramel		

Common terms

asado/a	roast		chocolate and spices –
barbacoa/pibil	wrapped in leaves and herbs and steamed/cooked in a pit		served with chicken or turkey
empanado/a	breaded	*a la parrilla*	grilled
frito	fried	*a la plancha*	grilled
al horno	baked	*a la Veracruzana*	usually fish, cooked with
al mojo de ajo	fried in garlic and butter*con*		tomatoes and onions
mole	the most famous of Mexican sauces containing chile,	*a la tampiqueña*	meat in thin strips served with guacamole and enchiladas

class of the salsa can even give some indication as to the quality of the restaurant – there are some tremendous raw salsas made with tomato, chilli, coriander and onion, or cooked salsas made with tomato, onion and chilli.

The most commonly eaten **meat** is chicken (*pollo*), with beef (*res*) and pork (*cerdo*) being a little less common. Steak is *bistec de res* and a hamburger is a *hamburguesa*. Every comedor or restaurant will have something for the committed carnivore. Meats are fried (*frito*), grilled/broiled (*a la plancha* or *a la parrilla*), roasted (*asado*) or breaded (*empanado*). In basic comedores the meat is generally tough, but in steakhouses some choice cuts are available. Other traditional Maya dishes include a superb range of **stews** – known as *caldos* – made with duck, beef, chicken or turkey.

You'll find **eggs** on almost every menu, most commonly fried, scrambled or poached, but there are also some uniquely Mexican combinations: *huevos rancheros* are fried eggs in a rich tomato-based salsa sauce and *huevos motuleños* are eggs cooked with tomato, salsa, cheese and peas on a bed of tortillas.

CREOLE FOOD

At its best, **Creole** food can be delicious, taking the best from the sea and mixing it with the smooth taste of coconut and mild spices. All along the eastern coast between Belize and Honduras you'll find the influence of Africa and the Caribbean is never far away, with plantain, cassava and breadfruit all part of culinary tradition, but sadly not always present in the region's restaurants. Conch soup, *pan de coco* (coconut bread) and *tapada* (fish, potatoes and vegetables including yucca) are all specialities. **Fish** is an essential part of the Creole diet: you'll find shark

steak, red snapper, barracuda and grouper all on the menu.

At its worst, Creole food can be something of a neglected art, conforming to a single recipe – the ubiquitous **rice and beans** – and a few other bland, starchy dishes. If you're lucky, your rice and beans may be injected with a bit more interest in the form of a little fish, chicken or beef and perhaps a side portion of fried plantain.

Seafood is almost always excellent, with superb fresh shrimp and crab. On San Pedro and Caye Caulker in Belize, the food is often exceptional, and the only worry is that you might get bored with **lobster**, which is served in an amazing range of dishes. You may want to avoid eating lobster in Honduras, however: over-collection has led to local divers having to spend more and more time underwater chasing fewer and fewer lobsters – a practice which has caused many deaths.

VEGETARIAN FOOD

Most people in the region eat as much meat as they can afford (which may be daily or just once a month) and vegetarianism is almost unknown anywhere in the region. To check if something is suitable, ask if it's *sin carne* (without meat); locals may not consider chicken to be a meat, however, so you may want to ask if it's *sin pollo* too. You'll certainly have no problem getting something to eat in any town or village, with eggs, beans, tortillas or rice and beans always available and fresh fruit everywhere. Popular **vegetarian dishes** include *chiles rellenos* (stuffed peppers) and *quesadillas*. Street food is often prepared without meat, so you could try pupusas, tostadas and tamales.

If things get a bit desperate, head for a Chinese restaurant or a pizzeria – both are common in the region. Mercifully, in the main tourist centres you won't usually have to explain your eating preferences and there will be many more cosmopolitan possibilities to enjoy, including salads, hummus and falafel.

DRINKING

The basic **drinks** to accompany food are water, fizzy drinks and beer. If you're drinking water, stick to bottled stuff (*agua mineral* or *agua pura*); it comes either plain (*sin gas*) or carbonated (*con gas*). Fizzy drinks (*refrescos* or *aguas*) such as Coca-Cola, Pepsi and Fanta are on sale everywhere.

JUICES AND SHAKES

Real fruit juices (*jugos*) and fruit shakes (*licuados*) are very common and a good healthy treat. **Juices** can be squeezed from anything that will go through the extractor. Orange (*naranja*) and carrot (*zanahoria*) are the staples, but you should also experiment with some of the more obscure tropical fruits. **Licuados** are made of fruit mixed with water (*con agua*) or milk (*con leche*) in a blender. They are always fantastic, but watch out for the five or six spoons of sugar that the locals normally take – you might want to ask for yours without sugar (*sin azúcar*). You could also try *limonada* (fresh lemonade) or *aguas frescas* – flavoured cold drinks: *agua de arroz*, a delicious drink like iced rice pudding, *agua de jamaica* (hibiscus) or *de tamarindo* (tamarind). The danger is that some of these drinks may not be made with purified water (*agua purificada*) – if you're suspicious, try a licuado made with milk.

COFFEE AND TEA

Coffee is the principal export crop of the Maya region, though, regretfully, this status is seldom reflected in the quality of the cup you'll be served. There are some exceptional coffee blends available, but you'll usually only get an export-quality brew in the very upmarket or foreign-owned establishments.

In its basic form, *café solo* or *negro*, coffee is strong, black, often sweet (ask for it *sin azúcar* for no sugar), and comes in small cups. For weaker black coffee, ask for *café americano*, though be warned that you may be given instant; if you do want instant, ask for Nescafé. White coffee is *café con leche* in most of the region, but known as *café cortado* or *con un pocito de leche* in Mexico. *Café con leche* in Mexico is made with all milk and no water (check if it's *hecho de leche*).

Espresso and cappuccino are occasionally available in Mexico and are extremely rare elsewhere.

Tea (*té*) can often be found, and you may well be offered a cup at the end of a comida. Usually it's some kind of herb tea like *manzanillo* (camomile) or *yerbabuena* (mint). If you get the chance to try traditional hot chocolate, "the drink of the Aztecs", then do so – it's an extraordinary, spicy, semi-bitter concoction, quite unlike the milky bedtime drink of your childhood.

ALCOHOL

Beer (*cerveza*) is generally good everywhere in the region. Mostly light, lager-style brews, bottles typically cost a dollar a bottle (US$1.75 in Belize). In Mexico the main **lager** beers are Bohémia, Superior, Dos Equis and Tecate (the last normally served with lemon and salt). The Belizean beer, Belikin, comes in three varieties. In Guatemala, Gallo has a near monopoly but is pretty bland; the premium Montelcarlo is better. All the four Honduran beers are made by the same company and tend to be refreshing rather than intoxicating, while El Salvador has maybe the best beers in the region, including Pilsner and Suprema. **Dark beer** (*cerveza obscura*) is available too. In Mexico there are three main varieties: Indio, Tres Equis and the excellent Negra Modelo. In Belize there is a good Belikin stout, and in Guatemala, Moza beer makes an interesting, flavoursome change from the ubiquitous Gallo.

Wine (*vino* – *tinto* for red, *blanco* for white) only makes an appearance in very upmarket restaurants, where a reasonable bottle will cost at least US$10; Chilean wines are usually the best value. In supermarkets, a reasonable bottle of Chilean or Argentinean wine will cost about US$5, though there are litre cartons of cheaper stuff on sale too. Mexico produces a fair number of perfectly good wines. You're safest sticking to the brand names like Hidalgo or Domecq.

As for **spirits**, the most famous is Mexico's **tequila**, derived from the maguey plant, though it is rarely drunk in any other country in the region. The best stuff is aged (*añejo* or *reposado*) for smoothness; try Sauza Hornitos, which is powerful, or Commemorativo, which is unexpectedly gentle on the throat. **Mescal** (often spelt mezcal) is basically the same drink, made from a slightly different type of maguey plant and younger and less refined. **Pulque**, a mildly alcoholic milky beer made from the same cactus, is the traditional drink of the poor and sold in special bars called *pulquerías*. Surprisingly, margaritas (tequila, orange liqueur, fresh lime juice) are seldom drunk outside the tourist bars.

Rum (*ron*) is the most important spirit outside Mexico and each country has a good brand or two. Prices are low, with a 75cl bottle costing as little as US$3 and a better-quality brand US$5. Flor de Caña from Honduras is many travellers' favourite, while some people favour the Guatemalan Zacapa Centenario and Ron Botran Añejo. Guatemala, Honduras and El Salvador all produce **aguardiente**, a fire-water made from sugar cane, whose power is at the heart of many

a fiesta; in Guatemala, Quezalteca is the most popular brand. In Honduras, Yuscarán is a national institution, often blended with herbs and plants. Drinking international liquor brands is extremely expensive anywhere in the Maya area; just ask for *nacional* if you want the local variety.

The best atmosphere for drinking any of these is in hotel bars or tourist areas. Traditional **cantinas** are for serious and excessive drinking, have a thoroughly threatening, macho atmosphere and are barred to women most of the time, though big-city cantinas can be more liberal.

MAIL, PHONES AND THE INTERNET

Mail and telecommunication services in Central America are very variable. Generally postal services are very cheap but unreliable, and even the locals use courier companies to send important packages and documents overseas; in Belize, however, things are more efficient. Local telephone and fax connections are very cheap throughout the region and long-distance national calls are not too pricey. International calls are extremely expensive, however, with rates way above what you'd pay in North America or Europe. On the other hand, Internet cafés and facilities are developing fast throughout the region and are increasingly evident wherever foreigners gather.

MAIL

When sending mail home, the best way to ensure speedy delivery is to use the **main post office** in

a capital city; this will also be the best place to send parcels. **Post boxes** are rare – you'll find them in the lobbies of big hotels and some tourist shops, but the best bet is to take mail to a post office. As a rule of thumb, an airmail letter to the US takes about a week and to Europe from ten days to two weeks. **Receiving mail** is less certain, but you can generally rely on the service in main post offices. Letters (with your surname underlined) should be sent to Lista de Correos (or General Delivery in Belize), Correo Central, name of city, country, and finishing with Central America. When looking to see if mail has arrived, ask to see the Lista de Correos, which is usually typed up each day, and search for your name (check whether mail is being held under your forename or surname). You'll need identification – a passport is best – and there's sometimes a small fee to collect your mail.

Always use some form of registration for **parcels**; it won't cost much more than the postage and you'll get a certificate to give you some sort of peace of mind. You can send parcels via surface mail but this takes months. Be prepared for the parcel to undergo some form of inspection, and there may also be some quirky labelling and wrapping regulations to observe.

Specialist **courier companies** (DHL, Federal Express etc) are establishing more and more offices throughout the region and even small towns now have offices. Obviously the charges involved are way above the standard postal rates, but they do represent the safest method of sending packages or documents home.

PHONES

Although telephone systems are gradually improving, local technology is still pretty primitive and connections are not always what they should be. **Local calls** are always cheap (some hotels in Mexico won't even charge you), but call boxes are not particularly widespread anywhere so it's often better to call from your hotel. Long-distance domestic calls are not too expensive either. In Mexico it's more cost-effective to use a telephone card for these.

Unfortunately, you'll have to pay a lot for **international calls**. In Mexico you'll be charged US$3 per minute to the US and an incredible US$7 a minute to call Europe. In Belize the same calls cost US$3.20 and US$6 a minute, respectively. In El Salvador and Guatemala, it's US$8 for a three-minute call to Europe. In Honduras, a three-minute call is US$19 to the UK or Australia, and US$8 to the US. Taking a telephone charge card or calling card with you is a good idea. Most North American cards work throughout the region, but at present UK-issued cards only function in Mexico and Belize.

A number of communication businesses have opened recently in tourist areas throughout the region, which can cut the cost of making international calls considerably; they often offer **email** and Internet services too. In Guatemala, for example, the soon-to-be-privatized Telgua company charges US$8 for a three-minute call to the UK, whereas private businesses charge from US$5.40 to US$6 for the same call. **Calling home collect** (*llamar por cobrar*) is fairly simple from most countries. North Americans are able to call collect from any country, but you can only call the UK collect from Mexico and Belize. Before leaving home, it's worth checking whether any phone company in your country has a number to call abroad which can connect you with the operator.

You should be able to send (and receive) a **fax** from any (largish) telephone office in the region, and it's often easier than making a phone call.

THE INTERNET

Online services are becoming more and more widespread in the Maya region. You'll find **cyber-cafés** in the capital cities and most of the major tourist centres, so if you have a service provider which allows you to pick up email anywhere, you can check your mail while abroad. Before you go, look at *www.netcafeguide.com* and click on the Latin America map to check out the locations.

THE MEDIA

The press in the Maya region tends to be somewhat limited in international coverage, though there are some **English-language publications** which provide useful information and are readily available everywhere except El Salvador. **Television** tends to be dominated by American broadcasts, though you might find some interesting local programmes.

The **BBC World Service** in English can be picked up by radios with short wave on 5975KHz in the 49m band, especially in the evening, on 15,220KHz in the 25m band, especially in the morning, and on 17,840KHz, especially in the afternoon. Other possible frequencies include: 6175KHz, 6195KHz, 9590KHz and 9895KHz. **The Voice of America** broadcasts on 15,210KHz, 11,740KHz, 9815KHz and 6030Khz.

MEXICO

There are two main **English-language newspapers** in Mexico. *The News* is a frumpy US-orient-ed organ which you'll find pretty much anywhere with a significant English-speaking presence. Far better is the broadsheet, *Mexico City Times*, which has the usual wire stories and incisive pieces from the *New York Times* and Britain's *Economist* and *Independent;* the Saturday issue even includes the Latin American edition of the *Guardian Weekly*. *Time* and *Newsweek* are easily available too.

Of the **domestic newspapers**, few carry much foreign news, and what there is is mainly Latin American; they are usually lurid scandal sheets, full of violent crime depicted in full colour. While each state has its own press, most are little more than government propaganda. The best national paper if you read Spanish is *La Jornada*, which is quite daringly critical of government policy, especially in Chiapas, and whose journalists regularly face death threats as a result.

On Mexican **TV** you can watch any number of US shows dubbed into Spanish, and cable and satellite are now widespread; even quite downmarket hotels offer numerous channels, many of them American.

Radio stations in the capital, Guadalajara and other major towns have programmes in English for a couple of hours each day, and in many places US broadcasts can also be picked up.

GUATEMALA

By far the most useful **English-language newspaper** published in Guatemala is the quite excellent (and free) *Siglo News,* which will give you an authoritative insight into this complicated country and help keep you informed of the current security situation. Two other free publications worth picking up are the monthly *Revue* and *Guatemala Weekly,* which are more lightweight and advertisement-driven, though both have their relative merits. The *Weekly* contains edited stories from Central American Report, the region's best news agency. You can pick up copies of all the above at the major hotels and many restaurants in Antigua, Guatemala City and Panajachel, as well as other tourist centres around the country. *Time, Newsweek* and occasionally the *Economist* are all sold in bookstores in Antigua and the top hotels in Guatemala City, and you may find the odd US newspaper too – *USA Today* or the *Miami Herald.* The best domestic Spanish-language daily newspapers are the outspoken *El Periódico* and the reliable *Siglo Veintiuno,* but both are less readily available than the mainstream, conservative *Prensa Libre.*

Television stations are in plentiful supply. Viewers can choose from five local channels and over a dozen satellite channels, all of them dominated by American programmes. CNN news is readily available. Guatemala has an abundance of **radio stations**, though variety is not their strong point: most transmit a turgid stream of Latin rock, cheesy merengue and evangelical rantings.

BELIZE

Belize's English-language media can make a welcome break in a world of Spanish, but this doesn't necessarily mean that it's very easy to keep in touch with what's happening in the rest of the world. Local news is reported in a very nationalistic manner but international events get very little attention. In Belize City, Belmopan, San Pedro and occasionally in some other towns, you should be able to get hold of some foreign newspapers. Satellite TV is widespread, and the best source of American news.

The four national **newspapers**: *The People's Pulse, The Reporter, The Belize Times* and *The Amandala* (all published weekly on Friday), mostly stick to a party line, and some are acutely xenophobic, though there's usually an interesting article or two. There are also free tourist newspapers: *The Belize Sun* (national), the *San Pedro Sun* (Ambergris Caye) and *Village Voice* (Caye Caulker).

There are two more-or-less national **television stations**: Channel 5, producing superb news and factual programmes, and the populist Channel 7, which shows an almost uninterrupted stream of imported American shows. Cable TV (mostly pirated from satellite) is the nation's preferred viewing medium, giving saturation coverage of American soaps, talk shows, sports, films and CNN. Of the main **radio** stations, Radio Belize (91.1 FM) is talk-based and transmits the BBC World Service from midnight to 6am. Friends FM (89.9FM) is music-based, as is Love FM (95.1FM), which also has a controversial phone-in.

HONDURAS

The most useful **publications** for travellers are *Honduras This Week,* a weekly English-language newspaper with in-depth coverage of events in Honduras, plus tourist and business information, and *Honduras Tips,* a free tourism magazine with plenty of good information and features. You'll find both in the big hotels in Copán, San Pedro Sula, La Ceiba and Roatán. Of local interest are two Bay Island-based publications, the *Utila Times* and the Roatán-based *Coconut Telegraph.*

Of the six daily Spanish-language newspapers, *El Tiempo,* based in San Pedro Sula is the most liberal and is regularly critical of the government and armed forces. The conservative *La Prensa* has the biggest circulation and the best international coverage.

There are over 150 **radio** stations in Honduras and numerous cable networks with US programmes, usually broadcast in English with Spanish subtitles.

EL SALVADOR

There's are no useful publications for travellers in El Salvador. Of the four national Spanish-language **newspapers**, the morning *La Prensa Gráfica* and *El Diario de Hoy* are widely read and very conservative; the afternoon *CoLatino* is the most left-wing.

There are over seventy **radio** stations, and seven national **television** channels, plus cable companies which broadcast programmes from the US, Spain and CNN news.

OPENING HOURS AND HOLIDAYS

Most offices, shops, post offices, museums and government offices are open Monday to Friday from 8.30am to 5pm throughout the region, though some take a break for lunch. On Saturdays, government offices are closed and some museums and post offices open from 9am until noon, but most shops are open all day.

Banking hours are generally similar, with most branches being open until 4pm (earlier in Mexico) and on Saturday mornings as well. In Guatemala, opening hours are extremely convenient, with many banks staying open until 7pm (and some as late as 8pm) from Monday to Friday and until 1pm on Saturdays.

On principal **public holidays** (see box below) almost all businesses close down, and in addition, each village or town will also have its own fiesta or saint's day when everything will be shut. These can last anything from one day to two weeks. The siesta tradition persists in the Yucatán, where some shops close for the hottest part of the day.

Archeological sites are open every day, usually from 8am to 5pm. At Tikal, the hours are even more relaxed (6am to 6pm, or 8pm with permission).

FIESTAS

Traditional fiestas are one of the great excitements of a trip to the Maya region, and every town and village, however small, devotes at least one day a year to celebration. The date is normally prescribed by the local saint's day and the main day is always marked by a climactic event, though the party often extends to a week or two around that date. On almost every day of the year there's a fiesta in some corner of the region, and with a bit of planning or a stroke of luck you should be able to witness at least one.

The format of fiestas varies between three basic models: ladino, Maya and Creole. In towns with a largely **ladino** population, fairs are usually set up and the days are filled with processions,

PUBLIC HOLIDAYS

January
1 New Year's Day
February
5 Anniversary of the Constitution (Mexico)
24 Flag Day (Mexico)
March
9 Baron Bliss Day (Belize)
21 Benito Juárez Day (Mexico)
Easter week (*Semana Santa*) in March or April
April
14 Day of the Americas (Honduras)
May
1 Labour Day
5 Battle of Puebla (Mexico)
24 Commonwealth Day (Belize)
June
30 Army Day (Guatemala)
August
3-6 El Salvador del Mundo (El Salvador)
September
1 Presidential address to the nation (Mexico)

10 National Day (Belize)
15 Independence Day (Guatemala, Honduras, El Salvador)
16 Independence Day (Mexico)
21 Independence Day (Belize)
October
3 Birth of Francisco Morazán (Honduras)
12 Discovery of America Day (El Salvador, Guatemala, Mexico, Belize)
20 Revolution Day (Guatemala)
21 Armed Forces Day (Honduras)
November
1 All Saints' Day (Mexico)
2 Day of the Dead (El Salvador, Mexico)
19 Garífuna Settlement Day (Belize)
20 Anniversary of the Revolution (Mexico)
December
12 Virgin of Guadalupe (Mexico)
24 Christmas Eve (Mexico)
25 Christmas Day
26 Boxing Day (Belize)

beauty contests and perhaps the odd marching band and plenty of fireworks, while the nights are dominated by dancing to merengue rhythms. In the Guatemalan and Chiapas highlands (and to a lesser extent in the Maya villages of Belize and Yucatán), where the bulk of the population is **Maya**, it's a different world. Here you'll see traditional dances, costumes and musicians, and a blend of religious and secular celebration that incorporates elements which predate the arrival of the Spanish. **Creole** celebrations are unabashedly hedonistic affairs, much more like a Caribbean carnival, with floats, earth-shaking reggae basslines, rum punch and plenty of grinding hips.

What they all share is an astonishing energy and an unbounded enthusiasm for drink, dance and fireworks, all three of which are virtually impossible to escape during the days of fiesta. One thing you shouldn't expect is anything too dainty or organized: fiestas are, above all, chaotic, and the measured rhythms of traditional dance

and music are usually obscured by the crush of the crowd and the huge volumes of alcohol consumed by participants. If you join in the mood, there's no doubt that fiestas are wonderfully entertaining and that they offer a real insight into the region's culture, ladino or *indígena*. Guatemala has some of the most spectacular fiestas, and the best include some specifically local element, such as the giant kites at **Santiago Sacatepéquez**, the religious processions in **Antigua** and the horse race in **Todos Santos**.

At certain times virtually the whole region erupts simultaneously: **Semana Santa** (Easter week) is perhaps the most important, but **November 1 and 2** (All Saints' Day and the Day of the Dead) and Christmas are also marked by partying across the area. **Independence Day** in Guatemala, Honduras and El Salvador is September 15 – another huge day for processions and celebrations.

MUSIC AND DANCE

Music and dance combine many different influences, but yet again they can be broadly divided between indigenous, ladino and Creole. For the ladinos, it's merengue, salsa and Latin house that get the punters grooving, and for the Creoles it's reggae and soca, but in many indigenous areas, dance is usually confined to fiestas, and in the highland villages this means traditional dances, heavily infused with history and symbolism.

At Maya fiestas, the drunken dancers may look out of control, but the process is taken very seriously and involves great expense on the part of the participants who have to rent their ornate costumes. The most common dance is the **Baile de la Conquista**, which re-enacts the victory of the Spanish, while at the same time managing to ridicule the conquistadors. According to some studies, the dance is based on pre-Columbian traditions. One of the most impressive dances is the **Palo Volador**, in which men swing by ropes from a thirty-metre pole. Today this is only performed in Chichicastenango, Joyabaj and Cubulco in Guatemala, and in isolated indigenous communities in Mexico, north of the Maya area.

Some of the best dancing you'll ever see is to the hypnotic drum patterns of **punta**, the music of the Garífuna, which betrays a distinctive West African heritage. Most Garífuna live on the Caribbean coast of Honduras, but there are also small communities at Lívingston in Guatemala and in Belize. If you get the chance to attend a punta party, be prepared for some explosively athletic shimmying and provocative hip movements – nineteenth-century Methodists were so outraged they called it "devil dancing". An excellent time to see Garífuna drumming and dance is November 19, Garífuna Settlement Day in Belize, and the best places to head for are either Dangriga or Hopkins.

Traditional music of either type is dominated by the **marimba**, a type of wooden xylophone that may well have originated in Africa (although many argue that it developed independently in Central America). The oldest versions use gourds beneath the sounding board and can be played by a single musician, while modern models, using hollow tubes to generate the sound, can need as many as seven players. The marimba is at the heart of traditional music, and marimba orchestras play at every occasion, for both ladino and indigenous communities. In the remotest of villages you sometimes hear them practising well into the night, particularly around market day. Other important instruments, especially in Maya bands, are the *tun*, a drum made from a hollow log; the *tambor*, another drum traditionally covered with the skin of a deer; *los chichines*, a type of maracas made from hollow gourds; the *tzijolaj*, a kind of piccolo; and the *chirimia*, a flute.

Ladino music is a blend of North American and Latin sounds, drawing on **merengue**, a rhythm that originally came from the Dominican Republic, which includes elements of Mexican music and the cumbia and salsa of Colombia and Cuba. There are also plenty of local bands producing their own version of the sound. It's fast-moving, easy-going and very rhythmic, and on any bus you'll hear many of the most popular tracks.

In Belize and the Bay Islands, **reggae** is the sound you'll hear on the street. Much of the music comes from Jamaica and the Caribbean islands, though Belize does have its own thriving domestic scene.

CRIME AND PERSONAL SAFETY

While political violence has decreased over recent years, crime rates throughout the region are rising alarmingly, especially in tourist locations. The majority of crime is petty theft – bag-snatching or pickpocketing – but some criminals operate in gangs and are prepared to use extreme violence to rob you.

Guatemala tops the list for tourist crime, closely followed by the north of **Honduras** and **El Salvador**; given the relatively small number of tourists in these last two, the probability of coming across trouble is that bit higher. **Mexico** and **Belize** are much safer in general, but incidents are rising in those countries too. Wherever you go you should take common-sense precautions, and if you've got valuables, make sure you insure them properly (see p.17).

AVOIDING CRIME

You're more likely to be a **victim** of crime when you've just arrived, especially when you're looking for a room after dark – getting to your hotel in daylight will add greatly to your safety. Keep your most valuable possessions in a moneybelt under your outer clothes and don't wear expensive jewellery. Trousers with zipped pockets are a good idea for deterring pickpockets. Surprisingly, border crossings, where you'll often have to change money, aren't that dangerous, as the presence of armed officials generally discourages thieves in the immediate area of the immigration post. If at all possible do the transaction and put your money away out of sight of other people, and once away from the post, be on your guard. You should also beware of people helping you find a bus and offering to carry your luggage; in many cases they will genuinely be offering a service in return for a tip, but at times like this you're easily distracted and might not see your luggage disappear.

Travelling on **public transport**, particularly by bus, you'll usually be separated from your main bag: it will go either in the luggage compartment underneath or in the rack on top. This is usually safe enough (and you have little option in any case), but keep an eye on it whenever you can. Although the theft of the bag itself is uncommon, opportunist thieves may dip their hands into zippers and outer pockets. You can buy small padlocks for backpacks, but for even greater security, put your pack into a coffee or flour sack (*costal*) and put that into a net (*red*). It might look a little outlandish but it's the way the locals transport goods and keeps your rucksack clean and dry too. Sacks and nets are sold in any market. Once on the bus it's best to keep your small bag on your lap. If you do put it on the inside luggage rack, keep it in sight and tie it (or preferably clip it with a carabiner) onto the rack to deter thieves who may try to snatch it and throw it out of the window to an accomplice.

In your **hotel**, make sure the lock on your door works from the inside as well as out: in many budget hotels the lock will be a small padlock (*candado*) on the outside. It's a good idea to buy your own, though, so you're the only one with keys; they're readily available on street stalls. Many hotels will have a safe or secure area for valuables. If you use it, make sure that whatever you put in is securely and tightly wrapped; a spare, lockable moneybelt is good for this.

Muggings and armed robberies are not common, but when they happen there's little you can do about it, so prevention is essential. Avoid obviously dangerous areas – deserted **city centres** and **bus stations** late at night – just like you would at home. Watch out for anyone who surreptitiously throws an obnoxious liquid over your pack or clothes – it's probably a ploy for a "passer-by" to help you clean it up, while another member of the gang snatches your bag. Much more serious are the planned armed robberies on tourist minibuses and luxury buses in Guatemala and Mexico. The robbers will usually go round the passengers collecting money and valuables, but occasionally victims are taken away and assaulted and even raped. For this reason some tour groups in Guatemala are accompanied by an armed guard.

POLICE

If you have anything stolen, report the incident immediately to the **police**. If there is a tourist police force, try them first, if only to get a copy of the report (*denuncia*) for insurance purposes (see p.17). The police in these parts are poorly paid and you can't expect them to do much more than make out the report – often you'll have difficulty getting them to do even this. You may have to dictate it to them and sometimes they'll demand a fee for their services. If you don't speak Spanish, try to bring along someone who does. If you can, you should also report the crime to your **embassy** – it helps the consular staff build up a higher-level case for better protection for tourists.

Obviously you want to avoid any **trouble** with the police whatsoever. Practically every capital city has foreigners incarcerated for **drug** offences who'd never do it again if they knew what the punishment was like. Drugs of all kinds are readily available, but if you do indulge, be very discreet – the pusher may have a sideline reporting clients to the police, and catching "international drug smugglers" gives the country concerned brownie points with the DEA. If you are arrested your embassy will probably send someone to visit you and maybe find an English-speaking lawyer, but they certainly can't get you out of jail.

WORK AND STUDY

There are opportunities to work and study in all the countries of the Maya region, with a huge number of development agencies and language schools based here. It's certainly possible to turn up and find a suitable language school without arranging things in advance, but if you're looking for development work it makes sense to plan ahead; some useful contacts are listed below. You should also check out the Web sites listed on p.27.

WORK

There are probably thousands of opportunities for **voluntary workers** in development projects throughout the region. In most cases you'll need to have a useful skill, speak at least basic Spanish and be able to commit yourself for a couple of months.

The first place to look is the on the Web: **CIAO** (Central Index of Appointments Overseas, *www.ciao-directory.org*) is an Internet-based organization which links companies looking for professionals and semi-skilled volunteers in Guatemala. In the UK, the **Central Bureau for Educational Visits**, which is at 10 Spring Gardens, London SW1A 2BN (☎0171/389-4880; *books@centralbureau.org.uk*), publishes two booklets, *Working Holidays* (updated annually) and *Volunteer Work*, both of which are packed with essential information, including contacts in Mexico and Central America. In the US, try **Volunteers for Peace**, 43 Tiffany Rd, Belmont,

VT 05730 (☎802-259-2759, fax 802-259-2922; *vfp@vermontel.com*; *www.vermontel.com/~vfp/home.htm*), a non-profit organization that organizes work camps in Honduras, Guatemala and Mexico.

In Guatemala, there's a good drop-in resource centre called **El Arco** at 5 Av Norte 25B Antigua (☎8320162), which links prospective volunteers with organizations throughout the country. **Casa Alianza** is a charity which helps street children in Guatemala and Honduras; the work is extremely demanding and volunteers need to give a minimum six-month commitment. You can contact them at Apartado Postal, 2704 Guatemala (☎2532965, fax 2533003; *bruce@casaalianza.org*), or in the US at SJO 1039, PO Box 025216, Miami, FL 33102-5216, or in the UK at the Coach House, Grafton Underwood, Northants, NN14 3AA. They also have a Web site (*www.casaalianza.org*)

There's very little **paid work** available in Central America. Your best bet is to approach language schools in the big cities for English teaching work (typically US$5–6 an hour); look for *academias de idomas* in the telephone directory. You're much more likely to get employed if you can show previous experience or, ideally a TEFL qualification. There are some opportunities for scuba-divers qualified to PADI divemaster level to work in the dozens of dive schools and resorts in the region – head for the Belize cayes and start asking around. Finally in the main tourist centres there always seems to be the odd position for bartenders; the money's terrible and you'll get very few tips, but so as long as you don't expect to make a living, it can be a lot of fun.

STUDY

The **Spanish-language-school** industry is a significant employer in a number of towns throughout the region, but especially in Guatemala. Most students opt for a study package that includes four or five hours' one-on-one daily tuition with a teacher and full board with a local family, but if you want to make your own accommodation arrangements or prefer to study for up to eight hours a day, this is usually possible. It's also possible to study in groups, though this is usually pre-arranged through a college or university.

The first consideration to make is **where to study**. If you're a complete beginner, it's best to choose a well-established centre such as Antigua or Quetzaltenango in Guatemala, San Cristóbal de las Casas in Chiapas, Mexico (see p.151), or Copán Ruinas in Honduras, where the culture shock is less extreme. However, the disadvantage with these towns is that there are significant numbers of foreigners in all of them and it's very easy to find yourself speaking English in your spare time. If you already speak some Spanish and really want to accelerate your learning, consider living somewhere more isolated from gringo influence – good places include Cobán (see p.396), Chimaltenango (see p.328), Huehuetenango (see p.360), San Andrés, near Flores, Petén (see p.407) in Guatemala and La Ceiba in Honduras.

Choosing a school is the next step. Standards of tuition vary markedly, with some "schools" consisting of little more than a desk in someone's front room and an unqualified, inexperienced teacher, while at the other end of the spectrum there are establishments with superb facilities, highly experienced and motivated teachers and excellent after-hours activities. The schools themselves vary considerably: some are purely profit-driven, while others donate a proportion of profits to local development projects such as funding village libraries or clean water initiatives.

It's your own commitment to study and the relationship with your **teacher** which are the most important factors determining your progress. If you are not happy with your teacher, ask to be given another. By Western standards it's extremely cheap to study Spanish in the Maya region, though **prices** vary a lot – you should expect to pay between $110 and $180 a week for five hours a day one-on-one tuition, full board and after-classes activities.

An international organization with substantial involvement in the region is the US-based **Amerispan**, PO Box 40007, Philadelphia PA 19106 (☎1-800/879-6640; *info@amerispan.com*; *www. amerispan.com*), which has a wide range of resources as well as information on language schools and volunteer opportunities.

PART TWO

SOUTHERN MEXICO

INTRODUCTION

outhern Mexico, comprising the **Yucatán peninsula** and the states of **Chiapas** and **Tabasco**, is both physically and culturally quite distinct from the rest of Mexico, its unique character reflecting the vast distance that separates it from the administrative centre of the country, both past and present. In this region are some of the longest inhabited parts of Mexico, where Maya traditions continue to be observed despite years of oppression and the encroaching demands of tourism. It is also home to some of the most spectacular of the ancient **Maya sites**, with temples bursting through a forest canopy that stretches to the horizon. The natural scenery is equally stunning: rugged mountains and steamy jungles give way to beaches of coral sand as fine as white pepper, warm tropical rivers where crocodiles bask in the sun and gently cascading waterfalls of a hundred different blues.

Sticking out from Central America like a thumb, the Yucatán peninsula comprises three states: touristic Quintana Roo, fringed with some of the world's most beautiful beaches; Yucatán, where most of the famous Maya sites are found; and wilder Campeche to the west, whose fortified capital is one of the peninsula's most picturesque cities. The resort of **Cancún** in northern **Quintana Roo** is where most travellers arrive. Despite the imitation Maya pyramids housing hotels and burger bars, the city owes more to Miami than Mexico, with its string of swanky high-rise hotels. Cancún's real attraction, however, is the twenty kilometres of blinding white sand that fronts the hotels, and the numerous opportunities to have fun in the sun, albeit at a price. Fired by Cancún's success, countless new resorts have sprung up to form a tourist corridor along Hwy-307, which runs south as far as Tulum. Formerly backpacker havens, the tiny island of **Isla Mujeres**, just offshore from Cancún, and the beach town of **Playa del Carmen**, some 100km further south, are becoming more expensive and more crowded every year. **Isla Cozumel**, a short ferry ride from Playa, is similarly pricey and, with fewer beaches than the mainland, it is of real interest only to divers, who gather here in shoals to plunge over its dramatic undersea coral walls. Those on a tight budget shouldn't despair, though, as there are more affordable beach destinations near **Tulum**, the most perfectly situated of all Maya ruins. Perched on shallow cliffs like a sentinel above the aquamarine of the Caribbean, it's at its most magical at dawn, when it catches the rays of the morning sun.

South of Tulum, tourism has not yet gained a foothold and the coast is dotted with small fishing villages rather than resorts. Only a few kilometres west of the highway tiny hamlets of plaster and palm are inhabited by indigenous Maya, who continue to practise many of the traditions of their ancestors. The coastline along here remains covered in mangroves, populated by myriad birds, crocodiles, turtles and even the occasional manatee. The main town in these parts is the dusty state capital, **Chetumal**, which in itself has little to offer visitors other than easy access to Belize, though nearby attractions include the vast **Laguna Bacalar**, a lagoon of a thousand shades of green and blue. Further inland, this southern part of the peninsula is covered in lush **tropical forest** that extends into Guatemala. This was once the domain of the lowland Maya, and their great ruined metropolises – notably **Calakmul**, **Kohunlich** and the moated city of **Becán** – litter the jungle.

The peninsula's **northern interior** is arid and flat, covered in scrubby jungle, with the only source of water being freshwater sinkholes known as **cenotes**. Here the legacy of the Spanish is evident in fine **colonial towns** such as **Mérida**, built with wealth generated by the hacienda system, and fortified **Campeche**, capital of the state that bears its name, originally built to protect the city from British and French pirates. Between Campeche and Mérida lies a host of Maya ruins. **Edzná**'s grand and lofty central pyramid looks out over a vast and empty central plaza to the endless flatness of the Yucatán. **Uxmal** and the **Puuc** sites are more subtle; their endlessly repeated intricate geometrical carvings, formed from tens of thousands of precisely positioned pieces of stone, are perhaps the Maya's most aesthetically satisfying architectural achievement. East of Mérida lies the best known and most visited of all Maya sites – **Chichén Itzá**. Thousands of tourists heave their way up the narrow steps of its perfectly symmetrical main temple every day, but after 4.30pm, when the streams of tour buses have left for Cancún and other Quintana Roo resorts, it's possible to have the place to yourself.

Southwest of the peninsula lies the state of **Chiapas**, home to some of Mexico's most diverse and spectacular landscapes. The great mountain ranges of the Sierra Madre Occidental and the Sierra Madre Oriental converge a little north of Chiapas, forming a ridge of peaks rising to over 2000m, clad with oak and pine and crested with volcanoes near Tapachula on the border with Guatemala. The remote slopes of these mountains form part of a protected national park, penetrated by roads only at its extremities. These roads lead inland from the Pacific coast – where the quiet of villages like Puerto Arista is disturbed only by the pounding of the surf – towards the Chiapas highlands, cutting across agricultural land where rich landowners still practise a form of feudalism, and on to the state capital, **Tuxtla Gutiérrez**. Tuxtla's mundane modernity feels almost out of place in Maya Chiapas, but it is a major transport hub and also boasts some excellent museums.

By contrast, the elegant Spanish city of **San Cristóbal de las Casas** is brimming with Maya from the surrounding communities. Anti-government graffiti are daubed on the walls of colonial houses, women in multi-coloured *huipiles* and shawls fill the street markets and vats of maize steam into the thin mountain air. A visit to the nearby villages of **San Juan Chamula** or **Zinacantán** may feel to you like a trip back in time, but remember that here, non-indigenous people – Mexican and tourist alike – are considered to be relics of an earlier, failed creation and regarded as primitive by the Maya.

Beyond San Cristóbal, the highland road descends through pine trees into the deep moss green of rainforest, as it heads towards **Ocosingo**, a sleepy, red-tiled, ranchers' town. Beyond here the road passes hundreds of clear blue waterfalls at **Agua Azul** on its way towards the haunting jungle ruins of **Palenque**. Perched on the side of a ridge overlooking the vast expanse of the Yucatán plain that extends across Tabasco, the ruins are best seen at dawn, when thick cloud evaporating from the rainforest clears to expose the elegant white limestone temples and palaces. Lost in the jungle not far away are the ruins of **Bonampak**, reached through the **Lacandón forest**, and **Yaxchilán**, near the border with Guatemala, on the bank of the lazy Río **Usumacinta**, which winds its way across northern Chiapas into the swamps of Tabasco. These cities were built in the Classic period between 300 and 900 AD, making them contemporary with Calakmul and the Río Bec sites in southern Yucatán. Both Palenque and Yaxchilán are famous for the quality of their paintings, which demonstrate a use of perspective that predates its appearance in Europe by hundreds of years. The sculpture, too, is unequalled in Mesoamerica; though the best pieces have been moved to Mexico City, there is still a beautiful bust in the Palenque site museum.

The state of **Tabasco** is for the most part hot and steamy, very flat, and undeveloped for tourists. Numerous rivers descend from the highlands of Chiapas, meandering

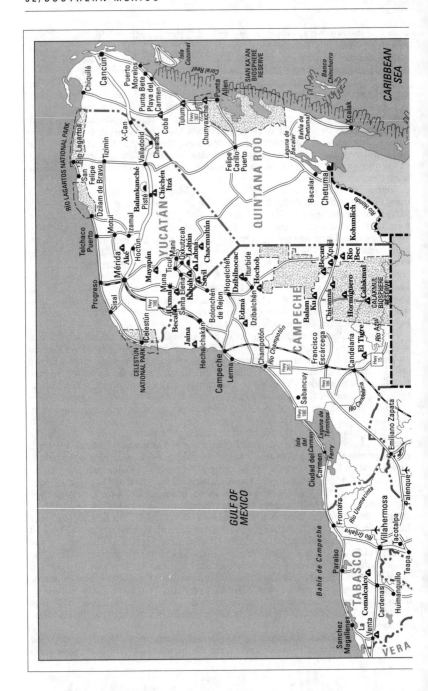

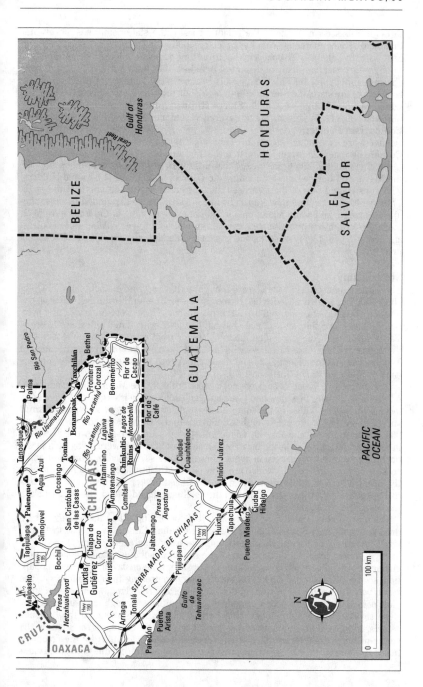

through Tabasco's marshes to the Atlantic coast – the state comprises more water than land. These marshes are a haven for crocodiles and numerous species of bird, best seen by taking river-boat trips or from tiny bankside villages like **Malpasito**. Though the coast has plenty of **deserted beaches**, they border a grey Atlantic whose charms cannot compete with the turquoise waters of the Yucatecan Caribbean. In the far south of the state, the **Sierra Puana** highlands provide a retreat from the heat and humidity, while further west, in the **Sierra Huimanguillo**, visitors can stay in remote highland villages in jagged, jungle-covered mountains as part of the **Agua Selva Ecotourism Project**.

There are no major sights in Tabasco, though the Chontal Maya city of **Comalcalco**, near Veracruz, is worth a visit for curiosity's sake – it is one of the only Maya cities built of kiln-fired brick. Tabasco's rivers were important trade routes for the Maya, and before them, the enigmatic **Olmec**, Mexico's first pyramid builders, who constructed one of their earliest cities at **La Venta** in the north of the state. There's little to see here now – apart from a grassy hillock surrounded by mosquito-infested jungle and some bits of unlabelled pottery – as most of the finds have been moved to **Villahermosa**, the state capital. An oil-boom town, Villahermosa is pleasant enough, with plenty of parks and greenery in addition to its small archeological museum.

Some history

The earliest inhabitants of Mexico are thought to have arrived in about 20,000 BC. By 5000–1500 BC, settled societies had formed, and shortly after this the first Mexican civilization, the **Olmecs**, emerged in southern Veracruz. These were America's first pyramid builders, creating an artificial volcano, complete with fluted sides, at La Venta, Tabasco. Olmec society provided the template for what was to follow, most famously the Zapotecs of the Oaxaca valleys who invented the calendar, the great civilization of Teotihuacán and the bloodthirsty and theocratic Aztecs whose self-prophesied demise came with the arrival of Cortés in 1519.

The greatest of Mexico's ancient people were probably the **Maya**, who have inhabited this area for over five thousand years and built some of their largest and most spectacular cities here. Those in the southern lowlands of the Yucatán, such as **Calakmul** and **Becán**, were at the height of their influence in the **Classic era**, between 300 and 900 AD, mysteriously and abruptly falling from power soon after. As they fell, new cities in a new architectural style, such as **Uxmal** and **Chichén Itzá**, were being built in the north. These in turn collapsed in about 1200 and were succeeded by **Mayapán** and a confederacy of other centres, which probably included Tulum and Cozumel. By the time the Spanish arrived, Mayapán's power, too, had been broken by revolt, and the Maya had splintered into tribalism – although they still maintained a long-distance sea trade that awed the conquistadors.

Hernan Cortés landed near Veracruz in 1519, beginning what was to be three hundred years of direct Spanish rule of Mexico (excluding Chiapas, which was administered separately as part of Guatemala until the early nineteenth century). Southern Mexico proved the most difficult part of the region to subdue. The Catholic Church, champions of indigenous rights, forbade the Spanish from enslaving the native population, so the colonists had to seek other means of controlling their labour force. The result was the **hacienda system** of debt peonage, whereby landowners rented small plots of land to the native people at rates that were sufficiently high to ensure that they were always owed a little money, paid back in the form of labour on the hacienda estates. Indigenous communities were broken up and the villagers resettled on the edges of huge estates controlled from mansions called haciendas by the colonists, many of whom were little more than peasants themselves. During this time grand cities such as Mérida developed into the architectural showcases you can see today, redolent of the landowners' power.

By the beginning of the nineteenth century, Spain's status as a world power was on the wane and the country's grip on its colonies was loosening. Mexico rebelled when Napoleon invaded the Iberian peninsula and placed his brother on the Spanish throne, using the excuse of loyalty to the deposed king, Fernando. The first leader of the movement for independence was a Catholic priest, Miguel Hidalgo y Costilla, who uttered the famous battle cry – "Mexicanos! Viva Mexico!" However, it was Vicente Guerrero and Agustín de Iturbide who finally secured **independence** in 1821. Little changed for the peasants, however – the hacienda system continued, the land was still in the hands of the small Spanish-born population, and even the **Mexican Revolution** of 1910–17, fought in the name of land redistribution, failed to redress the balance.

The hacienda system has not been altogether unresisted, though: small rebellions pepper the nation's history. The most successful was the 1847 Maya insurrection against plantation owners in the Yucatán peninsula, popularly known as the **Caste Wars**. Outraged at the system of debt peonage and the continued annexation of communal land, a Maya army rose against its oppressors, and within a year the Maya had the Spanish under siege in the peninsula's two largest towns, Campeche and Mérida. Then, as the Maya were on the brink of creating an independent state, swarms of black ants appeared on the horizon, presaging rain, and despite opposition from the Maya generals, each soldier started for home to harvest his cornfield.

History repeated itself in 1994 when a Maya army calling themselves the **Zapatista Army of National Liberation** (EZLN), after Emiliano Zapata, an indigenous hero of the Mexican Revolution, occupied several cities in Chiapas, including San Cristóbal de las Casas. The EZLN demanded an end to debt peonage and the repeal of a law introduced by President Salinas of the ruling PRI party permitting the sale of government-owned Maya communal land. Protracted negotiations over the intervening period have failed to arrive at a solution, and, despite widespread international condemnation, the PRI continues to wage a covert paramilitary war against the Maya peasants who support the Zapatistas' aims. For details see box on p.140.

FIESTAS IN MEXICO

JANUARY

1 New Year's Day: **San Andrés Chamula** (Chiapas) and **San Juan Chamula** (Chis), both near San Cristóbal, have civil ceremonies to install a new government for the year.

6 Fiesta de Polk Keken in **Lerma** (Campeche), near Campeche, with many traditional dances.

19 *El Pochó* dancers perform at **Tenosique** (Tab) dressed as jaguars and men to represent the struggle of good and evil. The celebration concludes on Shrove Tuesday with the burning of an effigy of El Pochó, god of evil.

20 Día de San Sebastián sees a lot of activity. In **Chiapa de Corzo** (Chis) a large fiesta with traditional dances lasts several days, with a re-enactment on the 21st of a naval battle on the Río Grijalva. A big day too in **Zinacantán** (Chis), near San Cristóbal.

FEBRUARY

2 Día de la Candelaria. Colourful Maya celebrations at **Ocosingo** (Chis).

11 Religious fiesta in **Comitán** (Chis).

27 In **Villahermosa** (Tabasco), a fiesta commemorates the anniversary of a battle against the French.

Week before Lent Carnival is at its most frenzied in the big cities – especially **Villahermosa** (Tab) and **Mérida**, though it's celebrated too in Campeche and Chetumal and on Isla Mujeres and Cozumel and in hundreds of villages throughout the area. **San Juan Chamula** (Chis) has a big fiesta.

continued oveleaf

FIESTAS contd
MARCH

Holy Week is widely observed – particularly big ceremonies in **San Cristóbal de las Casas**. **Ciudad Hidalgo** (Chis), at the border near Tapachula, has a major week-long market.

20 Feria de las Hamacas in **Tecoh** (Yuc), a hammock-producing village near Mérida.

21 Equinox. Huge gathering to see the serpent shadow at **Chichén Itzá**.

APRIL

1–7 A feria in **San Cristóbal de las Casas** (Chis) celebrates the town's foundation. A Spring Fair is generally held here later in the month.

13 The traditional festival of honey and corn in **Hopelchén** (Cam) lasts until the 17th.

29 Día de San Pedro celebrated in several villages around San Cristóbal, including **Amatenango del Valle** and **Zinacantán**.

MAY

3 Día de la Santa Cruz celebrated in **San Juan Chamula** (Chis) and in **Teapa** (Tab), between Villahermosa and San Cristóbal, **Hopelchén** (Cam), **Celestún** (Yuc) and **Felipe Carrillo Puerto** (QR).

12–18 Fiesta in **Chankán Veracruz** (QR), near Felipe Carillo Puerto, celebrating the Holy Cross which spoke to the Maya here.

15 Día de San Isidro sees peasant celebrations everywhere – famous and picturesque fiestas in **Huistán** (Chis), near San Cristóbal.

Variable dates A four-day nautical marathon **from Tenosique to Villahermosa** (Tab), when craft from all over the country race down 600km of the Río Usumacinta.

JUNE

24 Día de San Juan is the culmination of several days' celebration in **San Juan Chamula** (Chis).

JULY

7 Beautiful religious ceremony in **Comitán** (Chis), with candlelit processions to and around the church.

25 Día de Santiago provokes widespread celebration – especially in **San Cristóbal de las Casas** (Chis), where they begin a good week earlier (17th is Día de San Cristóbal), and in nearby villages such as **Tenejapa** and **Amatenango del Valle**.

Variable date At **Edzná** (Cam) a Maya ceremony to the god Chac is held, to encourage, or celebrate, the arrival of the rains.

AUGUST

30 Día de Santa Rosa celebrated in **San Juan Chamula** (Chis).

SEPTEMBER

14–16 Throughout Chiapas, celebration of the annexation of the state to Mexico, followed by independence celebrations everywhere.

14 Día de San Roman. In **Dzan** (Yuc), near Ticul, the end of a four-day festival with fireworks, bullfights, dances and processions – in **Campeche** (Cam) the Feria de San Roman lasts until the end of the month.

21 Equinox. Another serpent spectacle at **Chichén Itzá**.

29 Día de San Migual is celebrated with a major festival in **Maxcanu** (Yuc), on the road from Mérida to Campeche and in **Huistán** (Chis).

OCTOBER

First Sunday Día de la Virgen del Rosario is celebrated in **San Juan Chamula** and **Zinacantán** (Chis).

3 Día de San Francisco in **Amatenango del Valle** (Chis).

First two weeks Processions and celebrations associated with the miraculous statue of Cristo de las Ampillas in **Mérida**.

18 A pilgrimage centred on **Izamal** (Yuc) starts ten days of celebration, culminating in dances on the night of the 28th.

NOVEMBER

2 Day of the Dead is respected everywhere, with particularly strong traditions in **Chiapa de Corzo** (Chis).

DECEMBER

8 Día de la Inmaculada Concepción is widely celebrated, especially in **Izamal** (Yuc) and **Champotón** (Cam), each of which has a fiesta starting several days earlier.

12 Día de la Virgen de Guadalupe is an important one throughout Mexico. There are particularly good fiestas in **Tuxtla Gutiérrez** and **San Cristóbal de las Casas** (Chis), and the following day another in nearby **Amatenango del Valle** (Chis).

CHAPTER ONE

YUCATÁN AND CAMPECHE

he three states that comprise the interminably flat, low-lying plain of the Yucatán peninsula – **Yucatán** itself, **Campeche** and Quintana Roo (covered separately in the following chapter) – are among the hottest and most tropical-feeling parts of Mexico, though they in fact lie further north than you might imagine: the sweeping curve of southern Mexico means that Mérida is actually north of the capital. Tourism has made major inroads, of course, especially in the north around the great **Maya sites** and on the route from Mérida to the resorts of the Quintana Roo coast, but away from the big centres and especially in Campeche state much of the country has been barely touched. And even in and around Mérida, a city large enough to have plenty of life of its own, it's easy to escape the tourist trail and find colonial towns, lesser-known ruins and the beaches the locals use.

Inevitably it is the Maya sites that prompt the most interest, and indeed the extraordinary concentration of superbly preserved centres, their relative ease of access and the variety of different architectural styles are unrivalled. **Mérida**, capital of Yucatán state, is the obvious initial base for exploration, and a vibrant and enjoyable city in its own right, with an attractive colonial centre, excellent market and accommodation and food of every sort. Lying astride the chief **transport** artery of the region, Hwy-180, which heads east to Cancún via **Chichén Itzá** and southwest to Campeche and Villahermosa, Mérida also offers easy access to the northern coast and to **Uxmal** and a trove of smaller, less visited ruins in the south. Uxmal and Chichén Itzá, certainly, are must-sees, but don't ignore the smaller sites, such as **Kabáh**, a particular favourite, or **Edzná** near Campeche, or **Dzibilchaltún**, north of Mérida; less carefully cleared and maintained, but less overrun with tourists, they offer a very different experience.

The road that runs across **the south** of the peninsula, from **Francisco Escárcega** to Chetumal, is relatively new, passing through jungle territory rich in Maya remains, several of which have recently been opened to the public for the first time. Though largely unexplored, these are beginning to see a trickle of visitors as access improves; you can get accommodation and arrange tours at **Xpujil**, a village named after the nearby archeological site, on the border between Campeche and Quintana Roo states.

Along with some of the Maya World's finest pre-Columbian ruins, Yucatán and Campeche are scattered with the towns and haciendas built by their Spanish conquerors. This **colonial legacy** is everywhere. Many old haciendas and *henequen* (sisal) plantations are now open to the public as upmarket hotels, restaurants or simply tourist attractions in their own right, while almost every town and village has its church and arcaded square: Mérida itself is among the most impressive, or check out the impregnable fortifications of **Campeche**, the vast monastery dominating the Maya remains at **Izamal**, or the backwater of **Valladolid**.

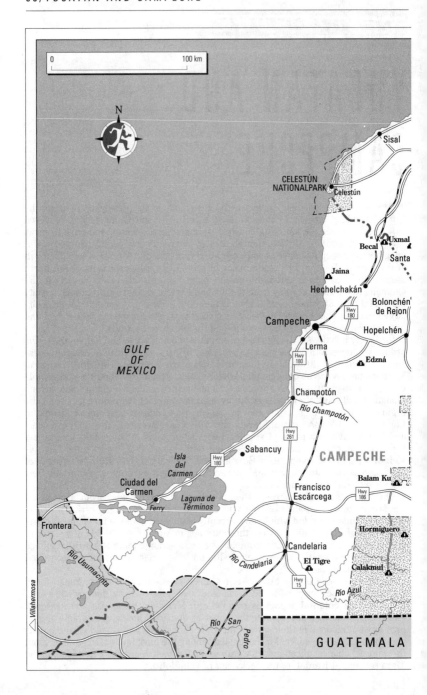

N

0   100 km

Sisal

CELESTÚN
NATIONALPARK Celestún

Uxmal
Becal
Santa

Jaina
Hechelchakán

Bolonchén
de Rejon

Campeche   Hwy
180

Hopelchén

Lerma
Hwy
180

Edzná

Champotón
Río Champotón

GULF
OF
MEXICO

Hwy
261

Isla
del
Carmen   Hwy
180   Sabancuy   CAMPECHE

Balam Ku

Ciudad del
Carmen   Francisco
Escárcega   Hwy
186

Laguna de
Términos

Ferry

Hormiguero

Frontera

Río Usumacinta   Candelaria

Río Candelaria   El Tigre   Calakmul

Hwy
15   *Río Azul*

Río San

Pedro   GUATEMALA

△ Villahermosa

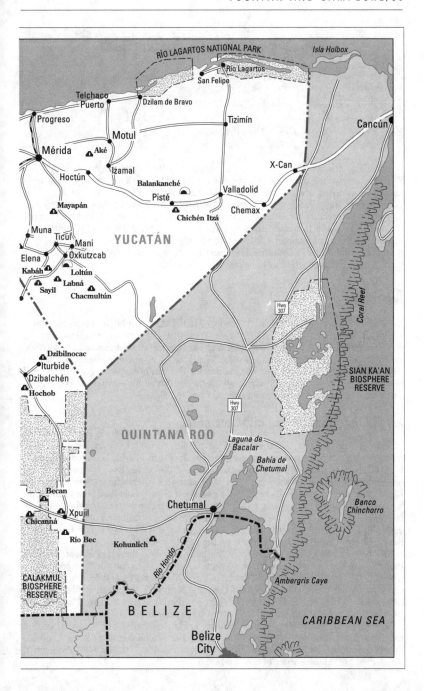

ACCOMMODATION PRICE CODES

All the accommodation listed in this book has been categorized into one of nine price bands, as set out below. The prices quoted are in US dollars and refer to the cheapest room available for two people sharing in high season.

① under US$5	④ US$15–25	⑦ US$60–80
② US$5–10	⑤ US$25–40	⑧ US$80–100
③ US$10–15	⑥ US$40–60	⑨ over US$100

Travelling around the peninsula, the changes in landscape are hard to miss. In Yucatán, the shallow, rocky earth gives rise to stunted trees – here, underground wells known as **cenotes** are the only source of water. At the opposite end of the scale, Campeche boasts a huge area of **tropical forest**, the Calakmul Biosphere Reserve, though this is steadily shrinking with the growing demand for timber and land for cattle ranching. While the **coastlines** of both states are great for spotting **wildlife** – notably the flocks of flamingos at Celestún and Río Lagartos – the **beaches** can't really compare with those in Quintana Roo. Best are the small-scale resorts on the Mérida coast around Progreso, mainly patronized by Mexicans.

Mérida

Even if practically every road didn't lead to **MÉRIDA**, it would still be an inevitable stop. The "White City", capital of the state of Yucatán, is in every sense the leading town of the peninsula, and remarkably calm and likeable for all its thousands of visitors. Every street in the centre boasts a colonial church or mansion, while the plazas are alive with market stalls and free entertainment. You can live well here and find good beaches within easy reach, but above all it's the ideal base for excursions to the great Maya sites of Uxmal (see p.72) and Chichén Itzá (p.78).

Arrival, information and city transport

Mérida is laid out on a simple **grid** of numbered streets: even numbers run north–south, odd from east to west, with the zócalo, **Plaza Mayor**, bounded by C 60, C 61, C 62 and C 63. Mérida's **bus stations** lie around the corner from each other on the west side of town. The brand new first-class **Cameon**, C 70 no. 55, between C 69 and 71, is sparkling and air-conditioned, with a *guardería*. Some short-haul buses use minor terminals, but you're most likely to arrive at the busy **second-class** terminal, on C 69 between C 68 and C 70. Inside is a **tourist information** counter, a hotel reservations desk and some phones. You'll also find a small **post office** at the side on C 70, and a Banpais **bank** (Mon–Fri 9am–1.30pm) on the nearby corner.

City buses don't go all the way from the bus stations to the Plaza Mayor. To walk (about 20min), turn right outside the second-class bus station and you'll be on the corner of C 68 and C 69; the Plaza Mayor is three blocks north and four blocks east. Colectivos from the smaller places off the main highways terminate in Plaza de San Juan, on C 69 between C 62 and C 64. To get to the Plaza Mayor, leave Plaza de San Juan by the northeast corner and walk three blocks north up C 62.

Mérida's Manuel Cresencio Rejón **airport** is 7km southwest of the city. There's a **tourist office** (daily 8am–8pm), post office, long-distance phones and car rental desks. To get downtown, take a colectivo (buy a ticket at the desk) or bus #79 ("Aviación"), which drops off at the corner of C 67 and C 60.

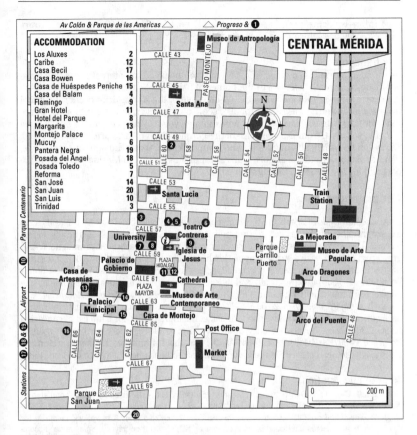

CENTRAL MÉRIDA

Av Colón & Parque de las Americas △   △ Progreso & ❶

ACCOMMODATION

Los Aluxes	2
Caribe	12
Casa Becil	17
Casa Bowen	16
Casa de Huéspedes Peniche	15
Casa del Balam	4
Flamingo	9
Gran Hotel	11
Hotel del Parque	8
Margarita	13
Montejo Palace	1
Mucuy	6
Pantera Negra	19
Posada del Angel	18
Posada Toledo	5
Reforma	7
San José	14
San Juan	20
San Luis	10
Trinidad	3

Information

Mérida's main **tourist office** is in the Teatro Peón Contreras, on the corner of C 60 and C 57 (daily 8am–8pm; ☎99/24-92-90). Pick up a copy of *Yucatán Today*, in English and Spanish, to find out what's going on in and around town. *Discover Mérida of Yucatán* offers information on the areas outside Mérida, while *Restaurants of Yucatán* gives detailed reviews. There are also plenty of leaflets available and you'll usually find some English-speaking staff. The **federal tourist office** is in the pink building marked *Gobierno del Estado Secretaria de Desarollo Economico*, C 59 no. 514, between C 62 and

THE PUUC ROUTE BUS

While at Mérida's second-class bus terminal you may want to buy a ticket for a transport-only **day-trip** by bus around the **Puuc Route**, which can be difficult to visit without your own transport. Ask at the Autotransportes del Sur counter. The trip costs US$5 and leaves at 8am every morning, visiting Uxmal, Labná, Sayil, Kabáh and Xlapak. You get just long enough at each site to form a general impression, but there's no guide or lunch included in the price.

C 64 (Mon–Fri 8am–2pm). Pronatura, at C 1-D no. 254 (99/44-22-90), organizes **tours** and also provides information on the ecology of the Yucatán.

City transport

As traffic in Mérida is so congested, and most of the places of interest are within walking distance, it really isn't worth the bother of using public transport to get around in the centre – though it can be fun to hop onto one of the **horse-drawn carriages** that trot up and down the Paseo de Montejo; see p.65. However, to get out to some of the more far-flung sites (Palacio Cantón, for example), you may need to catch a bus. A number of buses leave from C 59 just east of the Parque Hidalgo; fares are around US$0.50. **Taxis** can be hailed all around town and from ranks at Parque Hidalgo, the post office, Plaza de San Juan and the airport. **Car rental** offices abound in Mérida, both at the airport and in the city (see "Listings" on p.68).

Accommodation

There are hundreds of **hotels** in Mérida, many in lovely colonial buildings very near the centre, so that although the city can get crowded at peak times you should always be able to find a room. The very cheapest hotels are concentrated **next to the bus station**, a noisy and grimy part of town, with a string of upmarket hotels along **Paseo de Montejo**, just north of the centre, most of them ultra-modern and lacking in charm or personality; the best hotels lie in between, both geographically and in terms of value. A luxurious alternative is to stay outside town in a colonial hacienda: try the seventeenth-century *Hacienda Katanchel*, at C 35 no. 520 (☎99/20-09-97 or 20-09-85; ⑨), which is set in 750 acres and boasts individual pavilions and freshwater wading pools; or ask at the tourist office for a full list of converted haciendas all over Yucatán. Finally, *Rainbow Maya* **trailer park**, 8km on the road to Progreso (☎99/28-04-48, fax 24-77-84; ②–③), has about a hundred hook-ups, water and electricity. The head office is in the Canto Farmacía; to book ahead, write to C 61 no. 468.

Near the bus station

Casa Becil, C 67 no. 550-C, between C 66 and C 68 (☎99/24-67-64). Friendly place, popular with North Americans and convenient for the bus station. ③.

Casa Bowen, C 66 no. 521-B, between C 65 and C 67 (☎99/28-61-09). A travellers' favourite for years, this restored colonial house is set around a bright, pleasant courtyard. Spartan but acceptable rooms with baths (some with a/c), and two apartments with kitchens. ③–④.

Pantera Negra, C 67, no. 547-B, between C 68 and C 70 (☎ & fax 99/24-02-51). One of the most charming hotels in town for any budget, in an intimate, and idiosyncratically decorated colonial house, just a block from the bus station. The owners make you feel very welcome and you may end up staying here for longer than you planned. Prices include breakfast. ④.

Posada del Ángel, C 67 no. 535, between C 66 and C 68 (☎99/23-27-54). Quiet and comfortable, with parking and restaurant. ④.

In the centre

Caribe, C 59 no. 500, Parque Hidalgo (☎99/24-90-22, fax 24-87-33; toll free: in Mexico ☎800/71-2-00-03, in US: ☎1-888/822-6431). In a small plaza a block from the Plaza Mayor, this place has a lovely patio restaurant and views of the cathedral and plaza from the rooftop pool. Travel agency; parking. ⑥.

Casa de Huéspedes Peniche, C 62 no. 507, just off the zócalo (☎99/28-55-18). Shambling but fascinating grand colonial house, with original paintings, a staircase out of *Gone with the Wind* and huge, bare rooms (bring a padlock). The shared bathroom looks like it hasn't been cleaned since the place was built. ②.

Flamingo, C 58, corner of C 59 (☎99/24-77-55). One of the cheapest in town with a pool. The attached restaurant, *Tikal*, has good set meals. ③.

Gran Hotel, C 60 no. 496, Parque Hidalgo (☎99/24-77-30, fax 24-76-22). Colonnades, fountains, palms and statues all ensure that the *Gran* lives up to its name. Rooms, all with private shower, are well furnished, often with antiques. ⑥.

Hotel del Parque, C 60 no. 495, Parque Hidalgo (☎99/24-78-44, fax 28-19-29). Lovely old building just off the main plaza. Some rooms need improvement and those at the back are quieter. You can dine in intimate little balconies in the restaurant, *La Bella Epoca.* ⑥.

Margarita, C 66 no. 506, between C 61 and C 63 (☎99/23-72-36). Budget favourite; small but clean rooms and good rates for groups. ②.

Montejo Palace, Paseo de Montejo 483-C (☎99/24-76-44, fax 23-03-48; in US 1-800-624-8451). Eight-storey hotel, with fully-equipped rooms, including satellite TV, in an upmarket location. Restaurant, cafeteria and pool. ⑨.

Mucuy, C 57 no. 481, between C 56 and C 58 (☎99/28-51-93). Quiet, well-run and pleasant hotel, with clean, good-value rooms. English-speaking staff and a selection of books in English. ③.

Posada Toledo, C 58 no. 487 (☎99/23-16-90 or 23-22-56). Superb, beautifully preserved nineteenth-century building. The rooms, all with private shower and some with a/c, are filled with antiques and the courtyard is a delight. The food is good, too, served in a historic dining room. ⑤.

Reforma, C 59 no. 508 (☎99/24-79-22, fax 28-32-78). Long-established, recently restored hotel in a colonial building. Rooms are arranged around a cool courtyard and there's a relaxing poolside bar and parking. Good prices on guided day-trips to Uxmal and on the *Ruta Puuc.* ④.

San José, C 63 no. 503-C (☎99/28-66-57). The cheapest place in town. Very basic but clean, and just off the zócalo. Enter through the café. ②.

San Juan, C 62 no. 545a between C 69 and C 71 (☎99/23-6823). A variety of good-value rooms in a listed colonial house, run by a very knowledgeable and friendly Meridian. Free Internet, faxes, juice and coffee for guests plus fascinating tailor-made ecological and archeological tours. Prices include breakfast. ④.

San Luis, C 61, corner C 68 (☎99/47-588). Where the men from UNCLE would stay – fabulously kitsch, and deliberately so. The man on reception has worked there since it opened in the 1960s. A wonderfully retro pool, clean, spacious rooms with en-suite bathroom and a/c, and a restaurant. ④.

Trinidad, C 62 no. 46, between C 55 and C 57 (☎99/23-20-33). A wide range of rooms and a plant-filled courtyard. Decorated with modern paintings and antiques. Guests can use the pool at its sister hotel, the *Trinidad Galería* (☎99/21-09-35), nearby on the corner of C 60 and C 51. ③–④.

The City

Founded by Francisco de Montejo (the Younger) in 1542, Mérida is built over, and partly from, the ruins of a Maya city known as **Tihó**. Although, like the rest of the peninsula, it had little effective contact with central Mexico until the completion of road and rail links in the 1960s, trade with Europe brought wealth from the earliest days. In consequence the city looks more European than almost any other in Mexico – many of the older houses, indeed, are built with French bricks and tiles, brought over as tradeable ballast in the ships that exported henequen. Until the advent of artificial fibres, a substantial proportion of the world's rope was manufactured from Yucatecan henequen, a business that reached its peak during World War I.

In 1849, during the Caste Wars, the Maya armies besieging Mérida were within a hair's breadth of capturing the city and thus regaining control of the entire peninsula, when the Maya peasants left the fight in order to return to the fields to plant corn. It was this event, rather than the pleas of the inhabitants for reinforcements, that saved the élite from defeat and brought Yucatán under Mexican control. Around the turn of the century, Mérida was an extraordinarily wealthy city – or at least a city that had vast numbers of extremely rich landowners riding on the backs of a landless, semi-enslaved peonage – a wealth that went into the grandiose mansions of the outskirts (especially along the Paseo de Montejo) and into European educations for the children of the *hacendados.* Today, with that trade all but dead, it remains elegant and bustling, its streets filled with Maya going about their daily business.

Plaza Mayor

Any exploration of Mérida begins naturally in the **Plaza Mayor**. The hub of the city's life, it's ringed by some of Mérida's oldest buildings, dominated by the **Catedral de San Idelfonso** (daily 6am–noon & 5–8pm), which was built in the second half of the sixteenth century. Although most of its valuables were looted in the Revolution, the **Cristo de las Ampillas** (Christ of the Blisters), in a chapel to the left of the main altar, remains worth seeing. This statue was carved, according to legend, from a tree in the village of Ichmul that burned for a whole night without showing the least sign of damage; later, the parish church at Ichmul burned down and the statue again survived, though blackened and blistered. The image is the focal point of a local fiesta at the beginning of October. Beside the cathedral, separated from it by the Pasaje San Alvarado, the old bishop's palace has been converted into shops and offices.

Next door to the cathedral is the **Museo de Arte Contemporáneo de Yucatán** (daily 9am–5pm; US$1.50, free on Sun), the finest art museum in the state, with permanent displays of the work of internationally acclaimed Yucatecan artists such as Fernando Castro Pacheco, Gabriel Ramírez Aznar and Fernando García Ponce. There are often temporary exhibitions of ceramics from around the region, Yucatecan embroidery and metallic art. On the south side of the plaza stands the **Casa de Montejo**, a palace built in 1549 by Francisco de Montejo himself and lived in by his descendants until 1980. It now belongs to Banamex, and much of the interior is open to the public (Mon–Fri 9am–5pm). The facade is richly decorated in the Plateresque style, and above the doorway conquistadors are depicted trampling savages underfoot. The **Palacio Municipal**, on the third side, is another impressive piece of sixteenth-century design with a fine clock tower, but the nineteenth-century **Palacio de Gobierno** (daily 8am–10pm), completing the square, is more interesting to visit. Inside, murals depict the history of Yucatán and, on the first floor, there's a small historical chamber devoted to the same subject.

North of the Plaza Mayor

Most of the remaining monuments in Mérida lie north of the zócalo, with C 60 and later the Paseo de Montejo as their focus. Calle 60 is one of the city's main commercial streets, lined with several of the fancier hotels and restaurants. It also boasts a series of colonial buildings, starting with the seventeenth-century Jesuit **Iglesia de Jesús**, between the Plaza Hidalgo and the Parque de la Madre. Beside it on C 59 is the **Cepeda Peraza Library**, full of vast nineteenth-century tomes; a little further down C 59, the **Pinacoteca Virreinal** houses a rather dull collection of colonial artworks and modern sculptures in a former church. Continuing up C 60, you reach the **Teatro Peón Contreras**, a grandiose Neoclassical edifice built by Italian architects in the heady days of Porfirio Díaz and recently restored. The **university** is opposite.

The **Museo de Arte Popular** (Tues–Sat 8am–8pm, Sun 8am–2pm; free) in the former monastery of La Mejorada, C 59 between C 50 and C 48, displays a fine collection of the different styles of indigenous dress found throughout Mexico. The rich wood and glass cases show *huipiles* (the long white dresses embroidered with colourful flowers at the neck, worn by Maya women), jewellery and household items, while old black-and-white photos provide glimpses of village life and ceremonials. At the rear of the museum you can stock up on souvenirs at the really good artesanía shop.

One block north of the Teatro Peón Contreras, the sixteenth-century **Iglesia Santa Lucía** stands on the elegant plaza of the same name – a colonnaded square that used to be the town's stagecoach termina. Finally, three blocks further on, there's the **Plaza Santa Ana**, a modern open space where you turn right and then second left to reach the Paseo de Montejo.

Paseo de Montejo

The **Paseo de Montejo** is a broad, tree-lined boulevard lined with the magnificent, pompous mansions of the grandees who strove to outdo each other's style (or vulgarity) around the turn of the century. In one of the grandest, the Palacio Canton, at the corner of C 43, is Mérida's **Museo de Antropología** (Tues–Sat 8am–8pm, Sun 8am–2pm; US$5, free on Sun). The house was built for General Canton, state governor at the turn of the century, in a restrained but very expensive elegance befitting his position, and has been beautifully restored and maintained. Given the archeological riches that surround the city, the collection is perhaps something of a disappointment, but it's a useful introduction to the sites nonetheless, with displays covering everything from prehistoric stone tools to modern Maya life. Obviously there are sculptures and other objects from the main sites, but more interesting are the attempts to fill in the background and give some idea of what it was like to live in a Maya city; unfortunately, most labels are only in Spanish. Topographic maps of the peninsula, for example, explain how cenotes are formed and their importance to the ancient population; a collection of skulls demonstrates techniques of facial and dental deformation; and there are displays covering jewellery, ritual offerings and burial practices, as well as a large pictorial representation of the workings of the Maya calendar. The **bookshop** has leaflets and guidebooks in English to dozens of ruins in Yucatán and the rest of Mexico.

The walk out **to the museum** is quite a long one – you can get there on a "Paseo de Montejo" bus from C 59 just east of the Parque Hidalgo, or take a **calesa** (horse-drawn taxi) instead. This is not altogether a bad idea, especially if you fancy the romance of riding about in an open carriage, and if times are slack and you bargain well, it need cost no more than a regular taxi. Unfortunately, however, the horses are not always treated as well as they could be. Take some time to head a little further out on the Paseo de Montejo, to a lovely and very wealthy area where the homes are more modern and interspersed with big new hotels and pavement cafés. The **Monumento a la Patria**, about ten long blocks beyond the museum, is a titan, covered in neo-Maya sculptures relating to Mexican history – you'll also pass it if you take the bus out to Progreso. To do the Grand Tour properly, you should visit the **Parque de las Americas**, on Av Colón, which is planted with trees from every country on the American continent, and get back to the centre via the **Parque Centenario**, Av de los Itzaes and C 59, where there's a zoo, botanical gardens and a children's park.

Markets and handicrafts

Mérida's **market**, a huge place between calles 65, 67, 56 and 54, is for most visitors a major attraction. As far as quality goes, though, you're almost always better off buying in a shop – prices are no great shakes, either, unless you're an unusually skilful and determined haggler. Before buying anything, head for the **Casa de Artesanías** in the Edificio de Monjas, on C 63 west of the zócalo, where you'll get an idea of the potential quality and price of the goods. Run by the government-sponsored Fonapas organization, it sells crafts from the peninsula, which are of a consistently high quality, right down to the cheapest trinkets and toys.

The most popular purchase is a **hammock** – and Mérida is probably the best place in the country to buy one – but if you want something you can realistically sleep in, exercise a degree of care. There are plenty of cheap ones about, but comfort is measured by the tightness of the weave (the closer-packed the threads the better) and the breadth: since you're supposed to lie in them diagonally, in order to be relatively flat, this is far more crucial than the length (although obviously the central portion of the hammock should be at least as long as you are tall). A decent-sized hammock (*doble* at least, preferably *matrimonial*) with cotton threads (*hilos de algodon*, more comfortable and less likely to go out of shape than artificial fibres) will set you back at least US$20 – more if you get a fancy multicoloured version.

If you'd rather not mess about with vendors in the market, head for a **specialist dealer**. Tejidos y Cordeles Nacionales is one of the best, very near the market at C 56 no. 516-B. More of a warehouse than a shop, it has hundreds of the things stacked against every wall, divided up according to size, material and cost. Buy several and you can enter into serious negotiations over the price. Similar hammock stores near-by include El Campesino and El Aguacate, both on C 58, and La Poblana at C 65 no. 492.

Other good **buys** include tropical shirts (*guayaberas*), panama hats (known here as *jipis*) and *huipiles*, which vary wildly in quality, from factory-made, machine-stitched junk to hand-embroidered, homespun cloth. Even the best, though, rarely compare with the antique dresses that can occasionally be found: identical in style (as they have been for hundreds of years) but far better made and very expensive.

Eating

Good **restaurants** are plentiful in the centre of Mérida, though those on the Plaza Major can be quite expensive. Best head for the historic and atmospheric area around the **Plaza Hidalgo**, just north, along C 60 between C 61 and C 59, where you'll find plenty of good restaurants and pavement cafés, lively with crowds of tour groups and locals. Further afield, on **Paseo de Montejo**, the more expensive and sophisticated restaurants include lots of upmarket places popular with young locals.

There are a number of less expensive places around the junction of C 62 and C 61, at the northwest corner of the plaza, but cheapest of all are the *loncherías* in the **market**, where you can get good, filling comidas corridas. Around the Plaza Mayor several wonderful **juice bars** – notably *Jugos California* – serve all the regular juices and licuados, as well as more unusual local concoctions: try mamey or guanabana. Other branches are dotted about the city. Combine these with something from the **bakery** Pan Montejo, at the corner of C 62 and C 63, to make a great breakfast.

Los Almendros, C 50, between C 57 and C 59, in the Plaza Mejorada. One of Mérida's most renowned restaurants, popular with locals and visitors. Delicious, moderately priced Yucatecan food, especially at Sunday lunchtime. The original *Los Almendros*, in Ticul, claims to have invented *poc-chuc* (see box below).

Restaurante Amaro, C 59 no. 507, between C 60 and C 62. Set in a lovely stone-flagged and tree-shaded courtyard with a fountain. Some vegetarian menus, offering a welcome change for veggies who are tired of endless quesadillas.

La Bella Epoca, C 60 no. 495, Parque Hidalgo. Intimate dining in a building full of period ambience with black-tie waiters and balconies for two overlooking the Plaza Hidalgo. Surprisingly cheap.

Lonchería Milly, C 59 no. 520, between C 64 and C 66. Tiny café serving basic, inexpensive dishes to a largely local crowd. Daily 7am–11am & noon–5pm.

YUCATECAN CUISINE

Typical **Yucatecan specialities** include *puchero*, a stew of chicken, pork, carrot, squash, cabbage, potato, sweet potato and banana chunks with a delicious stock broth, garnished with radish, coriander and Seville orange; *poc-chuc*, a combination of pork with tomatoes, onions and spices; *sopa de lima* (not lime soup, exactly, but chicken broth with lime and tortilla chips in it); *pollo* or *cochinita pibil* (chicken or suckling pig wrapped in banana leaves and cooked in a *pib*, basically a pit in the ground, though restaurants cheat on this); *papadzules* (tacos stuffed with hard-boiled eggs and covered in red and green pumpkin-seed sauce); and anything *en relleno negro*, a black, burnt-chilli sauce. Little of this is hot, but watch out for the *salsa de chile habanero* that most restaurants have on the table – pure fire.

El Louvre, C 62 no. 499, corner of C 61. Popular eating place with tasty comidas corridas.

Marlin Azul, C 62 no. 488, near the zócalo. Best-value breakfast in town – great if you're on a tight budget.

Las Mil Tortas, C 62, between C 67 and C 65. Great Mexican-style sandwiches and tortas.

El Patio Español, *Gran Hotel*, C 60, Parque Hidalgo. Historic restaurant offering good, surprisingly well-priced food, and great service. As the name indicates, Spanish dishes are a speciality.

Pizzería de Vito Corleone, C 59 no. 508, corner of C 62. Inexpensive pizza restaurant that also does takeaway.

El Rincón, in the *Hotel Caribe*, C 60, next to Parque Hidalgo. Both this and the cheaper *Cafetería El Meson*, in the same building, are good, central places to eat in pleasant surroundings.

Entertainment and nightlife

Mérida is a lively city, and every evening you'll find the streets buzzing with revellers enjoying a variety of **free entertainment**. To find out what's happening, pick up a free copy of *Yucatán Today* from the tourist office or any hotel. **Venues** include the plazas, the garden behind the Palacio Municipal, the Teatro Peón Contreras (next to the tourist office) and the Casa de la Cultura del Mayab, C 63 between C 64 and C 66. Things can change, but typical performances might include energetic and fascinating **vaquerías** (vibrant Mexican folk dances, featuring different regional styles, to the rhythm of a *jaranera* band); Glen Miller-style **Big Band** music; the **Ballet Folklórico de la Universidad de Yucatán**, which performs a spectacular interpretation of Maya legends; **marimba** in the Parque Hidalgo; **classical music** concerts; and the very popular **Serenata Yucateca**, an open-air performance of traditional songs and music.

Perhaps the best time to see the Plaza Mayor and the surrounding streets is **Sunday**, when vehicles are banned from the area and day-long music, dancing, markets and festivities take over – a delight after the usual traffic roar. Street markets are set up along C 60 as far as the Plaza Santa Ana and there's a **flea market** in the Parque Santa Lucía.

There's plenty to do of a more commercial nature too, from **mariachi nights** in hotel bars to **Maya spectaculars** in nightclubs. Those aimed at tourists will be advertised in hotels, or in brochures available at the tourist office. Less obviously there are **video bars** and **discos** in most of the big hotels.

Apart from the hard-drinking *cantinas* (and there are plenty of these all over the city – including a couple of good ones on C 62, south of the plaza), many of Mérida's **bars** double as restaurants.

Bars, discos and live music

La Ciudad Maya, C 84 no. 502, corner of C 59 (☎91/24-33-13). Floor shows with Yucatecan and Cuban music. Daily 1–10pm.

La Conquista, inside the *Paseo de Montejo* hotel, C 56 no. 482, near C 41. Quiet, dark, romantic disco.

Estudio 58, C 58, between C 55 and C 57, next to and underneath the *Hotel Maya Yucatán*. Central disco and nightclub with no cover charge. Live music and a happy hour 9.30–10.30pm.

Los Juglares, C 60 no. 500. Live jazz, blues and rock until 3am.

Kalia Rock House, C 22 no. 282, near C 37. Flavour of the month at the time of writing; noisy and fun. 9pm–3am.

Pancho's, C 59, opposite the *Hotel Reforma*. A steak restaurant with a pricey Tex-Mex menu and a disco later, *Pancho's* is a magnet for Americans homesick for "Mexican" food. The fun theme, with giant photos of Mexican revolutionaries and bandolier-draped waiters in sombreros is ridiculously over the top. Try to hit the happy hour, 6–9pm.

La Prosperidad, C 56, corner of C 53. Earthier than the tourist bars, though becoming ever more popular. It's in a huge *palapa*, with live rock music in the afternoons and evenings. The beer's not cheap but it does come with substantial tasty snacks.

Listings

Airlines Aerocaribe/Aerocozumel/Mexicana Inter, Paseo de Montejo 500 (☎99/28-67-86; airport ☎99/46-16-78); Aeroméxico, Plaza Americana, Hotel Fiesta Americana (☎99/20-12-60; airport ☎99/46-14-00); Aviacsa, Prolongacion Montejo no. 130 (☎99/26-90-87; airport ☎99/46-13-78); Aviateca, Paseo de Montejo no. 475c (☎99/25-80-59; airport ☎99/46-13-12); Mexicana, Paseo de Montejo 493 (☎99/24-66-33; airport ☎99/46-13-92).

American Express Paseo de Montejo 95, between C 43 and C 45 (Mon–Fri 9am–2pm & 4–5pm, Sat 9am–noon; ☎99/28-42-22).

Banks and exchange Most banks are around C 65 between C 60 and C 64, and are open 9am–1.30pm. Banco Atlántico, C 65 no. 515, changes money 8am–1pm. Of the many casas de cambio around the centre, try Canto, C 61 no. 468, between C 54 and C 52 (Mon–Fri 8.30am–1.30pm & 4.30–7.30pm, Sat 8.30am–1pm), or Del Sureste, C 56 no. 491, between C 57 and C 59 (Mon–Sat 9am–5pm). Finex, C 60 and 59, in the corner of the Parque Hidalgo, is open longest (daily 8.30am–8pm).

Bookshops English-language guidebooks are sold at Dante Touristic Bookstore on the corner of C 57 and C 60. The *Holiday Inn*, Av Colón near the junction with Paseo de Montejo, has a small supply of English-language novels.

Car rental Hertz, at the airport (☎99/46-13-55); National, C 60 no.486-F (☎99/23-24-93, airport ☎99/46-13-94); Thrifty, C 60 no.446-C (☎ & fax 99/23-34-40).

Consulates Opening hours are likely to be fairly limited, so it's best to phone ahead and check. Belize/UK, C 58 no. 450 (☎99/28-61-52); Cuba, C 1-C no. 277A between C 38 and C 40 (☎99/44-42-15); Spain C 3-A, no. 237 (☎99/44-83-50); USA, Paseo de Montejo at Av Colón 453 (☎99/25-50-11).

MOVING ON FROM MÉRIDA

Mérida is a major transport hub, especially if you're travelling on **by bus**. Most major destinations are served from the main first- and second-class stations, but some places are better served from the multitude of different little stations dotted around town.

From the first-class **Cameon**, the most important routes run by **ADO** are to Campeche, México, Palenque and Villahermosa. **Caribe Express** provides a comfortable, a/c service with videos to Campeche and Villahermosa, as well as Cancún, Escárcega, Playa del Carmen and a number of other destinations. There are also services to Akumal, Villahermosa, Tulum and Playa del Carmen run by **Autotransportes del Caribe**. Both Caribe Express and Autotransportes del Caribe also have desks in the main first- and second-class buildings.

Buses from the **second-class** station, on C 69 between C 68 and 70, leave for **Campeche** (Autotransportes de Sureste; 4hr); **Cancún** (Expreso de Oriente; 6hr); **Escárcega** (Autotransportes de Sureste; 6hr); **Palenque** (Autotransportes de Sureste; 10–11hr); **Playa del Carmen** (Expreso de Oriente; 7hr); **Tuxtla Gutiérrez** (Autotranportes de Sureste; 20hr); **Valladolid** (Expreso de Oriente; 3hr); and **Villahermosa** (Autotransportes de Sureste; 10hr).

Of Mérida's **smaller bus stations**, C 50 on the corner with C 67 serves Autobuses de Occidente en Yucatán, for destinations west of Mérida, and Lineas Unidos del Sur de Yucatán: buses leave for **Celestún** (5am–8pm; 2hr), **Oxkutzcab** (hourly) and **Sisal** (2hr). Autobuses del Noreste en Yucatán leave from C 50 no. 529, between C 65 and C 67, for **Río Lagartos** (6hr), San Felipe (7hr) and Tizimín (4hr). Directly opposite, Autotransportes de Oriente leave for **destinations inland and east of Mérida**, with hourly buses to Cancún (6hr) and to Izamal, Pisté and Valladolid.

In addition, **colectivos** depart Plaza de San Juan, C 69 between C 62 and C 64, for Dzibilchaltún, Oxkutzcab and Ticul, among other destinations. On the northern side of the plaza there are departures to Progreso (1hr) and to Dzibilchaltún, Sierra Papacal, Komchén and Dzitya.

Flights from Mérida leave for most Mexican cities and some international destinations; to get out to the airport, catch bus #79 ("Aviación") going east on C 67.

Laundry If your hotel doesn't do laundry, try Lavamatica, C 59 no. 508 (Mon–Fri 8am–6pm, Sat 8am–2pm), which offers full-service washes.

Post office C 65, between C 56 and C 56-A (Mon–Fri 7am–7pm, Sat 9am–1pm). Has a reliable Lista de Correos that keeps mail for ten days.

Telephones Use one of the ubiquitous Ladatels or one of the many casetas dotted around town: Caseta Condesa, C 59 near C 62; Computel, Paseo de Montejo on the corner with C 37; or TelPlus, C 61 no 497, between C 58 and C 60.

Travel agencies Mérida boasts dozens of travel agencies. The best for archeological, cultural and natural history tours in the peninsula are Ecoturismo Yucatán, C 3 no. 235 between C 32-A & C 34 (☎99/25-21-87, fax 25-90-47). For trips to Cuba, try Cubamex, C 17 no. 198, between C 18 & 20 (☎99/44-43-14), Cumex, C 61 no. 499 (☎99/23-91-99), or Viajes Crisal C 56 no. 483 (☎99/26-30-44, fax 23-79-13).

North of Mérida: the coast

From Mérida to the port of **Progreso**, the closest point on the coast, is just 36km – thirty minutes on the bus. About halfway between the two, a few kilometres off the main road, lie the ancient ruins of **Dzibilchaltún**, with a cenote at the very middle of the city, fed with a constant supply of fresh water from a small spring, which you can swim in. The drive out of the city follows Paseo de Montejo through miles of wealthy suburbs and shopping malls before reaching the flat countryside where the henequen industry seems still to be flourishing. On the outskirts of Mérida there's a giant Cordemex processing plant, and a nearby shop run by the same company sells goods made from the fibre.

It's easy enough to visit both Dzibilchaltún and Progreso in one trip from Mérida if you start early: **buses** to Progreso leave from the terminal on C 62 between C 65 and C 67 and combis return to Mérida from the corner of C 80 and C 31 near the post office, on the north side of Progreso's parque central. Once you've visited the ruins, either walk, hitch or wait for the lunchtime bus back to the main road, where you can flag down a Progreso bus. Alternatively, combis for Chablecal stop at Dzibilchaltún; they leave when full (about every half-hour) from the Parque de San Juan at Mérida (corner of C 62 and C 69).

Dzibilchaltún

The importance for archeologists of the ruins of the ancient city of **Dzibilchaltún** (daily 8am–5pm; US$1.50, free on Sun) is, unfortunately, hardly reflected in what you actually see. There was, apparently, a settlement here from 1000 BC right through to the Conquest, the longest continuous occupation of any known site; more than eight thousand structures have been mapped and the city's major points were linked by great causeways – but little has survived, in particular since the ready-dressed stones were a handy building material, used in several local towns and in the Mérida–Progreso road.

In addition to providing the ancient city with water, the 44-metre-deep **Cenote Xlacah** was of ritual importance to the Maya: more than six thousand offerings – including human remains – have been discovered in its depths. A causeway leads from the cenote to a ramshackle group of buildings around the **Templo de las Siete Muñecas** (Temple of the Seven Dolls). The temple itself was originally a simple square pyramid, subsequently built over with a more complex structure. Later still, a passageway was cut through to the original building and seven deformed clay figurines (dolls) buried, with a tube through which their spirits could commune with the priests. In conjunction with the buildings that surround it, the temple is aligned with various astronomical points and must have served in some form as an observatory. It is also remarkable for being the only known Maya temple to have windows and for having a tower in place of the usual roof-comb. The dolls, and many of the finds from the cenote, can be seen in a small museum by the site entrance. Around Dzibilchaltún, five and half square kilometres have been declared an **Eco-Archeological Park**, partly to protect a unique species of fish found in the cenote. Nature trails take you through the surrounding forest and it's a great place for bird-watching.

Progreso

First impressions of **PROGRESO** – a working port with a vast concrete pier – are unprepossessing, but the beach is long and broad with fine white sand (though the water's not too clean) and it makes for a pleasant enough day out from Mérida. The shorefront behind the beach is built up all the way to **Puerto Chicxulub**, an unattractive fishing village some 5km away, and a walk between the two takes you past the mansions of the old henequen exporters, interspersed with modern holiday villas.

Streets in Progreso are confusingly numbered using two overlapping systems: one has numbers in the 70s and 80s, the other in the 20s and 30s. However, it's a small place, and not difficult to find your way around. There are a few moderately priced **places to stay** on Av Malecón, which runs along the seafront between the beach and the hotels. The less expensive hotels are a few roads back. Best bets include *Hotel Miralmar*, C 27 no. 124, on the corner of C 76 (☎993/5-05-52; ③); *Real del Mar*, Av Malecón, near C 20 (☎993/5-07-98; ③), which has clean simple rooms with bathrooms; and *Tropical Suites*, Av Malecón 143 (☎993/5-12-63; ④), which has some suites with kitchens. As for **eating**, try the seafood snacks served at *Sol y Mar*, Av Malecón at C 80, or buy **picnic food** at the market on C 27 and C 80.

Beaches around Progreso

There are stretches of **beach** in either direction from Progreso and, though this coast is the focus of much new tourism development, it's never crowded. Indeed, in winter, when the holiday homes are empty (and the rates come down), you'll have miles of sand to yourself. Check the numbers posted outside the villas and you may find bargain **long-term accommodation**.

The road east from Progreso runs through Puerto Chicxulub and continues to **Telchac**, one hour away, and the luxury *Hotel Maya Beach Resort* (☎99/24-95-55; ⑨). A little further on, at **Chabihau**, there's a small, unnamed **hotel** (③). With more time and a little perseverance, it's possible to get even further east, to **DZILAM DE BRAVO**, a remote fishing village at the end of the road, with no beach because of its ugly, though functional, sea defence wall. Here the *Hotel Los Flamencos* (④), on the main road, about ten minutes' walk west of the main square, offers basic rooms. You can rent boats (at least US$65) at the dock to visit **Bocas de Dzilam**, 40km away in the **San Felipe Natural Park**. Set in 620 square kilometres of coastal forests, marshes and dunes, the *bocas* (Spanish for mouths) are freshwater springs on the seabed; the nutrients they provide help to encourage the wide biological diversity found here. Bird- and wildlife-watching is superb: you'll see turtles, tortoises, crocodiles, spider monkeys and dozens of bird species.

A more direct way to get to Dzilam de Bravo is to catch a second-class bus in Mérida from the Autobuses del Noreste terminal. Four buses daily pass through on their way to and from Tizimín and Progreso, and one bus daily leaves for Izamal at 1pm.

Heading west, there are a number of new hotels and holiday homes along the road to **Yucalpetén**, a busy commercial port and naval base 4km from Progreso. Further west, the small but growing resorts of **Chelem** and **Chuburná**, respectively fifteen and thirty minutes from Progreso – and easy day-trips from Mérida – have clean, wide beaches and a few rooms and restaurants. It's hard to believe that the semi-deserted pueblo of **SISAL** was Mérida's chief port in colonial times. Change is in the air, though, as Sisal is earmarked for tourism. At present just a few North American duck-hunters

come for the shooting in winter, staying at the *Club de Patos*; the only other accommodation as yet is a couple of basic **budget hotels**, the *Los Corsarios* and the *Felicidades*
(both ③), near the zócalo. Beyond here the coast road is barely practicable, but there
are empty beaches all the way round to Celestún.

Celestún

CELESTÚN, at the end of a sandbar on the peninsula's northwest coast, would be little more than a one-boat fishing village were it not for its amazing bird-filled lagoon that
boasts a large flock of flamingos. To see them – as well as the blue-winged teals and
shovellers that migrate here in the winter to take advantage of the plentiful fish in these
warm, shallow waters – rent one of the boats from the bridge on the main road into
Celestún. The bus driver will drop you off here – ask for "*flamencos*" – or it's a twenty-
minute walk from the main square. Launches cost US$33 and take up to six people.
Bring your bathers with you as you may get the chance to swim in the rich red waters
among the mangroves.

Nominally protected by inclusion in the 1500-square-kilometre **Celestún Natural
Park**, the flamingos are nevertheless harassed by boats approaching too close in order
to give visitors a spectacular flying display, disturbing the birds' feeding. Try to make
it clear to your boatman that you don't wish to interrupt the birds' natural behaviour;
you will still get good photos from a respectable distance.

There are first-class **buses** from Mérida for Celestún every two hours (1hr 30min)
from the Cameon. Second-class services (2–3hr), which also stop at Sisal, leave from
the terminal on C 50, corner of C 67. There are half a dozen **lodgings** in the village: the
Hotel Gutiérrez, C 12 no. 107 (☎992/28-01-60; ④), which has some a/c rooms, and *Hotel
Maria Carmen*, C 12 no. 111 (☎992/28-03-13; ④), are both on the beach not far from the
main square. Further along the beach to the north is the *Hotel San Julio*, C 12 no. 93-A
(no phone; ③), more basic than the others but clean and comfortable. Several **seafood
restaurants** can be found on the dusty main street and on the beach – the ceviche in
Celestún is invariably good – and there's also a market, a bakery, a bank and a filling
station.

South of Mérida: Uxmal and the Ruta Puuc

About 80km south of Mérida in the **Puuc hills** lies a group of the peninsula's most
important archeological sites. **Uxmal** (pronounced oosh-mal) is chief of them, second
only to Chichén Itzá in size and significance, but perhaps greater in its initial impact and
certainly in the beauty and harmony of its extraordinary architectural style. Lesser
sites include **Kabáh**, astride the main road not far beyond; **Sayil**, nearby down a rough
side track; and **Labná**, further along this same track. Though related architecturally,
each site is quite distinct from the others, and each is dominated by one major structure. From Labná you could continue to **Oxkutzcab**, on the road from Muna to Felipe
Carillo Puerto, and head back to Mérida, via **Ticul** and **Mani,** or else take the longer
route past the Maya ruins of **Mayapán**.

Like Chichén Itzá, the Puuc sites are now regarded as being as authentically Maya as
Tikal or Palenque, rather than the product of invading Toltecs, as was once believed.
Though there are new stylistic themes both in the Puuc sites and at Chichén Itzá, there
are also marked continuities of architectural and artefactural technique, religious symbolism, hieroglyphic writing and settlement patterns. The newer themes are now believed to
have been introduced by the **Chontal Maya** of the Gulf Coast lowlands, who had become
the Yucatán's most important trading partners by the Terminal Classic period (800–1000
AD). The Chontal Maya themselves traded extensively with Oaxaca and central Mexico
and are thought to have passed on their architectural styles and themes to the Yucatán.

Getting to the sites

The sites are far enough apart that it's impractical to do more than a fraction of the them by bus, unless you're prepared to spend several days and endure a lot of waiting around. The cheapest and most practical way to visit the sites is to take the **"Ruta Puuc" day-trip bus** (US$5), run by Autotransportes del Sur from the bus station (see box on p.61), and though you don't get much time at the ruins, Uxmal is the last visited and it is possible to stay later and pay for a different bus back. Scores of Mérida travel agencies offer pricier Puuc route trips.

It's better still to **rent a car**: in two days you can explore all the key sites, either returning overnight to Mérida or finding a room in Muna, Ticul or, more expensively, at Uxmal itself. This way you could even include the Uxmal son et lumière – better than the one at Chichén Itzá. For details of car rental agencies, see p.68.

Uxmal

UXMAL – "thrice-built" – represents the finest achievement of the **Puuc architectural style**, in which buildings of amazingly classical proportions are decorated with broad

Uxmal emblem glyph

stone mosaic friezes of geometric patterns, or designs so stylized and endlessly repeated as to become almost abstract. As in every Maya site in the Yucatán, the face of **Chac**, the rain god, is everywhere. Chac must have been more crucial here than almost anywhere, for Uxmal and the other Puuc sites, almost uniquely, have no cenote or other natural source of water, relying instead on artificially created underground cisterns, jug-shaped and coated with lime, to collect and store rainwater. In recent years these have all been filled in, to prevent mosquitoes breeding.

Little is known of the city's history, but what is clear is that the chief monuments, and the city's peaks of power and population, fall into the Terminal Classic period, and though there are indications of settlement long before this, most of the buildings that you see date from this period. Some time after 900 AD the city began to decline and by 1200 Uxmal and all the Puuc sites, together with Chichén Itzá, were all but abandoned. The reasons for this are unknown, although political infighting, ecological problems and loss of trade with Tula may have played a part. Later, the **Xiu dynasty** settled at Uxmal, which became one of the central pillars of the League of Mayapán, and from here, in 1441, the rebellion originated that finally overthrew the power of Mayapán and put an end to any form of centralized Maya authority over the Yucatán. All the significant surviving structures, though, date from the Classic period.

The site

Entering **the site** (daily 8am–5pm; US$4), the back of the great **Pirámide del Adivino** (Pyramid of the Magician) rises before you. The most remarkable-looking of all Mexican pyramids, it soars at a startling angle from its oval base to a temple some 30m above the ground, with a broad but steep stairway up either side. It takes its name from the legend that it was magically constructed in a single night by a dwarf, though in fact at least five stages of construction have been discovered – six if you count the modern restoration, which may not correspond exactly to any of its earlier incarnations.

The rear (east) stairway leads, past a tunnel which reveals Templo III, directly to the top, and a platform surrounding the temple that crowns the pyramid. Even with the chain to help you, the climb up the high, thin steps is not for the unfit, nor for anyone who suffers from vertigo. The views, though, are sensational, particularly looking west over the rest of the site and the green unexcavated mounds that surround it. Here you're standing at the front of the summit temple, its facade decorated with interlocking geometric motifs. Below it, the west stairway runs down either side of a second, ear-

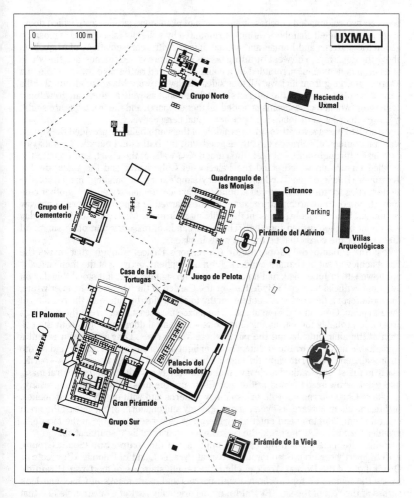

0   100 m

Grupo Norte

Hacienda
Uxmal

Quadrangulo de
las Monjas

Entrance

Parking

Pirámide del Adivino

Grupo del
Cementerio

Villas
Arqueológicas

Casa de las
Tortugas

Juego de Pelota

El Palomar

N

Palacio del
Gobernador

Gran Pirámide

Grupo Sur

Pirámide de la Vieja

lier sanctuary in a distinctly different style. Known as the **Edificio Chenes** (or Templo
IV), it does indeed reflect the architecture of the Chenes region (see p.92), the entire
front forming a giant mask of Chac. At the bottom of the west face, divided in half by
the stairway, you'll find yet another earlier stage of construction (the first) – the long,
low facade of a structure apparently similar to the so-called "Nunnery".

The **Quadrangulo de las Monjas** (Nunnery Quadrangle), a beautiful complex of
four buildings enclosing a square plaza, is one of many buildings here named quite erro-
neously by the Spanish, to whom it resembled a convent. Whatever it may have been, it
wasn't a convent; theories range from it being a military academy to a sort of earthly paradise where intended sacrificial victims would spend their final months in debauchery.
The four buildings are in fact from different periods and, although they blend superbly,
each is stylistically distinct. The **north building**, raised higher than the others and even
more richly ornamented, is probably also the oldest. Approached up a broad stairway

between two colonnaded porches, it has a strip of plain stone facade (from which doors lead into the vaulted chambers within) surmounted by a slightly raised panel of mosaics: geometric patterns and human and animal figures, with representations of Maya huts above the doorways. The **west building** boasts even more varied themes, and the whole of its ornamentation is surrounded by a coiling, feathered rattlesnake with the face of a warrior emerging from its jaws. All four sides display growing Maya architectural skills – the false Maya vaults of the interiors are taken about as wide as they can go without collapsing (wooden crossbeams provided further support), and the frontages are slightly bowed in order to maintain a proper horizontal perspective.

An arched passageway through the middle of the south building provided the square with a monumental entrance directly aligned with the **ball court** outside. Nowadays a path leads through here, between the ruined side walls of the court, and up onto the levelled terrace on which stand the Palacio del Gobernador and the **Casa de las Tortugas** (House of the Turtles). This very simple, elegant building, named for the stone turtles (or tortoises) carved around the cornice, demonstrates well another constant theme of Puuc architecture: stone facades carved to appear like rows of narrow columns. These probably represent the building style of the Maya huts still in use today – walls of bamboo lashed together. The plain bands of masonry that often surround them mirror the cords that tie the hut walls in place.

It is the **Palacio del Gobernador** (Governor's Palace), though, that marks the finest achievement of Uxmal's builders. John L. Stephens, arriving at the then virtually unknown site in June 1840, had no doubts as to its significance: "if it stood this day on its grand artificial terrace in Hyde Park or the Garden of the Tuileries," he later wrote, "it would form a new order . . . not unworthy to stand side by side with the remains of the Egyptian, Grecian and Roman art." The palace faces east, away from the buildings around it, probably for astronomical reasons – its central doorway aligns with the column of the altar outside and the point where Venus rises. Long and low, it is lent a remarkable harmony by the architect's use of light and shade on the facade, and by the strong diagonals that run right through its broad band of mosaic decorations – particularly in the steeply vaulted archways that divide the two wings from the central mass, like giant arrow-heads aimed at the sky. Close up, the mosaic is equally impressive, masks of Chac alternating with grid-and-key patterns and with highly stylized snakes. Inside, the chambers are, as ever, narrow, gloomy and unadorned; but at least the great central room, 20m long and entered by the three closer-set openings in the facade, is grander than most. At the back, the rooms have no natural light source at all.

Behind the palace stand the ruinous buildings of the **Grupo Sur** (South Group), with the partly restored Gran Pirámide (Great Pyramid), and El Palomar (Dovecote or Quadrangle of the Doves). You can climb the rebuilt staircase of the **Gran Pirámide** to see the temple on top, decorated with parrots and more masks of Chac, and look across at the rest of the site. **El Palomar** was originally part of a quadrangle like that of the Nunnery, but the only building to retain any form is this, topped with the great wavy, latticed roof-comb from which it takes its name.

Of the outlying structures, the **Pirámide de la Vieja** (Pyramid of the Old Woman), probably the earliest surviving building at Uxmal, is now little more than a grassy mound with a clearly man-made outline. The **Grupo del Cementerio** (Cemetery Group), too, is in a state of ruin – low altars in the middle of this square bear traces of carved hieroglyphs and human skulls.

Practicalities

Several **buses** a day run direct from Mérida to Uxmal, and any bus heading down the main road towards Hopelchén (or between Mérida and Campeche on the longer route) will drop you just a short walk from the entrance. Note that none runs late enough to get you back to Mérida after the son et lumière. At the modern **entrance to the site** (daily 8am–5pm; US$7, free on Sun) the **tourist centre** includes a small museum, a snack bar and a shop with guides to the site, souvenirs, film and suchlike. Uxmal's son et lumière (daily except Mon) is at 7pm in Spanish (US$2.50), 9pm in English (US$3); the commentary is pretty crass, but the lighting effects are undeniably impressive.

There are three expensive **hotels** nearby. The best value near the ruins is *Villas Arqueológicas* (☎ & fax 99/280-06-44; ⑦), right at the entrance, which has a/c rooms, a pool and a good library on the Maya. *Hacienda Uxmal* (☎99/23-47-44, fax 28-08-40; ⑨) is equally luxurious, with huge rooms, beautiful tiling and heavy wooden furniture, and *Rancho Uxmal* (☎999/2-02-77; ⑤) is a cheaper option, but still comfortable, with some a/c rooms; both are 4km north towards Muna. You can also **camp** at the *Rancho* (①).

Travelling from Uxmal to Kabáh, you'll pass the **Sacbe campsite and trailer park** (②). It's about fifteen minutes' walk south from the main square in the village of Santa Elena; if you're travelling by bus, ask the driver to drop you off at the entrance. Run by a Mexican–French couple, who have maps and can provide accurate information about the area, the site is a haven for backpackers, with tent sites dotted among the shady fruit trees. There are also some new cabañas (②), and limited space for your own hammock. There's nowhere to **eat** here or in Santa Elena, so bring supplies.

Kabáh

Some 20km south of Uxmal, the extensive site of **KABÁH** (daily 8am–5pm; US$1.50, free on Sun) stretches across the road. Much of it remains unexplored, but the one great building, the **Codz Poop** or Palace of Masks, lies not far off the highway to the left. The facade of this amazing structure is covered all over, in ludicrous profusion, with goggle-eyed, trunk-nosed masks of Chac. Even in its present state – with most of the long, curved noses broken off – this is the strangest and most striking of all Maya buildings, decorated so obsessively, intricately and repetitively that it seems almost insane. Even the steps by which you reach the doorways and the interior are more Chac noses. There are a couple of lesser buildings grouped around the Codz Poop, and on the other side of the road an unusual circular pyramid – now simply a green, conical mound. Across the road a sort of triumphal arch marks the point where the ancient causeway from Uxmal entered the city.

Leaving Kabáh, you may have to virtually lie down in the road to persuade a bus to stop for you – ask the guards at the site for the bus times. Hitching a ride with other visitors, though, is generally pretty easy, and with luck you may even meet someone touring all the local sites.

Sayil

A sober, restrained contrast to the excesses of Kabáh, the ruined site of **SAYIL** (daily 8am–5pm; US$1.50, free on Sun) lies some 5km along a minor road heading east from the highway, 5km beyond Kabáh. It is again dominated by one major structure, the extensively restored **Gran Palacio** (Great Palace), built on three storeys, each smaller than the one below, and some 80m long. Although there are several large masks of Chac in a frieze around the top of the middle level, the decoration mostly takes the form of bamboo-effect stone pillaring – seen here more extensively than anywhere. The interiors of the middle level, too, are lighter and airier than is usual, thanks to the use of broad openings, their lintels supported on fat columns. The upper and lower storeys are almost entirely unadorned, plain stone surfaces with narrow openings.

Few other structures have been cleared. From the Gran Palacio a path leads to the right to the large temple of **El Mirador**, and in the other direction to a stela, carved with a phallic figure and now protected under a thatched roof. On the opposite side of the road from all this, a small path leads uphill, in about ten minutes, to two more temples.

Xlapak, Labná and Chacmultún

The minor road continues, paved but in poor condition, past the tiny Puuc site known as **XLAPAK** (daily 8am–5pm; US$1, free on Sun). Its proximity to the larger sites of Labná and Sayil means that Xlapak (Maya for "old walls") is seldom visited, but if you have the time, stop to see the recently restored buildings with their carvings of masks and yet more Chac noses. **LABNÁ** (daily 8am–5pm; US$1.50, free on Sun) is about 3km further. Near the entrance to this ancient city is a palace, similar to but less impressive than that of Sayil, on which you'll see traces of sculptures including the inevitable Chac, and a crocodile (or snake) with a human face emerging from its mouth – symbolizing a god escaping from the jaws of the underworld. Remnants of a raised causeway lead from here to a second group of buildings, of which the most important is the **Arco de Labná**. Originally part of a complex linking two great squares, like the Nunnery at Uxmal, it now stands alone as a sort of triumphal arch. Both sides are richly decorated: on the east with geometric patterns; on the west (the back) with more of these and niches in the form of Maya huts or temples. Nearby is El Mirador, a temple with the well-preserved remains of a tall, elaborate roof-comb.

CHACMULTÚN, 50 km from Labná on a partially paved road off Hwy-184, is another interesting Puuc site, with a series of hilltop buildings built on artificial terraces. One of them, the Edificio de las Pinturas, contains various **wall paintings** of Maya adorned with feathers and brandishing spears or holding trumpets, parasols or pictures of the houses they once lived in. Other buildings preserve traces of the deep blues and reds that once covered Maya temples and the El Palacio building has an intricate columned facade typical of the Puuc style.

Oxkutzcab and around

From the village of **OXKUTZCAB** (also known as Huerta del Estado) on Hwy-184, 20km from Labna, you can head north back to Mérida via Ticul and Mani. Though there's little reason to overnight in Oxkutzcab, it's as good a place as any to stop for a while, with a huge **fruit market**, bustling and lively in the mornings, selling most of its produce by the crate or sack. Calles 51 and 50 edge the main park and the mercado, with a large Franciscan church cornering them. There are also some remote Puuc ruins at Kuiuc and Xkichmook, both of which lie off a minor road that runs south from the village of Oxkutzcab.

Buses to Mérida, via Ticul, leave about every hour (2hr) from the **bus station** at the corner of C 56 and C 51; colectivos come and go from beside the mercado on C 51. Of the two basic **hotels**, *Hospedaje "Trujeque"*, C 48, opposite the park (☎997/5-05-68; ③), is cleaner and more comfortable, though *Hospedaje Rosalia*, C 54 no. 103 (☎997/5-03-37; ③), has the advantage of being just around the corner from the bus station. The Banamex **bank** on C 50, opposite the park, can only exchange US dollars cash – not travellers' cheques. **Restaurants** and cafeterias skirt the market, but if you fancy a long, lazy lunch, try a few blocks back at the *Restaurante Su Cabaña Suiza*, C 54 no. 101, where comidas are served in the tranquillity of a spacious open-sided *palapa*.

The Grutas de Loltún

Just outside Oxkutzcab, hidden away near the road to Labná, the **Grutas de Loltún** (daily 9am–5pm; US$4, US$2 on Sun), studded with stalactites and stalagmites (one in the shape of a giant corn cob), were revered by the Maya as a source of water from a time long before they built their cities. At the entrance, a huge bas-relief of a jaguar warrior guards the opening to the underworld, and throughout there are traces of ancient paintings and carvings on the walls. Nowadays the caves are lit, and there are spectacular guided tours (officially at 9.30am, 11am, 12.30pm, 2pm & 3pm; in practice it depends on who turns up, and when; US$1.50). The surrounding jungle is visible through the collapsed floor of the last gallery and ten-metre-long tree roots find an anchor on the cavern floor. The *Restaurante Guerrero*, by the entrance to the caves, is welcome but expensive.

There's very little transport to the caves **from Oxkutzcab**: taxis exploit their monopoly by charging well over the odds for the short run. Colectivos and trucks that pass the caves leave from C 51 next to the market; if you get there by 8.30am you may be able to catch the truck taking the cave employees to work. Getting back is less easy, as the trucks are full of workers and produce, but, if you wait, something will turn up.

Ticul, Mayapán and Mani

Conveniently located 80km south of Mérida on Hwy-184, **TICUL** is another excellent base for exploring the Puuc region. You can head straight back to Mérida from here or else take the slightly longer route via the Maya sites of **Mani** and **Mayapán**. The town is an important centre of Maya shamanism as well as a pottery-producing centre and it's full of shops selling reproduction Maya antiquities, mostly too big to carry home. Visitors are welcome to watch the manufacturing process at the *fabricas*. Despite this, Ticul lives life at a slow pace, with more bicycles (and passenger-carrying *triciclos*) than cars.

On the main road between Mérida and Felipe Carrillo Puerto in Quintana Roo, Ticul is an important transport centre, well served by **buses** to and from Mérida and with services to Cancún. If you're arriving by bus from Mérida, you'll be dropped in C 24 on the corner with C 25, behind the church. Buses **from Campeche** don't go through Ticul so you'll have to get off at Santa Elena to catch one of the colectivos that leave from the main square between about 6am and 7pm; the trip takes about thirty minutes. **Trucks** for Oxkutzcab and surrounding villages set off when they're full from the side of the plaza next to the church; **combis** for Mérida leave from further down the same street.

Even-numbered roads run north to south, odd numbers east to west. Calle 23 is the main street, with the plaza at its eastern end at C 26. Half a block from the plaza, the *Sierra Sosa*, C 26 no. 199-A (☎997/2-00-08; ④), has basic **rooms**, with shower and fan (upstairs is better), and a few new a/c rooms with TV. The English-speaking manager, Luis Sierra, is a good source of information, and you can make international calls from reception. Alternatives include the plusher *Motel Cerro Inn*, C 23 no. 292, at the western edge of town (☎997/2-02-60; ④), in its own tree-shaded spacious grounds with an on-site *palapa* restaurant; and the newer *Hotel Bugambilias*, C 23 between C 44 and C 46 (☎997/2-07-61; ④), slightly closer to town than the *Cerro*, but with less character.

The best of the **restaurants** is the original *Los Almendros*, C 23 no. 207, which serves superb local dishes in pleasant surroundings. The *Restaurant Colorín*, next door to *Hotel Sierra Sosa* on C 26, does an inexpensive comida, or, if you fancy a large satisfying pizza, try *La Gondolia Pizzeria*, C 23 on the corner of C 26. As usual, the least expensive places are the *loncherías* near the bus station.

Mayapán and Mani

Forty-nine kilometres north of Ticul are the ruins of **MAYAPÁN**, the most powerful city in the Yucatán from the eleventh to the fifteenth century. Its history is somewhat vague but, according to Maya chronicles, it formed (with Chichén Itzá and Uxmal) one of a triumvirate of cities that as the **League of Mayapán** exercised control over the entire peninsula from around 987 to 1185. However, these dates, based on surviving Maya chronicles, are controversial, since archeological evidence suggests that Mayapán was not a significant settlement until the thirteenth century. The rival theory has Mayapán founded around 1263, after the fall of Chichén Itzá.

The league broke up when the **Cocom** dynasty of Mayapán attacked and over-whelmed the rulers of an already declining Chichén Itzá, establishing themselves as sole controllers of the peninsula. Mayapán became a huge city by the standards of the day, with a population of some 15,000 in a site covering five square kilometres, in which traces of more than four thousand buildings have been found. Here rulers of subject cities were forced to live where they could be kept under control, perhaps even as hostages. This hegemony was maintained until 1441 when Ah Xupan, a Xiu leader from Uxmal, finally led a rebellion that succeeded in overthrowing the Cocom and destroy-ing their city – thus paving the way for the disunited tribalism that the Spanish found on their arrival, which made their conquest so much easier.

What can be seen today is a disappointment – the buildings anyway were crude and small by Maya standards, at best poor copies of what had gone before. This has led to its widespread dismissal as a "decadent" and failing society, but a powerful case can be made for the fact that it was merely a changing one. Here the priests no longer domi-nated – hence the lack of great ceremonial centres – and what grew instead was a more genuinely urban society: highly militaristic, no doubt, but also far more centralized and more reliant on trade than anything seen previously.

After the fall of Mayapán, the Xiu abandoned Uxmal and founded **MANI**, 15km east of Ticul. It's hard to believe that what is now simply a small village was, at the time of the Conquest, the largest city the Spanish encountered. Fortunately for the Spanish, its ruler, Ah Kukum Xiu, converted to Christianity and became their ally. Here, in 1548, was founded one of the earliest and largest **Franciscan monasteries** in the Yucatán. This still stands, surrounded now by Maya huts, and just about the only evidence of Mani's past glories are the ancient stones used in its construction. In front of the church, in 1562, Bishop Diego de Landa held the notorious *auto de fe* in which he burned the city's ancient records (because they "contained nothing in which there was not to be seen the superstitions and lies of the devil"), destroying virtually all surviving original Maya literature.

Chichén Itzá

Chichén Itzá, the most famous, the most extensively restored and by far the most visited of all Maya sites, lies conveniently astride the main road from Mérida to Cancún and the Caribbean, about 120km from Mérida and a little more than 200km from the coast. There's a fast and very regular bus service all

along this road, making it perfectly feasible to visit as a day's excursion from Mérida, or en route from Mérida to the coast (or even as a day out from Cancún, as many tour buses do). The site, though, deserves better, and both to do the ruins justice and to see them when they're not entirely overrun by tourists, an overnight stop is well worth considering – either at the site itself or, less extravagantly, at the nearby village of **Pisté** or in Valladolid (see p.84).

Chichén emblem glyph

The route from Mérida: Izamal and Aké

If your route to Chichén Itzá is fairly leisurely, **IZAMAL**, 72km from Mérida, is the one place that does merit a detour. The town is something of a quiet backwater whose colo-nial air is denied by its inhabitants' allegiance to their traditional dress and lifestyle. It was formerly an important Maya religious centre, where they worshipped **Itzamna**, mythical founder of the ancient city and one of the gods of creation, at a series of huge pyramid-temples of the same name. Most are now no more than low hillocks in the sur-rounding country, but two survive in the town itself. One, **Kinich Kakmo** (daily

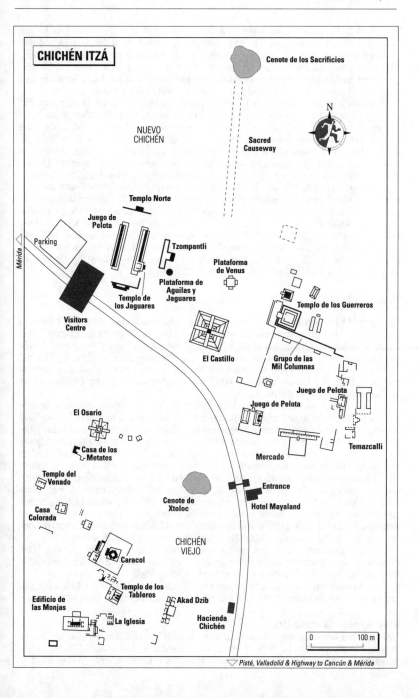

8am–8pm; free), just a couple of blocks from the central plaza and dedicated to the sun god, has been partly restored. The other had its top lopped off by the Spanish and was replaced with a vast monastery, the **convent of St Anthony of Padua** (daily; free), which was painted a deep yellow, like much of the town, for the pope's visit in 1993. The porticoed atrium is particularly beautiful and photogenic in the late afternoon, and inside it is a statue of the Virgin of Izamal, patron saint of the Yucatán.

There are a couple of very basic hotels in Izamal, both on the zócalo. Don't get caught out with no money here as there isn't a bank, though there is a **post office** on the main square. *Restaurant Portales* on the main square serves good Mexican **food**, as does the *Café Restaurant Los Norteños*, next to the bus station, one block back from the main square. **Buses to Izamal** leave every 45 minutes from Autotransportes de Oriente in Mérida (see p.68). They take a little over an hour and return to Mérida every 45 minutes. It's therefore possible to visit Izamal in a comfortable afternoon trip from Mérida.

The Maya city of **Aké**, which lies halfway between Izamal and Mérida, was probably in alliance with Izamal and is linked to it by one of the peninsula's largest *sacbes* (Maya roads). One of the most impressive buildings here is a large, pillared building on a platform, surrounded by a huge plaza of 20,000 square metres. There is also a ruined henequen hacienda, San Lorenzo de Aké, on the same site, whose church is built over one of the temples. The charm of this site lies partly in its tranquillity, as few visitors come here, but you'll need your own transport to get to it. Follow the signs from Tixkobob, the nearest village, which lies on the highway.

Practicalities

Arriving at Chichén Itzá you'll find that the highway, which once cut straight through the middle of the ruins, has been re-routed around the site. If you're on a through bus it may drop you at the junction of the bypass and the old road, about ten minutes' walk from the entrance – most, though, drive right up to the site entrance. Although blocked off by gates at each side of the fenced-in site, the old road still exists, conveniently dividing the ruins in two: **Chichén Viejo** (Old Chichén) to the south, **Nuevo Chichén** (New or "Toltec" Chichén) to the north.

The main **entry to the site** (daily 8am–5pm, though the process of getting everyone out starts at least an hour earlier; US$4, extra with video camera or tripod, free on Sun) is to the west, at the Mérida end. Keep your ticket, which permits re-entry, and check the timetable for admissions to the various buildings – most open only for a couple of hours each day, and you'll want to plan your wanderings around their schedules. There are bus and car parks here, and a huge **visitor centre** (open until 10pm) with a museum, restaurant, and shops selling souvenirs, film, maps and guides (best are the Panorama series). **Guided tours** of the ruins can be arranged at the visitor centre. Group tours (9am–3.30pm) for six to eight people, in Spanish or English, cost around US$8 per person. Private tours (8am–2.30pm) cost around US$33 per guide. There's a nightly **son et lumière** in English (9pm; US$4) and Spanish (7pm; US$2): worth seeing if you're staying nearby – it's no great shakes, but there's nothing else to do in the evening.

You can also buy tickets and get in at the **smaller eastern gate** by the *Hotel Mayaland* (see opposite), where there are fewer facilities. Book at the hotel reception for two-hour **horseback riding trips** around Chichén Viejo.

To make your way to the Caribbean coast from Chichén Itzá, it's best to take any bus you can as far as Valladolid (see p.84), and if necessary change there for a first-class service.

Staying near Chichén Itzá

Chichén Itzá boasts some excellent **hotels** virtually on site. The *Hacienda Chichén* (☎985/1-00-45; in Mérida: ☎99/24-88-44, fax 24-50-11; in US: ☎1-800/624-8451; ⑧), which has a couple of small ruins within its grounds, is the best; write to C 60 no. 488,

Mérida 97000. The even posher *Hotel Mayaland*, Carretera Mérida–Puerto Juárez Km 120 (☎985/1-01-28 or 1-00-77, fax 1-01-29; ⑨), has a gorgeous colonial-style dining room and rooms in luxurious thatched huts dotted about the gardens. Nearby Pisté has cheaper options.

Least aesthetically pleasing, but still pretty good, is *Villas Arqueologicas* (☎985/1-00-34, fax 1-00-18; ⑧), a modern place run by Club Med, with rooms set out round a patio enclosing a pool and cocktail bar: by night, its library of archeological and architectural tomes doubles as a disco (usually empty). All three hotels have pools, which are open to anyone who eats lunch there, though in the *Villas Arqueologicas* you could probably get away with just having a drink at the poolside bar.

Alternatively, you can take a taxi in the **other direction** (east) from the ruins and get to the tiny *Dolores Alba* (☎985/28-56-50, fax 21-37-40; in Mérida: ☎99/28-56-50; ⑤), just over 2km away, with a restaurant and rooms around a pool – the best value here if you don't mind being stuck by the road in the middle of nowhere (but still much less than an hour's walk from the site). The staff are very helpful and friendly and will provide transport to the site (but not back). Rooms can be booked in advance at the hotel of the same name in Mérida.

PISTÉ

Pisté is a tiny, unattractive village spread along the main road between Mérida and Valladolid, about twenty minutes' walk from the ruins. Its saving grace is that it enables visitors to get up early enough to miss the teeming hordes of package tourists who arrive at Chichén Itzá at about 10.30 am. **Buses** pass Pisté every thirty minutes for Mérida and about every hour for Valladolid. There are also services to Cancún and Playa del Carmen.

Most **hotels** are on the main road, between the village and the ruins, so it's easy to shop around for the best deal. *Hotel Misión Chichén Itzá*, Km 118 (☎985/1-00-22, fax 1-00-23; ⑥) has a/c rooms with bath and the best pool in Pisté. Budget travellers should head for the unglamorous, but clean and friendly *Posada El Carrousel* (☎985/1-00-78; ③); the best rooms are away from the road.

There are **restaurants** lining the road, alongside the hotels. The best value are the *Posada El Carrousel* and *Las Mestizas*, which does some good-value regional cuisine. The pricier hotels all have their own restaurants.

The site

Though in most minds **CHICHÉN ITZÁ** represents the very image of the Maya, in reality it is its very divergence from accepted Maya tradition that makes it so fascinating, and so important to archeologists. Even today, its history remains hotly disputed. Archeologists are fairly certain that the city rose to power in the Terminal Classic period (between 800 and 1000 AD), and was probably established about five hundred years before that, but what they are undecided about is exactly who built the city. Much of the evidence at the site – an emphasis on human sacrifice, the presence of a huge ball court and the glorification of military activity – points to a strong Mexican influence; considering the dates of Chichén's ascendancy, it seemed that this was the result of the city's defeat by the Toltecs, a theory reinforced by the resemblance of the Temple of the Warriors to the L-shaped colonnade at Tula, along with numerous depictions of the Toltec god-king, the feathered serpent, **Quetzalcoatl** (Kukulkán to the Maya).

However, recent work at Chichén Itzá has revealed some continuity between Chichén Itzá and earlier Maya sites in the southern lowlands. It's now thought that Chichén Itzá was never invaded by the Toltecs, but occupied by Maya throughout its history, with the Mexican influence coming via its chief trading partner, the Chontal Maya or Putun of the Gulf Coast lowlands. The Chontal were themselves influenced by Mexico and Oaxaca through a thriving network of trade and political allegiances. This new theory is not without its own puzzles, though, as the **Itzá** kings who ruled Chichén Itzá were referred to by the contemporary Maya as "foreigners". However, they may actually have been Maya who moved north after droughts caused the abandonment of the forest cities, and there is, indeed, a marked continuity of styles with the Maya sites of the southern lowlands.

Chichén Nuevo

If it's still reasonably early, head first for **El Castillo** (or the Pyramid of Kukulkán), the structure that dominates the site. This should allow you to climb it before the full heat of the day, and get a good overview of the entire area. It is a simple, relatively unadorned square building, with a monumental stairway climbing each face (though only two are restored), rising in nine receding terraces to a temple at the top. The simplicity is deceptive, however, as the building is in fact the **Maya calendar** made stone: each staircase has 91 steps, which, added to the single step at the main entrance to the temple, amounts to 365; other numbers relevant to the Maya calendar recur throughout the construction. Most remarkably, at sunset on the spring and autumn equinoxes, the great serpents' heads at the foot of the main staircase are joined to their tails (at the top) by an undulating body of shadow – an event of just a few hours that draws spectators, and awed worshippers, by the thousand.

Inside the present structure, an earlier pyramid survives almost wholly intact. An entrance has been opened at the bottom of El Castillo, through which you reach a narrow, dank and claustrophobic stairway (formerly the outside of the inner pyramid) that leads steeply to a temple on the top. In its outer room is a rather crude chac-mool, but in the **inner sanctuary**, now railed off, stands one of the greatest finds at the site: an altar, or throne, in the form of a jaguar, painted bright red and inset with jade "spots" and eyes – the teeth are real jaguar teeth. This discovery was one of the first to undermine the Toltec theory: though the sculpture is apparently Toltec in style, it predates their ostensible arrival.

THE "TOLTEC" PLAZA

The Castillo stands on the edge of the great grassy plaza that formed the focus of Nuevo Chichén Itzá: all its most important buildings are here, and from the northern edge a *sacbe*, or sacred causeway, leads to the great **Cenote de los Sacrificios**. The **Templo de los Guerreros** (Temple of the Warriors), and the adjoining **Grupo de las Mil Columnas** (Group of the Thousand Columns), take up the eastern edge of the plaza. These are the structures that most recall the great Toltec site of Tula, near México City, both in design and in detail – in particular the colonnaded courtyard (which would originally have been roofed with some form of thatch) and the use of atlantean columns, representing warriors in armour, their arms raised above their heads. Throughout, the temple is richly decorated with carvings and sculptures (originally with paintings, too) of jaguars and eagles devouring human hearts, feathered serpents, warriors and, the one undeniably Maya feature, masks of Chac. On top are two superb **chac-mools**: offerings were placed on the stomachs of these reclining figures, representing the messengers who would take the sacrifice to the gods, or perhaps the divinities themselves.

Once again, the Templo de los Guerreros was built over an earlier temple, in which (during set hours) some remnants of faded **murals** can be made out. The "thousand" columns alongside originally formed a square, on the far side of which is the building known as the **Mercado**, although there's no evidence that this actually was a marketplace. Near here, too, is a small, ruinous ball court.

Walking across the plaza towards the main ball court, you pass three small platforms. The **Plataforma de Venus** is a simple, raised, square block, with a stairway up each side guarded by feathered serpents. Here, rites associated with Quetzalcoatl in his role of Venus, the morning star, would have been carried out. Slightly smaller, but otherwise virtually identical in design, is the **Aquilas y Jaguares** platform, on which you'll see relief carvings of eagles and jaguars holding human hearts. Human sacrifices may even have been carried out here, judging by the proximity of the third platform, the **Tzompantli**, where victims' skulls were hung on display. This is carved on every side with grotesquely grinning stone skulls.

THE BALL COURT

Chichén Itzá's **Juego de Pelota** (ball court), on the western side of the plaza, is the largest known in existence – some 90m long. Its design is classically Maya: a capital I shape surrounded by temples, with the goals, or target rings, halfway along each side. Along the bottom of each side wall runs a sloping panel decorated in low relief with scenes of the game and its players. Although the rules and full significance of the game remain a mystery, it was clearly not a Saturday afternoon kick-about in the park. The players are shown processing towards a circular central symbol, the symbol of death, and one player (thought to be the winning captain – just right of the centre) has been decapitated, while another (to the left) holds his head and a ritual knife. Along the top runs the stone body of a snake, whose heads stick out at either end of this "bench".

At each end of the court stand small buildings with open **galleries** overlooking the field of play – the low one at the south may simply have been a grandstand, that at the north (the **Templo Norte**, also known as the Temple of the Bearded Man, after a sculpture inside) was almost certainly a temple – perhaps, too, the umpires' stand. Inside, there are several worn relief carvings and a whispering gallery effect that enables you to be heard clearly at the far end of the court, and to hear what's going on there.

The **Templo de los Jaguares** also overlooks the playing area, but from the side; to get to it, you have to go back out to the plaza. At the bottom – effectively the outer wall of the ball court – is a little portico supported by two pillars, between which a stone jaguar stands sentinel. Inside are some wonderful, rather worn, relief carvings of Maya priests and warriors, animals, birds and plants. Beside this, a very steep, narrow staircase ascends to a platform overlooking the court and to the **Upper Temple** (restricted opening hours), with its fragments of a mural depicting battle scenes.

The **Cenote de los Sacrificios** lies at the end of the causeway that leads off through the trees from the northern side of the plaza – about 300m away. It's a remarkable phenomenon, an almost perfectly round hole in the limestone surface of the earth, some 60m in diameter and more than 40m deep, the bottom half full of water. It was thanks to the presence of this natural well (and perhaps another in the southern half of the site) that the city could survive at all, and it gives Chichén Itzá its present name "At the Edge of the Well of the Itzá". This well was regarded as a portal to the "other world" and Maya would throw offerings into it – incense, statues, jade and especially metal disks (a few of them gold), engraved and embossed with figures and glyphs – and also human sacrificial victims. People who were thrown in and survived emerged with the power of prophecy, having spoken with the gods. A new cafeteria now overlooks the well, a distraction for anyone contemplating the religious and mystical significance of the cenote.

Chichén Viejo

The southern half of the site is the most sacred part for contemporary Maya, though the buildings here are not, on the whole, in such good condition: less restoration work has been carried out so far, and the ground is not so extensively cleared. A path leads from the road opposite El Castillo to all the major structures, passing first the pyramid known as **El Osario** (aka the High Priest's Grave), currently undergoing restoration. Externally it is very similar to El Castillo, but inside, most unusually, a series of **tombs** was discovered. A shaft, explored at the end of the last century, drops down from the top through five crypts, in each of which was found a skeleton and a trap door leading to the next. The fifth is at ground level, but here too there was a trap door, and steps cut through the rock to a sixth chamber that opens onto a huge underground cavern – the burial place of the high priest. Sadly the shaft and cavern are not open to the public.

Near here, also very ramshackle, are the **Templo del Venado** (Temple of the Deer) and the **Casa Colorada** (Red House), with a cluster of ruins known as the Southwest Group beyond them. Follow the path round, however, and you arrive at **El Caracol** (the Snail, for its shape; also called the Observatory), a circular, domed tower standing on two rectangular platforms and looking remarkably like a twentieth-century observatory in outline. No telescope, however, was mounted in the roof, which instead has slits aligned with various points of astronomical observation. Four doors at the cardinal points lead into the tower, where there's a circular chamber and a spiral staircase leading to the upper level, from where sightings were made.

El Caracol is something of a Maya–Toltec mix, and, in fact, this was one of the buildings that first led archeologists to postulate the Toltec invasion theory. It has few of the obvious decorative features associated with either, though, and the remaining buildings are pure Maya. The so-called **Edificio de las Monjas** (the Nunnery) is the largest and most important of them – a palace complex showing several stages of construction. It's in rather poor condition, the rooms mostly filled with rubble and inhabited by flocks of swallows, and part of the facade was blasted away by a nineteenth-century explorer, but it is nonetheless a building of grand proportions. Its **annexe** has an elaborate facade in the Chenes style, covered with masks of Chac which combine to make one giant mask, with the door as a mouth. **La Iglesia** (the Church), a small building standing beside the convent, is by contrast a clear demonstration of Puuc design, with a low band of unadorned masonry around the bottom surmounted by an elaborate mosaic frieze and a roof-comb. Hook-nosed masks of Chac again predominate, but above the doorway are also the figures of the four **bacabs**, mythological creatures that held up the sky – a snail and a turtle on one side, an armadillo and a crab on the other.

Beyond Las Monjas, a path leads in about fifteen minutes to a further group of ruins – among the oldest on the site, but unrestored. Nearer at hand is the **Akad Dzib**, a relatively plain block of palace rooms which takes its name ("Obscure Writings") from some undeciphered hieroglyphs found inside. There are, too, red palm prints on the walls of some of the chambers – a sign frequently found in Maya buildings, whose significance is not yet understood. From here you can head back to the road past El Caracol and the Cenote de Xtoloc.

Valladolid and around

The second town of Yucatán state, **VALLADOLID** is around 40km from Chichén Itzá, still close enough to beat the crowds to the site on an early bus, and of interest in its own right. Although it took a severe bashing in the nineteenth-century Caste Wars, the town has retained a strong colonial feel, and centres on a pretty, peaceful zócalo. The most famous of the surviving churches is sixteenth-century **San Bernardino**, 1km southwest of the zócalo (daily 9am–11pm; mass daily at 6pm). Built over one of the town's **cenotes**, **Sis-Ha**, the church is currently under restoration: the buildings are very impressive, but there's little left inside as, like so many of the Yucatán's churches, San Bernardino was sacked by the local Indians in the wars. Valladolid's other cenote, **Zací**, on C 36 between C 39 and C 37 (daily 8am–6pm; US$2), has become a tourist attraction, with a museum and an open-air restaurant at the entrance.

Arrival and information

Buses between Mérida and Cancún don't go into Valladolid, but stop at **La Isleta**, a small bus station on the highway, where you transfer to a local bus for the ten-minute run into town. Valladolid's **bus station** is located on C 37 between C 54 and C 56, seven blocks to the west of the zócalo. *De paso* buses run at least hourly to both Mérida and Cancún and there are at least ten daily departures for Playa del Carmen, most of which are via Cancún, though a few take the road past Cobá and call at Tulum (see following chapter). Some local second-class buses begin their journey here, too, for the above destinations and the smaller towns, including Tizimín, for Río Lagartos (see p.86).

To get to the centre from the bus station takes about ten minutes. Turn left onto C 37, then right after a couple of blocks, then left again, following C 39 to the pretty zócalo; you'll pass some of the cheaper **hotels** on the way. The **tourist office** is on the southeastern corner of the zócalo (daily 9am–noon & 4–6pm). Though in theory there's plenty of information available, including free maps of Valladolid, you'll be lucky to find the office attended. Best to head for **El Bazaar**, a collection of inexpensive restaurants on the corner of C 39 and C 40 on the zócalo; the souvenir shop here has maps and current information. The **post office** is on the zócalo, near the corner of C 39 on C 40 (Mon–Fri 8am–2.30pm), as is Bancomer, which changes travellers' cheques between 9.30am and 12.30pm. Banco de Sureste in Supermaz, a shopping plaza at C 39 no. 229, changes travellers' cheques every day (including weekends) until 8.30pm and cash until 9pm (closed 2pm–6.30pm). In the same plaza you'll find a shop with **Internet** facilities (*afa@mail.valladolid.net.mx*; US$5 an hour) and a **laundry**. For national and international **telephone calls** there are Ladatel casetas at the bus station and on the zócalo (daily 7am–10pm). You can **rent bikes** from Refaccionaría de Bicicletas Paulino Sliva at C 44 no. 191, between C 39 and C 41, for US$2 an hour.

Accommodation

Valladolid's budget hotels lie between the bus station and the centre, but for more atmosphere it's worth splashing out a bit to stay in colonial style on the zócalo.

María de la Luz, C 42, on the zócalo (☎ & fax 985/6-20-71). The rooms are less luxurious than the lobby, but comfortable and good value, with a/c. The restaurant, which serves huge inexpensive buffet breakfasts, opens onto the zócalo, and there's a pool. ④.

María Guadalupe, C 44 no. 198 (☎985/6-20-68). The best-value cheap hotel with clean, well-kept rooms with baths. Colectivos for the cenote at Dzitnup leave from outside. ③.

Maya, C 41 no. 231, four blocks west of the zócalo (no phone). Clean, cheap hotel, with rooms around a courtyard; some have a/c. ②–④.

El Mesón del Marqués, C 39 no. 203, on the zócalo (☎985/6-20-73 or 6-30-42, fax 6-22-80). Lovely hotel in a former colonial mansion, overlooking a courtyard with fountains and lush plants. There's a wonderful palm-fringed pool, and one of the best restaurants in town. ⑤.

Mendoza, C 39 no. 204, corner of C 46 (☎ & fax 985/6-20-02). The sole advantage of this place is its proximity to the bus station, but you'll find better quality if you press on towards the centre. ③–④.

San Clemente, C 42, corner of C 41 (☎985/6-31-61). Just off the zócalo, this very comfortable hotel has a restaurant and pool. Prices are similar to the *María de la Luz*, but the facilities are better. ④.

Zací, C 44 no. 193, between 39 and 37 (☎985/6-21-67). Pleasant hotel with a lovely, plant-filled courtyard and a small pool. Rooms have either a fan or, for a few dollars more, a/c and cable TV. ④.

Eating and drinking

Whatever your budget, to eat well in Valladolid you don't have to stray further than the zócalo, where you can get inexpensive snacks or treat yourself without going into debt.

El Bazaar, northeastern corner of the zócalo, C 39 and C 40. Inexpensive *loncherías* and pizzerias, always busy and open until late.

El Mesón del Marqués, C 39 no. 203, on the zócalo. Probably Valladolid's best restaurant, offering tranquillity in the centre of town and tables around the fountain of the hotel courtyard, though it's often packed with tour groups. Yucatecan specialities such as lime soup and *poc-chuc*.

Restaurante San Bernadino de Siena, C 49 no. 227, two blocks from Convento San Bernadino (☎985/6-27-20). Locally known as *Don Juanito's* and frequented mostly by Mexicans, this highly recommended, mid-price restaurant is a great place for a lazy lunch or dinner away from the hustle and bustle of the town centre.

Cenote Dzitnup

Seven kilometres west of Valladolid, the remarkable **Cenote Dzitnup** or X'Keken (daily 8am–5pm; US$1.50) is reached by descending into a cave, where a nearly circular pool of crystal-clear, turquoise water is illuminated by a shaft of light from a opening in the roof. A swim in the ice-cold water is a fantastic experience, but take a sweater as the temperature in the cave is noticeably cooler than outside.

There are direct colectivos to Dzitnup from outside the *Hotel María Guadalupe* in Valladolid (see p.85). Alternatively, any westbound second-class bus will drop you at the turn-off, 5km from Valladolid, from where it's a 2km walk down a signed track. You could also take a taxi or, best of all, cycle from Valladolid.

Around Valladolid

From Valladolid the vast majority of traffic heads straight on to Cancún and the Caribbean beaches. There are a few places worth taking time out to explore, however, and, if you have more time, an alternative is to head north via Tizimín to **Río Lagartos** or **San Felipe**. You'll need to make an early start if you want to co-ordinate your buses, go on a flamingo trip and get back to Valladolid in the same day – the last bus for Tizimín from Río Lagartos leaves at 5.30pm and the last bus for Valladolid leaves Tizimín at 7pm. You'll have to return to Valladolid to head on to the Caribbean coast.

Balancanché

34 kilometres from Valladolid, on the way to Chichén Itzá, you can visit the **Caves of Balancanché**, where in 1959 a sealed passageway was discovered leading to a series of caverns in which the ancient population had left offerings to Chac. "Guided tours" in English (daily 11am, 1pm & 3pm; US$7, US$2.50 on Sun) – in reality, a taped commentary – lead you past the usual stalactites and stalagmites, an underground pool and, most interestingly, many of the original Maya offerings still in situ. Be warned that in places the caves can be cold, damp and thoroughly claustrophobic. Charles Gallenkamp's *Maya* (see "Books" in Contexts) has an excellent chapter devoted to the discovery of the caves, and to the ritual of exorcism that a local *h-man* (traditional priest) insisted on carrying out to placate the ancient gods and disturbed spirits. Buses between Valladolid and Mérida will drop you at *las grutas*.

Río Lagartos and Las Coloradas

Travelling by bus from Valladolid north to Río Lagartos, you have to change at the elegant colonial town of **TIZIMÍN**, 51km from Valladolid. There's little to see, but the small **Parque Zoológico de la Reina** has animals from all over the peninsula, and the pretty plaza is peaceful enough for whiling away a few hours. The best of the modest but overpriced hotels in the centre is *María Antonia*, C 50 (☎986/3-23-84; ④). Tizimín also has direct bus services to and from Mérida and Cancún.

RÍO LAGARTOS, 100km north of Valladolid, stands on a lagoon in marshy coastal flatland, inhabited by vast colonies of **pink flamingos**. Despite talk of turning the area into a new tourist centre, so far it remains a backwater fishing village. It's easy enough to visit on a day-trip from Valladolid, but if you want to stay, try the very comfortable *Cabañas dos Hermanos*, at the back of a family home, by the beach, which sleep two or three people and have private bathrooms and pay-as-you-view cable TV. From the bus station, turn right and continue on to the water's edge. You can also **camp** on the lagoon shore almost anywhere near town. A boat trip over to the seaward shore of the spit that encloses the lagoon will bring you to a couple of **beaches**, but they're not up to much, and in the end it's the flamingos alone that make a visit worthwhile.

You're likely to be swamped by offers to take you out to see the flamingos as soon get off the bus or out of your car. If not, the best place to start is the friendly *Restaurante Isla Contoy*, on the waterfront, where you can leaf though a book of photos and visitors' comments while waiting for your boat to turn up. A **boat** to visit the many feeding sites costs around US$35, with a maximum of seven people, but the price and length of the trip are infinitely negotiable. Make sure that your guide understands that you don't want to harass the flamingos, as some will get too close if they think their passengers would prefer to see some action. If you want to be certain that you are getting a knowledgeable guide, controlled by the syndicate that protects the flamingos, prearrange a trip with Adrian Marfil, C 16 no. 100 (☎98/3-26-68), or from Cancún with EcoloMex Tours (☎98/84-38-05, fax 84-38-49). As well as flamingos, you're likely to see fishing eagles, spoonbills and, if you're lucky, one of the very few remaining crocodiles for which Río Lagartos was named.

The most spectacular flamingo colony is at **Las Coloradas**, on the narrow spit that separates the lagoon from the sea about 16km east of Río Lagartos. There's a small village and salt factory here, but you'll need your own transport, as the bus timetable does not give you a chance to stay long enough to see anything.

San Felipe

If it's beaches you're after, **SAN FELIPE**, 12km west of Río Lagartos, is a much better bet – many of the buses from Valladolid to Río Lagartos come out here. There are a few cheap rooms for rent, above the Marufo cinema, and at least one good restaurant, the *El Payaso*. However, most people get a boat across to the offshore spit to set up **camp** on one of a number of beaches. At Mexican holiday times these are positively crowded, the rest of the year quite deserted. If you do camp, be sure to bring protection against mosquitoes; if not, it's easy enough to arrange for the boat to collect you in the evening.

Isla Holbox

Although most traffic between Mérida and the coast heads directly east to Cancún, it is possible to turn north at Valladolid or Nuevo X-Can to **Chiquilá**, where you can board the ferry for **Isla Holbox**, a 25-kilometre-long island near the easternmost point of the Gulf coast. Sometimes touted as a new beach paradise to fill the place that Isla Mujeres once had in travellers' affections, it's by no means as attractive: the water is murkier than on the Caribbean coast and the sea can be rough. However, there are miles of empty beaches to enjoy, and anyone who's come from the more touristy resorts will find the island's relaxed, laid-back pace – and the genuinely warm welcome – something of a relief.

Practicalities

Buses for Chiquilá leave Valladolid (2hr 30min) and Tizimín (1hr 30min) a couple of times a day. Catch an early bus to make sure you get the afternoon ferry. Coming from the east, get a bus to the road junction just before Nuevo X-Can and wait for a colectivo (US$1) to Kantunilkin, about halfway to Chiquilá, where you can pick up the bus. The **Chiquilá ferry** for Holbox leaves twice a day, at 8am and 1pm (1hr; US$1.50), and returns at 5am and noon. Holbox is also served by a **car ferry**, leaving Chiquilá at 10am (daily except Thurs & Sun) and returning at 6am. Make sure you don't miss the boat: Chiquilá is not a place you want to get stranded. There's a restaurant and a store, but little else; if you need to stay the night in order to get the early ferry, you could camp under the *palapa* by the basketball court – mosquito netting is essential.

Isla Holbox has a few simple and inexpensive **hotels**; to contact them, call ☎988/7-16-68 and ask for the hotel by name or by its extension number. The first hotel you see, the *Posada Flamingo* (ext 102; ①), just to the right of the dock, has basic clean rooms with hot showers. It's handy for the early ferry and the friendly owners **rent scooters** and organize **boat trips**. To get nearer the **beach** you'll have to walk across the island, which takes about ten minutes. Here you'll find the *Posada Los Arcos* (①) on the plaza (ask at the *Tienda Dionora*), and, even nearer the sea, the cabañas at the *Posada Dingrid* (①). You'll also spot **houses for rent**, which can be worth it if you plan to stay a while. A couple of shops provide basic supplies and there are some good **seafood restaurants**, but little in the way of entertainment; have a drink and a chat with a fisherman, though, and you may get a chance to go fishing. Bring plenty of repellent as the mosquitoes here are some of the worst in Mexico.

From Mérida to Campeche

From Mérida to Campeche there's a choice of two routes. First-class buses, and all *directo* services, take the shorter road via **Hwy-180** – the colonial Camino Real, lined with villages whose plazas are laid out on the traditional plan around a massive old church. The Maya ruins at **Oxkintok**, around halfway on the highway, look fairly unimpressive today, but this was a city with a lifespan of a thousand years or more and was still thriving in the Postclassic – after 1000 AD. The site has some of the oldest hieroglyphs so far found in the Yucatán (dating from between 475 AD and 859 AD), and many of the buildings are earlier, belonging to the upper Preclassic (300 BC–300 AD). Their style, as well as that of ceramics found at the site, suggests a link with the Maya architecture of the Petén. **BECAL**, 10km further south and just inside Campeche state, is one of the biggest centres for the manufacture of basketware and the ubiquitous Yucatecan **jipis**, or "Panama" hats (real panama hats, as everyone knows, come from Ecuador). There's a *Centro Artesanal* by the road where you can buy them, but it's more interesting to go into the village and watch this cottage industry at work. **HECELCHAKAN**, about 80km before Campeche, has a small **archeology museum** on the main square (Mon–Sat 9am–6pm; free), with figures from Jaina and objects from other nearby sites.

The longer route **via Muna and Hopelchén**, passing the great sites of **Uxmal**, **Kabáh** and **Sayil** (see pp.72, 75), offers more to see if you have the time. With a car you could easily visit all three, perhaps stopping also at **BOLONCHÉN DE REJON**, with its nine wells (*bolonchén* means nine wells), and the nearby **Grutas de Xtacumbilxunan**, 3km south, and still get to Campeche within the day. By bus it's slightly harder, but with a little planning – and if you set out early – you should be able to get to at least one. Kabáh is the easiest since its ruins lie right on the main road.

Campeche

CAMPECHE, capital of the state that bears its name, is one of Mexico's less well-known colonial gems. Elegant eighteenth- and nineteenth-century houses painted in pastel shades and interspersed with the occasional church give it a distinctly European feel. At its heart, relatively intact, lies a colonial port still surrounded by hefty defensive walls and fortresses; around, the trappings of a modern city that is once again becoming wealthy. The seafront is a bizarre mixture of ancient and ultra-modern: originally the city defences dropped straight into the sea, but now they face a reclaimed strip of land on which stand the spectacular new Palacio de Gobierno and State Legislature (spectacularly ugly in the eyes of most locals), and the big hotels. Few tourists stop here, preferring to sweep by en route to Escárcega and Palenque or take Hwy-180 and the ferry along the beautiful coast route via Ciudad del Carmen to Villahermosa. This is strongly to Campeche's advantage (even if locals don't see it that way), for while the attractions in and around the city can't compare with Mérida's, it is at least spared the blight of tourist overkill.

A Spanish expedition under Francisco Hernandez landed outside the Maya town of Ah Kin Pech in 1517, only to beat a hasty retreat on seeing the forces lined up to greet them. It wasn't until 1540 that Francisco de Montejo founded the modern town, and from here set out on his mission to conquer the Yucatán. From then until the nine-teenth century, it was the chief port in the peninsula, exporting mainly logwood (source of a red dye known as *hematein*) from local forests. It also became an irre-sistible target for the pirates who operated with relative impunity from bases on the untamed coast round about. Hence the fortifications, built between 1668 and 1704 after a particularly brutal massacre of the population.

Arrival and information

Campeche's **Central Camionera**, with first- and second-class terminals, is 2km from the colonial centre, along Av Gobernadores. To get to the centre, turn left outside, cross the road and take a city bus marked "Centro" or "Gobernadores". Local buses leave from the market, just south of the city wall. If you arrive at the **airport**, about 10km southeast of town, you'll have to take a taxi.

Within the city, even-numbered **streets** run parallel with the sea, starting for some reason with C 8, just inside the ramparts; odd-numbered streets run inland. The zóca-lo, **Parque Principal**, is bordered by C 8, C 10, C 55 and C 57. Almost everything of interest is gathered within the old walls.

Campeche's **tourist office**, in the Plaza Moch Couoh on Av Ruiz Cortines, opposite the unsightly government palace (daily 9–8pm; ☎981/6-73-64 or 6-55-93, fax 6-67-67), is helpful and friendly and there's usually someone there who can speak English. Be sure to pick up the free tourist magazines, with articles about what's going on in and around town and in the state. They also have a list of independent **guides** (speaking various languages) who lead tours of the city and archeological zones; you may have to provide the transport. Other tourist **information booths** scattered around town at the major tourist sites and the bus station have a limited supply of maps and leaflets that you could just as easily pick up from the larger hotels.

Accommodation

Because Campeche is not on the tourist circuit, it boasts plenty of inexpensive **hotels**, though for the same reason they can be rather shabby. Avoid rooms overlooking the street, as Campeche's narrow lanes magnify traffic noise. The best bargains are to be found within a couple of blocks of the zócalo.

The **youth hostel**, on Av Agustín Melgar (☎981/1-18-08; ①), is clean and bustling, with single-sex dorms, and camping in the grounds, but it's a long way out. To get there, catch a bus ("Directo/Universidad") from the ADO station, or one marked "Lerma" or "Playa Bonita" heading west through the old part of the city.

America, C 10 no. 252, between C 59 and C 61 (☎981/6-45-88). Elegant colonial building with com-fortable rooms; the best ones overlook the courtyard. ④.

Baluartes, Av Ruíz Cortines, just south of the *Ramada* (☎981/6-24-10). The *Ramada*'s older and slightly cheaper rival, with a pool, TVs and a/c. ⑥.

Campeche, C 57 no. 2, opposite the cathedral (☎981/6-51-83). Basic rooms in a colonial house; the rooms overlooking the zócalo are noisy. ③.

Central, Av Gobernadores 462 (☎981/1-07-66). The name is hardly appropriate, as it's way out, opposite the bus stations, but it has perfectly adequate rooms. ③.

Colonial, C 14 no. 122 (☎981/6-22-22). The best-value place in town, in an old colonial building. ③.

Posada del Ángel, C 10 no. 307, corner of C 55 (☎981/6-77-18). Modern hotel, centrally located by the corner of the cathedral. Some rooms have a/c. ③.

Ramada Inn, Av Ruíz Cortines 51 (☎981/6-22-33, fax 6-76-18). Comfortable, upmarket hotel with a pool, restaurant and nightclub. There's also a travel agency and car rental facilities. ⑦.

The City

A visit to Campeche should begin with a wander through the city's delightful old streets, stopping along the way to visit La Mansión Carvajal on C 10 between C 51 and C 53, an elegant colonial house, reminiscent of Andalucian Moorish homes, that once belonged to one of the city's richest families. The **Cathedral**, overlooking the zócalo, was founded in 1540, making it one of the oldest churches on the peninsula – the bulk of the construction, though, took place much later, and what you see is not particularly striking Baroque. The city walls nearby, towards the seafront, are being rebuilt, and will eventually link all the eight bulwark fortresses (*baluartes*), most of which currently stand alone. The **Baluarte San Carlos**, is the most dramatic, with cannons on the battlement roof and, underneath, the beginnings of a network of ancient tunnels that undermines much of the town. The tunnels once provided a place of refuge for the populace from pirate raids and were probably used by the Maya before that. Now they are said to be haunted by evil ghosts who emerge at night through the countless entrances in the old colonial houses to steal children. If you want to continue the **tour of the walls**, the "Circuito Baluartes" bus will take you right round, stopping at regular intervals. The Baluarte San Pedro now houses a crafts exhibition and shop, while the Baluarte Santiago is surrounded by a small **Jardín Botanico** (Tues–Sat 9am–8pm, Sun 9am–1pm; free).

Other sights are a little further out. About twenty minutes' walk to the right (northeast) along the seafront is **Iglesia de San Francisco**, the only surviving remnant of a sixteenth-century Franciscan monastery. On this site, supposedly, the first Mass to be heard in Mexico was celebrated in 1517. Not far beyond lies the **Pozo de la Conquista** (Well of the Conquest), where the same Spanish expedition, under Francisco Hernandez, took on water to fill their leaking casks. In the other direction, again along the waterfront malecón, the **Fort San Miguel** houses Campeche's **archeological museum** (Tues–Sun 9am–2pm & 4–8pm; US$1). Objects from Edzná and Jaina predominate – some of the delicate Jaina figurines are cross-eyed, a feature that the Maya considered a mark of beauty. As with straightened noses and flattened foreheads, this was often brought about by deliberate deformation – Bernal Díaz noted that the first two prisoners taken by Hernandez were both cross-eyed. There are also some interesting Olmec and Maya pieces including some fine sculpture and some prehispanic gold, but the highlight is the treasure from the tombs at Calakmul. The jade death masks are awe-inspiring and every bit as impressive and beautiful as the death masks of Pacal from Palenque. Take a look at the views over the bulwarks, too, which are wonderful at sunset. The **Fort San José**, on a hill on the opposite side of the city has an armaments museum and a collection of items from the colonial era. There are plans to convert all the bulwarks into museums and the tourist office will have the latest details.

If you're desperate to be by the sea, a "Playa Bonita" bus along the waterfront will take you past Fort San Miguel and beyond to the **beaches** at **Playa Bonita** and **Lerma**, a fishing village just beyond the city. It's not a terribly attractive prospect, however, with the port and lots of factories probably spewing out pollutants, and there are better beaches out towards Ciudad del Carmen.

Eating and drinking

Restaurants abound in the centre of Campeche, especially along C 8 and C 10. **Seafood**, served almost everywhere, is a good bet; try the shark or shrimps in spicy sauce.

Centro Manic, C 59 no. 22 between C 12 & C 14. Vegetarian restaurant, patisserie and bookshop that also organizes spiritual workshops.

El Gato Pardo, C 49, between C 10 and C 12, just outside the city wall. Pizzeria and video bar, serving excellent pizzas to young rock fans. Nightly until 1am.

Marganzo Regional, C 8 no. 262. Seafood and regional dishes served in relaxed surroundings. The five-dollar breakfast buffet is especially popular. Daily 7am–midnight.

Nutri Vida, C 12 no. 167, near C 59. Good vegetarian restaurant serving fresh fruit, granola, yoghurt, juices, vegeburgers and other healthy food at reasonable prices. Closed Sat evening and Sun.

La Parroquia, C 55 no. 8. Traditional, family-run restaurant; good value and very popular with locals. Open 24hr.

Los Portales, C 55 no. 9. Across from *La Parroquia* and in much the same vein. Open 24hr.

Restaurant Miramar, C 8 and C 61. Campeche's best seafood; pricey, but worth it.

Restaurant del Parque, C 8 no. 251, corner of C 57 on the zócalo. Popular budget place for standard Mexican food. Daily 6am–midnight.

Listings

American Express Next to the Banco del Atlántico.

Banks Banco del Atlántico and Bancomer are next door to each other on Av 16 de Septiembre, opposite the Baluarte de la Soledad, both with ATMs. Banamex is on C 10, at the corner of C 53.

Car rental Autorent (☎981/6-27-14) in the *Ramada Inn*, or Hertz in the *Hotel Baluartes* (☎981/6-88-48).

Email and fax MultiPro (☎982/1-74-66, email *multipro41@hotmail.com*) C 63 no.7 between C 12 and C 14 has Internet facilities. You can fax from the Telecomm office on Av 16 de Septiembre (Mon–Fri 9am–8pm, Sat 9am–1pm).

Laundry The Tintoria Campeche (Mon–Sat 9am–4pm) on C 55, no. 26.

Post office Av 16 de Septiembre at C 53, in the Oficinas del Gobierno Federal (Mon–Fri 8am–8pm, Sat 9am–2pm).

Tours Destino Maya on Av Miguel Alemán, above the Cine Estelar (☎981/1-09-34 or 1-37-26), offers tours around the Maya sites in Campeche.

MOVING ON FROM CAMPECHE

Regular first-class ADO, Colon and second-class Autobuses del Sur **buses** (all from the same terminal - see p.89) leave for Ciudad del Carmen (hourly, 3hr), Mérida (more than 12 daily, 2hr), Chetumal via Escárcega and Xpujil (3 daily, 5–7hr), Villahermosa (10 daily, 6–7hr). There are also services to San Cristóbal (via Palenque), Playa del Carmen, Veracruz, México and Coatzalcoalcos (for southern Veracruz) and second-class buses direct to Uxmal. Minibuses leave from the market just outside the southern end of the old city (C53 and Circuito Baluartes Este) for local villages like the craft centres Becal and Calkini, and for Edzná. Aeroméxico (☎938/6-56-78 or 6-49-25) operates a variety of internal flights; Calakmul (☎938/6-31-09 or 1-36-50) flies to México only. A taxi out to the **airport** costs around US$7.

The Campeche coast

South of Campeche, Hwy-180 sweeps along the mostly deserted coast, passing several small resorts. Most tourists heading in this direction turn inland at **Champotón**, a growing fishing village and oil port at the mouth of the Río Champotón, on their way southeast towards Escárcega for Chetumal or Palenque. If you want to get anywhere reasonably quickly, even if you're heading to Villahermosa and beyond, this route is the best option. Alternatively, if you want to head towards Ciudad del Carmen and then into southern Veracruz, you could continue along the coast to **Sabancuy**, 83km before Ciudad del Carmen, a little village which has one of the best beaches in Campeche.

There are few tourists and only one hotel, the *Posada Bellavista* (②). At **Isla Aguada**, the Puenta de la Unidad, said to be the longest road bridge in Mexico, crosses the eastern entrance to the **Laguna de Terminos**, joining the **Isla del Carmen** to the mainland.

Ciudad del Carmen

CIUDAD DEL CARMEN, the only town of any size on the 35-kilometre-long Isla del Carmen, doesn't merit a special trip except perhaps during its lively **fiesta** in July. It's not unpleasant, but it's hot and crowded and has much less historical atmosphere than Campeche. The conquistadors landed here in 1518, but the first settlers were pirates in 1633. Nowadays it's home to a fishing fleet, catching, among other things, giant prawns for export. The oil boom has created new industries and forced prices up, so you won't find any accommodation bargains here. The town's environs also suffer from oil industry pollution. Just west of town is the **ferry dock** for **Zacatal**, where the road to Frontera continues. Buses don't necessarily make a direct connection.

Practicalities

ADO (first-class) and Sur (second-class) buses use the same station on Av Periferica Ote. To get to the centre, take a taxi or colectivo (5am–11pm; about 20min). The **tourist office**, in the Palacio Municipal on the corner of C 22 and C 31 (Mon–Fri 8am–3pm), has plenty of information (English and Spanish) on Campeche state, but little about Ciudad del Carmen. The **post office** (Mon–Fri 7am–7pm, Sat 7am–1pm) is tucked away at C 22 no. 57, between C 25 and C 27, while Banamex, on the corner of C 24 at the edge of the Parque General Ignacio Zaragosa, and Bancomer, C 24 no. 42 at the corner with C 29 (both Mon–Fri 9am–1.30pm), have ATMs and cajeros.

Most of the **accommodation** is on C 20, C 22 and C 24 near the waterfront. At fiesta time places fill up, so book ahead. Five minutes around the corner from the bus station, *Casa de Huéspedes Bugambilias*, Av Periferica Nte 4 (☎938/2-49-28; ③), has large clean rooms with baths away from the main road, though only five minutes from the bus station. The *Roma*, C 22 no. 110 between C27 and C29 (☎938/2-04-10; ②), is a good-value place across a small park from the waterfront; most luxurious of all is the *Hotel de Parque*, on the corner of C 33 between Parque General Ignacio Zaragosa and the waterfront (☎938/2-30-46 or 2-30-66; ⑦), where all rooms have a/c, TV and phone. **Food** in Ciudad del Carmen is a mixture of specialities from the Yucatán peninsula and the state of Tabasco, with a stress on shellfish. Many low-priced restaurants are grouped together along C 33 by the busy Parque General Ignacio Zaragosa, and there are two good places on the seafront opposite the *Roma*: *Cafetería La Fuente*, C 20 no.203 at C29, for basic Mexican snacks, and *La Ola Marina*, next door, which serves expensive, good seafood and shellfish in a relaxed atmosphere.

Edzná and the Chenes sites

Some 60km from Campeche lie the impressive ruins of **EDZNÁ** (daily 8am–5pm; US$2, free on Sun), the only local site almost accessible by bus. Though this is an area where the **Chenes** style of architecture (closely related to the Puuc of Uxmal – see p.72) dominated – *chen* means "well" and is a fairly common suffix to place names hereabouts – Edzná is far from a pure example of it, also featuring elements of Río Bec, Puuc and Classic Maya design. For the real thing, you have to venture further south.

Edzná was a large city, on the main trade route between the Maya of the highlands and the coast. The most important structure is the great **Templo de los Cinco Pisos** (Temple of the Five Storeys), a stepped palace/pyramid more than 20m high built on a vast acropolis. Unusually, each of the five storeys contains chambered "palace" rooms: while solid temple pyramids and multistorey "apartment" complexes are relatively common, it is rare to see the two combined in one building. At the front, a steep monumental staircase leads to a three-roomed temple, topped by a roof-comb. The view from here is one of the most impressive in the Yucatán. It is easy to imagine the power that the high priest or king commanded as you look out over two plazas, the more distant of which must have been capable of holding tens of thousands of people. Beyond lie the unexcavated remains of other large pyramids, and behind them, the vast flat expanse of the Yucatán shelf. A stela of the god of maize positioned here was illuminated by the sun twice a year, on the dates for the planting and harvesting of maize, and the whole temple is orientated to face to the rising sun.

Lesser buildings surround the ceremonial precinct. The **Casa Grande**, a palace on the northwest side, and some of the buildings alongside it, were cleared by archeologists in late 1986. Some 55m long, the Casa Grande includes a room used as a *temezcal*, with stone benches and hearths over which water could be boiled. There are two haunting stucco masks of the gods of day and night in the **Templo de los Mascarones** and, nearby, a small early Classic ball court in the Petén style and another ball court ring still in place along the west wall. The rest of the site – including a large system of drainage (and possibly irrigation) canals – remains unexcavated.

Buses for Pich or Bon Fil leave from the huge market in Campeche (C 53 and Circuito Baluartes Este) every half-hour and will take you within 1km of the entrance at Edzná. Getting back is harder: there are passing buses but they are erratic; ask the driver of your bus on the way out. Alternatively, you could join an **organized trip** from Campeche. Some small **cabañas** are being built near the ruins; bookings can be made through the Campeche tourist office.

Other Chenes sites

The examples of true Chenes style are accessible only with a car or exceptional determination. The chief sites are reached on a poor road from **HOPELCHÉN**, a village about 100km from Campeche on the long route to Mérida. A bus follows this road as far as **Dzibalchen** and **Iturbide**, but it's not much use for visiting the sites as it turns straight round on arrival. If you choose to **stay** in Hopelchén, *Los Arcos*, C 17 on the corner of the plaza, near where the buses stop (☎982/2-00-37; ③), is the only option.

The best of the ruins are some way from the paved road and substantially buried in the jungle. **Hochob**, just outside Dzibalchen, has an amazing three-roomed temple (low and fairly small, as are most Chenes buildings), with a facade entirely covered in richly carved, stylized snakes and masks. The central chamber is surmounted by a crumbling roof-comb, and its decoration creates the effect of a huge mask, with the doorway as a gaping mouth. The remains of **Dzibilnocac**, 1km west of Iturbide, demonstrate the ultra-decorative facades typical of the Chenes style and its restored western temple-pyramid makes a trip out here very worthwhile.

Francisco Escárcega to Xpujil

Heading south from Campeche on the inland route, Hwy-261 meets the east–west Hwy-186 at **FRANCISCO ESCÁRCEGA** (always referred to as Escárcega), a hot, dusty town straggling along the road and old train tracks for a couple of kilometres. There's little to detain you in town, but Escárcega does provide a jumping-off point for a number of relatively unexplored **Maya sites** that are now beginning to be developed for tourism. Known as the **Río Bec sites**, many of them are in the **Calakmul Biosphere Reserve**, a vast area of tropical forest, once heavily populated by lowland Maya, which stretches all the way into the Petén region of Guatemala. Though the region's most famous site lies over the border at **Tikal** (see p.409), others within Mexico, only recently accessible, are every bit as exciting as the sites of the northern Yucatán.

The ADO bus station is at the road junction; from there, walk 1500m east to the centre and the Sur bus station. If you need to **stay**, try the *Posada Escárcega* (☎981/4-00-79; ③), just two blocks from the second-class terminal; turn left and then second left. **Getting out of town** is relatively easy: at least ten buses run daily to Mérida, there's an hourly service to Campeche between 4am and 6pm, a 4.30am second-class bus to Palenque, and a couple to San Cristóbal; in addition, Escárcega is on the ADO first-class route between Chetumal and Villahermosa. Services to Xpujil and Chetumal run overnight or in the mornings only – nothing heads out in the afternoon.

However, the far from glamorous village of **XPUJIL** is a better place for exploring the region. Basically a one-street town straddling Hwy-186, it has a few simple places to stay. Try the *Hotel Calakmul* (☎983/2-91-62; ③–④) or the *Restaurant and Cabañas El Mirador Maya* (☎983/4-03-71; ③–④), which has simple, thatched cabañas with hammocks. There are a couple of restaurants, two Ladatel phones and a small post office, all easy to find.

Leaving Xpujil, there are, in theory, two ADO **buses** a day to Chetumal, and two to Escárcega and onward. Both of these are scheduled to leave in the morning, but staff at the bus station are not reliable with their timetable information. It is therefore best to buy your ticket first thing in the morning on the day you intend to leave. It is possible to catch a series of second-class buses through to Mérida via Dzibalchen, Hopelchén and the Ruta Puuc. This rough road passes through the northern half of the Calakmul Biosphere Reserve, and is an interesting and little travelled route north, if you have time to spare.

The Río Bec sites

The **Río Bec** style, characterized by long buildings with matching towers at each end and narrow roof-combs can be seen at a number of sites in this region. The most accessible is **Xpujil**, just 1500km back along the highway from Xpujil village (US$1, free on Sun). Dating from the Classic period, it is perhaps the least impressive of all the sites, though its three towers with almost vertical, and purely decorative stairways are very striking.

Trips to the sites and the forest are organized by Servidores Turisticos (☎983/2-33-04 or 2-44-88), a co-operative of locals, led by Fernando Sastre and Leticia Valensuela Santiago; ask for them at the *Calakmul* restaurant. Prices range from US$20 per person for a full-day guided tour to Becán, Chicanná, Xpujil and the Grutas del Sol to US$75 for a tour to Calakmul (between up to fifteen people). The guides are all local people from the cattle-ranching community, many of whom were once rapaciously cutting down the forest and killing the spotted cats for their pelts, but are now working to **preserve the forest**, which stands little chance of survival without initiatives such as this.

You can also take **taxis** to the sites. Expect to pay about US$40 for a taxi to Calakmul and Balam Ku, including waiting time and about US$15 to visit Chicanná and Becán.

Becán

Becán (US$2, free on Sun), 6km west of Xpujil then 500m north on a signed track, is unique among Maya sites in being entirely surrounded by a dry moat, 15m wide and 4m deep. This moat and the wall on its outer edge form one of the oldest known defensive systems in Mexico, and have led some to believe that this was the site of Tayasal, capital of the Itzá, rather than present-day Flores in Guatemala. The site was first occupied in 600 BC, reaching its peak between 600 and 1000 AD. Unlike many of the sites in the northern Yucatán, many of the buildings here seem to have been residential – note the unusual use of internal staircases. The style is a fusion of Río Bec and Chenes (see p.92), with its profusion of facades with fantastic stone masks.

Chicanná and Balamku

Chicanná (US$2, free on Sun), 3km further west than Becán, south of the highway, hosts the luxurious *Ramada Eco Village Resort* (☎91/535-24-66; ⑨). The buildings at the site recall the Chenes style in their elaborate decoration and repetitive masks of Chac; the great doorway in the **House of the Serpent Mouth** is especially impressive. **Balam Ku** (US$1, free on Sunday), 50km beyond Chicanná, just after the turn-off to Calakmul, would be completely forgettable were it not for the two huge cross-eyed red masks that adorn its central temple. These are larger than any you'll see in the north, though less impressive than the masks at Kohunlich in nearby Quintana Roo. Their significance is unknown.

Río Bec and Hormiguero

Río Bec, which gives its name to the region's dominant architectural style, and **Hormiguero** are accessible only by dirt road. To see all the scattered buildings of Río Bec (free) you need to go on an organized expedition, but you can see one small group independently: head east 13km from Xpujil, then south 6km to the *ejido* of 20 de Noviembre. The site is protected within the **Reserva de Fauna U'Luum Chac Yuc**, so you need to sign in at the small museum that acts as the reserve headquarters (☎982/4-03-73), who will fix you up with a guide from the village. You'll see that, as with Xpujil, the "steps" on the twin towers were never meant to be climbed: the risers actually angle outwards. Hormiguero (US$2, free on Sunday), also fuses the Chenes style with the Río Bec. There are only two buildings excavated, the largest having a huge gaping mouth for its central doorway, surrounded by elaborate carving.

Calakmul

The most impressive of the Río Bec sites, **Calakmul** lies 60km off Hwy-186, which cuts across the bottom of the peninsula. Though it is only partially restored, its location in the heart of the jungle and its sheer size make this Classic Maya city irresistible. This is probably the biggest archeological area in Mesoamerica, extending for some 70 km. It has seven thousand buildings in the central area alone and more stelae and pyramids than any other Maya city; the great pyramid here is the largest Maya building in existence, with a base covering five acres. The view of the rainforest from the top of the principal pyramids is stunning, bettered only at Tikal, and on a clear day you can even see the tallest Maya pyramid of all, Danta, at El Mirador in Guatemala. You're sure to see some wildlife too, especially if you arrive early – there are peccary, toucan, occasional howler monkeys and even jaguar here.

During the Classic period, the city had a population of about 200,000 people and was the regional capital of the northern part of Petén. A recently discovered *sacbe* (Maya road) running between Calakmul and El Mirador (another leads on to Tikal) has confirmed that these cities were in regular communication, as archeologists had long suspected. Calakmul reached its zenith between 500 and 850 AD but, like most cities in the area, it was mysteriously abandoned about fifty years later. The site was discovered in 1931, but excavations only started taking place in 1982 and only a fraction of the buildings have been excavated so far, the rest being earthen mounds.

The treasures of Calakmul are on display in the archeological museum at Campeche (see p.90) and include two hauntingly beautiful jade masks. You can also see the first mummified body to be found in Mesoamerica, from inside Structure no. 15, which was unearthed in 1995.

El Tigre

Another site worth visiting in this region is the Classic Maya city of **El Tigre**, 140km to the west of Calakmul on the **Río Candelaria**, though it is only accessible by launch – negotiate prices for the four- to six-hour journey with fishermen on the river in **Candelaria** town, which itself is connected by bus or train from either Escárcega or Campeche. Much of the forest on the banks of the Río Candelaria has been cleared by cattle ranchers, but the area is still excellent for birdlife, and if you're lucky you might see a crocodile. The ruins are only partially cleared and there are no tourists. Accommodation is very basic in Candelaria town and non-existent at the ruins, so bring a tent if you want to try to spend the night here. The tourist office in Campeche will have the latest details about camping possibilities.

travel details

Buses

There aren't many places that you can't get to by bus on the peninsula. Sometimes the timetabling isn't totally convenient but the service is generally efficient. Some places aren't served by first-class buses, but second-class buses and combis will get you around locally and to the nearest major centre. Such places include: Oxkutzcab, Progreso, Ticul and Tizimín. The following frequencies and times are for first-class services. Second-class buses usually cover the same routes running 10–20 percent slower.

Campeche to: Ciudad del Carmen (hourly; 3hr), Mérida (more then 12 daily; 2hr), Chetumal via Escárcega and Xpujil (3 daily, 5–7hr), Villahermosa (10 daily, 6–7hr). There are also services to San Cristóbal (via Palenque), Cancún, Playa del Carmen, Veracruz, México and Coatzalcoalcos (for southern Veracruz).

Mérida to: Campeche (every 30min; 3–4hr); Cancún (frequently; 5–6hr); Chetumal (7 daily; 9hr); México (6 daily; 28hr+); Palenque (2 daily; 10–11hr); Playa del Carmen (frequently daily; 8hr); Progreso (frequently; 45min); Tizimín (3 daily; 4hr); Tulum (8 daily; 6hr); Uxmal (13 daily; 2hr); Valladolid (hourly; 3hr); Villahermosa (6 daily; 10hr).

Tizimín to: Mérida (3 daily; 4hr); Río Lagartos (5 daily; 1hr); Valladolid (hourly; 1hr).

Valladolid to: Cancún (6 daily; 2hr); Chetumal (3 daily; 5hr); Cobá (4 daily; 2hr); Mérida (hourly; 3hr); Playa del Carmen (3 daily; 4hr); Tizimín (hourly; 1hr); Tulum (4 daily; 4hr).

Planes

Mérida has a busy **international airport** with several daily flights to México and regular connections to Miami and many other cities in the southern US. Campeche and Chetumal also have daily direct services to México.

CHAPTER TWO

QUINTANA ROO

The coastal state of **Quintana Roo** was a forgotten frontier for most of modern Mexican history – its lush tropical forests exploited for their mahogany and chicle (from which chewing gum is made), but otherwise unsettled, a haven for outlaws and pirates, and for Maya living beyond the reach of central government. In the 1970s, however, the stunning palm-fringed white-sand **beaches** of the Caribbean coast and its magnificent offshore **coral reefs** began to attract **tourists**: the first highways were built, new townships settled, and the place finally became a full state (as opposed to an externally administered Federal Territory) in 1974.

The stretch of **coast** beween Cancún and **Tulum** is the most heavily visited – and the focus of much recent, rapid hotel construction. Modern development is centred on the resorts of **Cancún** and **Playa del Carmen**, along with the islands of **Isla Mujeres** and **Cozumel**, which have become some of the world's most desirable package tour destinations and increasingly overdeveloped as a result. You'll see images of the Maya everywhere here, but while their culture is shamelessly used to promote tourism, little of this money ever reaches the Maya themselves, and where they haven't been forced out by developers, they continue to live in poverty in small communal villages in the scrub forest, growing maize and carving or weaving a few trinkets for tourists.

Further south things get quieter: the beaches within the **Si'an Ka'an Biosphere Reserve** are nesting sites for turtles, and behind them are areas of mangrove swamp, home to numerous animals including jaguar and even manatee. The vast and beautiful **Laguna de Bacalar** was an important stop on the Maya's pre-Columbian trade routes and was later used as an outpost for arms shipment from Belize during the Caste Wars. **Chetumal**, the state capital and a dull duty-free border town, is of chief importance as a gateway to and from Belize.

Inland, Quintana Roo is little visited. There are some spectacular **Maya sites** here, though they are not as accessible or as well restored as the pristine open-air museums of Yucatán. **Cobá**, a lakeside Maya city just off the road to Valladolid, has some of the Maya World's tallest temples, but is only partially excavated, hidden in jungle swarming with mosquitoes. The Early Classic site of **Kohunlich**, famous for its giant sculpted faces of the Maya sun god, lies in the heart of the Petén jungle that stretches into Guatemala and Belize; even more remote are the ruins of **Kinichna**, **Chacchoben** and **Dzibanche**.

ACCOMMODATION PRICE CODES

All the accommodation listed in this book has been categorized into one of nine price bands, as set out below. The prices quoted are in US dollars and refer to the cheapest room available for two people sharing in high season.

① under US$5	④ US$15–25	⑦ US$60–80
② US$5–10	⑤ US$25–40	⑧ US$80–100
③ US$10–15	⑥ US$40–60	⑨ over US$100

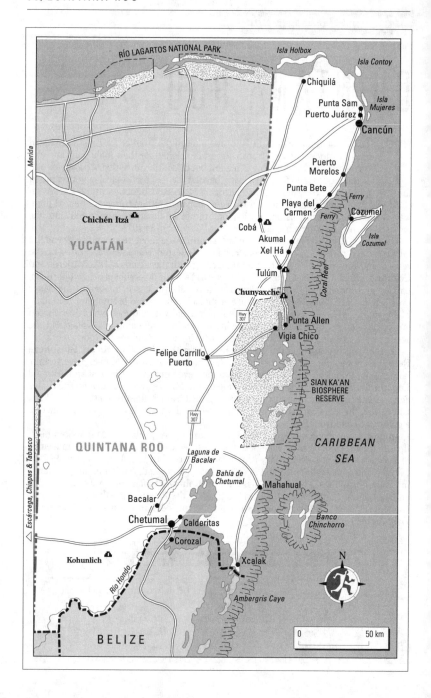

Hwy-307 skirts the coast all the way down to Tulum, where a dirt track leads on to Punta Allen in the Si'an Ka'an Biosphere Reserve. Heading west to Valladolid, Chichén Itzá and Mérida, you have a choice between the old road (*viejo*) or the new *cuota* highway, a toll road running a few kilometres north of the old road for most of its length.

Cancún

Hand-picked by computer, **CANCÚN** was a fishing village of 120 people as recently as 1970. Now it's a city with a resident population of half a million and receives almost two million visitors a year. To some extent the computer selected its location well. Cancún is marginally closer to Miami than it is to México, and if you come on an all-inclusive package tour the place has a lot to offer: striking modern hotels on white-sand beaches; high-class entertainment including parachuting, jet-skiing, scuba-diving and golf; a hectic nightlife; and from here much of the rest of the Yucatán is easily accessible. For the independent traveller, though, it is expensive, and can be frustrating and unwelcoming. You may well be forced to spend the night here, but without pots of money the true pleasures of the place will elude you.

There are, in effect, two quite separate parts to Cancún: the *zona commercial* downtown – the shopping and residential centre which, as it gets older, is becoming genuinely earthy – and the *zona hotelera*, a string of hotels and tourist amenities around "Cancún island", actually a narrow strip of sandy land connected to the mainland at each end by causeways. It encloses a huge lagoon, so there's water on both sides.

Arrival, information and city transport

Charter flights from Europe and South America, and direct scheduled flights from dozens of cities in Mexico and North and Central America, land at the **airport**, 15km south of the centre. Colectivos take you to any part of town for a fixed price of US$12 per person – buy your ticket from the desk by the exit. Taxis cost about US$20. Arriving by bus, you'll pull in at one of the two **bus stations**, next to each other in the heart of downtown, just by a roundabout at the major junction of avenidas Tulum and Uxmal; there's a *guardería* here (daily 7am–11pm).

Avenida Tulum, Cancún's main street, is lined with the bulk of the city's shops, banks, restaurants and travel agencies, as well as many of the hotels – up side streets, but in view. The **state tourist office** is a couple of blocks from the bus station at Tulum 26 (daily 9am–9pm; ☎98/84-80-73). For the **federal tourist office** (daily 9am–9pm; ☎98/84-32-38 or 84-34-38), continue along Tulum until the roundabout at Av Cobá, turn left and the office is at the furthest corner of the block with Av J.C. Nader. Both have free maps and leaflets and copies of the ubiquitous promotional listings **magazines** *Cancún Tips* and *Cancún Nights*: all information you can pick up at just about every travel agency and hotel reception. There are several other tourist information kiosks on Tulum and in the *zona hotelera*; some are genuine, but if you're asked if you want "tourist information" as you pass, it's almost certain you're being selected for a timeshare sales pitch. Many hotels arrange **trips to the chief Maya ruins** – most commonly Chichén Itzá, Tulum and Cobá. Check with the receptionist about the latest offers.

Downtown you'll be able to walk just about anywhere, but you need some sort of transport to get around the *zona hotelera*, which stretches for more than 20km. **Buses** marked "Tulum–Hoteles, Ruta 1" run along Av Tulum every few minutes. There's a fixed fare of US$0.50. Alternatively, **taxis** are plentiful and can be hailed almost anywhere – the trip between downtown and the *zona* costs around US$6. A car affords you more scope and makes day-trips as far as the ruins at Cobá perfectly feasible.

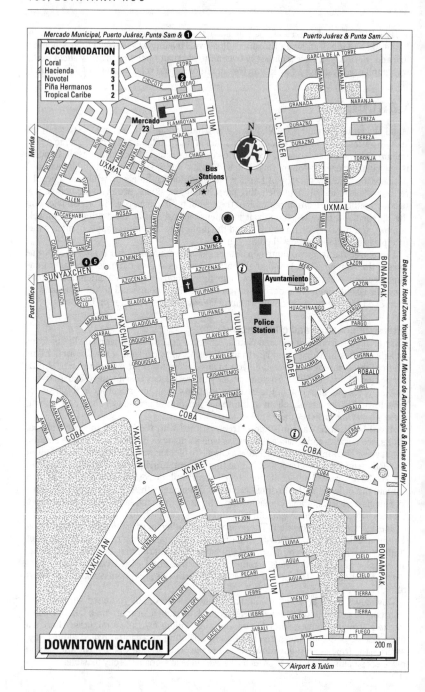

ACCOMMODATION

Coral	4
Hacienda	5
Novotel	3
Piña Hermanos	1
Tropical Caribe	2

DOWNTOWN CANCÚN

Accommodation

Cancún has plenty of accommodation, most of it very expensive for the casual visitor. **Downtown** holds the only hope of a decent budget room, while the glittering beach-front palaces of the **zona hotelera** offer exclusive luxury, many with extravagant interiors featuring waterfalls and cascades of tropical vegetation. All have excellent service, with colour TV and minibars in rooms, at least one immaculate pool, glitzy bars and restaurants, and, more often than not, shops and a travel agency. Many will also put on a show in the evening, a disco, or both. Of course, this is all rather expensive if you just drop by, but very much more reasonable as part of a **package**, and prices may be reduced considerably in the summer.

At the other end of the spectrum there is a 600-bed **youth hostel** out on the beach at the beginning of the *zona* on Av Kukulkán (☎98/83-13-37; ③). Single-sex dorms have bunks and lockers; the beach isn't great here, but there's a pool.

DOWNTOWN HOTELS

Coral, Sunyaxchen 30, near Grosella (☎98/84-05-86, fax 84-45-69). Very reasonably priced for Cancún; away from the busiest traffic, clean rooms, some with a/c, and a pool. ④.

Hacienda, Sunyaxchen 39 (☎98/84-36-72, fax 84-12-08). Good location and good value; rooms all have a/c and colour TV and there's a pool, café, travel agency and beach club. ⑤.

Novotel, Tulum 27, corner of Azucenas and across from the bus station (☎98/84-29-99, fax 84-31-62). Centrally located, clean and secure; the best hotel in its class. Rooms, with fan or a/c, are very comfortable; try to get one at the back. The cool patio restaurant overlooks a small garden. ⑤.

Piña Hermanos, C 7 Ote (☎98/84-21-50). The best of three budget hotels in a row, and one of the city's best deals; from the bus station, head north along Tulum (by bus or about fifteen minutes' walk) almost to the junction with Av López Portillo. Turn right at C 10 Ote, then take the third on the right. Clean rooms with hot showers. ③.

Tropical Caribe, C Cedro 30, five blocks north along Tulum from the bus station (☎98/84-14-42). Large place with plenty of clean basic rooms with hot showers – the cheapest budget option. ②.

BEACH HOTELS

Carisa y Palma, Km 9 (☎98/830211). The cheapest of the beach hotels, but hardly a rock bottom price. Pool, a/c and beach access, but rather anonymous. ⑧.

Club Las Velas, Blvd Kukulkán, Km 3.5 (☎98/83-22-22, fax 83-21-18; in US ☎1-800/223-9815). Overlooking the Nichupté Lagoon, this all-inclusive resort (the price covers meals and drinks, sports and evening entertainment) somehow manages to retain a village atmosphere. ⑨.

Kin Há, Blvd Kukulkán, Km 8 (☎98/83-23-77, fax 83-21-47). Near the main shopping and entertainment centres. Beautiful rooms and suites with spacious balconies. All the facilities and a great buffet breakfast at a reasonable price. ⑨.

Presidente Cancún, Blvd Kukulkán, Km 7.5 (☎98/83-02-00, fax 83-25-15; in US ☎1-800/468-3571). Luxury, first-class hotel with superb service. All rooms overlook the sea, and there are two pools and a jacuzzi. ⑨.

The Town and beaches

There's little to see in **downtown Cancún**. Most visitors head straight for the *zona hotelera* and the **beaches**. Though you're free to go anywhere, some of the hotels do their best to make you feel like a trespasser, and staff will certainly move you off the beach furniture if you're not a guest. To avoid being eyed suspiciously by hotel heavies, head for one of the dozen or so **public beaches**: all are free but you may have to pay a small charge for showers. Entertainment and expensive watersports are laid on all around the big hotels; if you venture further, where more sites await construction, you can find surprisingly empty sand and often small groups of nude sunbathers.

To catch a bit of culture while you're out here, the *Sheraton* boasts a small Maya ruin in its grounds, above the pool, while the **Museo de Antropología**, located behind the convention centre (Tues–Fri 9am–7pm, Sat & Sun 10am–5pm; US$2, free on Sun), has a small but absorbing outline of Mesoamerican and Maya culture and history, with information in English and Spanish. Cancún's largest Maya remains, the **Ruinas del Rey** (daily 8am–5pm; US$2, free on Sun), are at Km 17, overlooking the Nichupté Lagoon. They're not especially impressive – and, if you decide not to take one of the guides at the entrance, there's no information available to explain them – but the area is peaceful and very good for bird- and iguana-watching.

The best **snorkelling** in Cancún is at Punta Nizuc, next to *Club Med* territory. You aren't allowed to cross the grounds unless you're staying there, so you have to get off the bus at the *Westin Regina Resort*, cross their grounds to the beach, then turn right and walk for about twenty minutes until you reach the rocky point. Walk across the rocks and snorkel to your heart's content. To join a **snorkelling tour** or go **diving**, contact Aqua Tours (☎98/83-02-27) or Aquaworld (☎98/85-22-88). A one-tank dive costs about US$50 and a full PADI open-water certification course around US$400. To view the colourful underwater life in a more leisurely fashion, take a trip on Nautibus (☎98/83-10-04; US$38), a **glass-bottomed boat** that leaves from Playa Linda (every ninety minutes, 8am–3.30pm).

Eating

Cancún's **restaurants** outnumber hotels many times over, and competition is fierce. The bulk of the **tourist restaurants** line Av Tulum and its side streets: eat here and you can enjoy "fun" disco sounds with your meal. Though seafood and steak form the mainstay of many menus, you can also eat Arabic, Yucatecan, Italian, Chinese, French, Cajun and Polynesian, not to mention international fast food plus some local chains. All the **hotels** in the *zona* have at least one formal restaurant, some of which are very elegant indeed, surrounded by tropical foliage with fountains and music. Many also feature a more relaxed and relaxing beach or poolside dining room.

For **budget food**, follow the locals and make for the markets. From the bus station, walk a few blocks north along Tulum, turn down Flamboyan or Cerdo and you'll come to the **Mercado Municipal**, with plenty of food stalls and tiny restaurants. Further along, at the junction of Tulum and López Portillo, is a small plaza, complete with fountain, at the edge of another market. The little cafés here are packed with Mexican families and it's the nearest Cancún comes to having a zócalo.

DOWNTOWN

100 Percent Natural, Sunyaxchen 26, at the junction with Yaxchilán. Not entirely vegetarian, but it serves fruit drinks, salads, yoghurt and granola, as well as Mexican dishes, seafood and burgers. A pleasant enough place, if a little overpriced. There's also a branch in the Plaza Terramar in the *zona hotelera*.

Los Almendros, Bonampak 60, opposite the Plaza de Toros. This is the Cancún branch of the famous restaurant that originated in Ticul, and is justly renowned for its good-value Yucatecan specialities.

Gory Tacos, Tulipanes 26. Don't be put off by the name: this spotless and very friendly place serves good, inexpensive Mexican food, steaks, hamburgers and sandwiches, and a range of vegetarian meals.

La Habichuela, Margaritas 25, in front of the Parque Las Palapas. Long-established and fairly expensive restaurant set in a walled garden. The menu is excellent, featuring such dishes as *coco-bichuela*: half a coconut filled with lobster and shrimp in a curry sauce, accompanied by tropical fruits. Live jazz adds to the atmosphere.

La Placita, Yaxchilán 12. Highly recommended Mexican restaurant. Tacos, steaks and the like served in fairly authentic style.

El Tacolote, Cobá 19, across from the hospital. Popular with Mexicans and offering a wide range of good-value tacos.

THE ZONA HOTELERA

Doña Yola, inside the Plaza Terramar. Bargain all-you-can eat breakfast for US$4; the rest of the American-style menu is more expensive.

Faro's, Plaza Lagunas. Famed for fresh fish, lobster, shrimp, crab, mussels and clams; also serves steaks, pasta and tapas.

Mr Papa's, Terramar Plaza. Giant baked potatoes with dozens of fillings for around US$7.

Entertainment and nightlife

Since Cancún's whole rationale is to encourage almost two million visitors each year to have fun, the entertainment scene is lavish – or remorseless, depending on which way you look at it. There's everything from sports and gambling **bars** to romantic piano bars and fun bars, even just plain drinking bars: enough choice to ensure that you can find a place to have a good time without being ripped off. Most of the **nightclubs**, on the other hand, are pricey, with a "no shorts or sandals" dress code. A couple of **cinemas** show new American releases subtitled in Spanish: the largest downtown is the multi-screen Cine Royal on Tulum opposite the Amex Office; in the *zona*, there's a cinema in the Plaza Kukulkán.

BARS AND NIGHTCLUBS

La Boom, Blvd Kukulkán, Km 3.5, at the front of the *Hotel Aquamarina Beach* (☎98/83-16-41). High-tech disco in an "English setting" with continuous videos. No cover charge on Mon; check *Cancún Tips* and *Cancún Nights* for other events.

Cats, Yaxchilán 12. Downtown club with live Jamaican bands. Daily 9pm–5am.

Christine's, in the *Krystal*, Blvd Kukulkán, Km 9 (☎98/83-11-33, ext 499). The most sophisticated and expensive nightclub in town, famed for its light show. Thursday is 70s and 80s night: look in the free magazines or phone to check other weekly events. Don't turn up in shorts, jeans, sandals or without a shirt.

Daddy'o, Blvd Kukulkán, Km 9, opposite the convention centre. A 21st-century nightclub with a high-tech sound system and a light and laser show. Casual dress but no shorts.

Fat Tuesday, Blvd Kukulkán, Km 6.5, and in the Terramar Plaza in the *zona hotelera* (☎98/83-26-76 or 83-03-91). Restaurant-bar with an outside dance floor and a choice of 60 flavours of frozen drinks. Cover charge after 9pm; open until 4am.

Pat O'Brien's, Flamingo Plaza in the *zona hotelera* (☎98/83-08-32). Live rock, blues and jazz in a larger-than-life version of the famous New Orleans bar. Three bars: a piano bar, a video lounge and an outdoor patio. Open until 2am.

Señor Frogs, Blvd Kukulkán, Km 5.5. Live reggae bands and karaoke nights.

Tequila Rock, in the *Party Centre*, Blvd Kukulkán, Km 9 (☎98/84-81-32 or 90-98-45). Pop, rock and disco music with high-tech effects. Check for the daily events – open bar, two-for-one drinks, ladies night and the like. Casual dress, shorts allowed.

DINNER WITH LIVE MUSIC

Ballet Folklórico Nacional de México, at the *Continental Villas Plaza Hotel* in the *zona hotelera* (☎98/83-10-95). Buffet dinner nightly at 7pm with a professional ballet featuring 35 artists. Tickets cost around US$35.

La Fisheria, Plaza Caracol. Fresh seafood and pizza accompanied by live Caribbean music.

Iguana Wana, Plaza Caracol. Lively café with Mexican and seafood specialities. Live music every evening, happy hour from 5 to 7pm. Open until 2am.

Los Rancheros, Flamingo Plaza. Another Mexican restaurant with a lively atmosphere, mariachi and marimba music every night.

DINNER CRUISES

Cancún Queen, Blvd Kukulkán, Km 10.5 (☎98/83-30-07 or 83-17-63). Fish and chicken dinner on a traditional Mississippi paddle-boat. Live music followed by a fiesta and a variety of party games with prizes. Two daily departures at 6.30pm and 9.30pm, returning ninety minutes later.

Columbus, from the Royal Maya Marina at Blvd Kukulkán (☎98/83-32-68 or 83-32-71). Romantic cruise with lobster and steak dinners. Daily 4–7pm and 7.30–10.30pm.

MOVING ON FROM CANCÚN

If you're heading west by car to Valladolid, Chichén Itzá and Mérida, you have a choice between the old road (*viejo*) or the new *cuota* highway, running a few kilometres north of the old road for most of its length. Drive north on Av Tulum then turn left to join López Portillo: after a few kilometres you will have the choice of which road to join. You pay in advance, at the booths on the highway, for the sections you intend to travel along. The trip all the way to Mérida costs US$30.

The first- and second-class bus stations are next to each other on the corner of Tulum and Uxmal. For Mérida, choices include the ADO Mercedes Benz; UNO; first-class, directo or second-class (hourly; 5am–9pm). The journey takes between four and seven hours. Other destinations include Campeche on the deluxe ATS Plus (daily; 9.30am; 9hr); Chetumal on first-class (6.30am–midnight); first-class to México (6pm); Playa del Carmen on ADO Mercedes Benz (3 daily; 1hr), first-class (5 daily; 1hr) and second-class (every 30–45min; 1hr); Tizimín on first- and second-class (6 daily; 4hr); Tulum on first-class (5 daily; 2hr) and second-class (5 daily; 2hr); Valladolid on ADO Mercedes Benz and second-class (hourly; 3hr).

International flights leave regularly from Cancún; from downtown and the *zona hotelera* a taxi to the airport costs about US$8.

THE FERRY TO ISLA MUJERES
The passenger ferry for Isla Mujeres (see opposite) officially leaves from Puerto Juárez, to the north of Av Tulum in Cancún, every thirty minutes between 8am and 8pm, the fast ferry (15min) on the hour and the slow ferry (30min) at thirty minutes past. However, in reality they simply leave when full, often at the same time. To get to the ferry terminal, catch a bus ("Puerto Juárez" or "Punta Sam") heading north from the stop on Tulum, opposite the bus station (20min), or take a taxi from Tulum (around US$3).

The car ferry (US$10 for car, plus US$1.50 for each passenger) leaves from Punta Sam, a few kilometres north of Puerto Juárez. There are six departures daily between 7.15am and 8.15pm, returning from Isla Mujeres between 6am and 7.15pm. However, it isn't really worth taking a car over to the island, which is small enough to cycle around and has plenty of bicycles and mopeds for rent.

Listings

American Express Tulum 208, two blocks beyond the *Hotel America* (☎98/84-19-99).

Banks Most banks are along Tulum and in the *zona hotelera* (9am–1.30pm; foreign exchange 10am–1pm) and many have 24hr ATMs. Banco del Atlántico, Tulum 15, offers good rates and credit card advances over the counter; the branch in the *zona hotelera,* on the corner of the convention centre at Km 9, has a money exchange booth (Mon–Fri 11am–2pm & 4–9pm). Banamex, Tulum 19, and in Plaza Terramar in the *zona hotelera*, and Bancomer, Tulum 26, have convenient ATMs. There are many casas de cambio which change cash (including currencies other than US$) and travellers' cheques faster than the banks, but generally offer worse rates.

Car rental Available at most hotels and at the airport, or try Avis, Mayfair Plaza (☎98/86-01-47), or Budget, Tulum 214 (☎98/84-69-55).

Consulates Canada, Plaza Mexico 312, Av Tulum (Mon–Fri 10am–2pm; ☎98/84-37-16); UK, *The Royal Caribbean*, *zona hotelera* (Mon–Fri 9am–5pm; ☎98/85-11-66 ext 462); US, Edificio Marruecos 31, Av Nader 40 (Mon–Fri 9am–2pm & 3–5.30pm; ☎98/84-24-11 or 84-63-99, fax 84-82-22).

Laundry Lavendería Las Palapas, on Gladiolas, at the far side of the park (Mon–Sat 7am–8pm, Sun 8am–2pm); Lavendería Alborada, Av Nader, just south of City Hall.

Post office Av Sunyaxchen at the junction with Xel-Ha (Mon–Fri 8am–7pm, Sat 9am–1pm), with a reliable Lista de Correos (postcode 77501).

Shopping Mercado 23 (turn left off Av Tulum, three blocks north of the bus station), sells arts and crafts from all over the country and is a good place to pick up some reasonably priced souvenirs.

Travel agents There's an abundance of tour operators and travel agency desks at most hotels, which can easily fix you up with the standard trips to Xel-ha, the main ruins or sell tickets for a cruise. Marand Travel, Plaza Mexico, Av Tulum 200, Suite 208 (☎98/84-38-05, fax 84-38-49), owned by Martha and Richard Uscanga, who also run EcoloMex Tours, is the best travel agency if you want to see the wildlife of the Yucatán.

Isla Mujeres

ISLA MUJERES, just a couple of kilometres off the easternmost tip of Mexico in the startlingly clear Caribbean sea, is an infinitely more appealing prospect than Cancún. Its attractions are simple: first there's the beach, then there's the sea. And when you've tired of those, you can rent a bike or a moped to carry you around the island to more sea, more beaches, a coral reef and the tiny Maya temple that the conquistadors chanced upon, full of female figures, which gave the place its name. Unfortunately, however, Mujeres is no longer the desert island you may have heard about, and its natural attractions have been recognized and developed considerably in the last few years. There are now several large hotels and regular day-trips from Cancún, and the once beautiful El Garrafón coral reef is now almost completely dead. Inevitably, too, prices have risen and standards (in many cases) have fallen. All that said, it can still seem a respite to those who've been slogging their way down through Mexico and around the Yucatán – everyone you've met along the way seems to turn up here eventually.

Arrival, information and getting around

The passenger **ferry** arrives downtown, at the main pier at the end of Av Morelos on Av Rueda Medina, which runs northeast to southwest; the car ferry comes in further east on Medina at the end of Bravo. Avenida Madero, one block north from the passenger ferry dock, cuts northeast straight across the island; as you walk away from the dock, the first street you cross is Juárez, the second Hidalgo and the third Guerrero, both of which lead north to the North Beach and south to the zócalo. The boats leave from Puerto Juárez (ten minutes in a taxi from central Cancún), every half hour, the last at 8pm. There's also a more expensive **hydrofoil**, which leaves from Playa Linda in Cancún's *zona hotelera* a few times a day, returning about an hour later. Aerocaribe and other airlines also occasionally fly out in light planes to Cancún or Cozumel from the small airstrip at the centre of the island.

The zócalo is skirted by Morelos, N Bravo, Guerrero and Hidalgo. The **tourist office** (Mon–Fri 9am–2.30pm & 7–9pm) is on the top floor of the Plaza Isla Mujeres, Hidalgo 7 & 8, opposite *Hotel Xul Ha*. Here you can pick up leaflets, maps and copies of the free *Isla Mujeres* magazine (in Spanish and English). The **post office** (Mon–Fri 8am–7pm, Sat 9am–1pm) is at the corner of Guerrero and Mateos, about ten minutes' walk from the centre; mail is held at the Lista de Correos for up to ten days (postcode 77400). There are **long-distance phones** at Av Medina 6-B (9am–9pm). **Banks** are few: Banco del Atlántico, Medina 3 (Mon–Fri 9am–1pm), does currency exchange between 10am and noon, but to avoid the queues you could use the **casa de cambio** (daily 9am–9pm) on Hidalgo, opposite *Rolandis* restaurant between Madero and Abasolo. There's a **laundry** on Juárez at Abasolo.

The best way of getting around the island is by **moped or bicycle**: the island is a very manageable size with few hills. Operadora Turistica, Hidalgo 43 at Mateos (☎987/46-46-41), advertises golf carts, bikes, mopeds and snorkelling gear for rent. Kan Kin, Absalo at Hidalgo, also rents out bikes and mopeds.

The only PADI-affiliated **dive shop** on the island is Coral on Matamoros no.13-A (☎987/7-07-63). It offers a range of trips including some to the "Cave of the Sleeping Sharks", where tiger, bull, grey reef, lemon and nurse sharks are regularly encountered.

Accommodation

Isla Mujeres is short on good-value **budget places to stay**, and, though prices are lower than at Cozumel, so is the quality. Most of the reasonably priced options are on the northern edge of the island.

There is no official **campsite** on Isla Mujeres, but you can pitch your tent or hang your hammock under one of the *palapas* (US$2 per person paid to the restaurant) on Playa Indios, towards the southern end of the island, shortly before reaching El Garrafón National Park.

Hotel Berny, Juárez at Abasolo (☎987/84-36-72, fax 84-12-08). Good value with spacious, clean rooms and a swimming pool; near the centre and the seafront. ④.

El Caracol, Matamoros 5 (☎987/7-01-50). Two blocks from North Beach; rooms with or without a/c, and a restaurant serving typical Mexican food. ④–⑤.

Caribe Maya, Av Francisco I Madero 9 (☎987/7-06-84). More character than the average budget hotel and good value. Some a/c rooms. ④.

Hotel Cabañas María del Mar, Av Carlos Lazo 1 (☎987/7-01-79, fax 7-01-56). Next to North Beach, with deluxe cabañas on the beach or hotel rooms with a/c, refrigerator and private balcony or terrace. Lively restaurant, tours and car rental. ⑤.

Posada del Mar, Medina 15-A (☎987/7-00-44 or 7-03-00, fax 7-02-66). Spacious rooms or bungalows with a/c, plus a restaurant and a pool with its own bar. ⑤.

María José, Madero 25 (☎987/70-24-44 or 70-24-45). Well-kept family-run hotel. Some of the back rooms open onto next-door's roof, where you can hang your hammock. ④.

Osorio, Madero 22. Turn left from the ferry, take the first right, and the hotel is on your left (☎987/7-02-94). No frills, but clean and near the sea. ④.

Las Palmas, Guerrero 20 (no phone). The cheapest option on the island; basic but acceptable. ④.

Perla del Caribe, Madero 2 (☎987/7-01-20 or 7-05-07, fax 7-00-11). At the opposite side of town to the ferry, one of the smartest hotels on the island, with a pool, restaurant and sea-view rooms with verandas. Car rental. ⑦.

Poc Na, Matamoros 15 (☎987/7-00-90), near the junction with Carlos Lazo, is a kind of private youth **hostel**, with small rooms with bunks and hammock space. It's a great place for meeting people, and has a reasonable restaurant. Rates include mattress and sheet or hammock. ①.

Roca Mar, corner of Guerrero and Bravo, behind the church next to the zócalo (☎987/7-01-01). One of the island's oldest hotels, well maintained, with a restaurant overlooking the Caribbean. ⑤.

Xul-ha, Hidalgo 23 Nte (☎987/7-00-75). Recently rebuilt next to the old hotel, this new hotel is clean and comfortable. ⑤.

The island

Isla Mujeres is no more than 8km long, and, at its widest point, barely a kilometre across. A lone road runs its length, past the dead calm waters of the landward coast – the other side, east-facing, is windswept and exposed. There's a small beach on this side in the town, but the currents even here can be dangerous. The most popular beach, just five minutes' walk from the town plaza, is **Playa Los Cocos** – at the northern tip of the island, but protected from the open sea by a little promontory on which stands what was the lone luxury hotel, the *El Presidente Zazil-Ha*. The hotel now stands abandoned, ravaged by one of the hurricanes that periodically wreck this coast.

If you've had enough of the beach, windsurfing and wandering round town (the Grand Tour takes little more than thirty minutes), rent a bike or moped to explore the south of the island. **El Garrafón National Park** (daily 8am–5pm; US$2), where the road south stops, is a tropical reef, just a few metres offshore, though, unfortunately, the crowds of day-trippers here have frightened away a lot of the fish here and the coral is virtually dead as a result of damage from divers and the anchors of the tourist boats. You can rent diving equipment from Operadora Turistica (see p.105). El Garrafón is almost at the southern end of the island – beyond, the road continues to the lighthouse, and from there a short rough track leads to the **Maya temple** at the southernmost tip.

It's not much of a ruin, but it is very dramatically situated on low rocky cliffs, below which you can often spot large fish basking.

On the way back, stop at **Playa Lancheros**, a palm-fringed beach that is virtually deserted except at lunchtimes when the day-trippers pile in. There's a small restaurant here, specializing in seafood, and a clutch of souvenir stalls. Inland, in the jungly undergrowth, lurk the decaying remains of the **Hacienda Mundaca**: an old house and garden to which scores of romantic (and quite untrue) pirate legends are attached.

You could also take a day-long boat trip to the island bird sanctuary of **Contoy** (some, with special permission, stay overnight), where you can see colonies of pelicans and cormorants and occasionally more exotic sea birds, as well as a sunken Spanish galleon. These are organized by the dive shop Coral (see p.105).

Eating

The area along and around Hidalgo between Morelos and Abasolo, lined with **restaurants** and crafts shops, is the best place to spend an evening on Isla Mujeres. Simply wander through the laid-back music-filled streets and see what takes your fancy. For inexpensive, basic Mexican food and great low-priced fruit salads, head for the **loncherías** opposite *Las Palmas* hotel.

Le Bistro, Matamoros 29. Pseudo-French café with a varied menu at reasonable prices. Good breakfasts.

Restaurant Gomar, Hidalgo 5 on the corner with Madero. Good seafood and chicken, but not much atmosphere – and a very loud TV – in this rather expensive restaurant.

Miramar, Medina, next to the pier. Attractive place on the seafront, away from the centre. Seafood and meat dishes, a little on the expensive side.

Pizza Rolandis, Hidalgo, between Madero and Abasolo. One of a chain serving pizza, lobster, fresh fish and other Italian dishes with salads.

Tonyno's Pizza and Pasta, Hidalgo, between Madero and Morelos, opposite *Mexico Lindo*. The lowest-priced pizzas – delicious too.

The east coast: Cancún to Playa del Carmen

Resort development along the spectacular white-sand beaches south from Cancún to the marvellous seaside ruins of Tulum proceeds rapidly as landowners cash in on Cancún's popularity. The **Caribbean Barrier Reef** begins off **Puerto Morelos**, a quiet, though expensive, town with excellent beaches. Further south is **Punta Bete**, which is smaller and quieter, while the phenomenal growth of **Playa del Carmen**, the departure point for boats to Cozumel, has transformed a village with a ferry dock into a major holiday destination.

Finding a relatively deserted stretch of beach is increasingly difficult, though not impossible, and many visitors based in Cancún rent a car to explore the coast. Although a moped is feasible as far as Puerto Morelos, where the divided highway ends (and there's a filling station), it's a long trip for the underpowered bikes, and bus and truck drivers show scant respect as they pass. The bus is probably a better idea as the service along Hwy-307 is cheap and efficient.

Puerto Morelos and around

Leaving Cancún behind, the first town on the coast is **PUERTO MORELOS**, 20km south. Formerly of little interest except as the departure point for the car ferry to Cozumel, in recent years Puerto has seen a surge in popularity, becoming a base for tours and **diving trips**. The taxi ride from Cancún airport to Puerto Morelos is slightly cheaper than to Cancún itself, and many visitors on international flights bypass the city altogether, making this their first stop. It's as good a place as any to hang out for a while: despite a rash of new hotel and condo construction, it is a relaxing, laid-back alternative to the bustle of Cancún, with some lovely beaches and exceptionally fine watersports, though prices here have risen considerably in recent years.

Arrival and information

Interplaya **buses** leave Cancún's bus station every thirty to forty-five minutes between 5am and 10pm and drop you at the highway junction, where taxis wait to take you the 2km into town. There's a **long-distance telephone** by the police station on the corner of the plaza, a number of small shops, a supermarket and a **bank** (Mon–Fri 9.30am–1pm) that will cash travellers' cheques. The **car ferry to Cozumel** officially operates daily at 6am every day except Tuesday, when it goes at 9am, and Thursday, when it goes at 5am; on Monday an extra ferry is scheduled to leave at noon. You need to get to the terminal around three hours early to be sure of getting a space. The ferry returns from Cozumel at 2pm daily except for Monday, when it leaves at 10am and 5pm. The service is erratic, however, and it's best to check the times either in Cozumel or with the tourist office in Cancún.

Most of the town's **restaurants** are around the plaza. *Los Pelicanos* and *Las Palmeras* are good for seafood and the cosy restaurant at *Posada Amor* offers very good value in a friendly, informal atmosphere. It's also a great place to pick up information about what's going on in town. *Rancho Libertad* has some vegetarian food.

Accommodation

Almost all of the hotels in Puerto Morelos are right on the beach, but many of them are overpriced. You can **camp free** on the sand as long as you're not directly in front of a house or hotel or try the *Acamaya Reef Trailer Park* (☎987/1-01-32), a couple of kilometres away from the centre, down the first turning on the left, 2km after the turn-off from the main highway, near the entrance to Crococun.

Amar Inn, north of the plaza, 500m along the seafront (☎987/1-00-26). The best place in town; pretty rooms and cabañas with kitchenettes around a shaded garden. The staff are very friendly and also run a shop selling handicrafts made by local Maya women. (US$5 extra for breakfast). ⑥.

Caribbean Reef Club, fifteen minutes south of the plaza, beyond the car ferry dock (☎987/1-01-62). Luxury accommodation right on the beach, around a pool. Every room has a sea view and guests have free use of sailboats and windsurf boards. Prices soar in December and January. ⑧–⑨.

Hacienda Morelos, on the front, south of the plaza (☎ & fax 987/1-00-15). Bright, airy rooms. ⑥.

Ojo de Agua, north of the plaza (☎987/1-00-27). Sixteen beachfront rooms and a pool. ⑥.

Posada Amor, Rojo Romez, just south of the plaza (☎987/1-00-33). The least expensive option here. It's not on the beach, but it's friendly and comfortable, with plenty of character. ⑤.

Rancho Libertad, fifteen minutes south of the plaza, beyond the car ferry dock (☎987/1-01-81; in US ☎1-800/305-5225). Two-storey thatched cabañas in a beach and garden setting. Rates include substantial fruit and cereal breakfasts. Snorkel and bike rental and scuba instruction available. No children. ⑥.

The town

The turn-off from Hwy-307 ends at the small, modern **plaza** in the centre of Puerto Morelos: the only proper streets lead north and south for a few blocks, parallel to the beach. Ahead lies the **beach**, a wooden **dock** (the car ferry terminal is a few hundred metres south) and the **lighthouse**. There's a small wooden tourist booth in the plaza minded – sometimes – by Fernando during the mornings. You'll see signs advertising rooms, snorkelling, scuba-diving, and catamaran trips (US$40 per day, including lunch): with the reef only 600m offshore and in a very healthy condition, Puerto Morelos is a great place to learn to **dive**. *Rancho Libertad* (see above) offers two tank dives for US$60 as well as PADI certification. For **dive trips**, contact Fernando (☎987/1-02-44) at the little tourist hut on the ocean side of the town square.

If you want to learn more about the **natural and social history** of the area, contact Sandra Dayton (☎987/1-01-36, or leave a message at the *Amar Inn*), who runs **Maya Echo**, a group dedicated to the conservation of the area's natural beauty and the preservation of Maya culture and spirituality. They organize tailor-made one-day tours into the forest and to local Maya villages, where the Maya will teach you about their way of life and their beliefs.

Just south of the turn-off for the *Acamaya Reef Trailer Park* (see above), the **Jardín Botanico Dr Alfredo Barrera** (daily 9am–5pm; US$2.50) features the native flora of Quintana Roo and is definitely worth a visit if you have the time. Exhibits are labelled in Spanish and English and there are also guides who can explain the medicinal uses of the plants. Trails lead to a small Maya site and a reconstruction showing how *chicle* was tapped from the sap of the *zapote* (sapodilla) tree before being used in the production of chewing gum.

Punta Bete

Tucked away between the more touristed resorts of Puerto Morelos and Playa del Carmen, the sedate **PUNTA BETE** is little more than a beach, a restaurant and a few cabañas, though there's now a big, expensive resort further down the beach towards Playa del Carmen. The beach is long, white and palm-fringed and not too crowded; it's also wonderful for **snorkelling** when the sea is calm. You can rent equipment from the restaurant *Xcalacoco*, which dishes up reasonably priced basic Mexican **food** and superb fish from 7.30am until 8pm. To get there, it's a slow, careful drive or a hot, dusty four-kilometre walk down the untarmacked and pot-holed dirt track from the highway. There's room for around thirty people in the **cabañas** (⑤), and **campers** with tents or trailers are welcome (US$3 per person), although there are no water or electricity hook-ups.

Playa del Carmen

PLAYA DEL CARMEN, once a soporific, very Mexican fishing village, has mushroomed in recent years and its streets are now packed with tourists – from cruise liners, on packages and on day-trips from Cancún. Prices have been forced up as a result, and designer shops have started to move in. Nonetheless, it is lower key and on a smaller scale than Cancún, and attracts a predominantly younger crowd. Most of what happens here happens on the **beach**, where the sea is gloriously clear and the sand unfeasibly white; inland, the main centre of activity is one block back on Av 5, pedestrianized across five blocks from Playacar to C 6. Here, a multitude of dive shops offer diving and snorkelling trips and you can stock up on clothes, crafts and exquisite jewellery from all over Mexico and Guatemala – at a price.

Arrival and information

Buses pull in at the corner of Av 5 and Av Juárez, the main street running east–west from the highway to the beach; some second-class buses stop one or two blocks further inland on Juárez. For **tourist information**, head for the wooden booth in the corner of the plaza (Mon–Sat 7am–midnight) at the end of Juárez. It's run by the multi-lingual Ramón Nuñez Díaz, who is there every day except August 31, when the booth is closed in celebration of his birthday. Pick up a copy of the useful *Destination Playa del Carmen*, which has a map, hotel and restaurant listings. Beware the other tourist information booths scattered around town, as they're mostly tied up with some ulterior motive – selling timeshares, for example.

Accommodation

You'll have no difficulty finding a room in Playa del Carmen – hotels are being built all the time. Budget travellers will find the town very expensive, though, as there's little under US$40. The **youth hostel**, on Av 30 near C 8, ten minutes' walk from the centre in a quiet part of town, is probably your best bet. Bunks in tightly packed dorms cost US$10 per person, with a ten percent discount with an IYH card. Lockers are provided.

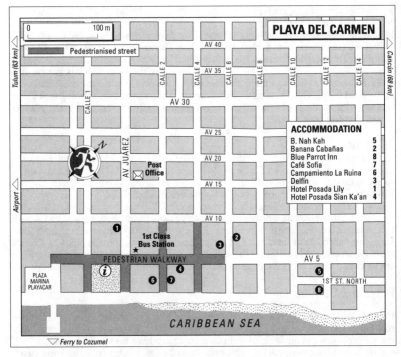

B. Nah Kah, C 12 between the beach and Av 5 (☎987/3-00-48). Very popular and relaxed Italian-run bed-and-breakfast. Individual and charming. ⑦–⑨.

Banana Cabañas, C 6 Nte between Av 5 and 10 (☎987/3-00-36). Comfortable cabañas surrounding a leafy garden. Mosquito nets provided. ⑥.

Blue Parrot Inn, on and slightly back from the beach (☎987/3-00-83, fax 3-00-49). Wide range of cabañas and rooms; the new Tucan annexe has suites with one or two bedrooms and kitchenettes. Can be noisy at night when the hugely popular beachfront *Dragon* bar is hopping. ⑤–⑨.

Campamiento La Ruina, C 2 Nte, between Av 5 and the sea (☎987/3-04-05). Playa's most sociable and economical place to stay, on the beach with its own ruin in the grounds. There are a variety of options: a few hook-ups; cabañas with or without private bath; camping space, and a huge *palapa* with lockers and room for 34 hammocks. ②–④.

Café Sofía, C 2 Nte, between Av 5 and the sea, the cheapest option, opposite the Ruina. ①–④.

Delfín, Av 5 on corner with C 6 Nte (☎ & fax 987/3-01-76). Relatively new hotel; rooms with fans and private bathrooms. ⑥.

Hotel Posada Lily, Juárez, between Av 5 and 10 (☎987/3-01-16). Good budget option just one block back from the beach. ③.

Hotel Posada Sian Ka'an, corner of Av 5 and C 2 Nte (☎987/3-02-02, fax 3-02-04). Small hotel built around a dried-up cenote. Clean and comfortable rooms, some with kitchenettes, others with private terraces. ⑥.

Eating

Playa del Carmen is heaving with **restaurants**, whether you want a romantic candlelit dinner or a low-priced traditional Mexican meal. The pedestrianized section of **Avenida 5** is edged end-to-end with dining tables where you can eat pizza, pasta, French food, burgers and chips, veggie – you name it. Probably the nicest places, though, are the **beach restaurants** and bars, where you can sift sand between your toes while eating fresh fish and sipping icy margaritas. Keep an eye open for the various happy hours.

Da Gabi, C 12, half a block from the beach near the *Blue Parrot Inn*. Italian-run restaurant serving delicious fresh pasta and pizza. A little pricey but recommended.

Deli Café, Av 5, between C 4 and C 6. Fresh juices, pastries, ice cream, burgers and other snacks. Great place for an inexpensive breakfast or to satisfy late-night munchies. Open all night.

Karen's, Av 5, between C 2 and C 4. Busy, moderately priced pizza restaurant in the heart of the pedestrianized zone. Live music on stage most nights and a happy hour 7–9pm.

Limones, Av 5, on the corner with C 6, just past the end of the pedestrianized area. Yucatecan and international specialities in romantic, leafy surroundings. Daily 6–11pm.

Mascaras, Juárez, near the beach. Thin-crust pizza, home-made pasta and seafood. Sip margaritas during the happy hour between noon and 6pm.

Media Luna, Av 5, opposite Plaza Rincon del Sol, near C 8. Vegetarian and seafood restaurant with delicious pasta and veg dishes. Hot crusty bread with fresh herb and garlic butter served with every meal. Small and popular; get there early. Daily except Tues; opens around 7pm.

Molcas, next to the pier. Pleasant setting for an expensive restaurant with an extensive menu. Live music Fri and Sat 6–9pm.

La Parilla, Av 5 at C 8. Wide selection of Mexican dishes, great margaritas and live music every night.

Sabor, Av 5, between C 2 and C 4. Great place for fresh juices, scrumptious cakes and vegetarian food at reasonable prices. The soya tortas are delicious.

Sergios, Av 5, on the corner of C 2. Good basic Mexican food in simple surroundings but still within the buzzy atmosphere of Av 5. Low prices for this part of town.

Bars and nightlife

You can wander through Playa del Carmen well into the night, following the happy-hour trail and listening to all sorts of music from salsa and reggae to 1970s classics. Drinks aren't cheap if you pay the full price, but it's a great way to meet people.

Caribe Swing Bar and Restaurant, on the beach near C 4. Totally laid-back: swing in a hammock on the beach while listening to live reggae, calypso and soca. 9pm–12.30am.

New Calypso House Bar, Av 5, between C 4 and 6. Live Caribbean music on Friday and Saturday, 5–11pm. Cosy atmosphere and a busy dance floor.

Siege's Disco, Juárez, near the beach. Popular disco that doesn't get going till after midnight. No cover charge most nights, except Saturday (US$5) and Wednesday, when US$15 buys unlimited drinks. Daily 10pm–4am.

Listings

Banks Bital is on Juárez between Av 10 and Av 15 (Mon–Fri 8am–1pm) and Bancomer is on Juárez between Av 25 and Av 30 (Mon–Fri 9am–1.30pm) with a 24hr ATM. There are a few casas de cambio around town but they offer very poor rates.

Car and bike rental Executive on Av 5 (☎987/30477) rent cars. Ciclissimo Sport (Mon–Sat only), opposite the ice factory on Juárez, near Av 30, and Copacabaña, Av 5 between C 10 and C 12, both rent bikes.

Email and fax There are a number of shops with Internet facilities on or around Av 5, including Caseta Telefonica (*phonefax@cancun.novenet.com.mx;* US$15 per hour) on C 4 Norte between Av 5 and Av 10.

Post office on Juárez, four blocks back from the beach (Mon–Fri 9am–7pm, Sat 9am–4pm); geared to dealing with tourists and has a stamp machine outside. The Lista de Correos (postcode 77710) keeps mail for ten days.

Telephones There are plenty of Ladatel phones and you can call long-distance at Computel caseta (daily 7am–10pm) next to the bus station.

Travel agents and tours The small airstrip a few hundred metres south of town handles short jaunts, chiefly to Cozumel, but also to Chichén Itzá and other key Maya sites; operators include

Aeroferinco (☎987/3-03-36), Aeroméxico (☎987/3-03-50) and Saab (☎987/3-08-04). Eurotravel at Rincon del Sol, Av 5 near C 8, or the travel agency at Molcas can organize tours to Maya ruins, along with horse-riding, boat trips, sky-diving and national and international flights.

Cozumel

ISLA COZUMEL is far larger than Mujeres and has, unfortunately, been developed beyond its potential. However, it offers the best **diving** in Mexico, with spectacular drop-offs, walls and swim-throughs, some beautiful **coral gardens** and a number of little-visited remote reefs where you can see larger pelagic fish and dolphins. The island is also good for **bird-watching** as it's a stopover on migration routes and has several species or variants endemic to Cozumel.

Before the Spanish arrived, the island appears to have been a major Maya centre, carrying on sea trade around the coasts of Mexico and as far south as Honduras and perhaps Panamá; after the Conquest it was virtually deserted for four hundred years. This ancient community – one of several around the Yucatán coast that survived the collapse of Classic Maya civilization – is usually dismissed as being the decadent remnant of a moribund society. But that was not the impression the Spanish received when they arrived, nor is it necessarily the right one. Architecture might have declined in the years from 1200 AD to the Conquest, but large-scale trade, specialization between centres and even a degree of mass production are all in evidence. Cozumel's rulers enjoyed a less grand style than their forebears, but the rest of an increasingly commercialized population were probably better off. And Cozumel itself may even have been an early free-trade zone, where merchants from competing cities could trade peaceably.

Whatever the truth, you get little opportunity to judge for yourself. A US air base, built here during World War II, has erased all trace of the ancient city, and the lesser ruins scattered across the roadless interior are mostly unrestored and inaccessible. The airfield did, at least, bring new prosperity – converted to civilian use, it remains the means by which most visitors arrive.

Arrival and information

Arriving by boat, you'll be right in the centre of town (officially **San Miguel**, but always known simply as Cozumel) with the zócalo just one block inland along Juárez; from the airport you have to take the VW combi service. The **tourist office** (Mon–Fri 9am–1pm) is upstairs inside the Plaza del Sol shopping centre on the zócalo; but there's nothing here that you can't get at hotels, restaurants and shop counters throughout the island. *Cozumel Tips* and the *Free Blue Guide to Cozumel* are crammed with discount cards and vouchers; the tabloid-sized, one-sheet *Insider's Guide to Diving and Snorkelling* can also be useful. The **post office** (Mon–Fri 8am–8pm, Sat 8am–5pm, Sun 9am–1pm) is about fifteen minutes' walk from the centre, on Av Melgar at the corner with C 7 Sur; for the Lista de Correos use the postcode 77600. Cozumel has many **banks** (Mon–Fri 9am–1.30pm), most of them with ATMs; currency is exchanged between 10am and 12.30pm. Outside these hours, Banco del Atlántico on the southeast corner of the zócalo has a money exchange counter (Mon–Fri 9am–8pm) separate from the main banking hall, and there's also a **casa de cambio** on the south side of the main square (daily 9am–8pm).

There are dozens of **dive shops** in town. The better shops use experienced instructors and small, fast boats. Deep Blue, Av 10 at Salas (☎ & fax 987/2-56-53; in the US ☎214/343-3034; *www.ipp.unicomp.net/deepblue*) is one of the best on the island. Run by an English/Colombian-American couple, it offers tailor-made tours to some of the most interesting and remote reefs on the island, in small groups and offers a full range of certification courses including PADI and IANTD (Nitrox) certifications. They can also help find accommodation, including house rental. There are plenty of other dive shops, but it's important to verify the certification of the divemaster leading your trip and to consider the number of other divers on the trip and safety aspects such as whether oxygen is carried.

Getting around

Cozumel town has been modernized and is easy enough to get around on foot – there's even a pedestrian zone. There's a distinct lack of buses, however, so to get further afield you'll have to go on a tour, take a taxi or rent a vehicle. **Cycling** is feasible on the tarmacked roads, but it can be a bit of an endurance test if you aren't used to long-distance pedalling, and positively unpleasant if you get caught in a sudden storm, likely from around July to October. **Mopeds** give you a bit more freedom and are easier to handle, and **jeeps** are available from numerous outlets (be sure to check the restrictions of your insurance if you want to go onto the dirt tracks). Prices vary little, but it's worth shopping around for special offers. Bikes cost around US$5 for 24 hours, mopeds three times that much, and jeeps around US$45 for a twelve-hour day.

Try Rentadora Cozumel, Av 10 Sur 172 (daily 8am–8pm; ☎987/2-11-20 or 2-14-29, fax 2-24-75), and in the lobby of *Hotel Flores*, Salas 72, which offers a full range of modern vehicles and will deliver the car to your hotel. Alternatively, try Rentadora Dorado, Juárez 181-C, which is a little cheaper.

Accommodation

Hotels in Cozumel are not cheap, most of them geared to divers. The affordable places are some way from the beaches, and you can find some bargains in the town centre, but the only truly budget option is to camp on the sands.

Aguilar, C 3 Sur 98, near the corner of Av 5 Sur (☎987/2-03-07, fax 2-07-69). Quiet rooms away from the road around a garden with pool and paddling pool. Fridges and cable TV are extra. ⑤.

Suites Colonial, Av 5 Sur 9, Aptdo 286 (☎987/2-05-42 or 2-05-06, fax 2-13-87). A/c rooms with baths, kitchenettes, cable TV and phones. ⑤–⑥.

Flores, Salas 72 (☎987/2-14-29). Basic rooms, fine for the price, and moped and bike rental in the lobby. ④.

Posada Letty, C 1 Sur, on the corner with Av 15 Sur (☎987/2-02-57). Clean, basic rooms; very light and airy on the first floor. ④.

El Marques, Av 5 Sur 180 (☎987/2-06-77, fax 2-05-37). Comfortable a/c rooms with fridges, close to the zócalo. ⑤.

Maya Cozumel, C 5 Sur 4 (☎987/2-00-11, fax 2-07-81). Less expensive than the seafront hotels, but just as good, with spacious garden and pool. The a/c rooms have TV, refrigerators and phones. ⑥.

Pepita, Av 15 Sur, on the corner with C 1 Sur (☎987/2-00-98). Basic option with a small pool. ④.

Saolima, Salas 268 (no phone). Rooms away from the road around a plant-filled courtyard. ④.

Villablanca Garden Beach Hotel, about 2km east of the zócalo (☎987/2-01-30 or 2-45-88, fax 2-08-65). More spacious than the town hotels, with a pool, tennis court and dive shop. Dive packages offered and good snorkelling from just across the road. ⑥.

Vista del Mar, Melgar 45, near the corner with C 5 Sur (☎987/2-05-45, fax 2-04-45). Comfortable, modern a/c rooms with sea views, private terraces and refrigerators. Small pool, restaurant, cafeteria, bar, private parking, diving shop and car or scooter rental on the premises. ⑥.

The island

Downtown Cozumel is almost entirely devoted to tourism, packed with restaurants, souvenir shops, tour agencies and "craft markets". **Black coral**, a rare and beautiful product of the reefs, is sold everywhere: until Jacques Cousteau discovered it off the island about twenty years ago, it was thought to be extinct. Even now there's not a great deal (it grows at little more than an inch every fifty years), so it's expensive and heavily protected – don't, under any circumstances, go breaking it off the reefs. A recent addition to the tourist attractions on the island is the **Archeological Park** (daily 8am–6pm; US$7) on Av 65 on the inland southern edge of town. The fee includes a guided tour that lasts around an hour, depending on your own pace and interest, leading you along a shady path through a garden filled with replicas of relics from the various ancient Mesoamerican cultures. You can also see demonstrations of hammock- and tortilla-making, in a replica of a Maya home, by Maya in traditional dress.

Cozumel's eastern shoreline is often impressively wild but, as on Isla Mujeres, only the west coast is really suitable for **swimming**, protected as it is by a line of reefs and the mainland. The easiest **beaches** to get to are north of the town in front of the older resort hotels. Far better, though, to rent a vehicle and head off down to the less exploited places to the south.

Heading **south**, you pass first a clutch of modern hotels by the car ferry dock; offshore here, at the end of the Paraiso Reef, you can see a rather alarming wrecked airliner on the bottom – it's a movie prop. There's accessible snorkelling by *Hotel Barracuda* and further along opposite the *Villablanca Garden Beach Hotel*. Carry on to the **Parque Chankanaab** or "Little Sea", recently designated a **National Park** (daily 7am–5.30pm; US$3), a beautiful if rather over-exploited lagoon full of turtles and lurid fish surrounded by botanical gardens. There's a beach and a tiny reef just offshore; also changing rooms, showers, diving and snorkelling equipment for rent, an expensive restaurant, and a protected children's beach. Further south, **Playa San Francisco** is the best spot for lounging and swimming, while at the southern tip, the **Laguna de Colombia** offers interesting snorkelling.

From here you can complete a circuit of the southern half of the island by following the road up the windswept eastern shoreline. There are a couple of good restaurants at **Punta Chiqueros** and **Punta Morena** and, on calm days, excellent deserted sands. The main road cuts back across the middle of the island to town, but if you have a jeep (not a moped, which probably won't have enough gas anyway) you could continue up a rough track to the northern point – off here is the small ruin of **Castillo Real**.

More accessible – halfway across the island from town, on the northern side of the road – the only excavated ruin on the island, **San Gervasio**, was built to honour Ixchel, the god of fertility. On the southern part of the island, the village of **CEDRAL** has a tiny Maya site near the old Spanish church; turn inland on the road shortly after passing San Francisco beach. If your vehicle is insured to go on dirt tracks, you can get to **Tumba de Caracol**, near the Punta Celarin lighthouse on the southernmost point of the island. It may have been built by the Maya as a lighthouse, and is worth visiting to hear the music produced when the wind whistles through the shells encrusted in its walls.

Eating

Eating tends to be expensive wherever you go on Cozumel, but there's plenty of choice if you've got money to spend. Most of the restaurants are downtown or along the island's west coast, but for a more laid-back atmosphere you can enjoy long, lazy lunches in the **palapas** dotted every few kilometres along the rugged eastern coast. Keep your eyes peeled for **discount vouchers** such as the Promo Tips Card given away with *Cozumel Tips*.

La Choza, corner of Av 10 and C Salas. Busy and popular, mid-priced restaurant serving Mexican home cooking. Good service and a buzzing atmosphere.

El Foco, Av 5 Sur 13, near C Salas. Long-established, busy restaurant, serving moderately priced Mexican dishes.

Joe's Lobster Pub, Av 10, between C Salas and C 3. Touristy restaurant serving Mexican food; the house speciality is lobster in garlic sauce. Nightly live music. Open 6pm–2am.

La Laguna, inside Parque Chankanaab. Busy, expensive restaurant with an extensive menu including superb seafood, typical Mexican dishes and cocktails. The park closes at 5.30pm.

Las Palmeras, on the zócalo (☎987/2-05-32). Seafood and Mexican cuisine by the main pier. Busy but mediocre considering the prices. Open 7am–11pm.

Mi Chabelita, Av 10, between C 1 and Salas. One of the few lower-priced restaurants left near the downtown area. A basic Mexican menu in simple surroundings.

Paradise Café. On an anticlockwise circuit of the island, it's where the tarmac road meets the east coast, half an hour from town. *Palapa*-roofed restaurant/bar in the middle of nowhere, dishing up moderately priced Mexican food to the accompaniment of reggae. Good place to swing in a hammock, sipping a margarita. Daily 10.30am–6.30pm.

Pepe's Grill, Av Melgar and C Salas (☎987/2-02-13). Seafood and steak in an elegant and relaxed atmosphere. Expensive but worth it. Daily 5–11pm.

Pizza Rolandi, Melgar 23. The best pizza on the island. Good service and great sangria.

Las Tortugas, Av 10 Nte, near C 2 Nte. Seafood, steaks and fajitas, as well as West Indian dishes, away from the hustle and bustle of the centre. Daily 11am–11pm.

From Playa south to Tulum

South of Playa del Carmen are a number of exquisite **beaches**, most of which have already been developed or are earmarked for exclusive hotels or condos within the next year or two. The first of note, 6km south of Playa, is **Xcaret**, tagged the "Incredible Eco-Archeological Park", but in fact a huge, somewhat bizarre **theme park** (daily April–Sept 8.30am–6pm; Oct–March 8.30am–5pm; US$25, free for under-5s). There's a museum, tropical aquarium, aviary, "Maya village", botanical garden, small archeological ruins, pools and beaches, and more than a kilometre of subterranean rivers down which you can swim, snorkel or simply float – along with scores of others – with the help of neon rubber rings.

Puerto Aventuras, 20km south of Playa, was originally planned to complement Cancún, with the five-star hotels, tennis and golf clubs and first-class service to show for it. There's a wide white-sand beach, a marina and a dive centre, but little worth stopping for apart from the **Cedam Museum** (Mon–Fri 10am–5pm), which gives an insight into the lives of the ancient mariners and pirates of this coast, displaying artefacts from ships wrecked on the reefs in the 1700s. Five kilometres south, the small fishing village of **XPU-HA** is known for its spectacular freshwater lagoons, **El Cenote Azul** and **El Cenote**, both of which are popular swimming spots.

AKUMAL – "the place of the turtles" – is 11km on: another resort area with high-class accommodation and top-notch facilities. As you enter from the highway, you're greeted by an arch across the road, to the right of which is the reception for the swanky *Hotel Club Akumal Caribe Maya Villas* (☎987/3-05-96; US ☎1-800/351-1622; ⑦–⑨). Apart from this, there's a variety of accommodation around the bay, ranging from beachfront bungalows to suites and condos, but none of it's cheap. Also on site are a couple of good, if expensive, restaurants and bars, limited shopping and the Akumal Dive Shop (☎987/4-12-59, fax 7-31-64).

Aventuras Akumal, another resort slightly further south, is dominated by the *Oasis Akumal* (☎987/2-28-28, fax 2-28-87; ⑨), an all-in resort with every facility you can think of. Also here is the *Villa de Rosa* (Postal 25, Tulum, Quintana Roo, 77780; ☎ & fax 987/4-12-71; ⑨), which specializes in **cave and cavern diving trips** along the Caribbean coast. A seven-night all-inclusive package starts at US$850 per person for a minimum of five people.

Six kilometres south of Akumal is another beautiful beach at **XCACEL** (US$2 fee), from where you can walk ten minutes south to a clean, cool cenote with a wooden platform for easy access (remember not to wear suntan lotion). Turtles lay their eggs here from May to September, when tourists are not encouraged: outside these times, you can see a few of the gentle creatures at the **turtle sanctuary**. The beach fills up occasionally with day-trippers from Playa del Carmen and Cancún, who flock to the large, expensive **restaurant** at the top of the beach (daily 10am–8pm), but otherwise this is a tranquil place to pitch your tent or park your trailer (no hook-ups), with clean showers and plenty of shade.

Xel-Ha Lagoon National Park (daily 8am–5.30pm; US$7), 13km north of Tulum and 45km from Playa, is somewhat over-exploited, with expensive restaurants and souvenir shops, and a comments book full of complaints from disgruntled Mexicans who feel that too much of the information is in English rather than Spanish. That said, it's a beautiful place, and the lagoon and the tropical fish that have not fled the crowds are beautiful, but get here early as after 9.30am you'll be fighting for space. You can rent snorkelling equipment on the spot and lockers are available. Across the other side of the highway, the small and only partly excavated **ruins** of Xel-Ha are of little interest but for the Temple of the Birds, where faded paintings are still visible in places.

Tulum

Tulum, 130km south of Cancún, is one of the most picturesque of all Maya sites – small, but exquisitely poised on fifteen-metre-high cliffs above the turquoise Caribbean. When the Spanish first set eyes on the place in 1518, they considered it as large and beautiful a city as Seville. They were, perhaps, misled by their dreams of Eldorado, by the glory of the setting and by the brightly painted facades of the buildings, for architecturally Tulum is no match for the great cities. Nevertheless, thanks to the setting, it sticks in the memory like no other. It is also an important Maya spiritual and cultural centre, and is one of the villages in the **Zona Maya**.

If you want to take time out for a **swim**, you can plunge into the Caribbean straight from the beach on site. There are limitless further possibilities strung out along the sandy road that runs south along the beautiful and deserted coastline. This track continues, though practicable only in a sturdy (and preferably 4-wheel-drive) vehicle, all the way to Punta Allen at the tip of the peninsula. The beginning of the old road has been blocked to protect the ruins from traffic damage, so you have to join it further south.

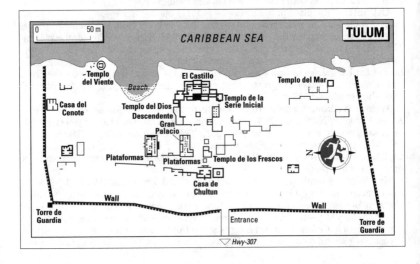

The site

The **Tulum site** (daily 8am–5pm; US$4, free on Sun) is about 1km from the main road – be sure to get off the bus at the turn-off to the ruins and not at the village. **Entrance** is through a breach in the wall that protected the city on three sides; the fourth was defended by the sea. This wall, some 5m high with a walkway around the top, may have been defensive, but more likely its prime purpose was to delineate the ceremonial and administrative precinct (the site you see today) from the residential enclaves spread out along the coast in each direction. These houses – by far the bulk of the ancient city – were mostly constructed of perishable material, so little or no trace of them remains.

As you go through the walls, the chief structures lie directly ahead of you, with the Castillo rising on its rocky prominence above the sea. You pass first the tumbledown **Casa de Chultun**, a porticoed dwelling whose roof collapsed only in the middle of this century, and immediately beyond it the **Templo de los Frescos**. The partly restored murals inside the temple depict Maya gods and symbols of nature's fertility: rain, corn and fish. They originally adorned an earlier structure and have been preserved by the construction around them of a gallery and still later (in the fifteenth century) by the addition of a second temple on top, with walls which, characteristically, slope outwards at the top. On the corners of the gallery are carved masks of Chac, or perhaps of the creator god Itzamna.

The **Castillo**, on the highest part of the site, commands imposing views in every direction. It may have served, as well as a temple, as a beacon or lighthouse – even without a light, it would have been an important landmark for mariners along an otherwise monotonously featureless coastline. You climb first to a small square, in the midst of which stood an altar, before tackling the broad stairway to the top of the castle itself. To the left of this plaza stands the **Templo del Dios Descendente**. The diving or descending god – depicted here above the narrow entrance of the temple – appears all over Tulum as a small, upside-down figure. His exact meaning is not known: he may represent the setting sun, or rain or lightning, or he may be the bee god, since honey was one of the Maya's most important exports. Opposite is the **Templo de la Serie Inicial** (Temple of the Initial Series) – so called because in it was found a stela (now in the British Museum) bearing a date well before the foundation of the city, and presumably brought here from elsewhere. Right below the castle to the north is a tiny cove with a beautiful white beach, and on the promontory beyond it the **Templo del Viento** (Temple of the Wind), a small, single-roomed structure. This is mirrored by a similar chamber – the **Templo del Mar** – overlooking the water at the southern edge of the site.

Staying near Tulum

There are a couple of hotels and restaurants in Tulum village, though there's no reason to try them unless you're stuck without a beach place. Everything of importance in the village is located along the highway. You can **change money** at two casas de cambio, one opposite the bus station and one next to it, and Joys Car Rental (☎987/1-20-81) rent cars and bikes at good rates.

By far the best places to stay, however, are in the **cabañas** and **campsites** scattered along the coast road to Punta Allen, south of the ruins, where you can rent huts or find space for a tent or a hammock. Dramatically situated on a cliff-top, these are some of the most popular places to stay in Quintana Roo: the view of the sunrise over the Caribbean sea in the morning is stunning, as is the sky at night. Even with the increased numbers of visitors, the gorgeous white-sand beach along this coast remains fairly empty, and the sea is warm and clear. If you're planning to stay at the cabañas near the ruins, be sure to turn up as early as you can – Christmas is the busiest period, but cabañas are hard to come by all year round. Although **camping on the beach** in Mexico is free, camping very near to one of the cabaña places could cause aggravation: it's best to pay the small fee or move further away. The places nearest the ruins are the most lively, with **restaurants**, and a **disco bar** at *Don Armando's*. There have been a number of **thefts** recently, so be sure to give your valuables in for safe-keeping and check the sturdiness of your cabaña. The following are listed in order of their distance from the ruins, going south.

El Mirador Cabañas, 1km from the ruins along the old Punta Allen road. Basic sandy-floor cabañas with hammock hooks only: bring your own or rent one of theirs. Shower *palapa* with running water. The restaurant is perched on the cliff, giving an idyllic view and wonderful cooling breezes. Snorkelling trips arranged. ③.

Santa Fe Cabañas, next door to *El Mirador*. Lively place with restaurant-bar. Cabañas have a bed and a hammock but no showers; you have to dredge your washing water from the well and toilets are primitive. Watch your valuables. Camping US$2.50. Snorkelling trips arranged. ③–④.

Don Armando's Cabañas, next door to *Santa Fe* (☎987/4-45-39 or 4-38-56). Sturdy, sandy-floored cabañas with security guards. The most popular of the inexpensive places near the ruins, so get there early. Camping US$3. ④.

Mar Caribe Cabañas, next to *Don's*. Rickety old cabañas for hammocks which were only intended for use by a fishing co-op, but there are plans to improve them. The restaurant does great fresh fish and has the broadest menu of all the cheaper places. ④.

Los Gatos Cabañas, 2km from the ruins. More laid-back than the places nearer the ruins; well-built thatched cabañas with mosquito-netted doubles and hammocks. A relatively private, shady spot, with a superb beach for swimming and snorkelling. Horse-riding can be arranged. Electricity in the restaurant and shower, and some cabañas have feeble battery light. ⑤.

La Perla Cabañas, the next along. Four basic cabañas and a restaurant with bar. ⑤–⑥.

Que Fresco, next to *La Perla*. Nice new cabañas, a restaurant and a communal shower with hot and cold water. ⑤–⑤.

Osho Oasis, 7km from the ruins (PO Box 99, Tulum, Quintana Roo; ☎ & fax 987/4-27-72). A comfortable retreat/resort with four standards of cabaña – some luxurious and spacious with private baths. The restaurant does a delicious veggie buffet, with fish by order. Electricity until about midnight. There's a meditation room, with yoga classes, massage sessions, Zen sittings and Kundalini meditation, and a TV with video for occasional film shows. ⑦.

Casa de Maleo, the only cheaper place in this section. Very basic cabañas right on the beach. ④.

Los Arrecifes, 500m further south along the road. Established twenty years ago, this is one of the oldest places on this coast. Cabañas with or without private bath in an idyllic setting with its own stretch of palm-fringed beach and a restaurant. ⑥.

Ana y José, a little further south (call Cancún for reservations: ☎98/80-60-21, fax 80-60-22). A variety of comfortable rooms, some close to the beach with hot and cold water, others set back slightly with cold water only. Good restaurant with a sedate and intimate atmosphere. You can also rent bikes and organize day-trips into the Si'an Ka'an Biosphere Reserve from here. ⑦.

Dos Ceibas, 9km from the ruins (☎987/12092). The last on this stretch, and the best of the lot, with very beautiful cabañas almost in the Si'an Ka'an Reserve, in front of a turtle egg-laying beach. ⑦.

Cobá

Set in muggy rainforest 50km northwest of Tulum, the crumbling city of **COBÁ** is a fascinating, if little-visited site. As it's scattered between two lakes and linked by a network of causeways, you'll need at least a couple of hours to see it all, wandering along poorly signposted paths through the jungle – but it's well worth the effort, as much for the **wildlife** as for the ruins. The jungle around Cobá is home to toucans, egrets, herons and myriad tropical butterflies including the giant electric blue morphidae. There are plenty of vicious mosquitoes too, so bring lots of repellent.

The city's most surprising characteristic is a resemblance not to the great ruins of the Yucatán, but to those of the Maya in lowland Guatemala and Honduras. Ceramic studies indicate that the city was occupied from about 100 AD, up until the advent of the Spanish, and the site is even mentioned in the *Chilam Balam*, a book of Maya prophecy written in the eighteenth century and drawn from earlier oral sources. Its zenith, however, was in the Classic and Late Classic (up until about 800 AD). Most of the larger pyramids were built in this period, including the giant, **Nocoh Mul**, tallest in the Yucatan and strikingly similar in its long, narrow and precipitous stairway to the famous Guatemalan ruins of Tikal. The city's influence and wealth during this period was derived from close links with the great cities of Petén, to the south, as the plethora of stelae, which are associated with Petén sites, and the style of almost all of the buildings and ceramics attest. Later, when the city maintained trade links with the Puuc cities to the west, the production of stelae ceased. In the Early Postclassic, from about 1000 AD, Cobá went into a brief decline, recovering in 1200 AD with a resurgence of new building which included the construction of the temple that crowns the Nocoh Mul pyramid.

Practicalities

There are four buses a day to Cobá from Tulum that continue on to Valladolid. They are all *de paso*, which means that by the time they reach Cobá they are often full. In the other direction, there is a bus at 1.30pm for Tulum from Cobá itself, as well as three *de paso* buses.

The **village** of Cobá, where the bus stops, is little more than a collection of shacks a few hundred metres from the site entrance. Should you be in the mood to blow a lot of money, you could do little better than **stay** at the *Villas Arqueologicas* (☎98/84-25-74; in US: ☎1-800/528-3100; ⑨), the only hotel anywhere near the site, and a wonderful bit of tropical luxury complete with swimming pool and archeological library. On the less expensive side, there are basic rooms to be had at *El Bocadito*, (③), which also has a decent restaurant. Other than this, you have little choice but to grab a drink and something to eat from one of the stalls by the entrance to the site. Don't swim in the lake here – it's full of crocodiles.

The Si'an Ka'an Biosphere Reserve

Created by presidential decree in 1986, the 13,675-square-kilometre **Si'an Ka'an Biosphere Reserve** is one of the largest protected areas in Mexico. The name means "the place where the sky is born" in the Maya language, and seems utterly appropriate when you experience the sunrise on this stunningly beautiful coast. It's a huge, sparsely populated region, with only around a thousand permanent inhabitants, mainly fishermen, *chicleros* and milpa farmers.

Approximately one-third of the area is **tropical forest**, one-third **fresh- and saltwater marshes and mangroves**, and one-third is marine environment, including a section of the longest **barrier reef** in the western hemisphere. The coastal forests and wetlands are particularly important feeding and wintering areas for North American migratory birds. Si'an Ka'an contains examples of the principal ecosystems found in the Yucatán peninsula and the Caribbean: an astonishing variety of flora and fauna. All five species of Mexican **cat** – jaguar, puma, ocelot, margay and jaguarundi – are present, along with spider and howler **monkeys**, tapir, deer and the West Indian manatee. More than three hundred species of **birds** have been recorded, including flamingo, roseate spoonbill, white ibis, crested guan, wood stork, osprey and fifteen species of heron. The Caribbean beaches provide nesting grounds for four endangered species of **marine turtle**: the green, loggerhead, hawksbill and leatherback, while Morelet's and mangrove **crocodiles** inhabit the swamps and lagoons.

The Biosphere Reserve concept, developed since 1974 by UNESCO, is an ambitious attempt to combine protection of natural areas and the conservation of their genetic diversity with scientific research and sustainable development. Reserves consist of a strictly protected **core area**, a designated **buffer zone** used for non-destructive activities and an outer **transition zone**, merging with unprotected land, where traditional land use and experimental research take place. The success of the reserve depends to a great extent on the co-operation and involvement of local people, and the Si'an Ka'an management plan incorporates several income-generating projects, such as improved fishing techniques, ornamental plant nurseries and, of course, tourism.

You can enter the reserve on your own (and at present there is no entrance fee) and there is accommodation at **Punta Allen**, the largest village in the reserve, but by far the best way to explore is on a **day-trip** with the **Amigos de Si'an Ka'an**, a Cancún-based, non-profit organization formed to promote the aims for which the reserve was established. The Amigos support scientific research and produce a series of guide and reference books on the natural history of Si'an Ka'an. You can be picked up either at your hotel **in Cancún, at Playa del Carmen** or at *Ana y José Cabañas* **in Tulum**. The weekly trip, led by bilingual Mexican biologists, begins at *Boca Paila Lodge*, where you will board a small launch and motor across the lagoon and upstream along through the mangroves canalized by the Maya. It's an amazing trip, with excellent opportunities for bird-watching and spotting crocodiles or manatees. At the inner lagoon you'll be shown where fresh water percolates up through the sandy lagoon floor. You'll also be given the choice to snorkel back along the channels through the mangroves, drifting with the current – that is, after a short talk on what to do if you meet a crocodile. Some day-trips include a visit to **Chunyaxche ruins** (see below), walking from the lagoon through the rainforest to the site. This is more likely if they start in Tulum rather than Cancún; ask when you're booking your trip.

To arrange a trip, for information on the work of the Amigos, or for details of how to receive their bulletin, call in at their office in Cancún at Av Cobá 5 between Nube and Brisa, on the third floor of the Plaza America (☎98/84-95-83, fax 87-30-80; *sian@cancun.rce.com.mx*), or write to Apartado Postal 770, Cancún 77500, Quintana Roo, Mexico.

Chunyaxche

The little-visited site of **Chunyaxche** (daily 8am–4pm; US$1.50, free on Sun) lies to the north of the reserve, about 25km south of Tulum. Some day-trips to the reserve include a trip to the ruins, but to **get there independently**, catch any second-class bus heading between Tulum and Chetumal and ask to be dropped at the entrance. A sign on the left of the highway points to a *palapa* that will one day be a visitor centre: for now you pay the caretaker.

Despite its size – probably the largest on the Quintana Roo coast – and proximity to Hwy-307, Chunyaxche is hardly developed for tourism, and you'll probably have the place to yourself. Archeological evidence indicates that Chunyaxche (also known as Muyil) was continuously occupied from the Preclassic period until after the arrival of the Spanish in the sixteenth century. There is no record of the inhabitants coming into direct contact with the conquistadors, but they were probably victims of depopulation caused by introduced diseases. Most of the buildings you see today date from the Postclassic period, between 1200 and 1500 AD. The tops of the tallest structures, just visible from the road, rise 20m from the forest floor. There are more than one hundred mounds and temples, none of them completely clear of vegetation, and it's easy to wander around and find dozens of buildings buried in the jungle; climbing them is forbidden, however.

The centre of the site is connected by a *sacbe* – a Maya road – to the small **Muyil lagoon** 500m away. This lagoon is joined to the large Chunyaxche lagoon and ultimately to the sea at **Boca Paila** by an amazing **canalized river**: the route used by Maya traders. If you travel along the river today you'll come across even less explored sites, some of which appear to be connected to the lagoon or river by **underwater caves**.

Leaving the site, particularly if you're making your way up to Tulum, should be easy enough, provided you don't leave it too late; continuing south could prove a little more difficult.

Punta Allen

Right at the tip of the peninsula, with a lighthouse guarding the northern entrance to the **Bahía de la Ascensión**, the Maya lobster-fishing village of **PUNTA ALLEN** is not a place you'd stumble across by accident. Some tourists from Cancún do get down this far in rented cars, but if you've only got one day virtually all you can do is turn around and head back.

Despite having a population of just four hundred, Punta Allen is the largest village within the reserve and is a focus of initiatives by both government departments and non-governmental organizations promoting sustainable development. During the summer, Earthwatch volunteers come here to assist scientists gathering data.

Entering the village, past the tiny naval station on the right and beached fishing boats on the left, you come to the first of the **accommodation** options: the *Cuzan Guest House* (☎983/4-03-58; ⑤), with tall conical cabañas and teepees, some with hot water. There's a **bar** and **restaurant** with information about the reserve, though you'll need to book meals if you're not staying there. On the beach, the *Let It Be Inn* (⑦) has three cabañas with private bath and a separate large thatched cabaña with a self-catering kitchen and dining room. *Chen Chomac Resort* (in Playa del Carmen: ☎987/2-20-20, fax 2-41-20; ⑦), a few kilometres north of the village, has some comfortable, modern thatched cabañas on the beach.

In theory there's a **long-distance phone** in the village shop, the Tienda Lili, but it can't be relied upon. A couple of small **restaurants**, the *Punta Allen* and the *Candy,* serve food. A **mobile shop** travels the length of the peninsula on Saturdays, selling meat, bread, fruit and vegetables, reaching Punta Allen about 2pm: useful if you're camping. Although there's no **dive shop**, the hotels generally have some form of watersport equipment for their guests and may let non-residents rent it. Fishermen can be persuaded to take you out into the reserve for a fee; they also go across the bay to the even tinier village of **Vigia Chico**, on the mainland.

From Tulum to Chetumal

The road from Tulum to Chetumal skirts around the Si'an Ka'an Biosphere Reserve and heads inland, past Felipe Carrillo Puerto, a major crossroads on the routes to Valladolid and Mérida, the beautiful **Laguna Bacalar**, and on to **Chetumal**, the gateway to Belize and a good point from which to explore **Kohunlich** and other Maya sites.

Felipe Carillo Puerto

FELIPE CARILLO PUERTO, formerly known as **Chan Santa Cruz**, is the capital of the "Zona Maya" and an important spiritual centre for the Maya. During the Caste Wars, Maya from the north gathered forces here and looked for guidance from a miraculous talking cross that told them to fight on against their oppressors. (Such talking crosses and statues are common in Maya mythology as conduits through which disincarnate spirits speak, or as manifestations of a soul, usually that of a shaman, when it has left the body during the state of trance; they are known as *way'ob* by the Yucatek Maya.) Presumably as an attempt to disguise its rebellious past, the town was renamed after a former governor of the Yucatán who was assassinated in 1924. However, a monument to the martyrs of the Caste Wars still stands in the town. There are several reasonable **hotels** around the main plaza – try the *Hotel Esquivel* (☎983/4-03-44; ③) on the zócalo, only 100m from the small bus station, but check the rooms first as some are significantly better than others.

Laguna Bacalar

Further south, some 35km north of Chetumal, is the beautiful **Laguna Bacalar**, the second largest lake in Mexico; 145km long and, on average, 1km wide, it links with a series of other lakes and eventually the Río Hondo and the sea. The village of Bacalar was a key point on the pre-Columbian trade route and unexcavated **Maya remains** surround the lake shore. The *Chilam Balam* of Chumayel, one of the Maya's sacred books, mentions it as the first settlement of the Itza, a Maya tribe originally from central Mexico. Near the village, there's a semi-ruinous **fort**: built by the Spanish for protection against British pirates from Belize (then British Honduras), it became a Maya stronghold in the Caste Wars, and was the last place to be subdued by the government, in 1901. There's a wide variety of **birdlife**, as well as huge fish that reach nearly two metres long. Nearby is the **Cenote Azul**, an inky-blue "bottomless" well that is crowded with swimmers and picnickers at weekends.

There are several lakeshore restaurants in the village, a couple of very basic pensiones and the splendidly grand and imposing *Hotel Laguna* (☎983/2-35-17; ⑨). Other options are outside the town: *Rancho Encantado* (☎ & fax 983/8-04-27, in the US 1-800 221 6509; ⑨ including breakfast and dinner) is a small resort on the lakeshore, with half a dozen cabañas, each with its own kitchen and dining room; it also organizes trips to Kohunlich and scuba-diving to Banco Chinchorro. *Paraiso Ranch* (☎983/7-10-26, fax 2-12-51; US$7 with their tent, US$5 with your own), 10km south of Bacalar (taxi US$3) is a family-owned **ecotourism and conservation project** and one of the most beautiful places to stay in Quintana Roo. Facilities are basic – there are no showers, accommodation is in tents, there's no bar and only one little restaurant – but guests come to enjoy the breathtaking natural beauty and participate in the conservation work that the very hospitable family organize. They also arrange canoe expeditions and tours of the little-visited Maya ruins in the south of Quintana Roo.

Chetumal and around

If you're heading south to Belize or Guatemala, you can't avoid **CHETUMAL**, capital of the state of Quintana Roo. The city is beginning to assert itself after decades of virtual stagnation, but there are still no "sights" to speak of. The best is the new **Museo de la Cultura Maya** (Tues–Sun 9am–7pm; US$4) on Héroes, near the corner of Mahatma Gandhi. Although it has very few original artefacts, the numerous interactive displays and models provide a fascinating insight into ancient Maya society, mathematics and cosmology. The courtyard outside the museum often hosts free exhibitions and there's a good **bookshop** selling guides and maps. Chetumal's broad, modern streets (the town was levelled by Hurricane Janet just over thirty years ago) are lined with rather dull, overpriced hotels and restaurants, and with shops doing a brisk trade in **low-duty goods** – Dutch cheese, Taiwanese hi-fis, American peanuts, reproduction Levis from the Far East, Scotch whisky – to be smuggled into Belize or back into Mexico. Chetumal's surroundings, however, do offer the opportunity for some beautiful excursions, and the **waterfront**, enlivened by free music in the plaza, has a certain sleazy tropical charm.

Practicalities

Chetumal's main bus station is a short taxi ride out of town and the **airport** is only 2km west of the centre, at the end of Av Revolución. **Avenida de los Héroes**, the town's main street, runs down from a big electricity-generating plant to the waterfront. The **information kiosk** (look for the small glass pyramid opposite the archeological museum) is very helpful with information on buses, hotels and maps; they can also give information on Belize. The **bus ticket office** in town is on Belice at Gandhi. There's a

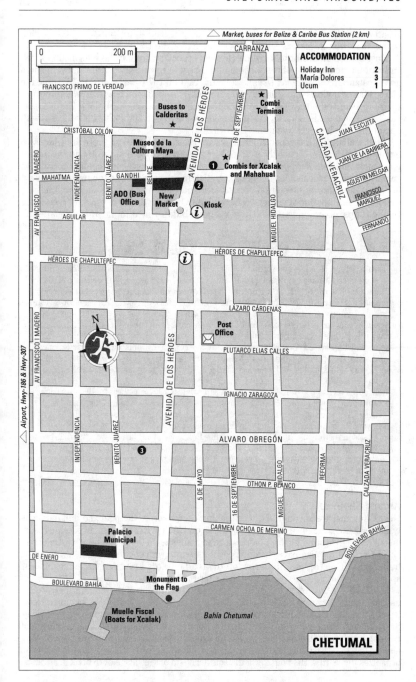

△ Market, buses for Belize & Caribe Bus Station (2 km)

CARRANZA

0   200 m

ACCOMMODATION
Holiday Inn   2
María Dolores   3
Ucum   1

FRANCISCO PRIMO DE VERDAD

JUAN ESCUTIA

Buses to
Calderitas
★

★ Combi
Terminal

CRISTÓBAL COLÓN

JUAN DE LA BARRERA

Museo de la
Cultura Maya

AGUSTIN MELGAR

AVENIDA DE LOS HÉROES

16 DE SEPTIEMBRE

CALZADA VERACRUZ

MAHATMA

INDEPENDENCIA

BENITO JUAREZ

GANDHI

BELICE

❶ Combis for Xcalak
and Mahahual

FRANCISCO
MARQUEZ

MADERO

❷

ADO (Bus)
Office

New
Market

Kiosk

ⓘ

FERNANDO

AV FRANCISCO

AGUILAR

MIGUEL HIDALGO

ⓘ

HÉROES DE CHAPULTEPEC

HÉROES DE CHAPULTEPEC

N

LÁZARO CÁRDENAS

AVENIDA DE LOS HÉROES

Post
Office
✉

MADERO

PLUTARCO ELIAS CALLES

AV FRANCISCO I MADERO

IGNACIO ZARAGOZA

Airport, Hwy-186 & Hwy-307 △

INDEPENDENCIA

BENITO JUAREZ

ALVARO OBREGÓN

❸

5 DE MAYO

16 DE SEPTIEMBRE

MIGUEL HIDALGO

OTHON P. BLANCO

REFORMA

CALZADA VERACRUZ

CARMEN OCHOA DE MERINO

BOULEVARD BAHÍA

Palacio
Municipal

DE ENERO

BOULEVARD BAHÍA

Monument to
the Flag

Muelle Fiscal
(Boats for Xcalak)

Bahía Chetumal

CHETUMAL

Guatemalan consulate at Héroes 358 (Mon–Fri 9am–4pm; ☎983/2-65-65), which issues visas (not necessary for citizens of the EC or the US).

Most of Chetumal's **hotels** are on Héroes, especially around the information kiosk and at the junction with Obregón. One of the best in town, with private showers and a good restaurant, is the *Hotel Ucum*, Mahatma Gandhi 167 (☎983/2-07-11; ③), while the nicest luxury option is the *Holiday Inn*, Héroes 171 (☎983/2-11-00; ⑦), which has a/c rooms, a pool and a travel agency. Obregón, which cuts east–west along Héroes, also has some good deals, such as the *María Dolores*, Obrégon 206 (☎983/2-05-08; ④), with one of the best budget restaurants in town.

Chetumal has nothing special in the way of restaurants, though there are **places to eat** all along Héroes, especially around Obregón – try *Sosilmar* at the *María Dolores* for good meat and fish. *Pantoja*, next to the *Hotel Ucum*, serves a good comida corrida – a favourite with the locals. For budget food, stick to the area around the **markets**, or eat in one of the stalls in the market opposite the museum. Vegetarians, as is so often the case, have few options. The best is *Sergio's* on Obregon no. 182, which serves some veggie soups, pizzas and salads. There's a good **bakery** next to the *María Dolores*.

MOVING ON FROM CHETUMAL

From Chetumal's main bus station you'll be able to travel to most destinations on first- or second-class buses. First-class services include: **Cancún** (eight daily via **Tulum**, **Playa Del Carmen**); **Mérida** (three daily); **Campeche** (six daily, most via **Escárcega**, two stop at **Xpujil**); **Villahermosa** (three daily) **Palenque and San Cristóbal** (one daily); **México** (two daily). There are second-class services that follow the same routes. Buses to **Flores in Guatemala** (one daily) also leave from the main terminal. Buses for towns in **Belize** leave hourly from the Venus Bus Line (mornings) or Batty's (afternoons) in **Lázaro Cárdenas** market, in the city centre. Combis for **Bacalar** (every 30 min), **Río Hondo** and **Mahahual/Xcalak** (one daily at 7am) leave from the Terminal de Combis on Hidalgo at Primo de Verdad. Other, smaller combis are scheduled to depart for Mahahual/Xcalak from C 16 de Septiembre at Mahatma Gandhi at 7am, but their departures are whimsical. **Boats for Xcalak** leave from the Muelle Fiscal (pier) off Boulevard Bahía every Friday, Saturday and Sunday at 8am and return at 3pm.

Taesa, Aviasca and Aeroméxico have daily **flights** to Mérida, Cancún and México; if you want to fly to Belize, you have to cross to Corozal, twenty minutes from the border, and take an internal flight. Crossing into Belize is straightforward: hand in your Mexican tourist card at the immigration office at the border and walk over the bridge to Belizean immigration; there's no charge. Moneychangers at the border offer fair rates and take travellers' cheques.

Around Chetumal

Near Chetumal are any number of refreshing escapes from the heat and dull modernity. At weekends, the town descends en masse on **CALDERITAS**, a small seaside resort just 6km north around the bay; there's a good campsite on the beach here, at *Amanacer en El Caribe*: they also have thatched cabañas, some with cooking facilities (⑤), and a trailer park. The **Laguna Milagros**, off the road towards Francisco Escárcega, is less spectacular than Bacalar, but is superb for bird-watching.

XCALAK is a tiny, very sleepy fishing community at the tip of the isthmus that stretches like a finger towards Belize on the other side of the huge Bahía de Chetumal. Boats leave from the Muelle Fiscal (pier) off Boulevard Bahía in Chetumal every Friday, Saturday and Sunday at 8am and return at 3pm.There are no spectacular beaches and nothing much to do in the village, but it is an excellent base for **bird-watching**, snorkelling and manatee safaris; contact the friendly and knowledgeable Carlos Vidal Batun, who organizes these trips. His house is at the southern end of the village or to book in advance, write in Spanish to him at domicilio conocido, Xcalak, Quintana Roo 77000. Adolfo Acevedo Young, a trained guide and conservationist (domicilio conocido, Xcalak, Quintana Roo 77940; ☎983/8-76-70) organizes **diving and boat trips** to Belize and to the vast coral atoll of **Banco Chinchorro**, 30km off the shore. There are few facilities in Xcalak: a couple of small restaurants and one basic but clean hotel, the *Caracol* (②).

MAHAHUAL, 35km north of Xcalak on a paved road, has more resident non-Mexicans, and a tiny beach. It's a very relaxing place, and is slightly closer to the Chinchorro atoll if you want to go diving. The Italian-owned cabañas, 400m after the *Piratos del Caribe* restaurant, 7km south of Mahahual village, are the best place to stay. Buses or combis will drop you there; otherwise you'll have to hitch as there are no taxis. If you want to **dive**, try Caribe Manatíes Dive centre in town (☎33 (0)491/40-18-78, *comets@infonie.fr*). These two villages have both been earmarked for tourism.

Local buses and combis run out frequently to all of these from the terminal at the junction of Verdad and Hidalgo, four blocks northwest of the information kiosk on Héroes. Buses to Calderitas leave from Cristóbal Colón, near the junction with Héroes. Travelling around this area, keep your passport and tourist card with you – as in all border zones, there are checkpoints on the roads.

Kohunlich and other Maya sites in the south

The most direct route from Chetumal back towards central Mexico is across the bottom of the peninsula via Francisco Escárcega along Hwy-186. Though the road enters the forests of the Calakmul Biosphere Reserve in Campeche state, in Quintana Roo most of the trees have been felled to ranch cattle for the beefburger industry. The only worthwhile stop along the road is the Classic Maya city of **KOHUNLICH**, some 60km from Chetumal, then another 9km off the road from the village of Fco Villa (daily 8am–5pm; US$4, free on Sun).

The ruins, which are seldom visited by anyone other than butterflies and birds, are beautifully situated, peering above the trees. The buildings date from the Late Preclassic to the Terminal Classic (100–900 AD) and are in the Río Bec architectural style characteristic of the region, featuring long rectangular buildings between towers decorated with non-functional stairways. Foliage has reclaimed most of them, and those which are cleared are little more than pyramid-shaped piles of rubble, looted by grave-robbers before archaeologists could preserve them. The exception is the Temple of the Masks, named after the four two-metre-high stucco masks which decorate its facade. Disturbing enough now, these wide-eyed, open-mouthed gods once stared out from a background of smooth, bright red stone.

You can also visit other Maya ruins in the south of Quintana Roo including the impressive Río Bec ruins at **Dzibanche**, **Chacchoben** and **Kinichna**. At present there is no transport to any of these ruins (including Kohunlich), but plans are afoot – check with the tourist office in Chetumal.

travel details

Buses

The most useful bus services are between Mérida and Cancún and those provided by Interplaya, which run at least every thirty minutes between Cancún and Tulum. Some places aren't served by first-class buses, but second-class buses and combis will get you around locally and to the nearest major centre. The following frequencies and times are for first-class services. Second-class buses usually cover the same routes running 10–20 percent slower.

Cancún to: Campeche (1 daily; 8hr); Chetumal (5 daily; 6hr); Mérida (frequently; 5–6hr); México (1 daily; 30hr+); Playa del Carmen (frequently; 1hr); Puerto Morelos (at least every 30min; 1hr); Tizimín (3 daily; 3hr); Tulum (at least every 30min; 2hr); Valladolid (6 daily; 2hr); Villahermosa (1 daily; 14hr).

Chetumal to: Cancún (8 daily via Tulum, Playa del Carmen; 5–8hr); Bacalar (every 30 mins; 30mins); Merida (3 daily; 8–10hr); Campeche (daily; 10hr; most via Escárcega, 2 stop at Xpujil); Villahermosa (3; daily) Palenque & San Cristóbal (1 daily; 10hr); Mexico (2 daily; 24hr); Mahahual/Xcalak (1 a day at 7.00am); Flores, Guatemala (1 daily; 12hr); Belize City via Orange Walk (hourly). There are second-class services that follow the same routes.

Playa del Carmen to: Cancún (frequently; 1hr); Chetumal (5 daily; 5–8hr); Cobá (4 daily; 2hr); Mérida (8 daily; 8hr); México (1 daily; 30hr+); Palenque (1 daily; 12hr); San Cristóbal de las Casas (1 daily; 14hr); Tulum (frequently; 1hr); Tuxtla Gutiérrez (1 daily; 16hr); Valladolid (3 daily; 4hr); Villahermosa (4 daily; 13hr).

Tulum to: Cancún (at least every 30min; 2hr); Chetumal (7 daily, 5 via Bacalar; 4–5hr); Cobá (4 daily; 1hr); Mérida (8 daily; 6hr); Playa del Carmen (frequently; 1hr); Valladolid (8 daily; 4hr); San Cristobal (1 daily via Palenque).

Planes

Cancún and Cozumel both have busy **international airports** with several daily flights to México and regular connections to Miami and many other cities in the southern US. Chetumal also has daily direct services to México. Around the Caribbean coast various small companies fly light planes – very frequently between Cancún and Cozumel, less often from these places to Isla Mujeres, Playa del Carmen and Tulum.

Ferries

There are frequent ferry services to **Isla Mujeres** and **Cozumel**. On both routes there is a choice between a low-cost slow boat or a more luxurious fast boat, which generally halves the crossing time. Although there is a car ferry to Isla Mujeres, it is hardly worth taking a vehicle over as the island is so small.

Passenger Ferries

Chiquilá to: Isla Holbox (2 daily; 1hr).

Playa del Carmen to: Cozumel (every 1–2hr; 30min–1hr).

Punta Juárez, Cancún to: Isla Mujeres (every 30min; 15–30min).

Car Ferries

Chiquilá to: Isla Holbox (1 daily, except Thurs & Sun; 1hr).

Puerto Morelos to: Cozumel – erratic, so check (1 daily, 2 on Mon; 2hr 30min).

Punta Sam to: Isla Mujeres (6 daily).

CHAPTER THREE

CHIAPAS AND TABASCO

E ndowed with a stunning variety of cultures, landscapes and wildlife, **Chiapas**,
Mexico's southernmost state, has much to tempt visitors. Deserted Pacific beaches, rugged mountains and ruined cities buried in steamy jungle offer a bewildering choice, added to which **indigenous traditions** continue to be observed –
albeit with a struggle – almost everywhere. Chiapas was actually administered by the
Spanish as part of Guatemala until the early nineteenth century, when it seceded to join

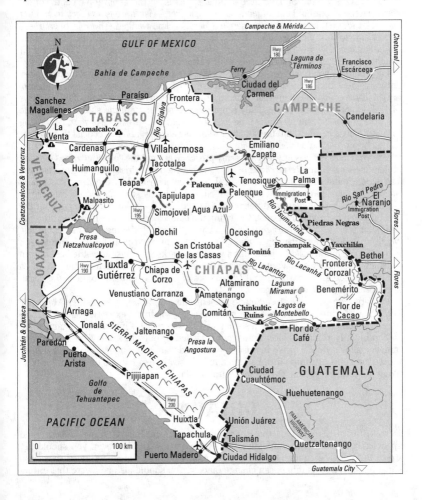

ACCOMMODATION PRICE CODES

All the accommodation listed in this book has been categorized into one of nine price bands, as set out below. The prices quoted are in US dollars and refer to the cheapest room available for two people sharing in high season.

① under US$5	④ US$15–25	⑦ US$60–80
② US$5–10	⑤ US$25–40	⑧ US$80–100
③ US$10–15	⑥ US$40–60	⑨ over US$100

---

newly independent Mexico, and today it has a higher proportion of Maya than any state except Oaxaca.

The villages around **San Cristóbal de las Casas**, in the geographic centre of the state, are the stronghold of indigenous Maya culture. A visit here is an entry to another age and, though tolerated, your presence is barely acknowledged. There is, of course, a darker side to this: picturesque as their life may seem to tourists, the indigenous population has long been bypassed or ignored by the political system, their land and their livelihood under constant threat from modernization or straightforward seizure.

Long before open revolt broke out on New Year's Day, 1994, a revived **Zapatista** peasant movement had carried out attacks on army patrols and, despite official denials of armed insurrection, the army had raided training camps in search of "subversives". News of such happenings was successfully suppressed, however, until the situation burst into the world's consciousness. At the time this book went to press, tourists were continuing to visit Chiapas in safety, but the situation remains sensitive, and it is crucial that you get as much information as you can before leaving home and check locally and with other travellers. There is currently a heavy army presence around the "**conflict zone**" – a fluid area in the far southeastern corner of the state between San Cristóbal, Palenque and the Lagos de Montebello – though, in general, the area controlled by the Zapatistas is well outside the usual tourist routes and their tactics don't involve urban guerrilla campaigns.

Tabasco is less obviously attractive than its neighbour – steamy and low-lying for the most part, with a major oil industry marring the landscape. Recently, however, the state has been seeking to encourage tourism, above all pushing the legacy of the **Olmecs**, Mexico's earliest developed civilization. The vibrant, modern capital, **Villahermosa**, on a bend in the mighty Río Grijalva, has a wealth of parks and museums, the best-known of which, the **Parque la Venta**, displays the famous Olmec heads from the site of La Venta. Tabasco also boasts several Maya sites of note – **Comalcalco**, near the coast, and **Pomoná**, in the southeast.

Perhaps Tabasco's most enigmatic ancient culture, however, is neither Maya nor Olmec, but **Zoque**, a people about whom little is known. In the extreme southwest, bordered by Veracruz and Chiapas, a section of Tabasco reaches into the mountains up to 1000m high. Here, in a region almost never visited by outsiders, a low-impact tourism initiative allows you to splash in pristine rivers and waterfalls and explore the astonishing Zoque ruins of **Malpasito**. La Palma in Tabasco is also the starting point for trips along the placid **Río San Pedro** into **Guatemala**.

CHIAPAS

Despite the rebellion of 1994, tourists continue to come to Chiapas; some, indeed, come specifically to witness the unfolding events. Before visiting, however, you should get **up-to-date advice**: though travel was apparently safe at the time of writing, in a volatile situation such as this things can change quickly. You should also be aware that **enter-**

ing Mexico in Chiapas (only possible from Guatemala), you'll almost certainly be given a maximum of fifteen days' stay — and to renew your passport stamp in the state you'll have to undergo a lengthy interview with an immigration official during which you'll need to convince him that you're neither a journalist, nor going anywhere in the conflict zone. The best bet if you want to stay longer in Chiapas (or Mexico) is to renew your tourist card in another state capital, such as Campeche or Mérida, and return if time permits.

The terrain of Chiapas ranges from the Pacific coastal plain, backed by the peaks of the Sierra Madre de Chiapas, through the mainly agricultural central depression, irrigated by the Río Grijalva, rising again to the highlands, **Los Altos de Chiapas**. Beyond the highlands the land falls away again: in the north to the Gulf coast plain of Tabasco, while to the east a series of great rivers, separated by the jungle-covered ridges of the **Lacandón rainforest**, flow into the Río Usumacinta, which forms the border with Guatemala.

The **climate**, too, can vary enormously. In one theoretical day you could be sweltering in the jungle at Palenque in the morning and spending the night by a fireside in the old colonial capital of San Cristóbal de las Casas. Generally the lowlands can be almost unbearably hot and humid, with heavy afternoon rainfall in summer, making a dip in the sea or river (or pool) a daily necessity. Days in the highlands can also be hot, and you'll need to carry water if you're hiking, though by evening you may need a sweater.

For its size, Chiapas has the greatest **biological diversity** in North America. A visit to the **zoo** in the state capital of **Tuxtla Gutiérrez**, which houses only animals native to the state, will whet your appetite for the region's natural wonders. In the huge **Montes Azules Biosphere Reserve**, reached from Palenque, a section of the largest remaining rainforest in North America has been preserved. This is also the home of the **Lacandón Maya**, who retreated into the forest when the Spanish arrived, and shunned contact until fifty years ago. There's **cloudforest** in the south, protected in the **El Triunfo Biosphere Reserve** and, far easier to visit, the beautiful lakes and hills of the **Parque Nacional Lagos de Montebello**.

The Classic period Maya site of **Palenque**, on the northern edge of the highlands, is one of Mexico's finest ancient sites and the focus of much recent restoration work. The limestone hills in this area are pierced by crystal-clear rivers, creating exquisite waterfalls – most spectacularly at **Agua Azul**. Palenque is also the best starting point for a trip down the **Usumacinta valley** to visit the remote ruins of **Bonampak** and **Yaxchilán**, continuing by boat to **Bethél** in **Guatemala** – an increasingly popular route to Flores and Tikal (see p.421). The **Carretera Frontera** pushes on south beyond these sites to the growing town of Benemérito, where you can also get a boat to Guatemala. Beyond here, however, is the conflict zone, and although the road around the border now almost links up with the road from Comitán and the Lagos de Montebello, foreigners are likely to be turned back by the army.

Other than in the conflict zone, travelling around Chiapas is not difficult. The main cities are connected by a network of good, all-weather roads and the **Carretera Interamericana** passes through some of the most spectacular scenery in the state. In the south, the coastal highway offers a speedy route from **Arriaga**, near the Oaxaca border, right through to **Tapachula**, almost on the frontier with Guatemala. Even the Carretera Frontera is now paved, making a day-trip from Palenque to **Bonampak** a possibility. Routes from the Yucatán to Chiapas are covered by good paved roads, though distances are long and the scenery fairly featureless. If time is short you might want to consider doing the journey on an **overnight bus** and save your time and energy for the great Maya sites ahead. In a few out-of-the-way places, particularly in the jungle, travel is still by dirt roads, which, though generally well maintained, can cause problems in the rainy season.

Palenque

PALENQUE is for many people the most extraordinary of the Maya sites. It's not large – you can see everything in a morning – but it is hauntingly beautiful, set in thick jungle screeching with insects. It is strongly linked to the Maya sites of Guatemala while keeping its own distinctive style. The town itself (officially Santo Domingo de Palenque) is of little intrinsic interest and is best viewed simply a base for exploring the ruins and the waterfalls in the nearby hills. However, you may prefer to stay in the new camping and cabaña places in the forest near the ruins, which are much more peaceful.

Arrival, orientation and information

Arriving by bus, you'll be on Juárez, where the highway comes into town. The **airport**, recently upgraded and with good connections throughout Mexico and to Flores, is 5km north of town in a dusty settlement called Pakal Ná.

Palenque's three **main streets**, Av Juárez, Av 5 de Mayo and Av Hidalgo, all run parallel and lead straight up to the zócalo, the parque central. For a **map** and lots of useful information, call in at the helpful **tourist office** in the Plaza de Artesanías on Juárez, a block below the zócalo (Mon–Sat 8am–8pm, Sun 9am–1pm; ☎934/5-03-56); the staff know all the bus times and give out plenty of free leaflets. The **post office** is on Independencia, a block from the plaza, and there's a **laundry** on 5 de Mayo, opposite the Hotel Kashlan. Cibernet offers an **email** service from the small office on Independencia near 20 de Noviembre (Mon–Sat 9am–2pm & 5–9pm; *cibernet@tnet.net.mx*).

The **banks** on Juárez are well used to changing travellers' cheques but service is as slow as ever – you're better off using the ATMs. Many of the **travel agencies** will

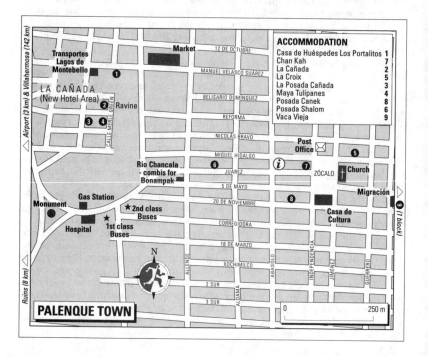

ACCOMMODATION

Casa de Huéspedes Los Portalitos	1
Chan Kah	7
La Cañada	2
La Croix	5
La Posada Cañada	3
Maya Tulipanes	4
Posada Canek	8
Posada Shalom	6
Vaca Vieja	9

PALENQUE TOWN

TOUR AND TRAVEL AGENCIES IN PALENQUE

The surge in the numbers of tourists visiting Palenque has encouraged at least a dozen **travel agencies** to offer tours to the surrounding attractions. Any of them can take you to the waterfalls at **Agua Azul** (see p.143) and **Misol-Há** (see p.142) and further afield to the ruins of **Bonampak** (see p.136) and **Yaxchilán** (see p.138), but none can sell you an international air ticket. Trips on the Río Usumacinta and guided horse-riding are also on offer, and some can organize rafting, light aircraft flights and river trips to Guatemala. Sample prices are: US$5 per person for an all-day trip to Misol-Há and Agua Azul; US$50 for a day-trip to Yaxchilán and Bonampak; and US$80 for an overnight trip to both sites, including camping near Bonampak, then a guided walk to the site. To visit both sites by plane will cost around US$120. A taxi to Bonampak costs around US$60. The agencies also offer transport to Flores (for Tikal) for US$35, via Bethél, but you can do the trip on your own *and* visit Yaxchilán on the way for less. Since the paving of the Carretera Frontera, leading to Bonampak and Yaxchilán, and the opening of inexpensive accommodation and restaurants nearby, it's easy enough to visit the sites on your own, and the "guides" who accompany you rarely offer any understanding of what you're seeing.

Having said that, **recommended agencies**, who usually have English-speaking guides, include: Viajes Misol-Há, Juárez 48 (☎934/5-04-88); Shumulhá, on Juárez next to the tourist office (☎934/5-03-56); and Viajes Yax-Há, Juárez 123 (☎934/5-07-98). Colectivos Chambalu run to Palenque ruins from their office on Allende, near the corner with Juárez, every fifteen minutes from 6am to 6pm. They also have two daily trips to Agua Azul. (See pp.136, 138 for details of how to get to Bonamapak and Yaxchilán on your own.)

change dollars or travellers' cheques; commission varies but it's considerably quicker than at the banks.

Accommodation

Palenque has seen a massive boom in hotel construction in recent years. There are plenty of places in the streets leading from the **bus stations** to the zócalo, especially Hidalgo (though the traffic noise means these are best avoided). The **La Cañada Rainforest Area**, west of the town centre, set among the relative quiet of the remaining trees, is generally more upmarket, though there is one excellent budget hotel there. You'll also find a host of new places, in addition to the *Mayabel* **campsite**, lining the **road to the ruins**.

IN TOWN

Casa de Huéspedes Los Portalitos, Mañuel Velasco Suárez, near the Transportes Lagos de Montebello bus station. Very ordinary place with rather less ordinary concrete beds, which are more comfortable than they sound. Private showers. ②.

Chan Kah, corner of Juárez and Independencia (☎934/5-03-18). A touch of luxury right on the zócalo, this very comfortable small hotel is under the same ownership as the *Chan Kah Resort Village* near the ruins. ⑤.

La Croix, Hidalgo, on the corner of the zócalo (☎934/5-00-14). A long-established favourite and, though past its best, still worth trying. Rooms are arranged around a plant-filled courtyard whose walls are decorated with murals of Palenque. Popular with motorcyclists. ③.

Posada Canek, 20 de Noviembre 43 (☎934/5-11-13). One of the best-value hotels if you're travelling alone and a popular travellers' place; some rooms have private baths and good views from the balcony; dorms are only US$3.50 per person. ②.

Posada Shalom, Juárez 156 (☎934/5-09-44). New hotel, with clean rooms and tiled private bathrooms; the best value in town in this price range. Luggage storage. ②.

Vaca Vieja, 5 de Mayo 42 (☎934/5-03-77). A couple of blocks beyond the zócalo, this is a comfortable hotel with private bathrooms, hot water and a decent restaurant. ②.

LA CAÑADA RAINFOREST AREA

La Cañada, Merle Green 14 (☎934/5-01-02). Spacious hotel rooms and cottages set in quiet, tree-shaded grounds; excellent value at this price. Good restaurant. ④.

Maya Tulipanes, Merle Green 6 (☎934/5-02-01, fax 5-01-04). Very comfortable a/c rooms with private baths. Shady grounds, a small pool and good restaurant. ⑤.

La Posada Cañada, behind the *Maya Tulipanes* (☎934/5-04-37). A very friendly place, popular with backpackers and good for information about trips into the jungle. Rooms are in a brightly painted two-storey building with private baths and hot water. Small new bar/restaurant. Discount for *Rough Guide* readers if staying more than one night. ③.

ON THE ROAD TO THE RUINS

The following hotels and campsites are listed **in order of their distance from town**.

Camping Chaac. Rustic place, but very inexpensive, with cabañas, camping, a small restaurant on the banks of two streams and a friendly owner. ①.

Chan Kah Resort Village, 6km along on the left, just before the national park entrance (☎934/5-03-18, fax 5-04-89). Luxury brick and stone cabañas in a lovely forest and river setting, humming with birdlife. Three stone-lined swimming pools and a restaurant. ⑦.

El Panchan, at the national park entrance, down a 200m track 3km from the ruins. Two places under different ownership: a budget, laid-back hammock and camping place and, next to it, comfortable, inexpensive rooms and thatched cabins, some with private bath. ①/③.

Mayabel Camping and Trailer Park, 2km from the site entrance. A great favourite with backpackers, *Mayabel* has a number of vehicle pads with electricity and water, and some cabañas (with hot water), in addition to *palapa* shelters for hammocks and tents. The site isn't crowded, and you can usually get a space. The path to the ruins through the back of the campsite is now closed, but magic mushroom aficionados continue to scour the fields in the morning mist. Lockers available. Hammock and tent rental ①, cabaña ③.

Eating and drinking

Food in Palenque is fairly basic and most restaurants serve up similar dishes, often pasta and pizza, to customers who've really only come for the ruins. Despite this there are bargains to be had from the many **set menus** available; compare what's on offer from the boards outside. Juárez has several **budget places** between the bus stations and the zócalo. Hidalgo has a more Mexican style of food, with several taco places, and at *Te'El*, a tiny café, you can drink delicious organic coffee from Chiapas. At the top of Hidalgo, on the corner of the zócalo, the *Restaurant Maya* has a wide choice and is popular but overpriced; *Virgo's*, across the street, is better value. *Las Tinajas*, on 20 de Noviembre, across from the *Posada Canek*, is a pleasant, family-run restaurant, with good food at fair prices. At *Granos Unidos*, on Guerrero, just behind the zócalo, you can get great cakes and **wholewheat bread**, ideal for taking on a trip; there's also a good Mexican **bakery**, Flor de Palenque, on Allende next to the colectivo terminal.

Palenque ruins

Palenque's style is unique. Superficially it bears a closer resemblance to the Maya sites of Guatemala than to those of the Yucatán, but its **towered palace** and **pyramid tomb** are like nothing else. The **setting**, too, is remarkable, surrounded by hills covered in jungle, while at the same time being right at the edge of the great Yucatán plain; if you climb to the top of any of the structures, you'll see an endless stretch of low, pale-green flatland across the dark green of the hills. The city flourished during the Classic period from around 300 to 900 AD, but its peak apparently came during a relatively short period of the seventh century, under two rulers – **Pacal** and **Chan Bahlum**. Almost everything you can see (and that's only a tiny, central part of the original city) dates from this era.

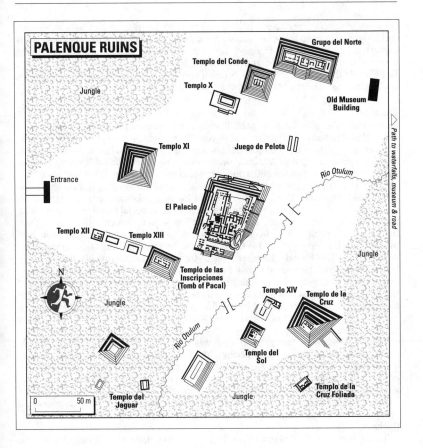

PALENQUE RUINS

Grupo del Norte

Templo del Conde

Templo X

Jungle

Old Museum Building

Templo XI

Juego de Pelota

Rio Otulum

Entrance

El Palacio

Templo XII

Templo XIII

Jungle

Templo de las Inscripciones (Tomb of Pacal)

Templo XIV

Templo de la Cruz

N

Jungle

Rio Otulum

Templo del Sol

0   50 m

Templo del Jaguar

Jungle

Templo de la Cruz Foliada

Path to waterfalls, museum & road

Practicalities

Getting to the site is no problem. The most regular combi service is operated by Colectivos Chambalu, on Allende near the corner with Hidalgo, and you'll never have to wait more than fifteen minutes. The combis will stop anywhere along the road, which is useful if you're staying at one of the hotels or campsites out here, though they stop running at 6pm. After that you'll either have to walk or take a taxi.

The ruins are in a **national park** (daily 8am–6pm, archeological zone daily 8am–5pm; US$2 including museum, free Sun). It's best to arrive early and climb the temples in the morning if you want to avoid the worst of the heat and the crowds. There's a small **café** by the entrance, where, for a fee, you can leave bags while you explore, and a toilet by the ticket office. There are ranks of souvenir stalls at the entrance to the site and you'll usually find a group of Lacandón in white robes (and wearing gold watches) selling bows and arrows and other artefacts. The **museum** on the road just before the entrance (Tue–Sun 10am–4.30pm), contains several carved panels removed from the site, and a good number of incense burners – large urns with elaborately stuccoed gods and mythological creatures – with explanations in Spanish and English. The map of the site shows that only a quarter of the structures have been excavated and an intricate model of the palace complex shows how it would have appeared in the Classic period, with the tops of the buildings adorned with roof combs. Signs inside the site are in English, Spanish and Tzeltal, though Chol is the language spoken by most modern Maya in this part of Chiapas.

The site

As you enter **the site**, the great palacio, with its extraordinary pagoda-like **tower** (currently closed to visitors), stands ahead of you. To the right, at the end of a row of smaller structures, comes the **Templo de las Inscripciones**, an eight-stepped pyramid, 26m high, built up against a thickly overgrown hillside. The broad, extremely steep stairway to the front and the paths up the hill lead to a sanctuary on top that contains a series of stone panels carved with hieroglyphic inscriptions relating to Palenque's history. Most remarkable, though, is the **tomb of Pacal** that lies at the heart of this pyramid. Discovered in 1952, this was the first such pyramid burial found in the Americas, and is still the most important and impressive. The smaller objects – the skeleton and the jade death mask – have been moved to the Museo Nacional de Antropología in Mexico City, but the crypt itself is still here, as is the massive, intricately carved stone sarcophagus. The **burial chamber** (10am–4pm), and the narrow, vaulted stairway leading down to it, are uncomfortably dank and eerie, but well worth the steep, slippery descent. You may not feel able to linger long at the bottom, however, as a long line of hot, claustrophobic visitors waits impatiently behind you. The deified king buried here died in 683 AD, and in order that he should not be cut off from the world of the living, a hollow tube, in the form of a snake, runs up the side of the staircase from the tomb to the temple.

In June 1994 another remarkable tomb was discovered in **Templo XIII**, a pyramid similar to the Templo de las Inscripciones, located just to the west. This burial, of a man of about forty, is considered by archeologists to be very similar chronologically to that of Pacal. In addition to a number of jade and obsidian grave goods, and food and drink vessels to sustain the deceased on his way to *Xibalbá*, the Maya underworld, the sarcophagus also contained the remains of two females, one adult and one adolescent. At present the tomb is not open to the public, but you can peer into the entrance through the bars.

The centrepiece of the site, **El Palacio**, is in fact a complex of buildings constructed at different times to form a rambling administrative or residential block. Its square **tower** (whose top was reconstructed in 1930) is quite unique, and no one knows exactly what its purpose was – perhaps a lookout post or an astronomical observatory. Bizarrely, the narrow staircase that winds up inside it starts only at the second level. Throughout you'll find delicately executed relief carvings, the most remarkable of which are the giant human figures on stone panels in the grassy courtyard.

From here, the lesser buildings of the **Grupo del Norte**, and the **Juego de Pelota** (ball court), are slightly downhill across a cleared grassy area. On higher ground in the other direction, across the Río Otulúm – lined with stone and used as an aqueduct in the city's heyday – lie the **Templo del Sol**, the **Templo de la Cruz** and the **Templo de la Cruz Foliada**, half-obscured by dense vegetation. All are tall, narrow mounds surmounted by a temple with an elaborate stone roof-comb, and each contains carved panels representing sacred rites. The cross found here is as important an image in Maya iconography as it is in Christian: for the Maya it's the **World Tree**, linking the heavens and the underworld with the land of the living.

The **Templo del Jaguar** is reached by a small path that follows the brook upstream – a delightful shaded walk. Beyond, more temples are being wrested from the jungle. If you want to penetrate a bit further, follow the path along the stream behind the

Templo de las Inscripciones and you're in the real jungle – or at least a pleasantly tame version of it. Tarzan creepers hang from giant trees, while all around there's the din of howler monkeys, strange bird calls and mysterious chatterings. The path leads to the *ejido* of Naranjo a little over an hour's walk away. It's easy to believe you're walking over unexcavated pyramids: the ground is very rocky and some of the stones certainly don't look naturally formed.

Downstream, the river cascades through the forest and flows over beautiful lime-stone curtains and terraces into a series of gorgeous series of pools – the aptly named **Bathing Pool of the Queen** is the most exquisite. The path leads down beside the river past more recently excavated buildings and crosses the river on a suspension bridge, eventually coming out on the main road opposite the museum; this is an official **exit** – but not an entrance.

MOVING ON FROM PALENQUE

Leaving Palenque on the **bus**, there are surprisingly few direct services to **Mérida** (9hr): ADO has departures via **Campeche** at 8am, 7pm and 10.30pm, and there are a couple of second-class services. There are two first-class departures at 5pm and 8pm from **Cancún** (12hr) and a couple of overnight buses to **México** (16hr). From **Tuxtla** there are first- and second-class departures at least hourly (7hr), all calling at **Ocosingo** and **San Cristóbal** (5hr). ADO has plenty of buses to the main transport hub of **Villahermosa** (2hr 30min) and you may find it easier to get there and change for desti-nations throughout Mexico.

Transportes Comitán y Lagos de Montebello, on Velasco Suárez, just past the market, has services down the Usumacinta Valley for **Bonampak** and **Frontera Corozal** (for Yaxchilán and **Bethél** in Guatemala), as does Combis Río Chancalá on 5 de Mayo. If you're taking the boat from **La Palma** to **El Naranjo**, Guatemala, bear in mind the boat usually leaves at 8am, so you may need to spend the night at **Tenosique**: if there's no direct bus take a Transportes Palenque colectivo from Allende near 20 Noviembre and change at **Emiliano Zapata**. Aerocaribe flies from Palenque to **Flores**, Mérida and Cancún; check with one of the recommended travel agents.

The Usumacinta valley and the Carretera Frontera

Palenque is the obvious starting point for trips to the Usumacinta valley sites of **Bonampak** and **Yaxchilán**, and several agencies in Palenque now offer overland or plane trips to the sites (see box on p.131), though you can easily do the trip indepen-dently. If you do decide to head out on your own, you'll need to be prepared to walk, and possibly also to camp, though **accommodation** is becoming increasingly available.

The Usumacinta valley and the Lacandón forest form Mexico's last frontier: new towns and farms are being carved out of the rainforest and the **Carretera Frontera** (Frontier Highway) provides access to a number of new settlements whose inhabitants are rapidly changing the forest to farmland. Despite what some maps indicate, the road is not yet complete all the way along the frontier, though the only "gap" is a 35km stretch of mountainous terrain between **Chajúl** on the Río Lacantún and **Flor de Café**, at the other end of the Carretera Frontera leading in from Comitán (see p.160); even this section may be complete by the time you read this. Several buses a day complete the nine-hour journey from Palenque to Chajúl, but you'll be discouraged from travel-ling beyond **Benemérito** by the Mexican army and there is also a real danger of armed

THE LACANDÓN

You may already have encountered the impressively wild-looking **Lacandón Maya** selling exquisite (and apparently effective) bows and arrows at Palenque. Still wearing their simple, hanging white robes and with their hair uncut, the Lacandón were until recently the most isolated of all the Mexican tribes. The ancestors of today's Lacandónes are believed to have migrated to Chiapas from Petén in Guatemala during the eighteenth century. Prior to that the Spanish had enslaved, killed or relocated the original inhabitants of the forest. The Lacandón refer to themselves as *Hach Winik* (true people); "Lacandón" was a label used by the Spanish to describe any group of Maya outside colonial control who lived in the Usumacinta valley and western Petén. Appearances notwithstanding, some Lacandón families are quite wealthy, having sold timber rights in the jungle, though most of the timber money has now gone. This has led to a division in their society and now most Lacandón live in one of two main communities: Lacanjá Chansayab, near Bonampak, where many of the villagers have become evangelical Protestants, and are developing low-impact tourism facilities (see below); and Nahá, where a small group still attempt to live a traditional life.

The best source of information on the Lacandón is the Casa Na Bolom in San Cristóbal de las Casas (see p.148), where you can find the manuscript of *Last Lords of Palenque* (Little Brown & Co, 1982) by Victor Perera and Robert Bruce.

robbery in this wild region. Plans for a series of **hydroelectric dams** on the Usumacinta, which would have inundated many archeological sites (as well as several new townships), appear to have been shelved, hopefully for good.

Exploring this route presents other options beyond Bonampak and Yaxchilán. From the riverbank settlement of **Frontera Corozal** you can get a boat a short distance upstream to **Bethél** in Guatemala, and from the fast-expanding town of Benemérito you can take a longer trip on a trading boat upstream to **Sayaxché**, on the Río de la Pasión (see p.420). The interior of this remote corner of Chiapas is the home of the **Lacandón Maya** and fortunately has some form of protection as the **Montes Azules Biosphere Reserve**.

Bonampak

The outside world first heard of the existence of **Bonampak** in 1946, when Charles Frey, an American conscientious objector taking refuge in the forest, was shown the site by the Lacandón, who apparently still worshipped at the ancient temples. Shortly after this American photographer Giles Healey was also led to the site by the Lacandón and was shown the famous murals – the first non-Maya ever to see these astonishing examples of Classic Maya art.

It's now possible to visit Bonampak on a day-trip **from Palenque** and, as always, it's best to get an early start: Transportes Lagos de Montebello, on Velasco Suárez, and Combis Río Chancala, on 5 de Mayo, have numerous departures to destinations along the Carretera Frontera, beginning at 4.30am. If you can, pick up an **information sheet** in the Casa Na Bolom in San Cristóbal (see p.148) before you set off.

Practicalities

For Bonampak you need to get off the bus from Palenque at **San Javiér** (about 3hr), where there's a whitewashed government control hut on the left and a basic comedor on the right. The large, thatched visitor centre here is not functioning at the moment. Take the track bearing right to **Lacanjá Chansayab** (it may be signposted), and after 4km, at a right-hand bend in the road, fork left. Most tour groups **camp** here for the night at *Camping Margarito* (①), where there is also a small restaurant. If you can't face the two-hour walk to Bonampak, Lacandón taxi-driver Chan Kin, who will probably be waiting outside the government control hut, will offer to take you in his taxi. The side road continues a few more kilometres to the Lacandón village, where you'll find several purpose-built **camping** shelters and hammocks available for rent. Ask for Kin Bor or Carlos Chan Bor, at the house where the paved road enters the village, either of whom will be able to fix you up with knowledgeable Lacandón guides to lead you through the forest. There are several rivers and waterfalls in the area, and you can reach the **Lacanjá ruins** in under two hours from here or Bonampak in three.

Lacandón boys may offer to guide you to the ruins and, though it's perfectly possible to follow the track on your own, you'll have a less apprehensive trip through the forest if you accept – and it won't cost much. The hiking is wonderful in the dry season (Jan–April), but muddy in the rain.

After taking the **entrance fee** (US$2; free Sun), the guard will probably not let you out of his sight. Day-trippers make their way back after a short visit, but the guards, who supplement their wages by selling cold drinks, may let you **camp** here, or possibly stay in one of the huts. Once you've seen the ruins, head back to the San Javiér junction, where you'll be able to catch a **bus** to Palenque until dusk or **hitch**.

The site
Set deep in the rainforest, the highlight of this site is the superb **Temple of the Frescoes**. Inside three separate chambers, on the temple walls and roof, are depicted vivid scenes of haughty Maya lords, splendidly attired in jaguar-skin robes and quetzal-plume headdresses, their equally well-dressed ladies, and bound prisoners, one with his fingernails ripped out, spurting blood. Musicians play drums, pipes and trumpets in what is clearly a celebration of victory. Dated to around 790 AD, the murals show the Bonampak elite at the height of their power. However, the collapse of the Classic Maya civilization was imminent: some details on the murals were never finished and Bonampak was abandoned shortly afterwards.

In **Room 1** the murals depict the heir apparent, an infant wrapped in white cloth, being presented to assembled nobility under the supervision of the lord of Yaxchilán, while musicians play trumpets in the background. **Room 2** contains a vivid, even gruesome, exhibition of power over Bonampak's enemies: tortured prisoners lie on temple steps, while above them lords in jaguar robes are indifferent to their agony. A severed head has rolled down the stairs and lord Chaan Muan, the king of Bonampak, grasps a prisoner (who appears to be pleading for mercy) by the hair – clearly about to deal him the same fate. **Room 3** shows the price paid for victory: Chaan Muan's wife, Lady Rabbit, prepares to prick her tongue to let blood fall onto the paper in a clay pot in front of her. The smoke from burning the blood-soaked paper will carry messages to ancestor-gods. Other gorgeously dressed figures, their senses probably heightened by hallucinogenic drugs, dance on the temple steps.

The best way to view the paintings is to lie down on the floor of the chamber and allow your eyes to adjust to the dim light filtering in through the doorway; you almost certainly won't be permitted to use a flashlight. Though time and early cleaning attempts have taken their toll on the murals, recent work has restored some of their glory. However, it has to be said that you'll get a better impression of the whole scene from the reproductions in the CICOM Museum of Anthropology in Villahermosa (p.172), or even from the lobby of the *Hotel Bonampak* in Tuxtla (p.158).

Frontera Corozal and Yaxchilán

Twenty kilometres beyond San Javiér, the turning for **FRONTERA COROZAL** is marked by a comedor and shop selling basic supplies. Corozal itself, another 19km down the side road and served by regular buses and combis from Palenque (last one back at 3pm), is on the bank of Río Usumacinta; to get to Yaxchilán, you need to catch a **boat** here.

There's a Mexican **immigration post** here: visitors to Yaxchilán will always be asked to show their passports, despite the fact that the site is in Mexico. On the right, past the immigration post, are the new cabañas of *Escudo Jaguar* (☎934/5-03-56 in Palenque; ③), named after Jaguar Shield, a king of Yaxchilán. The brightly painted, thatched cabañas have comfortable beds with mosquito nets, hot water in the tiled bathroom and full-length windows opening onto the porch – a touch of luxury at a bargain price. There's also a good **restaurant** and you can **camp** for under US$2. More basic accommodation is available at Corozal's two posadas: the *Yani* (①, with fan) on the right before the immigration post is marginally the better. There are a couple of comedores here too.

Entering Guatemala is relatively easy as there's plenty of river traffic between Corozal and **Bethél**, a thirty-minute boat ride upstream, where there's a Guatemalan immigration post. Heading **downstream from Yaxchilán** to the ruins of **Piedras Negras** (p.421) on the Guatemalan side is really only practicable as part of an organized white-water rafting expedition, as there are rapids above and below the site, and beyond the site the river speeds through two massive canyons: the **Cañon de San José**, with fearsome rapids between cliffs 300m high, and the slightly less dramatic **Cañon de las Iguanas**.

Yaxchilán: the site

To reach the site, you need to get a ride at Corozal in a boat heading downstream – ask around at the waterfront. It shouldn't prove too difficult as these are the boats used by tours from Palenque and the boatmen will be pleased to make some extra money; bargain carefully, though, since you need to be picked up again. The trip takes about an hour and, unless you have to charter your own boat, should cost less than US$10 per person.

A much larger site than Bonampak, **Yaxchilán** (daily 8am–4pm; US$2, free Sun), built strategically on a bend in the river, was an important centre in the Classic period. When the water is low, you can see (and climb) a **pyramid** built on a rock shelf on the river bed. Some archeologists suggest this was a bridge support, though this is unlikely as no corresponding structure has been found on the opposite bank, and the **altar** on top may indicate that it was used for religious ritual.

The first groups of numbered buildings and those around the **main plaza**, built on fairly level river terraces, are easy to view. The temples bear massive honeycombed roofs, now home to hundreds of bats, and everywhere there are superb, well-preserved stucco carvings. These panels, on lintels above doorways or on stelae, depict rulers performing ritual events, often involving bloodletting to conjure up spirit visions of ancestors. Some of the very best lintels have been removed to the British Museum in London, but the number and quality of the remaining panels are unequalled at any other Maya site in Mexico. Yaxchilán's most famous kings (identified by their nameglyphs) were **Shield Jaguar** and his son **Bird Jaguar**, who ruled at the height of the city's power, from around 680 AD to 760 AD. Under their command, Yaxchilán began the campaign of conquest that extended its sphere of influence over the other Usumacinta centres and led to alliances with Tikal and Palenque.

A path behind **Building 42** leads through the jungle, over several unrestored mounds, to three more tall temples. The guards won't always take you back here, as it's out of their way (and they insist you begin to return well before the 4pm closing time as camping is no longer allowed at the site), but the climb is worth the effort for the view of distant mountain ridges, in solitude. There's a real sense of a lost city as you explore the ancient, moss-covered stones, watched from the trees by toucans and monkeys. Butterflies flit around the forest glades, and so, unfortunately, do mosquitoes.

The southern Usumacinta

Continuing south a further 35km brings you to **BOCA LACANTÚN**, where a bridge carries the road over the enormous Río Lacantún. You can expect any bus along this road to be stopped by immigration officials or at army checkpoints, so keep your passport handy. At the confluence of the Lacantún and Usumacinta rivers is an unusual Maya remain, the **Planchon de Figuras**, a great limestone slab of unknown origin, carved with Maya glyphs, birds, animals and temples. If you're travelling by river, you'll see the beautiful **Chorro cascades** just downstream.

Benemérito and onward

The sprawling frontier town of **BENEMÉRITO**, 2km beyond Boca Lacantún, is the largest settlement in the Chiapas section of the Usumacinta valley, fast becoming an important centre for both river and road traffic. There's a hospital, market, shops, restaurants and a few basic **hotels**. The highway is the town's main street and in the centre, at the Farmacia Arco Iris, is the main road leading to the river, less than 2km away. **Arriving by boat** from Guatemala you'll find a restaurant and some none too cheap rooms by the dock. The other hotels, on the main street, are hardly any better: the *Hospedaje Montañero* (①) has rough beds with mattresses that feel like you're sleeping on a ploughed field, but there is electric light.

Getting to Palenque is no problem: buses and combis wait by the *Hospedaje El Tapanco*, and the restaurant opposite sells tickets. **Heading south**, a few buses a day go as far as the end of the road, which at the time of writing was Chajúl, on the Río Lacantún (5hr).

A side road, branching off to the southwest 8km beyond Benemérito leads to **Pico de Oro**, an amazingly clean, pleasant village on the south bank of the Lacantún. There are a couple of **restaurants**, but no hotels. Across the river the huge **Montes Azules Biosphere Reserve** stretches for miles along the opposite bank – you can hear the howler monkeys roaring. It's possible to stay in the reserve: continue on to **Reforma Agraria**, where *Las Guacamayas* (☎934/5-03-56; ③) rents out new thatched **cabañas** on the bank of the Lacantún and can also arrange guides to show you the wonders of the rainforest.

By river to Guatemala

If you hope to get **from Benemérito to Sayaxché** (8–12hr) by boat, you'll need patience or a good deal of money. **Trading boats** are the cheapest method, but with no proper schedule you just have to ask. To reach Sayaxché in one day you'll need to leave early. Fast boats, taking less than three hours, are now making the trip, stopping at the various sites en route, but you'll have to charter one and they cost at least US$150. **Entering Guatemala**, you'll get your passport stamped at the army post at **Pipiles**, at the confluence with the Río de la Pasión. There's no Mexican immigration here (or at Benemérito) so make sure you get an exit stamp in Frontera Corozal. Boats sometimes travel upriver beyond this, to Playa Grande in Guatemala, but this is an isolated area, with nothing like the traffic between Benemérito and Sayaxché. If you're **entering Mexico**, you'll certainly be stopped at army checkpoints on the road, and perhaps along the river too.

The Chiapas highlands

There is nowhere in Mexico so rich in scenery or indigenous life as highland Chiapas. Forested uplands and jungly valleys are studded with rivers and lakes, waterfalls and unexpected gorges, and flush with the rich flora and fauna of the tropics – wild orchids and brilliantly coloured birds and monkeys. The network of roads, though growing, is

THE ZAPATISTA REBELLION

On **January 1, 1994**, the day the NAFTA treaty came into effect (see p.493), several thousand lightly armed rebels, wearing their uniform of green or black army-style tunics and black balaclavas, occupied San Cristóbal de las Casas, the former state capital and Chiapas's major tourist destination. From the balcony of the Palacio Municipal, **Subcomandante Marcos**, the Zapatistas' enigmatic leader, or at least main spokesperson, read *La Declaración de la Selva Lacandona*, declaring war on the "seventy-year-old dictatorship . . . of traitors", and demanding the resignation of the Mexican president and the state governor and an overhaul of the country's archaic political structure. Simultaneously, in a series of bold, carefully executed strikes, the rebels, the Zapatista Army of National Liberation (EZLN), occupied the towns of Las Margaritas, Ocosingo and Altamirano, making the same demands.

After a thirty-hour occupation, during which they destroyed government equipment and municipal records, the EZLN withdrew from San Cristóbal. The next day, the army began its furious counter-attack with ground troops and aircraft. Dozens of civilians and Zapatistas were killed as the army retook **Ocosingo**; a series of isolated attacks by groups claiming to support the rebellion led the army to believe there was a serious possibility of a nationwide revolution, and for several days journalists were kept away from the conflict zone.

Meanwhile, penetrating and witty communiqués signed by Marcos, sent from a secret hideout in the Lacandón rainforest and published in the Mexican and international press, became a major feature of the battle to keep the struggle in the world spotlight. The war was waged by the Zapatistas with the pen and the **Internet** – and they were winning. Reports of widespread human rights abuses committed by the army – including summary execution of suspected rebels and the terrorizing of civilians – caused an international outcry, and on January 13 a **ceasefire** came into effect. In the meantime, dozens of indigenous organizations in Chiapas formed a representative body, **CEOIC** (later, **CONAI**), presided over by **Bishop Samuel Ruiz** of San Cristóbal, calling for an end to human rights abuses and the start of peace negotiations.

At first talks appeared to go well, but on March 23, the **assassination of Luis Donaldo Colosio**, the PRI presidential candidate – effectively the next Mexican president – sparked conspiracy theories and halted the peace process. The EZLN withdrew, believing the army was preparing an attack, but continued to consult with communities in the area, and in June announced a rejection of the proposals. Mexico's **general election** on August 21, 1994, passed relatively quietly, though when the results were announced, the main left-wing opposition party, the **PRD**, accused the PRI of fraud and organized a series of demonstrations in Chiapas. When the PRI candidate took office, the opposition candidate assumed the role of parallel governor, establishing with the support of the Zapatistas a **"Rebel Government in Transition"**. On September 28, the assassination of Ruiz Massieu, general secretary of the PRI, heightened tension, and the army kept a lookout at the ends of roads leading to Zapatista-controlled areas.

Within days of the new president, Ernesto Zedillo, taking office in **December 1994**, the Zapatistas made their first major foray through the army cordon, briefly occupying several towns. Despite the provocation, Zedillo's response was restrained, and no major offensive was ordered immediately, though reports of rebels on the move sent panic through Mexico's financial markets, leading to a massive **devaluation of the nuevo peso**.

In February 1995, however, President Zedillo asserted his strength of purpose as Mexico's leader by unmasking the mysterious "Subcomandante Marcos" as **Rafael Guillén**, a former university professor and veteran of 1970s guerrilla movements, and ordered the army to arrest him. This hardening of attitude was intended to boost the president's credibility rather than as a realistic attempt to subdue the uprising. Nevertheless, an **army offensive** temporarily reoccupied some of the Zapatista-controlled territory, spreading fear among the indigenous community and creating thousands of **internal refugees** as peasants fled to the mountains.

Despite these apparent setbacks, or even because of them, the Zapatistas continued to enjoy popular sympathy, and the government was forced to re-open negotiations. After detailed national and international consultations, the Zapatistas insisted that any solution to the conflict must include a recognition of indigenous rights. Eventually, in **February 1996**, amid mutual suspicion and a strengthening of the Mexican army's presence in Chiapas, the **San Andrés Accords on Rights and Indigenous Cultures** were signed. The Accords recognized the right to education in indigenous languages and guaranteed representation in national and state legislatures; in theory, a new beginning, which would attempt to remedy centuries of discrimination.

Immediately prior to this agreement, the Zapatistas proposed to establish a political front, the Zapatista Front of National Liberation (FZLN), but, since fighting elections or gaining political power are not part of its remit, it is difficult to gauge its effectiveness. Any hopes of a real settlement were premature, however, as the government failed to move on the constitutional and legal changes necessary to implement the Accords. The Zapatistas lost whatever faith they had in Zedillo's good intentions and in September the EZLN **suspended peace talks**. Despite the establishment of the Commission for Verification and Follow-up of the San Andrés Accords (COSEVER), which represents both sides in the conflict, negotiations have not resumed.

Although the Accords received widespread support throughout the country, the Mexican government dragged its heels over implementing them. Their unspoken policy appeared to be to marginalize the Zapatistas and contain political unrest within Chiapas, thereby avoiding a protracted **counter-insurgency war**, costly both in humanitarian terms and in the unfavourable international reaction this would cause. Each side accused the other of deliberately stalling the talks and of placing contradictory interpretations on what had been agreed so far.

The EZLN had by now lost any chance of regaining the initiative in an armed conflict and the Mexican government steadfastly refused to accept international arbitration. The Zapatistas' support was weakening as the forces ranged against them consolidated their power. The army gradually tightened the cordon around the Zapatista strongholds; roads and bases were built and troop numbers were increased. Right-wing **paramilitary groups**, financed by ranchers and landowners and affiliated to the PRI, long a feature of political oppression in Chiapas, grew in strength. Known collectively as *guardias blancas* (white guards) and able to act with apparent impunity, they have carried out an escalating campaign of terror against the indigenous population and anyone suspected of being a Zapatista sympathizer. Hundreds of people have been attacked and murdered, and thousands more driven from their homes, but the worst atrocity (which made headlines around the world) was the **massacre** of 45 displaced Tzotzil Indians in a church in the village of Acteal, north of San Cristóbal, on **December 22, 1997**. This provoked such a storm of outrage that the government was forced to act; dozens of paramilitaries and police suspected of taking part in the massacre were arrested and both Mexico's interior minister, Emiliano Chuayffett, and the Chiapas governor, César Ruiz Ferro, resigned.

The massacre and its aftermath once again placed Chiapas at the centre of the political agenda, and increased demands for implementation of the peace accords were made. The extra troops sent to Chiapas did nothing to halt the activities of the paramilitaries. Indeed, their incursions into EZLN strongholds, retaking and occupying several of the 38 *municipios rebeldes* (autonomous authorities) set up by the Zapatistas, caused Bishop Ruiz to resign as mediator in June 1998. CONAI was dissolved, **negotiations ceased completely**, and it now appears that the government's strategy is to overcome the rebels by military means.

In **1998**, the Zapatistas still control much of the land they took at the beginning of the conflict (over ten percent of Chiapas), but a peaceful end to the conflict seems more remote than at any time since the uprising began. In Mexico City and San Cristóbal **demonstrations** continue to be held in support of the Zapatistas, and in San Cristóbal Zapatista dolls and Marcos souvenirs, emblazoned with his masked features, sell in their thousands.

A word of warning, though, if your sympathies extend beyond giving economic assistance to the indigenous souvenir-makers: there is a concerted **anti-foreigner campaign** in Chiapas at present. Government officials, citing the "infestation of foreign activists who stir up and manipulate many indigenous groups contrary to constitutional order", claim that the presence of *simpatico* foreigners influences political opposition in the state. Although there are foreign observers in "civil peace camps" in the Zapatista areas, they are not recognized as such by the Mexican authorities. Being in, or even near, the **conflict zone** invites suspicion of taking part in political activities – illegal for foreigners – and several people have recently been deported.

If you do go, be as fully informed as you can: **SIPAZ**, the International Service for Peace (☎ & fax 408/425-1257 in US; *sipaz@igc.org*) has a volunteer programme in Chiapas and their **Web site** *www.nonviolence.org/sipaz* provides the best regular updates and analysis of the situation in Chiapas. The **EZLN supporters' Web site** (*www.ezln.org*) has superb links, including the relevant pages of *La Jornada*, and is an excellent source of information.

still skeletal, and for much of its history the state's isolation has allowed its **indigenous population** to carry on their lives little disturbed. In the villages you'll see the trappings of Catholicism and of economic progress, but in most cases these go no deeper than the surface: daily life is still run in accordance with ancient customs and beliefs.

As strong and colourful as the traditions are, away from the big towns Spanish is still very much a second language, and the economic and social lot of the Maya remains greatly inferior to that of ladinos. The **Zapatista rebellion**, centred in this area, did not appear from nowhere. The oppressive exploitation of the colonial *encomienda* system remained powerful here far longer than in parts of Mexico more directly in the government eye (there were local rebellions, quickly suppressed, in the early eighteenth and late nineteenth centuries), and despite some post-revolutionary land redistribution, most small villages still operate at the barest subsistence level. Not surprisingly, many of the customs are dying fast, and it's comparatively rare to see men in traditional clothing, though many women still wear it. Conversely, such traditions as do survive are clung to fiercely and you should be extremely sensitive about **photography** – especially of anything that might have religious significance – and donning **native clothing**, the patterns on which convey subtle social and geographic meaning.

Palenque to San Cristóbal

The journey from Palenque to San Cristóbal through the Chiapas highlands is an impressive and beautiful one, as the road winds up and around the spectacular mountain valleys, lush with greenery. Many people do the five-hour trip in one go, but there are some wonderful attractions to see (and stay at) along the way. The exquisite **waterfall** at Misol Há and the awesome cascades at **Agua Azul** deserve more than the quick glimpses offered on tours from Palenque; both places have some accommodation and it's more rewarding to stay and enjoy the morning and evening when the crowds have gone. It's also easier than ever to stop off to visit and stay at **Toniná** ruins. The only large town on the route, **Ocosingo** (and the surrounding area) has been the heartland of the **Zapatista rebellion**, so check on security before stopping in any of the villages along here, and be prepared to be searched by the Mexican army on the road. In the largely Tzeltal villages around here all of the women, if none of the men, still wear traditional clothing; something you'll see a lot more of later.

Misol Há and Agua Clara

At **Misol Há**, 20km from Palenque, a beautiful 30m waterfall provides a stunning backdrop to a pool that's safe for swimming (US$0.60). A fern-lined trail through lush rainforest filled with bird calls leads along a ledge behind the wide cascade where you can stand and enjoy the refreshing spray. It's an easy 1500m walk from the road and there's inexpensive **accommodation** in some of the most beautiful wooden cabañas anywhere in Mexico (☎ & fax in Palenque 934/5-12-10; ③). The cabins, and the **restaurant** catering to tour groups, are owned and run by the *ejido* of San Miguel. Each cabin has a private bathroom and electricity and some have kitchens.

Thirty kilometres past Misol Há and a few kilometres before the Agua Azul turn, a signed track on the right passes through the *ejido* of **AGUA CLARA** and leads down to the Río Shumulhá, here emerging from a gorge below Agua Azul. On the riverbank, the *Hotel Agua Clara* (☎934/5-11-30 in Palenque; ④ including continental breakfast) has comfortable, spacious rooms with shared bathrooms. Part of a project to bring economic benefits to the local people, the hotel and restaurant are managed by the villagers, who are genuinely keen to welcome you. A rickety (but safe) suspension bridge crosses the swirling river, which you can explore by renting **canoes and kayaks**.

Agua Azul

The series of beautiful waterfalls on the Río Shumulhá in the **Parque Nacional Agua Azul**, about 4km down a track from the road (54km from Palenque) has become a major tour-bus destination; there are microlight flights over the falls and horse-riding tours for the less adventurous. If you come by bus (not on a tour), you'll be dropped at the crossroads, from where it's a 45-minute walk down the track, and at least an hour's sweaty hike back up. At the end of the track you pay to enter the park (US$0.60), and there are several restaurants and a campsite (with hammock space). You can eat better at *Comedor & Camping Casa Blanca,* at the top of the main fall, where there are also **beds and hammock space** in a large barn-like building (①); the owners also hire out horses. Of course, you can camp free almost anywhere if you walk upstream a way: the best spot is a tiny beach by the entrance to a magnificent gorge. Be sure to keep a close eye on your belongings, though, and be warned that muggings have been reported. You should walk upstream anyway, to where perilous-looking bridges cross the river at various points, for this really is an area of exceptional beauty, with dozens of lesser falls above the developed area. At the right times of year, the river is alive with butterflies. Higher up, the swimming is safer, too – though watch out for signs warning of dangerous currents, as there are several tempting but extremely perilous spots, and people drown here every year; crosses mark the spots where they met their fate.

Ocosingo

OCOSINGO makes a good place to escape the tourist crowds of San Cristóbal or Palenque. It's not as pretty as San Cristóbal, but it's certainly a great deal more attractive than Palenque, its streets lined with single-storey, red-tiled houses and thick with the scent of wood smoke. It's a town that has stayed close to its country roots, with plenty of cowboys in from the ranches in their Stetsons and pickups. Ocosingo is also the jumping-off point for the stunning Maya site of **Toniná**.

 Buses all stop on or near the main road; walk down the hill and you can hardly miss the zócalo. It's surrounded by elegant *portales* and a big old country church, also an *ayuntamiento* with a thoroughly incongruous modern first floor, complete with tinted-glass office windows. The best of the **hotels**, the *Hotel Central* (☎967/3-00-24; ④), sits under a modern section of the *portales* by the *Restaurante la Montura.* You could also try the *Margarita* (☎967/3-02-80; ③), down the side street by the *Montura,* which has some a/c rooms. There are a couple of good budget recommendations including the *Hospedaje San José,* off to the left at the bottom of the zócalo (☎967/3-00-39; ②), and the *Agua Azul,* 1 Ote Sur (head right at the church; ☎967/3-03-02; ②), with comfortable rooms around a courtyard. Several other restaurants face the square: the *Rahsa,* the best in town, is on 3 Sur Ote, a side street southwest of the plaza, while *Los Portales* is also good but shuts very early. The **food market**, straight down Av Central from the zócalo, sells locally produced cheeses, including a round waxy variety and delicious cream cheese.

 Leaving Ocosingo is easy enough until mid-evening, with frequent buses and combis to San Cristóbal and Palenque. The last ATG buses in either direction officially leave at 7.30pm – though they're likely to be later as they're *de paso*.

Toniná

Considering how little known it is, the Classic period Maya site of **Toniná** (daily 9am–4pm; US$1.50), some 14km east of Ocosingo, is surprisingly big, and restoration is uncovering many more buildings. It centres on an enormous grassy plaza, once surrounded by buildings, and a series of seven artificial terraces climbing the hillside above it. At the bottom are two restored ball courts and an overgrown pyramid mound; as you climb the hill, passing corbel-arched entrances to two vaulted rooms on the right, you begin to get an impression of Toniná's vastness. The sixth and seventh terraces each have a number of small temples, while beyond are more huge mounds, currently under excavation. From the top there are fine views of the surrounding countryside.

There are also tombs on both the fifth and sixth levels, one of which contains an enormous mask of the Earth Monster, a powerful force in Maya cosmology. The most striking feature, however, is the enormous **Mural of the Four Suns**, on the sixth platform. This amazingly well-preserved stucco codex tells the story of Maya cosmology by following the four suns (or eras of the world) as they were created and destroyed. The worlds are depicted as decapitated heads surrounded by flowers; a grinning, skeletal Lord of Death presents a particularly graphic image as he grasps a defleshed human head. At the time of writing another mural (not open to visitors at present) had just been discovered and the new museum was about to open.

The **road from Ocosingo** is now paved, and colectivos and trucks leave frequently from market area, mainly heading for the large new army base by the turn-off to the site. From there it's only a 2km walk, and it's easy enough to persuade the driver to take you all the way to the site. A taxi from Ocosingo costs US$5 to the ruins or to the neat wooden **cabins** of the *Rancho Esmeralda*, signed just before the turn-off to the site (fax 967/3-07-11; ④, camping ①). The comfortable private cabins have no electricity and no private bath, but you'll be made very welcome by the American owners Glen and Ellen, even if you turn up without booking. The *Rancho* is just a ten-minute walk from the ruins; it's a wonderful, tranquil setting, and the food is plentiful and superb.

San Cristóbal de las Casas

Surrounded by rocky peaks and pine-forested mountains which have been slashed by horrendous erosion gullies, **SAN CRISTÓBAL DE LAS CASAS** nestles in a flat valley at an elevation of over 2000 metres. Its low, whitewashed red-tiled houses seem huddled together as if to keep out enemies, and indeed, the town was designed as a Spanish stronghold in a hostile area; the attack by Zapatista rebels in January 1994 was the latest in a long series of uprisings by the indigenous population. It took the Spanish four years to pacify the area sufficiently to establish a town here in 1528. Officially named Ciudad Real ("Royal City"), it was more widely known as Villaviciosa ("Evil City") for the oppressive exploitation exercised by its colonists. In 1544, **Bartolomé de las Casas** was appointed bishop, and promptly took an energetic stance in defence of the native population. His name – added to that of the patron saint of the town – was held in something close to reverence by the Maya. Throughout the colonial era, San Cristóbal was the capital of Chiapas, which was then administered as part of Guatemala; it lost this rank in 1892 as a result of its reluctance to accept the union with Mexico. Today it offers visitors a refreshing climate and an unrivalled provincial colonial charm, as well as a chance to visit Maya villages and buy unique souvenirs at great prices.

Though it's the local crafts and the indigenous way of life that draw people to San Cristóbal, this romanticization is not always appreciated by the indígenas themselves, who not surprisingly resent being treated as tourist attractions or objects of amateur anthropology. Nevertheless, the life of the town depends on the people from surrounding villages, who fill its streets and dominate its trade. Many of the salespeople are **expulsados** – converts to evangelical Protestantism expelled by the village leaders – now living in shanties on the edge of town and unable to make a living from farming. The women make crafts to sell to tourists and have taken advantage of the publicity generated by the Zapatistas: the most popular souvenirs they sell are now hand-made **Marcos dolls**, complete with ski mask, rifle and bandoliers. There's even a female

ACCOMMODATION

Casa Blanca	14
Casa Na Bolom	2
Ciudad Real	12
Don Quijote	7
El Paraíso	4
Posada B & B	11
Posada del Barón	9
Posada Casa Real	10
Posada Chilam Balam	16
Posada Diego de Mazariegos	5 & 6
Posada Gladys	1
Posada Margarita	8
Posada Morales Bungalows	15
Rancho Nicolás	17
Rincón del Arco	3
Santa Clara	13

SAN CRISTÓBAL DE LAS CASAS

Zapatista doll of Romana, who is reputed to be in a position of command in the movement.

Despite being the main focus of the Zapatista attack, the town was only occupied for thirty hours, and no tourists were harmed; many, in fact, took advantage of the opportunity to be photographed with the rebels. For the time being, San Cristóbal remains one of the most restful and enjoyable places in the republic to spend a few days doing very little, with an infrastructure set to cater for its young, predominantly European visitors.

Arrival and information

First impressions of San Cristóbal, with the modern parts of the city sprawling unattractively along the highway, are not the best. In the centre, though, there is none of this thoughtless development. Whether you come by first- or second-class **bus**, you'll almost certainly arrive just off the Carretera Interamericana at the southern edge of town. From the Cristóbal Colón **first-class terminal**, at the junction of Insurgentes and the Carretera Interamericana, walk straight along Insurgentes for about seven blocks up to the zócalo; **second-class** services stop along the Carretera Interamericana either side of Cristóbal Colón. There's no **left-luggage** service at the bus station, but you can rent lockers at the Tienda El Paso, one block up Insurgentes on the left. A taxi from the newly opened **airport**, 18km east of the town, costs US$5.

The helpful **tourist office**, just off the southwest corner of the zócalo at Hidalgo 2 (Mon–Fri 9am–9pm, Sat 9am–8pm, Sun 9am–2pm; ☎962/8-65-70), is one of the best in the country, with good free city maps and up-to-date lists of hotels in all price ranges, bus times and events. Staff know Chiapas well, and there's usually someone who speaks English (and possibly other European languages). Free **listings magazines** for information on hotels, restaurants and excursions are also usually available. There are more bulletin boards in and around the **municipal tourist office** in the Palacio Municipal at the northeast corner of the zócalo.

Accommodation

San Cristóbal boasts some of the best-value **budget and mid-price hotels** in Mexico. Walking up Insurgentes from the bus station to the zócalo, you'll pass examples in all price ranges. Press on a little further along Real de Guadalupe, off the northeast corner of the zócalo, and you'll find many more. All but the most basic places now have hot water, though not necessarily all the time. Nights can be pleasantly cool in summer, but cold in winter, so make sure there are enough blankets.

For **longer stays**, check out the many noticeboards in the bus stations and popular cafés, where you'll find rooms and even whole houses for rent. The closest official **campsite** is *Rancho San Nicolás* (see below).

Budget and mid-price accommodation

Bungalows Posada Los Morales, Ignacio Allende 17 (☎962/8-14-72). Whitewashed stone cabins with living room with a fireplace, bath (generally with hot water) and stove, in a hillside garden four blocks west of the zócalo. Authentic colonial atmosphere, right down to the ancient wooden furniture and flagstoned floor and wonderful views of the town. ④.

Posada del Barón, Belisario Domínguez 2 (☎ & fax 962/8-08-81). Well-run new hotel one block east of the zócalo. Each room has a spotless tiled bathroom with plenty of hot water. You can make international calls, and there's usually someone who speaks English. ④.

Posada Bed and Breakfast, two locations on the same street, at Madero 46 and 83 (☎962/8-04-40). The name says it all: good-value, inexpensive lodging, including a reasonable breakfast. Shared bathrooms. Use of kitchen for a small fee. ②.

Posada Casa Blanca, Insurgentes, on the right just before the zócalo (no phone). One of the best-value budget hotels, conveniently located. Rooms are basic but clean; private showers with hot water. ①.

Posada Casa Real, Real de Guadalupe 51 (☎962/8-13-03). Lovely, friendly hotel with a flower-filled courtyard. Large rooms all with very comfortable double beds and a place for washing and drying clothes on the sunny rooftop terrace. No private baths, but there is hot water. At US$4 per person, it's very good value for singles. ②.

Posada Chilam Balam, Niños Heroes 9 (☎962/8-43-40). Simple, friendly hotel, a few blocks west of the zócalo, with single-storey red-tiled rooms around a courtyard, and a *pila* in the tiny garden to hand-wash clothes. Hot water but no private bathrooms. ②.

Posada de Gladys, Real de Mexicanos 16 (☎962/8-57-75). A popular travellers' hangout with a friendly atmosphere. Dorms and private rooms. ②.

Posada Margarita, Real de Guadalupe 34 (☎962/8-09-57). Long-standing budget favourite. Rooms are bare but comfortable; no private showers, but communal ones are clean. Good, inexpensive café in the blue-and-white tiled courtyard, and the restaurant (next door) has live music most nights. Good travel agency and luggage storage. ②.

Rancho San Nicolás, 2km east of the centre, on the extension of Francisco León (☎962/8-00-57). Primarily a campsite and trailer park, but there are also a few rooms in a pleasant country setting. ③.

More expensive accommodation

Casa Na Bolom, Vicente Guerrero 33 (☎962/8-14-18, fax 8-55-86). Staying in this famous museum and research centre was formerly possible only for invited scholars and archeologists (see p.148) – now it's open to anyone. Comfortable rooms with fireplaces, decorated with village artefacts and original photos taken by Gertrude Blom. Non-residents can eat here if they book ahead – or just turn up for breakfast (7.30–10am) or Sunday lunch (1–4pm). ⑤.

Ciudad Real, Plaza 31 de Marzo 10 (☎962/8-04-64). Colonial mansion, superbly located overlooking the zócalo; popular with European tour groups. Most rooms rise above the covered courtyard (now a dining room, adorned with potted palms); quieter ones are at the back. Friendly, helpful staff. ⑤.

Don Quijote, Cristóbal Colón 7; turn left where Colón crosses Real de Guadalupe (☎962/8-09-20, fax 8-03-46). Newish hotel on a quiet street. Comfortable, well-lit, carpeted rooms with hot-water showers. The lobby is decorated with original costumes from Chiapas villages collected by the owner. Free morning coffee. English and French spoken. ④.

El Paraíso, 5 de Febrero 19 (☎ & fax 962/8-00-85). A wonderfully restored colonial-style house. Rooms are smallish but very comfortable and the restaurant is excellent. Great value. German and English spoken. ⑤.

Posada Diego de Mazariegos, 5 de Febrero 1 (☎962/8-18-25). San Cristóbal's top historic hotel, in two colonial buildings, either side of General Utrilla. Many rooms feature a fireplace and antique furniture; bathrooms are beautifully tiled. Often busy with tour groups. ⑥.

Rincón del Arco, Ejército Nacional 66, corner of Vicente Guerrero (☎962/8-13-13, fax 8-15-68). Lovely, well-priced luxury hotel. The large rooms with antique furniture, fireplaces and beautifully tiled bathrooms are set around a courtyard or in delightful gardens. About 1km northeast from the zócalo, it's just a block from Casa Na Bolom and affords gorgeous views of the surrounding hills. Restaurant and parking. ⑤.

Santa Clara, Insurgentes 1, corner of the zócalo (☎962/8-11-40, fax 8-10-41). A former colonial mansion, known locally as "La Casa de la Sirena" for the sixteenth-century carvings of mermaids on the outside walls. The large rooms have antique furniture, and public areas are adorned with colonial weapons and suits of armour. Heated pool and good restaurant. ⑤.

The City

There aren't that many specific things to do in San Cristóbal: the true pleasures lie in simply wandering the streets and in getting out to some of the nearby villages. If you've come here to study or buy textiles and weavings from the villages, several superb places offer the chance to preview indigenous crafts.

As always the **zócalo**, Plaza 31 de Marzo, is worth seeing, not so much for the relatively ordinary sixteenth-century cathedral (though it does have a nice *artesonado* ceiling and elaborate pulpit) as for some of the colonial mansions that surround it. For a full description of the city's colonial churches and monuments pick up a copy of Richard Perry's excellent book *More Maya Missions: Exploring Colonial Chiapas*, available in the bookstores listed on p.150. The finest of the mansions is **La Casa de la Sirena**, now the *Hotel Santa Clara*, which was probably built by the conquistador Andrés de la Tovilla in the mid-sixteenth century and has a very elaborate doorway around the corner on Insurgentes.

In the middle of the zócalo there's a bandstand, which now incorporates a café, but even when no band is playing the city authorities provide piped music for people strolling here. If you haven't already come across them, this is probably where you'll first encounter some of San Cristóbal's insistent **salespeople**, mostly women and girls from the villages, traditionally dressed and in no mood to take no for an answer. You must either learn to say no as if you really mean it, or else accept that they'll break your resistance eventually. Bear in mind that they really do need the income: many have been expelled from their villages for converting to Protestantism and live in desperate hardship.

Templo del Carmen

From the zócalo, Hidalgo leads south to the **Templo del Carmen**, by the Moorish-style (*mudéjar*) tower and arch across the road, which once served as the gateway to the city. The church is not particularly inspiring architecturally, but you can also visit the adjoining cultural complex, including the Casa de la Cultura and **Instituto de Bellas Artes**. Considering the amount of artistic activity in and around San Cristóbal, these are pretty disappointing – especially since a serious fire in 1993 destroyed several eighteenth-century religious paintings – but sometimes there's an interesting temporary exhibition, concert or recital. On the way here, at the corner with Niños Heroes, you pass the Tienda de los Artesanos de Chiapas (Tues–Sun 9am–2pm & 5–8pm), a state-run venture which provides an outlet for Chiapas textiles and crafts at fair prices. The **displays of weaving** and embroidery styles in the exhibitions here are as good as any museum and if you're planning to visit any of the villages have a look in here first to get an idea of what's on offer.

The museums and Santo Domingo

In the other direction, General Utrilla leads north from the zócalo towards the market. At no. 10, Plaza Siván, the small **Museo del Ambar** (daily 10am–6pm; free) displays amber found in the Simojovel Valley; you can buy authentic pieces here too. La Pared, on Hidalgo, also has a very good selection of genuine amber at reasonable prices.

Santo Domingo, further up the road, is perhaps the most intrinsically interesting of San Cristóbal's churches, with a lovely pinkish Baroque facade embellished with Hapsburg eagles. Inside it's huge and gilded everywhere, with a wonderfully ornate pulpit – see it in the evening, by the dim light of candles, and you can believe it's all solid gold. Being so close to the market, Santo Domingo is often full of traders and villagers, and the area in front of the church is filled with craft stalls – often the best place to **buy souvenirs**. Appropriately, then, part of the former *convento* next door has been converted into a craft co-operative (Sna Jolobil) selling textiles and other village products. The quality here is generally good, and prices correspondingly high.

A block behind the church, in another part of the monastery, the **Museo Etnografía y Historia** and the Centro Cultural de los Altos de Chiapas (Tues–Sun 10am–5pm; US$1.50) has gorgeous displays of textiles, as well as vivid portrayals of how the Maya fared under colonial rule. The **library** at the rear is a fascinating place to study old books and records of Chiapas, and the gardens are a relaxing place to rest.

The market

San Cristóbal's daily **market** lies beyond Santo Domingo along General Utrilla. It's a fascinating place, if only because here you can observe indigenous life and custom without causing undue offence. What's on sale is mostly local produce and household goods, although there are also good tyre-soled leather *huaraches* and rough but warm sweaters, which you might well feel the need of. The market is far bigger than at first you suspect, so make sure you see it all (though beware that the main covered part is full of really gross, bloody butchers' stalls). For other high-quality **crafts**, try the stores in town, especially on Real de Guadalupe – those furthest from the zócalo, like Artesanías Real at 44, and Artesanías Chiapanecas at 46-C, are the best.

Casa Na Bolom

From opposite Santo Domingo, Chiapa de Corzo leads east towards the **Casa Na Bolom** at Vicente Guerrero 33, a private home, museum and library of local anthropology (Tues–Sun 9am–1pm; ☎962/8-14-18), devoted especially to the isolated **Lacandón Maya** (see box on p.136). This was the home of Danish explorer and anthropologist Frans Blom, who died in 1963, and his Swiss wife, Gertrude Duby, an anthropologist and photographer who died in 1993, and is renowned as a centre for the study of the region. The **Museo Moxviquil** (tour of house, grounds and museum in English or Spanish Tues–Sun at 4.30pm, US$2.50 including film; guided tours in Spanish only at 11.30am, US$2) exhibits discoveries from the site as well as an excellent map. After the tour, a film about the life of the Bloms and the destruction of the Lacandón forest is shown, and sometimes a video on Lacandón agriculture. Na Bolom also hosts some volunteer cultural and agricultural projects; write or call for details. You can also stay here (see p.146).

Guadalupe and San Cristóbal
Further afield, two churches dominate views of the town from their hilltop sites: **Guadalupe** to the east and **San Cristóbal** to the west. Neither offers a great deal architecturally, but the climbs are worth it for the views – especially San Cristóbal, at the top of a dauntingly long and steep flight of steps. Be warned, though, that women have been subjected to harassment at both of these relatively isolated spots (especially San Cristóbal): don't climb up here alone or after dark. Just below Guadalupe is the wonderful *Café Dorado*, which is open in the afternoon for coffee, meals and stunning sunset views of the city.

Eating, drinking and entertainment

There's a huge variety of good **restaurants** along Insurgentes and in the streets immediately around the zócalo, especially on Madero. Where San Cristóbal really scores, however, is in lively places that cater to the disparate, somewhat bohemian crowd here, made up of university and language-school students, a permanent population of young Americans and a constant stream of travellers. Lots of the places are vaguely arty, with a coffee-house atmosphere and interesting menus that feature plenty of **vegetarian** options. There are a couple of good **bakeries** on Diego de Mazariegos, two blocks west of the zócalo.

As for **nightlife**, many of these same places host **live music** in the evenings, only rarely imposing a cover charge. There are even a couple of **discos** in the big hotels: one at the *Posada El Cid* on the Carretera Interamericana, another at the *Hotel Rincón del Arco*.

San Cristóbal also boasts three **cinemas**: the *Cine Las Casas*, Extensión Universitaria, Guadalupe Victoria 21, showing a wide selection of Mexican and international films; the *Cinema Santa Clara*, 16 de Septiembre 30, showing mainly Mexican films; and *El Puente*, Real de Guadalupe, which screens Latin American and foreign films. Check current listings in the tourist office on Hidalgo.

Cafés and restaurants
Café Altura, 20 de Noviembre 19. Best of several coffee shops around here, serving organic coffee and natural foods. Gentle music and poetry in the evenings.

Los Anafres, Flavio de Paniagua 2, near the corner with Utrilla. Friendly little Mexican restaurant where you can eat indoors or in a sunny courtyard. The speciality is grilled meats brought to your table on the *anafre*; also good vegetarian food and great soups.

Café Dorado, Real de Guadalupe, just below the church. Opens at 4pm to offer a welcome stop to visitors climbing the steps to Guadalupe church. Pasta, pizza and wonderful sunsets.

Café Restaurant Milán, Insurgentes 79 C. Opposite the Cristóbal Colón terminal. Very good little restaurant with the best-value breakfasts this side of town.

Café El Puente, Real de Guadalupe 55. Excellent café serving good inexpensive salads, soups, sandwiches and delicious cakes; also acts as a cultural centre, with newspapers and magazines, lectures, film shows and a good noticeboard. Closed Sun.

Café San Cristóbal, Cuauhtémoc 2, near the corner with Insurgentes. This tiny coffee house, subtly refurbished, is popular with the regulars who come to play chess and read the newspapers.

Casa de Pan, Dr Navarro 10 (closed Mon). Superb range of vegetarian food and baked goods, including bagels at very reasonable prices, made with locally grown organic ingredients; cookbook available. Owners Kip and Ronald Nigh are active in development projects for indigenous women and organic agriculture and this has become a meeting place for expatriate aid workers. Live music nightly.

Emiliano's Moustache, Cresencio Rosas 7, near Cuauhtémoc. Vast range of authentic tacos – the especiál is big enough for two. Some vegetarian choices too. Music in the evening.

Las Estrellas, Escuadron 201 6, opposite the bandstand outside Santo Domingo church. Inexpensive place for *artesanía* shoppers to break for lunch; eat indoors or in the shady courtyard. Wide choice of food, including some vegetarian dishes, and good service.

El Faisán, Madero 2, just off the zócalo. Pricey but excellent French food.

La Galería, Hidalgo 3, just south of the zócalo. Increasingly sophisticated restaurant where international food is served in the refined atmosphere of a colonial mansion, surrounded by some fairly expensive art. Only faint vestiges of its hippy origins remain. Evening music.

Latinos, C Diego de Mazariegos 19. More of a late-night music venue, but with good Mexican, vegetarian and international food. Many types of music: Latin (of course), salsa, reggae, jazz and rock.

Madre Tierra, Insurgentes 19, corner of Hermanos Domínguez. European-style restaurant in a colonial house, often with live salsa or classical music. Great, healthy food including homemade soup, salad, pasta and cappuccino. The next-door bakery and deli sells wholewheat bread and carrot cake until 8pm. Good views from the upstairs terrace bar.

El Mirador II, Madero 16. The best cheap Mexican restaurant on Madero; good comidas corridas.

La Parilla, corner of Belisario Domínguez and Dr Navarro, on a tiny square. Specializes in grilled meats, including *alambres al queso*, similar to a kebab with melted cheese; they also serve great pizza. Sit on one of the saddles used as bar stools to enjoy the atmosphere and great views. Closed Mon.

Paris-Mexico, Madero 20. Superb authentic French and Mexican cuisine, expertly cooked and not overpriced – try the daily lunch special, a three-course meal of soup, crêpe and dessert, always with a vegetarian option.

Plaza Mirador, Plaza 31 de Marzo 2. Surprisingly inexpensive considering the location overlooking the zócalo, and serving tasty filling meals, usually with a vegetarian choice.

Restaurante Normita II, corner of Juárez and José Flores, one block southeast of the plaza. A great little restaurant, serving Jaliscan specialities and inexpensive breakfasts.

Restaurante Tuluc, Insurgentes 5. Justifiably popular, with a good comida corrida and dinner specials, this the first place to open in the morning (6am); ideal if you have to catch an early bus.

El Teatro Café, 1 de Marzo 8 (☎962/8-31-49). Superb, moderately priced French and Italian food. Boasting the only rooftop dining area in San Cristóbal, this is definitely the best place to enjoy the sunset as you eat. French and English spoken.

Listings

Banks and exchange Most banks are around the zócalo; they usually exchange dollars and give cash advances (mornings only) and most have 24hr ATMs. Casa de Cambio Lacantún, Real de Guadalupe 12 (Mon–Sat 8am–2pm & 4–8pm, Sun 9am–1pm) offers better rates and quicker service.

Bike rental Los Pinguinos, 5 de Mayo 10–B (8-02-02). Well-maintained bikes for about US$2 per hour, US$8 per day; also tours to local attractions. German and English spoken.

Bookstores Librería La Pared, Hidalgo 2, next to the tourist office, has new guidebooks (including *Rough Guides*) and the largest selection of new and secondhand books in English and other languages in southern Mexico; you can rent, trade or buy books. Other bookstores include Librería Chilam Balam, on General Utrilla near Dr Navarro; Librería Soluna, Real de Guadalupe 13B; and Librería La Quimera, Real de Guadalupe 24B. The excellent Mapa Turistico de Chiapas (1:400,000 scale, 4km:1cm) is available at most of the bookstores in town. Casa Na Bolom, Vicente Guerrero 33, has a very good library (Mon–Thurs 9am–3pm, Fri 9am–11am) and sells some books and maps of the Lacandón forest.

Email and the Internet You can receive faxes and email at Librería la Pared, Hidalgo 2, next to the tourist office (☎962/8-72-32, fax 8-63-67; *lapared@sancristobal.podernet.com.mx*). To send email and get connected to the Web, go to the excellent *Cyberc@fé*, a new, well-equipped Internet café in the Pasaje Mazariegos mall, in the first block along Real de Guadalupe (Mon–Sat 9am–10pm, Sun 11am–9pm; ☎962/8-74-88; *cybercafé@sancristobal.podernet.com.mx*).

Language courses Centro Bilingüe, in Centro Cultural el Puente, Real de Guadalupe 55 (✆ & fax 962/8-37-23; *spanish@sancristobal.podernet.com.mx*), is the longest-established language school in San Cristóbal. Instituto Jovel, María Adelina Flores 21 (✆ & fax 962/8-40-69; *jovel@sancrisobal.podernet.com.mx*), is newer but highly recommended. Both offer courses at various levels, and can arrange accommodation with local families.

Post office At the corner of Cuauhtémoc and Crescencio Rosas, southwest of the zócalo (Mon–Fri 8am–7pm, Sat 9am–1pm). In addition, most hotels have Mexipost boxes and many of the larger ones sell stamps.

Telephones There are Ladatel phones on the zócalo, under the arches of the Palacio Municipal, and in the Cristóbal Colón terminal; hotels and restaurants have casetas. You can make and receive phone calls at Librería la Pared (see above).

Tours Viajes Lacantún, Madero 16 (✆962/8-25-88), Viajes Chinkultic in the *Posada Margarita*, Real de Guadalupe 34 (✆ & fax 962/8-09-57), and Viajes Pakal, Cuauhtémoc 6B (✆962/8-28-18). To buy international air tickets go to Santa Ana Tours, 16 de Septiembre 6 (✆962/8-02-98).

MOVING ON FROM SAN CRISTÓBAL

San Cristóbal is pretty well connected, and you can get directly to most destinations in the state and throughout the Yucatán. Check times at the **tourist office** on Hidalgo, which maintains an accurate and up-to-date list of *all* bus times. Ticket lines are long, so try to buy your onward ticket in advance. **Tuxtla Gutiérrez** (2hr) is served frequently by most companies, and in addition combis and taxis tout for customers outside the bus stations on the highway.

Villahermosa (7hr) is not so well served, though there are a few first-class services daily with Cristóbal Colón; it's easier to go any bus to Tuxtla and change there. For **Palenque** (5hr), there are plenty of first- and second-class departures, day or night. All buses going to Palenque call at **Ocosingo** (2hr 30min), and in addition there's plenty of passenger-van traffic: just go to the highway and someone will call out to you. Several first-class buses head for **Ciudad Cuauhtémoc** (via **Comitán**) on the **Guatemalan border**: Cristóbal Colón takes 3hr 30min, while Transportes Lombardo, on the Carretera Interamericana to the east of the junction with Insurgentes, runs second-class services beginning at 4.30am, most of which continue to **Tapachula** (7hr 30min). On the highway you'll also find any number of combis to Comitán.

For **Oaxaca** (12hr) there are two overnight services at 5pm and 7pm, with more departures from Tuxtla. The first-class companies all have at least two daily services to **Mexico City** (19hr). For **Campeche** (10hr) and **Mérida** (13hr), Transportes Lacandónia has a second-class bus at 1.15pm, while a first-class service leaves at 9.30pm. For the **Yucatan coast** Maya de Oro has a luxury service at 9.30pm, calling at **Chetumal** (10hr; for Belize), **Playa del Carmen** (14hr) and **Cancún** (17hr).

Aerocaribe operates **regional flights** five days a week to Palenque, Tuxtla, Villahermosa and Cancún and has connections throughout Mexico; there are also **international flights** to Flores, for Tikal.

Around San Cristóbal

Excursions to the villages around San Cristóbal should be treated with extreme sensitivity. Quite simply, you are an intruder, and will be made to feel so – be very careful about taking photographs, and certainly never do so inside churches (theoretically you need a permit from the tourist authorities in Tuxtla Gutiérrez for any photography in the villages; in practice you should always get permission locally). There's a well-worn travellers' tale, true in its essentials, of two gringos being severely beaten up for photographing the interior of the church at San Juan Chamula. You should also be careful about what you wear: cover your legs, and don't wear native clothing – it may have some meaning or badge of rank for the people you are visiting.

The best time to make your visit is on a Sunday, when most villages have a market, or during a fiesta. At such times you will be regarded as having a legitimate reason to come, and you'll also find some life – most villages are merely supply points and meeting places for a rural community and have only a very small permanent population.

Some kind of trip out of San Cristóbal is definitely worth it, though, if only for the ride into the countryside, even if on finally reaching a village you find doors shut in your face and absolutely nothing to do (or, conversely, you are mobbed by begging kids). The indigenous people in the immediate vicinity of San Cristóbal and to the west are generally **Tzotzil** speaking, while those a little further to the east are **Tzeltal**, but each village has also developed its own trademarks in terms of costumes, craft specialities and linguistic quirks: as a result, the people are often subdivided by village or groups of villages and referred to as Chamulas, Zinacantecos, Huistecos (from Huistán) and so on.

It's a good idea to find out about village life before you go; the Tienda de los Artesanos on Hidalgo (see p.148) has a good display on the villages, with pictures of the local dress in each, and the tourist office can supply details of tours and bus timetables where relevant.

Transport and tours

Inexpensive combis leave frequently from the end of Utrilla, just north of the market in San Cristóbal, for Chamula and Zinacantán, and less often, but still several times a day, for other villages. If you'd rather take an **organized tour** (around US$7–8 per person), there are several to choose from. Among the best are those led by **Mercedes Hernández Gómez**, who grew up in Zinacantán – her knowledge is so extensive that she never gives the same tour twice; meet by the kiosk in the zócalo at 9am – she'll be carrying her distinctive umbrella. **Alex and Raul's** "Culturally Responsible Excursions" leave from outside the tourist office on the zócalo at 9.30am (☎962/8-37-41).

THE SAN CRISTÓBAL AREA

You can also get details on **horseback tours** into the surrounding area from the tourist office; the *Posada Margarita* is one of several places that organizes them. Many of the organized tours go to the **Grutas de San Cristóbal** (also called Rancho Nuevo caves; daily 9am–5pm; US$0.50), an enormous cavern extending deep into a mountain about 10km away. This is quite far enough to get saddle-sore if you're not used to riding, though the horses are placid enough even for total beginners. Make sure you agree your itinerary before setting off: some guides expect you to turn round and head home as soon as you reach your destination. The caves can also be reached by bus since they're barely a kilometre from the main road to Comitán; look for the "Rancho Nuevo" sign on the right. A track leads for about 1km from the road through a pine-forested park with hiking trails often used by the army. If you want to go by **bike**, it's about a fifty-minute ride, uphill most of the way from San Cristóbal.

Another favourite trip is to **El Arcotete**, a large, natural **limestone arch** that forms a bridge over a river. To get there, follow Real de Guadalupe out of town, past the Guadalupe church, where it then becomes the road to Tenejapa; El Arcotete is down a signed track to the right, about 3.5km past the church.

San Juan Chamula

SAN JUAN CHAMULA is the closest of the villages to San Cristóbal and the most frequently visited. It's also the most commercialized – prices in the market are certainly no bargain and local kids will pester you for "presents" (whining *"regaleme"*) the whole time. The best way to deal with the situation without either party feeling insulted is to select just one or two children and buy a couple of the painted clay animals or braided bracelets they're selling, then tell all the others you've bought all you're going to and hope they'll go to someone else. To get the most out of a visit you really need to go on one of the organized tours (see opposite); questions are answered honestly and in full.

Chamula is little more than a collection of civic and religious buildings with a few houses – most of its population actually lives on isolated farms or *ejidos* in the countryside. Protestant converts among the villagers were driven out thirty years ago and only some of the Catholic sacraments are accepted. The rituals practised in the **church** at Chamula – a mixture of Catholic and traditional Maya practice – are extraordinary, and the church itself is a glorious sight, both outside and in, where worshippers and tourists shuffle about in the flickering light of a thousand candles. Before you enter, though, be sure to obtain permission (and buy a ticket; US$0.50) from the "tourist office", to the right-hand side of the plaza as you face the church. Do *not* take **photographs** inside, or even write notes.

A couple of comedores on the plaza provide simple, filling meals and in the cantina you can buy *pox* (pronounced "posh"), a wickedly strong cane alcohol used as an offering in the church and also simply to get celebrants blind drunk. There are fairly regular colectivo departures from San Cristóbal's market to Chamula, especially frequent for the Sunday market. If you take a bus up, the 10km back is an easy and delightful walk, almost all downhill.

Zinacantán and other villages

ZINACANTÁN is also reasonably close to San Cristóbal, some 15km, and accessible on public transport. It's an easy walk from Chamula (about 1hr 30min), slightly harder in the other direction. If you reach Zinacantán early enough on Sunday morning you'll have time to look around, visit the market, and still walk to Chamula before the market there has packed up. (Chamula's market stays open longer than the others, presumably in honour of its foreign visitors.) Zinacantán also has a **museum**, Museo Ik'al Ojov ("Our Great Lord"), with displays of costumes from different hierarchical groups and a tableau of a house interior (daily 8am–6pm; donation).

A number of other villages can be reached by early morning buses from the market area, although you may have difficulty getting back. **TENEJAPA**, about 28km northeast of San Cristóbal through some superb mountain scenery, is the closest easily accessible Tzeltal village, and has a particularly good Sunday market. Combis leave for Tenejapa from Bermudas, an unmarked side street running east from the market, near the corner with Yajalon, roughly hourly or when full (1hr). Last one back to San Cristóbal leaves Tenejapa at 3pm. **HUISTÁN**, some 36km out, just off the road to Ocosingo, is Tzotzil-speaking, and with more than the usual amount of villagers in traditional dress. **SAN PEDRO CHENALHÓ**, in a valley 36km north, is harder to get to but worth it for the Sunday market. It has a basic pensión and, perhaps because of fewer visitors, seems friendlier than most.

Moxviquil

Moxviquil, a completely deserted ruined **ancient site**, is a pleasant excursion from San Cristóbal of a few hours on foot; it's best, however, to study the plans at the Casa Na Bolom first, as all you can see when you get there are piles of rough limestone. To get there, find Av Yajalon, a few blocks east of Santo Domingo, and follow it north to the end (about 30min) at the foot of tree-covered hills, in a little settlement called Ojo de Agua. Head for the highest buildings you can see, two timber shacks with red roofs. The tracks are at times indistinct as you clamber over the rocks, but after about 300m a lovely side valley opens up on your left – suitable for camping. The main path veers gradually to the right, becoming quite wide and leading up through a high basin ringed by pine forest. After 3km you reach the village of **Pozeula**; the ruins are ahead of you across a valley, built on top of and into the sides of a hill.

Laguna Miramar

Further to the southeast is the **Laguna Miramar**, the largest lake in southeast Mexico, which you can visit as part of an organized trip from San Cristóbal. Lying in the centre of the Lacandón forest, Miramar is now a pristine part of the Montes Azules Biosphere Reserve and staying here enables you to experience the last true rainforest in North America. There are no settlements on the shore and an island in the lake has traces of a fortress which was a stronghold of the Maya until it was finally conquered in 1559. The high canopy forest here is home to abundant wildlife and there are rivers and caves to explore. A trip here is a unique expedition, costing around US$200. It usually involves flying in from Ocosingo, though you can get a combi from Ocosingo to the *ejido* of **Emiliano Zapata** (5hr), where you register with the village committee. For details contact Fernando Ochoa at the *Casa de Pan* in San Cristóbal (☎967/8-04-68).

San Cristóbal to Tuxtla Gutiérrez

The two-hour journey from San Cristóbal to **Tuxtla Gutiérrez** is one of the most spectacular in Mexico, as the road twists through the mountains, breaking through the cloud into cool pine forests to offer sweeping views of highland valleys, before descending into the heat of the Grijalva valley and Tuxtla. Most people come this way simply to take the boat trip through the astonishing **Cañon del Sumidero**, but the town of **Chiapa de Corzo**, on the riverbank from which the boats depart, has some colonial monuments as well as some little-visited but easily accessible **Maya ruins**. Tour agents in San Cristóbal offer good-value **day-trips** to the cañon (doing it on your own is only fractionally cheaper), but Tuxtla does have some sights worth seeing – **museums** and a fascinating **zoo** – so you might want to consider staying overnight.

Chiapa de Corzo

CHIAPA DE CORZO is an elegant little town overlooking the river, barely twenty minutes from Tuxtla. An important centre in Preclassic times, it's the place where the oldest Long Count date, corresponding to December 7, 36 BC, has been found on a stela (the remaining ruins are on private land behind the Nestlé plant, beyond the far end of 21 de Octubre). There are at least a dozen **places to eat** on the riverside here, and plenty to see: the most striking feature is an amazingly elaborate **sixteenth-century fountain**, which dominates the zócalo. A blend of Spanish and Moorish architecture, it is built of brick in the *mudéjar* style in the shape of the Spanish crown. A tribute to its painstaking restoration, it is one of the most spectacular surviving early colonial monuments in Mexico. The small **museum of regional handicrafts**, in a cobbled courtyard surrounded by the ancient brick arches of the Convento Santo Domingo (Tues–Sun 10am–4pm; US$0.50), features the local painted and lacquered gourds.

There are two **hotels** in town: the basic *Los Angeles*, on the southeast corner of the zócalo (②), and the new *Hotel la Ceiba,* Domingo Ruíz 300 (☎961/6-07-73; ⑤), three blocks west from the zócalo, which is more upmarket and very quiet and comfortable, with a/c rooms and a small pool.

To get to **Chiapa** from San Cristóbal, take any second-class bus or combi (few first-class services stop in the town), though you're likely to be dropped off by the highway; there's a steady stream of microbuses from Tuxtla passing to take you to the centre.

The ruins of Chiapa de Corzo

Strategically located on an ancient trade route high above the Río Grijalva, the ruins of **Chiapa de Corzo** comprise some two hundred structures scattered over a wide area of private property, shared among several different owners and sliced in two by the Carretera Interamericana. Mound 32, a small flat-topped pyramid, is clearly visible at the road junction as you head east of town. This is the longest continually occupied site in Chiapas, beginning life as a farming settlement in the early Preclassic period (1400–850 BC). By the late Preclassic (250 BC–250 AD), it was the largest centre of population in the region, trading all over Mesoamerica. What you see today are mainly low pyramids, walls and courtyards.

To **get to the site** from town, take any microbus heading east from the zócalo, get off at the junction with Hidalgo and follow the signs. After about ten minutes you'll come to an unmarked gate in a fence on the right; go to the house (officially closed Mon) and pay the US$0.75 **fee** to the family who farm among the ruins. On foot, it's about 3km northeast from the zócalo in Chiapa de Corzo, passing the beautifully located sixteenth-century church ruin of San Sebastián on the way.

The Cañon del Sumidero

Just downstream from Chiapa de Corzo, the Río Grijalva has carved the **Cañon del Sumidero**, a spectacular cleft through cliffs that in places reach almost 1500m in height. The most popular way to see the canyon is to take a boat from the *embarcadero*, just below the zócalo; **boats** leave when full and charge US$0.50 per person. The river is dead calm since the Netzahualcóyotl dam was constructed at the northern end of the canyon, where the boats turn around. The trip lasts a couple of hours, passing several waterfalls (best during the rains) and entering caves in the cliffs, and it's enlivened by a commentary that points out such detail as the place where hundreds of Chiapanec warriors flung themselves off the cliff rather than submit to the Spanish. The guides will also spot **crocodiles** large enough to make a dramatic impression with a long lens on your camera.

To appreciate the view from above, take the road that runs north from Tuxtla past a series of miradores, in a **national park** that includes the most scenic sections of the canyon. The best views are from the mirador known as **La Coyota**, or at the end of the road near the restaurant *La Atalaya*. There's no public transport other than tours, but to see at least the lower reaches you could take a "Km 4" combi from Tuxtla heading north along 11 Oriente Nte, past the Parque Madero, and get off at the turnaround point. From here it's a 25-minute walk to the first mirador, **La Ceiba**, for stunning views of the canyon and river. There's usually sufficient traffic to make hitching a possibility, though be sure to take water along.

Bochil, Simojovel and around

Just beyond Chiapa de Corzo, the **road to Villahermosa** (see p.169) – a spectacular wind down to the Gulf plain – cuts off to the north. Few tourists take this route, but it offers an interesting excursion to some little-visited highland villages; you can also return to San Cristóbal this way.

The road climbs through mountains wreathed in cloud to **BOCHIL**, some 60km from Tuxtla, where some buses pull over for a rest stop. It's a pleasant small town, a centre for the **Tzotzil Maya**, and a good base from which to explore the surrounding hills and villages. Most people still wear the traditional dress or *traje*, the women in white *huipiles* with red embroidery, pink ribbons in their hair and dark blue skirts, and maybe a few men in the white smock and trousers rolled up to the knee. You'll be stared at, usually covertly, and, as always, should be *very* wary of taking photographs: not merely out of simple courtesy, but because you may be taken for a government agent – these towns protested very strongly at the election result in August 1994 and in December 1994 were briefly occupied by the Zapatistas, who destroyed public records. There are a couple of simple **places to stay**, including the *Posada San Pedro* (②), whose basic rooms are set out around a courtyard on 1 Poniente Nte, a block from the plaza; head for Banamex at the top of the plaza and turn right. Bochil has a frequent second-class bus service to Tuxtla, with Autotransportes Tuxtla–Bochil. Five kilometres beyond Bochil at **Puerto Cate**, a side road leads down to the right to **San Andrés Larráinzar**, a Tzotzil village 23km down the dirt track; trucks cover the route. From San Andrés you can reach **San Juan Chamula** (p.153), 18km away, which is well connected by combis **to San Cristóbal**. This makes for an interesting route to or from San Cristóbal – but you'll need to check the current political situation and set off fairly early.

Combis run regularly up the minor road to **SIMOJOVEL**, 40km from Tuxtla at the head of a spectacular valley, the source of most of the amber you'll find sold in local markets. Should you want **to stay**, the *Casa de Huéspedes Simojovel*, one block south of the plaza on Independencia (②), has basic rooms around a flower-filled courtyard.

Tuxtla Gutiérrez

TUXTLA GUTIÉRREZ, the capital of the state and a fast-growing, modern city, does its best to deny most of Chiapas's attraction and tradition, but you may well end up having to stay the night here as it's the main gateway to central Mexico and a major transport hub. It's not a bad place – there's a fascinating **zoo** and some excellent **museums** to fill some time – but there's no call to stay longer than necessary.

The centre of town is arranged in the usual Chiapas grid of numbered streets fanning out from Av Central, which runs east–west, and C Central, which runs north–south; often you'll see the streets named not just as Av 3 Nte, but as Av 3 Nte Pte, which defines which quarter of the city you're in – it can be extremely confusing if you're looking for the junction of 3 Nte Pte with 3 Pte Nte. **Avenida Central** (also known as Av 14 de Septiembre and Blvd Belisario Domínguez) is the town's focus, with the **zócalo** right at the centre.

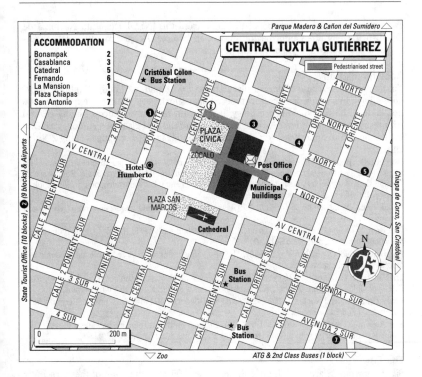

CENTRAL TUXTLA GUTIÉRREZ

Parque Madero & Cañon del Sumidero

ACCOMMODATION
Bonampak   2
Casablanca   3
Catedral   5
Fernando   6
La Mansion   1
Plaza Chiapas   4
San Antonio   7

Pedestrianised street

Cristóbal Colon
★ Bus Station

PLAZA CÍVICA

ZÓCALO

Hotel Humberto

Post Office

Municipal buildings

PLAZA SAN MARCOS

Cathedral

Bus Station

Bus Station

Zoo

ATG & 2nd Class Buses (1 block)

State Tourist Office (10 blocks), (9 blocks) & Airports

Chiapa de Corzo, San Cristóbal

0   200 m

Arrival and information

Tuxtla has two **airports**. The Aeropuerto San Juan, near Ocozocautla on a hill-top often shrouded in fog, 28km to the west of town, is generally used only in summer; colectivos run from here into the city. Aeropuerto Francisco Sarabia is a more convenient 7km west of the city; taxis or colectivos will bring you into the centre. First-class **buses** pull in to the ADO/Cristóbal Colón station on Av 2 Nte at C 2 Pte. To reach the centre (you can leave luggage at the juice bar *Miroslava* opposite), turn left from the entrance onto C 2 Pte Nte and left again when you reach Av Central. The main second-class terminal, used by Autotransportes Tuxtla Gutiérrez (ATG) and a couple of smaller companies, takes up half a block of 3 Sur Ote, near 7 Oriente, 1km southeast of the centre: for the zócalo, follow C 2 Sur west past the market area until you hit C Central Sur, then turn right.

The most central place to pick up maps and information is at the **municipal tourist office**, conveniently located in the underpass at C Central Nte and Av 2 Nte Ote; unfortunately opening hours are erratic. Tuxtla's **tourist office** proper is a good way west of the zócalo, across from the *Hotel Bonampak* in the Edificio Plaza de las Instituciones at Blvd Belisario Domínguez 950 (Mon–Fri 9am–3pm & 6–9pm; ☎961/3-93-96), but the staff have a good selection of maps and leaflets about all Chiapas's attractions. The main **post office** (Mon–Fri 8am–7pm, Sat 9am–1pm), just off the east side of the zócalo, has a reliable Lista de Correos.

Banks are everywhere. Banamex on 1 Sur Pte and Bancomer on Av Central Pte, both within a couple of blocks of the zócalo, have ATMs. A good **travel agent** is Viajes Miramar (☎961/2-39-30), off the northeast corner of the zócalo at Av 1 Ote Nte 310. You can obtain **topographic maps** of the state from the INEGI (Instituto Nacional de Estadística, Geografía y Información) office, on 1 Norte Ote, just past the post office – useful if you're travelling in out-of-the-way places.

Accommodation
Tuxtla has no shortage of decent places to stay, with plenty of budget options. Most hotels have hot water, but there are occasional shortages. Though inexpensive, the hotels near the bus stations are noisy. If you want the convenience of being central with less noise, head a few blocks east (left out of the first-class bus station, crossing the zócalo by the underpass) to find a clutch of hotels in all price ranges along 2 Norte Ote.

Bonampak, Belisario Domínguez 180 (☎961/3-20-50, fax 2-77-37). Fourteen blocks west of the zócalo, where Av Central becomes Blvd Domínguez. Part of the Best Western chain. Rooms are all a/c and there's a pool, restaurant, travel agency and car rental. It's worth dropping in for a look at the Bonampak mural reproductions (see p.137). ⑥.

Casablanca, Av 2 Nte Ote 25 (☎961/1-03-05). Friendly place offering good-value rooms, some with a/c and TV. Luggage storage. ③.

Catedral, Av 1 Nte Ote 367 (☎961/3-08-24). The best budget hotel in the city. Clean rooms, tiled bathrooms and even a bedside light. ②.

Fernando, 2 Nte Ote 515 (☎961/3-17-40). The best value in this area: large, comfortable rooms and helpful staff. Parking available. ②.

La Mansión, C 1 Pte Nte 221 (☎961/2-21-51). Only a block west of the zócalo and a block from Cristóbal Colón, this comfortable, affordable hotel has a lift and a good-value restaurant. ③.

Plaza Chiapas, Av 2 Norte Ote 299 (☎961/3-83-65). Modern hotel with great prices. All rooms have private bath and some have a balcony. ②.

San Antonio, 2 Av Sur Ote 540 (☎961/2-27-13). Clean, friendly, inexpensive hotel near the ATG terminal. Rooms are large with private bath. Good budget restaurant next door. ②.

The City
Sights downtown are few: the **zócalo**, or Plaza Cívica, is the chief of them, recently refurbished with much ostentatious marble, fountains and the very restrained, white-washed **Catedral de San Marcos**. Its bell tower is one of the leading local entertainments: every hour a mechanical procession of the twelve apostles goes through a complicated routine accompanied by a carillon of 48 bells. At the side of the cathedral, the **Plaza San Marcos** is full of life, its ever-growing **handicraft market** bustling with vendors from all over Chiapas. In the zócalo, across Av Central, there's often free live music, especially at weekends. West of the zócalo, between 9 and 10 calles, you pass the clean and very popular **Parque la Marimba**, a favourite evening gathering place for families to stroll and listen to the marimba bands.

Slightly further afield, you could also head out to the **Parque Madero**, northeast of the centre, where the small **Museo Regional de Chiapas** (Tues–Sun 9am–4pm; US$1.50) displays artefacts and maps detailing the pre-Columbian groups living in Chiapas – highlights include intricately carved human bones from the ruins of Chiapa de Corzo (see p.155). Botanical gardens and an *Orquideario* full of blooms native to the Chiapas jungle are in the same complex, reached along a shaded walkway. To get there, head north from the zócalo and then turn right onto Av 5 Norte Ote for 2km, or take a combi marked "Parque Madero" along Av Central.

The zoo
If you have half a day to spare, you could spend it at the **Zoológico Miguel Alvárez del Toro** or **ZOOMAT** (Tues–Sun 8.30am–5.30pm; free but donations welcome), on a forested hillside south of the city. There's a **bus** out there, #60, marked "Cerro Hueco" or "Zoológico", which you can catch on C 1 Oriente between avenidas 6 and 7 Sur, a bit

of a walk from the centre – it's very slow and roundabout, though, and a taxi (US$1) is a great deal easier.

The zoo claims to have every species native to Chiapas, from spiders to jaguars, and, by any standards, it's excellent, with good-sized cages, complete with natural vegetation and freshwater streams, and a conservationist approach. There is, for example, one dark cage with a label that announces the most destructive and dangerous species of all: peer in and you're confronted with a reflection of yourself. A number of animals, including *guaqueques negros* (agoutis) – rodents about the size of a domestic cat – and some very large birds, are free to roam the zoo grounds. Occasionally you'll witness bizarre meetings, as these creatures confront their caged relatives through the wire. This is particularly true of some of the pheasants – *ocofaisan* and *cojalita* – where the descendants of the caged birds are freed but make no attempt to leave because they naturally live in family groups. People of nervous disposition should avoid the *vivario*, which contains a vast and stomach-turning collection of all the snakes, insects and spiders you might meet on your travels.

Eating and drinking

The centre of Tuxtla has dozens of **restaurants**, and you need never wander more than a block or so either side of Av Central to find something in every price range. Juice bars are everywhere and there are also some great bakeries along Av Central. The very **cheapest** places are on 2 Sur, while between the second-class bus area and the centre you'll pass several tiny, family-run restaurants, each serving an excellent-value comida corrida. More cheap places to eat can be found in the Mercado Díaz Ordáz, C Central Sur, between avenidas 3 and 4 Sur.

All the larger hotels have a restaurant attached, and these are often good value. *Gringo's Chicken*, on C 2 Ote just south of Av Central, may satisfy a yen for cooking *estilo Americano*, though the combination of southern-fried chicken with chilli, tortillas and southern-fried potatoes is uniquely Mexican. Most popular for socializing and people-watching are the swish restaurants behind the cathedral, always packed with smartly dressed locals. Prices for the Mexican food at *La Parroquia* are not too high and there's a good breakfast buffet. Next door, the *Trattoria San Marco* serves good portions of pizza, Mexican food, and great gateaux at slightly higher prices. For **vegetarian** food,

---

MOVING ON FROM TUXTLA

Cristóbal Colón, ADO and Maya de Oro buses all depart from the **first-class station** at the corner of Av 2 Nte Ote and C 2 Pte Nte; Rapidos del Sur (RdS), a good second-class line, is adjacent. Main destinations include **Mexico City** (16hr), **Veracruz** (11hr), **Oaxaca** (9hr). RdS serve the **Chiapas coast**; and Maya de Oro run luxury services to Mexico City, **Mérida** (14hr) and **Cancún** (18hr).

The various **second-class terminals** are dotted around the city. The main one, at the junction of Av 3 Sur Ote and C 6 Ote Sur, is used by Autotransportes Tuxtla Gutiérrez (ATG) and serves Oaxaca, Villahermosa, Mérida and Palenque. There's even a service to Chetumal, Playa del Carmen and Cancún. Other local buses operate from the street outside. Getting **to San Cristóbal** is extremely easy: ATG have frequent departures and combis leave from outside the terminal whenever they have a full load; from a block away on Av 8 Ote, between 2 and 3 Sur, Omnibus de Chiapas runs a frequent and inexpensive service. A shared **taxi** to San Cristóbal (four people) will cost only US$4 each.

For **Chiapa de Corzo** hop on one of the microbuses that leave every five minutes from the Transportes Chiapa–Tuxtla office at 3 Oriente Sur and 3 Sur Ote in Tuxtla (there's another company round the corner at 2 Ote Sur and 2 Sur Ote). It's easy enough to get back: microbuses leave from the northeast corner of the zócalo in Chiapa.

try *Nah Yaxal*, just off Av Central at 6 Poniente Nte, west of the zócalo. It's clean and modern, though a little pricey. Opposite there's a good bread and cheese shop. The *Café Avenida*, next to the *Hotel Avenida*, at Av Central 224, is an authentic Mexican coffee shop. In the block west of it there are several **bakeries**.

San Cristóbal to Guatemala: Comitán and Montebello

Southeast of San Cristóbal, the Carretera Interamericana continues to the border through some of Chiapas's most scintillating scenery. You'll pass through **Amatenango del Valle**, a Tzeltal-speaking village with a reputation for good unglazed pottery, and **Comitán**, the only place of any size, which is the jumping-off point not only for Guatemala and the **Lagos de Montebello National Park**, but for the Classic period **Maya sites** of Junchavín and Tenam Puente. Beyond the Montebello lakes, the Carretera Frontera runs past **Tziscao** and over forested ridges almost to the Río Lacantún, soon to complete the long-planned highway paralleling the Guatemalan border, linking with the other end of the highway heading south from Palenque. At the time of writing tourists were discouraged (and at times prohibited) from taking this route – check first before you head out.

Comitán and around

An attractive town in its own right, **COMITÁN** is spectacularly poised on a rocky hillside and surrounded by country in which wild orchids bloom freely. Once a major **Maya centre** of population (Bonampak, Yaxchilán, and even Palenque are not far away as the parrot flies across the jungle), Comitán was originally a Maya town known as Balún Canán (Nine Stars, or Guardians), renamed Comitlán (place of potters) when it came under Aztec control. The final place of any note before the border (Ciudad Cuauhtémoc is no more than a customs and immigration post with a collection of shacks), today Comitán is a market and supply centre for the surrounding agricultural area. There's a **Guatemalan consulate** and a collection of reasonable **hotels**, and it's a good place to rest if you've some hard travelling through the Lacandón forest or into Guatemala ahead of you.

Comitán's zócalo, on several levels and with plenty of shady places to rest, is surrounded by municipal buildings, the Santo Domingo church, shops, restaurants and the theatre. Opposite the tourist office, adjoining the church on the corner of the plaza, the **Casa de Cultura** (daily 9am–8pm; free) features murals on the walls of its courtyard and has exhibits on local history, while the splendid little **Museo Arqueológico** (Tues–Sun 10am–5pm; free) presents an easily understandable chronology of the local Maya sites. The town also boasts a wealth of beautiful churches, many of them of historical and architectural interest, including the colonial Santo Domingo and San Sebastián.

Arrival and information

Buses stop along the Carretera Interamericana, a long six or seven blocks from the centre. Only Cristóbal Colón has a terminal (and a *guardería*); all other buses just pull in at the roadside.

Comitán's layout can be a little confusing at first, particularly as many streets have recently been renamed; pick up a free map from the **tourist office** in the Palacio Municipal on the zócalo (Sun 9am–2pm, Mon–Sat 9am–8.30pm; ☎961/2-40-47). They will also have the latest information on **Guatemalan visa** requirements. The **con-**

sulate itself is at the corner of C 1 Sur Pte and Av 2 Poniente Sur, a couple of blocks southwest of the zócalo (Mon–Fri 8am–4.30pm; ☎ & fax 961/2-26-69; US$10 fee for visa); if you need only a tourist card, pick one up at the border. Also on the zócalo is a Bancomer for **currency exchange**, dollar cash advances and ATM. The **post office** is one and a half blocks south on Central Sur (Mon–Fri 8am–7pm, Sat 8am–1pm). There's even an **Internet café**, *Internet Comitán*, behind the tourist office at Pasaje Morales 12 (daily 9am–2pm & 4–9pm; *sinco@comitan.podernet.com.mx*). The best **travel agent** is Viajes Balun Canan, Av 1 Nte 31 (☎961/2-03-07), though they can only arrange internal flights.

Apart from restaurants in the hotels, most of the best **places to eat** in Comitán are on the zócalo. For really good-value Mexican food served in clean surroundings, try *Helen's Enrique*, with tables under the arches, or the *Restaurant Nevelandia*; there are a couple of cheaper places too. The **market**, two blocks east of the zócalo, is filled with fruit stands and has some very good comedores.

Moving on from Comitán, there are plenty of buses and combis to Ciudad Cuauhtémoc for the border, and San Cristóbal and Tuxtla to the west. Heading for the **Lagos de Montebello**, buses or combis leave about every fifteen minutes from the terminal on Av 2 Pte Sur, between calles 2 and 3 Sur, about three blocks southwest of the zócalo. Otherwise, you can just wait for one to come along on the highway heading south.

Accommodation

Comitán has plenty of hotels, which are especially good value in the budget range. Nights are much cooler than days, so you'll need at least one blanket.

Hospedaje Colonial, C 1 Nte Ote 13 (☎961/2-50-67). Basic, clean rooms with private bath and secure parking. ②.

Hospedaje Montebello, 1 Poniente Nte 10, a block northwest of the zócalo (☎961/2-35-72). Great budget hotel. Large, clean rooms around a courtyard, some with private bath, and the communal shower is really hot. Clothes-washing facilities. ②.

Hospedaje Primavera, C Central Pte 4, just west from the zócalo (no phone). Basic but clean rooms round a courtyard, with several budget places to eat nearby. ②.

Lagos de Montebello, on the Carretera Interamericana at the junction with C 3 Norte Pte (☎961/2-10-92, fax 2-39-18). Modern, comfortable rooms round a shady courtyard. Convenient if you're travelling by car. ④.

Pensión Delfín, Av Central 19 A, right on the zócalo (☎933/2-00-13). Good value, with modernized rooms and dependable hot water. ③.

Posada del Virrey, Av Central Nte 13 (☎961/2-18-11). Bright, modern rooms around a courtyard, with private bath and TV. ④.

The ruins of Junchavín and Tenam Puente

The little-visited site of **Junchavín** (daily 7am–5pm; free) is about a 45-minute walk northwest from Comitán's zócalo: follow Av Central Nte for about 2km until you reach the church of Santa Teresita on the right, recognizable by its two tall bell towers. The road immediately past the church to the right, signposted **Quija**, will lead you out of town into hilly farming country. The entrance to the site is on the left after 1500m. Hundreds of steps lead up to a small flat-topped pyramid, flanked by two smaller structures. The best time to visit is early or late in the day to avoid the heat. Views are superb and it is said you can see Chinkultic (see p.162), 45km to the southeast. Combis from the zócalo run along the road to Quija; ask at the tourist office for times.

Tenam Puente is a much larger site, a few kilometres off the Carretera Interamericana, 15km to the south of Comitán. A bus leaves for the *ejido* of **Francisco Sarabia** from 3 Oriente Nte in Comitán at 8.30am, but you can take any bus heading south and get off at the junction 11km further on, then hitch or walk the 3km to the village. People here are friendly and will direct you to the ruins, which lie 1km beyond the school and playground. The path is difficult to find among the bushes and corn-fields, but you'll soon see stone terraces and mounds, and eventually several large structures, including a 20m pyramid. There are pleasant walks in the forested hills around here, but you'll need to take water.

Comitán to Lagos de Montebello

The **Parque Nacional Lagos de Montebello** stretches along the border with Guatemala down to the southeast of Comitán – beautiful wooded country in which there are more than fifty lakes, sixteen of them very large. The combination of pine for-est and lakes is reminiscent of Scotland or Maine, with miles of hiking potential: for the less energetic, roadside viewpoints provide glimpses of many of the lakes, including the **Laguna de Siete Colores**, lent different tints by natural mineral deposits and the sur-roundings. You could see quite a bit of the park in a long day-trip – buses cover the route all day from 5am, with the last bus leaving the park entrance around 7.30pm – but to really enjoy the beautiful lakes and forest, and to visit the small but spectacular **ruins of Chinkultic**, you're better off staying in or near the park. If you intend to head off the beaten track, you'll need to get hold of a good **map** before you arrive. The restaurant at the park headquarters displays an excellent topographic map of Chiapas, copies of which are sometimes available at the tourist offices in Comitán or bookshops in San Cristóbal, though by far the best source is INEGI in Tuxtla (see p.158).

Park accommodation and practicalities

The road leading to the lakes turns off the Carretera Interamericana 16km from Comitán at the village of **La Trinitaria**, with the park entrance 36km further on. In the recent past there were frequent **army checkpoints** along this road and you may still be asked for your passport at any time; the soldiers are invariably polite but make sure your tourist card is valid. There are several **places to stay** along the road. The most comfortable is the lovely *Parador Museo Santa María*, about 18km along on the right (☎967/8-09-88; ⑤), a former hacienda, furnished with antiques and oil paintings. Don't expect too many mod cons, though: the rooms are lit with oil lamps. Another 12km brings you to the best budget accommodation on the road, the *Hospedaje and Restaurant La Orquidea* (②), better known simply as *Doña María's*. Here there are half a dozen simple cabins with electric light, and showers in a separate building. It's a very *simpatico* place, run by Doña María Domínguez, who has given much help and support to Guatemalan refugees; you may find volunteers staying here. It's very peaceful too, set among the pines, just a short walk from the Chinkultic ruins, with a restaurant serv-ing good helpings of simple food; buses stop right outside.

The park entrance is 4km past *Doña María's*, and the paved road ends a few kilo-metres beyond the entrance at the **park headquarters**, after passing some of the more accessible and picturesque lakes; this is where the combis turn round. There's a free lakeshore **campsite** here, some simple cabañas (①) and a **restaurant**, the *Bosque Azul*, overlooking the lake of the same name. The small river flowing out of the lake (head for the bridge signed "paso de soldaldo") passes through an exquisitely beauti-ful, jungle-lined gorge and under a massive natural limestone arch before disappearing into a cave beneath a cliff face. Small boys will greet you and offer to guide you to the *grutas*, though you don't really need their help. **Horses** are available for hire.

The ruins of Chinkultic

Just before *Doña María's*, a 2km track leads off to the left to the Classic period Maya ruins of **Chinkultic** (US$2), which was probably occupied from about 200 to 900 AD. So far only a small proportion of the site has been cleared and restored, but it's well worth a visit for the setting alone. Climb the first large mound, and you're rewarded with a view of a small lake, with fields of maize beyond and forested mountain ridges in the background. Birds, butterflies and dragonflies abound, and small lizards dart at every step. A ball court and several stelae have been uncovered, but the highlight is undoubtedly the view from the top of the tallest structure, **El Mirador**. Set on top of a steep hill, with rugged cliffs dropping straight down to a cenote, the temple occupies a commanding position; though peaceful now, this was clearly an important centre in ancient times.

Tziscao and the Carretera Frontera

Near the entrance to the park, the **Carretera Frontera** turns off to the right. Still inside the park boundaries, it passes the village of **TZISCAO**, a tiny settlement on the shore of Laguna Tziscao. On the lakeshore here is the *Albergue Tziscao*, an unofficial youth **hostel** (no membership needed). While its location is great, and you can rent boats to paddle on the lake, the three-tiered concrete bunks (①) give the impression of being in a cave and you'll almost certainly need a sleeping bag. Food and cold beer is available. To follow the trail around the lake, go back to the junction beyond the church and turn right. Along the way you pass **Laguna Internacional**, where the border is marked by a white obelisk at either end of the lake; **entering Guatemala** here is not recommended. Beyond Tziscao, the Carretera Frontera (served by buses from Comitán) continues for another 70km through mountains and jungle with some spectacular views and precipitous drops, to the end of the line at Flor de Café. The largest settlement along the road is **LAS MARAVILLAS DE TENEJAPA**, a lovely village with a restaurant but no accommodation, about three and a half hours from Tziscao.

   FLOR DE CAFÉ stands at the foot of a steep limestone ridge formed by a finger of the Sierra la Colmena. The road goes no further at present (though construction is underway) and a track over the ridge connects with the village of Peña Blanca, two hours away, a neat, clean *ejido* where you can get food, drinking water and, if you want, a guide to **Nuevo San Andrés** on the Río Lacantún. From here there are occasional boats downstream to **Ixcán** or **Chajul** and from Chajul there are buses to **Benemérito** (see p.139). To make this journey you'll need camping equipment and should be prepared to wait for connections. Be aware that this route traverses the the area controlled by the Zapatistas and you may well be stopped by them or the Mexican army and forbidden to proceed.

Ciudad Cuauhtémoc and the Guatemalan border

A visit to the Lagos de Montebello is a good introduction to the landscapes of Guatemala, but if you want to see the real thing it's only another 60km or so from the La Trinitaria junction (plenty of passing buses) to the Mexican border post at **CIUDAD CUAUHTÉMOC**. There's nothing here but a few houses, the immigration post, a restaurant and the Cristóbal Colón bus station; the two hotels are not recommended.

   The **Guatemalan border** post is at **La Mesilla**, a 3km taxi ride away, about US$0.50 per person in a shared taxi. As always, the crossing is best attempted in daylight: the border is open until at least 10pm, but onward transport will be difficult if you leave it this late. If you need a **visa** (see p.15), you should really have one by now, though the chances are you'll be let in if you agree to pay the entry charge, which could be as much as US$10. Officially, if you have a visa or tourist card (or you're from the EU, in which case you need neither), there is **no charge** for entering Guatemala. However, the La Mesilla border post is the worst in the country for exacting illegal charges from tourists, with the customs officers sometimes joining in with demands for *inspección aduanal*. If you think you've been charged too much – anything over US$1 – politely but firmly refuse to pay or, failing that, demand a receipt and, if you feel up to it, report the incident.

Getting into Mexico is much easier: Mexican tourist cards are issued free and vans or buses will be waiting to take you to Comitán (passing La Trinitaria junction). The last direct bus to San Cristóbal is the Cristóbal Colón at 6.30pm (3hr 30min). **Buses** on to Huehuetenango, Quezaltenango and Guatemala City wait just over the border, leaving at least every hour until about 4pm. The **moneychangers** will give you reasonable rates for travellers' cheques or dollars, not so good for pesos. There are a couple of adequate bars on the Guatemalan side, and several **hotels** up the street from the border; see p.366 for more information.

The Chiapas coast

Hwy-200, much of it recently upgraded, provides a fast route from the Oaxaca border to Guatemala, with little to detain you on the way. However, the recent floods in September 1998 may mean that your journey will take longer than usual. **ARRIAGA**, the first town on the Chiapas coast road, is a dusty, totally uninteresting place, but its location at the junction of Hwy-195 (the road over the mountains to Tuxtla) means you may have to change buses here. **TONALÁ**, larger and marginally more inviting than Arriaga, is just a thirty-minute microbus ride away down Hwy-200, though if you want to break your journey you're better off heading to the beach at **PUERTO ARISTA**.

Continuing south, the highway traverses the steamy coastal plain of the **Soconusco**, running about 20km inland, with the 2400m peaks of the **Sierra Madre de Chiapas** always in view. The plain itself is a fertile agricultural area, mainly given over to coffee and bananas, though there are also many ranchos, where cattle grow fat on the lush grass.

Tapachula is the main city along this part of the coast, and with good connections to the border you can speed straight on, pausing only to change buses, or possibly to visit the ruins of **Izapa**, right by the roadside. It's not a bad place to spend the night, however, with several inexpensive hotels, and from here you can easily reach the cool coffee country around the delightful hill town of **Unión Juárez**, nestled at the foot of **Volcán Tacaná**, the highest peak in Chiapas.

Puerto Arista

Although this quiet village may not be everyone's idea of a perfect beach resort, **PUERTO ARISTA**, with its miles of clean sand and invigorating surf, does offer a chance to escape the unrelenting heat of the inland towns. There's little to see, and you have to stay under the shade of a *palapa* near the shore to benefit from the breezes, but it's a worthwhile stop if you've been travelling. While the waves are definitely refreshing, you need to be aware of the potentially dangerous **rip tides** that sweep along the coast – never get out of your depth. Combis and taxis to Puerto Arista (US$0.50) leave Tonalá at least every twenty minutes (or when full) from the corner of 5 de Mayo and Matamoros, a couple of blocks south of the zócalo in the market area, where the streets are crammed with fruit and vegetable stalls.

The road from Tonalá joins Puerto Arista's only street at the **lighthouse**, which is the centre of town. Walk a couple of kilometres left or right and you'll be on a deserted shoreline; ahead lies the beach, with **hotels** and inexpensive *palapa* **restaurants** packed closely together. It won't feel crowded, though, unless you arrive in Semana Santa, as there seem to be at least as many buildings abandoned or boarded up as there are occupied. **Prices** are difficult to determine and most places try to overcharge. The best bet is to have a refresco or a cold beer at a restaurant and ask if you can leave your bags while you have a good look around. The cheaper places are basic and not particularly good value; bargain with the owner and you may be able to knock the price down.

Turn right at the lighthouse for the more established hotels, such as *La Puesta del Sol*, the nearby *Brisas del Mar* and the *Agua Marina* (all ②), which are all clean and well run. Best here is the *Arista Bugambilias* (☎966/3-07-67 ext 116; ⑤), with a pool and private garden on the beach. Turn left at the lighthouse and you'll see signs for more hotels and several very basic cabaña places. The *Lucerito* (☎966/3-07-67 ext 152; ④), just back from the beach is a great bargain, with new tiled a/c rooms and a pool.

Tonalá to Tapachula

With your own vehicle, you can explore some of the side roads leading from Hwy-200 in the 220km between Tonalá and Tapachula, further south: either up into the mountains, where the heavy rain gives rise to dozens of rivers and waterfalls, or down to almost deserted beaches. Most coastal villages are actually on the landward side of a narrow lagoon, separated from the ocean by a sandbar. These sandbars block many rivers' access to the sea, causing marshes to form and providing a superb wetland habitat, the highlight of which is an **ecological reserve** protecting 45km of coastline near **Acacoyagua**: the state tourist authorities are building a hotel here. Travelling by bus, it's much more difficult (though still possible) to take in destinations off the main road, and you need to be prepared to hitch and camp. At **HUIXTLA**, 42km before Tapachula, Hwy-211 snakes over the mountains via Motozintla to join the Carretera Interamericana near Ciudad Cuauhtémoc and the Guatemalan border at **La Mesilla** (see p.163). This boneshaking road offers stupendous mountain views and is covered by buses running between Tapachula, Comitán and San Cristóbal.

Tapachula

Though most travellers see it as no more than an overnight stop en route to or from Guatemala, **TAPACHULA** does actually have something to offer, being a gateway to both the coast and the mountains, with a lovely setting at the foot of the 4000m Volcán Tacaná. A busy commercial centre, known as the capital of the Soconusco, the southeastern region of the state, it grew in importance in the nineteenth century with the increasing demand for coffee and bananas. Being a border city, it has a lively cultural mix, including not just immigrants from Central America, but also small German and Chinese communities. The **Museo Regional de Soconusco** (Tues–Sun 10am–5pm; US$0.50), in the same building as the tourist office, tells their story, as well as displaying scraps of excavated finds from local ruins.

Arrival and information

The city's layout is a little confusing, for while the streets are laid out in the regular numbered grid common in Chiapas, the zócalo, **Parque Hidalgo**, is not at its centre. It's not too far away, though: C Central meets Av Central three blocks east and a block south of the zócalo. All the main **bus stations** are north of the centre; the various second-class terminals are within walking distance of the zócalo, while first-class Cristóbal Colón is further out at C 17 Ote between Av 3 Nte and Av 5 Nte; taxis to the centre are cheap (under US$1) and walking takes about twenty minutes. Tapachula's **airport** (☎962/6-22-91), 18km south on the road to Puerto Madero, is served by Aeroméxico (☎962/6-20-50), Aviacsa (☎962/6-14-39), Taesa (☎962/6-37-32) and several smaller commuter airlines.

The **tourist office** (daily 9am–3pm & 6pm–9pm; ☎962/5-54-09) is on the ground floor of the old Palacio Municipal, on the west side of the zócalo. The helpful staff will call a hotel for you and give you a city map. The **post office** is a long way southeast of the zócalo at C 1 Ote, between 7 and 9 Nte (Mon–Fri 8am–6pm, Sat 8am–1pm). The main **banks** are one block east of the zócalo, but for changing cash and travellers' cheques you'll get a much quicker service from Cambios Tapa, in the Plaza Victoria shopping mall, a block east of the zócalo along C 5 Pte (Mon–Sat 8am–6pm, Sun 9am–

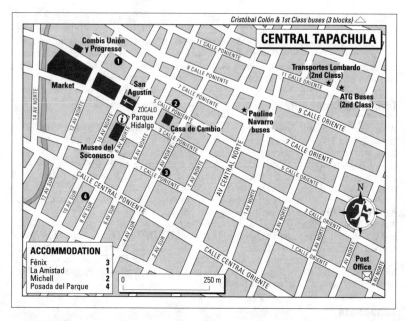

1pm). The **Guatemalan consulate** at C 2 Ote 33, between Av 7 and 9 Sur (Mon–Fri 8am–4pm; ☎962/6-12-52), issues Guatemalan visas.

ACCOMMODATION

There's at least one **hotel** near each of the bus stations, but ones around the second-class terminals can be sleazy. Calle 11 also has a few, and there's a whole clutch on Av 8 Nte, between calles 11 and 13 Pte. Some rather desperate-looking places can be found around the **market**, which straggles down the hill west of the zócalo, although there are also some surprisingly good-value hotels.

La Amistad, C 7 Pte 34, between 10 and 12 avenidas Nte (☎962/6-22-93). The best budget hotel in the city; clean, cool rooms around a flower-filled courtyard. ②.

Fénix, Av 4 Nte 19, near the corner of C 1 Pte (☎962/5-07-55). Good value at the price: rooms have a/c and there's a cooling fountain in the courtyard. ④.

Hospedaje Chelito, Av 1 Nte at the corner C 17 Ote (☎962/6-24-28). Handy location just around the corner from the Cristóbal Colón terminal (head left outside) with some a/c rooms. ③.

Michell, C 5 Pte 23-A (☎962/6-88-74). Modern hotel half a block east of the zócalo; all rooms have a/c and TV and doubles have balconies. ⑤.

Posada del Parque, Av 8 Sur 3, two blocks south of the zócalo (☎962/6-51-18). Clean, quiet and very good value. ②.

EATING AND DRINKING

There are more than enough **restaurants** around the zócalo to satisfy all tastes. Most are on the south side, where *Nuevo Doña Leo* has the best-value breakfast and comida corrida, together with tortas and tacos; *Los Comales* is similar, but a bit more expensive. The restaurant at the *Hotel Don Miguel*, C 1 Pte, off the southeast corner of the zócalo, is pretty fancy but does a great-value breakfast. As usual there are cheap places to eat and some fine bakeries to be found around the market area, beginning with the row of juice bars on 10 Av Pte, a block west of the zócalo.

MOVING ON FROM TAPACHULA

First-class buses for destinations throughout Mexico leave from the Cristóbal Colón terminal; any bus or combi from the centre to Talismán passes the entrance. Some of the better second-class services also leave from here. If you're heading directly **to Guatemala** you can take advantage of the twice-daily luxury Galgos service which takes you right through the border (US$28; 5-6hr). The main **second-class bus operators** are Rapidos del Sur, at 9 Pte and 14 Nte, for the coast as far as Salina Cruz, and Autobuses Paulino Navarro, 7 Pte between 2 and Central Nte, for the coast road, Ciudad Hidalgo and Puerto Madero. The most frequent bus service to San Cristóbal is with Lombardo (second-class) at 11 Ote and 3 Nte, with hourly services from 4am to 8pm (7hr 30min). Autotransportes Tuxtla Gutiérrez operate long-distance but comfortable second-class services from the same location. Union y Progreso, 5 Pte between 12 and 14 Nte, runs frequent combis to Unión Juárez and to the Talismán bridge for the Guatemalan border.

The ruins of Izapa

Though the road from Tapachula to the border passes right through the archeological site of **Izapa** (daily 8am–4pm; US$1), few visitors bother to stop, which is a pity, since as well as being easy to get to (any bus or combi to the Talismán border will stop), the site is large – with more than eighty temple mounds – and important for its evidence of both the Olmec and early Maya cultures. Izapa culture, in fact, is seen as a transitional stage between the Olmecs and the glories of the Classic Maya period; here you'll see early versions of the rain god Chac and others in elaborate bas-relief on the stone facings of the temples. Founded as early as 800 BC, Izapa continued to flourish throughout the Maya Preclassic period, until around 300 AD; most of what remains is from the later period, perhaps around 200 AD, although the site continued to be occupied until the Postclassic.

The **northern side** of the site (left of the road as you head to the border) is more cleared and accessible than the southern half. There's a ball court, and several stelae, which, though not Olmec in origin, are carved in a recognizable Olmec style, similar to monuments at other early Maya sites. The **southern side**, down a track about 1km back along the main road, is a good deal more overgrown, but you can spot altars with animal carvings – frogs, snakes and jaguars – and several unexcavated mounds.

Unión Juárez

The small town of **UNIÓN JUÁREZ**, high on the flank of the Tacaná volcano, 43km from Tapachula, offers a chance to escape the heat of the lowlands. The journey from Tapachula follows the valley of the Río Suchiate, which forms the border with Guatemala. There are some excellent day hikes to waterfalls and, with a guide, you can even reach the volcano's summit, at 4092m the highest point in Chiapas. This is a two-to three-day trip, with a cabin to sleep in at the top, though you'll need to bring a warm sleeping bag at least.

To get to Unión Juárez from Tapachula, catch a bus from the Unión y Progreso station in Tapachula (every 20 mins) to **CACAHOATÁN**, where you pick up a combi run by Transportes Tacaná: the whole journey takes around an hour and twenty minutes. There are just two **places to stay** in Unión Juárez: the budget but comfortable *Posada Aljoad*, half a block off the west side of the plaza (☎964/7-20-25; ②), which has rooms with private, hot-water bathrooms around a courtyard and a good inexpensive restaurant; and the good-value *Hotel Colonial Campestre*, which you pass as you enter the town from the south (☎964/7-20-00, fax 7-20-15; ⑤), with spacious, modern rooms, complete with TV and private bathrooms – a very friendly place with a good restaurant, *La Suiza Chiapaneca*, and a great base for exploring the volcano; Fernando, the owner's son, can **guide** you. On the north side of the plaza, the *Carmelita* and *La Montaña* are good, inexpensive **restaurants**. Combis leave for Cacahoatán (and Tapachula) from the east side of the plaza (every 30min until 8pm).

The Guatemalan border: the Talismán bridge and Ciudad Hidalgo

Both of these southern crossing points are easy places to enter Guatemala, but the **Talismán Bridge** is closer to Tapachula and better for onward connections. From Tapachula combis (Unión y Progreso) run frequently, taking about thirty minutes and passing the Cristóbal Colón bus station on the way. In theory there's a small toll to pay to cross the bridge, but immigration procedure is generally pretty slack and trouble-free. For those who need a visa, there are **Guatemalan and El Salvadoran consulates** in Tapachula. Changing money is best done in Tapachula, but there's no shortage of moneychangers at the border and you'll only get a slightly less favourable rate.

There are several **hotels** and **restaurants** at the border, some technically in Mexico, some in Guatemala, but almost all of them over the bridge in the no-man's land between the two border posts. None is particularly good value, but the *Buenavista* and the *Handall* (both ②) are the best of the bunch. Heading **onward**, Guatemala City is about five hours away; there's usually a bus waiting, but if not, take a bus or van to **Malacatán** and continue from there (see p.367). Travelling into Mexico from Guatemala, there's no shortage of combis to Tapachula and plenty of first-class buses from Tapachula onward. You'll probably have your passport checked many times along Hwy-200, so be prepared.

CIUDAD HIDALGO, on the border, is a very busy road crossing and the point where the train enters Guatemala, but it's less convenient if you're travelling by bus. There's a **casa de cambio** (and freelance moneychangers) at the corner of Av Central and C Central Sur, and several **hotels**; the *Hospedaje La Favorita*, C Central Ote (②), is best. Plenty of willing locals offer to pedal you across the Puente Rodolfo Robles to **Ciudad Tecún Umán** in Guatemala (p.367) but it's an easy walk. Cristóbal Colón runs a **bus** from Ciudad Hidalgo to México daily at 6pm, but it's much easier to take a bus or combi to Tapachula (45min) and change there. There's almost always one waiting by the casa de cambio.

TABASCO

The state of **Tabasco**, crossed by numerous slow-moving tropical rivers on their way to the Gulf, is at last making determined efforts to attract tourists. These rivers were used as trade highways by the ancient **Olmec** and **Maya** cultures, and the state boasts dozens of **archeological sites**. Few of these pre-Columbian cities have been fully excavated, though **Comalcalco**, north of Villahermosa, has been expertly restored and is certainly worth a visit.

Tabasco's **coast**, alternating between estuaries and sandbars, salt marshes and lagoons, is off the beaten track to most visitors. A road runs very close to the shore, however, enabling you to reach the deserted **beaches**. As yet these have somewhat limited facilities, and even the main coastal town, **Paraíso**, is a tiny place.

Much of inland Tabasco is very flat, consisting of the flood plains of a dozen or so major rivers; indeed, most of the state's borders are waterways. Enterprising tour operators are running **boat trips** along the main rivers, the Grijalva and the Usumacinta, which are the best way to see remote ruins and to glimpse the region's abundant birdlife. You can also travel by river into Petén in **Guatemala**, leaving from La Palma, near Tenosique, in the far eastern corner of the state.

In the far south of the state, around **Teapa** and Villa Luz, the Chiapas highlands make their presence known in the foothills known as the **Sierra Puana**. Overlooking the vast Gulf coast plain, these hills offer a retreat from the heat and humidity of the lowlands. Waterfalls spill down from the mountains and a few small spas (*balnearios*) have developed. Village tracks provide some great **hiking trails** and, despite the proximity to Villahermosa, you can enjoy a respite from the well-travelled tourist circuit. Nearby, in the remote **Sierra Huimanguillo**, southwest of Villahermosa, the **Agua Selva Project** is a superb example of ecotourism, aiming to bring small groups of visitors to enjoy these pristine mountains.

Villahermosa itself, the state capital and an almost unavoidable stop, has in recent years undergone an amazing transformation, with oil wealth financing the creation of spacious parks and several museums – the city at last lives up to its name. One excellent example is the **Parque Museo la Venta**, an outdoor archeological exhibition on the bank of a lagoon, which provides a glimpse of the otherwise barely accessible **Olmec** civilization.

Some history

Little is know about the **Olmec culture**, referred to by many archeologists as the mother culture of Mesoamerica. Its legacy of the Long Count calendar, glyphic writing, a rain god deity – and probably also the concept of zero and the ball game – influenced all subsequent civilizations in ancient Mexico, and the fact that it developed and flourished in the unpromising environment of the Gulf coast swamps 3200 years ago only adds to its mystery.

The Spanish conquistador **Hernan Cortés** landed at the mouth of the Río Grijalva in 1519, and at first easily defeated the local **Chontal Maya**. However, the town he founded, Santa María de la Victoria, was beset first by indigenous attacks and then by pirates, eventually forcing a move to the present site and a change of name to Villahermosa de San Juan Bautista in 1596. For most of the colonial period, Tabasco remained a relative backwater, since the Spanish found the humid, insect-ridden swamps distinctly inhospitable. **Independence** did little to improve matters as local leaders fought among themselves, and it took the **French invasion** of 1862 and Napoleon III's imposition of the unfortunate Maximilian as emperor of Mexico to bring some form of unity, with Tabasco offering fierce resistance to this foreign intrusion.

The industrialization of the country during the dictatorship of Porfirio Díaz passed agricultural Tabasco by, and even after the **Revolution** it was still a poor state, dependent on cacao and bananas. Though **Tomás Garrido Canabal**, Tabasco's governor in the 1920s and 1930s, is still respected as a reforming socialist whose implementation of laws regarding workers' rights and women's suffrage was decades ahead of the rest of the country, his period in office was also marked by intense **anticlericalism**. Priests were killed or driven out, all the churches were closed, and many of them, including the cathedral in Villahermosa, torn down. The region's **oil**, discovered in the 1930s but not fully exploited until the 1970s, provided the impetus to bring Tabasco into the modern world, enabling capital to be invested in the agricultural sector and Villahermosa to be transformed into the cultural centre it is today.

Villahermosa and around

VILLAHERMOSA, capital of the state, is a major and virtually unavoidable road junction: sooner or later you're almost bound to pass through here on the way from central Mexico to the Yucatán or back, especially if you hope to see Palenque (see p.130). It's a large and prosperous city, and at first impression it can seem as bad a case of urban blight as any in Mexico. However, the longer you stay, the more compensations you will

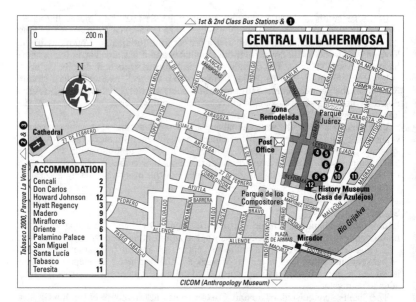

CICOM (Anthropology Museum) ▽

discover: quite apart from the **Parque la Venta**, there are the attractive plazas and quiet ancient streets, impressive ultramodern buildings, and sudden unexpected vistas of the broad sweep of the Río Grijalva. In the evening, as the traffic disperses and the city cools down, it begins to look really appealing, and strolling the pedestrianized streets around the zócalo – the *Zona Remodelada* or *Zona Luz* – where everything stays open late, becomes a genuine pleasure. You can also visit the archeological sites of Comalcalco and La Venta from Villahermosa.

Arrival and information

Arriving **by bus**, things are pretty hectic as the highway thunders through the concrete outskirts of the town and past the two bus stations. These are fairly close to each other: the second-class a busy, ramshackle affair actually on the highway, with constant buses to main destinations; the first-class (always known simply as El ADO – pronounced "El *Ah-day-o*"), an efficient modern building with a *guardería* (7am–11pm), just off the highway on Javier Mina. You'd be well advised to buy your outward ticket on arrival as it can be hard to get a seat on departing buses; you also avoid having to come back here more often than necessary.

From ADO, colectivos run into **the centre** from outside the building. There are also combis aplenty – look out for those labelled "Parque Juárez" or "Malecón". Otherwise, it's at least twenty minutes' walk to town: head up Merino or Fuentes, opposite the station, for six or seven long blocks, and then turn right at Madero, which will eventually get you to the zócalo (Plaza de Armas), past most of the cheap hotels. To get from ADO to the second-class terminal, turn left on Mina, walk three blocks down to the highway, Blvd Adolfo Ruíz Cortines, and cross it on the overpass – you can't miss the terminal. To get into town from **the second-class terminal**, cross the road by the footbridge and turn left to follow the highway by the footbridge to its junction with Madero. Though colectivos are plentiful, it's not easy to work out where they're going; asking a local is the best way to find out.

Taxis can be found at both bus stations, though more easily at ADO. Villahermosa is so humid that you might want to use them to get around town, too, especially since the set fare within the city is only US$1. Plenty of combis also ply the main streets – you'll soon get to recognize the destinations, and the drivers and fellow passengers are helpful.

The most convenient **airport** is the Aeropuerto Carlos A. Rovirosa, east of the centre at Carretera Villahermosa–Palenque Km 13; it's the closest airport to Palenque and consequently very busy with regional flights. No buses run to the centre but there are plenty of taxis, charging around US$7.

Information

Villahermosa's **tourist information** infrastructure is developing slowly. The small booths at the airport and at ADO can offer only a jumble of hotel leaflets, and though you can get hold of some excellent booklets and maps at the main state and federal **tourist office**, out near the modern **Tabasco 2000** shopping and business complex at Paseo Tabasco and Av de los Ríos (Mon–Fri 9am–3pm & 6–9pm; ☎93/16-36-33), it's not clearly signposted and is too far away from the centre to be of much use. There are branches of all major **banks** at the airport and in the centre, on Madero or Juárez, and you can easily change cash and travellers' cheques. The main **post office** is in the *Zona Remodelada* at the corner of Saenz and Lerdo (Mon–Fri 8am–7.30pm). **Travel agencies** are another boom industry, with dozens in the *Zona* and the bigger hotels, all of them arranging flights and trips to Palenque. Downtown, Viajes Villahermosa, 27 de Febrero 207 (☎93/12-54-56, fax 14-37-21), is recommended; while Creatur, Paseo Tabasco 715 (☎93/15-39-99, fax 15-39-88; *creatur@inforedmx.com.mx*), is the best in the region, with multilingual staff.

Accommodation

There are plenty of budget **hotels** along Constitución, and, if you look around carefully, you can find somewhere both comfortable and reasonable in the pedestrianized *Zona Remodelada*, on Madero or Lerdo de Tejada, close to the zócalo. Many budget places have rooms on several floors and most have no lift; bear this in mind as you're sweating with the humidity. In the downtown area it's possible to find rooms for very little, but the very cheapest are distinctly dodgy. The most upmarket hotels are around the Tabasco 2000 complex.

Cencali, Paseo Tabasco and Juárez (☎93/15-19-99, fax 15-66-00). Set in luxuriant gardens on the shore of a lagoon, this has a quiet location and a large inviting pool. ⑦.

Don Carlos, Madero 422 (☎93/12-24-92, fax 12-46-22). Thoroughly modern, comfortable a/c rooms that aren't outrageously expensive. Good restaurant and bar. ⑤.

Howard Johnson, Aldama 404 (☎ & fax 93/14-46-45). Just what you'd expect from the chain: modern, comfortable rooms with a/c and TV. Located in the *Zona Remodelada*, with great views from the rooftop terrace and a luxurious pavement café for reading the papers. ⑥.

Madero, Madero 301 (☎93/12-05-16). The city's best value in this range, with features often not found in a budget hotel; ask for a room away from the street. Private showers and some a/c rooms. ②–③.

Miraflores, Reforma 304 (☎93/12-00-22; fax 12-04-86). Excellent value on a pedestrian street in the heart of the *Zona Remodelada*. Colour TV and phone; a balcony café for people-watching; plus a restaurant and bar. Car rental in the lobby. ⑤.

Oriente, Madero 425 (☎93/12-11-01). Clean, tiled rooms with private bath, some with a/c. ②.

Palomino Palace, across from ADO (☎93/12-84-31). Decent hotel right by the bus station. Usually has rooms available with fan, private shower and TV. Bar and restaurant. ③.

San Miguel, Lerdo de Tejada 315 (☎93/12-15-06). Battered but serviceable rooms with clean sheets and private bath. ②.

Santa Lucía, Madero 418, next to the Don Carlos (☎93/12-24-99). Clean, well-furnished rooms with tiled bathrooms in a modern building. No views but there is a lift. ③.
Tabasco, Lerdo de Tejada 317 (☎93/12-05-64). Basic but good value with plenty of rooms. ②.
Teresita, Constitución 224 (☎93/12-34-53). The nicest budget accommodation along here, quite basic but friendly. Some rooms have private bath; the best are at the back, overlooking the river. ②.

The City

Though most visitors quite rightly head straight out to the Parque la Venta, the centre of Villahermosa warrants some exploration. The pedestrianized **Zona Remodelada**, with some vestiges of the colonial city, is as good a place as any to start your wandering. At its northern end, opposite the Parque Juárez, at the junction of Madero and Zaragoza, the **Centro Cultural de Villahermosa** (daily 10am–9pm; free) has changing exhibitions of art, photography and costume, and is a venue for films and concerts – as well as having an excellent café. The zócalo, **Plaza de Armas**, with its river views, is a pleasant place to while away some time, especially in the cool of the evening. Here, the imposing white-painted **Palacio del Gobierno**, with turrets at the corners, faces the pretty little church of La Concepción. The new footbridge at the corner of the Plaza de Armas allows you to stroll over the river and watch the fireflies glow in the bushes on the bank, and has an enormous mirador for splendid views. Parque Juárez, at the northern end of the *Zona*, is very lively in the evenings as crowds swirl around watching the street entertainers. The pedestrian area fills with window-shoppers enjoying frozen yoghurts or eating out at open-fronted restaurants or one of the many *coctelerias*.

The Casa de Azulejos and CICOM complex

Villahermosa's small **history museum**, at the corner of 27 de Febrero and Juárez (Tues–Sat 9am–8pm; US$0.70), gives a quirky, detailed account of Tabasco's history, illustrated by such diverse objects as an early X-ray machine, the printing press of *El Disidente* newspaper from 1863, together with archeological pieces from Comalcalco and other information on the Maya sites. The turn-of-the-century museum building is popularly known as the "Casa de Azulejos", and indeed there are **tiles** everywhere, forming an optical illusion in the lobby, with examples of patterns from all over Europe and the Middle East. Upstairs, wrought-iron balconies overlook the *Zona*, and above you statues of nymphs and classical figues perch on the railings around the roof.

An easy walk along the river from the *Zona Remodelada* brings you to Villahermosa's cultural centre, **CICOM** (Centro de Investigaciones de las Culturas Olmeca y Maya); small ferry boats cross the river at a couple of places. The complex includes a concert hall, a beautiful theatre, a research library and a fine restaurant, along with the **Centro de Estudios y Investigación de los Belles Artes** (Tues–Sun 10am–4pm; free), which hosts art and costume displays. The highlight for most visitors is undoubtedly the **Museo Regional de Anthropología Carlos Pellicer Cámara** (daily 9am–8pm; US$1.50), with artefacts and models displayed on four levels, in chronological order. In addition to the Olmec and Maya displays, you can also view a reproduction of the Bonampak murals. Carlos Pellicer, a poet and anthropologist born in Villahermosa, and the driving force behind the rescue of the stone carvings from the original La Venta, is commemorated by a bronze statue outside the complex. His house, at C Narcisco Sáenz 203, in the *Zona Remodelada*, has also been turned into a museum, the **Casa Museo Carlos Pellicer** (daily 9am–8pm; free).

Parque la Venta and the Museo de Historia Natural

Soon after they were discovered by Pemex engineers draining a marsh, most of the important finds from the Olmec **site of La Venta** (p.175) – some 120km west of the city, at the border with Veracruz state – were transferred to the **Parque la Venta** (daily 9am–5pm; US$2). Although hardly the exact reproduction it claims to be, Parque la Venta does give you a chance to see a superb collection of artefacts from the earliest Mexican civilization, in the beautiful jungly setting of the Parque Tomás Garrido Canabal.

You should visit the **museum** first, under an enormous thatched roof, to familiarize yourself with the known facts of the Olmec culture. The most significant and famous items are, of course, the gigantic **basalt heads**, which present such a curious puzzle with their flattened, negroid features. There's a whole series of other Olmec stone sculptures; follow the numbers as the path winds through the park. In their zeal to recreate an authentic jungle setting, the designers have deer and coatis (members of the raccoon family) wandering around freely, while crocodiles, jaguars, monkeys and others exist in sizeable enclosures. The mosquitoes are an authentic but unplanned touch.

Also in the park, opposite the entrance, the excellent **Museo de Historia Natural** (daily 9am–8pm; US$1) has displays on geography, geology, animals and plants. The museums are on the shores of a large lake, the Laguna de Ilusiones; you can rent boats or climb the Mirador de los Aguilas, a tower in the lake. **Combis** run to the park from along Madero in the city centre ("Tabasco 2000", "Circuito 1", "Parque Linda Vista" among others) and also along the highway from the second-class bus terminal. Beyond La Venta, many of the buses continue to Tabasco 2000.

Eating and drinking

The number of **restaurants** in Villahermosa has grown over the last few years, and some of the new ones are truly cosmopolitan. Most of the better hotels have improved their own dining rooms and, if you're staying near Tabasco 2000, your hotel restaurant will be among the best in the city.

Both **bus stations** have plenty of food joints nearby. Inside the second-class there are juice and coffee bars, a good bread shop and a less good restaurant. Across the street from ADO there's a row of inexpensive places, of which the *Café Turistico* is best. The *Bar Neptuno*, half a block from ADO down Fuentes, is great to while away some time if you're waiting for a bus. The sign on the door says "Turistico", but the atmosphere is distinctly Mexican, with live music and slow service. Women are admitted, though it's probably best not to go alone. As ever, the **market** is good for fruit, bread and cheap tacos: you'll find it several blocks east of the *Zona Remodelada*, at Pino Suárez and Zozoya. *Aquarius*, Zaragoza 513, behind the Parque Juárez, is an excellent **vegetarian restaurant** and **health food shop**, with delicious fresh wholemeal sandwiches and daily specials.

The best place in the *Zona* for an inexpensive, filling meal **at lunchtime** is the buffet at *La Bodegita del Centro*, on Lerdo, near the corner with Madero, where you choose from a variety of taco fillings, washed down with *horchata*, a vanilla or almond-flavoured rice drink. Or try the popular *El Tortito Valenzuela*, on the corner of 27 de Febrero and Madero, for filling tacos and tortas. *Café La Cabaña*, at the end of Juárez near the *Casa de los Azulejos*, serves good but pricey coffee in a prime location. Even better, and less touristy, is the *Café Selecto*, round the corner on 27 de Febrero, past the corner with Hidalgo, where you get great *pan dulces* in an arty atmosphere.

Beyond here, at the junction of Paseo Tabasco and the malecón, there are several **taco restaurants**, some of them quite fancy. More restaurants line Paseo Tabasco at intervals all the way up to the junction with Mina. Head up this way if you want to sample the best of *comida Tabasqueña* at the *Guaraguao*, on the corner of 27 de Febrero and Javier Mina (☎93/12-56-25). Specialities from the coasts and rivers of Tabasco include *pejelargarto*, a type of alligator gar (a pike-like fish, common to Tabasco's rivers), and great seafood. It closes early, though, about 8.30 or 9pm.

MOVING ON FROM VILLAHERMOSA

Villahermosa being the state capital, you should have no problems getting an **onward bus**. To get to the first-class terminal take a "Chedraui" combi – they go to a huge department store behind the terminal. Between them, ADO and Cristóbal Colón operate dozens of services to all the main destinations: Tuxtla (7hr), Veracruz (7hr), Tenosique (3hr), Mérida (9hr), Campeche (6hr), Cancún (12hr), Chetumal (7hr), Oaxaca (9hr), Mexico City (12hr), and even the US border and Pacific coast. From ADO there are several departures to **Palenque** (2hr 30min) and you can also easily get to Palenque from the second-class terminal, from where there are constant departures to all the same destinations, plus Comalcalco, Paraíso and Frontera. For **San Cristóbal** (8–9hr) there are a few direct services; otherwise change at either Tuxtla or Palenque. The **airport** is a major regional hub, served by dozens of flights throughout Mexico.

Comalcalco ruins

The Classic period site of **Comalcalco** (daily 8am–5pm; US$1.50) is an easy and worthwhile trip from Villahermosa and you can be fairly sure of having the carefully tended ruins virtually to yourself. The westernmost Maya site, Comalcalco was occupied around the same time as Palenque, with which it shares some features, and may even have been ruled by some of the same kings.

The area's lack of building stone forced the Chontal Maya to adopt a distinctive, almost unique, form of construction – kiln-fired brick (the site's name means house of bricks in Nauhatl). As if the bricks themselves were not sufficient to mark this site as different, the builders added mystery to technology: each brick was stamped with a geometric or representational design before firing, and the design was deliberately placed facing inwards, so that it could not be seen in the finished building.

There's a small **museum** at the site, and a restaurant. Take water with you, though, since the humidity is extremely high. If you're going to venture into the long grass or bushes, insect repellent is a must.

The **bus from Villahermosa** takes an hour and a quarter: ADO has several departures a day, and Transportes Somellera runs a service every thirty minutes from the second-class station. Both bus stations in Comalcalco are on Gregorio Méndez; walk the 150m back to the highway and catch a combi heading north (left) towards **Paraíso**. The ruins are on the right (signposted) after about five minutes. Some combis go all the way there; otherwise, the site is fifteen minutes' walk up the track, past some houses and a cacao plantation. If you get stuck in Comalcalco, there are a few basic **hotels** near the bus stations.

The site

Though there are dozens of structures, only around ten or so of the larger buildings have been subjected to any restoration. The first one you come to is the main structure of the **North Plaza Cluster**: Temple I, a tiered pyramid with a massive central stairway. Originally, the whole building (along with all of the structures here) would have been covered with stucco, sculpted into masks and reliefs of rulers and deities, and brightly painted. Now only a few of these features are left, the exposed ones protected from further erosion by thatched shelters, while some are deliberately left buried.

Opposite Temple I is the **Great Acropolis**: more mounds, mainly grass-covered, though there's a fine stucco mask of Kinich Ahau, the Maya sun god. Due to the fragile nature of the brick you're not allowed to climb most of the temples, but if you walk to the far end of the complex you'll come to **El Palacio**, where you can climb the mound and get a close view of the brickwork. There's a series of small arches here, faintly reminiscent of English Victorian railway architecture. You'll also get a good overview of the whole site, including many other mounds in the surrounding forest and farmland. **Cacao**, used as money by the Maya, is grown in the area, and you'll pass cacao bushes on the way in, their huge green bean pods sprouting straight from the trunk.

La Venta

The small town of **LA VENTA**, on the border between Tabasco and Veracruz, would be of little interest were it not for the **archeological site** (daily 10am–4.30pm; US$1.50, free Sun), where the huge Olmec heads displayed in Villahermosa were discovered. In the **museum** at the entrance, models show where the site was located, in a swamp surrounded by rivers, while glass cases are filled with unlabelled bits of pottery. Information panels on the wall give a good explanation of Olmec culture and history. The site itself has a few weathered stelae or monuments, but the highlight is the huge grass-covered mound, about 30m high – clearly a pyramid. The climb up is worth the effort for the views and the breeze. Paths below take you through the jungle – fascinating for plants and butterflies but haunted by ferocious mosquitoes.

La Venta is served by a steady stream of **buses** to Villahermosa and Coatzalcoalcos, so there's no need **to stay**; the *Hotel del Sol* (②), on the corner of the small plaza, is a friendly, pleasant option if you get stuck.

The Sierra Huimanguillo and the Agua Selva Project

More than 100km southwest of Villahermosa, between the borders of Veracruz and Chiapas, a narrow triangle of Tabasco thrusts into the highlands. Known as the **Sierra Huimanguillo**, from the town in the lowlands just to the north, this little-visited corner of the state is the focus of the **Agua Selva Ecotourism Project**. Designed to bring the benefits of small-scale tourism to the *ejidos* of the area through building cabañas and *albergues* in the villages, the project aims to bring economic benefits without sacrificing the abundant natural attractions. The mountains here are not that high, only up to 1000m, but they are rugged, and to appreciate them at their best you have to hike; not only to caves, canyons and waterfalls, but also to the **Zoque** ruins of Malpasito, with their astonishing **petroglyphs**.

Visiting the Agua Selva Project, you'll have to pass through **HUIMANGUILLO**, a mid-sized town 75km southwest of Villahermosa. Buses leave Villahermosa frequently during the day; if there isn't a direct one, go second-class to **Cárdenas** and change there. ADO buses stop right in the centre, on Escobar, half a block south of the plaza. Second-class buses arrive at the terminal on Gutiérrez, near the market, five blocks west along Libertad from the town centre. The bus for **Malpasito** leaves at 1pm (2hr 30min), returning from the village at 5am.

In the centre of town, the *Hotel del Carmen* on Morelos 39, two blocks south of the plaza (✆ & fax 937/5-09-15; ③) offers **accommodation** and **information**, with large well-furnished rooms, all with private bath. Downstairs, the *Cafétería Orquidias* serves good Mexican food, which you can eat surrounded by photographs of the mountains and waterfalls in the *sierra*. The owner, George Pagole del Valle, a leading light in the Agua Selva project, will be able to supply information and may even give you a lift if he's heading for Malpasito.

Malpasito and the Zoque ruins

Beyond Huimanguillo the road to Malpasito heads south, following the valley of the **Río Grijalva** (here called the Mezcalapa) for 60km, crossing into Chiapas at one point, before heading west onto a dirt road for 15km to reach the *ejido*.

By now you can see the peaks, with the great jungle-covered plateau of El Mono Pelón ("the bald monkey") dominating the skyline. This is the highest point in Tabasco, and the sheer sides look impossible to climb. In **MALPASITO** you can stay right by the river, in the simple, three-room *Albergue Ecológico* (②), managed by the Peréz Rincón family; you can eat with them or at the table by the river. Drinking and cooking water is piped in from a spring, pure and fresh, but you bathe in the river. Higher up, and nearer the waterfalls, the plusher *Albergue La Pava* (⑤, including meals) consists of large, oval thatched cabañas with bamboo sides, some with two storeys, giving you a bird's-eye view into the surrounding forest. The dirt road from Malpasito comes to within half a kilometre of the cabañas, then it's a forty-minute walk over a suspension bridge and along the side of a gorge between moss-covered boulders. This is an utterly beautiful, tranquil place, perfect for enjoying the abundant wildlife.

The ruins

A walk of just over 1km from the *albergue* in Malpasito brings you to the Postclassic **Zoque** ruins of the same name, overlooked by jagged, jungle-covered mountains and reminiscent of Palenque (see p.130). The Zoque, however, were not a Maya group, and little is known about them today. On the way in, you pass terraces and grass-covered mounds, eventually leading to the unusual **ball court**. At the top of the stone terraces forming the south side of the court a flight of steps leads down to a narrow room, with stone benches lining either side. Beyond this, and separate from the chamber, is a square pit 1.5m square and more than 2m deep. This room may have been used by the ball players, or at least one team, to effect a spectacular entrance as they emerged on to the top of the ball court. Beyond the ball court a grass-covered plaza leads to two flights of wide steps and another small plaza at the top, giving stunning views of mountains all around.

Perhaps the most amazing feature of this site are the **petroglyphs**. More than three hundred have been discovered so far: animals, birds, houses and what are presumably religious symbols etched into the rock. One large boulder has the most enigmatic of all: flat-topped triangles surmounted by a square or rectangle, and shown above what look like ladders or steps – possibly stylized houses or launching platforms for the chariots of the gods. The trail leads on to a clear pool beneath a 12m waterfall – too good to miss if the hike around the ruins has left you hot and dirty. More trails lead up into the mountains; one relatively easy one leads to the base of La Pava, on almost perpendicular pillars of rock; the top of it is said to resemble the head of a turkey.

Francisco J. Mujica and the Cascada Velo de Novia

Another *ejido* in the Agua Selva Project, **Francisco J. Mujica**, 18km northeast of Malpasito, has simple accommodation at the *Cabaña Raizes Zoque* (②). There's no public transport (though this could change soon), but it's connected by dirt road to Hwy-187 south of Huimanguillo, and you could get directions there or in Malpasito.

The hills around here are superb for walking and scrambling around canyons, and few outsiders have ever been here. The hills are also full of caves, many containing petroglyphs. To venture to the most scenic parts you'll need a guide – easily arranged by the *ejido*. An hour-long hike from Mujica takes you over several rivers, beyond the milpas, to **Cascada Velo de Novia** (Bridal Veil Falls) and to the edge of an enormous

PETER WILSON

Tulum, Quintana Roo, Mexico

JERRY DENNIS

Caracol observatory, Chichén Itzá, Mexico

JERRY DENNIS

El Castilo, Chichén Itzá, Mexico

Coral and diver, Caribbean coast, Mexico

Maize harvest, Chajul, Guatemala

Belltower, Izamal, Mexico

Pyramid of the Magician, Uxmal, Mexico

Fiesta costume, Guatemala

Temple of Five Levels, Edzna, Mexico

Main plaza and Agua volcano, Antigua, Guatemala

Maya fiddle player, Mexico

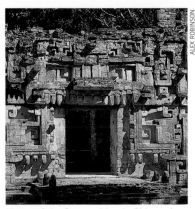
House of the Serpent Mouth, Chicanná

Vallodolid cenote, Yucatán, Mexico

canyon. The hike entails descending about 300m down an extremely steep slope – the guide will have a rope, but you'll still need to clutch at tree roots for support – then walking along a narrow rock ledge at the side of the river to get beneath the thundering cascade. Below the falls, the river winds between huge boulders before plunging over the edge of a sheer-sided, semicircular **gorge**. The only way out is to clamber up the way you came in.

Teapa and the southern hills

An hour's bus ride through banana country to the south of Villahermosa, the small, friendly town of **TEAPA** is a lovely base for the spas and caves nearby. Cristóbal Colón **buses** leave Villahermosa for Tuxtla every couple of hours, calling at Teapa, though buses back are *de paso* and it may be difficult to get a seat. Though some second-class buses stop at the terminal on Méndez, right in the centre, most pull in at the **market** (plenty of good fruit stalls) near the edge of town. To get to the centre, walk a couple of blocks down the hill and turn left at the green clock onto Méndez, which takes you past the hotels and onto the plaza. Teapa's **hotels** are good value: try the *Casa de Huéspedes Miye* (☎932/2-04-20; ②), a clean, family-run place with private showers and (sometimes) hot water, with rooms round a tiny plant-filled courtyard.

There's **swimming** in the Río Teapa here, but it's better at the *balneario* on the Río Puyacatengo, a few kilometres east (walk or take the bus for Tacotalpa). Six kilometres west of Teapa, almost on the Chiapas border, is the **El Azufre Spa**, where for a small fee you can bathe in clear pools or take the waters in the sulphur pool. **Camping** is free and there's a small restaurant. Again you can get here on foot, or catch a second-class bus towards **Pichucalco**. Colectivos run from the plaza in Teapa to the spectacular **Grutas de Coconá** (daily 8am–4pm; US$0.35). Eight chambers are open to tourists, and some for spelunking only. A stroll through the caves takes about 45 minutes. In one chamber there's a supposedly miraculous representation of the face of Christ, carved by nature into the rock. You could also walk (45min) to the caves from Teapa: from Méndez, head for the Pemex station and turn right, following the sign. When you get near the forested hills, the road divides; head left over the railway track.

The Sierra Puana: Tapijulapa and Oxolotán

Southeast from Teapa, you can get further away from the humidity of the lowlands by taking day-trips up the valley of the Río Oxolotán to Tabasco's "hill country". This is an extraordinarily picturesque area, with unspoilt colonial towns set in beautiful wooded valleys, and a turquoise river laden with sulphur cascading over terraced cliffs. You'll need to get a fairly early start to make the most of the day. The 6.30am bus to **Tacotalpa** from the second-class station on Méndez in Teapa (20min) connects with one to **TAPI-JULAPA**, the main settlement (45min), in time to have breakfast in the *Restaurant Mariquita*, in the corner of the shady plaza. The town is tiny, with narrow cobbled streets, red-tiled roofs and, unfortunately, no accommodation. Turn right at the end of the main street, Av López Portillo, where steps lead down to the Río Oxolotán. Here you may find boats to take you upstream to visit the **Parque Natural Villa Luz**, with its spa pools, rivers, cascades and caves. There are more boats during holidays, but it's easy enough to walk to the park: cross the tributary river on the suspension bridge, head left on the concrete path, across the football field, then follow the track over the hill, keeping close to the main river – about 35 minutes in all.

In the park (open daily; free), signed trails lead to caves, but the outstanding feature – not least for its powerful aroma – is the river, which owes its colour to dissolved minerals, especially sulphur. The Río Oxolotán exits from a cave and meanders for 1km or so until it reaches the cliff marking the river valley. Here it breaks up into dozens of cascades and semicircular pools. Thousands of butterflies settle on the riverbanks, taking nourishment from dissolved minerals, and jungle trees and creepers grow wherever they find a foothold. The **caves** are not really open to the public, but you can peer into their precipitous entrances; in Maya cosmology the openings are believed to lead to the underworld (*Xibalba*) and the abode of the Lords of Death. Beyond the caves are a couple of open-air **swimming pools** said to have therapeutic properties.

OXOLOTÁN is only 25 minutes from Tapijulapa and trucks and combis make the trip frequently. Here the ruins of a seventeenth-century Franciscan monastery host performances by the *Teatro Campesino y Indígena* (The Peasant and Indigenous Theatre), a company that has taken part in cultural festivals throughout Mexico and abroad. If you're in the area when a performance is scheduled, it's worth making an effort to go. **To get there from Tapijulapa**, climb the hill to the church, then descend to the road beyond, where there's a bus stop. The last bus back leaves at 6pm, but you're probably better off catching the 3pm bus if you're heading to Teapa.

East to the Usumacinta and Guatemala

Heading east from Villahermosa, Hwy-186 cuts across a salient of northern Chiapas before swinging north into Campeche to Francisco Escárcega, then east again as the only road across the base of the Yucatán peninsula to Chetumal. At Catazajá, in Chiapas, 110km from Villahermosa, is the junction for Palenque. If you've been there and want to see **Tikal** in Guatemala's Petén, the most direct route is via **Tenosique** on the **Río Usumacinta** (perhaps visiting the ruins of Pomoná en route), and on to **La Palma** on the **Río San Pedro**, then by boat upriver to **El Naranjo**, in Guatemala (see p.421). Several travel agencies in Palenque run minibuses to La Palma but it's very easy to do it yourself, though the journey always involves at least one very early start.

Coming from either Palenque or Villahermosa, you'll pass through the dull town of **EMILIANO ZAPATA**, hopefully only to change buses. The **bus stations** are in the same building on the edge of the town and there are plenty of first- and second-class services to Villahermosa and Tenosique, tailing off rapidly in the evening. If you do get stuck, try the *Hotel Ramos* (☎934/3-07-44; ③), opposite the bus station, which is at least comfortable and saves you going into town. It also has the only proper **travel agent** for a long way: Creatur (☎ & fax 934/3-15-30).

Tenosique

The Río Usumacinta is crossed by the road and railway at Boca del Cerro, a few kilometres from **TENOSIQUE**, where the now placid river leaves some pretty impressive hills. **Buses** arrive at a small terminal close to the highway, just out of town. Inexpensive colectivos run frequently to the centre; get off when you see a large white church with blue trim on the right of the main street, C 26 (also known as C Pino Suárez). If you have **to stay**, the *Azulejos* (②), opposite the church, has friendly staff; slightly better is the *Rome* (☎934/2-01-51; ②), a block closer to the plaza, on C 28.

If you're staying overnight and you've exhausted what limited sightseeing Tenosique has to offer (such as visiting the house where Pino Suárez was born and admiring his bust and monument), you'll want to head for the zócalo and calles 26 and 28, the main areas for shopping and **eating**. There's a juice bar which prepares good licuados on the corner of the plaza, a good coffee shop just past the plaza on C 28 and, opposite, the **market**, with a row of inexpensive comedores. *La Palapa* restaurant overlooks the broad river, where the boat traffic heads constantly back and forth.

If you're going to Guatemala you'd be wise to stock up on provisions: there's a good **bakery** opposite the *Hotel Rome* and fruit stalls everywhere. The banks in Tenosique aren't interested in changing money, but Bancomer has an ATM. For **Guatemalan**

quetzales ask around in the shops on C 28 where you should find someone who will give better rates than the boatmen. **Moving on**, there are plenty of bus services to Villahermosa during the day, a first-class service to Mexico City at 5pm and a 6pm bus to Escárcega and points east, with services finishing off around 7pm.

Pomoná ruins

On the road from Emiliano Zapata, about 30km west of Tenosique the ruins of **Pomoná** (daily 8am–4pm) are reached 4km down a signed track; ask the bus driver to drop you off. Although the site, located in rolling countryside with views of forested hills to the south, makes a pleasant diversion, a visit is really only for the dedicated. The restored structures date from the Late Classic period; the site's largest building is a stepped pyramid with six levels and there are several smaller ones. Pomoná was a subject of the much larger city of Piedras Negras (p.421), further up the valley of the Usumacinta. The modern little **museum** houses some interesting carved panels and stelae – made even more mysterious by the complete omission of any explanations of what you're seeing.

La Palma and the Río San Pedro to Guatemala

Buses for **LA PALMA** leave Tenosique every two hours from 4.30am to 4.30pm; there's no terminal, just follow C 31 down the side of the church for five blocks. They head due east through flat farming and ranching country and after an hour reach the Río San Pedro, stopping at the *Parador Turístico* restaurant, by the dock for the **boat trip to El Naranjo**. The usual departure time is 8am, returning at 1pm from El Naranjo (4hr; US$20), but you may have to wait until sufficient passengers turn up. The trip is interesting, but frankly overpriced, and if you want to take a river route to Guatemala you'll see far more (and better) Maya sites crossing to **Bethél**, and visting Bonampak (see p.136) and Yaxchilán (see p.138) en route to Flores. There are some basic **rooms** at La Palma; ask at the restaurant.

If you're **entering Mexico** here you might just be in time for the last bus to Tenosique; if not you'll probably be offered an overpriced truck ride. Bear in mind that the last buses onward from Tenosique leave around 7pm. **Leaving for Guatemala** you hand in your Mexican tourist card at the immigration post at El Pedregal, about halfway through the journey. Border formalities are hardly rigorous, though your luggage might be searched on leaving Mexico, and possibly again by the Guatemalan army on arrival at **EL NARANJO** (see p.421), where the immigration official will usually demand a fee.

Entry to Guatemala is free for most Europeans; North Americans may be asked to buy a tourist card (US$5). There's a small, basic hotel and restaurant, the *Quetzal* (②), overlooking the river in El Naranjo, and 1km upstream from the ferry in the town proper, the *Posada San Pedro* has rustic bungalows (③); alternatively, no one will mind if you **camp**. Just up from the riverbank are some large, overgrown **ruins** with the bigger pyramids surmounted by machine-gun posts. At least five daily **buses** leave El Naranjo for **Flores** (4hr 30min; US$4).

travel details

Buses

Departures given are for first-class services; there are likely to be at least as many second-class buses to the same destinations.

Palenque to: Campeche (3 daily; 6hr); Cancún (3 daily; 12hr) Mérida (3 daily; 9hr); México (2 daily; 16hr) San Cristóbal (hourly; 5hr); Tuxtla Gutiérrez (hourly; 7hr); Villahermosa (at least 8 daily; 2hr

30min). Plenty of second-class buses run along the Carretera Frontera for the junctions to **Bonampak** and **Yaxchilán**.

San Cristóbal to: Ciudad Cuauhtémoc, for Guatemala (at least 8 daily; 3hr 30min); Comitán, for Lagos de Montebello or the Guatemalan border (at least hourly; 2hr); México (5 daily; 20hr); Palenque (9 daily; 5hr); Tapachula (4 daily; 9hr);

Tuxtla Gutiérrez (constantly; 2hr); Villahermosa; some direct, otherwise via Tuxtla or Palenque (6 daily; 8-9hr).

Tuxtla Gutiérrez to: Ciudad Cuauhtémoc, for Guatemala (6 daily; 6hr); Comitán, for Lagos de Montebello or the Guatemalan border (hourly; 4hr); Mérida (4 daily; 14 hr); México (at least 9 daily; 16hr); Palenque (hourly; 7hr); San Cristóbal (first-class hourly, others constantly; 2hr); Tapachula (15 daily; 7hr); Tonalá (hourly; 3hr 30min); Villahermosa (9 daily; 7hr).

Tapachula to: Arriaga (12 daily; 4hr); México (10 daily; 18hr); Oaxaca (1 daily; 12hr); San Cristóbal (2 daily; 9hr); Tuxtla Gutiérrez (15 daily; 7hr); Veracruz (1 daily; 14hr); Villahermosa (2 daily; 13hr).

Villahermosa to: Campeche (at least 12 daily; 6hr); Cancún (5 daily; 12hr); Chetumal (5 daily; 7hr); Mérida (at least 12 daily; 9hr), México (at least hourly; 11hr); Palenque (8 daily; 2hr 30min); San Cristóbal; some direct, otherwise via Tuxtla or Palenque (6 daily; 8–9hr); Tapachula (2 daily; 13hr); Tuxtla Gutiérrez (9 daily; 7hr); Veracruz (12 daily; 7hr).

International Buses

Tapachula to: Guatemala City: (2 daily at 9am & 2pm; 5–6hr).

International Boats

La Palma (near Tenosique) to **El Naranjo**, Guatemala (1 daily; 4hr).

Frontera Corozal (Yaxchilán) to **Bethél**, Guatemala (several daily, no schedule; 30min).

Planes

Air services throughout the region are expanding as new airports open up, and services will almost certainly have increased from those listed in the text. For the latest information check with one of the recommended travel agents mentioned in the text.

Villahermosa has several daily flights to the capital, but there are also daily direct services from Tuxtla Gutiérrez, Ciudad del Carmen, Coatzacoalcos and Tapachula. Aerocaribe (☎93/16-31-32 in Villahermosa) has scheduled services between Palenque, San Cristóbal, Flores (Guatemala), Mérida and Cancún.

Servicios Aéreos San Cristóbal, based in Ocosingo (☎967/3-10-88) operates **light aircraft** – from Palenque or San Cristóbal to Yaxchilán or Bonampak, for example.

PART THREE

BELIZE

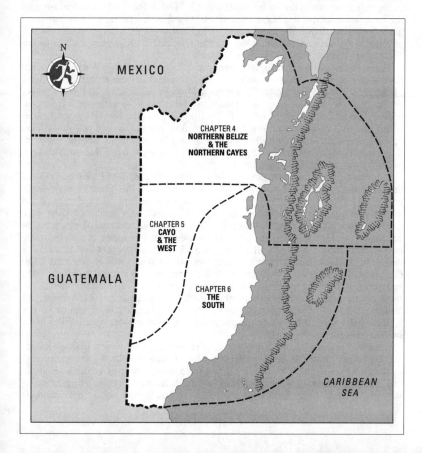

MEXICO

CHAPTER 4
NORTHERN BELIZE
& THE
NORTHERN CAYES

CHAPTER 5
CAYO
& THE WEST

GUATEMALA

CHAPTER 6
THE SOUTH

CARIBBEAN SEA

INTRODUCTION

Wedged in by the Yucatán peninsula to the north and the forests of Petén to the west, **Belize** offers some of the most breathtaking coastal scenery – both above and below water – anywhere in the Maya World. Add to this magnificent inland landscapes, Maya ruins and wildlife to rival any destination in the region, and it's easy to see why the number of visitors to this tiny country increases every year. Despite its small size – roughly that of Wales or Massachusetts – Belize has the lowest population density in Central America, a fact that contributes to its easygoing, friendly and, with the exception of bustling Belize City, noticeably uncrowded character. With far less of a language barrier to overcome than elsewhere in the region, Belize's numerous small hotels and restaurants, and reliable public transport, make it an ideal place to travel independently, offering visitors plenty of scope to explore the heartland of the ancient Maya. Though largely independent since the break-up of the Maya civilization in around 900 AD, Belize's early history is impossible to separate from that of the surrounding areas in Mexico and Guatemala, and some of the most fascinating of the **Maya sites** can be found here. Traces of the culture have been discovered all over the country and, though only a few sites have been as restored as those in the Yucatán, many are just as extensive, and in their forest settings you're likely to see more wildlife and fewer tour buses.

Today, Belize is the only **English-speaking** country in the Maya World, as much a Caribbean nation as a Latin one, with a blend of cultures and races that includes Maya, Mestizo, African and European. The **modern Maya** in Belize are from three separate groups: Yucatec, who fled from the Caste Wars in the mid-nineteenth century; Mopan, who arrived in southern and western Belize from Petén in the late 1800s; and Kekchí who came to Toledo in southern Belize from Alta Verapaz around the same time. Spanish is at least as widely spoken as English, but the rich, lilting **Creole**, based on English but typically Caribbean, is the language understood and used by every Belizean, whatever their native tongue.

Belizean territory comprises marginally more sea than land, and for many visitors the sea is the main attraction. Lying just offshore is one of the country's most astonishing natural wonders – the dazzling turquoise shallows and cobalt depths of the longest **barrier reef** in the Americas. Beneath the surface, a brilliant, technicolour world of fish and corals awaits divers and snorkellers, while scattered along the entire reef, like emeralds set in sapphire, a chain of islands, known as **cayes**, protect the mainland from the ocean swell and offer more than a hint of tropical paradise. Beyond the reef lie the real jewels in Belize's natural crown – three of only four **coral atolls** in the Caribbean. Dawn here is a truly unforgettable experience, as the red-gold disk of the sun glides up over the foaming white reef crest. These reefs and islands, among the most diverse marine ecosystems on the planet, are increasingly under threat, but Belize is at the forefront of practical research to develop effective protection for the entire coastal zone; for visitors, this means a chance to explore some of the finest **marine reserves** in the world.

Belizeans' recognition of the importance of conserving their natural heritage means that the country now has the greatest proportion of **protected land** (over 35 percent) in the hemisphere. As a result, the **densely forested interior** remains relatively untouched, boasting abundant natural attractions, including the region's highest waterfall and the world's only **jaguar reserve**. Rich tropical forests support a tremendous range of **wildlife**, including howler and spider monkeys, tapirs and pumas, jabiru storks and scarlet macaws; spend any time inland and you're sure to see the national bird, the unmistakeable keel-billed toucan.

The rugged, almost impenetrable **Maya Mountains**, rising to over 1100m, dominate Belize's south-central region. This is where the country's main rivers rise, flowing north and east to the Caribbean. The ancient Maya grew rich on cacao (used as currency) grown in these valleys and developed powerful city-states by controlling river and coastal trade routes. Over the millennia, the rivers and their tributaries have dissolved the limestone bedrock to form some of the largest **cave systems** in the Americas. Few of these have been fully investigated, though all the ones explored so far contain numerous **Maya ceremonial artefacts**. All the caves are registered archeological sites and each year more become accessible to visitors.

Almost every visitor will have to spend at least some time in **Belize City**, even if only passing through, as it's the hub of the country's transport system. First-time visitors may be shocked initially by the decaying buildings and the pollution of the river, but it is nonetheless possible to spend several pleasant hours in this former outpost of the British Empire. In contrast, Belize's capital, **Belmopan**, is primarily an administrative centre, with little to offer visitors.

Northern Belize is relatively flat and often swampy, with a large proportion of agricultural land, though as everywhere in Belize there are **Maya ruins** and **nature reserves**. In the northwest, adjacent to the Guatemalan border, is the vast **Rio Bravo Conservation Area**, where hunting has been banned for over a decade, allowing unusually close encounters with the wildlife. The forests here hide dozens of Maya sites, the largest of which, **La Milpa**, is just one of many in the country currently being examined by archeological teams. **Lamanai**, near Orange Walk, is one of the most impressive Maya sites in the country, while the lagoons at **Sarteneja** (Shipstern Nature Reserve) on the northeast coast and inland at **Crooked Tree** provide superb protected habitats for wildlife, particularly birds.

The mainland coast is almost entirely low-lying and swampy – wonderful for wildlife, but for swimming and underwater activities you need to visit the **cayes**, the largest of which, **Ambergris Caye**, draws over half of all tourists to Belize, with the tiny resort town of **San Pedro** their main destination. Here, in **Bacalar Chico National Park**, you can wander around the ports of the ancient Maya. **Caye Caulker**, to the south, is the most popular of the islands with independent travellers. Many of the other cayes are becoming easier to reach, and organized day-trips are available for divers and snorkellers to **Turneffe Islands** and **Lighthouse Reef** atolls.

In the west, **San Ignacio** has everything the ecotourist could want: Maya ruins and rainforest, rivers and caves, and excellent accommodation in every price range. On the way here you should make every effort to visit what is one of the two best **zoos** in the Maya region (the other being in Tuxtla Gutiérrez). **Caracol**, the largest Maya site in Belize, is now a routine day-trip from San Ignacio, and the magnificent ruin of **Xunantunich** is just to the west, on the way to the Guatemalan border. Right on the border (and extending across it) is **El Pilar**, the largest Maya site in the Belize River valley.

Dangriga, the main town of the south-central region, serves as a jumping-off point for visitors to the central cayes and atolls (little developed at present, but becoming more accessible every year) and for trips to the **Cockscomb Basin Wildlife Sanctuary**. Further down the coast, the quiet Garífuna village of **Hopkins** sees more visitors every year, and the delightful, laid-back **Placencia**, at the tip of a long, curving peninsula, has some of the country's best **beaches**. Most visitors to **Punta Gorda**, the main town of Toledo District, are on their way to or from **Puerto Barrios** in Guatemala by boat. Venture inland, however, and you'll find the villages of the **Mopan** and **Kekchí**

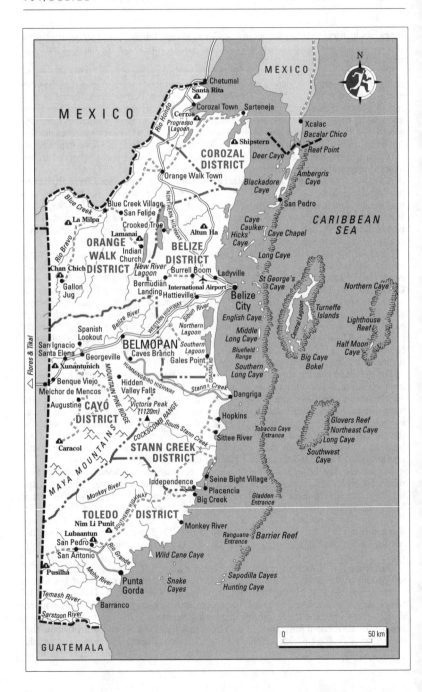

N

MEXICO

Chetumal
Santa Rita
Corozal Town
Sarteneja
Cerros
Rio Hondo
Progresso Lagoon

Xcalac
Bacalar Chico
Reef Point

COROZAL DISTRICT
Shipstern
Deer Caye

Orange Walk Town
Blackadore Caye
Ambergris Caye

San Pedro

CARIBBEAN SEA

Blue Creek Village
San Felipe
Crooked Tree
Blue Creek
La Milpa
Lamanai
Indian Church
ORANGE WALK DISTRICT
Chan Chich
Gallon Jug

Altun Ha
Caye Caulker
Hicks Caye
Caye Chapel

BELIZE DISTRICT
New River Lagoon
Burrell Boom
Ladyville
Long Caye

Bermudian Landing
International Airport
Hattieville
St George's Caye

Belize City

Northern Caye

Rio Bravo

Spanish Lookout
Belize River
WESTERN HIGHWAY
Sibun River
English Caye
Middle Long Caye
Central Lagoon
Turneffe Islands
Lighthouse Reef

San Ignacio
Santa Elena
Georgeville
BELMOPAN
Caves Branch
Northern Lagoon
Southern Lagoon
Bluefield Range
Half Moon Caye

Flores & Tikal

Xunantunich
HUMMINGBIRD HIGHWAY
Gales Point
Southern Long Caye
Big Caye Bokel

Benque Viejo
Melchor de Mencos
Hidden Valley Falls
MOUNTAIN PINE RIDGE
Stann Creek
Dangriga

Augustine
CAYO DISTRICT
Victoria Peak (1120m)
COCKSCOMB RANGE
South Stann Creek
Hopkins
Glovers Reef
Northeast Caye
Long Caye

Caracol
MAYA MOUNTAINS
Sittee River
Tobacco Caye Entrance
Southwest Caye

STANN CREEK DISTRICT

Independence
Seine Bight Village
Placencia
Big Creek
Gladden Entrance

Monkey River
SOUTHERN HIGHWAY
TOLEDO DISTRICT

Nim Li Punit
Monkey River
Ranguana Entrance
Barrier Reef

Lubaantun
San Pedro
Rio Grande
Wild Cane Caye

San Antonio
Moho River
Sapodilla Cayes
Hunting Caye

Pusilhá
Punta Gorda
Snake Cayes

Temash River
Barranco

Sarstoon River

GUATEMALA

0   50 km

Maya, set in some of the most stunning countryside in Belize and surrounded by the only true **rainforest** in the country. Here are yet more caves, rivers and ruins, including **Lubaantun**, source of the enigmatic Crystal Skull.

Some history

Exactly how Belize came by its name is something of a mystery; it could be a corruption of "Wallace", the name either of a notorious English pirate who is reputed to have landed here in 1638, or of Peter Wallace, a Scotsman who may have founded a colony here in 1620. However, those preferring a more ancient origin believe the name to be derived from the **Maya** term *belekin*, meaning "towards the east".

The general assumption that Belize was practically deserted by the time Europeans arrived is now widely discredited. The Maya population in 1500 AD is estimated to have been around 200,000 — almost as high as it is today — and the Maya towns and provinces were still vigorously independent, as the Spanish found to their cost on several occasions. Although the Maya had abandoned their central cities by the tenth century, the political entity of Xunantunich survived to about 1000 AD, albeit in a fairly primitive state. The Maya cities in northern Belize also survived and indeed prospered, with Lamanai, amongst others, remaining occupied throughout the **Postclassic** period (850–1540 AD) and beyond.

From the Early Postclassic to the time of the Spanish Conquest, the Yucatán peninsula and northern Belize consisted of over a dozen rival provinces, bound up in a cycle of competition and conflict. Northern Belize was part of the wealthy, independent Maya province of **Chactemal** (later Chetumal), with its capital possibly being Santa Rita, near Corozal. Chetumal was a wealthy province producing cacao and honey, while trade, alliances and wars kept it in contact with surrounding Maya states up to and beyond the Spanish conquest of Aztec Mexico. Further south in Belize was the province known to the Maya of Chetumal as Dzuluinicob ("Land of Foreigners"), whose capital, **Tipu**, lay on the Macal River south of San Ignacio.

The first contact with **Europeans** was in 1511, when shipwrecked Spanish sailors landed on the southern coast of Yucatán: five were immediately sacrificed, and the others taken as slaves. When Spanish envoys came to ask for the release of their countrymen, one of them, **Gonzalo Guerrero**, refused to go, preferring life among his former captors. He had married the daughter of the chief of Chetumal, adopting Maya ways, and later became a crucial military adviser to the Maya in their resistance to the Spanish. His knowledge of Spanish tactics meant that attempts in the 1520s and 1530s to subdue the Maya of Chetumal were disastrous failures.

Late in 1543, however, Gasper Pacheco began another chapter in the sickeningly familiar tale of Spanish atrocities; advancing on Chetumal, he destroyed crops and food stores and ruthlessly slaughtered the inhabitants. By 1544, Pacheco had subdued Maya resistance sufficiently to found a town on Lake Bacalar and claim **encomienda** (tribute) from villages around Chetumal. It is likely that he also conquered parts of Dzuluinicob, though the Maya still strenuously resisted Spanish domination. During the second half of the sixteenth century, the Spanish gradually strengthened their hold over northern Belize, establishing missions at Lamanai and Tipu.

The Maya resentment that was always present beneath the surface boiled over into total **rebellion** in 1638, forcing Spain to abandon Chetumal and Tipu completely. However, it is likely that the Maya of Belize were under some form of Spanish influence even if they were not under direct rule. The Maya struggle to remain independent was to continue with simmering resentment until 1707, when the population of Tipu was forcibly removed to Lago de Petén Itzá. This act effectively ended Spanish attempts to settle the west of Belize, as it was impossible to establish a successful colony without people to work for the Spanish *encomenderos*.

The failure of the Spanish to occupy southern Yucatán allowed buccaneers or **pirates** (primarily British) preying on the Spanish treasure fleets to find refuge along the coast of Belize. Spanish forces mounted several expeditions to dislodge the buccaneers (or **Baymen** as they called themselves), but these were never more than partially successful. These expeditions continued until in 1798, when the settlers (with British naval help) achieved victory in the **Battle of St George's Caye** – a success that reinforced the bond with the British government. In 1862, Belize became a colony of **British Honduras** and in 1871 it was officially declared a Crown Colony, becoming an integral, though minor part of the British empire.

For the people of Belize, the twentieth century has been dominated by uncertainty over their relationship with the "mother country". In both 1914 and 1939, thousands of Belizeans volunteered to assist the war effort, but each time the returning soldiers faced poverty and humiliation – events which marked the onset of black consciousness and the beginning of the **independence movement**. By the 1950s, the days of the British empire were numbered and the 1954 general election, in which all literate adults could vote, was won with an overwhelming majority by the People's United Party (PUP), led by George Price, with a manifesto to achieve independence from Britain.

Guatemala, however, as inheritor of the Spanish colonial jurisdiction of that name, had never entirely let go of its claim to Belize, despite agreements and treaties with the British government allowing British settlers to cut wood in Belize. The British government never took the claim very seriously and Belize was granted internal self-government in 1964 – the first step on the road to full independence. The prospect of what was, according to Guatemala's constitution, the department of "Belice" becoming independent outraged Guatemalan national pride and the government moved troops to the border several times, threatening to invade.

Throughout the 1970s, the situation remained tense, but gradually international opinion shifted in favour of Belizean independence, underlined most significantly by a UN resolution passed in 1980 which demanded Belize's independence with all territory intact by the following year. Although further negotiations with Guatemala did not fully resolve the territorial dispute, Belize achieved full **independence** on September 21, 1981, with Queen Elizabeth II as head of state. The present Guatemalan government, while restating its historic claim to at least some of Belize's territory, claims to be committed to solving any dispute through negotiation, and the two countries now exchange ambassadors.

Belize's democratic credentials are beyond dispute: at each general election since independence, the voters have kicked out the incumbent government and replaced it with the opposition. In practice, this has meant that the left-of-centre PUP has alternated with the more market-led United Democratic Party (UDP). This pattern was dramatically illustrated in 1998, when the UDP government's neo-liberal policies (under pressure from the World Bank) resulted in thousands of public sector redundancies – and a catastrophic defeat at the last general election, with even Prime Minister Manuel Esquivel losing his seat. The PUP, with Said Musa as prime minister, now forms Belize's government.

Despite a booming **tourist industry**, bringing in almost US$100 million a year, **agriculture** remains the mainstay of Belize's economy, accounting for 25 percent of GDP. Figures are obviously not available for income from the lucrative drug transhipment business, but this illicit economy is at least as large as the official one. Per capita income, at over US$2500 per year, is the highest in the region, boosted by the money many Belizeans receive from abroad. This apparent advantage is offset by the fact that many of the brightest young people leave the country, fitting in relatively easily in English-speaking North America.

CHAPTER FOUR

NORTHERN BELIZE AND THE NORTHERN CAYES

Many visitors to Belize are drawn here by the natural and cultural attractions of the northern half of the country – the impressive **Maya sites** and several large expanses of strictly protected land – but, without doubt, the most appealing and popular features of the country lie offshore along the **Barrier Reef**. Here the islands of the generally upmarket **Ambergris Caye** and the more budget-oriented **Caye Caulker** offer relaxing bases to enjoy the reef. They also provide a springboard to the two northern atolls, **Turneffe Islands** and **Lighthouse Reef**, each boasting world-renowned dive sites. The astonishingly diverse ecosytems of the reef and the cayes are protected in a network of **Marine Reserves** and National Parks stretching from the border with Mexico, visits to which are easily arranged.

Belize City, the country's largest urban area and former capital, is not usually a highlight on the itineraries of many visitors, but its many historic buildings and several new museums deserve a visit. As it's the transport hub of the country, you'll certainly pass through at some point and should allow time for one of the twice-daily city tours, which take in the Marine Terminal, home of the marvellous **Coastal Zone Museum**, and the Image Factory, Belize's only true **art gallery**.

Physically, the northern half of the country is relatively low-lying, with large areas of swamp in the east. The only towns in the north are **Orange Walk** on the New River, jumping-off point for trips to the ruins of **Lamanai**, and **Corozal**, a peaceful settlement on the shore of Corozal Bay, just a short distance from the Mexican border. Although much of the land is given over to agriculture, there are also extensive nature reserves. **Shipstern Nature Reserve** protects a system of lagoons and lowland forest in the extreme northeast, and in the far northwest, the **Rio Bravo Conservation Area** covers a range of habitats from lagoons and savannah to higher, forested ridges. All the nature reserves offer accommodation, and community-based projects in the villages of **Bermudian Landing** and **Crooked Tree** combine conservation and tourism; staying in one of these offers a much more enjoyable experience than you'll get on a brief day-visit.

ACCOMMODATION PRICE CODES

All the accommodation listed in this book has been categorized into one of nine price bands, as set out below. The prices quoted are in US dollars and refer to the cheapest room available for two people sharing in high season.

① under US$5	④ US$15–25	⑦ US$60–80
② US$5–10	⑤ US$25–40	⑧ US$80–100
③ US$10–15	⑥ US$40–60	⑨ over US$100

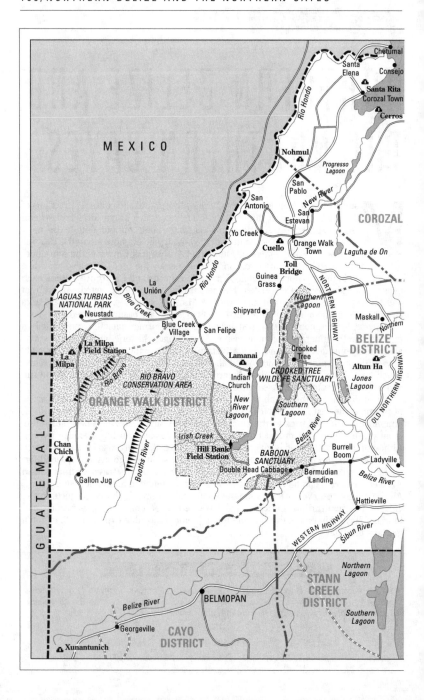

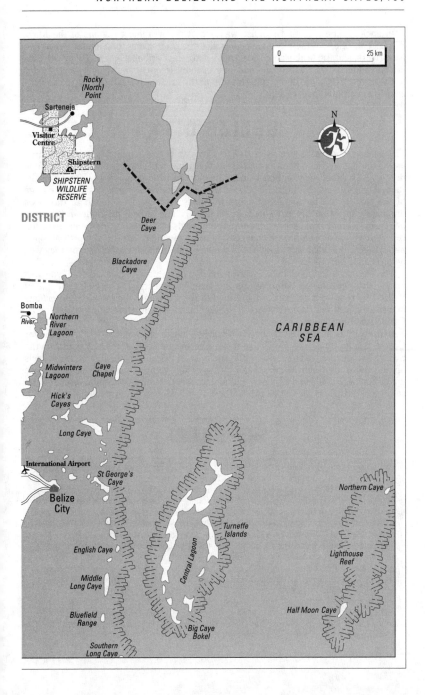

0   25 km

N

Rocky
(North)
Point

Sarteneja

Visitor
Centre

Shipstern

SHIPSTERN
WILDLIFE
RESERVE

DISTRICT

Deer
Caye

Blackadore
Caye

Bomba

River

Northern
River
Lagoon

CARIBBEAN
SEA

Midwinters
Lagoon

Caye
Chapel

Hick's
Cayes

Long Caye

International Airport

St George's
Caye

Belize
City

Northern Caye

English Caye

Turneffe
Islands

Lighthouse
Reef

Middle
Long Caye

Central Lagoon

Bluefield
Range

Half Moon Caye

Southern
Long Caye

Big Caye
Bokel

In ancient times, northern Belize was one of the wealthiest regions of the Maya World. The rulers of the city-states controlled the trade along the Hondo, Belize and New rivers, and the seaborne coastal trade along the Caribbean coast. Today the area is well connected by roads inland and an ever more frequent and reliable boat service to the cayes. There are some superb tours of the area on offer, though it's also very easy to get around independently.

BELIZE CITY

The narrow, congested streets of **Belize City** can seem daunting to anyone at first, especially if they have been prepared by the usual travellers' tales of crime-ridden urban decay. Admittedly, at first glance, the city can be unprepossessing and chaotic. Its buildings – many of them dilapidated wooden structures – stand right at the edge of the road or on the banks of stagnant canals (still used for much of the city's drainage), and there are few sidewalks to offer refuge to pedestrians from the ever-increasing numbers of cars and trucks. The hazards of Belize City, however, are often reported by those who have never been here. If you approach the city with an open mind, meet the inhabitants, and take in the new museums and galleries, you may well be pleasantly surprised.

The city has a distinguished history, a handful of sights and, particularly if you visit during the **September celebrations**, an astonishing energy. The 60,000 people of Belize City represent every ethnic group in the country, with the **Creole** descendants of former slaves and Baymen forming the dominant element, generating an easygoing Caribbean atmosphere.

Belize City is divided neatly into two halves – north and south – by the **Haulover Creek**, a delta branch of the Belize River. The pivotal point of the city centre is the **Swing Bridge**, always busy with traffic and opened twice a day to allow larger vessels up and down the river. **North** of the Swing Bridge things tend to be slightly more upmarket; here you'll find expensive hotels, most of the embassies and consulates and some very luxurious homes. **South** of the Swing Bridge is the commercial zone, with

---

HASSLE

Walking in Belize City in daylight is perfectly safe if you observe common-sense rules. The introduction of specially trained tourist police in 1995 made an immediate impact on the level of **hassle** and this, coupled with the legal requirement for all tour guides to be licensed, has driven away the hustlers and reduced street crime. That said, it's still sensible to proceed with caution: most people are friendly and chatty, but quite a few may want to sell you drugs or bum a dollar or two. The best advice is to stay cool. Be civil, don't provoke trouble by arguing too forcefully, and never show large sums of money on the street. Women wearing short shorts or skirts will attract verbal abuse from local studs.

Marijuana might be readily available, but it is illegal, and busting tourists can help a policeman get promoted – buying **drugs** on the street can mark you out as an easy target. The virtual absence of nightlife, apart from the bars and discos in the more expensive hotels (most ordinary bars and restaurants are closed by 9.30pm), means there's little reason to walk the streets after dark. If you do venture out, bear in mind that anyone on their own is in danger of being mugged: it's far safer to take a taxi at night. You'll soon learn to spot dangerous situations and in the city centre you can always ask the tourist police for advice or directions; they'll even walk you back to your hotel if it's near their patrol route. For more on security, see p.44.

banks, offices and supermarkets; the foreshore here is the city's most prestigious district, home to the colonial governor's residence, which is now a museum. Belize City is small enough to make **walking** the easiest way to get around, at least in daylight.

A brief history

When the **Spanish** conquered southern Yucatán and Belize in 1544, historians estimate there were around 200,000 Maya living in Belize (a close approximation of the country's total population today) and, even if there is scant proof of a Maya settlement beneath the present-day city, there is abundant evidence that Moho Caye, just off the river mouth, was a Maya fishing and transhipment port. Although Spanish friars founded missions inland and the secular authorities sent military expeditions upstream to force the scattered Maya villages into paying tribute to *encomenderos* (colonial landlords) in Yucatán, they built no large towns in Belize, a remote region in a remote province of New Spain. The imperial Spanish Crown may have reigned but it exercised little effective rule in this far frontier.

By the late sixteenth century the Spanish treasure fleets in the Caribbean attracted British (and other European) **pirates**, or buccaneers, who took advantage of the refuge offered by the reefs and shallows of Belize, using the cayes as bases for further plundering raids. Ever the opportunists, the buccaneers made money between raids by cutting the valuable **logwood** (used for textile dyes) which grew abundantly in the tropical swamps and building a number of camps from Campeche to Honduras. The settlement at the mouth of the Belize River, constructed by consolidating the mangrove swamp with wood chips, loose coral and rum bottles gradually became more permanent, and by the eighteenth century **Belize Town** was well established as a centre for the **Baymen** (as the settlers called themselves), their families and their slaves, though the capital of the Bay settlement was on St George's Caye. After the rains had floated the logs downriver, the men returned to Belize Town to drink and brawl. There were also huge Christmas celebrations which went on for weeks.

Spain was still the dominant colonial power in the region, however, and mounted several expeditions aimed at demonstrating control over the territory. In 1779, a Spanish raid captured many of the settlers, the rest fleeing, though most returned in 1783, when Spain agreed to recognize the rights of the British settlers. As a result of this, Belize Town grew into the main centre of the logwood and mahogany trade on the Bay of Honduras. Spanish raids continued until the **Battle of St George's Caye** in 1798, when the settlers achieved victory.

The increasing influence of British expatriates in the nineteenth century resulted in **colonial-style wooden housing** dominating the shoreline, as the "Scots clique" began to clean up the town's image and take control of its administration. Belize also became a base for Anglican missionaries: in 1812 the Anglican cathedral of St John was built to serve a diocese that stretched from Belize to Panamá. Despite fires and epidemics, the town and settlement grew with immigration from the West Indies and refugees from the Caste Wars in the Yucatán. In 1862, Belize became a colony of **British Honduras**, with Belize City as the administrative centre, and in 1871, Belize was officially declared a Crown Colony, with a resident governor appointed by Britain.

The early twentieth century saw the beginnings of the independence movement, which was given added momentum by the effects of the Depression and a massive **hurricane** on September 10, 1931. The city was celebrating the anniversary of the Battle of St George's Caye when the hurricane hit, uprooting houses, flooding the entire city and killing about a thousand people – ten percent of the population. Disaster relief was slow to arrive and many parts of the city were left in a state of squalid poverty. In 1961, the city was once again ravaged by a hurricane: 262 people died, and the

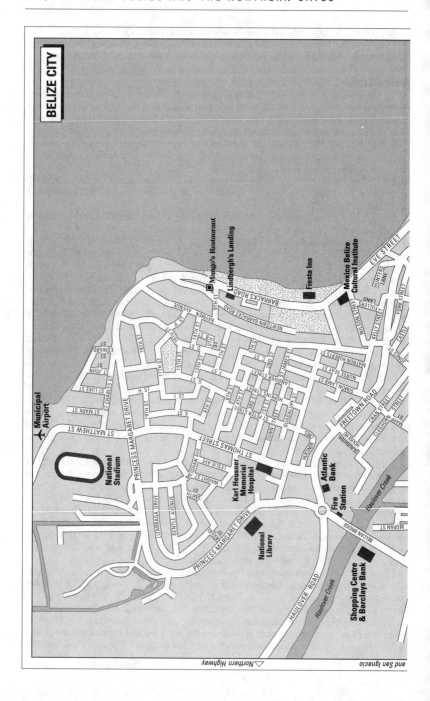

BELIZE CITY

Mango's Restaurant
Lindbergh's Landing
Fiesta Inn
Mexico Belize Cultural Institute

EVE STREET
HUNTERS LANE
BARRACKS ROAD
NEWTOWN BARRACKS ROAD
BAYMEN AVENUE
FULLERS LAND
WILSON STREET
KELLY STREET
YORK STREET
CASTLE LANE
JONES ST

16TH ST
15TH ST
14TH ST
13TH ST
12TH ST
11TH ST
10TH ST
SHELL ST
EDWARD ST
18TH ST
19TH ST

Municipal Airport

National Stadium

ST MATTHEW ST
ST CHARLES DRIVE
ST MARK ST
ST LUKE ST
ST JOHN ST

PRINCESS MARGARET DRIVE

D ST
C ST
5TH ST
ST JAMES ST
NURSE SEAY ST
MATRON ROBERTS ST
SIMON LAMB ST

HOPKINS STREET
HANOVER STREET
CURL STREET
ST PETER STREET
DUNN STREET
GLADUPE ST

IZARRAGA DRIVE
GENTLE AVENUE
SMITH ST
MEGHAN AVE
L WAIGHT ST
LESLIE AVE

ST THOMAS STREET

FREETOWN ROAD
CRAN STREET
CLEGHORN STREET
SANDHIRE HOUSE
MARK

Karl Heusner Memorial Hospital

Atlantic Bank

Fire Station

National Library

Hauliver Creek
Hauliver Creek
HAULOVER ROAD

MOPAN ST
BELCAN BRIDGE

Shopping Centre & Barclays Bank

△Northern Highway

and San Ignacio

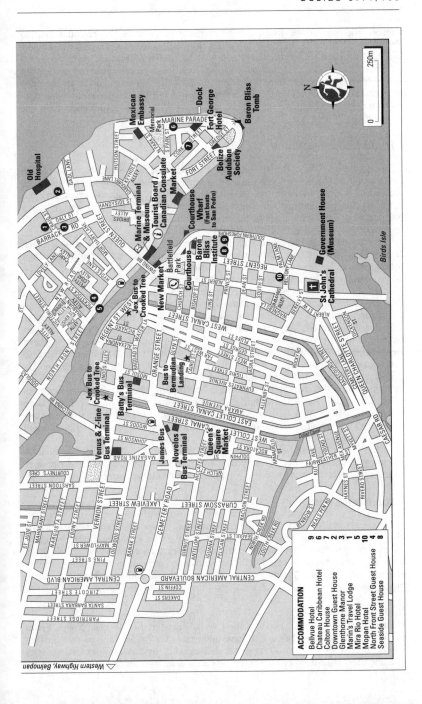

damage was so serious that plans were made to relocate the capital inland to Belmopan. (Hattieville, on the Western Highway, began life as a refuge for those fleeing the hurricane.) The official attitude was that Belize City would soon become a redundant backwater as Belmopan grew, but in fact few people chose to leave for the sterile "new town" atmosphere of Belmopan, and Belize City remains by far the most populous place in the country. Since **independence** in 1981, the rise of foreign investment and tourism has made an impact, and Belize City is now experiencing a major construction boom.

Arrival and information

Although Belize City is by far the largest urban area in the country (the capital, Belmopan is less than one tenth the size), getting from the transport terminals to the centre is very easy, and once you get downtown you'll find that almost everything you need is within a kilometre of the Swing Bridge. **Taxis**, identified by their green licence plates, charge Bz$5 for one or two passengers within the city. A **city bus** operates to a few residential areas, but is of little use to the visitor.

The four main **bus companies** in Belize have their terminals in the same western area of the city, around the Collet Canal and Magazine Road, a fairly derelict part of town known as Mesopotamia. It's only 1km from the centre and you can easily walk – or, especially at night, take a taxi – to any of the hotels listed opposite.

Most scheduled **boats returning from the cayes** pull in at the Marine Terminal on the north side of the Swing Bridge, though some use Courthouse Wharf on the south side, from where it's a fairly short walk or taxi ride to any of the hotels or bus depots.

Belize City has two **airports**. International flights land at the **Philip Goldson International Airport**, 17km northwest of the city at Ladyville, just off the Northern Highway. Belize's **domestic airlines** also make stops at the international airport, so you might want to pick up an onward flight right away: prices to all destinations are US$15 more than from the main domestic base at the **municipal airport**, a few kilometres north of the city centre, on the edge of the sea. There's no bus service from either airport to Belize City. Landing at the international airport, you can either take a taxi into the city (US$15), or walk to the Northern Highway (25min) and flag down one of the frequent passing buses; from the municipal airport, a taxi costs US$2.50 and walking takes 25 minutes.

At the Belize **tourist board**'s main office, 83 N Front St (Mon–Fri 8am–noon & 1–5pm; ☎02/77213), you can pick up free bus timetables, a hotel guide and city map, nature reserve brochures and copies of the free **tourist newspapers**.

Accommodation

There are about fifty **hotels** in Belize City, around a third of which cost US$15–25 double, with at least another half-dozen in the US$25–40 range. The selection below covers all price ranges. For a more comprehensive list, pick up a copy of *Destination Belize* from the tourist board or any hotel. There's usually no need to book (unless you're eager to stay in a particular hotel) as you'll almost always find something in the price range you're looking for.

North of the river

Most of the budget hotels north of the river are clustered on or near **North Front Street**, and those listed below also have good rates for singles. The more upmarket hotels (most take credit cards) are generally located in the historic **Fort George area** or along the **seafront**, where the residents can benefit from the sea breezes.

BUDGET ACCOMMODATION

Dim's Mira Rio, 59 N Front St (☎02/34147), across the road from the *North Front Street Guest House*. Reasonable rooms with washbasin and toilet overlooking the river, though the shared bathroom is cramped. The bar below is good for information, as boat owners often call in for a beer, and there's also simple but tasty Creole food available. ③.

Downtown Guest House, 5 Eve St, near the end of Queen St (☎ & fax 02/32057). Best-value budget place in the city. Small, very friendly, clean and secure; even the shared bathrooms have reliable hot water. You can receive a fax, get laundry done and the owner, Miss Kenny, will cook a bargain breakfast. ③.

Freddie's Guest House, 86 Eve St, on the city edge near the waterfront (☎02/33851). Three clean, secure and peaceful rooms (one with an immaculate private bathroom); the shared bathrooms also gleam. The best value in this price range. ④.

Marin's Travelodge, 6 Craig St, towards the old hospital (☎02/45166). Another very good budget option; comfortable, clean and really quiet. The rooms are well furnished and the showers excellent. ③.

North Front Street Guest House, 124 N Front St (☎02/77595). A budget travellers' favourite: friendly, helpful and just two blocks from the boats to Caye Caulker.

MODERATE TO EXPENSIVE

Chateau Caribbean, 6 Marine Parade (☎02/30800, fax 30900). Comfortable, colonial-style hotel with a/c, cable TV and some sea views. Good restaurant (see p.199). The spacious public areas, with wicker furniture and balconies overlooking the sea, are a favourite of visiting film crews, and the chateau has often been used as a movie set. ⑦.

Colton House, 9 Cork St (☎02/44666, fax 30451). Beautifully kept colonial house in the Fort George area, dating from the 1920s; easily the best guest house in Belize. The five a/c rooms are individually decorated in English country-house style, each with an immaculate bathroom and balcony. Free coffee is available in the mornings though no meals are served. Owners Alan and Ondina Colton keep an extensive book and video library on Belize and can arrange substantial discounts on tours. No children under nine. ⑤.

The Great House, 13 Cork St (☎02/533400, fax 33444). Six spacious and well-equipped, a/c rooms in a recently modernized and expanded private house, originally built in 1927. All rooms have a balcony, private bathroom, coffee-maker, TV, phone and dedicated fax line. There's also a fine restaurant in the courtyard. ⑧.

Glenthorne Manor, 27 Barrack Rd, off Queen St (☎02/44212). A large, comfortable colonial-style house with individually designed (and named) rooms with balconies; a/c rooms available. A delicious Belizean-style continental breakfast is included and there's secure parking, a sitting room, laundry facilities and use of the kitchen. ⑤.

Radisson Fort George, 2 Marine Parade, north side of the harbour mouth (☎02/33333, fax 73820). The luxurious flagship of the city's hotels, and by far the most expensive (though you can expect substantial discounts). All rooms have huge cable TV, fridge and minibar and those in the club wing, reached by the only glass elevator in Belize, have unbeatable sea views. There's an excellent restaurant and the grounds (with pool) are an oasis of calm on the edge of the sea. ⑨.

South of the river

Bellevue Hotel, 5 Southern Foreshore (☎02/77051, fax 72353). The top hotel on the south side of the Swing Bridge, right on the seafront with a private dock. Modern, a/c rooms in a converted and extended colonial house; those at the back open onto a balcony overlooking the relaxing courtyard, adorned with palms and pool. The upstairs Harbour Room bar is a popular Belizean meeting place, especially during the Friday evening happy hour, and the Mayan Tavern disco is a focal point of the city's nightlife, with live music at weekends. Good restaurant, too. ⑥.

Mopan Hotel, 55 Regent St (☎02/77351; fax 75383). Large wood-fronted building at the quiet end of the street near Government House Museum. Run by avid conservationist Jean Shaw, this is a popular place for naturalists, writers and scientists to stay. Rooms all have private bath and some have a/c, but some are dimly lit. Very good-value breakfasts, and lunch and dinner can be ordered. Jean also runs Mopan Travel, is the agent for Aerovias and can arrange flights to Guatemala. ⑤.

Sea Side Guest House, 3 Prince St (☎02/78339), half a block from the southern foreshore. A clean, well-run and very secure hotel that's become a bustling meeting place for travellers – and you really can see the sea. One room has seven hostel-style dorm beds (US$9); private rooms (without bath) are available too. Good hot shared showers, a pay phone, email service, loads of information and a relaxing, orchid-filled garden. Meals can be ordered and you get a key for access at all times. ③.

The City

Richard Davies, a British traveller in the mid-nineteenth century, wrote of the city: "There is much to be said for Belize, for in its way it was one of the prettiest ports at which we touched, and its cleanliness and order . . . were in great contrast to the ports we visited later as to make them most remarkable." Many of the features that elicited this praise have now gone, though some of the distinctive **wooden colonial buildings** have been preserved as heritage showpieces, converted into hotels, restaurants or museums. Even in cases where the decay is too advanced for the paintwork, balconies and carved railings to be restored, the old wooden structures remain more pleasing than the concrete blocks that have replaced so many of them.

Before the construction of the first wooden bridge in the early 1800s, cattle were winched over the waterway that divides the city – hence the name Haulover Creek. Its replacement, the present **Swing Bridge**, made in Liverpool and opened in 1923, is the only manually operated swing bridge left in the Americas. Every day at 5.30am and 5.30pm the endless parade of vehicles and people is halted by policemen, and the process of turning begins. Using long poles inserted into a capstan, four men gradually lever the bridge around until it's pointing in the direction of the harbour mouth. During the few minutes that the bridge is open, the river traffic is busier than that on the roads, and traffic is snarled up across the whole city. There's a possibility, however, that the bridge may be demolished, since a new drawbridge has been built a few blocks upriver, relieving some of the congestion. A vocal preservation campaign has been mobilized.

If walking around the sights sounds too tiring then take a **city tour** with Captain Nicolas Sanchez (mobile ☎014/8777) in his open-sided bus. Nick's historical knowledge is so phenomenal and extensive that no two tours are alike: daily tours (2hr 30min; US$12.50) leave punctually from the Marine Terminal at 9am and 3pm.

The north side

Immediately on the **north side** of the Swing Bridge is the **Marine Terminal**, the place to catch boats for the northern cayes. In the same building, the beautifully restored former Belize City Fire Station, built in 1923, are two of Belize's new museums, both superbly designed. The **Coastal Zone Museum** contains fascinating displays and explanations of reef ecology, the highlight being a 3-D model of the entire reef system including the cayes and atolls. Upstairs, the **Marine Museum** exhibits an amazing collection of models and documents relating to Belize's maritime heritage (both Mon–Sat 8am–4.30pm; US$2). Opposite the Marine Terminal is the three-storey wooden **Paslow Building**, which houses the post office on the ground floor. A block east of the Marine Terminal, at 91 N Front St, **The Image Factory** (Mon–Fri 9am–6pm; ☎02/34151; free but donations welcome) is home to Belize's hottest contemporary artists. The gallery puts on outstanding and often provocative exhibitions and you can sometimes get a chance to discuss the work with the artists themselves. Continuing east along N Front Street, past the "temporary" market (which often has a greater variety of produce than the official market south of the Swing Bridge), you pass the **National Handicraft Centre** (Mon–Fri 8am–5pm; ☎02/33636), which sells high-quality Belizean crafts at fair prices.

Beyond here the road follows the north shore of the river mouth – an area that was Fort George Island until 1924, when the narrow strait was filled in – reaching the point marked by **Bliss Lighthouse**, a memorial to Baron Bliss, Belize's greatest benefactor (see below). Walking around the shoreline you pass **Memorial Park**, which honours the Belizean dead of World War I. In this area you'll find several **colonial mansions**, many of the best-preserved now taken over by embassies and upmarket hotels; a fine example is the Mexican embassy on the north corner of the park.

Natural history enthusiasts will benefit from a visit to two of Belize's foremost conservation organizations in the Fort George area. The **Belize Audubon Society** at 12 Fort St (☎02/35004) has information, books, maps and posters relating to all the country's wildlife reserves, and is very prominent in conservation education. Nearby, at 2 S Park St (☎02/75616), facing Memorial Park, are the offices of the **Programme for Belize**, which manages the Rio Bravo Conservation Area (see p.210); call in for news on progress and information on access from the enthusiastic staff.

Further along, at the corner of Hutson Street and Gabourel Lane, set back one block from the sea, is the **US Embassy**, another superb example of an apparently colonial building, though it was actually constructed in New England in the nineteenth century, then dismantled and shipped to Belize. It's also notable for being the only US embassy in the world not guarded by US Marines.

The south side

The **south side** is generally the older section of Belize City. In the early days, the elite lived in the seafront houses while the backstreets were inhabited by slaves and labourers. These days it's the commercial centre, containing the main shopping streets, banks and travel agencies. Right by the Swing Bridge is the three-storey **covered market**, which opened in 1993 on the site of the rather decrepit old market from 1820. Though the new one is much cleaner, it's not popular with either traders or shoppers, most of whom have carried on using the "temporary" market, on the north side of the river.

Albert Street, running south from the Swing Bridge, is the main commercial thoroughfare, with banks, supermarkets and good value T-shirt and souvenir shops – Sings, at no. 35, has some of the best bargains. On the parallel **Regent Street**, a block closer to the sea, are the former colonial administration and court buildings, known together as the **Court House**. These well-preserved examples of colonial architecture, with their columns and fine wrought iron, were completed in 1926 after an earlier building on the same site was destroyed by fire. The Court House overlooks a patch of grass and trees with an ornamental fountain in the centre, ambitiously known as Central Park until it was renamed **Battlefield Park** in the early 1990s, commemorating the heated political meetings which took place there before independence.

A block behind the Court House, on the waterfront, is the **Bliss Institute**, which looks like a squat airport control tower but is in fact the cultural centre of Belize City (Mon–Fri 8.30am–noon & 2–8pm, Sat 8.30am–noon). The Bliss building is the home of the **National Arts Council** and hosts a small exhibition from the National Art Collection. Many other exhibitions, concerts and plays are put on here, and it's worth checking with the tourist board if there's anything happening during your visit. Just inside the entrance are stelae and altars from Caracol – priceless examples of Maya art that seem to have been dumped in a corner while somewhere is found to display them; a small plaque gives an account of the scenes depicted on the stones.

The Institute was funded by the legacy of Baron Bliss, an eccentric Englishman with a Portuguese title. A keen fisherman, he arrived off the coast of Belize in his yacht *Sea King* in 1926 after hearing about the tremendous amount of game fish in local waters. Unfortunately, he became ill and died without ever having been ashore. Despite this, he left most of his considerable estate to benefit the people of the colony. This became the Bliss Trust, which has been used on various projects, helping to build markets and improve roads and water supplies. In gratitude the authorities declared March 9 (the date of his death) as Baron Bliss Day, an official public holiday commemorated by boat races funded partly by his legacy.

At the end of Albert Street is **St John's Cathedral**, the oldest Anglican cathedral in Central America and one of the oldest buildings in Belize. Work began on it in 1812 and was completed in 1820, the red bricks for its construction brought over as ballast in British ships. Complete with a square, battlemented tower, it looks more like a large English parish church than anything you might expect to find in Belize; the main structure, roof and mahogany beams have survived almost 180 years of tropical heat and hurricanes. Here, in great pomp, the kings of the Mosquito Coast, tribal chiefs of the Miskito Indians, keen to keep their links with Britain to avoid Spanish colonial rule, were crowned between 1815 and 1845, taking the title to a British Protectorate extending along the coast of Honduras and Nicaragua.

Opposite the cathedral, in a breezy seafront setting, is the well-preserved **Government House Museum** (Mon–Fri 8.30am–4pm; US$2.50), painted white and surrounded by a green lawn and palm trees. Built in 1814, it was the residence of the governor when Belize was a British colony. At midnight on September 20, 1981, the Belize flag was hoisted here for the first time as Belize celebrated independence. Today, Government House is still used for some official receptions, particularly on Independence Day, but the present governor general, Sir Colville Young, a Belizean, wanted to make this superb example of Belize's colonial heritage available to everyone and designated it a museum in 1996. The collection on show includes silverware, glasses and furniture used during the colonial period, as well as colonial archives. A plush red carpet leads down the hall to the great mahogany staircase, the walls lined with prints of sombre past governors. The upstairs, however, is less grand, with bedroom furniture that is more typical of a middle-class British home of the 1960s. In the grounds, the carefully restored *Sea King*, the tender of Baron Bliss's yacht of the same name, stands as testimony to the craftsmanship of Belizean boatbuilders.

West of the cathedral is **Yarborough Cemetery**, which was used until 1881, when it reached full capacity. The graves have fallen into disrepair but a browse among the stones will turn up fascinating snippets of history. The cemetery is named after the magistrate who owned the land and allowed the burial of prominent people here from 1781; most of the occupants were members of the elite, with commoners only being admitted after 1870. At the seaward end of this strip of land, connected to the mainland by a narrow wooden causeway, is the island known as **Bird's Isle**, a venue for reggae concerts and parties.

Eating, drinking and nightlife

The multitude of **restaurants** in Belize City doesn't offer very much in the way of variety. There's the tasty but monotonous **Creole** fare of rice and beans, plenty of seafood and steaks, and a preponderance of **Chinese** restaurants, usually the best bet for vegetarians. Greasy fried chicken is available as a takeaway from small restaurants all over the city: a Belizean favourite known as "dollar chicken", whatever the price. If you're really in a hurry, try *HL's Burger*, Belize City's answer to *McDonald's*, which has a growing number of outlets. The big hotels have their own restaurants, naturally quite expensive, but with much more varied menus and good service.

If you're shopping for food, the main **supermarkets** – Brodie's and Romac's – are worth a look; they're on Albert Street, just past the park, and their selection of food is good if expensive, reflecting the fact that much is imported. Milk and dairy products, produced locally by Mennonite farmers (see p.207), are delicious and good quality. Naturally enough, local **fruit** is cheap and plentiful, though highly seasonal; Belizean citrus fruits are among the best in the world.

In the listings below we have quoted a phone number in places where it is recommended you should **reserve a table**, or for those places which offer a **delivery service**.

Restaurants and cafés north of the river

The Ark, 109 N Front St (☎02/77820). Very tasty Belizean dishes at great prices. A good choice for a quick meal as the food is already cooked; also does deliveries. Mon–Sat 7am–11pm.

Chateau Caribbean, 6 Marine Parade. For undisturbed views of blue sea and offshore islands, head up the steps to this cool first-floor restaurant, with gleaming white linen and cutlery, where prices are more reasonable than you'd expect. Order something inexpensive and forget for a while the heat and noise of the city.

Chon Sing, N Front St, opposite the Texaco station. Large portions of Chinese food, unfortunately accompanied by violent kung-fu videos on the TV.

Mango's, 164 Newtown Barracks Rd (☎02/34021). Away from the centre, near the *Fiesta Inn*, this was formerly *The Grill*, and continues to be one of the best restaurants in the city. Seafood is a speciality, but there are also well-prepared steak and pasta dishes and a vegetarian option.

Mar's Belizean Restaurant, 118 N Front St. Great, clean place serving really tasty Belizean food at good prices. Handy for anyone at *North Front Street Guest House*; opens at 6am.

Pepper's Pizza, 2215 Baymen Av. Decent pizza restaurant that also delivers. Mon–Thurs 5–11pm, Fri & Sat 5–12.

Sea Rock, 190 Newtown Barracks Rd. Extremely good Indian food in a quiet, clean restaurant. You'll need to take a taxi as it's a long way from the centre.

The Smoky Mermaid, 13 Cork St. The in-house restaurant of the *Great House* and the best new restaurant in the city, with tables around a fountain in the courtyard and a popular Friday evening happy hour.

Restaurants and cafés south of the river

La Cocinita, 56 Regent St. Wonderful Belizean restaurant, with great daily breakfast and lunch specials. You can eat indoors or at a table on the veranda overlooking the street. Mon–Fri 7.30am–2.30pm.

Dit's, 50 King St. Great pastries and inexpensive Creole food such as cowfoot soup.

Macy's, 18 Bishop St (☎02/73419). Long-established, reasonably priced Creole restaurant that's popular with locals and extremely busy at lunchtimes.

Marlins, 11 Regent St West, next to the *Belcove Hotel*. Good, inexpensive, local food in large portions, with some tables on a veranda overlooking the river.

River Side Patio, at the rear of the market. Good place to relax with a drink as you watch the bridge swing. Mexican-style food, and entertainment on Friday and Saturday evenings.

Drinking, nightlife and entertainment

Belize City's more sophisticated, air-conditioned **bars** are found in the most expensive establishments, and there aren't many of those. At the lowest end of the scale are dimly lit dives, effectively men-only, where, though there's the possibility that you'll be offered drugs or be robbed, it's more likely that you'll have a thoroughly enjoyable time meeting easygoing, hard-drinking locals. There are several places between the two extremes, most of them in restaurants and hotels – for example, *Marlins* restaurant (see above) and *Dim's Mira Rio* hotel. One of the best is *Lindbergh's Landing*, facing the seafront park, just past the *Fiesta Inn*, a quiet bar located at the spot where Charles Lindbergh landed the *Spirit of St Louis* in 1927 (the first aircraft to land in Belize), decorated with photographs of the famous aviator.

Nightlife, though not as wild as it used to be, is becoming more reliable and the quality of live bands is improving all the time. If you're after **live music**, the *Calypso Bar* at the *Fiesta* frequently hosts top local bands, the *Radisson Fort George* and the *Bellevue* hold regular dances, and there's **reggae** at the *Lumba Yaad Bar*, on the riverbank just out of town on the Northern Highway.

Listings

Airlines International: Aerocaribe, Belize Global Travel, 41 Albert St (☎02/77185); Aerovias, Mopan Travels, 55 Regent St (☎02/75446); American, corner of New Rd and Queen St (☎02/32522); Continental, 32 Albert St (☎02/78309); Taca, Belize Global Travel (☎02/77185). Domestic: Maya Island Air (☎02/31140 or 026/2345); Tropic Air (☎02/45671 or 026/2012).

American Express Belize Global Travel, 41 Albert St (☎02/77363).

Banks The main banks are on Albert St (Mon–Thurs 8am–2pm, Fri 8am–4.30pm). Barclays has no surcharge for Visa and MC cash advances (Belize Bank charges US$7.50), and you can use foreign-issued credit and debit cards in Barclays ATMs. Cash in US dollars is usually readily available from the banks. Many shops, hotels and restaurants change travellers' cheques and cash dollars, and you can also spend US dollars and receive change in Belize dollars.

Bookstores The Book Centre, 2 Church St (opposite the BTL office), has the best selection of titles, including Rough Guides; Tubroos Tree Gift Shop, in the arcade below *Great House*, also sells Rough Guides. For good books on Belize check out the SPEAR library on Pickstock Street and New Road (☎02/31668). Many of the larger hotels also sell books, magazines and papers (including Caribbean editions of US newspapers and *Time, Newsweek*, etc), and some budget hotels operate book exchanges.

Car rental The following have offices in the city and desks at the international airport: Avis (☎02/34619); Budget (☎02/32435); Crystal (☎02/31600); National (☎02/31650).

Embassies and consulates Though the official capital is at Belmopan, some embassies remain in Belize City and are normally open Mon–Fri mornings. Several EU countries have consulates (mainly honorary) in Belize City; current addresses and phone numbers are listed in the green pages of the telephone directory. Canada (cannot issue passports), 83 N Front St (☎02/31060); Guatemala, 8 A Street, Kings Park (☎02/33150); Honduras, 91 N Front St (☎02/45889); Mexico, 20 Park St (☎02/31388); US, 29 Gabourel Lane (☎02/77161).

Immigration office In the government complex on Mahogany St, near the junction of Central American Blvd and the Western Highway (Mon–Thurs 8.30–11.30am & 1–4pm, Fri 8.30–11.30am & 1–3.30pm; ☎02/24620). Thirty-day extensions of stay (the maximum allowed) cost US$12.50.

Laundry Central America Coin Laundry, 114 Barrack Rd (Mon–Sat 8.30am–9pm; reduced hours Sun), and in many hotels.

Medical care Dr Gamero, Myo-On Clinic, 40 Eve St (☎02/45616); Karl Heusner Memorial Hospital, Princess Margaret Drive, near the junction with the Northern Highway (☎02/31548).

Photography For good-quality print and slide developing, and fast passport photos, try Spooners, 89 N Front St.

Police The main police station is on Queen Street, a block north of the Swing Bridge (☎02/72210). Or contact a member of the tourist police (see p.190), or the tourist board (see p.194) during opening hours.

Post office The main post office is in the Paslow Building, on the corner of Queen St, immediately north of the Swing Bridge (Mon–Fri 8am–noon & 1–4.30pm). The parcel office is next door on N Front St.

Telephone office You can make international calls from the main BTL office at 1 Church St (Mon–Sat 8am–6pm), who also offer an efficient fax and email service. Payphones and cardphones are dotted around the city.

Travel and tour agents The best agents for booking international and regional flights are Belize Global Travel, 41 Albert St (☎02/77185) and Jal's, 148 North Front St (☎02/45407). Most inland day tours from Belize City visit two or more of the following: the Belize zoo, the Bermudian Landing Baboon Sanctuary, the Crooked Tree Wildlife Sanctuary, Altun Ha ruins and Lamanai ruins. All but the last two of these places are very easy to visit independently and you're likely to save money doing it on your own, even when you include the cost of accommodation, but if time is short and you'd prefer a guided tour, contact one of the following: Belize Travel Adventures, 168 N Front St (☎02/33064, fax 33196; *bzetravel@btl.net*); Discovery Expeditions, 126 Freetown Rd (☎02/30748, fax 30750; *discovery@btl.net*); Melmish Mayan Tours (☎02/35399, fax 31531); or David Cunningham (☎ & fax 02/24400; mobile ☎014/9892), an independent naturalist tour guide, who can also be contacted through the *Mopan Hotel*.

MOVING ON FROM BELIZE CITY

Moving on from Belize City **to all towns** in the country, across the borders **to Chetumal** in Mexico and **to Melchor** in Guatemala, and **to the main northern cayes** is very simple **during daylight**. While a few buses continue to run on the main routes during the evening, there are no **night flights** (international or domestic) in Belize, nor do any **scheduled boats** operate at night.

Most of the **bus companies** and bus departure points are in the same area, along the Collet Canal and Magazine Road, a short walk from the centre of town. While the main bus companies have their own depots, there are numerous smaller operators with regular departures but no contact address or telephone number. The abbreviations used below follow the name of the company.

BUS COMPANIES AND DEPOTS

Batty (BA), 15 Mosul St (☎ 02/72025); for the Northern and Western highways.

James Bus (JA), leaves for Punta Gorda (via Belmopan) from Shell station, Cemetery Rd, near Collet Canal, at 7am daily.

Jex Bus (JX), (☎025/7017) leaves for Crooked Tree from Regent St West and Pound Yard, Collet Canal.

McFadzean's Bus (MF), leaves for Bermudian Landing (via Burrell Boom) from the corner of Cemetery Rd and Mosul St, near the Batty bus depot, at noon.

Novelos (NV), 19 West Collet Canal (☎02/77372); for the Western Highway.

Perez Bus (PE), leaves for Sarteneja from the Texaco station on North Front St at noon.

Ritchie's Bus (RI), leaves from Collet Canal, near Cemetery Rd. Direct bus for Placencia at 2.30pm.

Russell's Bus (RU), leaves for Bermudian Landing from Cairo St, near the corner of Cemetery Rd and Euphrates Ave at noon & 4.30pm.

Venus (VE), Magazine Rd (☎02/73354); for the Northern Highway.

Z-Line (ZL), Magazine Rd (☎02/73937); for the Hummingbird and Southern highways and Coastal Rd to Dangriga, Placencia and Punta Gorda.

BUS SERVICES FROM BELIZE CITY

Where **express services** (exp), are available these are faster and a fraction more expensive than regular services.

BY AIR

There are **direct international flights** from Belize international airport to Miami, New Orleans, Houston and LA in the US; to Cancún in Mexico; and to San Salvador, Guatemala City, Flores, San Pedro Sula and Roatán in other Central American countries (see pp.3, 30 in Basics for more on this). If you're **leaving** from the international airport, arrive early, and don't forget the US$15 departure taxes. Most **domestic flights** originate from Belize City's municipal airport:

To **Caye Caulker** (15–20min) and **San Pedro** (10min from Caye Caulker; both US$24), at least hourly from 7am to 5pm; to **Dangriga** (8–10 daily, 25min; US$28); **Placencia** (further 20min; US$53); to **Punta Gorda** (another 25min; US$68).

BY BOAT

Scheduled boats to Caye Caulker leave from the Marine Terminal (☎02/31969), on N Front St, by the Swing Bridge (every 2 hours from 9am–5pm; 45min; US$7.50). For **San Pedro** on **Ambergris Caye**, scheduled boats leave from Courthouse Wharf, south of the Swing Bridge (3 daily, calling at Caye Caulker; 1hr 25min; US$12.50). Any scheduled boat will also stop on request at **St George's Caye**.

THE NORTH

Northern Belize is an expanse of relatively level land, where lagoons, swamps and savannahs are mixed with rainforest and farmland. The largest town in the north is **Orange Walk**, the country's main centre for sugar production. Further to the north, **Corozal**, just fifteen minutes from the border, is a small and peaceful Caribbean town with a strong Mexican element. Most of the original settlers here were refugees from the Caste Wars in Yucatán, and as a result, Spanish is as common as Creole throughout the north.

Most visitors to northern Belize are here to see the **Maya ruins** and **wildlife reserves**. The largest site, **Lamanai**, features some of the most impressive pyramids in the country. **Altun Ha**, reached by the old Northern Highway, is usually visited as part of a day-trip from Belize City or San Pedro. Other sites include **Cuello** and **Nohmul**, respectively west and north of Orange Walk, and **Santa Rita** and **Cerros**, both near Corozal.

The four main **wildlife reserves** in the region each offer a different approach to conservation and an insight into different environments. At the **Bermudian Landing Community Baboon Sanctuary** in the Belize River valley, a group of farmers have combined agriculture with conservation, much to the benefit of the black howler monkey, while at the **Crooked Tree Wildlife Sanctuary** a network of rivers and lagoons offers protection to a range of resident and migratory birds, including the endangered jabiru stork. By far the largest and most ambitious conservation project, however, is the vast **Rio Bravo Conservation Area**: 970 square kilometres of tropical forest and river systems in the west of Orange Walk district, adjoining the border with Guatemala. The most northerly protected area is the **Shipstern Nature Reserve**, preserving a large area of tropical forest and wetland.

Travelling around the north is fairly straightforward if you stick to the main roads, with buses running at least hourly along the Northern Highway between Belize City and Santa Elena on the Mexican border, calling at Orange Walk and Corozal, and continuing across the border to the market in **Chetumal**.

Belize City to Orange Walk

Regular, fast buses run the 88km along the **Northern Highway** from Belize City to Orange Walk in less than an hour and a half. To get to the **Bermudian Landing Baboon Sanctuary**, **Crooked Tree Wildlife Sanctuary** or the ruins of **Altun Ha** by public transport, you'll need to take one of the local buses detailed in the text.

Leaving Belize City you pass spreading suburbs, where expensive houses are constructed on reclaimed mangrove swamps; look to the east and you'll get a glimpse of the sea. Seven kilometres from the city a metal-framed bridge carries the road over the mouth of the Belize River at the point where the Haulover Creek branches away to the south. For the next few kilometres the road stays very close to the river and is prone to flooding after heavy rain. At **Ladyville**, 15km from Belize City, you pass the turning to the international airport.

The Bermudian Landing Community Baboon Sanctuary

The **Community Baboon Sanctuary**, established in 1985 as a collaboration between primate biologist Rob Horwich and a group of local farmers (with help from the Worldwide Fund for Nature), is one of the most interesting conservation projects in Belize. A mixture of farmland and broadleaved forest, the sanctuary stretches along

30km of the Belize River valley – from Flowers Bank to Big Falls – and comprises a total of eight villages and over a hundred landowners. Farmers here have adopted a voluntary code of practice to harmonize their own needs with those of the wildlife in a project combining conservation, education and tourism.

The main focus of attention is the **black howler monkey** (locally known as a baboon), the largest monkey in the New World. The baboons live in troops of between four and eight, and spend the day wandering through the leafy canopy feasting on leaves, flowers and fruits. At dawn and dusk they let rip with the famous howl, a deep and rasping roar that carries for miles. The sanctuary is also home to around two hundred bird species, plus anteaters, deer, peccaries, coatis, iguanas and the endangered Central American river turtle. Special **trails** are cut through the forest so that visitors can see it at its best; you can wander these alone or with a guide from the village. Another option is to take a guided canoe trip from *Jungle Drift Lodge* (see below).

Practicalities

At the heart of the area, 43km northwest of Belize City, lies **BERMUDIAN LANDING**, a Creole village and former logging centre that dates back to the seventeenth century. The turn-off to the village is 23km along the Northern Highway; the rest of the journey is along a good unpaved road, also used to access Hill Bank Field Station (see p.211). There are two to three buses from Belize City to the village every day except Sunday. Bear in mind that all buses for Belize City leave Bermudian Landing early – between 5.30 and 6.30am. Day-visitors should register at the **visitor centre** (8am–4pm; US$5) at the western end of the village; the fee includes a short guided trail walk and entrance to Belize's first natural history museum inside the centre, with exhibits and information on the riverside habitats and animals you're likely to see.

You can **camp** at the visitor centre (US$5), and just behind here the *Baboon Guest House* (☎014/9286; ④) has two beautiful rooms with electric lights in a simple thatched cabin with a separate, clean tiled bathroom. Alternatively, a number of local families offer **bed-and-breakfast** rooms (④), a wonderful way to experience village life; check at the visitor centre or ask the sanctuary manager, Fallet Young, who lives nearby. The best place to stay, however, is the friendly *Jungle Drift Lodge* (☎014/9578, fax 02/78160; ③–⑤), just beyond the centre of the village, on the left, 75m from where the bus stops. The neat wooden, thatched cabañas, each with a porch, electric light and fan, are set right above the riverbank, shaded by trees festooned with howler monkeys, and surrounded by a profusion of tropical plants in the gardens. Some cabins have private bathrooms and even those with shared bath have hot water; camping is US$5. Meals (vegetarian and vegan on request) are eaten with the family, and the food, some of the best you'll find anywhere in the country, is plentiful. There's a trail along the riverbank, and *Jungle Drift* also rents out canoes and kayaks, and organizes superb river floats and night trips to spot crocodiles in nearby Mussel Creek.

There are a few **restaurants and bars** in the village: *Russell's Restaurant*, in the centre on the left-hand side (also the place where the bus parks for the night), and *Edna's Cool Spot* on the right, both serve simple meals of beans and rice.

The ruins of Altun Ha

Fifty-five kilometres north of Belize City and just 9km from the sea is the impressive Maya site of **Altun Ha** (daily 8am–4pm; US$5), occupied for around twelve hundred years until the Classic Maya collapse in 900–950 AD. The site was also occupied at various times throughout the Postclassic era, though no new monumental building took place during this period. Its position close to the Caribbean coast suggests that it was sustained as much by trade as agriculture – a theory upheld by the discovery of trade objects such as jade from the Motagua valley in Guatemala and obsidian from the Mexican and

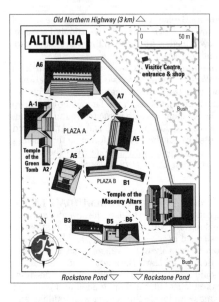

Guatemalan highlands – both very important in Maya ceremony.

Around five hundred buildings have been recorded at Altun Ha, but the core of the site is clustered around two Classic period plazas. Entering from the road, you come first to **Plaza A**, enclosed by large temples on all four sides. A magnificent tomb has been discovered beneath Temple A-1, the **Temple of the Green Tomb**. Dating from 550 AD, this yielded a total of three hundred items of grave goods, including jade, jewellery, stingray spines, skin, flints and the remains of a Maya book. Temple A-6, which has been particularly badly damaged, contains two parallel rooms, each about 48m long and with thirteen doorways along an exterior wall.

The adjacent **Plaza B** is dominated by the site's largest temple, B-4, the **Temple of the Masonry Altars**, the last in a sequence of buildings raised on this spot. If it seems familiar, it's because you might already have seen it on the Belikin beer label. Several tombs have been uncovered within the main structure but only two were found intact; most of the others were probably desecrated during the political turmoil that preceded the abandonment of the site. In 1968, archeologists discovered a carved jade head of **Kinich Ahau**, the Maya sun god, in one of the tombs. Standing just under 15cm high, it is the largest carved jade found anywhere in the Maya World; today it's kept in the vaults of the Belize Bank, as there's no national museum to display it.

Outside these two main plazas are several other areas of interest, though little else has been restored. A short trail leads south to **Rockstone Pond**, a literal translation of the Maya name of the site and also the present-day name of a nearby village. The pond was dammed in Maya times to form a reservoir and today it's home to a large crocodile; at the eastern edge stands another mid-sized temple. Built in the second century AD, this contained offerings that came from the great city of Teotihuacán in the Valley of Mexico.

Practicalities

Altun Ha is fairly difficult to reach independently. There is a daily afternoon bus from Cinderella Plaza in Belize City (call ☎03/22041 to check times) to the village of **MASKALL**, passing the turn-off to the site at the village of **LUCKY STRIKE** (community phone ☎02/44249), just 3km from Altun Ha. Any travel agent in Belize City will arrange a tour and increasingly visits are taken as part of a day-trip from San Pedro (see p.224). There's no accommodation at the site, but you can ask the caretaker for permission to **camp** nearby. If money's no object, however, you can submit to the therapeutic pleasures of the *Maruba Resort and Jungle Spa*, near Maskall at Mile 40, Old Northern Highway (☎03/22199; in US ☎713/799-2031, fax 795-8573; ⑨), with luxurious rooms and cabins with hand-built wooden furniture and feather beds (there are alternatives if you're allergic). The food is excellent, and you'd need to stay a week to take advantage of all the health and beauty treatments.

Crooked Tree Wildlife Sanctuary and village

Further along the Northern Highway, roughly midway between Belize City and Orange Walk, a well-signed branch road heads west 5km to **Crooked Tree Wildlife Sanctuary**, a reserve that takes in a vast area of inland waterways, logwood swamps and lagoons. The sanctuary's greatest treasure are the tens of thousands of migrating and resident birds; over 250 species have been recorded, including snail kites, tiger herons, snowy egrets, ospreys and black-collared hawks. The most famous visitor is the **jabiru stork**, the largest flying bird in the New World, with a wingspan of 2.5m. Belize has the biggest nesting population of jabiru storks at one site; they arrive in November, the young hatch in April or May, and they leave just before the summer rainy season gets under way. The **best time to visit** for bird-watchers is from late February to June, when the lagoons shrink to a string of pools, forcing wildlife to congregate for food and water.

In the middle of the reserve, connected to the mainland by a causeway, the village of **CROOKED TREE** straggles over a low island in the wetlands. One of the oldest inland villages in the country, its existence is based on fishing, farming and, more recently, tourism. Some of the mango and cashew trees here are reckoned to be more than a hundred years old, and during January and February the air is heavy with the scent of cashew blossom. It's worth coming just to enjoy the unbelievably tranquil pace of life in the village. Even without going on a boat trip through the lagoons you'll see plenty of birds as you stroll through the sandy, tree-lined lanes and along the lakeshore. Guides here are supremely knowledgeable, imparting their expertise with understated enthusiasm.

Practicalities

There are four daily **buses** to Crooked Tree from Belize City. The Jex service (☎025/7017) leaves once daily from Regent St West (Mon–Sat 10.30am), and twice-daily from the Pound Yard bridge (Mon–Fri 4.30pm & 5.30pm); there's also a daily Batty service (Mon–Fri 4pm, Sat noon & Sun 9am). There's enough traffic along the side road from the Northern Highway to make hitching an option, and any non-express bus will drop you off at the junction. As always, it's a good idea to check the times with the bus company (details on p.201), or by calling the village community phone on ☎02/44101 or ☎021/2084. Returning buses leave daily for Belize City (Mon–Sat between 6am & 7am; Sun 4pm). Private telephones are just coming online in Crooked Tree; at present you can use the **telephone** at the Jex store – the best stocked in the village – just past the end of the causeway, or the payphone in the centre of the village. The US$4 visitor fee is payable in the **Sanctuary Visitor Centre** near the end of the causeway. Steve and Donald Tillet and the other reserve wardens are excellent guides, providing a wealth of information on the area's flora, fauna and rural culture.

ACCOMMODATION

Most of the accommodation at Crooked Tree is in resort-type lodgings. If this is not your scene, there's also reasonably priced **bed-and-breakfast** accommodation (*Molly's* is recommended; ④) or check at the visitor centre. Otherwise, there's a dorm room at *Bird's Eye View Lodge* (see below), and most of the resort lodges also have space for **camping** (US$5 per person). All the places listed can arrange superb guided boat tours through the reserve.

Bird's Eye View Lodge (☎02/32040, fax 24869; in US ☎718/845-0749). Comfortable rooms with private bath right on the lakeshore, plus a dorm (US$10 per person) and camping. The food is excellent and the tiny bar on the upstairs deck is a good place to catch the evening breeze. ⑦ including breakfast.

Chau Hiix Lodge (☎02/73787; in US ☎407/322-6361, fax 322-6389). Five well-appointed cabins set in comfortable isolation amid 4000 acres of forest and wetlands at Sapodilla Lagoon, near Chau Hiix ruins, on the southern edge of the sanctuary. Just getting here is an adventure, as the boat (no road access) navigates broad lagoons and tiny creeks. Packages include transport from the airport, meals, guided trips and use of boats and canoes. Two people pay US$525 each for three nights or US$935 for a week.

Crooked Tree Resort (☎02/75819, fax 74007). Neat wood-and-thatch cabins on the lakeshore. ⑤.

Paradise Inn (☎021/2084, fax 02/32579; in US ☎888/875-8453). Simple but beautiful thatched cabins at the north end of the village just paces from the lake, built by the owner Rudy Crawford; his sons Glen and Robert are two of the best guides in the village. The hospitality is wonderful and the home-cooked food is great. Camping available. ⑤.

Sam Tillet's Hotel (☎ & fax 021/2026; in US ☎1-800/765-2611, fax 407/322-6389). Near the village centre, on the bus route, this is the best-value hotel in the village. Rooms (including a budget room downstairs) are in a large, thatched cabaña, each with a private bathroom, and the deck is a good place to relax in the evenings; there's also a shelter for camping. The garden attracts an amazing variety of birds and Sam, known locally as the "king of birds" for his knowledge, is a great host. Superb restaurant too. ④.

Around Crooked Tree

Visitors to Crooked Tree can benefit from a couple of projects carried out nearby by volunteers from two British-based conservation development organizations, each aiming to promote bird-watching around the lagoon. Both are usually accessible only by boat. The first, 3km north of the village, is an amazing 700m long **boardwalk**, supported 1.5m above the swamp on strong logwood posts. Built in 1997 by a Raleigh Expeditions team, the walkway allows access through the otherwise impenetrable low forest at the edge of the lagoon, and a seven-metre-high observation tower affords panoramic **views** – a great place to enjoy the sunset.

Chau Hiix ("small cat"), a Maya site on the western shore of the lagoon, is currently being excavated by a team from the University of Indiana, and, as it has escaped looting, may yield potentially revolutionary discoveries to them. A number of burials have been discovered and the findings are currently being analysed. Climbing the nearby **observation tower** (also with a boardwalk), built in 1998 by volunteers from Trekforce Expeditions, will give you a clearer idea of the site, though admittedly much of what you see is just great, forested mounds. Most of the exposed stonework is covered over at the end of the season, but there are plans to consolidate the structures and make them more accessible to visitors.

Orange Walk and around

With a population approaching 20,000, **ORANGE WALK** is the largest town in the north of Belize and the centre of a busy agricultural region. Like Corozal to the north, Orange Walk was founded by Mestizo refugees fleeing from the Caste Wars in Yucatán in 1849, who chose as their site an area that had long been used for logging camps and was already occupied by the local Icaiché (Chichanha) Maya. Throughout the 1850s and 1860s the Icaiché, led by Marcos Canul, were in conflict with both the Cruzob Maya, who were themselves rebelling against Mestizo rule in Yucatán, and with the British settlers and colonial authorities in Belize. Canul organized successful raids against British mahogany camps and even briefly occupied Corozal in 1870. In 1872 the Icaiché launched an attack on the barracks in Orange Walk. The West India Regiment, which had earlier retreated in disarray after a skirmish with Canul's troops, this time forced the Icaiché to flee across the Rio Hondo, taking the fatally wounded Canul with them. A small monument opposite the park in Orange Walk commemorates the last (officially the only) battle fought on Belizean soil.

Though not unattractive, the town boasts few tourist attractions and Corozal (see p.213), less than an hour to the north, is a preferable place to spend the night. The centre of town is marked by a distinctly Mexican-style formal plaza, shaded by large trees, and the town hall across the main road is called the Palacio Municipal, reinforcing the strong historic links to Mexico. The tranquil, slow-moving **New River**, a few blocks east of the centre, was a busy commercial waterway during the logging days; now it provides a lovely starting point for a visit to the ruins of **Lamanai**, to which several local operators offer tours (see p.209).

Practicalities

Hourly **buses** from Belize City and Corozal pull up on the main road in the centre of town, officially Queen Victoria Avenue but always referred to as the Belize–Corozal Road. Services to and from Sarteneja (see p.212) stop at Zeta's store on Main Street, two blocks to the east, while local buses to the surrounding villages (including Indian Church, for Lamanai) leave from the crossroads by the fire station in the centre of town.

The Belize–Corozal Road is lined with hotels, restaurants and filling stations, so there's no need to walk far. There are no recommended budget **hotels**; if you do have to stay, then the best options are either the *Victoria*, 40 Belize–Corozal Rd, at the southern end of town (☎03/22518, fax 22847; ⑤), where most of the rooms have balconies, some are a/c, and there's a pool, or, better still, the new *St Christopher's*, 10 Main St (☎ & fax 03/21064; ⑤), which has beautiful rooms (some a/c) with private bathrooms, set in grounds sweeping down to the river.

The majority of **restaurants** in Orange Walk are Chinese, though there are a few Belizean-style places serving simple Creole or "Mexican" food. *Lover's Restaurant*, tucked away in the far corner of the park at 20 Lover's Lane, offers the best Belizean food (and is the meeting place for the Novelo's Jungle River Tours), while *Juanita's*, on Santa Ana Street, by the Shell station towards the south end of town, has the best

---

MENNONITES IN BELIZE

The **Mennonites** arose from the radical Anabaptist movement of the sixteenth century and are named after the Dutch priest Menno Simons, leader of the community in its formative years. Recurring government restrictions on their lifestyle, especially regarding their pacifist objection to military service, forced them to move repeatedly. Having removed to Switzerland, they travelled on to Prussia, then in 1663 to Russia, until the government revoked their exemption from military service, whereupon some groups emigrated to North America, settling in the prairies of Saskatchewan. World War I brought more government restrictions, this time on the teaching of German (the Mennonites' language). This, together with more widespread anti-German sentiments in the dominion and the prospect of conscription, drove them from Canada to Mexico, where they settled in the arid northern state of Chihuahua. When the Mexican government required them to be included in its social security programme, it was time to move on again. An investigation into the possibility of settling on their own land in British Honduras brought them to the British colony of Belize in 1958.

They were welcomed enthusiastically by the colonial authorities, eager to have willing workers to clear the jungle for agriculture. Perseverance and hard work made them successful farmers, and in recent years prosperity has caused drastic changes in their lives. The Mennonite Church in Belize is increasingly split between the **Kleine Gemeinde**, a modernist section who use electricity and power tools and drive trucks, tractors and even cars, and the **Altkolonier**, traditionalists who prefer a stricter interpretation of their beliefs. Around Orange Walk the land around Blue Creek, to the north, has been developed by the progressives, while the Mennonites in Shipyard, on the New River, follow a more traditional way of life. Members of the Mennonite community, easily recognizable in their denim dungarees, can be seen trading their produce and buying supplies every day in Orange Walk and Belize City.

Mexican dishes. For Mexican-style *pan dulces* (sweet bread and pastries) and fresh bread, try the Panificadora la Popular, on Beytias Street, off the northeast side of the park. Nightlife boils down to either the weekend **discos** in the *Mi Amor* or *Victoria* hotels or the numerous bars and clubs dotted around town.

The best place to **change money** and get cash advances is the Scotia Bank, just east of the plaza. Caribbean Holidays, on Beytias Street (☎03/22803), is able to book international flights. The **post office** is on the right of the main road at the north end of town.

Maya sites around Orange Walk

Although the **Maya sites** in northern Belize have been the source of a number of the most important archeological finds anywhere in the Maya world, they are not (with the notable exception of Lamanai) as monumentally spectacular as some in the Yucatán. Today, the area around Orange Walk has some of the most productive arable farmland in Belize, and this was also the case in Maya times – aerial surveys in the late 1970s revealed evidence of raised fields and a network of irrigation canals, showing that the Maya practised skilful intensive agriculture. In the Postclassic era this region became part of the powerful Maya state of Chactemal (or Chetumal), controlling the trade in cacao beans (used as currency) grown in the valleys of the Hondo and New rivers. For a while the Maya here were even able to resist the conquistadors, and long after nominal Spanish rule had been established in 1544 there were frequent Maya rebellions, including one in 1638 when they drove the Spanish out and burned the church at Lamanai.

Cuello and Nohmul

Cuello, a small site 5km west of Orange Walk dates back to 1000 BC, making it one of the earliest sites in the Middle Preclassic Maya lowlands. However, the site is more interesting to archeologists than to the casual visitor; there's not much to look at except a single small stepped pyramid (structure 350), rising in nine tiers – a common feature of Maya temples – and several earth-covered mounds. The ruins are behind a factory where Cuello rum is made and the site is on the Cuello family land, so you should ask permission to visit by phoning ☎03/22141; you can also get a tour of the distillery if you ask. A taxi from Orange Walk costs about US$5 each way.

Nohmul (Great Mound), 17km north of Orange Walk and just west of the village of San Pablo, was a major ceremonial centre with origins in the early Preclassic period, perhaps as early as 900 BC. The city was abandoned before the end of the Classic period, to be reoccupied by a Yucatecan elite during the Early Postclassic (known here as the Tecep phase, around 800–1000 AD). The ruins cover a large area, comprising the east and west groups, connected by a *sacbe* (causeway), with several plazas around them. The main feature (structure 2) is an acropolis platform surmounted by a later pyramid which, owing to the site's position on a limestone ridge, is the highest point in northern Belize. As at so many of Belize's Maya sites, looters have plundered the ruins and, tragically, at least one structure has been demolished for road fill.

Nohmul lies amid sugar-cane fields, 2km west of **San Pablo**, on the Northern Highway; any bus between Corozal and Orange Walk goes through the village. To visit the site, contact Estevan Itzab, whose land it's on and who lives in the house on the west side of the highway, across from the village water tower at the north end of the village; his son Guillermo will probably be your guide.

Lamanai

Though they can't match the scale of the great sites in Mexico and Guatemala, the **ruins of Lamanai** (daily 8am–4pm; US$5) are perhaps the most impressive in Belize, and their setting on the New River Lagoon, in a 950-acre archeological reserve, gives them a special quality that is long gone from the sites that are served by a torrent of tourist buses.

Lamanai is one of only a few sites whose original Maya name *Lamanyan* is known; it translates as "Submerged Crocodile", hence the numerous representations of crocodiles. *Lamanai*, however, is a seventeenth-century misunderstanding of *Lamanyan*, and actually means "Drowned Insect". The site was continually occupied from around 500 BC up until the sixteenth century, when Spanish missionaries built a church – the location of Indian Church village. More than seven hundred structures have been mapped here by teams led by David Pendergast of the Royal Ontario Museum, the majority of them still buried beneath mounds of earth. Seven troops of black howler monkeys make Lamanai their home and you'll certainly see a couple of them peering down through the branches as you wander the trails.

The site

The most impressive feature at Lamanai, prosaically named N10-43, but informally called "El Castillo", is a massive **Late Preclassic temple**, towering 35m above the forest floor – and offering magnificent views across the surrounding forest. When first built, around 100 BC, it was the largest structure in the entire Maya World, though it was extensively modified later on. On the way to El Castillo you pass N10-27, a much smaller, unreconstructed pyramid, at the base of which lies **Stela 9**, bearing some of the best-preserved carvings at Lamanai. Dated to 625 AD, it shows the magnificently attired Lord Smoking Shell participating in a ceremony – probably his accession. At the northern end of the site, structure N9-56 is a sixth-century pyramid with two stucco masks of a deity (probably Kinich Ahau, the sun god) carved on different levels. The lower mask, 4m high, is particularly well-preserved, showing a clearly humanized face wearing a crocodile headdress and bordered by decorative columns. The temple overlies several smaller, older buildings, the oldest of which is a superbly preserved temple from around 100 BC and there are a number of other well-preserved and clearly defined glyphs.

The small **archeological museum** at the site houses an amazing collection of artefacts, arranged in chronological order, mostly figurines depicting gods and animals, particularly crocodiles. The most beautiful exhibits are the delicate eccentric flints – star and sceptre-shaped symbols of office – skilfully chipped from a single piece. The most unusual item is a drum the size and shape of a pair of binoculars. Nazario Ku, the friendly head caretaker at the site, is very knowledgeable about Maya culture and is the best guide at the site.

Traces of later settlers can be seen around the nearby village of **INDIAN CHURCH**: to the south of the village are the ruins of two churches built by Spanish missionaries, and to the west are the remains of a nineteenth-century sugar mill, built by Confederate refugees from the American Civil War.

Practicalities

Getting to Lamanai is relatively easy. Three buses a week (Mon, Wed & Fri; 2hr) leave at 4pm from the side of the fire station in Orange Walk for **Indian Church**. The bus is based in the village, leaving for Orange Walk at 6am on the same days, so you'll have to stay overnight; you can check bus times by calling the community phone in Indian Church on ☎031/2015. The most pleasant way to get here, though is by river, and a number of operators organize **day-trips** for US$30–50 per person. By far the most informative are those of Jungle River Tours, run by Antonio, Wilfrido and Herminio Novelo at the *Lover's Restaurant* in Orange Walk (☎03/22293, fax 23749). In addition to their extensive knowledge of Maya sites, the Novelos are also wildlife experts, and will point out the lurking crocodiles and dozens of species of bird, including snail kites, that you might otherwise miss. Another good, regular tour is aboard the *Lamanai Lady*, which departs daily at 9am from the toll bridge 11km south of Orange Walk; book through Discovery Expeditions in Belize City (☎02/31063). For independent travellers on a budget, the best bargain can usually be arranged by Barbara or Tanya at Tower Hill Maya Tours, on the right immediately north of the toll bridge; call ahead to check availability (☎03/23839). To make your own way to the toll bridge, take the Batty bus that leaves Belize City at 7am for Chetumal; the driver will drop you at the right place for the 9am start.

To get to Lamanai **by road** in your own vehicle, head to the south end of Orange Walk and turn right (west) by Dave's Store, where a signpost gives the distance to Lamanai as 35 miles. Continue along the Yo Creek road as far as San Felipe, where you should bear left for the village of Indian Church, 2km from the ruins.

If you want **to stay** in Indian Church (and you'll have to if you're travelling by bus), there are a couple of places offering **rooms** (④), though they're rather overpriced. Speak to Nazario Ku at the site and he'll let you **camp** at his house or rent you a hammock very cheaply; you can eat with the family. You can also visit the Xochil Ku (Sacred Flower) project in his grounds (daily; donation), a butterfly-breeding educational centre where you can see the butterflies develop through the stages of their life cycle. More **upmarket accommodation** is available nearby in the thatched cabañas at *Lamanai Outpost Lodge* (☎ & fax 02/33578; in US ☎1-888/733-7864; ⑧), set in extensive gardens sweeping down to the lagoon. You can arrange to take part in Maya research here under the supervision of archeologist Laura Howard, who is based at the lodge.

The Rio Bravo Conservation Area

In the far northwest of Orange Walk district, the **Rio Bravo Conservation Area** is a 24-square-kilometre tract designated for tropical forest conservation, research and sustained-yield forest harvests. This conservation success story actually began with a disastrous plan in the mid-1980s to clear the forest, initially to fuel a wood-fired power station and later to provide Coca-Cola with frost-free land to grow citrus crops. Environmentalists were alarmed, and their strenuous objections forced Coca-Cola to drop the plan, though the forest remained threatened by agriculture.

An imaginative project to save the threatened forest, the **Programme for Belize** was initiated by the Massachusetts Audubon Society in 1988. Funds were raised from corporate donors and conservation organizations, but the most widespread support was generated through an ambitious "adopt-an-acre" scheme, enthusiastically taken up by schools and individuals in the UK and North America. Coca-Cola itself, anxious to distance itself from the charge of rainforest destruction, has donated more than nine square kilometres. Today, rangers with powers of arrest patrol the area to prevent illegal hunting and logging and to stop farmers encroaching onto the reserve with their milpas. The guarded boundaries also protect dozens of Maya sites, most of them unexcavated and unrestored, though many have been looted. Thanks to the ban on hunting, the forest teems with **wildlife**, including all five of Belize's cat species, tapirs, monkeys and crocodiles and more than three hundred species of bird.

Adjoining the Rio Bravo Conservation Area to the south, the privately owned land of **Gallon Jug** also contains a large area of protected land, in the centre of which is the fabulous *Chan Chich Lodge,* regarded as one of the best eco-lodges in the world. There's no **public transport** to the Rio Bravo Conservation Area, but it's possible to arrange a stay at either of the **field stations**, or at *Chan Chich* (see below).

La Milpa and Hill Bank field stations

One of the aims of the Programme for Belize is environmental education, and **field stations** have been built at La Milpa and Hill Bank to accommodate both visitors and students. Each field station has comfortable (though expensive) **dorms** (US$75 per person), and the facilities utilize the latest "green" technology, including solar power and composting toilets. Prices, though high (discounts for student groups), include three meals and two excursions or lectures a day. La Milpa also has beautiful **cabañas** which sleep up to six (US$90 per person). To visit or stay at either station contact the station manager through the PFB office, 2 South Park St, Belize City (☎02/75616, fax 75635) who may be able to arrange transport, or write to PFB, Box 749, Belize City. **La Milpa Field Station**, set in a former milpa clearing in the higher, northwestern forest, has a tranquil, studious atmosphere. Deer and ocellated turkeys feed contentedly around the cabins and there are binoculars and telescopes for spotting birds. Anyone can stay, but guests are mainly students on tropical ecology courses. A day-visit to the field station, which includes a guided tour of La Milpa ruins or one of the trails costs US$20, but getting there on public transport is not easy; you'll have to get a bus from Orange Walk to San Felipe, 37km away, and arrange to be picked up there – the PFB office has details.

Hill Bank Field Station, at the southern end of the New River Lagoon, is a former logging camp which has been adapted to undertake scientific forestry research and development, and there are often students and scientists working here, including archeological teams from the University of Texas. There's plenty of wildlife around too, particularly birds and crocodiles, and butterflies abound.

La Milpa ruins
Five kilometres west of the field station is the huge Classic Maya city of **La Milpa**, the third largest site in Belize. The **ceremonial centre**, built on top of a limestone ridge, is one of the most impressive anywhere, with at least 24 courtyards and two ball courts; while the **Great Plaza**, flanked by four temple-pyramids (the tallest stands 24m above the plaza floor), is one of the largest public spaces in the Maya World. After centuries of expansion, La Milpa was abandoned in the ninth century, though Postclassic groups subsequently occupied the site and the Maya here resisted both the Spanish conquest in the sixteenth century and British mahogany cutters in the nineteenth century. Recent finds have included major elite burials with many jade grave goods.

Gallon Jug and Chan Chich Lodge

Forty kilometres south of the La Milpa field station, the former logging town of **GAL-LON JUG**, set in neat fenced pastures, is the home of Barry Bowen, reportedly the richest man in Belize. In the 1980s, his speculative land deals led to an international outcry against threatened rainforest clearance. The experience apparently proved cathartic as Bowen is now an ardent conservationist and most of the 125,000 acres here are strictly protected. The focal point is the luxurious, world-class **Chan Chich Lodge** (☎ & fax 02/34419; in US ☎1-800/343-8009; ⑨), with twelve large thatched cabañas set in the plaza of the Classic Maya site of Chan Chich, surrounded by forest. It is a truly awe-inspiring setting: grass-covered temple walls crowned with jungle tower up from the lodge, and the forest explodes with a cacophony of bird calls at dawn. The **guided**

trails are incomparable, with consistently high wildlife sightings, day or night. You can drive here from Orange Walk through Blue Creek and La Milpa, but most guests fly in to the airstrip at Gallon Jug.

Sarteneja and the Shipstern Nature Reserve

The largely uninhabited **Sarteneja peninsula**, jutting out towards the Yucatán in the northeast of Belize, is covered with dense forests, swamps and lagoons that support an amazing array of wildlife. The only village here is **Sarteneja**, a mainly Spanish-speaking lobster-fishing centre that's just beginning to experience tourism. A couple of new hotels have been built, there's also accommodation at the reserve headquarters (see practicalities, below), and guides are available to take you to the lagoons and beyond. Although Sarteneja itself, and especially its shoreline, are pretty enough, it's the **Shipstern Nature Reserve**, 5km before the village (daily 8am–5pm; US$5 including guided walk), established in 1981 and covering eighty square kilometres, which is the main attraction. All **buses** to Sarteneja pass the entrance to the reserve; the head-quarters and **visitor centre** are just 100m from the road.

The bulk of the reserve is made up of what's technically known as "tropical moist forest", although it contains only a few mature trees as the area was wiped clean by Hurricane Janet in 1955. It also includes some wide belts of savannah – covered in coarse grasses, palms and broad-leaved trees – and the shallow Shipstern Lagoon, dotted with mangrove islands. Taking the superb guided walk along the **Chiclero Trail** from the visitor centre, you'll encounter more named plant species in one hour than on any other trail in Belize. It's also a bird-watcher's paradise: the lagoon system supports blue-winged teal, American coot, thirteen species of egret and huge flocks of lesser scaup, while the forest is home to fly-catchers, warblers, keel-billed toucans, collared aracari and at least five species of parrot. In addition, there are crocodiles, manatees, coatis, jaguars, peccaries, deer, raccoons, pumas and an abundance of insects, particularly butterflies. Though the reserve's butterfly farm didn't prove as lucrative as hoped, the wardens still tend the butterflies carefully, releasing them into the forest when mature. You can **stay** here in neat four-bed dorms (US$10 per person) with cooking facilities, and there's a two-roomed house for rent (US$40 per day). For information, call the Belize Audubon Society (BAS) in Belize City (☎02/34987), though there will almost certainly be room if you just turn up.

Sarteneja village practicalities

Three daily **buses** leave Belize City for Sarteneja: the Perez bus leaves the Texaco station on N Front St at 11.30am and 1pm, and Venus leaves at 12.30pm (all times Mon–Sat), passing through Orange Walk (stopping at Zeta's store on Main Street ninety minutes later); buses return to Belize City from Sarteneja at 4am, 5am, and 6am.

There's no shortage of **accommodation** in Sarteneja. The long-established *Diani's Hotel* (☎04/32084; ④), right in the centre of town facing the shore, is inexpensive but rather run-down; better options are *Fernando's Seaside Guest House* (☎04/32085; ⑤), on the seafront, which has spacious, thatched rooms with private bath, or *Sayab Cabañas* (④), towards the back of the village by the water tower, which has two lovely thatched cabins with private bath set in a small garden filled with tropical plants. All the places to stay also serve **food**; the thatched *Mira Mar* restaurant on the seafront is also the most obvious bar, and there are several more dotted around the village. Fernando Alamilla, who runs *Fernando's*, is an excellent **fishing guide** and can take you across to Bacalar Chico National Park, on Ambergris Caye (see p.222).

Corozal and around

COROZAL, 45km north of Orange Walk along the Northern Highway, is Belize's most northerly town, just twenty minutes from the Mexican border. Corozal's location near the mouth of the New River enabled the ancient Maya to prosper here by controlling river- and seaborne trade, and two sites – Santa Rita and Cerros – are within easy reach. The present town was founded in 1849 by refugees from the massacre in Bacalar, Mexico, who were hounded south by the Caste Wars.

Today's grid-pattern town is a neat mix of Mexican and Caribbean, its appearance largely due to reconstruction in the wake of Hurricane Janet in 1955. There's little to do in Corozal, but it's an agreeable place to spend the day on the way to or from the border, and is hassle-free, even at night. There's a breezy shoreline park shaded by palm trees, while on the tree-shaded main plaza, the **town hall** is worth a look inside for the vivid depiction of local history in a mural by Manuel Villamar Reyes. In two of the plaza's corners you can see the remains of small forts, built to ward off Indian attacks.

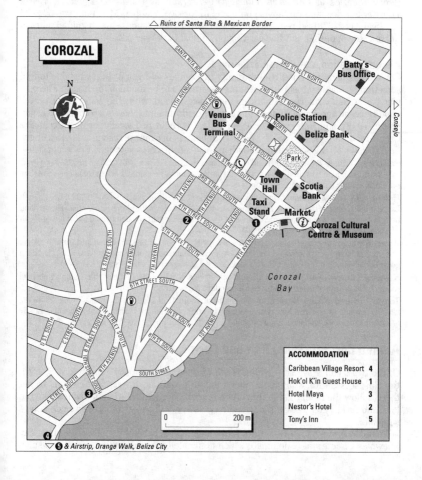

ACCOMMODATION

Caribbean Village Resort	4
Hok'ol K'in Guest House	1
Hotel Maya	3
Nestor's Hotel	2
Tony's Inn	5

On October 12, **Columbus Day** – or PanAmerica Day, as it is now known – celebrations in Corozal are particularly lively, a combination of Mexican fiesta and Caribbean carnival.

Arrival and information

All **buses** between Belize City and Chetumal pass through Corozal, roughly hourly in each direction. Maya Island Air and Tropic Air operate daily **flights** between Corozal and San Pedro on Ambergris Caye. Jal's travel agency (☎04/22163) at the south of town, beyond *Tony's Inn*, can organize both domestic and international flights.

For reliable tourist **information**, visit the **Corozal Cultural Centre** (☎04/23176; Tues–Sat 9am–noon & 1–4.30pm), housed in the restored colonial market building in the waterfront park, just past the new market. Inside, there's a museum (US$1.50) with imaginative displays depicting episodes in Corozal's history. Scotia Bank, on the plaza, is the best place for **cash advances**, and the **post office** is on the west side of the plaza. For organized **tours** to local nature reserves and archeological sites, contact Henry Menzies at *Caribbean Village* (☎04/22725); he's also the agent for Belize Transfer Service, and can advise on travel to Mexico. Stephan Moerman (☎04/22833 or 22539, fax 22278), a French biologist and naturalist, arranges superb guided tours to Cerros (see opposite) and Bacalar Chico National Park (see p.222).

Accommodation, eating and drinking

Corozal has plenty of hotel **rooms** in all price ranges and you'll always be able to find something suitable. Most of the best **meals** are also to be found in the hotels. The popular bar at *Nestor's* serves American and Belizean food, while the *Hotel Maya* serves good Belizean and Jamaican food in a quieter environment. There's a wonderful restaurant at *Tony's*, and *Haley's* in *Caribbean Village* is renowned locally for its inexpensive Creole food. Corozal also has the usual complement of Chinese restaurants. Amazingly, *Le Café Kela*, on the seafront just north of the centre, serves authentic French pastries.

Caribbean Village Resort, south end of town, across from the sea (☎04/22045, fax 23414). Good-value, whitewashed, thatched cabins, with hot water, among the palms. Plus an inexpensive restaurant, trailer park (US$12) and camping (US$5). ④.

Hok'ol K'in Guest House, facing the sea a block south of the market (☎04/23329, fax 23569). Large, tiled rooms with hammocks on the balcony and private bath, plus some suites. The ground floor is completely wheelchair-accessible, and there's a restaurant, gardens and a guest lounge with a book exchange and videos of Belize. ⑤.

Hotel Maya, south end of town, facing the sea (☎04/22082, fax 22827). Clean and friendly place. The rooms have been renovated and all have private bathrooms; new rooms have a/c. There's a good restaurant, and the owner, Rosita May, is the local agent for Maya Island Air. ④–⑤.

Nestor's, 5th Ave South, between 4th and 5th streets (☎04/22354). Reasonable budget hotel; all rooms have private showers and there's a popular sports bar and restaurant. ④.

Tony's Inn and Beach Resort, on the seafront, about 1km south of the plaza (☎04/22055, fax 22829). A touch of well-run luxury in a superb location with secure parking. The spacious, mostly a/c rooms overlook landscaped gardens and a pristine beach bar. Excellent restaurant. ⑦.

Around Corozal: Santa Rita and Cerros

Of the two small Maya sites within reach of Corozal (both daily 8am–4pm; US$2.50), the closest is **Santa Rita**, about fifteen minutes' walk northwest of the town. To get there, follow the main road in the direction of the border and when it divides take the left-hand fork; Peter Ponce, the friendly caretaker, will show you around once you've signed in.

Founded around 1500 BC, Santa Rita was in all probability the powerful Maya city known as **Chactemal** (Chetumal), which dominated the trade of the area. It was still a

GETTING TO AND FROM AMBERGRIS CAYE

Flying to San Pedro is the easiest and most popular approach: from Belize City Municipal and Belize International airports, Maya Island Air (☎02/31140 or 026/2345 in San Pedro) and Tropic Air (☎02/45671; 026/2012 in San Pedro) between them have flights at least hourly from 7am to 5pm (25min). Both airlines also fly from San Pedro to Corozal (see p.214), so you could head into Mexico without returning to Belize City.

Though **boats** from Belize City to San Pedro (1hr 15min; US$12.50 one way) are less frequent than those to Caye Caulker (see box on p.225), there are a few regular fast services. The *Triple J* (☎02/44375) is the best boat on the run and one of the first to leave, at 9am from Courthouse Wharf, returning at 3pm. Another boat, run by the Caye Caulker Water Taxis, leaves from the Marine Terminal by the Swing Bridge at 9am, leaving San Pedro at 2.30pm. In the afternoons the *Thunderbolt* leaves the Swing Bridge at 1pm, returning at 7am, the *Andrea* leaves Courthouse Wharf at 3pm, returning from San Pedro at 7am, and the *Seascape*, leaves from the dock in front of the Bellevue Hotel at 4pm, calling at Caye Caulker and returning from San Pedro at 8am.

Travelling from San Pedro to other cayes, any of the above scheduled boats also stop at Caye Caulker (and there are regular departures from San Pedro to Caye Caulker from 8am to 4.30pm), and they'll also call at St George's Caye or Caye Chapel if you ask.

restaurants and bars are here; the few budget places are in the original village of San Pedro. Despite development, the town just about manages to retain elements of its Caribbean charm with two-storey, clapboard buildings still predominating in the centre. One of the most interesting (and hectic) times to be in San Pedro is during the **International Costa Maya Festival**, a week-long celebration featuring cultural and musical presentations from the five Mundo Maya countries, held annually in the third week of July. The festival began as a way to drum up visitors during the off season; it's now so popular you may need to book rooms.

Arrival and information

Arriving in San Pedro, boats usually dock at the *Coral Beach* or Texaco piers on the front (reef) side of the island. Both are within a block or so of the centre of town, marked by the seafront Central Park. Landing at San Pedro's **airport**, at the north end of Coconut Drive, only 500m south of the centre, is almost as convenient. It's within walking distance of any of the hotels in town, though golf buggies and **taxis** will be waiting. You can leave luggage near the airport while you look for somewhere to stay – see the staff in the Travel and Tour Belize office a few steps north of the terminal; they can also give good advice and information on hotels (including budget options), or indeed anything else in San Pedro.

San Pedro's official **tourist office** (daily 9am–5pm; ☎026/2298) shares its location with the new Ambergris Museum (see p.220) in the Island Plaza Mall on Barrier Reef Drive; the travel or tour agencies recommended on p.224 can also provide accurate information. It's always worth picking up a copy of the island's free tourist newspaper, the *San Pedro Sun*, available from most hotels and restaurants. Finally, as befits Belize's premier tourist destination, Ambergris Caye has one of the best Belizean **Web sites** – *www.ambergriscaye.com*.

Orientation and getting around the island

The three **main streets** of the town centre run parallel to the beach. Formerly (and more prosaically) called Front, Middle and Back streets, they have now been given names more

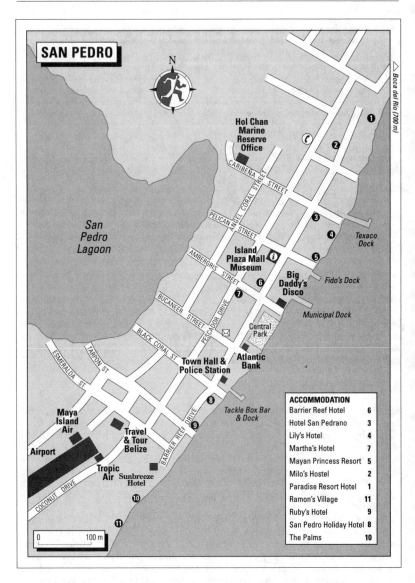

SAN PEDRO

N

San Pedro Lagoon

Hol Chan Marine Reserve Office

CARIBENA STREET

PELICAN STREET

ANGEL CORAL STREET

AMBERGRIS STREET

Island Plaza Mall Museum

Big Daddy's Disco

BUCANEER STREET

PESCADOR DRIVE

BLACK CORAL ST.

TARPON ST.

ESMERALDA ST.

Central Park

Town Hall & Police Station

Atlantic Bank

Maya Island Air

Travel & Tour Belize

Airport

Tropic Air

Sunbreeze Hotel

COCONUT DRIVE

BARRIER REEF DRIVE

Tackle Box Bar & Dock

Boca del Rio (700 m)

Texaco Dock

Fido's Dock

Municipal Dock

0   100 m

ACCOMMODATION	
Barrier Reef Hotel	6
Hotel San Pedrano	3
Lily's Hotel	4
Martha's Hotel	7
Mayan Princess Resort	5
Milo's Hostel	2
Paradise Resort Hotel	1
Ramon's Village	11
Ruby's Hotel	9
San Pedro Holiday Hotel	8
The Palms	10

in keeping with the new upmarket image – Barrier Reef Drive, Pescador Drive and Angel Coral Street. Most locals stick to the old names; in any case it's impossible to get lost.

The town centre is small enough to get around on foot; pleasant enough at any time, it's particularly enjoyable on weekend evenings, when Barrier Reef Drive is closed to vehicles. However, in recent years, the town has expanded rapidly to the north and south, so you might want to **rent a bike**, a **moped** or a very expensive **golf cart** from one of the travel agencies, in order to explore the sometimes rough roads further out.

Several hotels out of the centre have **courtesy bikes** for guests – something you might want to bear in mind when choosing a place to stay. On some occasions you might need a **water taxi**, especially if you're staying in the northern resorts; you'll often find them by the dock in front of Fido's Courtyard, a group of shops and restaurants on Barrier Reef Drive just north of the park. Armando, with his skiff *Jean Luc*, is very reliable, though at US$20 a ride, it's expensive for fewer than four people (call ☎014/9448 to check the fare). There's also a **fast ferry** to and from the north – the comfortable *Island Express* (US$4 each way), leaving from Fido's every two hours between 7.15am and 11.15pm, returning from 8.15am to 10.15pm.

Accommodation

Most of the **hotels**, including all the budget options, are in San Pedro itself, though there are increasing numbers of more expensive places north and south of the town. You shouldn't have any problem finding somewhere to stay in the high season (December to Easter), with the exception of Christmas and Easter weeks when booking ahead is definitely advisable. **Prices** are higher in general than in the rest of Belize but **discounts** on the quoted rates are often available, especially in the low season, so it's worth calling ahead to ask. Almost everywhere takes credit cards.

Budget to mid-range accommodation

Changes in Latitudes, 1km south of town, near the Belize Yacht Club (☎ & fax 026/2986). Very friendly small B&B set in gardens half a block from the sea with immaculately clean rooms, some a/c. Canadian owner Lori Reed is a mine of information, and offers free pickup from the airport. Good low-season discounts. ⑦ including breakfast.

Del Rio Cabañas, ten-minutes' walk north of the centre (☎ & fax 026/2286; in US ☎318/984-9655). Friendly place with a range of accommodation: *Las Cabañas*, comfortable wood-and-thatch cabins with fans, facing the sea; *Casa Blanca*, modern a/c rooms; *Los Cuartos*, budget rooms with shared bath. ④–⑦.

Hideaway Lodge, 1km or so south of the town, (☎026/2141, fax 2269). Large, recently renovated, rooms with fan or a/c; especially good value for groups. Relaxing pool area and good restaurant. Guests can rent bicycles. ⑥.

Laidy's Apartments, along the beach north of the town centre (☎026/2682). Well-furnished rooms, all with private bath and hot water; good value if you're sharing. ⑤–⑥.

Martha's, Pescador Drive across from *Elvie's Kitchen* (☎026/2053). Clean, comfortable rooms with fan, bedside lights and private bathroom. ④.

Milo's, at the north end of Barrier Reef Drive, on the left just before the *Paradise Hotel* (☎026/2033, fax 2198). The best-value budget hotel on the caye; basic but clean rooms, some with private bath. Shared bathrooms have hot water. No credit cards. ④.

Ruby's, Barrier Reef Drive, a very short walk from the airstrip (☎026/2063, fax 2434). Clean, comfortable, family-run hotel right on the seafront. Rooms get better views and increased rates the higher up you go; all are good value. ④–⑤.

More expensive hotels

Barrier Reef Hotel, in the centre of town, opposite the park (☎026/2075, fax 2719). Distinctive, white-painted colonial-style building with a pool. The bright, clean rooms all have a/c and there's a good restaurant. ⑦.

Capricorn Resort, on the beach 5km north of town (☎026/2809, fax 021/2091). Most people come here for the incredibly good restaurant (see p.223), but there are also three delightful, secluded, wooden cabins with porches, and a beautiful upper-storey suite with a/c, overlooking a pristine beach. Breakfast is included, as is transport by water taxi from town on arrival and departure; free bike rental for guests. ⑨.

Caribbean Villas Hotel, 2km south of town (☎026/2715, fax 2885). Spacious, very comfortable rooms and well-equipped suites, all with ocean views, set in a garden on the beachfront; the best-value smaller hotel in this range. Free guest bikes. ⑧–⑨.

Coconuts, on the beach 1500m south of town (☎026/3500, fax 3501). A comfortable, modern hotel with clean, well-decorated tiled rooms, all with a/c. Very helpful and informative owners, who provide free bikes for guests and pay the taxi fare when you arrive. ⑦–⑧.

Mata Chica Beach Resort, on the beach 7km north of town (☎ & fax 021/3012). The most beautiful and spacious beach cabañas in the country, designed by French/Italian owners Philippe and Nadia and painted in pastel colours that change with the light. Each interior is unique, with murals by French artist Lionel Dumas. The reef is just 600m away; guests can sail there aboard the resort's luxurious catamaran. US$165 for a double cabaña. ⑨.

Mayan Princess Resort, Barrier Reef Drive, just north of the centre (☎026/2778, fax 2784). Very comfortable, spacious, well-equipped beachfront suites, each with a large balcony overlooking the sea; the best value suites in town for the price. ⑨.

Paradise Resort Hotel, at the north end of Barrier Reef Drive (☎026/2083, fax 2232). A well-run hotel in a great beachside location. Accommodation ranges from thatched double rooms and spacious cabañas to modern villas sleeping up to six. ⑦–⑨.

The Palms, Coconut Drive, just south of the town centre (☎026/3322, fax 3601). Luxury, well-furnished a/c suites overlooking the beachfront in a quiet location, but conveniently near the town. Lots of extras here, including fully equipped kitchens, daily maid service and a beautiful private pool. US$158 for a one-bedroom suite. ⑨.

San Pedro Holiday Hotel, Barrier Reef Drive, just south of the town centre (☎026/2014, fax 2295). San Pedro's oldest hotel, but with all modern facilities, including a/c. There's a very good restaurant, plus *Celi's Deli* which serves good-value snacks. ⑧.

Victoria House, 3km south of town (☎026/2067, fax 2429; in US ☎1-800/247-5159). A range of luxury villas, cabañas and hotel rooms set in a stunning beachfront location and an obvious hit with honeymooners. Service is excellent and there's a fine restaurant. Prices start at US$130 for a double room in high season, and go up to US$545 for a two-bed villa. ⑨.

Exploring the caye and the reef

Although there are a few places you can visit on land, it's the water which is the focus of daytime entertainment on Ambergris Caye, from sunbathing on the docks to windsurfing, sailing, fishing, diving and snorkelling. Many hotels will rent snorkelling equipment and there are several specialist **dive shops** offering instruction. A word of **warning**: there have been a number of accidents in San Pedro in which speeding boats have hit people swimming off the piers. A line of buoys, not always clearly visible, indicates the "safe area", but speedboat drivers can be a bit macho; be careful when choosing where to swim.

Before going snorkelling or diving, whet your appetite for the wonders of the reef with a visit to the excellent **Hol Chan Marine Reserve office and visitor centre** (Mon–Fri 8am–noon & 1–5pm; ☎026/2247) on Caribeña St. They have photographs, maps and other displays on the marine reserves (see p.222), and the staff will be pleased to answer your questions; you may even be able to get a ride with the ranger up to Bacalar Chico. Equally worthwhile is a visit to the new **Ambergris Museum** in the Island Plaza Mall on Barrier Reef Drive (daily 2–6pm; US$2.50). Maya pottery comprises some of the oldest exhibits, with colonial weapons and old photographs illustrating the island's history right up to the 1960s.

South of San Pedro, the road continues for several kilometres to the Maya site of **Marco Gonzalez**, but the further you go the swampier and more mosquito-infested the terrain becomes. The site is hard to find and there's not a lot to see, but studies have shown that it was once an important trade centre, with close links to Lamanai (see p.209). Archeological teams are still investigating here, so check at the museum to see if work is going on during your visit. A kilometre or so **north of San Pedro**, the **Boca del Rio**, sometimes called "The River" but actually a widening erosion channel, is crossed during daylight by a tiny ferry (US$0.50 per person) just big enough to take a golf cart (US$2.50); on the other side a rudimentary road (also navigable by golf cart) leads to the northern resorts. The northernmost section of the caye, now accessible on organized day-trips, boasts the spectacular **Bacalar Chico National Park and Marine Reserve** and several **Maya sites**.

Diving

For anyone who has never dived in the tropics before, the **reefs near San Pedro** are fine, but experienced divers looking for high-voltage diving will be disappointed. This is a heavily used area which has long been subjected to intensive fishing, and much of the reef has been plundered by souvenir hunters. To experience the best diving in Belize you need to take a trip out to one of the **atolls**.

Dive instruction and **local dives** are best done with smaller, independent operators rather than the bigger dive shops, as both the instruction and guiding will be more tailored to your needs. In general, a PADI or NAUI **open-water certification**, which takes novices up to the standard of a fully qualified sport diver, costs around US$350; a more basic, introductory **resort course** costs around US$125. For **qualified divers** a two-tank dive costs around US$50, including tanks, weights, air and boat. The best dive shops in San Pedro recommend you make a voluntary contribution of US$1 per tank to help fund the town's **hyperbaric chamber**: this covers you for treatment if you need it, so make sure you fill out the agreement when you sign on to dive.

Among the best local operators are Amigos del Mar, at the well-signed dock just north of the centre (☎026/2706, fax 2648). Two **live-aboard dive boats** are also based in San Pedro, giving you the opportunity to stay out at the atolls for two to three days. Both vessels are crewed by professionals, carry safety equipment and sleep five or six, though usually you'll be **camping** on one of the remote cayes of Lighthouse Reef (see p.230). The *Caye Explorer* (☎026/5019), a charter-only boat, costs US$125 per person per day; the *Offshore Express* (☎026/2817) runs a couple of two-day trips per week, charging US$250 for five dives. Finally, the *Blue Hole Express* (☎026/2982) runs **day-trips** to the Blue Hole, which cost US$165 for divers, US$110 for snorkellers. The boats are popular and space is limited, so book well in advance if possible: any of the above boats pick up passengers at Caye Caulker on request, at no extra charge. For the best **advice** on any aspect of diving from San Pedro, or to book the dive boats recommended above, contact Chris Allnatt at the Blue Hole Dive Center, on Barrier Reef Drive.

Snorkelling

Just about every hotel in San Pedro offers **snorkelling** trips, costing around US$15 for three hours, plus about US$5 to rent equipment. If you've never used a snorkel before, practise the technique from a dock first; you might prefer to snorkel in a life jacket – this will give you greater buoyancy and prevent you from bumping into the coral. Generally, the options available mean you can either head north to the spectacular **Mexico Rocks** or Rocky Point or, more commonly, south to the **Hol Chan Marine Reserve** (see p.222). **Night snorkelling**, a truly amazing experience, is also available, and usually costs a little more than a daytime trip. Several boats take snorkellers out for a day-trip to Caye Caulker, employing a mix of motor and sail, and comprising two leisurely snorkelling stops and lunch on the caye, returning to San Pedro around sunset: the *Rum Punch II* (US$40), a ten-metre sailboat, and the 22-metre motor-powered *Winnie Estelle* (US$55), with an open bar and a spacious, shaded deck to spread out on are the best overall value.

In addition to the boat trips to **Caye Caulker** there are increasingly popular **day-trips** on land from San Pedro to the ruins of **Altun Ha** (see p.203) and even **Lamanai** (see p.209). Rounding the southern tip of the island in a fast skiff, you head for the mainland at the mouth of the Northern River, cross the lagoon and travel up the river to the tiny village of Bomba. With a good guide this is an excellent way to spot wildlife, including **crocodiles** and **manatees**, and the riverbank trees are often adorned with **orchids**. Two of the best **guides** are Daniel Nuñez (☎026/2314) and Fido Badillo (☎026/2286).

The south: Hol Chan Marine Reserve

The **Hol Chan Marine Reserve**, 8km south of San Pedro, at the southern tip of the caye, takes its name from the Maya for "little channel", and it is this break in the reef that forms the focus of the reserve. Established in 1987, its three zones – covering a total of around thirteen square kilometres – preserve a comprehensive cross-section of the marine environment, from **coral reef** through **seagrass beds** to **mangroves**. All three habitats are closely linked: many reef fish feed on the seagrass beds, and the mangroves are a nursery area for the juveniles. As your boat approaches, you'll be met by a warden who explains the rules and collects the entry fee (US$2.50). You'll see plenty of marine life here, including some very large **snappers**, **groupers** and **barracuda**. However, its very popularity brings problems, and much damage has already been caused by snorkellers standing on the coral or holding onto outcrops for a better look – on all the easily accessible areas of the reef you will see the white, dead patches, especially on the large brain coral heads. **Never touch** the coral – not only will that damage the delicate ecosystem, but it can also cause you agonizing burns; even brushing against the razor-sharp ridges on the reef top can cause cuts that are slow to heal.

Near Hol Chan, but outside the reserve, is the extremely popular (but controversial) **shark-ray alley**, where you can swim with **nurse sharks** and **stingrays** in water only 2–3m deep. Despite their reputations, these creatures are not that dangerous, and watching them glide effortlessly beneath you is an exhilarating experience. Biologists, however, claim that the practice of feeding the fish to attract them alters their natural behaviour, exposing both the fish and humans to danger – at times the area is so crowded that any hope of communing with nature is completely lost amongst the flailing bodies of the snorkellers.

The north: Bacalar Chico National Park and the Maya sites

A visit to the remote and virtually pristine northern section of Ambergris Caye is an unmissable highlight, not only for the obvious attractions of the **Bacalar Chico Marine Reserve and National Park**, but also for the chance to see a number of previously inaccessible **Maya sites** on the northern coast. On a day-trip from San Pedro you can visit several areas of the reserve and take in two or three of the ten or more Maya sites; the best **guide** to Bacalar Chico is Daniel Nuñez (☎026/2314). Travelling by boat through Boca del Rio and up the west coast, you might briefly stop to observe colonies of seabirds roosting on some small, uninhabited cayes; there are several species of herons and egrets and you might even spot the **roseate spoonbill**.

The reserve itself covers the entire northern tip of Ambergris Caye – the largest protected area in the northern cayes. Its 110 square kilometres extend from the reef, across the seagrass beds to the coastal mangroves and **caye littoral forest**, and over to the salt marsh and lagoon behind. The reserve is patrolled by rangers based at the headquarters and **visitor centre** at San Juan, on the northwest coast, where you register and pay the US$2.50 park fee. There's a surprising amount of **wildlife** up here, including crocodiles, deer, peccary and, prowling around the thick forests, several of the wild cats of Belize. Birdlife is abundant and **turtles** nest on some beaches: contact the Belize Audubon Society (see p.197) or the Hol Chan Reserve office (see p.220) if you want to help patrol the beaches during the turtle nesting season.

Some of the **Maya sites** in the north of the caye are undergoing archeological investigation and there's a real air of adventure and discovery as you explore the ancient ruins now buried in thick bush and jungle. **Santa Cruz**, about two-thirds of the way up the west coast of Ambergris Caye, is a very large site, known to have been used for the shipment of trade goods in the Postclassic era, though the true function of most of the stone mounds here remains uncertain. Further north, the beach at **San Juan** was another transhipment centre for the ancient Maya; here you'll be crunching over literally thousands of pieces of Maya pottery. But perhaps the most spectacular site is **Chac Balam**, a ceremonial and administrative centre; getting there entails a walk through mangroves to view deep burial chambers, scattered with thousands more pottery shards.

On the way back, you navigate **Bacalar Chico**, the narrow channel dug by the Maya about 1500 years ago to allow a shorter paddling route for their trading canoes between their cities in Chetumal Bay and the coast of Yucatán. At the mouth of the channel the reef is close to the shore; the boat has to cross into the open sea, re-entering the leeward side of the reef as you approach San Pedro, so completing a circumnavigation of the island.

Eating, drinking and entertainment

There are plenty of places to **eat** in San Pedro, including some of the best restaurants in the country. Although prices are generally higher than elsewhere in Belize, you'll usually get good service – comparatively rare in much of the country. **Seafood** is prominent at most restaurants; you can also rely on plenty of steak, shrimp, chicken, pizza and salads. Many **hotels** have their own dining room, and in many cases also do **beach barbecues**. There are several **Chinese** restaurants, too, the cheaper ones representing the best value on the island. In the evening several **fast-food stands** open for business in front of the park on Barrier Reef Drive.

Buying your own food isn't particularly cheap here: there's no market and the grocery stores are stocked with imported canned goods. The range and quality of groceries is improving all the time, however: Rock's **supermarket** – one on Pescador Drive and one south of town in San Pablo – has the widest selection, while Milo's, at the north end of Barrier Reef Drive, offers the best value. At the luxury end of the scale, there's the Sweet Basil deli, just north of Boca del Rio, with a great selection of imported cheeses, wine and paté. La Popular **bakery**, on Pescador Drive has a wide selection of breads, including Mexican-style *pan dulces*. *Manelly's Ice Cream Parlour*, on Pescador, is the best place in town for a sit-down **ice cream** treat.

Restaurants

Big Daddy's Fast Food, just past the park, in front of *Big Daddy's Disco*. The best and cheapest indoor fast food in town, serving large portions of very good Belizean and Mexican-style dishes at great prices in a new a/c restaurant. Open lunchtime until late in the evening.

Capricorn Restaurant, on the beach in *Capricorn Resort* (☎026/2809). Unbeatable gourmet food in a beautiful location; try the French crêpes, stone-crabcakes or filet mignon/seafood combo. Book for dinner in high season.

Celi's Restaurant, in the *Holiday Hotel*. Good seafood and evening barbecues. Closed Wed. *Celi's Deli* does delicious breakfasts and snacks, including the best *tamales* in town.

El Patio, a couple of kilometres south of the centre, next to the Rock's supermarket. Fine dining at very reasonable prices in a lovely courtyard with fountains. Open for all meals.

Elvie's Kitchen, on Pescador, across from *Martha's* (☎026/2176). Long an institution in San Pedro, and always serving good burgers and fries, *Elvie's* has now zoomed upmarket, with an expanded menu featuring soups, Caesar salad, steaks, chicken and, of course, lobster. Good food and service with gentle live music in the evenings; you may need to book for dinner.

Jade Garden, Coconut Drive, south of town. The best Chinese restaurant on the island, and good value too.

Little Italy, in the *Spindrift Hotel* (☎026/2866). San Pedro's finest Italian restaurant. Excellent food and service, and a good wine list. Their great-value Mexican-style lunch buffet (11.30am–2pm) has lots of choice. You may need to book for dinner in high season.

Mambo, on the beach 7km north of town (☎021/3010). The dining room of the *Mata Chica Beach Resort* and Ambergris Caye's top restaurant, with superb food and wine and a classy, romantic atmosphere. The menu changes daily but it is always fabulous; try Nadia's exquisite homemade fettuccini or the original paella. Dinner reservations are essential: guests are picked up from *The Palms* hotel for dinner at 6.30pm; call for lunch.

Rasta Pasta Pizza Amor, in the *Sunbreeze Hotel*, at the south end of Barrier Reef Drive. Another wonderful San Pedro restaurant, serving a range of dishes at reasonable prices, all carefully seasoned with Maralyn and Albert's unique, home-prepared spices. A great place for nightlife too.

The Reef, near the north end of Pescador. Really good Belizean food, including delicious seafood, at great prices in a simple restaurant cooled by a battery of fans.

Ruby's Café, Barrier Reef Drive, next to *Ruby's Hotel*. Delicious homemade cakes, pies and sandwiches, and freshly brewed coffee served from 6am.

Bars and nightlife

Entertainment in San Pedro becomes more sophisticated every year, and the best way to find out what's on (and what's hot) is to ask at your hotel or check the listings in the *San Pedro Sun*; what follows is a brief mention of a few of the highlights. Many of the hotels have fancy bars, several of which offer **happy hours** – usually two for the price of one on local drinks – while back from the main street are a couple of small **cantinas** where you can buy a beer or a bottle of rum and drink with the locals.

Sandals Bar, on Ambergris Street, next to *Martha's Hotel*, is a friendly bar with less outrageous prices than most and a cool sand floor that's a treat for your feet; *ceviche*, a delicious seafood cocktail, is served every day, and it's worth checking to see if Mike's doing a barbecue. *Big Daddy's* **disco**, in and around a beach bar just past the park, has early evening piano, and a lively reggae band later on. Happy hour here runs from 5 to 9pm and there's a daily beach barbecue. *Genesis Bar*, at the *Sunbreeze Hotel*, has a daily happy hour (5–7pm), with free wine tasting, and live reggae and jazz several evenings a week (karaoke on Fridays). For the best beachside happy hour (5–7pm), head for *Crazy Canuk Bar* at the *Playador Hotel* where you can get in the party mood to the sounds of the resident band Barefoot Skinny. The extremely popular *Tarzan's Disco and Nite Club*, opposite the park, has a very lively dance floor.

Listings

Airlines Maya Island Air (☎026/2345) and Tropic Air (☎026/2012) each have flights at least every hour to Belize municipal and international airports.

Banks and exchange No need to change money as US dollars are accepted – even preferred – everywhere. The Atlantic Bank on Barrier Reef Drive (Mon–Fri 8am–2pm, Sat 8.30am–noon) is the best place for cash advances, despite the US$5 charge.

Conservation Apart from the Hol Chan office (see p.220), contact Green Reef (☎026/2838, email *greenreef@btl.net*) for information on the marine reserves and ecology of Ambergris Caye.

Laundry Two places in Pescador Drive; washing costs US$3, drying another US$3.

Police Emergency ☎911; police station ☎2022.

Post office On the corner of Buccaneer Street and Barrier Reef Drive, at the side of the Alijua (Mon–Thurs 8am–noon & 1–5pm, Fri 1–4.30pm).

Shopping and souvenirs Belizean Arts in Fido's Courtyard has the island's best selection of paintings by Belizean artists, and a fine range of Central American arts and crafts. Rainforest Rescue, on Barrier Reef Drive, sells beautifully designed, high-quality T-shirts and speciality Belizean foods. At Iguana Jack's, opposite the primary school on Barrier Reef Drive, John Wetserhold creates fascinating ceramic iguanas and lizards. For the best-quality wood carvings and more fine ceramics, go to the Best of Belize, near the south end of Pescador Drive.

Travel and tour agencies Your hotel will be able to book any of the tours mentioned in the text; for local trips around the caye and to the mainland, Tanisha Tours (☎026/2314) is the best. For international and regional flights the best place to check is Travel and Tour Belize, on Coconut Drive, near the airport (☎026/2031, fax 2185), or try Amigo Travel, on Barrier Reef Drive, a block before the park (☎026/2180, fax 2192); both have great expertise in arranging trips throughout Belize and Central America.

Caye Caulker

South of Ambergris Caye and 35km northeast of Belize City, **Caye Caulker**, a little over 7km long, is the most accessible island for the independent traveller. In 1961 Hurricane Hattie destroyed most of the houses and tore a gash through the island at a point just north of the village. Now widened by mangrove destruction and erosion, "The Split", as it's known, is a popular spot for swimming.

Until recently, tourism existed almost as a sideline to the island's main source of income, **lobster fishing**, which has kept the place going for decades, but today lobster numbers are dangerously low and islanders have had to diversify. Fishermen have become hoteliers, and fishing boats now offer snorkelling trips; new hotels and bars are being built, older ones improved, and prices – low for years – have begun to rise. For the moment, however, Caye Caulker remains relaxed and easy-going. As yet there is little air-conditioning on the island, which is fine most of the time when a cooling breeze blows in from the sea, but it can mean some very sticky moments if the breeze dies. **Sandflies and mosquitoes** can cause almost unbearable irritation on calm days. Sandflies are the worst: inactive in breezy conditions, at other times they make a good insect repellent essential, though even that doesn't seem to last long (some swear by Avon's Skin-So-Soft). The success of a lengthy campaign by many islanders and others in Belize's environmental community has resulted in the protection of the northern tip of the island and a section of the barrier reef as the **Caye Caulker Marine Reserve**, upholding the country's reputation as a leader in the field of natural area conservation.

GETTING TO AND FROM CAYE CAULKER

Flights on the San Pedro run stop at the Caye Caulker airstrip, 1.5km south of the village centre – call the airlines' main offices (p.200) for information. On the island the offices are at the airstrip (Maya Island Air ☎026/2012; Tropic Air ☎026/2040). However, most visitors to Caye Caulker still arrive **by boat**. There are departures every two hours from 9am to 5pm (45min; US$7.50) from the Marine Terminal in Belize City (☎02/31969). All scheduled boats to San Pedro (see box on p.201) also call at Caye Caulker. Boats from **Caye Caulker to San Pedro** depart every three hours from 7am to 4pm (check at the Caye Caulker water taxi office; ☎022/2992) and return roughly every three hours from 8am to 4.30pm. Leaving **for Belize City**, boats depart roughly every two hours from 6.30am to 3.30pm. It's best to check in at the water taxi office and book a place in a boat the day before you leave; the staff will also know the times that the boats on the San Pedro–Belize City run call at Caye Caulker; make sure it's clear which dock the boat is leaving from.

Arrival and information

Arriving by air, golf cart taxis can take you to your hotel, though hotels south of the main dock are only a ten-minute walk. **By boat** you'll be dropped off at one of the main piers on the island; either the "front" (east) dock or the "back" (west) dock – easily recognizable as they're longer than the others. From either dock you simply walk straight ahead to the **water taxi office**, effectively the centre of the village. They can give **information** and will probably hold your luggage while you look for a place to stay.

As yet, there are no street names on the caye, but the street running along the shore at the front of the island is effectively "**Front Street**", with just one or two streets running behind it in the centre of the village. Staff at Caye Caulker's **travel agency**, Dolphin Bay Travel (☎ & fax 022/2214), on "Front Street" just north of the centre, have outstanding local knowledge, and can arrange domestic and international flights, tours and trips; you can also pick up a copy of *Village Voice*, the island's fortnightly free newspaper here.

There are several **payphones** in the centre and the BTL office is opposite the water taxi office. The **post office** is on the back street, south of the village centre. The Atlantic Bank (Mon–Fri 8am–noon & 1–2pm) gives Visa **cash advances** (US$5 fee), and an increasing number of businesses accept plastic for payment.

Accommodation

Most of the year it's easy enough to find an inexpensive room in one of the small, mostly clapboard **hotels**, but to arrive at Christmas or New Year without a reservation could leave you stranded. Even the furthest hotels are no more than ten minutes' walk from the front dock: the listings below are given roughly in the order you'd come to them walking from the dock. Most places now accept credit cards.

North from the front dock

Sandy Lane Hotel, a block back from the front (☎022/2217). Small, quiet, and inexpensive with rooms in the original building and newer, more expensive concrete cabins in the grounds. ③–⑤.

Martinez Caribbean Inn, on the seafront (☎022/2133). Secure and well run; all rooms with private bath and hot water and some have a/c. The best rooms are at the front. ③–④.

Barbara's Guest House, towards the north end near the Split (☎022/2025). Friendly, secure, Canadian-run place, with simple, clean rooms, away from the bars. ③.

Island Sun Guest House, on the seafront, just past *Barbara's* (☎022/2215). Simple but well-furnished rooms in a great location, with an upstairs deck on which to enjoy breakfast. ④.

South from the front dock

Daisy's (☎022/2150). Simple, budget rooms just back from the sea, run by a friendly family. ②.

Morgan's Inn, opposite Galería Hicaco (☎022/2178, fax 2239). Three quiet, roomy cabins in private grounds, set just back from the beach. ⑤.

Jimínez Cabañas (☎022/2175). Five clean, comfortable wood-and-thatch cabins – the best value on the island – surrounded by a delightful garden; towards the back of the island. ④.

Tree Tops Hotel, south from the cemetery, just before *Tom's* (☎022/2008, fax 2115). Easily the best hotel on the island (indeed the country) at this price, just 50m from the water. Five comfortable rooms, with fridge, cable TV and powerful ceiling fan. Although only one room has private bath, the shared bathroom is immaculate. Booking is advisable. ⑤.

Anchorage Resort, on the shore 300m south of *Tom's* (☎ & fax 022/2304). New, two-storey hotel in palm-shaded grounds. Comfortable, clean, tiled rooms with private bathrooms and balconies overlooking the sea. Great value. ⑥.

Lorraine's Guest House, next to the *Anchorage* (☎022/2002). Simple but comfortable cabins with hot water, run by a friendly lady. A bargain and near the beach. ④.

Exploring the reef and the caye

The **reef** lies only 1500m from the shore and the white foam of the reef crest is always visible. It's certainly an experience not to be missed: swimming along coral canyons surrounded by an astonishing range of fish, with perhaps even the odd shark or two (almost certainly harmless nurse sharks). Here as everywhere, snorkellers should be aware of the fragility of the reef and be careful not to touch any coral – even sand stirred up by fins can cause damage.

The northern part of the island is long and narrow, covered in mangroves and thick vegetation that extends right down to the shore: the rare and threatened caye littoral forest habitat. At the very northern tip is the **Caye Caulker Marine Reserve**, designated a protected area in 1998 and now visited on boat trips (see below). As always your **trip to the reef** will be more enjoyable if you have some idea of what you're seeing. A couple of places offer interpretative **slide shows** of reef and island ecology: at Seaing is Belizing, next to Dolphin Bay Travel, Dorothy Beveridge shows slides covering all aspects of Belize's flora and fauna; in the **gift shop** you can buy slides, films (and get them developed), and books. At the Galería Hicaco, toward the south end of the front street, marine biologist Ellen McRae, one of the driving forces behind the establishment of the Caye Caulker Marine Reserve, can explain exactly what it is you're seeing in this amazing underwater world. She can also conducts **Audubon bird walks**, an introduction to the dozens of bird species of the caye.

Swimming, snorkelling and diving

Swimming isn't really possible from the shore as the water's too shallow. You have to leap off the ends of piers or go to "The Split" at the north end of the village. **Trips to the reef** from Caye Caulker are easily arranged and cost around US$8–20 per person, depending on where you go. Most last several hours and take in a number of sites, often including Caye Caulker's own marine reserve. You can usually rent decent **equipment** (US$3 for snorkel, mask and fins) from the place where you book your trip; always check it fits well and try to practise from a dock before you go to the reef. The best trips and guides are generally offered by Meldie and Barbara of Driftwood Snorkelling, to the north of the main dock (☎022/2011). There are also some recommended **independent guides**, with one of the best trips offered by Ras Creek in his dory *Heritage* (US$15). Ras leaves from the main front dock around 11am and takes you out to the reef right in front of the caye, showing you nurse sharks and eagle rays in their element as you float above them, arriving back as the sun is setting – the perfect end to an utterly relaxing day. Carlos, of Carlos Tours (☎022/2093), is a very conscientious guide who takes small groups on snorkelling or sailing trips; contact him at *Cindy's Café*. Frenchie's (☎022/2234, fax 2074), at the northern end of the village, is the longest-established **dive shop** on the caye and offers safe and very knowledgeable trips, with some great reef diving, night dives and day-trips to Lighthouse Reef and the Blue Hole. For the best dive **instruction** on the island (up to divemaster level), go to the Caye Caulker School of Scuba (☎022/2292, fax 2239), just south of *Edith's Hotel*; a four-day open-water PADI course costs US$250.

Other activities and trips to other islands

Belize has the largest surviving population of the West Indian manatee and you can take trips **manatee-watching at Swallow Caye**, south of Caye Caulker, where the gentle animals congregate around a hole in the shallows just offshore; the skipper turns off the motor and poles towards the hole in order not to disturb them. You're almost certainly guaranteed a sighting, often of whole family groups. These trips also usually include a visit to **Goff's Caye**, **English Caye** or **Sergeant's Caye** – tiny specks of sand and coral with a few palm trees. If you want to go around the caye on your own you can rent a **kayak** for around US$15–20; try *Daisy's* hotel or ask at the Galería Hicaco, where you can also rent a **sailboard** and receive instruction. Caye Caulker is a good base for **day-trips to the atolls** of the Turneffe Islands and Lighthouse Reef. For snorkellers the best is Jim and Cindy Novelo's expedition to the exquisite **Half Moon Caye** (see p.230), the most easterly of Belize's islands, on the skiff *Sunrise* (US$70 including lunch; ☎022/2195). The trip leaves at 6am and you speed across the shallows to the gap in the reef between Caye Caulker and Caye Chapel, heading for the deep blue of the open sea. The route takes you across the northern tip of Turneffe atoll, possibly stopping to snorkel along the eastern edge, before continuing on to Lighthouse Reef and the wonders of the Blue Hole.

Eating, drinking and entertainment

Good cooking, large portions and very reasonable prices are features of all the island's **restaurants**, half of which you'll pass while looking for a room. **Lobster** (in season) is served in every imaginable dish, from curry to chow mein; other **seafood** is generally good value, accompanied by rice or potatoes and sometimes salad. Along Front Street are a couple of **fast-food** stands, serving tacos and burritos. There's a good **bakery** on the street leading to the football field and as you walk around you might see children selling bread or pastries from bowls balanced on their heads. You can also buy food at several **shops and supermarkets** on the island,

Restaurants and cafés

Cindy's Café, on Front Street, serves mainly breakfasts and snacks – but wonderful ones, with good coffee and fresh fruit juices and superb homemade bagels, yoghurt and carrot cake.

Glenda's, at the back of the island. Justly famous for delicious cinnamon rolls and breakfasts.

Marin's Restaurant, towards the south end of Middle Street. A very long-established restaurant, serving really good seafood at great prices either indoors or at a table in the shady courtyard.

Martinez Restaurant, just before *Martinez Inn*. Reasonable Belizean food at very good prices.

Oceanside, next to *Martinez Inn*. Tasty, well-presented seafood at good prices.

The Sand Box, by the main front dock. The best restaurant on the island, serving great Italian/American food and local dishes in large portions and fairly swiftly too. Open from 7am for a coffee and roll before the boat. Tables inside or in the shady garden with volleyball court.

Tropical Paradise, at the south end of front street serves good-quality Belizean and American-style food at reasonable prices in a comfortable a/c dining room.

Bars and nightlife

Caye Caulker's **social scene** oscillates around several bars and restaurants, and frequently there's **live music** to add atmosphere to the evening. Few places are strictly bars, though the three-storey *I&I's*, between the *Tropical Paradise* and *Edith's*, is more bar than restaurant. Away from the music, evening entertainment mostly consists of relaxing in a restaurant over dinner or a drink. Most people are friendly enough, but as the evening wears on and drink takes its toll, it can get rowdy. Be careful with your money too – Caye Caulker has a criminal element and a drug problem, but only three policemen.

Shopping and souvenirs

Although **shopping** won't be your main consideration on Caye Caulker, there are a few places where you can buy some unique **gifts**. At *Cindy's Café* (see above) you can get locally produced **music** and **books**, including Rough Guides; Wendy Nuñez also sells Belizean music and Garífuna **drums**, as well dazzling hand-painted T-shirts from her house next to Dolphin Bay Travel. Traci's Gifts, next to *Martinez Inn*, has a good selection of original **art** and other good-quality locally produced gifts at affordable prices, and further north, at Island Designs, Cindy Novelo has the widest range of art, crafts and clothing from throughout Central America.

Other northern cayes and the atolls

Although Caye Caulker and San Pedro are the only villages anywhere on the reef, there are several other islands that can be visited. Caye Caulker is within day-trip distance of some of these and there are a few superbly isolated hotels – called **lodges** – on some reefs and cayes. The attraction of these lodges is the "simple life", usually focusing on diving or fishing; staying at them is generally part of a package that includes transfers from the airport, accommodation, all meals and the sports on offer. Buildings are low-key, wooden and sometimes thatched, and the group you're with will probably be the only people staying there. Views of palm trees curving over turquoise water reinforce the sense of isolation.

Caye Chapel

As a diversion during a snorkelling trip you could visit **Caye Chapel**, immediately south of Caye Caulker. Quite different from Caye Caulker, privately owned Caye Chapel has an airstrip, golf course, marina and (usually deserted) hotel. The beaches are cleaned daily and the bar is usually open all day – perfect for a cold beer after a hard day's snorkelling. It was on Caye Chapel that the defeated Spanish fleet paused for a few days after the Battle of St George's Caye in 1798, and, according to legend, some of their dead are buried here.

St George's Caye

Tiny **St George's Caye**, around 15km from Belize City, was the capital of the Baymen in the eighteenth century and still manages to exude an air of colonial grandeur; its beautifully restored colonial houses face east to catch the breeze and their lush green lawns are enclosed by white picket fences. The sense of history is reinforced by the eighteenth-century cannons mounted in front of some of the finer houses; for another glimpse into the past you could head for the small graveyard of the early settlers on the southern tip of the island. Today, the island is home to the villas of Belize's elite, an adventure training centre for British forces in Belize and a few fishermen, who live toward the north end in an area known, appropriately enough, as "Fishermen Town".

There's not much here for the casual visitor, but some fishing and snorkelling trips do call at St George's Caye. If you come, you may meet Karl and Angelika Bishof, an Austrian couple who run Bela Carib (☎02/49435), a company that carefully collects and exports tropical fish. The tanks contain a fascinating display of reef creatures and you're welcome to look around; the couple plan to open a **marine aquarium** soon. **Accommodation** on the caye is luxurious: *Cottage Colony* (☎02/77051, fax 73253; ⑨) has the most beautiful location. Rooms are in extremely comfortable colonial-style, wooden houses with modern facilities set in palm-shaded grounds.

The Bluefield Range

In the **Bluefield Range**, a group of mangrove cayes 35km southeast of Belize City, you can stay on a remote **fishing camp**. *Ricardo's Beach Huts* (☎02/78469) offer simple, comfortable accommodation right on the water, in huts built on stilts. At US$165 per person for three days and two nights it's not cheap, but the price includes transport to and from Belize City, all meals – including, as you might imagine, fresh fish and lobster – and a fishing or snorkelling trip to Rendezvous Caye, right on the reef; Rough Guide readers get a discount. Ricardo Castillo is a reliable, expert fishing guide, scrupulously practising conservation of the reef.

The Turneffe Islands

The virtually uninhabited **Turneffe Islands**, 40km from Belize City, are an oval archipelago of low-lying mangrove islands 60km long, enclosed by a beautiful coral reef. A few places offer all-inclusive **accommodation**, but the construction of resorts in this remote, fragile environment has involved cutting down mangroves and is the cause of much controversy among conservationists. Halfway down the eastern side, *Blackbird Caye Resort* (☎02/33504, fax 30268) has accommodation in ten wood-and-thatch cabañas, charging from US$1400 for a week of diving or fishing. South of Blackbird Caye, **Calabash Caye** is the base for Coral Caye Conservation, where volunteers take part in a research project to complete a systematic investigation of the entire atoll, with a view to establishing a marine reserve. Participants stay in dorm cabins at the University College of Belize Marine Research Centre. *Turneffe Island Lodge* (☎ & fax 021/2011; in US ☎1-800/874-0118), on **Caye Bokel**, a sandy island at the southern tip of the archipelago, has wood-and-thatch cabins with hot water and 24-hour electricity. It costs US$1100 per person for a week at the resort; another US$150 or so for diving, more for fishing (both are superb).

Lighthouse Reef, the Blue Hole and Half Moon Caye

About 80km east of Belize City is Belize's outer atoll, **Lighthouse Reef**, with the Blue Hole and Half Moon Caye natural monuments forming the main attractions. The **Blue Hole**, protected as a Natural Monument, is technically a "karst-eroded sinkhole", a shaft about 300m in diameter and 135m deep, which opens out into a complex network of **caves and crevices**, complete with stalactites and stalagmites. It was formed over a million years ago when Lighthouse Reef was a sizeable island – or even part of the mainland. Its great depth gives it a peculiar deep blue colour, and even swimming across is disorienting as there's no sense of anything beneath you. Unsurprisingly, the Blue Hole and Lighthouse Reef are major magnets for **divers**, offering incredible walls and dropoffs. Several **shipwrecks** form artificial reefs; the most prominent is the *Ermlund*, which ran aground in 1971 and looms over the reef just north of Half Moon Caye.

The **Half Moon Caye Natural Monument**, the first marine conservation area in Belize, was declared a national park in 1982 and became a World Heritage Site in 1996. Visitors must register with the ranger on arrival, and pay the US$5 **fee**, which includes entry to the Blue Hole. The **visitor centre**, built by volunteers from Raleigh and Trekforce expeditions, has displays on the ecology of the caye.

The 45-acre caye is divided into two distinct ecosystems: in the west, guano from thousands of seabirds fertilizes the soil, allowing the growth of dense vegetation, while the eastern half has mostly coconut palms growing in the sand. A total of 98 bird species has been recorded here, including frigate birds, ospreys, mangrove warblers, white-crowned pigeons and – most important of all – a resident population of four thousand **red-footed boobies**, one of only two nesting colonies in the Caribbean. The boobies came by their name because they displayed no fear of humans, enabling sailors to kill them in their thousands, and they still move only reluctantly when visitors stroll among them. Their nesting area is accessible from a platform and the birds are not in the least bothered by your presence. Apart from birds, the island supports iguanas and lizards, and both loggerhead and hawksbill turtles nest on the beaches, which also attract the biggest hermit and land crabs in Belize.

There's no accommodation on the caye, but **camping** is allowed with the permission of the Belize Audubon Society (see p.197), who manage the reserve; many of the overnight diving expeditions camp here.

travel details

Buses

Bus company addresses and details of **services from Belize City** are given the box on p.201.

Bermudian Landing to: Belize City (2–3 Mon–Sat; 1hr 15min), via Burrell Boom.

Chetumal to: Belize City (hourly; 3hr 30min, express services 3hr), via Corozal and Orange Walk; Sarteneja (Mon–Sat at 1.30pm; 3hr 30min), via Orange Walk.

Corozal to: Belize City (hourly; 2hr 30min), via Orange Walk (1hr); to Chetumal (hourly; 1hr including border crossing).

Crooked Tree to: Belize City (4 daily; 1hr 30min).

Orange Walk to: Belize City (hourly; 1hr 30min); to Corozal (hourly 1hr); Indian Church, for Lamanai (3 weekly on Mon, Wed, Fri at 4pm; 2hr).

Sarteneja to: Belize City (Mon–Sat 2–3 daily; 3hr 30min); Chetumal (Mon–Sat; 1daily).

Planes

Maya Island Air (☎026/2345) and Tropic Air (☎026/2012) each operate three daily flights between Corozal and San Pedro. For a rundown of **flights** to the cayes from Belize City and between the cayes themselves, see the boxes on pp.201, 217 and 225.

Boats

For a rundown of **boats** to the cayes from Belize City and between the cayes themselves, see the boxes on pp.201, 217 and 225.

CHAPTER FIVE

CAYO AND THE WEST

Heading west from Belize City to the Guatemalan border, you travel through a wide range of landscapes, from open grassland and rolling hills to dense tropical forest. A fast paved road, the **Western Highway**, connects Belize City with the Guatemalan border, a route that takes you from the heat and humidity of the coast to the lush foothills of the Maya Mountains. Before reaching Belize's tiny capital, **Belmopan**, the road passes several places of interest: the **Belize Zoo**, the **Monkey Bay Wildlife Sanctuary and National Park**, and **Guanacaste National Park**, a small reserve at the junction with the Hummingbird Highway to Dangriga.

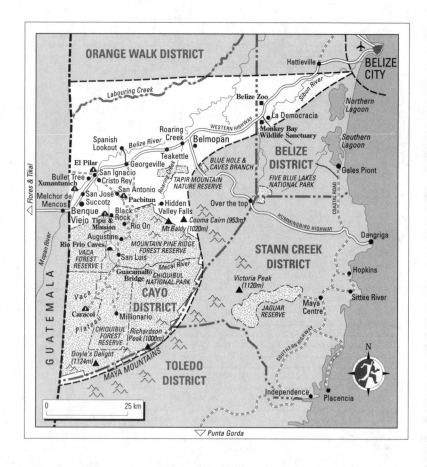

Heading further west, following the Belize River valley, you start to climb into the foothills of the Maya Mountains, where most of the landscape, including the entire mountain range, is under official protection in a vast network of national parks, wildlife sanctuaries and forest and archeological reserves. South of the highway, the **Mountain Pine Ridge Forest Reserve** is a pleasantly cool region of hills and pine woods boasting some of the finest lodge accommodation in the country. **San Ignacio**, on the Macal River, and only 15km from the Guatemalan border, is the busy main town of Cayo District and the ideal base for exploring the forests, rivers and ruins of western Belize. The ruins of **Caracol**, the largest Maya site in Belize and a focus for current archeological research, lie deep in the jungle of the Vaca plateau, south of San Ignacio.

Between San Ignacio and the Guatemalan border, the road climbs past the hilltop ruin of **Cahal Pech**, then descends, following the valley of the **Mopan River** to the frontier bridge. A few kilometres before the frontier itself, at the village of **San José Succotz**, an ancient ferry crosses the river, allowing access to another hilltop Maya site, **Xunantunich**, whose highest structures offer stunning views over to Guatemala's department of Petén. Belize's westernmost Maya site, **El Pilar**, 18km northwest of San Ignacio, actually extends into Guatemala, and is the first **International Archeological Reserve** anywhere in the Maya World.

Belize City to San Ignacio

Served by frequent buses between Belize City and San Ignacio, the Western Highway leaves the city through the middle of the Lord's Ridge cemetery, then skirts the shoreline, running behind a tangle of mangrove swamps. After 10km the road crosses the **Sir John Burden Canal**, an inland waterway, now a nature reserve and valuable wildlife corridor, that connects the Belize River with the **Sibun River**. At HATTIEVILLE, 26km further on, named after the 1961 hurricane that created the refugees who initially populated it, there's a turning north to **Burrell Boom** and **Bermudian Landing** (see p.203), a short cut to the Northern Highway. If time permits you should allow an hour or two to visit the **Belize Zoo**, probably the finest zoo in Central America. Just beyond the zoo, the unpaved **Coastal Road** to Dangriga offers a short cut to the south. At **Monkey Bay Wildlife Sanctuary** you'd need to stay at least a day or two to fully appreciate what's on offer, but **Guanacaste National Park** is a worthwhile stop right by the roadside just before Belmopan.

The Belize Zoo

Twenty kilometres beyond Hattieville, at Mile 29, the **Belize Zoo** (daily 9am–4.30pm; ☎081/3004; US$7.50; half price for children, Peace Corps & VSO) is the first point of interest out this way and easily visited on a half-day trip from Belize City. All buses between Belize City and Belmopan pass the entrance and there's a sign on the highway. A 200m walk brings you to the entrance and the **Gerald Durrell Visitor Centre**, with displays of children's art and exhibits on Belize's ecosystems.

Long recognized as a phenomenal conservation achievement, the zoo originally opened in 1983 after an ambitious wildlife film left Sharon Matola, the film's production assistant, with a collection of semi-tame animals no longer able to fend for themselves in the wild. The zoo is actively involved in conservation education and captive breeding and has achieved international recognition in these fields. For locals and visitors alike this means the chance to see the native animals of Belize at close quarters, housed in spacious enclosures which closely resemble their natural habitat.

The zoo is organized around the theme of "**a walk through Belize**", with a trail that takes you into the pinelands, the forest edge, the rainforest, lagoons and the river forest. The residents include a **Baird's tapir** (known locally as a mountain cow) called April, well known to the schoolchildren of Belize, who visit in their hundreds on her birthday (in April) to feed her a huge vegetable birthday cake. All the Belizean cats are represented and some, including the **jaguars**, have bred successfully. There's also a wide range of birds, including toucans, macaws, parrots, jabiru storks, a spectacled owl and several vultures; other inhabitants include deer, spider and howler monkeys, peccaries, agouti (which sometimes appears on menus as "gibnut"), crocodiles and various snakes.

Two kilometres beyond the zoo the **Coastal** (or Manatee) **Road** provides an unpaved short cut (marked by a sign and a couple of bars), served by buses, to Gales Point and **Dangriga**. A further 2km past the junction, *Cheers* (☎ & fax 014/9311) is a friendly **bar** run by Canadians Anita, Mike and Chrissy Tupper, where you can get good food at reasonable prices as well as tourist **information**. Should you need to book accommodation somewhere ahead, you can use their cellular phone and fax service.

Monkey Bay Wildlife Sanctuary

Half a kilometre past *Cheers* and 400m off to the left of the highway (signposted at Mile 31 1/2), the **Monkey Bay Wildlife Sanctuary** (☎08/23180) is a 44-square-kilometre protected area extending to the Sibun River and offering birding and nature **trails** through five distinct vegetation and habitat types. Adjoining the sanctuary across the river is the nine-square-kilometre **Monkey Bay National Park**. The two protected areas serve as a wildlife corridor spanning the Sibun valley south through karst limestone hills to the Manatee Forest Reserve. Government agencies and NGOs are currently working on an ambitious project to extend this corridor to connect protected areas in northern Belize, across the rapidly developing Western Highway, with those in the south.

The sanctuary headquarters includes a **field research station**, which serves as library, museum and classroom, and is the Belize base for Conservation Corridors. Although the field station specializes in hosting academic programmes in natural history, it's also a wonderfully relaxing **place to stay** for anyone; either in the bunkhouse (US$7.50) or camping (US$5). Monkey Bay is a viable experiment in "off the grid" sustainable living, utilizing solar power, rainwater catchment and biogas fuel for cooking; the **food**, some of it grown in the station's organic gardens, is excellent and plentiful. From Monkey Bay you can take guided **canoe trips** on the Sibun River and it's also a perfect base to explore little-visited **caves** in the Sibun Hills to the south – all of which have evidence of use by the ancient Maya.

Monkey Bay is also home to the **Wildlife Care Center** (WCC), a holding facility for confiscated and rescued wild animals, often kept illegally as pets, aiming eventually to repatriate those animals which would survive in the wild. The WCC is not open to the public but there are training opportunities for foreign students and **conservation vol-**

unteers – you'll need to be self-funded and be able to commit for at least three months. If you're interested, write to the director Robin Brockett, c/o Belize Audubon Society, PO Box 1001, Belize City.

Onward to Guanacaste Park

Five hundred metres beyond Monkey Bay, **JB's Bar** is an old favourite with the British Army, whose mementos deck the walls, alongside a word of thanks from Harrison Ford and the crew of *The Mosquito Coast*. The restaurant serves good food and there are comfortable, well-priced **rooms** (☎014/0898; ⑤) with electricity and hot water, and the owner can arrange **tubing** on the Sibun River. Twenty-five kilometres beyond *JB's*, and 2km before the turning for Belmopan, opposite the airstrip at Mile 46, a track leads off to the right to **Banana Bank Lodge** (☎ 081/2020, fax 2026; ⑧ including breakfast – no service charge), on the north bank of the Belize River, crossed by foot-passenger boat. The **accommodation**, with views sweeping down to the Belize River, consists of five beautifully furnished wood-and-thatch cabañas and five rooms. This 4000-acre ranch, half of which is still primary forest, owned by John and Carolyn Carr, offers great horse-riding and a chance to visit dozens of Maya mounds, some quite large. The natural history is astonishing: almost two hundred bird species have been recorded here, and there's a beautiful **lagoon** with resident Morelets crocodiles.

Guanacaste National Park

Right by the highway, 73km from Belize City at the junction for Belmopan and the Hummingbird Highway, **Guanacaste National Park** (daily 8am–4.30pm; US$2.50, including a free short tour with a ranger) is Belize's smallest national park and the easiest to visit. Here you can wander through a superb area of lush tropical forest at the confluence of Roaring Creek and the Belize River. **Buses** stop right outside the park. The **visitor centre**, near the entrance, has maps and information on the park ecology (including a superb exhibit on the life cycle of the leaf-cutter ants, which you'll see all over Belize), and there's an orchid display in the courtyard. Outside, four or five short **trails** take you through the park and along the banks of the Belize River.

The main attraction is a huge **guanacaste** or tubroos tree, a forty-metre-high, spreading hardwood that supports some 35 species; hanging from its limbs are a huge range of bromeliads, orchids, ferns, cacti and strangler figs, which blossom spectacularly at the end of the rainy season. The trunk of the guanacaste is traditionally favoured for use as dugout canoes. Other botanical attractions include young mahogany trees, *cohune* palms, a cotton tree and quamwood, while the forest floor is a mass of ferns, mosses and vines, and wild orchids grow everywhere on trunks and branches. As the park is so close to the road, your chances of seeing any four-footed **wildlife** are fairly slim, but recently a small number of howler monkeys have used the park as a feeding ground. **Birds**, however, abound, with over fifty species, among them blue-crowned motmots, black-faced ant-thrushes, black-headed trogons, and squirrel cuckoos.

Belmopan

From Guanacaste Park the Western Highway pushes on towards San Ignacio and the Guatemalan border, while a paved branch road turns south 2km towards Belize's capital, **BELMOPAN**, beyond which it becomes the Hummingbird Highway, continuing all the way to the coast at Dangriga. For most people the capital is no more than a break in the bus ride to San Ignacio, though if you're heading to Dangriga or Placencia this is the place to change buses.

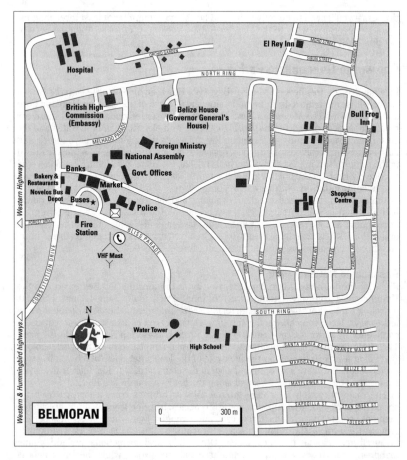

BELMOPAN

0 ————— 300 m

Belmopan was founded in 1970 after Hurricane Hattie swept much of Belize City into the sea. The government decided to use the disaster as a chance to move to higher ground and, in a Brasília-style bid to focus development on the interior, chose a site in the geographical heart of the country. The name of the city combines the words Belize and **Mopan**, the language spoken by the Maya of Cayo. The layout of the main government buildings, designed in the 1960s, is supposedly modelled on a Maya city, with structures grouped around a central plaza; the National Assembly building even incorporates a version of the traditional roof comb. Belmopan was meant to be a classic New Town, symbolizing the dawn of a new era, with tree-lined avenues, banks, a couple of embassies and telecommunications worthy of a world centre. Today it has all the essential ingredients of a successful town bar one – people.

Unless you've come to visit a government department, there's no particular reason to stay any longer in Belmopan than it takes your bus to leave. The Archeological Vault once provided the only other real reason for any tourist to visit Belmopan, but that closed a few years ago, leaving no permanent venue to display the outstanding range of archeological artefacts found in Belize. However, the theatre opposite the market square sometimes has temporary displays, and a new exhibition area is currently under construction; to find out what's available for viewing call the **Archaeology Department** on ☎08/22106. The **Archives Department** (Mon–Fri 8am–noon & 1–4.30pm; free; ☎08/22247), 26–28 Unity Blvd, also welcomes visitors and has photographs and documents providing a fascinating glimpse of old Belize.

Practicalities

Buses from Belize City to San Ignacio and Dangriga all pass through Belmopan, and Shaws run a frequent service between Belmopan and San Ignacio, so there's at least one bus an hour in either direction all day; the last bus from Belmopan to Belize City leaves at 6.30pm, to San Ignacio at 10pm and to Dangriga at 6pm. The buses all pull up in an unpaved square in front of the small **market**, with several food and fruit stands.

The nearest **restaurant** is the *Caladium*, beside the Novelos bus terminal (where you can leave luggage), which is good for Belizean dishes. *Mom's Place*, in Harlem Square (the block behind the *Caladium*), is a friendly, inexpensive place where you can always get a vegetarian meal. Nearby, to the left of the market, you'll find the Canadian-run *International Café* (closed Wed & Sat), serving sandwiches, soups, salads and snacks – always with a daily special and vegetarian choices. It's also good for **information** and you can pay to use their phone for local calls.

Just beyond the market are the **banks**, and to the right of the market square is the Ministry of Natural Resources, where you can buy **maps**; the **post office** is just behind here. The **British High Commission** (☎08/22146) is situated on the North Ring Road, behind the National Assembly building. The BTL **telephone** office is beside the large satellite dish, and the **immigration** office is in the main building beside the theatre.

Hotels in Belmopan cater for the needs and expense accounts of diplomats and aid officials; San Ignacio, less than an hour away, is far more interesting and less expensive. If you do have to stay here, the *El Rey Inn*, 23 Moho St (☎08/23438; ④), is a pleasant and reasonably inexpensive option. The best place in town is *Bull Frog Inn*, 23 Half Moon Ave (☎22111, fax 23155; ⑦); its comfortable rooms have a/c and TV, and a there's a very pleasant restaurant and bar.

Belmopan to San Ignacio

Beyond Belmopan the scenery becomes more rugged, with thickly forested ridges always in view to the south. The Western Highway stays close to the valley of the Belize River, crossing numerous tributary creeks and passing through a series of villages – Roaring Creek, Teakettle, Ontario, Unitedville – and **Santa Elena**, San Ignacio's sister town on the eastern bank of the Macal River. There's been something of an accommodation boom along this route, with a couple of long-established cottage-style **lodges** now joined by several newer enterprises. Alternatively, with your own vehicle you can turn south at Georgeville, 26km from the Belmopan junction, and head along the unpaved **Chiquibul Road** into the Mountain Pine Ridge.

Tapir Mountain Nature Reserve and Pook's Hill Lodge

South of the highway, between Roaring and Barton creeks, the **Tapir Mountain Nature Reserve** protects 28 square kilometres of the northern foothills of the Maya Mountains, a rich, well-watered habitat covered in high-canopy tropical moist forest and home to all of Belize's national symbols: Baird's tapir, the keel-billed toucan, the black orchid and the mahogany tree. The reserve is accorded Belize's highest category of protected land and, as one criterion of this is to "maintain natural processes in an undisturbed state", Tapir Mountain can only be visited by accredited researchers.

Although you generally cannot enter the reserve, you can enjoy spectacular views of it by staying nearby at one of the best new lodges, **Pook's Hill Jungle Lodge**

(☎081/2017, fax 08/23361; ⑧, no service charge); the turning to it is clearly signpost-ed at Mile 52 at the village of **Teakettle**, 8km west of Belmopan. The nine-kilometre track up to the lodge is bumpy but in good condition. If you're travelling by bus, you should call ahead and one of the owners, Ray and Vicky Snaddon, will pick you up from the junction.

Accommodation is in nine thatched cabañas, grouped in a small clearing over-looking the thickly forested Roaring River valley and with breathtaking views across the Tapir Mountain Reserve to the Mountain Pine Ridge beyond. Delicious meals are served in the dining room at the edge of the forest and upstairs a thatched, open-sided deck serves as a bar in the evenings. This spectacular location clearly held attractions for the ancient Maya too – the lodge sits on a Maya platform and there's a plaza and some small structures behind the cabañas. There are wonderful **nature trails** and superb **horse-riding trails**, and you can hike or ride to more substantial ruins and caves further up the valley. You don't have to go far to see the **wildlife** either – bird-watching here is in a league of its own and there will almost always be a raptor of some kind, perhaps a bat falcon hunting or feeding. To cool off, you can go **tubing** in the river.

Warrie Head Lodge and Caesar's Place

Beyond Teakettle, at Mile 54, just over the Warrie Head Creek bridge, is the entrance to **Warrie Head Ranch and Lodge** (☎02/75317, fax 75213; ⑦), formerly a logging camp and now a working farm offering very comfortable wooden cabins and rooms set back a few hundred metres from the road. Owners Johnny and Elvira Searle have gone to great lengths to provide visitors with a glimpse of Belize's colonial heritage – the rooms have modern facilities but are filled with authentic period furniture, and colonial artefacts abound, including a restored 1904 steam engine once used to haul logs. The grounds, filled with fruit and native trees, slope down to the creek, where an exquisite series of travertine terraces forms turquoise pools – perfect for swimming.

On the bank of Barton Creek to the right of the highway at Mile 60, **Caesar's Place** (☎09/22341, fax 23449; ⑤) is Caesar and Antonieta Sherrard's café and guest house, with comfortable, attractive rooms, trailer hookups (US$7.50) and space for camping (US$3.75). The *Patio Café* is a good place to stop for lunch and serves delicious **home cooking**, with Belizean and American dishes mingling with the flavours of other Central American countries. The **gift shop** is one of the best in Belize: Caesar makes great wood carvings using wood properly dried in his solar kiln, and there are slate carvings, Guatemalan textiles and silver jewellery from Taxco in Mexico. It's also a great place to pick up information about Guatemala and Mexico, and Caesar's son Julian can organize canoe or caving trips along the Macal River. Beyond *Caesar's*, just over the Barton Creek bridge, the two prominent, grass-covered **pyramids** mark the unexcavated Maya site of **Floral Park**; you'll see virtually all there is to see as you pass by in the bus.

The Chiquibul Road

Six kilometres beyond the Barton Creek bridge you come to the **Georgeville** junction, from where (with your own transport) you can head south along the **Chiquibul Road** to the **Mountain Pine Ridge** (see p.247). You should get off at this junction if you're hitching to **Augustine/Douglas Silva**, headquarters of the Mountain Pine Ridge Forest Reserve, though you really need 4-wheel drive, or a mountain bike, to properly explore this fascinating and exciting area of hills, caves and jungle. The road – well used by villagers, foresters and tourists – reaches deep into the forest, crossing the Macal River at the Guacamallo bridge before heading for Caracol (see p.250).

MOUNTAIN EQUESTRIAN TRAILS AND GREEN HILLS BUTTERFLY HOUSE
Eleven kilometres along the road, at **Mountain Equestrian Trails** (☎09/23310, fax 23361;
in US ☎1-800/838-3918; ⑨), you'll find very comfortable accommodation in a tropical forest setting on the edge of the Pine Ridge. There are four thatched cabañas with hot water,
lit by oil lamps, and the tasty meals served in the *Cantina* restaurant feature large portions
of Belizean and Mexican-style food. If you want to get even closer to nature, *MET* also has
an idyllic **tented camp**, *Chiclero Trails* (⑥ including all meals), the base for low-impact
wildlife safaris that take you deep into the Chiquibul forest. As the name implies, *MET* is
primarily oriented towards **horse-riding** vacations and is unquestionably Belize's premier
riding centre, with superb riding on nearly 100km of forest trails.

On the opposite side of the road to *MET*, the Green Hills Butterfly House (Christmas
to Easter daily 8am–5pm, rest of year appointment only; ☎09/23310; US$2.50, minimum
two people) is Belize's best butterfly exhibit, run by Dutch biologists Jan Meerman and
Tineke Boomsma. The main attraction is the enclosed flight area, where scores of gorgeous butterflies flutter around, settling occasionally on the flowers to sip nectar. This
is a breeding centre too and you can watch one of nature's wonders as the caterpillars
emerge from their chrysalises. There's lots more to see too – the botanical garden is
home to Belize's National Passionflower Collection and a renowned collection of epiphytes (air plants).

On to San Ignacio: Santa Elena
Nine kilometres beyond Georgeville, the highway passes through San Ignacio's sister
town of **SANTA ELENA**, on the eastern bank of the Macal River. Though quite a large
town, Santa Elena has few of the attractions of San Ignacio, but it is the site of the turn-
off to the **Cristo Rey road** (see p.248) towards Augustine/Douglas Silva and the
Mountain Pine Ridge. Most visitors choose to stay in San Ignacio, but there are a few
hotels in Santa Elena. By far the best is the *Snooty Fox Guest House* (☎09/22150, fax
3556; ⑤–⑥), high above the Macal River at 64 George Price Ave, where the spotless
rooms are very good value, and there's a good restaurant, secure car parking, and
owner Michael Waight offers the best value **canoe rental** in the area – just US$20 per
day. At Santa Elena the Macal River is crossed by the **Hawksworth Bridge**, built in
1949 and still the only road suspension bridge in Belize.

San Ignacio and Cayo District

On the west bank of the Macal River, 35km from Belmopan, **SAN IGNACIO** is a friendly, relaxed town that draws together much of the best in inland Belize. Surrounded by
fast-flowing rivers and forested hills, it's an ideal base from which to explore the region,
offering good food, inexpensive hotels and restaurants, and frequent bus connections.
The evenings are cool and the days fresh, and there's a virtual absence of mosquitoes
and other biting insects. The **population** is typically varied: most people are Mestizos,
and Spanish is the main language, but you'll also hear plenty of Creole and English.

Some history
The name the Spanish gave to this area was **El Cayo**, the same word they used to
describe the offshore islands. San Ignacio town is usually referred to as **Cayo** by locals,
and this is the name you'll often see indicated on buses. It's an apt description of the
area, in a peninsula between two converging rivers, and also a measure of how isolated
the early settlers felt, surrounded by the forest. It wasn't just the jungle they had to fear;
the forest was also home to a Maya group who valued their independence. **Tipu**, a
Maya city that probably stood at Negroman on the Macal River, about 9km south of the

present town, was the capital of the province of **Dzuluinicob**, where for years the Indians resisted attempts to Christianize them. The early wave of conquest, in 1544, made only a little impact here, and the area was a centre of rebellion in the following decades. Two **Spanish friars** arrived in 1618, but a year later the entire population was still practising idolatry. Outraged, the friars smashed the idols and ordered the native priests flogged, but by the end of the year the Maya had once again driven out the Spaniards. Four years later, Maya from Tipu worked as guides in an expedition against the Itzá and in 1641, the friars returned, determined to Christianize the inhabitants. To express their defiance of the Spanish clerics, the Maya priests conducted a mock Mass, using tortillas as communion wafers, and threw out the friars. From then on Tipu remained an outpost of Maya culture, providing refuge to other Maya fleeing Spanish rule and apparently retaining a good measure of independence until 1707, when the population was forcibly removed to Lake Petén Itzá in Guatemala.

Like many places in Belize, San Ignacio probably started its present life as a **logging camp**. A map drawn up in 1787 simply states that the Indians of this general area were "in friendship with the Baymen". Later it was a centre for the shipment of chicle, the sap of the sapodilla tree and basis of chewing-gum. The self-reliant *chicleros*, as the collectors of chicle were called, knew the forest intimately, including the location of most, if not all, Maya ruins. When the demand for Maya artefacts sent black-market prices rocketing in the twentieth century, many of them turned to looting.

Until the Western Highway was built in the 1930s, local transport was by mule or water, and it could take ten days of paddling to reach San Ignacio from Belize City; later, small steamers made the journey. Nowadays, river traffic, which had almost died out, is enjoying something of a revival as increasing numbers of tourists take river trips.

San Ignacio

San Ignacio's main street is Burns Avenue; along here, or nearby, you'll find almost everything you need, including the best market in Belize. However, the town's best feature is its location – it's an excellent base for day-trips. The river and the surrounding countryside are equally inviting, and there are many ways to enjoy them – on foot, by boat, on a mountain bike or on horseback.

Arrival and information

Buses stop in the marketplace just behind Burns Avenue. To check times of onward services call Batty on ☎09/22058 or Novelos on ☎09/32054, or ask at the Batty's office in the market area (you can **leave luggage** there too). There's no official tourist office in San Ignacio, but Bob Jones, owner of the long-established *Eva's* bar and restaurant at 22 Burns Ave (☎09/22267), is renowned for providing first-class **tourist information**. *Eva's* was also Belize's first **Internet café** (*evas@btl.net*), and you can pick up the local newspaper *The Cayo Trader* here and buy **books** and **maps** at the gift counter.

All the **banks** are on Burns Avenue, though if you need Guatemalan quetzales you can save time at the border by using the services of the reliable **moneychangers** who'll approach you. The **BTL office** (Mon–Fri 8am–noon & 1–4pm, Sat 8am–noon) is on Far West St, and the **post office** right in the centre, next to Court's furniture store. **Laundry** can be dropped off at *Martha's*, on West Street behind *Eva's*. **Car rental** is available at Western Auto Rental (☎09/23134). For domestic and international **air tickets** go to Universal Travel, 8 Mossiah St (☎09/23884, fax 23885). The Arts and Crafts of Central America, two doors from *Eva's*, sells reasonably priced Guatemalan **gifts**, books (including Rough Guides) and maps. Past here, Caesar's Gift Shop sells the same jewellery and wood carvings as at his place on the Western Highway; you can also find out about *Black Rock River Lodge*, in the Macal River valley (see p.246).

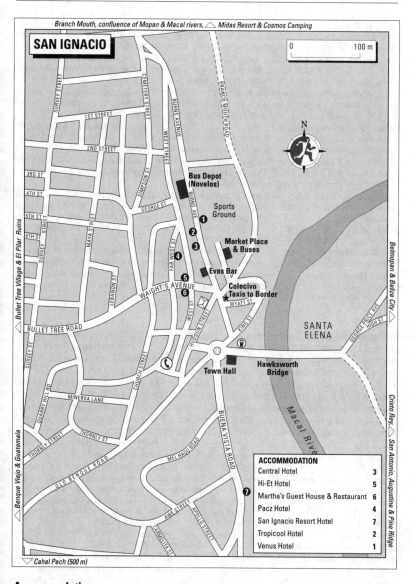

SAN IGNACIO

Branch Mouth, confluence of Mopan & Macal rivers, △ Midas Resort & Cosmos Camping

Bus Depot (Novelos)

Sports Ground

Market Place & Buses

Evas Bar

Colecivo Taxis to Border

Town Hall

Hawksworth Bridge

SANTA ELENA

Macal River

Bullet Tree Village & El Pilar Ruins

Benque Viejo & Guatemala

Belmopan & Belize City

Cristo Rey, San Antonio, Augustine & Pine Ridge

Cahal Pech (500 m)

ACCOMMODATION	
Central Hotel	3
Hi-Et Hotel	5
Martha's Guest House & Restaurant	6
Pacz Hotel	4
San Ignacio Resort Hotel	7
Tropicool Hotel	2
Venus Hotel	1

Accommodation

The **hotels** in San Ignacio offer the best-value budget accommodation in the country, and you'll almost always find space. For **camping** near town see the *Cosmos* and *Midas* entries.

Central Hotel, 24 Burns Ave (☎09/24179). Simple, clean budget hotel with hot water and shared baths, and a comfortable balcony with hammocks. Good local information. ③.

Cosmos Campground, a 15min walk from town along the road to Branch Mouth (☎09/22116). Full camping facilities, including decent showers, flush toilets and a kitchen area. Tent space (US$3), and there are also eight clean, simple cabins, some with private bath. ②–③.

Hi-Et Hotel, West St, behind *Eva's* (☎09/22828). Friendly, family-run budget hotel with one downstairs room and four basic rooms upstairs, each with a tiny balcony, all sharing a cold-water bathroom. The least expensive hotel in town, and phenomenally popular. ②.

Martha's Guest House, West St, behind *Eva's* (☎09/23647). Three comfortable and very popular rooms in Martha and John August's home, with shared hot-water bathroom. The restaurant below is a favourite meeting place, with good information available. Accepts Visa. ④.

Midas Resort, Branch Mouth Rd (☎09/23172, fax 23845). The only resort actually in town, and the best-value cabaña place in Cayo. Very comfortable Maya-style thatched cabañas with private bathroom, set in peaceful grounds on the riverbank; camping also available. Accepts Visa. ④.

PACZ Hotel, 4 Far West St, (☎09/22110, fax 22972). Five clean, comfortable rooms with hot water in the shared bathrooms. Owner Pete Zubrzycki runs amazing cave tours and gives reliable information. Good restaurant below. Accepts Visa. ④.

San Ignacio Resort Hotel, 18 Buena Vista St (☎09/22034, fax 22134), a 10min walk uphill from the town centre. San Ignacio's premier hotel and in a superb location, with views over the Macal River valley. Rooms (some a/c) are spacious and comfortable and the dining room terrace overlooks the pool. The restaurant is one of the best in the area and the *Stork Club* bar has a happy hour on Fridays. Nature trails lead down to the river. ⑦–⑧.

Tropicool Hotel, Burns Ave, 75m past *Eva's* (☎09/23052). Bright, clean, budget rooms (the best value in town) with ceiling fan and shared hot-water bathrooms and a sitting room with TV. ③.

Venus Hotel, 29 Burns Ave (☎09/23203, fax 22225). Good rates and the best deal around if you want to stay a week, but rooms vary in quality, so check before you take one; some have a private bath and a few have a/c and TV. Accepts Visa/MC. ③–④.

Eating

Along with its budget hotels, San Ignacio has several good, inexpensive **restaurants**, and there are a number of **fast-food stalls** in the market area. **Fruit stands** in the centre of town are laden with bananas, oranges and papayas. The Saturday **market** is the best in Belize, with local farmers bringing in fresh-picked produce and it's also a good place to stock up on provisions for trips – see Chris Lowe here for his *Fruit-A-Plenty* trail mix and granola bars. For general groceries, Celina's Store, two blocks from *Eva's* down Burns Avenue, has the widest selection and best prices. You can get fresh **bread** and baked goods from La Popular bakery on West Street, behind *Eva's*, and most afternoons small boys will be around selling tasty, freshly cooked and very inexpensive empanadas and tamales.

Eva's Bar, 22 Burns Ave. Good, reasonably priced, filling meals, including chilli, chicken, tasty Creole dishes and some vegetarian options. Also has email (*evas@btl.net*) and Internet service, a public phone and a gift shop – a great place to meet fellow travellers and local tour operators.

Martha's Kitchen and Pizza Parlour, West St, behind *Eva's*. Under the guest house of the same name and just as well run, with good service. Great breakfasts with strong, locally grown coffee, main dishes of traditional Creole food and pizza (always a vegetarian choice) and delicious cakes for dessert. The patio tables (candle-lit in the evenings) are a popular place to meet and it's also becoming well-known as an information centre and a place to meet your tour guides.

The Running W Restaurant, at the *San Ignacio Hotel*, 18 Buena Vista St. Excellent food in tranquil surroundings, and not at all expensive. Breakfasts are especially good value.

Sandcastle Bar, an open-sided, American-style sports bar on the riverbank, behind the market square, serving good steak and seafood, and you can get good nachos and other bar snacks.

Serendib Restaurant, 27 Burns Ave. Excellent Sri Lankan curries and seafood at very reasonable prices. Good service too.

Around San Ignacio

Although you can easily use San Ignacio as a base for day-trips, if you'd like to stay in the countryside, numerous guest houses and ranches in the area offer **cottage-style** accommodation and organized trips. On the whole, standards are very high and most of them cater to visitors who come here after a week on the reef, a phenomenon known as a "surf and turf holiday". However, there are some really good-value places in all price ranges. Many are booked up during peak season (Christmas to Easter), but can offer reduced prices in low season if open. Most offer horse-riding, bird-watching, canoeing, good home cooking and various trips into the surrounding area. All can reached by road and are well signposted from San Ignacio, though to get to a couple of them you'll have to cross the river in a canoe or small boat.

The countryside around Cayo is ideal for exploring on **horseback** which, as with canoeing, can be arranged by the big resorts at a price. The best deal, though, is offered by Charlie Collins, who runs Easy Rider (☎09/22203 or 014/8276) and knows the area well; her horses are cared for and she carefully matches riders to the right horse. A **mountain bike** is another great way to explore Cayo; ask at *Eva's* for details. **Caving** is increasingly popular in Cayo; the most experienced caving guide around, Pete Zubrzycki of *PACZ Hotel* (☎09/22110), leads truly amazing trips into the Maya underworld, and can also arrange **rafting** on the Macal River. For the **Maya sites** around San Ignacio, and expertly guided trips to Tikal (see p.409) the most reliable and recommended people are Ramon Silva, who runs International Archaeological Tours, 23 Burns Ave (☎09/23991, fax 22760), and Tessa Fairweather (☎08/22412), a very experienced private tour guide; Tessa lives in Belmopan but will meet you in San Ignacio.

Branch Mouth

Perhaps the easiest introduction to this region is to take the twenty-minute walk to **Branch Mouth**, where the Macal and Mopan rivers merge to form the Belize River. The track leads north from the football field, past rich farmland, with thick vegetation, tropical flowers and butterflies on either side. At the confluence of the rivers is a huge tree, with branches arching over the jade water. A rusting iron mooring ring in the trunk is a reminder of the past importance of river transport; now there are swallows skimming the surface, parrots flying overhead and scores of tiny fish in the water. The scar of raw earth on the opposite bank is evidence of the severe flooding of recent years, when the river rose within metres of the suspension bridge and even inundated the streets of San Ignacio.

Cahal Pech

Twenty minutes' walk uphill out of town to the southwest, clearly signposted along the Benque road, lie the ruins of **Cahal Pech** (daily 8am–4pm; US$2.50); there's also a small **museum** (in theory open daily from 8am–4pm; US$2.50). Cahal Pech means "place of ticks" in Mopan Maya, but that's certainly not how the elite families who ruled here in Classic times would have known it. Entering the site through the forest you arrive at Plaza B, surrounded by temple platforms and the remains of dwellings; your gaze is soon drawn to **Structure 1**, the Audiencia. If you're used to seeing finely executed, exposed stonework at reconstructed Maya sites then the thick overcoat of lime-mortar on buildings here may come as a bit of a shock. The Classic Maya, however, viewed bare stone facings as ugly and unfinished, and covered all surfaces with a thick coat of plaster or stucco. Cahal Pech was the royal acropolis-palace of an elite Maya family during the Classic period, and there's evidence of monumental construction from at least as early as the Middle Preclassic (400 BC) when the city probably dominated the central Belize River valley. However, most of what you see dates from the late ninth century AD.

For a cultural experience of an entirely different nature, you can stroll across to the adjacent hilltop for a drink at the *Cahal Pech Tavern*. The best of the nearby **accommodation** choices are the well-designed, good-value wood-and-thatch cabañas of *Cahal Pech Village* (☎09/23740, fax 22225), overlooking San Ignacio. Each cabaña – named after a Belizean Maya site – has electricity and private bath with hot water, and the interiors are decorated with Guatemalan textiles.

Barton Creek Cave

Of the many **cave trips** available in Cayo, one of the most fascinating is to **Barton Creek Cave**, accessible only by river, and only on a tour (around 4–5hr; US$22.50 per person); contact David or Connie at *Martha's Guest House* preferably the day before you'd like to go. David is a very responsible guide and a multilingual Belizean who will point out the astonishing Maya artefacts in the cave. The trip begins with a drive through the traditional Mennonite settlement of **Upper Barton Creek** to the cave entrance, framed by jungle at the far side of a jade-green pool, where you board the canoe. The river is navigable for about 1600m, though in a couple of places the roof comes so low you have to crouch right down in the canoe, and ends in a gallery blocked by a huge rockfall. The clear, slow-moving river fills most of the cave width, though the roof soars 100m above your head in places. **Maya burials** line the banks, the most awe-inspiring indicated by a skull set in a natural rock bridge used by the Maya to reach the sacred site, surrounded by pottery vessels. Like all caves in Belize, Barton Creek Cave is a registered archeological site and nothing must be touched or removed. If it's been raining, a **subterranean waterfall** cascades over the rocks at the end of the navigable passage – a truly unforgettable sight. Beyond, lie many more kilometres of passageways, accessible only on a fully equipped expedition.

The Macal River

If the idea of a day or more on the **Macal River** appeals, then any of the resorts can **rent canoes** to paddle on your own (very good value from the *Snooty Fox*, see p.239), but by far the best-value **guided canoe trip** is offered by *Tony's River Adventures* (☎09/23292 or contact Tony at *Eva's*). For US$12.50 per person you will be expertly paddled upriver to *Chaa Creek* (see below) in the morning and float down in the afternoon, and you'll see far more wildlife under his guidance than you could alone.

The Rainforest Medicine Trail

A canoe trip is the best way to visit the **Rainforest Medicine Trail** (daily 8am–noon & 1–5pm; US$5.50; ☎09/23870), next to *Chaa Creek Cottages*. The trail is dedicated to Don Eligio Panti, a Maya bush doctor (*curandero*) from San Antonio village who passed on his skills to Dr Rosita Arvigo, director and founder of the **Ix Chel Tropical Research Station**, where the trail begins: Don Eligio died in 1996, at the age of 103.

The medical knowledge of the Maya was extensive, and the trail takes in a wide range of **traditional healing plants**, many of them now used in modern medicine. It's a fascinating experience; there are vines that provide fresh water like a tap; poison-wood, with oozing black sap, its antidote always growing nearby; and the bark of the negrito tree, once sold for its weight in gold in Europe as a cure for dysentery. You'll also see specimens of the tropical hardwoods of the jungle that have been exploited for economic reasons. The more mundane, but very welcome, products of the forest range from herbal teas to blood tonic: Traveller's Tonic, a preventative for diarrhoea, really works, as does Jungle Salve for insect bites, and there are many more cures and tonics available.

Chaa Creek Natural History Centre

A visit to the marvellous **Chaa Creek Natural History Centre** (daily 8am–5pm; US$6), in the grounds of *Chaa Creek Cottages*, is the best introduction to Cayo's history, geography and wildlife. If you're spending more than a couple of days in the area, try to see this first. With fascinating and accurate displays of the region's flora and fauna, vivid archeological and geological maps, and a scale model of the Macal valley, it's worth a visit in its own right; it also has the **Butterfly Breeding Centre** (included in entry fee) where you can admire the magnificent blue morpho. Call to check on the current events programme (☎09/22037).

The Belize Botanic Gardens

Located at *duPlooy's* (see below), south of *Chaa Creek*, the **Belize Botanic Gardens** (daily 8am–5pm; US$5; ☎09/23101) is an ambitious new project established in 1997 on fifty acres of former farmland and forest. The garden is the brainchild of *duPlooy's* owners and avid plant lovers, Ken and Judy duPlooy. There are already around four hundred tree species and 130 orchids, a nursery with over a thousand seedlings, two ponds and several kilometres of interpretative **trails**. The aim is to create a first-class biological educational and study resource for Belizean and overseas researchers, and to conserve many of Belize's native plant species in small areas representative of their natural habitats; they've already gone a long way to achieving this on the ground. The diversity created by these different ecosystems attracts an ever-increasing number of **birds** – and you can be guided around the gardens by **expert naturalist** guide Philip Mai. The garden can be reached by road or river, but it's best to call ahead if you need a guided tour.

Accommodation on the Macal River

Most accommodation along the Macal River is in upmarket **cabaña-style resorts**, beautifully located in the forest above the riverbank, though some do have slightly cheaper options, and all will give discounts to Rough Guide readers. There is one budget place, also in a wonderful location. The listings below are in the order that you approach them travelling upriver, though all are accessible by road; for a couple you also have to cross the river by boat. Any of these places can organize superb **horseback tours** to nearby Maya ruins and some also have **mountain bikes** for rent.

Crystal Paradise Resort, in the village of Cristo Rey, on the east bank of the river, and on the bus route to San Antonio (☎ & fax 09/22772). A friendly place with a range of accommodation, including private cabañas and simple rooms, owned and built by the Belizean Tut family. The thatch-roofed dining room overlooks the valley. Cabaña price includes two delicious meals. ⑤–⑨.

Chaa Creek Cottages, on an unpaved turn-off 10km along the road to Benque (☎09/22037, fax 22501). Beautiful, whitewashed wood-and-stucco cabañas in gorgeous grounds high above the Macal River, with a justly deserved reputation for luxury and ambience. The cottages have tiled floor and bathroom, and range from delightful cabins to a luxury suite. There's a fine restaurant and bar with spacious outdoor deck. A trail map guides you through the forest and over the hills to several nearby Maya sites. Good off-season discounts. ⑨.

Macal River Campsite, on the east bank, just below *Chaa Creek* (☎09/2037, fax 2501). The brainchild of Mick Flemming of *Chaa Creek*, with roomy tents under tarps on raised wooden bases. It's camping in comfort, with hot water in clean, tiled bathrooms, and oil lamps in the evening. There's access to all the *Chaa Creek* trails. US$50 per person, including meals.

duPlooy's, further along the *Chaa Creek* track (☎09/23101, fax 23301). Spacious private bungalows (US$150) beautifully located in farmland and forest on the west bank of the Macal River, and home to the new Belize Botanic Garden (see above). Rooms in the Pink House are less expensive at US$40, each with a double and single bed. The deck, extending from the bar, overlooks the river cliffs, providing a walkway into the forest and a superb bird-watching site. Getting here without a vehicle is difficult, but there's a shuttle service from the airport leaving at 1pm; free if you're staying for three nights. ⑤–⑨.

Guacamallo Jungle Camp, on the east bank of the river. No phone; contact David or Connie at *Martha's* in San Ignacio (☎09/23647). Simple cabins high above the river, which you cross in a canoe, located at the edge of a huge and mysterious Maya site. Good, plentiful food and a wonderful sense of timelessness as you sit on a Maya mound outside your cabin watching the stars at night. US$25 per person, including transport, dinner and breakfast. ⑥.

Ek Tun (☎091/2002; in US ☎303/442-6150), in a remote location on the east bank of the Macal River, not directly accessible by road. Two stick-and-thatch cabañas in sublime isolation – the most luxurious in the country. Each cottage has two bedrooms, hot-water shower and deck overlooking the garden. Gourmet dinner is served under the thatch overlooking the river. Trails lead through the forest and along the river cliffs, dotted with cave entrances, and there is much evidence of Maya occupation in the area. ⑨.

Black Rock River Lodge (☎09/22341, fax 23449); it's possible to drive here, or you can take a trip from *Caesar's Place* on the Western Highway (see p.238). Set high above the west bank of the Macal River with stunning views of the jungle-clad limestone cliffs of the upper Macal valley, the solidly-built deluxe cabañas have private hot showers and floors made of smooth stones from the river. Shared bath cabins are also available. Solar power provides electricity. You can hike from here to Vaca or Flour Camp **caves**, each containing some amazing Maya pottery. ⑤–⑦.

The Mopan River

The main tributary creeks of the **Mopan River** rise in the Maya Mountains and flow into Guatemala, re-entering Belize at the border before the final, and most picturesque, 25km stretch to its confluence with the Macal River at Branch Mouth (see p.243). There are some attractive and not too serious **white-water rapids** along this stretch, and it's easy enough to arrange kayak or rafting trips on the Mopan; check at any of the resorts listed below (*Clarissa Falls* is best), or with Pete Zubrzycki at *PACZ Hotel* in San Ignacio (☎09/22110).

Five kilometres west of San Ignacio (leaving town along the Bullet Tree Road) is the small village of **Bullet Tree Falls**, where a bridge crosses the river and, as with the Macal River, there are Maya ruins in the vicinity; **El Pilar** and **Buenavista del Cayo** are described below, Xunantunich, the easiest of Belize's major sites to visit, is covered on p.251. For **accommodation** on the Mopan River see opposite.

El Pilar and Buenavista del Cayo

From Bullet Tree Falls you can visit **El Pilar**, the largest Maya site in the Belize River valley, covering forty hectares and including seventy major structures grouped around 25 plazas. Although there's no public transport to the site, 14km northwest of the village, a rough, motorable road climbs the escarpment, and if the archeologists are working there you will probably be able to get a lift. Alternatively you could go on horseback or by mountain bike – check at *Eva's*. The site is open daily (no admission charge at present) and Teo Williams, the caretaker, will show you around; his book, *Teo's Way*, is a fascinating account of his life and work, which is on sale at the site – transcribed from taped interviews by Alison Anderson Davies and written largely in Creole.

El Pilar's long sequence of construction began in the Preclassic period, around 450 BC, and continued right through to the Terminal Classic, around 1000 AD, when some of the largest existing temples were completely rebuilt. The most impressive structures – four large pyramids between fifteen and twenty metres high and a ball court – are grouped around Plaza Copal, from whose west side a flight of steps leads down to a thirty-metre-wide causeway running to **Pilar Poniente** in Guatemala. In an unprecedented move, the two countries have overcome generations of mutual suspicion to create the **El Pilar Archeological Reserve for Maya Flora and Fauna**, covering an area of nine square kilometres on both sides of the border. Several hiking **trails** lead you around the reserve focusing on both the archeology and natural history of El Pilar, and the site is considered one of the finest bird-watching areas in Cayo.

On the east bank of the Mopan River, halfway between San Ignacio and the border, the small Maya site of **Buenavista del Cayo** was once the centre of a wider political region of which Cahal Pech is known to have been a satellite. The ruins are on private land and you need permission from the owner to visit; perhaps the best way to get there is on horseback – Easy Rider (see p.243) runs tours. Archeologists have uncovered a palace, ball courts, carved stelae, plazas and courtyards. A number of important burial items were also found here, including the famous Jauncy vase, now in Belmopan. There's also evidence that the Maya established workshops to mass-produce pottery on the site. Since excavation most of the structures have been covered over, but there is a charming palace and courtyard in a glade.

Accommodation on the Mopan River

There is less accommodation along the Mopan River than there is along the Macal, but what's available is more within the reach of the budget traveller and no less special. The resorts below are listed in order of increasing distance from San Ignacio.

Parrot Nest, just past Bullet Tree Falls, 5km from San Ignacio (☎09/23702). Five fantastic thatched cabins, one sitting very securely up a tree. Shared bathroom with hot shower. Horses can be rented to visit the ruins of El Pilar. Phone ahead for transport. ④.

Clarissa Falls, along a signed track to the right off the Benque road, just before the *Chaa Creek* turn (☎09/23916), and right by a set of rapids. There's a wide range of accommodation: simple, clean, stick-and-thatch cabins, some with private bath; a "bunkhouse" cabin with hammocks and shared hot-water showers(US$7.50 per person), and space for camping (US$3.75). Owner Chena Gálvez serves great home cooking. Horse-riding, rafting and tubing at reasonable rates. ③–⑤.

Nabitunich, down a track just beyond the *Clarissa Falls* turn, off the Benque road (☎09/32309, fax 33096). Run by friendly Rudy and Margaret Juan, this is the best of the resorts on the Mopan River, with beautiful thatched stone cottages set in 400 acres of forest and farmland, and the gardens have spectacular views of El Castillo at Xunantunich. Camping (②) also available. ⑦.

The Mountain Pine Ridge

South of San Ignacio, the **Mountain Pine Ridge Forest Reserve** is a spectacular range of rolling hills and jagged peaks formed from some of the oldest rocks in Central America. In amongst these granite outcrops there are also some sections of limestone, riddled with superb caves, the most accessible of which are the **Rio Frio Caves** in Augustine/Douglas Silva. For the most part the landscape is semi-open, a mixture of grassland and pine forest growing in nutrient-poor, sandy soil, although in the warmth of the river valleys the vegetation is thicker gallery forest, giving way to rainforest south of the **Guacamallo Bridge**. The rains feed a number of small streams, most of which run off into the Macal and Belize rivers. One of the most scenic rivers is the **Rio On**, rushing over cataracts and forming a gorge – a sight of tremendous natural beauty within view of the picnic shelter. On the northern side of the ridge are the **Thousand-Foot Falls** (actually over 1600ft (490m) and the highest in Central America).

The Pine Ridge is virtually uninhabited but for four or five tourist lodges and one small settlement, **Augustine/Douglas Silva**, site of the forest reserve headquarters. The whole area is perfect for **hiking** and **mountain biking**, but **camping** is allowed only at Augustine/Douglas Silva and at the Mai Gate, beyond San Antonio village. It's fairly hard – though rewarding – to explore this part of the country on your own, and unless you have a car, a mountain bike or come on an organized tour, you may have to rely on hitching.

Getting to the reserve

There are two **entrance roads** to the reserve, one from the village of **Georgeville**, on the Western Highway (see p.238), and the other from **Santa Elena**, along the Cristo Rey road and through the village of **San Antonio**, served by four Mesh **buses** a day from San Ignacio. If you're up to it, the best way to get around is to rent a **mountain bike** in San Ignacio; the bus to San Antonio takes bikes, or you could put them in the back of a passing pickup truck. Any travel agent or resort can arrange **organized tours**: if you're staying at any of the Cayo resorts, a full-day tour of the Pine Ridge costs around

US$45–50 per person for a group of four; more if you want to go to Caracol. If you're **on a budget**, contact Rafael August of Western Adventure Tours through *Martha's*, or Tommy of Tommy's Tours through *Eva's*, who can take you on a superb tour for around half the price. Recent road improvements in the Pine Ridge, particularly on the road to Caracol, make a trip in a **rental jeep** perfectly feasible (most of the year), but always check road conditions first and heed the advice of the forestry officials.

The Cristo Rey Road to San Antonio

The **road to Cristo Rey** village begins in Santa Elena, 150m on the right after crossing the Hawksworth Bridge. Two kilometres along this road is the excellent *Maya Mountain Lodge* (☎09/22164, fax 22029; ⑤–⑦), run by Bart and Suzi Mickler and set in rich tropical forest. Accommodation is in colourfully decorated individual cabañas, each with a private bath, electricity and hot water; the larger and slightly cheaper Parrot's Perch cabin is ideal for groups. The lodge sometimes hosts student groups and has a library and lecture area; they especially welcome families and have plenty of activities for kids, including the best illustrated trail guide in Belize. After another few kilometres you come to **CRISTO REY**, a pretty village of scattered wooden houses on a high bank above the Macal River. Near the beginning of the village, you'll come to *Sandals Restaurant*, run by Orlando Madrid, which also has a few simple **cabins** (☎014/7446; ④). Orlando can take you on guided canoe or cave trips and **rents canoes** at reasonable prices.

San Antonio and Pacbitún ruins

In **SAN ANTONIO**, 10km further on from Cristo Rey, the villagers are descendants of Maya (Uxcawal is their name, in their own language) refugees, who fled the Caste Wars in Yucatán in 1847 and most people still speak Yucatec. Their story is told in a fascinating written version of San Antonio's oral history, *After 100 Years* by Alfonso Antonio Tzul. Nestled in the Macal River valley, surrounded by scattered milpa farms, with the forested Maya Mountains in the background, the village was home to the late Don Eligio Panti, the famous *curandero* (see p.244). It's a superb place to learn about traditional Maya ways, not least by going to see the Garcia sisters, who grew up in the village determined not to let Maya culture be swamped by outside influence. They run the *Chichan Ka Guest House* (☎09/23310, fax 22057; ④) and **Tanah Museum** (US$3), at the approach to the village (the bus stops right outside), which has simple but comfortable **rooms** (some with private bath). It's a very relaxing place to stay; meals are prepared in the traditional way – often using organic produce from the garden – and courses are offered in the gathering and use of medicinal plants. The sisters are also renowned for their slate carvings, and their **gift shop** has become a favourite tourgroup stop. The Mesh **bus to San Antonio** (Mon–Sat only; 1hr) departs from the market in San Ignacio four times a day between 10.30am and 5pm, returning from San Antonio between 6am and 3pm.

Three kilometres east of San Antonio, on the road to the Pine Ridge, lie the ruins of **Pacbitún** ("stones set in the earth"), a major ceremonial centre with at least 24 temple pyramids, a ball court and several raised causeways. One of the oldest known Preclassic sites in Belize (1000 BC), it continued to flourish throughout the Classic period, and Maya farming terraces and farmhouse mounds can be seen in the hills all around. Only Plaza A and the surrounding structures are cleared. This is the highest point in Pacbitún, created when the Maya re-shaped an entire hilltop. The tombs of two elite women yielded the largest haul of Maya musical instruments ever found in one place: drums, flutes, ocarinas (wind instruments) and the first discovery of Maya maracas. Though the site is not always open to casual visitors, José Tzul, who lives on the right just before the entrance, runs Blue Ridge Mountain Rider (☎09/22322) and can arrange horseback tours of the area, taking in Pacbitún (US$50 per day).

The forest reserve

Not far beyond Pacbitún, and 25km before Augustine, the entrance roads meet and begin a steady climb towards the **entrance to the reserve** proper. One kilometre beyond the junction is a **campsite** (①) run by Fidencio and Petronila Bol, a delightful couple and owners of Bol's Nature Tours. Fidencio used to work as a caretaker at several Maya sites, including Pacbitún and Caracol, and Petronila has compiled *A Book of Maya Herbs*. Fidencio can guide you to several nearby **caves** – the aptly named Museum Cave holds dozens of artefacts, including intact bowls. About 5km uphill from the campsite is the **Mai Gate**, a forestry checkpoint (where visitors register), which has reserve information as well as toilets and drinking water. Once you've entered the reserve, the dense, leafy forest is quickly replaced by pine trees.

After 3km a branch road heads off to the left, running for 7km to a point overlooking the **Thousand-Foot Falls** (US$1.50). The setting is spectacular, with rugged, thickly forested slopes across the steep valley – almost a gorge. The long, slender plume of water becomes lost in the valley below, giving rise to their other, more poetic name – Hidden Valley Falls. The waterfall itself is about 1km from the viewpoint, but try to resist the temptation to climb around for a closer look: the slope is a lot steeper than it first appears and, if you do get down, the ascent is very difficult.

One of the reserve's main attractions has to be the **Rio On Pools**, a gorgeous spot for a swim, 11km further on. Here the river forms pools between huge granite boulders before plunging into a gorge, right beside the main road. Another 8km from here and you reach the reserve headquarters at **AUGUSTINE/DOUGLAS SILVA**. If you're heading for **Caracol**, this is where you can get advice on road conditions. You can **stay** at the **campsite** or the **bunkhouse** (②), for which you need camping gear. The village shop sells basic supplies and cold beer, but there are no phones.

The **Rio Frio Cave** is a twenty-minute walk from Augustine, following the signposted track from the parking area through the forest to the main cave, beneath a small hill. The Rio Frio flows right through and out of the other side of the hill here and if you enter the foliage-framed cave mouth, you can scramble over limestone terraces the entire way along and into the open again. Sandy beaches and rocky cliffs line the river on both sides.

Accommodation in the Mountain Pine Ridge

The **resorts** in the Pine Ridge include some of the most exclusive accommodation in the interior of Belize. These lodges, mostly cabins set amongst pines, surrounded by the undisturbed natural beauty of the forest reserve, and with quiet paths to secluded waterfalls, are ideal places to stay if you're visiting Caracol. The listings below are in the order in which you approach them from the entrance road.

Hidden Valley Inn, on the Cooma Cairn road to Thousand-Foot Falls (☎08/23320, fax 23334; in US ☎1-800/334-7942). Twelve roomy, well-designed cottages with fireplaces stacked with logs to ward off the evening chill, at the highest elevation of any accommodation in Belize, and set in a seventy-square-kilometre private reserve which includes Thousand-Foot Falls. Meals are in the spacious main house, with the ambience of a mountain lodge with wood-panelled walls and a well-stocked library. Prices (US$180 double) include breakfast, dinner, tax and service charge. ⑨.

Pine Ridge Lodge, on the road to Augustine, just past the Cooma Cairn junction to Thousand-Foot Falls (☎09/23310, fax 22267; in US ☎216/781-6888). Small resort on the banks of Little Vaqueros Creek, with a choice of Maya-style thatched cabins or more modern ones with red-tiled roofs. The grounds and trees are full of orchids and trails lead to pristine waterfalls. ⑨ including breakfast.

Blancaneaux Lodge, 1km beyond Pine Ridge Lodge, then 2km down a track to the right, by the airstrip (☎09/23878, fax 23919). A sumptuous lodge with rooms, cabins and villas overlooking Privassion Creek. Owned by Francis Ford Coppola, it features a few Hollywood excesses, not least the prices, though these are considerably lower during the off season. Villas (up to US$450) have two enormous rooms decorated with Guatemalan and Mexican textiles. Cabañas (US$160) and lodge rooms (US$95 with shared bath) are perhaps more affordable. Meals feature home-grown organic vegetables, pizza and fine Italian wines. ⑧–⑨.

Five Sisters Lodge, at the end of the road past *Blancaneaux* (☎091/2005, fax 09/23081). Set on the hillside among the granite and pines overlooking Five Sisters waterfalls cascading over Privassion Creek, this has the best location in the Pine Ridge. There are eleven comfortable palmetto-and-thatch cabañas, each with hot shower and a deck with hammocks, and less expensive rooms in the main building. The grounds are a profusion of flowers and a trail leads through broadleaf forest to Little Vaqueros Falls. Electricity is provided by a small, unobtrusive hydro but the oil lamps are wonderfully romantic. Rates include breakfast; other meals are good value if you're on a day-trip. ⑤–⑦.

Caracol and around

Beyond Augustine, the main ridges of the Maya Mountains rise up to the south, while to the west is the Vaca plateau, a fantastically isolated wilderness. Here the ruins of **Caracol** (daily 8am–4pm; US$5), the largest known Maya site in Belize, were lost in the rainforest for several centuries until their rediscovery by *chicleros* in 1936. They were first systematically explored by A.H. Anderson in 1938, who named the site Caracol – Spanish for "snail" – because of the large numbers of snail shells found there. Other archeologists visited and made excavations in the 1950s, but early reports took a long time to reach the public domain as many documents were destroyed by Hurricane Hattie in 1961. In 1985 the first detailed, full-scale excavation of the site, the "Caracol Project", began under the auspices of Drs Arlen and Diane Chase of the University of Central Florida. Initially expected to take at least ten years, research continues to unearth a tremendous amount of material on the everyday life of all levels of Maya society. Apparently there was a large and wealthy middle class among the Maya of Caracol and dates on stelae and tombs suggest an extremely long occupation. At its greatest extent, around 700 AD during the Late Classic period, Caracol covered 88 square kilometres and had a population estimated to be around 150,000, with over 30,000 structures – a far greater density than at Tikal. What continues to puzzle archeologists is why the Maya built such a large city on a plateau with no permanent water source – and how they managed to maintain it for so long; the Maya-built reservoir is still used when the archeologists are in residence.

It's an amazing experience to be virtually alone in this great abandoned city, the horizon bounded by jungle-covered peaks, through which it's only three hours on foot to Guatemala. Caracol is a **Natural Monument Reserve**, a haven for wildlife as well as archeologists, and you may catch sight of ocellated turkeys feeding in the plazas and tapirs dining at night on the succulent shoots growing on cleared areas. The site is so isolated that in the past it was badly looted; today, a permanent team of caretakers are on guard all year, and the British Army and Belize Defence Force make frequent patrolling visits. During your visit you'll be guided by one of the guards, or, if excavation is in progress, by one of the researchers. Before you set off you should drop in to the new **visitor centre**, built by Raleigh volunteers.

The ruins

Only the core of the city, covering 38 square kilometres and containing at least 32 large structures and twelve smaller ones around five main plazas is currently open to visitors – though this is more than you can effectively see in a day. The largest pyramid, **Canaa**, is the tallest Maya structure in Belize at 42m and still one of the tallest buildings in the country, while several others are over 20m high. At the top of this immense restored structure is a small plaza, with three more sizeable pyramids; an altar here has revealed signs of a female ruler. Beneath Canaa, a series of looted tombs still have traces of the original painted glyphs on the walls. Archeological research has revealed some superb tombs, with lintels of iron-hard sapodilla wood supporting the entrances and painted texts decorating the walls.

Other glyphs carved on altars tell of war between Caracol and Tikal (see p.411), with power over a huge area alternating between the two great cities. One altar dates

Caracol's victory over Tikal at 562 AD – a victory that set the seal on the city's rise to power. Several altars and stelae were deliberately broken by logging tractors in the 1930s, including Altar 23, the largest at Caracol, dated to 810 AD, which clearly depicts two bound captive lords with a row of glyphs above and between them. One of the most awe-inspiring sights in this fantastic city is an immense, 700-year old **ceiba tree** – sacred to the Maya – with enormous buttress roots twice as high as a human being.

The Chiquibul Cave System

Fifteen kilometres beyond Caracol is the vast **Chiquibul Cave System**, the longest cave system in Central America, containing what is reputed to be the largest cave chamber in the western hemisphere. The entire area is dotted with caves and sinkholes, which were certainly known to the ancient Maya and probably used for ceremonies; as yet there has been no cave found in Belize which does not contain Maya artefacts. You need to come on a properly organized expedition if you want to explore. Further south, **Puente Natural** is an enormous natural limestone arch; if you're lucky you could get a lift in with the researchers from the new research station nearby.

Succotz and the ruins of Xunantunich

Back on the Western Highway, the village of **SAN JOSÉ SUCCOTZ** lies about 10km west of San Ignacio, right beside the Mopan River, just before Benque Viejo. It's a very traditional village in many ways, inhabited largely by Mopan Maya, who celebrate fiestas here on March 19 and May 3. Under colonial administration, the Maya of Succotz sided with the British – a stance that angered other groups, such as the Icaiché, who burnt it to the ground in 1867. The villagers here still identify strongly with their Maya culture, and many of the men work as caretakers of other Maya sites in Belize. The Magaña family's art gallery and **gift shop** (signed from the main road) sells superb wood and slate carvings, and there's very basic **accommodation** at the *Xunantunich Hotel* (②) across from the ferry.

Outside fiesta times, Succotz is a quiet village, and the main reason most people visit is to see the Classic period ruins of **Xunantunich** (pronounced Shun-an-tun-ich), "the Stone Maiden", up the hill across the river. Any bus or shared taxi running between San Ignacio and the border will drop you by the venerable, hand-winched **cable ferry** (daily 8am–5pm, lunch break around noon; Mon–Sat free, Sun US$1.50) which carries foot passengers and vehicles across the river. From the riverbank a steep track leads through the forest for a couple of kilometres to the ruins. If you're carrying luggage you can safely leave it in the *Plaza* restaurant (which is also a good source of information), opposite the ferry.

Xunantunich

Xunantunich (Mon–Fri 8am–5pm; weekends and holidays 8am–4pm; US$5) was explored in the 1890s by Dr Thomas Gann, a British medical officer, and in 1904 Teobalt Maler of the Peabody Museum took photographs and made a plan of the largest structure, A–6, commonly known as El Castillo. Gann returned in 1924, excavated large numbers of burial goods and removed the carved glyphs of Altar 1, the whereabouts of which are now unknown. British archeologist J. Eric S. Thompson excavated a residential group in 1938, unearthing pottery, obsidian, jade, a spindle, seashells, stingray spines and hammers. Recent excavations have found evidence of Xunantunich's role in the power politics of the Classic period – it was probably allied as a subordinate partner, along with Caracol, to the regional superpower Calakmul, against Tikal. By the Terminal Classic, Xunantunich was already in decline, though still apparently populated until around 1000 AD, after the so-called Classic Maya "collapse".

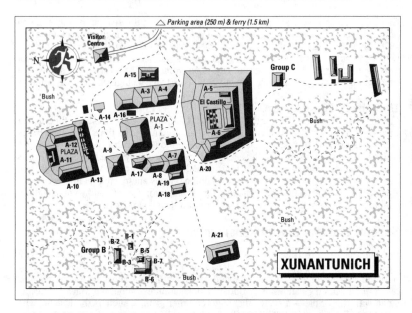

Your first stop should be the marvellous new **visitor centre**, easily the best at any Maya site in Belize. There's a superb scale-model of the city and the labels on exhibits will answer most questions. One of the highlights is a fibreglass replica of the famous hieroglyphic frieze, from which you get a much better idea of the significance of the real thing. Nearby, the original small museum has several well-preserved stelae from the site. If you want a **guide** to show you around try asking one of the caretakers, Ruben Penados or Ramon Archila, if they have time; they are very knowledgeable, having worked on recent excavations and reconstruction.

The site is built on top of an artificially flattened hill and includes five plazas, although the remaining structures are grouped around just three of them. The track brings you out into Plaza A–2, with large structures on three sides. Plaza A–3, to the right, is almost completely enclosed by a low, acropolis-like building, and Plaza A–1, to the left, is dominated by **El Castillo**, the city's largest structure, 40m high, and a prominent symbol of Belize's national identity. As is so often the case, the building is layered, with later versions built on top of earlier ones. It was once ringed by a decorative **stucco frieze** carved with abstract designs, human faces and jaguar heads, depicting a king performing rituals associated with assuming authority, and has been extensively restored. The climb up El Castillo is daunting, but the views from the top are superb, with the forest stretching out all around and the rest of the ancient city mapped out beneath you. The Preclassic ruins of **Actuncan** are a couple of kilometres north.

Benque Viejo and the border

The final town before the Guatemalan border is **BENQUE VIEJO DEL CARMEN**, less than half an hour from San Ignacio, where Guatemala and Belize combine in almost equal proportions and Spanish is certainly the dominant language. It's a quiet little place with little to offer the passing traveller, and there's a constant stream of taxis to and from the border post. **Hotels** are basic at best, and you're much better off staying in San Ignacio. **Crossing the border** is straightforward; see p.423 for details.

If you've time to kill, and are interested in the cultural aspects of Mestizo traditions, you might want to visit the small El Ba'lum Art Gallery, 43 Churchill St (Mon & Tues 1–4pm, Wed–Sat 9am–noon & 2–4.30pm; US$1.50). There are displays of old photographs and documents, logging and chicle-gathering equipment, paintings and musical instruments. Cubola, Belize's foremost **book and music publishers,** have an interesting gift shop at 35 Elizabeth St (☎09/32241), which sells unusual crafts, including brightly painted models of Belize's colonial-style houses, as well as recordings of the country's top bands.

travel details

The Western Highway from Belize City to the Guatemalan border is served by hourly buses from 5am to 8pm (3hr 30min), most of which continue over the border to Melchor de Mencos. Bus companies, main destinations and journey times are covered in the Belize City section (see box on p.201), with Batty operating until 10am and Novelos taking over at 11am; each has express buses on some journeys.

From Benque and the border to Belize City buses leave hourly from 4am to 4pm; additionally, Shaws run a service between Belmopan, San Ignacio and Melchor (Mon–Fri 7am–5pm), which increases the frequency along this route.

San Antonio to: San Ignacio (Mon–Sat at 6am, 7am, 1pm & 3pm; 1hr).

San Ignacio to: Belize City (Batty and Novelos run regular services, including expresses, hourly until 5pm; 3hr); Belmopan (Batty, Novelos and Shaws buses; hourly; 50min); San Antonio (Mon–Sat 4 daily from 10.30am–5pm; 1hr); the border (Batty, Novelos and Shaws run frequent services going every 30min during peak times 7.30am–4pm; 30min) most continue to the market in Melchor de Mencos). Buses for the border pass through San José (20min) and Benque Viejo (25min), though if you're headed this way it's often easier and quicker to take a shared taxi for US$2 per person.

CHAPTER SIX

THE SOUTH

To the **south of Belmopan** Belize is at its wildest. Here the central area is dominated by the **Maya Mountains**, sloping down towards the coast through a series of forested ridges and valleys carved by sparkling rivers. As you head further south the climate becomes more humid, promoting the growth of dense **rainforest**, rich in wildlife. The forests here have evolved to cope with periodic hurricanes sweeping in from the Caribbean and have in the past been selectively logged for mahogany. Among the broadleaf forests there are also large stands of Caribbean pine, looking strangely out of place in the tropics. The **coastal strip** south of Belize City is a band of savannah, swamp and lagoon, while beyond Dangriga the shoreline is composed of sandy bays, peninsulas and mangrove lagoons. In the far south the estuaries of the slow-moving Temash and Sarstoon rivers, lined with the tallest **mangrove forest** in Belize, form the country's southernmost national park, adjoining protected land in Guatemala.

Population density in this part of Belize is low, with most of the towns and villages located on the coast. **Dangriga**, the largest settlement, is home of the **Garífuna** people – descended from Carib Indians and shipwrecked, enslaved Africans. The villages of **Gales Point**, on Southern Lagoon, north of Dangriga, and **Hopkins**, on the coast to the south, are worth visiting to experience their tranquil way of life. Further south, the **Placencia peninsula** has become established as the focus of coastal tourism in southern Belize; from here and Dangriga you can visit a number of idyllic **cayes** sitting right on top of the reef, or go further out to pristine **Glover's Reef** atoll.

Inland, the Maya Mountains remain unpenetrated by roads, forming a solid barrier to land travel except on foot or horseback. The Belize government, showing supreme foresight, has placed practically all of the mountain massif under some form of legal protection, whether as national park, nature reserve, wildlife sanctuary or forest reserve. The most accessible area of this rainforest, though still little-visited by tourists, is the **Cockscomb Basin Wildlife Sanctuary**, a reserve designed to protect the sizeable jaguar population and a good base for exploring the forest.

The Southern Highway, the only road heading south of Dangriga, comes to an end in **Punta Gorda**, where you can visit Kekchí and Mopan **Maya villages** in the lush southern foothills of the Maya Mountains. Maya sites in the south are just as numerous as in the rest of the country, though generally smaller and certainly less well-known. **Nim Li Punit**, just off the highway, is worth a visit to see the largest and one of the best-preserved stelae in the country, and **Lubaantun**, near San Pedro Columbia,

ACCOMMODATION PRICE CODES

All the accommodation listed in this book has been categorized into one of nine price bands, as set out below. The prices quoted are in US dollars and refer to the cheapest room available for two people sharing in high season.

① under US$5	④ US$15–25	⑦ US$60–80
② US$5–10	⑤ US$25–40	⑧ US$80–100
③ US$10–15	⑥ US$40–60	⑨ over US$100

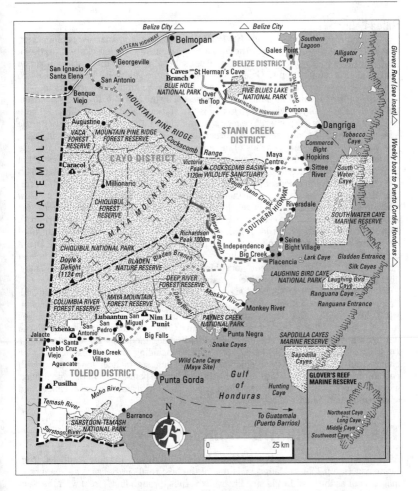

was where the enigmatic **Crystal Skull** came to light. From Punta Gorda you can easily reach **Puerto Barrios** (and possibly Lívingston) in Guatemala in one of the skiffs which leave each morning.

The Coastal Road and Gales Point

To head south from Belize City you first need to go west; either to Belmopan for the Hummingbird Highway (see p.235), or to the start of the unpaved **Coastal** (or Manatee) **Road shortcut to Dangriga**, heading southeast from Mile 30 on the Western Highway. The road is usually in good condition and is served by around five buses a day (Z-Line and Ritchie's) on the Belize City–Dangriga route. Along the way the scenery is typical of southern Belize: citrus plantations, pine ridge and steep limestone hills covered in broadleaf forest.

Gales Point

The tranquil Creole village of **GALES POINT** straggles along a narrow peninsula jutting into the shallow, placid **Southern Lagoon**, connected by creeks to **Northern Lagoon**, an even larger body of water. **Buses** heading along the Coastal Road to Dangriga pass the junction to Gales Point, 4km from the village itself; some buses go all the way into the village, others are usually met by a van to take passengers in.

The mangrove-cloaked lagoons, linked to the sea by the Manatee River, are an essential breeding area for rare wildlife including jabiru storks, manatee, crocodiles and both freshwater and marine turtles. Scenery and wildlife are the big attractions here: the lagoon system is the largest manatee breeding ground in the entire Caribbean basin, and Belize's main nesting beaches of the endangered **hawksbill turtle** lie either side of the mouth of the Manatee River. The villagers have formed the Gales Point Progressive Cooperative to protect their wildlife and encourage tourists to visit. With help from international conservation organizations and volunteers, they guard the turtles' nesting beaches and have installed signs and buoys warning boatmen to slow down to avoid harming the manatees. Renting a dory (traditionally a dugout canoe) for about US$10 per day allows you to explore the waterways, or you can take a trip with Moses Andrewin, an expert local **guide**. Gales Point is also a centre of **traditional drum-making**; you can learn to make and play drums at Emett Young's Creole Drum School. Emett often performs elsewhere so it's best to check ahead to see if he's at home. You'll also learn a lot about local history and culture – made even more enjoyable while sipping the home-produced cashew wine in the evenings.

In the village you'll see several signs pointing to houses offering simple bed-and-breakfast **accommodation** (④); to book ahead call the community telephone on ☎021/2031. *Gentle's Cool Spot*, a small bar and restaurant at the point where the buses turn around also has a few simple, clean rooms (③), and recently a couple of basic **campsites** have opened. The most luxurious accommodation is *Manatee Lodge* (☎08/23320, fax 23334; in US ☎1-800/334-7942; ⑨ including dinner, breakfast, service charge and tax), a two-storey, colonial-style building set in lush lawns lined with coconut trees in a beautiful location right at the tip of the peninsula. On the upper floor, a wooden deck offers great views at sunrise and sunset. Guests have use of canoes and small sailboats to enjoy the lagoon.

The Hummingbird Highway

After recent resurfacing work, the **Hummingbird Highway**, heading southeast from Belmopan (see p.235) to Dangriga, is one of the best roads in Belize. The scenery is magnificent as the road heads steadily over the hills through lush forest with the eastern slopes of the **Maya Mountains**, coated in greenery, rising to the right. The hills form part of a ridge of limestone mountains, riddled with underground rivers and caves, many of which you can visit on guided trips to explore the Maya underworld. About 19km out of Belmopan the road crosses the **Caves Branch River**, a tributary of the Sibun River. Further on, just past the highest point on the road is the stunningly beautiful **Five Blues Lake National Park**; beyond here the road follows the **Stann Creek valley**, lined with citrus groves, virtually all the way to Dangriga.

St Herman's Cave and the Blue Hole National Park

Just beyond the Caves Branch River, by the roadside on the right, is **St Herman's Cave** (daily 8am–4pm; US$4, valid also for the Blue Hole), one of the most accessible caves in Belize. Any bus between Belmopan and Dangriga will drop you at the cave or the Blue Hole, making an easy day-trip, but to really appreciate the mysteries of caving in Belize you need to stay nearby, at the *Caves Branch Jungle Lodge*.

Follow the marked trail behind the **visitor centre** for ten minutes to the cave entrance, squashed beneath a dripping rock face. To enter, down steps that were originally cut by the Maya, you'll need a flashlight. Inside, you clamber over the rocks and splash through the river for about twenty minutes, admiring the stunning formations, before the cave appears to end. To continue beyond, and emerge from one of the other entrances, you need to go on a tour – one of the best is organized by Pete Zubrzycki of *PACZ Hotel* in San Ignacio (see p.242). A new **interpretative trail**, with a spectacular observation platform, leads over the cave for 4km to a **campsite** (①).

Another signed trail leads 3km from the cave, over the ridge, to the **Blue Hole National Park**, which you can also reach by continuing along the highway for 2km. The Blue Hole is actually a short but deep stretch of underground river whose course is revealed by the collapse of a karst cavern, flowing on the surface for about 50m before disappearing beneath another rock face. Its cool, fresh turquoise waters, surrounded by dense forest and overhung with vines, mosses and ferns are perfect for a refreshing dip.

CAVES BRANCH JUNGLE LODGE
The best place **to stay** near the Blue Hole (and indeed along the whole Hummingbird Highway) is *Caves Branch Jungle Lodge* (☎ & fax 08/22800,), halfway between St Herman's Cave and the Blue Hole and about 1km from the road; it's easily accessible and signed from the highway. Set in a huge area of superb, high-canopy forest on the banks of the beautiful Caves Branch River, the lodge, run by Canadian Ian Anderson, offers a range of comfortable, rustic accommodation to suit all budgets. The highlights are the spacious, screened cabaña suites, with private bathroom with hot shower (⑨); there are great private cabañas too (⑦). For budget travellers even the bunkhouse (US$15 per person) has flush toilets and showers, and finally there's camping and hammock space (US$5); all prices include tax, and there's no service charge. Delicious and filling meals, served buffet-style, are eaten together in a simple dining room. Try to plan at least two nights here; even if you don't take any of the trips on offer, one day just won't seem enough.

Ian, together with the expert local guides, leads truly amazing **guided tours** through some of the area's most spectacular **caves** and along crystal-clear rivers running through the limestone hills. All the caves contain Maya artefacts – ceramics, carvings and the like – with abundant evidence of Classic period ceremonies. **Rafting trips** on the Sibun River, both by day and night, take you silently through the forest, or you can float on **inner tubes** 9km along a subterranean river, your headlamp piercing the intense darkness. The cave and river trips are not cheap (on average about US$65 per person) but well worth it, as the guest-book entries testify.

Over the Top and Five Blues Lake National Park

Beyond the Blue Hole, the Hummingbird Highway is well paved, undulating smoothly through the increasingly hilly landscape, eventually crossing a low pass. This is the highest point on the road, and the downhill slope is appropriately called **Over the Top**. On the way down, the road passes through **St Margaret's Village**, where a women's co-operative arranges bed-and-breakfast **accommodation** in private houses (☎081/2005; ③). A few kilometres past the village, the *Over the Top Restaurant* stands on a hill at Mile 32, overlooking the junction of the track to **Five Blues Lake National Park**, seventeen square kilometres of luxuriantly forested karst scenery, centred around a beautiful lake. Named for its constantly changing colours, the lake is another cenote or "blue hole", caused by a cavern's collapse. It's about an hour's walk to the lake and the road is passable in a good vehicle; trails enable you to explore the practically deserted park. Continuing south for 3km on the highway from Over the Top, there's cabaña and bed-and-breakfast **accommodation** at *Palacio's Mountain Retreat* (⑤), overlooking a river; buses stop right outside.

On towards Dangriga

Palacio's marks the start of the **Stann Creek valley**, the centre of the Belizean citrus fruit industry. Bananas were the first crop to be grown here, and by 1891 half a million stems were being exported through Stann Creek (now Dangriga) every year. However, this banana boom came to an abrupt end in 1906, when disease destroyed the crop, and afterwards the government set out to foster the growth of **citrus fruits**. Between 1908 and 1937 the valley was even served by a small railway – many of the highway bridges were originally rail bridges – and by 1945 the citrus industry was well established. Today it accounts for about thirteen percent of the country's exports and, despite widely fluctuating prices, is heralded as one of the nation's great success stories – although for the largely Guatemalan labour force, housed in rows of scruffy huts, conditions are little better than on the oppressive coffee fincas at home. The Hummingbird Highway officially comes to an end at **Middlesex**, 18km past Over The Top, continuing as the Stann Creek Valley Road, lined with citrus plantations.

Dangriga

DANGRIGA, formerly called Stann Creek, is the district capital and the largest town in southern Belize. It's also the cultural centre of the **Garífuna**, a people of mixed indigenous Caribbean and African descent. Since the early 1980s Garífuna culture has undergone a tremendous revival; as a part of this movement the town was renamed Dangriga, a Garífuna word meaning "sweet waters" – applied to the North Stann Creek flowing through the centre.

The most important day in the Garífuna calendar is November 19, **Garífuna Settlement Day**, when Dangriga is packed solid with expatriate Belizeans returning to their roots, and the town erupts into wild celebration. The party begins the evening before, and the drumming and *punta* dancing pulsate all night long. In the morning there's a re-enactment of the arrival from Honduras, with people landing on the beach in dugout canoes decorated with palm leaves. Christmas and New Year are also celebrated in unique Garífuna style. At this time you might see the *wanaragu* or *Jonkunu* (John Canoe) dance, where **masked and costumed dancers** represent figures consisting of elements of eighteenth-century naval officers and Amerindian tribal chiefs wearing feathered headdresses and with shell rattles on their knees. Dangriga is also home to some of the country's most popular artists and performers, including painter Benjamin Nicolas, painter and guitarist Pen Cayetano, drum-maker Austin Rodríguez, and the Warribagaga Dancers and Turtle Shell Band; the artists have small galleries here, and you may catch a live dance performance. Fine **crafts** are produced as well; distinctive brown and white basketware, woven palm leaf hats and baskets and dolls in Garífuna costume.

During quieter times the atmosphere is enjoyably laid-back, though there's little to do during the day. As the south of the country becomes more accessible, however, Dangriga is becoming increasingly useful as a base for visiting south-central Belize, the cayes offshore and the mountains, ruins and jaguar reserve inland.

Arrival, orientation and information

In addition to **buses** heading just for Dangriga, all buses between Belize City and Punta Gorda call here (see p.201 for details of bus companies and services in Belize City). On arrival, all buses enter Dangriga at the south end of town: Z-Line have a modern terminal about 1km south of the centre, while Ritchie's office is a few blocks further north; you can leave luggage at either. Dangriga's **airstrip**, by the shore, just north of the *Pelican Beach Hotel* is served by flights on Tropic Air (☎02/45671) and Maya Island Air (☎05/22659), every couple of hours to and from Belize City, and south to Placencia and

△ **❶** & *Airstrip*

DANGRIGA

GRAPEFRUIT RD KUYLEN'S ALLEY
COURT HOUSE ROAD
COCONUT RD
**Police
Station**
Hospital
CITRON ST
OBINTI ALLEY
LEMON STREET
PLUM STREET
ORANGE ST
RECTORY RD
Town Hall
HANS AVE
RAMOS ROAD
DOCTOR'S ALLEY
Market
WEST ST
NORTH RIVERSIDE DRIVE
North Stann Creek
COMMERCE STREET
❷
Gulf

Boats to Tobacco Caye
**Boat to
Puerto Cortés**
❸
of
■ River Cafe

BLUEFIELD ROAD
KNOPP'S STREET
CHATUYE ST
Honduras
❹
CASTILLO ALLEY
PINE STREET
CANAL STREET
CEDAR STREET
OAK STREET
MAGOON ST
HEAR PINE ST.
ALEJO BENI AVENUE
**Ritchie's
Bus ★ ❺**
MOHO ROAD
ECUMENICAL DRIVE
ST VINCENT STREET
GANEY STREET
MAGOON ST
HOWARD STREET
MADRE CACAO RD
MAHOGANY RD
SALMWOOD ROAD
TUBROOSE STREET
N
POLACK STREET
YEMERI ROAD
SHARP STREET

**Stann Creek
Ecumenical College**
ZERICOTE STREET
MANGROVE ROAD
❻

Hummingbird & Southern Highways

Havana *Creek*
**Havana
Hotel**
ISLA ROAD
STANN CREEK VALLEY ROAD
SAMPSON'S ST
DANIEL'S ST
UNITY STREET
**Z-Line Bus
Depot**
HAVANA STREET
CABBAGE ROAD

ACCOMMODATION
Bluefields Lodge   4
Chaleanor Hotel   5
Jungle Huts Hotel   3
Pal's Guest House   6
Pelican Beach Hotel   1
Riverside Hotel   2

0   200 m

Punta Gorda. For both domestic and **international flights** check at Treasured Travels, 64 Commerce Street (☎05/22578).

The centre of town is marked by the **road bridge** over the South Stann Creek, with the main thoroughfare leading north as Commerce St and south as St Vincent St. Almost everything you're likely to need, including **hotels**, **restaurants**, **banks** and **boat transport**, is on or near this road. **The post office** is on Caney St, in the southern half of town, a block back from the sea. There's no official tourist office in Dangriga, but for reliable **tourist information** and friendly service call in at Aquamarine Adventures (☎ & fax 05/23262), run by English/Belizean couple Derek and Debbie Jones, in *Soffie's Hotel*, 1 Chatuye St, on the south bank of the river. They're also about to open Belize's second **Internet café** (*djones@btl.net*). The walls are filled with details of tours, you can use the **payphone** and the gift shop sells Rough Guides. Also worth checking for details of boats is the *River Café*, on the south side of the bridge.

Accommodation

Dangriga has experienced something of a hotel-building boom in the last few years, resulting in an ample choice of **places to stay** and – with some real bargains on offer – no need to stay in a cheap dive.

Bluefield Lodge, 6 Bluefield Rd (☎05/22742). Clean, secure and well-run, it's everything a budget hotel should be, with good-value rooms and really comfortable beds. ④.

Chaleanor Hotel, 35 Magoon St (☎05/22587, fax 23038). Newish and very good value with very clean, spacious rooms, all with private bath. Meals with views in the rooftop restaurant. ⑤.

A BRIEF HISTORY OF THE GARÍFUNA

The **Garífuna** trace their history back to the island of **St Vincent**, one of the Windward Islands in the eastern Caribbean. At the time of Columbus's landing in the Americas the islands of the Lesser Antilles had recently been settled by people calling themselves *Kalipuna*, or *Kwaib* (from which we get the terms Garífuna and Carib) from the South American mainland, who had subdued the previous inhabitants, the Arawaks. The admixture of African blood came in 1635 when two Spanish ships, carrying slaves from Nigeria to their colonies in America, were wrecked off St Vincent and the survivors took refuge on the island. At first there was conflict between the Caribs and the Africans, but the Caribs had been weakened by wars and disease and eventually the predominant race was Black, with some Carib blood, becoming known by the English as the **Black Caribs** – in their own language they were *Garinagu*, or *Garífuna*.

For most of the seventeenth and eighteenth centuries St Vincent was nominally under British control, but in practice it belonged to the Caribs (Garífuna), who successfully fended off British attempts to gain full control of the island until 1796. The colonial authorities could not allow a free Black society to survive amongst slave-owning European settlers, and the Garífuna population was hunted down and transported to **Roatán**, one of the Bay Islands (see p.456), where the British abandoned them. Perhaps in response to pleas for help from the Garífuna, who continued to die on Roatán, the Spanish commandante of Trujillo, on the Honduran mainland, took the 1700 survivors to Trujillo where they were in demand as labourers. The Spanish had never made a success of agriculture here and the arrival of the Garífuna, who were proficient at growing crops, benefited the colony considerably. The boys were conscripted and the Garífuna men gained a reputation as sailors, soldiers and mercenaries.

In the early nineteenth century small numbers of Garífuna moved up the coast to **Belize**, and although in 1811, Superintendent Barrow of Belize ordered their expulsion, it had little effect. When European settlers arrived in Stann Creek in 1823, the Garífuna were already there and were hired to clear land. The largest single migration to Belize took place in 1832 when vast numbers, under the leadership of Alejo Benji, fled from Honduras (by then part of the Central American Republic) after they had supported the wrong side in a failed revolution to overthrow the republican government. It is this arrival which is today celebrated as **Garífuna Settlement Day**, though it seems likely many arrived both before and after.

Throughout the nineteenth and twentieth centuries the Garífuna travelled widely in search of work. To start with they confined themselves to Central America (where they can still be found all along the Caribbean coast from Belize to Nicaragua), but in World War II Garífuna men supplied crews for both British and US merchant ships. Since then trips to the US have become an important part of the local economy, and there are small Garífuna communities in New York, New Orleans, Los Angeles and even in London. Belize has a National Garífuna Council, and its scholars are attempting to create a written language. The council has already published *The People's Garífuna Dictionary* and some school textbooks. *The First Primer on a People Called Garífuna* by Myrtle Palacio is in English and available in Belize. There's an excellent US-based Garífuna **Web site** (*www.garifuna-world.com*) listing cultural events and current developments in the entire Garífuna community.

Jungle Huts, on the riverbank upstream from the town centre bridge (☎05/23166). Pleasant thatched cabañas and hotel rooms with private bath and hot water, some with TV. ⑤.

Pal's Guest House, 868 Magoon St, by the bridge over Havana Creek (☎ & fax 05/22095). Good-value accommodation in two buildings, one right on the beach. ③–⑥.

Pelican Beach Resort, on the beach north of the town, next to the airstrip (☎05/22024, fax 22570). Rooms at the front are in a wooden colonial-style building; there's a concrete building behind, but the best beachfront rooms, while beautiful, are overpriced. The dining room features a large marine aquarium. Top-class tours inland and to the cayes. ⑦–⑨.

Riverside Hotel, right beside the bridge (☎05/22168). Clean rooms (some with bath) in a good location with a vantage point over the river. Prices are per person; a good deal for singles. ②.

Soffie's, 1 Chatuye St, south bank of the river, heading towards the sea (☎0522789, fax 23262). A range of rooms and all good value, most with private bath and a balcony with fine sea and river views; some suites and some budget rooms too. Good information. ②–⑤.

Eating, drinking and nightlife

If you're going to try **Garífuna food** in Belize, Dangriga is the place to do it. There are a few **food stalls** around the Z-Line station, and some are fine, but the best place for Garífuna cooking is *Pola's Kitchen*, 25 Tubroose St, at the south end of town. The walls are decorated with Garífuna artefacts and it has a no-smoking policy that is probably unique in Belize. Dishes such as *hudut* (also called *fufu*) feature plantain cooked in coconut sauce, and there's *sere*, a delicious fish and vegetable stew, also flavoured with coconut. The restaurant at the *Pelican Beach* is the top place in town – resident chef Bill is skilled in preparing all of Belize's cultural specialities. The *River Café*, on the south bank of the river, just over the bridge, is a good restaurant serving Creole food and great breakfasts, catering for local boatmen and visitors waiting for boats to Tobacco Caye. *King Burger* (not what you might think), under the *Riverside Hotel*, serves good rice, chicken, burgers, fruit juices, fish and conch soup (a Belizean delicacy), and the restaurant at *Soffie's* is good value. Of the several Chinese restaurants on the main street, the *Starlight* is the best value. For picnic supplies you could try the **market** on the north bank of the river, by the sea, but it's very small – for other groceries it's best to head for the Southern Pride supermarket by Barclays Bank. Opposite the bank, the Dangriga **bakery** has good bread and buns.

There's no shortage of **bars** in Dangriga, though some, particularly those calling themselves clubs, like *The Kennedy Club*, *The Culture Club* and the *Harlem Club*, are particularly dubious-looking, both inside and out. Along the beach to the north of the centre, the *Round House* is a good place to meet the locals and dance on the sand.

MOVING ON FROM DANGRIGA

Returning to Belize City, Z-Line **buses** (☎05/22732) leave at 5am, 6am, 8.30am, 9am, 10am, 10.15am, 1.30pm and 4pm. Ritchie's (☎ 05/23132) leave at 5.30am & 8.30am, both using the Coastal Road. If you're continuing south bear in mind that buses to Punta Gorda don't necessarily originate here; Z-Line leaves at noon, 4pm and 7pm, and there's also one James bus around noon; the journey takes five hours over dirt roads. All buses to Punta Gorda stop at Independence (2hr) – also known as Mango Creek – where you can pick up boats to Placencia (see box on p.270), and there's also a Z-Line bus daily at 2.30pm.

There are always at least three daily services from Dangriga to Placencia (2hr), but departure times are continually changing as the two rivals, Ritchie's and Z-Line, battle it out: currently they depart daily at 11.30am, 12.30pm and 4.30pm; at least one calls at Hopkins (40min) and Sittee River – usually the 11.30am Ritchie's service.

For Puerto Cortés in Honduras a fast **skiff** leaves each Saturday at 9am (US$50; around 3hr) from the north bank of the river, two blocks up from the bridge; be there at least an hour before departure (preferably book the day before) with your passport, so that the skipper, Carlos Reyes (☎05/23227), can take care of the formalities.

Offshore: Tobacco Range Cayes and Columbus Reef

The **Tobacco Range** is a group of mangrove cayes (some of which have accommodation) just behind the beautiful **Tobacco Reef**, about 16km east of Dangriga. **Mayan Island**, just north of the Man-O'-War Caye **bird sanctuary** in the Tobacco Range, offers good-value new **accommodation** in spacious, wooden cabañas, each with a double bedroom, a living room with a veranda facing the reef, and a private bathroom with hot water (⑧ including all meals, no service charge). There's also a dive centre. Contact Aquamarine Adventures in Dangriga (see p.259).

At the southern tip of Tobacco Reef sits the slightly larger **South Water Caye**, while to the northeast, **Columbus Reef** is another superb section of the barrier reef with some small cayes scattered along its length, including the tiny **Tobacco Caye** perched on its southern tip. Each caye has a number of delightful places to stay – sunsets out here can be breathtakingly beautiful, outlining the distant Maya Mountains with a purple and orange aura.

Tobacco Caye

Tobacco Caye, ideally situated right on the reef, is easy to reach and has the least expensive accommodation. **Boats** (US$15; 40min) leave every day from near the bridge, but there are currently no regular departures; check for information at *Soffie's* or the *River Café* in Dangriga. The most prompt and reliable service is operated by Captain Buck, though any of the hotel owners on the island will take you, and maybe arrange a package deal. Tobacco Caye is tiny – just five acres in area. If you stand in the centre you're only a couple of minutes from the shore in any direction, with the unbroken reef stretching north for miles. The island's **dive shop**, Second Nature Divers (☎05/37038) is excellent and offers good-value PADI courses, equipment rental and trips to the atolls. A single-tank local dive (plus equipment) costs US$25; a dive course is US$225.

Accommodation here is simple but comfortable, and generally good value; you'll be staying either in wooden buildings on the sand or cabins right over the sea. In most cases the price includes all meals, but here more than anywhere it's essential to check what you're paying for – and whether the price is quoted in US or Belize dollars. *Gaviota Coral Reef Resort* (☎05/22294 or 014/9763, fax 23477; ⑥–⑦) is the least expensive place to stay, with cabins on the sand and over the water, and budget rooms in the main building, all with shared bath. Meals (included in price) are wonderful and there's discount transport for guests if you call ahead. *Island Camps Caye Resort* (☎ 02/72109 or ☎014/7160, fax 02/70350; ⑥–⑧; meals around US$15 per day extra) has seven small double cabins and three larger cabins, one with private bath. *Lana's on the Reef* (☎05/22571 or 014/7451; ⑦ including meals) has simple rooms with shared bathroom in a lovely wooden house, and Lana serves great food. Finally you can stay right on the shore in a cabin room or in one of a pair of private cabañas, all with private bath at *Reef's End Lodge* (☎05/22419, fax 22828; ⑥–⑦ including meals). The restaurant here is built over the sea on the tip of the reef, and the bar is a fantastic place to enjoy the sunset.

South Water Caye

Eight kilometres south of Tobacco Caye and about three times the size, **South Water Caye** is arguably one of the most beautiful islands in Belize. Like Tobacco Caye it sits right on the reef and offers fantastic, very accessible snorkelling and scuba-diving in crystal-clear water. South Water Caye is now the focus of a large new **marine reserve**, and the southern end of the island is part of a small nature reserve. Turtles sometimes nest in the sand here, and the reef curves around offshore protecting the pristine beach. Most resorts have their own very good **dive shop** and there's also the Living Reef Dive Centre (☎05/22214), which offers PADI dive courses and trips to Glover's

Reef, where there's a resort on Long Caye (p.265). The island's **accommodation** is upmarket and expensive and has to be booked in advance. The *Pelican Beach Resort* in Dangriga (☎05/22024) has a range of idyllic options in a stunning location at the south end of the island, including some beautiful wooden houses and a two-storey wooden hotel; rates (including meals) are in the range of US$150–170. They also operate *The Pelican's University*, which houses groups, often students, in a two-storey building with five bunk-bedded rooms – definitely a fine place to study: US$60 per person per day including meals.

The Southern Highway to Placencia

To the south of Dangriga the country becomes more mountainous, with settlements mainly restricted to the coastal lowlands. The **Southern Highway**, running from Dangriga to Punta Gorda, is still mostly unpaved with the exception of the far southern section. However, paving is progressing steadily, the road surface is frequently graded and strong bridges have been built, high above the river levels, so it should be passable except during the very worst rainstorms. For its entire length the highway is set back from the coast, running beneath the peaks of the Maya Mountains, often passing through pine forest and vast citrus and banana plantations. Several branch roads lead off to settlements, such as **Hopkins**, a Garífuna village on the coast, and the nearby Creole village of **Sittee River**, where you can catch the boat to the idyllic cayes of **Glover's Reef**. From the village of **Maya Centre**, 36km south of Dangriga, a road leads west into the Cockscomb Basin Wildlife Sanctuary, generally referred to as the **Jaguar Reserve**.

Hopkins and Sittee River

Stretching for more than 3km along a shallow, gently curving bay, and thickly shaded by palm trees, **HOPKINS** is home to around a thousand Garífuna people, who, until recently, made their living from small-scale farming and fishing, often paddling dugout canoes to pull up fish traps, or using baited handlines. Garífuna Settlement Day on November 19 is celebrated enthusiastically with singing, dancing and above all the beating of drums – an integral part of the Garífuna culture. A few kilometres south of the Hopkins turn-off is the junction of the road to the Creole village of **Sittee River**, a pleasant place in its own right, but most useful as a jumping-off point for Glover's Reef (see p.264).

Hopkins practicalities

Hopkins is a pleasant place to spend a few days relaxing, with food and accommodation in all price ranges, and you can rent kayaks, windsurf boards and bicycles. It's possible (though not always easy) to organize trips to the reef and cayes further out; the view back towards the village from the sea, with the high ridges of the Maya Mountains in the background, is breathtaking.

The **bus service** to Hopkins is a little unpredictable, but there's at least one daily run to and from the village; currently the 11.30am Ritchie's service from Dangriga to Placencia calls in en route: once there, check at your hotel for the current situation. As there are no street names in Hopkins, the best way to locate anything is to describe its position in relation to the point where the road from the Southern Highway enters the village, dividing it roughly into northern and southern halves. At the time of writing only a few places have private telephones but you can make calls on the two **community telephones**: ☎05/22033 in the Nuñez store at the roadside in the south of the village or ☎05/22803 in the BTL office.

A few simple **restaurants** and **bars** have opened up in Hopkins in recent years, though by now there are sure to more than those listed here. *Over the Waves*, on the beach in the village centre, is recommended; if you ask you'll be allowed to leave luggage here while you look for a room. *Swinging Armadillos*, 120m to the north, is a great little restaurant billed as a "hammock lounge" by owner Mike Flores, where you can swing in the shade and enjoy the sea breeze while sipping a cold drink.

ACCOMMODATION

There's plenty of **accommodation** in the village. Some places now have private phones, so you can book ahead if you want, though this is rarely necessary.

Hopkins Inn, south of the centre, on the beach (☎05/37013). Three immaculate white-washed cabins with hot showers and a fridge. Friendly owners Rita and Greg Duke can arrange trips on their Hobie-cat. Continental breakfast included. ⑥.

Jaguar Reef Lodge, on the beach, 1km or so beyond the south end of the village (☎ & fax 021/2041; in US ☎1-800/289-5756). Luxury resort with large, thatched cabañas in beautifully landscaped grounds and in a superb location; often used by top nature-tour companies. The restaurant, under a huge thatched roof overlooking the beach, has great food and service. Trips to the Maya ruins of Mayflower, currently being excavated by Tulane University can be organized. Kayaks and bikes are available for guests, and there's a dive shop with instruction. US$150 double; no service charge. ⑨.

Lebeha, at the north end of the village. Inexpensive rooms and hammock spaces in a brightly painted, thatched house surrounded by plants. Good food, including fresh bread. ③.

Ransome's Seaside Cabaña (☎05/22889 in Dangriga). Wonderful two-bedroom, fully furnished cabin set in a tropical garden south of the centre. Kayaks and bicycles for rent. ⑥.

Sandy Beach Lodge, on the beach at the south end (☎05/37006). Six simple, spacious, good-value rooms in wood-and-thatch cabins (most with private bath), run by the only women's co-operative in Belize. Meals feature seafood cooked in Creole and Garífuna style. ④.

Swinging Armadillos, on the beach 150m north of the centre (☎05/37016). Two small and comfortable rooms perched over the sea just beyond the small bar and restaurant of the same name (see above). Friendly owner Mike Flores rents bikes. ④.

Sittee River

Sittee River and its banks offer great opportunities for spotting wildlife; apart from the dozens of bird species there are freshwater turtles and crocodiles. It is served by the same buses as Hopkins on the Dangriga/Placencia route, the road from Hopkins passing through the village to connect with the Southern Highway. Most visitors here are on their way to *Glover's Atoll Resort* (see opposite), but there are a few **places to stay**. The great-value *Toucan Sittee* (☎05/37039), set in a beautiful riverbank location is by far the best accommodation option. It's owned by the extremely hospitable Neville and Yoli Collins, who provide some of the best budget accommodation in the country, in solidly built, well-furnished, wooden cabins (④) with electric light and hot showers; there are also very comfortable dorm beds (US$8) and camping (US$3). The food is really good, with lots of fresh fruit and vegetables, and they rent **canoes** and **bikes**. In the village there's the rather basic *Glover's Guest House* (④), and *Isolene's*, on the riverbank, also offers rooms (④) and has a good restaurant serving simple meals. If you need to stock up on **supplies** for your trip to Glover's Reef, Hill Top Farm sells vegetables and Reynold's Store sells most other basic goods.

Glover's Reef

The southernmost of Belize's three coral atolls, **Glover's Reef** lies between 40 and 50km off Dangriga. Named after British pirate John Glover, the atoll is roughly oval in shape, about 35km north to south, and its only cayes are in the southeastern section. Glover's Reef is the best developed and most biologically diverse atoll in the Caribbean, rising from ocean depths of over 600m, with some of the best **wall diving** in the world. Inside the beautiful aquamarine lagoon are hundreds of **patch reefs** – a snorkelling wonderland. All the cayes have nesting ospreys, and Belize's marine turtles nest on the beaches. There are also vitally important grouper spawning grounds on the northeast of the atoll, and immense **whale sharks** – the largest fish in the world – pass through on their southward autumn migration.

These unique features helped to bring about the decision in 1993 to declare the whole atoll a protected area – **Glover's Reef Marine Reserve** – and in 1996 it was designated a World Heritage Site. The atoll is divided into management zones, and no fishing is allowed from any of the cayes. All of the cayes here offer some **accommodation**, mostly in purpose-built camps and cabins for **sea-kayaking** groups, though there is one upmarket diving lodge, and on Northeast Caye there are cabins within the reach of budget travellers.

The cayes

Covered in thick coconut and broadleaf forest, and with evidence of Maya fishing camps, **Northeast Caye** is home to *Glover's Atoll Resort* (☎05/23048 or 014/8351). The resort has ten simple, self-catering **beach cabins** overlooking the reef (US$149 per person per week, including transport from Sittee River) and space for **camping** (US$80 per week). Unless you're in a pre-booked group (in which case you can arrange to be catered for), you'll have to bring your own food and make your own meals; cooking is done on a kerosene stove, or on the barbecue pit nearby. Activities (paid for separately) include sea kayaking, fishing, snorkelling, scuba-diving with PADI or NAUI certification, and sailing to the other cayes. The resort's motor/sail boat, *Christmas Bird*, picks up guests in Sittee River each Sunday morning, and leaves the caye the following Saturday; the trip takes up to four hours, longer if under sail.

Long Caye, just across the channel from Northeast Caye, is the base for the sea-kayak expeditions run by Slickrock Adventures (see "Basics", p.6); accommodation is mostly in wooden cabins on stilts. Four kilometres to the southwest, **Middle Caye** is in the wilderness zone of the reserve, and has a marine research and monitoring station run by the Wildlife Conservation Society; you can visit with permission, and there are some interesting displays on the ecology of the atoll. **Southwest Caye**, 5km beyond Middle Caye, is the base for the sea-kayak groups of *Island Expeditions* (p.7 in "Basics"), where guests stay in spacious, comfortable white tents.

The Cockscomb Basin Wildlife Sanctuary

Back on the mainland, the jagged peaks of the **Maya Mountains** rise to the west of the Southern Highway, their lower slopes covered in dense rainforest. The tallest summits are those of the Cockscomb range, which includes Victoria Peak, at 1120m the second highest mountain in Belize and a dramatic sight on a clear day. Beneath the sharp ridges is a sweeping bowl, part of which was declared a **jaguar reserve** in 1986; it has since been expanded to cover an area of over four hundred square kilometres – the **Cockscomb Basin Wildlife Sanctuary**.

The area was inhabited in Maya times, and the ruins of **Kuchil Balam**, a Classic period ceremonial centre, still lie hidden in the forest. In more recent times the residents of Quam Bank, a logging camp and Maya village moved out of the Cockscomb when the reserve was established, relocated to the present village of **MAYA CENTRE** on the Southern Highway.

Technically, this is a **tropical moist forest**, with an annual rainfall of up to 300cm that feeds a complex network of wonderfully clear streams and rivers, most of which eventually run into the Swasey River and the South Stann Creek. The forest is home to a sizeable percentage of Belize's **plant and animal species**. Among the mammals are tapir, otter, coati, deer, anteater, armadillo and, of course, jaguar, as well as all other cat species. Over 290 species of bird have also been recorded, including the endangered scarlet macaw, the great curassow, the keel-billed toucan and the king vulture. It is particularly important as a refuge for the largest raptors, including the solitary eagle and the white hawk eagle. And there's an abundance of reptiles and amphibians, including the red-eyed tree frog, the boa constrictor and the deadly fer-de-lance snake (known as tommy-goff in Belize). The forest itself is made up of a fantastic range of plant species, including orchids, giant tree ferns, epiphytes (air plants) and trees such as *banak*, *cohune*, mahogany and ceiba.

Practicalities: Maya Centre

All **buses** heading south from Dangriga pass Maya Centre village (45min), from where a rough ten-kilometre track leads to the sanctuary headquarters. You need to sign in and pay the reserve entrance fee (US$5) at the thatched **craft centre** at the road junction. Just beyond, the small **shop** sells basic supplies and cold drinks, including beer, and there's a small restaurant behind. The shop is run by Julio Saqui, a skilled guide who operates Julio's Cultural and Jungle Tours (☎051/2020) – the best way to organize a guide if you're thinking of attempting the hike to Victoria Peak, or indeed anywhere in the Cockscomb. The people of Maya Centre know the reserve intimately, and are by far the best **guides** around. You can easily walk in to the reserve from Maya Centre – it takes a couple of hours or so along the gentle uphill slope, and you can leave any excess luggage with Julio. If you've come without transport and don't fancy the walk you can ride in with Julio's brother, Ernesto, the former director of the reserve, in his pickup for US$12.50.

If you need somewhere **to stay** in Maya Centre, Ernesto and his wife Aurora run *Nu'uk Che'il* (Maya for "in the middle of the forest") *Cottages* (☎051/2021; ③): simple but delightful thatched cabañas, with shared bathroom and hot water. The **restaurant**, serving Maya and Belizean food, is a great place to get a filling meal on your way to or from the reserve. Aurora is one of the Garcia sisters (see p.248), and has developed a medicinal trail (US$2) in the forest next to the cottages and makes **traditional herbal medicines**, for sale in the H'men Herbal Centre. The Saquis and other families in Maya Centre are a few of the totally genuine proponents of the concept of ecotourism, and staying here is a perfect way to learn about the life of the forest and experience Maya culture.

The Jaguar Reserve

At the sanctuary headquarters, in a cleared grassy area surrounded by beautiful tropical foliage, there's an excellent **visitor centre**, with a model of the Cockscomb Basin, displays on the area's ecology, and maps and trail guides; you can also pick up a copy of *Cockscomb Basin Wildlife Sanctuary*, a superb and detailed guide to the history, flora and fauna of the reserve. If you want to stay in the reserve, there's comfortable dorm **accommodation** in two styles: the old huts for US$6, and a newer, purpose-built dorm (US$10 per person) behind the main buildings; there are also comfortable rooms (⑤) and a **campground** (US$2.50) a little further on. If you're not on a group tour you'll have to bring your own food and cook it on the gas stove.

Although the basin could be home to as many as fifty of Belize's six-hundred-strong **jaguar population**, your chances of seeing one are very slim. However, it's an ideal environment for plant-spotting, serious bird-watching or for seeking out other elusive wildlife, and the trail system in the Cockscomb is the best developed in any of Belize's protected areas. **Inner tubes** are available from the ranger's office; walk upstream and float down for an amazingly tranquil view of the forest. The **Ben's Bluff Trail** is a strenuous but worthwhile 4km hike from the riverside to the crest of a forested ridge –

where there's a great view of the entire Cockscomb Basin – with a chance to cool off in a delightful rocky pool on the way back. If you're suitably prepared, you can climb Victoria Peak – a two-day hike each way – with backcountry **campsites** prepared by Raleigh volunteers.

Sapodilla Lagoon Wildlife Refuge and Black Cat Lodge

Continuing on the Southern Highway for 3km past Maya Centre, you'll reach the turn-off for the privately owned **Sapodilla Lagoon Wildlife Refuge** (signed on the left-hand side of the road; buses will stop here), where you'll probably have a better chance of actually spotting a **jaguar** or a nesting jabiru stork than anywhere else in the country. The refuge, owned by American Larry Staley, stretches along both sides of the highway, from the eastern foothills of the Maya Mountains to the coast at Sapodilla Lagoon, bounded in part by the Sittee River, and includes a range of habitats. Larry has built trails and observation platforms and converted the main house into *Black Cat Lodge*, which is run like a very relaxed youth **hostel**. It's a 25-minute walk in from the road, and accommodation is in bunk beds and hammocks, with shared bathroom. The price (US$20 per person) includes three meals (food is supplied, guests cook for themselves, bring your own drinks), horse-riding and use of the canoe. **Camping** is free, and you pay only for food. There's no need to book; just show up, even at night, though you can write to Larry, c/o Sittee River Village.

The Placencia peninsula

Sixteen kilometres south of Maya Centre, a good dirt road heads east from the Southern Highway through pine forest and banana plantations for 13km, reaching the sea at the tiny settlement of **Riversdale**. This marks the start of the **PLACENCIA PENINSULA**, a narrow, sandy finger of land separating the Caribbean and Placencia Lagoon and curving down 26km to **Placencia**, a small, laid-back fishing village, light years from the hassle of Belize City, and now catering to an increasing number of tourists. As you travel south down the peninsula you'll pass a dozen or so (mostly upscale) **resorts and hotels**, most of them owned and operated by expatriate North Americans. Accommodation is usually in cabins with private bathrooms and electricity. In addition to the pleasures of a Caribbean beach just a few steps away, most of the resorts also have access to Placencia Lagoon, and can arrange diving trips and tours inland to the Jaguar Reserve and several Maya ruins.

Maya Beach and Seine Bight

At the time of writing, the first of the peninsula's resorts were in **MAYA BEACH**, a beautiful stretch of coast with wide, white sand beaches, halfway to Placencia. The *Green Parrot Beach Houses* (☎ & fax 06/ 224880; ⑨) are spacious wooden houses raised on stilts. Each house has a living room, a loft bedroom with a queen-size and a single bed, a superb kitchen and a deck with hammocks. There's also an excellent restaurant and the rates include continental breakfast and transport from Placencia airstrip. Just south of the *Green Parrot* are the six lovely wood-and-thatch cabins of *Singing Sands Inn* (☎ & fax 22243; ⑧), where there's a good restaurant and bar and a pool for dive training.

Three kilometres beyond Maya Beach the Garífuna village of **SEINE BIGHT** now has several (mostly overpriced) resorts and hotels, some of which look out of place alongside the dilapidated shacks in the village. One of the best places is the *Hotel Seine*

Bight (☎06/23536, fax 23537; ⑧–⑨), with well-designed, wood-and-thatch cabañas and suites (some two-storey) decorated with Garífuna artefacts and set around a pool on the beach. It also has a good restaurant; you may have to book a table in high season. The only other reasonably priced accommodation is *Aunt Chigi's Place* (④), a distinctive collection of brightly painted green and yellow buildings set back from the road near the school.

The village is certainly worth a visit even if you're not staying; you can play pool in the *Sunshine Bar* and listen to Garífuna music in the *Kulcha Shak* (which also has basic but overpriced rooms). At the south end of the village you can visit *Lola's Art Gallery and Laguñedu Cafe*, where Lola Delgado displays her superb (and affordable) oil and acrylic paintings of village life – in great demand to decorate the rooms of the resorts. Lola's husband Edward is also an artist, producing fine wood carvings. Lola is a great cook and serves superb Creole or Garífuna dinners followed by drumming, singing and dancing. Call in first to check when she's cooking.

Resorts from Seine Bight to Placencia

Beyond Seine Bight another series of resorts offers upscale **accommodation**; the list below is in the order you approach them from the north. Even though they're pricey, most places will give Rough Guide readers worthwhile discounts.

Luba Hati, 1km south of Seine Bight (☎06/23402, fax 23403). The name is Garífuna for "House of the Moon", and the rooms, featuring original tiles and artwork and designed with Italian flair, are named after the word for moon in several languages. The terraces on two levels are a perfect place to savour the evening breezes – and the moonlight. Price includes continental breakfast and transfer from the airstrip. ⑨.

Serenity Resort, 2km south of Seine Bight (☎06/23232, fax 23231). Twelve large, comfortable, sky-blue cabins with patio, and a ten-bedroom hotel with a conference centre, often used by church and study groups. Has an excellent restaurant and great views from the roof. ⑦.

Rum Point Inn, just north of the airstrip, 4km from Placencia (☎06/23239, fax 23240; in US ☎1-800/747-1381). The most sumptuous (and expensive) rooms on the peninsula; unique, giant mushroom-shaped whitewashed cabins, with windows cut into the roof and plants growing inside, which are spacious, cool and very comfortable, and there are some new suites. There's also a pool, to help with dive instruction, and the *Auriga II*, one of the best dive boats in the country, with a highly professional crew. With emphasis on archeology, science and natural history, the library is the best of any hotel in the country, and the restaurant is first-class (non-residents must book). US$225 double, including all meals. ⑨.

Kitty's Place, just south of the airstrip (☎06/23227, fax 23226). Conveniently near the village and one of the nicest options in this area, with a variety of really comfortable accommodation including apartments, beach cabañas, garden rooms, a studio and rooms in a couple of colonial-style houses on the beach. The atmosphere is sublime, and the grounds and views are unbeatable. The restaurant serves delicious Belizean and international food and breakfast is included in the room price. ⑧–⑨.

Turtle Inn, 1km north of the village (☎06/23244, fax 23245). Seven wood-and-thatch cabañas on a gorgeous, palm-lined beach. Skip White, the American owner, has built a superb, relaxed resort for diving, fishing and jungle tours. No added service charge; tips are optional. Guests can use sea kayaks and bicycles. Rates include breakfast. ⑨.

Placencia

Perched on the tip of the peninsula, shaded by palm trees and cooled by the sea breeze, **PLACENCIA** is a welcome stop after the bus ride from Belize City or Dangriga. It is also one of the few places in mainland Belize with proper beaches, and this, together with the abundant, inexpensive accommodation makes it a great place to relax. Unfortunately its remote location and distance from the reef put many of the tours out of the reach of travellers on a low budget, though more options are becoming available.

The easiest way to reach Placencia is on one of the regular Maya Island or Tropic Air **flights** from the international or municipal airports (about 45min). Much cheaper are the direct **buses from Dangriga**, which leave between 11.30am and 4.30pm. You can also hop over easily on the regular **boat service** from **Independence/Mango Creek**, the small town just across the lagoon, where residents come to buy supplies and the older children go to school. For full transport details in Independence, see p.270.

Arrival, orientation and information

Buses from Dangriga end up at the beachfront gas station, right at the end of the peninsula (they return between 5am and 7am – check at your hotel for exact times, or at the *Seaspray*, where they sell tickets). If you're **flying** in, there's usually a taxi (US$10, and you can share the cost) waiting to take you to the village; if not it's only a three-minute walk to *Kitty's* where you can call Brad's Taxi (☎014/7307). Boats from Independence (see p.270) usually arrive at the main dock, by the gas station. If you're looking for **budget rooms** you should get off the bus when you see the sign for the *Seaspray Hotel*, about halfway through the village, on the left-hand side of the road. Head for **the sidewalk**, a concrete walkway that winds through the palms like an elongated garden path, and you'll be at the centre of a cluster of hotels and restaurants.

There's no official **tourist office**, but locals, most of whom (or their family) will have some interest in a tourist business, are glad to answer questions; the Orange Peel Gift Shop, across from the soccer field, supplies hand-drawn **maps** of the village and peninsula. Another good source of information is the office of Placencia Tours next to the gas station (with a reliable **public telephone** outside). The **post office** is currently across from Olga's Store, near the gas station, and the new **BTL office** is by the sidewalk in the centre of the village. The Atlantic **bank**, across from the main dock by the gas station, is open at least three mornings a week, and there's a branch of Barclays in Independence (open Friday mornings only); both can give cash advances. If your hotel doesn't do **laundry**, try Willie's Laundry, at the north end of the village.

Accommodation

In Placencia village proper there's a wide choice of **accommodation**, and you should have no problem finding a room provided you don't arrive at Christmas, New Year or Easter without a booking. Possibilities begin at the sidewalk, and as you wend your way down it seems as though every family is offering **rooms**.

Barracuda and Jaguar Inn, signed just past the market, towards the south end of the village (☎06/23330, fax 23250). Two varnished wooden cabins with two double beds and coffee-maker, plus a large deck with lounge chairs and a hammock; Placencia's best value in this range. Good information and trips, and discounts for Rough Guide readers. ⑤.

Coconut Cottage, on the beach, just south of the centre (☎ & 06/fax 23234). Two gorgeous, well-decorated and immaculately clean cabins in a quiet location, equipped with fridge, coffee-maker and hot-water shower; booking necessary in high season. ⑥.

Conrad and Lydia's Rooms, near the north end of the sidewalk (☎06/23117). Very good-value, clean, secure rooms run by a friendly family, who'll cook breakfast on request. ④.

Deb & Dave's Last Resort, on the road, the bus will stop outside (☎06/23207, fax 23334). The nicest budget place in the village: lovely, very comfortable wooden rooms with a shared, clean bathroom with hot water. Bikes and kayaks can be rented. ④.

Julia's Hotel, in the centre of the village, just south of the *Seaspray* (☎06/23185). Small hotel, with clean, simple rooms on the beach, between the sidewalk and the sea. ③.

Merlene's Apartment, west from the south dock, turn right at the gas station (☎06/23264). The best studio apartment in the village, with two comfortable beds, a huge fridge and a stove. A balcony runs along the front and you can watch the sunrise over Placencia Caye. ⑤.

Paradise Vacation Resort, follow the path to the right from the end of the sidewalk, at the main dock (☎06/23179, fax 23256). Two-storey hotel where most of the rooms have private bath and hot water. Large deck upstairs where you can enjoy the breeze. Very good value. ④.

Ranguana Lodge, on the beach in the centre of the village (☎ & fax 06/23112). Very friendly and well run, with beautiful white cabañas featuring hardwood interiors. All have hot water, fridge and coffee-maker, plus a balcony and hammocks. ⑥.

Seaspray Hotel, on the beach in the centre of the village (☎ & fax 06/23148). A popular, well-run hotel with a range of accommodation, all with bath, hot water and all recently renovated. Also provides reliable information and sells tickets for Ritchie's bus. ④–⑥.

Trade Winds, on the south point (☎06/23122, fax 23201). Five cabins with fridge, coffee-maker, hot water and deck, and five newer rooms, all on a spacious plot that gets the sea breezes. Run by Janice Leslie, Placencia's former postmistress and a mine of local knowledge. ⑤–⑥.

Traveller's Inn, signed from the sidewalk, just south of the centre (☎06/23190). Decent, basic rooms (the cheapest in the village) some with private bath, run by a friendly couple. ②.

Eating, drinking and nightlife

There are plenty of good **restaurants** in Placencia, though, even more than elsewhere in Belize, places change management fast, so it's always worth asking around; some of the best are listed below. There are also a number of good restaurants at the resorts along the peninsula, and it may be worth sharing a cab to try somewhere different. Most places close early; you'll certainly have a better choice if you're at the table by 8pm. Fresh **bread** is available from John The Bakerman, just north of the market, and from a number of local women who bake Creole bread and buns. There are also several reasonable **shops**; try The Market, opposite the soccer field, or Olga's Store, near the gas station, but get there early as fresh goods are soon sold out.

The evenings in Placencia are as relaxed as the days and there are plenty of **bars**, ideal for drinking rum and watching the sun set; increasingly many have **live music** to enhance the party mood. One of the best beachfront locations is the *Cozy Corner* (formerly a disco of the same name), with a deck and tables under the palms, while nearby, on the sidewalk, the *Sunrise* has a band at weekends. Turn right at the sign by the soccer field for *Lagoon Saloon*, a favourite meeting place at the south end of the village; it closes early though, so is best for an early evening drink.

Chili's, at the south point, near the main dock. A bargain food counter in what Bill, the owner, calls, a "chicken shed"; try the enormous vegetarian burrito. Best at lunchtime.

Daisy's Ice Cream Parlour, set back from the sidewalk, just south of the *Seaspray*. Deservedly popular place for ice cream, cakes and snacks, and now serving complete meals.

INDEPENDENCE TRAVEL CONNECTIONS

Just across the lagoon from Placencia, **Independence**, though of little intrinsic interest, is a useful travel hub and is served by all **buses** between Dangriga and Punta Gorda. Buses leave Dangriga daily at about 2.30pm (2hr) or you can take any service to or from Punta Gorda. There's a regular **boat to Placencia** – the *Hokey Pokey* (☎06/22376; 35min; US$7.50) – which leaves at 8.30am and 2.30pm, returning from Placencia at 10am and 4pm; the boatman usually meets the arriving buses. Otherwise, if you wait around for a while, you may be able to get a lift on a boat with a Placencia local for around the same price.

Heading north from Independence, Z-Line buses leave for **Dangriga** (2hr) at 8am, noon and 3pm, and south to **Punta Gorda** (3hr) at 2pm, 6pm and 9pm. The James bus also passes through once daily, heading south about 2.30pm. Z-Line buses take a rest/meal stop at the *Cafe Hello* in Independence; the James bus stops at *Marita's* (the better restaurant), across the way on Hercules Avenue.

With all these transport connections you should be able to avoid getting stuck **overnight** here. If you do, the *Hello Hotel* (☎06/22428; ⑥), mainly used by business people, has some a/c rooms; you could also try the clean, simple *Ursula's Guest House* (③) on Gran Main St. Barclays **bank** (Fri am only) gives cash advances.

Merlene's Restaurant, just past Brenda's (☎06/23264). Great for breakfast (usually the first to open), serving good coffee and fantastic homemade bread and cakes. Lunch and dinner are equally good, especially for fish, but it's tiny so you may have to book.

Omar's Fast Foods, on the sidewalk, just south of the centre. Really inexpensive, and sometimes even fast, but the quality can vary. Great, filling burritos.

La Petite Maison, just south of The Market (☎06/23172). Classic French cuisine superbly served in a romantic, candlelit atmosphere. The set menu changes daily and you get a wonderful five-course dinner. At US$23 it's pricey by Placencia standards, but worth it for a special occasion. Only serves eight dinners, so you need to book. Open Tuesday to Saturday between December and April.

Pickled Parrot Bar & Grill, at the Barracuda and Jaguar Inn. Very friendly place under a big thatched roof, which is consistently the best restaurant in the village, serving fresh seafood, great pizza, pastas and salads. The bar has wonderful tropical blender drinks.

Around Placencia, offshore and inland

In general, trips from Placencia can be tailor-made to your preference and perhaps your pocket, and you can arrange anything from an afternoon on the water to a week of camping, fishing, snorkelling and sailing. The main **reef** lies about 30km offshore; this distance means that snorkelling and diving trips are more expensive here than many other places in Belize. Here are the exquisitely beautiful **Silk Cayes**, where the Barrier Reef begins to break into several smaller reefs and cayes. Other coral-fringed islands include the **Bugle Cayes** and **Lark Caye**, while many trips take in uninhabited **Laughing Bird Caye**, a recently expanded National Park. **Diving** on any of these places is excellent, with fringing and patch reefs and booking your scuba-diving through a dive shop (rather than an independent guide) is usually the least expensive option. Placencia Dive Shop at the southern end of the sidewalk (☎06/23313) has friendly, safety-conscious service, excellent guides and the best dockside facilities; it's also good value at US$60 for a two-tank dive. Also worth trying, especially for PADI courses, is Aquatic Adventures, on the dock at the end of the village (☎06/23182).

   Placencia lagoon is ideal for exploring in a **canoe** (US$10 per day), available from Dave Dial at the gas station, who also rents a small **sailboat** (US$25). **Kayaks** and **bikes** (US$15 per day each) can be rented from Sundowner Tours, in the post office, or from Dave Vernon at *Deb & Dave's*. The best **fishing guides** in the village are Martin Westby of Gone Fishing (☎06/23330) and Bernard Leslie, who runs Ocean Motion (☎06/23162), near the southern end of the sidewalk. It's also worth **heading inland** from Placencia – up the thickly forested banks of the **Monkey River** or to the Jaguar Reserve (see p.266).

The Monkey River

One of the best day-trips from Placencia takes you by boat 20km southwest to the almost pristine **Monkey River**, teeming with fish, birdlife and, naturally enough, howler monkeys. Dave Dial of Monkey River Magic (☎06/23208, fax 23291) runs the best **tours**, his wildlife expertise complemented by the experienced local guides from Monkey River village. Tours (US$40, including a continental breakfast), leave from the dock by the gas station at 7am. A thirty-minute dash through the waves is followed by a leisurely glide up the river and a walk along forest trails. Lunch is usually taken on a sandbank on the river or you can get a meal in *Alice's Restaurant* in **MONKEY RIVER TOWN** (in reality a small village), where there's also time to enjoy a drink in the *Driftwood Bar*, at the river mouth, on the widest beach in Belize. If you want **to stay**, try *Enna's Hotel* (⑤), which has decent basic rooms and 24hr electricity, though it's overpriced; there may be other places by now. For local information call Monkey River community telephone on ☎06/22014, and for a guide call Eloy Cuevas (☎06/22014), or ask at *Enna's* for Evaristo Muschamp.

On the coast just north of the mouth of the Monkey River, a couple of new places (only accessible by boat) offer **accommodation**. *Bob's Paradise*, 2km north of the river (☎014/8206; in US ☎954/429-8763; ⑧ including breakfast), has three good wooden cabins with comfortable beds and hot shower, near the water's edge; just south of here, *The Monkey House* (☎014/8912; ⑦) also has three very pleasant wooden cabins with private bathrooms, each with a screened porch; the dining room is just yards from the sea and the food is great.

The far south: Toledo District

South of the Placencia and Independence junctions, the Southern Highway leaves the banana plantations and the grim settlements squashed beside the plantation roads, twisting at first through pine forests, and crossing numerous creeks and rivers. There are only a few villages along the way, and new citrus plantations are always in view, the neat ranks of trees marching over the hills. The mountains to the west are all part of the country's system of forest reserves, national parks and nature reserves, though conflicts over the status of some protected areas are emerging as Toledo District (whose residents often feel they live in Belize's "forgotten district") becomes more developed.

Although the **Maya** of Belize are a fairly small minority within the country as a whole, in Toledo the two main groups – **Mopan** and **Kekchí** – make up about half the population. For the most part they live in simple villages, very similar in appearance to their Guatemalan counterparts; the verdant, mountainous landscape of the far south resembles that of Guatemala's Alta Verapaz and southern Petén, where the ancestors of many of Belize's Maya came from. The biggest of the Maya villages are **San Antonio** and **San Pedro Columbia**, reached by a good side road heading west from the highway; both have hotels, and there are many other villages in the vicinity with simple guest houses.

There's plenty of evidence that the ancient Maya lived here too, with ruins scattered in the hills around the villages. The best-known site is **Lubaantun**, where the famous Crystal Skull was "discovered", but **Nim Li Punit**, with some impressive stelae, is an easy visit from the highway. The Southern Highway ends in **Punta Gorda**, the southernmost town in Belize and the only town in Toledo. It's the base for visits to both the inland villages and the southernmost cayes, and is connected to **Puerto Barrios** in Guatemala by several daily skiffs.

South to Punta Gorda: Nim Li Punit

About 73km from the Placencia junction, near the Maya village of **Indian Creek**, are the ruins of **Nim Li Punit**, a Late Classic period Maya site possibly allied to nearby Lubaantun. The site is only 1km west of the highway and the track is signposted. Although it's an easy visit from the road, few people bother to stop – a pity since it's home to the largest and one of the best-preserved stelae in Belize. The ruins, discovered in 1976, lie on a ridge with views over the maize fields of the village and the entire southern coastal plain beyond – a scene largely unchanged since ancient times. A total of 25 stelae were found here, eight of them carved; **Stela 14**, at almost 10m high, is the tallest in Belize, and one of the tallest anywhere in the Maya World. Unfortunately, the site was badly looted soon after its discovery and in 1997 several of the stelae were again badly damaged – this time by fire and machete. You enter through a plaza with walls and buildings of cut stones, a characteristic of sites in southern Belize, and pass through the ball court to the South Group, which holds most of the carved stelae. Although Stela 14 lies on the ground – in fact it was never erected – it's still an impressive sight, with panels of glyphs above and a richly attired ruler below: it's his elaborate headgear that gives Nim Li Punit its name, being Kekchí for "big hat". **Stela 15**, dated to 721 AD and the earliest stelae here, is smaller yet even more impressive. Carvings on this great sandstone slab depict a larger-than-life figure in the act of dropping an offering – perhaps *copal* incense or kernels of corn – into an elaborately carved burning brazier supported on the back of a monster. To his right, a much smaller figure also makes an offering into the brazier, while on his left side a column of very clear glyphs separates the main figure from an attendant, or guard; all three figures are almost entirely surrounded by panels of glyphs. At the moment there's no entry fee to the site, but there are plans to charge one; ask caretaker Placido Ash to show you around.

The junction from the Southern Highway to **San Antonio and the Maya villages** is 17km south of Indian Creek – marked by a gas station at a place called "The Dump"; beyond here the road is smooth and fast all the way into Punta Gorda, 21km to the south.

Punta Gorda

The Southern Highway eventually comes to an end in **PUNTA GORDA** (commonly known as PG), the heart of the isolated Toledo District. However, the first section of the highway north from Punta Gorda is now paved and the few visitors who make it out here are rewarded by spending a few days at the Maya villages inland (see p.277), where you can experience a way of life far removed from the rest of Belize. Offshore, the **Sapodilla Cayes** form the focus of Belize's newest **marine reserve**. Punta Gorda's position on low sea cliffs allows cooling breezes to reduce the worst of the heat, but there's no denying that this is the wettest part of Belize. The trees are heavy with mosses and bromeliads, their lush growth encouraged by heavy rains which can last for days.

To the north of Punta Gorda are the remains of the Toledo settlement, which was founded in 1867 by Confederate emigrants from the US. Many of the original settlers soon drifted home, discouraged by the torrential downpours and the rigours of frontier life, but their numbers were later boosted by Methodists from Mississippi. The Methodists were deeply committed to the settlement, and by 1870 sugar was the main product, with twelve separate estates running their own mills. The settlement reached its peak in 1890, after which it was threatened by falling sugar prices.

Today's town has a population of around four thousand – a mixture of Mestizos, Garífuna, Maya and Creoles, with a few Lebanese and Chinese as well – and is the focal point for a large number of villages and farming settlements. Saturday is the busiest day, when people from the surrounding villages come in to trade. Despite the recent minor building boom, Punta Gorda remains a small, unhurried, friendly town and you won't encounter any hassle.

Arrival and information

Buses from Belize City, via Dangriga, take around eight or nine hours to reach Punta Gorda; Z-Line (☎07/22165) go all the way through the town to their depot at the south end of town while James buses (☎07/22049) stop at their office near the main dock. **Skiffs to and from Puerto Barrios** in Guatemala use the main dock by the immigration office, roughly in the centre on the seafront. The airstrip, served by five or six daily **flights** from Belize City, is only five blocks west of the centre. For details of moving on from PG, see the box on p.276.

Despite having relatively few visitors, Punta Gorda is practically awash with **information centres**: the privately run Toledo Visitors Information Center (TVIC; ☎07/22470), by the ferry dock, offers homestay accommodation in the Maya Villages and runs a guest house in San Pedro Columbia (see p.280). The **Belize Tourist Board** has a very informative office on Front Street (Tues–Sat 9am–noon & 1–4.30pm, Sun 9am–noon; ☎07/22531); check here for times of all the buses to the Maya villages.

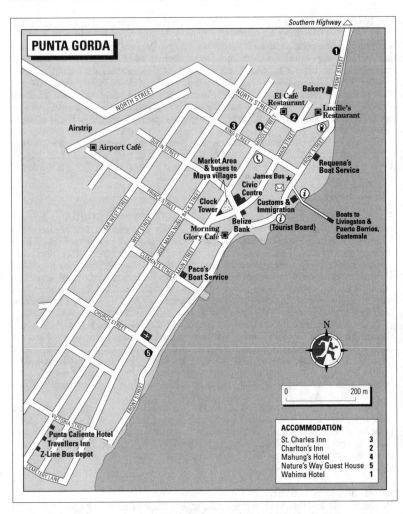

The group of government buildings opposite the main dock houses the **post office** and a **public phone**; the BTL office is a block further on. The only **bank** is the Belize Bank (Mon–Fri 8am–1pm, Fri also 3–4pm), at the top corner of the main square, across from the Civic Center. There will usually be a **moneychanger** outside the immigration office when the international boats are coming and going – it's best to get rid of your Belize dollars before you leave.

Accommodation

During the last couple of years there has been a spate of **hotel** building in the village, in the expectation of a rapid rise in the number of visitors enjoying the area's many attractions. While numbers have increased, however, few people spend long here, and there are plenty of bargains.

Charlton's Inn, 9 Main St (☎07/22197, fax 22471). This two-storey concrete building has rooms (some a/c) with private bath, hot water and TV; there's also cold water to drink. The *Inn* has safe parking and owner Duwane Wagner can arrange car hire and sell domestic air tickets. ③–⑤.

Mahung's, corner of North and Main streets (☎07/22044). Reasonable, inexpensive rooms with hot water; some private baths, a/c and TV. Bicycle rental available. ③.

Nature's Way Guest House, 65 Front St (☎07/22119). The best budget place in Punta Gorda; renowned as a meeting place and information point. Private rooms and clean, comfortable dorm accommodation (US$8), overlooking the sea. Good meals served in the wholefood restaurant. Owner William "Chet" Schmidt, a committed environmentalist, has been in PG for thirty years and is a driving force behind the Toledo Ecotourism Association. ③.

Punta Caliente, 108 José María Nuñez St (☎07/22561), next to the Z-Line terminal. Clean, comfortable rooms with private bath, fan and cable TV. There's a good restaurant, which has virtually been made into a museum of Garífuna culture by owner and historian Alex Arzú. ④.

St Charles Inn, 23 King St (☎07/22149). Clean and quiet, with carpeted rooms with TV. At the top end of the scale for Punta Gorda, and recommended. ④.

Tate's Guest House, 34 José María Nuñez St, two blocks west of the town centre (☎07/22196). A quiet, friendly, family-run hotel with some a/c rooms. ④–⑤.

Wahima, 11 Front St (☎07/22542). Inexpensive, basic and friendly hotel, right on the seafront; buses pass the door. Some rooms have a/c, fridge and TV. ②–⑤.

Eating and drinking

Restaurants in Punta Gorda are basic but the situation is improving; there are several newer places where the quality is better, and it's certainly easy to get a filling meal at a reasonable price. The *Punta Caliente Hotel* has one of the best restaurants in town, with Creole and Garífuna dishes, and a daily special. The *Morning Glory Café* (closed Mon) on Front Street serves seafood, burgers and snacks in clean, bright surroundings. You can get the good old Creole staples of rice and beans in the pleasant surroundings of *Lucille's*, by the Texaco station further north along Front Street. Just beyond here, *Mangrove* is a bright, new place serving seafood, burgers, steaks, and vegetarian options. *El Café*, behind *Charlton's Inn*, does the best coffee in town and opens for breakfast at 6am. There's a good **bakery** on Front Street, past the Texaco station, and you can get excellent bread and buns at the little shop just past the *Morning Glory Café*.

The best place to enjoy an early evening drink is *Waluco's*, though it's 2km from the centre; follow Front Street north over the metal bridge. It's popular with expats (there's a surprising number in PG), there's a deck to enjoy the breeze and the beers are at normal prices. Otherwise **nightlife** is either a quiet drink with a meal or a visit to one of several **bars and clubs**, such as the *Starlight* on Main Street.

Staying around Punta Gorda: Toledo's ecotourism projects

Ecotourism is a buzzword throughout Belize, and several projects in Toledo are poised to reap the benefits. Their aim is to achieve a balance between the need for economic development and the need to preserve the rich natural and cultural heritage of the area. It is hoped that small numbers of "low-impact" visitors will provide additional income to villages without destroying the communities' traditional way of life. One interesting project is the cultivation of cacao beans, to produce **chocolate**; almost all of the crop around here is used to make the delicious Maya Gold organic chocolate sold in the UK. Belize was a great centre of cacao production in ancient times and the Maya used cacao beans as money, which were traded over great distances. You'll often see cacao beans drying on special concrete pads as you travel through the villages.

Many Maya villages in Toledo are sited in **Indian Reservations**, designated as such in colonial times to protect the Maya subsistence lands. Title, however, remained with the government (which leases logging concessions), not the Maya who actually occupied the reserves. Recent developments in forestry policy have alarmed community leaders, who fear that so-called "conversion forestry", which allows all trees over a certain size on the reservations to be cut down for timber production, will cause further severe erosion and silt up previously clear streams used for drinking. The **Toledo Ecotourism Association**, 65 Front St, Punta Gorda (☎07/22680, fax 22119) aims to combat the destruction of the forest where the participants make their livelihood by offering visitors a **Guest House and Eco Trail Program**. Thirteen villages in southern Toledo are involved in the project; each has an eight-bed guest house (US$9 per person) and meals are taken at different houses to allow distribution of the income. Each village has its own attraction, be it a cave, waterfall, river or ruin, and there are guided walks or horse rides (around US$3.50 per hour; 4hr minimum); there may also be canoes to rent. The villagers have an extensive cultural knowledge of the medicinal uses of plants and the ancient Maya myths and this can be an excellent way to find out about Maya culture and experience village life without feeling like an intruder. The programme has also raised the consciousness of the villagers themselves as they learn to use both the concept of ecotourism and the political process to protect their forest; its efforts were rewarded in 1997 with a tourism industry prize for "Socially Responsible Ecotourism". The guest houses detailed in the text on pp.279 and 281 are part of the programme.

As an alternative to the guest house programme, the TVIC (☎07/22470) promotes the **"host family network"**, in which visitors stay in a village with a Mopan or Kekchí Maya family, participate in village work – grinding corn, chopping firewood, cooking tortillas and the like – and sleep in a hammock. In either programme you'll find few modern conveniences like electricity and flush toilets (though most villages have community telephones, operating on a solar panel), but if you go with an open mind you'll have a fascinating and rewarding experience and the villagers will be happy to teach you some Maya words.

MOVING ON FROM PUNTA GORDA

Z-Line **buses** leave for Belize City (8–9hr) at 5am, 9am and noon; the James bus departs at either 4.30am, 6am or 11am, depending on the day of the week. Buses for the **Maya villages** leave between noon and 1pm (on the days they run) from the streets next to the Civic Center; the tourist office will have full details. Most bus companies are literally one-man operations and Sunday is their day off. **San Antonio** is the biggest village and has two buses, Chun's and Prim's – at least one of them will continue to **Jalacté** on the Guatemalan border (not a legal crossing for visitors). There are **departures** at noon (Mon, Wed, Fri & Sat) for **San Pedro Columbia** (for Lubaantun) and you can usually get here any day with rides in pickup trucks. Most other villages have just one bus, which travels at least on **market days** (Wed & Sat) and sometimes other days as well. Returning from the villages all buses leave early – around 3.30–5.30am.

To **Puerto Barrios** in Guatemala there are several regular daily **skiffs** (US$12.50; 1hr in good weather). It's preferable (though not essential) to buy your ticket the day before you travel, so the skipper can get the paperwork ready. The best boats are Paco's (leaves at 8.30am; ☎07/22246); Requena's (leaves at 9am; ☎07/22070); and Carlos Carcamo's (leaves at 4pm). You will have to pay the PACT exit fee (US$3.75). Some boats will call at **Lívingston** if there's sufficient demand. Returning, boats leave Barrios at 8am or 10am, 1pm & 2pm.

For **flights** check the airlines' offices at the airstrip: Maya Island (☎07/22856); Tropic (☎07/22208).

Out to sea: the cayes and the coast

The cayes and reefs off Punta Gorda mark the southern end of Belize's Barrier Reef. The main reef has started to break up here, leaving several clusters of islands, each surrounded by a small independent reef. Though visited by specialist sea-kayaking tours, the whole area gets relatively little attention from international tourism and is very interesting to explore. At the moment there are few tour operators in Punta Gorda who can reliably run trips to the reef, but if you check with the information centres on p.273, or with Chet at *Nature's Way*, you can find out the latest news.

The closest cayes to Punta Gorda are the **Snake Cayes**, hundreds of tiny islands in the mouth of a large bay, where the shoreline is a complex maze of mangrove swamps; the area is proposed as a marine reserve, partly to protect the many **manatees** living in this shallow water habitat. On **Wild Cane Caye**, archeologists, with the assistance of Earthwatch volunteers, have found evidence of a Maya coastal trade centre. Further out, in the Gulf of Honduras, are the **Sapodilla Cayes**, the largest of which, **Hunting Caye**, has an immigration post to deal with visitors from Guatemala and Honduras. Other cayes in this group, notably **Lime Caye**, **Franks Caye** and **Nicolas Caye** have some tourism development planned, and will consequently face increasing visitor pressure in the near future. The designation of the **Sapodilla Cayes Marine Reserve** means that these cayes now receive some protection, though the influx of day-trippers can mean a difficult job for the already thinly stretched conservation agencies. The reserve's management plan is still under development; Will Maheia, one of PG's hard-working environmentalists and director of the Toledo Institute for Development and Education, is devising a plan to train net fishermen to become fly-fishing guides. TIDE is involved with many other practical projects; if you're interested in **volunteering**, contact Will at PO Box 150, Punta Gorda (☎07/22274).

From Punta Gorda you can see range upon range of mountains in Guatemala and Honduras, but the Belizean **coastline south** of here is flat and sparsely populated. Tidal rivers meander across a coastal plain covered with thick tropical rainforest that receives over 350mm of rain a year, forming a unique ecosystem in Belize. The Temash River is lined with the tallest mangrove forest in the country, the black mangroves towering over 30m above the riverbanks, while in the far south, the Sarstoon River, navigable by small boats, forms the border with Guatemala; the land between these rivers is now the **Sarstoon-Temash National Park**. These rivers are sometimes paddled on tours run by sea-kayaking companies (see "Basics", pp.6–7), this time using inflatable river kayaks.

The only village on the coast down here is **BARRANCO** (community phone (☎07/22138), a small, traditional Garífuna settlement of two hundred people, which you can visit through the village guest house programme (see opposite). A rough seasonal road connects the village with the Southern Highway, but most people rely on traditional dories, now motor-powered, to get to Punta Gorda.

Towards the mountains: Maya villages and ruins

Heading inland from Punta Gorda towards the foothills of the Maya Mountains, you meet yet another uniquely Belizean culture. Here **Mopan Maya** are mixed with **Kekchí** speakers from the Verapaz highlands of Guatemala. For the most part each group keeps to its own villages, language and traditions, although both are partially integrated into modern Belizean life and many speak English. Guatemalan families have been arriving here for the last hundred years or so escaping repression and a shortage of land at home, and founding new villages deep in the forest. Several families a year still cross the border to settle in land-rich Belize, along routes that have been used for generations. The villages are connected by road and all have a basic bus service from Punta Gorda (see box opposite), although moving around isn't all that easy and in many places you'll have to rely on hitching, despite the fact that there isn't much traffic. A good option is to rent a bike from *Mahung's* (see p.275). The people here are of course used to walking, and the villages are also connected by an intricate network of footpaths.

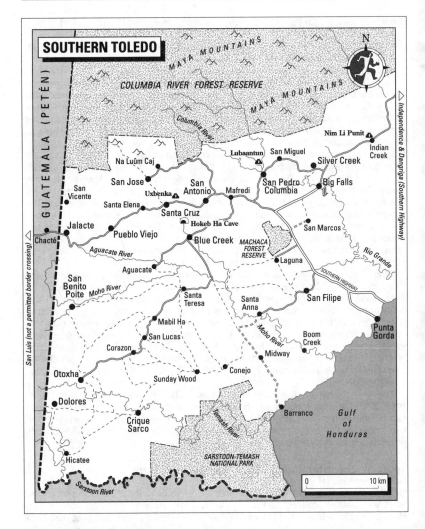

San Antonio and Uxbenka

The Mopan Maya village of **SAN ANTONIO**, perched on a small hilltop, is the easiest settlement to reach, as it's served by daily buses from Punta Gorda. It also has the benefit of *Bol's Hill Top Hotel* (community phone ☎07/22124; ④), which has simple **rooms** with electric light and superb views. There are a couple of shops in the village, and you can get **meals** at Theodora's or Clara's houses, behind *Bol's*. The area is rich in wildlife, surrounded by jungle-clad hills and swift-flowing rivers. Further south and west are the villages of the Kekchí Maya, fairly recent immigrants who still retain strong cultural links with Guatemala.

The founders of San Antonio were from the Guatemalan town of San Luis just across the border, and they maintain many age-old traditions. Among other things the Indians of San Luis brought with them their patron saint – opposite *Bol's Hotel is* the beautiful **stone-built church** of San Luis Rey, currently looked after by an American Jesuit order. The church is the third to stand on the site (two previous versions were destroyed by fire) and its most remarkable feature is a set of superb stained-glass windows depicting the twelve apostles and other saints, donated by the people of St Louis, Missouri. The villagers also adhere to their own pre-Columbian traditions and fiestas – the main one takes place on June 13, and features marimba music, masked dances and much heavy drinking.

Seven kilometres west from San Antonio, 1km before the village of **Santa Cruz**, are the ruins of **Uxbenka**, a fairly small Maya site, superbly positioned on an exposed hilltop, with great views towards the coast. Uxbenka's existence only became known to archeologists in 1984 after reports of looting in the area: there's now a site caretaker, who lives in Santa Cruz. As you climb the hill before the village you'll be able to make out the shape of two tree-covered mounds to your left. Though the site has not been fully excavated, you can still make out a couple of pyramids and a plaza, and there are several badly eroded stelae, protected by thatched shelters. There's a **guest house** at the entrance to the village, and several buses a week; some continue to **Jalacté** on the border. All around are **trails** through the forest to rivers and waterfalls, and you can walk over to **San José** (with a guest house and on a bus route; community phone ☎07/22972) in about three hours.

Blue Creek and Pusilha

At Mafredi, about 4km before San Antonio, a branch road (served by buses from PG) heads off south and west to **BLUE CREEK**, where the main attraction is the village's namesake – a beautiful stretch of water that runs through magnificent rainforest. The junction is marked by *Roy's Cool Spot*, where you can get a meal and a drink. Four kilometres down the road to Blue Creek you can **stay** in the simple bamboo-and-wood cabins of *Roots and Herbs* (③), where Pablo and Sonia Bouchub can teach you about the medicinal plants of Toledo. The food is excellent and Pablo is a great **guide**; the birdwatching is fantastic and he knows routes to ruins, lagoons and caves.

Another 3km brings you to Blue Creek itself, and whether you're walking or driving you won't miss the river, as the road crosses it in the middle of the village; the **guest house** is across the bridge and to the left. For the best **swimming** spot, walk upriver along the right-hand bank (facing upstream), and in about ten minutes you'll come to a lovely turquoise pool and the wooden cabins of *Blue Creek Rainforest Lodge*, set among the trees (⑤ including meals). The lodge is under the same ownership as *Leslie Cottages* on South Water Caye. The **aerial walkway** here, 25m above the river and extending into the forest on the opposite bank, is unique in Belize. It was built to study the ecology of the forest canopy but visitors can use it by arrangement; you're strapped into a harness before climbing ladders fixed to a large tree on the riverbank. Back at ground level, the **source of Blue Creek**, where the water gushes from beneath a mossy rock face, is about another fifteen minutes' walk upriver. Alongside is the entrance to the **Hokeb Ha cave**, which is fairly easy to explore. The entire area is made up of limestone bedrock honeycombed with caves, many of which were sacred to the Maya, and doubtless there are still plenty of others waiting to be rediscovered. If you want to experience the cave in solitude don't come on a Sunday: it's starting to get crowded. Sylvano is the best guide in Blue Creek and can take you to Maya altars deep in the Blue Creek cave, accessible only by boat.

About 7km west of Blue Creek is the Kekchí village of **Aguacate**, beyond which the road climbs a ridge leading to the valley of the Moho River, near the border with Guatemala. Further up the valley are the ruins of **Pusilha**, a large Maya ceremonial centre. The city is built alongside the river on a small hilltop and although many of the buildings are quite extensive, none is very tall, reaching a maximum height of just 5 or

6m. The site has yielded an astonishing number of carved monuments and stelae, including zoomorphs in a style similar to those at Quiriguá in Guatemala, leading archeologists to suggest that at some stage Pusilha may have been under Quiriguá's control. The site's most unusual feature is the remains of a stone bridge. The ruins are accessible by boat, on foot or on horseback, which could make the whole business rather expensive.

San Pedro Columbia and Lubaantun

To visit the ruins of Lubaantun (daily 8am–4pm; US$4) from San Antonio, get a bus or lift along the road to the Southern Highway and turn left at the track leading to **SAN PEDRO COLUMBIA**, a Kekchí village. The bus to San Antonio drops you at the entrance road, about 4km from the village – there's sometimes a truck waiting to ferry passengers over the final section of the journey, and the village also has its own bus service. To get to the site, head through the village and cross the bridge over the Columbia River, just beyond which you'll see the track to the ruins, a few hundred metres on the left.

Lubaantun, which means "Place of the Fallen Stones" – not its original name – is a major Late Classic ceremonial centre which at one time covered a large area. The site is on a high ridge and from the top of the tallest building you can (just) see the Caribbean, over 30km away. Maya architects shaped and filled the hillside, with retaining walls as much as 10m high. Some restoration has now begun and the pyramids are quite impressive, as is the surrounding forest.

It now seems that the site was only occupied briefly, from 700 to 890 AD, very near the end of the Classic period. There are five main plazas with eleven major structures and three ball courts. The architecture is unusual in a number of ways: there are no stelae or sculpted monuments other than ball court-markers, and the whole site is essentially a single acropolis, constructed on a series of low ridges. Another unusual feature is the absence of mortar; the stone blocks are carved with particular precision and fitted together, Inca-style, with nothing to bind them. The plainness and monumentality

THE CRYSTAL SKULL OF LUBAANTUN

Perhaps Lubaantun's most enigmatic find came in 1926, when the famous **Crystal Skull** was unearthed here. The skull, made from pure rock crystal, was found beneath an altar by Anna Mitchell-Hedges, the adopted daughter of the British Museum expedition's leader, F.A. Mitchell-Hedges. By a stroke of luck the find happened to coincide with her seventeenth birthday, and the skull was then given to the local Maya, who in turn presented it to Anna's father as a token of their gratitude for the help he had given them. It is possible that the "discovery" was a birthday gift for Anna, placed there by her father who had acquired it on his previous travels, although she strenuously denies the allegation. Anna Mitchell-Hedges still owns the skull; she recalls how she spotted sunlight glinting off it during the excavation of a rubble-filled shaft and promises to reveal more in the course of time.

While mystery and controversy still surround the original skull, London's British Museum has another crystal skull which – according to Dr G.M. Morant, an anthropologist who examined both skulls in 1936 – is a copy of the one found at Lubaantun. He also concluded that both of the life-size crystal skulls are modelled on the same original human head but could give no answer as to their true age and origin. While on display in the Museum of Mankind, its label was suitably vague: "Possibly from Mexico, age uncertain . . . resembles in style the Mixtec carving of fifteenth-century Mexico, though some lines on the teeth appear to be cut with a jeweller's wheel. If so it may have been made after the Spanish Conquest." There is a similar, smaller crystal skull in the Musée de l'Homme in Paris, and others exist too; all attract great interest from "New Age" mystics, who believe that crystal has supernatural properties.

of Lubaantun's architecture is again similar to the later buildings at Quiriguá in Guatemala, and there may have been some connection between the two sites.

Lubaantun was brought to the attention of the colonial authorities in 1903, and the governor sent Thomas Gann to investigate. A survey in 1915 revealed many structures, and three ball-court markers were removed and taken to the Peabody Museum. The British Museum expedition of 1926 was joined in 1927 by J. Eric S. Thompson, who was to become the most renowned Maya expert of his time. No further excavations took place for over forty years until Norman Hammond mapped the site in 1970, producing a reconstruction of life in Lubaantun which showed the inhabitants' links with communities on the coast and inland. Lubaantun's wealth was created by the production of cacao beans, used as money by the civilizations of Mesoamerica.

PRACTICALITIES

Several places in and around San Pedro (community phone ☎07/22303) offer **accommodation**. Alfredo and Yvonne Villoria have a bright, clean **bed-and-breakfast** room on their sustainable technology farm, *Dem Dats Doin'* (☎07/22470; ④), on the right a kilometre before the village. Check at the TVIC by the dock in Punta Gorda. There's a **guest house** in the village and a small hotel is under construction. Through the village and 3km beyond the turn-off to the ruins (follow the signs), a steeply undulating road leads to *Fallen Stones Butterfly Ranch* (☎07/22167; ⑧ including breakfast), which has comfortable wooden cabins on a hilltop with superb views over the Columbia River Forest Reserve to the Maya Mountains beyond. The cabins all have a private shower with hot water and electricity, and the dining room juts over a ridge, offering good food and even more gorgeous views at dawn and dusk.

travel details

The Southern Highway doesn't have as many buses running along it as the Northern and Western highways, and bus schedules are not as reliable. However, as road improvements take effect, journey times will shorten and timetable reliability will improve. The main routes are listed below; other buses to the smaller villages are covered in the text. Bus company offices and departure frequencies from Belize City to Dangriga, Placencia and Punta Gorda are covered in the box on p.201.

Buses

Dangriga to: Belize City (10 daily; 2–3hr); Hopkins and Sittee River (1–2 daily; 45min); Placencia (2–3 daily; 2hr); Punta Gorda (5 daily; 5hr). All buses between Dangriga and Punta Gorda stop at Independence/Mango Creek.
Hopkins and Sittee River to: Dangriga (daily around 7am).

Placencia to: Dangriga (2–3 daily; 2hr), all connecting with departures to Belize City.
Punta Gorda to: Dangriga (5 daily; 5hr); Belize City (5 daily; 8–9hr).

Flights

Maya Island Air (☎02/31362) and Tropic Air (☎02/45671) each have at least four daily flights from Belize City to Dangriga (25min); most continue to Placencia (a further 20min) and Punta Gorda (20min beyond Placencia).

International Boats

Dangriga to: Puerto Cortés, Honduras (weekly skiff, on Sat; 3hr).
Punta Gorda to: Puerto Barrios, Guatemala (at least 3 daily; 1hr).

PART FOUR

GUATEMALA

N

BELIZE

MEXICO

CHAPTER 9
**THE NORTH
& EAST**

CHAPTER 8
**THE WESTERN
HIGHLANDS
& PACIFIC COAST**

CHAPTER 7
**GUATEMALA CITY
& ANTIGUA**

HONDURAS

EL SALVADOR

INTRODUCTION

At one time the heart of the ancient Maya World, Guatemala has an exceptional wealth of archeological remains, with giant temples and rainforest cities scattered around the country, and it is this outstanding legacy that makes the country so compelling for visitors. Though the cities have long been abandoned, the descendants of the ancient **Maya** remain, having survived almost five hundred years of cultural attack. Today, they comprise over half of Guatemala's twelve million population and it is their vibrant culture, perhaps the strongest in Latin America, that is Guatemala's most definitive characteristic. Countering this is a powerful **ladino** society, a blend of Latin machismo that is decidedly urban and commercial in its outlook.

The Guatemalan landscape is astonishingly diverse. Separated from the steamy flatlands of the Pacific coast by a spiky backbone of volcanoes, the Maya **highlands** offer some of the most beautiful scenery. High ridges, pine forests, sweeping valleys, tiny cornfields and gurgling streams provide a backdrop for sleepy, traditional villages where amazing fiestas and markets take place. Traditional weavings and handicrafts are made in this region by the Maya and one of the best places to buy them is at the famous twice-weekly market at **Chichicastenango**. The huge highland lake, **Lago de Atitlán**, is unmissable: ringed by sentinel-like volcanoes, its shores are dotted with some of the most traditional indigenous villages in the country. **Panajachel**, on the northern shore, is where most people stay, an attractive resort with some excellent restaurants, cafés and textile stores, but **San Pedro La Laguna**, on the opposite shore of the lake, is an alternative base, with a more bohemian travellers' scene.

There is more bewitching scenery around the country's second city of **Quetzaltenango** (also called Xela), an excellent place for a series of day-trips to nearby hot springs, market towns and volcanoes. Further north, deep in the mountains of the **Cuchumatanes**, there are scores of extremely traditional and isolated villages. Perhaps the two best places to head for are **Nebaj**, in the Ixil triangle, and **Todos Santos**, to the north of Huehuetenango; both are intensely rewarding places to visit, with excellent walking amidst superb scenery, and plenty of cheap guest houses.

The **Pacific coast** is generally hot and dull – a strip of black volcanic sand and a smattering of mangrove swamps that blend into the country's most productive farmland. The beaches here are not as you imagine a Pacific beach to be, except at the wildlife reserve of **Monterrico**, which boasts a maze of swamps to explore and a fine stretch of sand where three species of turtle nest.

If it's real adventure and exploration you seek, nothing can compete with the hidden archeological wonders of **Petén**. This unique lowland area, which makes up about a third of the country, is covered with dense rainforest – only recently threatened by development – that harbours the remains of vast Maya cities and a tremendous array of wildlife, including jaguar, howler and spider monkeys, the lumbering tapir, toucans and scarlet macaws. The only town of any size here is **Flores**, from where you can easily reach **Tikal**, the most impressive of all Maya sites. Other dramatic ruins, such as the monumental triadic temples of Preclassic **El Mirador**, require days of tough travel to reach.

To the east of the Petén is another highland region, the **Verapaces**, with stunning alpine scenery and the sleepy coffee centre of **Cobán**, while further east are the spectacular gorge systems of the **Río Dulce**, the ruins of **Quiriguá** and, on the Caribbean coast, the funky town of **Lívingston**, home to Guatemala's only black community.

Guatemala City is of little interest to travellers except for a couple of museums: it's much better to stay in the quintessentially colonial city of **Antigua**, just an hour away, which has a unique architectural heritage and the country's best selection of hotels, restaurants and cafés. Antigua also has a number of good language schools and is an ideal place to **study Spanish**.

Some history

By the time the Spanish arrived in Guatemala in 1523, **the Maya** were in crisis. The Classic Maya culture, which had reached degrees of sophistication in architecture, astronomy and art unequalled by any other pre-Columbian society, had collapsed over six hundred years previously. The spectacular cities of Petén – Tikal, Ceibal, Piedras Negras and Río Azul – had been long abandoned to the jungle and most Maya lived in the highlands to the south. When the conquistadors entered the Guatemalan region, the situation could not have been more favourable to them: the highland Maya tribes were warring amongst themselves and an exploding population had outstripped its food supply.

Pedro de Alvarado, the conquistador despatched by Cortés to explore Guatemala, could hardly have been better suited to the job – ambitious, cunning, intelligent, dashingly handsome and brutally cruel. By 1525, just two years after his arrival, he had conquered all the main tribes with a series of utterly ruthless military manoeuvres and savvy tactical alliances. At the most significant battle, near modern-day Quetzaltenango, the Spanish defeated a 30,000-strong Quiché force with a few hundred horsemen, soldiers and Mexican allies. Legend has it that Alvarado himself slew the Quiché leader **Tecún Umán** in hand-to-hand combat. After being driven from Iximché, the capital of their Cakchiquel Maya allies, the Spanish moved to a site (now called Ciudad Vieja), near Antigua, where they established their first permanent capital on November 22, 1527.

The early years of **colonial rule** were marked by a catalogue of uprisings, natural disasters and disease, with waves of plague, typhoid and smallpox killing around ninety percent of the Maya population. In 1541, following a massive earthquake, the capital was devastated by a mud slide. A new city was established at nearby **Antigua**, which grew to control the provinces of Guatemala (present-day Costa Rica, Nicaragua, El Salvador, Honduras, Guatemala and Chiapas) and was the region's centre of political and religious power for two hundred years, until another catastrophic earthquake in 1773 forced the capital to move again to its present-day site of **Guatemala City**. With no gold or silver to plunder, colonial society was based on agriculture: livestock, cacao, tobacco, cotton and, most valuable of all, indigo, were all farmed using indentured indigenous labour and presided over by a Spanish-born ruling class and the Catholic Church.

Two centuries of colonial rule totally reshaped Guatemalan society, giving it new cities, a new religion, a transformed economy and a racist hierarchy. Nevertheless, the indigenous culture was never completely eradicated as in other parts of the continent. In the relative isolation of the highlands, the Maya simply absorbed the symbols and ideas of the new regime, fusing Maya and Catholic traditions to create a unique synthesis of old and new world beliefs.

The event that precipitated **independence** was Napoleon's invasion of Spain, after which a mood of reform swept through the colonies, leading to the signing of the Act of Independence in 1821. Guatemala soon joined the liberal **Central American federation**, which had a US-style constitution and set about abolishing religious orders, the death penalty and slavery. This era was brought to a swift end, however, by a religious

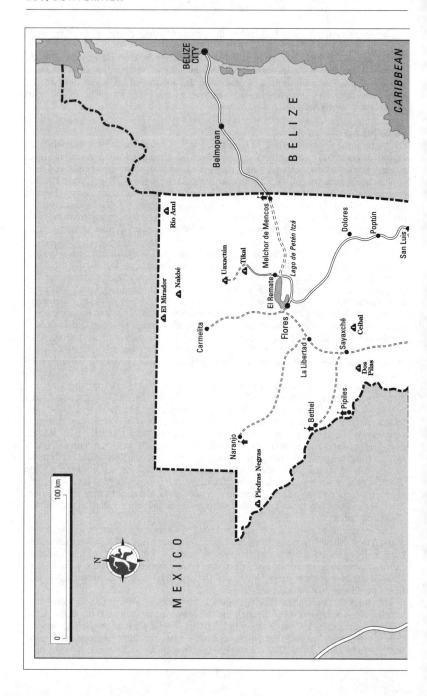

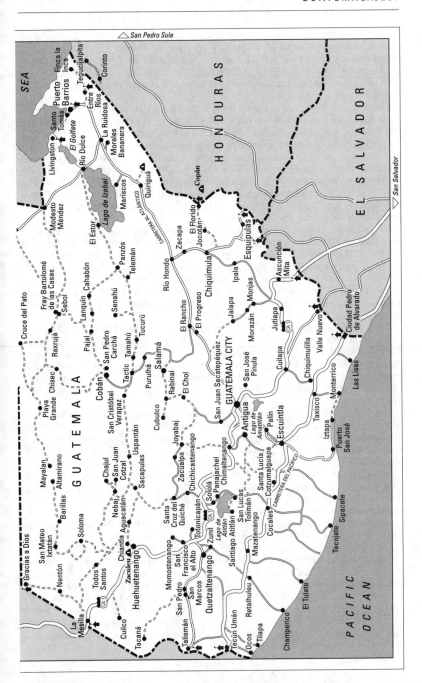

revolt from the mountains, led by a charismatic, conservative 23-year-old, Rafael Carrera, who would accept no authority other than the Catholic Church. There was another major turning-point in Guatemalan politics, with the election of president Rufino Barrios in 1871, an arrogant man with tyrannical tendencies, who revolutionized the country's agriculture, encouraging **coffee** farming, and increasing foreign trade twenty-fold as a result.

The economic boom was based upon a system of forced labour and land confiscation: up to one quarter of the male population was despatched to work on the fincas at harvest time and vast swathes of productive farmland were sold to the highest bidder. By the early twentieth century, **bananas** were also becoming increasingly important, their cultivation controlled by an exceptionally powerful player, the **United Fruit Company**, who had already amassed great profits in Costa Rica. The power of the Fruit Company became so pervasive that the company earned itself the nickname "El Pulpo" (the octopus), its yellow tentacles controlling all Guatemala's railways and the main port, Puerto Barrios. One president, who threatened to terminate United Fruit Company contracts, lasted barely more than a year.

Jorge Ubico, who became president in 1930, was more calculating, and though he embarked on a high-profile programme of reform, he sided firmly with big business and the Fruit Company. When the peasants revolted, they were still compelled to work the fincas by a **vagrancy law**. However, opposition from professionals and young military officers grew, until a wave of student violence finally forced Ubico to resign after fourteen years of tyrannical rule, in an event dubbed the **1944 revolution**. As a result, a new constitution was drawn up, the vote given to all adults and the president prevented from running for a second term.

Juan José Arévalo, a teacher, won the 1945 presidential elections with 85 percent of the vote, with a political doctrine which was christened "**spiritual socialism**". Extensive social welfare programmes were introduced: schools and hospitals were built, an ambitious literary campaign launched, the vagrancy law abolished and unions legalized. Unsurprisingly, though, these progressive reforms angered conservative interests, including the army, and there were repeated coup attempts during this time.

The next presidential elections, in 1950, were won with ease by **Jacobo Arbenz**, who immediately introduced controversial **land reforms**. His redistribution of 8840 square kilometres to the peasants outraged the Fruit Company, which lost half its land. Nor were the CIA (whose director was on the Fruit Company's board) or the US government impressed and they got to work setting up a small military invasion of Guatemala. A ragtag of exiles was put together who successfully managed to overthrow Arbenz in 1954. The army immediately stepped in to fill the power vacuum, all reforms were reversed, land was returned to its previous owners and large numbers of unionists and agrarian reformers were executed.

The thirty years following the CIA-backed coup were perhaps the darkest period in Guatemala's history since the Conquest. The armed forces unleashed a brutal reign of terror during which elections were rigged, thousands of political opponents were killed and thousands more "disappeared". Inevitably, a **guerrilla war** began. Indigenous campesinos, caught in the crossfire between the military and the guerrillas, suffered terribly, and thousands fled to become refugees in Mexico. In 1977, President Carter suspended all military aid to Guatemala because of its appalling human rights record – though Israeli military aid soon replaced that of America. The Catholic Church decided to withdraw all its clergy from the Quiché diocese after a number of its priests were murdered, and in the towns, death squads targeted students, journalists, academics, politicians, lawyers, teachers and unionists.

In 1982, **Ríos Montt**, an evangelical army officer, seized power, determined to restore law and order, eradicate corruption and defeat the guerrillas. Repression eased in the towns but the war intensified in the highlands, aided by a successful (but locally detested) Civil Defence Patrol (PAC) system, which forced the villagers to patrol the countryside, armed with ancient rifles.

Democratic reform remained elusive until 1985, when the first legitimate elections in thirty years were held. However, political and economic power remains very much concentrated in the hands of the **ladino** half of the population, with presidents severely restricted by the shadow of the dominant Guatemalan oligarchy of landowners, generals and big business. Land reform is still untackled (it's estimated that close to seventy percent of the cultivable land is owned by less than five percent of the population), human rights abuses continue and some 85 percent of the population remains in poverty, with little access to health care or education.

Fighting these fundamental inequalities is an increasingly well-organized and confident opposition. The most prominent activist fighting for change is undoubtedly the Quiché Maya woman, **Rigoberta Menchú**, who won the Nobel Peace Prize in 1992 for her work on behalf of indigenous people. Today, the stirrings of a cultural reawakening are unmistakable: hundreds of new schools are being established so that indigenous children can learn in their own language, and there is a resurgence of interest in *costumbres* (traditional religious ways). In 1996, **Peace Accords** signed by President Arzú and the guerrilla leaders brought to an end the 36-year civil war, with a fanfare of promises of indigenous rights, human rights investigations and socio-economic development for all Guatemalans: political violence appeared to be a thing of the past.

In April 1998, however, Guatemala was stunned by the murder of **Bishop Juan Gerardi**, who had just published an exhaustive investigation into the human rights abuses of the civil war. His report blamed the army for most of the atrocities, and it is generally believed that his murder was sanctioned by a military intent on preserving its dominant power base. Whether Geradi's assassination represents an isolated incident or a return to more sinister times remains to be seen, but it certainly demonstrates the acute fragility of Guatemalan democracy. The future seems extremely precarious, with the core issues of land reform and Maya rights untackled and the military still controlling events – in many ways the work to reshape Guatemala has just begun.

FIESTAS IN GUATEMALA

JANUARY
1–5 Santa María de Jesús, near Antigua (main action on the 1st and 2nd).
19–25 **Rabinal**, in the Verapaces (main day 21st).
22–26 **San Pablo La Laguna**, Lake Atitlán (main day 25th).

MARCH
Second Friday in Lent **Chajul**, in the Ixil triangle.

APRIL
24 **San Jorge La Laguna**, Lake Atitlán.
25 **San Marcos La Laguna**, Lake Atitlán.

MAY
6–10 **Uspantán** (main day 8th).
8–10 **Santa Cruz La Laguna** (main day 10th).

JUNE
12–14 **San Antonio Palopó**, near Panajachel (main day 13th).
21–25 **Olintepeque**, near Quetzaltenango.
22–25 **San Juan Cotzal**, near Nebaj.
22–26 **San Juan Atitlán** (main day 24th).
27–30 **San Pedro La Laguna** (main day 29th).
28–30 **Almolongo**, near Quetzaltenango (main day 29th).

continued oveleaf

FIESTAS contd

JULY

21–Aug 4 **Momostenango** (most interesting on July 25 and Aug 1). Plenty of interesting celebrations and traditional rituals in this centre of *costumbres*.

23–27 **Santiago Atitlán** (main day 25th).

25 **Antigua**. Live bands and salsa and merengue in the main plaza.

25 **Cubulco**, in the Verapaces. Riotous fiesta with spectacular dances including the Palo Volador.

31–Aug 6 **Cobán**. City celebrations followed by the national folklore festival.

AUGUST

1–4 **Sacapulas** (main day 4th).

9–15 **Joyabaj**, west of Santa Cruz del Quiché (main day 15th). Very unusual fiesta with many pre-Columbian dances.

12–15 **Nebaj** (main day 15th).

15 **Guatemala City**. Bank holiday in the capital celebrated with marching bands and city-wide indulgence.

SEPTEMBER

12–18 **Quetzaltenango** (main day 15th).

17–21 **Salamá** (main day 17th).

24–30 **Totonicapán** (main day 29th).

OCTOBER

1–6 **San Francisco el Alto** (main day 4th).

2–6 **Panajachel** (main day 4th).

29–Nov 1 **Todos Santos**.

NOVEMBER

1 (All Saints Day) Celebrations all over the country, but most dramatic in **Todos Santos** with the epic drunken horse race and in **Santiago Sacatepéquez**, where massive paper kites are flown.

23–26 **Nahualá** (main day 25th).

22–26 **Zunil** (main day 25th).

25 **Santa Catarina Palopó**, Lake Atitlán.

30 **San Andrés Xecul**, near Quetzaltenango.

30 **San Andrés Itzapa**, near Antigua.

DECEMBER

7 Bonfires (the Burning of the Devil) throughout the country

7 **Ciudad Vieja**, near Antigua.

13–21 **Chichicastenango** (main day 21st). Many interesting dances in this well-attended fiesta.

CHAPTER SEVEN

GUATEMALA CITY, ANTIGUA AND AROUND

Situated just forty kilometres apart in Guatemala's highlands, the two cities of **Guatemala City** and **Antigua** could hardly be more different. The capital, Guatemala City, fume-filled and concrete-clad, is a maelstrom of industry and commerce. There are few attractions or sights here to detain the traveller,

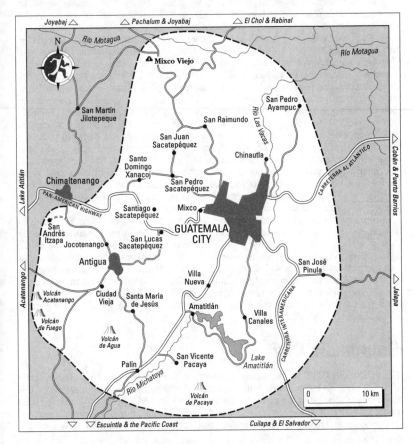

ACCOMMODATION PRICE CODES

All the accommodation listed in this book has been categorized into one of nine price bands, as set out below. The prices quoted are in US dollars and refer to the cheapest room available for two people sharing in high season.

① under US$5	④ US$15–25	⑦ US$60–80
② US$5–10	⑤ US$25–40	⑧ US$80–100
③ US$10–15	⑥ US$40–60	⑨ over US$100

---

though a day or two spent visiting the museums and exploring the markets and shops won't be wasted. Antigua is everything the capital is not: tranquil, urbane and resplendent with spectacular colonial buildings and myriad cosmopolitan cafés, restaurants and hotels. Unsurprisingly, it is the town where most travellers choose to base themselves, finding the relaxed atmosphere a welcome break after the frenzied pace of life in Guatemala City.

Guatemala City is actually the fourth capital of the country. The Spanish conquistadors made their first base at Iximché in 1523, but when they were driven out by the Cakchiquel tribe, they retreated to another site close to today's village of Ciudad Vieja. In 1541, however, this was destroyed by a cataclysmic flood, and the capital was moved to Antigua. The new site grew steadily from small beginnings to become the centre of Spanish colonial power and one of the most important cities in the Americas, but when a series of devastating earthquakes all but destroyed it in 1773, it was decided to move the capital to present-day Guatemala City. The new capital, although slow to develop at first, began growing at an unbelievable rate at the start of the twentieth century and now dominates the country, forming the political and economical heart of the nation.

The countryside around Antigua and Guatemala City – an astonishing landscape of volcanoes, pine forests, meadows, milpas and coffee farms, punctuated with villages – is well worth exploring. Looming over the capital is the **Volcán de Pacaya**, one of the most active volcanoes in Latin America. In the last few years, it has been spewing a spectacular fountain of sulphurous gas and molten rock and, in May 1998, a small eruption doused Guatemala City in ash so that flights to and from the city had to be suspended for a couple of days. However, it's usually possible to climb the peak as well as the neighbouring dormant cones of **Agua** and **Fuego**, close to Antigua.

There are countless interesting villages to visit in this area, including **San Andrés Itzapa**, where there is a pagan shrine to the "evil saint" Maximón, **Santa María de Jesús**, a Maya village where the trail to the Volcán de Agua begins, and the small, atmospheric village of **Santiago Sacatepéquez**. The one **Maya ruin** in the region that can compete with the lowland sites further north is **Mixco Viejo**; it's tricky to get to unless you have your own transport, but its setting, in splendid isolation, is tremendous. Little evidence remains of the former splendour of **Kaminaljuyú**, today almost buried in the capital's suburbs, but this was once one of the largest and most important cities of the Maya World.

Guatemala City

GUATEMALA CITY sprawls across a sweeping highland basin, surrounded on three sides by low hills and volcanic cones. Congested and polluted, it is, in many ways, the antithesis of the rest of the country. The capital was moved here in 1776 after the seismic destruction of Antigua, but the site had been of importance long before the arrival of the Spanish. These days, its shapeless and swelling mass, ringed by shanty towns, ranks as the largest city in Central America. It is home to around three million people, about a quarter of Guatemala's population, and is the undisputed centre of politics, power and wealth.

The city has an intensity and vibrancy that are both its fascination and its horror, and for many travellers a trip to the capital is an exercise in damage limitation, as they struggle through a swirling mass of bus fumes and crowds. The centre is now run-down and polluted and the affluent middle classes have long since fled to the suburbs. It is certainly not somewhere you visit for its beauty or architectural attractions, but it does have a sight or two and a couple of good museums.

Like it or not – and many travellers don't – Guatemala City is the crossroads of the country, and you'll certainly end up here at some time, if only to hurry between bus terminals or negotiate a visa extension. Once you get used to the pace, it can offer a welcome break from life on the road, with cosmopolitan restaurants, cinemas, shopping plazas and metropolitan culture. And if you really can't take the pace, it's easy enough to escape: buses leave every few minutes, day and night.

Some history

The pre-conquest Maya city of **Kaminaljuyú**, whose ruins are still scattered amongst the western suburbs, was well established here two thousand years ago. As a result of an alliance with the great northern power of Teotihuacán (near present-day Mexico City) in early Classic times (250–550 AD), Kaminaljuyú came to dominate the highlands and eventually provided the political and commercial backing that fostered the rise of Tikal (see p.410). The city was situated at the crossroads of the north–south and east–west trade routes and at the height of its prosperity it was home to a population of some 50,000. However, following the decline of Teotihuacán around 600 AD, Kaminaljuyú was surpassed by the great lowland centres that it had helped to establish, and soon after their rise, some time between 600 and 900 AD, the city was abandoned.

Seven centuries later, when Alvarado entered the country, the fractured tribes of the west controlled the highlands and preoccupied the conquistadors. The Spanish ignored the possibility of settling here until the devastating 1773 earthquake that forced them to flee disease-ridden Antigua and establish a new capital. The new city was named **Nueva Guatemala de la Asunción** by royal decree and was officially inaugurated on January 1, 1776.

The new city's growth was slow initially, as many chose not to flee Antigua, despite endless decrees and repeated waves of smallpox and cholera. An 1863 census listed just 1206 residences and the earliest photographs show the city was still little more than a large village with a theatre, a government palace and a fort. Another factor retarding the city's growth was the existence of a major rival, Quetzaltenango, but when it too was razed to the ground by a massive earthquake in 1902, many wealthy families moved to the capital, finally establishing it as the country's primary city.

Just fifteen years after the Quetzaltenango earthquake, the capital itself was badly hit by a series of **earthquakes** in 1917 and 1918, which caused widespread devastation and necessitated substantial reconstruction. However, since these tremors, Guatemala City has grown at an incredible rate, mainly due to an influx of rural immigrants. The steady flight from the fields, characteristic of all developing countries, was aided and abetted by a chronic shortage of land and, in the 1970s and 1980s, by internal refugees escaping the military's "scorched earth" offensives and widespread rural violence. Many of these displaced people, for the most part Maya, feel unwanted and unwelcome in the city and the divisions that cleave Guatemalan society are at their most acute in the capital's crumbling streets. While the wealthy elite sip coffee in air-conditioned shopping malls and plan their next visit to Miami, the heart of the city, Zona 1, has been left to disintegrate into a threatening tangle of fume-choked streets, largely devoid of any kind of life after dark. A small army of **street children** lives rough, scratching a living from begging,

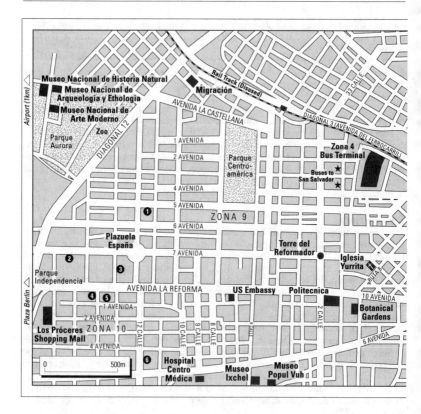

prostitution and petty crime, and there is strong evidence of "social cleansing" by the security forces. Glass skyscrapers rise alongside colonial churches, and shoeless widows peddle cigarettes and sweets to designer-clad nightclubbers.

Arrival and information

Arriving in Guatemala City for the first time, it's easy to feel overwhelmed by its scale, with suburbs sprawled across some twenty-one **zones**, but you'll find that the central area, which is all that you need to worry about, is really quite small.

Broadly speaking, the city divides into two distinct halves. The northern section, centred on **Zona 1**, is the old part of town, containing the parque central, most of the budget hotels, shops, restaurants, cinemas, the post office and many of the bus companies. This part of the city is cramped, congested and polluted, but bustling with activity. The two main streets are 5 and 6 avenidas, both thick with street traders, fast-food joints and copious neon. Directly north of the parque central is **Zona 2**, a largely residential suburb, with the sole attraction of the **Parque Minerva**, where there is a relief map of the country, a popular local attraction. Two kilometres further east along the city ring road is the new long-distance **Meta del Norte** bus terminal, for all departures north and east.

South of Zona 1, acting as a buffer between the two halves of town, is **Zona 4**, home of the administrative centre or Centro Cívico, the national theatre and the **tourist**

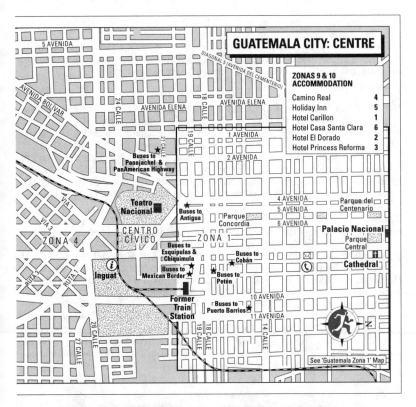

GUATEMALA CITY: CENTRE

ZONAS 9 & 10 ACCOMMODATION

Camino Real	4
Holiday Inn	5
Hotel Carillon	1
Hotel Casa Santa Clara	6
Hotel El Dorado	2
Hotel Princess Reforma	3

office, Inguat, at 7 Av 1–17 (Mon–Fri 8.30am–4.30pm, Sat 8.30am–1pm; ☎3311333, fax 3318893). The information desk is on the ground floor and here you can buy a half-decent map of the country and city; there's usually someone who speaks English. For detailed hiking maps, go to the Instituto Geográfico Militar, Av Las Américas 5–76, Zona 13 (Mon–Fri 8am–4pm). The other great "landmark" in Zona 4 is the **bus terminal**, a crazy world of peripatetic humanity, exhaust fumes and the city's largest fruit and vegetable market.

The southern half of the city, **Zona 9** and **Zona 10**, is the modern, wealthy part of town, split in two by Avenida la Reforma. Here you'll find exclusive offices, apartment blocks, hotels and shops and Guatemala's most expensive nightclubs, restaurants and cafés. Many of the embassies and two of the country's finest museums are also here.

ADDRESSES IN GUATEMALA CITY

The system of street numbering in the capital may seem a little confusing at first and it is complicated by the fact that the same calles and avenidas can exist in several different zones. Always check the zone first and then the street. For example "4 Av 9–14, Zona 1" is in Zona 1, on 4 Avenida between 9 and 10 calles, house number 14.

Continuing south, the neighbouring Zonas 13 and 14 are rich, leafy suburbs and home to the airport, zoo and more museums and cinemas.

There is little of interest in the west side of the city except the new **Central de Mayoreo** long-distance bus terminal in Zona 12 and the sparse remains of the ruins of **Kaminaljuyú**, which have been mostly erased by the city's suburbs.

By air

Aurora airport is on the edge of the city in Zona 13, some way from the centre, but close to Zona 10. The domestic terminal, though in the same complex, is separate, and entered by Av Hincapié. In the complex, you'll also find a Banco del Quetzal for exchange, a tourist office open daily from 6am to 9pm, a Telgua office and a post office (both open 24hr).

Much the easiest way to get to and from the airport is by taxi: you'll find plenty of them waiting outside the terminal. The fare to or from Zona 1 is around US$10, to Zona 10 around US$6, to Antigua around US$25. Buses also leave from directly outside the terminal, across the concrete plaza, dropping you in Zona 1, either on 5 Av or 9 Av.

By bus

If you're travelling by **first-class** (pullman) bus, you'll arrive either at the company's own terminal – most of them are in Zona 1 – or at one of the two new purpose-built terminals, which should be fully functioning by 1999. The new **Meta del Norte** terminal in Zona 18 will serve all routes to Petén, Cobán and the Caribbean; the **Central de Mayoreo** terminal in Zona 12 will be the base for routes to the western highlands, the Pacific coast and to Mexico. Brand-new Volvo cross-city buses will connect the two with each other and the centre of town.

If you've arrived by **second-class** "chicken bus" from Antigua, you'll arrive in Zona 1 at the junction of 18 C, between 4 and 5 Av. The Zona 4 terminal operates second-class buses to the western highlands, the Pacific coast and some towns in the eastern highlands. The Zona 1 "terminal" near the old train station continues to send second-class services to the north and east of the country, and pullman buses to the Mexican border along the Carretera al Pacifico.

BUS COMPANIES IN THE CAPITAL

The main bus companies, their addresses and departure times, are all given in the box on pp.306–7.

City transport

As in any big city, coping with the public transport system takes time. Even locals can be bamboozled by Guatemala's seemingly anarchic web of **bus routes**. In Zona 1 buses #82 and #83 stop on 10 Av, while buses to many different parts of the city run along 4 Av. Destinations are posted on the front of the bus. Buses run from around 6 or 7am until about 10pm. Guatemala City has a ferocious rush hour and many roads throughout the city are jammed between 7.30am and 9am and from 4.30pm to 7pm.

There are currently both metered and non-metered **taxis**. If you can't face the complexities of the bus system or it's late at night, the excellent new metered taxis are comfortable and cheap. Amarillo (☎3321515; 24hr) are highly recommended and will pick you up from anywhere in the city; the fare from Zona 1 to Zona 10 is US$4–5. There are plenty of non-metered taxis around too – you'll have to use your bargaining skills with these and fix the price beforehand. You may also see the odd Thai **tuk-tuk** buzzing around the city streets, Bangkok-style – these are very quick and cheap.

USEFUL BUS ROUTES

#71 Starts on 10 Av, Zona 1, and goes to the Centro Cívico and the immigration office on Av La Castellana.

#82 Starts in Zona 2 and continues through Zona 1 along 10 Av, then past the Centro Cívico in Zona 4 and on to Av la Reforma before turning left at the Obelisco. The route passes many of the embassies, the American Express office, the Popol Vuh and Ixchel museums and the Los Próceres shopping centre.

#83 Starts on 10 Av, Zona 1, and goes to the airport.

Any bus marked **"terminal"**, and there are plenty of these on 4 Av in Zona 1, will take you to the main bus terminal in Zona 4.

Any bus with **"Bolívar"** or **"Trébol"** written on will take you along the western side of the city, down Av Bolívar and to the Trébol junction for connections to the western highlands.

Accommodation

The majority of the budget and mid-range hotels are conveniently grouped in central and eastern Zona 1, with the luxury hotels mostly clustered in Zona 10. Zona 1 is not a great place to be wandering around in search of a room, especially at night. Book ahead and make sure you take a taxi if you arrive after dark.

Budget hotels

Hotel Fenix, 7 Av 15–81, Zona 1 (☎2516625). Safe, friendly and vaguely atmospheric, set in an old, warped, wooden building. There's a café downstairs and some rooms have private bathrooms. ②.

Hotel Hernani, corner 15 C and 6 Av A, Zona 1 (☎2322839). Comfortable old building with good, clean rooms, all with their own shower. Close to being the best budget deal in town. ②.

Hotel Monteleone, 18 C 4–63, Zona 1 (☎2382600, fax 2382509). Rooms are attractively decorated, with quality mattresses and bedside lamps, and some with private baths. The best value in town, extremely clean and safe and right by the Antigua terminal, but not the best area to be in after dark. ②–③.

Hotel San Martin, 16 C 7–65, Zona 1 (☎2380319). Very cheap, clean and friendly, this is among the best deals at the lower end of the scale. Some rooms with private bath. ②.

Hotel Spring, 8 Av 12–65, Zona 1(☎2326637, fax 2320107). An excellent deal here and a safe location, though it's often full of Peace Corps volunteers. Rooms are set around a pretty colonial courtyard and some have private bath. Breakfast available and free mineral water. ②–③.

Mayan Guest House, 11 Av B 7-03, Colonia Nueva Monserrat, Zona 7 (☎5910884). New youth hostel set up with bunk beds, kitchen facilities and luggage storage. The main disadvantage is the location, which though safe, is 3km from the centre, off Calzada Roosevelt. Take any bus bound for the western highlands or Antigua. ②.

Pensión Meza, 10 C 10–17, Zona 1 (☎2323177 or 2534576). Infamous budget travellers' hangout; cheap and laid-back, with plenty of 1960s-style decadence. Fidel Castro and Che Guevara stayed here – the latter in room 21. Dorms and doubles, some with private shower. Noticeboard, ping-pong, music all day, and the owner, Mario, speaks good English. ①–②.

Mid-range hotels

El Aeropuerto Guest House, 15 C A 7–32, Zona 13 (☎3323086). Five minutes' walk from the international airport. Call for a free pickup or else walk across the grass outside and follow the road to the left. A pleasant, convenient and very comfortable hotel; all rooms have private showers, hot water and fluffy towels. ⑤.

Chalet Suizo, 14 C 6–82, Zona 1 (☎2513786, fax 2320429). Friendly, comfortable and very safe, as it's right opposite the police headquarters. Nicely designed, spotlessly clean and all very Swiss and organized, with left luggage and a new café that's open all day. No double beds. ④–⑤.

Hotel Carillon, 5 Av 11–25, Zona 9 (☎ & fax 3324036). If you'd rather not enter the turmoil of Zona 1, this place is good value for the location. It is wood-panelled throughout and the rooms are well appointed. ⑤.

Hotel Colonial, 7 Av 14–19, Zona 1 (☎2326722, fax 2328671). Well-situated colonial-style hotel with dark wood, wrought iron and attractive tiles in the lobby. Tasteful and comfortable, but slightly old-fashioned; the rooms come with or without private bathroom. ④.

Hotel Hincapié, Av Hincapié 18–77, Zona 13 (☎3327771, fax 3374469). Under the same management as the *El Aeropuerto* and conveniently located for the domestic terminal. Rates include local calls, continental breakfast, and transport to and from the airport. ⑤.

Hotel PanAmerican, 9 C 5–63, Zona 1 (☎2326807, fax 2518749). The city's oldest smart hotel, very formal and civilized, with a strong emphasis on Guatemalan tradition. Cable TV, continental breakfast and airport transfer included. Brilliant for Sunday breakfast. ⑥.

Hotel Posada Belén, 13 C A 10–30, Zona 1 (☎2534530, fax 2513478). Tucked down a side street in a beautiful old building. Supremely quiet, safe and very homely, with its own restaurant. No children under five. ⑥.

Luxury hotels

Camino Real, Av la Reforma and 14 C, Zona 10 (☎4484633, fax 3374313). The favoured address for visiting heads of state and anyone on expenses, this hotel continues to lead in the luxury category, in spite of increasing competition from newer places. Rooms cost US$180. ⑨.

Holiday Inn, 1 Av 13–22, Zona 10 (☎3322555, fax 3322584). First-class hotel, within walking distance of the city's best upmarket shops, bars and restaurants. Rooms cost US$140. Best value in this category. ⑨.

Hotel Casa Santa Clara, 12 C 4–51, Zona 10 (☎3391811, fax 3320775). Small, beautifully appointed hotel that also boasts a quality in-house Middle Eastern restaurant. ⑦.

Hotel El Dorado, 7 Av 15–45, Zona 9 (☎3317777, fax 3321877). In the same category as the *Camino Real*; luxurious and comfortable, rooms cost US$140. ⑨.

Hotel Princess Reforma, 13 C 7–65, Zona 9 (☎3344545, fax 3344546). Pleasant mid-sized hotel with small pool, sauna, gym and tennis courts. Rooms from US$134. ⑨.

Hotel Royal Palace, 6 Av 12–66, Zona 1 (☎ & fax 3324036). Comfortable, Best Westin-owned landmark right in the heart of Zona 1; avoid the noisy streetside rooms. Seasonal bargain rates. ⑦.

The City

Guatemala City is hardly over-endowed with sights, but there are some places that are worth visiting while you're here. The Ixchel, Popol Vuh and Archeological museums are particularly good, and there are a few impressive buildings in Zona 1 as well as some more outlandish modern ones dotted across the southern half of the city.

If you're interested to see how the rich let their hair down, head for the Zona Viva in Zona 10, while Zona 1 is the place to see the big city streetlife – hawkers, market vendors, evangelical preachers and prostitutes are all here in abundance.

The old city: zonas 1 and 2

The hub of the old city is **Zona 1**, which is also the busiest and most claustrophobic part of town. This is a squalid world of faceless concrete blocks, broken pavements, car parking lots and plenty of noise and dirt. However, 5 and 6 avenidas, the city's principal shopping area, harbour a certain brutal fascination and are the most exciting part of the capital, thick with street vendors and city bustle.

The heart of the capital, the windswept plaza called the **parque central**, is also the country's political and religious centre and the point from which all distances in Guatemala are measured. It is a soulless place patronized by bored taxi-drivers, *limpiab-otas* (shoeshiners) and pigeons, that only really comes alive on Sundays and public holidays when a tide of Guatemalans descend on the square to stroll, chat and snack or to visit the *huipil* market. There is a new national spirit detectable here now, as soldiers chat

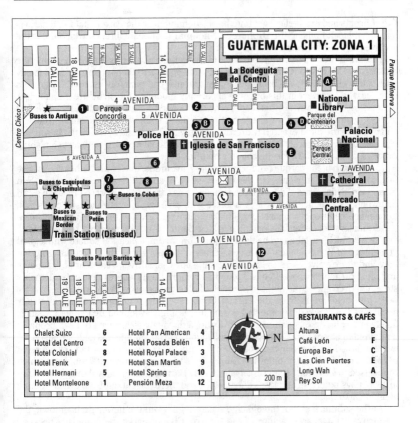

GUATEMALA CITY: ZONA 1

19 CALLE · 18 CALLE · 17 CALLE · 16 CALLE · 15A CALLE · 15 CALLE · 14 CALLE · 13 CALLE · 12A CALLE · 12 CALLE · 11 CALLE · 10 CALLE · 9 CALLE · 8 CALLE · 7 CALLE · 6 CALLE · 5 CALLE

Parque Minerva

Centro Cívico

La Bodeguita del Centro

4 AVENIDA

Parque Concordia

5 AVENIDA

★ Buses to Antigua ❶

❷

❸ B   C

Police HQ   6 AVENIDA

6 AVENIDA A

❺

❻

✝ Iglesia de San Francisco

National Library

Parque del Centenario ❹ D

Palacio Nacional

Parque Central

7 AVENIDA

7 AVENIDA

Buses to Esquipulas & Chiquimula ❼ ❽
★ ❾ ★ Buses to Cobán

8 AVENIDA

✉

✝ Cathedral

★ ★ ★
Buses to Mexican Border   Buses to Petén

❿ ☎

9 AVENIDA

Mercado Central

Train Station (Disused)

10 AVENIDA

Buses to Puerto Barrios ★

⓫

⓬

11 AVENIDA

19 CALLE · 18 CALLE · 17 CALLE · 16 CALLE · 15A CALLE · 15 CALLE · 14 CALLE

ACCOMMODATION

Chalet Suizo	6	Hotel Pan American	4
Hotel del Centro	2	Hotel Posada Belén	11
Hotel Colonial	8	Hotel Royal Palace	3
Hotel Fenix	7	Hotel San Martin	9
Hotel Hernani	5	Hotel Spring	10
Hotel Monteleone	1	Pensión Meza	12

N

0   200 m

RESTAURANTS & CAFÉS

Altuna	B
Café León	F
Europa Bar	C
Las Cien Puertes	E
Long Wah	A
Rey Sol	D

with Maya girls, and you may even hear politics being discussed – something almost unthinkable a decade or so ago. Next to the giant Guatemalan flag in the centre of the square is a small box containing an **eternal flame** dedicated to "the anonymous heroes for peace", which has made the parque a place of pilgrimage for many Guatemalans.

The most striking building here is the **Palacio Nacional**, a grandiose stone-faced structure started in 1939 under President Ubico. For decades it housed the executive branch of the government, and from time to time its steps have been fought over by assorted coupsters. The palace is currently undergoing conversion into an interactive museum of the history of Guatemala. If you can get inside, it's worth a look at its most imposing features – two Castillian-style interior courtyards and the stained glass windows of the former **Salas de Recepción** on the second floor.

On the east side of the plaza, the blue tile-domed **Catedral** (daily 8am–1pm & 3–7pm) was completed in 1868. Its solid, squat design was intended to resist the force of earthquakes and has, for the most part, succeeded. Inside there are three main aisles, all lined with arching pillars, austere colonial paintings and intricate altars supporting an array of saints. Opposite the cathedral, the western side of the parque central merges into the **Parque del Centenario**, former site of the Palacio de los Capitanes Generales, which was destroyed by the 1917 earthquake. The parque is unremarkable in the extreme, with an ugly bandstand which is occasionally used for live concerts and evangelical get-togethers. Looming over the Parque del Centenario is a modern block housing the **Biblioteca Nacional** (National Library), which holds the archives of Central America.

Heading to the east, around the back of the cathedral, there's the sunken concrete bulk of the **Mercado Central** (Mon–Sat 6am–6pm, Sun 9am–noon), painted sickly blue and yellow, with a miserable mini-plaza and car park on its roof. Taking no chances, the architect of this building apparently modelled the structure on a nuclear bunker, sacrificing any aesthetic concerns to the need for strength. Inside, you'll find textiles, leatherware and jewellery on the top floor; fruit, vegetables, snacks, flowers and plants in the middle; and **handicrafts**, mainly basketry and *típica*, in the basement. Unexpectedly, the market is a good spot to buy traditional weaving, with an astonishing range of cloth from all over the country on offer.

To the south of the parque central are **6 and 7 avenidas**, thick with clothes shops, fast-food joints and neon signs. On the corner of 6 Av and 13 C is the **Iglesia de San Francisco**, dating from 1780, a church famous for its carving of the Sacred Heart. It's said that when it was built, the mortar was mixed with cane syrup, egg whites and cow's milk to enhance its strength against earthquakes. Another block to the south is the **police headquarters**, an outlandish-looking mock castle with imitation medieval battlements.

The next block is taken up by the **Parque Concordia**, a pleasant square with a good percentage of Zona 1's very few trees. Plenty of people spend their time hanging out here and there's always a surplus of shoeshine boys, taxi-drivers, amateur philosophers and rabid preachers on weekends. More disturbingly, this is where many of Guatemala's street children spend the night – the smell of glue can be overpowering at times.

As you head south from the Parque Concordia, things go into a slow but steady decline as the cracked pavements become increasingly swamped by temporary stalls, finally emerging in the madness of **18 Calle**, a distinctly sleazy part of town probably best avoided day or night. An assorted collection of grimy nightclubs and "streap-tease" joints, this is the street that most of the city's petty thieves, prostitutes and low-life seem to call home. At the junction of 18 C and 9 Av is the former **train station**, from which trains used to leave for Tecún Umán and Puerto Barrios. It was badly damaged by a fire in 1996, days before an audit was due to start, and there are currently no trains running at all in Guatemala.

At the southern end of the old city, separating it from the newer parts of town, the distinctively 1960s architecture of the **Centro Cívico** marks the boundary between Zonas 1 and 4. Here you'll find the main office of **Inguat** (see p.295) and the lofty **Teatro Nacional**, also referred to as the Miguel Asturias cultural centre, one of the city's most prominent and unusual structures, completed in 1978. Designed along the lines of an ocean liner, painted blue and white with portholes as windows, it has superb views across the city. Cultural events are regularly staged in the theatre's auditorium and an adjoining open-air space, and there's also a little-visited museum dedicated to the Guatemalan military that's really only of interest to would-be *comandantes*.

The new city

The southern half of the city is far more spacious, with broader streets, and is, rough-ly speaking, divided into two by **7 Avenida**. To the south of the Centro Cívico over in Zona 4, at the junction of 7 Av and 2 C, is the landmark **Torre del Reformador**, Guatemala's answer to the Eiffel Tower. This was built in honour of President Barrios, whose liberal reforms transformed the country between 1871 and 1885. Unfortunately you can't go up it. Just to the south on the junction with Ruta 6 is the **Yurrita Church**, built in an outlandish neo-Gothic style more reminiscent of a horror movie set than the streets of Guatemala City.

Continuing southeast down Ruta 6 from the Yurrita church, you approach **Av la Reforma**, the new city's main transport artery, which divides Zonas 9 and 10. Many of the new city's important sites and buildings are to be found on or just off this tree-lined boulevard, including the **Botanical Gardens** (Mon–Fri 8am–5pm) of the San Carlos University; the entrance is on 0 C. Inside you'll find a beautiful small garden with quite a selection of species, all neatly labelled in Spanish and Latin. There's also a small, not terribly exciting natural history museum, with a collection of stuffed birds including a quetzal and an ostrich as well as geological samples, wood types, live snakes and some horrific pickled rodents.

Far more worthwhile are the two privately owned museums in the campus of the University Francisco Marroquín, reached by following 6 C Final off Av la Reforma to the east. **Museo Ixchel** (Mon–Fri 8am–5.50pm, Sat 9am–12.50pm; US$2) is strikingly housed in its own purpose-built cultural centre. Probably the capital's best museum, the Ixchel is dedicated to Maya culture, with particular emphasis on traditional weaving. There's a stunning collection of hand-woven fabrics, including some very impressive examples of ceremonial costumes, with explanations in English. There's also information about the techniques, dyes, fibres and weaving tools used, and the way in which costumes have changed over the years. Don't miss the very good miniature *huipil* collection next to the basement café.

Right next door, on the third floor of the *auditorio* building, is the city's other private museum, the excellent **Popol Vuh** Archeological Museum (Mon–Fri 9am–5pm, Sat 9am–1pm; US$2), boasting an outstanding collection of artefacts from sites all over the country. The small museum is divided into Preclassic, Classic, Postclassic and Colonial rooms, and all the exhibits are top quality. In the Preclassic room are some stunning ceramics, stone masks and *hongo zoomorfo* (mushroom heads); the Classic room has an altar from Naranjo, some lovely incense burners and a model of Tikal; the Postclassic contains a replica of the Dresden Codex; and the colonial era is represented by various ecclesiastical relics and processional crosses.

Back on Av la Reforma, the smart part of town is to the south, a collection of leafy streets filled with boutiques and travel agents, the American embassy, banks, office blocks and sleek hotels. This part of town has clearly escaped the Third World. A little to the east, around 10 C and 3 Av, is the so-called **Zona Viva**, a tight bunch of upmarket hotels, restaurants and nightclubs and, at the bottom of La Reforma, the upmarket Los Próceres shopping mall. If you've spent some time in the impoverished highland villages, the ostentation on show in this little enclave will come as quite a shock to the system. To get to Av la Reforma from Zona 1, take bus #82, which runs along 10 Av in Zona 1, past the Yurrita Church and all the way along Av la Reforma, which is a two-way street so you can return by the same means.

WEST OF 7 AVENIDA

Out to the west of 7 Avenida it's quite another story, and while there are still small enclaves of upmarket housing, and several expensive shopping areas, things are really dominated by commerce and transport, including the infamous **Zona 4 bus terminal**, at 1 C and 4 Av. This area is probably the country's most impenetrable and intimidating jungle – a brutish swirl of petty thieves, hardware stores, bus fumes and sleeping vagrants. Around the terminal the largest **market** in the city spreads across several blocks. To get to the bus terminal from Zona 1, take any of the buses marked "terminal" from 4 Av or 9 Av, all of which pass within a block or two.

Further to the south, in Zona 13, the **Parque Aurora** houses the city's remodelled **zoo** (Tues–Sun 9am–5pm; US$1.40), with a collection that includes African lions, Bengal tigers, crocodiles, giraffes, Indian elephants, hippos, monkeys and all the Central and South American big cats, including some well-fed jaguar. Most of the larger animals have a reasonable amount of space, many smaller animals do not.

On the other side of the Parque Aurora is a collection of state-run museums (all Tues–Fri 9am–4pm, Sat & Sun 9am–noon & 1.30–4pm). The best of these is the **Museo**

Nacional de Arqueología y Etnología (US$5), which has a selection of Maya artefacts to rival the Popul Vuh. The collection has sections on prehistoric archeology and ethnology and includes some fantastic stelae, spectacular jade masks from Abaj Takalik and a ball-court marker from Tikal. There are also several vast pieces of Maya stonework on show, some of them from the more remote sites such as Piedras Negras, and a display on indigenous culture, with traditional masks and costumes. In comparison, the city's **Museo Nacional de Arte Moderno** (US$1.70) is a little disappointing, though there are some impressively massive murals, as well as an abundance of twee images of Maya life. **The Museo Nacional de Historia Natural** (US$1.70) seems the most neglected of the trio, featuring a range of mouldy-looking stuffed animals from Guatemala and elsewhere and a few mineral samples. Beside the park, there's a seldom-used bullring and a running track. Close by, on 11 Av, is a touristy handicraft market, while to the south is Aurora airport. To get here, take bus #63 from 4 Av or #83 from 10 Av.

Kaminaljuyú

Way out west on the edge of the city, beyond the stench of the city rubbish dump, is the long thin arm of Zona 7, which wraps around the ruins of Kaminaljuyú (Mon–Fri 8am–4pm, Sat 8am–1pm; US$4). Archeological digs on this side of the city have revealed the astonishing proportions of a Maya city that once housed around 50,000 people and includes more than three hundred mounds and thirteen ball courts. Unlike the massive temples of the lowlands, these structures were built of adobe, and most of them have been lost to centuries of erosion and a few decades of urban sprawl. Today, the archeological site, incorporating only a tiny fraction of the original city, is little more than a series of earth-covered mounds, a favourite spot for football and romance, and it's virtually impossible to get any impression of Kaminaljuyú's former scale and splendour.

To get to the ruins, take bus #29 or #72 from the parque central or any bus that has a small "Kaminaljuyú" sign in the windscreen.

Eating, drinking and entertainment

Despite its status as the capital and the largest city in Central America, Guatemala City isn't a great place for indulging. Most of the population hurry home after dark and it's only the very rich who eat, drink and dance until the small hours. There are, however, restaurants everywhere in the city, invariably reflecting the type of neighbourhood they're in. Nightclubs and bars are concentrated in Zona 10.

Movie-watching is also popular and there is a good selection of cinemas. Most movies are shown in English with Spanish subtitles. There are four cinemas on 6 Av between the main plaza and the Parque Concordia. Of the others, the very best for sound quality is the Magic Place on Av las Américas, Zona 13. Also recommended are Cine Las Américas, Av las Américas, between 8 and 9 C, Zona 13 and Cine Tikal Futura, Tikal Futura, Calzada Roosevelt, Zona 11. Programmes are listed in the two main newspapers, *El Gráfico* and *Prensa Libre*.

Restaurants and cafés

When it comes to eating cheaply in Guatemala City, stick to Zona 1, where there are some good comedores and dozens of fast-food chains. In the smarter parts of town, particularly Zonas 9 and 10, the emphasis is more on upmarket cafés and glitzy dining, though there is more choice here including Mexican, Middle Eastern, Chinese and Japanese options.

ZONA 1

Altuna, 5 Av 12–31, Zona 1. Spanish/Basque food in a wonderfully civilized, old-fashioned atmosphere. Very strong on fish and seafood. Not cheap, but affordable.

Café Astoria, 10 C 6–72, Zona 1. Very German deli and café – excellent sausages and ham.

Café León, 8 Av 9–15, Zona 1. Spanish-owned café in the heart of things; ideal for *café y churros*.

Café Penalba, 6 Av 11–71, Zona 1. Inexpensive set meals.

Europa Bar, 11 C 5–16, Zona 1. The most popular expat hangout in Zona 1, set inauspiciously beneath a multistorey car park. Primarily a bar, with CNN and sports on screen, but there are also cheapish eats. Owner Judy is a mine of local information. You can trade US dollars here and make local calls. Closed Sun.

Fu Lu Sho, 6 Av and 12 C, Zona 1. Popular, inexpensive Chinese restaurant with an Art Deco interior, opening onto the bustle of 6 Av.

El Gran Pavo, 13 C 4–41, Zona 1; 6 C 3–09, Zona 9; and 15 Av 16–72, Zona 10. Three restaurants all serving massive portions of genuinely Mexican, moderately priced food.

Long Wah, 6 C 3–75, Zona 1, west of the Palacio Nacional. Good Chinese restaurant, not at all expensive.

Rey Sol, south side of Parque Centenario. "Aerobic" breakfasts (sic), very good selection of vegetarian dishes and licuados. The shop sells wholemeal bread, granola and veggie snacks.

Tao Restaurant, 5 C 9–70, Zona 1. The city's best-value three-course veggie lunch. There's no menu; you just eat the meal of the day at tiny tables around a plant-filled courtyard.

ZONAS 9 AND 10

Los Alpes, 10 C 1–09, Zona 10. A haven of peace, where superb pastries and a fine range of drinks make for the best place to relax in the city. Closed Mon.

Los Antojitos, Av la Reforma 15–02, Zona 9. Good, moderately priced Central American food – try the chiles rellenos or guacamole.

Antro's, 4 Av 15–53, Zona 10. Excellent vegetarian restaurant with some Middle Eastern dishes. Closed Sun.

El Arbol de la Vida, 7 Av 13–56, Zona 9. The city's best vegetarian restaurant; reasonably priced.

Burger Warehouse, 4 Av 15–70, Zona 10, serving well-priced burgers, fried chicken dishes and pitchers of beer. Moderately priced for the area.

Jake's, 17 C 10–40, Zona 10. Lunch and dinner from an international menu, very strong on fish and with terrific sweets. Pleasant, candle-lit atmosphere, excellent service and correspondingly high prices. Closed Sun & Mon.

Luigi's Pizza, 4 Av 14–20, Zona 10. Very popular, moderately priced Italian restaurant, serving delicious pizza, pasta and baked potatoes.

Maitreya's Deli, 13 C 4–44, Zona 10. Top-quality, delicious sandwiches, freshly prepared in house. Wide range of drinks and full meals also offered. Expensive.

Olivadda, 12 C 4–51, Zona 10. Very smart, authentic Middle Eastern fare. Feast on falafel, hummus and taboulleh for around US$10 a head.

Palace, 10 C 4–40, Zona 10. Pasta and snacks, cakes and pastries, in a cafeteria atmosphere.

Piccadilly, Plaza España, 7 Av 12–00, Zona 9. One of the most popular continental restaurants with tourists and Guatemalans alike. Decent range of pastas and pizzas, served along with huge jugs of beer. Moderate prices. Also in Zona 1 on 6 Av and 11 C.

Puerto Barrios, 7 Av 10–65, Zona 9. Excellent, pricey seafood in a boat-like building.

Sushi, 2 Av 14–63, Zona 10. Very popular Japanese restaurant, which rather bizarrely advertises itself as a "rock café" too. Reasonable prices.

Vesuvio Pizza, 18 C 3–36, Zona 10. Huge pizzas with plenty of mouth-watering toppings, cooked in a traditional, wood-burning oven.

Bars and clubs

The best bet for a night out in **Zona 1** is to start somewhere like *Las Cien Puertes* (see below) or one of the bars nearby and then check out what's on at *La Bodeguita*. In the

Zona Viva (Zona 10), there are several Western-style nightclubs and bars. If you crave the low life, then stroll on down 18 C, to the junction with 9 Av, and you're in the heart of the red-light district, where the bars and clubs are truly sleazy.

Zona 10 is where the wealthy go to have fun and it's anything but an egalitarian experience. Techno has now hit Guatemala, though you'll be lucky to get anything other than the standard, commercial "handbag" strain. Most city DJs spin a mix of pan-Latin and Eurohouse, with the merengue of the Caribbean often being spiced up with raggamuffin vocals; plus there are specialist clubs for salsa fanatics. The city's greatest reggae club is *La Gran Comal* on Via 4 between 6 Av and Ruta 6, Zona 4. Radiating rhythm, it's relaxed, but not as worn out as the clubs of Zona 1. It's a favourite haunt of black Guatemalans from Lívingston and the Caribbean coast, and well worth a visit.

La Bodeguita del Centro, 12 C 3–55, Zona 1 (☎2302976). Large, leftfield venue with live music, comedy, poetry and all manner of arty events. Free entry in the week, around US$4 at weekends. Definitely worth a visit for the Che Guevara memorabilia alone.

Las Cien Puertes Pasaje Aycinena, 9 C between 6 &7 Av. Funky, leftfield bar in a beautiful run-down colonial arcade. Good Latin sounds, very moderate prices and some imaginative Guatemalan cooking. Recommended.

Crocodilo's, 16 C and 2 Av, in the Los Próceres shopping mall in Zona 10. A restaurant that doubles up as a cocktail bar, with a happy hour daily 6–9pm.

El Establo, Av la Reforma 14–34, Zona 9. Cosy bar with polished wood interior, bookstore, good food and pool tables round the back.

Kahlua, 15 C & 1 Av, Zona 10. Currently one of the most happening clubs in town with two dance floors and a chill-out room. Music is a reasonable mix of dance and Latin pop.

Shakespeare's Pub, 13 C 1–51, Zona 10. Small basement bar catering to middle-aged expat North Americans.

Tapioca Azul, 3 Av & 13 C, Zona 10. Stylish bar with a convivial atmosphere and good food.

Listings

Airlines Airline offices are scattered throughout the city, with many along Av la Reforma. It is fairly straightforward to phone them and there will almost always be someone in the office who speaks English. Aerovias, Av Hincapié 18 C, Zona 13 (☎3325686, airport ☎3327470); Air Canada 12 C 1–25, Zona 10 (☎3353341); American Airlines, Av la Reforma 15–54, Zona 9 (☎3347379); Aviateca (also for Taca, Inter, Lacsa and Nica), Av Hincapié 12–22, Zona 13 (☎3347722); British Airways, 1 Av 10–81, Zona 10, 6th floor of Edificio Inexa (☎3327402); Continental, 12 C 1–25, Zona 10, Edificio Geminis 10, Torre Norte (☎3313341); Delta, 15 C 3–20, Zona 10, Centro Ejecutivo building (☎3370642); Iberia, Av la Reforma 8–60, Zona 9 (☎3370911, airport ☎3325517); Inter, see Aviateca above; Lacsa, see Aviateca above; Mexicana, 13 C 8–44, Zona 10, Edificio Edyma (☎3336001); Nica, see Aviateca above; TWA, Av la Reforma 12–81 Zona 10 (☎3346240); Taca, see Aviateca above; United Airlines, Av la Reforma 1–50, Zona 9, Edificio el Reformador (☎3322995, fax 3323903).

American Express Main office in the Banco del Café, Av la Reforma 9–00, Zona 9 (Mon–Fri 8.30am–4.30pm; ☎3340040, fax 3311928). Take bus #82 from 10 Av, Zona 1.

Banks and exchange Opening hours vary wildly, with some banks shutting as early as 3pm and others staying open until after dark. At the airport, Banco Del Quetzal (Mon–Fri 7am–8pm, Sat & Sun 8am–8pm) gives a good rate and also takes most European currencies. For cashing travellers' cheques, try Banco Industrial, 7 Av 11–52, Zona 1 (Mon–Fri 8.30am–7pm, Sat 8.30am–5.30pm), which also gives Visa cash advances with passport, or Lloyds Bank, 8 Av 10–67, Zona 1 (Mon–Fri 9am–3pm). At Credomatic, on the corner of 5 Av and 11 C, you can get Visa and Mastercard cash advances (Mon–Fri 8.30am–7pm, Sat 9am–1pm).

Books For a reasonable selection of English fiction, try Arnel, in the basement of the Edificio El Centro on 9 C, corner of 7 Av, in Zona 1; Librería del Pensativo, 7 Av and 13 C, Edificio La Cúpula, Zona 9 (Mon–Fri 10am–7pm, Sat 10am–1.30pm); Geminis, 3 Av 17–05, Zona 14; and Sol y Luna on 12 C and 3 Av, Zona 1. A selection of secondhand English books can be bought from the El Establo, Av la Reforma 14–34, Zona 10, and the Europa Bar on 11 C 5–16, Zona 1.

Car rental Renting a car in Guatemala is expensive and you should always keep a sharp eye on the terms. Jeeps can be rented for a little under US$100 a day and cars start from US$70. Avis, 12 C 2–73, Zona 9 (☎3312734, fax 3321263); Budget, Av la Reforma 15–00, Zona 9 (☎3322591, fax 3342571); Dollar, airport (☎3317185); Hertz, 7 Av 14–76, Zona 9 (☎3322242, fax 3317924); National Car Rental, 14 C 1–24, Zona 10 (☎3664670, fax 3370221); Rental, 12 C 2–62, Zona 10 (☎3610672, fax 3342739) – the only company to rent motorbikes; Tabarini, 2 C A 7–30, Zona 10 (☎3319814, fax 3341925).

Embassies Most of the embassies are in the southeastern quarter of the city, along Av la Reforma and Av las Américas, and they tend to open weekday mornings only unless otherwise indicated.

Belize, Av la Reforma, Edificio el Reforma 1–50, Zona 9, 8th Floor, Suite 803 (Mon–Fri 9am–1pm & 2–5pm; ☎3345531 or 3311137); Brazil, 18 C 2–22, Zona 14 (☎3370949); Canada, 13 C 8–44, Zona 10, Edificio Edyma Plaza (Mon–Thurs 8am–4.30pm, Fri 8am–1.30pm; ☎3336102); Chile, 14 C 15–21, Zona 13 (☎3321149); Colombia, 12 C 1–25, Zona 10 (☎3353602); Costa Rica, Av la Reforma 8–60, 3rd floor, Zona 9, Galerias Reforma Torre 1, (☎ & fax 3320531); Ecuador, 4 Av 12–04, Zona 14 (☎3372902); El Salvador, 4 Av 13–60, Zona 10 (☎3662240); Honduras, 9 Av 16–34, Zona 10 (☎3374344); Mexico, 15 C 3–20, Zona 10 (Mon–Fri 9am–1pm & 3–6pm; ☎3337254 or 3337255); Nicaragua, 10 Av 14–72, Zona 10 (☎3680785); Panama, 5 Av 15–45, Zona 10 (☎3372445); Peru, 2 Av 9–67, Zona 9 (☎3318558); United Kingdom, Torre II, 7 Av 5–10, 7th floor, Zona 4 (9am–12noon & 2–4pm; ☎3321604); United States, Av la Reforma, 7–01, Zona 10 (Mon–Fri 8am–5pm; ☎3311541); Venezuela, 8 C 0–56, Zona 9 (☎3316505).

Immigration Main immigration office (*Migración*) is at 41 C 17–36, Zona 8 (☎4751302, fax 4751289; Mon–Fri 8am–4pm). Come here to extend your tourist card up to a maximum total of ninety days, or extend a visa for a month. Take bus #71 from 10 Av in Zona 1 or 6 Av in Zona 4.

Laundry Lavandería Obelisco, Av la Reforma 16–30, next to Samaritana supermarket (Mon–Fri 8am–6.45pm, Sat 8am–5.30pm) charges around US$3 for a self-service wash and dry, and there's also a self-service laundry at 4 Av 13–89, Zona 1.

Libraries The best library for English books is in the IGA (Guatemalan American Institute) at Ruta 1 and Via 4, Zona 4. There's also the National Library on the west side of the Parque del Centenario and specialist collections at the Ixchel and Popol Vuh museums.

Medical care Your embassy should have a list of bilingual doctors, but for emergency medical assistance dial ☎125 for the Red Cross, or there's the Centro Médico, a private hospital with 24hr cover, at 6 Av 3–47, Zona 10 (☎3323555). Central Dentist de Especialistas, 20 C 11–17, Zona 10 (☎3371773), is the best dental clinic in the country, and superb in emergencies.

Pharmacies Farmacia Osco, 16 C & 4 Av, Zona 10.

Photography Colour transparency and both colour and monochrome print film is easy to buy, though expensive. There are several camera shops on 6 Av in Zona 1. Foto Sittler, 12 C 6–20, Zona 1 and La Perla, 9 C and 6 Av, Zona 1, repair cameras and offer a three-month guarantee on their work.

Police The main police station is in a bizarre castle-like structure on the corner of 6 Av and 14 C, Zona 1. In an emergency dial ☎120.

Post office The main post office, 7 Av and 12 C (Mon–Fri 9am–5.30pm) has a Lista de Correos, where they will hold mail for you.

Telephone You can make long-distance phone calls and send faxes from Telgua, one block east of the post office (daily 7am–midnight).

Tours Mesoamerica Explorers, 7 Av 13–01, Zona 9 (☎3325045), organizes nature and archeological trips around Petén and Alta Verapaz. Maya Expeditions 15 C 1–91, Zona 10 (☎3634955, fax 3634164) is the leading ecotourism specialist and especially good for rafting trips. For flight tours to Copán in Honduras and other Maya sites, try Jungle Flying, Av Hincapié and 18 C, domestic terminal, Hangar 21, Zona 13 (☎ 3604917, fax 3314995).

Travel agents There are plenty in the centre and along Av la Reforma in Zonas 9 and 10. Flights to Petén can be booked through all of them. Clarke Tours, Diagonal 6 10-01, Zona 10, Las Margaritas Torre 2, 7th floor(☎3392888, fax 3392909), operates city tours and organizes trips to many parts of the country; Discovery Tours, 12 C 2–04, Zona 9, Edificio Plaza Del Sol (☎3392281, fax 3392285), organizes visits to remote ruins; Maya Expeditions, 15 C 1–91, Zona 10 (☎3634955, fax 3634164), specializes in ecotourism adventure.

Work Hard to come by. The best bet is teaching at one of the English schools, most of which are grouped on 10 and 18 calles in Zona 1. Check the classified sections of the *Siglo News*, *Guatemala Weekly* and *Revue*.

MOVING ON FROM GUATEMALA CITY

To get to the **international terminal** of **Aurora airport** from Zona 1, either take bus #83 from 10 Av (30min) or take a taxi (around US$10); from Zona 10 a taxi is around US$6. There's a US$25 departure tax on all international flights payable in either quetzals or dollars. The **domestic terminal** is in the same complex but only reached via Av Hincapié; you'll need to take a taxi.

If you're leaving by **first-class bus**, departures are either from the office of the bus company or from the new purpose-built terminals on the edge of the city. These new terminals are due to become fully operational in 1999, but as most companies have refused to move out of the centre you will probably be able to choose from a terminal in the city and another outside. The new Zona 12 **Centro de Mayoreo** terminal will serve routes to Mexico, the Pacific coast (and El Salvador) and the western highlands via the Carretera Interamericana. The Zona 18 **Meta del Norte** terminal is to serve routes east and north including Petén (for Belize), the Caribbean and Cobán. Presently, **Zona 1 terminal** is spread out around the streets surrounding the old train station at 18 C and 9 Av, where there are first-class departures to Puerto Barrios, Cobán, the Pacific highway, the Mexican border and Petén.

Moving on by **second-class bus**, the main centre is the chaotic **Zona 4 terminal**, where services run to all parts of the country. To get there, take any city bus marked "terminal"; you'll find these heading south along 4 Av in Zona 1.

BUSES FROM GUATEMALA CITY

Note that there are two **new terminals** being built on the outskirts of town, which will no doubt affect bus departure points (see above for more details).

The abbreviations we've used for the bus companies are as follows:

KQ	King Quality	**SJ**	San Juanera	**TG**	Transportes Galgos
L	Lituega	**TB**	Ticabus	**TM**	Transportes
LA	Líneas Américas	**TA**	Transportes Alamo		Marquensita
LD	Línea Dorada	**TD**	Transportes Dulce	**TR**	Transportes Rebuli
LH	Los Halcones		María	**TV**	Transportes Velásquez
MI	Melva Internacional	**TE**	Transportes Escobar y		
RO	Rutas Orientales		Monja Blanca		*see table opposite*

Around Guatemala City

Escaping from the urban extremes of the capital is fairly straightforward and, fortunately, there is some superb scenery and some interesting villages within a hour or two of the centre. If you can, avoid travelling on a Sunday when everyone else seems to be day-tripping too.

South of the capital

Heading south towards the Pacific, just 25km south of Guatemala City, is **Lago de Amatitlán**. The lake, nestled at the foot of the Volcán de Pacaya and encircled by forested hills, enjoys an undeniably superb setting, though its waters are now very polluted. Amatitlán's very proximity to the capital has been its downfall and every weekend its shores are swamped by day-trippers and holiday-home owners. However, there are some **thermal baths**, where you can take a revitalizing dip, and boats, which can can be hired for around US$2 an hour. Buses run every fifteen minutes or so to the village of **Amatitlán**, 1km off the highway, from 20 Calle and 3 Av, Zona 1 (45min).

To	Company	Bus stop	Frequency	Journey time
Antigua	various (2nd)	18 C & 4 Av, Zona 1	15min	1hr
Chichicastenango	various (2nd)	Zona 4 terminal	30min	3hr 30min
Chiquimula	RO	19 C & 9 Av, Zona 1	15 daily	3hr 30min
Cobán	TE	8 Av 15–16, Zona 1	14 daily	4hr 30min
Cubulco	TD (2nd)	19 C & 9 Av, Zona 1	13 daily	5hr
Escuintla	various (2nd)	Zona 4 terminal	30min	1hr 15min
Esquipulas	RO	19 C & 9 Av, Zona 1	15 daily	4hr
Flores	various (1st/2nd)	17 C & 8 Av, Zona 1	12 daily	12–14hr
	LD (1st)	16 C 10–55, Zona 1	1 daily	12hr
Huehuetenango	LH (1st)	7 Av 15–27, Zona 1	3 daily	5hr
	TV (1st)	20 C 1–37, Zona 1	11 daily	5hr
La Mesilla	TV (1st)	20 C 1–37, Zona 1	5 daily	7hr
Monterrico	various (2nd)	Zona 4 terminal	5 daily	4hr 30min
Panajachel	TR (2nd)	21 C 1–54, Zona 1	11 daily	3hr
Puerto Barrios	L (1st)	15 C 10–40, Zona 1	19 daily	5hr 30min
Quetzaltenango	LA (1st)	2 Av 18–74, Zona 1	6 daily	4hr
	TA (1st)	21 C 1–14, Zona 1	5 daily	4hr
	TM (1st)	1 Av 21–31, Zona 1	8 daily	4hr
	TG (1st)	7 Av 19–44, Zona 1	6 daily	4hr
	SJ (2nd)	Zona 4 terminal	9 daily	4hr 30min
Rabinal	TD (2nd)	19 C & 9 Av, Zona 1	13 daily	4hr 30min
Salamá	TD (2nd)	19 C & 9 Av, Zona 1	13 daily	3hr 30min
San Salvador	MI (1st)	3 Av 1–38, Zona 9	11 daily	5hr
	TB (1st)	11 C 2–72, Zona 9	1 daily	5hr
	KQ (1st)	16 C 1–30, Zona 10	2 daily	5hr
Santa Cruz del Quiché	various (2nd)	Zona 4 terminal	30min	4hr
Tecún Umán	various (1st)	19 Av & 8 C, Zona 1	30min	5hr
Talismán	various (1st)	19 Av & 8 C, Zona 1	30min	5hr
Zacapa	RO	19 C & 9 Av, Zona 1	15 daily	3hr

A further 10km down the highway, a turn-off heads into the hills through an aromatic network of coffee and tobacco plantations to the small village of **SAN VICENTE PACAYA**, from where trails lead to the **Volcán de Pacaya**. This volcano has been in a constant state of eruption since 1965 and is the most active in the Maya

SAFETY ON THE VOLCÁN DE PACAYA

Before setting out on the climb to the peak of Pacaya, you should bear in mind that the volcano has been the scene of a number of **attacks**, rapes, murders and robberies. Some serious incidents took place in early 1997 and tours now come complete with armed guards. While most people climb the volcano without encountering any trouble, it is worth checking the current security situation with your embassy or at the tourist offices in Guatemala City or Antigua and keeping an eye on the Antigua noticeboards, where recent incidents are usually publicized. Though there is a small risk of trouble no matter who you go with, try Quetzal Volcano Expeditions who advertise in Dona Luisa's, Gran Jaguar Tours, 4 C Poniente 30 (☎8322712), or Adventuras Vacacionales, 5 Av Sur 11B (☎8323352), both in Antigua. We've received complaints about Popeye and Yaxcha Expeditions.

region. A trip to the smoking cone is an unforgettable experience, but as there have been a number of attacks around Pacaya (see box on p.307) in recent years and given the volcano's extremely active nature, witnessing the spectacle does involve a degree of risk.

The best time to watch the eruptions is **at night**, when the sludge that the volcano spouts can be seen in its full glory as a plume of brilliant orange. Though it is possible to climb the cone independently, virtually everyone now chooses to join a group with a guide and an armed guard. Antigua is the best place to organize a trip, most of which cost around US$15 a head, leave in the early afternoon and return about 11pm.

Northwest of the capital

Leaving the city through Zona 7 and a suburb called El Florida, the road starts to climb into the hills, through an area that, apart from one or two luxury mansions, is oddly uninhabited. The first village you come to is **SAN PEDRO SACATEPÉQUEZ**, where the impact of the earthquake is still painfully felt. The Friday market here is small, but still worth a browse. Another six kilometres takes you over a ridge and into the village of **SAN JUAN SACATEPÉQUEZ**. As you approach, the road passes a number of makeshift greenhouses where flowers are grown, an industry that has become the local speciality. By far the best time to visit is for the Friday market, when the whole place springs into action and the village is packed. Keep an eye out for the *huipiles* worn in San Juan, which are unusual and impressive, with bold geometric designs of yellow, purple and green. **Buses** to both villages run every half-hour or so from the Zona 4 terminal in Guatemala City.

Beyond San Juan the road divides. If you follow the branch heading for **MIXCO VIEJO**, the scenery changes dramatically, leaving behind the pine forests and entering a huge dry valley scattered with small farms. Mixco Viejo was the capital of the Pokoman Maya, one of the main pre-conquest tribes, whose language has all but died out. The site, thought to date from the thirteenth century, is in a magnificent position: protected on all sides by deep ravines, it can be entered only along a single-file causeway. When the Spanish arrived in 1525, this was one of the largest highland centres, with nine temples, two ball courts and a population of around nine thousand. After an initial failure by the Spanish to gain control here, Alvarado attacked the city himself with the aid of two hundred Mexican allies, but his armies were attacked from behind by a force of Pokoman warriors who arrived from nearby Chinautla. The ensuing battle was won by the Spanish cavalry, but the city remained impenetrable. According to legend, Alvarado then learnt of a secret entrance to the city; he entered Mixco virtually unopposed and then massacred all the inhabitants.

Today the site has been impressively restored, with its plazas and temples laid out across several flat-topped ridges. Like all the highland sites the structures are fairly low – the largest temple reaches only about 10m in height – and devoid of decoration. It is, however, an interesting site in a spectacular setting and, during the week, you'll probably have the ruins to yourself, which gives the place all the more atmosphere.

Mixco Viejo is by no means an easy place to reach, and if you can muster enough people it's worth **renting a car** (see p.305). Alternatively, Swiss Travel, in the *Chalet Suizo* in Guatemala City, can organize **tours** of the site (see p.297). If you're determined to travel by **bus**, there is one leaving the Zona 4 terminal in Guatemala City at 9.30am every day, which passes the site on the way to Pachalum. Make sure that the one you take passes *las ruinas*, as there are buses that go to the village without doing so; also make sure you don't get on a bus saying "Mixco", which is not the right place at all. If you do opt to travel by bus, then you'll have to **hitch** back on a truck to San Juan Sacatepéquez, which may be very slow-going, unless you're prepared to hang around until 3am when the bus returns. Far better to **camp** at one of the attractive shelters overlooking the ruins.

Antigua

Superbly sited in a sweeping highland valley and suspended between the cones of Agua, Acatenango and Fuego volcanoes is one of the Guatemala's most enchanting colonial cities – **ANTIGUA**. In its day, it was one of the great cities of the Spanish empire, ranking alongside Lima and Mexico City, and serving as the administrative

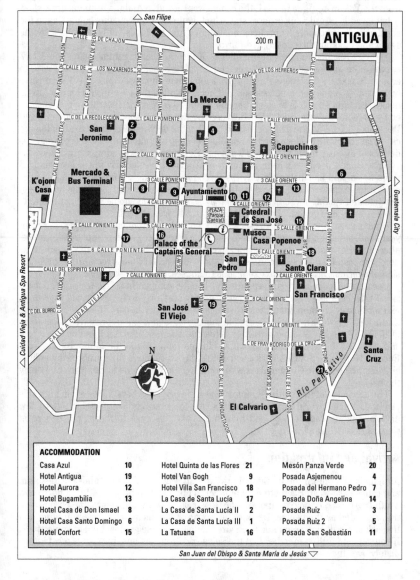

ANTIGUA

ACCOMMODATION					
Casa Azul	10	Hotel Quinta de las Flores	21	Mesón Panza Verde	20
Hotel Antigua	19	Hotel Van Gogh	9	Posada Asjemenou	4
Hotel Aurora	12	Hotel Villa San Francisco	18	Posada del Hermano Pedro	7
Hotel Bugambilia	13	La Casa de Santa Lucía	17	Posada Doña Angelina	14
Hotel Casa de Don Ismael	8	La Casa de Santa Lucía II	2	Posada Ruiz	3
Hotel Casa Santo Domingo	6	La Casa de Santa Lucía III	1	Posada Ruiz 2	5
Hotel Confort	15	La Tatuana	16	Posada San Sebastián	11

San Juan del Obispo & Santa María de Jesús ▽

centre for all of Central America and Mexican Chiapas. Built by Spanish architects and Maya labourers, it is a classically designed city of elegant squares, churches, monasteries and grand houses, and this magnificent colonial legacy has ensured Antigua's continuing prosperity as one of Guatemala's premier tourist attractions.

Antigua was actually the third capital of Guatemala. The Spanish settled first at the site of **Iximché** (see p.328) in July 1524 and then at a site a few kilometres from Antigua, now called Ciudad Vieja, but when this was devastated by a massive mud slide from the Volcán de Agua in 1541, the capital was moved to Antigua. Antigua grew slowly but steadily as religious orders established themselves one by one, competing in the construction of schools, churches, monasteries and hospitals, all largely built by the sweat and blood of the conscripted Maya.

The city reached its peak in the middle of the eighteenth century, after the **1717 earthquake** prompted an unprecedented building boom, and the population rose to around 50,000. By this stage, Antigua was a genuinely impressive place, with a university, a printing press and a newspaper. But, as is so often the case in Guatemala, earthquakes brought all of this to an abrupt end. For the best part of a year the city was shaken by tremors, with the final blows delivered by two severe shocks on September 7 and December 13, 1773. The damage was so bad that the decision was made to abandon the city in favour of the modern capital. Fortunately, despite endless official decrees and epidemics of disease, many refused to leave and Antigua was never completely deserted.

Since then, the city has been gradually repopulated, particularly in the last hundred years or so, and as Guatemala City has become increasingly congested, many of the city's middle classes have moved to Antigua. They've been joined by a large number of resident and visiting foreigners, attracted by its relaxed and sophisticated atmosphere, lively cultural life, benign climate and largely traffic-free streets.

Efforts have been made to preserve the architectural grandeur of the past in recent years and, although some of the buildings of the colonial legacy lie in splendidly atmospheric ruin or else steadily decaying, many more have been impeccably restored as hotels or restaurants. Local conservation laws also protect the streets from the intrusion of overhanging signs and extensions to houses.

Because of its relaxed atmosphere and beauty, Antigua is a favoured hangout for jaded travellers to refuel and recharge. The bar scene is always lively and there's an extraordinarily cosmopolitan choice of restaurants. If you can make it here for **Semana Santa** (Easter week), you'll witness the most extravagant and impressive processions in all Latin America. Another attraction is the city's **language schools**, some of the best and cheapest in the continent, drawing students from around the globe. Expats from Europe, North and South America and even Asia contribute to the town's cosmopolitan air, mingling with the Guatemalans who come here at weekends to eat, drink and enjoy themselves.

The downside of this settled, comfortable affluence is perhaps a loss of vitality – this civilized, isolated world can seem almost a little too smug and comfortable. After a few days of sipping cappuccinos and munching cake, it's easy to forget that you're in Central America at all.

Arrival and information

Antigua is laid out on the traditional grid system, with avenidas running north–south, and calles east–west. Each street is numbered and has two halves, either a north and south (*norte/sur*) or an east and west (*oriente/poniente*), with the plaza, the parque central, regarded as the centre. Despite this apparent simplicity, poor street lighting and the lack of street signs combine to ensure that most people get lost here at some stage. If you get confused, remember that the Volcán de Agua, the one that hangs most immediately over the town, is to the south.

Arriving by bus, you'll end up in the main bus terminal, a large open space beside the market. The street opposite (4 C Poniente) leads directly to the plaza. The **tourist office** (daily 8am–6pm; ☎8320763) on the south side of the plaza dispenses reasonable, if overcautious, information. You'll find the newly formed **tourist police** just off the parque central on 4 Av Norte; they should be able to escort you to the Cerro de la Cruz for a panoramic view of Antigua and the surrounding volcanoes and help you with any difficulties.

Antigua is one of the most popular places in Latin America to **study Spanish**. For a full list of recommended schools see p.317, or you can consult the noticeboards in various tourist venues which advertise private language tuition – as well as apartments, flights home and shared rides. Probably the most read are those at *Doña Luisa's* restaurant, 4 C Oriente 12, and the Rainbow Reading Room, 7 Av Sur 8.

For **tours** of the city, contact Geovany at Monarcas, 6 Av Norte 60A (☎8323343), who looks at Maya influence on Antiguan architecture and the flora around the city, or Elizabeth Bell (☎8320140 ext 341), who leads excellent historical walking tours around the town.

Accommodation

Hotels in Antigua are in plentiful supply although, like everything else, they can be a bit hard to find due to the absence of overhanging signs. Be warned that rooms get scarce (and prices increase) around Holy Week.

Casa Azul, 4 Av Norte 5 (☎8320961 or 8320962, fax 8320944). One of the best locations in town, just off the plaza, with huge, atmospheric rooms in a converted colonial mansion. Facilities include sauna, jacuzzi and a small swimming pool. ⑧.

La Casa de Santa Lucía, Alameda Santa Lucía Sur 5 (☎8326133). Secure, spacious and attractive rooms decorated with dark wood, all with bathrooms and hot water. Best value in town in this price category, hence very popular. You'll have to ring the bell to get in; guests are given a key. ②.

La Casa de Santa Lucía 2, Alameda Santa Lucía Norte 21 & **La Casa de Santa Lucía 3** 6 Avenida Norte 43 A (no phones). Almost carbon copies of the original. Spacious rooms all with hot showers and both extremely well priced. Neither are signposted. Ring the bell for entry. ②.

Hotel Antigua, 8 C Poniente 1 (☎8320288, fax 8320807). Tasteful colonial decor and a ruined church practically on the premises. Swimming pool, excellent restaurant, beautiful gardens and pleasant rooms with open fires to ward off the chill of the night. US$132 including breakfast. ⑨.

Hotel Aurora, 4 C Oriente 16 (☎ & fax 8320217). Attractive colonial building with rooms set around a pleasant grassy courtyard and fountain. Rooms are a little old-fashioned, but comfortable enough. ⑥.

Hotel Bugambilia, 3 C Oriente 19 (☎8325780). Quiet location, clean and safe, but rooms are a little plain. English-speaking owners are very helpful and hospitable. Snacks available. ③.

Hotel Casa Santo Domingo, 3 C Oriente 28 (☎8320140, fax 8320102). Spectacular colonial convent, sympathetically converted into a hotel and restaurant at a cost of several million dollars. Rooms and corridors are bedecked in ecclesiastical art and paraphernalia and there's no lack of luxury. Probably the most atmospheric hotel in Guatemala. Off season, there can be almost fifty percent discounts. US$150 for a double room. ⑨.

Hotel Confort, 1 Av Norte 2 (☎8320566). Attractive family-run guest house with a pleasant garden in a quiet street. Though the rooms are attractive, none has a private bath. ④

Hotel la Casa de Don Ismael, 3 C Poniente 6 (☎8321932). Attractively presented rooms with towels and soap provided, a lovely little garden, free mineral water and free tea or coffee in the morning. Communal bathrooms are brightly painted and kept spotless. Very fair prices. ②.

Hotel Quinta de las Flores, Calle del Hermano Pedro 6 (☎8323721, fax 8323726). A little out of town, but the attractive, tastefully decorated rooms and the spectacular garden, with a swimming pool and many rare plants, shrubs and trees, make it a wonderful place to relax. ⑦.

Hotel Van Gogh, 6 Av Norte 14 (☎ & fax 8320376). Homely atmosphere, attractive rooms, a nice bar/TV lounge with log fires in winter, a café, and email and fax services. ④.

Hotel Villa San Francisco, 1 Av Sur 15 (☎8323383). Well-run, Swiss-owned hotel with secure, pleasant rooms, a rooftop terrace and very competitive email, fax and phone services. ②–③.

SEMANA SANTA IN ANTIGUA

Antigua's Semana Santa (Holy Week) celebrations are perhaps the most extravagant and impressive in all Latin America. The celebrations start with a procession on Palm Sunday, representing Christ's entry into Jerusalem, and continue through to the really big processions and pageants on Good Friday. On Thursday night the streets are carpeted with meticulously drawn patterns of coloured sawdust, and on Friday morning a series of processions re-enacts the progress of Christ to the Cross accompanied by sombre music from local brass bands. Setting out from La Merced, Escuela de Cristo and the village of San Felipe, teams of penitents wearing peaked hoods and accompanied by solemn dirges and clouds of incense carry images of Christ and the Cross on massive platforms. The pageants set off at around at 8am, the penitents dressed in either white or purple. After 3pm, the hour of the Crucifixion, they change into black.

It is a great honour to be involved in the procession, but no easy task as the great cedar block carried from La Merced weighs some 3.5 tonnes, and needs eighty men to lift it. Some of the images displayed date from the seventeenth century and the procession itself is thought to have been introduced by Alvarado in the early years of the Conquest, imported directly from Spain.

Check the exact details of events with the tourist office who should be able to provide you with a map detailing the routes of the processions. During Holy Week hotels in Antigua are often full, and the entire town is always packed on Good Friday. But even if you have to make the trip from Guatemala City or Panajachel, it's well worth coming here for, especially on the Friday.

Mesón Panza Verde, 5 Av Sur 19 (☎ & fax 8322925). Small, immaculately furnished hotel in a colonial-style building that is also home to one of Antigua's premier restaurants. Supremely comfortable suites, some with four-poster beds. Faultless service. Breakfast included. ⑥–⑧.

Posada Asjemenou, 5 Av Norte 31 (☎8322670, fax 8322832). Good value, comfortable rooms with a colonial feel; either with or without private bathroom. ④–⑤.

Posada de Doña Angelina, 4 C Poniente 33 (☎8325173). Popular budget option. Rooms are a bit gloomy, but there are plenty of them, some with private bath. Close to the bus terminal, so not the most tranquil place in town. Run by a dynamic señora. ②–③.

Posada del Hermano Pedro, 3 C Oriente 3 (☎8322089, fax 8322087). Comfortable hotel in a tastefully converted colonial mansion. Good location. When the rooftop bar opens, the views will be stunning. ⑥.

Posada Ruiz, Alameda Santa Lucía 17 & **Posada Ruiz 2**, 2 C Poniente 25 (no phones). Small rooms with no frills, but rates are extremely cheap and both are a short stumble from the bus terminal. ①.

Posada San Sebastián, 3 Av Norte 4 (☎ & fax 8322621). Charming establishment. Each room is individually decorated with antiques, there's a gorgeous little bar and the location is very convenient. Excellent value. ⑥.

La Tatuana, 6 Av Sur 3 (☎8320537). Small hotel with imagintively decorated rooms, all with private bath. Extremely good value for the price. ④.

The City

Antigua has an incredible number of ruined and restored colonial buildings, and although these constitute only a fraction of the city's original architectural splendour, they do give an idea of its former extravagance. However, the prospect of visiting them all can seem overwhelming; if you'd rather just see the gems, make **La Merced**, **Las Capuchinas**, **Casa Popenoe** and **San Francisco** your targets.

If Antigua seems to you a little too sanitized and over-oriented to the tourist dollar, head for the area around the bus terminal and the **marketplace**, which has a little more

Guatemalteco character and myriad cheap stalls selling snacks, juices and licuados, flowers, fruit and vegetables and secondhand clothes and shoes.

The parque central

The shady **parque central** is a favoured meeting place and civic focal point – though its calm atmosphere is relatively recent. For centuries the central plaza was the focus of the colonial city, bustling with constant activity. A huge market spilled out across it, which was cleared only for bullfights, military parades, floggings and public hangings.

The most imposing of the surrounding structures is the **Catedral de San José**, on the eastern side. The first cathedral was begun in 1545, but an earthquake brought down much of the roof and, in 1670, it was decided to start on a new cathedral worthy of the town's role as a capital city. The scale was astounding: a vast dome, five naves, eighteen chapels and an altar inlaid with mother-of-pearl, ivory and silver. But in 1773, it was destroyed yet again by an earthquake. Today, two of the chapels have been restored, and inside is a figure of Christ by the colonial sculptor, Quirio Cataño. Behind the church, entered from 5 C Oriente, are the remains of the rest of the original structure – a mass of fallen masonry and some rotting beams, broken arches and hefty pillars. Buried beneath the floor are some of the great names of the Conquest, including Alvarado, his wife Beatriz de la Cueva, Bishop Marroquín and the historian Bernal Díaz del Castillo.

Along the entire south side of the square runs the squat two-storey facade of the **Palace of the Captains General**, with a row of 27 arches along each floor. It was originally constructed in 1558, but rebuilt after earthquake damage. The palace was home to the colonial rulers and also housed the barracks of the dragoons, the stables, the royal mint, law courts, tax offices, great ballrooms, a large bureaucracy, and a lot more besides. Today it contains the local government offices, the headquarters of the Sacatepéquez police department and the tourist office. Directly opposite is the **Ayuntamiento**, the city hall, which dates from 1740 and remained undamaged until the 1976 earthquake. It holds a couple of minor museums, the Museo de Santiago (Tues–Fri 9am–4pm, Sat & Sun 9am–noon & 2–4pm; US$1.60), which holds a collection of colonial artefacts in the old city jail, and the Museo del Libro Antiguo (same hours; US$1.60), in the rooms that held the first printing press in Central America. A replica of the press is on display, alongside some copies of the works produced on it.

South and east of the parque central

Across the street from the ruined cathedral, in 5 C Oriente, is the **Museo de Arte Colonial** (Tues–Fri 9am–4pm, Sat & Sun 9am–noon & 2–4pm; US$4), formerly the site of a university. The deep-set windows and beautifully ornate cloisters make it one of the finest architectural survivors in Antigua. The museum contains a good collection of dark and brooding religious art, sculpture, furniture and murals depicting life on the colonial campus.

Moving down 5 C Oriente, at the corner with 1 Av Sur is the **Casa Popenoe** (Mon–Sat 2–4pm; US$1), a superbly restored colonial mansion that gives an interesting insight into domestic life in colonial times. Originally owned by a Spanish judge, it was abandoned for some time until its painstaking restoration by Dr Wilson Popenoe, a United Fruit Company scientist. Among the paintings are portraits of Bishop Marroquín and the menacing-looking Alvarado himself. The kitchen and servants' quarters have also been carefully renovated: you can see the original bread ovens, the herb garden and the pigeon loft, which would have provided the mansion's occupants with their mail service. Go up to the roof for great views of the city and Volcán de Agua.

A little further down 1 Av Sur is the imposing church of **San Francisco** (daily 8am–6pm). One of the oldest churches in Antigua, dating from 1579, it grew into a vast religious and cultural centre that included a school, a hospital, music rooms, a printing press and a monastery. All of it was lost, though, in the 1773 earthquake. Inside the church are buried the remains of Hermano Pedro de Betancourt (a Franciscan from the Canary Islands who founded the Hospital of Belén in Antigua). Pilgrims come here from all over Central America to ask for the benefit of his powers of miraculous intervention. The ruins of the monastery, which are among the most impressive in Antigua, have pleasant grassy verges with good picnic potential.

One block west and one block north of San Francisco, two churches face each other at opposite ends of a pretty palm-tree lined plaza, which doubles as an open-air *típica* textile street market. Women travel from as far away as Lago de Atitlán and even the Ixil triangle to sell their wares here, returning home after a day or two, hopefully with a little cash gained. At the western end is the **San Pedro Church** dating from 1680, and at the eastern end **Santa Clara**, a former convent. In colonial times it was popular for aristocratic ladies to take the veil here; the hardships were not too extreme and the nuns gained a reputation for their fine cooking. The convent was twice destroyed in the earthquakes of 1717 and 1773, but the current building with its ornate facade survived the 1976 tremors intact. In front of Santa Clara is a large *pila* or washhouse where village women gather to scrub, rinse and gossip.

For a list of **language schools** in Antigua, see p.317.

North and west of the parque central

At the junction of 2 C Oriente and 2 Av Norte is the site of **Las Capuchinas** (Tues–Sun 9am–5pm; US$1.60), the largest and most impressive of the city's convents, dating from 1726, whose ruins are some of the best preserved but least understood in Antigua. The Capuchin nuns who lived here were not allowed any visual contact with the outside world: food was passed to them by means of a turntable and they could only speak to visitors through a grille. The ruins are the most beautiful in Antigua, with fountains, courtyards and massive earthquake-proof pillars. The most unusual point is the tower or "retreat", with eighteen tiny cells set into the walls on the top floor and a lower floor incorporating seventeen small recesses, some with stone rings.

A couple of blocks to the west, spanning 5 Av Norte, the arch of **Santa Catalina** is all that remains of the original convent founded here in 1609. The arch was built in order for the nuns to walk between the two halves of the establishment without being exposed to the pollution of the outside world. Somehow it has managed to defy the constant onslaught of earthquakes and is now a favoured, if clichéd, spot for photographers as the view to the Volcán de Agua is unobstructed from here.

Walking under the arch and to the end of the street, you reach the church of **La Merced**, which boasts one of the most intricate facades in the entire city. Look closely and you'll see the outline of a corn cob, a motif not normally used by the Catholic Church and probably added by the original Maya labourers. The church is still in use, but the cloisters and gardens lie in ruins, exposed to the sky.

Continue west down 1 C Poniente to the junction of the tree-lined street, Alameda Santa Lucía, and you reach the spectacular remains of **San Jerónimo**, a school built in 1739. Well-kept gardens are woven between the huge blocks of fallen masonry and crumbling walls. On the other side of the bus station is an imposing monument to Rafael Landivar (1731–93), a Jesuit composer who is generally considered to be the finest poet of the colonial era. In an unlikely spot, behind the bus station at C de Recoletos 55, the **K'ojom Casa de la Música** (Mon–Fri 9am–12.30pm & 2–5pm, Sat closes at 4pm; US$1), is a small but delightful museum devoted to indigenous music and ceremony, with some fascinating photographs of Maya life.

Eating and drinking

In Antigua the choice of food is even more cosmopolitan than the population. You can munch your way around the world in a number of reasonably authentic restaurants for a few dollars a time, or dine in real style for around US$10 a head. The only thing that seems hard to come by is authentic Guatemalan comedor food – which will be quite a relief if you've been subsisting on eggs and beans in the mountains.

Cafés

Bagdad Café, 1 C Poniente 9. Simple courtyard café that bakes its own bread. Healthy snacks and tasty sandwiches and cakes. Also has in-house email, fax and phone facilities.

Café Condesa, west side of plaza; pass through the Casa del Conde bookshop. Extremely civilized place to enjoy an excellent breakfast, coffee and cake or full lunch. The gurgling fountain and period charm create a nice tone for the long, lazy Sunday brunches favoured by Antiguan society.

Café la Fuente, in La Fuente, 4 C Oriente 14. Vegetarian restaurant/café where you can eat stuffed aubergine and falafel or sip coffee in one of the most attractive restored courtyards in the city.

Pasteleria Okrassa, 6 Av Norte 29. Great for croissants, cinnamon rolls and healthy drinks – try the raspberry juice.

Jugocentre Peroleto, Alameda Santa Lucía 36. Brilliant budget hole-in-the-wall cabin with excellent and cheap healthy breakfasts, fruit juices and yummy cakes.

Restaurants

El Asador de Don Martín, 4 Av Norte 16. Suberb colonial setting. Beautiful dining rooms and a lovely roof terrace with some of the finest views in Antigua. Three ambitious menus and a huge wine list. Expensive but well worth a splurge.

Beijing, 6 Av Sur and 5 C Poniente. Antigua's best Chinese and East Asian food, prepared with a few imaginative twists. Good noodle dishes, soups and Vietnamese spring rolls. Fairly expensive.

Café Flor, 4 Av Sur 1. Highly commendable Thai, Indonesian and Indian cuisine. While the cooking is not a hundred per cent authentic, dishes are still well executed and the atmosphere relaxed and convivial. Reasonable prices.

Café Panchoy, 6 Av Norte 1B. Good-value cooking with a real Guatemalan flavour – top steaks and some traditional favourites like chiles rellenos. Excellent margaritas. Closed Tues.

Café-Pizzeria Asjemenou, 5 C Poniente 4. A favourite for its legendary breakfasts. Also very strong on pizza and calzone, but the service can be erratic. Daily 9am–10pm.

Casa de las Mixtas, 3 C Poniente & 7 Av Norte. A basic comedor, but nicely set up with attractive decor and cooking that is executed with more flair than most. Open early until 7.30pm. Inexpensive.

Doña Luisa's, 4 C Oriente 12. One of the most popular places in town. The setting is relaxed but the menu could do with a revamp – the basic line-up of chilli con carne, baked potatoes, salads and hamburgers is looking a little tired. An adjoining shop sells bread and pastries baked on the premises.

La Escudilla, 4 Av Norte 4. Tremendous courtyard restaurant, usually extremely busy on account of the excellent-value, good-quality food. The pasta is good, the US$3 all-day, all-night set meal is exceptional value and the delicious salads are unequalled in Antigua. Vegetarians have plenty of tasty choices too. You may have a wait, though, when it's busy.

La Fonda de la Calle Real, upstairs at 5 Av Norte 5; there's also a smarter new restaurant in a beautiful colonial house at 3 C Poniente 7. Probably the most famous restaurants in Antigua. Try the excellent Guatemalan specialities, including *pepián* (spicy meat stew) and *caldo real* (chicken soup). Moderate to expensive. Closed Wed.

Frida's, 5 Av Norte 29. Lively atmosphere and the best Mexican food in town – a tasty selection of enchiladas, fajitas etc. Decorated with 1950s Americana.

Panza Verde, 5 Av Sur 19. One of Antigua's most exclusive restaurants. Exemplary European cuisine, professional service and a nice setting, with well-spaced tables grouped around a courtyard garden. Try the trout or sea bass meunière.

Los Pollos, 7 Av and 4 C Poniente. The restaurant everyone loves to hate, home to assorted nocturnal Antiguan low-life. The soggy fries and deep, deep-fried chicken may not seem that tempting, but wait until you stumble out of a bar at midnight. Open 24hr.

Quesos y Vinos, 5 Av Norte 32. Very stylish Italian-owned restaurant with a reliable reputation for good homemade pasta and pizza, and wines from Europe and South America. Another branch, at 2 C Oriente and 2 Av Norte, is more atmospheric, and serves the same menu in a stunning location. Moderate.

Rainbow Café, 7 Av Sur 8. Relaxed bohemian atmosphere in this favourite travellers' hangout. Great vegetarian menu of creative salads and pasta dishes, epic smoothies and decent cappuccinos matched by friendly, prompt service. Also home to one of Antigua's best travel agents, a good secondhand bookshop, and regular musical jams.

Weiner, Alameda Santa Lucía 8. Especially good for a well-priced, filling breakfast, this restaurant also does lunchtime specials, serves good coffee and herbal teas and has an extensive selection of bottled European beers. Moderate.

Drinking and nightlife

Evening activity is officially curtailed in Antigua by a "dry law" which forbids the sale of alcohol after 1am. The places listed below on 5 and 7 Av Norte are particularly popular with the gringo crowd and all open at around 7pm. Antigua's club scene is limited to two venues; both tend to be quiet Monday to Wednesday, busy Thursday and heaving at weekends.

There are a number of small video cinemas that show a range of Western films on a daily basis – *Trainspotting*, *Salvador* and *Reservoir Dogs* are on almost permanently. Fliers with weekly listings are posted on noticeboards all over town. The main cinemas are: Cinemaya, 2 C Oriente 2; Cinema Bistro, 5 Av Norte 28; Cinema Tecún Umán, 6 C Poniente 34a; and inside the Proyecto Cultural El Sitio, 5 C Poniente 15.

Bars and clubs

La Canoa, 5 C Poniente between 4 & 5 avenidas. A small, unpretentious club where people come to dance to mainly Latin sounds. Merengue is the main ingredient, spiked with a dash of salsa and reggae; they also play a few tracks of western and Latin pop/rock. Good mix of locals and foreigners and reasonable drink prices. US$2 at weekends, free in the week.

La Casbah, 5 Av Norte 30. The most controversial place in town, attracting a well-heeled crowd from Antigua and Guatemala City. The venue, in the ruins of an ancient church, is spectacular and the music can occasionally match the site, with deep bassline-driven dance mixes. Now has a sister club in Guatemala City. Drinks are expensive. Mon–Thurs free, Fri & Sat around US$4.

La Chimanea, 7 Av Norte 7. One of the more popular bars, though the music selection is disturbingly eclectic – expect everything from Rod Stewart to Black Sabbath.

Macondo's, 5 Av Norte and 2 C Poniente. Probably the closest thing Antigua has to a pub, though the constant visual barrage of music videos spoils things somewhat. Closed Mon.

Picasso's, 7 Av Norte 16. Good drinking-hole that can get quite lively in high season. Usually closed Sun.

Riki's Bar, 4 Av Norte 4. Unquestionably the most happening place in town due to the excellent site inside *La Escudilla*, the jazz-only music policy and the unrivalled happy hour (7–9pm), which means this place is rammed most nights.

Listings

Banks and exchange Banco Industrial, 5 Av Sur 4, just south of the plaza (Mon–Fri 8.30am–7pm, Sat 8am–5pm), with a 24hr ATM for Visa cardholders; Banco del Agro, north side of the plaza, (Mon–Fri 9am–8pm, Sat 9am–6pm); Lloyds, in the northeast corner of the plaza (Mon–Fri 9am–5pm), which changes sterling travellers' cheques.

Bookstores Casa Andinista, 4 C Oriente 5A (☎8320161); Casa del Conde, on the west side of the plaza (☎8323322); Un Poco de Todo, also on the west side of the plaza. The Rainbow Reading Room, 7 Av Sur 8, has by far the largest selection of secondhand books.

Car and bike rental Tabarini, 2 C Poniente 19A (☎ & fax 8323091); Avis, 5 Av Norte 22 (☎ & fax 8322692). Both have similar prices with cars from around US$60 a day and jeeps from US$80, including unlimited mileage and insurance. Jopa, 6 Av Norte 3 (☎8320794), will rent motorbikes.

STUDYING SPANISH IN ANTIGUA

Antigua's **language-school** industry is big business, with a couple of dozen established schools, and many more less reliable set-ups, some operating in the front room of someone's house. Whether you're just stopping for a week or two to learn the basics, or settling in for several months in pursuit of total fluency, there can be no doubt that this is one of the best places in Latin America to learn Spanish: it's a beautiful, relaxed town, lessons are cheap and there are several superb schools. In addition, Guatemalan Spanish is clearly pronounced and has few local dialects. The only major drawback is that there are so many other students and tourists here that you'll probably end up spending your evenings speaking English. If this worries you then you might want to consider studying in a less touristy town – Quetzaltenango, Huehuetenango, Cobán and nearby Chimaltenango all have Spanish schools and fewer visitors.

Before making any decisions, you could drop into **Amerispan**, 6 Av Norte 40 (✆ & fax 8320164; in US ✆1-800/879-6640, fax 215/985-4524), which selects schools throughout Latin America to match the needs and requirements of students, and provides advice and support.

CHOOSING A SCHOOL

Though you can sign up for tuition only, most schools offer a weekly package that includes up to eight hours' one-on-one tuition a day and full board with a local family. Prices vary tremendously, from US$170 a week for the above deal at the top schools, down to as little as US$70 at a smaller school, though most schools will negotiate, particularly in the low season. Generally speaking you get what you pay for, with the more expensive schools offering the best programmes and most professional teachers.

The enthusiasm and aptitude of your teacher, of course, is paramount, and, even in the better schools, the quality of teaching staff can vary widely. If you are not happy with your teacher, ask for another; some programmes offer a different teacher each week. Before choosing a school, check how many other students will be sharing your house, as some schools pack as many as ten foreigners in with one family. It is also possible for students and teachers to go private, having met through a school: this brings the price down and enables the teacher to earn more, although it should only be done with the utmost discretion. Expect to pay US$5 an hour for a private lesson.

The tourist office in Antigua has a list of "approved schools", but this is as much a product of bribery and influence as a reflection of professional integrity. Note that the *Rigoberta Menchú* school has no connection at all with the Rigoberta or her foundation. The following schools are well-established, recommended and towards the top end of the price scale :

Tecún Umán Linguistic School, 6 C Poniente 34 (✆ & fax 8312792);
Projecto Lingüístico Francisco Marroquín, 7C Poniente 31 (✆8322886);
Centro Lingüístico Maya, 5 C Poniente 20 (✆ & fax 8320656);
Instituto Antigueno de Español, 1 C Poniente 33 (✆8322685);
Christian Spanish Academy, 6 Av Norte 15 (✆ & fax 8320367);
Sevilla, 1 Av Sur 8 (✆ & fax 8320442);
San José El Viejo, 5 Av Sur 34 (✆8323028, fax 8323029).

The following are little less expensive, but still professional and recommended:

APPE, 6 C Poniente 40 (✆8320720);
La Unión, 1 Av Sur 21 (✆ & fax 8320424);
Probigua, 6 Av Norte 41B (✆ & fax 8320860).

Finally, if you'd rather study with a private teacher, try one of the following:

Julia Solis – see noticeboard in *Doña Luisa's* at 4 C Oriente 12; **Rossalinda Rosales**, 1 C Poniente 17; **Gladys de Porras**, 7 Av Sur 8.

The Posada San Vincente, 6 Av Sur 6 (☎ & fax 8323311), and Aviatur, 5 Av Norte 27 (☎ & fax 8322642), both rent mountain bikes and charge around US$8 a day or US$25 weekly.

Laundry Rainbow Laundry at 6 Av Sur 15 (Mon–Sat 7am–7pm). A wash typically costs around US$2.

Libraries and cultural institutes El Sitio, 5 C Poniente 15 (☎8323037), has an active theatre, library and art gallery, and regularly hosts exhibitions and concerts; see the *Revue* or *Guatemala Weekly* for listings.

Medical care 24hr emergency service at the Santa Lucía Hospital, Calzada Santa Lucía Sur 7 (☎8323122). Also, Doctor Aceituno, who speaks good English, has his surgery at 2 C Poniente 7 (☎8320512).

Pharmacies Farmacia Santa María, west side of plaza (8am–10pm).

Police The police HQ is on the south side of the plaza, next to the tourist office (☎8320572). The tourist police are just off the plaza on 4 Av Norte.

Post office Alameda de Santa Lucía opposite the bus terminal (Mon–Fri 8am–4.30pm). DHL are at 6 C Sur 16 (☎8323718 or 8323732), and Quick Shipping is at 3 Av Norte 26 (☎8322595).

Supermarkets La Bodegona at 4 C Poniente, Alameda Santa Lucía.

Taxis On the east side of the plaza close to the cathedral, or call ☎8320526.

Telephones The Telgua office is half a block south of the plaza on 5 Av Sur (7am–10pm), but rates are higher here than anywhere else and you'll have to queue. For all communication services, including email, Conexión, in the La Fuente cultural centre at 4 C Oriente 14 (☎8323768), is probably the best-organized place in town. *Hotel San Francisco*, 1 Av Sur 15 (☎8323383; 24hr), also has competitive rates for email, fax and overseas phone calls. The very cheapest place in town to make international phone calls is at the CSA language school on 6 Av Norte 15 (☎8323922). Several offices, cafés, hotels and language schools will send your email. Try the internet café, *Cybermannia*, at 5 Av Norte 25B (☎8320162).

Travel agents There are dozens of travel agents in Antigua; the following are the most professional and reliable. The Rainbow Travel Center, 7 Av Sur 8 (Mon–Sat 9am–6pm; ☎8324202 or 8324203, fax 8324206) has some of the best deals in town, is fully computerized and the staff are friendly and efficient. Tivoli, at 5 Av Norte 10A, on the west side of the plaza (Mon–Sat 9am–1pm & 3–5.30pm; ☎8323041) is another recommended all-rounder. Monarcas, 6 Av Norte 60A (☎ & fax 8323343) is a highly recommended specialist agency with some fascinating Maya culture and ecology tours and trips to Semuc Champey and Copán. Adventure Travel Center Viareal, 5 Av Norte 25B (☎ & fax 8320162), is another excellent agent, particularly for adventure and sailing trips. Speak to them too if you need a shuttle bus.

Around Antigua

The countryside around Antigua is superbly fertile and breathtakingly beautiful. The valley is dotted with small villages, ranging from the ladino coffee centre of Alotenango to the traditional indígena village of Santa María de Jesús. None of them is more than an hour away and all make interesting day-trips. For the more adventurous, the volcanic peaks of Agua, Acatenango and Fuego offer strenuous but superb hiking, best done through a specialist agency. For details on climbing Pacaya, near Guatemala City, see p.307.

Santa María de Jesús and the Volcán de Agua

Up above Antigua, a smooth new sealed road snakes through the coffee bushes and past the village of San Juan del Obispo before arriving in **SANTA MARÍA DE JESÚS**, starting point for the ascent of the Volcán de Agua. Perched high on the shoulder of the volcano, the village is some 500m above Antigua, with magnificent views over the Panchoy valley and east towards the smoking cone of Pacaya. The village was founded at the end of the sixteenth century and is of little interest, though the women wear beautiful purple *huipiles*. Buses run from Antigua to Santa María every hour or so from 6am to 5pm, and the trip takes thirty minutes.

Agua is the easiest and by far the most popular of Guatemala's big cones to climb: on some Saturday nights hundreds of people spend the night at the top. It's an exciting ascent with a fantastic view to reward you at the summit. The trail starts in Santa María de Jesús (see opposite). To reach it, head straight across the plaza, between the two ageing pillars, and up the street opposite the church doors. Take a right turn just before the end and then continue past the cemetery and out of the village. From here on it's a fairly simple climb on a clear path, cutting across the road that goes some of the way up. The climb can take anything from four to six hours and the peak, at 3766m, is always cold at night. There is shelter (though not always room) in a small chapel at the summit, however, and the views certainly make it worth the struggle.

Ciudad Vieja and San Antonio Aguas Calientes

To the south of Antigua, the Panchoy valley is a broad sweep of farmland, overshadowed by three volcanic cones and covered with olive-green coffee bushes. A single road runs out this way, eventually reaching Escuintla and the Pacific coast, and passing a string of villages as it goes. **Minibuses** from the terminal in Antigua run a regular service to Ciudad Vieja, San Antonio and Santa Catarina.

The first place of interest, 5km from Antigua, is **CIUDAD VIEJA**, a scruffy and unhurried village with a distinguished past: it was near here that the Spanish established their second capital, **Santiago de los Caballeros**, in 1527. Within twenty years the new capital had a cathedral, monasteries, farms and a school, but while the rest of the conquistadors were settling in, their leader, Alvarado was off seeking wealth in Mexico, Peru and Spain. In 1541 he set out for the Spice Islands, travelling via Jalisco where he met his end, crushed to death beneath a rolling horse. When news of his death reached his wife **Doña Beatriz**, at home in Santiago, she plunged the capital into an extended period of mourning, staining the entire palace with black clay, inside and out. On the morning of September 9, 1541, she became the first woman to govern in the Americas, but before the night of her inauguration was out, an earthquake struck, and from the crater of the Volcán de Agua a great wave of mud and water slid down, sweeping away the capital and killing Doña Beatriz.

Today there's no trace of the original city, and all that remains from that time is a solitary tree, in a corner of the plaza, which bears a plaque commemorating the site of the first mass ever held in Guatemala. The plaza also boasts an eighteenth-century colonial church that has recently been restored. The exact centre of the original city is still the subject of some debate, but the general consensus puts it about 2km to the east of Ciudad Vieja.

Down a branch road, 3km west from Ciudad Vieja, the village of **SAN ANTONIO AGUAS CALIENTES** is set to one side of a steep-sided bowl beneath the peak of Acatenango. San Antonio is famous for its weaving, characterized by complex floral and geometric patterns, and on the stalls in the plaza you can find a complete range of the local output. This is also a good place to learn the traditional craft of back-strap weaving; if you're interested, the best way to find out about possible tuition is by simply asking the women in the plaza.

Adjoining San Antonio is the village of **SANTA CATARINA**, which has a superb ruined colonial church. Out on the edge of the village there's also a small **swimming pool** (Tues–Sun 9am–6pm) – the perfect place for a chilly dip. To get to the pool, walk along San Antonio's main street until you come to the plaza in Santa Catarina and continue up the street that goes up the far side of the church. Turn left at the end and you'll come to the pool on the right, in five minutes or so.

San Andrés Itzapa

The main road from Antigua to Chimaltenango ascends from the Panchoy valley, past dusty farming villages, before a dirt track branches off to **SAN ANDRÉS ITZAPA**, one of the many villages badly hit by the 1976 earthquake. San Andrés is home to to the cult of **San Simón** (or Maximón), the "evil saint", who is housed in his own pagan chapel. Despite San Andrés being just 18km from Antigua, few tourists visit this shrine, and you may feel less intrusive and more welcome here than his other places of abode, Zunil (see p.356) and Santiago Atitlán (p.347). Once you've tracked him down, you'll find that Maximón lives in a fairly strange world, his image surrounded by drunken men, cigar-smoking women and hundreds of burning candles, each symbolizing a request: red for love, white for health, and so on. Local stores stock candles and incense and there are also books on witchcraft for sale. Uniquely in Guatemala, this San Simón attracts a largely ladino congregation and he is particularly popular with prostitutes.

If you want to visit San Simón you have to do so between sunrise and sunset, as the Maya believe he sleeps at other times. Head for the central plaza from the dirt road into the village, turn right when you reach the church, walk two blocks, then up a little hill and you should spot street vendors selling charms, incense and candles. If you get lost, just ask for the "Casa de San Simón".

Inside the dimly lit shrine, the walls are adorned with hundreds of plaques from all over Guatemala and Central America, thanking San Simón for his help. You may be offered a *limpia*, or soul cleansing, which, for a small fee, involves being beaten by one of the resident women workers with a bushel of herbs. A bottle of the firewater *aguardiente* is also demolished: some is offered to San Simón, some of it you'll have to drink yourself and the rest is consumed by the attendant, who sprays you with alcohol (from her mouth) for your sins – all in all, quite an experience.

To get to **San Andrés Itzapa** from Antigua, take any bus heading to Chimaltenango from the terminal (every 20min, 5.30am–7pm) and get the driver to drop you off where the dirt road leaves the highway. From there you can hitch or else it's a thirty-minute walk.

MOVING ON FROM ANTIGUA

Because of its small size, and due to its position off the Interamericana, few bus routes originate in Antigua. If you're heading to anywhere in the east of the country, take the first bus to Guatemala City and change there. If you're heading into the western highlands it's usually best to catch the first bus to Chimaltenango (see p.328) and get another connection there. The main bus destinations are as follows:

Guatemala City (1hr). A constant flow of buses leaves for the capital (4am–7pm, except Sun 6am–7pm)

Ciudad Vieja (20min)

Chimaltenango (40min)

Escuintla via El Rodeo (2 daily; 2hr 30min)

Panajachel (1 daily at 7am; 2hr 30 min)

San Antonio Aguas Calientes (every 30min; 30min)

Santa María de Jesús (every 30 min; 20 min)

SHUTTLES

Bus services between Antigua, Guatemala City, Panajachel and Chichicastenango are supplemented by several "tourist shuttle" services, the best of which are organized by the Turansa and Adventure Travel Viareal travel agencies (see Listings, p.318, for details). Shuttles are a lot more expensive than the public buses but much more comfortable and quicker. There are frequent airport and Guatemala City shuttles for around US$7; Chichicastanango (around US$12) is well served on market days (Thursday and Sunday); and there less frequent services to Panajachel (around US$18). For Copán in Honduras (around US$35), try Monarcas (see p.318). Shuttles to the Río Dulce (around US$25) and Monterrico (US$25) run at weekends when there is enough demand. Just about any travel agent in Antigua will book you a shuttle; other recommended agencies are also detailed in Listings on p.318.

CHAPTER EIGHT

THE WESTERN HIGHLANDS AND PACIFIC COAST

The **western highlands** are considered by most visitors – and most Guatemalans – to be the most beautiful and captivating part of the entire country. Stretching from the outskirts of the capital to the Mexican border, the area is defined by two main features: the awesome chain of sentinel-like volcanoes that define the southern side and the towering bulk of the **Cuchumatanes** mountain range that rises from the tropical plains to the north. Between the two is a bewitching pattern of twisting, pine-forested ridges, lakes, gushing streams and deep valleys. These highlands are the heartland of the **Maya**, who have lived here for over two thousand years, and it is their incredibly rich culture that gives the region its unique identity.

Beneath the volcanoes, a world away from the cool mountain air and unhurried pace of the highlands, is the steamy **Pacific coast**, known to Guatemalans as La Costa Sur. This is ladino country, a flat featureless landscape of huge farm plantations, bustling towns and largely disappointing beach resorts. The sticky lowland climate, dangerous sea currents and poor facilities unsurprisingly attract few tourists, but there are a couple of important archeological sites and also one pleasant resort, **Monterrico**, with a network of swamps, home to all kinds of wildlife including sea turtles.

The western highlands and Pacific coast may be poles apart climatically and culturally, but historically both regions have been interlinked since the earliest times. With the lofty peaks of the highlands blocking an easy entry route into Guatemala to the north, anyone trying to invade the country, from the first hunter-gatherers to the **Spanish conquistadors**, entered to the south, along the coast. The early ancestors of the Maya moved down the narrow Pacific coastal plain from Mexico and settled in villages along the coast before heading inland and establishing the first city of the Maya World, **Kaminaljuyú**, at a site close to Guatemala City. Alvarado and the conquistadors followed a similar path into Guatemala in 1523, before defeating the Quiché Maya near the highland town of Quetzaltenango.

The Spanish had little time for the hostile climate of the Pacific coast and the region remained largely undeveloped until independence, when the land was cleared for farming and huge agricultural **fincas** were established. Coffee bushes were planted on the lower slopes of the mountains and cotton and sugar cane in the lowlands. With insufficient local labour to work the fincas, thousands of highland Maya were forcibly recruited (by presidential decree) to toil in the coastal heat in appalling conditions. Today their

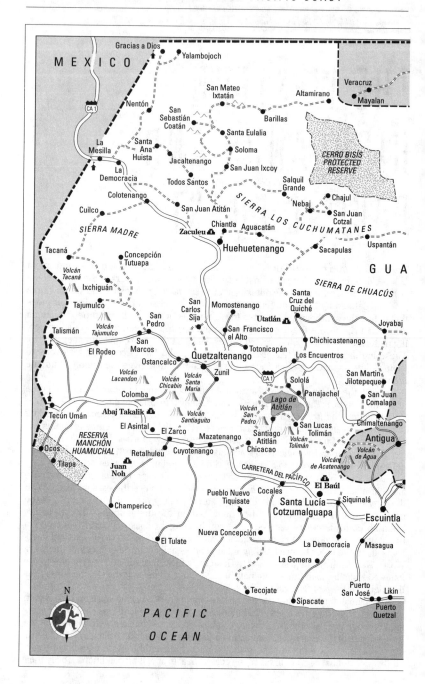

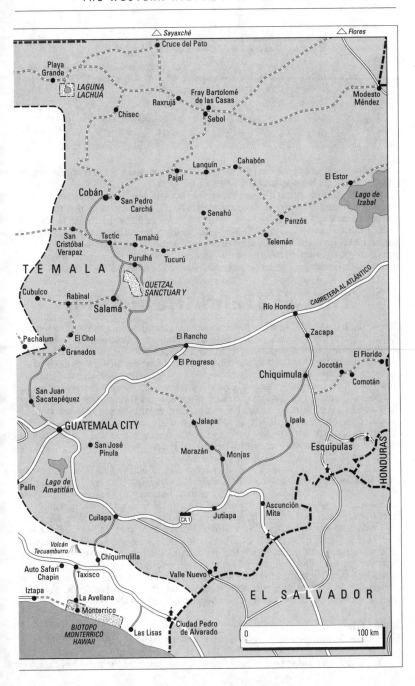

ACCOMMODATION PRICE CODES

All the accommodation listed in this book has been categorized into one of nine price bands, as set out below. The prices quoted are in US dollars and refer to the cheapest room available for two people sharing in high season.

① under US$5	④ US$15–25	⑦ US$60–80
② US$5–10	⑤ US$25–40	⑧ US$80–100
③ US$10–15	⑥ US$40–60	⑨ over US$100

---

descendants still migrate to the Pacific coast for seasonal work out of economic necessity, and many die from malaria and pesticide poisoning.

Two main **highways** cut through the region, both thick with thundering trucks and buses, so getting around is very easy. In the south, the nation's fastest route, the **Carretera al Pacífico** runs close to all the major lowland towns between the border with El Salvador and the town of Tecún Umán on the Mexican frontier. The **Carretera Interamericana** to the north is of more interest to travellers as it scythes a serpentine path through some spectacular mountain scenery, passing on the way, the major junctions of Chimaltenango, Los Encuentros and Cuatro Caminos.

THE WESTERN HIGHLANDS

The strength of the Maya culture in the western highlands and its outstanding beauty, studded with volcanoes, deep river valleys and possibly the most beautiful lake in the world, **Lago de Atitlán**, make this region Guatemala's primary attraction. It's a land blessed with tremendous fertility but cursed by instability: the hills are regularly shaken by earthquakes and occasionally showered by volcanic eruptions. Of the thirteen cones that loom over the western highlands, three volcanoes are still active: **Pacaya**, **Fuego** and **Santiaguito**. Two major **fault lines** also cut through the area, making earthquakes a regular occurrence. The most recent major quake in 1976 was centred around **Chimaltenango** – it left 25,000 dead and around a million homeless. But despite its sporadic ferocity, the landscape is outstandingly beautiful and the atmosphere is calm and welcoming, with irrigated valleys and terraced hillsides carefully crafted to yield the maximum potential farmland.

The highland landscape is controlled by many factors, all of which affect its appearance. Perhaps the most important is **altitude**. At lower levels the vegetation is almost tropical, supporting dense forests, **coffee**, **cotton**, **bananas** and **cacao**, while higher up, the hills are often wrapped in cloud and the ground is sometimes hard with frost. Here trees are stunted by the cold, and **maize** and potatoes are grown alongside grazing herds of sheep and goats. The **seasons** also play their part. In the rainy season, from May to October, the land is superbly green, with young crops and lush forests of **pine**, **cedar** and **oak**, while during the dry months the hillsides gradually turn to a dusty yellow. You'll find no matter what the time of year that the climate is benign: the days are pleasurably warm, but rarely hot, and the evenings are mild. In a few spots the climate is decidedly different, though, such as in the high-altitude town of Quetzaltenango, where it gets very chilly between November and February.

Some history

The earliest known people to settle in the western highlands are thought to have arrived from the arid Mexican lands to the north, establishing small villages in the region by 2500 BC. These people were farmers, who cultivated the same basic staples as today's **Maya** – corn, beans, squash and chillies – and who almost certainly spoke a proto-Maya language. This area was to remain peripheral and sparsely populated throughout the Classic era, while in the northern lowlands (today's Petén), glorious monuments were constructed and scientific and artistic achievements accomplished.

The highlands were undoubtedly dominated by **Kaminaljuyú** (see p.302), just outside today's Guatemala City, which controlled trade routes and was closely aligned with the mighty city of Teotihuacán to the north. Towards the end of the eleventh century, the highlands were invaded by **Toltecs** from the north, who established themselves as an elite ruling class. Under Toltec domination, a number of rival centres emerged, based on tribal and linguistic divisions. The most powerful tribes were the **Quiché**, with their capital at Utatlán; the **Mam** centred at Zaculeu and the **Cakchiquel**, based at Iximché.

Though pre-conquest life was certainly hard, the **arrival of the Spanish** in 1523 was a total disaster for the Maya population. In the early stages, **Alvarado** and his army met with a force of Quiché warriors in the Quetzaltenango basin and defeated them in open warfare. Alvarado is said to have slain the great Quiché warrior, **Tecún Umán**, himself. The Spanish made their first permanent base at **Iximché**, the capital of their Cakchiquel Maya allies, but this uneasy alliance was to last only a few years. Alvarado then moved to a site near the modern town of Antigua, today called Ciudad Vieja, from where the Spanish gradually brought the rest of the highlands under a degree of control. The damage done by Spanish swords, however, was nothing when compared to that of the **diseases** they introduced. Waves of smallpox, typhus, plague and measles swept through the indigenous population, reducing their numbers by as much as ninety percent in the worst-hit areas.

In the long term, the **Spanish administration** of the western highlands was no gentler than the Conquest, as indigenous labour became the backbone of the Spanish empire. Guatemala offered little of the gold and silver that was available in Peru or Mexico, but there was still money to be made from **cacao** and **indigo**. As well as being the heart of Spanish Guatemala, Antigua served as the administrative centre for the whole of Central America and Chiapas (now in Mexico). In 1773, however, it was destroyed by a massive earthquake and the capital was subsequently moved to its modern site.

The departure of the Spanish in 1821 and subsequent **independence** brought little change at village level. Ladino authority replaced that of the Spanish, but Maya were still required to work the coastal plantations, and when labour supplies dropped off they were simply press-ganged and forced to work, often in horrific conditions. It's a state of affairs that has changed little even today, and remains a major burden on the indígena population.

In the late 1970s, **guerrilla movements** began to develop in opposition to military rule, seeking support from the indigenous population and establishing themselves in the western highlands. The Maya became the victims in this process, caught between the guerrillas and the army. A total of 440 villages were destroyed; thousands died and thousands more fled the country, seeking refuge in Mexico. In recent years indigenous society has also been besieged by a tidal wave of American **evangelical churches** whose influence undermines local hierarchies, dividing communities and threatening to destroy Maya culture.

Today, with the signing of the 1996 **Peace Accords**, tensions have lifted and there is evidence of a new spirit of self-confidence within the highland Maya population. Some fundamental problems still remain – poverty, racism and the still unsettled issue of **land reform** – but there is a reawakened sense of pride in Maya identity. Despite intense pressure, the traditional structures of society are still in place. Rejecting ladino commercialism, the Maya see trade as a social function as much as an economic one. Conservative and inward-looking, they live in a world centred on the village, with its

MARKET DAYS

Make an effort to catch as many market days as possible – they're second only to local fiestas in offering a glimpse of a way of life unchanged for centuries.

Monday: San Juan Atitán; Zunil.

Tuesday: Chajul; Patzún; San Lucas Tolimán; San Marcos; Totonicapán.

Wednesday: Cotzal; Huehuetenango; Momostenango.

Thursday: Aguacatán; Chichicastenango; Chimaltenango; Jacaltenango; Nebaj; Panajachel; Sacapulas; San Mateo Ixtatán; Santa Cruz del Quiché; Soloma; Totonicapán; Uspantán.

Friday: Chajul; San Francisco el Alto; Santiago Atitlán; San Andrés Itzapa; Sololá.

Saturday: Cotzal; Santa Clara La Laguna; Santa Cruz del Quiché; Todos Santos; Totonicapán.

Sunday: Aguacatán; Chichicastenango; Huehuetenango; Jacaltenango; Joyabaj; Momostenango; Nebaj; Nahualá; Panajachel; Sacapulas; San Juan Comalapa; San Pedro Sacatepéquez; Santa Cruz del Quiché; Santa Eulalia; Soloma; Uspantán.

own civil and religious hierarchy. Subsistence farming of maize and beans remains at its heart, and the land its life-blood.

Where to go

Almost everywhere in the western highlands is of interest to the traveller. The landscape is exceptionally beautiful, dotted with highland villages of adobe houses and whitewashed colonial churches. **Lago de Atitlán** is unmissable – a lake of astounding natural beauty ringed by volcanoes and some of the most traditional Maya villages in all Guatemala. **Chichicastenango**, a sleepy highland town steeped in Maya/Catholic tradition, has perhaps the most famous market in the country. At the **markets of Sololá** and **San Francisco el Alto** there is little for the Western traveller to buy, but the pleasure is in the sights and smells and in soaking up the atmosphere. It's also worth trying to check out a few of the smaller-scale markets throughout the region (see box above), if only to buy some fruit, take a photograph or two and enjoy the relaxed atmosphere.

For real adventure, spectacular scenery and myriad hiking possibilities, the **Ixil triangle** in northern Quiché and the countryside around **Todos Santos** in the Cuchumatanes are unmatched. Both are remote, intensely traditional areas that lie at the end of tortuous bus journeys; both suffered terribly in the civil war. Much easier to get to are the villages around **Quetzaltenango** (Xela), Guatemala's second city. Though Xela itself is a fairly unexciting provincial centre, it has some first-class **Spanish schools** and, within easy reach, you'll find the villages of Zunil and San Francisco el Alto, the hot springs of Fuentes Georginas and the climbable near-perfect cone of the Santa María volcano. Trekking trips to the beautiful crater lake on top of the Chicabal volcano and to Tajumulco, Guatemala's highest peak, can also be arranged in Quetzaltenango.

The scenery, villages and Maya culture are the main attractions in the highlands, but there are also interesting **historical Maya ruins**: Iximché, the pre-conquest city of the Cakchiquel, the Quiché stronghold of **Utatlán**, and the Mam city of **Zaculeu**. There are also hundreds of assorted smaller sites, many still actively used for Maya religious ritual and ceremony. These ancient cities don't bear comparison to Tikal, Copán and the lowland centres, but they're fascinating nevertheless.

The **Carretera Interamericana** is the main transport artery, served by a constant flow of buses. If you want to get to more remote areas, however, you'll have to use the

TOURIST CRIME

While there is no need to be paranoid, visitors to the highlands, especially the heavily touristed areas should be aware that **crime against tourists** – including robbery and rape – is a problem. Pay close attention to security reports from your embassy and follow the usual precautions with extra care. Though there have been very few attacks on hikers in the Lago de Atitlán area recently, it's still safer to walk in a group. Similarly, don't amble around Panajachel alone late at night. In the more remote highlands, where foreigners are a much rarer sight, attacks are extremely uncommon.

slow and uncomfortable dirt roads, especially in northern Quiché and Huehuetenango. Fortunately there is always the the mountain scenery to help cushion the ride. The most practical plan of action is to base yourself in one of the larger places and then make a series of day-trips to markets and fiestas, although even the smallest of villages will usually offer some kind of accommodation.

The Carretera Interamericana

Leaving Guatemala City, the serpentine Carretera Interamericana cuts right through the western highlands as far as the border with Mexico. In its entirety this road stretches from Alaska to Chile (with a short break in southern Panamá), and here in Guatemala it forms the main artery of transport in the highlands. As you travel around, the highway and its junctions will inevitably become familiar, since, wherever you're going, it's invariably easiest to catch the first local bus to the Carretera Interamericana and then flag down one of the buses heading along the highway. Along the route you'll see kerbside stalls set up by subsistence farmers selling surplus fruit and vegetables and you'll pass giant billboards brandishing tobacco company slogans – "*Para ganadores*" (For winners) – and assorted political graffiti.

Heading west from the capital, you'll climb steadily up a three-laned highway to San Lucas Sacatepéquez, from where a well-maintained side road descends to Antigua. There are three further major junctions on the Carretera Interamericana, which you'll soon get to know well. The first of these is **Chimaltenango**, an important town and capital of its own department; from its ugly sprawl along the highway you can also make connections to or from Antigua. Continuing west, **Los Encuentros** is the next main junction, where one road heads off to the north for Chichicastenango and Santa Cruz del Quiché and another branches south to Panajachel and Lago de Atitlán. Beyond this the highway climbs high over a mountainous ridge before dropping to **Cuatro Caminos**, from where side roads lead to Quetzaltenango, Totonicapán and San Francisco el Alto. The Carretera Interamericana continues on to Huehuetenango before it reaches the Mexican border at La Mesilla. Virtually every bus travelling along the highway will stop at all of these junctions and you'll be able to buy fruit, drink and fast food from a resident army of vendors, some of whom will storm the bus looking for business, while others are content to dangle their wares in front of your window.

After leaving Guatemala City, the first place of interest is **SANTIAGO SACATEPÉQUEZ**, 1km or so to the north of the highway. The road branches off from San Lucas Sacatepéquez and buses shuttle back and forth along the branch road. If you're in Guatemala at the right time of year, the day to visit Santiago is November 1, when there is a local fiesta to honour the **Day of the Dead**. Massive kites made from paper and tobacco are flown in the cemetery to release the souls of the dead from their agony. The festival is immensely popular, and hundreds of Guatemalans and tourists come every year to watch the spectacle. Teams of young men struggle to get the kites aloft while the crowd looks on with bated breath, rushing for cover if a kite comes crashing to the ground. There is also a **market** in Santiago on Tuesday and Sunday.

Chimaltenango

Founded by Pedro de Portocarrero in 1526, on the site of the Cakchiquel centre of Bokoh, **CHIMALTENANGO** was later considered as a possible site for the new capital. It has the misfortune, however, of being positioned on the continental divide and it suffered terribly from the earthquake in 1976, which shook and flattened much of the surrounding area. Today's town, its centre just to the north of the main road, is dominated by that fact, with dirt streets, breeze-block walls and an air of weary desperation. The town extracts what little business it can from the stream of traffic on the Carretera Interamericana, and the roadside is crowded with cheap comedores, mechanics' workshops, and sleazy bars that become brothels by night. "Chimal" is also home to a good new **Spanish school** where you can live and study away from the gringo scene of Antigua, but within firing range if you need to catch a film or have a meal. The Spanish and Maya Language School of Chimaltenango, 9 C final, Lote 23, Quintas Los Aposentos 1 (☎ & fax 8391492), is staffed by ex-Peace Corps teachers and supports good local causes. **Buses** passing through Chimaltenango run to all points along the Carretera Interamericana. For Antigua they leave every twenty minutes between 5.30am and 6.30pm from the market in town – though you can also wait at the turn-off on the highway.

To the north of Chimaltenango a rough dirt road runs through 19km of plunging ravines and pine forests to the village of **SAN MARTÍN JILOTEPEQUE**. The village remains badly scarred by the 1976 disaster, but the sprawling Sunday market is well worth a visit and the weaving here, the women's *huipiles* especially, is some of the finest you'll see – with intricate and ornate patterning, predominantly in reds and purples. **Buses** to San Martín leave the market in Chimaltenango every hour or so from 4am to 2pm, the last one returning at about 3pm, and the trip takes around an hour.

Tecpán and the ruins of Iximché

Continuing west along a fast section of the Carretera Interamericana, the next site of interest lies close to the small town of **TECPÁN**, ninety minutes or so from Guatemala City. This may well have been the site chosen by Alvarado as the first Spanish capital, to which the Spanish forces retreated in August 1524 after they'd been driven out of Iximché. Today it's a place of no great interest, though it has a substantial number of restaurants and guest houses. It caters for a mainly Guatemalan clientele who come to picnic at the ruins and drink and eat in town.

The **ruins of Iximché** (daily 8am–5pm; US$4), the pre-conquest capital of the Cakchiquel, are about 5km south of Tecpán on a beautiful exposed hillside, protected on three sides by steep slopes and surrounded by pine forests. From the early days of the Conquest, the Cakchiquel allied themselves with the conquistadors, so the structures here suffered less than most at the hands of the Spanish. Since then, however, time and weather have taken their toll and the majority of the buildings that housed a population of 10,000 have disappeared, leaving only a few stone-built pyramids, clearly defined plazas and a couple of ball courts. Nevertheless, the site is strongly atmospheric and its grassy plazas, ringed with pine trees, are marvellously peaceful, especially during the week, when you may well have the place to yourself. The ruins are still actively used as a focus for Maya worship: sacrifices and offerings take place down a small trail through the pine trees behind the final plaza. There is also a small **museum** (same hours, no additional charge) at the entrance to the site with a jumbled collection of stone carvings, photographs and information (in Spanish only) about Iximché.

To **get here**, you can take any bus travelling along the Carretera Interamericana between Chimaltenango and Los Encuentros and ask to be dropped at Tecpán; the centre of the town is about 1km from the main highway. To get to the ruins, simply walk through Tecpán and out the other side of the plaza, passing the *Centro de Salud*, and follow the road through the fields for 5.5km – an hour or so on foot. With any luck you'll be able to hitch some of the way, particularly at weekends when the road can be fairly busy. There's **camping** at the site, but bring your own food as the small shop sells little other than drinks. Iximché's shady location is perfect for a picnic or barbecue. If you're not planning to camp, be back on the Carretera Interamericana before 6pm to be sure of a bus onwards.

Chichicastenango

The road for Chichicastenango and the **department of El Quiché** leaves the Carretera Interamericana at the **Los Encuentros** junction, another 30km past the Iximché turn-off. Heading north from Los Encuentros, the highway drops down through dense, aromatic pine forests, plunging into a deep ravine before bottoming out by a tributary of the Motagua river.

Continuing upwards around endless switchbacks, the road eventually reaches **CHICHICASTENANGO**, Guatemala's "*mecca del turismo*". If it's market day, you may get embroiled in one of the country's very few traffic jams – a rare event outside the

capital – as traders, tourists and locals all struggle to reach the town centre. In this compact and traditional town of cobbled streets, adobe houses and red-tiled roofs, the calm of day-to-day life is shattered on a twice-weekly basis by the **Sunday and Thursday markets** – Sunday is the busiest. The market attracts hordes of tourists and commercial traders, as well as Maya weavers from throughout the central highlands.

The market is by no means all that sets Chichicastenango apart, however. For the local Maya population it's an important centre of culture and religion. The area was inhabited by the Cakchiquel long before the arrival of the Spanish and, over the years, Maya culture and folk-Catholicism have been treated with a rare degree of respect – although inevitably this blessing has been mixed with waves of arbitrary persecution and exploitation. Today, the town has an incredible collection of Maya artefacts, parallel indígena and ladino governments and a church that makes no effort to disguise its acceptance of unconventional pagan worship. Traditional weaving is also adhered to here and the women wear superb, heavily embroidered *huipiles*. The men's costume of short trousers and jackets of black wool embroidered with silk is highly distinguished, although it's very expensive to make and these days most men opt for Western dress.

However, for the town's **fiesta** (December 14–21), at Easter and on Sundays, a handful of *cofradías* (elders of the religious hierarchy) still wear traditional clothing and carry spectacular silver processional crosses and incense burners. The fiesta, while not the most spontaneous, is certainly one of the most spectacular, and has attractions including a massive procession, live bands, traditional dances, clouds of incense, gallons of *chicha* (a home-brewed alcohol), endless deafening fireworks and the *Palo Volador* (in which men dangle by ropes from a twenty-metre pole). On the final day, all babies born in the previous year are brought to the church for christening.

Arrival and information

There's no bus station in Chichi, but the corner of 5 C and 5 Av operates loosely as a terminal. **Buses** heading between Guatemala City and Santa Cruz del Quiché pass through Chichicastenango every half-hour, stopping in town for a few minutes to load up with passengers. In Guatemala City, buses leave from the terminal in Zona 4, from 4am to about 5pm. Coming from Antigua, you can pick up a bus easily in Chimaltenango. From Panajachel, you can take any bus up to Los Encuentros and change there; or on market days there are several direct buses, supplemented by a steady flow of special tourist shuttles run by various companies. There are also special shuttle services from Antigua on market days.

If you're bitten by market fever and need to **change money**, there's no problem in Chichi, even on a Sunday. Try Banco Ejercito on 6 C (Tues–Sun 9am–5pm) or, almost opposite, Banco Industrial (Mon 10–2pm, Wed–Sun 10am–5pm) for Visa card holders. *Hotel Santo Tomás* also offers exchange. The **post office** (Mon–Fri 9am–5.30pm) and **Telgua** (daily 7am–8pm) are both on 6 Av, up behind the church.

Accommodation

Hotels can be in short supply on Saturday nights, but you shouldn't have a problem on other days. Prices can also be inflated on market days, but at other times you can usually negotiate a good deal.

Hospedaje Girón, 6 C 4–52 (☎7561156). Rooms are pretty, clean and well priced, either with or without private bath. Good value for single travellers. ③.

Hospedaje el Salvador, 5 Av 10–09 (☎7561329). Best budget deal in town, with a vast warren of rooms, a bizarre external colour scheme, and cheap prices. Insist that the owners turn on the hot water. ②.

Hotel Bella Vista 4 Av, heading north out of town (☎2041097). New small-scale pensión with spotless rooms and adjoining bathrooms. ③.

Hotel Chugüilá, 5 Av 5–24 (☎ & fax 7561134). Attractive rooms, all on different levels and some with fireplaces. Lovely greenery and pot plants everywhere. Secure parking. ④–⑤.

Hotel Posada Belen, 12 C 5–55 (☎7561244). Not the most attractive rooms, though half have private bathrooms; the views are good from the back. ②.

Hotel Santo Tomás, 7 Av 5–32 (☎7561061, fax 7561306). Very comfortable, well-appointed rooms set around two colonial-style courtyards. Rooms 29–37 are the ones to book if you can – they have great mountain views. Restaurant, swimming pool, sauna and jacuzzi. ⑦.

Maya Inn, 8 C and 3 Av (☎7561176, fax 7561212). Chichi's oldest tourist hotel offers very comfortable rooms with old-fashioned period charm. Though its character is undeniable, prices are a bit steep. ⑧.

The Town

Though most visitors come here for the market, Chichicastenango also offers an unusual insight into traditional religious practices in the highlands. At the main **Santo Tomás Church**, in the southeast corner of the plaza, the Quiché Maya have been left to adopt their own style of worship, blending pre-Columbian and Catholic rituals. The church was built in 1540 on the site of a Maya altar, and rebuilt in the eighteenth century. It's said that indigenous locals became interested in worshipping here after Francisco Ximénez, the priest from 1701 to 1703, started reading their holy book, the **Popol Vuh**.

Don't enter the building by the front door, which is reserved for *cofrades* and senior church officials; use the **side door** instead and be warned that taking **photographs** inside the building is considered deeply offensive – don't even contemplate it. Before entering the church, it's customary to make offerings in a fire at the base of the steps or to burn incense in perforated cans, a practice that leaves a cloud of thin, sweet smoke hanging over the entrance. Inside is an astonishing scene of avid worship. A soft hum of constant murmuring fills the air as the faithful kneel to place candles on low-level stone platforms for their ancestors and the saints. For these people, the entire building is alive with the souls of the dead, each located in a specific part of the church. Ronald Wright described the scene in his fascinating book, *Time Among the Maya*:

> A large semicircular flight of stone steps leads to the front door; and these steps are a sacred stage like the huge stairways of the ancient pyramids. Here the senior shaman-priests burn clouds of incense and arrangements of candles to Mundo and the ancestors. These men are "chuchkahau" (mother-fathers), heads of their lineages, guardians of calendrical knowledge, and rememberers of the dead. Many of their forebears are buried beneath this church: every portion of the steps and the floor inside is dedicated to the founders of families, going back in some cases to the ancient Quiché kings.

Beside the church is a former monastery, now used by the parish administration. It was here that the Spanish priest Francisco Ximénez became the first outsider to be shown the Popol Vuh. His copy of the manuscript is now housed in the Newberry Library in Chicago: the original was lost some time later in the eighteenth century. The text itself was written just to the north of here, in Utatlán, shortly after the arrival of the Spanish, and is a brilliant poem of over nine thousand lines that details the cosmology, mythology and traditional history of the Quiché.

On the south side of the plaza, on market day often hidden by stalls, the **Rossbach Museum** (Tues, Wed, Fri & Sat 8am–noon & 2–4pm, Thurs & Sun 8am–1pm & 2–4pm, US$0.20) houses a broad-ranging collection of pre-Columbian artefacts, mostly small pieces of ceramics, jade jewellery and stone carvings, some as old as two thousand years, that had been kept by local people in their homes.

THE CEMETERY AND THE SHRINE OF PASCUAL ABAJ

The town **cemetery**, down the hill behind El Calvario, offers further evidence of the strange mix of religions that characterizes Chichicastenango. The graves are marked by anything from a grand tomb to a small earth mound and in the centre is a Maya shrine where the usual offerings of incense and alcohol are made.

The church and cemetery are certainly not the only scenes of Maya religious activity: the hills that surround the town, like so many throughout the country, are topped with shrines. The closest of these, less than a kilometre from the plaza, is known as **Pascual Abaj**. Although the site is regularly visited by tourists, it's important to remember that any ceremony you witness is deeply serious and you should keep your distance and be sensitive about taking any photographs. The shrine is laid out in a typical pattern with several small altars facing a stern pre-Columbian sculpture. Offerings are usually overseen by a *brujo* (a type of shaman) and range from flowers to sacrificed chickens, always incorporating plenty of incense, alcohol and incantations.

To get to Pascual Abaj, walk down the hill beside the Santo Tomás church, take the first right, 9 Calle, and follow this as it winds its way out of town. You'll soon cross a stream and then a well-signposted route takes you through the courtyard of a workshop that churns out wooden masks. If you look up, you might see a thin plume of smoke if there's a ceremony in progress. The path continues uphill for ten minutes through a dense pine forest.

Eating

If you've come from Panajachel or Antigua, the dining scene here may come as a bit of a shock to the system. You won't find sushi or Thai curries in Chichi, just simple, good-value Guatemalan comedor food. The plaza on **market day** is the place to come for authentic highland eating: try one of the makeshift food stalls, where you'll find cauldrons of stew, rice and beans.

Buenadventura, upper floor, inside the Centro Comercial. Bird's-eye view of the vegetable market; simple, no-nonsense food and the breakfasts are the cheapest in town.

Café La Villa de Los Cofrades, in the Centro Comercial on the north side of the plaza. Good set meals – soup, a main dish and salad, fries and bread – for under US$4. The breakfasts are also superb.

Comedor Gumarcaj, opposite the *Hotel Santo Tomás*. Simple, cheap and friendly comedor that serves up a mean chicken and chips and lush licuados.

La Fonda del Tzijolaj, upper floor in the Centro Comercial. Yes, the name's unpronounceable, but the food is probably the best in town and the balcony views of the church of Santo Tomás and the market are excellent. Try the delicious chiles rellenos.

Santa Cruz del Quiché and around

The capital of the Department of El Quiché, **SANTA CRUZ DEL QUICHÉ** lies half an hour north of Chichicastenango. A good paved road connects the two towns, running through pine forests and ravines, and past the **Laguna Lemoa**, a lake which, according to local legend, was originally filled with tears wept by the wives of Quiché kings after their husbands had been slaughtered by the Spanish. Santa Cruz del Quiché itself is a fairly uneventful place where not a lot happens. It is, however, the transport hub for the department and the most direct route to the Ixil triangle, as well as being the only practical place to base yourself for a visit to the nearby ruins of **Utatlán**.

On the central plaza, there's a large colonial church, built by the Dominicans with stone from the ruins of Utatlán. The Catholic Church suffered terribly in Quiché in the late 1970s and early 1980s, when priests, who were often connected with the cooperative movement, were singled out and murdered. The situation was so serious that Bishop Juan Gerardi withdrew all his priests from the department in 1981. They have since returned to their posts, but the bishop himself was later assassinated in April 1998.

Beside the church, the large clock tower is also said to have been built from Utatlán stone, stripped from the temple of Tohil. In the middle of the plaza, a defiant statue of the Quiché hero, Tecún Umán, stands prepared for battle, though his position is undermined somewhat by an ugly urban tangle of hardware stores, *panaderías* and trash that surrounds this corner of the square and the spectacularly ugly, looming presence of the tin-roof-topped, breezeblock-built mercado.

Arrival and information

The **bus terminal**, a large, open affair, is about four blocks south and a couple east of the central plaza. Connections are generally excellent from Quiché. There's a constant stream of second-class **buses** to Guatemala City, going every half-hour between 3.30am and 5pm; all pass through Chichicastenango and Los Encuentros. There are also regular services to Nebaj between 8.30am and 4pm, to Uspantán, four times a day between 9am and 2pm (5hr), and to Quetzaltenango, regularly between 3am and 1pm.

The street directly north of the terminal is **1 Av**, which takes you up into the heart of the town. Two **banks** will change your travellers' cheques: Banco Industrial at the northwest corner of the plaza (Mon–Fri 8.30am–5.30pm, Sat 8.30am–12.30pm), which also advances cash on Visa, and Banco G&T, 6 A 3–00 (Mon–Fri 9am–7pm, Sat 9am–1pm), which doesn't. If you're heading into the Ixil Triangle (see p.336), you may want to stock up on **film**: try Kodak or Fuji, both one block northeast of the central church.

Accommodation

There's a limited range of **hotels** in Quiché, none of them luxurious. The cheapest are right beside the bus terminal. Most of the others are between the terminal and the plaza.

Hotel Rey K'iche, 8 C 0–39, Zona 5 (☎2325834). Two blocks north, one east from the terminal. Well-run, extremely clean and welcoming place with 26 rooms, most with cable TV and private bathroom. ③–④.

Hotel Maya Quiché, 3 Av 4–19, Zona 1 (☎7551464). A friendly place with big clean rooms, some with bathroom. ②–③.

Posada San Antonio, 2 Av, two blocks from the terminal (no phone). Brand new in 1997 and the best budget deal in town. Rooms are smallish but very clean and the bathrooms (with hot water) are scrubbed with evangelical zeal. Decent in-house restaurant. ②.

Hotel San Pascual, 7 C 0–43, Zona 1 (☎7551107). Walk up 1 Av, and turn left into 7 C. Large, clean rooms and equally well-kept communal bathrooms. ②–③.

Hospedaje Tropical, 1 Av and 9 C. Extremely basic place; no hot water but dirt cheap. ①.

Eating and drinking

There's very little to get excited about in Quiché. Most restaurants and cafés are grouped around the plaza. *El Torito Steakhouse*, 7 C 1–73, just southwest of the plaza, is the smartest place in town, with kitsch cowboy decor and a menu that's a real carnivore's delight – try the tasty sausages and fried chicken. On the west side of the plaza is *La Pizza de Ciro*, which dispenses reasonable pizzas that taste fine if you've come from remote Nebaj and pretty poor if you've journeyed from cosmopolitan Antigua. Close by are several uninspiring bakeries, with dry pastries and cakes, and also *Café La Torré*, a friendly place for a coffee, snack or a delicious piece of cheesecake. For a no-nonsense comedor meal try *Restaurante Las Rosas*, 1 Av, 1–28.

The ruins of Utatlán (K'umarkaaj)

Early in the fifteenth century, riding on the wave of successful conquest, the Quiché king Gucumatz (Feathered Serpent) founded a new capital, K'umarkaaj. A hundred years later, the Spanish arrived, renamed the city **Utatlán**, and then destroyed it. Today you can visit the ruins, about 4km to the west of Santa Cruz del Quiché.

According to the Popol Vuh, Gucumatz was a lord of great genius, assisted by powerful spirits, and there's no doubt that his capital was once a great city, with several separate citadels spread across neighbouring hilltops. It housed the nine dynasties of the tribal elite, including the four main Quiché lords, and contained a total of 23 palaces. The splendour of the city embodied the strength of the Quiché empire, which at its height boasted a population of around a million.

By the time of the Conquest, however, the Quiché had been severely weakened and their empire fractured. They first made contact with the Spanish on the Pacific coast, suffering a heavy defeat at the hands of Alvarado's forces near Quetzaltenango, with the loss of their hero, Tecún Umán. The Quiché then invited the Spanish to their capital, but the suspicious Alvarado captured the Quiché leaders, burnt them alive and then destroyed the city.

The site (daily 8am–5pm; US$2) is not as dramatic as some of the ruins in Petén, but is impressive nonetheless, surrounded by deep ravines and pine forests. This setting and the fascinating historical significance of the site make up for the lack of huge pyramids and stelae. There has been little restoration since the Spanish destroyed the city and only a few of the main structures are still recognizable; most are buried beneath grassy mounds and shaded by pine trees. The small **museum** has a scale model of what the original city may once have looked like.

The central plaza is almost certainly where Alvarado burned alive the two Quiché leaders in 1524. Nowadays, it's where you'll find all the remaining three **temple buildings**, the great monuments of Tohil, Auilix and Hacauaitz, all of which were simple pyramids topped by thatched shelters. In the middle of the plaza there used to be a circular **tower**, the Temple of the Sovereign Plumed Serpent, and its foundations can still be made out. The only other feature that is still vaguely recognizable is the **ball court**, which lies beneath grassy banks to the south of the plaza.

Perhaps the most interesting thing about the site today is that *brujos*, the traditional Maya priests, still come here to perform religious rituals, practices that predate the arrival of the Spanish by thousands of years. The entire area is covered in small burnt circles – the ashes of incense – and chickens are regularly sacrificed in and around the plaza. Beneath the plaza is a long **tunnel** that runs underground for about a hundred metres. Inside are nine **shrines**, coincidentally or not, the same number as there are levels of the Maya underworld, *Xibalbá*. Each is the subject of prayer and attention, but it is the ninth, housed inside a chamber, that is the most actively used for sacrifice, incense and alcohol offerings. Why the tunnel was constructed remains uncertain, but some local legends have it that it was dug by the Quiché to hide their women and children from the advancing Spanish whom they planned to ambush at Utatlán. Others believe it represents the seven caves of Tula mentioned in the Quiché masterpiece, the Popol Vuh (see p.331). Whatever the truth, today the tunnel is the focus for active Maya rituals and a favourite spot for sacrifice, the floor carpeted with chicken feathers, and candles burning in the alcoves at the end. To get to the tunnel follow the signs to *la cueva* (the cave); the entrance is usually littered with empty incense wrappings and *aguardiente* liquor bottles. If there is a ceremony taking place, you'll hear the mumbling of prayers and smell incense smoke as you enter the tunnel, in which case it's wise not to disturb the proceedings by approaching too closely. Tread carefully inside the tunnel, as some of the side passages end abruptly with precipitous drops.

To get to Utatlán, you can walk or take a taxi there from Santa Cruz del Quiché. To walk, head south from the plaza along 2 Av, and then turn right down 10 C, which will take you all the way out to the site – it's a pleasant forty-minute hike. You're welcome to **camp** close to the ruins, but there are no facilities or food. A taxi there and back, with an hour at the ruins, costs around US$8.

East to Joyabaj

An astonishingly good paved road runs east from Santa Cruz del Quiché, beneath the impressive peaks of the **Sierra de Chuacús**, through a series of interesting villages set in beautiful rolling farmland. The first of the villages is **CHICHÉ**, a sister village to Chichicastenango, with which it shares costumes and traditions, though the market here is on Wednesday. Next is **CHINIQUE**, followed by the larger village of **ZACUAL-PA**, which has Thursday and Sunday markets in its beautiful broad plaza. The village's name means "where they make fine walls", and in the hills to the north are the remains of a pre-conquest settlement. There's a pensión down the street beside the church, should you want to stay.

The last place out this way is the small town of **JOYABAJ**, again with a small archeological site to its north. During the colonial period, Joyabaj was an important staging post on the royal route to Mexico, but all evidence of its former splendour was lost when the earthquake in 1976 almost totally flattened the town and hundreds of people lost their lives: the crumbling facade of the colonial church that stands in front of the new prefabricated version is one of the few physical remains. In recent years the town has staged a miraculous recovery, however, and it is now once again a prosperous traditional centre: the Sunday **market**, which starts up on Saturday afternoon, is a huge affair well worth visiting, as is the **fiesta** in the second week of August – five days of unrelenting celebration that includes some fantastic traditional dancing and the spectacular *Palo Volador*, in which "flying" men or *ángeles* spin to the ground from a huge wooden pole, a pre-conquest ritual now performed in only three places in the entire country. The pole represents the Maya world tree, with its top in the heavens and its base in *Xibalbá*, the underworld. Though the fiesta is in many ways a hybrid of Maya and Christian traditions, the *ángeles* symbolize none other than the wizard twins of the Popol Vuh (see p.331), who descend into the underworld to do battle with the Lords of Death.

It's possible to **walk** from Joyabaj, over the Sierra de Chuacús, to Cubulco in Baja Verapaz (see p.391). It's a superb but exhausting hike, taking at least a day, though it's perhaps better done in reverse as transport connections are far better in Joyabaj.

Practicalities

Buses run between Guatemala City and Joyabaj, passing through Santa Cruz del Quiché, every hour or so (from 8am to 2.30pm from the capital and 5am to 3pm from Joyabaj). There's a good but very basic **pensión**, the *Hospedaje Mejia* (①), on the plaza in Joyabaj, and plenty of scattered **comedores** – one of the best is just off the main street beside the filling station.

For Panajachel and connections to the Pacific coast, **buses leave Joyabaj** twice daily in the morning, heading for Cocales. It's also possible to get back to the capital along a rough and seldom-travelled route via **San Martín Jilotepeque** (see p.329) on the daily bus that leaves Joyabaj at 2am.

To the Cuchumatanes: Sacapulas and Uspantán

The land to the north of Santa Cruz del Quiché is sparsely inhabited and dauntingly hilly. About 10km out of town, the single rough road in this direction passes through San Pedro Jocopilas, and from there struggles on without tarmac, eventually dropping to the isolated town of **SACAPULAS**, two hours from Quiché. In a spectacular position on the Río Negro, beneath the foothills of the Cuchumatanes, Sacapulas has a small colonial church and a good market every Thursday and Sunday beneath a huge ceiba tree in the plaza.

With its strategic position, Sacapulas should be a transport hub but, alas, it's not. To **get to Sacapulas** is not too difficult; you can catch any of the buses that leave Santa Cruz del Quiché for Uspantán or Nebaj. **Leaving Sacapulas** is far more difficult: bus departure times are 1am and 3am for Quiche, so you'll probably have to **hitch**. Wait by the bridge as traffic heading for Quiché can turn left or right after crossing the river. There are also buses to Huehuetenango and to Uspantán, but all services in this remote region are erratic and subject to delays and cancellations. Hitchhike whenever possible and expect to pay the same rate as you would on the bus.

At least if you get stuck there's a half decent place to **stay**: the *Restaurant Río Negro* offers basic but clean rooms (①). The cook, Manuela, serves up good **meals** and excellent banana, pineapple and papaya milkshakes.

East of Sacapulas, a dirt road rises steeply, clinging to the mountainside and quickly leaving the Río Negro far below. As it climbs, the views are superb, with tiny Sacapulas dwarfed by the sheer scale of the landscape. Eventually the road reaches a high valley and arrives in **USPANTÁN**, a small town lodged in a chilly gap in the mountains and often soaked in steady drizzle. Rigoberta Menchú (see p.488), the Quiché Maya woman who won the 1992 Nobel Peace prize is from Chimel, a tiny village in this region, but probably the only reason you'll end up here is in order to get somewhere else. With buses for Cobán and San Pedro Carchá leaving at around 3am, the best thing to do is go to bed. (The return buses leave San Pedro Carchá for Uspantán at 10am and noon.) There are two friendly pensiones, the *Casa del Viajero* (①) and the *Galindo* (①). **Buses** for Uspantán, via Sacapulas, leave Quiché at 9am, 11am, noon and 2pm, returning at 7pm, 11.30pm, 1am and 3am – a five-hour trip.

The Ixil triangle

High up on the spine of the Cuchumatanes, in a landscape of steep hills, bowl-shaped valleys and gushing rivers, is the **Ixil triangle**. Here the three small towns of Nebaj, Chajul and Cotzal, remote and extremely traditional, share a language spoken nowhere else in the country. This triangle of towns forms the hub of the **Ixil-speaking region**, a massive highland area which drops away towards the Mexican border and contains at least 100,000 inhabitants. These lush and rain-drenched hills are hard to reach and notoriously difficult to control, and today's relaxed atmosphere and highland charm conceal a bitter history of protracted conflict. It's an area that embodies some of the very best and the very worst characteristics of the Guatemalan highlands.

On the positive side is the beauty of the landscape and the strength of indigenous culture, both of which are overwhelming. When Church leaders moved into the area in the 1970s, they found very strong communities with women included in the process of communal decision-making. The people were reluctant to accept new authority for fear that it would disrupt the age-old structures. Counterbalancing these strengths are the horrors of the human rights abuses that took place here over the last few decades, which must rate as some of the worst anywhere in Central America.

Before the **Conquest**, the town of Nebaj was a sizeable centre, producing large quantities of jade and possibly allied in some way to Zaculeu (see p.361). The Spanish Conquest was particularly brutal in these parts, however. After many setbacks, the Spaniards managed to take Nebaj in 1530 and by then they were so enraged that not only was the town burnt to the ground, but the survivors were condemned to slavery as punishment for their resistance. Things didn't improve with the coming of independence, when the Ixil people were regarded as a source of cheap labour and forced to work on the coastal plantations; many never returned. Even today large numbers of local people are forced to migrate in search of work and conditions on many of the plantations remain appalling. In the late 1970s and early 1980s, the area was hit by waves of horrific violence as it became the main theatre of operation for the **EGP** (the Guerrilla Army of the Poor). Caught up in the conflict, the people have suffered enormous losses, with the majority of the smaller villages destroyed by the army and their inhabitants herded into "protected" settlements. With the peace accords, a degree of normality has returned to the area and new villages are being rebuilt on the old sites.

Despite this terrible legacy, the fresh green hills are some of the most beautiful in the country and the three towns are friendly and accommodating, with a relaxed and distinctive atmosphere.

Nebaj

NEBAJ is the centre of Ixil country, a beautiful old town, by far the largest of the three, with white adobe walls and cobbled streets. The weaving done here is unusual and intricate, its greatest feature being the women's *huipiles*, which are an artistic tangle of complex geometrical designs in superb greens, yellows, reds and oranges, worn with brilliant red *cortes* (skirts). On their heads, the women wear superb headcloths decorated with pompom tassles that they pile up above their heads; most men no longer wear traditional dress. You'll find an excellent shop selling goods produced by the Ixil weaving co-op on the main square.

The small **market** is worth investigation, a block to the east of the church. On Thursday and Sunday numbers swell and traders from out of town visit with secondhand clothing from the US, stereos from Taiwan and Korea and chickens, eggs, fruit and vegetables from the Guatemalan highlands. The town church is also worth a look, although it's fairly bare inside. If you're here for the second week in August, you'll witness the **Nebaj fiesta**, which includes processions, dances, drinking and fireworks.

Arrival and information

The **plaza** is the focal point for the community, with the major shops, municipal buildings and police station all encircling the square. The market and brand new **bus terminal** are on 7 C nearby. There is a **bank**, Bancafé, 2 Av 46, near the market (Mon–Fri 8.30am–4pm, Sat 8am–1pm), which exchanges both cash and travellers' cheques.

Getting to Nebaj is straightforward with **buses** from Santa Cruz del Quiché every hour and a half between 8.30am and 4pm (4hr), plus a daily service from Huehuetenango every morning (6hr), or you can take a bus to Sacapulas and change there. **Leaving Nebaj** is more problematic, with the schedules being subject to frequent changes, so check at the terminal before you want to leave. **Pickups and trucks** supplement the buses; the best place to hitch south is on the road out of town, a little further past the *Hotel Ixil*.

Accommodation

You'll find little in the way of luxury in Nebaj, although what there is does have an inimitable charm and prices here are some of the lowest in the country. There are few street signs, so you'll probably have to rely on the gang of children who act as guides – none of the hotels in town is more than a few minutes' walk from the terminal.

Hospedaje Esperanza, northwest of the plaza. Friendly, simply and basic. Ask the owner's daughter if you want to learn to weave. ①.

Hospedaje Ilebal Tenam, three minutes from the plaza on the road to Chajul/Cotzal. Brand new in 1997, this tremendous hospedaje has a double deck of very simple but very clean rooms and exhilaratingly hot showers. ①.

Hospedaje Las Tres Hermanas, a block northwest of the plaza. Despite its damp rooms, ancient mattresses and shabby apperance, this is one of the most famous hotels in Guatemala and still has real character. During the troubles of the 1970s and 1980s this place put up a virtual who's who of international and Guatemalan journalists including Victor Perera, George Lovell and Ronald Wright (see p.510). It is still run by two of the original three sisters, who must have some stories to tell. ①.

Hotel Ixil, on the main road south out of town. The large, bare rooms are a little on the damp side, though the setting is pleasant, around a courtyard in a nice old colonial house. Functional, warmish shower and friendly staff. ②.

Hotel Posada de Don Pablo, one block west of the plaza, opposite *Irene's* comedor. Another new hotel, this is one of the smartest in town, with spotless, pine-trimmed rooms, comfortable beds, private bathrooms and safe parking. ③.

Eating

As for **eating**, the best comedor in town is *Irene's*, just off the main square, with several others in the plaza itself. The *Maya-Inca* on 5 C is owned by a friendly Peruvian/Guatemalan couple and serves delicious Peruvian and local dishes, though the portions are small. In addition, there is always something to eat at the market. For entertainment, most of the raving in town is courtesy of Nebaj's burgeoning neo-Pentecostal church scene, with four-hour services involving much wailing and gnashing of teeth.

Walks around Nebaj

In the hills that surround Nebaj there are several beautiful **walks**, with one of the most interesting ones taking you to the village of **ACUL**, two hours away. Starting from the church in Nebaj, cross the plaza and turn to the left, taking the road that goes downhill between a shop and a comedor. At the bottom of the dip it divides and here you take the right-hand fork and head out of town along a dirt track. The track switchbacks up a steep hillside, and heads over a narrow pass into the next valley, where it drops down into Acul.

The village was one of the original so-called "model villages" into which people were herded after their homes had been destroyed by the army. If you walk on through the village and out the other side, you arrive at the Finca San Antonio, run by an Italian family who have lived here for more than fifty years and make some of the country's best cheese, which they sell at pretty reasonable prices.

A second, shorter walk takes you to a beautiful little **waterfall**, La Cascada de Plata, about an hour from Nebaj. Take the road to Chajul and turn left just before it crosses the bridge, a kilometre or two outside Nebaj. Don't be fooled by the smaller version you'll come to shortly before the main set of falls.

San Juan Cotzal and Chajul

To visit the other two towns in the Ixil triangle, it's best to coincide your visit with **market days** when there is more traffic on the move: Cotzal is on Wednesday and Saturday, Chajul on Tuesday and Friday, Nebaj on Sunday. **Buses** run to an irregular schedule, but on Sunday transport returns to both the other towns from Nebaj after 10am. Pickups supplement the buses. Look out, too, for aid agency and MINUGUA (United Nations) 4-wheel drives. It's certainly possible to visit both towns as part of an interesting day-trip from Nebaj if you get an early start.

SAN JUAN COTZAL is closer to Nebaj, up to an hour and a half away, depending on the state of the road. The town is set in a gentle dip in the valley, sheltered somewhat beneath the Cuchumatanes and often wrapped in a damp blanket of mist. Cotzal attracts very few Western travellers so you may find many people assume you're an aid worker or attached to a fundamentalist church.

Intricate turquoise *huipiles* are worn by the Maya women in Cotzal, who also weave bags and rope from the fibres of the maguey plant. There is little to do in the town itself, but there is some great hill-walking close by. If you want to **stay**, there is a small, very basic unmarked pensión called *Don Polo* (②), two blocks from the church, or you may find the *farmacia* in the corner of the plaza will rent you a room. *La Maguey* **restaurant**, in someone's front room, a block behind the church, serves up reasonable, if bland, food. **Buses** should return to Nebaj daily at 6am and 1am; you'll have to hitch at other times.

Last but by no means least of the Ixil settlements is **CHAJUL**. Made up almost entirely of old adobe houses, with wooden beams and red-tiled roofs blackened by the smoke of cooking fires, it is also the most determinedly traditional and least bilingual of the Ixil towns. The women of Chajul wear earrings made of old coins strung up on lengths of wool and dress entirely in red, filling the streets with colour – you'll see them washing their scarlet *cortes* and *huipiles* at the stream that cuts through the middle of the village. Here boys still use blowpipes to hunt small birds, a skill that dates from the earliest of times but is now little used elsewhere.

The colonial church, a massive structure with huge wooden beams and gold leaf decoration, is home to the **Christ of Golgotha** and the target of a large pilgrimage on the second Friday of Lent – a particularly good time to be here. The dirty *Hospedaje Cristina* (①) is a depressing option if you want somewhere to **stay** for the night; ask instead at the post office where one of the workers rents out rooms. Some other families also rent out beds in their houses to the steady trickle of travellers now coming to Chajul; you won't have to look for them, they will find you. For **eating**, there's an assortment of simple comedores and food stalls scattered around the marketplace.

If you want to walk off your lunch, it's possible to **hike from Cotzal to Chajul**, two to three hours away through the spectacular Ixil countryside. Retrace your steps down the Nebaj–Cotzal road to the edge of town and follow the dirt road that branches off to the right; the road is in good condition and it's impossible to get lost. The final uphill part of the walk is quite tough, especially if the sun is shining.

A number of unscheduled trucks bump along the two-hour route between Nebaj and Chajul on **market** days (Tuesday and Friday) and there are regular morning **buses** from 4am. Return buses leave at 11.30am and 12.30pm and there's usually a **truck** at 3.30pm. (You'll share the covered trailer with firewood and vegetables – not recommended for anyone who is claustrophobic.)

Lago de Atitlán

Lake Como, it seems to me, touches the limit of the permissibly picturesque; but Atitlán is Como with the additional embellishments of several immense volcanoes. It is really too much of a good thing. After a few days of this impossible landscape one finds oneself thinking nostalgically of the English Home Counties.
                              Aldous Huxley, *Beyond the Mexique Bay* (1934)

Whether or not you share Huxley's refined sensibilities, there's no doubt that Lago de Atitlán is astonishingly beautiful and most people find themselves captivated by its scenic excesses. Indeed, the effect is so overwhelming that a handful of gringo devotees have been rooted to its shores since the 1960s.

The lake itself is an irregular shape, with three main inlets. It measures 18km by 12km at its widest point and shifts through an astonishing range of blues, steely greys and greens as the sun moves across the sky. Hemmed in on all sides by steep hills and massive volcanoes, it's at least 320m (nearly 1000 feet) deep.

Another astonishing aspect of Atitlán is the strength of Maya culture still evident in the lakeside villages. Despite the thousands of tourists that pour in from Europe and North America every year, you can still find some of the most intensely traditional villages in Guatemala here. **San Antonio Palopó**, **Santiago Atitlán** and, above the lake, **Sololá** are some of the very few villages in the entire country where Maya men still

LAGO DE ATITLÁN

0   5 km

Cocales (25 km) & Carretera del Pacífico ▽

wear *traje* – traditional costume. Two languages, **Tzutujil** and **Cakchiquel**, are spoken on the shores, and a third, **Quiché**, a few kilometres away.

There are thirteen villages on the shores of the lake, with many more in the hills behind, ranging from the cosmopolitan resort-style **Panajachel** to tiny, isolated **Tzununá**. The villages are mostly subsistence farming communities and it's easy to hike and boat around the lake staying in a different one each night. The area has only recently attracted large numbers of tourists and for the moment things are still fairly undisturbed, but some of the new pressures are decidedly threatening. The increase in population has also had a damaging impact on the shores of the lake, as the desperate need to cultivate more land leads to deforestation and accompanying soil erosion.

You'll probably reach the lake through Panajachel, which makes a good base for exploring the surrounding area. "Pana" has an abundance of cheap hotels and restaurants and is well served by buses. To get a real sense of a more typical Atitlán village, however, travel by boat to Santiago Atitlán or San Antonio Polopó. **San Pedro La Laguna** is now the village where the marijuana smokers head for, with the most active travelling "scene" and a surplus of extremely cheap hotels. **Santa Cruz** and **San**

Marcos are the places to head for if you're seeking real peace and quiet and there are good hikes on this side of the lake.

Sololá

Perched on a natural balcony overlooking the lake, Sololá is a fascinating place, ignored by the majority of travellers. In common with only a few other towns, it has parallel indígena and ladino governments and is probably the largest Maya town in the country, with the vast majority of the people still wearing traditional costume.

The town itself isn't much to look at: a wide central plaza with a recently restored clock tower on one side and a modern church on the other. However, its **Friday market** is one of Central America's finest – a mesmeric display of colour and commerce. From as early as 5am the plaza is packed, drawing traders from all over the highlands, as well as thousands of rural Sololá Maya, the women covered in striped red cloth and the men in their outlandish "**space cowboy**" shirts, woollen aprons and wildly embroidered trousers. The town's symbol, an abstraction of a bat, can still be seen on the back of the men's jackets; it refers to the royal house of Xahil, who were the rulers of the Cakchiquel at the time of the Conquest. The pre-conquest site of **Tecpán-Atitlán**, which was abandoned in 1547 when Sololá was founded by the Spanish, is to the north of town.

If you can't make it for the Friday market, there's another smaller version on Tuesdays. Another interesting time to visit Sololá is on Sunday, when the **cofradías**, the elders of the Maya religious hierarchy, parade through the streets in ceremonial costume to attend the 10am Mass.

Panajachel

Ten kilometres beyond Sololá and separated by a precipitous descent is **PANA-JACHEL**. Over the years, what was once a small Maya village has become something of a resort, with a sizeable population of long-term foreign residents whose numbers are swollen in the winter by an influx of North American seasonal migrants and a flood of tourists. Panajachel was a premier hippie hangout back in the 1960s and 1970s and developed a bad reputation amongst some sections of Guatemalan society as a haven for drug-taking gringo drop-outs. Today "Pana" is much more integrated into the tourism mainstream and is as popular with Guatemalans, Mexicans and Salvadoreans as Westerners. The lotus-eaters and crystal-gazers have not all deserted Panajachel however. Many have reinvented themselves as (vaguely) conscientious capitalists who own restaurants and export *típica* clothing. Today there is much talk about the lake being one of the world's few "vortex energy fields", along with the Egyptian pyramids and Machu Pichu. Though you are unlikely to see fish swimming backwards or buses rolling uphill to Sololá, the lake does have a undeniable power and attracts a perennial population of healers, therapists and masseurs to Panajachel. In many ways it's this **gringo** crowd that gives the town its modern character and identity – vortex energy centre or not.

Not so long ago (although it seems an entirely different age), Panajachel was a quiet little village of **Cakchiquel** Maya, whose ancestors were settled here after the Spanish crushed a force of Tzutujil warriors on the site. Today the old village has been enveloped by the new building boom, but it still retains a traditional feel, and most of the Maya continue to farm in the river delta behind the town. The Sunday market, bustling with people from all around the lake, remains oblivious to the tourist invasion.

For travellers, Panajachel is one of those inevitable destinations and, although no one ever owns up to actually liking it, everyone seems to stay for a while, particularly as it's a comfortable base for exploring the lake and the central highlands. The old village is still attractive and although most of the new building is fairly nondescript, its lakeside

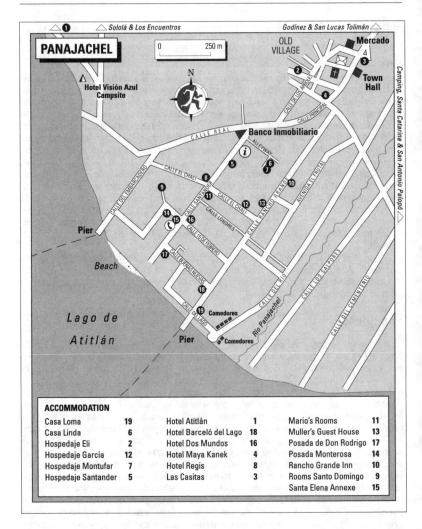

ACCOMMODATION

Casa Loma	**19**	Hotel Atitlán	**1**	Mario's Rooms	**11**
Casa Linda	**6**	Hotel Barceló del Lago	**18**	Muller's Guest House	**13**
Hospedaje Eli	**2**	Hotel Dos Mundos	**16**	Posada de Don Rodrigo	**17**
Hospedaje García	**12**	Hotel Maya Kanek	**4**	Posada Monterosa	**14**
Hospedaje Montufar	**7**	Hotel Regis	**8**	Rancho Grande Inn	**10**
Hospedaje Santander	**5**	Las Casitas	**3**	Rooms Santo Domingo	**9**
				Santa Elena Annexe	**15**

setting is superb. The main **daytime activity** is hanging out, either wandering the streets, shopping, eating and drinking, or swimming and sunbathing at the **public beach**, where you can also rent a kayak and explore the lake for a few hours (mornings are usually much calmer). Scuba-divers can also dive the lake with ATI Divers. **Weaving** from all over Guatemala is sold with daunting persistence in the streets here, but you'll need to bargain hard as prices can be high.

Arrival, information and accommodation

The bus drops you beside the Banco Inmobiliario, very close to the main drag, C Santander, which runs down to the lake shore. Straight ahead, up Calle Principal, is the old village. The **tourist office** is on C Santander (Mon–Sat 9am–5pm; ☎7621392). **Boat and bus schedules** are posted on the door. **Taxis** usually wait outside the post office, or you can call one on ☎7621571.

The streets of Panajachel are overflowing with cheap **hotels**, and there are plenty of "**rooms**". If you have a tent, first choice is the new **campsite** (☎7622479; US$2 per person), on the corner of the road to Santa Catarina and C del Cementerio over the river bridge (just off the map). Here happy campers will find kitchen and storage facilities and there are also sleeping bags and tents for hire. Don't bother camping at the public beach: your stuff will be ripped off.

Casa Linda, down an alley off the top of C Santander. Popular backpackers' retreat where the central garden is undeniably beautiful but the rooms are a shade pricey for a hospedaje. ②.

Casa Loma C Rancho Grande, near the lake (☎7621447). New place with very inviting pine-trimmed rooms, some with kitchen and TV. Best value in town in this price category. ③–④.

Las Casitas, at the back of the old village, near the market (☎7621224). Very clean, friendly, safe and quiet. Rooms have private bathrooms and hot water. ③.

Hospedaje Eli, Callejeón del Pozo, off C de los Arboles (☎7620148). Eight clean, cheap rooms overlooking a pretty garden in a quiet location.①.

Hospedaje García, C el Chali (☎7622187). Plenty of featureless but perfectly reasonable budget rooms. ②.

Hospedaje Montufar, down an alley off the top of C Santander(☎7620406). Quiet location and the rooms are cleaned with true evangelical zeal by a very accommodating family. Doubles and triples available. ②.

Hospedaje Santander, C Santander (☎7621304). Leafy courtyard, friendly owners and clean, cheap rooms, some with private bathrooms. Recommended. ①–②.

Hotel Atitlán, on the lakeside, 1km west of the centre (☎ & fax 7621441 or 7621416). The nicest hotel in the Panajachel area with a stunning lakeside location, lovely gardens and a swimming pool. Rooms are very comfortable and tastefully decorated. A double costs US$120. ⑨.

Hotel Barceló del Lago, right on the lakeshore (☎7621555, fax 7621562). Luxury colossus complete with pool, jacuzzi and gym. Very corporate "international" flavour, though great volcano views help remind you you're in Guatemala. US$110 double. ⑨.

Hotel Dos Mundos, C Santander (☎ & fax 7622078). Italian-owned hotel, just off the main drag, offering comfortable rooms set in a private garden, where there's also a small swimming pool. The attached *Lanterna* restaurant is recommended for authentic Italian cuisine at moderate prices. ⑤.

Hotel Maya Kanek, C Principal, near the church (☎7621104). Comfortable rooms, all with private showers, set around a cobbled courtyard that doubles as a car park. ③.

Hotel Posada de Don Rodrigo, C Santander, facing the lake (☎ & fax 7622322 or 7622329). Colonial-style hotel where the rooms, though on the small side, have a little more character than most. Pool and ugly waterslide overlook the lake. ⑧.

Hotel Regis, C Santander 3–47 (☎7621149, fax 7621152). Age-old establishment with lovely outdoor thermal pools. Individual bungalows are pleasant and come with cable TV. ⑥.

Mario's Rooms, C Santander (☎7621313). Basic, clean rooms, some with private bathrooms. Hot water on request for a few quetzales. ②–③.

Muller's Guest House, C Rancho Grande (☎7622442). Extremely tasteful Swiss-owned luxury guest house with quality modern European furnishings and a garden. Recommended. ⑤.

Posada Monterosa, C Monterrey (☎7620055). Brand new in 1997, this small place has spotless rooms with bathrooms and safe car parking. ④.

Rancho Grande Inn, C Rancho Grande (☎7621554, fax 7622247). A long-standing Panajachel institution with very attractive, nicely appointed bungalows, superbly kept gardens and helpful staff. Breakfast included. ⑤–⑥.

Rooms Santo Domingo, down a path off C Monterrey. One of the very cheapest places in town, set well away from the hustle. Wooden rooms all face a charming little garden or else there are more expensive options upstairs with private baths. ①–③.

Santa Elena Anexe, C 15 de Febrero. Safe, pleasant and ramshackle place with an abundance of children and parrots. One of the cheapest places in Pana, though hot showers are extra. ①.

BOATS

There are two **piers** in Panajachel. The pier near the *Hotel Barceló del Lago* serves Santa Catarina, San Antonio Palopó, San Lucas Tolimán, Santiago Atitlán and lake tours. The second pier at the end of C del Embarcadero is for all villages on the northern side of the lake: Santa Cruz, San Marcos, San Juan and San Pedro. Confusing matters somewhat, some of the boats for the northern lakeside start from the *Hotel Barceló del Lago* pier, but all will call at the C del Embarcadero pier to pick up passengers. Unfortunately, **rip-offs** are the rule for tourists. You'll be asked for triple or quadruple what the locals normally pay. The Inguat office has a list of boat schedules and prices. Another scam is charging more for the last boat of the day. **Tours of the lake** run by the Santa Fe company leave the Hotel del Lago pier at 8.30am; Santiago depart at 10.30am. Both visit San Pedro, Santiago Atitlán and San Antonio Palopó.

Panajachel to Santiago Atitlán (1hr) at 5.45am, 8.35am, 9.30am, 10.30am, 1pm, 3pm & 4.30pm. Returning at 6am, 7am, 11.45am, 12.30pm, 2pm, 3pm & 4.30pm.
Panajachel to San Pedro (1hr 30min) at 6am, 7am, 8.20am, 10am, 11am, noon, 2pm, 3pm, 4pm, 6pm, 7pm. Returning at 4.45am, 5.30am, 6am, 8am, 8.45am, 10am, noon, 12.30pm, 2pm, 3.45pm, 5pm.

Santiago Atitlán to San Pedro (40min) at 7am, 9am, 10am, 11am, noon, 1pm, 2pm, 3.30pm & 5pm.
Panjachel to Santa Catarina (20min) **San Antonio** (40min) and **San Lucas** (1hr 30min) 9.30am & 2pm. Returning San Antonio at 1pm and Santa Catarina at 1.30pm.

Eating, drinking and entertainment

Panajachel has an abundance of **restaurants**, all catering to the cosmopolitan tastes of its floating population. You'll have no trouble finding tasty Chinese, Indian, Italian, Mexican and Mediterranean dishes. For really cheap and authentically Guatemalan food there are plenty of comedores on and just off the new beach promenade and close to the market in the old village.

CAFÉS AND RESTAURANTS

Bombay, in the shopping arcade just past *Al Chisme*, C de los Arboles. Eclectic vegetarian food which, despite the name, has nothing Indian about it. Indonesian *gado-gado,* epic pitta bread sandwiches (try the falafel), and organic coffee. Closed Mon.

Las Chinitas, halfway down C Santander. Excellent pan-Asian cuisine in a pretty patio. Menu raids Indonesia, China, Thailand, and Japan for influence. Moderate prices. Closed Mon.

Al Chisme, C de los Arboles. A smart, European-style restaurant and bar adorned with black and white photographs of former customers that is very popular with gringos. Delicious food including sandwiches, crêpes, steaks, curried shrimps, and pasta, but all a little pricey. Closed Wed.

Comedor Costa Sur, near the church in the old town. Clean and attractive comedor, loudly bedecked with Mexican blankets. Great breakfasts, lunchtime dishes and licuados.

Deli, C Principal. Excellent range of salads, sandwiches, pastries, bagels, cakes, wine and tea. Also a nice garden and classical music. Two more branches on C Santander, *Deli 2* and *Delicafé*.

The Last Resort, C el Chali. Looks vaguely like an English pub, but serves the best American buffet breakfasts in town. Also a vast menu of pasta, steaks and vegetarian dishes – portions are huge.

Mario's, C Santander. A limited range of low-cost food: huge salads, delicious yoghurt and pancakes.

Restaurante Jhanny, halfway down C Rancho Grande. Ignore the fairylights and head inside for a superb Guatemalan-style *menú del día* (US$2.50); tables are nicely arranged around a little garden.

La Terraza, above Inguat at the top of C Santander. This is the finest restaurant on the lake and one of the best in the country, serving a captivating collection of European and Asian-influenced cuisine. Expensive.

Yalanki, C Santander. This is the best streetside bar/café with excellent snacks, barbecued meats, beer and good musical vibes.

NIGHTLIFE

There are three **video bars**, each showing English-language films: the *Grapevine* on C Santander, one in the *Carrot Chic* restaurant at the top end of C de los Arboles and, on the same street, *Cafe Cinema*. For **drinking**, try *The Last Resort* on C el Chali, where you can also play table tennis, or *Ubu's Cosmic Cantina*, behind the *Sevananda* restaurant on C de los Arboles, where there's a big screen for sports fans, movie buffs and news addicts. On C de los Arboles you'll also find the long-running *Circus Bar* and the new *El Aleph* bar/café for **live music**, and across the road the *Chapiteau* **nightclub**. Other clubs have a habit of opening and closing rapidly. Finally there's a **pool hall** in the old village, near the post office.

Listings

Banks and exchange Banco Inmobiliario at the junction of C Santander and C Principal (Mon–Fri 9am–7pm Sat 9am–noon), or Banco Industrial on C Santander, which has a 24hr ATM for Visa card holders. Try the AT travel agency or *Hotel Regis*, both on C Santander, for Mastercard transactions.

Bicycle rental Moto Servicio Queche, C de los Arboles & C Principal, rents mountain bikes for US$1 an hour, US$5 a day.

Bookstores Delante, down an alley off C Buenas Vistas, has a comprehensive selection of second-hand titles. Galería Bookstore, upper floor, C de los Arboles, stocks a reasonable choice of second-hand books and a few interesting new books in English.

Laundry Lavandería Automatico, C de los Arboles (Mon–Sat 7.30am–6pm). US$4 for a full load washed, dried and folded.

Medical care Dr Edgar Barreno speaks good English; his surgery is down the first street that branches to the right off C de los Arboles (☎7621008).

Motorbike rental Moto Servicio Queche, C de los Arboles and C Principal, rents 185cc bikes for US$6 an hour, US$25 for 24 hours, US$100 for the week.

Pharmacy Farmacia La Union, C Santander.

Police On the plaza in the old village (☎7621120).

Post office In the old village, down a side street beside the church (Mon–Fri 8am–4.30pm).

Telephone To make a phone call or send a fax, check first with businesses in C Santander for the best rates; many advertise discounted calls. Otherwise, Telgua (daily 7am–midnight) is near the junction of C Santander and C del Chali. *C@fenet*, in the same building as Telgua, at street level, will send and receive email.

The eastern shore

On the eastern shore, backed up against the slopes of the crater, are a couple of villages, the first of which, **SANTA CATARINA PALOPÓ**, is just 4km from Panajachel. The people of Santa Catarina used to live almost entirely by fishing and trapping crabs, but the introduction of black bass into the lake to create a sport-fishing industry has put an end to all that as the bass eat the smaller fish. They've now turned to farming and migratory work, with many of the women travelling to Panajachel and Antigua to peddle their weaving. The women wear stunning *huipiles*, in vibrant turquoise and purple zigzags.

Much of the shoreline as you leave the village has been bought and developed, and great villas, ringed by impenetrable walls and razor wire, have come to dominate the environment. Very much a part of this invasion is the new hotel *Villa Santa Catarina* (☎7621291; ⑦) which has opened on the lakeshore, complete with 32 rooms, two banqueting halls, a pool and superb views of the lake.

Another 5km brings you to **SAN ANTONIO PALOPÓ**, a larger and more traditional village, squeezed in beneath a steep hillside. It is on the tour-group itinerary, so the villagers have become a bit pushy in selling their weavings, but despite this, the village is quite interesting and the situation is beautiful. The hillsides above San Antonio are well irrigated and terraced, reminiscent of rice paddies, and most men wear the village *traje* of red shirts with vertical stripes and short woollen kilts. Women wear almost identical shirts, made of the same fabric with subtle variations to the collar design. The whitewashed central church is also worth a look; just to the left of the entrance are two ancient bells.

A single **bus** leaves Panajachel for San Antonio at 9.15am, but a number of pickups also ply this route (approximately every hour; last one returns to Panajachel from San Antonio at 5pm) and of course **boats** (see p.344). If you decide **to stay**, there are two options: the fairly upmarket *Hotel Terrazas del Lago* (☎7621288; ⑤), down by the water, which has comfortable rooms and beautiful views, or the very simple but clean pensión (①) owned by Juan Lopez Sánchez, near the entrance to the village. Try the comedor below the church for a cheap **meal**.

If you want to continue to circumnavigate the lake from San Antonio, you'll have to catch a boat, as shortly beyond the village a steep section of the Atitlán crater prevents the construction of a road. The next village, **SAN LUCAS TOLIMÁN** is probably the least attractive of the lot, a busy ladino-dominated coffee production centre. Though the setting under the Volcán de Tolimán is tremendous, in San Lucas the easygoing atmosphere of the lake is tempered by the influence of the Pacific coast. Both the Tolimán and Atitlán **volcanoes** can be climbed from here, though taking a guide is recommended as the trails are difficult to locate; ask at your hotel or the town hall. The main **market day** here is on Friday, which is certainly the best time to drop by, although it unfortunately clashes with the market in Santiago.

If you need to somewhere to **stay**, there is the pretty comfortable *Hotel Villa Real Inter* on 7 Av 1-84 (☎7220102; ③–④), with hot showers, safe parking and a restaurant, or the *Hotel Brisas del Lago* (③), down by the lake, which has similar facilities. For a good cheap deal, the best place is the friendly, clean and good-value *Cafetería Santa Ana* (①). There are a number of straightforward places to eat: *Café Tolimán* is probably the best.

San Lucas is the junction of the coast road and the road to Santiago Atitlán, and **buses** regularly thunder through in both directions. On the whole, buses head out towards Cocales and the coast in the early morning, with the last bus at about 2.30pm, making their way back to Santiago in the afternoon with the last bus passing through San Lucas at around 5.30pm. There are also five daily buses between here and Panajachel (1hr 30min) running mostly in the morning; the last one leaves at 2pm. **Boats** leave San Lucas for Panajachel at noon and 4pm (1hr 30min; US$2.50), calling in at San Antonio and Santa Catarina on the way, but always check schedules at the dock first – there may be an early morning service too.

Santiago Atitlán

On the other side of the Tolimán volcano, **SANTIAGO ATITLÁN** is set to one side of a sheltered horseshoe inlet, overshadowed by the twin cones of Atitlán and Tolimán. It's the largest and most important of the lakeside villages, and also one of the most traditional, being the main centre of the Tzutujil-speaking Maya. At the time of the Conquest, the Tzutujil had their fortified capital, **Chuitinamit-Atitlán**, on the slopes of San Pedro, while the bulk of the population lived spread out around the site of today's village. Alvarado and his crew, needless to say, destroyed the capital and massacred its inhabitants, assisted this time by a force of Cakchiquel Maya, who arrived at the scene in some three hundred canoes.

Today, Santiago is an industrious but relaxed sort of place. During the day the town becomes fairly commercial, its **main street**, which runs from the dock to the plaza, lined with weaving shops. There's nothing like the Panajachel overkill, but the persistence of underage gangs here can still be a bit much. By mid-afternoon, once the ferries have left, things revert to normal and the whole village becomes a lot more friendly. There's not a lot to do in Santiago other than stroll around soaking up the atmosphere or go to the market on Friday morning.

The old colonial Catholic **church** is well worth a look, however. The huge altarpiece, which was carved when the church was under *cofradía* control, culminates in the shape of a mountain peak and a cross. The cross symbolizes the Maya world tree, which supports the source of all life, including people, animals and the corn ears that you can see on the cross. In the middle of the floor is a small hole which Atitecos believe to be the centre of the world. The church is also home to a stone memorial commemorating Father Stanley Rother, an American priest who served in the parish from 1968 to 1981. Father Rother was a committed defender of his parishioners in an era when, in his own words, "shaking hands with an Indian has become a political act". Branded a Communist by President García, he was assassinated by a paramilitary death squad like hundreds of his parishoners before and after him. His body was returned to his native Oklahoma for burial, but his heart was removed and buried in the church.

As is the case in many other parts of the Guatemalan highlands, the Catholic Church in Santiago is locked in bitter rivalry with several evangelical sects, who are building churches here at an astonishing rate. Their latest construction, right beside the lake, is the largest structure in town. Folk-Catholicism also plays an important role in the life of Santiago and the town is well known as one of the few places where Maya still pay homage to **Maximón**, the drinking and smoking saint (see p.320 and p.356). Any child will take you to see him; just ask for the "Casa de Maximón". If you can get to Santiago at **Easter**, there's a huge religious procession through the town culminating in a symbolic and highly charged confrontation between an effigy of Christ, borne by the town's Catholics, and the image of Maximón, complete with a cigar in his mouth.

The traditional **costume** of Santiago, still worn a fair amount, is both striking and unusual. The men wear long shorts which, like the women's *huipiles*, are striped white and purple and intricately embroidered with birds and flowers. The women also wear a *xk'ap*, a band of red cloth approximately 10m long, wrapped around their heads, which has the honour of being depicted on the 25-centavo coin. Sadly this headcloth is going out of use and on the whole you'll probably only see it at fiestas and on market days, worn by the older women.

Practicalities

Boats to Santiago leave from the beach in Panajachel seven times a day between 5.45am and 4.30pm, returning between 6am and 4.30pm – the trip takes about an hour. The village is also astonishingly well connected by **bus** with almost everywhere except Panajachel (see below).

As for **accommodation**, a backpackers' favourite is the *Hotel Chi-Nim-Ya* (☎7217131; ②), on the left as you enter the village from the lake. The good value *Hotel Tzutuhil*, in the centre of town (☎7217174; ②), is a five-storey concrete building with spectacular views from the top floor and a restaurant. For something special, there are two good options: the *Posada de Santiago*, on the lakeshore 1km south of the town (☎7028462, fax 7217167; ⑥), a fine American-owned luxury hotel and restaurant with rooms in stone cabins, each with its own log fire, and the new *Hotel Bambú* (☎2018913; ⑤), with beautiful thatch-roofed stone bungalows and rooms, plus an excellent restaurant with Spanish specialities, just a ten-minute walk or canoe ride north of the main Santiago dock.

There are three **restaurants** at the entrance to the village, just up from the dock, all fairly similar. In the centre of the village you can eat at the *Hotel Tzutuhil* or, if you really want to dine in style, head out to the restaurant in the *Posada de Santiago* or *Hotel Bambú*.

Leaving Santiago, buses depart from the central plaza and head via San Lucas Tolimán and Cocales towards Guatemala City, leaving six times daily between 2.30am and 2pm. For San Pedro, seven boats leave Santiago every day from 7am until 4pm (40min).

San Pedro La Laguna

Around the other side of the Volcán de San Pedro is the village of **SAN PEDRO LA LAGUNA**, which has now usurped Panajachel to become the pivotal centre of Guatemala's travelling "scene". Generally, this status involves little more than playing host to the few dozen colourful foreigners who have set up home here and providing a plentiful supply of marijuana to keep the young gringo visitors happy. This isn't Goa, but San Pedro does have a distinctively bohemian flavour. Things certainly seem very mellow here but it hasn't always been so. Crack cocaine arrived in San Pedro in the early 1990s and the locals got so fed up with the wasted gringos in their midst that they wrote to a national newspaper demanding that the freaks get out of town. Today things seem to have settled down again and, despite the obvious culture clash between locals (most of whom are evangelical) and travellers, everyone seems to get on reasonably well.

Again, the setting is spectacular, with the San Pedro volcano rising to the east and a ridge of steep hills running behind the village. To the left of the main beach, as you look towards the lake, a line of huge white boulders juts out into the water – an ideal spot for an afternoon of swimming and sunbathing.

The **Volcán de San Pedro**, which towers above the village to a height of some 3020m, is largely coated with tropical forest and can be climbed in four to five hours. Any of the underage guides will be able to show you the trail. Andrés Adonias Cotuc Cite, who makes a living collecting wood on the volcano, is highly recommended. Get an early start in order to see the views at their best and avoid the worst of the heat. If you'd rather do something a little more relaxing, **horses** can be rented for around US$2.50 an hour and **canoes** for a great deal less.

Accommodation

San Pedro has some of the cheapest accommodation in all Latin America, with a number of basic, clean guest houses that almost all charge less than US$2 a person per night. There's nothing in the way of luxury. If you plan to stay around for a while then you might want to consider **renting a house**, which works out incredibly cheap. To locate any of the hotels listed below, let one of the local children guide you through the coffee bushes; a tip of a quetzal or two is appropriate.

Hospedaje Xocomil, turn left from the Panajachel dock and it's on the right. Spotless rooms around a little garden. ①.

Hotel Puerto Bello, turn left after Nick's Place, by the docks. Excellent budget hotel with really cheap rates, hot showers and a friendly owner. Good deal for solo travellers. ①.

Hotel Sakari, between the piers. The smartest place in town – modern and clean with four tiled rooms all with private bath and hot water. ②.

Hotel San Pedro, close to the Santiago dock, next door to the *Villa Sol*. Clean rooms grouped around a central courtyard, some with private bath. ②.

Hotel Ti'Kaaj, near the Santiago dock. Rooms are the same as everywhere else, but they are set in a beautiful garden with orange trees and hammocks. ①.

Hotel Valle Azul, turn right at the Panajachel dock. Ugly new addition on two floors, but the views are excellent and the rooms are plain, clean and good value, some with private bathrooms. ①.

Hotel Villa Sol, beside the Santiago Atitlán dock. Twin-deck concrete block with plain clean rooms, some with bathroom. Palm trees and a nice lawn add a little green relief. ①–②.

Eating and drinking

The steady flow of gringo travellers has given San Pedro's **cafés** and **restaurants** a decidedly international flavour and most places are excellent value for money.

Vegetarians are well catered for, especially at the **thermal baths** between the two docks where, after a revitalizing soak, you can eat some fine organic food (late afternoon and early evening only). There are a few typical Guatemalan comedores in the centre of the village and by the Santiago dock. For a **drink**, try the upstairs café at *Nick's Place* or the *Ti'Kaaj*.

Comedor Francés, between the docks. Reasonably priced Gallic fare – coq-au-vin at less than US$2 and yummy crêpes.

Nick's Place, by the Pana docks. Free movies upstairs and good-value grub (chicken and chips at US$2) make this the most popular place in town.

Pinocchio, between the two docks. Good Italian where you can feast on bruschetta and pasta.

Restaurant al Mesón, close to the Panajachel dock. Thatched cabañas shelter a good restaurant serving chicken platters and sandwiches. Favoured daytime haunt where you can sit on the grassy verges and watch the boats come and go.

Restaurant Rosalinda, a short walk uphill from Santiago dock. Excellent comedor – fresh lake fish, grilled meats and a warm welcome.

Restaurant Ti'Kaaj, opposite the eponymous hotel. Stunning views of the lake and volcanoes from the upper floor and a lovely garden out front too. Great breakfasts, pasta and a bar.

Restaurant Valle Azul, overlooking the lake. Popular daytime place for snacks and drinks.

The western shore

The **western side** of the lake is the only part that remains largely inaccessible to cars. From San Pedro, a rough dirt road runs as far as Tzununá and from there a spectacular path continues all the way to Sololá. Most of the boats between San Pedro and Panajachel call at all the villages en route, but the best way to see this string of isolated settlements is **on foot**: it makes a fantastic day's walk. A narrow strip of level land is wedged between the water and the steep hills most of the way, but where this disappears the path is cut into the slope providing dizzying views of the lake below. To walk from San Pedro to Santa Cruz takes between five and six hours and if you want some really rewarding hiking, this is the section of the lake to head for. San Pedro attracts the most visitors but there are also some excellent **places to stay** in San Marcos and Santa Cruz.

From San Pedro you follow a dirt road to **SAN JUAN LA LAGUNA**, just 2km or so away at the back of a sweeping bay surrounded by shallow beaches. The village of San Juan specializes in the weaving of *petates*, mats made from lake reeds, and there's also a large weaving co-op, *Las Artesanas de San Juan*; if you walk from the dock it's signposted on the left. On the other side of the street a brand new hospedaje has been built.

Leaving San Juan, you'll pass the small settlement of **San Pablo La Laguna**. After this, the villages start shrinking considerably. At **SAN MARCOS LA LAGUNA**, about two hours from San Pedro, a group of hotels have been sensitively established amongst a thick foliage of banana, mango, jocote and avocado trees. San Marcos has a decidedly New Age feel, thanks to the influence of the *Pirámides* yoga and meditation retreat (fax 7622080; US$8 per person per day including courses). The grounds of the retreat are beautiful, the pyramid cabañas comfortable and the vegetarian food delicious.

There are a number of other **accommodation** possibilities in San Marcos, including the excellent *Posada Schumann* (Guatemala City ☎3604049 or 3392683, cell phone 2022216; ④), run by the charming Olga Robinson. It is solar-powered and has four rooms and three beautiful stone bungalows with some stupendous volcano and lake views. *Hotel Paco Real* (fax 7629168; ②) also has a superb choice of well-priced chalets and rooms, a restaurant and immaculate communal bathrooms with hot water. The cheapest beds in the San Marcos jungle are at the *Hotel San Marcos* (②), where you'll find six perfunctory rooms in a concrete block; or at the *Unicornio* (①), where there are basic huts, a kitchen and a sauna. For somewhere **to eat**, though there are no comedores, most of the hotels above have restaurants and there is also a brilliant **bakery** that pumps out wholemeal bread and supplies many of the hotels. To **get to** any of the places listed above, turn left (west) from the jetty and walk along the lakeshore path for 300m until the *Posada Schumann;* signposts will direct you from here.

In the next lakeside village, **TZUNUNÁ**, the women often run from oncoming strangers, sheltering behind the nearest tree in giggling groups. Here the road indisputably ends, giving way to a narrow path cut out of the steep hillside, which can be a little hard to follow as it descends to cross small streams and then climbs up again around the rocky outcrops. The next village is **Jaibalito**, a ragged-looking place lost amongst the coffee bushes; from here it's two more hours to Santa Cruz along a glorious easy-to-follow path that grips the steep hillside.

Set well back from the lake on a shelf 100m or so above the water is **SANTA CRUZ LA LAGUNA**, the largest in this line of villages. If you arrive here by boat it may appear to be just a collection of **hotels**, as the village is higher up above the lake. There isn't much to see in Santa Cruz, apart from a fine sixteenth-century church, and most people spend their time here walking, swimming or just chilling out with a book. There are **no phones** in Santa Cruz; use the communal fax number instead (☎7621196), and try and book accommodation a few days ahead.

On the shore, opposite a line of wooden jetties, you'll find the *Iguana Perdida* (①–②), owned by Mike and Deedle, a very special place with undoubtedly the most convivial atmosphere in Lago de Atitlán. The rooms are fairly basic, ranging from a dorm to twin bed doubles, but it's the gorgeous, peaceful site overlooking the lake and volcanoes that really makes this place. Dinner is a three-course communal affair (US$5) and the *Iguana* is also home to Lago de Atitlán's only **dive school**, ATI Divers, a professional PADI outfit that can train all levels up to assistant instructor. Next door is another good place, the *Hotel Arca de Noé* (④), slightly more expensive and comfortable with attractive rooms and home cooking. Just behind the *Iguana* are the simple, clean rooms at the *Hospedaje García* (②); and on the other side, the *Posada Abaj* (③), which has a beautiful peaceful garden but lacks atmosphere.

Beyond Santa Cruz there are two ways to reach Panajachel. **Boats** travelling between Panajachel and San Pedro stop at Santa Cruz hourly in the day, or you can rent a boat to Panajachel for around US$4. The path that runs directly to Panajachel is very hard to follow, and distraught walkers have been known to spend as long as seven hours scrambling through the undergrowth. Alternatively, you could **walk to Sololá**, up through the village along a spectacular and easy-to-follow path that takes around three hours, and from there catch a bus back to Panajachel.

Quetzaltenango (Xela) and around

To the west of Lago de Atitlán, the highlands rise to form a steep-sided ridge topped by a string of forested peaks. On the far side of this is the **Quetzaltenango basin**, a sweeping expanse of level ground that forms the natural hub of the western highlands. It was here that the conquistador Pedro de Alvarado first struggled up into the highlands from the Pacific coast and came upon the abandoned city of Xelajú (near Quetzaltenango), entering it without any resistance. Six days later, he and his troops fought the Quiché in a decisive battle on the nearby plain, massacring the Maya warriors.

Totally unlike the capital and only a fraction of its size, Guatemala's second city, **QUETZALTENANGO**, has the subdued provincial atmosphere that you might expect in the highlands, its edges gently giving way to corn and maize fields. Bizarre though it may seem, it's character and appearance is vaguely reminiscent of an industrial town in northern England – grey, cool, slightly dour and culturally conservative. Ringed by

high mountains and bitterly cold in the early mornings, the city wakes slowly, only getting going once the warmth of the sun has made its mark.

Some history

Under colonial rule, Quetzaltenango flourished as a commercial centre, benefiting from the fertility of the surrounding farmland and good connections to the port at Champerico. When the prospect of independence eventually arose, the city was set on deciding its own destiny and Quetzaltenango declared itself the capital of the independent state of **Los Altos**. But the separatist movement was unsuccessful and the city has had to accept provincial status ever since. During the coffee boom at the end of the last century, Quetzaltenango's wealth and population grew so rapidly that it began to rival the capital in status.

All this, however, came to an abrupt end when the city was almost totally destroyed by the massive **1902 earthquake**. Rebuilding took place in a mood of high optimism: all the grand Neoclassical architecture dates from this period. A new rail line was built to connect the city with the coast but after this was washed out in 1932–33 the town never regained its former glory, gradually falling further and further behind the capital.

Today, Quetzaltenango has all the trappings of wealth and self-importance: the grand imperial architecture, the great banks and a list of famous sons. But it is completely devoid of the rampant energy that binds Guatemala City to the all-American twentieth century. The city has a calm and dignified air and Quetzaltecos have a reputation for formality and politeness; if the chaos of Guatemala City gets you down then Quetzaltenango is an ideal antidote.

Arrival and information

Unhelpfully for the traveller, virtually all buses arrive and depart Quetzaltenango from nowhere near the centre of town. If you arrive by **second-class bus** you'll almost certainly end up in the chaotic **Minerva bus terminal** on the western edge of Xela. Walk through the covered marketplace to 4 C and catch a local bus marked "parque" to get to the plaza from there. An extremely useful transport hub is a roundabout called the **rotunda** at the far end of Calzada Independencia, where virtually all long-distance buses stop on their way to and from the city. Three main companies operate **first-class** buses to and from the capital, each with their own private terminal: Líneas Américas terminal is just off Calzada Independencia at 7 Av 3–33, Zona 2, Quetzaltenango (☎7612063 or 7614587), Alamo is at 14 Av 3-76, Zona 3 (☎ 7612964), and Galgos is at C Rodolfo Robles 17–43, Zona 1 (☎7612248).

Quetzaltenango is laid out on a standard grid pattern, somewhat complicated by a number of steep hills. The oldest part of the city, focused around the plaza, is made up of narrow streets, while in the newer part, reaching out towards the Minerva terminal, the blocks are larger. The city is also divided up into **zones**, although for the most part

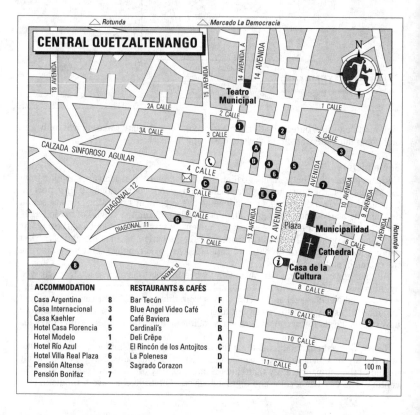

CENTRAL QUETZALTENANGO

ACCOMMODATION		RESTAURANTS & CAFÉS	
Casa Argentina	8	Bar Tecún	F
Casa Internacional	3	Blue Angel Video Café	G
Casa Kaehler	4	Café Baviera	E
Hotel Casa Florencia	5	Cardinali's	B
Hotel Modelo	1	Deli Crêpe	A
Hotel Río Azul	2	El Rincón de los Antojitos	C
Hotel Villa Real Plaza	6	La Polenesa	D
Pensión Altense	9	Sagrado Corazon	H
Pensión Bonifaz	7		

you'll only be interested in 1 and 3, which contain the plaza area and the bus terminal respectively. Most places are within easy walking distance. To get to the Minerva terminal you can take any bus that runs along 13 Av between 8 C and 4 C in Zona 1. For the eastern half of town, along 7 Av, catch one of the buses that stops in front of the Casa de la Cultura, at the bottom end of the plaza.

The official **tourist office** is on the main plaza (Mon–Fri 8am–1pm & 2–5pm, Sat 8am–noon; ☎7614931). They are helpful and have maps and local information. Quetzaltenango is an excellent place to study Spanish, with dozens of schools, many of a high standard.

Accommodation

A bit like the city itself, most accommodation in Quetzaltenango tends to be on the dour and gloomy side. Once you've made it to the plaza, all the places (but one) listed below are within ten minutes' walk.

Casa Argentina, 12 Diagonal 8–37 (☎7612470). Probably the best budget place in town with comfortable rooms, a reasonable dorm, kitchen and very friendly owners who are an excellent source of information. Home of Quetzaltrekkers (see p.356) and assorted long-term gringos. ②.

Casa Internacional, 3 C 10–24 (☎7612660). Excellent budget choice and often booked solid. Safe and friendly with a kitchen and hot water. ②.

Casa Kaehler, 13 Av 3–33 (☎7612091). Lovely place with spotless rooms around a leafy courtyard; hot showers and some private baths. Very secure, but be sure to book ahead as it's very popular. ②.

Hotel del Campo, Carretera a Cantel Km 224, 4km from the town centre (☎ 7611663, fax 7610074). Big, modern hotel with a swimming pool and a decent restaurant. Though it's good value, it's only really an option if you have your own transport. ⑤.

Hotel Casa Florencia, 12 Av 3–61 (☎7612811). The lobby isn't going to win any design awards, but the nine rooms are comfortable enough and all come with private bath. Cheap breakfasts too. ④.

Hotel Modelo, 14 Av A 2–31 (☎7612529, fax 7631376). Civilized and quiet, but a bit gloomy for the price and decidedly old-fashioned. The nicest rooms face a small garden courtyard, or try the separate annexe which is better value. ④–⑤.

Hotel Río Azul, 2 C 12–15 (☎ & fax 7630654). Very reminiscent of an English boarding house, but spotless and welcoming and all rooms have private bathrooms. ③.

Hotel Villa Real Plaza, 4 C 12–22 (☎7614045, fax 7616780). Quetzaltenango's second hotel, across the plaza from the *Bonifaz*, to which it is a modern(ish) rival. Comfortable enough, but lacks atmosphere. ⑥

Pensión Altense, 9 C 8–48 (☎7612811). Just above the budget range, this place has plenty of clean rooms, all with private bathrooms. ③.

Pensión Bonifaz, northeast corner of the plaza (☎7612182, fax 7612850). The hotel, founded in 1935, has character and comfort, a decent restaurant and a quirky bar. Very much the backbone of Quetzaltenango society, with an air of faded upper-class pomposity, but still the best place in town. ⑥.

The City

There aren't many things to do or see in Quetzaltenango, but if you have an hour or two to spare then it's well worth wandering through the streets, soaking up the atmosphere and taking in the museum. The hub of the place is the **central plaza**, officially known as the **Parque Centro América**. A mass of mock-Greek columns and imposing banks, it has an atmosphere of dignified calm. The buildings have a look of defiant authority, although there's none of the buzz of business that you'd expect.

The northern end of the plaza is dominated by the grand Banco del Occidente, complete with sculptured flaming torches. On the west side is Bancafé and the impressive but crumbling **Pasaje Enriquez**, which was planned as a sparkling arcade of upmarket shops. It was derelict for many years but has now been partially revived. Inside you'll find the *Salon Tecún Bar*, the hippest place in town, and a good place for meeting other travellers.

At the bottom end of the plaza, next to the tourist office, is the **Casa de la Cultura** (Mon–Fri 8am–noon & 2–6pm, Sat 9am–1pm; US$1), the city's most blatant impersonation of a Greek temple, with a bold grey frontage. The main part of the building is given over to an odd mixture of local exhibits. On the ground floor, to the left-hand side, you'll find a display of assorted documents from the liberal revolution and the State of Los Altos (see p.351), sports trophies and a museum of marimba. Upstairs there are some interesting Maya artefacts, a display about local industries and a fascinating collection of old photographs.

Along the other side of the plaza is the **Cathedral**, with the new cement version set behind the spectacular crumbling front of the original. There's another piece of classical grandeur, the **Municipalidad** or town hall, a little further up. Take a look inside at the courtyard, which has a neat little garden set out around a single palm tree. Back in the centre of the plaza are rows and circles of redundant columns, a few flowerbeds, and a monument to Rufino Barrios, president of Guatemala from 1873 to 1885.

Away from the plaza, the city spreads out, a mixture of the old and new. 14 Avenida is the commercial heart, complete with pizza restaurants and neon signs. At the top of 14 Avenida, at the junction with 1 Calle, stands the **Teatro Municipal** (undergoing some restoration), another spectacular Neoclassical edifice. Further afield, the city's role as a regional centre of trade is more in evidence.

Out in Zona 3 is the **Mercado la Democracia**, a vast covered complex with stalls spilling out onto the streets. There's another Greek-style structure right out on the edge of town, the **Templo de Minerva**. It was built to honour President Barrios's enthusiasm for education and makes no pretence at serving any practical purpose. Beside the temple is the fairly miserable **zoo** (Tues–Sun 9am–5pm; free), where there is also a children's playground. Below the temple are the sprawling **market** and **bus terminal** and it's here that you can really sense the city's role as the centre of the western highlands, with indígena traders from all over the area doing business.

Eating, drinking and entertainment

There are more than enough **restaurants** to choose from in Quetzaltenango, with four reasonable pizza places on 14 Avenida alone. Note that almost nowhere opens before 8am in the morning, so forget early **breakfasts**. It is very sleepy after dark, too, and **nightlife** is not easy to come by. Hedonists will have to catch a taxi to the best **clubs**, which are all out of town.

Cafés and restaurants

Artura's Restaurant, 14 Av 3–09, Zona 1. Dark, cosy atmosphere, with traditional, moderately priced food and a separate, fairly civilized bar for drinking.

Blue Angel Video Café, 7 C 15–22, Zona 1. Another popular gringo hangout with a daily video programme. An intimate, friendly place where you can eat great vegetarian food. Daily 2.15pm–11pm.

Café Baviera, 5 C 12-50, Zona 1, a block from the plaza. Spacious pine-panelled coffee house, dripping with photographic nostalgia. Quality cakes and unquestionably the best coffee in town. Daily 8am–8pm.

Cardinali's, 14 Av 3–41, Zona 1. Without doubt the best Italian food outside the capital, at reasonable prices. Make sure you are starving when you eat here because the portions are huge.

Deli Crêpe, 14 Av, Zona 1. Looks a bit gloomy from the outside, but wait till you try the licuados, pancakes and delicious sandwiches.

Pan y Pasteles, 18 Av and 2 C, Zona 1. The best bakery in town, run by Mennonites whose fresh pastries and breads are used by all the finest restaurants. Tues & Fri only, 10am–4pm.

Pensión Bonifaz, corner of the plaza, Zona 1. Always a sedate and civilized spot for a cup of tea and a cake, or a full meal, and for rubbing shoulders with the town's elite. Expensive.

La Polonesa, 14 Av 4–55, Zona 1. An unbeatable selection of set lunches (with daily specials) all at under US$2, served on nice solid wooden tables.

El Rincon de los Antojitos, 15 Av and 5 C, Zona 1. Despite being run by a French–Guatemalan couple, this friendly little restaurant has a purely Guatemalan menu, with specialities such as *pepián* (spicy chicken stew) and *hilachas* (beef in tomato sauce).

Sagrado Corazon, 9 C 9-00, Zona 1. Excellent little comedor, great-value breakfasts, meals and very friendly service.

Shanghai, 4 C 12–22, Zona 1. Some of the best Chinese food in town, and not too expensive.

Drinking and nightlife

There's not much to do in the evenings in Quetzaltenango, and the streets are generally quiet by about 9pm. A couple of **bars**, though, are worth visiting. At the popular *Tecún*, on the west side of the plaza, you can down *cuba libres*, sip the beer on tap and listen to the latest sounds imported by the gringo bar staff. At the more sedate but classy *Don Rodrigo*, 1 C and 14 Av, you'll find leather-topped bar stools, draught beer and good but pricey sandwiches. The *Greenhouse Café Teatro*, 12 Av 1–40 (☎7630271), has a lively cultural programme including theatre, dance and poetry readings.

Quetzaltenango is a good place to catch movies, with a number of **cinemas** including the new screen inside the shopping mall, Plaza Polonco, just off the central plaza, for pure Hollywood; and Cadore at 7 C and 13 Av, for violence, horror and soft porn. For art house films, the brand new Paraíso on 14 Av, near the Teatro Municipal, is excellent.

Listings

Banks and exchange Banco Inmobiliario, Banco del Occidente and Banco del Café (with the longest opening hours – Mon–Fri 8.30am–8pm, Sat 10am–2pm) are all in the vicinity of the plaza and will change travellers' cheques. Banco Industrial, also in the plaza, has an ATM that takes Visa.

Bike and car rental Guatemala Unlimited, 12 Av and 1 C, Zona 1 (☎7616043). Mountain bikes are around US$6 a day; or try the Vrisa bookstore (see below).

Bookstore Vrisa, 15 Av 3–64, opposite Telgua and the post office, has over 3000 used titles, plus a newsroom with *Newsweek*, *The Economist*, a message board, espresso coffee and bike rental.

Consulates Mexican Consulate, 9 Av 6–19, Zona 1 (Mon–Fri 8–11am & 2.30–3.30pm). A Mexican tourist card costs US$1. Hand in paperwork in the morning and collect in the afternoon.

Laundry MiniMax, 4 Av and 1 Zona 1 (Mon–Sat 7am–7pm). US$2 for a full-load wash and dry.

Medical care Doctors Cohen and Molina at the Policlinica, A C 13–15, speak some English. For emergencies, the Hospital Privado is at C Rudolfo Robles 23–51, Zona 1.

Photography For camera repairs try Fotocolor, 15 Av 3–25, or one of the several shops on 14 Av.

Post office At the junction of 15 Av and 4 C.

Telephone office The Telgua office (7am–10pm daily) is just opposite the post office. Maya Communications, above *Tecún Bar* on the central plaza (daily 10am–7pm; ☎ & fax 7612832), offers all communication services, including email.

Around Quetzaltenango

Quetzaltenango (Xela) is the obvious place to base yourself to explore the surrounding countryside, with bus connections to all parts of the western highlands. It's easy to spend a week or two here, making day-trips to the markets and fiestas, basking in hot springs or hiking in the mountains. The valley is heavily populated and there are numerous small towns and villages in the surrounding hills, mostly indigenous agricultural communities and weaving centres. If you want to go **hiking**, the most obvious climb is the **Santa María volcano**, towering above Quetzaltenango itself, but there's also **Laguna Chicabal**, a small lake set in the cone of an extinct volcano and **Tajumulco**, the highest peak in Central America. Casa Iximulew, 15 Av and 5 C, Zona 1, runs **organized trips** to most of the volcanoes around Xela and to Zunil and Fuentes Georginas; or try Guatemala Unlimited, 12 Av and C 35, Zona 1 (☎ & fax 7616043). Quetzaltrekkers, based inside the *Casa Argentina* hotel (see p.353) runs regular hikes to the Tajumulco volcano, an amazing three-day trek between Todos Santos and Nebaj.

To the south, straddling the coast road, lie **Zunil** and the hot springs of **Fuentes Georginas**, 18km away, overshadowed by volcanic peaks. To the north are **San Andrés Xecul**, Totonicapán, capital of the department of the same name, and **San Francisco el Alto**, a small town perched on an outcrop overlooking the valley. Thirty-five kilometres beyond lies **Momostenango**, the country's principal wool-producing centre and a focus of Maya culture.

Volcán de Santa María

Due south of Quetzaltenango, the perfect cone of the **Santa María volcano** rises to a height of 3772m. From the town only the peak is visible, but seen from the rest of the valley the entire cone seems to tower over everything around. The view from the top is, as you might expect, spectacular, and if you're prepared to sweat out the climb you certainly won't regret it. It's possible to climb the volcano as a day-trip, but to really see it at its best you need to be on top at dawn, either sleeping on the freezing peak, or camping at the site below and climbing the final section in the dark by torchlight. Either way you need to bring enough food, water and stamina for the entire trip; and you should be acclimatized to the altitude before attempting it.

Take a local bus from the Minerva terminal to the village of **Llanos del Pinal** (hourly, 30min), get off at the crossroads and walk down the dirt road towards the volcano's base. After 45 minutes a marked path leads to the left, soon becoming a rocky trail, and another hour later you'll reach a flat grassy area ideal for **camping**. From here the trail cuts to the right and then straight up the side of the cone; it's another two to three hours to the top. At the summit the views are incredible if you get a clear day, with the Xela valley below, the volcanoes of Tacaná and Tajumulco to the west and four more to the east. Immediately to the south is the (very) active cone of **Santiaguito**, which has been in a state of constant eruption since 1902.

Zunil and Fuentes Georginas

Heading southwards to the Pacific, you come to the traditional village of **ZUNIL**, a vegetable-growing market town surrounded by steep hills and a sleeping volcano. The plaza is dominated by a beautiful colonial church with an intricate silver altar protected behind bars. The women of Zunil wear vivid purple *huipiles* and carry bright shawls, and for the Monday market the plaza is awash with colour. Just below the plaza is a **textile co-op** where hundreds of women market their beautiful weavings. Zunil is also one of the few remaining places where **Maximón** (or San Simón), the evil saint, is still worshipped (see p.320). In the face of disapproval from the Catholic Church, the Maya are reluctant to display their Judas, who also goes by the name Alvarado, but his image is usually paraded through the streets during Holy Week, dressed in Western clothes and smoking a cigar. Virtually any child in town will take you to his abode for a quetzal.

In the hills above Zunil are the **Fuentes Georginas**, a spectacular set of luxurious hot springs. A turning to the left off the main road, just beyond the entrance to the village, leads up into the hills to the baths, 8km away. You can walk it in a couple of hours, or rent a pickup from the plaza in Zunil for about US$5, though if you're not staying the night you'll have to arrange the return trip (another US$5) a few hours later with the driver. The baths are surrounded by fresh green ferns, thick moss and lush forest, and to top it all there's a restaurant and bar beside the main pool. You can swim in the pool for US$1 or rent a **bungalow** for the night (②) complete with bathtub, double bed, fireplace and barbecue. In the rainy season it can be cold and damp, but with a touch of sunshine it's a fantastic place to spend the night.

Buses to Zunil run from Quetzaltenango's Minerva bus terminal every half-hour or so, with the last bus back from Zunil leaving at around 6.30pm. Most buses will travel via the rotunda on the east side of town.

San Andrés Xecul

Heading to the Interamericana from Quetzaltenango, a kilometre before you reach the junction of Cuatro Caminos, is a branch road that leads to possibly the wildest church in the Maya World. Bypassed by almost everything, **SAN ANDRÉS XECUL** is to all appearances an unremarkable farming village but for the **village church**, a beautiful old building with incredibly thick walls. Its facade is painted an outrageous mustard yellow, with vines dripping plump, purple fruit and podgy little angels scrambling across the surface. The village is also rumoured to act as a "university" for students of shamanism, though there is little evidence of this save the scores of small altars in the hills around. Buses leave for San Andrés from the Minerva terminal in Quetzaltenango several times daily, or take any bus bound for Cuatro Caminos and get the driver to drop you off at the dirt road to San Andrés and either hitch or walk the 4km.

San Francisco el Alto

The small market town of **SAN FRANCISCO EL ALTO** overlooks the Quetzaltenango valley from a magnificent hillside setting. It's worth a visit for the view alone, with the great plateau stretching out below and the cone of the Santa María volcano marking the opposite side of the valley. But another good reason for visiting the village is the **Friday market**, which is possibly the biggest in Central America. Traders from every corner of Guatemala make the trip, many arriving the night before, and some starting to sell as early as 4am, by candlelight. Throughout the morning a steady stream of buses and trucks fill the town to bursting; by noon the market is at its height, buzzing with activity.

The town is set into the hillside, with steep cobbled streets connecting the different levels. Two areas in particular are monopolized by specific trades. At the very top is an open field used as an **animal market**, where everything from pigs to parrots changes hands. The teeth and tongues of animals are inspected by the buyers and at times the scene degenerates into a chaotic wrestling match, with pigs and men rolling in the dirt. Below this is the town's plaza, dominated by textiles. On the lower level, the streets are filled with vegetables, fruit, pottery, furniture, cheap comedores, and plenty more. These days most of the stalls deal in imported denim, but under the arches and in the covered area opposite the church you'll find a superb selection of traditional cloth. For a really good **photographic** angle and for views of the market and the surrounding countryside, pay the church caretaker a quetzal and climb up to the **church roof**. By early afternoon the numbers start to thin out, and by sunset it's all over – until the following Friday.

There are plenty of **buses** from Quetzaltenango to San Francisco, leaving every twenty minutes or so from the rotunda; the first is at 6am, and the last bus back leaves at about 5pm (45min).

Momostenango

A further 22km from San Francisco, down a dirt road that continues over a ridge behind the town then drops down through lush pine forests, is **MOMOSTENANGO**, a small, isolated town and the centre of wool production in the highlands. Momostecos travel throughout the country peddling their blankets, scarves and rugs; years of experience have made them experts in the hard sell and given them a sharp eye for tourists. The wool is also used in a range of traditional costumes, including the short skirts worn by the men of Nahualá and San Antonio Palopó and the jackets of Sololá. The ideal place to buy Momostenango blankets is in the **Sunday market**, which fills the town's two plazas.

A visit at this time will also give you a glimpse of Momostenango's other feature: its rigid adherence to tradition. Opposite the entrance to the church, people make offerings of incense and alcohol on a small fire, muttering their appeals to the gods. The town is famous for this unconventional folk-Catholicism, and it has been claimed that there are as many as three hundred Maya **shamans** working here. Momostenango's religious **calendar**, like that of only one or two other villages, is still based on the 260-day *Tzolkin* year – made up of thirteen twenty-day months – that has been in use since ancient times.

A good time to visit Momostenango is for the fiesta on August 1, or else for the start of the Maya new year. If you decide to stay for a day or two then you can take a walk to the *riscos*, a set of bizarre sandstone pillars, or beyond to the **hot springs** of Pala Chiquito, about 3km away to the north.

The best **place to stay** in Momostenango is the *Hotel Estiver*, 1C 4–15, Zona 1 (☎7365036; ②). It has clean rooms, some with private bathrooms, great views from the roof and safe parking. For **eating**, there are plenty of small comedores on the main plaza. Momostenango is also home to ADIFAM, a development agency that concentrates on educating children in the municipality. Volunteers are needed and, if your Spanish is good enough, you can contact them at the *Hotel Estiver*.

Buses run here from Quetzaltenango, passing through Cuatro Caminos and San Francisco el Alto on the way. They leave the Minerva terminal in Quetzaltenango every hour or so from 10am to 4pm (1hr 30min) and from Momostenango between 6am and 3pm. On Sunday, special early-morning buses leave Quetzaltenango from 6am: you can catch them at the rotunda.

Totonicapán

Capital of one of the smaller departments, **TOTONICAPÁN** is reached down a direct road leading east from Cuatro Caminos. Surrounded by rolling hills and pine forests, the town stands at the heart of a heavily populated and intensely farmed little region. There is only one point of access and the valley has always held out against outside influence, shut off in a world of its own. Totonicapán is a quiet place, ruffled only by the Tuesday and Saturday **markets**, which fill the two plazas to bursting. Until fairly recently a highly ornate traditional costume was worn here, but this has now disappeared and the town has instead become one of the chief centres of commercial weaving. On one side of the main plaza is a workshop where young men are taught to weave on treadle looms; visitors are always welcome to stroll in and take a look around. This same plaza is home to the municipal **theatre**, a grand Neoclassical structure echoing the one in Quetzaltenango.

There are good connections between Totonicapán and Quetzaltenango, with buses shuttling back and forth every half-hour or so. Totonicapán is very quiet after dark, but if you want to stay, the best **hotel** is the *Hospedaje San Miguel*, a block from the plaza at 8 Av and 3 C (②–③). It is pretty comfortable and some rooms have bathrooms, but beware p rice rises before market days. The *Pensión Blanquita* (①) is a friendly and basic alternative opposite the filling station at 13 Av and 4 C. **Buses** for Totonicapán leave Quetzaltenango between 6am and 5pm, passing the rotunda and Cuatros Caminos, or else take any bus to Cuatros Caminos and change there.

Huehuetenango

HUEHUETENANGO, capital of the department of the same name, lies in the corner of a small agricultural plain, 5km from the Carretera Interamericana at the foot of the mighty Cuchumatanes. Though Huehue is the focus of trade and transport for a vast area, its atmosphere is provincial and relaxed. Before the arrival of the Spanish, it was the site of one of the residential suburbs that surrounded the Mam capital of Zaculeu

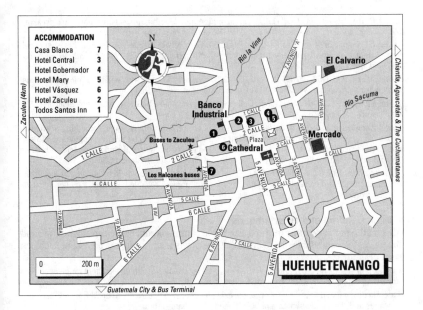

ACCOMMODATION

Casa Blanca	7
Hotel Central	3
Hotel Gobernador	4
Hotel Mary	5
Hotel Vásquez	6
Hotel Zaculeu	2
Todos Santos Inn	1

HUEHUETENANGO

(see p.361). Under colonial rule, it was a small regional centre with little to offer other than a steady trickle of silver and a stretch or two of grazing land and, though the supply of silver dried up long ago, other minerals are still mined, and coffee and sugar have been added to the area's produce.

Today's Huehuetenango has two quite distinct functions – and two contrasting halves – each serving a separate section of the population. The large majority of the people are ladinos, and for them Huehuetenango is an unimportant regional centre far from the hub of things. Here the mood is summed up in the unhurried atmosphere of the attractive **plaza** at the heart of the ladino half of town, where shaded walkways are surrounded by administrative offices. Overlooking it, perched above the pavements, are a shell-shaped bandstand, a clock tower and a grandiose Neoclassical church, a solid whitewashed structure with a facade that's crammed with Doric pillars and Grecian urns.

A few blocks to the east, the town's atmosphere could hardly be more different. Around the **market**, the hub of the Maya part of town, the streets are crowded with traders, drunks and travellers from Mexico and all over Central America. This part of Huehuetenango, centred on 1 Avenida, is always alive with activity, its streets packed with people from every corner of the department and littered with rotten vegetables.

Arrival, information and accommodation

Huehue is fairly small so you shouldn't have any real problems finding your way around, particularly once you've located the plaza. You'll arrive at the purpose-built **bus terminal** halfway between the Carretera Interamericana and town. Minibuses make constant trips between the town centre and the bus terminal.

Virtually all Huehue's **hotels** are within a short stroll of the plaza and tend to be good value for money, though there's nothing at the top end of the scale.

Casa Blanca, 7 Av 3–41 (☎ & fax 7642586). The town's newest upmarket hotel, built in colonial style. The fine restaurant and spacious garden terrace are well worth a visit too. ⑨.

Hotel Central, 5 Av 1–33 (☎7641197) Classic budget hotel, with large, scruffy rooms in a creaking old wooden building and a fantastic comedor. No singles or private baths. ①.

Hotel Gobernador, 4 Av 1–45 (☎ & fax 7641197). Formerly known as the Astoria, this is an excellent budget hotel run by a very friendly family, with attractive rooms, with or without bath, hot showers and a good comedor. ②.

Hotel Mary, 2 C 3–52 (☎7641618, fax 7641228). Centrally located with small but pleasant rooms, some with a private shower and loads of steaming hot water. ②–③.

Hotel Vásquez, 2 C 6–67 (☎7641338). Cell-sized rooms around a bare courtyard, but clean and safe, with secure parking. ②.

Hotel Zaculeu, 5 Av 1–14 (☎7641086, fax 7641575). Large, comfortable hotel, something of an institution. Some of the older rooms surrounding a leafy courtyard are a bit musty and gloomy, while in the more expensive new section they are larger and more spacious. All come complete with cable TV and private bathroom. There's also parking and a reasonable restaurant. ④–⑤.

Todos Santos Inn, 2 C 6–74 (☎7641241). The best budget hotel in town. Rooms seem far too attractive for the price and come with bedside lights for reading and reliable hot water. Excellent deal for single travellers. ②–③.

Eating, drinking and entertainment

Most of the better **restaurants** are, like the accommodation, in the central area, around the plaza. **Films** are shown two or three times a week at the cinema on 3 C, half a block west of the plaza.

La Cabana del Café, 2 C, opposite *Hotel Vásquez*. Logwood café with an excellent range of coffees (including cappuccino), great cakes and a few snacks.

Café Jardin, 4 C and 6 Av. Friendly place serving inexpensive but excellent breakfasts, milkshakes, pancakes and the usual chicken and beef dishes. Open 6am–11pm.

La Fonda de Don Juan, 2 C 5–35. Attractive place with good if pricey pizzas and a reasonable range of beers, but the pasta portions are too small.

Hotel Central, 5 Av 1–33. Very tasty, inexpensive set meals. Particularly good breakfast.

Mi Tierra, 4 C 6–46. Superb new resturant with nice decor including plants and a fountain. Good atmosphere and the flavoursome menu is more imaginative than most – great for house salads, *churrascos* (barbecued meat) and cheesecake. Plus the beer's cheap. Closed Wed.

Listings

Banks Banco G&T is on the plaza (Mon–Fri 9am–8pm, Sat 10am–1pm); Banco del Café, a block to the south (Mon–Fri 8.30am–8pm, Sat 9am–3pm); and there's a Banco del Ejercito at the junction of 5 Av and 4 C (Mon–Fri 9am–7pm, Sat 9am–1pm). Note that you may have problems getting cash or changing travellers' cheques on a Saturday.

Language schools Huehuetenango is a good place to learn Spanish as you don't rub shoulders with many other gringos. As almost everywhere, schools offer a package of tuition and accommodation with a family for around US$110 a week. One of the best is El Portal, 1 C 1–64, Zona 3 (☎ & fax 7641987), closely rivalled by Fundación 23, 6 Av 6–126, Zona 1 (☎7641478), and Xinabajul, 6 Av 0-69 (☎ & fax 7641518). Abesaida Guevara de López gives good private lessons (☎7642917).

Laundry The best is in the Turismundo Commercial Centre at 3 Av 0–15 (Mon–Sat 9.30am–6.30pm).

Mexican consulate In the Farmacia El Cid, on the plaza at 5 Av and 4 C (8am–noon & 2–7pm). They'll charge you US$1.80 for a tourist card that's usually free at the border though few nationalities now need one at all.

Post office 2 C 3–54 (Mon–Fri 8am–4.30pm).

Telephone Telgua is at 4 Av 6-54 (daily 7am–10pm), though it may move back to its former location next to the post office.

Shopping Superb weaving is produced throughout the department and can be bought in the market here or at Artesanías Ixquil, on 5 Av 1–56, opposite the *Hotel Central*, where both the prices and quality are high. If you have time, though, you'd be better advised to travel to the villages and buy direct from the producers.

Zaculeu

A few kilometres to the west of Huehuetenango are the ruins of **ZACULEU** (daily 8am–6pm; US$4), capital of the **Mam**, who were one of the principal pre-conquest highland tribes. The site includes several large temples, plazas and a ball court, but unfortunately it has been restored with an astounding lack of subtlety (or accuracy). Its appearance – more like an ageing film set than an ancient ruin – is owed to a latter-day colonial power, the **United Fruit Company**, under whose auspices the ruins were reconstructed in 1946–7. The walls and surfaces have been levelled off with a layer of thick white plaster, leaving them stark and undecorated. There are no roof-combs, carvings or stucco mouldings, and only in a few places does the original stonework show through. Even so, the site does have a peculiar atmosphere of its own. Surrounded by trees and neatly mown grass, with fantastic views of the mountains, it's also an excellent spot for a picnic. There's a small **museum** on site (daily 8am–noon & 1–6pm), with examples of some of the unusual burial techniques used and some interesting ceramics found during excavation.

The site is thought to have been a religious and administrative centre housing the elite, while the bulk of the population lived in small surrounding settlements or else scattered in the hills. Zaculeu was the hub of a large area of Mam-speakers, its boundaries reaching into the mountains as far as Todos Santos. However, to put together a history of the site means relying on the records of the Quiché, their more powerful

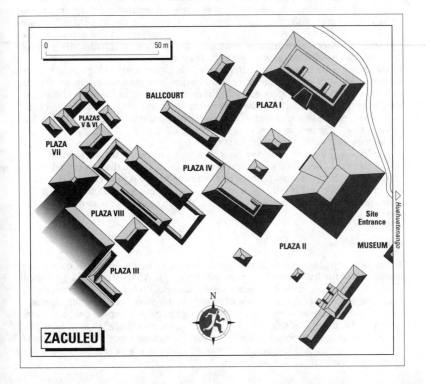

neighbours. According to their mythology, the Quiché conquered most of the other highland tribes, including the Mam, some time between 1400 and 1475. Following the death of the Quiché leader, Quicab, in 1475, the Mam managed to reassert their independence, but no sooner had they escaped the clutches of one expansionist empire than the Spanish arrived with a yet more brutal alternative.

Pedro de Alvarado despatched an army under the command of his brother, Gonzalo, which was met by about five thousand Mam warriors. The Mam leader, Caibal Balam, quickly saw that his troops were no match for the Spanish and withdrew them to the safety of Zaculeu, where they were protected on three sides by deep ravines and on the other by a series of walls and ditches. The Spanish army settled outside the city and besieged the citadel for six weeks until starvation forced Caibal Balam to surrender.

To get to Zaculeu from Huehuetenango, take one of the pickups or buses that leave from close to the school on 7 Av between 2 and 3 calles – make sure it's a Ruta 3 heading for Ruinas Zaculeu (not Zaculeu Central).

The Cuchumatanes

The largest non-volcanic peaks in Central America, the **Cuchumatanes** rise from a limestone plateau close to the Mexican border and reach their full height above Huehuetenango. This area is bypassed by the majority of visitors, though the mountain scenery is magnificent, ranging from wild, exposed craggy outcrops to lush, tranquil river valleys. The upper parts of the slopes are almost barren, scattered with boulders and shrivelled cypress trees, while the lower levels, by contrast, are richly fertile and cultivated with corn, coffee and sugar. Between the peaks, in the deep-cut valleys, are hundreds of tiny villages, isolated by the scale of the landscape. A visit to these mountain villages, either for a market or fiesta (and there are plenty of both), offers one of the best opportunities to see Maya life at close quarters.

The arrival of the Spanish had surprisingly little impact in these highlands, despite the initial devastation, and some of the communities here are amongst the most traditional in the Maya World. More recently, the mountains were the scene of bitter fighting between the army and guerrillas. In the late 1970s and early 1980s, a wave of violence and terror in this area sent thousands fleeing across the border to Mexico, but nowadays, with the fighting over, things are much calmer.

The most accessible of the villages in the vicinity, and the only one yet to receive a steady trickle of tourists, is **Todos Santos**. The horse-race fiesta on November 1 is one of the most interesting and outrageous in Guatemala. To the east a road struggles through the mountains, past the interesting village of **Aguacatán**, on its way to Cobán in Alta Verapaz. If you seek a real adventure, a remote road leads north to the ladino town of **Barillas** via some of the least visited, most traditional villages in the country.

Aguacatán

To the east of Huehuetenango, a dirt road turns off at Chiantla to weave through dusty foothills along the base of the Cuchumatanes to **AGUACATÁN**. This small agricultural town is strung out along two main streets, shaped entirely by the dip in which it's built. The language of Aguateca is spoken only in this village and its immediate surrounds by a population of around 15,000. During the colonial period, gold and silver were mined in the nearby hills and the Maya are said to have made bricks of solid gold for the king of Spain to persuade him to let them keep their lands. Today, the town is steeped in tradition and the people survive by growing vegetables, including huge quantities of garlic, much of it for export.

Aguacatán's huge Sunday **market** gets under way on Saturday afternoon, when traders arrive early to claim the best sites. On Sunday morning a steady stream of people pours down the main street, cramming into the market and plaza and soon spilling out into the surrounding area. Around noon the tide turns as the crowds start to drift back to their villages, with donkeys leading their drunken drivers. Despite the scale of the market, its atmosphere is subdued and the pace unhurried; for many it's as much a social event as a commercial one.

The traditional costume worn by the women of Aguacatán is unusually simple: their skirts are made of dark blue cotton and the *huipiles*, which hang loose, are decorated with bands of coloured ribbon on a plain white background. This plainness, though, is set off by the local speciality – the *cinta*, or headdress, in which they wrap their hair, an intricately embroidered piece of cloth combining blues, reds, yellows and greens, and finished off with pompom tassels.

Aguacatán's other attraction is the source of the Río San Juan, which emerges fresh and cool from beneath a nearby hill, making a good place for a chilly dip. To get there, walk east along the main street out of the village for about a kilometre, until you see the sign. From the village it takes about twenty minutes.

Eight daily **buses** run from Huehuetenango to Aguacatán between 6am and about 2.45pm (1hr). Stay at either the *Nuevo Amanecer* (②) or the *Hospedaje Aguateco* (①). Both are small and very simple. **Beyond Aguacatán** the road runs out along a ridge, with fantastic views stretching out below, eventually dropping down to the riverside town of **Sacapulas** (see p.335).

Huehuetenango to Barillas

It's an eight-hour bus trip to Barillas, travelling through beautiful scenery and stopping at several villages en route. Heading north out of Huehuetenango, the road for the mountains passes through the suburb of Chiantla before starting to climb the arid hillside and, as the bus sways around the switchbacks, the view across the valley is superb. In the distance you can sometimes make out the perfect cone of the Volcán de Santa María, towering above Quetzaltenango some 60km to the south. At the top of the slope the road slips through a pass into the *región andina*, a desolate grassy plateau suspended between the peaks; you'll find the *Comedor de los Cuchumatanes* here, where buses stop for a chilly lunch before pressing on through **Paquix**, the junction for the road to Todos Santos.

Beyond Paquix the road runs through a couple of magical valleys, grazed by sheep and populated by a few hardy highlanders. Great grey boulders lie scattered among ancient-looking oak and cypress trees, their trunks gnarled by the bitter winds. The road emerges at the top of an incredibly steep valley, where it clings to the hillside, cut out of the sheer rock face that drops hundreds of metres to the valley floor. This northern side of the Cuchumatanes contains some of the most dramatic scenery in the entire country, and the road is certainly the most spine-chillingly precipitous.

The first village reached by the road is **SAN JUAN IXCOY**, an apple-growing centre drawn out along the valley floor. There's no particular reason for breaking the journey here, but there is a small pensión (①), where you can get a bed and a meal. In season, around the end of August, passing buses are besieged by an army of fruit-sellers. Over another range of hills and down in the next valley is **SOLOMA**, largest, busiest and richest of the villages in the northern Cuchumatanes, with a population of around three thousand – a good place to break the trip. Its flat valley-floor was once the bed of a lake, and the steep hillsides still come sliding down at every earthquake or cloudburst. Soloma translates (from Kanjobal, the dominant language on this side of the mountains) as "without security", and its history is blackened by disaster: it was destroyed by earthquakes in 1773 and 1902, half burnt down in 1884, and decimated by smallpox in 1885. The long white *huipiles* worn by the women of Soloma are similar to those of San Mateo Ixtatán and the Lacandones, and are probably as close as any in the country to the style worn before the Conquest. These days they are on the whole donned only for the **market** on Thursday and Sunday, which again is by far the best time to visit. The *Río Lindo* is a good, friendly **hotel** (②) that also does food, or there's the cheaper *Hotel Central* (①) and, as a last resort, the *Hospedaje San Juan* (①).

Leaving Soloma the road climbs again, on a steadily deteriorating surface, over another range of hills, to the hillside village of Santa Eulalia. Beyond, past the junction to San Rafael La Independencia, it heads through another misty, rock-strewn forest and emerges on the other side at **SAN MATEO IXTATÁN**, the most traditional, and quite possibly the most interesting, of this string of villages. Little more than a thin sprawl of wooden-tiled houses on an exposed hillside, it's strung out beneath a belt of ancient forest and craggy mountains. The people here speak **Chuj** and form part of a Maya tribe who occupy the extreme northwest corner of the highlands and some of the jungle beyond, bordering that of the Lacandón (see p.136).

The only time to visit, other than for the fiesta on September 21, is on a market day, Thursday or Sunday. The rest of the week the village is virtually deserted. The women here wear unusual and striking *huipiles*, long white gowns embroidered in brilliant reds, yellows and blues, radiating out from a star-like centre. The men wear short woollen tunics called *capixay*, often embroidered with flowers around the collar and quetzales on the back. Below the village is a beautiful Maya ruin, the unrestored remains of a small pyramid and ball court, shaded by a couple of cypress trees. If you decide to **stay**, there are several extremely basic pensiónes – don't expect sheets – the best of which is the *El Aguila* (①), run by the very friendly family who also operate the *Comedor Ixateco*.

Beyond San Mateo the road drops steadily east to **BARILLAS**, a ladino frontier town in the relative warmth of the lowlands. Further on still, the land slopes into the Usumacinta basin through thick, uninhabited jungle. Rough tracks penetrate a short distance into this wilderness (and a local bus runs out as far as San Ramón), opening it up for farming, and eventually a road will run east across the **Ixcán** (the wilderness area that stretches between here and the jungles of Petén) to Playa Grande (see p.400). The cheapest place **to stay** in Barillas is the *Tienda las Tres Rosas* (①), and the best, the *Hotel Monte Cristo* (①), costs not much more.

Pullman buses to Barillas, passing through all the villages en route, are operated by Flor Solomera and leave Huehuetenango at 10pm and 9.30am, taking around four hours to reach Soloma and at least eight hours to Barillas. San Pedrito, Autobuses del Norte and Rutas Barillenses also run services; check at the bus terminal for details. All buses leave from Huehue main bus terminal, and it's well worth buying your ticket in advance as they operate a vague system of seat allocation. It's a rough and tortuous trip, the buses usually filled to bursting and the road invariably appalling. Buses leave Barillas for Huehuetenango at 5am, 6am, 10am, 11am, 11.45am and 11.30pm.

Todos Santos

Backtracking towards Huehuetenango, a road veers to the west from the **Paquix** junction, through high-altitude ladino-farmed land. After 12km or so the road starts to drop, the temperature slowly rises, and you'll start to see the explosively coloured *traje* costume of the Todosanteros. The road continues to decline, gripping the mountains, and you'll soon get a glimpse of the magical village of Todos Santos.

Spectacularly sited in its own remote deep-cut river valley, **TODOS SANTOS** is many travellers' favourite place in Guatemala. Though the sheer beauty of the alpine surroundings is one attraction, it's the unique culture that is really astounding. The *traje* worn here is startling: the men wear red-and-white candy striped trousers, black woollen breeches and pinstripe shirts, decorated with dayglo pink collars, while the women wear dark blue *cortes* and superbly intricate purple *huipiles*. The Todosanteros are perhaps the proudest of all Guatemala's Maya people – there is a distinctive swagger in the step of the men – and the **fiesta** (on November 1) is one of the most famous in the country. For three days the village is taken over by unrestrained drinking, dancing and marimba music. The whole event opens with an all-day horse race and there is a massive stampede as the inebriated riders tear up the course, thrashing their horses with live chickens, their pink capes flowing out behind them. On the second day, "The Day of the Dead", the action moves to the cemetery, with marimba bands and drink stalls set up amongst the graves. It is a day of intense ritual that combines grief and celebration. On the final day of the fiesta, the streets are littered with bodies and the jail packed with brawlers. The Saturday **market**, although nothing like as riotous, also fills the village.

The village itself is pretty – a modest main street with a few shops, a plaza and a church – but it is totally overshadowed by the looming presence of the Cuchumatanes mountains, insulating Todos Santos from the rest of the world. Above the village – follow the track that goes up behind the *Comedor Katy* – is the small Maya site of **Tojcunanchén**, where you'll find a couple of mounds sprouting pine trees. The site is occasionally used by *brujos* for the ritual sacrifice of animals.

Todos Santos is home to one of Guatemala's most interesting **language schools**, where you can study Spanish or Mam. A percentage of the profits goes to local development projects. For reservations, contact Proyecto Lingüístico Quetzalteco de Español, 5 C 2–40, Zona 1 (or Apdo Postal 114), Quetzaltenango (☎7612620).

Practicalities

Buses leave Huehuetenango for Todos Santos from the main bus terminal at 12.30pm and 3pm – get there early to mark your seat and buy a ticket. Some carry on through the village, heading further down the valley to Jacaltenango and pass through Todos Santos on the way back to Huehuetenango at 4am and 10.30am. Ask around for the latest schedule.

One of the best places **to stay** is *Hospedaje Casa Familiar* (②), 30m above the main road past *Comedor Katy*, where views from the terrace café are breathtaking. There is another good place, *Hospedaje las Ruinas* (①), further up the track on the right, in a large twin-storey concrete structure that may now be signposted. Turning left just before you reach the *Casa Familiar* brings you to *Hotel Mam* in an orange house; this is another good option with hot showers (①). There are two other "hotels" in Todos Santos, both very inexpensive but extremely rough, the *Hospedaje La Paz* (①) and *Las Olguitas* (①).

The best place to **eat** is the delightful *Comedor Katy*, though you can also find good meals at the *Casa Familiar*. There is a new logwood gringo-geared restaurant/café called *Ixcanac* in the centre of town, where you'll find spaghetti, good barbecued meats, wine and videos.

Though most of the fun of Todos Santos is in simply hanging out, it would be a shame not to indulge in a traditional smoke sauna (*chuc*) while you're here. Most of the guest houses will prepare one for you. If you want to take a shirt, pair of trousers or *huipil* home with you, you'll find an excellent co-op selling quality weavings next to the *Casa Familiar*.

Walks around Todos Santos

The village of **SAN JUAN ATITÁN** is around five hours from Todos Santos across a beautiful isolated valley. Follow the path that bears up behind the *Comedor Katy*, past the ruins and high above the village through endless muddy switchbacks, until you get to the ridge overlooking the valley where, if the skies are clear, you'll be rewarded by an awesome view of the Tajumulco and Tacaná volcanoes. Take the central track from here, heading downhill past some ancient cloud forest to San Juan Atitán, four to five hours further on; it's easy to follow. There's a hospedaje (①) if you want to stay and morning **pickups** return to Huehue from 6am (1hr). Market days are Monday and Thursday.

Alternatively, you can walk down the valley along the road from Todos Santos to **San Martín** and on to **Jacaltenango**, a route which also offers superb views. There's a basic hospedaje (①) in Jacaltenango, so you can stay the night and then catch a bus back to Huehuetenango in the morning. Some buses from Huehue also continue down this route.

West to the Mexico border

From Huehuetenango the Carretera Interamericana runs for 79km to the Mexican border at **La Mesilla**. There are hourly buses between 5am and 6pm (2hr). If you do get stuck at the border there's **accommodation** at the new *Hotel Maricruz* (②–③), a clean place with private bathrooms and a restaurant, or the cheaper *Hospedaje Marisol* (②). The two sets of customs and immigration are 3km apart. There are taxis, and on the Mexican side you can pick up buses running through the border settlement of **Ciudad Cuauhtemoc** to **Comitán** or even direct to **San Cristóbal de las Casas**. Heading into Guatemala, the last bus leaves La Mesilla for Huehuetenango at around 4pm.

THE PACIFIC COAST

Beneath the chain of volcanoes that mark the southern side of the highlands is a strip of sweltering, low-lying land, some 300km long and on average 50km wide, known by Guatemalans simply as **La Costa Sur**. This featureless yet supremely fertile coastal plain – once a wilderness of swamp, forest and savannah – is today a land of vast fincas, scattered with indifferent commercial towns and small seaside resorts.

The Pacific coast was once as rich in wildlife as the jungles of Petén, but while Petén has lain largely undisturbed, the Pacific coast has been ravaged by development. Its large-scale agriculture – including sugar cane, palm oil, cotton and rubber plantations – accounts for a substantial proportion of the country's exports. Only in some isolated sections, where mangrove swamps have been spared the plough, can you still get a sense of the way it once looked: a maze of tropical vegetation. The **Monterrico Reserve** is the most accessible protected area, a swampy refuge for sea turtles, iguanas, crocodiles and an abundance of bird life.

As for the archeological sites, they too have largely disappeared, though you can glimpse the extraordinary art of the **Pipil** (see below) around the town of **Santa Lucía Cotzumalguapa**. These small ceremonial centres, almost lost in fields of sugar-cane, reveal a wealth of carvings, and some of them are still regularly used for religious rituals. The one site that ranks with those elsewhere in the country is **Abaj Takalik**, outside Retalhuleu, where the ruins are well worth a detour on your way to or from Mexico, or as a day away from Quetzaltenango Xela (or Retalhuleu).

Unfortunately, nature has cursed the coast here with mosquitoes, unpredictable waves and currents and man has added filthy palm huts, pig pens and garbage, so that the **beach** is not the attraction it should be. The hotels are also some of the country's worst, so if you're desperate for a dip and a fresh shrimp feast, it's far better to visit on a day-trip from the capital or Quetzaltenango. The one glorious exception to this rule is the nature reserve of **Monterrico**, harbouring a fairly attractive village and possibly the country's finest beach, with a superb stretch of clear, clean sand.

The main transport route in this region is the Carretera al Pacífico that runs between the border with Mexico at Técún Umán and El Salvador at Cuidad Pedro de Alvarado. There's a regular flow of buses along the highway and you shouldn't have to wait long for a ride.

Some history

Before the arrival of the **Ocós** and **Itzapa** tribes from the west, little is known of the history of the Pacific coast. By 1500 BC, however, these Mesoamerican tribes had developed village-based societies with considerable skills in the working of stone and pottery. Between 400 and 900 AD, the whole coastal plain was again overrun by Mexicans; this time it was the **Pipil**, who brought with them sophisticated architectural and artistic skills and built ceremonial centres.

The first Spaniards in Guatemala arrived here on the Pacific coast, having travelled overland from the north, and their first confrontation with the Maya occurred in the heat of the lowlands. Once they had established themselves to the north in Quetzaltenango, the Spanish despatched a handful of Franciscans to convert the Pipil coastal population. In **colonial times**, the land was a miserable disease-ridden backwater used for the production of indigo and cacao, or for cattle ranching. It was only after **independence** that commercial agriculture began to dominate this part of the country.

Today the coastal strip is the country's most intensely farmed region – where entire villages are effectively owned by vast fincas, and coffee is grown on the volcanic slopes. Much of the nation's income is generated here, and the main towns are alive with commercial activity and dominated by the assertive machismo of ladino culture. Since the development of large-scale agriculture, the highland Maya have performed much of the hard physical labour: though no longer forcibly recruited, many thousands still come to the coast for seasonal work and continue to be exploited by the fincas.

From the Mexican border to Coatepeque

The coastal border with Mexico is the busiest of Guatemala's frontiers, with two crossings, Talismán and Tecún Umán, open 24 hours. The northernmost of the two border posts is the **Talismán Bridge**, also referred to as **El Carmen**, where there's little more than a few huts, a couple of basic pensiones (both ①) and a round-the-clock flow of buses to Guatemala City. If you're heading towards Quetzaltenango or the western highlands, take the first bus to **Malacatán** and change there. On the Mexican side, over the bridge, there's a constant flow of minibuses leaving for Tapachula.

The **Tecún Umán** crossing is favoured by most Guatemalans and all commercial traffic. It has an authentic frontier flavour, with all-night bars, lost souls, contraband and moneychangers. There are some cheap hotels: the *Hotel Vanessa 2* (②) and the *Hotel Don José*, 2 C 3–42 (☎7768164; ②) are two of the best, but it's probably a much better idea to get straight out of town – everyone else is. Once again, there's a steady stream of buses to Guatemala City along the Pacific Highway via Coatepeque and Retalhuleu. If you're Mexico-bound, once you're over the border, there are very frequent bus services to Tapachula (30min).

As you head east from the Mexican border, **COATEPEQUE** is the first place of any importance on the main road, a town that's in many ways typical of the coastal strip. A furiously busy, purely commercial centre, this is where most of the coffee produced locally is processed. The action is centred on the **bus terminal**, an intimidating maelstrom of sweat, mud and energetic chaos. Buses run every thirty minutes from here to the two border crossings, hourly between 4am and 5pm to Quetzaltenango and hourly from 2.30am to 6pm to Guatemala City.

The best place to **stay** in Coatepeque is the *Hotel Villa Real*, 6 C 6–57 (☎7751308, fax 7751939; ④), a modern hotel with clean rooms and secure parking. A bit cheaper is the family-run *Hotel Baechli*, 6 C 5–35 (☎7751483; ④), which has plain rooms with fan and TV, plus secure parking. There are two banks that will change your travellers' cheques on the plaza and a Telgua office (daily 7am–10pm) at 5 Av and 7 C.

Retalhuleu to Cocales

About 40km beyond Coatepeque is the largest town in the region, **RETALHULEU**, usually referred to as **Reu**, pronounced "Ray-oo". Set away from the highway and surrounded by the walled homes of the wealthy, Retalhuleu has managed to avoid the worst excesses of the coast and has a relaxed easy-going air. It was founded by the Spanish in the early years of the Conquest and remains something of an oasis of civilization, with a plaza featuring towering Greek columns and an attractive colonial church. If you have time to kill, pop into the local **Museum of Archeology and Ethnology** in the plaza (Tues–Sun 9am–noon & 2–6pm; US$1), where you'll find an amazing collection of anthropomorphic figurines, mostly heads, and some photographs of the town dating back to the 1880s.

Budget **accommodation** is in short supply in Retalhuleu. The cheapest place in town is the *Hotel Pacífico* at 7 Av 9–29 (☎7711178; ①), which is scruffy and fanless. Otherwise rates go up steeply: *Hotel Astor*, 5 C 4–60 (☎7710475; ③), has rooms with fan, TV and bath, set around a pleasant courtyard, and is very good value for money; or across the road there's the *Hotel Modelo*, 5 C 4–53 (☎7710256; ③). If you want a bit more luxury, try the modern *Hotel Posada de Don José*, 5 C 3–67 (☎7710180; ④), which has good rooms, a reasonable restaurant and a pool.

The **plaza** is the hub of activity. Here you'll find three **banks**, including the Banco del Agro and, close by, the Banco Industrial with a 24-hour Visa ATM, the **post office** (Mon–Fri 8am–4.30pm) and the Cine Morán; the **Telgua** office (daily 7am–10pm) is just around the corner. The best **restaurants** are also on the plaza. Try the *Cafetería la Luna*, or, for cakes and pastries, *El Volován*.

Buses running along the coastal highway almost always pull in at the Retalhuleu terminal on 7 Av and 10 C, a ten-minute walk from the plaza. There's an hourly service to and from Guatemala City, the Mexican border and Quetzaltenango and there are also regular buses to Champerico and El Tulate. Retalhuleu has the only **Mexican consulate** on the Pacific coast, at 5 C and 3 Av (Mon–Fri 4–6pm).

Abaj Takalik

Near El Asintal, a small village 15km to the east of Retalhuleu, the site of **Abaj Takalik** (daily 9am–4pm; US$4) is currently being excavated and has already provided firm evidence of an **Olmec** influence reaching the area in the first century AD. Excavations have so far unearthed enormous stelae, several of them very well preserved, dating the earliest monuments to around 126 AD. This is a large site, with four main groups of ruins and around seventy mounds in the main part of the site. The remains of two large **temple platforms** have also been cleared, and what makes a visit to this obscure site really worthwhile are the carved sculptures and stelae and altars found around their base. In particular, you will find rare and unusual representations of frogs and toads (monument 68) – and even an alligator (monument 66). Amongst the finest carving is stela 5, which features two standing figures separated by a hieroglyphic panel, dated to 126 AD. Look out for a giant Olmec head, too, showing a man of obvious wealth with great hamster cheeks.

There is a small building which acts as the site **musuem** containing a model of Abaj Takalik and assorted carvings and ceramics. You should be able to get a warm *agua* near the entrance, but there is no food available.

To **get to Abaj Takalik**, take a local bus from Reu to **El Asintal**, from where it's a 4km walk through coffee and cacao plantations. If using your own transport, take the highway towards Mexico from Reu, and turn right at the sign. Drive through the village of El Astinal passing the entrance to Finca Santa Margarita, where there is a stone carving.

Zunil market, Guatemala

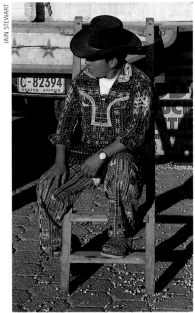

Sololá man, Guatemala

Basketball, San Juan Atitán, Guatemala

Huipil, San Mateo Ixtatán, Guatemala

Scarlet Macaw

Creole man, Lívingston, Guatemala

Stela H, Copán, Honduras

Lake Atitlán, Guatemala

Santo Thomás Church, Chichicastenango, Guatemala

Temple complex, Tikal, Guatemala

Lubaantun, Belize

Hunting Caye, South Belize

Champerico, Mazatenango and Cocales

Some 42km south of Retalhuleu, a paved road reaches to the beach at **CHAMPERICO**, which, though it certainly doesn't feel like it, is the country's third port. The town enjoyed a brief period of prosperity when it was connected to Quetzaltenango by rail, but there's little left now apart from a rusting pier. The **beach** is much the same as anywhere else, although its sheer scale is impressive (watch out for the dangerous undertow). Delicious fried shrimp and fish **meals** are widely available; try the *Restaurant Monte Limar*. The best **place to stay** is the friendly, Spanish-owned *Miramar* at 2 C and Av Coatepeque (☎7737231; ②), a lovely old building with a fantastic wooden bar and dark windowless rooms. **Buses** run between Champerico and Quetzaltenango every two hours or so passing through Retalhuleu. The last bus for Retalhuleu leaves Champerico at 6pm.

Back on the highway, heading east, the next place of any size is the unremarkable town of Cuyotenango, where a side road heads off to the featureless beach of El Tulate. The next stop on the highway is **MAZATENANGO**, another seething commercial town, which also has a quieter, calmer side centred around the plaza. *Maxim's*, at 6 Av 9–23, serves excellent Chinese food and barbecued meats, or try *Croissants Pastelería* on the plaza for coffee and cakes. There are also a couple of cinemas, plenty of **banks**, a few run-down pensiones and, on the main highway, the decent, clean *Hotel Alba* (☎8720264; ④), which has secure parking.

About 30km beyond Mazatenango is **COCALES**, a crossroads from where a road runs north to Santiago Atitlán, San Lucas Tolimán and Lago de Atitlán. If you're heading this way you can wait for a connection at the junction, but don't expect to make it all the way to Panajachel unless you get here by midday. The best bet is to take the first pickup or bus for Santiago and catch a boat from there to other points on the lake. The last transport to Santiago Atitlán leaves Cocales at around 5pm.

Santa Lucía Cotzumalguapa and around

Another 23km brings you to **SANTA LUCÍA COTZUMALGUAPA**, another uninspiring Pacific town a short distance north of the highway. The main reason to visit is to explore the **archeological sites** that are scattered in the surrounding cane fields. Pullman **buses** passing along the highway will drop you at the entrance road to town, ten minutes' walk from the town centre, while second-class buses from Guatemala City go straight into the terminal, a few blocks from the plaza. Buses to the capital leave the terminal hourly until 4pm, or you can catch a pullman from the highway.

As usual, the **plaza** is at the centre of things. Santa Lucía's shady square is disgraced by possibly one of the ugliest buildings in the country (in a very competitive league), a memorably horrific green and white concrete municipal structure. Just off the plaza you'll find several cheap and scruffy **hotels**, the *Pensión Reforma*, 4 Av 4–71 (①), and the *Hospedaje El Carmen*, around the corner on 5 Calle (①). The nearest upmarket place is the *Caminotel Santiaguito* (☎8825435; ④), a slick motel on the main highway, which has a swimming pool and restaurant.

Back in town at least three **banks** will change your travellers' cheques. Try Banco Corpativo in the plaza which accepts most varieties. For **food**, the *Comedor Lau* on 3 Av does reasonable Chinese meals or there's a huge new *Pollo Campero* on the north side of the square and *Sarita* ice creams on 3 Av. For a drink, *Cevicheria La Española* on 4 Av, south of the plaza, is the best bet.

Pipil sites around Santa Lucía Cotzumalguapa

Getting to the sites isn't easy unless have your own transport or rent a taxi. Drivers loiter with intent in the main plaza – you should reckon on US$10 to visit all the sites.

Children will guide on foot as well – ask in your pensión or in the plaza – though a walking tour can be an exhausting and frustrating process, taking you through a sweltering maze of cane fields. If you want to see just one of the sites, choose Bilbao, just 1km or so from the centre of town, which features some of the best carving. If you get lost at any stage, ask for "*las piedras*", as they tend to be known locally.

In 1880, more than thirty Late Classic stone monuments were removed from the Pipil site of **Bilbao**, and nine of the very best were shipped to Germany. Four sets of stones are still visible in situ, however, and two of them perfectly illustrate the magnificent precision of the carving, beautifully preserved in slabs of black volcanic rock. To **get to** the site, walk uphill from the plaza, along 4 Av, and bear right at the end, where a dirt track takes you past a small red-brick house and along the side of a cane field. About 200m further on is a fairly wide path leading left into the cane for about 20m. This brings you to two large stones carved in bird-like patterns, with strange circular glyphs arranged in groups of three: the majority of the glyphs are recognizable as the names for days once used by the people of southern Mexico. In the same cane field, further along the same path, is another badly eroded stone, and a final set with a superbly preserved set of figures and interwoven motifs.

The second site is about 5km further afield in the grounds of the **Finca El Baúl**, down the only tarmacked road (3 Av) that heads north out of town. The hilltop site has two huge stones that date from the Classic period. The first is propped against a tree, carved in low relief, and depicts a standing figure wearing a skirt. The skirted figure bears a spectacular headdress, possibly that of Huhuetéotl, the fire god of the Mexicans, who supported the sun. Surrounding the figure are a number of carved circles, one seemingly bearing the date 8 deer. The second stone is a massive half-buried head, in superb condition, with wrinkled brow, huge cheesy grin and patterned headdress, which probably again represents Huehuetéotl. The site itself is still actively used for pagan ceremonies, particularly by women hoping for children or safe childbirth. In front of the stones is a set of small altars on which local people make animal sacrifices, burn incense and leave offerings of flowers.

The next place of interest is the **finca** itself, a few kilometres further away from town, where the carvings include more superb heads, a stone skull, a massive jaguar and an extremely well-preserved stela of a ball-court player (monument 27) that dates from the Late Classic period. Alongside all this antiquity is the finca's old steam engine, a miniature machine that used to haul the cane along a system of private tracks. As the finca has its own bus service you may be able to get a ride there. Buses leave from the *Tienda El Baúl*, a few blocks uphill from the plaza, four or five times a day, the first at around 7am and the last either way at about 6pm.

On the other side of town is the final site at **Finca las Ilusiones**, where there's another private collection of artefacts and some stone carvings. To get there, walk east along the highway for about 1km and turn left by the second Esso station. Perhaps the most striking figure here is a pot-bellied statue (monument 58) that is probably from the middle Preclassic era. There are several other original carvings, including some fantastic stelae, plus some copies and a small museum crammed with literally thousands of small stone carvings and pottery fragments.

La Democracia

Continuing down the highway to Siquinalá, a rundown sort of place, there's another branch road that heads to the coast. Nine kilometres south, on the branch road, **LA DEMOCRACIA** is of particular interest as the home of another collection of archeological relics. To the east of town lies the site of **Monte Alto**, many of whose best pieces are now spread around the town plaza under a vast ceiba tree. These so-called "fat boys" are massive stone heads with simple, almost childlike faces. Some are attached to smaller rounded bodies and rolled over on their backs clutching their swollen stomachs. Some theorists reckon the statues predate almost all other archeological finds in Guatemala and could well be as much as four thousand years old, while others suggest a more recent date of between 800 and 200 BC. Also on the plaza, the town **museum** (Tues–Sun 8am–noon & 2–5pm) houses carvings, ceremonial yokes worn by ball-game players, pottery, grinding stones and a few more carved heads.

Escuintla and south to the coast

At the junction of the two principal coastal roads from the capital, **ESCUINTLA** is the largest and most important of the Pacific towns. There's nothing to do here, but you do get a good sense of life on the coast, its pace and energy and the frenetic commercial activity that drives it. Escuintla lies at the heart of the country's most productive region, both industrially and agriculturally, and the department's resources include cattle, sugar, cotton, light industry and even a small Texaco oil refinery.

Below the plaza a huge, chaotic **market** sprawls across several blocks, spilling out into 4 Av, the main commercial thoroughfare, which is also notable for a lurid blue mock castle that functions as the town's police station.

There are plenty of cheap **hotels** near 4 Av, most of them sharing in the general air of dilapidation. The *Hospedaje Oriente*, 4 Av 11–30 (①), is cheap and pretty clean, or for a/c and secure parking, head for the recommended *Hotel Costa Sur*, 4 Av and 12 C (☎8881819; ③). For **changing money**, there's a Banco Industrial at 4 Av and 6 C, and Lloyds at 7 C 3–07. The best deal for **eating** is at *Pizzeria al Macarone*, 4 Av 6–103, which has US$1.70 lunch specials. There are also two **consulates** in town, Honduras at 6 Av 8–24 and El Salvador at 16 C 3–20.

Buses to Escuintla leave from the Treból junction in Guatemala City frequently until 7pm, returning from 8 C and 2 Av in Escuintla. For other destinations there are two terminals: for places **en route to the Mexican border**, buses run through the north of town and stop by the Esso station opposite the Banco Uno (take a local bus up 3 Av); buses for the **coast road and inland route to El Salvador** are best caught at the main terminal on the south side of town, at the bottom of 4 Av (local bus down 4 Av). From the latter, buses leave every thirty minutes for Puerto San José, hourly for the eastern border, and daily at 6.30am and noon for Antigua, via El Rodeo.

Puerto San José

South from Escuintla the coast road heads through acres of cattle pasture to **PUERTO SAN JOSÉ**, which, in its prime, was Guatemala's main shipping terminal, funnelling goods to and from the capital. It has now been made virtually redundant by Puerto Quetzal, a container port a few kilometres to the east. Today both town and port are somewhat sleazy and the main business is local tourism: what used to be rough sailors' bars pander to the needs of the day-trippers from the capital who fill the beaches at weekends.

The shoreline is separated from the mainland by the **Canal de Chiquimulilla**, which starts near Sipacate, west of San José, and runs as far as the border with El Salvador, cutting off all the beaches in between. Here in San José, the main resort area is on the other side of the canal, directly behind the beach. This is where all the bars and restaurants are, most of them crowded at weekends with big ladino groups feasting on seafood. The **hotels** nearby are not so enjoyable, catering as they do to a largely drunken clientele, but try *Casa San José Hotel*, Av del Comercio (☎7765587; ③), where you'll find a pool and restaurant. Or, for a really cheap option, *Hospedaje Viñas de Mar* (②), which is basic but right by the beach.

Buses between San José and Guatemala City run every hour or so all day. From Guatemala City they leave from the terminal in Zona 4 (or the new Zona 12 terminal when operational) and from the plaza in San José.

Monterrico

The setting of **MONTERRICO**, further east along the coast, is one of the finest on the Pacific coast, with the scenery reduced to its basic elements: a strip of dead straight sand, a line of powerful surf, a huge empty ocean and an enormous curving horizon. The village is friendly and relaxed, separated from the mainland by the waters of the Chiquimulilla canal, which in this case weaves through a fantastic network of mangrove **swamps**. Mosquitoes can be a problem during the wet season.

Beach apart, Monterrico's chief attraction is the **nature reserve**, which embraces the village, the beach – an important **turtle** nesting ground – and a large slice of the swamps behind, forming a total area of some 72 square kilometres. Sadly, however, the protected status the reserve officially enjoys does not stop the dumping of domestic rubbish and the widespread theft of turtle eggs. That said, it's well worth making your way to Monterrico, if only for the fantastically beautiful ocean. This is certainly the best place on the coast to spend time by the sea.

You can also visit the **Biotopo Monterrico-Hawaii**, a mangrove swamp with dark, nutrient-rich waters and four distinct types of mangrove that form a dense mat of branches, interspersed with narrow canals, open lagoons, bullrushes and water lilies. The tangle of roots acts as a kind of marine nursery, offering small fish protection from their natural predators, while above the surface the dense vegetation and ready food supply provide an ideal home for hundreds of species of bird and a handful of mammals, including racoons, iguanas, alligators and opossums. The best way to travel is in a small *cayuco*; ask around at the dock for a boatman.

Practicalities

The best way to **get to Monterrico** is via the coastal highway at **Taxisco**. From here trucks and buses run the 17km paved road to **LA AVELLANA**, a couple of kilometres from Monterrico on the opposite side of the mangrove swamp, where boats shuttle passengers and cars back and forth. There's a steady flow of traffic between Taxisco and La Avellana, the last bus leaving Taxisco at 6pm and La Avellana at 4.30pm. Several direct buses run between La Avellana and the Zona 4 bus terminal in Guatemala City, taking around three and a half hours; alternatively, get on any bus heading for Taxisco and change there.

Accommodation

There's a pretty good range of **accommodation** in Monterrico, with almost everything concentrated right on the beach. As there are **no phones** it isn't easy to book in advance; you'll do best if you try those that have reservation numbers in Guatemala City. As elsewhere on the coast, prices can increase by around fifty percent at weekends.

Hotel Baule Beach, next door to the *Kaiman* (Guatemala City ☎4736196, fax 4713390). The most enduring gringo guest house on the entire Pacific coast, run by American Nancy Garver, a former Peace Corps volunteer. All rooms have their own bathroom and mosquito net; there's a pool and decent food. Good deal for single travellers. ③.

Hotel El Mangle, behind the *Baule Beach* (Guatemala City ☎3603336). Five simple rooms all with private bathroom. No pool or food. ④.

Johnny's Place, turn left when you reach the ocean and it's the first place you'll come to (Guatemala City ☎3374191). Self-catering bungalows sleeping four. Three small pools. ④–⑤.

Kaiman Inn, the next option as you head east down the beach. Here large rooms have mosquito nets and fans and there's a pool and a variable Italian restaurant. ④.

Paradise Hotel, 2km outside the village, on the road heading for Itzapa (Guatemala City ☎4784202, fax 4784595). Best reached with your own transport. Spacious bungalows with two double beds and private bath. There's a swimming pool and a decent, though expensive restaurant. ⑦.

Pez de Oro, the last place as you head east down the beach (Guatemala City ☎3683684). The nicest cottages in Monterrico – well-spaced, comfortable and tastefully decorated with a small swimming pool and a good Italian restaurant with excellent pasta and wine by the glass. ⑤.

Pig Pen, 20m on the right when you reach the beach. Excellent budget base with the cheapest beds in town. Rooms are bare but clean and you can also cook your own food. Alternatively, hook up a hammock for a dollar a night. ①.

Eating and drinking

When it comes to **eating** in Monterrico, you can either dine at one of the hotels on the beach, or at a comedor in the village, the best being the *Divino Maestro*, where they do a superb shark steak with rosemary. For a relaxing **drink** with great music, head for the *Pig Pen*, run by Michael, a friendly Canadian. He can also point you in the right direction if you want to rent surfboards and boats or find a guide.

travel details

Buses

Chichicastenango to: Guatemala City (every 30min between 5am and 4.30pm; 3hr); Quetzaltenango (7 daily; 2hr 30min); Santa Cruz del Quiché (every 30min; 30min).

Coatepeque to: Retalhuleu (every 30min; 50min); Talismán and Tecún Umán (12 daily; 40min).

Cocales to: Escuintla (14 daily; 30min).

Escuintla to: Antigua (2 daily; 2hr 30min); Guatemala City (18 daily; 1hr 15min).

Guatemala City to: Mexican border at Tecún Umán and Talismán via all towns on Pacific Highway (19 daily; 5hr); Tapachula, Mexico (2 daily; 6hr); Puerto San José (8 daily; 2hr); Monterrico (4 daily; 4hr).

Huehuetenango to: Aguacatán (8 daily; 1hr); Guatemala City (14 daily); La Mesilla (12 daily; 2hr); Todos Santos (2–3 daily; 2hr 30min).

Joyabaj to: Guatemala City (11 daily; 4hr 30min); San Martín Jilotepeque (1 daily; 2hr).

La Avellana to: Guatemala City (3 daily; 3hr 30min).

Monterrico to: Pueblo Viejo, for Itzapa (3 daily; 2hr).

Panajachel to: Antigua (1 daily; 3hr); Chichicastenango (7 buses daily Thurs and Sun, fewer on other days; 1hr 30min); Cocales (5 daily; 2hr 30min); Guatemala City (9 daily; 3hr 30min); Quetzaltenango (6 daily; 2hr 30min); Santa Catarina (hourly; 30min); San Antonio Palopó (hourly; 45min). There are also tourist shuttles to Antigua and Guatemala City, and to Chichicastenango on market days.

Quetzaltenango to: Chichicastenango (7 daily; 2hr 30min); Guatemala City (19 daily; 4hr); Huehuetenango (20 daily; 2hr); Momostenango (hourly; 1hr 30min); Panajachel (6 daily; 2hr 30min); San Francisco el Alto (every 30min; 45min); Totonicapán (every 30min;1hr); Santa Cruz del Quiché (7 daily; 3hr); Tecún Umán (10 daily; 2hr 30min); Zunil (every 30min; 25min).

Retalhuleu to: Guatemala City (18 daily; 4hr); Cocales (14 daily; 50min); Mazatenango (12 daily; 30min); Champerico (8 daily; 1hr); Quetzaltenango (10 daily; 1hr 15min).

Santa Cruz del Quiché to: Guatemala City (every 30min; 3hr 30min); Nebaj (6 daily; 4hr); Quetzaltenango (7 daily; 3hr); Sacapulas (4 daily; 2hr); Uspantán (4 daily; 5hr).

Talismán to: Guatemala City (10 daily; 5hr).

Tecún Umán to: Guatemala City (14 daily; 5hr); Quetzaltenango (10 daily; 2hr 30min).

CHAPTER NINE

THE NORTH AND EAST

The area to the north and east of the capital is an incredibly diverse and beautiful area, where you'll find some of Guatemala's most spectacular Maya sites. The vast northern department of **Petén** is largely lowland jungle, abundant with wildlife and harbouring the ruins of ancient cities with their towering ceremonial centres of temples, pyramids and stelae. Further south, the spectacular alpine scenery of the **Verapaces** offers outstanding hiking possibilities, vast networks of caves to explore and the sublime tranquillity of the pools at Semuc Champey to enjoy. The far south is the most diverse area, comprising both arid and rain-sodden mountain ranges, the near-desert of the central **Motagua valley** and a permanently humid, tropical Caribbean coastline.

This is a very sparsely populated land – there isn't one city in the entire region and no town has a population above fifty thousand – but its lack of people has enabled dozens of **national parks** and reserves to be established. Some are small-scale, designed to safeguard the habitat of a particular species, such as the manatee or the quetzal, while others, such as the Maya Biosphere Reserve, which covers the whole of northern Petén, are gigantic. It's this vast rainforest, much of it still intact despite the attentions of loggers, which offers the ultimate challenge for would-be pioneers in search of some serious adventure. If you're after some less demanding exploration, however, the aquatic splendour of **Lago de Izabal** and the **Río Dulce** gorge area are much more accessible, and have plenty of comfortable accommodation options.

For all the scenic delights of this region, its greatest attraction is the cultural legacy of the **Maya**. Vast temple-rich cities remain buried in the jungles of Petén, some, such as Nakbé, first settled as long ago as three thousand years. The most rewarding site to visit is **Tikal**, perhaps the most magnificent of all Maya sites, which has been partially cleared and is easily reached by air or road. There are scores of other huge temple cities which remain almost unexcavated, such as Río Azul and El Mirador, and which doubtless conceal secrets about the continent's greatest pre-Columbian culture – a civilization able to construct seventy-metre-high buildings long before the birth of Christ.

Today the region's culture is largely **ladino** and, though there are pockets of people speaking Maya languages, they mostly adhere much less strictly to traditional customs and dress than in the western highlands. Guatemala's black Carib population, known as the Garífuna, also live in this region, near **Lívingston**.

ACCOMMODATION PRICE CODES

All the accommodation listed in this book has been categorized into one of nine price bands, as set out below. The prices quoted are in US dollars and refer to the cheapest room available for two people sharing in high season.

① under US$5	④ US$15–25	⑦ US$60–80
② US$5–10	⑤ US$25–40	⑧ US$80–100
③ US$10–15	⑥ US$40–60	⑨ over US$100

EAST TO THE CARIBBEAN

The region to the east of Guatemala City is the most disparate part of the country – a heady mix of desert, rainforest, mountains, lakes and huge plantations, peopled by ladinos, Creoles and isolated pockets of Maya. Connecting Guatemala City with the Caribbean is the **Motagua valley**, a broad corridor of land between two high mountain ranges: the Sierra de las Minas and the Sierra del Espíritu Santo. The upper part of the valley is near-desert, but as the Motagua river approaches the coast, the climate becomes increasingly humid and tropical, and at the Caribbean port of Puerto Barrios, it can rain at any time of year.

To the north of the Motagua valley is **Lago de Izabal**, Guatemala's largest lake, a vast expanse of fresh water, ringed by lonely settlements, swamps, hot springs, waterfalls and caves. The largely unpopulated shores are home to a tremendous variety of wildlife including alligators, turtles, iguana and manatees; the best base for exploring the area is the town of Río Dulce. Just inland from the funky town of Lívingston, home to the black Garífuna people, are the towering gorge systems of the Río Dulce, richly covered in jungle.

The **eastern highlands**, known by Guatemalans as "el Oriente", are dry ladino lands, scarred intermittently by ancient, eroded volcanoes and dusty, featureless towns that offer little for the traveller. If you are passing through this area en route to the top-drawer ruins of **Copán**, just over the border in Honduras, you may choose to divert your journey and visit the ancient pilgrimage town of Esquipulas.

The Motagua Valley

Heading east from the capital's suburbs, the Carretera al Atlántico shadows the **Motagua river valley** as it flows from the highlands towards the Caribbean sea. This upper section of the valley, though never densely populated, has long been a pivotal trade route between the highlands and the Caribbean. In Maya days, salt, shells, cacao, obsidian and the most precious commodity of all, jade, were humped and floated up and down the valley – now it's container trucks loaded with textiles, coffee beans, cotton, sugar and bananas that thunder down this ancient trade route. Quiriguá was the only significant Maya settlement in the valley, closely connected with Copán, which lies 50km to the south.

After the collapse of the Maya civilization, this area was largely abandoned to the jungle and mosquitoes, but at the end of the nineteenth century, the United Fruit Company hatched a scheme to clear the land. They built a railway and planted thousands of acres of banana trees, which spawned profits and influence so great that the company dominated trade for over fifty years and even had a hand in bringing down two Guatemalan governments. Today bananas still dominate the region's economy, though it's Del Monte which now controls the Fruit Company's yellow empire, exporting over two billion bananas a year.

Today, the first place of any concern as you head east along the highway is the **El Rancho** junction, from where a branch road heads north up to Cobán and the Verapaces, where much of Guatemala's coffee and cardamom crops are grown. Continuing east along the Motagua valley, the scenery becomes progressively drier until the junction of **Río Hondo**, where the hills are spiked with cacti. Here a road heads through countless Pepsi-sponsored comedores and an army of food sellers to the **eastern highlands** (see p.386), a quintessentially ladino land of hot dusty towns and expended volcanic cones. This is also the route you need to take if you're heading for Copán in Honduras, or Esquipulas and the El Salvador border.

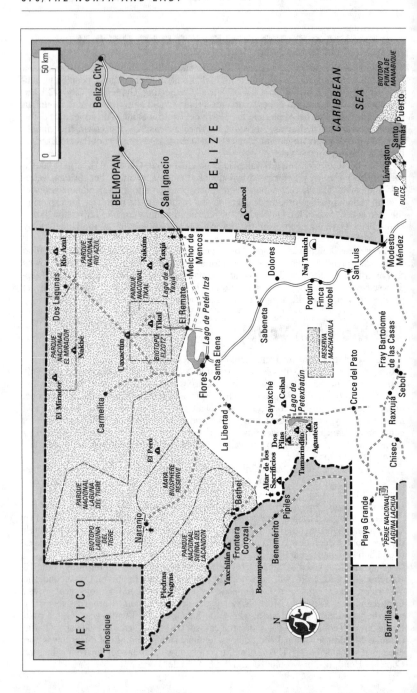

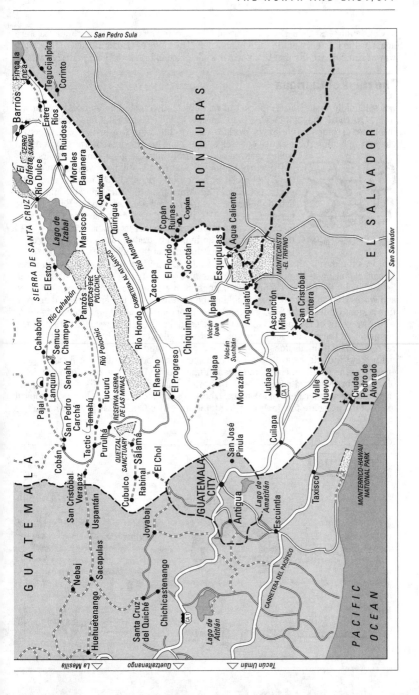

Continuing east along the Carretera al Atlántico, the terrain starts to gather moisture again as the influence of the Caribbean is felt. The ruins of **Quiriguá**, just off the highway at Km 205, are the first really worthwhile place to break the long journey east.

The ruins of Quiriguá

Set splendidly in an isolated pocket of rainforest, surrounded by an ocean of banana trees, **Quiriguá** may not be able to match the scale of Tikal, but it does have some of the finest carvings in the Maya World. Only neighbouring Copán (see p.434) comes close to matching the magnificent stelae, altars and so-called zoomorphs, covered in well-preserved and superbly intricate glyphs and portraits.

The **early history** of Quiriguá is still fairly vague, but during the Late Preclassic period (250 BC–250 AD), migrants from the north, possibly Putun Maya from the Yucatán peninsula, established themselves as the rulers here. Later, in the Early Classic period (250–600 AD), the centre was dominated by Copán, just 50km away, and doubtless valued for its position on the banks of the Río Motagua, an important trade route, and as a source of jade, which is found throughout the valley.

Quiriguá emblem glyph

It was the during the rule of the great leader **Cauac Sky** that Quiriguá challenged Copán, capturing its leader Eighteen Rabbit in 737. Dominating the lower Motagua valley and its highly prized resources for a century, it was able to assert its independence and embark on an unprecedented building boom: the bulk of the great stelae date from this period. Under **Jade Sky**, who took the throne in 790, Quiriguá reached its peak, with fifty years of extensive building work, including a radical reconstruction of the acropolis. At the end of Jade Sky's rule, in the middle of the ninth century, the historical record fades out, as does the period of prosperity and power.

Entering the site beneath the ever-dripping ceiba, jocote, palm and fig trees, you emerge at the northern end of the **Great Plaza**. To the left of the path from the ticket office is a badly ruined pyramid, with the untidy bulk of the **acropolis** dominating the site from the southern end of the plaza. Liberally scattered around the luxuriant tropical grass of the plaza are the finely carved **stelae** for which Quiriguá is justly famous. The

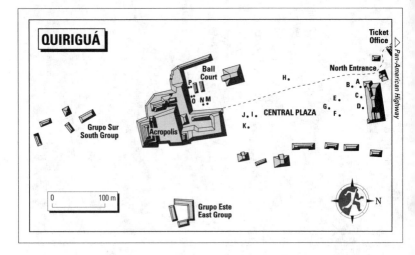

nine stelae are among the tallest in the Maya world, and all are similarly studded with portraits and glyphs, and topped by thatched palm roofs. The figures represent the city's rulers, with Cauac Sky depicted on no fewer than seven (A, C, D, E, F, H and J). Two unusual features are particularly clear: the vast headdresses, which dwarf the faces, and the beards. Largest of the stelae is E, which rises to a height of 8m and weighs 65 tons.

As you head down the path towards the acropolis, you can just make out the remains of a **ball court** on your right before you reach the other features that have earned Quiriguá its fame. Squatting at the base of the raised acropolis are six bizarre **zoomorphs**: globular-shaped blocks of stone carved with interlacing animal and human figures; look out for the turtle, frog and jaguar. The best of the lot is P, which shows a figure seated in Buddha-like pose, interwoven with a maze of other detail.

Practicalities

The **ruins** (daily 7.30am–5pm; US$4) are situated some 70km beyond the junction of Río Hondo, and 4km from the main road, reached by a dirt track that serves the banana industry. All **buses** running between Puerto Barrios (2hr) and Guatemala City (4hr) pass by. There's a fairly regular bus service from the highway to the site itself, plus assorted motorbikes and pickups. Leaving the ruins, you shouldn't have to wait too long to get a ride back to the main highway, or you can walk it in less than an hour.

There are a couple of good, simple places to **stay** in the village of **QUIRIGUÁ**, 5km from the ruins, reached either by following the old railtrack west for 3km or heading back to the highway and getting a ride from there. Alongside the old hospital for tropical diseases is the *Hotel y Restaurante Royal* (②), while the *Hotel el Eden* (②), next to the old station, just off the tracks, is another excellent budget option, which also serves tasty **meals**.

It's another 90km down the Carretera al Atlántico from Quiriguá to the Caribbean Sea and the town of Puerto Barrios. The only place of any significance on the route is the **Ruidosa junction** at Km 245, where the highway splits and a road turns north for the Río Dulce and Petén.

Puerto Barrios

Named for the president, who founded it in the 1880s, the port of **PUERTO BARRIOS** was the main port for most of the twentieth century. It soon fell into the hands of the United Fruit Company, who used its control of the railroad to ensure that the bulk of the trade passed this way and also managed to exempt itself from almost all tax.

These days the boom is over and the town distinctly forlorn, with some sleazy strip clubs, all-night bars and brothels. The streets are wide, but they're poorly lit and badly potholed, and the handful of fine old Caribbean houses are now outnumbered by grimy hotels and hard-drinking bars. The only reason that most travellers come here is to get somewhere else: to Honduras via the "jungle route", to Livingston, or to Punta Gorda in Belize by boat.

Arrival and information

There is no purpose-built bus station in Puerto Barrios. Litegua **buses**, which serve all destinations along the Caribbean Highway, have their own terminal in the centre of town on 6 Av, between 9 and 10 C. All second-class buses – to Chiquimula (for Honduras) and Esquipulas (for El Salvador) – arrive and depart close by from several bays grouped around the central market opposite. **Taxis** seem to be everywhere in Barrios – drivers toot for custom as they drive through the streets.

As there is no Inguat tourist office in town, check at the Litegua terminal for bus schedules and at the **dock** at the end of 12 C for boat departures to Livingston and to Punta Gorda in Belize. You have to clear **immigration** before you can buy a ticket to

Belize, which is best done the day before departure: the immigration office is at the end of 9 C, two blocks north of the dock (daily 7am–noon & 2–5pm). There are also daily **flights** connecting Puerto Barrios with Guatemala City (1hr; US$60); call Inter Airlines (☎3347722, fax 3612159) for more details. The airstrip is about 3km northeast of the centre of town.

The **Telgua** office is at the junction of 8 Av and 10 C (daily 7am–midnight) and the **post office** at 6 C and 6 Av (Mon–Fri 8am–4.30pm). There are a number of **banks** in Puerto Barrios: you'll find Lloyds Bank on the corner of 7 Av and 15 C (Mon–Fri 9am–3pm, Sat 9am–1pm), Banco G&T (for Mastercard) at 7 C and 6 Av (Mon–Fri 9am–7pm, Sat 9am–1pm), and Banco Industrial (with a 24hr Visa-friendly ATM) at 7 Av and 7 C.

Accommodation

Cheap **hotels** are plentiful in Puerto Barrios and, in amongst the squalor, there is a slice of Caribbean charm. This is a very hot and sticky town so you'll definitely need a fan or a/c in your room.

Hotel Caribeña, 4 Av between 10 C and 11 C (☎9480384). This large friendly place has very good value rooms, with doubles, triples and quadruples available. Friendly management and a top-notch seafood restaurant which also does cheap breakfasts. ②.

Hotel Cayos del Diablo, across the bay, reached by a regular free boat service from the jetty (☎9480361 or 9480362, fax 9482364). Lovely hideaway hotel, discreetly set above a secluded beach. Beautiful thatched cabaña accommodation, swimming pool and good restaurant. The definitive luxury option on this stretch of coastline. ⑧.

Hotel Europa 2, 3 Av & 12 C (☎9481292). Ideally placed for the ferry to Lívingston, this is a clean, safe, friendly place and all rooms have fans and private showers. Good prices for single travellers. An almost identical twin, *Hotel Europa 1*, is at 8 Av and 8 C (☎9480127). Both ③.

Hotel Internacional, 7 Av and 16 C (☎9480367). Very well priced motel-style set-up, with a small, heat-busting swimming pool. Rooms all have private showers and TV, and come with a choice of either a/c or fan. ③–④.

Hotel Lívingston, 7 Av between 8 C and 9 C (☎9482124). Above a small shopping mall, this funky marine-green-painted hotel is fair value for money, safe, and the rooms all have TV and private bathrooms. Not so well priced for solo travellers. ③.

Hotel del Norte, 7 C & 1 Av (☎ & fax 9480087). An absolute gem of a hotel – a magnificent colonial time-warp built entirely from wood. The clapboard rooms aren't especially comfortable or very private, but there is a nice swimming pool, and the location, overlooking the Caribbean, is magnificent. Best of all is the incredibly classy, mahogany-panelled restaurant and bar – though the food doesn't quite match the decor. ③–⑤.

Hotel Xelajú, 9 C, between 6 Av and 7 Av (☎9480482). Reasonable budget place. Looks a little rough from the outside, but the rooms are clean, the place is safe and no visiting señoritas are allowed. ②–③.

Eating, drinking and nightlife

When it comes to **eating**, there is an abundance of cheap **comedores** around the market, such as *Cafesama* and *El Punto*. The best place in town, however, is the *Rincon Uruguayo* (closed Mon), where meat is cooked on a giant *parrilla* (grill), South American style, and there are also vegetarian dishes like barbecued spring onions and *papas asados*. It's a ten-minute walk south of the centre at 7 Av and 16 C. Another popular place is the *Safari*, ten minutes north of the centre, right on the seafront at the end of 5 Av, which specializes in fish and seafood. Also worth trying is *Restaurant La Caribeña*, 4 Av between 10 C and 11 C, which does good fish and a superb *caldo de mariscos* (seafood soup); or, in the centre of town, the upmarket *La Fonda de Enrique* on 9 C, right opposite the market/bus terminal, where you'll find great seafood, a nice relaxed atmosphere and a/c. Finally, there is the unique period charm of the *Hotel del Norte* restaurant (see above).

Puerto Barrios also has more than its fair share of **bars**, pool halls and nightclubs, offering the full range of late-night sleaze. None of these is hard to find, with a lot of the action centring around 6 and 7 Av and 6 and 7 C. **Reggae** and **punta rock** are the sounds on the street in Puerto Barrios, and you'll catch a fair selection at weekends in *La Canoa*, 5 Av and 2 C, a small club popular with Garífuna. It's a bit of a hike from the town centre, so you may want to take a taxi.

The jungle route to Honduras

Heading into Honduras from Puerto Barrios, there are two very different options: either the long haul by bus via Chiquimula (see p.386), or the adventurous **jungle route**, involving a combination of buses, pickups and boats through swamps and banana plantations.

If you set out early from Puerto Barrios, you'll certainly get to San Pedro Sula (see p.440) the same day, and it's even possible to make the late afternoon flight out to one of the Bay Islands. The route is actually pretty straightforward; the first stage involves taking an early bus (6am and 7.45am, then every 45min) from Puerto Barrios to **Finca la Inca** (see map); buses leave from a bay next to the market on 8 C, between 6 and 7 Av, and take two hours. After an hour you pass **immigration** at the village of **Entre Ríos** (24hr; unofficial exit "tax" around US$1.75). After another hour trundling slowly through the banana plantations, the driver will pull over by the Río Motagua, where there should be a **boat** ready and waiting, plus the odd moneychanger lurking with intent. The twenty-minute boat ride takes you to a tiny village just inside Honduras, from where a Honduran *lancha* will take you on the fifty-minute trip up the Río Tinto; look out for kingfishers and terrapins on the way. Some sections of this river trip can be difficult in the dry season. Finally a pickup will drive you to the village of **Tegucigalpita** (20min), where there is a basic comedor and the simple *Hospedaje Rosita* (①) if you get stuck.

From Tegucigalpita there are regular buses to **Puerto Cortés** (2hr) via the pretty Caribbean town of Omoa (1hr 30min); both have **immigration** posts. San Pedro Sula is extremely well connected with Puerto Cortés by Citul buses (every 30min 5am–7.30pm; 1hr 15min); Citul is located just across the plaza from immigration.

If your route doesn't follow the exact pattern described above, don't panic; it's probably because there is insufficient water to make the river route to Tegucigalpita. In this case, you may well end up travelling via the Honduran village of **Cuyamelito**, a little further on from Tegucigalpita on the same road.

Lívingston, Río Dulce and Lago de Izabal

At the mouth of the Río Dulce and only accessible by boat, **LÍVINGSTON** is a very funky town that not only enjoys a superb setting but also offers a unique fusion of Guatemalan and Caribbean culture, where marimba mixes with Marley. Along with several other villages in Central America, Lívingston provides the focus for the displaced **Garífuna** or black Carib people, who are now strung out along the Caribbean coast between southern Belize and Honduras. Their history begins on the island of St Vincent, where their African slave ancestors intermarried with shipwrecked sailors and native Carib islanders. In 1795 they rebelled against British rule, and were resettled on the island of Roatán, off Honduras, from where they migrated to the mainland (see p.260). To a lesser extent, Lívingston also acts as a focal point for the Kekchí Maya, many of whom moved into the area to escape the fighting during the guerrilla war.

Lívingston is undoubtedly one of the most fascinating places in Guatemala and many visitors find the languid rhythm of life here hypnotic. The town is just as popular with weekending Guatemalans as it is with international travellers, and offers a welcome break from mainstream Guatemalan culture. Carib **food** is generally excellent and more varied than the usual comedor dishes, and Garífuna punta rock and reggae make a pleasant listening diversion from the standard merengue beat.

While there's not really that much to do in town itself other than relaxing in local style, there are a few places nearby that are worth a visit. The Garífuna **museum** (in theory Mon–Fri 8am–noon & 2–4pm) is worth a look for its collection of Garífuna art and handicrafts; it's in a lovely wooden house just of the main drag to the dock, close to the *Bahía Azul* restaurant. Sadly, the local **beaches** are not of the Caribbean dream variety but swimming is safe at least. It is not safe for women to walk alone along the beaches, however, as a number of rapes have been reported in recent years.

The most popular trip out of town is to **Las Siete Altares**, a waterfall about 5km away, but as there have been **attacks on tourists** walking to the falls, you should ask about the current situation before setting out; if you decide to go, don't take anything of value. The safest option is to hire a local guide or visit as part of a tour – try Exotic Travel in the *Bahía Azul*. If you decide to go it alone, continue down the street past the *Ubafu* bar and turn right by the *African Place* hotel to the beach, then follow the sand away from town. After a couple of kilometres, wade across a small river and, just before the beach eventually peters out, take a path to the left. Follow this inland and you'll soon reach the first of the falls; to reach the others, scramble up, and follow the water. All of the falls are idyllic places to swim, but the highest one is the best of all.

Arrival and information

The only way to get to Livingston is **by boat**, either from Puerto Barrios, the Río Dulce, Belize, or Omoa in Honduras. Livingston is a small place with only a handful of streets, and you can see most of what there is to see in an hour or so. You'll arrive at the main dock on the south side of town; straight ahead, up the hill, is the main drag with most of the restaurants, bars and shops. The **immigration office** (daily 7am–9pm) is on the left as you walk up the hill, a block or so before the *Hotel Río Dulce*.

Exotic Travel, in the same place as the *Bahía Azul* restaurant, is the best **travel agent** in town. The helpful owners will arrange a variety of **trips** around the area: up the Río Dulce (US$8); along the coast to a lovely white-sand beach called, appropriately enough, Playa Blanca (US$9); to the Sapodilla Cayes off Belize (see p.277) for **snorkelling** (US$30); and to the Punta Manabique reserve for game **fishing** (US$14). As these trips only depart if there are sufficient people, prices may vary. Sign up early and be prepared to wait a day or two.

For **changing money**, try the Banco de Comercio, down the road to the left as you walk up the hill from the docks (Mon–Fri 9am–5pm & Sat 9am–1pm), or the Almacen Koo Wong in the centre of town. **Telgua** is on the right, up the main street up from the docks (daily 7am–midnight), and the **post office** is next door.

Scheduled **boats** leave for Puerto Barrios daily at 5am and 2pm (1hr 30min), supplemented by **speedboats**, which leave when full – roughly half-hourly. There are also boats to Punta Gorda in **Belize** on Tuesdays and Fridays at 8am (1hr) and to Omoa in **Honduras** on the same days at 7.30am (minimum four people; 2hr 30min). You can buy tickets at Exotic Travel.

Accommodation

There is a pretty decent selection of hotels in town and though rooms fill up at weekends and during holidays, you should always be able to find a bed.

Hotel California, turn right just before the *Bahía Azul* restaurant. Clean hotel painted a very vivid green. Reasonable rooms all with private bathroom. ②.

Hotel Caribe, along the shore to the left of the dock as you face the town (☎9481073). Basic, budget hotel with bare rooms, some with private shower and fan. Doubles only. ①–②.

Hotel Casa Rosada, about 300m left of the dock (☎ & fax 9027014). Cabins right on the water, with nice hand-painted details, beautiful views and an intimate relaxed atmosphere. Immaculate shared bathrooms, very friendly management and excellent vegetarian meals. ③.

Hotel Garífuna, turn left off the main street towards the *Ubafu* bar, then first right (☎9481091). Squeaky clean, with spotless rooms and very safe. All rooms have fans and private shower. ②.

Hotel El Viajero, turn left after the dock, past the *Hotel Caribe*. Safe, budget hotel with slightly shabby rooms, all with fans and some with private bathroom. ①.

Tucán Dugú, first on the right uphill from the jetty (☎ & fax 9481073). Lívingston's only luxury hotel, with great views of the bay, a pleasant bar and swimming pool (small fee for non-residents). ⑦–⑧.

Eating and drinking

There are plenty of places to **eat** in Lívingston, one of the best being *The African Place*, in a Moorish-style building past the *Ubafu* bar, which serves superb seafood and Spanish dishes. For a memorable **vegetarian** meal, check out the *Casa Rosada* (see above), though it's not priced for budget travellers. The *Bahía Azul*, on the main street, is probably the most popular place in town, with an excellent terrace for watching Lívingston streetlife. There are also plenty of cheap, small comedores on the main street, all selling decent **fried fish**: try *Comedor Coni* or the *Lívingston*.

For evening **entertainment** there are plenty funky bars, of which *Ubafu* is usually the most lively, and a disco on the beach where you'll hear the deep bass rhythms of Jamaican reggae and pure Garífuna punta rock.

The Río Dulce

Another very good reason for coming to Lívingston is to venture up the **Río Dulce**, a truly spectacular trip that eventually leads to the town of the same name about 30km upriver. From Lívingston the river heads into a system of **gorges**, between sheer rock faces 100m or so in height, with a wall of tropical vegetation and cascading vines clinging to the sides. Here and there you might see some white herons or flocks of squawking parakeets and you'll pass an excellent place for a swim, where warm sulphurous waters emerge from the base of the cliff. There's a nature reserve along the way, the **Biotopo de Chocón Machacas** (daily 7am–4pm; US$5), designed to protect the **manatee** – though the huge mammals are extremely timid and you'll be very lucky to see one.

The reserve also protects the forest that still covers much of the lake's shore, and there are some specially cut trails where you might catch sight of a bird or two, or, if you've plenty of time and patience, even a tapir or jaguar. Heading on upstream, across the small **Golfete** lake, the river closes in again and passes the marina and bridge at the squalid town known as **Río Dulce** (or sometimes El Rellano). This part of the Río Dulce is a favourite playground for wealthy Guatemalans, with boats and hotels that would put parts of California to shame. The area is also popular with European and North American yachties because of its sheltered waters, its stores and its repair workshops. The road for Petén crosses the river here and the boat trip comes to an end, although you should certainly include a stop at the *castillo*, on the other side of the bridge. West of here is the **Lago de Izabal**, a vast freshwater expanse bordered by isolated villages, swamps, hot springs, waterfalls and caves.

Río Dulce town

The town of **RÍO DULCE** is little more than a truck stop, where traffic for Petén pauses before the long stretch to Flores. Río Dulce is actually the new name for a couple of older settlements, El Rellano to the north and Fronteras to the south, which have been connected by a monstrous concrete road bridge, obliterating almost any sense of tranquillity in this formerly beautiful area. The road is lined with cheap comedores and stores and you can pick up buses here in either direction. Though the urban ugliness of Río Dulce is initially very offputting, if you escape the immediate area around the bridge you'll find plenty to explore: the Río Dulce gorge itself, the *castillo* close by, the Biotopo Chocón Machacas nature reserve and, venturing further west, Lago de Izabal.

An excellent **place to stay** for those on a tight budget is *Hotel Backpackers* (☎2081779, fax 3319408; ①–③), a new set-up underneath the bridge, on the south side, with dorm beds, private doubles and hammock space. Marie, the manager, is a great source of information, and there's a noticeboard with lots of good stuff about yacht crewing opportunities and sailing courses; they also rent canoes. *Hotel Río Dulce*, on the north side of the bridge (③), is a comfortable place with nice, clean double rooms with fans and showers. At the *Hacienda Tijax*, two minutes by water taxi from the bridge (☎9027825; ①–②), you can pitch a tent or stay in one of the rustic self-catering lodges, which comfortably sleep up to eight. This is a working farm with a large-scale rubber plantation and reforestation project underway. For something a little more upmarket, try *Suzanna's Laguna*, on the southwestern waterfront (fax in Guatemala City 3692681; ⑤), which has beautiful polished-wood rooms, an open-air bar and a restaurant; or *Hotel Vinas del Lago* near the *castillo* (☎9027505, fax 4763042; ⑦), which offers great views across the lake from several terraces and also has its own private beach. Both the above need to be reached by a water taxi from the jetty in Río Dulce town.

As for **restaurants**, *Bar/Restaurant Hollymar*, on the north side of the bridge, is a great place to meet other travellers (and yachties), eat good food and drink the night away. You can also make radio contact with most places around the river and lake from here. *Bruno's*, a couple of minutes' walk from the *Hollymar*, offers the chance to catch up with the latest news and watch movies and North American sports events – it's very popular with the American sailing fraternity.

Moving on from here, if you're heading towards Guatemala City or Puerto Barrios, take the first bus or minibus to La Ruidosa junction (every 30min) and pick up a connection there. There are frequent buses to Flores until 5pm (4hr), and then hourly until 11pm, but as it's highly inadvisable to travel at night, you may want to sleep in Río Dulce and move on in the morning. If you're heading for Lívingston via the Río Dulce gorge, check at the *Hollymar* first (see above) for the next boat departure; there are several daily (around US$10). In the next year or so a new road should open on the north side of the lake, connecting Río Dulce town with the Finca el Paraíso, heading on to El Estor (see p.399) for the trip up the Polochic valley towards Cobán and the Verapaces.

Finally, there are **flights** connecting Río Dulce with Guatemala City on Fridays, Saturdays and Sundays. Telephone Inter Airlines (☎3347722) for details, but be warned that cancellations are frequent.

Castillo de San Felipe

If you have an hour or so to spare then it's worth heading out to the **Castillo de San Felipe**, 1km upstream from the bridge (daily 8am–5pm; US$1), which looks like a miniature medieval castle. The castle, which marks the entrance to Lago de Izabal, is a tribute to the audacity of British pirates, who used to sail up the Río Dulce to raid supplies and harass mule trains. The Spanish were so infuriated by this that they built the fortress to seal off the entrance to the lake, and a chain was strung across the river. Inside there's a maze of tiny rooms and staircases, and there are panoramic views of the lake.

A kilometre from the castle, close to the waterside village of **SAN FELIPE**, is the *Rancho Escondido* (☎ & fax 3692681; ②–③), a friendly American-Guatemalan guest house and backpackers' retreat, with hammock space and a restaurant. If you call or radio from the *Hollymar*, they'll come and pick you up.

Lago de Izabal

Beyond the *castillo*, the broad expanse of **Lago de Izabal** opens up before you, with great views of the highlands beyond the distant shores; local boatmen run trips from Río Dulce town to various places around the lake. On the north shore, about 25km from Río Dulce, is **Finca el Paraíso**, where there's plenty to explore, including an amazing hot waterfall cascading into pools cooled by fresh river water, and a series of caves whose interiors are crowded with extraordinary shapes and colours – made even more memorable by the fact that you have to swim by torchlight to see them. At the finca itself there are six beautiful cabañas on the waterfront (⑨). To book, either radio them on VHF73, or phone Guatemala City on ☎2532397 and speak to Sra Gabriella de la Vega Rodriguez. The finca is very soon to be connected by a new bus or pickup service from Río Dulce and El Estor; in the meantime you can hire a boat or hitch a bumpy ride on a tractor-drawn trailer.

MARISCOS is the main town on the south side of the lake. The main reason that people head this way is to catch the ferry across the lake to **El Estor** (see p.399), from where early morning buses run to Cobán in Alta Verapaz. It's pretty much a one-street town, with three cheap, pretty scruffy **hotels**, a police station, a pharmacy, and of course the passenger **ferry** that leaves at noon, returning at 6am (1hr). Small *lanchas* supplement the ferry service at other times when there are enough passengers (1hr; US$3.50). There's one bus a day from Guatemala City and one from Puerto Barrios; both return after the arrival of the boat from El Estor at 7am. At other times take any bus along the Carretera al Atlántico, ask to be dropped at La Trinchera, and a pickup will take you from there to Mariscos. The best place to stay in Mariscos is *Hotel*

Karinlinda (②–③), where some rooms have private bathrooms. *Hospedaje Los Almendras* (①) is more basic, but reasonably clean.

The other reason to head this way is to reach *Denny's Beach* (Guatemala City ☎ & fax 3692681; VHF 09; ④), an ideal place to get away from it all. As well as pleasant cabañas overlooking the sandy beach, there's camping space and room to sling a hammock. The open-air bar and restaurant are a bit expensive so bring as many provisions as you can from the well-stocked supermarket at Mariscos pier. Hire a *lancha* from the pier for the fifteen-minute trip or call Dennis Gulck, the owner, and someone will come and get you. On the other side of the lake from Mariscos is another attractive, usually deserted beach, Playa Dorada. It's a 4km hike away, or you can take a water taxi from the dock at Mariscos.

The eastern highlands

The **eastern highlands**, lying to the southeast of the capital, have to rank as the least-visited part of Guatemala. The population is almost entirely latinized, speaking Spanish and wearing Western clothes, although many are pure Maya by blood. The ladinos of the east have a reputation for behaving like cowboys and supporting right-wing politics – violent demonstrations of macho pride are not uncommon. Not surprisingly, the military recruits much of its personnel here.

The landscape here lacks the immediate appeal of the western highlands: the mountains are lower and the volcanoes less symmetrical. There are plenty of blunted peaks to explore, however, and if you want to climb one, the **Volcán de Ipala** is the best to make for, with an idyllic crater lake at its summit. The region's towns are almost all pretty featureless and perennially hot and dusty, so you're unlikely to want to hang around for long. **Esquipulas** is worth a visit, though, for its colossal church, the most important pilgrimage site in Central America. You can head into either Honduras and El Salvador from here, though if you're making your way to the ruins of Copán there's a quicker route via neighbouring **Chiquimula**.

Chiquimula

Set to one side of the broad Río San José valley, the town of **CHIQUIMULA** is an unattractive, bustling ladino stronghold surrounded by parched near-desert cacti-pierced terrain. If you've just arrived from Honduras, things only get better from here. The town has long been an important transport terminal, but there is little to see here apart from a massive ruined colonial church on the edge of town beside the highway. Most travellers are in town to get to Honduras or to visit the top-drawer Maya site of Copán, just over the border (see p.434).

Everything you're likely to need in Chiquimula is east of the **plaza**, and close to the bus terminal, on 3 Calle, which leads towards the main highway. Of the **hotels** in town, *Pensión Hernandez* at 3 C 7–41 (☎ & fax 9420708; ②) is the first place to try, with plenty of very clean, simple rooms, all with fan and some with private shower. It has safe parking, a small pool, **email** facilities and the owner speaks good English. A little further down the same road, at 3 C 8–30, *Hotel Central* (☎9420118; ④) has five pleasant rooms all with with private bathroom and cable TV. Still on the same street, *Pensión España* at 3 C 7–81 (①) is very cheap and basic. *Hotel Victoria*, half a block west of the bus terminal at 2 C 9–99 (☎9422238; ③), is reasonable value and all rooms have private shower and cable TV.

When it comes to **eating**, there are plenty of good, inexpensive comedores in and around the **market**, which is centred on 3 C and 8 Av, as well as *Magic Burger* and *Cafe Paíz*, both on 3 C, for predictable fast food and good fruit juices. For something a little more ambitious, try *Bella Roma*, 7 Av 5–31, which specializes in pizza and pasta. *Las Vegas*, on 7 Av off the plaza, with fairly high prices and garish decor, is where the town's upwardly mobile gather – you can forget the cocktails here, but the food's reasonable. Otherwise the only evening entertainment in Chiquimula is at the Cine Liv on the plaza.

For **changing money** there's a branch of the Banco G&T at 7 Av 4–75 (Mon–Fri 9am–7pm, Sat 10am–2pm), or try the largest of the sombrero shops in the daily market, which is always worth a look. Telgua is on the corner of the plaza (daily 7am–midnight). The **bus terminal** is at 1 "A" C, between 10 Av and 11 Av, midway between the plaza and the highway. There are frequent **buses** from here to Guatemala City (every 30min; 5.30am–3.30pm; 3hr), Esquipulas (every 15min; 5.30am–7pm; 1hr), Jalapa via Ipala (hourly; 6am–4pm) and Puerto Barrios (hourly; 3hr 30min). For Copán, catch one of the eight daily buses to the border at El Florido (2hr 30min).

The Volcán de Ipala

Reached down a side road off the main highway between Chiquimula and Esquipulas, the **Ipala volcano** (1650m) may seem a little disappointing at first, as it looks rather like a rounded hill, unlike the near-perfect conical peaks of the western highlands. However, it's well worth heading for if you yearn for some real solitude. Very few visitors make it out this way and the chances are that if you visit on a weekday you'll have the place to yourself. The eroded cone, inactive for hundreds of years, is now filled by a beautiful little **crater lake**, ringed by dense tropical forest. You can walk round the entire lake in a couple of hours. The lake waters are said to contain a unique species of fish, the *mojarra*, with six prominent spines on its back. It's very peaceful up here and the lake makes a wonderful place to **camp**, though you'll have to bring all your own supplies as there are no shops or other facilities. To **get to** the lake it is possible to climb the volcano from the village of Ipala itself, a distance of around 10km, but the easiest ascent (2hr) is from the south, setting out from close to the village of Agua Blanca (see below). If you have your own transport, head for the tiny settlement of Sauce, at Km 26.5 on the Ipala–Agua Blanca road, park close to the small store and follow the dirt track up to the summit.

AGUA BLANCA is a ladino moustache-and-cowboy-hat kind of place, with a good little hospedaje, the *Maylin* (①), and a couple of comedores, the best of which is the *El Viajero*. It's a pretty straightforward route to the lake; ask the way to the Finca el Paxte and continue to the top from there. The village of **IPALA**, 20km to the north of Agua Blanca down a new sealed road, is connected by bus with Jutiapa to the south, Jalapa to the west, Chiquimula to the north and Esquipulas to the east. The village itself is a pretty forlorn place with a few shops and three hotels, the best of which is the basic *Hotel Ipala Real* (☎9237107; ②), where rooms have en-suite showers and toilets; cable TV is available too.

Esquipulas

The final town on this eastern highway, **ESQUIPULAS**, has a single point of interest: it harbours the most important Catholic shrine in Central America, a carving of the Black Christ that dates from colonial times. It's a beautiful ride from Chiquimula through the hills, beneath craggy outcrops and forested peaks, emerging suddenly at the lip of a huge bowl-shaped valley, with Esquipulas itself below.

The town is entirely dominated by the four perfectly white domes of the **church**, brilliantly floodlit at night. Beneath these the rest of the town is a messy sprawl of cheap hotels, souvenir stalls and restaurants. The year-round pilgrimage has generated numerous sidelines, creating a booming resort where people from all over Central

America come to worship, eat, drink and relax, in a bizarre combination of holy devotion and indulgence. The principal day of **pilgrimage**, when the religious significance of the shrine is at its most potent, is January 15. Even the smallest villages will save enough money to send a representative or two on this occasion, filling the town to bursting point. The town has also played an important role in modern-day politics: it was here that the first **peace accord** initiatives to end the civil wars in El Salvador, Nicaragua and Guatemala were signed in 1987.

As a religious shrine, Esquipulas probably predates the Conquest. When the Spanish arrived, the Maya chief surrendered rather than risk bloodshed; the grateful Spaniards named the town in his honour and commissioned the famed colonial sculptor Quirio Cataño to carve an image of Christ for the church. Perhaps in order to make it more appealing to the local Maya, he chose to carve it from balsam, a dark wood. In 1737, the bishop of Guatemala, Pardo de Figueroa, was cured of a chronic ailment on a trip to Esquipulas, and consequently ordered the construction of a new church. This was completed in 1758, and his body was buried beneath the altar.

Inside the church today there's a constant scurry of hushed devotion amid clouds of smoke and incense. In the nave, pilgrims approach the image on their knees, while others light candles, mouth supplications or simply stand in silent groups. The image itself is approached by a side entrance; join the queue to shuffle past beneath it and pause briefly in front before being shoved on by the crowds behind. Back outside you'll find yourself among swarms of souvenir and relic hawkers, and pilgrims who, duty done, are ready to head off to eat and drink away the rest of their stay.

Practicalities

When it comes to staying in Esquipulas, you'll find yourself amongst hundreds of visitors whatever the time of year. **Hotels** probably outnumber private homes but bargains are in short supply and the bulk of the budget places are grubby and bare. Prices are rarely quoted in writing and are always negotiable, depending on the flow of pilgrims. Avoid Saturday nights, when rooms cost double.

Many of the **budget** options are clustered together in the streets off the main road, 11 C. The family-run *Hotel Villa Edelmira* (②–③) is one of the best, or look for a room at *La Favorita* on 10 C and 2 Av (②). For a touch more luxury, head for 2 Av, beside the church, where you'll find the *Hotel los Ángeles* (☎9431254; ③), some of whose rooms have private bathrooms, and the *Hotel Esquipulao* (④), a cheaper annexe of the *Hotel Payaqui* (☎9431143, fax 9431371; ⑤), which has TV and fan in all the rooms and a pool.

There are also dozens of **restaurants** and **bars**, most of them overpriced by Guatemalan standards. Breakfast is a great deal in Esquipulas; you shouldn't have to pay more than US$1.50 for a good feed. There's a decent range of lunch specials later on, though dinner can be expensive. The *Hacienda Steak House*, a block from the plaza at 2 Av and 10 C, is one of the smartest places in town, while many of the cheaper places are on 11 C and the surrounding streets. Banco Industrial have a branch with a 24-hour ATM at 9 C and 3 Av, and there's also a Banco G&T (Mon–Fri 9am–7pm, Sat 10am–2pm).

Rutas Orientales run a superb hourly **bus** service between Guatemala City and Esquipulas; their office is on the main street at 11 C and 1 Av. There are also buses across the highlands to Ipala and regular minibuses to the borders with **El Salvador** (every 30min; 6am–4pm; 1hr) and **Honduras** at Aguacaliente (every 30min 6am–5.30pm; 30min). If you want to get to the ruins of Copán, you'll need to catch a bus to Chiquimula and change there for the El Florido border post (see p.433). There's a **Honduran consulate** (Mon–Fri 9am–5pm) in the *Hotel Payaqui*, beside the church.

THE VERAPACES

The twin departments of the Verapaces presently attracts only a trickle of tourists, yet they harbour some of the most spectacular mountain scenery and highland towns in Guatemala. Though both Alta (upper) and Baja (lower) Verapaz border the western highlands, their climates are distinctly different. In the south, the low-altitude terrain of **Baja Verapaz** gets very little rainfall and largely consists of sparsely populated cactus country. To the north, the increasing altitude gradually traps more moisture and the mist-soaked hills around Cobán in **Alta Verapaz** are the wettest, greenest mountains in Guatemala. Locals say it rains for thirteen months a year.

Though Maya traditions and costume are less evident than in the mountains further west, if you've time to spare you'll find these highlands are astonishingly beautiful, with their unique limestone structure, moist, misty atmosphere and boundless fertility. The hub of the area and the capital of Alta Verapaz is **Cobán**, an attractive mountain town with some good accommodation, coffee houses and restaurants. It is a little subdued once the rain really settles in but it's still the best base for exploring the area, particularly in August, when it hosts the National Folklore Festival. In **Baja Verapaz**, the towns of **Salamá**, **Rabinal** and **Cubulco** also have famous fiestas where incredible costumes are worn and traditional dances performed. If you head out to the north of Cobán, you can reach the exquisite natural bathing pools of **Semuc Champey**, surrounded by lush tropical forest and fed by the azure waters of the Río Cahabón.

The **history** of the Verapaces is in many ways quite distinct from the rest of Guatemala. Long before the Conquest, local **Achí Maya** had earned themselves a unique reputation as the most bloodthirsty of all the tribes, said to sacrifice every prisoner that they took. Their greatest enemies were the **Quiché**, with whom they were at war for a century. So ferocious were the Achí that not even the Spanish could contain them by force. Alvarado's army was unable to make any headway against them, and eventually he gave up trying to control the area, naming it *tierra de guerra*, the "land of war".

The Church, however, couldn't allow so many heathen souls to go to waste, and under the leadership of **Fray Bartolomé de las Casas**, they made a deal with the conquistadors. If Alvarado would agree to keep all armed men out of the area for five years, the priests would bring it under control. In 1537 Las Casas and three Dominican friars set out into the highlands, befriended the Achí chiefs, learnt the local dialects and translated devotional hymns. By 1538 they had made considerable progress and had converted large numbers of Maya. At the end of the five years, the famous and invincible Achí were transformed into Spanish subjects, and the king of Spain renamed the province Verapaz (True Peace).

Since the colonial era the Verapaces have remained isolated and, in many ways, independent. All their trade bypassed the capital, taking a direct route to the Caribbean along the Río Polochic and out through Lago de Izabal. The area really started to develop with the **coffee boom** at the turn of the century, when German immigrants flooded into the country to buy and run fincas, particularly around Cobán in Alta Verapaz. The Germans quickly prospered, exporting huge quantities of coffee back to Europe, until their expulsion during World War II, when the US insisted that Guatemala remove the enemy presence. Today, the Verapaces are still dominated by the huge coffee fincas and the wealthy families that own them, and there are also architectural hints of the Germanic influence here and there. Taken as a whole, however, the Verapaces remain very much indígena country: Baja Verapaz has a small **Quiché** population around Rabinal, and in Alta Verapaz the Maya population is largely **Pokomchí** and **Kekchí**. The production of coffee and more recently the spice **cardamom** for the Middle Eastern market has cut deep into their land and their way of life, the fincas driving

MARKET DAYS IN THE VERAPACES	
Monday Senahú; Tucurú.	**Saturday** Senahú.
Tuesday Chisec; El Chol; Cubulco; Lanquín; Purulhá; Rabinal; San Cristóbal Verapaz; San Jerónimo.	**Sunday** Chisec; Cubulco; Lanquín; Purulhá; Rabinal; Salamá; San Jerónimo; Santa Cruz; Tactic.

many people off prime territory and on to marginal plots. Though the people are predominantly Maya, traditional costume is worn less here than in the western highlands.

The northern, flat section of Alta Verapaz includes a slice of Petén rainforest, and in recent years Kekchí Maya and landless Mestizos from the south have expanded into this region. Here they carve out sections of the forest and attempt to farm, a process which offers little security for the migrants and also threatens the future of the rainforest.

The main **transport** route into the Verapaces climbs up from the El Rancho junction on the Carretera al Atlántico, past the turn-off at La Cumbre and skirts the Quetzal Sanctuary before arriving at Cobán – a journey very well served by frequent pullman buses. As all other routes in the region are unsealed and only covered by a limited service of second-class buses and pickups, the going can be slow.

Baja Verapaz

The main approach to both departments is from the Carretera al Atlántico, where the road to the Verapaz highlands branches off at the **El Rancho** junction. This road, lined with scrub bush and cacti, climbs steadily into the hills, the dusty browns and dry yellows of the Motagua valley soon giving way to an explosion of greens as dense pine forests and alpine meadows grip the mountains. Some 48km beyond the junction is **La Cumbre de Santa Elena**, where the road for the main towns of Baja Verapaz turns off to the west, immediately starting to drop towards the floor of the **Salamá valley**. Surrounded by steep hillsides, with a level flood plain at its base, the valley appears entirely cut off from the outside world.

Salamá, Rabinal and Cubulco

At the western end of the valley is **SALAMÁ**, capital of the department of Baja Verapaz. The town has a relaxed and prosperous air and, like many of the places out this way, its population is largely ladino. There's not much to do here other than browse in the Sunday market, though the crumbling colonial bridge on the edge of town and the old church, with its huge altars, darkened by age, are worth a look. The **fiesta** in Salamá runs from September 17 to 21. If you decide **to stay**, the pick of the hotels is the *Hotel Tezulutlan* (☎9400141;④), a gorgeous old building just off the parque, with rooms set around a leafy courtyard. *Pensión Juarez* (☎9400055; ②), a basic budget hotel at the end of 5 C, past the police station, is cheaper and provides hot water. For **eating**, try one of the places around the plaza: *El Ganadero* is the best restaurant and *Deli-Donus* scores for coffee and snacks. There's also a Banco del Café (Mon–Fri 9am–5pm, Sat 10am–2pm) and a post office (Mon–Fri 8am–4.30pm).

RABINAL is an hour or so from Salamá, another isolated farming town that's also dominated by a large colonial church. Here the proportion of indígena inhabitants is considerably higher, making both the Sunday market and the fiesta well worth a visit.

Founded in 1537 by Bartolomé de las Casas himself, Rabinal was the first of the settlements established during his peaceful conquest of the Achi nation.

Rabinal's **fiesta**, running from January 19 to 25, is renowned for its dances. The most famous of these, an extended dance drama known as the "Rabinal Achi", was last performed in 1856, but many other unique routines are still performed. The *patzca*, for example, is a ceremony to call for good harvests, using masks that portray a swelling below the jaw, and wooden sticks engraved with serpents, birds and human heads. If you can't make it for the fiesta, the Sunday market is a good second-best. Rabinal has a reputation for producing high-quality artesanía, including carvings made from the *árbol del morro* (the calabash tree) and traditional pottery. There are several fairly basic **hotels** in Rabinal, the best of which is the excellent *Posada San Pablo* (②), a superb budget hotel with spotless rooms. If you can't get in there, try the *Hospedaje Caballeros*, 1 C 4–02 (①).

Another hour of rough road brings you down into the next valley and to **CUBULCO**, an isolated ladino town, surrounded on all sides by steep, forested mountains. Cubulco is again best visited for its **fiesta**, this being one of the few places where you can still see the **Palo Volador**, a pre-conquest ritual in which men throw themselves from a thirty-metre pole with a rope tied around their legs, spinning down towards the ground as the rope unravels, and hopefully landing on their feet. It's as dangerous as it looks: most of the dancers are blind drunk and deaths are not uncommon. The fiesta still goes on, though, as riotous as ever, with the main action taking place on January 23. The best place to stay is in the large *farmacia* (①) in the centre of town, and there are several good comedores in the market.

There are hourly **buses** from Guatemala City to Salamá, Rabinal and Cubulco from 9 Av and 19 Av in the capital, returning from Cubulco until 2.30pm. If you're only going as far as Salamá, there's a steady shuttle of minibuses to and from La Cumbre for connections with pullman buses between Cobán and Guatemala City.

If you'd rather not leave the valley the same way that you arrived, there is another option. One bus a day, leaving Cubulco at around 9am, heads back to Rabinal and then, instead of heading for La Cumbre and the main road, turns to the south, crossing the spine of the Sierra de Chuacús and dropping directly down towards Guatemala City. The trip takes you over rough roads for at least eight hours, but the mountain views and the sense of leaving the beaten track help to take the pain out of it all.

The Biotopo del Quetzal

Back on the main highway towards Alta Verapaz and Cobán, the road sweeps around endless tight curves below forested hillsides. Just before the village of Purulhá (Km 161) is the **Biotopo del Quetzal** (daily 6am–4pm; US$5), an eleven square kilometre nature reserve designed to protect the habitat of this endangered bird. The forest is also known as the Mario Dary Reserve, in honour of one of the founders of Guatemala's environmental movement, a lecturer from San Carlos University in Guatemala City, who pioneered the establishment of nature reserves in Guatemala and campaigned for years for a cloudforest sanctuary to protect the quetzal. He was murdered in 1981, possibly as a result of his upsetting powerful timber interests. The reserve he instituted is a steep and dense rain- and cloudforest, pierced by waterfalls, natural pools and the Río Colorado, which cascades through the reserve towards the valley floor. **Buses** from Cobán pass the entrance hourly, but make sure they know you want to be dropped at the reserve as it's easy to miss.

Paths through the undergrowth from the road complete a circuit that takes you up into the woods and around above the reserve headquarters (maps available). There are reasonable numbers of quetzals hidden in the forest but they're extremely elusive. The **best time** to visit is at sunrise, just before or just after nesting season (March–June).

THE RESPLENDENT QUETZAL

The **quetzal**, Guatemala's national symbol – and with the honour of lending its name to the currency – has a distinguished past but an uncertain future. The feathers of the quetzal were sacred from the earliest of times, and in the strange cult of Quetzalcoatl, whose influence spread throughout Mesoamerica, the quetzal was incorporated into the plumed serpent, a supremely powerful deity. To the Maya the quetzal was so sacred that killing one was a capital offence, and the bird is also thought to have been the *nahual*, or spiritual protector, of the Indian chiefs. When Tecún Umán faced Alvarado in hand-to-hand combat his headdress sprouted the long green feathers of the quetzal, and when the conquistadors founded a city adjacent to the battleground they named it **Quetzaltenango**, the place of the quetzals.

In modern Guatemala the quetzal's image saturates the entire country, appearing in every imaginable context. Citizens honoured by the president are awarded the Order of the Quetzal, and the bird is also considered a symbol of freedom, since caged quetzals die from the rigours of confinement. Despite all this, the sweeping tide of deforestation threatens the existence of the bird, and the sanctuary is about the only concrete step that has been taken to save it.

The more resplendent of the birds, and the source of the famed feathers, is the male. Their heads are crowned with a plume of brilliant green, the chest and lower belly is a rich crimson, and trailing behind are the unmistakable oversized, golden-green tail feathers, though these are only really evident in the mating season. The females, on the other hand, are an unremarkable brownish colour. The birds nest in holes drilled into dead trees, laying one or two eggs at the start of the rainy season, usually in April or May. They can also be quite easily identified by their strange jerky, undulating flight.

A favoured feeding tree of the quetzals is the broad-leaved *aguacatillo* which produces a small avocado-like fruit. Whether or not you see a quetzal, the forest itself, usually damp with a perpetual mist the locals call *chipi-chipi*, is well worth a visit: a profusion of lichens, ferns, mosses, bromeliads and orchids, spreads out beneath a towering canopy of cypress, oak, walnut and pepper trees.

A kilometre or so past the entrance is the rustic *Hospedaje Los Ranchitos del Quetzal* (☎3313579; ②–③), where you can **stay** in wooden cabins or stone houses. There's no electricity and the comedor's menu is usually limited to eggs and beans, but a major compensation is that quetzals are often seen in the patch of forest around the hotel; staff sometimes insist on charging an entrance fee even if you just want to come in and look around. If you're after more luxurious accommodation, try the *Hotel Posada Montaña del Quetzal* (☎3351805; ⑤), 4.5km before the reserve on the way from Guatemala City, which offers pleasant rooms with warm private showers and has its own restaurant, bar and pool.

Alta Verapaz

Beyond the quetzal sanctuary, the main road crosses into the department of Alta Verapaz, and another 13km takes you beyond the forests and into a luxuriant alpine valley of cattle pastures, hemmed in by steep, perpetually green hillsides. The first place of any size is **TACTIC**, a small, mainly Pokomchí-speaking town adjacent to the main road, which most buses pass straight by.

The colonial **church** in the village is worth a look, as is the Chi-ixim chapel, high above the town. If you fancy a cool swim, head for the *Balneario Cham-che*, a crystal-clear spring-fed **pool**, on the other side of the main road, opposite the centre of town.

The simple *Pensión Central,* on the main street north of the plaza(①), is a reasonable budget bet, or for a little more comfort try *Hotel Villa Linda* close by (☎9539216; ③), where the rooms have private baths.

Continuing towards Cobán, about 10km past Tactic is the turn-off for San Cristóbal, a pretty town almost engulfed by fields of coffee and sugar cane, set on the banks of the Lago de Cristóbal. From here a rough road continues to **Uspantán** in the western highlands (see p.336), from where buses run to Santa Cruz del Quiché, via Sacapulas, for connections to Nebaj and Huehuetenango. To head out this way you can either hitch from San Cristóbal or catch one of the buses that leaves San Pedro Carchá (see p.396) at 10am and noon, passing just above the terminal in Cobán ten minutes later, and reaching San Cristóbal after about another half-hour.

Cobán and around

The heart of this misty alpine land and the capital of the department is **COBÁN**, where the paved highway comes to an end. If you're heading up this way, stay in town for a night or two and sample some of the finest coffee in the world in one of Cobán's genteel cafés. Cobán is not a large place; suburbs fuse gently with nearby meadows and pine forests, giving the town the air of an overgrown mountain village. When the rain settles in, it can have something of a subdued atmosphere and in the evenings the air is usually damp and cool. That said, the sun does put in an appearance most days, and the town makes a useful base to recharge, eat well and sleep well. It also acts as a hub for all kinds of **ecotourism** possibilities in the spectacular mountains and rivers nearby.

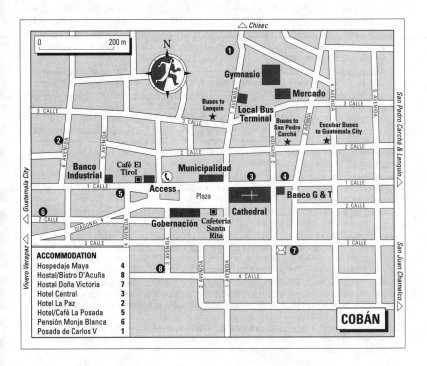

ACCOMMODATION

Hospedaje Maya	4
Hostal/Bistro D'Acuña	8
Hostal Doña Victoria	7
Hotel Central	3
Hotel La Paz	2
Hotel/Café La Posada	5
Pensión Monja Blanca	6
Posada de Carlos V	1

Arrival and information

Transportes Escobar Monja Blanca, one of Guatemala's best **bus** services, operates hourly departures between Guatemala City and Cobán, a journey of four to five hours; their office is on the corner of 2 C and 4 Av, Zona 4 (☎9521536 or 9521498). Buses to **local destinations** such as Senahú, El Estor, Lanquín and Cahabón leave from the terminal down the hill behind the town hall. There are also regular long-distance departures to and from San Pedro Carchá (see p.396), a few kilometres away.

It's also possible to **fly** between Guatemala City and Cobán: Inter Airlines have daily flights (30min) to and from the capital from the small airstrip a few kilometres southeast of the centre of town. There are also occasional charter flights to the remote departmental airstrips of Playa Grande (Ixcán) and Chisec.

Inexcusably, Inguat currently choose not to grace Cobán with a tourist office, but luckily a couple of hotels more than adequately fill the **information** gap. First place to try is the *Hostal d'Acuña* (see below), which has helpful staff, a good folder with maps and bus times and also a useful noticeboard. *Hostal Doña Victoria* also provides good information. Another source is the Access office, in the same complex as *Café Tirol,* where both the owners are bilingual.

Cobán is divided into number of **zonas** like many other Guatemalan towns, with the northeast corner of the plaza at 1 C and 1 Av as the dividing point. Zona 1 is in the northwest, Zona 2 in the southwest, Zona 3 to the southeast and Zona 4 to the northeast.

Accommodation

Unless you're here for one of the August fiestas you'll probably only pause for a day or two before heading off into the hills, out to the villages, or on to some other part of the country. There are, however, plenty of **hotels** in town, and there's free **camping** at the Parque las Victorias on the northwest side of town, which lacks showers, though there are toilets and running water.

Hospedaje Maya, 1 C 2–33, Zona 4, opposite the Cine Norte (☎9522380). Large, basic hotel used by local travellers and traders. Bargain rates, warm showers and friendly staff but smelly toilets. ①.

Hostal d'Acuña, 4 C 3–17, Zona 2 (☎9521547). Undoubtedly the most popular budget choice, offering spotless rooms with comfortable bunks. Dorms are built in the garden of a colonial house and guests can enjoy excellent home cooking on the veranda. Highly recommended. ②.

Hostal Doña Victoria, 3 C 2–38, Zona 3 (☎9522214, fax 9522213). Beautiful refurbished colonial house dripping with antiques and oozing character. Commodious bedrooms are individually furnished and all come with hot water and private bathroom; the streetside rooms are rather noisy, though. Lovely garden and good café/bar and restaurant. ⑤.

Hotel Central, 1 C 1–74, Zona 4 (☎9521442). Germanic decor and friendly staff, but the rooms, set round a nice little garden, are a little gloomy for the price – though they do have hot water and private bathrooms. ④.

Hotel la Paz, 6 Av 2–19, Zona 1 (☎9521358). Safe, pleasant budget hotel run by a very vigilant *señora*. Some rooms have private bathroom. ②.

Hotel la Posada, 1 C 4–12, Zona 2, at the sharp end of the plaza (☎ & fax 9521495). Probably the city's finest hotel, in an elegant colonial building, with a beautiful, antique-furnished interior. The rooms, many with wooden Moorish-style screens and some with four-poster beds, are set around two leafy courtyards and offer all the usual luxuries. Excellent restaurant and café. ⑤.

Pensión Monja Blanca, 2 C 6–37, Zona 2 (☎9521358). A wonderfully old-fashioned atmosphere and a variety of rooms, all set around a stunning courtyard garden. The older ones are a little rundown but the others have been nicely refurbished and come with private bath; all are very quiet. ②–③.

Posada de Carlos V, 1 Av 3–44, Zona 1 (☎ & fax 9521780). Mountain chalet-style hotel close to the market, with pine-trimmed rooms and modern amenities. Comfortable but not memorable. Check out the lobby photographs of old Cobán. ④.

The Town

Cobán's imperial heyday, when it stood at the centre of its own isolated world, is long gone, and the glory faded. The elevated **plaza**, however, remains an impressive triangle, dominated by the cathedral, from which the town drops away on all sides. Check inside to see the remains of a massive, ancient, cracked church bell. A block behind, the **market** bustles with trade during the day and is surrounded by food stalls at night. Life in Cobán revolves around **coffee**: the sedate restaurants, tearooms, trendy nightclubs and overflowing supermarket can be attributed to the town's affluent elite, while the crowds that sleep in the market and plaza, assembling in the bus terminal to search for work, are migrant labourers heading for the plantations. Hints of the days of German control can also be found here and there in the architecture, incorporating the occasional suggestion of Bavarian grandeur.

The most interesting sight in Cobán is the church of **El Calvario**, a short stroll from the town centre. Head west out of town on 1 Av and turn right up 7 Av until you reach a steep cobbled path. You'll pass a number of tiny **Maya shrines** on the way up – crosses blackened by candle smoke and decorated with scattered offerings. There's a commanding view over the town from the church and also the green expanse of the Parque las Victorias next door. Another place worth a look is just outside town: the **Vívero Verapaz** is a former coffee finca now dedicated to the growing of orchids, which flourish in these sodden mountains. The plants are carefully grown in a shaded environment, and a farmworker will show you around and point out the most spectacular blooms, which are at their best between November and January. The farm is on the old road to Guatemala City, which you reach by leaving the plaza on Diagonal 4, the road that runs past the *Pensión Familiar*; at the bottom of the hill you turn left, go across the bridge and follow the road for 3–4km. Any taxi driver will be able to take you.

Eating, drinking and entertainment

When it comes to **eating** in Cobán you have a choice between fancy European-style restaurants and very basic, cheap comedores. For really cheap food, your best bet, as always, is the **market**, but remember that it's closed by dusk, after which street stalls set up in the plaza selling barbecued meat and warm tortillas.

Bistro Acuña, 4 C 3–17, Zona 2. The most relaxed place to eat in town – stunning period setting, uplifting classical music, attentive service and a good place to meet other travellers. A full-scale blow-out will cost around US$8 a head but there are many cheaper options, including great cannelloni. Make sure you leave room to sample something from the cake cabinet.

Café Tirol, 1 C, on the north side of the plaza. Relatively upmarket by Guatemalan standards, though cheaper than the *Posada*. Serves 22 different types of coffee, pretty good breakfasts, hot chocolate, pancakes and sandwiches. Service can be distracted. Tues–Sun 7am–8.30pm.

Cafetería Santa Rita, 2 C, on the plaza, close to the cathedral. Good comedor with friendly service and decent nosh. Very Guatemalan, in the unlikely event you're sick of all those European-style cafés.

Hotel la Posada, 1 C 4–12, Zona 2, at the sharp end of the plaza. The smartest restaurant in town with traditional Guatemalan specialities as well as international cuisine. The café on the veranda outside serves superb breakfasts, coffee, tea and snacks.

Kam Mun, 1 C & 9 Av, Zona 2. Excellent, hyper-hygienic Chinese restaurant. Good line-up of economical oriental choices. Daily noon–9.30pm.

NIGHTLIFE

Generally speaking Cobán is a pretty quiet place, particularly so in the evenings. There are two **cinemas**, the CineTuria in the plaza, and the Cine Norte, on 1 C. In addition to the usual cantinas, there are two half-decent **bars**: *La Tasca* in the *Hostal Doña Victoria*, which has a good happy hour, and *Kikoe's* on 2 Av, close to the *Hostal d'Acuña*. Strange though it may seem, the town also has several **nightclubs**. Try *Oasis*, on 6 Av, just off 1 C, or *Le Bon* on 2 C and 3 Av. Both serve up the usual disco soup of cheesy merengue and handbag house, laced with a dash of salsa.

Listings

Banks and exchange Banco Industrial at 1 C and 2 Av (Mon–Fri 8.30am–7pm, Sat 8.30am–5.30pm) with Visa facilities, or Banco G&T, 1 C and 2 Av (Mon–Fri 9am–7pm, Sat 9am–1pm).

Car rental Tabarini, 7 Av 2–27, Zona 2 (☎ & fax 9521504), and Geo Rentals, a local company, in the same building as *Café Tirol* and Access (☎9521650).

Laundry La Providencia, at the sharp end of the plaza on Diagonal 4 (Mon–Sat 8am–noon & 2–5pm).

Post office 2 C and 2 Av (Mon–Fri 8am–4.30pm).

Spanish schools If you enjoy Cobán's slightly subdued atmosphere you could spend some time studying Spanish at the Instituto Cobán Internacional (INCO Int) at 2 C 6–23, Zona 2 (☎ & fax 9521727). It costs around US$110 per week for twenty hours of teaching, two excursions and full board. There is also the Active Spanish School on 3 C 6–12 Zona 1 (☎9521432), which is extremely cheap at US$85 a week, including full board.

Telephones and email Telgua has its main office in the plaza (daily 7am–midnight) and you can send email from Access, in the same building as the *Café Tirol*.

Tours Epiphyte Adventures, on 2 Av and 2 C (☎9522213), offers highly informative tours around Alta Verapaz, including Semuc Champey, Laguna Lachuá, and a French-owned eco-lodge near the remote Candelaria caves. The *Hostal d'Acuña* and *Hostal Doña Victoria* both run trips to Semuc Champey and other destinations.

San Pedro Carchá

A few kilometres away, connected by regular buses, **SAN PEDRO CARCHÁ** is a smaller version of Cobán, with a stronger Maya character and silver instead of coffee money firing the economy. These days the two towns are merging into a single urban sprawl, and many of the buses that go on towards Petén, or even over to Uspantán, leave from Carchá. Local buses between the two leave from the terminal in Cobán and from the plaza in Carchá.

If you've an hour to spare, the **regional museum** in a street beside the church (Mon–Fri 9am–noon & 2–5pm; small charge) is worth a look. There's a collection of Maya artefacts and dolls dressed in local costumes, as well as a mouldy collection of stuffed birds and animals including the inevitable moulting quetzal. A little further afield, the **Balneario las Islas** is a stretch of cool water that's popular for swimming; you can also **camp** here. It's a couple of kilometres from the town centre: walk along the main street beside the church and take the third turning on the right, then follow the street for about 1km and take the right-hand fork at the end.

If you want **to stay** here, the *Hotel la Reforma*, 4 C 8–45 (☎9521448; ②), is a good option. For **changing money**, there's a branch of the Banco del Ejercito on the plaza (Mon–Fri 9am–1pm & 2.30–5.30pm, Sat 10am–2pm). **Buses** to local destinations such as Senahú, El Estor, Lanquín and Cahabón leave from the plaza. Two buses a day (10am & noon) leave from beside the fire station **to Uspantán**, for connections to Sacapulas, Nebaj and Quiché.

San Juan Chamelco

A few kilometres southeast of Cobán, easily reached by regular local buses from the terminal, **SAN JUAN CHAMELCO** is the most important Kekchí settlement in the area. Most of your fellow bus passengers are likely to be women dressed in traditional costume, wearing beautiful cascades of old coins for earrings and speaking Kekchí rather than Spanish. Chamelco's focal point is a large colonial **church**, whose facade is rather unexpectedly decorated with a Maya version of the Hapsburg double eagle –

undoubtedly a result of earlier German presence in the region. Inside the belfry is hidden the village's most significant treasure: a church bell that was given to the Maya leader Juan Matalbatz by the Holy Roman Emperor Charles V.

The best time to visit the village is for its annual **fiesta** on June 16. Participants in the wild processions dress up in a variety of outfits including pre-conquest Maya costumes and representations of local wildlife in celebration of the local Kekchí culture and environment.

Not far from Chamelco is a great **place to stay**, *Don Jerónimo's* (⑤ for full board), a vegetarian guest house/retreat run by an eccentric American, who has been living off the land for a good twenty years. You'll find him either by walking 5km from Chamelco to the Aldea Chajaneb, or by catching a bus from outside the Tienda Maranatha, on the street running behind the church. Ask to be dropped off at the appropriate footpath.

Lanquín and Semuc Champey

Northeast of Cobán, a rough, badly maintained road heads off into the hills, connecting a string of coffee fincas. The road soon drops down into rich land to the north as the valleys open out; their precipitous sides are patched with cornfields and the level central land is saved for the all-important coffee bushes. As the bus lurches along, clinging to the sides of the ridges, there are fantastic views of the valleys below.

The road divides after 43km at the **Pajal** junction, three hours from Cobán, where one branch turns north to Sebol and Fray Bartolomé de las Casas and the other cuts down deep into the valley to **LANQUÍN**, 12km away (45min), a very sleepy, modest Kekchí village sheltered beneath towering green hills. Don't count on practising your Spanish here – the language has yet to gain much influence. There's a good, cheap hospedaje-cum-store-cum-comedor, the *Divina Providencia* (①), which offers good grub, steaming hot showers and the only cold beers in town. The clapboard-built rooms are comfortable enough, though you'll probably get to know all about your neighbours' nocturnal pursuits. More luxurious is the *Hotel El Recreo* (☎9522160, fax 9522333; ④), on the entrance road, with a choice of rooms in wooden huts, a restaurant and a pool. There is electricity only between 6pm and 9pm, though, and prices rise at weekends.

Just a couple of kilometres from the village on the road back to Cobán are the **Lanquín caves** (US$2), a maze of dripping, bat-infested chambers stretching for at least 3km underground. An illuminated walkway, complete with ladders and chains, cuts through the first few hundred metres, but it's very slippery so take care. Before you set out from the village ask in the *municipalidad* (town hall) if they can turn on the lights. It's also well worth dropping by at dusk when thousands of bats emerge from the mouth of the cave and flutter off into the night. A small car park near the entrance to the caves has a covered shelter where you're welcome to **camp** or sling your hammock.

Semuc Champey

The other attraction around Lanquín are the extraordinary pools of **Semuc Champey** (US$1), which are a great deal more spectacular than the caves. The problem can be **getting there**, however. If you're very lucky and there are enough tourists in town, you can catch a pickup at about 8am, returning around noon. Otherwise you can book a tour from Cobán (around US$30 per person) or take the *Hostal d'Acuña* shuttle bus (Wed & Sat, when sufficient demand). Hiring Rigoberto Fernandez's pickup for US$10 return trip, including two hours at the pools is another option. You can find him in the unnamed shop painted vivid green beneath the central park.

The hard way is to walk. It takes nearly three hours and can be extremely tough going if the sun is shining, so take plenty of water. Leave the village along the gravel road that climbs the hill to the south, then drops into another valley. From here the track wanders through thick tropical vegetation where bananas, coffee and the spear-leafed cardamom plants grow beside scruffy thatched huts. After crossing a suspension bridge, the road climbs uphill again to the car park where you may be asked for the entry fee. Finally, follow the muddy track that brings you, at long last, to the pools. The effort of getting here is rewarded by a natural staircase of turquoise waters suspended on a limestone bridge, with a series of idyllic **pools** in which you can swim. The bulk of the Río Cahabón runs underground beneath this natural bridge, and by walking a few hundred metres upstream over a slippery obstacle course of rocks and roots you can see the aquatic frenzy for yourself. The river water plunges furiously into a cavern, cutting under the pools to emerge downstream. If you have a tent or a hammock it makes sense to **stay** the night. There's a thatched shelter here and the altitude is sufficiently low to keep the air warm in the evenings. Be warned, though, it is not safe to leave your belongings unattended.

Beyond Lanquín

Beyond Lanquín the road continues to **Cahabón** (which has a basic pensión), another 24km to the east, and from there a very rough road heads south to Panzós (see p.399), cutting high over the mountains through superb scenery. In the unlikely event of the road being in a good enough state of repair, there's an occasional bus between these two places, but normally transport is by pickup – although even these are increasingly rare.

    Buses to Cahabón, passing through Lanquín, leave Cobán four times daily (6am, 12.30pm, 1pm & 3pm; 4hr; returning at 5am, 7am and 3pm). On Sundays there may only be the 3pm service to Cobán and it will be packed. Buses pass Pajal for **Fray Bartolomé de las Casas** and **Raxrujá** (see p.400) twice each morning (around 6.30am & 8.30am).

The Polochic valley

If you're planning to head out towards the Caribbean from Cobán, or simply interested in taking a short trip along backroads, then the **Polochic valley** is an ideal place to spend the day being bounced around inside a bus. Hourly buses leave Cobán for El Estor, trundling slowly down the valley along a dirt road passing several villages on the way. Travelling the length of the valley, you witness an immense transformation as you drop down through the coffee-coated mountains and emerge in the lush, tropical lowlands. The scenery is pure Alta Verapaz: V-shaped valleys where coffee commands the best land and fields of maize cling to the upper slopes wherever they can. The villages are untidy-looking places where the Kekchí and Pokomchí Maya are largely latinized and seldom wear the brilliant red *huipiles* that are traditional here.

    The first village at the upper end of the valley is **Tamahú**, and below it is **TUCURÚ**. High above Tucurú in the mountains to the north is the **Chelemá Reserve**, a large protected area of pristine cloudforest which contains one of the highest concentrations of quetzals anywhere in the world, not to mention an array of other birds and beasts, including some very vocal howler monkeys. The forest is extremely difficult to reach; to visit, contact the reserve's office in Cobán opposite the *Hotel La Paz*, at 6 Av, Zona 1 (☎9513238).

    Beyond Tucurú the road plunges abruptly and cattle pastures start to take the place of the coffee bushes. Both the villages and the people here have a more tropical look about them. Next comes **La Tinta**, and then **Telemán**, the largest of the squalid trading centres in this lower section of the valley. From Telemán a side road branches off to the north to **SENAHÚ**, climbing high into the lush hills past row upon row of neatly ranked coffee bushes. Set behind the first ridge of hills, Senahú is a small coffee centre set in a verdant, steep-sided bowl and an ideal starting point for a short wander in the Alta Verapaz hills. Three **buses** a day run from Cobán to Senahú, the first return-ing at 4pm (check with the drivers for the latest times); or you could easily hitch a ride on a truck from Telemán. There are a couple of simple pensiónes, and also the *Hotel Senahú* in the centre of the village (☎9522160; ④), with six pleasant rooms. It's possi-ble to **trek** to Semuc Champey and Lanquín from here in two to three days – ask for a guide at the *Hotel Senahú*. Another stunning hike is to Cahabón, which you can also do in a 4-wheel drive, weather permitting.

Heading on down the Polochic valley you reach **PANZÓS**, the largest of the valley villages. Its name means "place of the green waters", a reference to the swamps that surround the river, swarming with alligators and birdlife. In 1978, Panzós made the international headlines when a group of campesinos attending a meeting to settle land disputes were gunned down by the army and local police in one of the earliest and most brutal massacres of General Lucas García's military regime. García had a personal interest in the matter, since he owned 78,000 acres of land around Panzós. Over 100,000 people attended a protest rally in Guatemala City after news of the massacre broke and the event is generally regarded as a landmark in the history of political violence in Guatemala.

El Estor

Beyond Panzós the road pushes on towards Lago de Izabal, passing a huge and desert-ed nickel plant, yet another monument to disastrous foreign investment. A kilometre or so further on, **EL ESTOR** had settled back into provincial stupor after the nickel boom but is now undergoing a revival as a centre of a regional development. Fresh farmlands are being developed all the time and a new road to the east will shortly open up a route to the Río Dulce along the north shore of Lago de Izabal. The town's name is thought to have derived from the English pirates who came up the Río Dulce to buy supplies at "The Store". Now the only boat that drops by is the **ferry for Mariscos**, which leaves daily at 6am, returning at noon. On the other side, the ferry is met by two buses, one to Guatemala City and the other for Puerto Barrios.

The best **hotel** in El Estor is the *Hotel Vista del Lago* (☎9497205; ②), a beautiful colonial-style wooden building by the dock, which the owner claims was the original store that gave the village its name. All rooms have private bathrooms, and second-floor rooms have superb views of the lake. A little cheaper, but still very pleasant, is the *Hotel Villela* at 6 Av 2–06 (②), a block up from the *Vista del Lago*, which is sur-rounded by a beautiful garden and has private showers. Simpler still, the *Hospedaje Santa Clara* at 5 Av 2–11 (☎9487244; ②) has basic, clean rooms, some with their own shower. For a delicious and not too expensive French **meal**, check out *Restaurante El Dios del Sol*, on the eastern side of town, or try *Hugo's Restaurant*, on the main plaza.

There's not a lot to do in El Estor, although it does have a friendly, relaxed atmos-phere, particularly in the warmth of the evening when the streets are full of activity. Don't miss the pool in the plaza, which harbours fish, turtles and alligators. You could, however, spend a few days exploring the surrounding area, much of which remains undisturbed. If you find yourself with an afternoon to spare, you could hike out of town to the **El Boquerón** canyon, 8km away in the hills to the east, which is an excellent place for a swim. There are **bikes** to rent at 6 Av 4–26, or you can arrange to have some-one take you there by boat. The delta of the **Río Polochic** (which has recently been given wildlife reserve status) is particularly beautiful, a green maze of swamp, marsh and forest that's home to alligators, monkeys, tapirs and an abundance of birdlife, while the lake itself abounds with fish, including tarpon and snook.

The best place to enquire about **tours** around El Estor is *Hugo's Restaurant*, whose owner will take you up the river to the canyon for around US$10 a person (minimum two people). In addition, the irrepressible Oscar Paz, who runs the *Hotel Vista del Lago*, is an enthusiastic promoter of the area and will arrange a boat and guide to explore any of the surrounding countryside, go fishing in the lake or visit the hot springs at *Finca Paraíso*.

North towards Petén

In the far northern section of Alta Verapaz, the lush hills drop away steeply onto the limestone plain that marks the frontier with the department of Petén. At present, two rough roads head north: the first from Cobán via **Chisec** and the second from San Pedro Carchá via Pajal, which passes the turn-off for Lanquín and Semuc Champey. From the **Pajal** junction it's a very slow, very beautiful journey north through typical Verapaz scenery – a verdant green landscape of impossibly green mountains, tiny adobe-built hamlets, pasture and pine forests. After three hours or more of twists and turns, you'll reach **Sebol**, a beautiful spot on the Río Pasión where tributary waterfalls cascade into the main channel; here a road heads off for Poptún and **FRAY BARTOLOMÉ DE LAS CASAS**. For some reason this village has been left off most maps, though it boasts three simple **hotels** – the best is *Pensión Ralíos* (①) – and buses to San Pedro Carchá (8hr) and Cobán. Back on the main road, the next stop is the small settlement of **Raxrujá**, where the buses from Cobán finish; currently only pickups and trucks head north for **Cruce del Pato** and beyond, either up to Sayaxché and Petén or west into the Ixcán.

Raxrujá and the Candelaria caves

RAXRUJÁ is the best place to get a pickup, truck or, if you're very lucky, a bus north to Sayaxché and Flores or west to Playa Grande and the Ixcán. Little more than a few streets and an army base straggling round the bridge over the Río Escondido, a tributary of the Pasión, it has the only **accommodation** for miles around, so you may end up staying here. *Hotel Raxruhá* (①), next to the Texaco garage, is the best on offer and there are plenty of quite reasonable places to **eat** in town. Buses leave for Cobán at 4am and 8am. Heading north, you can only travel by pickup. There's no timetable – they just leave when the driver has enough passengers – but you shouldn't have to wait more than a hour or so.

The limestone mountains to the west of Raxrujá are full of caves. Some of the best are the **Candelaria caves**, 10km west. The most impressive cave mouths are on private property, a short walk from the road, jealously guarded by Daniel Dreux, who has built the **Complex Cultural de Candelaria** conservation area. There is wonderful **accommodation** here but it's often block-booked by French tour groups. One of the Cobán travel agents (see p.396) may be able to organize a trip.

The area beyond Raxrujá, where the rolling foothills of the highlands give way to the flat expanse of southern Petén, is known as the **Northern Transversal Strip**, dubbed the "Generals' Strip" as huge parcels of land, complete with their valuable mineral resources, were dispensed to military top brass instead of to needy campesinos in the 1970s.

Playa Grande and around

Continuing west from Raxrujá, trucks make the 90km journey over rough roads to **PLAYA GRANDE** (at least 6hr), the bridging point of the Río Negro. The town is an authentic frontier settlement with cheap hotels, rough bars and brothels. If you need to **stay**, the best option is the basic but clean *Hospedaje Reyna* (①).

One point of interest in this area is the **Parque Nacional Laguna Lachuá**, a beautiful little lake 4km off the main road east of Playa Grande. One of the least visited national parks in Central America, this is a beautiful, tranquil spot, the clear, almost circular lake completely surrounded by dense tropical forest. Though it smells slightly sulphurous, the water is good for swimming, with curious horseshoe-shaped limestone formations by the edge that make perfect individual bathing pools. You'll see otters and an abundance of birdlife, but watch out for mosquitoes. There's a large thatched *rancho* (shelter) by the shore, ideal for camping or slinging a hammock. Fireplaces and wood are provided, but you'll need to bring food and drinking water. You can also rent canoes.

You can get to Playa Grande **from Cobán** on one of a stream of trucks and pick-ups setting out from the corner of the bus terminal – a journey of at least eight hours. Heading south **from Sayaxché** you need to catch a bus or pick-up to Playitas via Cruce del Pato and take another pickup or truck from there. There are also charter **flights** from the airstrip in Cobán.

Into the Ixcán

The Río Negro marks the boundary between the departments of Alta Verapaz and Quiché; the land to the west is known as the **Ixcán**. This huge swampy forest, some of which was settled in the 1960s and 1970s by peasants migrating from the highlands, became a bloody battleground in the 1980s. In the past few years the Ixcán has become a focus for repatriado settlement, as **refugees** who fled to Mexico in the 1980s are resettled in a string of "temporary" camps west of the the river.

Travelling further west across the Ixcán and into northern Huehuetenango, though no longer hazardous, is still very arduous – it takes at least two or three days to get from Playa Grande to Barillas (see p.364). **Veracruz**, 20km (1hr 30min) from Playa Grande, is the first place of note, a settlement at the crossroads beyond the Río Xalbal. Some buses continue to Mayalan, 12km away, across the presently unbridged Río Piedras Blancas. Here the road ends and you'll have to walk 15km (4–5hr) to **Altamira** on the far bank of the Río Ixcán, past several tiny villages; the path is easy to follow. At the last village, **Rancho Palmeras**, ask for directions to the crossing point on the Ixcán, where boys will pole you across the flowing river. Once across, Altamira is still a few kilometres away, up the hill. From here a regular flow of trucks make the 30km (4hr) journey to Barillas over some of the worst roads in the country. It's a spectacular journey, though, especially as you watch the growing bulk of the Cuchumatanes rising ever higher on the horizon. You can also get trucks over the border into **Mexico**, taking you to Chajul on the Río Lacantún in Chiapas (see p.63), but you need a Guatemalan exit stamp first, probably best obtained in Cobán or Flores.

PETÉN

The vast northern department of **Petén** covers about a third of Guatemala but contains less than three percent of the country's population. This huge expanse of swamps, dry savannahs and tropical rainforest forms part of an untamed wilderness that stretches into the Lacandón forest of southern Mexico and across the Maya Mountains to Belize. Totally unlike any other part of the country, much of it is all but untouched, with ancient ceiba and mahogany trees that tower 50m above the forest floor. Undisturbed for so long, the area is also extraordinarily rich in **wildlife**. Some 285 species of bird have been sighted at Tikal alone, including a great range of hummingbirds, toucans, blue and white herons, hawks, buzzards, wild turkeys, motmot (a bird of paradise) and even the elusive quetzal, revered since Maya times. Beneath the forest canopy are many other species that are far harder to locate. Among the mammals are the massive tapir or mountain cow, ocelots, deer, coatis, jaguars, monkeys, plus crocodiles and thousands of species of plants, snakes, insects and butterflies.

Recently, however, this position of privileged isolation has been threatened by moves to colonize the country's final frontier. Waves of **settlers**, lured by offers of free land, have cleared enormous tracts of jungle, while oil exploration and commercial logging have cut new roads deep into the forest. The population of Petén, just 15,000 in 1950, is today estimated at 350,000, a number which puts enormous pressure on the remaining forest. Various attempts have been made to halt the tide of destruction, and in 1990, the government declared that forty percent of Petén would be protected by the **Maya Biosphere Reserve**, although little has been done to enforce this. In late 1997 a new move was made to highlight the threat to the remaining jungle, with a series of conferences and concerts by an all-star international cast including Bianca Jagger and backed by President Arzú.

The new interest in the region is in fact something of a reawakening as Petén was once the heartland of the **Maya civilization**, which reached here from the highlands some 2500 years ago. Maya culture reached the height of its architectural, scientific and artistic achievement during the Classic period (roughly 250–925 AD), when great cities rose out of the forest. The ruins at Tikal and El Mirador, among the most spectacular of all **Maya sites**, represent only a fraction of what was once here. At the close of the tenth century the cities were mysteriously abandoned, and many of the people moved north to the Yucatán where Maya civilization continued to flourish until the twelfth century.

By the time the Spanish arrived, the area had been partially recolonized by the **Itzá**, a group of Toltec-Maya who inhabited the land around Lago de Petén Itzá. The forest proved so impenetrable that it wasn't brought under Spanish control until 1697, more than 150 years after they had conquered the rest of the country. The Spanish had little enthusiasm for Petén, however, and under their rule it remained a backwater. Independence saw no great change and it wasn't until 1970 that Petén became genuinely accessible by car. Even today the network of roads is skeletal, and many routes are impassable in the wet season.

The hub of the department are the twin lakeside towns of **Flores** and **Santa Elena**. You'll probably arrive here, if only to head straight out to the ruins of **Tikal**, Petén's prime attraction, though the town is also the starting point for adventures to more distant ruins – **El Mirador**, **Nakbé** and **Río Azul**. **El Remate** is a tranquil alternative location, halfway between Flores and Tikal. The caves and scenery around **Poptún**, on the main highway south, justify exploration, while down the other road south, **Sayaxché** is surrounded by yet more Maya sites. From Sayaxché you can set off down the Río Pasión to **Mexico** and the ruins of **Yaxchilán** (see p.138), or take an alternative route back to Guatemala City – via Cobán in Alta Verapaz.

Getting to Petén

Many visitors arrive in Petén by bus or plane directly from **Guatemala City**: by air it's a short fifty-minute hop to Flores; **by bus** it can take anywhere between ten and fifteen gruelling hours. A number of domestic airlines fly the route daily and **tickets** can be bought from virtually any travel agent in the country; in 1998 a cut-throat price war saw flight prices dropping as low as US$60 return, though if tariffs return to previous levels you can expect to pay double that. Flights are heavily in demand and overbooking is common. Six **bus companies** provide around twenty services a day from Guatemala City to Flores. If you don't want to do the 554km trip in one go, it's easy enough to do it in stages – the best places to break the journey are at **Quiriguá** (see p.378), **Río Dulce** (see p.383) and **Poptún** (see opposite).

Coming from the Guatemalan highlands, you can reach Petén along the backroads **from Cobán** in Alta Verapaz, which is a long, adventurous route. **From Belize or Mexico**, you can enter the country through Petén. The most obvious route is from Belize through the border at Melchor de Mencos, but there are also two river routes that bring you through from Palenque or Tenosique in Mexico. All of these are routes are described on pp.420–2.

Poptún and around

Heading north from the Río Dulce, the main route to Flores cuts through a degraded landscape of small milpa farms and cattle ranches that were untouched jungle a decade or two ago. Some 95km from the Río Dulce, at an altitude of 500m, the first settlement of any interest is the small town of **POPTÚN**. For many travellers this dusty frontier settlement is the unlikely embodiment of rustic bliss and organic food, thanks to the proximity of the *Finca Ixobel* (see below). There's no particular reason to stay in the town itself, but you may well stop by to use the Telgua office or banks. If you do get stuck here, you can **stay** at the friendly *Hotel Posada de los Castellanos* (②), where you get a bathroom and hot water. The best food in town can be had at the *Fonda Ixobel 2*, which bakes good bread and cakes.

For a more rural setting, head 4km north of Poptún, to *Cocay Camping* (①), set in peaceful isolation on the banks of the river just past the village of Machaquilá. The site provides camping space, very simple huts and vegetarian food. Over the bridge to the right, set nicely in a patch of forest, are the new cabañas of the *Villa de los Castellanos* (☎9277541, fax 9277542; ⑤, but ask about special backpacker rates), offering a comfortable base for adventurous visitors to explore the forests, rivers and caves of central Petén. Carlos, the owner, is an excellent source of information – botanical, historical and logistical.

Finca Ixobel

A couple of kilometres' walk south of Poptún, surrounded by aromatic pine forests in the cool foothills of the Maya Mountains, the *Finca Ixobel* (☎9277363) is a working farm that provides **accommodation** to passing tourists. The farm was originally run by Americans Mike and Carole DeVine, but on June 8, 1990, Mike was murdered by the army. This prompted the American government to suspend military aid to Guatemala and, after a drawn-out investigation which cast little light on their motives, five soldiers were convicted of the murder in September 1992. Others involved have managed to evade capture and their commanding officer, Captain Hugo Contreras, escaped from jail shortly after his arrest. Carole fought the case for years and remains at the finca.

Finca Ixobel is a supremely beautiful and relaxing place, where you can swim in the pond, walk in the forest, dodge the resident "attack" parrots and stuff yourself stupid with healthy home-grown food. There are **hikes** into the jungle, horse-riding trips, rafting, 4-wheel-drive jungle jaunts, and short excursions to nearby caves. There was an armed attack on a group visiting the caves in late 1997, so you should check the current security situation with finca staff. Accommodation is in attractive bungalows with private bathroom (④), regular rooms (②–③), or dorms (②), and there's also camping and hammock space (①) and tree houses (②). You run up a tab for accommodation, food and drink, paying when you leave – which can be a rude awakening. To get to the finca, ask the bus driver to drop you at the gate (marked by a large sign), from where it's a fifteen-minute walk through the pine trees.

Flores

FLORES, the capital of Petén, has an easy pace and a sedate, old-world atmosphere diametrically opposite to the commerce and bustle that typifies most towns in Petén. Its genteel cobbled streets, ageing houses and twin-domed church are set on a small island in Lago de Petén Itzá, connected to the mainland by a short (manmade) causeway. The frontier mentality lies just across the water in **SANTA ELENA**, a chaotic, featureless town that's dusty in the dry season and mud-bound during the rains.

FLORES & SANTA ELENA

0   300 m

Lago de Petén Itzá

CALLE FRATERNIDED

① Cincap   Teatro
Parque
⊕ Catholic Church
Gobernación Departmental   Banco Hipotecario
Central   ① Inguat ProPetén

PASAJE PROGROSO

CALLE DE JUNIO
AV REFORMA
AV BARRIOS
AVENIDA SANTA ANA
CALLE 15 DE SEPTIEMBRE

EL CRUCERO
CALLE CENTRO AMÉRICA

Lanchas to San Benito, San Andrés & San José

Restaurant El Tucán

★ Bus to airport/ Santa Elena/ San Benito

ACCOMMODATION

Hospedaje Doña Goya	2
Hotel La Casona de la Isla	4
Hotel Alonzo	11
Hotel Jade	9
Hotel La Jungla	6
Hotel la Casita de Flores	7
Hotel Sac-Nicte	8
Hotel San Juan	10
Hotel Santana	5
Hotel Sabana	1
Jaguar Inn	12
Posada Tayazal	3

Source: ProPetén

▽ Causeway to Santa Elena 750 metres (approx.)

1 CALLE
2 CALLE
3 CALLE
3 CALLE
4 CALLE (CALLE PRINCIPAL)
4 CALLE A
5 CALLE

SAN BENITO

SANTA ELENA
3 AVENIDA
5 AVENIDA
6 AVENIDA

Buses to Guatemala City & Poptún ★
★ Bus Station
Mercado

▷ Airport

The **lake** was a natural choice for settlement, and its shores were heavily populated in Maya times, with the capital of the Itzá, **Tayasal**, occupying the island that was to become modern Flores. Cortés passed through here in 1525, on his way south to Honduras, and left behind a sick horse which he promised to send for later. A horse-worshipping cult started as a result, and later visitors were sacrificed to the equine deity. Tayasal was eventually destroyed by Martín de Ursúa and an army of 235 in 1697.

For the entire colonial period (and indeed up to the 1960s) Flores languished in virtual isolation, having more contact with neighbouring Belize than with the capital. Today,
despite the steady flow of tourists passing through en route to Tikal, the town retains
an urbane air. It has little to detain you and is small enough to explore in an hour or so,
but it does offer some attractive places to stay and spectacular lake views.

Arrival and information

Arriving by **bus** from Guatemala City or Belize, you'll be dropped a block or two from
the causeway to Flores. The **airport** is 3km east of the causeway; taxis into town
charge US$2 per person. **Local buses** cover the route, crossing the causeway about
every ten minutes, but they entail a time-consuming change halfway; returning to the
airport, they leave from the Flores end of the causeway every twenty minutes or so.

The staff at the **Inguat** desk in the arrivals hall at the airport (Mon–Sat 6–10am &
3–6pm, sometimes also on Sun) can give you reasonable maps and **information**.
There's another office on the plaza in Flores (Mon–Fri 8am–4pm; ☎9260669), where
the helpful staff will most likely direct you across the plaza to **CINCAP**, a very useful
resource centre with exhibitions on historical and contemporary life in Petén
(Tues–Sat 9am–1pm & 2–8pm, Sun 2–6pm) to examine their more detailed maps,
books and leaflets. If you're planning to go on a trip to remote parts of the Maya
Biosphere Reserve, check with **ProPetén** on C Central (Mon–Fri 8am–5pm;
☎9261370, fax 9260495) for current information on route conditions, accommodation
and guides. They also do **organized trips**, including the "Scarlet Macaw Trail", a five-
day expedition by truck, horse and boat along rivers and through primary forest, taking in the remote ruins of El Perú and the largest concentration of scarlet macaws in
northern Central America.

If you're interested in doing some **voluntary work**, ARCAS (*Asociación de Rescate y
Conservación de Vida Silvestre*), the Wildlife Conservation and Rescue Association
(☎9260077 or ☎ & fax 5914731 in Guatemala City) runs a rescue service for animals
taken illegally as pets from the forests and always needs volunteers. The work, while
rewarding, can be very demanding and you'll need to sign up for at least three weeks.
You can obtain information from their office in Santa Elena, two blocks south of Telgua.

Accommodation

Accommodation in Flores/Santa Elena has undergone a boom in recent years and the
sheer number of new **hotels** keeps prices competitive. There are several good budget
places in Flores itself, making it unnecessary to stay in noisier and dirtier Santa Elena
unless your budget is extremely tight.

FLORES

La Casita de Flores, cross the causeway and it's on the right (☎3600000, fax 9260032). Small,
attractive rooms with very good rates in the low season. ③.

Hospedaje Doña Goya, at the north end of of the island (no phone). Excellent family-run budget
guest house, with the best prices on the island. Clean, light rooms with fans, some with private
baths; the ones at the front have balconies. Good rates for single travellers. Also organizes trips to
nearby caves. ②.

Hotel la Casona de la Isla, Calle 30 de Junio (☎9260692, fax 9260593). The one with the arresting citrus and powder-blue paint job. Attractive, modern rooms with private bath and a/c, swimming
pool and spectacular sunset views from the terrace bar-restaurant. ⑤.

Hotel la Jungla, in the southwest corner of the island (☎9260634). The best value in this price
range, with gleaming tiled floors and private baths with hot water. Also has rooftop views over the
town and lake and a good restaurant. ③.

Hotel Sabana, at the northern tip of the island (☎ & fax 9261248). Large modern place with a small
pool and nice lake views, especially from the restaurant. Some rooms have a/c; all are good value. ④.

Hotel Santana, in the southwest corner of Flores (☎9260492, fax 9260662). Recently modernized three-storey building with a small pool and patio overlooking the lake. Very comfortable, spotless rooms with fan and private bath; first-floor rooms have private lakeside terraces and a/c. ⑤.

Posada Tayazal, C la Unión near the *Doña Goya* (☎ & fax 9260568). Well-run budget hotel with decent rooms, some with private baths. Shared bathrooms have hot water. Roof terrace, information service and tours to Tikal. Best budget bet if *Doña Goya* is full. ②–③.

SANTA ELENA

Hotel Alonzo, 6 Av 4–99 (☎9260105). Clean rooms, some with balcony, and a few with private bathrooms. Public telephone and reasonable restaurant. On the Fuente del Norte bus route from Guatemala City. ②.

Hotel Jade, 6 Av. A backpackers' stronghold. Shambolic but the cheapest place in town. ①.

Hotel Jaguar Inn, Calzada Rodríguez Macal 8–79 (☎9260002). Comfortable rooms with choice of a/c or fan, but situated a little out of town towards the airport. ④

Hotel Sac-Nicte, 1 C 4–45 (☎ & fax 9260092). Clean rooms with fans and private shower; second-floor rooms have views of the lake. Breakfast possible before the 4am trip to Tikal. ②.

Hotel San Juan, 8 C, a block from the causeway (☎ & fax 9260042). Conveniently doubles as the Pinita bus terminal but it's not particularly friendly or good value. Most guests are captives straight off the bus.

Eating and drinking

Flores unquestionably offers the most cosmopolitan dining scene in Petén and there are a number of good restaurants, many with delightful lakeside views, though prices are a little higher than elsewhere in Guatemala. Santa Elena has a very limited selection of comedores so even if you're staying here you may want to cross the causeway for a little more atmosphere.

FLORES

La Canoa, C Centro América. Popular, good-value place, serving pasta, great soups, and some vegetarian and Guatemalan food, as well as excellent breakfasts.

The Chaltunhá, opposite *Hotel Santana*, right on the water. Great spot for lunch, snacks and sandwiches, and not too expensive.

Pizzeria Picasso, across the street from the *Tucán* and run by the same family. Serves great pizza under cooling breezes from the ceiling fans.

Las Puertas, signposted on C Santa Ana. Paint-splattered walls and live music as well as very good pasta and healthy breakfasts. Worth it for the atmosphere.

Restaurant Gran Jaguar, Av Barrios. Guatemalan restaurant geared up for tourists. Good-value meals include soup, salad, tea, coffee and a pastry.

El Tucán, a few metres east of the causeway, on the waterfront. Excellent fish, enormous chef's salads, Mexican food and the best waterside terrace in Flores.

SANTA ELENA

Restaurant Petenchel, 2 C, past the park. Simple, good food. The nicest place to eat within two blocks of the main street and you can leave your luggage here.

El Rodeo, 2 C & 5 Av. It's not going to win any Michelin stars but it's good value even if the service is slow.

Listings

Banks Banco de Guatemala, two blocks west of the plaza in Flores; in Santa Elena, Bancafé, Banco G&T (for Mastercard) and Banco Industrial (with Visa ATM) are all on 4 Av.

Car and bike rental Several firms, including Budget, Hertz and Koka, operate from the airport. All offer cars, minibuses and jeeps, with prices starting at around US$70 a day for a jeep. Bikes can be rented from Cahuí, 30 de Junio, Flores, for US$1 per hour (daily 7am–7pm; ☎ & fax 9260494).

Laundry Lavandería Amelia, behind CINCAP in Flores; Lavandería Emanuel on 6 Av in Santa Elena.

Post office Two doors away from the Inguat office in Flores; at 2 C and 7 Av, two blocks east of the *Hotel San Juan*, in Santa Elena (Mon–Fri 8am–4.30pm).

Telephones and email Telgua is in Santa Elena on 5 C, but you're better off using one of the private telephone and fax services at the *Hotel Alonzo* in Santa Elena, or Cahuí, 30 de Junio in Flores (daily 7am–7pm; ☎ & fax 9260494). For email, check out *C@fénet* on Av Barrios (daily 9am–9pm) or Arpa on C Centro America, both in Flores. Make sure any messages you want to send are sent while you're there.

Travel agents The most helpful is Arco Iris on C Centro América, Flores (☎9260786), which sells flights and has the best prices for tours to the ruins and around the lake. Expedicion Panamundo, 2 C 4–90, Santa Elena (☎ & fax 9260501), sells fairly pricey tours, but the guides have archeological expertise. Explore, C Centro América, Flores (☎9260665, fax 9260550), has specialist knowledge of the Petexbatún area. The Hotel San Juan travel agency in Santa Elena is not recommended.

Around Flores

If you have a few hours to spare in Flores, the most obvious excursion is a **trip on the lake**. Boatmen can take you around a circuit that takes in a mirador, a small ruin on the peninsula opposite and the **Peténcito zoo** (daily 8am–5pm), 3km east of Santa Elena, with its small collection of sluggish local wildlife, and pause for a swim along the way. Beware the concrete waterslide by the zoo – it's caused at least one death. Boatmen loiter behind the *Hotel Yum Kax* or around the start of the causeway. If you'd rather paddle around under your own steam you can rent a canoe for around US$2 an hour.

Of the numerous **caves** in the hills behind Santa Elena, the most accessible is **Aktun Kan** (daily 8am–5pm; US$1.20). Simply follow the Flores causeway through Santa Elena, turn left when it forks in front of a small hill, and then take the first right. Otherwise known as *La Cueva de la Serpiente*, the cave is the legendary home of a huge snake. The guard may explain some of the bizarre names given to the various shapes inside, some of which resemble animals and even a marimba.

San Andrés and San José

Though accessible by bus and boat, the traditional villages of **San Andrés** and **San José**, across the lake from Flores, have until recently received few visitors. Sloping steeply up from the shore, the streets are lined with one-storey buildings, some of palmetto sticks and thatch, some coated with plaster and others with brightly painted concrete. Pigs and chickens wander freely. **Getting to the villages** is best achieved by using the *lanchas* that leave regularly from the beach next to the *Hotel Santana* in Flores and from **San Benito**, a suburb of Santa Elena. A chartered *expreso* from Flores or San Benito will cost around US$8. Regular morning **buses** leave for San Andrés from the market in Santa Elena; if they don't continue to San José, it's an easy 2km walk downhill. **Returning** in the mornings is simple, with *lanchas* at 6am, 7am and noon, and there are regular buses throughout the day.

Most outsiders in **SAN ANDRÉS** are students at the only **language school** in Petén, the Eco-Escuela. Since nobody in the village speaks English, a course here is an excellent opportunity to immerse yourself in Spanish without distractions, though it may be daunting for absolute beginners; full board and five hours of tuition is US$120 a week. For more information, check at ProPetén in Flores or call ☎9288106 (Spanish only) or ☎9261370 (Spanish and English) or contact Conservation International Eco-Escuela in the US (☎202/9732264, fax 8875188). There are currently no hospedajes in the village, but 3km to the west is the attractive *Hotel Nitún* (☎9288132, fax 9288113; ⑤ including transport from Flores), with **accommodation** in thatched stone cabañas with hardwood floors and private bathrooms and a restaurant serving superb food. *Hotel Nitún* is the base for Monkey Eco Tours, which organizes expeditions to remote archeological sites.

SAN JOSÉ, perched above a lovely bay, just 2km east along the shore from San Andrés, is even more relaxed than its neighbour. The village is undergoing something of a cultural revival: Itzá, the pre-conquest Maya tongue, is being taught in the school, and you'll see signs in the language dotted all around. Over the hill beyond the village is a secluded rocky beach where there's a shelter to sling a hammock and a couple of cabins to rent.

Beyond San José a signed track on the left leads 4km to the Classic period **ruins of Motúl** (free). The site is fairly spread out and little visited (though there should be a caretaker about), with four plazas, stelae and pyramids. It's a secluded spot, ideal for bird-watching, and probably best visited by bicycle from either of the villages – either borrow one from a villager or rent a bike in Flores.

El Remate

On the eastern shore of Lago de Petén Itzá, 30km from Santa Elena on the road to Tikal, **EL REMATE** offers a pleasant alternative to staying in Flores. It's a quiet, friendly village, growing in popularity as a convenient base for visits to Tikal. **Getting to El Remate** is easy: every minibus to Tikal passes through the village, or catch any bus heading for the Belize border, get off at the village of **Puente Ixlú** (also called El Cruce) and it's a 2km walk down the Tikal road. **Returning to Flores**, local buses pass through El Remate at 5.30am, 7.30am and 8am and a swarm of minibuses from Tikal ply the route from midday onwards.

On the north shore of the lake, 3km along the dirt road that heads west from the centre of El Remate, the **Biotopo Cerro Cahuí** (daily; US$5) is a six-and-a-half-square-kilometre wildlife conservation area comprising lakeshore, ponds and some of the best examples of undisturbed tropical forest in Petén. The smallest and most accessible of Petén's reserves, it contains a rich diversity of plants and animals and is especially recommended for bird-watchers. There are hiking trails, a couple of small ruins and two thatched miradores on the hill above the lake; pick up maps and information at the gate where you sign in, close to the *El Gringo Perdido* hotel.

Accommodation and eating

All the places listed here have a distinctive charm and they're well spaced, with no sense of overcrowding. There are no private **phone numbers**: to book ahead you need to leave a message (in Spanish) on the community telephone (☎9260269). There are no restaurants per se in El Remate, but most of the hotels provide meals; *Don David's*, in particular, is highly recommended. The following hotels are listed in the order you approach them from Puente Ixlú.

El Mirador del Duende, high above the lake, reached by a stairway cut into the cliff. An incredible collection of globular whitewashed stucco cabañas decorated with Maya glyphs, plus space for hammocks and tents. The owner is an expert on jungle lore, leading hikes to all Petén's archeological sites, and the restaurant serves cheap vegetarian food. ①–②.

La Mansión del Pajaro Serpiente, just below *El Mirador del Duende* (☎ & fax 9260065 in Flores). The most comfortable accommodation on the road to Tikal. Stone-built and thatched two-storey cabañas in a tropical garden and smaller cabañas at about a third of the price, all with superb lake views. Good food. ④–⑦.

La Casa de Don David, 300m beyond *La Mansión*, right on the junction. Probably the most atmospheric place in El Remate. Great home cooking and near-legendary after-dinner "tarantula tours" and "Tikal tips" lectures from owner David Kuhn, who is a mine of information about Petén. New restaurant premises next door (book ahead for dinner). If you need a lift from Puente Ixlú, send a kid on a bicycle and David will come and pick you up. ③.

Casa Mobego (formerly *Casa Roja*), 500m down the road to Cerro Cahuí on the right. Good budget deal right by the lake. Simple, well-constructed stick-and-thatch cabañas, plus camping, canoe rental, a good, inexpensive restaurant and swimming. ②.

El Gringo Perdido, on the north shore, 3km from *Don David's* (contact Viajes Mundial in Guatemala City: ☎2320605, fax 2538761). Long-established place in a supremely tranquil setting offering rooms with bath, a mosquito-netted bunk and some excellent-value basic cabañas. Also offers camping, a fine restaurant and guided canoe tours. ②–⑤.

El Hotel Camino Real Tikal, beyond Cerro Cahuí, 5km from the Tikal highway (☎9260209; in Guatemala City ☎3334633, fax 3374313). Luxury option in extensive lakeside grounds with excellent views of the lake and a private beach. Rooms are a bit unimaginative and corporate, with attendant luxury trappings like buggies and a souvenir shop. Free use of kayaks and a guided tour of the Biotopo Cerro Cahuí. US$132 for a double. ⑨.

Tikal

Towering above the rainforest, **Tikal** is possibly the most magnificent of all Maya ruins. The site is dominated by five enormous temples, steep-sided granite pyramids that rise up to 60m from the forest floor, while around them are literally thousands of other structures, many semi-strangled by giant roots and still hidden beneath mounds of earth. The site itself is deep in the jungle of the **Parque Nacional Tikal**, a protected area of some 370 square kilome-

Tikal emblem glyphs

tres on the edge of the even larger Maya Biosphere Reserve and adjoining another large *biotopo*. The trees around the ruins are home to hundreds of species including howler and spider monkeys, toucans and parakeets. The sheer scale of the place is overwhelming and its atmosphere spellbinding. Whether you can spare as little as an hour or as long as a week, it's always worth the trip.

Plane and bus schedules are designed to make it easy to visit the ruins as a day-trip from Flores or Guatemala City, but if you can spare the time it's well worth **staying overnight**, partly because you'll need the extra time to do justice to the ruins themselves but, more importantly, to spend dawn and dusk at the site, when the forest canopy bursts into a frenzy of sound and activity. The air fills with the screech of toucans and the roar of howler monkeys, while flocks of parakeets wheel around the temples and bats launch themselves into the night. With a bit of luck you might even see a grey fox sneak across one of the plazas.

Arrival and information

The best way to reach the ruins is in one of the **tourist minibuses** that meet flights from the capital and are operated by just about every hotel in Flores and Santa Elena, starting at 4am to catch the sunrise. In addition a **local bus** (Pinita) leaves the market at 1pm, passing the *Hotel San Juan* and arriving at Tikal about two hours later; it then continues to Uaxactún (see p.415), returning to Santa Elena at 6am. If you're travelling from Belize to Tikal, there is no need to go all the way to Flores; get off instead at **Puente Ixlú** – the three-way junction at the eastern end of Lago de Petén Itzá – to change buses. The local bus from Santa Elena to Tikal and Uaxactún passes at about 2pm and there are passing minibuses all day long, at their most frequent in the mornings.

Entrance to the national park costs US$8.50 a day and you're expected to pay again if you stay overnight, although this is not always strictly enforced. If you arrive after dusk you will automatically be issued with a ticket for the next day. The ruins themselves are **open** daily from 6am to 5pm and extensions to 8pm can be obtained from the *inspectoría* (7am–noon & 2–5pm), a small white hut on the left at the entrance to the ruins.

The one-room **Tikal Museum** (Mon–Fri 9am–5pm, Sat & Sun 9am–4pm; US$1.80), between the *Jungle Lodge* and *Jaguar Inn* hotels (see below), houses some of the arte-facts found in the ruins, including tools, jewellery, pottery, obsidian and jade, and the remains of Stela 29. There's also a **post office**, shops and a **visitor centre** containing a selection of some the finest stelae and carvings from the site, a scale model of Tikal and a café. Two **books** of note are usually available: Coe's *Tikal: A Handbook to the Ancient Maya Ruins* is the best guide to the site, while *The Birds of Tikal*, although by no means comprehensive, is useful for identifying some of the hundreds of species.

Accommodation, eating and drinking

There are three **hotels** at the ruins, all of them fairly expensive and not especially good value, though they offer discounts out of season. The largest and most luxurious is the *Jungle Lodge*, which offers bungalow accommodation (⑥), some "budget" rooms (④), which are often booked up, and a pool; reservations can be made in Guatemala City (☎4768775, fax 4760294). Next door is the overpriced *Jaguar Inn* (☎9260002; ⑥), and close by the better *Tikal Inn* (☎ & fax 9260065; ⑤–⑥), where there are thatched bun-galows, pleasant rooms and a heat-busting swimming pool.

Alternatively, for US$6 you can **camp** or sling a **hammock** under one of the thatched shelters in a cleared space used as a campsite. Hammocks and mosquito nets (essen-tial in the wet season) can be rented either on the spot or from the *Comedor Imperio Maya* opposite the visitor centre. At the entrance to the campsite there's a shower block, but water is sporadic. The *Jaguar Inn* also has some tents, complete with mat-tresses and drinking water (②). It is possible to camp within the ruins, although this is, strictly speaking, against the regulations.

The three simple **comedores** at the entrance to the ruins and a couple more inside offer a limited menu of traditional Guatemalan specialities – eggs, beans, grilled meat and chicken. For more extensive and expensive menus, there's an adequate restaurant in the *Jaguar Inn* and an overpriced café in the new visitor centre. It's essential to buy some water before setting out, though cold drinks are sold at a number of spots within the ruins.

The rise and fall of Tikal

According to archeological evidence, the first occupants of Tikal arrived around 700 BC, probably attracted by its position above the surrounding seasonal swamps and by the availability of flint for making tools and weapons. The first definite evidence of build-ings dates from 500 BC, and by about 200 BC ceremonial structures had emerged, including the original version of the **North Acropolis**. Two hundred years later, at around the time of Christ, the **Great Plaza** had begun to take shape and Tikal was already established as a major site with a large permanent population. Despite devel-opment and sophisticated architecture, Tikal remained very much a secondary centre, dominated, along with the rest of the area, by **El Mirador**, a massive city about 65km to the north (see p.417).

The closing years of the **Preclassic** era were marked by the eruption of the Ilopango volcano in El Salvador, which smothered huge areas of Guatemala in a thick layer of volcanic ash. Trade routes were disrupted and the ensuing years saw the decline and abandonment of El Mirador, creating a power vacuum disputed bitterly between the cities of Tikal and Uaxactún. Tikal eventually won under the inspired leadership of Great Jaguar Paw, probably with the aid of the powerful highland centre of **Kaminaljuyú** – on the site of modern Guatemala City – which was itself allied with **Teotihuacán**, the ancient metropolis that dominated what is now central Mexico.

The victory over Uaxactún enabled Tikal's rulers to control central Petén for the next three centuries, as Tikal grew into one of the most elaborate and magnificent of all

Maya city-states. This extended period of prosperity saw temples rebuilt, the city's population grow to somewhere between 50,000 and 100,000, and its influence reach as far as Copán in Honduras.

In the middle of the sixth century, however, Tikal suffered a major setback. In the Maya Mountains of Belize, **Caracol** was emerging as a major regional power, and conquered Tikal in 557 AD under the ambitious leader Lord Water. The effect of Caracol's assault was to free many smaller centres throughout Petén from Tikal's influence, creating fresh and disruptive rivalry. By the middle of the seventh century, however, Caracol's stranglehold had begun to relax and Tikal embarked upon a dramatic renaissance under the formidable leadership of **Ah Cacaw**, Lord Chocolate. During his reign the main ceremonial areas, the East Plaza and the North Acropolis, were reclaimed from the desecration suffered at the hands of Caracol and completely remodelled. Tikal regained its position under Ah Cacaw and, as a tribute, his son Caan Chac had the leader's body entombed in the dazzling Temple 1. Ah Cacaw's strident approach gave birth to a revitalized and powerful ruling dynasty: the site's five main temples were built in the hundred years following his death, and magnificent temples were still under construction at Tikal as late as 889 AD.

What brought about Tikal's final **downfall** remains a mystery, but what is certain is that around 900 AD almost the entire lowland Maya civilization collapsed. Possible causes range from an earthquake to popular uprising, with the latest theories indicating that an environmental disaster caused by overpopulation may have triggered the collapse. We do know that Tikal was abandoned by the end of the tenth century.

Little is known of Tikal again until 1848, when it was **rediscovered** by a government expedition led by Modesto Méndez. Later in the nineteenth century a Swiss scientist visited the site and removed the beautifully carved wooden lintels from the tops of temples 1 and 4 – they are currently in a museum in Basel – and in 1881 the English archeologist Maudslay took the first photographs of the ruins. Until 1951 the site could only be reached on horseback and the ruins remained mostly uncleared. The Guatemalan army then built an airstrip, paving the way for a cultural invasion of archeologists and tourists. The gargantuan project to excavate and restore the site started in 1956, and involved teams from the University of Pennsylvania and Guatemala's Institute of Anthropology. Most of the major work was completed by 1984, but thousands of minor buildings remain buried in roots, shoots and rubble. A five-year project to restore Temple 5 (at 58m the second highest structure at Tikal) is currently being coordinated with help from the Spanish government.

The ruins

The sheer scale of the ruins at Tikal can at first seem daunting. The **central area**, with its five main temples, forms by far the most impressive section; if you start to explore beyond this you can ramble seemingly forever in the maze of smaller, **unrestored structures** and complexes. Compared to the scale and magnificence of the main area, they're not that impressive, but armed with a good map (the best is in Coe's guide to the ruins), it can be exciting to search for some of the rarely visited outlying sections. Don't even think about exploring the more distant structures without a map; every year at least one tourist gets lost in the jungle. Tikal is certain to exhaust you before you exhaust it.

From the entrance to the Great Plaza

Following the path to the right of the **map** you pass **Complexes Q and R**, twin pyramids built by **Chitam**, Tikal's last known ruler, to mark the passing of a *katum* (twenty 360-day years). Set to one side is a copy of the superbly carved Stela 22 (now in the visitor centre). Bearing to the left after Complex R you approach the **East Plaza**; in its

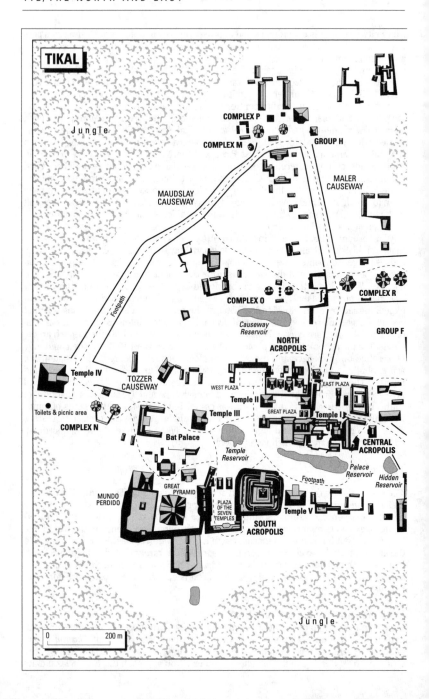

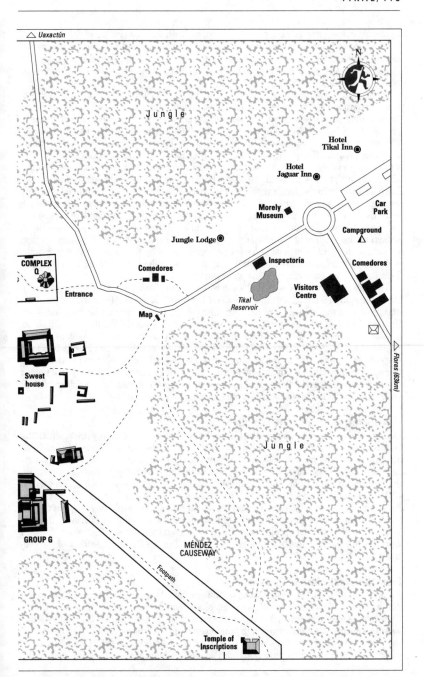

southeast corner stands an imposing temple, beneath which were found the remains of several severed heads, the victims of human sacrifice. Behind the plaza is the **sweat house**, which may have been similar to those used by highland Maya today. It's thought that Maya priests would take a sweat bath in order to cleanse themselves before conducting religious rituals.

From here a few short steps bring you to the **Great Plaza**, the heart of the ancient city. Surrounded by four massive structures, this was the focus of ceremonial and religious activity at Tikal for around a thousand years. Beneath the grass lie four layers of paving, the oldest of which dates from about 150 BC and the most recent from 700 AD. **Temple 1**, towering 44m above the plaza, is the hallmark of Tikal – it's also known as the Temple of the Grand Jaguar because of the jaguar carved in its door lintel (now in a museum in Basel). This is the temple built as a burial monument to contain the magnificent tomb of **Ah Cacaw** (Lord Chocolate, 682–721 AD) by his son and successor Caan Chac. Within the tomb at the temple's core, the skeleton was found facing north, surrounded by an assortment of jade, pearls, seashells and also stingray spines, which were used in bloody body-piercing rituals. A reconstruction of the tomb is on show at the site museum. Standing opposite, like a squat version of Temple 1, is **Temple 2**, known as the Temple of the Masks for the two grotesque masks, now heavily eroded, that flank the central stairway. As yet no tomb has been found beneath this temple, which now stands 38m high, although with its roof-comb intact it would have equalled Temple 1. It's an easy climb up the staircase to the top.

The **North Acropolis**, which fills the whole north side of the Great Plaza, is one of the most complex structures in the entire Maya world. In true Maya style it was built and rebuilt on top of itself, and beneath the twelve temples that can be seen today are the remains of about a hundred other structures. As early as 100 BC the Maya had constructed elaborate platforms supporting temples and tombs here. Archeologists have removed some of the surface to reveal these earlier structures, including two four-metre-high **masks**. One facing the plaza, protected by a thatched roof, is clearly visible; the other can be reached by following the dark passageway to the side – you'll need a torch. In front of the North Acropolis are two lines of **stelae** with circular altars at their bases, all of which were originally painted a brilliant red.

The central acropolis and Temple 5

On the other side of the plaza is the **Central Acropolis**, a maze of tiny interconnecting rooms and stairways built around six smallish courtyards. The buildings here are usually referred to as palaces rather than temples, although their precise use remains a mystery. Possibilities include law courts, temporary retreats, administrative centres, and homes for Tikal's elite. Behind the acropolis is the palace reservoir, which was fed with rainwater by a series of channels from all over the city. Further behind the Central Acropolis is the 58-metre-high **Temple 5**, which supports a single tiny room at the top thought to be a mortuary shrine to an unknown ruler. The temple is currently the subject of a huge restoration project, due to be completed by the year 2000, when the view from the top will be superb, with a great profile of Temple 1 and a side view of the central plaza.

From the West Plaza to Temple 4

Behind Temple 2 is the **West Plaza**, dominated by a large Late Classic temple on the north side, and scattered with various altars and stelae. From here the Tozzer Causeway – one of the raised routes that connected the main parts of the city – leads west to **Temple 3** (55m), covered in jungle vegetation. A fragment of Stela 24, found at the base of the temple, dates it at 810 AD. Around the back of the temple is a huge palace complex, of which only the **Bat Palace** has been restored. At the end of the

Tozzer Causeway is **Temple 4**, the tallest of all the Tikal structures at a massive 64m. Built in 741 AD, it is thought by some archeologists to be the resting place of the ruler Coon Chac, whose image was depicted on wooden lintels built into the top of the temple. To reach the top you have to scramble over roots and rubble, and finally up a metal ladder around the side of the pyramid. Slow and exhausting as this is, one of the finest views of the whole site awaits. All around you the forest canopy stretches out to the horizon, interrupted only by the great roof-combs of the other temples.

The Mundo Perdido, the Plaza of the Seven Temples and the Temple of the Inscriptions

To the south of the Central Acropolis, reached by a trail from Temple 3, you'll find the **Plaza of the Seven Temples**, which forms part of a complex dating back to before Christ. There's an unusual triple ball court on the north side of the plaza, and to the east is the unexcavated South Acropolis. To the west, the **Mundo Perdido**, or Lost World, is another magical and very distinct section of the site with its own atmosphere and architecture. Little is known about the ruins in this part of the site, but archeologists hope that further research will help to explain the early history of Tikal. The main feature is the **great pyramid**, a 32-metre-high structure whose surface hides four earlier versions, the first dating from 700 BC. The top of the pyramid offers awesome views towards Temple 4 and the Great Plaza and makes an excellent base for the visual dramatics of sunrise or sunset – minus the crowds.

Finally, there's the **Temple of the Inscriptions**, reached along the Méndez Causeway from the East Plaza behind Temple 1. The temple (only discovered in 1951) is about 1km from the plaza. It's famous for its 12m roof-comb, at the back of which is a huge but rather faint hieroglyphic text.

Uaxactún and the far north

Away to the north of Tikal, lost in a sea of jungle, are several other very substantial **ruins** – unrestored and for the most part uncleared, but with their own unique atmosphere. The village and ruins of Uaxactún lie 24km north of Tikal, strung out by the side of a disused airstrip. With three places to stay, several comedores and a daily bus to Santa Elena, the village is an ideal jumping-off point for the more remote sites of **El Zotz**, **Río Azul** and **El Mirador**, where the bulk of the temples are coated in an anarchic tangle of vegetation and only the tallest roof-combs are visible. **Dirt tracks** go as far as Río Azul and El Zotz, though doubtless they'll soon be reached by road. For the moment, however, they remain well beyond the reach of the average visitor – perfect if you're in search of an adventure and want to see a virtually untouched Maya site.

Uaxactún

UAXACTÚN is substantially smaller than Tikal, but thought to date from the same era. During the Preclassic period Uaxactún and Tikal coexisted in relative harmony, dominated by El Mirador, but by the first century AD, with El Mirador in decline, a fierce rivalry ignited between Tikal and Uaxactún. The two finally clashed in 378 AD when Tikal's warriors conquered Uaxactún, forcing it to accept subordinate status.

The overall impact of Uaxactún may be a little disappointing after the grandeur of Tikal, but you'll probably have the site to yourself, giving you the chance to soak up the atmosphere. The most interesting buildings are in **Group E**, east of the airstrip, where three reconstructed temples, built side by side, are arranged to function as an observatory. Viewed from the top of a fourth temple, the sun rises behind the north temple on the longest day of the year and behind the southern one on the shortest day. Beneath one of these temples the famous **E-VII** was unearthed, the oldest building ever found in Petén, with the very earliest foundations possibly dating back as far as 2000 BC. The original pyramid had a simple staircase up the front, flanked by two stucco masks, and post holes in the top suggest that it may have been covered by a thatched shelter. Over on the other side of the airstrip is **Group A**, a series of larger temples and residential compounds, some of them reconstructed, and some impressive stelae.

Practicalities

A **bus** from Flores passes through Tikal en route for Uaxactún at around 3.30pm; alternatively, you could take one of the **tours** run by a number of companies based in Flores. **Staying** overnight you have three options. The *EcoCampamento* (☎9260077 in Flores) has tents and hammocks, protected by mosquito nets, under a thatched shelter (①–②), the welcoming *Hotel El Chiclero* (③) offers clean rooms without bath, or you can camp or sling a hammock for US$2.50 a head. Owner Antonio Baldizón also organizes 4-wheel-drive trips to Río Azul, and his wife Neria prepares excellent food. *Tecomate* (①–②) is a similar camping, cabaña and hammock place at the entrance to the village, run by Manuel Soto, who can guide you to any of the more remote Maya sites.

Uaxactún's **guide association** has a small **information office** at the end of the airstrip and will organize **camping trips** to any of the remote northern sites, into the jungle or east to Nakúm and Yaxhá. Equipment is carried on horseback and the price (US$30 per person per day for a group of three or more) includes a guide, horses, camping gear and food. Check at CINCAP or ARCAS in Flores who can give advice and help you put together excursions.

El Zotz

Thirty kilometres west of Uaxactún, along a rough jeep track sometimes passable in the dry season (by 4-wheel drive) is **El Zotz**, a large Maya site set in its own *biotopo* reserve adjoining the Tikal national park. To **get there** you can rent vehicles in Uaxactún, or hire a packhorse, guide, food and camping equipment from Uaxactún's guide association. After about four hours – almost halfway – you come to **Santa Cruz**, where you can camp if necessary. At the site itself you'll be welcomed by the guards who look after the *biotopo* headquarters. You can camp here and, with permission, use their kitchen and drinking water; remember to bring some food to share with the guides.

Totally unrestored and smothered by vegetation, El Zotz has been systematically looted, although there are guards on duty all year. Zotz means "bat" in Maya and each evening at dusk you'll see tens, perhaps hundreds, of thousands of **bats** of several species emerge from a cave near the campsite. It's especially impressive in the moonlight, the beating wings sounding like a river flowing over rapids – one of the most remarkable natural sights in Petén.

Walking on, it takes about four and a half hours to get to **Cruce dos Aguadas**, a crossroads village on the bus route to Santa Elena (the bus leaves at 7am). Here you'll find shops and the *Comedor Patojas*, where they'll let you sling a hammock or camp. Northwards, the road goes to Carmelita for El Mirador; there's also a track westwards towards El Perú, though this is not passable in the rainy season.

Río Azul

The remote site of **Río Azul**, almost on the tripartite border where Guatemala, Belize and Mexico meet, was only rediscovered in 1962. The city and its suburbs had a population of around five thousand and probably reached a peak in the Preclassic era, but remained an important site well into the Classic period. Although totally unrestored, the core of the site is similar to a small-scale Tikal, with the tallest temple (AIII) standing some 47m above the forest floor, surfacing above the treetops and giving magnificent views across the jungle.

Several incredible **tombs** have been unearthed here, lined with white plaster and painted with vivid red glyphs. Tomb 19 is thought to have contained the remains of one of the sons of Stormy Sky, Tikal's great early Classic expansionist ruler (who ruled Tikal shortly after it conquered Uaxactún), suggesting that the city may have been founded by Tikal to consolidate the borders of its empire. Nearby tombs contained bodies of warriors dressed in clothing typical of Teotihuacán in central Mexico – further supporting evidence of links between Tikal and the mighty ancient city.

Extensive **looting** occurred after the site's discovery, with a gang of up to eighty men plundering the tombs and removing some of the finest murals in the Maya world once the archeological teams had retreated to Flores in the rainy season. Río Azul supplied the international market with unique treasures including some incredible green jade masks and pendants. Mercifully, despite its chamber being looted in 1981, Tomb 1's walls remain almost intact. Today there are two resident guards.

The **road** that connects Tikal and Uaxactún continues for another 95km north to Río Azul. This route is only passable in the dry season, and even then it's by no means easy. The three-day round-trip by **jeep** (a day each way and a day at the site) involves frequent stops to clear the road. **Walking** or on **horseback** it's four days each way – three at a push. Trips (around US$300 per person) can be arranged through the *Hotel el Chiclero* in Uaxactún or, more expensively, through a number of agents: check with Inguat, CINCAP or ProPetén in Flores. Once you arrive at Río Azul you'll be welcome to **stay** at the guard's camp (bring some supplies).

El Mirador

El Mirador is perhaps the most exotic and mysterious of all Petén's Maya sites. Still buried in the forest, this massive city matches Tikal's scale, and may even surpass it. Rediscovered in 1926, it dates from an earlier period than Tikal, flourishing between 150 BC and 150 AD, and was almost certainly the first great city in the Maya World. It was unquestionably the dominant city in Petén, occupying a commanding position above the rainforest, at an altitude of 250m, and was home to tens of thousands of Maya. Little archeological work has been done here but it's clear that the site represents the peak of Preclassic Maya culture, which was far more sophisticated than was once believed.

The core of the site covers some sixteen square kilometres, stretching between two massive pyramids that face each other across the forest. The site's western side is marked by the massive **Tigre Complex**, made up of a huge single pyramid flanked by two smaller structures, a triadic design that's characteristic of El Mirador's architecture. The base of this complex alone would cover around three football fields, while the height of the 2000-year-old main pyramid touches 70m, equivalent to an eighteen-storey building and making the structure the tallest anywhere in the Maya world. In front of the Tigre Complex is El Mirador's sacred hub: a long narrow plaza, the **Central Acropolis**, and a row of smaller buildings. Burial chambers unearthed in this central section contained the bodies of priests and noblemen, surrounded by the obsidian lancets and stingray spines used to pierce the penis, ears and tongue in ritual bloodletting ceremonies. The spilling of blood was seen by the Maya as a method of summoning and sustaining the gods, and was clearly common at all the great ceremonial centres.

To the south of the Tigre Complex is the **Monos Complex**, another triadic structure and plaza, named after the resident howler monkeys. To the north the **León pyramid** and the **Casabel Complex** mark the edge of the site. Heading away to the east, the Puleston Causeway runs to the smaller East Group, the largest of which (about 2km from the Tigre Complex) is the **Danta Complex**. This is another triadic structure, rising in three stages to a height just below that of the Tigre pyramid, but with an even better view since it was built on higher land.

The area **around El Mirador** is riddled with smaller Maya sites, and as you look out across the forest from the top of either of the main temples you can see others rising above the horizon on all sides – including the giant Calakmul in Mexico (see p.95). Among the most accessible are **Nakbé**, some 10km to the southeast, with origins as early as 1000 BC, probably predating all other Maya sites in the area. Some initial excavation work has been done at Nakbé, uncovering several pyramids from as early as 600 BC, some reaching 45m in height. A huge Maya mask (5m by 8m) was also found in September 1992, and doubtless much more will follow. Far Horizons run expeditions to Nakbé; see "Basics" p.6 for details.

El Tintal, a massive site 21km to the southwest of El Mirador, was connected by a causeway to its neighbour, and the ruins, though severely looted, make an ideal campsite. Climb to the top of the largest pyramid and there are spectacular views, including El Mirador in the distance.

Getting to El Mirador is a substantial undertaking, involving an arduous 60km pickup or truck ride north from San Andrés to **Carmelita**, a chicle- and *xate*-gathering centre, followed by two days of hard jungle hiking – you'll need a horse to carry your food and equipment. The journey – impossibly muddy in the rainy season – is best attempted from mid-January to August; February to April is the driest period. It offers an exceptional chance to see virtually untouched forest, and perhaps some of the creatures that inhabit it. Whether you take a tour or go independently, you're advised to examine the information and maps in ProPetén and CINCAP first. ProPetén offers five-day **tours** (around US$200 for two people) from Carmelita to El Mirador, including guide, packhorse and digs in Carmelita – you need to bring your own food and water purification system. It's also possible to travel **independently**, arranging a guide and horse in Carmelita (about US$30 a day), and bringing your own food, water and camping gear. It's essential to bring some supplies for the guards, who spend forty days at a time in the forest, subsisting on beans and tortillas. **To get to Carmelita**, take a bus from Santa Elena to San Andrés (see p.407), then hitch via Cruce Dos Aguadas (see p.416). ProPetén in Flores often have vehicles going to Carmelita, so it's worth checking with them before setting out. When you arrive at Carmelita, ask for Luís Morales, president of the Tourism Committee, who will arrange guides for the trip.

Sayaxché and around

Southwest of Flores, on a lazy bend in the Río Pasión, the easygoing frontier town of SAYAXCHÉ makes an ideal base for exploring the surrounding forest and its huge collection of archeological remains. The town is the supply centre for a vast surrounding area that is being steadily cleared and colonized. The complex network of rivers and swamps that cuts through the forested wilderness here has been an important trade route since Maya times, and there are several interesting ruins in the area. Upstream is **Ceibal**, a small but beautiful site in a wonderful jungle setting; to the south is **Lago de Petexbatún**, on the shores of which are the small ruins of **Dos Pilas** and **Aguateca**. Both sites offer great opportunities to wander in the forest and watch the wildlife.

Sayaxché practicalities

Getting to Sayaxché from Flores is very straightforward, with several Pinita **buses** (6am, 9am, 10am, 1pm and 4pm; 2hr) and one Del Rosio service (5am) plying the fairly smooth 62km dirt road. At other times hitching a ride in a **pickup** is not too difficult. A ferry takes you over the Río Pasión, directly opposite Sayaxché.

   Hotels in Sayaxché are on the basic side. The *Guayacan* (☎9268777; ②), right beside the river, is the best, with plain but clean rooms, some with private bath, and lovely sunset views from the terrace. For a cheaper room, head left down the street above the *Guayacan* to the cleanish *Hospedaje Mayapan* (①), where you may be able to rent a **bike** for visiting Ceibal. There are plenty of reasonable places to **eat**, the best being the *Restaurant Yaxkin,* which is a little pricey, though the portions are huge (closes 8pm). There is also decent food at *Guayacan* and at *La Montaña,* which is owned by the knowledgeable and helpful Julián Mariona, who can arrange **trips** to the nearby ruins (around US$40 a day). Plenty of **boatmen** are eager to take you up- or downriver, though they tend to see all tourists as walking cash-dispensers and quote prices in dollars. Try Pedro Méndez Requena of Viajes Don Pedro (☎ & fax 9286109), who offers **tours** of the area from his office on the riverfront. You can change travellers' cheques at Banora, a block up from the *Guayacan*.

The ruins of Ceibal

The most accessible and impressive of the sites near Sayaxché is **Ceibal**, which you can reach by land and river. It's easy enough to make it there and back in an afternoon **by boat**; haggle with the boatmen at the waterfront and you can expect to pay around US$40 (for up to six people). The beautiful hour-long boat trip is followed by a thirty-minute hike uphill through towering rainforest to the ruins. **By road**, Ceibal is just 17km from Sayaxché. Any transport heading south out of town towards Cruce del Pato passes the entrance track to the site, from where it's an 8km walk through fields and then jungle to the ruins. Travel agents in Flores also run day-trips to Ceibal (around US$30 per person); see p.407 for recommended companies.

Ceibal emblem glyph

   Surrounded by forest and shaded by huge ceiba trees, **the ruins** of Ceibal are a mixture of cleared open plazas and untamed jungle. Though many of the largest temples lie buried under mounds, Ceibal does have some outstanding carving, well preserved by the use of hard stone. The two main plazas are dotted with lovely **stelae**, centred around two low platforms. During the Classic period Ceibal was a relatively minor site, but it grew rapidly between 830 and 930 AD, apparently after falling under the control of colonists from what is now Mexico, becoming a large lowland site, with an estimated population of around ten thousand. Outside influence is clearly visible in the carving here: speech scrolls, straight noses, waist-length hair and serpent motifs are all decidedly non-Maya. The monkey-faced Stela 2 is particularly striking, beyond which is Stela 14, another impressive sculpture straight ahead down the path. If you turn right here and walk for ten minutes you'll reach the only other restored part of the site, set superbly in a clearing in the forest – an unmissable massive circular stone platform which was either an altar or **observation** deck for astronomy.

Lago de Petexbatún: Aguateca and Dos Pilas

A similar distance to the south of Sayaxché is **Lago de Petexbatún,** a spectacular expanse of water ringed by dense forest and containing plentiful supplies of snook, bass, alligator and freshwater turtle. The shores of the lake abound with wildlife and Maya remains and, though the ruins themselves are small and unrestored, their sheer number suggests that the lake was an important trading centre for the Maya. **Aguateca,** perched on a high outcrop on the southern tip of the lake, is the most accessible site (although it's the furthest from Sayaxché) as a boat can get you to within twenty minutes' walk of it.

Encompassed by dense tropical forest and with superb views of the lake, Aguateca has a magical atmosphere. You can clearly make out the temples and plazas, dotted with well-preserved stelae. The carving is superbly executed, the images including rulers, captives, hummingbirds, pineapples and pelicans. Aguateca is also the site of the only known **bridge** in the Maya world, which crosses a narrow gash in the hillside, but although it's unique it's not that impressive. If you ask the guards who live here, they may give you an enthusiastic and well-informed tour of the site, and if you want to **stay** they'll find some space for you to sling a hammock or pitch a tent – bring along a mosquito net and some food.

Slightly closer to Sayaxché is **Dos Pilas**, another unreconstructed site, buried in the jungle to the west of the lake. Dos Pilas was the centre of a formidable empire in the early part of the eighth century, with a population approaching ten thousand. The ruins are quite unusual, as the major structures are grouped in an east–west linear pattern. Around the central plaza are some tremendous stelae, altars and four **hieroglyphic stairways** decorated with glyphs and figures.

To **get to Dos Pilas** from Sayaxché, it's a 45-minute speedboat trip (or up to 3hr in a cargo boat) to *Rancho El Caribe*, at the northern tip of the lake, and then a further 12km trek on foot to the ruins. About 7km from the lake you pass the small site of **Arroyo de Piedra**, where you'll find a plaza and two fairly well-preserved stelae. It's cheapest to **stay** at the site itself, camping or sleeping in a hammock, but if you desire more comfort, the *Posada Caribe* (☎ & fax 9286114; ⑦ including full board) offers an alternative of clean, screened cabins, reasonable food and boat trips to Aguateca; negotiate rates in advance. It may be possible to get to both sites **by mule** (or even truck) during the dry months.

South to the Ixcán

South of Sayaxché the road skirts the edge of the **Parque Nacional Ceibal**, at first slicing through a stretch of jungle, then through a flat, degraded land of scrub, lone tree stumps, cattle pasture and thatched cabañas full of indigenous families. These Kekchí, some returning refugees, attempt to eke out a meagre existence in this poor, largely treeless landscape. Half an hour before **Cruce del Pato** (see p.400), where the road splits, the magnificent bulk of the Cuchumatanes mountain range comes into view, the looming, forested peaks rising abruptly from the plain. A Del Rosio bus runs down this road to **Playitas** every morning.

Routes to Mexico

There are a number of possible routes **into Mexico** from Petén, all of which offer a sense of adventure and a glimpse of the rainforest – and involve shuttling between buses, boats and immigration posts. However, travellers should bear in mind that at the time of writing, Mexican border officials were only giving **two-week visas** to travellers entering the state of Chiapas from Guatemala, due to the armed conflict in the region.

From Sayaxché to Benemérito

Downriver from Sayaxché, the **Río Pasión** snakes its way through an area of forest, swamp and small settlements to **Pipiles**, which marks the point where the rivers Salinas and Pasión merge to form the Usumacinta. All boats stop here for **immigration**, and exit stamps can be obtained. Not far from Pipiles is the small Maya site of **Altar de los Sacrificios**, commanding an important river junction. This is one of the oldest sites in Petén, but these days there's not much to see beyond a solitary stela.

Following the **Usumacinta** downstream you arrive at **Benemérito** in Mexico (see p.139), a sprawling frontier town at the end of a dirt road from Palenque. It's about US$8–10 for this eight-hour trip, though cargo boats can take a couple of days to get this far. There are basic hotels and restaurants in Benemérito and you can head on to Yaxchilán from here directly by boat or, much more cheaply, by bus to Frontera Corozal (where there are basic bedrooms and camping) and then by boat.

From Bethel to Frontera Corozal

Currently the cheapest and most straightforward route to Mexico is along the rough road to **BETHEL** on the Río Usumacinta, where there is a new Guatemalan **immigration** post. Two buses a day leave Flores for Bethel (5am & 1pm; 4hr), passing the junction north of Sayaxché about a couple of hours later. At Bethel it's relatively easy to find a *lancha* heading downstream, or you can hire one (US$25 to Frontera Corozal; 30min). If you need to stay, Bethel itself is a pleasant village where you can **camp** above the riverbank and there are several **comedores** and shops. The **Bethel ruins**, 1.5km from the village, are today little more than tree-covered mounds, but there's an excellent **eco-campamento** here called the *Posada Maya*, with hammocks (①) or tents (including mattresses and clean sheets) under thatched shelters (②), on top of a wooded cliff high above the river. Over the border in Frontera Corozal there is an **immigration post**, plus some comedores and very basic hotels. From here there are regular **buses**, shared minibuses and tour buses to Palenque until 3pm (4hr). For further adventure, the spectacular ruins of **Yaxchilán** (see p.138), grouped around a great loop in the Usumacinta, are 15km away; **hiring a boat** for this beautiful trip costs around US$60 return.

El Naranjo to La Palma

Another popular route **from Flores to Mexico** takes you by a bad road to **EL NARAN-JO** (several buses a day until 2.30pm; 4–5hr). El Naranjo is a rough spot, consisting of little more than an army base, an **immigration** post, where you'll be asked for a US$5 "leaving tax", stores (offering poor exchange rates) comedores and basic hotels. The best place to **stay** is the friendly, family-run *Posada San Pedro* across the river (☎9261276 in Flores; ④). The other places in town are pretty filthy. The river-trip down the San Pedro starts here; there's usually a **boat** (US$20 per person; 4hr) for Mexico at around 1pm, returning from La Palma at 8am. Your first port of call is the Mexican immigration post, about an hour away, and beyond that is the small riverside village of **La Palma** in Mexico (see p.179). La Palma is a good transport hub with basic rooms to rent and bus connections to Tenosique (last bus 5pm).

Piedras Negras

On the Guatemalan side of the Usumacinta, downstream from Yaxchilán, the ruins of **Piedras Negras** are some of the most inaccessible and least visited of all the major Maya ruins. Though many of the very best carvings are on display in the Museo Nacional de Arqueología y Etnología in Guatemala City, where they're a great deal easier to see, there's still plenty to experience on site. Piedras Negras, whose name refers to the stones lining the river bank here, was closely allied with Yaxchilán and probably under its rule at various times.

Piedras Negras emblem glyph

Upon arrival, the most immediately impressive monument is a large rock jutting over the riverbank with a carving of a male seated figure presenting a bundle to a female figure. This was once surrounded by glyphs, now badly eroded and best seen at night with a torch held at a low angle. Continuing up the hill, across plazas and over the ruins of buildings, you get some idea of the city's size. Several buildings are comparatively well preserved, particularly the **sweat baths**, used for ritual purification. The most imposing of all is the **Acropolis**, a huge complex of rooms, passages and courtyards towering 100m above the riverbank. A **megalithic stairway** led down to the river at one time, doubtless a humbling sight to visitors (and captives) before the forest invaded the city. Another intriguing sight is a huge double-headed turtle glyph carved on a rock overhanging a small valley. This is a reference to the end of a *katun*; inside the main glyph is a giant representation of the day sign Ahau (which also means Lord), recalling the myth of the birth of the maize god. During research carried out at Piedras Negras in the 1930s, the artist and epigrapher Tatiana Proskouriakoff noticed that dates carved on monuments corresponded approximately to a human life span, indicating that the glyphs might refer to events in one person's lifetime, possibly the rulers of the city. Rejected for decades by the archeological establishment, her theory was later proved correct.

Traditionally, the presence of FAR guerrillas in the region protected the ruins from systematic looting – neither looters nor the army dared enter. Now that the guerrillas have gone and access from the Mexican bank is becoming easier, it remains to be seen how long Piedras Negras can maintain its relatively untouched state. The site is currently being researched by a joint American-Guatemalan team of Maya academics – the first serious investigation of Piedras Negras since 1939.

There's no easy way to **get to** Piedras Negras, as the site is only accessible by boat. Several tour operators run trips down the Usumacinta, with the best-organized being Maya Expeditions (see p.305), a specialist white-water rafting operation based in Guatemala City.

From Flores to Belize

The hundred kilometres from Flores to the border with Belize takes you through another sparsely inhabited section of Petén, a journey of up to three hours by bus down a pretty smooth dirt road. You'll need to set out early in order to get to San Ignacio or Belize City the same day; if you catch the 5am express service you can even make it straight through to Chetumal, in Mexico. Along the way the bus passes through **Puente Ixlú** (see p.408), halfway between Tikal and Flores, so if you're coming directly from the site or El Remate you can pick up a ride there.

Lago de Yaxhá and the ruins of Nakúm

About halfway between Puente Ixlú and the border is **Lago de Yaxhá**, a shallow limestone depression ringed by dense rainforest and home to two isolated Maya sites. The lake is around 8km from the main Flores–Belize road, a sweltering two-hour walk. The main track bears off to the right towards a finca, but to make it to **the ruins of Yaxhá** you want to head to the left, along a smaller track. The ruins, rediscovered in 1904, are spread out across nine plazas on the north shore of the lake. Though clearing and restoration work has recently begun, don't expect any of the manicured splendour of Tikal, but do count on real atmosphere as you attempt to discover the many features still half hidden by the forest. **Topoxte**, another small site on an island close to the west shore of the lake is not particularly impressive, but very unusual in that everything is built on a miniature scale, including tiny temples and stelae. You can **stay** at the wonderful *El Sombrero Eco-Campamento* (☎9265299, fax 9265198; in Guatemala City ☎4482428; in San Ignacio, Belize ☎092/3508; ④), on the south side of the lake, a wooden jungle lodge run by solar power. It has space for **camping** (①), a library of books on wildlife and the Maya, and organizes boat and horseback trips to Nakúm, though meals are on the pricey side. There's also free camping on the north shore beneath a thatched shelter close to the ruins.

The unrestored **ruins of Nakúm**, a somewhat larger site, are about 20km north of Lago de Yaxhá, though the road is rarely passable so you'll probably have to walk. The most impressive structure is the residential-style palace, which has forty rooms and is similar to the North Acropolis at Tikal. There are two guards here who will show you where to camp or sling a hammock. It's also possible to **walk to Tikal** in a day from Nakúm (around 25km), though you'll need to persuade a guard to act as a **guide**, or bring one with you – speak to Inguat or see CINCAP in Flores.

The border: Melchor de Mencos

Despite the differences between Guatemala and Belize, border formalities are fairly straightforward: you have to pay a small departure tax on leaving Guatemala. **Moneychangers** will pester you on either side of the border and give a fair rate. There's also a **bank** (Mon–Fri 8.30am–2pm) just beyond the immigration building, next to the *Hotel Frontera Palace* (☎ & fax 9265196; ④), which has rooms in pleasant thatched cabins, hot water and a restaurant.

Buses to the border from Flores/Santa Elena leave from the *Hotel San Juan* in Santa Elena at 5am, 8am and 11am, while Rosita buses leave from the market at 5am, 7am, 9.30am, 11am, 2pm, 3pm and 6pm. Linea Dorada/Mundo Maya also operate a 5am **express service** to Belize City (5hr; US$20) and on to Chetumal (8hr; US$30), leaving from their offices on C Principal in Santa Elena. More than twice as expensive as the public bus, this service is quicker and smoother and also connects with services to Cancún. The *Hotel San Juan* operates a similar express bus service, leaving at 5am. Buses leave **for Belize City** every hour or so (3hr) right from the border. Indeed, most actually begin their journey from the market in Melchor; for other destinations you may have to take a shared taxi to Benque Viejo or to San Ignacio (US$2 per person; 20min).

travel details

Buses

Agua Blanca to: Guatemala City (3 daily; 5hr).

Chiquimula to: El Florido (6am–4.30pm; 2hr 30min); Esquipulas (every 15 min; 1hr); Guatemala City (14 daily; 3hr 30min); Ipala (8 daily; 1hr); Puerto Barrios (10 daily; 3hr).

Cobán to: Cahabón (4 daily; 4hr); El Estor (11 daily; 8hr); Guatemala City (14 daily; 4–5hr);Lanquín (4 daily, 3hr); San Cristóbal Verapaz (hourly; 45min); San Pedro Carchá (every 15 min; 20min); Senahú (3 daily; 7hr); Tactic (hourly, 45min).

Cubulco to: Guatemala City via El Chol (1 daily; 9hr); Guatemala City via la Cumbre (hourly; 5hr 30min); Rabinal (hourly; 1hr 30min); Salamá (hourly; 2hr 30min).

Esquipulas to: Aguacaliente for Honduras (every 30 min; 30min) and for El Salvador (every 30min; 1hr); Chiquimula (every 15 mins; 1hr); Guatemala City (hourly 2am–6pm; 4hr).

Flores to: Belize City (2 daily; 5hr); Bethel (2 daily; 5hr); Chetumal (2 daily; 9hr); Cruce del Pato (2 daily; 4hr); El Naranjo (8 daily; 4–5hr);Guatemala City (20 daily; 10–15hr); Melchor de Mencos (10 daily; 3hr); Sayaxché (7 daily; 2hr); Tikal (1 daily; 2hr); Uaxactún (1 daily; 3hr).

Mariscos to: Guatemala City (1 daily at 7am; 4hr 30min); Puerto Barrios (1 daily; 2hr).

Poptún to: Flores (around 20 daily; 2hr); Río Dulce (around 20 daily; 2hr 30min).

Puerto Barrios to: Chiquimula (10 daily; 3hr); Mariscos (1 daily at 3pm); Guatemala City (19 daily; 5hr); Esquipulas (4 daily;4hr); Finca la Inca for Honduras (12 daily; 2hr); Mariscos (1 daily at 3pm).

Poptún to: Flores (around 20 daily; 2hr); Río Dulce (around 20 daily; 2hr 30min).

Salamá to: Cubulco (hourly; 1hr 30min); Guatemala City (hourly; 3hr); Rabinal (hourly; 1hr).

San Pedro Carchá to: Cobán (every 15min; 20min); Fray Bartolomé de las Casas (3–4 daily; 6hr); Raxrujá via Sebol (2 daily; 7 hr); Uspantán via Cobán (2 daily; 5hr).

Rabinal to: Cubulco (hourly; 1hr 30min); Guatemala City via El Chol (1 daily; 8 hr);

Guatemala City via La Cumbre (hourly; 4hr); Salamá (hourly; 1hr).

Sayaxché to: Cruce de Pato (2 daily; 2hr); Flores (7 daily; 2hr).

Tikal to: Flores (1 daily; 2hr), plus numerous minibuses (1hr); Uaxactún (1 daily; 3hr).

Pickups

Cobán to: Playa Grande via Laguna Lechuá (early morning most days; around 8hr); Chisec (most days; 5hr).

Raxrujá to: Cruce del Pato: first pickup to village of Canleche (1hr), second pickup to Cruce del Pato (20min).

Boats

El Naranjo to: La Palma Mexico (daily; 1pm).

Sayaxché to: Benemérito, Mexico: a trading boat leaves most days (at least 12hr, could be much longer); rented speedboats take 2hr 30min–3hr.

Flores/San Benito to: San Andrés: boats (25min) leave when full, in daylight hours only.

Puerto Barrios to: Lívingston: ferry twice daily at 10.30am and 5pm (1hr 30min; US$1.50), plus speedboats (approx hourly; 45min); Punta Gorda, Belize daily at 1pm (1hr 30min).

Lívingston to: Río Dulce (daily; around 3hr); Puerto Barrios (5am and 2pm; 1hr 30min); Punta Gorda, Belize (Tues and Fri, minimum 4 people; 8am; 1hr); Omoa, Honduras (Tues and Fri, 7.30am, minimum 6 people; 2hr 30min).

Mariscos to: El Estor (daily at noon; 1hr), plus speedboats.

Río Dulce to: Guatemala City (Fri, Sat, Sun; 1hr 20min).

Sayaxché to: Rancho el Caribe on the Río Petexbatún: there should be a daily boat (2hr).

Planes

Cobán to: Guatemala City (daily; 30min); Playa Grande (irregular flights).

Flores to: Guatemala City (daily; 50min); Belize City (daily; 30min); Cancún (5 a week); Palenque (3 a week); Chetumal (3 a week).

Puerto Barrios to: Guatemala City (daily; 1hr).

You can also charter flights to Uaxactún, Dos Lagunas, El Naranjo, Sayaxché, Poptún, Río Dulce, Lívingston and to the Honduras border.

PART FIVE

HONDURAS & EL SALVADOR

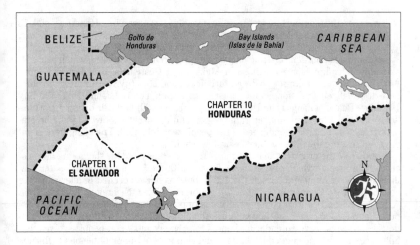

BELIZE

Golfo de Honduras

Bay Islands (Islas de la Bahía)

CARIBBEAN SEA

GUATEMALA

CHAPTER 10
HONDURAS

CHAPTER 11
EL SALVADOR

PACIFIC OCEAN

NICARAGUA

N

HONDURAS & EL SALVADOR

Lying at the southernmost fringe of the old Maya empire, Honduras and El Salvador seem, at first glance, to have little to recommend them to visitors. Covered in this book are just the Maya parts of these two countries, near the Guatemalan border. Boasting only a handful of archeological sites, which pale considerably in comparison with those in Mexico and Guatemala, this part of Central America is better known for civil war, turbulence and abject poverty. Foreign visitors here are relatively few, stopping off only to visit **Copán**, before heading on to the **Bay Islands** – Roatán, Guanaja and Utila – a string of cayes with fantastic diving opportunities. Yet those who spend longer in the region find themselves swayed by the breathtaking scenery and the friendliness of the people who inhabit it. Travelling here is not easy, but making the effort to do so is well worth it.

Honduras, the original Banana Republic, is more renowned for staggering levels of corruption than anything else. A close alliance with the US prevented the bitter conflicts that beset its neighbours in the 1980s, but has not succeeded in alleviating the country's acute economic and **social problems**. After Nicaragua, this is Latin America's second poorest nation, with levels of poverty that can be disturbing to witness. Yet the open generosity and genuine friendliness displayed by those who have little else are what leave an enduring impression. The country and people are wonderfully diverse, with the rugged landscapes and character of the mountainous highlands contrasting strongly with the vivid scenery and laid-back atmosphere of the Caribbean north coast and islands.

To the south of Honduras, tucked along the Pacific edge of the isthmus, lies **El Salvador**, the smallest country in Central America, which is chiefly remembered for its devastating **civil war** in the 1980s. Throughout the lost decade, atrocity followed atrocity in a seemingly unstoppable escalation. Then in 1992, with both sides having fought each other to a standstill, peace accords were signed, and the attention of the world's press moved elsewhere, while El Salvador was faced with the complex task of rebuilding itself. Today, few tourists visit the country, deterred by an ever-present reputation for violence and danger. Those that do, however, are often overwhelmed by the sheer beauty of the country, stretching from lush, tropical Pacific lowlands to sweeping rugged mountain chains, dotted with the omnipresent cones of extinct volcanoes. The people of El Salvador are some of the most engaging and interesting in the region. With a well-deserved reputation for hard work and business acumen, they live life with a vigour that would be hard to match, and confront the dangers of a still uncertain future head on.

A brief history of Honduras

Before the arrival of the Spanish, Honduras was populated by a number of different tribes, of whom the Maya are the best documented. Archeologists believe that **Maya settlers** began moving south into the Río Copán valley from around 1000 BC. Construction of the city of **Copán** began around 100 AD and by the time of the founding of the royal dynasty in 426 AD, Copán exerted control as far north as the Valle de Sula, east to Lago Yojoa and west into what is now Guatemala. Home to the governing and religious elite, and supporting a total population of around 24,000, the city was the pre-eminent Maya centre for scientific and artistic development. When, for reasons which are not entirely clear, Maya civilization began to collapse around 900 AD, Copán was abandoned, although the area it previously controlled remained inhabited.

Columbus landed on the island of Guanaja on July 30, 1502, during his fourth and final voyage, before exploring the Central American coastline visible on the horizon. Sailing east along the coast, the fleet first stopped at Punta Caxinas, close to present-day Trujillo, where the first Catholic Mass in Latin America was held on August 14, 1502. A further twenty years elapsed before the conquistadors returned to take possession of the new territory, with the first **Spanish settlement**, Triunfo de la Cruz on the Bahía de Tela, founded in 1524 by Cristóbal de Olid.

With Honduras under control, the Spanish began to focus their attention on the interior of the country, largely because of the inhospitable climate of the coastal settlements and their vulnerability to pirate attacks. The discovery of **gold** in the Valle de Comayagua in 1539, and **silver** around Tegucigalpa over the following forty years, seemed to promise untold riches. For the indigenous inhabitants, the consolidation of Spanish power was catastrophic. Contemporary population records are notoriously inaccurate, but from an estimated 400,000 in 1524, the population had probably fallen as low as 15,000 by 1571. Those who survived the diseases of the Old World were enslaved and either shipped overseas or sent to the mines. Social structures collapsed and communities were forcibly dispersed, with the most affected peoples being the highland tribes, since they had most contact with the colonists. Incredibly, considering their impact, the number of colonists numbered fewer than 300 throughout the seventeenth century.

For the Spanish, the steep **decline in population** was, above all, a severe hindrance to economic development. Though, at their peak, the mines provided a comfortable living for their owners, from the seventeenth century onwards the labour shortage made working deeper seams impracticable, and profits dropped sharply as a result. By the early nineteenth century, Honduras was an **economy in crisis**: mining was virtually defunct and a series of severe droughts hit both agriculture and livestock. Society was sharply divided, with a narrow layer of the relatively wealthy – state functionaries, merchants, a handful of mine- and hacienda-owners – above the poor mass of Mestizo and indigenous peoples. There was no middle class, nor any kind of unifying national infrastructure and by the time of independence in 1821, Honduras still had no national printing press, newspapers or university.

News of **independence** reached Honduras on September 28, 1821, and the provinces of Central America declared themselves an independent republic on July 1, 1823, only to plunge almost immediately into civil war. The Honduran Francisco Morazán, elected president of the republic in 1830, was unable to persuade even his own countrymen of the potential of a united republic. Faced repeatedly with uprisings he was unable to crush, Morazán resigned in 1839, when Honduras and Nicaragua went to war against El Salvador. The Central American Republic was finished, and the five independent republics, among them the **Republic of Honduras**, came into existence.

The newly independent country stumbled through successive political and economic crises, much of it occasioned by rivalry between Liberal and Conservative political forces. Not until 1876 did the country begin to assume the aspects of a modern state, under the premiership of **Dr Marco Aurelio Soto**, a Liberal, and his successor Luis Bográn. These two men reformed the judiciary, Church and armed forces and put into place unified communications and education infrastructures. Believing that foreign capital was the key to economic development, **foreign investment** by US, British and European companies was encouraged. This developed industries, but crucially allowed most of the country's resources to be controlled by foreign concerns. In the banana industry, for example, three companies – United Fruit, Vacarro Bros (later Standard Fruit) and the Cuyamel Fruit Company (bought out by United Fruit in 1929) – soon

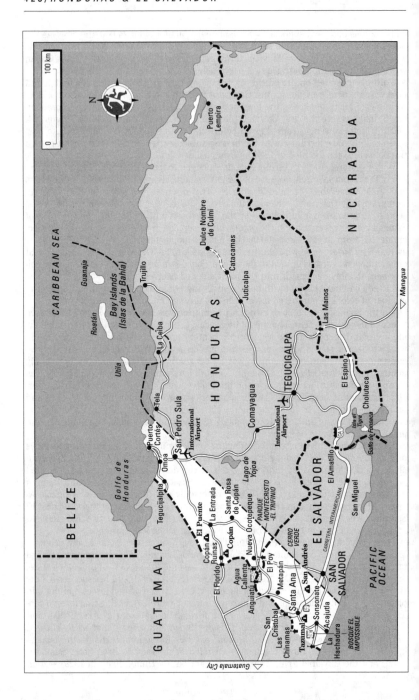

became dominant, all but wiping out small-scale producers. Government concessions allowed the companies to steadily increase their holdings, which, by 1924, amounted to half a million acres of land on the north coast and control of seventy percent of Honduras's total exports, with subsequent expansion into and control of railways, energy and banking sectors and substantial political influence. A succession of weak and shortlived governments struggled to keep control in the face of the dominant interests of the fruit companies and, behind them, the US, along the virtually autonomous north coast.

Over the next thirty years, the foundations of the modern state were laid and a new national cohesion was formed, with a central bank, a public service and increased export. A **coup** in October 1956 introduced the **military** as a new element into the hierarchy of power, with the 1957 constitution giving the armed forces the right to disregard governmental action they regarded as unconstitutional. In October 1963, a second coup installed Colonel Oswaldo López Arellano as provisional president, and during his first period of office one of the more bizarre conflicts of modern Central America occurred, the so-called **"Football War"**. The conflict stemmed from tensions generated by a steady rise in illegal migration of campesinos from El Salvador into Honduras in search of land. The two countries began a series of qualifying matches for the 1970 World Cup, and at the second match, won 3–0 by El Salvador, spectators booed the Honduran national anthem and attacked visiting Honduran fans. On July 14, 1969, the Salvadorean army bombed targets within Honduras and advanced into Honduran territory. After three-days, around two thousand deaths and a complete rupture of diplomatic relations, the Organization of American States (OAS) negotiated a ceasefire and established a three kilometre-wide demilitarized zone along the border. Only in 1992 did both sides accept an International Court of Justice ruling demarcating the border in its current location.

Another coup restored Lopéz to power in December 1972. His attempted new industrialization programme was – given the by now endemic **corruption** at senior levels of government, in the military and in business – a recipe for disaster; millions of dollars of national and international loans and aid money were siphoned off to private bank accounts. Forced from office through the **"Bananagate"**, López was succeeded in April 1975 by Colonel Juan Melgar Castro. During his tenure and that (1978–81) of his successor General Policarpo Paz García, agrarian reform slowed to a trickle, repression of civil rights and freedom of speech increased, and corruption among military and government personnel grew to almost laughable levels.

Following the **Sandinista revolution** in Nicaragua in July 1979, Honduras found itself at the centre of US geo-political strategy – the "fourth border of the US". Honduras became the focus for the US-backed Contra war in Nicaragua, accepting in return over US$1.5bn of direct economic and military aid during the 1980s. Domestically, the relationship between the military and government grew ever closer. **Human rights** violations rose alarmingly, with the army implicated in at least 184 "disappearances" of activists from labour organizations and peace movements. In 1984, army officers, increasingly anxious over Alvarez's actions, forced him into exile. Honduras's role in US affairs diminished after Reagan left office and both the Contra war and the civil war in El Salvador were resolved, focusing attention on the country's worsening economic and social problems. Under **Rafael Leonardo Callejas** (in office 1989-93), neo-Liberal austerity measures were introduced, leading to a sharp rise in poverty levels, and although jurisdiction over legal and government affairs was slowly wrestled back from the military, human rights abuses were still common. In 1993, the widely respected Liberal candidate, businessman turned politician **Carlos Roberto Reina**, was elected president, on a platform of engineering moral renewal through tackling governmental and business corruption. Though acting successfully on the most overt cases, he was not able to prevent the economy sliding further into recession, or to halt a steadily worsening spiral of social instability, affecting the north coast in particular.

Carlos Flores Facussé took office in November 1997. Continuing with the free-market economics of his predecessor, he also promised a **programme of national conciliation**, with investment to reverse the cycle of deepening poverty and social despair. The potential for growth remains uncertain, however. As throughout Honduras's history, economic development is still tied to foreign investment. The economic and political power of the fruit companies has to a certain extent diminished – only to be supplanted by the growing influence of Far East *maquiladora* plants and the tourist industry.

A brief history of El Salvador

The first settled peoples of El Salvador were **the Maya**, who had arrived in the territory by at least 1200 BC, and from 500 BC had developed several large settlements in the west and centre of the country. During the early Classic period (300–900 AD), important cities developed and thrived at San Andrés, Tazumal, Cara Sucia and Quelepa, though these cities were abandoned around 900 AD, when the Maya empire began to crumble. During the early Postclassic period (900–1200 AD), a succession of Nahuatl-speaking groups, known as Pipils, began to migrate south from Mexico. Final waves of Nahuatl speakers arrived in the thirteenth and fourteenth centuries.

After an exploratory visit by Andrés Niño in May 1522, **the Spanish** arrived in force in El Salvador in June 1524. Pedro de Alvarado, commanding a force of around 250 Spanish and 5000 indigenous soldiers, entered what is now the department of Ahuachapán from Guatemala. Initial progress was slow – it is thought that the Pipil forces were up to twice as large as those of the Spanish – and domination of western El Salvador was secured only in April 1528. Only in 1538 was the Spanish hold upon the whole of the territory secure.

During the colonial rule, the conquistadors established the *encomienda* system and developed **haciendas** for those Spaniards wishing to take advantage of the abundant agricultural resources. Basalm and cocoa became increasingly important export crops, with an huge demand from Europe. However, from the early eighteenth century, there was growing demand for *añil* (indigo), and landowners rejected cocoa in favour of producing this superior dye. By the mid-eighteenth century, indigo had become the primary export crop, with the main beneficiaries being the hacienda owners and *comerciantes* – the middle men handling the sale and shipping. El Salvador became a rigidly stratified society, whose European elite consisted of the small number of Spanish-born Crown functionaries and priests and a few hundred Creole (Latin American-born) hacienda owners and *comerciantes*; of available agricultural land, around half was held in private haciendas. The vast majority of the population, Mestizo and indigenous, existed at subsistence level, cultivating maize.

Following independence in 1841 El Salvador was in an almost perpetual state of turmoil as rival Liberals and Conservatives battled for power. Not until the presidency of Rafael Zaldívar did the country achieve any measure of stability. Economically, the production of coffee became the driving force from 1860 onwards, fuelled by the collapse in demand for indigo and the growing popularity of coffee on the tables of Europe and North America. This **coffee boom** created the conditions for the development of a "coffee elite" and land became concentrated into fewer and fewer hands – a tiny but powerful oligarchy, with three quarters of all land eventually held by less than two percent of the population. The oligarchy monopolized coffee production and trade, extending its interests into other agricultural sectors, industry and finance. Over the next decades, until a military coup in 1898, private interests were the motivating force behind all changes in government, but in the first decades of the twentieth century, the coffee boom also brought relative economic stability and consolidation of the state. Transport links, including railways, and a communications system were put into place, education expanded and a functioning civil judicial system established. At the same time, it was a period of deepening social polarization. The elite dominated business and the state machine, while the vast majority lived in the most basic of conditions. Despite regular elections, democracy was a concept in name only, with the bulk of the population excluded from both the political process and the profits from coffee. Growing civil violence was dealt with by increasing repression from the government.

Plans for democratic development set in place by President Bosque at his election in 1927, were brought to an abrupt end by the **Wall Street Crash** in 1929, which decimated the market in coffee, the crop that generated 95 percent of El Salvador's total exports. Worst affected by the collapse were the landless poor, whose living conditions deteriorated appallingly. **Social unrest** was exacerbated by growing repression, and on the night of January 22, 1932, thousands of campesinos rebelled. Armed mainly with machetes, they attacked military installations and haciendas in the west of the country, assassinating hundreds of civilians including government functionaries. Mainly because plans to rebel had been publicly widely known in the days before the event, government forces rapidly quashed the rebellion and the ringleaders were arrested and later executed.

The scale of government action in the wake of the failed rebellion was unprecedented in the history of the country. The army, the police, the *guardia nacional* and the private forces of the hacienda owners engaged in a week-long orgy of killing. During "**La Matanza**" (the massacre), as it became known, anyone suspected of connections to the rebellion, anyone wearing indigenous dress or anyone simply perceived to be guilty was shot. In some cases, whole villages disappeared. The death toll was estimated at up to 30,000 people, although the government itself insisted that only two thousand were killed. For El Salvador's indigenous population, the effects of the massacre went far beyond the immediate death toll: it became suspect to be identified as *indio* (Indian) and, as a result, traditional dress, language and customs largely disappeared.

The rebellion and its bloody aftermath ushered in a era of **military rule** as the oligarchy, desperate to defend its interests, handed political power to the army while retaining economic control. For the next fifty years, the two groups worked together in a symbiotic relationship. Successive groups of military officers assumed power, usually removed from office by coup and counter-coup while the economic business of state was handled by the oligarchy, who relied on the army to protect its interests.

After World War II, the economy diversified into production of sugar, cotton and beef for export. Profits and benefits deriving from this expansion remained firmly in the hands of the oligarchy, while the vast majority of the population had no access to land. The census of 1971 recorded that 64 percent of agricultural land was held by four percent of landowners. A downturn in external markets in the 1970s again led to a steep deterioration, followed by growing, militant pressure for change. The elections of 1972, won by the Christian Democratic Party (PDC) advocating a peaceful road to reform, should have heralded this change. The army, however, installed its own candidate, Colonel Arturo Molina, exiled Duarte and other opposition leaders, and cracked down on trade union and reform activists.

Throughout the 1970s repression continued. In 1977, news programmes around the world showed footage of the army firing upon unarmed civilians during a protest in front of the cathedral in central San Salvador; up to three hundred died. In 1980, Archbishop Oscar Romero was assassinated on the orders of a serving army officer, Roberto D'Aubuisson. Though preliminary reforms were implemented and agreement secured for a transfer of power from military to civilian hands, these were insufficient to halt a deepening cycle of extra-judicial violence. Many were convinced that change could only come through violence. At both ends of the spectrum far-right paramilitary death squads and left-wing guerrilla groups began to mobilize.

In October 1980, the formal integration of all the left-wing guerrilla organizations led to the foundation of the Frente Faribundo Martí de Liberación Nacional (**FMLN**). Three months later, in January 1981, the FMLN launched its first general offensive, gaining territory in the eastern and northern departments of the country and forcing the government into defensive action. The newly-installed US Reagan administration began to pump aid to the government, to expand and to equip fighting forces. Despite this, however, the army remained hampered by insufficient organization, leadership and endemic corruption, unable to confront the guerrillas' ambush tactics and targeted attacks. During the course of the war, 80,000 people were killed and more than 500,000 fled the country as refugees. Against a background of continuing fighting, the promised transfer of power from military to civilian hands was completed, with parliamentary elections in 1982 and a new constitution introduced in 1983. The FMLN, however, remained outside the political process and sporadic attempts at peace talks foundered upon the seemingly irresolvable demands for fundamental changes in the role and structure of the army.

Widely perceived as incompetent and corrupt, Duarte was succeeded in 1989 by Alfredo Cristiani, candidate of the right-wing ARENA party founded by Roberto D'Aubuisson. The FMLN renewed offensives against the government, most spectacularly during its "last offensive" of November 1989 when areas of major cities, including San Salvador, were occupied. In turn, the death squads and the military, intensified their activities. Suspected FMLN sympathizers, trade unionists and Church activists were intimidated and assassinated.

In April 1990, representatives of both the FMLN and the government, under the chairmanship of the UN, met and talked in Geneva in the first of a series of negotiations that would lead to peace. **The Chapultepec Accords**, signed on January 16, 1992, were followed on February 1 by a formal ceasefire. The FMLN agreed to the demobilization of its forces, the government to a purge of the armed forces and reduction in their size. A land transfer programme, expected to transfer ten percent of agricultural land to demobilized combatants and refugees, was inaugurated, and a tripartite commission, including the government, workers and private sector, was set up to formulate further social and economic policies. On December 15, 1992, the day the FMLN registered as an official political party, the civil war was formally ended.

The elections held in March 1994 resulted in Armando Calderón Sol of the ARENA party assuming the presidency. However, **dissatisfaction** has increased, primarily because of the government's perceived failure to comply with the Chapultepec Accords and disquiet over alleged corruption. Members of the armed forces alleged to have participated in human rights abuses have more often been offered amnesty or early retirement rather than prosecution, while the land transfer programme remains incomplete. Although there exists a genuine desire for reconciliation and reconstruction, the majority of Salvadoreans continue to fight daily against the deeply ingrained divisions that sparked the original conflict.

CHAPTER TEN

HONDURAS

N orthwestern Honduras offers some of the country's most spectacular tourist attractions, including Copán, one of the finest sites of the Maya world, and the glorious white beaches of the Bay Islands, the country's most visited destination. Added to these, the inspiring, untouched natural beauty of the country and the open generosity and friendliness of the people make this a fascinating and enjoyable region to visit.

Copán is the site that most people head for first, just a short distance from the Guatemalan border. It may not be as impressive as Tikal or Chichén Itzá in terms of architecture, but the carvings and stelae here are outstanding. Further north, **San Pedro Sula**, Honduras's second city, is a useful transport hub and an excellent base for exploring one of the country's finest cloudforest reserves, the **Parque Nacional el Cusuco**. While ecotourism is a relatively new concept here, more and more Hondurans are becoming aware of the role the country's extensive network of **national parks** and reserves plays in protecting irreplaceable natural resources. The remoter parts of the parks host an astonishing array of flora and fauna, amid some of the finest stretches of virgin **cloud-** and **tropical forest** in Central America.

The lively coastal town of **La Ceiba** is a convenient stop-off en route to the Bay Islands; if you've time to stay a while, there are also some good beaches just outside the town and one of the most accessible cloudforest reserves in the country, **Pico Bonito**. Less than 60km from the north coast are the **Bay Islands** – Roatán, Guanaja and Utila – whose palm-fringed beaches and clear, Caribbean waters make for the ultimate in beach holidays and provide world-class snorkelling and diving.

Into Honduras from Guatemala

The border post of **El Florido** in Guatemala is 50km from Chiquimula, a slow and rough journey through the Sierra de Espíritu Santo, on a not particularly good road. Eight second-class buses (6am–4.30pm; at least 2hr 30min) make the journey daily. The crossing here is straightforward, with backpackers en route to and from the ruins forming most of the traffic. Border guards will charge you around $1 to leave Guatemala and US$2.50 to enter Honduras. If you are entering Honduras only to visit Copán and intend to re-enter Guatemala almost immediately, ask the Honduran guards for a temporary entrance stamp. This is given to you on a separate piece of paper, thus keeping your

---

ACCOMMODATION PRICE CODES

All the accommodation listed in this book has been categorized into one of nine price bands, as set out below. The prices quoted are in US dollars and refer to the cheapest room available for two people sharing in high season.

① under US$5	④ US$15–25	⑦ US$60–80
② US$5–10	⑤ US$25–40	⑧ US$80–100
③ US$10–15	⑥ US$40–60	⑨ over US$100

Guatemalan visa valid. There is no bank at the post, but the ever-present moneychangers handle dollars, lempiras and quetzales, though not at particularly good rates. From El Florido, **buses** run every thirty minutes to the town of Copán Ruinas, taking around half an hour; the last leaves at 4pm. Coming the other way, the last bus leaves town at 3pm, though it's sensible to cross as early in the day as possible to ensure onward connections in Guatemala.

Copán and around

Twelve kilometres east of the Guatemalan border crossing of El Florido, in the serene,

rolling landscape of Honduras's western highlands, lies the ancient site of **Copán**. One of the most impressive of all the Maya sites, its pre-eminence derives not from size – in scale it's far less imposing than Tikal or Chichén Itzá – but from the overwhelming legacy of artistic craftsmanship that has survived here over hundreds of years. Not surprisingly, the site is heavily promoted by the Honduran government and tour operators, and now ranks as the second most visited spot in the country after the Bay Islands.

Copán emblem glyph

Copán Ruinas: the town

The archeological site of Copán lies one kilometre south of the small town of **COPÁN RUINAS**, generally simply referred to as Copán, a charming place of steep cobbled streets and red-tiled roofs, set among green hills. Despite the weekly influx of hundreds of visitors, which now contributes a large part of the town's income, it has managed to remain largely unspoilt and genuinely friendly.

A thirty-minute stroll around Copán, taking in the clean air and relaxed atmosphere, encompasses virtually all the town's attractions. Somewhat eclipsed by the new sculpture museum at the site itself, though still worth a visit, is the **Museo Regional de Arqueología** (Mon–Sat 8am–noon & 1–4pm; US$1.50) on the west side of the parque central. Displayed inside are statuettes, sculptures and other Maya artefacts. The small municipal **market** is in the block behind the museum; turn right beyond Hondutel. For

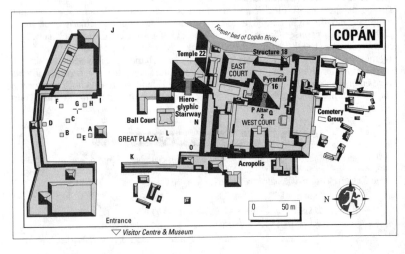

COPÁN

Fomer bed of Copán River

Temple 22
Structure 18
EAST COURT
Pyramid 16
Hiero-glyphic Stairway
Ball Court
P Altar Q
WEST COURT
Cemetery Group
GREAT PLAZA
Acropolis
Entrance
▽ Visitor Centre & Museum
0   50 m
N

a view over the town and surrounding countryside, walk north from the parque central for about five blocks, to the old military barracks up the hill.

Catering to the growing tourist trade are a number of **souvenir shops** on or close to the parque central, selling ceramic, wood and leather crafts from the region and elsewhere in the country; all are broadly similar in terms of price and range. Tabacos y Recuerdos, next to the *La Posada* hotel, has a wide selection of Honduran cigars.

Arrival and information

Buses from El Florido enter town from the west, running up to circle the parque central. Buses from other destinations in Honduras enter town from the east, by the small football field. Banco Atlántida on the parque changes dollars, travellers' cheques and Guatemalan quetzales, and advances cash on Visa cards. **Hondutel** and the **post office** are next door to each other, just off the southwest corner of the parque. A block further southwest is Justo a Tiempo Lavandería (Mon–Sat 7.30am–5.30pm), a laundry that also offers an English and German book exchange.

Two blocks west of the parque, next door to the Spanish school, Go Native Tours arranges day-trips in the area, plus excursions further afield.

Accommodation

Many of the town's **hotels** have recently undergone refits to compete for the ever-booming organized tour market. Prices, consequently, are higher than in much of Honduras, though there's still enough of a range to suit most budgets.

Casa de Café B&B, at the southwest edge of town, overlooking the Río Copán Valley (☎552 7274). A charming place, with a fabulous garden where you could lie in a hammock and enjoy the views all day. Comfortable, airy rooms all have bath and hot water. Breakfast is included and there's free coffee all day, plus a library and TV. ⑤.

Hotel Brisas de Copán, one block north of the parque central (☎651 4118). Clean, good-sized rooms, all with bath, hot water and TV. ④.

Hotel California, one block northeast of the square (no phone). A new, laid-back place with clean rooms around a courtyard. Free drinking water. ②.

Hotel Camino Maya, southwest corner of parque central (☎651 4446, fax 651 4518). Newly renovated, adequately sized rooms, all with bath and hot water. Some have a balcony overlooking the parque. ⑥.

Hotel Los Gemelos, across from the *California* (☎651 4077). The backpackers' favourite, still going strong. Very friendly place, with basic but spotless rooms, all with shared bath. The owners provide hot water if enough people ask. ①.

Hotel Marina Copán, east side of the parque central (☎651 4070, fax 651 4477). The most luxurious place in town by a long shot. Stylish rooms have a/c and TV, and there's a small pool, sauna, gym and bar on site. ⑧–⑨.

Iguana Azul, next to the *Casa de Café* and under the same ownership. Private rooms and a newly refurbished and decorated dormitory, all with shared bath. Communal area and laundry facilities. Dorms ①, doubles ②–③.

La Posada, just north of the parque central (no phone). Recently renovated large, comfortable rooms, some with bath. Good value. ②–③.

Eating and drinking

Copán has a wide range of places to **eat** and **drink**, some of them catering specifically to the tourist market. Virtually all restaurants stop serving at 10pm.

Café Elisa, in the *Hotel Camino Maya*. Excellent local and European-style breakfasts, including fruit salads and waffles.

Café Isabel, one block west of the parque. Unpretentious place serving a range of well-prepared local dishes; the vegetable soup is particularly good.

Café Welchez, northwest corner of the parque. Pleasant European-style café, serving fairly pricey coffees, juices, alcoholic drinks and light meals. The tables upstairs by the window are a good spot for people-watching.

Llama del Bosque, two blocks west of the parque. Wide menu including local breakfasts, meat and chicken dishes, baleadas and snacks.

Tres Locos Bar, at the *Hotel California*. A fun bar and a good place to catch up on local news and information. Closes at 9pm.

Tunkul Bar and Restaurant, across from the *Llama del Bosque*. Popular, foreign-owned restaurant, serving large portions of meat, pasta and vegetarian dishes for reasonable prices. The bar stays open until midnight.

Vamos a Ver Café, one block south of the parque. Delicious European-style soups, sandwiches, cheeses and snacks. The courtyard eating area is always busy. English-language videos shown every night.

A brief history of Copán

Once the most important **city-state** on the southern fringes of the Maya empire, Copán was largely cut off from all other cities except **Quiriguá**, 64km to the north in Guatemala (see p.378). Archeologists now believe that settlers began moving into the Río Copán valley from around 1000 BC, although construction of the city is not thought to have begun until around 100 AD.

By the sixth century, Copán had emerged as a powerful centre, although information on its early history and rulers is sparse. A stela discovered in the Papagayo temple in 1988 refers to **Yak K'uk Mo'**, the first ruler and founder of the dynasty, who governed from at least 426 AD to 435 AD; the stela itself was erected by the third ruler, **Mat Head**. Little is known about the six subsequent rulers, although both the third and fourth are mentioned on Monument 26 at Quiriguá.

The **golden era** of Copán began with the accession to the throne of **Moon Jaguar**, the tenth ruler, in 553 AD, and continued through the reigns of **Smoke Serpent** (578–628 AD), **Smoke Jaguar** (628–695 AD) and **Eighteen Rabbit** (695–738 AD). This period of stable, long-lasting governments allowed for unprecedented political, social and artistic growth. The carved relief style for which Copán is famous developed during the reign of Eighteen Rabbit, who also oversaw the construction of the Great Plaza, the final version of the ball court and Temple 22 in the East Court.

Following Eighteen Rabbit's capture and decapitation by Cauac Sky, ruler of an ascendant and increasingly threatening Quiriguá, Copán entered a long decline, halted briefly during the rule of **Smoke Shell**, the fifteenth ruler (749–763 AD), who was responsible for the construction of the **Hieroglyphic Stairway**, one of the most impressive pieces of Maya architecture. Smoke Shell's son, **Yax Pac** (763–820 AD), constructed **Altar Q**, which illustrates the dynasty from its beginning. During his rule, however, the city continued to decline: skeletal remains indicate that the main pressure came from inadequate food resources. The seventeenth and final ruler, **U Cit Tok'**, took the throne in 822 AD – two years after Yax Pac is thought to have died – but the date and reason for the ending of his reign are unknown.

The site was known to the Spanish, although they took little interest in it. A court official, Don Diego de Palacios, in a letter written in March 1576, mentions the ruins of a magnificent city "constructed with such skill that it seems that they could never have been made by people as coarse as the inhabitants of this province". Not until the nineteenth century and the publication of *Incidents of Travel in Central America, Chiapas and Yucatán* by **John Lloyd Stephens** and **Frederick Catherwood** did Copán become known to the wider world. Stephens, the then acting US ambassador, had succeeded in buying the ruins in 1839 and, accompanied by Catherwood, a British architect and artist, spent several weeks clearing the site and mapping the buildings. The instant success of the book on publication and the interest it sparked in Mesoamerican culture ensured that Copán became a magnet for **archeologists**.

British archeologist **Alfred Maudsley** began a full-scale mapping, excavation and reconstruction project in 1891 under the sponsorship of the Peabody Museum,

Harvard. A second major investigation was begun in 1935 by the Washington Carnegie Institute, which involved diverting the Río Copán to prevent it carving into the site. A breakthrough in understanding, not only of Copán but the whole Maya World, came in 1959 and 1960, when archeologists Heinrich Berlin and Tatiana Proskouriakoff first began to decipher **hieroglyphs**, leading to the realization that they record the history of the cities and the dynasties. Since 1977, the Instituto Hondureño de Antropología e Historia has been running a series of projects, with the help of archeologists from around the world.

The site

The ruins lie 1km north of town, a fifteen-minute walk along a raised footpath. Entrance to the site is through the **visitor centre** (daily 8am–4pm; US$10), on the left-hand side of the car park, where a small exhibition explains Copán's place in the Maya empire; 200m beyond the centre is the warden's gate, the entrance to the site proper. On the right-hand side of the car park is the **Museum of Mayan Sculpture** (daily 8am–4pm; US$10), which is dominated by a full-scale, brightly painted replica of the **Rosalila Temple**, built in 591 and discovered intact under Structure 16 only in 1989. There is a ground floor exhibition on aspects of Maya beliefs and cosmology, while the upper floor houses many of the finest original sculptures from the site, comprehensively displaying the ability and skill of the Maya craftsmen. Opinions vary on whether the museum should be visited before or after the site itself: visiting it first enables you to witness how the original carvings have withstood the test of time.

The east and west courts

Turn right after passing through the warden's gate and a short walk takes you into the **West Court**, a confined area that forms part of the main acropolis. **Altar Q**, at the base of Pyramid 16, is the most famous feature here. Carved in 776 AD, it is thought to celebrate **Yax Pac**'s accession to the throne on July 2, 763. The top of the altar is carved with six hieroglyphic blocks, while the sides are decorated with sixteen cross-legged figures, all seated on cushions, who are believed to represent previous rulers of Copán. All are pointing towards a portrait of Yax Pac which shows him receiving a ceremonial staff from the city's first ruler, Mah K'ina Yax K'uk Mo, thereby endorsing Yax Pac's right to rule. Behind the altar is a small crypt, discovered to contain the remains of a macaw and fifteen big cats, possibly sacrificed in honour of Yax Pac.

Pyramid 16, behind Altar Q, was found to contain the intact facade of the Rosalila Temple, apparently purposely buried within it. The temple served as a centre for worship during the reign of Smoke Serpent, or Butz'Chan, Copán's eleventh ruler (578–628 AD), a period that marked the apogee of political, social and artistic growth. Generally, it was Maya custom to ritually deface or destroy obsolete temples or stelae, so the discovery of the Rosalila has been one of the most exciting finds of recent years. Once scientific studies are completed, the temple will be re-sealed against the outside world.

Climbing the stairs behind Altar Q brings you into the **East Court**, which is slightly larger than the West and bears more elaborate carvings. The best of these are life-sized jaguar heads, with hollow eyes which would have once held pieces of jade or polished obsidian. In the middle of the staircase, flanked by the jaguars, is a rectangular Venus mask, carved in superb deep relief. At the southern end of this court is **Structure 18**, a small square building with carved panels. The floor of this structure has been dug up to reveal a magnificent tomb, possibly that of Yax Pac. The tomb was empty when excavated by archeologists and is thought to have been looted on a number of occasions. South of Structure 18, the **Cemetery Group** was once thought to have been a burial site, although current thinking is that it was a residential complex, possibly home to the ruling elite. To date, however, little work has been done on this part of the site.

To the north, separating the East Court from the Great Plaza, is one of Copán's most impressive buildings, **Temple 22**. Some of the stonework is astonishingly simple, while other sections – particularly around the door frames – are superbly intricate and decorated with outlandish carving. Above the door is the body of a double-headed snake, its heads resting on two figures, which in turn are supported by skulls. The corners of the temple bear portraits of the long-nosed rain god **Chac**, a favourite Maya deity. The quality of the carving on this temple has led archeologists to suggest that the East Court may have been Copán's most important plaza. The decoration here is unique in the southern Maya region, with only the Yucatán sites such as Kabáh and Chicanna having carvings of comparable quality.

The Great Plaza

Beyond Temple 22 lies the **Great Plaza**, strewn with the magnificently carved and exceptionally well-preserved stelae that are Copán's outstanding features. The style of carving is similar to that of Quiriguá, and at both sites the portraits of assorted rulers dominate the decoration, with surrounding glyphs giving details of events during their rule.

Pressed up against the Central Acropolis, at the southern end of the plaza, is the **Hieroglyphic Court**, on the left-hand side of which is the famed **Hieroglyphic Stairway**, perhaps the most astonishing work of all at Copán. Made up of some 63 stone steps, every block is carved to form part of the glyphic sequence – a total of between 1500 and 2200 glyphs. It forms the longest known Maya hieroglyphic text, but, unfortunately, attempted reconstruction by early archeologists left the sequence so jumbled that a complete interpretation is still some way off. The easiest part to understand is the dates, and these range from 544 AD to 744 AD. At the base of the stairway **Stela M** records a solar eclipse in 756 AD.

The **Ball Court**, one of the few Maya courts still to have a paved floor, lies just north of the stairway. Originally the entire plaza would have been paved like this and probably painted as well. The court dates from 775 AD, and beneath it are two previous versions. The rooms that line the sides of the court, overlooking the playing area, were probably used by priests and members of the elite as they observed the ritual of the game.

Facing the ball court is the **Temple of the Inscriptions**, a towering stairway, and at its base is **Stela N**, another classic piece of Copán carving with portraits on the two main faces and glyphs down the sides. The depth of the relief has protected the nooks and crannies, and in some of these you can still see flakes of paint; originally the carvings and buildings would have been painted in a whole range of bright colours, but for some reason only the red has survived.

Dotted all around the Great Plaza are Copán's famed **stelae**, made from andesite, a fine-grained, even-textured volcanic rock, particularly suited to retention of intricate detail in carvings. Most of the stelae represent **Eighteen Rabbit**, Copán's "King of the Arts" (Stelae A, B, C, D, F, H and 4). **Stela A**, dating from 731 AD, has incredibly deep carving, although much is now eroded. Its sides include a total of 52 glyphs, better preserved than the main faces. **Stela B** is one of the more controversial stones, with a figure that some see as oriental in appearance, supporting theories of mass migration from the east. **Stela C** (730 AD) is one of the earliest stones to have faces on both sides and, like many of the central stelae, it has an altar at its base, carved in the shape of a turtle. Two rulers are represented here: facing the turtle (a symbol of longevity) is Eighteen Rabbit's father, who lived well into his eighties, while on other side is Eighteen Rabbit himself.

Las Sepultras

Two kilometres northeast of Copán is the smaller site of **Las Sepultras** (daily 8am–4pm; entrance on the same ticket as for Copán), the focus of much archeological interest in recent years because of the information it provides on daily domestic life in Maya times. Eighteen of some forty residential compounds at the site have been excavated, yielding one hundred buildings that would have been inhabited by the elite. Smaller compounds on the edge of the site are thought to have housed young princes, as well as concubines and servants. It was customary to bury the nobility close to their residences, and around the compounds more than 250 tombs have been excavated, allowing insights into the Maya way of life. Given the number of women found in the tombs it seems likely that they practised polygamy. One of the most interesting finds – the tomb of a priest or shaman, dating from around 450 AD – is on display in the museum in Copán Ruinas.

Around Copán

There are a couple of places within easy reach of Copán that make an extra day or two's stay here worthwhile. Closest is the small Maya site of **Los Sapos**, a delightful walk south from town. Ten kilometres or so in the opposite direction, the picturesque waterfall of **El Rubí** is the perfect spot for a picnic. Copán is also a convenient spot to cross over into Guatemala, with the **El Florido** border crossing just 12km to the west.

Los Sapos, dating from the same era as Copán, is set in the hills to the south of town, less than an hour's gentle walk away. The site, whose name derives from a rock carved in the shape of a frog, is thought to have been the place where Maya women came to bear children; unfortunately, though, time and weather have eroded much of the carving. To get there, follow the main road south out of town, turn left onto a dirt track just past the river bridge and follow this as it begins to climb gently into the hills. The views across the tobacco fields of the river valley are beautiful, and there are plenty of spots for swimming along the way.

Pickups leave Copán regularly throughout the day for the peaceful town of **Santa Rita**, 9km north. At the river bridge, just before entering the town, a path leads up to **El Rubí**, a pretty double waterfall on the Río Copán, about 2km away. Surrounded by shady woods, this is the perfect spot for a swim in the clear, cold water, followed by a picnic. Follow the path as it climbs along and above the right-hand bank of the river for about twenty minutes; just past a steep stretch and small bend to the right, the narrow path running down through the pasture on the left leads to a pool and high rock, on the other side of which is El Rubí.

Leaving Copán: north to San Pedro Sula

If, on leaving Copán, your destination is San Pedro Sula or any of the Honduran coastal cities, you will inevitably find yourself passing through **LA ENTRADA**, a distinctly unlikeable junction town 55km north, whose only redeeming feature is that plenty of buses leave it. The journey along CA-11, winding its way through lightly wooded mountains and fertile pasture lands, is undeniably scenic, though usually painfully slow. There are some direct buses from Copán to San Pedro Sula, but since these leave at an unfeasibly early hour of the morning it's often more convenient to take any of the local buses running to La Entrada and change to an express running along CA-4 from Santa Rosa. Should you get stuck here, *Hotel San Carlos* (☎898 5228; ④), at the junction of CA-11 and CA-4, is the best of the available **accommodation**.

Breaking the journey in this way gives you, with a few hours to spare, a chance to visit the archeological site of **El Puente** (daily 8am–4pm; US$3.80); a signed turn on CA-11 4km before La Entrada gives access to the site, 6km away. Opened in 1994, El Puente receives comparatively few visitors, which makes its location – amid the grassy fields flanking the Río Chinamito – all the more enjoyable, although after the glories of Copán, the scale of the site is inevitably disappointing.

Once a sizeable **Maya** settlement, dating back to the Late Classic period and under the authority of Copán, El Puente contains over two hundred structures. To date, only a small number in the centre have been excavated, including religious buildings and buildings for the use of the elite, built around what was the main plaza. The most important of these (Structure 1) is an eleven-metre-high, six-stepped pyramid, oriented east–west and thought to be a funerary temple; the long, lower pyramid along its lower edge contains burial chambers. The small **museum** at the entrance to the park, about 1km from the restorations, has an informative exhibition on the site itself and on Maya culture in general.

No public transport runs up the road to the site, but hitching is considered safe; traffic is more frequent in the mornings. A round-trip taxi fare from La Entrada will cost around US$10.

San Pedro Sula

Honduras's second city, and the country's economic focus, **SAN PEDRO SULA** sprawls across the fertile Valle de Sula, at the foot of the Merendón mountain chain, just an hour from the coast. Flat and uninspiring to look at, and for most of the year uncomfortably hot and humid, this is not a city for sightseeing. However, it's the transport hub for northern and western Honduras, making a stay here, however short, usually unavoidable. On a more positive note, in terms of **facilities**, San Pedro ranks alongside the capital, Tegucigalpa, with its own international airport, foreign consulates, and a wide range of hotels, restaurants and shopping outlets, so that travellers coming from the north rarely need to visit the capital. If you do choose to stick around for a day or two, it's not difficult to organize a trip out to one of the country's finest **cloudforest reserves**, the Parque Nacional el Cusuco (see p.445).

One of the first Spanish settlements in the country, founded by Pedro de Alvadaro in 1536, today's San Pedro bears almost no trace of its pre-twentieth-century incarnation. Burnt out by French corsairs in 1660 and virtually abandoned during a yellow fever epidemic in 1892, the city struggled to maintain a population of more than five thousand; today only a few wooden buildings remain as proof of its long past. Its fortunes began to rise with the growth of the **banana** industry in the late nineteenth century, when the city rapidly cemented its role as Honduras's commercial centre. With its outer reaches continuing to sprout factories, many of them foreign-owned, and a population currently in the region of 500,000, San Pedro today ranks as one of the fastest-growing cities in Central America.

Arrival and information

The **Aeropuerto Internacional Villeda Morales**, the point of entry for both domestic and international flights, including daily flights to La Ceiba, lies 12km southeast of the city. As yet, there is no public transport between the airport and the city centre; **taxis** charge around US$8. **Buses** arrive at their own separate terminals, most within a few blocks of each other in central San Pedro. There are frequent bus departures for cities inland and all destinations along the north coast. If you're heading for the **Bay Islands** (see p.450), you'll need to take a Cotraibal bus from 1 Av, 7–8 C SO (☎552 3822) to La Ceiba, from where boats run daily.

San Pedro's regular grid layout makes navigation easy: avenidas run north–south and calles east–west, numbered in ascending order from the central 1 Avenida and 1 Calle, which intersect two blocks east of the cathedral. The city is further divided into quadrants, whose labels – southwest (SO), southeast (SE), northwest (NO) and northeast (NE) – are always used in directions. The bus terminals, many hotels and the main

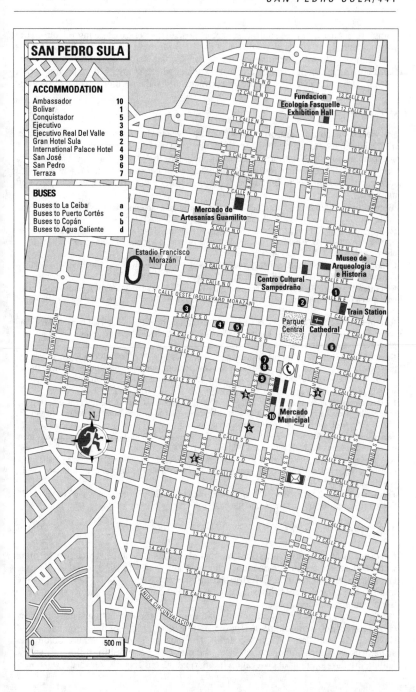

SAN PEDRO SULA

ACCOMMODATION

Ambassador	10
Bolivar	1
Conquistador	5
Ejecutivo	3
Ejecutivo Real Del Valle	8
Gran Hotel Sula	2
International Palace Hotel	4
San José	9
San Pedro	6
Terraza	7

BUSES

Buses to La Ceiba	a
Buses to Puerto Cortés	c
Buses to Copán	b
Buses to Agua Caliente	d

Fundacion Ecología Fasquelle Exhibition Hall

Mercado de Artesanías Guamilito

Estadio Francisco Morazán

CALLE OESTE (BOULEVARD MORAZAN)

Centro Cultural Sampedraño

Museo de Arqueología e Historia

Train Station

Parque Central

Cathedral

Mercado Municipal

AVENIDA CIRCUNVALACION

N

0   500 m

commercial area are in the southwest sector, close to the centre. Running west from the parque central, 1 Calle is also known as the Blvd Morazán for the first twelve blocks until it meets the **Av Circunvalación** ring road, which separates the city centre from San Pedro's wealthier residential districts; this is where many of the more upmarket restaurants are located. Beyond the Circunvalación, 1 Calle becomes Blvd los Próceres.

Accommodation

San Pedro's **accommodation** ranges from the five-star luxury of the *Gran Hotel Sula*, a city landmark, to sleazy, dollar-a-night dives. Expect to pay at least US$10 for an acceptable room with bath in a secure hotel; double that, and TV and air conditioning become standard. The area south of the market can get rough at night, and although foreigners are unlikely to be targeted, it is not really a place to be wandering around after dark.

Ambassador, 7 C, 5 Av SO (☎557 6825). Reasonably comfortable rooms, all with bath. Not a particularly pleasant area at night, but convenient for many of the bus terminals. ②–③.

Bolívar, 2 C, 2 Av NO (☎553 3224, fax 553 4823). Good-value hotel with an upmarket feel about it. The large rooms all have bath, a/c and TV. Downstairs there is a small pool and terrace, and a rather characterless bar and restaurant. ⑤.

Conquistador, 2 C SO, 7–8 Av (☎552 7605). Small and very friendly place, four blocks west of the parque central. Rooms are small but clean and all have bath, a/c and TV. ④.

Ejecutive Real del Valle, Edificio Maria Emilia, 6 Av, 4–5 C SO (☎553 0366). A comfortable place with a welcoming atmosphere. The front door is always kept locked. All rooms have a/c, bath, hot water and TV. ④.

Ejecutivo, 10 Av, 2 C SO (☎552 4289, fax 552 5868). Friendly, well-run hotel set in a quiet residential area, a 15min walk from the centre or 5min in a taxi. Rooms all have a/c, bath and TV and the price includes breakfast. ⑤.

Gran Hotel Sula, 1 C O, at the parque central (☎552 9999, fax 552 7000). A city landmark and, at present, the only real luxury option, though soon to face competition from a number of international chains. Rooms have everything you would expect for the price, including balconies with views over the city. ⑨.

Internacional Palace Hotel, 8 Av, 3 C SO (☎550 3838, fax 550 0969). Recently refurbished hotel offering high-level accommodation at reasonable prices. All rooms have bath, hot water, a/c and TV. The rooftop pool and bar are a good place to cool off. ⑤.

San José, 6 Av, 5–6 C SO (☎557 1208). One of the better hotels in the lower price range. Clean, good-sized rooms with bath and a choice of fan or a/c. ②.

San Pedro, 3 C, 1–2 Av SO (☎553 1513, fax 553 2655). Large, rambling place that's popular with travellers. The choice of rooms ranges from basic ones with shared bath to ones with large beds, private bath, a/c and TV. ①–③.

Terraza, 6 Av, 4–5 C SO (☎550 3108). Good value and convenient for the centre and bus terminals. Rooms all have bath and hot water and the café downstairs serves decent breakfasts. ③.

The City

Parque Barahona, large and recently repaved, is the focus of the city centre, teeming with vendors, shoe-shine boys, moneychangers and general malcontents. On its eastern edge, the colonial-style **Catedral Municipal** was actually only completed in the mid-1950s; facing it across the parque is the unremarkable Palacio Muncipal, home to the city administration.

San Pedro has few tourist attractions, but one place that is worth a visit is the first-class **Museo de Arqueología e Historia**, a few blocks north of the parque at 3 Av, 4 C NO (Tues–Sun 10am–4.15pm; US$0.40). The museum's collection of pre-Columbian sculptures, ceramics and other artefacts, the majority recovered from the Sula valley, outline the development of civilization in the region from 1500 BC onwards; weaponry and paintings from the colonial period continue the theme. While you're in this area, check out what's on at the **Centro Cultural Sampedrano**, 3 C, 3–4 Av NO (☎553 3911), which regularly hosts concerts and plays. Continue north away from the centre along 3 Av to reach the ecological foundation **Fundación Ecologista Hector Rodrigo Pastor Fasquelle**, at the junction with 11 C NO (Mon–Fri 9am–4pm), which has an exhibition hall on the ecology of Honduras. Displays feature pictorial and written explanations of the development of cloudforests and the wildlife encountered in the country's varied habitats, including the nearby Parque Nacional Cusuco (for details of Cusuco's **information** office, see p.445).

San Pedro has a good selection of places to buy **handicrafts** produced throughout the country. Ten or so blocks northwest of the parque central, the **Mercado Guamilito**, 9 Av, 6–7 C NO, is an indoor market with numerous stalls selling hammocks, ceramics, leatherwork and wooden goods. If you can carry them, the cotton hammocks are a good buy; gentle bartering should get you better prices. A couple of shops on the Calle Peatonal, just off the parque central, sell similar stuff, though prices are higher and the range not as wide. For the more eclectically minded, Le Merendon, a taxi ride out of the centre at 18 Av, 6 C SO, is a thatch-roofed display area cum beer garden, with an offbeat selection of works from artisans around the country; look out for the huge straw animals and the ceramic garden decorations. Danilo's, a couple of streets away at 18 Av B, 9 C SO, is an outlet for one of the best leather goods producers in the country, selling excellent-value bags, purses and belts, among other items. Finally, the vast general market, the **mercado municipal**, is between 4–5 Av SO and 5–6 C SO, though stalls spill onto the streets around for several blocks.

Eating, drinking and entertainment

As you'd expect in such a business-oriented, wealthy city, there's a good selection of **places to eat** and a diverse range of evening entertainment. The more down-to-earth places can be found in the centre, while the Av Circunvalación, south of 1 C, is the so-called Zona Viva, the place to go for upmarket restaurants, bars and clubs. A couple of modern two-screen **cinemas**, the Cine Tropicana, at 2 C, 7 Av SO, and the Cine Geminis, 1 C, 12 Av NO, are within easy walking distance of the centre; both show new US films, and the occasional Latin American offering.

Cafés and restaurants

Café Pampelona, parque central. Always crowded with locals, this place has an extensive menu and reasonable prices. Don't expect too much in the way of service but soak up the noisy atmosphere (closes 8pm).

Café Skandia, in the *Gran Hotel Sula*. Air-conditioned and open 24hr, the *Skandia* is something of a San Pedro institution, offering sandwiches, light meals and snacks, which are not as expensive as you might expect.

Cafetería Mayan Way, 6 Av, 4–5 C SO, next to *Hotel Terraza*. Good breakfasts and set lunches at down-to-earth prices.

Don Udo's, 1 C, 20 Av SO (☎553 3106). Held to be one of city's finest, offering a broad range of European and local dishes and a decent wine list. Prices are not cheap, but worth it for a splurge; expect to pay from US$15 a head for a full meal with wine. Sunday brunches are less formal. Mon–Sat evenings, Sun 10am–2pm.

Italia y Mas, 1 C, 8 Av NO. Excellent pasta, risotto and other Italian dishes for lunch or dinner, with tables inside and in a back courtyard. Prices reflect the upmarket clientele.

Pizzería Italia, 1 C, 7 Av NO. Cosy little place serving good pizza and a small selection of pasta dishes. The service is informal, and prices fairly low.

Restaurante Shanghai, Calle Peatonal. Reasonably authentic Chinese food served in huge portions.

Restaurante la Tejana, Av Circunvalación, 9 C SO. Popular place for lunch and dinner, with a wide selection of well-prepared seafood, as well as meat and chicken dishes.

Shauky's Place, 18 Av, 8 C SO. Now moved from the outskirts of the city, this easygoing bar and restaurant has tables set around an open-air gravelled garden. Delicious steak and meat dishes costing around US$7 and a few vegetarian choices too. Mon–Sat from 4pm.

Bars and clubs

After dark, the *Café Internacional*, Blvd Morazán, 14–15 Av SO, attracts a young, moneyed crowd; the drinks are reasonably priced and there is a small restaurant. The three bars at *Frog's Sports Bar*, Blvd los Próceres, 19–20 C SO, have pool tables and giant TV screens. Later in the evening, *Johnny's*, by the market, is an idiosyncratic spirits-only bar, where locals go to shoot the breeze to the accompaniment of 1950s be-bop. The nearby *Black and White* disco, a local favourite, is hot and frenetic at the weekends, while *Henry's* and *Confetti's* in the Zona Viva play Latin American and Euro-disco rhythms for a younger crowd.

Listings

Airlines American Airlines, Centro Comercial Firenze, 16 Av, 2 C (☎558 0518 or 558 0521, fax 558 0527); British Airways, Edificio Sempe, Carretera a Chamelecon (☎556 6952 or 552 3942, fax 556 8764); Continental, *Gran Hotel Sula*, 4 Av, 1–2 C (☎557 4141, fax 557 4146); COPA, Centro Comercial Prisa, 1 C, 9–10 Av (☎550 9654, fax 550 8641); Iberia, 3 C, 4–5 Av (☎557 5311, fax 553 4297); Isleña, Edifico Trejo Merlo, 7 Av, 1–2 C (☎552 8322); Lacsa, Edificio Romar, 8 Av, 1–2 C (☎550 6649, fax 550 8641); Taca International, Centro Comercial Prisa 1 C, 9–10 Av (☎550 5649, fax 550 8641).

American Express Agencia de Viajes Mundirama, Edificio Martinez Valenzuela, 2 C, 2–3 Av SO (☎553 0192, fax 557 9092).

Banks and exchange Banco Atlántida has a number of branches in the downtown area for exchange and visa advances; Banco de Occidente, 6 Av, 2–3 C SO, changes cash and travellers' cheques; Credomatic, 5 Av, 1–2 C NO, advances cash on Visa and Mastercard.

Bookshops The cigar shop in the *Gran Hotel Sula* has a small assortment of English-language fiction as well as US magazines and newspapers.

Car rental Avis, Blvd Morazán 58 (☎552 2872); Budget, Aeropuerto Villeda Morales (☎566 2267, fax 553 3411); Dollar, 3 Av 3–4 C NO (☎552 7626); Molinari, *Gran Hotel Sula* (☎553 2639, fax 552 2704) and at the airport (☎566 2580).

Consulates Belize, Km 5, road to Puerto Cortés (☎551 0124, fax 551 1740); El Salvador, 12th floor, Edificio Bancatlan (☎557 5851; Mon–Fri 9am–noon & 2.30–3.30pm); Guatemala, 8 C, 5–6 Av NO (☎553 0653; Mon–Fri 8am–2pm); Mexico, 2 C, 20 Av SO, 205 (☎553 2604; Mon–Fri 8.30–11.30am); UK, 13 Av, 11–12 C SO, No 62 (☎557 2046; Mon–Fri 9am–noon).

Immigration Direcion General de Migracíon, Calle Peatonal, above the Moreira Honduras souvenir shop (Mon–Fri 8.30am–4.30pm).

Laundry Lavandería Express 9 Av, 3 C NO (Mon–Sat 8am–5pm).

Medical care Emergency department at Clínica Bendaña, Av Circunvalación, 9–10 C SO (☎553 1618).

Police ☎552 3128.

Post office At 9 C, 3 Av SO.

Telephone office Hondutel, at 4 C, 4 Av SO, is open 24hr; fax service is available 8am–5pm.

Travel agents and tours Agencia de Viajes Mundirama, Edificio Martinez Valenzuela, 2 C, 2–3 Av SO (☎553 0192, fax 557 9092) is efficient and well-organized for booking or changing international air tickets. Transmundo de Sula, 5 Av, 4 C NO (☎550 1140), is also a reputable company. One of the most reputable tour companies is Cambio CA, Edificio Copal, 1 C, 5–6 Av SO (☎552 0496; *cambio@mayanet.hn*), which runs tours to Cusuco and other destinations. Explore Honduras, Edificio Posada del Sol, 1 C, 2 Av SO (☎552 6242, fax 552 6093), is recommended if you want an organized trip to the Bay Islands.

Around San Pedro: Parque Nacional el Cusuco

Only 20km or so west of San Pedro in the Sierra del Merendón, the stunning **Parque Nacional el Cusuco** (daily 6am–5pm; US$10) supports an abundant range of animal and plant life, much of it rare and threatened. Though inevitably affected by the proximity of human settlement, Cusuco is still a joy to visit and not too difficult to reach from San Pedro. To see as much as possible, the best plan is to arrive in the afternoon, camp overnight and walk the trails early in the morning.

The lower reaches of the park have long been inhabited and were heavily logged during the 1950s, contributing to disastrous floods during the 1970s. Here the mixed pine and broadleaf forest is secondary regrowth. At around 1800m the **cloudforest** begins, its dense oaks and liquidambars reaching to 40m in some places, stacked over avocados and palms, all supporting mosses, vines, orchids and numerous species of heliconias, recognizable by the red or orange brackets holding the blossoms. Studies carried out in the park in 1992–95 revealed the existence of at least seventeen species of plant hitherto unknown in Honduras.

Four **trails**, ranging between 1km and 2.5km, have been laid out among the lower sections of cloudforest (there is no access to the highest, steepest sections of the reserve), taking you through a hushed world of dense, dripping, multi-layered vegetation. If you're incredibly lucky, you might spot the reserve's namesake, the *cusuco* (armadillo), as well as salamanders, monkeys and even a jaguar, but the dazzling range of birdlife is likely to be more rewarding in terms of sightings. Quetzals can be spotted from April to June, and trogons, kites and woodpeckers are among the more numerous of the hundred-plus species of bird living here.

Practicalities

Cusuco is managed by the Fundación Ecologista Hector Rodrigo Pastor Fasquelle, whose office is above the *Pizzería Italia*, 1 C, 7 Av NO, in San Pedro (☎552 1014) Information leaflets are usually available and they can also advise on getting to the reserve. The main point of **access** is via the small town of **COFRADÍA**, 18km southwest of San Pedro off CA-4. From here, a dirt road continues for another 26km to the village of **BUENOS AIRES**, 5km beyond which is the park **visitor centre**. Getting there independently is time-consuming: you need to take a westbound bus to Santa Rosa de Copán, alighting in the village of Cofradía (1hr), and then wait for onward transport. Other options include renting a car – a 4-wheel drive can make the whole journey in about two hours, depending on the state of the road – or taking a tour from San Pedro (see opposite). At the visitor centre there are displays on the wildlife, trail maps, a dormitory (①) and a campsite.

La Ceiba

One hundred and ninety kilometres east along the coast from San Pedro Sula, **LA CEIBA**, the lively capital of the department of Atlántida, is in many ways one of the most approachable Honduran cities. Set beneath the stunning backdrop of the steep, green slopes of the Cordillera Nombre de Dios, the city is bustling and self-assured by day; at night it's a whole different story, when people gather to sample the excellent nightlife for which the city is renowned across the country. Things really come to a head during La Ceiba's **Carnaval** in May, when 200,000 revellers descend on the town.

La Ceiba owes its existence to the **banana** industry: the Vaccaro Bros (later Standard Fruit and now Dole) first laid plantations in the area in 1899 and set up their company headquarters in town in 1905. Although fruit is no longer shipped out through

La Ceiba, the plantations are still important to the local economy, with crops of pineapple and African palm now as significant as bananas.

Though for many travellers La Ceiba is no more than a stop-off en route to the Bay Islands (see p.450), there are some good beaches just 10km or so outside town. Alternatively, with more time and a little planning – or the services of a tour operator – you can explore the cloudforest of the nearby Parque Nacional Pico Bonito or the mangrove swamps of the Refugio Vida Silvestre (see p.449).

Arrival and information

Long-distance and local **buses** arrive at the main terminal, 2km west of the centre; taxis downtown, usually shared, charge US$0.50 per person. Those arriving by **air** will find themselves at **Aeropuerto Internacional Golosón**, 9km from the centre, off the main highway west to San Pedro Sula. From the terminal, the taxi fare into the centre is US$3, around half that if you flag one down on the highway, where you can also pick up buses heading into the city. The **ferry** to and from **Roatán** and **Utila** in the Bay Islands uses the Muralla de Cabotaje municipal dock, about 5km to the east of the city – taxis charge US$2 per person.

FUCSA, which manages the Refugio de Vida Silvestre Cuero y Salado (see p.449), has an office in the Edificio Ferrocarril Nacional, two blocks west of the parque central (Mon–Fri 8–11.30am & 1.30–4.30pm, Sat 8–11.30am; ☎ & fax 443 0329).

Accommodation

Given La Ceiba's status, both as a provincial and party centre, there is a wide range of **places to stay**. The only problem will be in deciding whether you want to be near the centre, or closer to the nightlife along 1 C. Prices inevitably tend to rise around Carnaval time in May, when reserving ahead becomes essential.

Colonial, Av 14 de Julio, 6–7 C (☎443 1953, fax 443 1955). One of the more upmarket places and a good deal for the price. Rooms all have bath, TV and phone, and facilities include a good restaurant, a bar and a sauna. ④.

Dan's Hotel, C 3, Barrio la Isla (☎ & fax 443 4219). Very friendly and quiet family-run place in a private house. The rooms, all with bath, are comfortable and some have TV. The owners cook breakfasts and other meals on request. ③–④.

Gran Hotel Paris, parque central (☎443 2391, fax 443 1614). A central landmark and still considered to be the classiest place in town, although now a little past its heyday. Rooms all have a/c, phone and TV, and there is a pool, a quiet bar and a restaurant. ⑤.

Iberia, Av San Isidro, 5–6 C (☎443 0401). A very friendly place and a bargain for the price. The rooms with a balcony overlooking the street are the nicest, but all have bath, a/c and TV. ③.

Italia, Av 14 de Julio, next to the *Colonial* (☎443 0150). Rooms are large and clean, but somewhat sparsely furnished; all have baths, however, and the place is secure. ②.

Parthenon Beach, 1 C, Av Bonilla, Barrio la Isla (☎443 0404, fax 443 0434). A somewhat eclectic place with a great beachfront location at the eastern edge of town. Room prices vary depending on whether they're a/c or not and in the old or new building. There is a good restaurant, outdoor bar and a pool, though the water is not changed with great frequency. ④–⑤.

Plaza Flamingo, 1 C, Av 14 de Julio (☎443 3149). Modern place with a friendly management, right in the centre of the Zona Viva. The large rooms have well-kept bathrooms, a/c, TV and fridge, but only a few have sea views. ④.

Rotterdam, 1 C, Av Barahona, Barrio la Isla (☎443 2859). New, Dutch-run hotel, just up from the beach. Adequate rooms, all with bath, which are good value for the price. ②.

The Town

Most things that are of interest to visitors lie within a relatively small area of the city, around the shady and pleasant **parque central**, six or so blocks back from the seafront. The unremarkable cathedral sits on the southeast corner, the *Gran Hotel Paris* on the northern edge. Running north from the parque almost to the seafront, Av

San Isidro, Av Atlántida and Av 14 de Julio form the main commercial district, lined with shops, banks and a couple of supermarkets. The main general **market** sprawls along the streets around the old wooden, market building on Av Atlántida.

Night action takes place along 1 C, which parallels the length of the seafront. Nicknamed the "Zona Viva" due to the preponderance of bars and clubs, 1 C extends west from the old dock and over the river estuary into **Barrio la Isla**, a quieter residential district, mainly home to Garífuna, once it leaves the seafront.

All the **beaches** within the city limits are, sadly, too polluted and dirty for even the most desperate to want to brave the rough water. Better by far is to head east to the much cleaner beaches a few kilometres out of town (see p.448).

Eating, drinking and entertainment

Not for nothing does La Ceiba have a reputation as the place to party. The **Zona Viva** hums every night of the week, with a profusion of places to drink, dance and be merry. A steady trickle of tourists and a growing number of resident ex-pats, both in front of and behind the bar, have helped to create a buoyant, distinctly non-threatening, international atmosphere. While the range of **places to eat** is not that extensive, excellently prepared Honduran and European food is not hard to find. Restaurants generally stop serving at around 10pm. For more cerebral entertainment, the **cinema**, just off the parque central, shows the usual subtitled Hollywood fare.

If you can make it, the most exciting time to be in La Ceiba is **Carnaval**, a week-long bash held every May to celebrate the city's patron saint, San Isidro. Dances and street events in various barrios around town culminate in an afternoon parade on the third Saturday of the month. Led by a float carrying the Carnaval Queen, the parade moves slowly down the gaudily decked Av San Isidro. Bands on stages placed along the avenida then compete to outplay each other throughout the evening and into the early hours. The 200,000 or so partygoers who attend Carnaval every year flock between the stages and the clubs on 1 C where the dancing continues until dawn.

RESTAURANTS AND CAFÉS

Café Cobal, 7 C, Av San Isidro. A fast-turnaround place serving breakfasts and lunch, mainly to office workers. The food is good, as are the juices, and the portions large.

Café Le Jardín, Av la Bastilla 767, near the Esso station. French-run bistro with seating in the garden, serving what's possibly the best food in Honduras. The steak and the chicken in cream sauce are particularly recommended. The wine list, featuring plenty of South American wines, is equally good. Two courses with wine costs around US$16 per person.

Café Tropical, Av Atlántida, 4–5 C. Cheerful café serving from early morning to around 10pm. Good pollo frito features heavily in the daily set menus.

La Casa, 9 C, Av San Isidro–Av 14 de Julio. One of the nicest restaurants in the centre, with tables set around an open courtyard. Wide range of Honduran food, with main courses costing around US$6.

Centro Cultural Satuye, 4 C, Av Herrera, Barrio la Isla. Light-hearted and informal Garífuna restaurant. Loud live music in the evenings.

La Concha, 1 C, three blocks east of the river. Laid-back German-owned restaurant with a meat-heavy menu; the potato soup is excellent.

Cri Cri Burger, Av 14 de Julio, 3 C. Good burgers, steak sandwiches and other snacks are served to the accompaniment of very loud music. The side tables are a good place to watch comings and goings in the street.

Expatriate's Bar and Grill, 12 C, two blocks east of Av San Isidro. Airy, North-American-owned thatched bar with a good range of vegetarian, chicken and meat dishes. Popular with resident foreigners and a good source of local information. Mon & Thurs–Sun 4pm–midnight.

Pupuseria Salvadoreña Tonita, Barrio la Isla, opposite the *Parthenon Beach*. Unpretentious and friendly; a good place to sample the national snack of El Salvador, the *pupusa*, a grilled tortilla, containing beans, cheese or meat, or varieties of the three.

Restaurante Elvir, Av San Isidro, beneath the *Iberia*. New place tucked away in a little courtyard and serving reasonably good pizza and pasta, as well as burgers and sandwiches. Closed Sun.

Restaurante Palace, Av 14 de Julio, 8 C. Big barn of a place serving delicious and authentic Chinese dishes.

BARS AND CLUBS

African Dani's, 1 C, two blocks east of the river, Barrio la Isla. A Garífuna dance hall, with live music and dancing most nights of the week.

Bar el Canadiense, Av 14 de Julio at 1 C. A relaxed French-Canadian-owned bar attracting a good mix of locals, resident foreigners and tourists. The pool table is always popular and the music is eclectic.

Cherry's, on the beach, at the end of Av 14 de Julio. A popular club, open all week and packed at the weekend. Plays a mixture of Latin American rhythms, reggae and country music.

Deutsch Australien Club, Av 14 de Julio at the beach. A quiet bar for mellow drinking and conversation.

D'Lidos, on 1 C, just east of the river in Barrio la Isla. Just as loud and just as popular as *Cherry's*.

Safari, opposite *D'Lidos*. Another popular club, attracting a predominantly local crowd.

Zanzibar, 1 C at Av 14 de Julio. The dark interior of this bar plays European rock turned up high. The stools on the street front are good for people-watching.

Listings

Airlines On the parque central are Isleña (☎443 2683), Sosa (☎443 1399) and Taca (☎443 1915); all three also have ticket desks at the airport, as do Rollins Air (☎443 4181) and Caribbean Air (☎445 1933).

Banks Banco Atlántida and Credomatic, among others, are located on Av San Isidro and Av Atlántida.

Car rental Molinari, *Gran Hotel Paris* (☎443 2391, fax 443 0055).

Immigration Av 14 Julio, 1–2 C.

Laundry Lavandería Plaza Copán, Av San Isidro, and Lavandería 2001, Barrio la Isla.

Police ☎438 0241.

Post office Av Morazán and 13 C, south of the parque.

Telephones Hondutel, at Av Ramón Rosa, 5–6 C, is open 24hr.

Tour operators For trips to Pico Bonito (see opposite), try one of the following: La Moskitia Ecoaventuras, Av 14 de Julio at 1 C (☎442 0104); Euro Honduras Tours, Av Atlántida at 1 C (☎443 3893, fax 443 0933); La Ceiba Eco Tours, Av San Isidro at 1 C (☎443 4420). La Moskitia Eco-Lodge, Plaza Aurora (☎440 0076, fax 440 0077), has three- to seven-day packages to Mosquitia. Harry's Horse Back Tours, contacted through the *Bar el Canadiense*, organizes horse-riding in Pico Bonito.

Around La Ceiba

The broad sandy **beaches** and clean water at Playa de Perú and the village of Sambo Creek are easy to reach as day-trips from the city; both are a short distance east along the coast. A trip to explore the **cloudforest** within the Parque Nacional Pico Bonito requires more planning, although the eastern edge of the reserve, formed by the Río Cangrejal, is more easily accessible, offering opportunities for swimming and white-water **rafting**.

The beaches: Playa de Perú and Sambo Creek

Ten kilometres east of the city, **Playa de Perú** is a wide sweep of clean sand that's popular at weekends. Any bus running east up the coast will drop you at the turn-off on the highway, from where it's a fifteen-minute walk to the beach. About 2km past the turning for Playa de Perú, on the Río María, there's a series of **waterfalls** and **natural pools** set in lush, shady forest. A path leads from Río María village on the highway,

CRIME AND DRUGS ON THE NORTH COAST

Increasing use of **drugs** has led to a significant rise in **crime** rates along the north coast. Muggings, bag-snatchings and personal attacks have all been reported and while the chances are that nothing will happen to you, it's sensible to take some precautions. Make sure you are never visibly carrying large amounts of cash, or expensive-looking bags or cameras; avoid walking around the centre of town late at night; and never go onto the beaches after dark – advice that holds for the whole of the north coast.

winding through the hills along the left bank of the river. It takes around thirty minutes to walk to the first cascade and pool; some sections are muddy and a bit of a scramble during the wet season.

There are further deserted expanses of white sand at the friendly Garífuna village of **SAMBO CREEK**, 8km beyond Río María. You can eat excellent fresh fish at a couple of restaurants in the village and there's also a small, basic hotel (①). Olanchito or Jutiapa buses from La Ceiba will drop you at the turn-off to Sambo Creek on the highway, a couple of kilometres from the village; slower buses run all the way to the village centre from La Ceiba's terminal every 45 minutes.

Parque Nacional Pico Bonito

Directly south of La Ceiba, the Cordillera Nombre de Dios shelters the **Parque Nacional Pico Bonito** (daily 6am–4pm; US$2.30), a remote expanse of tropical broadleaf forest, cloudforest and – in its southern reaches, above the Río Aguan valley – pine forest. Taking its name from the awe-inspiring bulk of Pico Bonito (2435m) itself, the park is the source of twenty rivers, including the Zacate, Bonito and Cangrejal, which cascade majestically down the steep, thickly covered slopes, and it provides sanctuary for an abundance of wildlife including armadillos, howler and spider monkeys, pumas and tigrillos. This abundance is due in large part to the inaccessibility of much of the park. The lower fringes are the most easily penetrable, with a small number of trails laid out through the dense greenery. The best of these is the four- to five-hour circular walk that winds, steeply in sections, up through the tree cover to a lookout over the Caribbean. Tour companies in La Ceiba operate day- and overnight trips to Pico Bonito, from around US$40 per person (see opposite). The **Río Cangrejal**, forming the eastern boundary of the park, boasts some of the best Class III and IV rapids in Central America; **white-water rafting trips** are organized by some of the tour companies listed on p.448. There are also some magnificent swimming spots, backed by gorgeous mountain scenery along the river valley. To get there, follow the dirt road that turns off the highway about 2km east of La Ceiba, and head south along the valley. *Balneario las Mangas*, about 12km from the highway, has small cabins for rent (③).

Refugio de Vida Silvestre Cuero y Salado

Thirty kilometres west from La Ceiba, the **Refugio de Vida Silvestre Cuero y Salado** (daily 7am–4pm; US$10) is one of the last substantial remnants of wetlands and mangrove swamp along the north coast. The reserve is home to a large number of animal and bird species, many of which are endangered, including manatees, jaguars, howler and white-faced monkeys, sea turtles, hawks and seasonal influxes of migratory birds. Though nominally protected since 1987, the edges of the reserve are under constant pressure from local farmers wanting to drain the land for new pastures.

The best way to see the reserve is to take a **guided tour**, not least because the guides know the spots where you're likely to see some wildlife. FUCSA, the body that manages the reserve, has an office in La Ceiba (see p.446) and organizes regular tours

(US$10 per boat), which you need to book in advance. They also run a small hostel at the reserve, where you can **stay** (①).

To get to the reserve **independently**, catch one of the hourly buses from La Ceiba's terminal to the village of La Unión, 20km or so west. From here, you can either make your way on foot through the fruit plantations – it takes around an hour and a half to walk the 8km – or travel by _burra_, a flat, poled railcar, along the railway tracks. The last bus back to La Ceiba leaves La Unión mid-afternoon.

The Bay Islands

Strung in a gentle curve less than 60km off the north coast of Honduras, the **Bay Islands (Islas de la Bahía)**, with their clear, calm waters and abundant marine life, are the country's main tourist attraction. Resting along a coral reef, the islands are a perfect destination for cheap diving, sailing and fishing; less active visitors can sling a hammock and relax in the shade on the many palm-fringed, soft-sand beaches. Comprising three main islands and some 65 smaller cayes, this sweeping 125-kilometre island chain lies on the **Bonacca Ridge**, an underwater extension of the mainland Sierra de Omoa mountain range. **Roatán** is the largest and most developed of the islands, while **Guanaja**, to the east, is an upmarket resort destination with some wonderful dive sites, and **Utila**, the closest to the mainland, is a target for budget travellers from all over the world.

Even old hands get excited about **diving** the waters around the Bay Islands, where lizard fish and toadfish dart by, scarcely distinguishable from the coral, eagle rays glide through the water like huge birds flying through the air, and parrotfish chomp steadily away on the coral; checking you out from a distance, barracuda and harmless nurse sharks circle the waters. In addition, the world's largest fish, the whale shark, which can reach up to 16m long, is a regular visitor to the channel between Utila and Roatán in October and November; dive shops on both islands run trips to look for this marine giant.

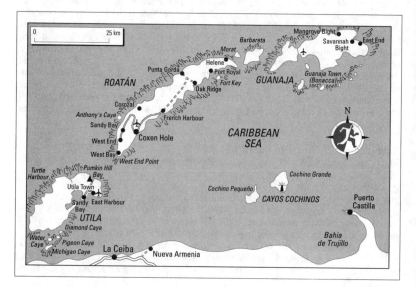

The best **time to visit** the islands is between March and September, when water visibility is best; October and November are the wettest months, and there is some rainfall from December to February. Daytime temperatures range between 25 and 29°C year round, though the heat is rarely oppressive, thanks to almost constant east–southeast trade winds. **Mosquitoes** and **sandflies** are endemic on all the islands, at their worst when the wind dies down; lavish coatings of baby oil help to keep the latter away.

Some history

The Bay Islands' history of conquest, pirate raids and constant immigration has resulted in a society that's unique in Honduras. The islands' original inhabitants are thought to have been the **Pech**, recorded by Columbus on his fourth voyage in 1502 as being a "robust people who adore idols and live mostly from a certain white grain from which they make fine bread and the most perfect beer". After the **Conquest**, the indigenous population dropped rapidly as a result of enslavement and forced labour. The islands' strategic location, as a provisioning point for the Europe-bound Spanish fleets, ensured that they soon became targets for **pirates**, initially Dutch and French, and latterly English. The Spanish decision to evacuate the islands, eventually achieved in 1650, left the way open for the pirates to move in. Port Royal, Roatán, became their base until the mid-eighteenth century, from where they launched sporadic attacks on ships and against the mainland settlements.

After the pirates left, Roatán was deserted until the arrival of the **Garífuna** in 1797. Forcibly expelled from the British-controlled island of St Vincent following a rebellion, most of the three-thousand-strong group were persuaded by the Spanish to settle in Trujillo on the mainland, leaving a small settlement at Punta Gorda on the island's north coast. Further waves of settlers came after the abolition of slavery in 1830, when white Cayman Islanders and freed slaves arrived on Utila, later spreading to Roatán and Guanaja. These new inhabitants fished and built up a very successful fruit industry, which exported to the US – until a hurricane levelled the plantations in 1877.

Honduras acquired rights to the islands following **independence** in 1821, yet many – not least the islanders themselves – still considered the territory to be British. In 1852, Britain declared the islands a Crown Colony, breaking the terms of the 1850 Clayton-Bulwer Treaty, an agreement not to exercise dominion over any part of Central America. Forced to back down under US pressure, Britain finally conceded sovereignty to Honduras in the Wyke-Cruz Treaty of 1859.

Today, the islands retain their **cultural** distinction from the mainland, although with both Spanish-speaking Hondurans and North American and European expats settling in growing numbers, there is ongoing re-shaping and adaptation. A unique form of **Creole English** is still spoken on the street, but due to the increasing number of mainlanders migrating here, Spanish – always the official language – is becoming just as common. This government-encouraged migration engenders mixed feelings, as does the huge growth in tourism since the early 1990s, a trend that shows no signs of abating; the islands' income, which traditionally came from fishing or working on cargo ships and oil rigs, is coming to rely more and more on tourism. Concern is also growing about the environmental impact of the industry and the question of who, exactly, benefits most from the boom.

Getting to the islands

The growth in tourism to the islands over the past few years means that all three are served by regular air and boat connections. Most flights and the scheduled ferry service leave from the coastal city of **La Ceiba** (see p.445), from where there are also occasional unscheduled boats.

Flying to the islands is uncomplicated, with locals treating the twin-propeller light aircraft almost like buses. From La Ceiba the flight to Guanaja takes around forty minutes,

---

RESPONSIBLE TOURISM IN THE BAY ISLANDS

While tourism has given the Bay Islands a higher standard of living than exists on the mainland, it's impossible not to notice the substantial gap between the level of facilities provided by the luxury resorts and the local way of life. Over the last three or four years the islands' resources have been put under growing strain but, fortunately, ways in which visitors can help are relatively simple. Tourists on average use three times as much **water** as locals, so try not to run taps or flush toilets needlessly. To conserve **power**, switch off lights, fans and other electrical appliances when not in your room. **Waste** disposal facilities tend towards the primitive, so if you can, use water purifiers instead of repeatedly buying plastic bottles for drinking water, and re-use plastic bags.

---

to Roatán around thirty minutes and to Utila about twenty minutes. There are also some direct flights to Roatán from San Pedro Sula (1hr) and Tegucigalpa (1hr). Schedules change at short notice and flights are sometimes cancelled altogether; bear in mind there might be delays to your arrival and, more crucially, departure. There are over twenty flights a day to Roatán and, outside peak season (Dec–April), you can usually buy tickets on the spot at the airport; reservations are required for Utila and Guanaja, which are served by a smaller number of flights – see p.463 for details of flight schedules. The domestic **airlines**, Isleña, Taca and Sosa, have offices on the central square in La Ceiba and at the airport; Isleña and Taca also fly to San Pedro Sula and Tegucigalpa. Two further carriers, Rollins Air and Caribbean Air, have offices at the airport.

The scheduled **ferry service** from La Ceiba to Roatán and Utila runs twice a day Monday to Saturday and once on Sunday. You do not have to buy tickets in advance, unless it's a holiday.

Utila

Smallest of the three main Bay Islands, **UTILA** is a key destination for budget travellers intent on learning to **dive** at some of the cheapest prices in the world. Even if you don't want to don tanks, the superb waters around the island offer great swimming and snorkelling possibilities. Utila is still the cheapest island, with the cost of living only slightly higher than on the mainland, although prices are gradually rising. The atmosphere is laid-back and people are on the whole friendly, although opportunistic crime is on the increase. As elsewhere, respect local customs in dress and don't walk around in your bathing suit. Note also that drinking from glass bottles on the street is prohibited.

Arrival and information

The **airstrip** is at the southeastern end of the island, at one end of the large, curved harbour around which the main settlement, **East Harbour**, is built. Jutting out into the sea, the main dock neatly bisects the bay; the area around the airport is known as **The Point**, while the west part of town, on the other side of the dock, is called **Sandy Bay**. A paved road runs right the way through town, from the airstrip to Sandy Bay, a distance of around 2km. **Cola de Mico Road**, the island's only other paved road, heads north from the dock across the width of the island.

Wherever you arrive, you'll be met by representatives from the dive schools, armed with **maps** and information on special offers, but it's worth checking out all the various options before signing up. For more objective **information**, the Utila branch of BICA (Bay Islands' Conservation Association) has a visitor and information office on the main street between the airstrip and the dock, though its opening hours are erratic (usually Mon–Fri 9am–noon and a couple of hours in the afternoon). Since 1996 they have been operating a **Visitor Pass** programme, with the proceeds funding community and conservation projects; the US$5 fee is supposed to be paid on arrival, although no one seems to check. For information on events and an insight into local feelings, pick up a copy of the monthly *Utila Times*, available from the office near BICA.

Everything in town is within easy walking distance; it takes around twenty minutes to stroll from the airstrip to the far western end. **Bikes** can be rented from the house next to Henderson's grocery store, just west of the centre, and from other places around town – look out for the signs. Current rates are around US$2 a day. Some locals use four-wheeled motorbikes to get around and occasionally pick up hitchers.

Accommodation

There is a profusion of **hotels**, **guest houses**, **rooms** and self-contained **houses** for rent, some very basic, some of excellent quality. Many places offer discounts for monthly stays. Electricity on the island is provided by two main generators, which supply power from 6am until midnight, with occasional cut-outs in the evening. This doesn't mean it's impossible to run a fan at night, since most hotels now have their own generators, but it's worth checking before taking a room. All the places reviewed below are on one of the two roads in town, listed in the order you come to them when walking from the airstrip.

FROM THE AIRSTRIP TO THE MAIN DOCK

Cooper's Inn, next to the *Utila Times* office (☎425 3184). One of the best cheap places on the island, with airy, clean rooms. *Delaney's Kitchen* downstairs serves good food. ①.

Sharkey's Cabins, behind *Sharkey's Restaurant*, close to the airstrip (☎425 3212). Set in a peaceful garden with a/c, private bath, big beds and a deck with views over the lagoon. ④.

Rubi's Inn, next to the *Mermaid* restaurant (☎425 3240). Very clean, with airy rooms and views over the water; kitchen facilities are available. ②.

Trudy's, about 200m down from the bridge (☎425 3103). A very popular place, with large, clean rooms, and a large deck to swim from at the back. ③.

COLA DE MICO ROAD

Blueberry Hill, across from Thompson's bakery. Characterful cabins with basic cooking facilities and friendly owners. ①.

Mango Inn, about 300m up from the crossroads (☎425 3335). A new, well-run place, where the accommodation, set around a shady garden, ranges from dorms to doubles with private bath. There is a book exchange and laundry service, and the attached *Mango Café* serves good food. ①–③.

SANDY BAY

Hotel Utila, just past Hondutel (☎425 3340). Rooms with bath and TV and some with a/c, in a large, modern building. ③–⑤.

Margaritaville Beach Hotel, about 200m out of town (☎425 3266). It's a bit of a walk to get here, but there are ample rewards: large airy rooms and a very quiet, seafront location. All rooms have bath and there's free coffee. ②.

Seaside Inn, opposite Gunter's, about 100m past the *Hotel Utila* (☎425 3150). Very popular with younger travellers and often full. Reasonable, good-value rooms. Those in the newer section have private bath. ①–②.

Utila Lodge, behind Hondutel (☎425 3143). This dive resort is the best hotel in town, offering daily rates as well as weekly packages. Also arranges fishing trips. ⑦.

Diving

Most visitors come to Utila specifically for the **diving**, attracted by the low prices, the clarity of water and the abundant marine life. Even in winter, the water is generally calm; common sightings include nurse and hammerhead sharks, turtles, parrotfish, stingrays, porcupine fish and an increasing number of dolphins. On the north coast of the island, Blackish Point and Duppy Waters are both good sites, while on the south coast, the best spots are Black Coral Wall and Pretty Bush. The good schools will be happy to spend time talking to you about the merits of the various sites.

Rather than signing up with the first dive school representative who approaches you, it's worth spending a morning walking around checking out all the schools. **Price** is not really a consideration, with the dozen or so dive shops all charging US$125–140 for a three- to five-day PADI course; advanced and divemaster courses are also on offer, as are fun dives, from US$25. **Safety** is a more pertinent issue: for peace of mind, you should make sure that you understand – and get along with – the instructors, many of whom speak a number of languages. Also, before signing up, check that classes have no more than six people, that the equipment is well maintained and that all boats have working oxygen and a first-aid kit. Anyone with asthma or ear problems should not be allowed to dive. A worthwhile investment is the diving **insurance** sold by BICA for US$2 a day, which covers you for medical treatment in an emergency.

It is important to bear in mind that the coral reef dies every time it is touched. BICA has been installing buoys on each of the sites to prevent boats anchoring on the reef and all the reputable schools will use these. **Recommended schools** include Alton's (☎425 3108), just over the bridge from the airstrip; Underwater Vision (☎425 3103), based in *Trudy's Hotel*; and Gunter's Dive Shop (☎425 3113), about 300m past the dock in Sandy Bay. Salty Dog's (☎425 3363), just past the dock in Sandy Bay, offers underwater photography equipment rental and instruction. Many of the dive shops also have snorkelling equipment for rent, and Gunter's rents out sea kayaks. West of town and only accessible by boat the *Laguna Beach Resort* (☎425 3239) and, further down the coast, the *Utila Reef Resort* (☎425 3254), run weekly dive packages, including all meals and daily dives.

Swimming, snorkelling and walking

The best swimming near town is at the **Blue Bayou**, about thirty minutes' walk west round the bay, where you can bathe in chest-deep water. Hammocks are slung in the shade of coconut trees and there's a food stand selling burgers and beers; snorkelling gear is also available for rent. East of town, **Airport Beach**, at the end of the airstrip, offers good snorkelling just offshore, as does the little reef beyond the **lighthouse**. The path from the end of the airstrip up the east coast of the island leads to a couple of small coves, the second of which is good for swimming and sunbathing, though piles of dumped garbage dilute the pleasure somewhat. There's an interesting, if tiring, walk to **Ironshores**, five minutes beyond the coves – a mile-long stretch of low volcanic cliffs with lava tunnels cutting down to the water.

Cola de Mico Road deteriorates into a dirt track as it continues across the island, all the way to **Pumpkin Hill** and beach, about an hour's walk from town. Here, the 82m hill gives good views across the island, while down on the beach, lava rocks cascade into the sea, forming underwater caves. There is good snorkelling here when the water is calm, although it's not safe to enter the caves. On clear days any point on the southern edge of the island offers great views across to the mainland and the dark bulk of Pico Bonito (see p.449).

The Cays

Eleven tiny outcrops strung along the southwest edge of the island, **Utila Cays** have been a designated wildlife refuge since 1992. Only **Suc Suc (Jewel) Cay** and **Pigeon Cay**, connected by a narrow causeway, are inhabited, and the pace of life here is slower even than on Utila. Small launches regularly cross the 8km from Utila, or can be privately hired to take you across for a day's snorkelling. *Vicky's Rooms* (①) on Suc Suc is the only **accommodation** at present; for **eating**, there are a couple of restaurants, and a good fish market. Most of the other cays are privately owned, though houses on Morgan and Sandy Cays can be rented through George Jackson (Pigeon Key; ☎425 3161). Camping is allowed on **Water Cay**, however – an idyllic stretch of white sand, coconut palms and a small coral reef, which is a popular spot for weekend and full-moon parties. A caretaker turns up every day to collect a nominal US$1 fee; he also rents out hammocks, though you'll need to bring all food and water with you.

Eating

Lobster and **fish** are obviously staples on the islands, along with the usual rice, beans and chicken. With the tourists, however, have also come **European** foods – pasta, pizza, pancakes and granola. Since most things have to be brought in by boat, **prices** are higher than on the mainland: main courses start at around US$4, and beers cost US$1. For eating on the cheap, head for the evening stalls on the road by the dock, which do a thriving trade in baleadas. Note that many of the restaurants stop serving at around 10pm.

Bahía del Mar, just before the bridge by the airstrip. Good steaks and fish dinners, and a popular bar.

Bundu Café, opposite the *Utila Times* office. Big European-style breakfasts, light snacks and lunches, and a book exchange. Mon–Wed, Fri & Sat 9am–3pm.

Golden Rose, just past the 7–11 store, 150m west of the dock. Held by dive instructors and locals to be the best on the island. Large portions of the usual chicken, fish and meat staples served in a friendly atmosphere.

Island Café, about 50m west of the dock. Good coffee, large sandwiches and light meals. The street-side balcony eating area is good for people-watching.

Jade Seahorse, 200m up Cola de Mico Rd. A popular gathering spot for travellers. Large plates of lobster, shrimp and other seafood for around US$5. Good licuados, too.

Mango Café, in the *Mango Inn*. A friendly, open-sided bar-restaurant in the courtyard of the hotel. The menu is heavy on European-style dishes, such as burgers, fishcakes and fries. The bar is popular in the evenings. Closed Mon.

Mermaid's Corner, next to the *Utila Times*. A popular, noisy pasta and pizza restaurant, where service can sometimes be slow. Dishes cost around US$3–4.

Sharkey's Reef Restaurant, opposite the *Bahía del Mar*. The nearest Utila gets to gourmet cuisine, with an eclectic selection of Californian- and Caribbean-style daily specials. Expect to pay around US$9 for an excellent meal with drinks. Wed–Sun, dinner only.

Thompson's Bakery, 50m up Cola Mico Rd. An institution among foreign tourists. Large cooked breakfasts of eggs and toast, plus a wide choice of baked goodies. Daily 6am–noon.

Utila Reef, about 200m past the bridge. A small restaurant with tables set on an upstairs deck, overlooking the water. Large portions of local food with a European twist; the lobster and rice is delicious.

Utila's Cuisine, 50m before the dock. An unpretentious place catering to locals. Chicken and meat dishes are well cooked and cheap.

Nightlife

Utila has a thriving weekend **nightlife**, with a mellower feel during the week when there are fewer visitors in town. Most days, the waterfront *Seabreaker* bar, just past the *Bundu Café*, is good for a quiet drink, but on Tuesday, Thursday and Saturday nights there's a cocktail hour, happy hour and loud Euro-indie and reggae until 11pm. On Saturdays the party continues at *07*, next to the *Mermaid* restaurant, whose happy hour runs from midnight to 1am, accompanied by disco and techno. *Casino*, by the dock, is more of a local hangout, playing reggae and a dash of salsa and merengue. Halfway up Cola de Mico Road, *The Bucket of Blood* is an island institution with regular happy hours and late-night drinking; more relaxed is the *Mango Café*, which closes at 10pm. Should you fancy a game of pool, there's a hall behind *The Bucket of Blood*, which stays open until 11pm. English-language videos are shown nightly at the *Bundu Café*.

Listings

Banks and exchange Banco Atlántida and Bancahsa, on the main road by the dock, exchange money and advance cash on Visa cards until 3pm.

Bookstores The *Bundu Café*, on the main street, east of the dock, has a book exchange.

Immigration office Next to Hondutel, in Sandy Bay.

Medical care There's a clinic just across from Immigration and Hondutel in Sandy Bay; open weekday mornings only.

Post office In the large building on the dock.

Telephones Hondutel is 200m along from the dock in Sandy Bay.

Travel agents Utila Tour Travel Centre (agents for Isleña), close to the airstrip, or Tropical Travel, further along the road to the dock, both book flights back to the mainland.

Roatán

Some 50km from La Ceiba, **Roatán** is the largest of the Bay Islands, a curving ridged hump almost 50km long and 5km across at its widest point. Geared towards tourism at the upper end of the scale, the island's accommodation mostly comes in the form of all-in luxury **resort packages**, although there are some good deals to be found. Like Utila, Roatán is a suberb **diving** destination, but also offers some great hiking, as well as the chance to do nothing except laze on a beach. **Coxen Hole** is the island's commercial centre, while **West End** is the place to head for absolute relaxation.

Arrival and getting around

Regular flights from La Ceiba and San Pedro Sula – and some from further afield – land at the new **international airport**, 3km east of Coxen Hole, the island's main town. Collective taxis into the centre charge US$1.50; alternatively, walk to the main road just outside the terminal building and wait for one of the public minibuses. In the airport there's an information desk, a hotel reservation desk, car rental agencies and a bank. Coming by **ferry** from the mainland, you'll arrive at the main **dock**, in the centre of Coxen Hole.

A paved road runs west to east along the island, connecting all the major communities. **Minibuses** leave regularly from the main street in Coxen Hole, running west to **Sandy Bay** and **West End** every thirty minutes until late afternoon. East up the island, buses run to **Brick Bay**, **French Harbour**, **Oak Ridge** and **Punta Gorda**, where the paved road ends, every hour or according to demand, until late afternoon. Fares are US$0.50–1.15, depending on distance.

To explore thoroughly, you're best off **renting a car**. In addition to the rental agencies at the airport, Sandy Bay Rent a Car has offices at Sandy Bay and West End, charging from US$45 per day. Hiring a **taxi** for the day is likely to be expensive, but it's worth bargaining to get a better rate. In and around West End village, you can also rent **bicycles**; take care cycling on the main routes, since the roads are narrow and drivers can be reckless.

Coxen Hole

Dusty and rundown **COXEN HOLE** is the island's main town and the departmental capital. Most visitors come here to change money or to shop, and unless you're on a very early flight there's no reason **to stay**. If you do need to, try the *Hotel Cayview* on the main street (☎445 1222; ⑤), which has comfortable rooms with a/c and bath. For **eating**, there are a number of cheap comedores around the centre, and the friendly *Pava Pizza* on the main street serves decent pizzas and sandwiches. The new *Que Pasa Café* in Librería Casi Todo II, on the western edge of town, ten minutes' walk from the centre, does European-style breakfasts and snacks.

All the town's facilities can be found on a 200m stretch of the main street, near where the buses stop. The four-storey Cooper Building holds the headquarters of **BICA**, the islands' conservation organization, where you can pick up leaflets on the flora and fauna of the islands and information on conservation projects. In the same building is the office of the *Coconut Telegraph*, an informative **magazine** about Roatán and its events, which comes out sporadically. Of the **banks** along here, Bancahsa changes travellers' cheques and offers cash advances on Visa; Credomatic also handles Visa transactions. Both the **post office** and **immigration** are by the small square halfway along the main street, while **Hondutel** is behind Bancahsa. For shopping, H.B. Warren is the largest **supermarket** on the island, with a wide stock of groceries and foodstuffs and a basic range of cheap clothes. Yaba Ding Ding and Mahchi are souvenir shops, selling postcards, T-shirts and jewellery.

Sandy Bay

About 7km west of Coxen Hole, halfway to West End, **SANDY BAY** is an unassuming village community, set between the road and the sea. There isn't as wide a choice of places to stay as in West End, but there are a couple of interesting attractions in the village, as well as some excellent snorkelling, since the water around here is protected as the **Sandy Bay Marine Reserve**.

The **Institute for Marine Sciences** (9am–5pm, closed Wed; US$4), based in *Antony's Key Resort*, has exhibitions on the marine life and geology of the islands and a museum with information on local history and archeology. You can also watch bottle-nosed **dolphin shows** (daily except Wed, 10am & 4pm, Sat & Sun also 1pm; US$4), or dive or snorkel amongst the dolphins: a half-hour dive (for qualified divers only) costs US$115, and half an hour's snorkelling US$75. Across the road from the institute, several short nature trails weave through the jungle of the **Carambola Botanical Gardens** (daily 8am–5pm; US$3), a riot of thick, lush vegetation, trees, flowers, ferns and orchids. A twenty-minute walk from the gardens up Monte Carambola brings you to the Iguana Wall, a section of cliff that serves as a breeding ground for iguanas and parrots.

The cheapest **accommodation** in Sandy Bay is *Beth's Place*, a large wooden building located off the dirt road to the beach (☎445 1266; ②); all rooms are non-smoking, with shared bath and use of the kitchen. By the sea is the *Oceanside Inn* (☎445 1552; ⑥), with large, comfortably furnished rooms and an attached restaurant. If you can afford it, the nicest place to stay is *Antony's Key Resort* (☎445 1003, fax 445 1140), where the cabins are set among the trees on the hillside above the water and on a small cay offshore; bookings are restricted to all-inclusive dive packages, starting at US$600. For **eating**, *Rick's American Café*, on the hillside above the main road, is a popular bar and restaurant, open daily for dinner and for Sunday brunch.

West End

Curving round a shallow bay at the southwest corner of the island, 14km from Coxen Hole, **WEST END** makes the most of a glorious setting. Though its calm waters and soft, white beaches are drawing a steady flow of foreigners and mainlanders alike, the village has retained its laid-back charm and the gathering pace of tourist development seems to have done little to dent the friendliness of the villagers.

The paved road from Coxen Hole finishes at the northern end of the settlement, by **Half Moon Bay**, one of the best **beaches** in the village. A sandy track runs down along the water's edge, ending in a small bridge at the far end of the village, beyond which is another lovely beach. The Coconut Tree store, just by the end of the paved road, has the best selection of groceries; 50m beyond, Librería Casi Todo is both a book exchange and a **travel agency**, where you can book or change flights. The little stall under the trees just beyond **rents bicycles**, motorbikes, inflatable boats, snorkelling gear and anything else needed for a good time in the water, while Joanna's Gift Shop, towards the far end of the village, has handicrafts and swimwear for sale. The *Online Café* (closed Sun), about ten minutes' walk along the road to Coxen Hole, can send and receive **faxes** and **email** and has a small book exchange.

ACCOMMODATION

The range of **accommodation** in West End has widened considerably in recent years, with many more places catering for the budget market. During low season (May–Nov) it's worth negotiating for a discount, particularly for longer stays. Accommodation is listed in the order you come to it entering the village from the main road.

Coconut Tree Cabins, on the paved road at the entrance to the village (☎445 1648). Comfortable, spacious cabins all with covered porches, fridges and hot water. ⑥.

Chilie's, about 100m to the right at the end of the paved road (no phone). A new, English-owned place with dorm beds and private rooms in a two-storey house, with a kitchen at the back for guests' use. There's also camping space in the garden. ②.

Dolphin Resort, about 100m past *Valerie's* (no phone). Small but clean rooms in a new brick building; all have a/c, private bath and hot water. ④.

Half Moon Bay Cabins, at the northern edge of Half Moon Bay, across from the village; follow the track for about 300m past *Chilie's* (☎445 1075). One of the original upmarket places to stay, with a lively restaurant attached. Secluded cabins are scattered around the wooded grounds, close to the water's edge, and all have fan or a/c. ⑥.

Jimmy's Lodge, at the far end of the village, 10min walk from the paved road (no phone). Extremely basic backpackers' institution, with mattresses on the floor in a large dorm and a hose shower; hammocks can also be slung, if there's space. Fantastic beach location. ①.

Keifito's Beach Plantation, about 10min walk along the beach past *Jimmy's* (fax 445 1648). Quiet and secluded, set on the hillside just above the shoreline. There is a small dock to swim off, and the restaurant serves reasonably priced meals.

Valerie's, about 100m to the left down the dirt track, behind Tyll's Dive Shop (no phone). Good budget option, with a relaxed atmosphere. Clean dorm beds or double rooms and use of the kitchen. ①–③.

Trish's Wish, about 150m past the *Dolphin Resort*, up the hill – follow the signed turn on the left (☎445 1205). A breezy wooden house, with apartments for two to five people. ④–⑤.

Pinochio's, turn left at the signed turn for *Stanley's Island* restaurant, 150m past the *Dolphin Resort* (fax only 445 1841). This new wooden building, set on the hillside 100m above the village, has clean and airy rooms with bath and hot water. The owners are very friendly and there's a good restaurant downstairs. ④.

DIVING AND WATER SPORTS

Diving courses for all levels are on offer, at slightly higher prices than on Utila. An open-water PADI course costs around US$200, with fun dives for around US$30. Optional dive insurance, at US$2 per day, is also available; see p.454 for more on safety precautions. A couple of the more popular shops, with good safety records, are Tyll's Dive, about 100m down from the end of the paved road, and West End Divers, virtually next door. Native Sons, on the beach at the end of the village, is a newer, locally owned school, while Sueño del Mar, 50m beyond West End Divers, rents underwater filming equipment.

The reef just offshore presents some superb **snorkelling** spots, the best being at the mouth of Half Moon Bay and just offshore from *Jimmy's Lodge*. You can rent **sea kayaks** from Sea Blades, at the Librería Casi Todo (half-day US$12, full-day US$20). Belvedere's, on the waterfront about 30m south of Librería Casi Todo, runs hour-long glass-bottomed boat tours for US$8 per person, while Flame & Smoke, on the beach past *Jimmy's Lodge*, charters boats for **fishing trips**.

EATING AND DRINKING

There is a more than adequate range of **places to eat** in West End, with fish featuring heavily on many menus, although pasta and pizza are increasingly popular. Eating here is not particularly cheap, with main courses starting at US$5–6. Drinking can also drain your pocket fast in West End – best seek out the half-price **happy hours** at many of the restaurants and bars. The new *Blue Mango Bar*, on the seafront about 200m down from Librería Casi Todo, has a nightly happy hour from 5pm to 7pm. *Foster's Restaurant/Bar*, built over the sea opposite Joanna's Gift Shop, is the scene for a party every Thursday night, and at other times a good place for a quiet drink with superb views over the ocean. The *Cool Lizard*, on the beach past *Jimmy's*, is also perfect for watching the sunset. On Saturdays, the *Online Café* organizes a weekly "Utila Party Boat", which returns on Sundays.

Cannibal Café, in front of the *Dolphin Resort*. One of the cheapest places to eat, serving mostly snacks. The baleadas and quesadillas are good value and filling.

Pinocchio's, below the hotel of the same name. Serves an eclectic range of meat, fish and pasta dishes at reasonable prices; the risotto is delicious. Closed Wed.

Rudy's Coffee Stop, on the road just before Joanna's Gift Shop. Great breakfasts of banana pancakes, omelettes, fresh coffee and juices. Closed Sun.

Salt and Pepper, above the Coconut Tree Store. A wide-ranging gourmet menu featuring French, Italian, Indian and Mexican cuisine, plus daily specials. US$10 and upwards for a meal with wine, but worth every penny.

Seaview Restaurant, about halfway along the main drag. A popular joint, with a nicely laid-out eating area. The large, thin-crust pizzas with a range of toppings are good value, through service can be slow.

Stanley's Island Restaurant, up the hill behind *Pinocchio's*. A locally owned restaurant serving good food at reasonable prices. The *tapado* (fish stew) and coconut bread are delicious.

West Bay

About 4km west of West End, towards the tip of Roatán, is **West Bay**, a stunning, white sand beach, fringed by coconut palms. Its water is crystal clear, and there's great snorkelling at the southern end of the beach, where the reef meets the shore. Both beach and water come under the protection of the Sandy Bay and West End Marine Reserve, though this hasn't been able to prevent a rash of cabañas and restaurants being built in the vicinity over recent years. Most are low-key, however, only slightly detracting from the tranquillity of the place, and, provided you avoid the sandflies by sunbathing on the jetties, you'll be as near to paradise as you can get.

West Bay beach is a pleasant 45-minute walk from West End, along the sand and over a few rock outcrops; or you can take small launches that leave regularly from *Foster's Restaurant*, with the last one returning at around 9pm. A dirt road, accessible to cars, has also been opened up; take the first right turning off the road to Coxen Hole.

At West Bay itself, the *Bite on the Beach* (Wed–Sun only) and *Neptuno's Seafood Grill* serve good, seafood **meals** for around US$8 a main course. About halfway along the beach, the Bananarama Dive School has pleasant **cabins** for rent (no phone; ⑤), while those at *Cabaña Roatana* are equipped with hot water and microwave ovens (☎445 1271; ⑥–⑦).

Eastern Roatán

From Coxen Hole, the paved road runs east along the shore, offering occasional glimpses of wrecked ships, and passing the small, secluded cove of **Brick Bay**. After about 10km it reaches **FRENCH HARBOUR**, a busy port and fish-packing town, which is more attractive than Coxen Hole and offers accommodation right in the centre of town. The *Harbour View Hotel*, about ten minutes' walk down from the bus stop, has reasonable rooms with bath and hot water (☎455 5390; ④). A further five minutes down the road, the more upmarket *Buccaneer Hotel* has a pool, a large wooden deck overlooking the water and a disco at the weekends (☎455 5032; ⑦). The best place to eat is *Gio's*, on the harbourfront close to the *Harbour View*, where you can feast on excellent, if pricey, seafood and soups.

From French Harbour the road cuts inland, running along a central ridge with superb views of both the north and south coasts. Much of the original forest cover here has gone, giving way to pasture, farmland and secondary growth. About 14km past French Harbour the road heads south to **OAK RIDGE**, a quaint fishing port with wooden houses built up the hillsides. There are some lovely unspoilt beaches to the east of town, accessible by launches from the main dock. The best place to stay is the *Hotel San José*, on a small cay just offshore from the dock (☎435 2328; ④). Rather pricey meals are served up at the terrace restaurant in the nearby *Reef House Resort*, but the sea views are fabulous. Launches run to the cay on demand (US$0.50).

About 5km from Oak Ridge on the northern coast of the island is the village of **PUNTA GORDA**, the oldest Garífuna community in Honduras and the oldest settlement on Roatán. The best time to visit is for the anniversary of the founding of the settlement (April 6–12), when Garífuna from all over the country attend the celebrations. If you want to **stay**, *Ben's Dive Resort* on the waterfront (☎445 1916; ⑤) has comfortable cabins, while *Los Cincos Hermanos* (no phone) in the centre has basic, clean rooms (①). Nearby, *Hello Hello* serves the standard fish or rice, beans and meat at good prices, while the *Paradise Bar* at the entrance to the village is the place to come for Sunday lunch barbecues.

From the end of the paved road at Punta Gorda, a dirt track, accessible to vehicles, continues east along the island, passing the turn-off for the secluded **Paya Beach** after around 1.5km. A further 5km or so along here is **Camp Bay Beach**, an unspoilt stretch of white sand. The road ends at the village of **PORT ROYAL**, on the southern edge of the island, where the remains of a fort built by the English can be seen on a cay offshore. The village lies in the **Port Royal Park and Wildlife Reserve**, the largest refuge on the island, set up in 1978 in an attempt to protect endangered species such as the yellow-naped parrot, as well as the watershed for eastern Roatán.

The eastern tip of Roatán is made up of mangrove swamps, with a small island, **Morat**, just offshore. Beyond is **Barbareta**, another cay, and one that has retained much of its virgin forest cover. The *Barbareta Beach Resort* runs inclusive packages from US$230 (minimum three nights), with diving, windsurfing and fishing tours available (☎445 1255). The reef around Barbareta and the nearby **Pigeon Cays** offers good snorkelling; launches can be hired to reach these islands from Oak Ridge, for around US$10 for a return trip.

Guanaja

The easternmost Bay Island, declared a nature reserve in 1961, **Guanaja** is the most beautiful, undeveloped and expensive of the islands, still heavily forested with hardwoods and the Caribbean pines that led Columbus, landing here on his fourth voyage in 1502, to name it Isla de Pinos. More than 50km long, and about 6km wide, Guanaja actually consists of two main islands, separated by a narrow canal, with the main settlement – **Bonacca** or Guanaja Town – on a small cay a few hundred metres offshore from the larger island. It's here that you'll find the island's shops and main residential area, as well as the bulk of the reasonably priced accommodation. All the houses in Bonacca are built on stilts above the water – a style that harks back to early settlement by Cayman islanders – and the only way to get around is by water taxi. Other, smaller settlements are **Mangrove Bight**, on the west coast of the main island, and **Savannah Bight**, on the east coast.

Arrival and information

Guanaja's **airstrip** is on the main island, by the canal; aside from a couple of dirt tracks there are no roads, the main form of transport being small **launches**. All flights are met by launches bound for the main dock in Bonacca. From here there are scheduled services to Savannah Bight at 7am and 11am; to get to Mangrove Bight, you can hitch a ride on a private boat for a nominal fee. The Capitania de Puerto on the main pier has **information** on unscheduled boat departures for the other islands and points on the Honduran mainland.

Bonacca itself is built on wooden causeways over the canals, many of which have now been filled in. The main causeway, running for about 500m east–west along the cay, with a maze of small passages branching off it, is where you'll find all the shops, **banks** and businesses. You can change dollars and travellers' cheques at Banco Atlántida (left from the dock) and Bancahsa (right from the dock); Bancahsa also gives cash advances on Visa.

Accommodation

Most of the hotels on Guanaja are luxury all-inclusive **dive resorts**, offering weekly packages that need to be booked in advance. Bonacca has a small number of more reasonably priced **hotels**, and there's a private house, just before the *Hotel Alexander*, which rents out a couple of rooms for under US$10 per person.

BONACCA

Casa Sobre el Mar, on Pond Cay, just south of Bonacca (☎453 4269). Three bright and breezy rooms, with all meals included in the price of US$85 per person. ⑨.

Hotel Alexander, at the eastern end of the main causeway, right from the dock (☎453 4326). The best location in Bonacca; large, comfortable rooms with private bath and balconies overlooking the water. ⑤.

Hotel Miller, midway along the main causeway (☎453 4327). The building is slightly run-down, but the rooms are OK. Hot water is available, and, for slightly more, a/c. ③.

Hotel Rosario, opposite the *Hotel Miller* (☎453 4240). Modern building, with comfortable rooms, all with private bath, a/c and TV. ⑤.

LARGE ISLAND

Unless otherwise stated, all prices are per person for a week-long package.

Bahía Resort, on the south side of the island across from Bonacca (☎453 4212). One of the smaller resorts, with a pool and accommodation in comfortable bungalows. Packages from US$800.

Bayman Bay Club, on the north side of the island (☎453 4179). Well-furnished cabins set on a wooded hillside above the beach. Packages including dives, all meals and other facilities are US$700–750.

Hillton Hotel, by the airstrip (☎453 4299). Clean rooms all have private bath and TV. This is the cheapest option on the main island, though not as scenically located as some of the resorts. ⑤.

The Island House Resort, on the north side of the island (☎453 4196). A very pleasant resort, close to expanses of beautiful beach. Packages from US$590.

Posada del Sol, on the south side of the island (☎453 4186). Cabins are scattered across sixty acres of ground and amenities include a pool, tennis court, sea kayaks and snorkelling equipment. Packages from US$340 for three nights.

SMALL ISLAND

West Peak Inn, towards the western tip of the small island (fax 453 4219). Relaxed place with comfortable cabins close to beautiful, deserted beaches and a trail up to the 94m West Peak. Price includes all meals. ⑥.

Around the island

The larger island boasts the highest point of the entire chain, **Michael's Peak** (412m), covered with Caribbean pine forest and hardwoods. A superb trail leads from

Mangrove Bight up the peak and down to Sandy Bay, affording stunning views of the island and surrounding reef; fit walkers can do the trail in a day, although it is possible to camp at the summit, provided you bring all food and water with you.

Launches can be hired privately from local fishermen to go **snorkelling** on the reef, though you'll need to bring your own equipment. On the main island, **Michael's Rock**, west of *Island House*, is a small rocky headland surrounded by stretches of beautiful white beach, with good snorkelling close to the shore. **Soldado Beach**, between the canal and the *Bayman Bay Resort*, is the supposed site of Columbus's landing; an unfinished memorial marks the spot. Off the south edge of the island lies the wreck of the *Jado Trader*, 28m below the surface, surrounded by coral.

Diving is excellent all around Guanaja, but can quite difficult to arrange if you're not signed up to a resort package. Dive Freedom, in the *Coral Café* building in Bonacca, can rent equipment for dives and runs courses for PDIC certification, a newer, North American rival to PADI.

Eating and drinking

There are several restaurants in Bonacca, most of which stay open until around 9pm and close on Sundays. Nowhere is particularly cheap, though, since most supplies have to be shipped in, and any truly gourmet eating experiences are likely to be restricted to the **package resorts** on the large island.

In Bonacca, *Bonacca's Garden*, about halfway along the main causeway, and the restaurant at the *Hotel Alexander* both serve reasonably priced local dishes. Decent pizza and pasta can be had at the *Up and Down Restaurant*, close to *Bonacca's Garden*, while the *Coral Café* is a good place for snacks and drinks.

Cayos Cochinos

Lying 17km offshore from the mainland, the **Cayos Cochinos (Hog Islands)** comprise two, thickly wooded main islands – **Cochino Grande** and **Cochino Pequeño** – and thirteen cays, all of them privately owned. The small amount of effort it takes to get here is well worth it for a few days' utter tranquillity. Fringed by a reef, the whole area has been designated a marine reserve, with anchoring on the reef and commercial fishing both strictly prohibited. The US Smithsonian Institute, which manages the reserve, has a research station on Cochino Pequeño. The hills are studded with hardwood forests, palms and cactus, and Cochino Grande has a number of trails across its interior, and a small peak rising to 145m.

Organized **accommodation** on the islands is limited to the *Plantation Beach Resort* on Cochino Grande (☎442 0974), which does weekly dive packages for around US$800, including all meals and three dives a day; they collect guests by launch from the Muralla de Cabotaje in La Ceiba (Saturday; US$30 one-way). It can be more rewarding, however, to stay in the Garífuna fishing village of **CHACHAUATE** on Lower Monitor Cay, south of Cochino Grande. Here, the villagers have allocated a hut for visitors to sling their hammocks for a minimal charge, and will cook meals for you. Basic groceries are available in the village, though you should bring water and your main food supplies with you from the mainland.

Unless you're staying at the *Plantation Beach*, the only way to the Cayos is by launch from the village of **Nueva Armenia**, 40km east of La Ceiba; these leave in the early mornings unless the weather's bad. One bus a day runs to Nueva Armenia (2hr) from La Ceiba; more frequent buses to Trujillo, Tocoa and Olanchito all pass through Jutiapa, 8km inland from Nueva Armenia, from where you can hitch or walk. There is a basic hotel (①) in Nueva Armenia and a few simple eating places.

travel details

Buses

Copán to: El Florido (every 30min; 30min); La Entrada (every 45min; 1hr 30min); San Pedro Sula (four daily, all early morning; 2hr).

La Ceiba to: Nueva Armenia (11am; 2hr); San Pedro Sula (3 daily; 3hr).

La Entrada to: San Pedro Sula (every 30min, 1hr 30 min; three direct services a day; 1hr).

San Pedro Sula to: Copán (four daily until 7am; 3hr); La Ceiba (Catisa-Tupsa, 12 daily; 3hr).

Flights

La Ceiba to: Roatán (Isleña, 8 daily Mon–Sat; Sosa, 4 daily; Rollins Air, 7 daily; Caribbean Air, 4 daily); Utila (Isleña, 2 daily Mon–Sat; Rollins, 2 daily Mon–Sat; Sosa, 3 daily Mon–Sat); Guanaja (Isleña, 2 daily Mon–Sat, 1 on Sun; Sosa, 1 daily Mon–Sat; Caribbean, 1 daily).

San Pedro to: La Ceiba (Isleña, 2 daily; Caribbean Air, 2 daily); Roatán (Isleña, 2 daily).

Boats

MV Tropical runs between La Ceiba and Roatán (2hr) and Utila (1hr 30min) on weekdays, Saturdays and Sundays (Roatán only); fares to both are around US$10 one-way.

La Ceiba to: Roatán Mon 5am and 3.30pm, Tues–Fri 3.30pm, Sat 11am, Sun 7am.

Roatán to: La Ceiba Mon 7.30am, Tues–Fri 7am, Sat 7am and 2pm, Sun 3.30pm.

La Ceiba to: Utila Mon–Fri 10am.

Utila to: La Ceiba Mon 11.30am, Tues–Fri 11.30pm.

The *MV Starfish* cargo supply boat runs between La Ceiba and Utila; passages can be bought at the dock.

La Ceiba to: Utila Tues 11am.

Utila to: La Ceiba Mon 5am.

CHAPTER ELEVEN

EL SALVADOR

n western El Salvador you'll find beautiful mountain scenery, relaxing towns and Maya ruins, and, on the Pacific coast, some of the cleanest and most remote beaches of the region. Easily accessed from Guatemala through several border crossings, this area offers a perfect introduction to El Salvador for travellers.

The **Pacific coast** is a sweep of remote, sandy, tropical beaches backed by fertile coastal lowlands. Towns and villages all along the coast are linked by the **Carretera Littoral**, the main paved highway. This is a beautifully scenic journey with the slopes of the Cordillera Apaneca rising to the north and rolling green pasture lands to the south. Public transport runs regularly to many places, but private transport is the best way to reach some of the more remote and beautiful beaches. While there are clusters of **tourist facilities** here and there, don't expect the facilities of international resorts. Instead, the beauty of this part of the country lies in relaxing on clean beaches or spending time in the relatively untouched fishing villages of the coast.

Travelling east along the coast from the Guatemalan border, you'll come to some of the nicer beaches in the country at **Los Cóbanos** and **Barra de Santiago**. To really get off the beaten track, though, you can visit the remote forest reserve of **El Bosque Impossible**, while the small city of **Sonsonate** is the first major stop with accommodation, banks and restaurants. From Sonsonate, buses leave regularly for the capital San Salvador and for Ahuachapán, Santa Ana and other points north.

More muted than in the north, the landscapes of **western El Salvador** also offer a perfect introduction to the country. Soft mountain chains edge back from the valleys, which are dominated by the dull, green expanses of the coffee plantations that bring the area its wealth. Spared from the most violent hardships of the 1980s conflict, the friendly towns and cities here are more amenable to visitors than in many places, and a relatively well-developed tourist infrastructure makes travelling fairly easy.

The joy of this part of the country consists largely of soaking up the atmosphere. The mountain towns of **Apaneca** and **Juayúa** and the tranquil city of **Ahuachapán** are perfect for a few days spent relaxing, perhaps taking a gentle hike through the rolling countryside; Ahuachapán in particular is a great little place to acclimatize yourself to El Salvador. The large city of **Santa Ana**, lying to the northeast, is a mellow contrast to the capital, with the nearby peaks of **Cerro Verde**, **Volcán Santa Ana** and **Volcán Izalco**, and the pre-Columbian site of **Tazumal**, short hops away. Only slightly further afield are the pre-eminent archeological sites in El Salvador, **San Andrés** and **Joya de Cerén**. Near the northern border crossing with Guatemala at Anguiatú, the accommodating small town of **Metapán** gives access to the remote **Bosque Montecristo**, set amid serene, remote mountain peaks.

East from Guatemala

The Pacific Coast border crossing between Guatemala and El Salvador is at **La Hachadura**, a busy crossing used by the international buses heading from Talismán, on the Mexican/Guatemalan border, to San Salvador. There is a small hospedaje on the Guatemalan side and the crossing is regularly served by buses from Escuintla and

Guatemala City. There is no tax for entry to El Salvador; neither are there any banks at this crossing, but the hordes of **moneychangers** will be happy to service your every need. You should change all Guatemalan quetzales here as it gets increasingly difficult to do so the further away you are from the border. The closest accommodation to the border on the El Salvador side is in the city of Sonsonate, 46km and a two-hour bus journey away, so it's wise to try and cross by early afternoon at the latest.

Cara Sucia and El Bosque Impossible

The first point of any interest, once over the border, is **CARA SUCIA**, a small village some 10km from La Hachadura on the Carretera Littoral. Dusty and somewhat bedraggled as it stretches along the highway, the village is chiefly important for its vicinity to the **archeological site** of Cara Sucia and one of El Salvador's greatest hidden glories, the forest reserve of **Bosque Impossible**.

The Cara Sucia **archeological site**, lying 1km or so south of the highway, was in its heyday a substantial **Maya settlement** made wealthy by trade in salt. However, for those who have come straight from the glories of Guatemala, be prepared – as so often in El Salvador – for some disappointment. The excitement here lies not in gasping in awe over a laboriously uncovered historical gem, but rather in engaging in a little detective work as you attempt to gain some idea of what the place might have looked like from what little has been rescued. Initial excavations at Cara Sucia uncovered a number of structures including two ball courts, but today, all work has been halted in the ever hopeful anticipation of new funds arriving. However, it makes for a very peaceful place for a picnic, and the walk to the site is very relaxing. There is no public **transport** to the site; from the crossroads 50m before the bridge at the western end of the village, take the road leading right, opposite *Comedor Nohemy*, and walk for about twenty minutes until you reach the Cooperativa Cara Sucia buildings on the right. Ask the guard to let you through and follow the track round the buildings, taking the right-hand fork to the ruins.

El Bosque Impossible
The road leading left at the crossroads in Cara Sucia village is a point of access to one of El Salvador's greatest hidden glories, the forest reserve of **El Bosque Impossible**. Supposedly named because of the difficulty of traversing the mountain tracks to get into it, the reserve covers 31 square kilometres and rises through three climatic zones across the mountain range of the Cordillera de Apaneca. Almost unique in the deforested, ecological disaster zone that is El Salvador today, it is one of the last remaining examples of the tropical forest that covered this part of Mesoamerica in pre-Columbian times. It is also the source of eight rivers, some of which play an important role in sustaining the mangrove swamps along the coast. The reserve contains over four hundred species of tree and 1600 species of plant, some of which are unique to the area. Birdwatchers may glimpse some of the more than two hundred species including emerald toucans, trogons, hummingbirds and eagles, while the park provides a secure habitat for a range of animals, including anteaters, white-tailed deer, ocelots and tigrillos.

As yet, there is no formal provision for staying in El Impossible and getting there without a private vehicle is rather time-consuming. The reserve is managed by a non-governmental organization, SalvaNatura (77a Av Nte and 7a C Pte, Col. Escalón, San Salvador; ☎263 1111), which is doing some sterling work in the areas of preservation and the creation of an ecotourist infrastructure in the face of considerable difficulties, most notably financial. You need to get permission from them to enter the sections of El Impossible that are open to visitors and, if you're not actually going to visit San Salvador in person, be prepared for some lengthy discussions over the phone. As of mid-1998, the organization was in the process of setting up loans to enable local villages to open visitor facilities, including a guest house and restaurants; check with them on the progress made in this area.

The main **access** to the reserve is through the village of **San Francisco Menéndez**, the turning for which is on the highway 4km west of Cara Sucia. Foreign visitors have to pay a fee of US$6 to enter El Impossible which, if you manage to negotiate permission over the phone, can be paid to the small SalvaNatura office in the village. Some of the **buses** running from the border to Sonsonate go via San Francisco.

The coast to Acajutla

Some 17km or so southeast of Cara Sucia is one of El Salvador's most remote and cleanest beaches, **Playa Barra de Santiago**. Long, wide and usually empty, it lies beside a small mangrove estuary, fringed on one side with palm trees and lapped on the other by the Pacific waves. A rough road, 10km past Cara Sucia, leads the 7km from the highway to the estuary, from where you should bargain with a fishing boat to take you across to the fishing village of Barra de Santiago, where the beach starts. One bus a day leaves in the morning for the city of Sonsonate; otherwise your only hope is to wait for one of the sporadic pickups.

Fifteen kilometres further east along the highway and another dirt road turning to the left, at the hamlet of Metalío, gives access to **Playa de Metalío**, a couple of kilometres away. Another palm-fringed expanse of sand – in this case more grey than golden – the beach is deserted during the week but, because of its greater accessibility, busy at weekends. Its beauty is somewhat marred by the refuse washed up from the port of Acajutla, just east down the coast.

Historically important for being the site of Pedro de Alvarado's first encounter with the Pipils in 1524, **ACAJUTLA** today is a hot, seedy and distinctly edgy place. The major town on this section of the coast, it lies 4km from the Carretera Littoral at the end of a spur road. Though El Salvadoreans flock here at weekends, it has little to recommend it to tourists and staying in Sonsonate is a far better option. If you do decide to come here, buses run from Sonsonate to Acajutla every half-hour, stopping to pick up passengers from coastal highway buses at the junction.

Sonsonate and south

The hub of the western coastal region of El Salvador is the small, flat and invariably hot city of **SONSONATE**. Though lying 18km or so inland, it is a place you will inevitably have to pass through. Set in rich tobacco and cattle-ranching country, Sonsonate is a bustling, commercial place with little of tourist interest. However, it does offer the first decent accommodation on the way to or from the border, and if you're in El Salvador at the end of January, it's worth making an effort to be here for the annual festival of **Verbena de Sonsonate**, when a host of music and drama performances are laid on. Even more colourful are the Easter celebrations during Holy Week, **Semana Santa**, when crowds flock to join the street processions and intricate pictures are drawn in coloured sawdust on the pavements. Sonsonate is also the **transport hub** for connections to the western beaches, the mountain town of Apeneca and the city of Santa Ana (see p.470).

Buses arrive at the main terminal, on C 15 de Septiembre, seven blocks east of the centre, and fifteen minutes' walk from the parque central. Of the limited **accommodation** in the centre, the *Hotel Orbe* on Av Fray Mucci Sur and 4a C Ote, two blocks east of the parque, has reasonably clean rooms with private bath (☎451 1416; ②). On the outskirts of town, on the road to San Salvador, is the much nicer *Hotel Agape* (☎451 1456; ④), set in beautiful gardens with comfortably furnished rooms; somewhat bizarrely the landscaped grounds also encompass an old people's home, which seems to be under the same ownership. Across the road from the *Agape* is the cheaper but acceptable *Hotel Fontana* (☎451 2631; ②). There are a number of **restaurants** along this road and, in the centre, a row of comedores overlooks the river by the rather attractive white bridge, on 4a Av Nte. There are **banks** in the centre, but since they are extremely reluctant to accept foreign credit cards, make sure you have some cash dollars to change.

Los Cóbanos and Los Remedios

Los Cóbanos, 25km due south of Sonsonate, is a favourite beach for Salvadorean holiday makers and consequently somewhat crowded at the weekends. Although rather rocky, this pretty, gently curved beach makes a nice contrast to the lengthy, broad expanses of sand that one normally associates with the Pacific coast; here the sea is gentle and the swimming good. There are a couple of places with **cabañas** for rent, of which *Solimar* (②) is the nicest, although it's closed during the week. Set slightly back from the seafront, the *Mar y Plata* (②) is slightly run-down, though if you are here midweek you'll have it virtually to yourself. A number of small shacks serve fresh fish and other **meals**. If you walk round the headland and over the rocks at the west end of the small bay, you'll come to the quieter beach of **Los Remedios**. **Buses** leave Sonsonate every hour for Los Cóbanos, with the last heading back to the city at 5pm.

Moving on from Sonsonate, **buses** run regularly for San Salvador, or north across the Cordillera de Apaneca to the cities of Ahuachapán and Santa Ana. The latter is the best base for visiting the Maya sites of Tazumal, San Andrés and Joya de Cerén.

The Cordillera de Apaneca to Ahuachapán

Stretching east for more than 70km from the Guatemalan border, the **Cordillera Apaneca-Ilamatepec** is an unbelievably green range of rolling mountains, patchworked coffee plantations and stands of pine forests, set under a clear, golden light. **NAHUIZALCO**, perched on the southern edge of the range, about 10km north of Sonsonate, is a predominantly Maya village, although few people wear traditional dress any longer. The town thrives on the manufacture of wicker, with workshops lining the main street. Some of the pieces, such as baskets, are small enough to take home; gentle bargaining is acceptable.

Beyond Nahuizalco, the air cools and freshens as the road winds its way up into the mountains proper; there are superb vistas down to Sonsonate and across the plains to the coast. Fourteen kilometres from Sonsonate is **SALCOATITÁN**, a sleepy little mountain village with some beautiful walks in the surrounding area. You can **stay** at the small clean *Hotel Oasis* (②) and there are a couple of simple places to eat. The village is also the nearest place to spend the night to the neighbouring town of **JUAYÚA** (pronounced "wai-u-a"), 2km further on down a spur road. Here the magnificent **Templo de Señor de Juayúa**, built in 1955 in colonial style, and with stained-glass windows depicting the saints, houses the **Black Christ of Juayúa**, carved by Quiro Cataño, sculptor of the Black Christ of Esquipulas in Guatemala (see p.387). The town is consequently something of a pilgrimage site, particularly during the January festival, which makes it all the more surprising that there is no accommodation.

Apaneca and the Laguna Verde

A short leg further along the road from Salcoatitán is another quiet, charming mountain town, **APANECA**, founded by Pedro de Alvarado in the mid-sixteenth century. Popular with weekend visitors, and home to one of the best-known restaurants in the country, drawing wealthy San Salvadoreans and foreign residents alike, the town nonetheless retains an air of friendly tranquillity. During the week, you're likely to have the place – and the surrounding mountain scenery – to yourself. The town is easily accessible by **bus** from both Sonsonate (1hr 30min) and Ahuachapán (1hr), so you can come for the day or just for a meal. The only **accommodation** is the *Cabañas de Apaneca,* which has six comfortable wood cabins set in lush gardens overlooking the mountain slopes, and a good on-site restaurant (☎450 5106; ⑥; reserve restaurant at weekends and holidays). The best place to **eat**, however, is *La Cocina de mi Abuela* (☎450 5203 ext 301; Sat & Sun only 11.30am–5pm), housed in a beautifully decorated colonial-era house. The nicest tables are on the covered veranda at the back, with scenic views. Fresh lake fish will set you back about US$8, and you can also have lasagne, meat and chicken. Otherwise, eating options in town are limited to the row of friendly little comedores opposite the church.

Laguna Verde

There is little to do in Apaneca itself, but it's an enjoyable, not too strenuous walk through woods and fincas to the **Laguna Verde**, a small crater lake 4km to the north-east of town. Fringed by reeds and surrounded by mist-clad pine slopes, the lake is a popular destination, and at the weekends you're likely to share the path with numerous families and walking groups.

From the highway on the edge of town, follow the dirt road to the right of the Jardín de Flores garden centre, which winds up and round the mountain, passing several fincas and a couple of small hamlets, overlooked by the weekend retreats of wealthy San Salvadoreans. An enjoyable short cut is to walk up the dried-up stream bed through the woods, which links the bends of the road. This is quite a scramble, though, and it's easy to get lost – ask directions from anyone you meet. The hamlet just above the lake, reached after about ninety minutes, has sweeping views on clear days. The white city sheltering in the valley below is Ahuachapán, while to the north the peak of Cerro Artilleria on the Guatemalan border is visible. The grassy slopes around the lake make a good spot for a picnic and you can also swim here. Closer to town, to the north, the smaller, less impressive **Laguna Las Ninfas**, is an easy forest walk of about 45 minutes.

Ahuachapán and around

From Apaneca the road winds 10km down through the scrubby little town of Ataco to the city of **AHUACHAPÁN**. This area, and the lands further north, are some of the oldest inhabited regions of what is today El Salvador, due in large part to the extremely fertile soil. Artefacts found in the region date back to the first Maya around 1200 BC. Ahuachapán is also one of the oldest Spanish settlements in the country, achieving city status in 1862, and has generally been a place of quiet bourgeois comfort; two attacks by Guatemalan troops – in 1863 and 1864 – were both firmly repulsed. In the early twentieth century the British visitor Percy Martin noted: "The people as a whole seemed to me to be very well-to-do and evidences of refinement and solid comfort were to be met with on all sides . . . I was also impressed with the absence of the usual number of drinking shops, of which I counted scarcely more than six in the whole town. The town is a quiet, sleepy and eminently peaceful place of residence where one might dream away one's life contentedly enough."

Today the city's main industry is geothermal electricity generation, at one time supplying seventy percent of the country's grid; consequently there are usually a number of European and Japanese technicians stationed here.

To get **to Guatemala** from here, a reasonably good and very scenic road runs the 20km or so to the border just past **Las Chinamas**; local buses leave every fifteen minutes, taking about an hour. International buses from Santa Ana (see p.476) also pass through at about 5.30am. There is no ticket office: stand on 6a C Pte more or less opposite the *Hotel San José* to flag down the buses. On the Guatemalan side, buses run from Valle Nuevo to Guatemala City.

Heading northeast from Ahuachapán, the road winds down through the last spurs of the Cordillera to **Chalchuapa**, situated on a scenic broad plain, that contains the archeological site of Tazumal. It's an easy trip from either Ahuachapán or Santa Ana.

Arrival and accommodation

Buses arrive at the terminal on Av Commercial, 10a–12a C Pte, eight blocks from the parque central. **Antel** is at 3a C Pte and 2a Av Sur by the parque, while the **post office** is at 4a C Ote and 1a Av Nte. Banco Salvadoreño, on C Barrios at 1a Av Nte, changes cash dollars.

Of the **accommodation**, *La Casa Blanca*, on 2a Av Nte at C Barrios, a couple of blocks from the parque, is housed in a well-decorated colonial building; the large, clean rooms all have bath, hot water and TV. The restaurant, set around a small courtyard is slightly overpriced, but good for sitting with a coffee or a beer (☎443 1505, fax 443 1503; ④). For those on a budget, *Hotel San José* on 6a C Pte between Av Commercial and 2a Av Nte, close to the market (☎443 1820; ③), has clean, dark rooms. The nicest place to stay, however, is *Hotel El Parador*, 2km out of town on the road to the Guatemalan border post at Las Chinamas (☎443 0331; ③). All rooms have bath, hot water and TV; there's also a restaurant (10am–9pm) and a small pool open to the public. About 500m further down the road, *Auto Hotel Los Amigos* (②) has bare but adequate rooms.

The city and around

Apart from its quiet, gently fading streets, and the lively daily **market** around the bus station, the main things to see in Ahuachapán are its **churches**. From the parque central, the imposing white edifice of the **Iglesia Parrocia de Nuestra Señora de la Asuncíon** dominates the centre of the city and acts as the focus for the annual fiesta in the first week of February. The spare 1950s-built **El Calvario**, with a fine, carved crucifix, is on 6a C Pte at 2a Av Nte.

Immediately south of the city, the hump of **Cerro Ataco** is a not too difficult, safe climb of about two hours; follow 2a Av Sur out of town and pick any one of the small paths going up to the summit. The body of water visible to the northwest, off the road to Las Chinamas, is the **Lago de Llano**, a small, lily-fringed lake fished extensively by locals. It's a thirty-minute stroll along the main road from the centre of town to the lake, or you can catch bus #60 to the rather depressing village of Las Brisas, set 2km back from the highway and about 500m from the lake shore; buses leave regularly from the market.

Some 5km east of town near the hamlet of El Barro, the **ausoles**, or geysers, form the basis of the local geothermal industry. The plumes of steam forced up from the earth hang impressively over the lush green vegetation and bright red soil, and look particularly stunning in the golden light of the early morning sun.

Eating and drinking

Like most Salvadorean provincial cities, Ahuachapán is not overly blessed with **places to eat**. All restaurants tend to close relatively early, around 9pm, except for the *El Parador*, *El Paso* and *La Posada* restaurants, in a row on the Las Chinamas road. These serve meat and seafood standards, and occasionally have live music at the weekends. In the centre, *Tacos El Zocalo* and *Jardín de China*, next door to each other on 1a Av Sur at 1a C Ote and with the same owner, offer Ahuachapán's version of Mexican and Chinese cuisine respectively; both are relaxed places, good for a drink as well as a meal. *La Estancia*, housed in a rather rundown white building on 1a Av Sur at C Barrios, has well-prepared standards at average prices. *Pizza Attos* on Av Menendez Nte at 2a C Ote serves big pizzas, while *Las Mixtas,* 2a Av Sur by the parque, is more of a fast food place, with a range of simple meals and snacks. For sitting and people-watching, stands in the parque serve coffee and snacks.

Chalchuapa and Tazumal

In addition to its faded but beautiful colonial church, **CHALCHUAPA** contains the most important site in El Salvador, **Tazumal** (Tues–Sun 9am–5pm; US$3). The ruins are, by comparison with sites in Honduras and Guatemala, rather small, although they do have their own, impressive beauty. **Buses** drop off at a small plaza a few blocks from the centre of town, from where you walk uphill for about four blocks and turn left at the sign; there is nowhere to stay. An informative (Spanish-language) museum at the site explains the development of the civilizations and displays artefacts discovered during excavations.

What is now the town of Chalchuapa was the seat of power for a strong and thriving Maya population from 900 BC onwards. The inhabitants produced "Usulutan" ceramics, key items of commerce in the Maya zone, and also controlled the trade in obsidian from Guatemala. This early society was literate – evidence suggests that they had both calendar and writing systems – and highly stratified, and artefacts indicate strong links with Olmec civilizations in Mexico. The catastrophic eruption of Volcán Ilopango in around 250 AD, which covered an area of 10,000 square kilometres in ash, did not affect Chalchuapa as badly as the central zone of the country; the area was quickly repopulated and Tazumal gradually became the main settlement.

Of the nine structures identified here, only two remain in reasonable condition, with a third partially excavated; the rest have been destroyed by the expansion of the town. The central, largest structure – a stepped ceremonial platform, influenced by the style of Teotihuacán in Mexico – dates back to the Classic period (300–900 AD). Altogether, thirteen different building stages took place over 750 years, mostly during the Late Classic period (600–900 AD) and beneath the structure are traces of a platform dating back to between 100 and 200 AD. Originally a number of smaller temples were attached to the main structure. At the base of its northern edge, a number of tombs (Late Classic period) have yielded artefacts such as Tiquisate ware from Guatemala, jade jewellery, items for religious rites and a flask containing powdered iron oxide. This last was used for decorating a ceremonial stone *hacha* or head, used during ball games. The ball court itself lay on the southern edge of the structure.

Tazumal was abandoned around the end of the ninth century, at the collapse of the Classic Maya culture. Unusually for abandoned Maya cities, however, immigrating Pipils (a Nahuatl-speaking group, migrants from Mexico around the tenth century AD, who established themselves in west, northwest and central El Salvador) then occupied the site. Structure 2, to the west of the main platform, is a Pipil pyramid dating back to the Early Postclassic period (900–1200 AD). The new residents also constructed another ball court, to the northwest corner of the site. Tazumal was finally abandoned around 1200 AD, with the focus of settlement in the area moving towards the centre of the current town.

Past Chalchuapa, the road runs for a further 10km, flanked by serene, green coffee plantations, before intersecting with the Carretera Interamericana (CA-1). Head northwest here and you reach the Guatemalan border at San Cristóbal (see p.476). Continue straight on, however, for a couple of kilometres further if Santa Ana is your destination.

Santa Ana

Self-possessed **SANTA ANA**, the second most important city in El Salvador, lies in a superb location in the Cihautehuacán valley. Surrounded by green peaks, with the slope of Volcán Santa Ana rising to southwest, the gently decaying colonial streets exude a certain bourgeois complacency. Far mellower than San Salvador and regarding itself as above the unseemly commercial bustle of both the capital and San Vicente, El Salvador's third city, it makes a very good and relatively relaxed introduction to El Salvador's "big town" life. Pleasures here, though, are very low-key, consisting in the main of admiring the handful of grandiose buildings or simply walking the streets soaking up the atmosphere and observing provincial mores. Easy day-trips away are the natural attractions of **Lago Coatepeque**, the forest reserve of **Cerro Verde** and the summit of the volcanoes **Santa Ana** and **Izalco**, as well as the sites of **San Andrés** and **Joya de Cerén**.

Some history

The conquistadors passed through the valley soon after their arrival in El Salvador, discovering a Pipil town of about three thousand inhabitants more or less where Santa Ana now stands. A Spanish settlement, however, was not founded until July 1569, when the disgraced Bishop Bernardino de Villapando arrived in the valley, en route from Guatemala. Commenting on the beauty and fertility of the area, he ordered work to begin on a church dedicated to **Nuestra Señora de Santa Ana**, the saint of the day of his arrival. This, completed in 1576, was on the site where the cathedral now stands, but was destroyed in the early twentieth century to make way for the new building. The settlement grew relatively quickly; a census of 1770 records that the population was almost as large as San Salvador at the time, made up of 589 Spanish and ladino families, and 138 indigenous families.

Ranching and agriculture, particularly sugar cane and latterly coffee, contributed to the city's wealth, and by the end of the nineteenth century Santa Ana was secure in its position of second city in El Salvador, numbering around 30,000 inhabitants. Buildings that befitted the city's perceived status, such as the theatre and cathedral, sprang up. Today, with a population of over 200,000, the city retains an air of restrained, provincial calm, generally only ruptured during the **July fiesta**, when a host of events brings the streets to life.

Arrival and information

Buses arrive at the main terminal on 10a Av Sur between 13a and 15a C Pte, nine or so blocks southwest of the central district; city bus #51 runs to the centre from the terminal. If you decide to go on foot, it's an easy walk of around twenty minutes.

The **Antel** phone office is on C Libertad at 5a Av Sur, just down from the parque central and the **post office** on 7a C Pte between Av Independencia and 2a Av Sur. **Banks**, which cluster around 2a Av Nte behind the Alcaldía, include BanCo, Credisur and Banco Hipotecario; there are also a couple of casas de cambio around here, though the exchange rates are the same as at the banks. There's a small, mainly fruit and vegetable **market** around the bus terminal, and a larger general market on 8a Av Sur, 1a–3a C Pte; there is also a Multi Mart supermarket on the parque.

Accommodation

Santa Ana's second-city status is not reflected in its range of **accommodation**, although there are a couple of reasonably comfortable hotels, one convenient for the bus terminal and the other closer to the general market. This area, around 8a and 10a Av Sur, has a concentration of cheap and basic accommodation, but walking around here alone at night is not recommended. As in all Salvadorean cities, street lighting is extremely weak, and this is considered to be one of the rougher parts of the city. The hotels listed here, however, are acceptable to stay in.

Hotel la Libertad, 4a C Ote at 1a Av Nte (☎441 2358). Perhaps the nicest budget place in the city with clean, basic rooms, some with bath, and in a great location right by the cathedral; bring your own padlock for the doors. ②.

Hotel Livingston, 10a Av Sur between 7a and 9a C Pte (☎441 1801). Safe, but rooms are small and box-like with shared baths. ①.

Hotel Maya, 11a C Ote at 11a Av Sur (☎441 3612). Another good, secure place, with motel-style rooms, some with bath; a 20min walk from the centre. ④.

Hotel Sahara, 3a C Pte between 8a and 10a Av Sur (☎ & fax 447 8865). The city's best, with large comfortable rooms, good service, a bar and a restaurant that's open until 10pm. ⑤.

Hotel Roosevelt, 8a Av Sur between 5a and 7a C Pte (☎441 1702). Clean and safe, although the rooms, all with bath, are rather dark. ③.

International Hotel Inn, 25a C Pte and 10a Av Sur (☎440 0810, fax 440 0804). Convenient for the bus terminal and international buses. The rooms are rather small, but comfortable, all with TV and bath. Watch out for the cockroaches. ④.

The City

The heart of Santa Ana is the **Parque Libertad**, a neatly laid-out plaza with a small bandstand, where people gather to sit and chat in the early evenings and on into the night. The main intersection (Av Independencia Sur/Nte and C Libertad Pte/Ote) skirts its southwest corner. On the eastern edge of the parque is the **Cathedral**, an imposing neo-Gothic edifice completed in 1905. Inside, brick arches soar upwards, and chapels, some containing images dating back 400 years and originally contained in the first church on the site, line the walls to the altar. Inset into the walls are plaques from local worshippers giving thanks to various saints for miracles performed. On the northern edge of the plaza, the **Teatro Nacional**, completed in classic Renaissance style in 1910, was funded by taxes on local dignitaries. Once the proud home of the country's leading theatre companies, the building became a movie theatre before falling into disuse. The building harks back to a relative age of plenty at the end of the nineteenth century when the local coffee barons began to look to Europe for inspiration as to how to spend – and display – their wealth. From the same era is the **Alcaldía**, facing the cathedral on the western edge of the plaza. Another fine Renaissance-style piece of architecture and, at the time of building, the largest of its type, the facade is lavishly decorate in a style that travel-writer Paul Theroux noted as the "colonnaded opulence of a ducal palace".

Another important church, **El Calvario**, lies five blocks west of the parque on 10a Av Nte by Parque Menéndez. Completed in 1885, the building has since been destroyed and rebuilt twice; the letters D.O.M. on the Doric-style facade stand for "Dios Omnipotente y Misericordioso" (God, omnipotent and merciful). A magnificent carving of Christ on the cross stands behind the altar. South of the parque central, on 1a Av Sur, sits the **Parroquía de Nuestra Señora del Carmen**, built in 1822; in 1871 it was briefly occupied by peasant rebels from the area around the Volcán Santa Ana, who, spurred on by Guatemalan president Rafael Carrera's calls for the indigenous peoples to reclaim their land, ran riot through the city. After the uprising fizzled out, those who refused to give themselves up were hunted through the mountains and killed.

Eating and entertainment

Santa Ana has a reasonable number of moderately priced places to eat around the centre; nightlife, however, is not high on the city's list of priorities. Most restaurants tend to shut around 10pm, even at the weekends. The **cinema** on C Libertad at 3a Av Sur is virtually the only place to go after nightfall; it shows standard first-run Hollywood films, subtitled.

Adriana's, 25a C Pte, one block down from International Hotel Inn. Simple place, serving well-prepared steak, meat and seafood.

Café Cappuchino, Av Independencia at C Libertad Pte. A relaxed, leafy café just off the plaza serving coffees, good juices, beers and simple meals (daily until 8pm).

Café Centro, 2a Av Sur between 1a and 3a C Pte. Good for large breakfasts and cheap lunches.

Los Horcones, next to the cathedral on Parque Libertad. The best views in the city, with seats on the open terrace facing over the cathedral and the plaza. The usual standards are well prepared and the juices are great.

Kiko's Pizza, Av Independencia between 7a and 9a C Pte. Huge pizzas: the regular size is more than enough for two.

K'y'Jau, C Libertad between 4a and 6a Av Sur. Popular restaurant, serving large, authentic portions of Chinese food.

Los Patios, 21a C Pte between Av Independencia and 2a Av Sur. One of the smartest places in the city. Good meals in a nice courtyard setting at reasonable prices.

Around Santa Ana

West from Santa Ana, the three **volcanic peaks** of Cerro Verde, Santa Ana and Izalco together form a concise, living example of geological evolution. The oldest, **Cerro Verde**, is now a softened, densely vegetated mountain harbouring a national park. **Volcán Santa Ana**, nominally active, has cultivated lower slopes giving way to the bare lava of the summit, while juvenile **Volcán Izalco**, one of the youngest volcanoes in the world, is an almost perfectly bare lava cone.

Some 30km southeast from Santa Ana, just off the Carretera Interamericana, lie two of the most important archeological excavations in El Salvador, the Maya sites of **San Andrés** and **Joya de Cerén**. Around an hour's bus journey from Santa Ana, both can easily be visited in a day-trip from the city.

Cerro Verde

From the El Congo junction, 15km southeast of Santa Ana, a narrow road winds up through the coffee plantations, maize fields and pine woods of the ancient volcano Cerro Verde to the **Parque Nacional Cerro Verde**. Lying 2000m above sea-level on what was the crater of the long-extinct volcano, this is the most accessible reserve in the country; consequently you're unlikely to be able to walk the short trails in solitude, particularly at the weekends. The dense, mature forest shelters numerous species of **plants** including pinabetes and more than fifty types of orchids. Animal life tends, wisely, to stay out of sight; most likely to be spotted are **birds**, including the native xara – with a shimmering blue body and black head – hummingbirds and toucans. Armadillos, deer and cuzuco are also sheltered in the park.

Cerro Verde is relatively well managed with clear trails and lookouts over Volcán Santa Ana and, far below, Lago de Coatepeque. However, the large numbers of visitors it receives cannot help but make an impact and there are growing calls for the management to be taken out of the hands of the government tourist service and be given to a private organization. From the entrance gate (daily until 5.30pm; US$0.60) a short track leads up to the car park, to the left of which is a small orchid garden. The main trail, the **sendero natural**, leads from the top of the car park, looping clockwise through the reserve. Despite the weekend crowds this is an enjoyable walk of around 45 minutes through the green calm of the forest. Smaller trails branching through the trees are variously closed off for conservation work.

By the car park are basic **cabañas** (①), although you have to bring your own food and water; check with the wardens as to where you can pitch a **tent**. The *Hotel del la Montaña* which lies just by the car park, was originally a government-run luxury resort, built to take advantage of the superb views of the stark, black cone of Volcán Izalco. Closed for refurbishment in 1997, there are as yet no indications as to when it will reopen.

Unless you're driving, **getting to Cerro Verde** requires a bit of planning, so it's probably worth hiring a taxi for a few hours. Otherwise, three buses a day run directly from

Santa Ana to the car park, the last leaving the city mid-afternoon (1hr 30min). The last bus back leaves from the car park at 5pm, but only runs as far as El Congo. Buses to Sonsonate pass the turn-off to the park, 14km from the entrance, from where you have to walk.

Volcán Santa Ana

From a signed turn about ten minutes into the *sendero natural*, a path branches down to the left, leading eventually to the summit of the **Volcán Santa Ana**, known also as "Llamatepec" or "father hill". The highest volcanic peak in the country at 2365m, Santa Ana is still considered active, although it hasn't erupted since the early twentieth century. The process of reforestation is far less advanced here than in Cerro Verde, and the outlines of the volcano far starker. The walk to the summit takes two or three hours altogether.

Heading downhill from the signed turn for about twenty minutes brings you to the Finca San Blas; the path continues past here and begins to wind up though woodlands. After about 45 minutes, the gradient gets steeper and woodland cover gives way to rock and, towards the summit, lava. Three newer craters sit inside the older larger one, which takes about an hour to circumnavigate, and at the bottom of the newest crater is a small, green sulphur lake.

Volcán Izalco

Just below the Cerro Verde is a lookout west over the visually stunning **Volcán Izalco**. Beginning as a small hole in the ground in 1770, the volcano was formed when lava began to pour continuously over the next two centuries. Clearly visible from the ocean, the "lighthouse of the Pacific" was used by sailors to navigate by until the volcano finally stopped erupting in the 1960s. Looming up from the breast of a hill, the bleak, black volcanic cone of the 1900-metre Izalco is a startling and spectacular contrast to the green slopes on which you're standing. It is possible to walk up the cone, although locals advise against it – robberies are not unknown. A marked trail leads from the lookout down for about thirty minutes to a saddle between the two volcanoes. From here it takes at least an hour to climb the completely bare slopes of volcanic scree to the summit.

Lago Coatepeque

East from the El Congo junction, a winding branch road descends a couple of kilometres to the crater lake of **Lago Coatepeque**, shadowed by the three peaks. From the road there are great views of the stunning deep blue waters, fed by natural hot springs – perfect for photo opportunities. Inevitably the lake is a popular weekend destination, both for the rich and not so rich; much of the shore is bounded by private houses and access to public stretches of water is difficult. Follow the road round to the left when it reaches the lake and you come to *Hotel Torremolinos* (☎446 9437; ⑤), which charges a small fee for day use of a semi-public beach; rooms in the hotel are large and clean and you can also rent boats. Much nicer is the *Hotel de Lago* (☎446 9511;⑤) just up the road, with large, shady gardens and a restaurant overlooking the lake. **Buses** leave Santa Ana every thirty minutes for the lake, running past the two hotels.

San Andrés and Joya de Cerén

Set among rolling fertile agricultural land, **San Andrés** (daily 9am–4pm; US$3) is initially visually disappointing, being much smaller than sites in Guatemala or Honduras.

Nonetheless, it is one of the largest pre-Columbian sites in El Salvador, originally covering around three and a half square kilometres and supporting a population of about 12,000. The site reached its peak in the Late Classic era, between around 650 and 900 AD, establishing itself as the regional capital for the settlements in the Zapotitán valley.

Only sections of the ceremonial centre have been excavated and the remains of seven major structures are visible; sadly, these have been preserved with the help of concrete, spoiling their beauty somewhat and visibly driving home the message that large amounts of cash are a necessity in the preservation of sites like this. Ruins from what would have been the surrounding residential districts, still visible up to fifty years ago, have now also been lost to farming activity. However, you can wander freely around the site, and it is a popular spot for picnicking family groups at the weekends. The informative museum (labelling in Spanish only) has a small replica of what the site would have looked like in its prime.

Of what is on view, the **Acropolis** (or south plaza) forms the major part of the centre, a raised platform supporting a number of pyramids and annexes. Structure 1, on the south edge, was a temple and on its north face are the remains of an altar. Access to these pyramids was restricted to the governing elite, whose living quarters (Los Aposentos) lay along the north and west edges of the acropolis; the bases of two of these have been reconstructed. The pyramids along the east edge of the acropolis were possibly burial chambers. North of the acropolis lay another plaza, used for markets and communal events. The largest pyramid (Structure 5) lies on the eastern edge of this plaza, but has not yet been excavated. Following the collapse of the Maya empire from around 900 AD, San Andrés was not taken over by incoming Pipils, although the remains of a small farm dating from the Early Postclassic era (900–1200 AD) have been found close to Los Aposentos.

Any San Salvador-bound bus will drop you off on the highway at the marked access road to the site, from where it is about five minutes' walk to the entrance. If you wish to visit **Joya de Cerén** (daily 9am–4pm; US$3), continue on the bus for a further 5km to a junction on the left marked for the town of San Juan Opico. Those accustomed to the imposing, ceremonial edifices of the sites in Guatemala will initially be sorely disappointed, yet Joya de Cerén was designated a World Heritage Site in 1993; its importance comes from the wealth of detail provided about the daily lives of the Maya.

The site was originally a prosperous Maya village, supporting its population in a style far superior than that enjoyed by many Salvadoreans today. Around 600 AD, however, the village was destroyed in a volcanic eruption, and lava from this and subsequent eruptions buried the site under up to five metres of ash until its accidental discovery in 1976.

To date, eighteen structures have been discovered, of which ten have so far been excavated. These include houses, storage rooms and one believed to be used for religious rituals or communal events; not all are open to the public, however. Artefacts found at the site, including jars containing petrified beans, utensils and ceramics, and the discovery of gardens for growing a wide range of plants including maize, beans, agave and chilli peppers has helped to confirm a picture of this society as well organized and stable, relatively wealthy and with networks of trade links throughout the Central American isthmus. There is a small but informative **museum** at the site, detailing the development of the Maya empire and outlining the course of excavations, though there's no English labelling.

It is possible to walk between San Andrés and Joya de Cerén, but you shouldn't attempt it alone. A path leads across the fields behind San Andrés, emerging about 4km northeast at an old rail track and abandoned station, just off the San Juan Opico road. From here it is a further 3km or so to Joya de Cerén.

Santa Ana to San Cristóbal and the Guatemalan border

At the junction with the road from Chalchuapa, the Carretera Interamericana heads northwest for 30km, through the small town of **Candalería de la Frontera** and on through gentle, green rolling countryside to the Guatemalan border at **San Cristóbal**. There are frequent buses from Santa Ana (1hr) to the crossing, which is efficient and not too busy, and has no exit or entry charges. There is no bank at the border, but numerous moneychangers offer reasonable rates for dollars, colones and quetzales. On the Guatemalan side, buses run to Asuncíon Mita, with connections to Guatemala City.

From Santa Ana to Metapán

Leaving Santa Ana, CA-12 heads north through agricultural plains and badly deforested hills, becoming wilder after it passes through the dusty town of **Texistepeque**, once a pre-Columbian Pok'oman settlement, and a Spanish town from 1556. Sixteen kilometres further on, at the hamlet of Desagüe, a dirt road leads 2km or so to serene **Lago de Güija**, surrounded by low hills; Río Ostúa, flowing through the lake forms the border with Guatemala. On the **Las Figuras** arm of land – accessible on foot during the dry season – stretching out on the left side of the lakeshore are a number of faint pre-Columbian rock carvings; the area around the lakeshore was populated exclusively by indigenous groups until well into the seventeenth century. You can rent boats from here to the small island of **La Tipa** in the lake.

Ten kilometres beyond the lake, the small, friendly town of **METAPÁN** is scenically set on the edge of the mountains of the Cordillera Metapán-Alotepeque, which run east along the border with Honduras. Having survived a number of setbacks, including two devastating fires which nearly destroyed the town, Metapán was one of only four communities which supported Delgado's first call for independence in 1811; rioting citizens opened the jail and attacked representatives of the Spanish Crown.

The **Iglesia de la Parroquía**, completed in 1743, is considered to be one of El Salvador's finest colonial churches, with a beautifully preserved facade. Inside, the main altar is flanked by small pieces worked in silver from a local mine, while the ornately decorated cupola features paintings of SS Gregory, Augustine, Ambrose and Jerome.

Long gone are the days when its citizens were forced to defend themselves against Guatemalan troops sweeping through the town. Today Metapán is a charming, friendly place, slumbering for the most part beneath the sun. Luckily for the casual visitor, someone decided to build the comfortable *Hotel San José* (☎442 0556; ④), on the edge of town by the bus terminal, a few blocks from the centre, where rooms all have bath and TV and the restaurant stays open until 9pm. **Accommodation** is otherwise limited to the basic *Hospedaje Central* on 2a Av Nte at C 15 de Septiembre in the centre of town (②). For **eating**, *El Rincon de la Pelon* on C Benjamin Mancia, in the centre, is a casual little place in the front room of a private house, serving delicious chicken and meat (until around 8.30pm).

Around Metapán: Bosque Montecristo

The main reason for staying in Metapán is for access to the international reserve of **Bosque Montecristo**. Established in 1986, with funding received from, among others, the European Union, the reserve rises through two climatic zones and is managed as part of the **El Trifinio International Biosphere**, administered by the governments of El Salvador, Honduras and Guatemala. The reserve centres on the **Cerro Montecristo** (2418m), at whose summit the borders of the three countries converge.

In the higher reaches of Montecristo, beginning at around 2100m, there are twelve square kilometres of **virgin cloudforest**. Orchids and pinabetes, typical of cloud-forests, thrive in the climatic conditions of an average annual rainfall of two metres and a hundred percent humidity. Huge oaks, pines and cypresses, some towering to over 20m, swathed in creepers, lichens and mosses, form a dense canopy preventing sunlight from reaching the forest floor. The numerous species of wildlife – which tend to be shy of humans – include mountain foxes, howler and spider monkeys and the occasional jaguar. The abundant birdlife includes quetzals, hummingbirds, striped owl and Elliot's colibri. On the lower slopes of the reserve, the forest cover is mainly mixed pine and broadleaf woods, much of it secondary growth, replanted since the early 1970s; acute deforestation and consequent severe flooding had provided the impetus for the creation of a reserve. This lower zone is inhabited, with a fragile equilibrium being reached between the demands of the inhabitants and those of conservation.

Getting to Montecristo

The untouched beauty of the upper heights of Montecristo is due in large part to its remoteness; the only road in is a dirt track running northeast from Metapán. If you're driving (4-wheel drive necessary), the road from Metapán branches right off the high-way just before the *Hotel San José*. You're not allowed to enter on foot. Occasional pick-ups also make the journey; otherwise you'll have to arrange transport at the hotel or the market. Montecristo is managed by the **National Parks and Wildlife Service** at MAG (Col Santa Lucía, El Matazano, Ilopango; ☎227 0622), from whom authorization should be sought to enter. Again, as in the case of El Impossible, if you're fixing this up by phone, you'll need to be persistent. Note that the cloudforest is **closed** to visitors from May to October.

The park entrance (US$1 fee) is 4km from Metapán; after another 2km you come to the Hacienda San José, or *Casco Colonial*, where the Ministry of Agriculture has its park office. The right-hand fork just before this leads to **Los Planes** (1890m), 18km inside the park, a well-organized recreation area with a small restaurant, camping area and orchid garden; if **camping**, bring food and water. These are the only facilities for staying in the park and – not surprisingly, given the fragile balance of conservation – attempts to camp elsewhere are heavily frowned upon.

From Los Planes a marked trail leads to **Punto Trifinio**, the summit of Cerro Montecristo, where the three countries meet. Walking straight to the summit will take around three hours; the path leads through the cloudforest, however, and you can branch off in any direction (be careful not to get lost). You must bring warm clothing and good footwear. Trails also lead from just below Los Planes to the peaks of Cerro el Brujo and Cerro Miramundo.

Crossing into Guatemala: north to Anguiatú

Regular buses (around 30min) make the 13km trip from Metapán along CA-12 to **Anguiatú** and the **Guatemalan border**. This is the most convenient crossing if you're heading for Esquipulas in Guatemala (see p.387), and the formalities are straightforward. If coming in the other direction, note that the last bus to Metapán leaves at 6.30pm. There are no banks, but lots of moneychangers.

travel details

Buses

Ahuachapán to: Chalchuapa (#210, every 15min until 6pm; 1hr); Las Chinamas (#263, every 15min until 5.30pm; 1hr); Santa Ana (#210, every 15min until 6pm; 1hr 30min).

La Hachadura to: Sonsonate (#259, every 10min until 6.30pm; 2hr).

Metapán to: Anguiatú (#211A, every 30min until 6.30pm; 30min).

Santa Ana to: Cerro Verde (#248 to Sonsonate runs via the car park; 3 daily; 1hr 30min); Chalchuapa (#277, #218, every 10 min; 40min); Lago Coatepeque (#220 ("El Lago"), every 30min until 5.30pm; 1hr); Metapán (#235, every 30min until 6.30pm; 1hr 30min); San Andrés (#201 every 15min until 6pm; 1hr; for Joya de Cerén take the same bus to the junction for San Juan Opico and change); San Cristóbal (#236 every 15min until 5.30pm; 50min).

Sonsonate to: Acajutla (#207, #215a, #252, every 10min until 7pm; 30min); Ahuachapán (#249, every 30min until 5.30pm; 2hr 30min); Apaneca (#249, every 30min until 5.30pm; 1hr 45min); Barra de Santiago (#285, 1 daily; 1hr 30min); Cerro Verde (take the Santa Ana bus #216, which passes the turn-off (1hr 30min); Juayúa (#249, every 30min until 5.30pm; 1hr 30min); La Hachadura (#259, every 10min until 5.30pm, passing the access roads for Metalío and Barra de Santiago and running through Cara Sucia, 2hr; or #286, via San Francisco Menéndez, 4 daily, 2hr 30min); Los Cóbanos (#257, hourly until 5pm; 45min); Nahuizalco (#249, every 30min until 5.30pm; 30min); Salcoatitán (#249, every 30min until 5.30pm; 1hr 15min); Santa Ana (#216, every 15min until 5.45pm; 2hr).

International buses

Santa Ana to: Guatemala City (Melva International, 25a C Pte, 6a–8a Av Sur; ☎440 1608) hourly from 5.30am to 2.30pm (7hr)

CHRONOLOGY: THE MAYA

14,000 BC		Waves of Asian hunter-gatherers cross the Bering land bridge into the American continent, though parts of the Maya region may have been colonized as far back as 20,000 BC, according to some scholars. These people probably hunted mammoths; their early culture is known as the **Clovis**.
7500–1500 BC	**Archaic (Proto-Maya) period**	The Pacific littoral region between Chiapas and western El Salvador is the most intensely inhabited part of the Maya region, though there are well-established villages throughout. Central and northern Maya regions, though thinly populated, are a relative backwater. Villagers farm maize and beans (and possibly cassava), make pottery and fish. Clay idol figures discovered from this period may be the first religious figurines. A proto-Maya language is thought to have been spoken.
1500 BC–250 AD	**Preclassic period**	
1500–1000 BC	Early Preclassic	Strong influence of **Olmec** culture, the first emergent civilization of Mesoamerica in the Maya region, bringing an early calendar and new gods. Trade in jade, salt and cacao increases between villages, and by the end of the period, the central region is developing very quickly, making pottery, and establishing the first substantial buildings.
1400 BC		First settlement in Copán valley.
1200 BC		Olmec civilization emerges on Gulf coast, just outside the Maya region.
1000 BC		Early architectural platforms constructed at **Cuello** in Belize.
1000–300 BC	Middle Preclassic	Recent discoveries of relatively sophisticated Middle Preclassic building construction at Nakbé in northern Petén have led to intense debate about whether the city could have existed in isolation. Many of the earliest foundations of the central region's sites could also have originated in this period. Olmec culture dominates other parts of Maya World.
750 BC		**Nakbé** is flourishing. Possibly the very first Maya "city", it is dominated by eighteen-metre-high temples. Maya culture eclipses Olmec influence in Petén.
500 BC		First evidence of buildings at **Tikal**.
400 BC		Olmec cultural influence ends throughout the region. Izapan artistic styles start to influence the south.
300 BC–250 AD	Late Preclassic	Early development of the foundations of Maya civilization: calendar, writing, architectural design and sophisticated artistic style. Monumental temple cities emerge. Causeways (*sacbes*) are built and trade links flourish. Evidence of enormous constructions in the Yucatán emerge: temple foundations at **Edzná** and canals and moat systems at **Yaxuná**.
300 BC		Nakbé temples rebuilt to 45-metre height and colossal stucco masks constructed. Early building work at **El Mirador**.
200 BC		Miraflores culture thrives on Pacific coast and Guatemalan highlands, centred at Kaminaljuyú; elaborate stelae carved. First ceremonial structures built at **Tikal**, **Uaxactún** and possibly **Calakmul**.
150 BC		The first great Maya city-state, **El Mirador**, emerges; seventy-metre-high temples are built, framed by giant masks.

c.1 AD		Major pyramids, platforms and giant stucco masks constructed at Uaxactún, Tikal and Cerros, but the region is dominated by El Mirador. Emergence of Teotihuacán in Mexico.
37 AD		Maya calendar dated stelae carved at **El Baúl** on Pacific coast.
150 AD		**El Mirador** abandoned, possibly due to disease or environmental collapse.
199 AD		Earliest recorded use of Long Count date in central region.
250 AD		**Kaminaljuyú** all but abandoned.
	Classic period	
250–600 AD	Early Classic	Maya region and much of Mexico dominated by the metropolis of Teotihuacán close to modern-day Mexico City. Dated inscriptions emerge in the lowlands. Elaborate carved stelae erected throughout central region after 435 AD. Extensive trade network along Caribbean coast between Yucatán and Honduras.
292 AD		Stela 29 carved at **Tikal**, with Long Count calendar date.
378 AD		Tikal defeats Uaxactún.
400 AD		Guatemalan highlands under Teotihuacán control; Kaminaljuyú rebuilt in its style.
435 AD		Copán dynasty founded; population and building work at **Copán** accelerates.
534–593 AD		Middle Classic hiatus: dearth of stelae carving and building throughout central region except at **Caracol**.
550 AD		**Becan** first occupied.
556–562 AD		Caracol (allied to Calakmul) challenges and defeats Tikal.
c.600 AD		Teotihuacán collapses. Population density in core region reaches an estimated 965 people per square kilometre. **Uxmal** first occupied.
600–800 AD	Late Classic	Golden age of the Maya, as civilization reaches intellectual and artistic peak and numerous powerful city-states emerge in central region, though the mighty superpowers of Calakmul and Tikal dominate. Monumental construction of temples, plazas, pyramids and palaces. Puuc, Río Bec and Chenes cities all flourish in northern area and there is spectacular construction throughout the Yucatán peninsula.
615 AD		Pacal's reign begins at **Palenque**; construction of palace starts.
628 AD		Smoke Imix's reign begins at **Copán**.
645 AD		Flint Sky's reign begins at **Dos Pilas**.
679 AD		Flint Sky sacrifices Tikal's ruler Shield Skull.
682 AD		Ah Cacaw's reign at **Tikal** prompts its resurgence: series of successful military campaigns against Calakmul and vast construction projects undertaken. Shield Jaguar's reign begins at **Yaxchilán**.
683 AD		Pacal buried at **Palenque**; Chan Bahlum succeeds.
695 AD		Smoke Imix dies, Eighteen Rabbit's reign begins at **Copán**.
c700 AD		**Yaxchilán** dominates the Usumacinta region. Population of Caracol estimated at over 100,000. Structure 1 at **Río Bec** built.
734 AD		Ah Cacaw of Tikal dies.
735 AD		Dos Pilas attacks **Ceibal**.
738 AD		Copán's Eighteen Rabbit killed by Cauac Sky of Quiriguá.
c.750 AD		Population peaks in central region. Temples 1, 2 and 5 built at **Tikal**.
c.760 AD		**Xpujil**'s Structure 1 and **Chicanná**'s Structure 2 built.

771 AD		Stela E completed at **Quiriguá**.
783 AD		Last dated monument at **Palenque**.
c.790 AD		**Bonampak** murals painted, but site abandoned shortly afterwards. **Dos Pilas** overrun. End of the *katun* celebrated across the Maya world with carved stelae.
799 AD		Mexicans invade Palenque.
800–925 AD	Terminal Classic	Overpopulation and intense agricultural cultivation in region, possibly leading to environmental collapse. Ceibal flourishes briefly in isolation. Most main cities almost abandoned by 900 AD except in the northern area. Sea trade continues along the Belizean coast.
810 AD		Temple 3 completed at **Tikal**. Last dated inscription at **Quiriguá**.
830 AD		Completion of Baktun 9.
849 AD		Putún dominate **Ceibal**; five stelae erected.
c.860 AD		Population of central region down to a third of previous level.
c.900 AD		**Uxmal** and **Chichén Itzá** abandoned.
909 AD		Erection of the last stela (to commemorate a Katun) in Maya region at **Toniná**.
	Postclassic period	
925–1200 AD	Early Postclassic	Maya collapse sees cities abandoned throughout the region. The Toltec from Central Mexico invade Yucatán region bringing a new religious cult and architectural styles such as the *chacmool*. Itzá influence replaces Toltec.
987 AD		The Toltec invade Puuc hills.
1100 AD		**Chichén Itzá** reoccupied by Toltec; new construction begins.
1200 AD		Itzá driven from Campeche coast.
1200–1500 AD	Late Postclassic	Toltec influence fades in Yucatán, and Itzá invade. Later years see Yucatán divided into sixteen small states. Cobá and Tulum thrive. Toltec elite from Putun area invade Guatemalan highlands.
c.1250		Toltec enter Guatemala. **Utatlán** founded.
c.1270		Itzá establish **Mayapán**.
1283		**Mayapán** becomes capital of Yucatán.
c.1300		Itzá establish **Tayasal** on Lago de Petén Itzá.
c.1420		**Tulum** built.
1450		Quiché state dominates warring highlands.
1470		**Iximché** founded.
1500		Continual conflict in Guatemalan highlands between the main tribal groups.
1519		Cortés lands in Mexico.
1521		Aztec capital of Tenochtitlán falls to Spanish.
1523		Alvarado arrives in Guatemala.

THE MAYA ACHIEVEMENT

For some three thousand years before the arrival of the Spanish, Maya civilization dominated Mesoamerica, leaving behind some of the most impressive architecture in the entire continent. The scale and grandeur of some Maya cities, such as El Mirador, built around 100 BC, was greater than those of anything that existed in Europe at the time, and the artistry and splendour of Maya civilization at the height of the Classic era arguably eclipsed those of its Old World contemporaries. The Maya culture was complex and sophisticated, fostering the highest standards of engineering, astronomy, stone carving and mathematics, as well as an intricate writing system.

To appreciate all this you have to see for yourself the remains of the great centres. Despite centuries of neglect, abuse and the throttling attentions of the jungle, they are still astounding – the biggest temple-pyramids tower up to seventy metres above the forest floor, well above the jungle canopy. Stone monuments, however, leave much of the story untold, and there is still a great deal that we have to learn about Maya civilization. What follows is the briefest of introductions to the subject, hopefully just enough to whet your appetite for the immense volumes that have been written on it; some of these are listed in "Books" on p.511.

THE MAYA SOCIETY

By the Early Classic period, the Maya cities had become organized into a hierarchy of power, with cities such as Kaminaljuyú, Tikal and Calakmul dominating vast areas and controlling the smaller sites through a complex structure of **alliances.** The cities jostled for power and influence, occasionally erupting into open warfare, which was also partly fuelled by the need for sacrificial victims. The distance between the larger sites averaged around 30km, and between these were myriad smaller settlements, religious centres and residential groups. The structure of the alliances can be traced through the use of emblem glyphs. Only the glyphs of the main centres are used in isolation, while the names of smaller sites are used in conjunction with those of their larger patrons. Of all the myriad Classic cities, the dominant ones were clearly Tikal, Calakmul, Palenque, Copán, Caracol, Piedras Negras, Dos Pilas and Yaxchilán. Trade, marriages and warfare between the large centres were commonplace as the cities were bound up in an endless round of competition and conflict.

By the Late Classic period, **population densities** across a broad swathe of territory in the central region were as high as 965 people per square kilometre – an extraordinarily high figure, equivalent to densities in rural China today. It's thought there were strict divisions between the classes, with perhaps eighty percent being preoccupied with intensive cultivation to feed these vast numbers. The peasant farmers, who were at the bottom of the social scale, also provided the labour necessary to construct the monumental temples that decorate the centre of every city (the Maya did not have the wheel) as well as perform regular "military service" duties. Even in the suburbs where the peasants lived, there are complexes of religious structures with simple, small-scale temples where ceremonies took place.

While the remains of the great Maya sites are a testament to the scale and sophistication of Maya civilization, they offer little insight into daily life in Maya times. To reconstruct the lives of the **ordinary Maya** archaeologists have turned to the smaller residential groups that surround the main sites, littered with the remains of household utensils, pottery, bones and farming tools. These groups are made up of simple structures made of poles and wattle-and-daub, each of which was home to a single family. The groups as a whole probably housed an extended family, who would have farmed and hunted together and may well have specialized in some trade or craft. The people living in these groups were commoners, their lives largely dependent on agriculture. Maize, beans, cacao, squash, chillies and fruit trees were cultivated in raised and irrigated fields, while wild fruits were harvested from the surrounding forest. It's not certain whether the land was privately or communally owned.

Until the 1960s, Mayanists had long shared the view that the ordinary Maya were ruled by a scholarly astronomer-priest elite, who were preoccupied with religious devotion and the study of calendrics and the stars. They were thought to be men of reason, with no time for the barbarity of war and conquest, and were often compared to the ancient Greeks. However, this early utopian vision could not have been further from the truth: the decipherment of Maya glyphs has proved that the Maya rulers were primarily concerned with the glories of battle and conquest and preserving their royal bloodlines; human sacrifice and bloodletting rituals were also a pivotal part of elite Maya society. The rulers considered themselves to be god-humans and thought that the line of royal accession could only be achieved by sacred validation in the form of human blood.

There were two **elite classes**: *ahau* and *cahal*, who between them probably made up two or three percent of the population. The *ahau* title was reserved exclusively for the ruler and extremely close blood relatives – the top echelon of Maya society; membership could only be inherited. One step down was the *cahal* class, most of whom would have shared bloodlines with the *ahau*. The *cahal* were mainly governors of subsidiary settlements which were under the control of the dominant city-state and their status was always subordinate to the *ahau*. Although *cahal* lords commissioned their own stelae, the inscriptions always declared loyalty to the regional ruler.

The rulers lived close to the ceremonial centre of the Maya city, in imposing palaces, though the rooms were limited in size because the Maya has never mastered the use of the arch. Palaces doubled as administrative centres and were used for official receptions for visiting dignitaries, with strategically positioned thrones where the ruler would preside over religious ceremonies.

The "**middle class**" of Maya society consisted of a professional class (*ah na:ab*) of architects, senior scribes (*ah tz'ib*), sculptors, bureaucrats and master artisans, some of whom were also titled, and probably young princes and important court performers. Priests and shamans can also be included in this middle class, though, surprisingly, no title for the priesthood has yet been recognized. It's possible that not giving the priests a title may have been a method used by a fearful ruler to limit their influence. Through their knowledge of calendrics and supernatural prophecies, the priests were also relied upon to divine the appropriate time to plant and harvest crops.

There's no doubt that **women** played an influential role in Maya society, and in the late Classic period there were even some women rulers – Lady Ahpo Katun at Piedras Negras, Lady Ahpo-Hel at Palenque and a Lady Six Sky at Naranjo. Women also presided at court and were given prestigious titles – Lady Cahal of Bonampak, for example. More frequently, however, as in Europe, dynasties were allied and enhanced by the marriage of royal women between cities. One of the best documented strategic marriages occurred after the great southern city of Copán had suffered the humiliation of having its leader captured and sacrificed by upstart local rival Quiriguá in 738 AD – a royal marriage was arranged with a noblewoman from Palenque over 500km away.

Maya **agriculture** was continuously adapting to the needs of the developing society, and the early practice of slash and burn was soon replaced by more intensive and sophisticated methods to meet the needs of a growing population. Some of the land was terraced, drained or irrigated in order to improve its fertility and ensure that fields didn't have to lie fallow for long periods, and the capture of water became crucial to the success of a site. This was especially true in the more arid Yucatán peninsula where utilizing natural underground sinkholes (*cenotes*) and the construction of man-made wells were critical to survival.

The large lowland cities, today hemmed in by the forest, were once surrounded by open fields, canals and residential compounds, while slash-and-burn agriculture probably continued in marginal and outlying areas. Agriculture became a preoccupation, with the ordinary Maya trading at least some of their food in markets, although all households still had a kitchen garden where they grew herbs and fruit.

Maize has always been the basis of the Maya **diet**, in ancient times as much as it is today. Once harvested it was made into *saka*, a cornmeal gruel, which was eaten with chilli as the first meal of the day. During the day labourers ate a mixture of corn dough and water, and we know that tamales were also a popular speciality. The main meal, eaten in the evenings, would have been similarly maize-based, although it may well have included meat and vegetables. As a supplement to this simple diet, deer, peccary, wild turkeys, duck, pigeons and quail were all hunted with bows and arrows or blowguns. The Maya also made use of dogs, both for hunting and eating. Fish were also eaten, and the remains of fish hooks and nets have been found in some sites, while there is evidence that those living on the coast traded dried fish far inland. As well as food, the forest provided firewood, and cotton was cultivated to be dyed with natural colours and then spun into cloth.

THE MAYA CALENDAR

One of the cornerstones of Maya thinking was an obsession with **time**. For both practical and mystical reasons the Maya developed a highly sophisticated understanding of arithmetics, calendrics and astronomy, all of which they believed gave them the power to understand and predict events. All great occasions were interpreted on the basis of the Maya calendar, and it was this precise understanding of time that gave the ruling elite its authority. The majority of the carvings, on temples and stelae, record the exact date at which rulers were born, ascended to power and died.

The basis of all Maya **calculation** was the vigesimal counting system, which used multiples of twenty. All figures were written using a combination of three symbols – a shell to denote zero, a dot for one and a bar for five – which you can still see on many stelae. When calculating calendrical systems the Maya used a slightly different notation known as the head-variant system, in which each number from one to twenty was represented by a deity, whose head was used to represent the number.

When it comes to the Maya **calendar** things start to get a little more complicated as a number of different counting systems were used, depending on the reason the date was being calculated. The basic unit of the Maya calendar was the day, or *kin*, followed by the *uinal*, a group of twenty days roughly equivalent to our month; but at the next level things start to get more complex as the Maya marked the passing of time in three distinct ways. The **260-day almanac** (16 *uinals*) was used to calculate the timing of ceremonial events. Each day was associated with a particular deity that had strong influence over those born on that particular day. This calendar wasn't divided into months but had 260 distinct day names.

(This system is still in use among some Cakchiquel and Mam Maya who name their children according to its structure and celebrate fiestas according to its dictates.) A second calendar, the so-called "**vague year**" or *haab*, was made up of 18 *uinals* and five *kins*, a total of 365 days, making it a close approximation of the solar year. These two calendars weren't used in isolation but operated in parallel so that once every 52 years the new day of the solar year coincided with the same day in the 260-day almanac, a meeting that was regarded as very powerful and marked the start of a new era.

Finally the Maya had another system for marking the passing of history, which is used on dedicatory monuments. The system, known as the **long count**, is based on the great cycle of 13 *baktuns* (a period of 5128 years). The current period dates from August 13, 3114 BC and is destined to come to an end on December 10, 2012. The dates in this system simply record the number of days that have elapsed since the start of the current great cycle, a task that calls for ten different numbers – recording the equivalent of years, decades, centuries etc. In later years the Maya sculptors obviously tired of this exhaustive process and opted instead for the short count, an abbreviated version.

ASTRONOMY

Alongside their fascination with time, the Maya were obsessed with the sky and devoted much time and energy to unravelling its patterns. Several large sites such as Copán, Uaxactún and Chichén Itzá have **observatories** carefully aligned with solar and lunar sequences.

The Maya showed a great understanding of **astronomy** and with their 365-day "vague year" were just half a day out in their calculations of the solar year, while at Copán, towards the end of the seventh century AD, Maya astronomers had calculated the lunar cycle at 29.53020 days, not too far off our current estimate of 29.53059. In the Dresden Codex their calculations extend to the 405 lunations over a period of 11,960 days, as part of a pattern that set out to predict eclipses. At the same time they had calculated with astonishing accuracy the movements of Venus, Mars and perhaps Mercury. Venus was of particular importance to the Maya as they linked its presence with success in war, and there are several stelae that record the appearance of Venus prompting the decision to attack.

RELIGION

Maya **cosmology** is far from straightforward as at every stage an idea is balanced by its opposite and each part of the universe is made up of many layers. To the Maya this is the third version of the earth, the previous two having been destroyed by deluges. The current version is a flat surface, with four corners, each associated with a certain colour; white for north, red for east, yellow for south and black for west, with green at the centre. Above this the sky is supported by four trees, each a different colour and species, which are also sometimes depicted as gods, known as *Bacabs*. At its centre the sky is supported by a ceiba tree. Above the sky is a heaven of thirteen layers, each of which has its own god, while the very top layer is overseen by an owl. Other attested models of the world include that of a turtle (the land) floating on the sea. However, it was the underworld, *Xibalbá*, the "Place of Fright", which was of greater importance to most Maya, as it was in this direction that they passed after death, on their way to the place of rest. The nine layers of hell were guarded by the "Lords of the Night", and deep caves were thought to connect with the underworld.

Woven into this universe the Maya recognized an incredible array of **gods**. Every divinity had four manifestations based upon colour and direction and many also had counterparts in the underworld and consorts of the opposite sex. In addition to this there was an extensive array of patron deities, each associated with a particular trade or particular class. Every activity from suicide to sex had its representative in the Maya pantheon.

RELIGIOUS RITUAL

The combined complexity of the Maya pantheon and calendar gave every day a particular significance, and the ancient Maya were bound up in a demanding **cycle of religious ritual**. The main purpose of ritual was the procurement of success by appealing to the right god at the right time and in the right way. As every event, from planting to childbirth, was associated with a particular divinity, all of the main events in daily life demanded some kind of religious ritual and for the most important of these the Maya staged elaborate ceremonies.

While each ceremony had its own format there's a certain pattern that binds them all. The correct day was carefully chosen by priestly divination, and for several days beforehand the participants fasted and remained abstinent. The main ceremony was dominated by the expulsion of all evil spirits, the burning of incense before the idols, a sacrifice (either animal or human), and blood-letting.

In divination rituals, used to foretell the pattern of future events or account for the cause of past events, the elite used various **drugs** to achieve altered states of consciousness. Perhaps the most obvious of these was alcohol, either made from fermented maize or a combination of honey and the bark of the balnche tree. Wild tobacco, which is considerably stronger than the modern domesticated version, was also smoked. The Maya also used a range of hallucinogenic mushrooms, all of which were appropriately named, but none more so than the *xibalbaj obox*, "underworld mushroom", and the *k'aizalah obox*, "lost judgement mushroom".

MAYA TIME: THE UNITS

1 *kin* = 24 hours
20 *kins* = 1 *uinal*, or 20 days
18 *uinals* = 1 *tun*, or 360 days
20 *tuns* = 1 *katun*, or 7200 days
20 *katuns* = 1 *baktun*, or 144,000 days

20 *baktun* = 1 *pictun*, or 2,880,000 days
20 *pictuns* = 1 *calabtun*, or 57,600,000 days
20 *calabtuns* = 1 *kinchiltun*, or 1,152,000,000 days
20 *kinchiltuns* = 1 *alautun*, or 23,040,000,000 days

THE MAYA TODAY

Despite the suggestions of numerous New Age books on the secrets of the "Ancient Maya", neither the Maya nor their tradition-al beliefs have vanished. Like most of the indigenous people of America, they have survived, though few peoples in the world can have been more persecuted. Since the Spanish Conquest in 1524, they have endured continuous subjugation under a feudal system, the banning of their religion and compulsory conversion to Christianity, and the shattering of their culture.

These ravages left the twentieth-century Maya people as scattered and introspective trib-al communities, divided into two geographical groups – the Highland Maya of Guatemala and Chiapas, and the Lowland Maya of Eastern Mexico, Guatemala and Belize, with little com-munication between them. However, in the 1980s and 1990s, the savage persecution and widespread killing of the Highland Maya began to foment a new solidarity between the two groups and a new sense of nationhood. This bore literary fruit when Rigoberta Menchú, a survivor of the army's worst excesses and the daughter of an assassinated Maya community leader, pub-lished her autobiography in 1983, subtitled "Asi Me Nacio La Conciencia" (This is How my Consciousness was Born). Her Nobel Peace Prize, awarded in 1992, brought international attention to the Maya and, for the first time, Maya voices were heard in the United Nations.

MAYA IDENTITY: A POLITICAL ISSUE

It is a great paradox that in terms of physical characteristics and associated genetic make-up, there is little to separate an indigenous Mexican or Central American from a ladino. Though most of the people today known as Maya are descen-dants of the ancient Maya, so too are the major-ity of the region's non-indigenous people. Some anthropologists have claimed that cultural crite-ria and language are the things that distinguish Maya from non-Maya, but even in the Maya heartlands of the Yucatán, Chiapas and highland Guatemala, only a minority of Maya men wear indigenous dress, and many speak perfect

Spanish. Ultimately, though, the question of indigenous identity is a political and not an anthropological problem. People should be able to define themselves, yet, since the Conquest, the Maya have only been defined by people other than themselves. An official explained the system used in Guatemalan censuses in the 1980s as follows: "We ask the subject's neigh-bours if they're indigenous, then consider dress, language, and general socio-economic condi-tion." Today, however, as Maya are becoming more politically aware, they are beginning to see themselves differently. "We need to recover not only our own identity, but the right to define that identity ourselves. It should not be left to some European or North American academic," pro-claims Alberto Esquit, a Guatemalan Maya activist in *The Maya of Guatemala* by Phillip Wearne.

In Guatemala, a sense of what it is to be Maya is becoming increasingly widespread and the definition of this is known as **Mayanidad**. It is difficult to express exactly what this encap-sulates, but a few elements of it can be gleaned from Rigoberta Menchú's autobiography and from *Perpectivas y Propuestas de los Pueblos Mayas de Guatemala* (Views and Proposals of the Maya People of Guatemala), prepared by the Fundacion Vicente Menchú of Guatemala. Mayanidad is primarily characterized by a **devotion to the land**, not for private owner-ship – an idea which arrived with the Spanish – but for communal sharing. "We never think of taking all for ourselves and leaving our brothers and sisters with nothing," explained one Maya. Other characteristics are **traditional forms of dress**, which express symbolic meanings, and the **consumption of maize** as the basic ele-ment of a staple diet, prepared in the form of tortillas baked by hand on a comal.

The ceremonies and symbols of what is essentially a **holistic religion**, administered by a shamanic priest are another important ele-ment. This concentrates on the sacredness of the earth, which is seen as a mother constantly providing for us, and of the sun, seen as a father channelling life energy to the earth. Religion also involves a symbolic link between **cardinal points**, colour and the livelihood of the Maya people; the burning of **incense**, **ritual dance** and the practice of traditional **shamanic heal-ing**; and a set of **mythological stories** involv-ing patterns in the sky and features of the landscape. Religion touches every aspect of life, including **social decision-making**, a process that relies on consensus. "In order to decide which day to have a meeting we look at the calendar and search for a good day which will augur well for our deliberations. Before an important meeting we prepare our hearts with a Maya ceremony. After that we are ready to share our problems and ideas, ready to listen to all and to try and understand what each has to say. Later we have a period of conciliation to enable us to reach a commonly held position."

Recent archeological work has shown that a vast number of these beliefs and traditions

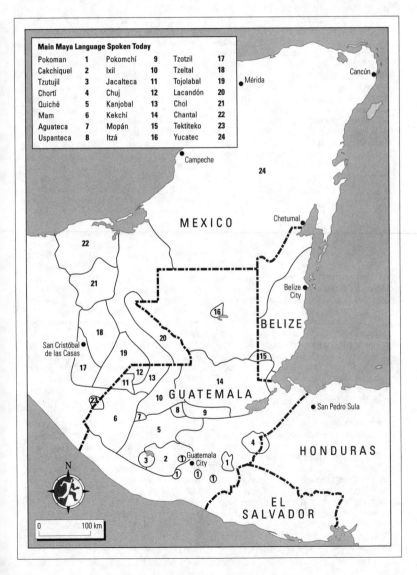

Main Maya Language Spoken Today

Pokoman	1	Pokomchí	9	Tzotzil	17
Cakchiquel	2	Ixil	10	Tzeltal	18
Tzutujil	3	Jacalteca	11	Tojolabal	19
Chortí	4	Chuj	12	Lacandón	20
Quiché	5	Kanjobal	13	Chol	21
Mam	6	Kekchí	14	Chantal	22
Aguateca	7	Mopán	15	Tektiteko	23
Uspanteca	8	Itzá	16	Yucatec	24

MAYA SPIRITUALITY AND SHAMANISM

Shamanism is difficult for Westerners to understand because it looks at the world in a way very different from that of Western science or philosophy. While science teaches us that our experience of ourself is a product of the material of which we are made, so that our thoughts, for example, are the properties of our brains, shamanism teaches that our thoughts and our brains are manifestations of a deeper inner reality which lies behind our experience of ourselves as thinkers: the material world is an aspect of the spiritual, not vice versa. This is true not just for human beings, but for everything animate and inanimate, from a crocodile to a mountain. The primordial forces that control the relationship between the material and the spiritual (death, life, time), are the gods.

Human beings are crucial in maintaining the balance in this relationship between the material and the spiritual. Their agent is the **shaman**, who abandons body and thoughts to enter a state of trance. He or she then journeys into the archetypal spirit world, redressing imbalances which manifest in the material world as, for instance, disease or drought. If the shaman is successful in altering the spirit world to favourably affect the material, then his activity must be paid for so that the balance is preserved. Thus **sacrifice** is often required before or after a shamanic ritual.

This shamanic legacy was adapted and elaborated by the great civilization that preceded the Maya, the **Olmecs**. The Olmecs were to pre-Columbian Mexico and Central America what the Greeks are to Western civilization. They began to elaborate the precepts of shamanism into a more complex mythology, building a replica of the volcano where the world was created by the gods – the first pre-Columbian **pyramid**. In front of this they built a rectangular plaza, where rituals were conducted, and near it a sunken court decorated with water plants, symbolic of the spirit world. The city was ruled over by a shamanic king, sometimes portrayed in carved stelae, who administered the rituals and the politics of the city and propitiated the gods through human sacrifice or ritual blood-letting.

The Maya pyramids were also seen as sacred mountains, and the temples on their summits were conceived as mouths to the spirit world. Like everything else in the shamanic world, these mountains were spiritually alive, and the Maya symbolized this by carving the mouths of mountain spirits known as **"Witz"** monsters around the temple doors (most dramatically at Chicanná, Hormiguero and the Chenes sites), or on their

sides (for example, at Tikal). These mountain temples were administered by priests or shamanic kings who had a special relationship with the spirit world – their source of power. This relationship was often indicated by the representation of entwined feathered serpents in close proximity to depictions of the Maya lords on stelae or other carvings. These "vision serpents" were symbolic conduits for souls travelling between the material and the spirit world. They are also portrayed rearing up in front of people in deep trance states, and opening their mouths to emit the heads of the dead or other beings from the other world – as in the famous lintel of Lady Xoc of Yaxchilán, now in the British Museum in London. Like the Olmec rulers, the Maya lords also practised blood-letting and human sacrifice to propitiate the gods.

It wasn't merely the mountain temples that were sacred in Maya cities. The spaces in between were used for prolonged rituals or festivals administered by the Maya lords, who re-enacted the myths of creation, ritually transferring power from the spirit world to the material; a modern parallel would be Catholic sacraments. Maya myths were often played out in the movement of the stars; the passage of the Milky Way across the night sky, for instance, was symbolic of the raising of a great tree (the World Tree) that separates the spirit world and the material world. Architecture was often oriented to the astral bodies for this reason and buildings were arranged in triangular form to represent the three stones of the **cosmic hearth** – the place where humans were cooked into creation by the Lords of Maize, marked in the sky by the three stars of Orion's Belt.

The famous pre-Columbian **ball game** also had ritual significance. Like the sunken court of the Olmecs, the ball court was decorated with symbols of the border between the material and spirit world, and within it, teams of players competed, re-enacting a game played by the Hero Twins, mythological characters who defeated the Lords of Death, then rescuing their parents, the Lords of Maize, who went on to create the present world.

Many of these shamanic traditions have been preserved by the modern Maya. Yucatec Maya *xmen* (shamans) still mediate between the material and spiritual worlds when they invoke the spirit of rain, the god Chac, during times of drought. The Maya of San Lorenzo Zinacantán still venerate the spirits of the mountains that overlook their valley home, and all over the Maya World communities still affirm the myths of creation in elaborate annual festivals and celebrations.

were held and practised by the Maya's pre-Columbian ancestors, further enabling modern Maya to reclaim their heritage.

A HISTORY OF THE MODERN MAYA

More than any other factor, it was the political events of the 1980s and 1990s in Guatemala and across the border in Mexico's Chiapas state that were crucial in establishing a new sense of Maya solidarity and, subsequently, identity. Both conflicts were part of the age-old problem of **land distribution**. After they conquered Mexico and Central America, the Spanish, who were forbidden from enslaving the native population by the Catholic Church and the Reyes Católicos, Fernando and Isabel, sought other means of controlling the people. The result was the "**hacienda system**", whereby the indigenous communities were broken up and the villagers resettled on the edges of huge estates owned by colonists from Spain, many of whom were little more than peasants themselves, from the poorest regions of the country, such as Extremadura and Castilla La Mancha. The landowners then rented small plots of land to the indigenous people at rates that were sufficiently high to ensure that they were always owed a little money, paid back in the form of labour on the hacienda estates. After independence, this system was perpetuated, and even today, in the late twentieth century, most of the peasants of Latin America are controlled in this way. In Guatemala, the successors to the haciendas are the coastal coffee and sugarcane **fincas**, to which Highland Maya peasants, unable to sustain a living on their poor lands in the mountains, are ferried at harvest time. In Mexico, huge farms are run by wealthy estate owners, known in Chiapas as *caciques*. In the Yucatán, however, fewer Maya labour under debt peonage as the plantations that produced *henequen* (sisal) collapsed with the introduction of nylon. This domination by the landowners looked as if it would continue indefinitely, until two factors brought it to a head in the 1980s: Catholic Liberation Theology and the threatened or actual appropriation of the little communal land worked by the Maya.

Liberation Theology was conceived in 1967 at a conference of South American bishops in Medellín in Colombia, who decided that the Church's priority should be to help the poor, rather than the rich. The theology demanded a "**preferential option for the poor**" through the erosion of unjust class structures and the establishment of base communities to empower both the urban and rural poor at a grass-roots level, by addressing their basic needs and teaching them about their rights.

This new theology spread quickly throughout Latin America. In Guatemala, it was practised by **Catholic Action**, a movement that taught the Maya about the root causes of their poverty and gave them a belief that they could change the unjust social structure that perpetuated it. However, there were often brutal consequences for its practitioners, and countless priests were murdered throughout the 1980s by US-backed or -installed military regimes, paranoid about Communism. In El Salvador, **Archbishop Romero** was shot dead while denouncing the exploitation of the poor to his parishioners during a sermon. In Mexico, the bishop of San Cristóbal de las Casas in Chiapas, **Samuel Ruiz**, was dubbed "the red bishop" by Mexico's dictatorship, the PRI, and blamed by them for fomenting the Zapatista movement.

Liberation Theology helped the Highland Maya of Guatemala and Chiapas to understand why they were poor, but when threats to take away the little land still worked by the Maya followed, they provoked first resistance and then insurrection.

ETHNIC CLEANSING IN GUATEMALA

The 1970s and 1980s saw increased incursions into Maya **communal lands** in the Guatemalan highlands by wealthy ladinos, which led eventually to wide-scale rebellion among the Maya community.

Land has been confiscated from the Maya ever since the Conquest: tourists visiting Guatemala City invariably pass along Avenida La Reforma, named in commemoration of a "reform" which abolished Maya ownership of communal lands in the nineteenth century. The revolts which followed this decision, which were crushed with characteristic brutality, were mirrored one hundred years later. This time, however, the Maya communities, consolidated by the work of Catholic Action, began to resist.

During the recession of the 1970s, growing numbers of urban Maya had taken leading roles in unions and community groups, and as

Highland Maya began to journey to the capital to protest their land rights and hire lawyers to defend their land, these groups met and exchanged ideas. Recognizing their joint aims and concerns, they began to work together more closely. However, they were met with repression, combined with the failure of the corrupt legal system and the government to address their demands. As the Maya protested more forcefully, the repression increased. According to an Oxfam report, the mutilated, dismembered and sexually abused bodies of 168 community leaders were found by or returned to Maya villagers between February 1976 and February 1977.

After **General Lucas García** came to power in a blatantly rigged election, the violence increased. Troops opened fire on a group of seven hundred peaceful demonstrators in **Panzós** in 1978, and death squads were given a free hand to rape, torture and kill potential "subversives". Maya villagers, becoming increasingly desperate, began to look for protection elsewhere. Inspired by the Cuban Revolution, **guerrilla groups**, such as **ORPA** (the Organization of the People in Arms) and **EGP** (the Guerrilla Army of the Poor) had been working amongst tribal groups in the highlands since the early 1970s and, by the end of the decade, frightened Maya were joining them in droves, hoping for protection from the brutalities of the army. The guerrillas, however, were ladino Marxists, with little interest in the Maya except as a means to bring about a proletarian revolution. By the early 1980s the split between ladinos and indigenous people in the guerrilla movements was at crisis point and increasing numbers of Maya felt that the guerrillas, too, had failed them. While the guerrillas fled to the mountains, villagers were left to face the army guns – and the systematic brutality of Guatemala's most cruel dictator, born-again Christian, General **José Efrain Ríos Montt**, who claimed his power "by God's Will".

Montt pledged to eradicate the guerrillas and set about a programme of ethnic cleansing – **The National Plan of Security and Development** – which would involve "changes in the basic structure of the state". The army was briefed and given maps with the positions of villages marked with pins. Under operation **"preventative terror"**, the villages with pink or yellow pins were burnt to the ground and the fleeing populations relocated in **model villages** and given the choice of being fed or killed. Those who chose to be fed were then organized into "civilian patrols" headed by military commissioners, whose job was to spy out possible subversives and fight against the guerrillas. The aim was to force the Maya to become ladinos and blur their identity by mixing the various communities.

Operation **"scorched earth"** dealt with those villages marked with red pins. After resident ladinos and landowners had been persuaded to leave "for their own safety" (because the army had been instructed to allow no survivors), troops swept through these highland villages, burning homes, destroying everything they could find and killing villagers as they fled. In the ensuing carnage, up to forty percent of some tribal groups were wiped out, and millions of displaced people who had somehow survived fled across the border to Mexico or chanced their luck in the mountains.

This method of reconquering the Maya through suppression, murder and relocation was continued by Montt's successor, **General Victores**, and the army, backed by civilian president, **Vinicio Cerezo**. Culturally, the scorched earth programme seemed devastating, but by the late 1980s, it became clear that it had in fact heightened **Maya self-awareness**, rather than subsumed it. Maya people came to regard themselves not merely as members of different tribes but as a people with a common heritage and traditions. The repression continued under **President Serrano**, who sanctioned death squads and extra-judicial killings, but could not prevent the formation of the **Mutual Support Group** (GAM) which, despite the assassination of a number of its leaders, worked to bring international attention to Guatemala's appalling human rights scandals. In 1990, villagers in Santiago Atitlán expelled the army after troops had murdered thirteen people, inspiring other highland villages to demand the closure of military bases.

In 1996 the new government of **Alvaro Arzú**, bowing to international pressure, was forced to commit itself to an **Indigenous Rights Accord** – a programme of reform for the Maya, encouraging education in native tongues, greater political participation, the preservation of sacred areas and the establishment of a **UN-presided Truth Commission**, looking into human rights abuses. So far, however, this has not produced anything of note. Political violence and military repression have waned under Arzú, though the assassination of human rights campaigner Bishop **Juan Gerardi** makes it clear that they have not completely disappeared. The Maya still work the fincas and remain poor and marginalized, with 75 percent illiteracy and the lowest life expectancy in the western hemisphere. The little that they have gained, they have paid for dearly; yet as Rigoberta Menchú herself puts it: "After so many years of struggle, this period seems to be the end of five hundred years of injustice, five hundred years of night. We are moving into the light of a new era for our peoples. After so many years of waiting for a new dawn, we believe our voices will make themselves heard..."

OPPRESSION AND INSURRECTION IN CHIAPAS

On January 1, 1994, the day the **North American Free Trade Agreement** (NAFTA) took effect, a predominantly Maya militia wearing balaclavas occupied several cities in Chiapas, including the capital, **San Cristóbal de las Casas**, proclaiming *Basta Ya!* (That's Enough!) to the government. Calling themselves the **Zapatista Army of National Liberation (EZLN)**, they were, like their Guatemalan counterparts, protesting against debt peonage and the further erosion of indigenous land rights.

Emiliano **Zapata**, from whom the Zapatistas take their name, was an indigenous guerrilla leader who became a key player in the Mexican Revolution of 1910, helping to draw up a constitution in 1917 that included pledges to dismantle the hacienda system and redistribute land to the indigenous community. Though Zapata's dream was never fully realized and he was to proclaim shortly before he was assassinated, that "the old landownings have been taken over by new landowners... and the people mocked in their hopes", under **Article 27** of the Constitution, some communal holdings known as **ejidos** were set aside for indigenous people. Though, strictly speaking owned by the state, the *ejidos* were held in common, and the farming and produce shared between village communities. However, in the early 1990s, **President Carlos Salinas de Gortari**, leader of the **PRI**, the world's most popular democratic political party, decided to modernize the Mexican economy in preparation for NAFTA. This plan involved the shedding of public ownership, according to

the Reagan-Thatcher blueprint. Article 27 was repealed and the *ejidos* were up for grabs.

It is hardly surprising, then, that the reinstatement of Article 27 was, and still is, one of the Zapatistas' key demands, together with the repeal of NAFTA and the abolition of debt peonage. The state's perception of the uprising, as well as the continuing response to it, was neatly expressed by a cartoon which appeared in the Mexican press shortly after the Zapatistas had made their demands. A detained Maya stands in front of a police official who says, "So, you don't speak Spanish? First charge then, treason."

The army reacted to the Maya rebellion with a use of force only exceeded by their Guatemalan counterparts. After expelling foreign journalists, they bombed Maya villages regarded as EZLN strongholds, murdered captured civilians suspected of being sympathizers and began a campaign of preventative terror. As the justice of the Zapatista cause received international attention, threatening to expose Mexico as being a one-party state, Salinas stepped in and called for negotiations. **Manuel Camacho Solis** was appointed Commissioner for Peace and Reconciliation in Chiapas, while the mysterious balaclava-clad, pipe-smoking **Subcomandante Marcos** spoke for EZLN. In an intermediary role was **Samuel Ruíz**, bishop of San Cristóbal de las Casas, a campaigner for indigenous rights. Some **concessions** were offered to the guerrillas and they retreated to consult with their communities – a three-month process during which all documents were translated into the various Maya languages and distributed to every community from which the EZLN drew their support. This three-month consultation period gave ample time for the message of the Zapatista uprising to spread. Although the rebellion directly affected only a small part of Chiapas, Maya peasant groups, who had long backed other political parties, denounced the PRI, accusing it of vote-rigging and of supporting the corrupt *caciques* (landowners), who kept them in bonded labour. By May, peasants had occupied nineteen municipal headquarters, and by June, over three hundred farms had been seized from *caciques*. This figure tripled over the following two years. In July, the EZLN reported that the base communities (established through Liberation Theology; see p.491) had rejected the proposals by 98 percent. However, they called a truce and retreated.

In the **August elections**, the PRI managed to hang onto not only national power, but also the governership of Chiapas. Though there are peasants within Chiapas who strongly support the PRI, the state election was almost certainly a fraud, and, in protest, the defeated opposition candidate, **Amado Avendano Figueroa**, declared himself "rebel governor". Half the municipalities in the state backed him, refusing to pay taxes to the government, and the EZLN warned that if the PRI candidate assumed power in Chiapas then they would call an end to their truce. After the army had surrounded the EZLN, the new President Zedillo attended the inauguration of the governor of Chiapas. The Zapatista response was immediate. Without firing a shot, the guerrillas showed their strength and discipline, perforating the army cordon and expanding their position from four municipalities to 35. Shortly afterwards, again undetected and without any gunfire, they retreated to the mountains, where they began a long stand-off with the government. The army responded in 1995 by launching an offensive and revealing that Subcomandante Marcos was, in fact, Rafael Sebastian Guillen Vicente, a professor of communications from the Metropolitan Autonomous University of Mexico City and a former Sandinista brigadier. The army offensive backfired, however: while the EZLN avoided confrontation and retreated deeper into the Lacandón jungle, where they remain to this day, the army terror campaign which forced 20,000 villagers to flee for their lives received national and international condemnation. A hundred thousand people protested in the capital, crying "Guillen for President", heightening the popularity and profile of the EZLN leader.

In the lengthy period of negotiation that continues to this present day, the small enclaves liberated from the wealthy landowners by the Zapatistas and their Maya peasant supporters have been left to govern their own affairs — something that they have done very successfully. Every **rebel Maya village** has a shortwave radio, operated round the clock, that feeds into a regional network tracking army movements. The ostentatious haciendas have become schools, and wooden shacks and communal agricultural land (milpas) now cover the airstrips where wealthy *caciques* once landed their private planes. The Maya have introduced traditional systems of social organization, adminis-

tration of justice and agricultural production, and though the government in Mexico City insists that the Zapatistas have made life worse for the Maya, things are very different on the ground. Michael McCaughan, a British journalist who visited the villages in June 1998, described what he saw: "The peasant farmers . . . seem bewildered by the fulfilment of a centuries-old dream . . . The day's labour is still a rough physical challenge, but at least the fruits belong to them . . . there is a new confidence. Indian men and women used to walk with heads bowed; now they look you in the eye and discuss world politics."

However, the stalemate that has allowed the villages to remain autonomous may not persist for much longer. It is an embarrassment for Mexico's government, which stands accused of feigning dialogue while stalling for a military solution. In April 1997, Human Rights Watch published a report exposing state responsibility for mounting rural violence against pro-Zapatista Maya in Chiapas, and against other indigenous peoples and campesinos, unhappy with their exploitation at the hands of rich landowners throughout Mexico. They concluded not only that the PRI had failed to bring local *caciques* to justice, but that they had supported paramilitary groups known as **guardias blancas** (white guards). They also reported that they had "conclusive evidence that they [the paramilitaries] . . . work in co-ordination with the police". White guards have operated in Chiapas for decades and are paid for by *caciques* to protect private property and the political infrastructure controlled by the PRI, which the *caciques* support. Along with other paramilitary groups, they have been responsible for a number of disappearances and murders in Chiapas in the past three years, as well as shootings against civilian protesters and priests. The PRI, however, has steadfastly refused to admit the existence of paramilitaries in Chiapas, let alone brought them to justice.

Until recently, the relationship between the PRI, *caciques* and peasant-based armed groups such as **Peace and Justice** and the **Chinchulines**, which are responsible for widespread murder and intimidation of pro-Zapatista peasants, was less clear. In their 1997 report, Human Rights Watch concluded that though there was no clear evidence, the fact that members of these groups were never brought to justice for their violence suggested links; there were also widespread reports that they were trained by the army. However, evidence finally emerged in December 1997, when 21 women, 14 children and 9 men from **La Sociedad Civil Las Abejas** (The Bees – a pro-Zapatista civil group that does not support the use of violence) were shot dead by armed peasants while attending Mass in **Acteal**. State police, only 200m away did nothing to prevent the attack, and in the outcry that followed, the government was forced to arrest a police commander and the local PRI mayor.

The few changes that occurred after Acteal were little more than window-dressing, and 1998 saw increased tension in the region and a steady build-up of troops. In January 1998, PRI delegate **Samuel Sanchez Sanchez** announced that he was in command of a para-military group that called themselves **Desarollo, Paz y Justicia** (Development, Peace and Justice) and would carry out attacks until EZLN disbanded. All paramilitary groups escalated their activities in 1998, murdering community leaders and forcing members of The Bees to flee their villages under threat of death. Moreover, they now seemed to be turning a blind eye on the activities of the army, whose deployment was also increasing in Chiapas. In January, troops opened fire on a crowd in **Ocosingo**, killing a woman and wounding two children.

By June, tension had risen to further heights. The third state governor to be elected in rigged elections in four years, **Roberto Albores Guillen**, described the autonomous municipalities as "the greatest threat to democracy" in Mexico and pledged to dismantle them one by one. Foreign journalists were once more expelled and 60,000 troops, paramilitaries and police, now under army control, surrounded the Zapatista villages. So far Guillen has proved to be a man of his word – Taniperlas, Tierra y Libertad and San Juan de la Libertad have been razed to the ground, and in the hills the EZLN is mounting arms and preparing for war. The European Community, the United Nations Committee Against Torture and Committee for the Elimination of Racial Discrimination, the Vatican, Amnesty International and numerous smaller NGOs have all condemned Zedillo's government for its handling of the Chiapas situation. Zedillo still has the support of the US, how-

ever, and as long as this continues, it looks as if his presidency is assured.

DEFORESTATION IN BELIZE AND MEXICO

The Maya of Belize and Mexico have also been subjected to land confiscation, mainly though government-backed **logging schemes**.

In September 1995, the Belize government granted a licence to a Malaysian company to log the Maya homeland. During the Spanish conquest, the Maya retreated to the jungle where they were subsequently allowed to stay within designated **reservation areas**. These comprise about 77,000 acres of government-owned land in the Toledo district of Belize, but now even that is under threat. According to Belize law, only protected areas are closed to loggers; "Indian Reservations" are not, and since the Maya do not actually own the land, the government can do as it pleases.

Logging began in 1996, in **Conejo Landing**. Bulldozers moved in, pushing down almost everything in their path, despite government assurances that only larger trees were to be selected for logging, and turning the Maya's principal source of drinking water into mud soup. In 1997 the bulldozers headed for the **Hinchasones** and **Xpichilha** reservations, where their "selective logging" resulted in floods that devastated Maya milpas and wrecked homes. Maya protests were rebuffed, the government arguing that Belize could not be divided up along ethnic lines, and logging still continues. The building of the new Southern Highway threatens to exacerbate the problem by making access to these areas even easier and, therefore, encouraging land settlers.

The Maya have taken their cause to an international level, following Rigoberta Menchú's example, and lobbying the **United Nations** and international NGOs. In the absence of any government maps of their lands, tribal groups have produced an illustrated **Maya Atlas**, a beautiful book with plans of every village and information about each community's culture and traditions. As one community leader explains: "Through our Atlas, our voices can be heard as we relate the history of our villages, as we describe our culture, folklores and way of life. Our aim is to protect our unique way of life for the people of Belize and the world, and for the appreciation and respect of indigenous rights.

We believe our Atlas will help press our claim for legal rights to our land. As an African proverb goes 'Until lions have their own historians, histories of the hunt will always glorify the hunter".

Battling for the same cause in Mexico are five hundred or so longhaired, white-robed **Lacandón Maya** of the southeastern Chiapas jungles. Lacandón methods of rainforest agriculture are some of the most advanced and efficient in the world, recycling the forest from garden plot through regrowth, partially forested milpa and eventually back to forest again. Each milpa can produce over eighty kinds of food and fibre crops above and below the soil, including fruit, nuts and maize, material for rope and clothing, and vines for baskets. The milpas are also bait for rainforest animals like agouti, which are trapped by the Lacandón for food. However, the Lacandón are dying out: in less than half a century, they have lost eighty to ninety percent of their forest to mahogany loggers, oil prospectors and settlers, who continue the onslaught despite ostensible government protection of the Lacandón lands. Since the 1950s, the population of settlers in the Lacandón rainforest has exploded from a few thousand to over 200,000. Second-generation settlers who need new land for subsistence, practise slash and burn, leaving the infertile soil exhausted and beyond recovery. Recently even these settlers have been dispossessed and their land appropriated by rich cattle-ranching landowners, whose huge fincas produce the meat for America's favourite junk food – the burger.

THE YUCATEC MAYA

Until recently, the least persecuted Maya group were those of Mexico's Yucatán peninsula. After the collapse of the market in *henequen* (used for making high-quality rope) earlier this century, the Maya who had until that point been subjugated under a system of debt peonage were more or less left to their own devices. The Yucatán became a quiet backwater and Mérida didn't even have road connections to the rest of Mexico. In the 1960s, though, the government decided to transform **Cancún**, a Maya fishing village, into a major tourist resort.

There is something distasteful about the way in which Maya images are used to sell dream holidays to package tourists destined for Cancún. Pictures of cute, sanitized Maya chil-

dren smile from brochures and billboards welcoming visitors to the Maya world, and vast ugly hotels mimic the designs of their ancestors' temples. Though a few commendable ecotourism projects, particularly in Campeche state, are attempting to channel a little money to the Maya, most of this new-found wealth doesn't reach them; instead it falls into the pockets of the wealthy ladino landowning group who have for so long exploited them.

That aside, the Yucatán is still a healthier area for the Maya than almost any other in the Maya world. Maya children are not allowed to learn their own language in schools, for example, but mass tourism has thankfully yet to oust the majority of the peninsula's villagers. Many still grow maize on milpas and continue to practice traditional lifestyles. Maya **xmen** (shamans) operate throughout the peninsula, even in larger centres like Ticul and Mérida, though they are most concentrated in the countryside, particularly around the important spiritual centre of **Felipe Carillo Puerto** in Quintana Roo. Here, like their ancestors, they still invoke **Chac**, the god of rain, and use their crystals to scry the future.

THE FUTURE

The indigenous peoples of the Americas have faced a stark choice since the time of the Conquest – assimilate or accept oppression. For five hundred years many have chosen the path of oppression and been marginalized by their rulers, who called them **Indians**, after Columbus's mistake. "Mexicans make no connection between their Aztec ancestors and the poor Indian selling vegetables on the pavement," notes a member of the country's National Indigenous Institute. "For most . . . one represents historic pride, the other contemporary shame."

Today, however "Indian" has become a pejorative term, and awareness of Native American culture, philosophy and rights is increasing. For over a decade, the UN Working Group on Indigenous Peoples has been drawing up a draft declaration on the rights of the world's indigenous peoples. However, as the story of the Maya illustrates, this is occurring alongside continued and vigorous oppression by the descendants of the conquerors. Nonetheless, the Maya are optimistic, and their spirit, it seems, is indestructible. "Little by little we are moving forward," claims

Rigoberta Menchú. "We have carried on a broad struggle for many years, and many people, many stalwart hearts in many parts of the world have accompanied us. We have always said that solidarity is a product of consciousness, a product of love, of love for life and for other people."

FURTHER INFORMATION AND RESOURCES

The Guatemalan Indian Centre, 94 Wandsworth Bridge Rd, London SW6 2TF, UK (☎0171/271 5291). Provides information on the Maya of Guatemala and elsewhere. A very useful source of contacts.

The Rigoberta Menchú Tum Foundation: *our-world.compuserve.com/homepages/rmtpaz/pro-eng.htm* Rigoberta Menchú's homepage detailing the work of her organization and providing links to other sites.

SIPAZ Web site: *www.nonviolence.org/sipaz/index.htm* Provides information about the Zapatistas.

EZLN *www.ezln.org* The homepage of the EZLN.

Minority Rights Group, 379 Brixton Rd, London SW9 7DE (☎0171/978 9498). Published an article on the plight of the Guatemalan Maya in 1994: *The Maya of Guatemala* by Philip Wearne.

Human Rights Watch, 485 Fifth Avenue, NYC NY 10019-6014 (*www.hrw.org*). Their Web site is regularly updated with information on the Chiapas conflict.

LANDSCAPE AND WILDLIFE

The countries of the Maya World embrace an astonishingly diverse collection of environments, ranging from the world's second longest coral reef along the Caribbean coast, through the lowland rainforests of Mesoamerica and the upland pine forests of the Guatemalan highlands, to the exposed volcanic peaks of Guatemala, and down to the often sweltering Pacific coast. The wildlife here is, if anything, even more varied than might be expected, due to the location of this region at the northern end of the land bridge between the temperate life zones to the north (the Nearctic) and the Neotropics to the south, and there are a number of local endemic species found nowhere else in the world.

This diversity of natural environments makes the Maya World an ideal location for wildlife enthusiasts and, though the main reason for visiting the **archeological sites** may be to understand more about the ancient Maya, the sites themselves also provide a vital refuge for the plants and animals of the region. This section aims to provide a general overview of the main ecosystems of the Maya World and give examples of some of the flora and fauna you might find there.

LANDSCAPE

The distinct geographical and climatic patterns found in any region create a series of **biomes** (life zones or habitats), each with its own characteristic flora and fauna. These are effectively an ecological map, with temperature and rainfall being the main co-ordinates. The range of elevation found in the countries of the Maya World means there are around ten biomes: from **subtropical dry forest** on the northwest coast of Yucatán to **tropical montane forest** found on the highest slopes of the volcanoes. Some of the main ones are covered below.

YUCATÁN AND THE GULF COAST LOWLANDS

The **Yucatán peninsula** is a limestone plateau, generally low-lying but gradually increasing in elevation from north to south. Although rainfall is plentiful, the dry season is more pronounced in the extreme northwest, and precipitation also gradually increases from north to south. Due to the permeable nature of limestone there is almost no surface water: most rain immediately soaks through and dissolves the rock, creating a **subterranean drainage** system, with great underground rivers flowing through caverns, and often entering the sea just offshore in upwellings of fresh water. Inland, **sinkholes** (cenotes) are formed when a cave roof collapses, where the water level is many metres below the surface of the land. In the north the vegetation is predominantly dry, tangled scrub and bush, although large areas have been cleared for cultivation. To the south are lusher subtropical forests, where the effects of agriculture are less obvious and the dense forest of **acacia**, **albizias**, **gumbo limbo** and **ceiba** is in parts almost impenetrable. The **sapodilla** tree grows here too, and **chicle**, used in the preparation of chewing gum, is harvested from its latex.

The **Gulf of Mexico coast** is low-lying and marshy in the north and west (protected in the Río Lagartos and Celestún national parks), giving way to a swampy, **alluvial plain** in Tabasco. Dotted with lagoons and crossed by the lower reaches of the Usumacinta, the Grijalva and a number of other rivers, the plain drains a huge volume of water from the Chiapas and Guatemalan highlands. Here much of the original **rainforest** has disappeared, replaced by banana plantations and cattle pasture; the climate is also ideal for **cacao**, which has grown here for thousands of years.

THE TROPICAL RAINFORESTS

Between north-central Yucatán and the northern foothills of the central highlands, and from the Gulf of Mexico to the Caribbean coast, the natural vegetation is either **tropical moist forest** or, with rainfall over 4000mm on some mountain slopes and in some coastal locations, true **tropical rainforest**. Formerly, this forest would have covered the whole of the region outlined above, but under continued pressure from agriculture and logging much of it has been reduced to a central "core", comprising southern Campeche and Quintana Roo, northern Petén, western and south-central Belize and the Lacandón forest of Chiapas. This area is still sufficiently large to support the whole range of wildlife described in the following section, and indeed much of it is under official protection in reserves and national parks, though their edges are constantly being nibbled away.

So diverse is the forest that scientists have identified seventy different forest types here, dependent on factors including (but not limited to) soil category, elevation and distance from the coast. However, it is the **broadleaved**, usually deciduous, trees, palms and vines which form the tropical rainforest (or moist forest) once the right conditions of temperature and moisture are met. The rainforest is characterized by the presence of several layers (though these will probably not be obvious from the ground), often connected by lianas and creepers: the **canopy**, perhaps 30–60m high, through which individual **emergent** trees rise; the **understorey** typically 10–20m high; and the **shrub** or ground layer. Many trees have only shallow tap roots, so **buttress roots**, flaring out from the trunk up to 6m above the ground, provide extra support.

The combination of a year-round growing season, plenty of moisture and millions of years of evolution have produced a unique environment. While temperate forests tend to be dominated by a few species – fir, oak or beech, for example – diversity characterizes the tropical forest. Each species is specifically adapted to fit into a particular ecological niche, where it receives a precise amount of light and moisture. It's a **biological storehouse** that has yet to be fully explored, although it has already yielded some astonishing discoveries. Steroid hormones, such as cortisone, and diosgenin, the active ingredient in birth control pills, were developed from wild yams found in these forests; and tetrodoxin, which is derived from a species of frog, is an anaesthetic 160,000 times stronger than cocaine.

Despite its size and diversity the forest is surprisingly **fragile**. It forms a closed system in which nutrients are continuously recycled and decaying plant matter fuels new growth. The forest floor is a spongy mass of roots, mosses and fungi, in which nutrients are broken down with the assistance of insects, bacteria and other micro-organisms, and chemical decay, before being released to the waiting roots and fresh seedlings. The thick canopy prevents much light reaching the forest floor, ensuring that the soil remains damp but warm – a hotbed of decomposition. The death of a large tree prompts a flurry of growth as new light reaches the forest floor, but once the trees are removed the soil is highly vulnerable, deprived of its main source of fertility. Exposed to the harsh tropical sun and direct rainfall, an area of cleared forest soon becomes prone to flooding and drought. Recently cleared land will contain enough nutrients for a few years of good growth, but its fertility declines rapidly. If the trees are stripped from a large area, soil erosion will silt the rivers and parched soils will disrupt local rainfall patterns. In its undisturbed state, however, the forest is superbly beautiful and is home to an incredible range of wildlife.

THE HIGHLANDS

The **highlands** occupy a broad region south of the main rainforest belt, stretching continuously from western Chiapas through the western and eastern highlands of Guatemala to the Maya Mountains of Belize. In Mexico the non-volcanic **Sierra Madre de Chiapas** run parallel to the coast, forming a steep barrier between 2500–2900m high to routes inland. Their sharp escarpments create a vast rain shadow, contributing to the relative aridity of the central depression of Chiapas.

The Sierras continue through Guatemala as a chain of 33 **volcanoes**, each peak within view of the next, beginning with Tacaná at over 4000m, straddling the Mexico–Guatemala border, right through to Izalco in El Salvador, the highest being **Tajumulco** at 4220m, just inside Guatemala. There are also three active cones: **Fuego**, **Pacaya** and **Santiaguito**, all of which belch sulphurous fumes, volcanic ash and the occasional fountain of molten rock. Beneath the surface their subterranean fires heat the bedrock, resulting in a number of **hot springs**.

On the northern side of the Sierra Madre and the volcanic ridge are the **central valleys** of the highlands, a complex mixture of sweeping bowls, steep-sided valleys, open plateaus and jagged peaks. This central area is home to the highland Maya population and all the available land is intensively farmed, with hillsides carved into workable terraces and portioned up into a patchwork of small fields. Traditionally, the land is rotated between milpa (slash-and-burn) fields and a fallow period, but in most areas it's now under constant pressure; the fertility of the soil is virtually exhausted and only with the assistance of fertilizer can it still produce a worthwhile crop. The pressure on land is immense and each generation is forced to farm more marginal territory, planting on steep hillsides where exposed soil is soon washed into the valley below.

Some areas remain off-limits to farmers, however: the peaks of the volcanoes, protected as national parks, are too steep to plant, and vast tracts of the highlands are still **forested**, with pine trees dominating, intermixed with oak, cedar and fir. At the higher elevations (2000–3000m) and under the right conditions **tropical montane forests** occur in isolated patches, some of which can be described as **cloudforests**. This scarce habitat features some evergreen trees, with branches draped in thick mosses, bromeliads and vines, and is home to one of the region's rarest and most spectacular birds, the resplendent **quetzal**, found in the cloudforests of the Sierra Madre and the Verapaces. Heading on to the north, the land rises to form several **mountain ranges**, the largest of which are the **Sierra de los Cuchumatanes**, a massive chain of granite peaks that reach a height of 3790m above Huehuetenango; further to the east there are several smaller ranges such as the Sierra de Chuacús, the Sierra de las Minas and the Sierra de Chama. The high peaks support stunted trees and open grassland, used for grazing sheep and cattle, but are too cold for maize and most other crops.

THE CARIBBEAN COAST AND THE BARRIER REEF

The unique environment of the **Caribbean Barrier Reef** is an almost continuous chain of **coral** beginning just south of Cancún and running 600km to the far south of Belize. East of the barrier reef are the only four **atolls** in the Caribbean: roughly oval-shaped reefs rising from the seabed surrounding a central lagoon. The largest, **Banco Chinchorro**, off the coast of southern Quintana Roo, is still infrequently visited; the others (relatively more accessible) are in Belize. All are under some form of protection as national parks or marine reserves; **Glover's Reef** is considered by scientists to be the best developed and the most pristine atoll in the Caribbean. **Offshore islands**, from Isla Contoy in the north, down through Isla Mujeres and **Cozumel** (off Quintana Roo) and Belize's hundreds of **cayes**, south to the **Bay Islands**, all have their own coral reefs and provide superb wildlife refuges, home to several endemic species.

Immediately inland from the coast and on the cayes, occupying slightly higher ground, the **littoral forest** is characterized by salt-tolerant plants, often with tough, waxy leaves which help conserve water. Species include red and white **gumbo limbo**, **black poisonwood**, **zericote**, **palmetto** and of course the **coconut**, which typifies Caribbean beaches, though it's not actually a native. The littoral forest supports a very high density of fauna, especially migrating birds, due to the succession of fruits and seeds, yet, due to its location, it also faces very high development pressure.

The shoreline is still largely covered with **mangroves**, which play an important economic role, not merely as nurseries for commercial fish species but also for their stabilization of the shoreline and their ability to absorb the force of hurricanes: each kilometre of mangrove shoreline is valued at several thousand dollars per year. The cutting down of mangroves, particularly on the cayes, exposes the land to the full force of the sea and can mean the end of a small and unstable island. The dominant species of the coastal fringe is the **red mangrove**, although in due course it undermines its own environment by consolidating the sea bed until it becomes more suitable for the less salt-tolerant black and white mangroves. The basis of the shoreline food chain is the nutrient-rich mud, held in place by the mangroves, whose roots are home to **oysters** and **sponges**. In the shallows, "meadows" of **seagrass beds** provide nurseries for many fish and invertebrates, and pasture for conch, manatees and turtles.

The extensive root system of seagrasses also protects beaches from erosion by holding the fragments of sand and coral together.

The reef is a world of astounding beauty, where fish and coral come in every imaginable colour. The corals look like an brilliant underwater forest, but in fact each coral is composed of colonies of individual **polyps**, feeding off plankton wafting past in the current. There are basically two types of coral: the hard, calcareous, reef-building corals, such as **brain coral** and **elkhorn coral** (known scientifically as the **hydrocorals**; 74 species), and the soft corals such as **sea fans** and **feather plumes** (the **ococorals**; 36 species). On the reefs you'll find the **chalice sponge**, which is a garish pink, the appropriately named **fire coral**, the delicate **feather-star crinoid** and the **apartment sponge**, a tall thin tube with lots of small holes in it.

In 1995 a major **coral reef bleaching** event occurred throughout the Caribbean. Coral bleaching occurs when the coral polyp loses some or all of the symbiotic **microalgae** (zooxanthellae) which live in its cells. This usually happens in response to stress, the most common cause of which is a period of above average sea temperatures, and it has been suggested that the increased occurrence of coral bleaching may be an indication of global warming.

THE PACIFIC COAST

The **Pacific coastline** is marked by a thin strip of grey or black volcanic sand, pounded by the surf. The **beach** itself mainly takes the form of large sandbanks, dotted with palm trees, which are ideal nesting sites for marine turtles. Behind these and before the mainland proper, lagoons and mangrove swamps create a maze of waterways that are an ideal breeding ground for young fish, waterfowl and a range of small mammals. Between the shore and the foothills of the highlands, the **coastal plain** is an intensely fertile and heavily farmed area, where the volcanic and alluvial soils are ideal for cultivating sugar cane, cotton and palm oil, for rubber plantations and cattle ranches. There's little land that remains untouched by the hand of commercial agriculture so it's hard to imagine what this must once have looked like, but it was almost certainly very similar to Petén – a mixture of savannah and rainforest supporting a rich array of wildlife.

Approaching the highlands, the volcanic soils, high rainfall and good drainage conspire to make it ideal for growing **coffee**, and it's here that both Mexico and Guatemala produce excellent crops, with rows of olive-green bushes ranked beneath shady trees. Where the land is unsuitable for coffee, lush tropical forest still grows, clinging to the hills. As you head up into the highlands, through deeply cleft valleys, you pass through some of this superb forest, dripping with moss-covered vines, bromeliads and orchids.

WILDLIFE

With far more species of plants and animals than the whole of North America, Central America is in many ways a paradise for visiting naturalists, above all for **botanists** and **birdwatchers**, with over 4500 species of flowering plants and over six hundred bird species. **Mammals**, too, are very diverse, ranging from the **jaguar**, the largest land predator, to tiny forest shrews, though both are equally elusive. The most common sighting is likely to be of **bats**, which make up almost half of all mammal species here. To give a complete listing of even the main species in each animal family, and the places you're likely to find them, would be impossible, so the ones mentioned below are necessarily just a small sample.

If you are keen on **seeing wildlife**, or even signs of it, there are a few things you can do to improve your chances. First, consider buying a specialist **wildlife guide** (see pp.511–12 for a selection) and consider bringing it along. Second, stay in or near one of the **protected areas**, which are covered in the guide. This might sound obvious, but all too often tourists are taken into a nature reserve during the day, when many animals are resting in the shade, in order to spend a few hours wandering about in the heat before trundling back to a hotel in the town. *Nothing* can increase your chances of spotting wildlife more than spending a whole day and a night in a reserve. Thus, the golden rule is never go on a day-trip to a reserve if you can spend the night there. Although many of the jungle lodges used by tour companies are very expensive, there are usually some budget options not far away. Finally, whether you're on an organized tour or travelling alone, go on a trail with a recommended **local guide**: you'll see more wildlife and glean more astonishing facts about the forest ecosystems under their guidance than you ever could alone.

Dozens of wildlife sites, national parks and reserves are covered in this guide. Some of the best, covering a range of habitats and which have several nearby accommodation choices, include: in Quintana Roo, the **Si'an Ka'an Biosphere Reserve**; in Chiapas, the **Montes Azules Biosphere Reserve**; in Guatemala, **Parque Nacional Tikal** and the Biotopo Mario Dary (the **Quetzal Reserve**); and in Belize, **Crooked Tree Wildlife Sanctuary** and the **Cockscomb Basin Wildlife Sanctuary**.

BIRDS

Birdlife is plentiful throughout the entire region. You'll see a variety of **hummingbirds**, flocks of screeching Aztec **parakeets**, **swifts**, **egrets** and the ever-present black and turkey **vultures** (*zopilote*), and in the forests you might be lucky and see the larger and more strikingly coloured **king vulture**. The forest is also home to three species of **toucan**: the collared aracari, the emerald toucanet and the keel-billed toucan – in some parks you can even see all three in one tree. One particularly interesting lowland species is the **oropendola**, a large oriole which builds a long woven nest hanging from trees and telephone wires. They tend to nest in colonies and a single tree might support fifty nests. You'll probably notice the nests more than the birds, but they thrive everywhere. At the archeological site of **Palenque** birding is unrivalled and local specialities include **chestnut-headed oropendola**, **scaled ant pitta**, **white-whiskered puffbird**, **slaty-tailed trogon**, **green shrike vireo** and **masked tanager**.

As the top predators in many places, **raptors** are often indicative of the overall health of a particular ecosystem. In the wetlands and on the coast **ospreys** are very common, and you'll often see one swooping on a fish. **Snail kites** are frequently seen on tree stumps along slow-moving rivers and, as its name implies, the **roadside hawk** is often seen sitting on fence posts along rural roads. The Mountain Pine Ridge of Belize is the habitat of the rare **orange-breasted falcon**; it's very similar cousin, the **bat falcon**, is more widespread. The largest raptors, such as the **harpy eagle**, the **solitary eagle**, the **black and white hawk eagle** and the **ornate hawk eagle** are rarely seen, but with perseverance and luck

they may be spotted in the protected highland forests.

Particularly striking are the brilliantly coloured **trogons**, including Guatemala's national bird, the resplendent **quetzal**. This magnificent bird once inhabited the cloud-forests from Chiapas to Costa Rica but, since the days of the Maya when it was hunted for its fantastic green tail-feathers, which snake behind it through the air as it flies, quetzal numbers have been significantly reduced and its current status is severely endangered. In Chiapas it is protected in the El Triunfo Biosphere Reserve and in Guatemala, in the Biotopo de Quetzal in Baja Verapaz (see p.391). Much more common are several species of **parrot**, including **red-lored**, **white-fronted** and **yellow-headed**, and the endangered **scarlet macaw** can still be seen in the mid-elevation forests. In the trees and on the ground, amongst the dense vegetation, it is also possible to see the larger game birds, such as **curassow**, **crested guan**, **chachalaca** and the splendidly coloured **ocellated turkey** – rare in most places but common at Tikal.

The abundant **wetlands** are wonderful places for bird-watching, and you're likely to see more species in and around these habitats than anywhere else. Inland, lagoons and rivers offer a great chance to spot a variety of birds, including several species of kingfisher and heron. One of the most common, the **belted kingfisher**, the region's largest, is very common, as is the smallest, the **pygmy kingfisher**. Members of the heron family include **tri-coloured herons**, **boat-billed herons**, **great egret**, **white ibis**, **roseate spoonbill**, and in some areas **wood storks** and **jabiru storks** – the last is the largest flying bird in the Americas. Other wetland birds include the **sungrebe**, **spotted rail**, **ruddy crake**, **northern jacana**, often seen stepping delicately on lily pads, and the **anhinga** – a cormorant-like bird which captures fish by spearing them with its dagger-like bill.

The coastal lagoons provide both feeding and breeding grounds for a huge variety of aquatic birds. The northern edge of the Yucatán Peninsula is famous for its fabulous collection of **migrating birds**, on their way to or from the eastern seaboard of North America, and its most famous residents are the large flocks of **greater flamingo**. Offshore, **Cozumel**, Mexico's largest island, provides some rewarding opportunities to sight seabirds such as **royal** and **Caspian terns**, **black skimmer**, and **Mexican sheartails**. Inland, the sparse woodland provides shelter for many typical endemics, such as the **Caribbean dove**, **lesser nighthawk**, **Yucatán vireo**, **Cozumel vireo**, **bananaquit** and a variety of **tanagers**. **Half Moon Caye**, right out on the eastern edge of Lighthouse Reef, Belize's outermost atoll, is a wildlife reserve designed to protect a breeding colony of four thousand **red-footed boobies**. Here you'll also see **frigate birds**, **brown pelicans**, **mangrove warblers** and **white-crowned pigeons**.

MAMMALS

Although mammals are widespread, they are almost always elusive, and your best chance of seeing them is at the bigger archeological sites, where they may have lost some of their fear of humans. At many forest sites you'll almost certainly see **howler** or **spider monkeys**, and at Bermudian Landing in the lower Belize River valley (see p.202), you can be almost guaranteed close-up views of troops of black howler monkeys – and you'll certainly hear the famous deep-throated roar of the males.

The largest land animal in the region is **Baird's tapir**, weighing up to 300kg, and usually found near water. Tapirs are endangered throughout most of their range but are not rare in Belize – though you're not likely to see one without a guide. Two species of peccary (New World wild pigs), the **collared** and the **white-lipped**, wander the forest floors in large groups, seeking out roots and palm nuts. The smaller herbivores include the **paca**, a rodent about the size of a piglet, which is hunted everywhere for food. It goes under several other names – *tepescuintle*, *agouti* and, in Belize, *gibnut*. You'll often see **coati**, inquisitive and intelligent members of the raccoon family, foraging in the leaf litter around the ruins with their long snouts, usually in family groups. Coatis and small **grey foxes** are frequently seen at Tikal, and in many places you can see **opossums** or **armadillos**.

Five species of wild cats are found in the region, though most are now rare outside the protected areas. **Jaguars** formerly ranged widely over the whole region, but the densest population is found in the lower elevation forests in the central area. **Pumas** usually keep

to remote highland and forest areas; less rare but still uncommon are the **ocelot** and the **margay**. The **jaguarundi** is the smallest and commonest of the wild cats, and you might spot one on a trail as it hunts during the day.

The coastal zone is home to the **West Indian manatee**, which can reach 4m in length and weigh up to 450kg. These placid and shy creatures move between the freshwater lagoons and the open sea. They were once hunted for their meat but are now protected and the places where they congregate have become tourist attractions. Belize has the largest manatee population in the Caribbean, estimated at between three hundred and seven hundred individuals.

REPTILES AND AMPHIBIANS

Reptiles might not be high on anyone's list of reasons to visit the Maya World, but they are plentiful and some are spectacular, even beautiful. Take a trip along almost any river and you'll see **green iguanas**; their very similar cousin the **spiny-tailed iguana** is very common at archeological sites in Yucatán. Even the small ones look like miniature dinosaurs and the big ones appear very fearsome, but they're all vegetarians. Other **lizards** are very common and you'll often see **geckos** lurking on a wall or ceiling hunting flies, or gaze in astonishment as a **basilisk** dashes upright across a creek or lagoon; hence its name in Belize – the "Jesus Christ lizard". Drift quietly along a river and you'll see **mud turtles** or **Central American river turtles** sunning themselves on logs.

Along the lower courses of rivers draining to the Gulf coast and the Caribbean are **Morelet's crocodiles**, which are common in almost any body of water, and not dangerous to humans unless they are very large – at least 3m long – but heed the warnings of locals if they advise against swimming in a particular lagoon. Previously hunted almost to extinction, they have made a remarkable comeback since being protected, and are now frequently spotted in Belize, Petén and Tabasco. The **caiman** is a smaller cousin, found in lagoons on the Pacific coast. The largest and rarest of the crocodilians is the **American salt-water crocodile**, found in places along the Yucatán coast, but most numerous on Turneffe Atoll in Belize.

Although there are at least 65 species of **snake** in the region, only a few are venomous and you're actually unlikely to see any snakes at all. One of the commonest is the **boa constrictor**, which is also the largest, growing up to 4m, though it poses no threat to humans. Others you might see are **coral snakes** (which are venomous) and **false coral snakes** (which are not); in theory they're easily distinguished by noting the arrangement of adjacent colours in the stripes, but it's best to admire all snakes from a distance unless you're an expert.

At night in the forest you'll hear the characteristic chorus of frog mating calls and you'll frequently find the **red-eyed tree frog** – a beautiful pale green creature about the size of the top joint of your thumb – in your shower in any rustic cabin. Less appealing perhaps are the giant **marine toads**, the largest toad in the Americas, weighing in at up to 1kg and growing to over 20cm. Like most frogs and toads it has toxic glands and the toxin of the marine toad has hallucinogenic properties – a property the ancient Maya exploited in their ceremonies by licking these glands and interpreting the resultant visions.

FISH

The Caribbean Barrier Reef is home to an incredible range of fish, including **angel**- and **parrotfish**, several species of **stingrays** and **sharks** (the most common are the relatively harmless nurse shark), **conger** and **moray eels**, **spotted goatfish**, and small striped **sergeant-major**. The sea and islands are also home to **grouper**, **barracuda**, **marlin** and the magnificent **sailfish**. Dolphins are frequently seen just offshore, mostly the **Atlantic bottle-nosed dolphin**, though further out large schools of the smaller **spotted dolphin** are sometimes found, and **whale sharks** pass by far out to sea in the autumn.

The reef has been harvested by fishermen for millennia, catching manatees and turtles as well as fish, but these days the **spiny lobster** and **queen conch** are the main catch, which are exported to the US. In the last two decades the fishing industry has been booming and the numbers of both of these have now gone into decline. Three species of **marine turtles**, the **loggerhead**, the **green** and the **hawksbill**, occur throughout the reef, nesting on isolated beaches, but they are seen infrequently as they

are still hunted for food. Recent changes in legislation and international agreements have provided them with greater protection, however.

INSECTS

Finally, one thing you'll realize pretty soon is that you're never far from an **insect** of some sort. Mostly you'll be trying to avoid them or even destroy them, particularly the common (though by no means ever-present) mosquitoes and sandflies. Some of the most beautiful insects, however, are the **butterflies**, which you'll frequently see feeding in clouds at the edges of puddles on trails. The caterpillars, too, are fascinating – and sometimes enormous. The largest and most spectacular are the members of the morpho family, of which the **blue morpho**, found in lowland forests, is a gorgeous electric blue. There are many more you can see on a visit to one of a growing number of **butterfly exhibits** in Belize.

Ants are the most numerous insects on the planet; something you can certainly believe on any walk in the forest here. The most impressive are perhaps **army ants**, with the whole colony ranging through the forest in a narrow column, voraciously hunting for insects. Don't be misled by the horror movies – they can't overpower you and rip the flesh from your bones – though they will give you a nasty bite if you get too close. People in rural areas welcome a visit as the ants will clear pests from their houses. **Leafcutter ants** have regular trails through the forest along which they carry sections of leaves often much larger than their bodies – the source of their alternative name, "parasol ants". The leaves are not food for the ants, but provide a growing medium for a unique type of **fungus** which the ants do eat. Evolution has linked ant and fungus, and neither can now survive without the other. **Spiders** (not strictly insects but arachnids) are also very common: take a walk at night with a flashlight anywhere in the countryside and you'll see the beam reflected back by the eyes of dozens of **wolf spiders** – remarkably bright for such small creatures. **Tarantulas** too, are found everywhere – and they really are as big as your hand. The sharp fangs look dangerous but tarantulas won't bite unless they're severely provoked.

CONSERVATION AND ECOTOURISM

The **environmental problems** facing the Maya World today are considerable. This century, the governments of the five countries have all followed a rigorous development strategy favouring industrialization and urbanization. Rapid population growth, political instability and war have also contributed to the widespread depletion of natural resources, while environmental pollution and overexploitation of natural resources persist. Over the past two decades, the region's presidents, responding to the diminishing forest cover and the pressure exerted from environmental groups, have often hinted at their concerns for conservation, but have rarely put any emphasis on creating environmental laws and policies.

The Maya world is rich in **biodiversity** and there are considerable pressures both from local people and from large foreign organizations with outside economic interest to exploit its natural wealth. Multinational timber companies clamber for a piece of the Maya forest to sustain the ever-strong cedar and mahogany trade. Coffee, cotton and banana cash-cropping and the illegal use of damaging pesticides have also led to extensive clearing of lands. On a regional level, the sale of local land for timber and ranching is seen as a means to short-term economic gain and little consideration given to the environmental consequences that may ultimately follow.

More recently it has been accepted that the largest single problem now affecting many areas of natural beauty is the overexploitation of the region by the mass tourism industry, in places such as **Cancún** in Mexico and the Honduran **Bay Islands**. A lack of education about what constitutes good environmental practice prevails in these parts, and the natural environment and in particular the forested areas of the Maya World have frequently been seen as an expendable resource for development. In recent years, however, there's been some recognition of the importance of finding a balance between conservation and development.

CONSERVATION EFFORTS

With the exception of Belize, the five nations of the Maya World have been slow to adopt **envi-**ronmental legislation** to protect their remaining natural ecosystems. **Mexico** was the one of the first countries to put into practice an idea that allowed for the protection of the environment alongside sustainable use of its resources, creating in 1974 the first **Biosphere Reserve**, at Montes Azules. An idea that originated at the UNESCO Conference in 1968, Biosphere Reserves are divided into zones, each with different ecological functions, uses and management structures. Over the past two decades the design has been fine-tuned, resulting in a model of three zones: an **outer transition** zone, in which the sustainable use of resources by locals is permitted; a **buffer zone**, where activities are severely limited; and a **conservation zone**, where access is strictly limited to qualified people for research and education purposes. Biosphere reserves involve NGOs and local community groups who work together with the government to promote sustainable development at a local level, a strategy that has been successfully implemented at the **Si'an Ka'an Biosphere Reserve** in **Quintana Roo** (see p.119).

The first strides towards conservation in **Guatemala** came in the 1980s as a result of the international reaction to satellite pictures of the Petén rainforest. The photos highlighted the problem of deforestation in the region, showing a sharp contrast in forest cover just across the border in Mexico. In an attempt to avoid this devastation, the Guatemalan government was prompted to set aside large areas of natural forest for conservation projects. In 1990 the **Maya Biosphere Reserve** was created in Petén to preserve 16,000 square kilometres of tropical lowland forests and wetlands. The reserve is administered, along with other national parks, by CONAP (National Council of Protected Areas); Guatemala's best chance of combining development and conservation is considered to be the creation of ecotourism initiatives in the region.

With a longstanding focus on biodiversity preservation, **Belize** has gained recognition as one of the most conservation-aware nations of the Americas. More than seventy percent of the forest remains and over 35 percent of Belize's territory is now covered by some sort of environmental legislation. The country also boasts an impressive network of national parks, nature reserves and wildlife sanctuaries. Various national and international voluntary organizations and conservation groups have been active in conservation in Belize for many years and have built up experience by practical work and by attending and hosting environmental conferences. Belize has also become a popular destination for working vacations, with organizations such as Coral Caye Conservation directly involving groups of young people in the conservation of delicate natural habitats.

Smallest of the five nations of the Maya World, **El Salvador** has one of the highest rates of deforestation in the world. Intensive cultivation of the land for cash crops, urban pressures and war have been responsible for the depletion of much of the country's virgin forest, to the extent that only six percent remains. The country also suffers from serious river pollution and erosion, and from the use of pesticides for cash crops has left much of the land infertile. Despite all of this, El Salvador remains an intensely beautiful country, but it is also the only nation of the Maya World without any serious environmental protection laws. Efforts are now underway to protect existing forested areas with reforestation campaigns and plans to encourage ecotourism. Recently, the country took a giant step forward with the designation of areas such as **Cerro Verde** as national parks.

Honduras has suffered from similar problems as its tiny neighbour, leading to deforestation and soil erosion. The first environmental law was passed here in 1993 and in recent years environmental groups have come together to jointly administer the country's protected areas and parks and to tackle issues from both a local and a national perspective. There are now over a hundred biological reserves and protected areas, though the more critical environmentalists have described these as nothing more than "paper parks" and claim that the government has neither the political will nor the financial backing to curb the destruction of the forest by multinational timber companies.

On an **international** level, there has recently been a move towards a cross-border conservation effort that looks very promising. The **MesoAmerican Biological Corridor**, backed by US and European governments and large donations from the World Bank, is planned to be the world's longest natural corridor, stretching from North America to South and allowing

---

CONSERVATION ORGANIZATIONS IN THE MAYA WORLD

The Belize Aubudon Society, PO Box 1001, 12 Fort St, Belize City (☎02/34987). Founded in 1969, this is the oldest conservation organization in Belize and is responsible for managing many of the country's reserves. Also provides useful information for travellers on visiting the reserves.

The Belize Zoo (see p.233). Has an excellent reputation for conservation and education. It actively participates in education projects with local schools and is also a growing ecotourism destination.

Ix Chel Medicine Farm (see p.244). An important centre for medical plant research and a popular destination for ecotourists.

Amigos de Si'an Ka'an (see p.120). A non-profit-making organization running ecological tours into the Si'an Ka'an reserve. The tours are well run and informative and all tourist revenues are used for conservation projects and local education programmes, which stress the importance of sustainable use of resources.

Pronatura Yucatán This is a group dedicated to the conservation of Mexico's protected areas. It is currently working projects in Río Lagartos, Celestún and the Calakmul Biosphere Reserve and

is actively involved in environmental management, community development, research and environmental education.

The Biotopo del Quetzal (see p.391). Protects 7,000 acres of cloud and forest area and acts as a safe haven for Guatemala's endangered quetzal, the nation's symbol. It also encourages scientific research and ecotourism within its boundries.

Wildlife Conservancy Society, 185th St, South Boulevard Building A, New York, NY 10460. Part of the New York Zoological Society, this organization is currently active in conservation projects in Petén, Guatemala.

Conservation International/ProPetén (see p.405). Promotes natural forestry management and conservation projects in the Maya Biosphere Reserve in Petén. It is also involved in fighting a long and sometimes violent battle against illegal activities that to date still go on this area.

SalvaNatura (see p.465). A non-profitmaking group working to safeguard the few remaining areas of natural beauty in El Salvador. The group has launched an environmental education programme and backs local community development.

wildlife a safe haven for the entire length of the Americas. It supersedes the Paseo Pantera, an ambitious regional plan devised by the governments of the Central American nations to link up protected areas – a plan that ultimately faltered due to lack of funding. In 1992 the presidents of participating nations signed the **Convention for the Conservation of Biological Diversity and the Protection of Natural Areas**. According to CCAD (Central American Commission for Environment and Development), the project will "put protected areas together using biodiversity-friendly forms of land use". It will use certain forms of development such as environmentally friendly tourism and carry out important research and development into alternative forest uses as a way of raising the necessary funds to keep these areas protected. At the time of writing, the corridor project remains very much in the planning stage and while many remain sceptical of the future success of the project, it does seem to offer a viable strategy for helping to conserve the region's natural wealth.

ECOTOURISM

Tourists have been visiting resorts like Acapulco since as far back as the 1920s, but it wasn't until the 1960s that **tourism** really took off in the Maya world. Like so many other countries with failing economies, the governments of the five countries sat up and took notice of the masstourist "phenomenon" sweeping through the western developed world. However, over the past twenty years, as tourism has continued to spread further into the Maya heartland, observations began to be made about its responsibility for the heightening environmental problems.

As a result, the Maya world has begun to experience a new trend in world tourism. Nature tourism, or **ecotourism**, now represents the fastest growing subsector of the industry, generating billions of dollars annually. Estimates on its exact value vary a great deal, but it is believed to account for about seven percent of international tourist receipts and is continuing to grow rapidly. The nations of the Maya World, like so many other developing countries, have latched onto the idea of ecotourism as the answer to the problems caused by mass tourism. And it's true that, if implemented properly, ecotourism would allow the region to capitalize on its resources and earn badly needed foreign revenue without destroying the environment.

Where the problem lies is that ecotourism means different things to the different groups involved in the tourism and conservation industries. If it is to be recognized as a legitimate sector of the tourist industry, then it has to have a workable, universally recognized **definition**. Ideally, it should be a community-based form of tourism that focuses on the wildlife and landscape of the region and shows respect for the local culture and history. It should aim to minimize the harmful effects of tourism on the natural environment, and better still, promote conservation. On a financial level, ecotourists can help to generate money for conservation and community projects, while local communities should benefit from new job opportunities. This type of **responsible tourism** should also provide local people with economic incentives to safeguard their environment.

There are many **examples** of projects throughout the Maya world which are trying to implement this new style of tourism. An excellent example is Mexico's **Yaxche – Arbol de la Vida**, a community-based ecotourism project that aims to bring tourism development to local communities in Yucatán, Quintana Roo and Chiapas. Tourists stay with families, eating traditional foods and experiencing true Maya culture and the natural environment. In **Belize**, the Toledo Ecotourism Association in Punta Gorda is also working with local communities to encourage eco-practice and ecotourism (see p.276).

ECO-EXPLOITATION

Whatever its benefits, ecotourism is not a panacea for all the deep-rooted environmental and social problems that mass tourism has created over the years. Perhaps the biggest problem is the misuse of the term itself. Large, mainly foreign, companies are taking advantage of this new niche in the market to sell more or less the same old tourism product, repackaged under the "eco" label – a practice that environmentalists have termed **eco-exploitation**.

The proliferation of eco-tours, eco-adventure and eco-travel over recent years has resulted in ecotourism being perceived as a type of environmental opportunism. It calls the credibility of ecotourism into question, with it running the risk of falling into the same trap as conventional tourism did before it. Until a common definition is arrived at, and guidelines set out for ecotourism objectives, true ecotourists will have to question the motives for ecotourism development and judge for themselves whether a project is using market interest in all things "green" to make a quick profit or is genuinely involved in conservation.

Unfortunately the Maya World has suffered more than most from the hijacking of the "eco" prefix – to the extent that hotel chains building new resorts in previously untouched areas are describing them as ecological. It is a problem that has particularly affected the Yucatán peninsula in Mexico. In 1997, the sacred paradise of **Bacalar** was brought into the sphere of international tourism when **Club Las Velas Gold** built its new "ecological" resort to "resemble a Maya village" – as their adverts claimed. However, any advocate for nature tourism will be quick to question how many authentic Maya villages contain eighteen-hole golf courses, marinas and luxury swimming pools.

Further north up the Quintana Roo coastline is the Eco-adventure Park **Xcaret** – known by environmentalists as the "Mexican Theme Park Painted Green". The owners of the park are, in fact, committed to a number of environmental research projects financed by the park revenues and a concerted effort is made to avoid the everyday environmental damage caused by visitors. However, despite the fact that Xcaret and others like it would appear to be conforming to the rules of ecotourism, it has come under severe criticism from several quarters. It is hard to fault the park's intentions, but strolling around the purpose-built attractions or across the man-made beach (with its imported sand) highlights the distinction between this type of project and grass-roots local initiatives.

Perhaps the biggest problem commonly associated with ecotourism development in the Maya World is that previously untouched regions with delicately balanced physical and cultural environments are being discovered and consequently overwhelmed by ecotourists. All tourism comes at a price in terms of environmental degradation, and no matter how aware we may be, the sheer presence of visitors can have a damaging effect on the natural environment and local culture. This has been the case in many so-called ecotourism destinations. In the **Hol Chan Marine Reserve** in Belize, ever-increasing numbers of ecotourists visiting the endangered reef ecosystems are in fact jeopardizing the very thing that they are coming to visit.

On an international level the **Mundo Maya Intergovernmental Plan for Tourism** has provoked concern amongst advocates of nature tourism. In October 1988 government members met in Guatemala City to discuss common problems relating to conservation and regional development. The outcome was an ambitious regional tourism plan called **La Ruta Maya** (later renamed **Mundo Maya**), which aims to promote environmentally sensitive tourism and sustainable development, creating employment opportunities, particularly in rural areas, and stimulating regional development.

As part of the project, research programmes are being set up to establish ecotourism projects that involve the direct participation of local rural communities. To date the plan is succeeding in minimizing damage caused to the environment, though there is no active involvement by tourists in the protection of the natural resources which are being visited. There is a positive attempt to apply rules and regulations to new hotels and resorts, and the Mundo Maya Organization does claim to carry out quality environmental assessments for these new developments. Unfortunately, though, it seems that these good intentions are not being carried out as planned. As a result, the project has come under criticism by many involved in ecotourism and conservation.

The project is seriously undermined by the promotion of **Cancún** (the most perfect example of the devastation caused by tourism development) within the plan, and **MayaPass**, a project that aims to increase the flows of tourists into previously untouched areas by improving the transport system. As one critic comments:"The Maya's sacred treasures have become public property in a Latin Disneyland style atmosphere."

The Ruta Maya project highlights a problem that has long affected developing regions: like so many other so-called ecotourism developments that are dominated by wealthy entrepreneurs, tour operators and hotel chains, a large proportion of the economic benefits may in fact bypass the needy local economies, ending up instead in the pockets of wealthy foreign investors in the developed world. There is still hope for the project, however, and it is helping to stimulate development in many needy areas, but it must be recognized that the plan still has a long way to go before it can be considered to be true ecotourism.

THE FUTURE

These problems aside, ecotourism shouldn't be seen as mass tourism's evil twin. Despite ideological difficulties, it does represent a more attractive alternative to mass tourism, and if developers choose not to opt for ecotourism initiatives, natural areas will invariably be destroyed through other uses. Ecotourism now offers the Maya World an amazing potential to link development and conservation. Not only will this allow these five countries the unique chance to preserve their environment and heritage for generations to come, it will allow them to capitalize on these resources and create new development opportunities for the future.

Tourists with a genuine interest in basing their trip on the natural environment are now able to choose from a wide variety of ecotourism experiences throughout the Maya World, many of which are noted throughout the guide. As the industry moves closer to setting out guidelines and rules and clarifying the true meaning of ecotourism, the region will hopefully see a rise in community-based ecotourism that will play an important part in taking conservation and development in the Maya World into the twenty-first century.

BOOKS

Until recently the Maya World has provoked limited literary attention, but the armed confrontations of the 1980s and recent Mayanist advances have seen an upsurge in the number of publications. However, there are no books currently available that take a contemporaneous look at politics in the Maya World as a whole – books are divided between those covering Central America as a region or individual countries, though many of the travel-based accounts delve fairly deeply into the subject. Books covering the Maya World and Central America are listed first, followed by sections on each country. Publishers are given in the format UK/US; where only one publisher is listed, this covers both the UK and US, unless specified.

TRAVEL

Peter Canby *Heart of the Sky – Travels Among the Maya* (HarperCollins). The author treads a familiar path through the Maya World, encountering an interesting collection of expats, Mayanists, priests, Guatemala City's idle rich and a female shaman. Though not as erudite as Ronald Wright's masterful account (see below), it's still an accessible and informative read.

Thomas Gage *Travels in the New World* (University of Oklahoma Press). Unusual account of a Dominican friar's travels through Mexico and Central America between 1635 and 1637, including some fascinating insights into colonial life, as well as some great attacks on the greed and pomposity of the Catholic Church abroad.

Aldous Huxley *Beyond the Mexique Bay* (Flamingo, UK). Huxley's travels took him, in 1934, from Belize through Guatemala to Mexico; swept on by his fascination for history and religion, he sprouted bizarre theories on everything he saw. Some great descriptions of Maya sites and culture, with superb one-liners summing up people and places. Some editions are illustrated with some interesting photographs of the ruins, people and markets.

Patrick Marnham *So Far From God* (Penguin). A saddened and vaguely right-wing account of Marnham's travels through the Americas from the US to Nicaragua (missing out Belize), including a fair chunk in the Maya region. Dotted with amusing anecdotes and interesting observations, the book's descriptions are dominated by the civil wars in Guatemala and El Salvador.

Nigel Pride *A Butterfly Sings to Pacaya* (Constable; o/p). An account of the author's travels, accompanied by his wife and four-year-old son, south from the US border in a jeep, heading through Mexico, Belize and Guatemala. A large section of the book is set in Maya areas, and it is illustrated by the author's drawings of people and animals. Though the travels took place 25 years ago, the pleasures and privations they experience rarely appear dated.

John Lloyd Stephens *Incidents of Travel in Central America, Chiapas, and Yucatán* (Dover). Stephens was a classic nineteenth-century traveller. Acting as American ambassador to Central America, he indulged his own enthusiasm for archeology; while the republics fought it out among themselves, he was wading through the jungle stumbling across ancient cities. His journals, written with superb Victorian pomposity punctuated with sudden waves of enthusiasm, make great reading. Some editions include fantastic illustrations by Catherwood of the ruins overgrown with tropical rainforest.

Ronald Wright *Time Among the Maya* (Abacus/Henry Holt). A vivid and sympathetic account of travels from Belize through Guatemala, Chiapas and Yucatán, meeting the Maya and exploring their obsession with time. The book's twin points of interest are the ancient Maya and the violence of the 1970s and 1980s. The author's knowledge is evident in the superb historical insight he imparts throughout the book, and an encyclopedic bibliography offers ideas for exploration. Certainly one of the very best travel books on the area.

ANCIENT MAYA CIVILIZATION

Michael Coe *The Maya* (Thames & Hudson). Now in its fifth edition, this clear and comprehensive introduction to Maya archeology is certainly the best on offer. Coe has also written several more weighty, academic volumes. His *Breaking the Maya Code* (Penguin/Thames & Hudson), a very personal history of the decipherment of the glyphs, owes much to the fact that Coe was present at many of the most important meetings leading to the breakthrough. This book demonstrates that the glyphs did actually reproduce Maya speech.

T. Patrick Culbert *Maya Civilization* (Smithsonian Press in US). Well-structured introduction to the subject written by a prominent Mayanist, which includes the latest theories on the collapse of the Classic civilization; colour illustrations and photographs throughout. *Classic Maya Political History* (Cambridge University Press), edited by the same author, is far more academic in tone and content.

M.S. Edmonson (translator) *The Book of Chilam Balam of Chumayel* (Agean, US). The *Chilam Balam* is a recollection of Maya history and myth, recorded by the Spanish after the Conquest. Although the style is not easy, it's one of the few insights into the Maya view of the world.

Mary Ellen Miller and Karl Taube *The Gods and Symbols of Ancient Mexico and the Maya: An Illustrated Dictionary of Mesoamerican Religion* (Thames & Hudson). A superb modern reference tool for studying ancient Mesoamerica, written by two leading scholars. Taube's *Aztec and Maya Myths* (British Museum Press) is perfect as a short accessible introduction to the region's mythology.

Jeremy A. Sabloff *Cities of Ancient Mexico* (Thames & Hudson). Though only a proportion of the book is devoted to the Maya World, the book is still the best introduction to ancient Mexico currently available. Also worth checking out is his *New Archeology and the Ancient Maya* (W.H. Freeman).

Linda Schele and David Freidel et al. The authors, in the forefront of the "new archeology", have been personally responsible for decoding many of the glyphs. While the writing style, which frequently includes "recreations" of scenes inspired by their discoveries, is controversial, it has nevertheless inspired a devoted following. *A Forest of Kings: The Untold Story of the Ancient Maya* (Quill, US), in conjunction with *The Blood of Kings* by Linda Schele and Mary Miller, shows that, far from being governed by peaceful astronomer-priests, the ancient Maya were ruled by hereditary kings, lived in populous, aggressive city-states, and engaged in a continuous entanglement of alliances and war. *The Maya Cosmos* (Quill, US) by Schele, Freidel and Joy Parker, is perhaps more difficult to read, dense with copious notes, but continues to examine Maya ritual and religion in a unique and far-reaching way. *The Code of Kings* (Scribner, US), written in collaboration with Peter Matthews and illustrated with Justin Kerr's famous "rollout" photography of Maya ceramics, examines in detail the significance of the monuments at selected Maya sites. It's her last book – Linda Schele died in April 1998 – and sure to become a classic of epigraphic interpretation.

Robert Sharer, *The Ancient Maya* (Stanford University). The classic, comprehensive (and weighty) account of Maya civilization, now in a completely revised and much more readable fifth edition, yet as authoritative as ever. Required reading for archeologists, it provides a fascinating reference for the non-expert.

Dennis Tedlock (translator) *The Popol Vuh* (Scribner/Touchstone). The epic poem of the Quiché Maya of Guatemala, written shortly after the Conquest and intended to preserve the tribe's knowledge of its history. It's an amazing swirl of ancient mythological characters and their wandering through the Quiché highlands, tracing Quiché ancestry back to the beginning. Though there are other versions, Tedlock's is the definitive publication.

J. Eric S. Thompson *The Rise and Fall of the Maya Civilization* (University of Oklahoma). A major authority on the ancient Maya during his lifetime, Thompson produced many academic studies, of which this is one of the more approachable. Although recent researchers have overturned many of Thompson's theories, his work provided the inspiration for the post-war surge of interest in the Maya and he remains a respected figure.

WILDLIFE AND THE ENVIRONMENT

Catherine Caulfield *In the Rainforest* (Knopf, US; o/p). Still, after a decade in print, one of the best introductory volumes to rainforests, dealing in an accessible, discursive fashion with many of the issues covered in the more academic or specialized titles. Much of the book is directed at the Amazon, but could easily be transposed to Honduras, Belize or Guatemala.

Louise H. Emmons *Neotropical Rainforest Mammals* (University of Chicago). Supported by François Feer's colour illustrations, this highly informative book is written by experts for non-scientists. Local and scientific names are given, along with plenty of interesting snippets.

Steve Howe and Sophie Webb *The Birds of Mexico and Northern Central America* (Oxford University Press). A tremendous work, the result of years of research, this is the definitive book on the region's birds. Essential for all serious birders.

John C. Kricher *A Neotropical Companion* (Princeton University Press). Subtitled "An Introduction to the Animals, Plants and Ecosystems of the New World Tropics", this contains an amazing amount of valuable information for nature lovers. Researched mainly in Central America, so there's plenty that's directly relevant.

GUIDEBOOKS

Bruce Hunter *A Guide to Ancient Maya Ruins* (University of Oklahoma Press in US and UK). Useful accompaniment to all the major sites in the Maya World, though many of the more obscure ruins are omitted.

Joyce Kelly *An Archaeological Guide to Northern Central America* (University of Oklahoma). Detailed and practical guide to 38 Maya sites and 25 museums in Guatemala, Belize, Honduras and El Salvador; an indispensable companion for anyone travelling through these countries. The second volume, *An Archeological Guide to Mexico's Yucatán Peninsula,* is an equally essential purchase for real exploration of the Mexico's Maya ruins and includes over ninety sites and eight museums. Kelly's star ratings – based on a site's archeological importance, degree of restoration and accessibility – may affront purists, but it does provide a valuable opinion on how worthwhile a particular visit might be.

CENTRAL AMERICAN HISTORY AND POLITICS

Tom Barry *Central America Inside Out* (Grove Atlantic in US). Well-informed summary of the entire region by an author who has also written or co-written books on every country in the Maya World.

Peter Dale-Scott and Jonathan Marshall *Cocaine Politics: Drugs, Armies and the CIA in Central America* (University of California). Polemical but well-researched exposé of CIA involvement in cocaine trafficking and political oppression in Central America in the 1980s. Reveals the truth behind the Iran–Contra scandal and gives the lie to the rhetoric of the war on drugs.

James Dunkerley *Power in the Isthmus* and *The Pacification of Central America* (Norton/Verso). Detailed accounts of the region's politics (excluding Belize) that offer a good study of recent events, particularly the region's civil wars, albeit in academic style. Well researched with plenty of statistics and charts.

William Weinberg *War on the Land: Ecology and Politics in Central America* (Zed Books/ Humanities Press). The author tells a story of intertwining conflicts and causes between conservation (and to a small extent ecotourism), land rights and politics in the individual Central American countries in a volume that deftly straddles the gap between academic interest and the general reader.

Ralph Lee Woodward Jr *Central America: A Nation Divided* (Oxford University Press). More readable than Dunkerley, this is probably the best book for a general summary of the Central American situation, despite its daft title.

BELIZE

HISTORY, POLITICS AND SOCIETY

Rosita Arvigo with Nadia Epstein *Sastun.* A rare glimpse into the life and work of a Maya *curandero,* the late Elijio Panti of San Antonio, Belize. Dr Arvigo has ensured the survival of many generations of accumulated healing knowledge, and this book is a testimony both to her perseverance in becoming accepted by Mr Panti and the cultural wisdom of the indigenous people. Arvigo has also written and co-authored several other books on traditional medicine in Belize, including *Rainforest Remedies.*

The Maya Atlas (North Atlantic Books, Berkley). As much a collection of personal accounts compiled by the contemporary Maya of southern Belize as it is a geography book, this is a fascinating co-production between university researchers and the Maya of Toledo. Trained by Berkely cartographers, teams of villagers surveyed their lands, completed a census and then wrote a history of each community. The regional maps accurately show the position of each village and drawings and photographs show scenes from everyday life. Available in Belize from the Toledo Maya Cultural Council, PO Box 104, Punta Gorda, Belize.

Tom Barry and Dylan Vernon *Inside Belize* (Resource Center in US). Excellent summary of the social economic and political affairs, published in 1995.

Infocus: Belize (LAB in UK; due to be published in 1999). Another addition to a concise, reliable country guide series that covers much of Latin America and the Caribbean.

Gerald S. Koop *Pioneer Years in Belize* (Country Graphics, Belize). A history of the Mennonites in Belize, written in a style as stolid and practical as the lives of the pioneers themselves. A good read nonetheless.

Assad Shoman *Thirteen Chapters of a History of Belize* (Angelus Press, Belize). A long overdue treatment of the country's history written by a Belizean who's not afraid to examine colonial myths with a detailed and rational analysis. Primarily a school textbook, but the style will not alienate non-student readers. Shoman, active in politics both before and since independence, also wrote *Party Politics in Belize*, a short but highly detailed account of the development of party politics in the country.

ARCHEOLOGY

Byron Foster (ed) *Warlords and Maize Men – A Guide to the Maya Sites of Belize* (Cubola, Belize). An excellent handbook to fifteen of the most accessible sites in Belize, compiled by the Association for Belizean Archeology and the Belize Department of Archeology.

J Eric S Thompson *The Maya of Belize – Historical Chapters Since Columbus* (Cubola, Belize). Interesting study of Belizean history in the first two centuries of Spanish colonial rule. It's a little-researched area of Belizean history and casts some light on the groups that weren't immediately conquered by the Spanish.

FICTION, POETRY AND AUTOBIOGRAPHY

Zee Edgell *Beka Lamb* (Heinemann). A young girl's account of growing up in Belize in the 1950s, in which the problems of adolescence are described alongside those of the Belizean independence movement. The book also explores everyday life in the colony, describing the powerful structure of matriarchal society and the influence of the Catholic Church. *In Times Like These* (Heinemann) is a semi-autobiographical account of personal and political intrigue set in the months leading up to Belize's independence.

Zoila Ellis *On Heroes, Lizards and Passion* (Cubola, Belize). Seven short stories written by a Belizean woman with a deep understanding of her country's people and their culture.

Felicia Hernandez *Those Ridiculous Years* (Cubola, Belize). A short autobiographical book about growing up in Dangriga in the 1960s.

Emory King *Belize 1798* (Tropical Books, Belize). Rip-roaring historical novel peopled by the charcters involved in the Battle of St George's Caye. King's enthusiasm for his country's history results in the nearest thing you'll get to a Belizean blockbuster, yet it's based on meticulous research in archives on both sides of the Atlantic. Wonderful holiday reading.

Shots From The Heart (Cubola, Belize). Slim anthology of the work of three young Belizean poets: Yasser Musa, Kiren Shoman and Simone Waight. Evocative imagery and perceptive comment relate experiences of a changing society. Musa's *Belize City Poem* (published separately) is a sharply observed, at times vitriolic, commentary on the impact of the simultaneous arrival of independence and US-dominated television on Belizean society.

WILDLIFE

Alan Rabinowitz *Jaguar* (Arbor House, UK). Account of the author's experiences studying jaguars for the New York Zoological Society in the early 1980s and living with a Maya family in the Cockscomb Basin, Belize. Rabinowitz was instrumental in the establishment of the Jaguar Reserve in 1984.

SPECIFIC GUIDES

Kirk Barrett *Belize by Kayak*. The most detailed book on this increasingly popular activity, though not widely available; contact *Reef Link Kayaking*, 3806 Cottage Grove, Des Moines, Iowa, US.

Ned Middleton *Diving in Belize* (Aqua Quest, US). The most readable book on the subject, expertly written and illustrated with excellent photographs taken by the author. Covers in detail all the atolls and many of the reefs and individual dive sites. Includes a section on Mexico's Banquo Chinchorro, just north of Belize.

GUATEMALA

HISTORY, POLITICS AND SOCIETY

Tom Barry *Guatemala: A Country Guide* (Resource Centre). A comprehensive and concise account of the political, social and economic situation in Guatemala, with a mild left-wing stance. Currently the best source for a good overview of the situation though the latest edition, published in 1992, excludes the Peace Accords.

Edward F Fisher and R McKenna Brown (eds)*Maya Cultural Activism in Guatemala* (University of Texas Press). Effectual summary of the indigenous movement in Guatemala, with strong chapters on clothing and identity and the revival of interest in Maya language and hieroglyphic writing.

Jim Handy *Gift of the Devil* (South End Press in US). Excellent history of Guatemala, concise and readable with a sharp focus on the Maya population and the brief period of socialist government. Don't expect too much detail on the distant past, which is only explored in order to set the modern reality in some kind of context, but if you're interested in the history of Guatemalan brutality then this is the book to read. By no means objective, it sets out to expose the development of oppression and to point the finger at those responsible.

Rigoberta Menchú *Rigoberta Menchú – An Indian Woman in Guatemala* and *Crossing Borders* (Verso). Momentous story of one of Latin America's most remarkable women, Nobel Peace Prize winner, Rigoberta Menchú. The first volume is a horrific account of family life in the Maya highlands, recording how Menchú's famly were targeted, terrorized and murdered by the military. The book also reveals much concerning Quiché Maya cultural traditions and the enormous gulf between ladino and indigenous society in Guatemala. The second volume docu-

ments Menchú's life in exile in Mexico, her work at the United Nations fighting for indigenous people and her return to Guatemala. An astounding tale of a woman's spirit, courage and determination.

Víctor Perera *Unfinished Conquest* (University of California Press in US and UK). Superb, extremely readable account of the civil war tragedy, plus comprehensive attention to the political, social and economic inequalities affecting the author's native country. Immacutely researched, the book's strength comes from the extensive interviews with both ordinary and influential Guatemalans and incisive analysis of recent history. The best introduction to the subject.

Jean-Marie Simon *Eternal Spring – Eternal Tyranny* (Norton in US and UK). Of all the books on human rights in Guatemala, this is the one that speaks with the utmost clarity. Combining the highest standards in photography with crisp text, there's no attempt to persuade you – the facts are allowed to speak for themselves, which they do with amazing strength. If you want to know what happened in Guatemala over the last twenty years or so there is no better book. Again, Simon clearly takes sides, aligning herself with the revolutionary left: there's no mention of any abuses committed by the guerrillas.

TRAVEL

Anthony Daniels *Sweet Waist of America* (Arrow/Trafalgar Square; o/p). A delight to read. Daniels takes a refreshingly even-handed approach to Guatemala and comes up with a fascinating cocktail of people and politics, discarding the stereotypes that litter most books on Central America.

FICTION

Miguel Angel Asturias *Hombres de Maíz* (Macmillan). Guatemala's most famous author, Nobel Prize winner Asturias, is deeply indebted to Guatemalan history and culture in his work. "Men of Maize" is generally regarded as his masterpiece, classically Latin American in its magic realist style, and bound up in the complexity of indigenous culture. His other works include *El Señor Presidente*, a grotesque portrayal of social chaos and dictatorial rule, based on Asturias's own experience; *El Papa Verde*, which explores the murky world of the United Fruit

Company; and *Weekend en Guatemala*, describing the downfall of the Arbenz government.

Francisco Goldman *The Long Night of White Chickens* (Grove Atlantic Faber). Drawing on the stylistic complexity of Latin American fiction, this novel tells the tale of a young Guatemalan orphan who flees to Boston, US, and works as a maid. When she finally returns home to Guatemala City she is murdered. It's a tremendously interesting and ambitious story, flavoured with all the bitterness and beauty of Guatemala's natural and political landscape. The novel inspired the film *Men With Guns*.

Gaspar Pedro Gonzáles *A Mayan Life* (Yax Te' Press, US). Absorbing story of the personal and cultural difficulties affecting a K'anjobal Maya from the Cuchumatanes mountains. The conflict between indigenous and ladino values becomes acutely evident as the central character seeks a higher education. Rich in ethnological detail and highly autobiographical, the book claims to be the first novel ever written by a Maya writer.

SPECIALIST GUIDES
William Coe *Tikal: A Handbook to the Ancient Maya Ruins*. Superbly detailed account of the site, usually available at the ruins. The detailed map of the main area is essential for in-depth exploration.

EL SALVADOR

HISTORY, POLITICS AND SOCIETY
Robert Armstrong and Janet Shenk *El Salvador: The Face of Revolution*. Accessible history of the root causes and development of the civil war of the 1980s.

Charles Clements *Witness to War* (Bantam Press). Fascinating account of a year spent working in the guerilla zone of Guazapa in the early 1980s by a volunteer US doctor. A vivid portrayal of how the civil war affected a specific area, which allows the reader a greater insight into what conditions were like across El Salvador.

Larry Dowell and Mark Deinner *El Salvador* (Norton). Evocative and compelling collection of photographs taken during 1986, sharply deliniating the progress of the civil war and its impact.

Kevin Murray and Tom Barry *El Salvador –a Country Guide* (Resource Center). Concise study of contemporary political, economic and social

affairs, with historical background, detailing the initiatives made in the years following the 1992 peace accords.

FICTION AND POETRY
Roque Dalton *Taberna y Otras Lugares*; *Poemas Clandestinas and Pobrecito Poeta que era Yo*. Perhaps the most famous Salvadorean poet, Dalton was also a journalist and revolutionary, and in constant open conflict with successive governments. Born in 1935, he was imprisoned and exiled on various occasions, always returning to the land of his birth. He was a member of the People's Revolutionary Army (ERP) in the early 1970s, along with founder members of the FMLN. After differences of opinion led to his departing the movement he was assassinated on ERP orders in May 1975 near Guazapa; his death remains a landmark in Salvadorean literary history and still remains unsolved. *Taberna y Otras Lugares* and *Poemas Clandestinas* are both collections of poetry, while *Pobrecito Poeta que era Yo* is a novella.

Mirrors of War (Zed Books). Wide-ranging collection of modern poetry and prose by Salvadorean writers, focusing on the causes and impact of the civil war.

Salarrué *Eso y Más, Cuentos de Barro* and *La Espada y Otras Narraciones*. Born Salvador Salazar Arrué in 1899, Salarrué was a writer, painter and commentator, and is one of the most widely known Salvadorean writers. His short stories and novellas focus upon the lives and realities of campesinos and non-metropolites.

HONDURAS

HISTORY, POLITICS AND SOCIETY
Tom Barry and Kent Norsworthy *Honduras – a Country Guide* (Inter-Hemispheric Education Resource Center). Concise but comprehensive study of contemporary political, economic and social affairs, with some historical background.

William V. Davidson *Historical Geography of the Bay Islands, Honduras* (South University Press, US). A study of physical and cultural geographical development of the islands. Useful for pieces of interesting background information.

TRAVEL AND IMPRESSIONS
Peter Ford *Tekkin a Waalk along the Miskito Coast* (Flamingo Press). Ford gives himself the

task of walking along the Caribbean coast from Belize to Nicaragua in the mid-1980s. A nice tale, with snippets of information on Garífuna history and contemporary development.

FICTION

Paul Theroux *The Mosquito Coast* (Penguin). Well-known tale of the collapse of a man in the steaming heat of Mosquitia. Though entertaining, Theroux only touches upon a remote corner of Honduras and the novel does little to enlighten the reader about the country as a whole. The movie, with Harrison Ford and Helen Mirren, was filmed in Belize.

Guillermo Yuscarán is the pen name of expatriate William Lewis, a long-time resident of Honduras. His novels and short stories, illustrating contemporary Honduran life can be bought (Spanish and English-language; Nuevo Sol, Tegucigalpa) in bookshops in Tegucigalpa and San Pedro Sula.

SPECIALIST GUIDES

William L. Fash *Scribes, Warriors and Kings* (Thames & Hudson). The definitive guide to the ruins of Copán with the complete historical background, superb maps and lavishly adorned with drawings and photographs.

Cindy Garoute *Diving the Bay Islands* (Aqua Quest, US). Glossy book with lots of great photos outlining the best places to dive off all the islands. Consider it essential if you're going to spend much time diving here.

MEXICO

HISTORY, POLITICS AND SOCIETY

Tom Barry (ed) *Mexico: A Country Guide* (LAB/Resource Center). A comprehensive account of contemporary Mexico: Barry and ten other contributors impart their expertise to make this the best single-volume survey on the issues facing Mexico in the 1990s.

Inga Clendinnen *Ambivalent Conquests: Maya and Spaniard in Yucatán 1517 to 1570* (CUP). A product of meticulous research which documents the methods and consequences of the Spanish Conquest of the Yucatán. The ambivalence in the title reflects doubts about the effectiveness of the Conquest in subjugating the Maya, and the book provides insights into postconquest rebellions: over three hundred years

after the Conquest the Maya rose in revolt during the Caste Wars, and almost succeeded in driving out their white overlords, while in January 1994, Maya peasants in Chiapas stunned the world and severely embarrassed the Mexican government by briefly capturing and controlling cities in the southeastern area of the state.

Bernal Díaz *The Conquest of New Spain*, translated by J.M. Cohen (Penguin/Linnet Books). This abridged version is the best available of Díaz's classic *Historia Verdadera de la Conquista de la Nueva España*. Díaz, having been on two earlier expeditions to Mexico, accompanied Cortés throughout his campaign of Conquest, and this magnificent eye-witness account still makes compulsive reading.

John Ross *Rebellion from the Roots* (Common Courage Press, US). A fascinating early account of the build-up to and first months of the 1994 Zapatista rebellion, and still the definitive book on the subject. Ross's reporting style provides a really detailed and informative background, showing the uprising was no surprise to the Mexican army. He's also the author of *Mexico in Focus* (LAB/Interlink), a short but authoritative guide to modern Mexican society, politics and culture – worth reading before a visit.

FICTION

Carlos Fuentes *The Death of Artemio Cruz* (Penguin/Farrar, Straus & Giroux; o/p), *The Old Gringo* (Picador/HarperCollins). Fuentes is by far the best-known Mexican writer outside Mexico, influenced by Mariano Azuela and Juan Rulfo, and an early exponent of magic realism. In *The Death of Artemio Cruz*, the hero, a rich and powerful man on his deathbed, looks back over his life and loves, from an idealist youth in the Revolution through disillusion to corruption and power; in many ways an indictment of modern Mexican society. His latest offering, *The Crystal Frontier* (Bloomsbury), is a collection of stories examining the way personal contacts colour Mexicans' experiences of their unequal relationship with the US.

Graham Greene *The Power and the Glory* (Penguin). Inspired by his investigative travels, this story of a doomed whisky priest on the run from the authorities makes a great yarn. It was a wonderful movie too.

D.H. Lawrence *The Plumed Serpent* (Penguin/McKay). One of Lawrence's own favourites, the novel reflects his intense dislike of the country – which followed on the brief honeymoon period of *Mornings in Mexico*. Fans of his heavy spiritualism will love it.

Malcolm Lowry *Under the Volcano* (Pan/NAL-Dutton). A classic since its publication, Lowry's account of the last day in the life of the British consul in Cuernavaca – passed in a mescal-induced haze – is totally brilliant. His *Dark as the Grave Wherein my Friend is Laid* is also based on his Mexican experiences.

Juan Rulfo *Pedro Páramo* (Serpent's Tail/Grove Atlantic). Widely regarded as the greatest Mexican novel of the twentieth century and a precursor of magic realism. The living and spirit worlds mesh when, at the dying behest of his mother, the narrator visits the deserted village haunted by the memory of his brutal patriarch father, Pedro Páramo. Dark, depressing and initially confusing but ultimately very rewarding.

Rulfo's short-story collection *The Burning Plain and Other Stories* (University of Texas), is rated by Gabriel García Marquez as the best in Latin America.

OTHER GUIDES

Richard Perry *Mexico's Fortress Monasteries* (Espadaña Press, US). One in a series of expertly written guides to the sometimes overlooked treasures of Mexico's colonial religious architecture. This volume covers more than sixty cathedrals, churches and monuments in Central Mexico, from Hidalgo to Oaxaca; *Maya Missions* deals with colonial Yucatán and *More Maya Missions* covers Chiapas; all are illustrated by the author's simple but beautiful drawings. These specialist offerings, ideal for travellers who want more information than most guidebooks can provide, are not widely available, though you can find them in tourist bookshops in the areas they cover.

LANGUAGE

There are over thirty languages spoken in the Maya World, but the *lingua franca* is Spanish, except in Belize and the Bay Islands of Honduras where English predominates. Almost everyone will speak some Spanish (even Belizean creoles), though it must be remembered it is the first language of perhaps only seventy percent of the region's people. In the Guatemalan highlands it's a second language for almost everyone and both locals and travellers struggle with grammar and verbs.

It is possible to survive speaking little or no Spanish if you confine yourself to the more touristy areas but you'll be in for a frustrating time – and if you plan to get off the beaten path some Spanish is essential. Just learning some basic conversational terms will open lots of doors, help prevent misunderstandings and enable you to bargain much more effectively. Simply learning the numbers will help immeasurably in hotels, restaurants, shops and at the marketplace. Many people choose to study Spanish in Central America; it's undoubtedly an excellent place to learn and courses are priced extremely competively.

SPANISH

The good news is that the Spanish spoken in Latin America is generally spoken much less rapidly and is much easier to decipher than in the rapid-fire, lispy intonations of Castile and Andulasia. Gone is the soft s, replaced by a crisp and clear version, and there's no need to learn the second person plural (*vosotros*) endings – they're not used in Latin America. People are generally incredibly patient, and you'll find the locals very willing to make an effort to understand you. Once

you get going you'll find that Spanish is one of the easiest languages to pick up – most of the complicated words are derived from Latin and are very similar in English and Spanish.

The rules of **pronunciation** are pretty straightforward once you get to know them, and strictly observed. An acute accent means that the stress falls on the accented syllable. Unless there's an **accent**, words ending in d, l, r and z are stressed on the last syllable, all others on the second last. All **vowels** are pure and short.

A somewhere between the "A" sound of back and that of father.

E as in get.

I as in police.

O as in hot.

U as in rule.

C is soft before E and I, hard otherwise: *cerca* is pronounced serka.

G works the same way, a guttural "H" sound (like the *ch* in loch) before E or I, a hard G elsewhere – *gigante* becomes higante.

H is always silent.

J the same sound as a guttural G: *jamón* is pronounced hamon.

LL sounds like an English Y: *tortilla* is pronounced torteeya.

N is as in English unless it has a tilde (accent) over it, when it becomes NY: *mañana* sounds like manyana.

QU is pronounced like an English K.

R is rolled, RR doubly so.

V sounds more like B, *vino* becoming beano.

X in the Maya world is pronounced SH – *Xela* is pronounced shela.

Z is the same as a soft C, so *cerveza* becomes servesa.

Below is a list of a few essential words and phrases (and see pp.35–7 for food lists), though if you're travelling for any length of time a dictionary and a **phrasebook** are worthwhile investments: the *Rough Guide to Mexican Spanish* is the best practical guide for the region. When choosing a **dictionary** it's better to buy a Latin American one – the University of Chicago version (Pocket Books) is good. When using a dictionary, remember that in Spanish CH, LL, and Ñ count as separate letters and are listed after the Cs, Ls, and Ns respectively.

A SPANISH LANGUAGE GUIDE

BASICS

Yes, No	*Sí, No*	Open, Closed	*Abierto/a, Cerrado/a*
Please, Thank you	*Por favor, Gracias*	With, Without	*Con, Sin*
Where?, When?	*¿Dónde?, ¿Cuándo?*	Good, Bad	*Buen(o)/a, Mal(o)/a*
What?, How much?	*¿Qué?, ¿Cuánto?*	Big, Small	*Gran(de), Pequeño/a*
Here, There	*Aquí, Allí*	More, Less	*Más, Menos*
This, That	*Este, Eso*	Today,Tomorrow	*Hoy, Mañana*
Now, Later	*Ahora, Más tarde*	Yesterday	*Ayer*

GREETINGS AND RESPONSES

Hello, Goodbye	*Hola, Adiós*	What (did you say)?	*¿Mande?*
Good morning	*Buenos días*	My name is . . .	*Me llamo . . .*
Good afternoon/night	*Buenas tardes/noches*	What's your name?	*¿Cómo se llama usted?*
See you later	*Hasta luego*	I am English	*Soy/inglés(a)*
Sorry	*Lo siento/discúlpeme*	American	*americano (a)*
Excuse me	*Con permiso/perdón*	Australian	*australiano(a)*
How are you?	*¿Cómo está (usted)?*	British	*británico*
I (don't) understand	*(No) Entiendo*	Canadian	*canadiense*
Could you speak more slowly?	*¿Podría hablar más lento?*	Dutch	*holandés (a)*
		Irish	*irlandés(a)*
Not at all/You're welcome	*De nada*	from New Zealand	*neozelandés(a)*
		Scottish	*escosés(a)*
Do you speak English?	*¿Habla (usted) inglés?*	South African	*sudafricano(a)*
I don't speak Spanish	*(No) Hablo Español*	Welsh	*galés(a)*

NEEDS – HOTELS AND TRANSPORT

I want	*Quiero*	Is there a hotel nearby?	*¿Hay un hotel aquí cerca?*
I'd like	*Quisiera*	How do I get to . . . ?	*¿Por dónde se va a . . . ?*
Do you know . . . ?	*¿Sabe . . . ?*	Left, right, straight on	*Izquierda, derecha, derecho*
I don't know	*No sé*		
There is (is there)?	*(¿)Hay(?)*	Where is . . . ?	*¿Dónde está . . . ?*
Give me . . . (one like that)	*Deme . . . (uno así)*	. . . the bus station	*. . . el terminal de camionetas*
Do you have . . . ?	*¿Tiene . . . ?*	. . . the nearest bank	*. . . el banco más cercano*
. . . the time	*. . . la hora*		
. . . a room	*. . . un cuarto*	. . . the post office	*. . . el correo/la oficina de correos*
. . . with two beds/ double bed	*. . . con dos camas/ cama matrimonial*	. . . the toilet	*. . . el baño/sanitario*
It's for one person (two people)	*Es para una persona (dos personas)*	Where does the bus to . . . leave from?	*¿De dónde sale la camioneta para . . . ?*
. . . for one night (one week)	*. . . para una noche (una semana)*	I'd like a (return) ticket to . . .	*Quisiera un boleto (de ida y vuelta) para . . .*
It's fine, how much is it?	*¿Está bien, cuánto es?*	What time does it leave (arrive in . . .)?	*¿A qué hora sale (llega en . . .)?*
It's too expensive	*Es demasiado caro*	What is there to eat?	*¿Qué hay para comer?*
Don't you have anything cheaper?	*¿No tiene algo más barato?*	What's that?	*¿Qué es eso?*
Can one . . . ?	*¿Se puede . . . ?*	What's this called in Spanish?	*¿Cómo se llama este*
. . . camp (near) here?	*¿ . . . acampar aquí (cerca)?*		

continued overleaf

A SPANISH LANGUAGE GUIDE contd

NUMBERS AND DAYS

0	cero	22	veintidós	first	primero/a
1	un/uno/una	30	treinta	second	segundo/a
2	dos	31	treinta y uno	third	tercero/a
3	tres	40	cuarenta	fourth	cuarto/a
4	cuatro	50	cincuenta	fifth	quinto/a
5	cinco	60	sesenta	sixth	sexto/a
6	seis	70	setenta	seventh	séptimo/a
7	siete	80	ochenta	eighth	octavo/a
8	ocho	90	noventa	ninth	noveno/a
9	nueve	100	cien	tenth	décimo/a
10	diez	101	ciento uno		
11	once	200	doscientos	Monday	lunes
12	doce	201	doscientos uno	Tuesday	martes
13	trece	500	quinientos	Wednesday	miércoles
14	catorce	1000	mil	Thursday	jueves
15	quince	2000	dos mil	Friday	viernes
16	dieciséis	1000000	un millión	Saturday	sábado
20	veinte	1999	mil novocientos	Sunday	domingo
21	veintiuno		noventa y nueve		

ENGLISH

The English spoken in Belize and the Honduran Bay Islands is delightfully melodic, unmistakeably Caribbean in rhythm and tone and sounds very similar to Jamaican patois. Initially this rich Creole dialect is difficult to understand – you will be able to pick up familiar phrases and expressions but complete comprehension is just out of reach. Creole is loosely based on English, but also uses elements of French, Spanish, African and Maya languages. Fortunately, almost everyone who speaks Creole also learns standard English at school, so they can dilute the patois if necessary. Here's a brief taster of some simple phrases.

Bad ting neda gat owna – Bad things never have owners.

Betta belly burst than good bikkle waste – It's better that the belly bursts than good victuals go to waste.

Cow no business eena haas gylop – Cows have no business in a horse race.

For more words of wisdom, there are usually copies of Creole Proverbs of Belize available in Belize City.

MAYA LANGUAGES

After years of state-backed castellanización programmes when Spanish was the only language of tuition and Maya schoolchildren were left virtual classroom spectators, a network of Maya schools has now been established, with hundreds alone in Kekchí areas of Guatemala. A strong indigenous cultural movement has now developed throughout the region, intent on preserving the dozens of different Maya languages still spoken (for a comprehensive map see p.489). Because the Maya birthrate is much higher than the ladino, there is now every chance that the main languages like Quiché, Yucateca and Mam will survive, though the fate of the more isolated tongues is far from secure.

Maya words do not easily translate into Spanish (or English) so you may see the same place spelt in different ways: K'umarkaaj can be spelt K'umarcaah or even Gumarcaj.

Nearly all Maya words are pronounced stressing the final syllable, which is often accented: Atitlán is A-tit-LAN, Calakmul is Ca-lak-MUL.

C is always hard like a K, unlike Spanish.

J is a guttural H, as in Spanish.

U like a W at the beginnning of a word and like an OO in the middle of a word – Uaxactún is pronounced washaktoon.

X sounds like SH – Xela is pronounced shela.

GLOSSARY

AGUARDIENTE Raw alcohol made from sugar cane.

AGUAS Bottled fizzy drinks such as Coca Cola, Sprite or Pepsi.

ALCALDE Mayor.

ALDEA Small settlement.

ALTIPLANO Highland area of western Guatemala.

AYUNTAMIENTO Town hall.

BALEADA Stuffed tortilla street snack (Honduras only).

BARRANCA Steep-sided ravine.

BARRIO Neighbourhood or district.

BAYMEN Early white settlers in Belize.

BIOTOPO Protected area of national ecological interest, usually with limited tourist access.

BRUJO Maya priest able to communicate with the spirit world.

CAKCHIQUEL Indigenous highland tribe occupying an area between Guatemala City and Lago de Atitlán, who, historically, collaborated with the conquistadors to defeat their rivals the Quiché and Tzutujil.

CAMIONETA Second-class bus in Guatemala. Small truck or van in other parts of Latin America.

CANTINA A hard-drinking bar where the machismo and beer run freely.

CENOTE Large natural wells found in the Yucatán that connect with the water table via a network of drains in the limestone. Also used for ceremonial purposes.

CHAC Maya rain god.

CHAPÍN Nickname for a Guatemalan.

CHICLE Sapodilla tree sap from which chewing gum is made.

CLASSIC Period during which ancient Maya civilization was at its height, usually given as 300–900 AD.

CODEX Maya manuscript made from the bark of the fig tree and written in hieroglyphs. Most were destroyed by the Spanish, but a copy of the Dresden Codex can be found in the Popol Vuh museum in Guatemala City (see p.301).

COFRADÍA Religious brotherhood dedicated to the protection of a particular saint. These groups form the basis of religious and civil hierarchy in traditional Guatemalan society and combine Catholic and pagan practices.

COLECTIVO Collective minibus transport, usually more expensive than the bus.

COLONIA City suburb.

COMEDOR Basic restaurant, usually with just one or two things on the menu. Always the cheapest place to eat.

CORTE Traditional Maya skirt, often elaborately embroidered.

COSTUMBRE Traditional customs of the highland Maya, usually of religious and cultural significance. Often refers to traditions that owe more to paganism than Catholicism.

CREOLE Of mixed Afro-Caribbean descent.

CUADRA Street block.

DON/DOÑA Sir/Madam. Mostly used to address a professional person or employer.

EFECTIVO Cash.

EVANGÉLICO Christian evangelist or fundamentalist; often missionaries. Used to denote numerous Protestant sects seeking converts.

EZLN The Zapatista Army of National Liberation, lead by Subcomandante Marcos and active in Chiapas since 1994 (see p.140).

FERIA Fair.

FINCA Plantation-style farm.

GARÍFUNA Black Carib with a unique language and strong African heritage living in village communities along the Caribbean coast between Belize and Nicaragua.

GRINGO/GRINGA Any white-skinned foreigner, but particularly North Americans. Not necessarily a term of abuse.

HENEQUEN Fibre from the agave (sisal) plant, grown in Yucatán and Guatemala to make rope.

HOSPEDAJE Small basic hotel.

HUIPIL A Maya woman's traditional blouse, usually woven or embroidered. In Guatemala and Chiapas most indigenous villages still have a unique design.

INDÍGENA Indigenous person of Maya descent.

ÍNDIO/A Racially abusive term to describe someone of Maya descent. The word *indito/a* is equally offensive.

INGUAT Guatemalan tourist board.

ITZÁ Tribal group who constructed Chichén Itzá; small pockets still live near Flores, in Petén, and continue to speak the Itzá language.

I.V.A. Sales tax.

IXIL Highland tribe grouped around the three towns of Guatemala's Ixil triangle – Nebaj, Chajul and San Juan Cotzal.

KEKCHÍ Guatemalan Maya tribal group based around Cobán, the Verapaces highlands and Lago de Izabal.

KUKULCÁN The Maya name for Quetzalcoatl, the plumed serpent. The most powerful, enigmatic and widespread of all the gods.

LADINO A vague term – at its most specific defining someone of mixed Spanish and indigenous blood, but more commonly used to describe a person of "Western" culture, or one who dresses in "Western" style, be they pure blood Maya or mixed blood.

LICUADO Blended fruit juice made with water or milk.

MAM Maya tribe occupying the far west part of Guatemala's highlands, around Huehuetenango.

MARIMBA Huge xylophone-like instrument used in traditional music. Also signifies the style of music played on this instrument.

MAYA General term for the large tribal group who inhabited Guatemala, southeastern Mexico, Belize, western Honduras and a slice of El Salvador since the earliest times, and still do.

MESTIZO Person of mixed native and Spanish blood.

METATE Flat stone for grinding maize into flour.

MIGRACIÓN Immigration office.

MILPA Maize field, usually cleared by slash and burn.

MINUGUA United Nations mission in Guatemala to oversee the peace process.

MIRADOR Lookout point.

NATURAL Another term for an indigenous person.

PALAPA Thatched palm-leaf hut.

PENSIÓN Simple hotel.

PILA Font or wash basin; either domestic or communal.

PISTO Guatemalan slang for cash.

PIPIL Indigenous tribal group which occupied much of the Guatemalan Pacific coast at the time of the Conquest. Only their art survives, around the town of Santa Lucía Cotzumalguapa.

POPOL VUH The Quiché Maya's epic story of the creation and history of their people (see p.511).

POSTCLASSIC Period between the decline of Maya civilization and the arrival of the Spanish, 900–1530 AD.

PRECLASSIC Archeological era preceding the blooming of Maya civilization, usually given as 1500 BC–300 AD.

PULLMAN Fast and comfortable bus, usually an old Greyhound.

PUNTA ROCK The music of the Garífuna.

QUICHÉ Largest of the Guatemalan Maya tribes, centred on the town of Santa Cruz del Quiché. Their ancient capital is close by at Utatlán.

SIERRA Mountain range.

TECÚN UMÁN Last king of the Quiché tribe, defeated in battle by Alvarado.

TEMPORADA Season. *La temporada de lluvia* is the rainy season.

TEOTIHUACÁN First major urban power in Mesoamerica, just north of today's Mexico City, that dominated the Maya region until the mid-Classic era.

TIENDA Shop.

TÍPICA Literally "typical". Guatemalan-made clothes woven from multicoloured textiles, usually geared towards the Western customer. Also used to describe a local dish - *comida típica*.

TRAJE Traditional Maya costume.

TZOLKIN The Maya's 260-day calendar that acts as an almanac and horoscope.

TZUTE Headcloth or scarf worn as a part of traditional Maya costume.

TZUTUJIL Indigenous tribal group occupying the land to the south of Lago de Atitlán.

XATE Decorative palm leaves harvested in the Petén for export to the US, to be used in flower arrangements.

ZÓCALO The main plaza in any Mexican town.

MAYA ARCHITECTURAL TERMS

ALTAR Elaborately carved altars, often of a cylindrical design, were grouped round the fringes of the main plaza. Used to record historical events, they probably also functioned as sacrificial stones. Some of the most fascinating are at Caracol (see p.250). See also **zoomorphs**.

BALL COURT Narrow, stone-flagged rectangular court with banked sides where the Maya ball game was played. The courts symbolized a stage between the real and supernatural worlds and for the ball players it could be a game of life and death – losers were sometimes sacrificed. The ball court at Chichén Itzá (see p.83) is 90m long but most are around 30m.

CHACHMOOL Reclining stone figure of Toltec origin that probably functioned as a sacrificial stone altar. Found from central Mexico to El Salvador but best-known examples are at Chichén Itzá.

CHENES Yucatecan Maya architectural style, related to the Puuc. The ruins of Hochob and Dzibilnocac (see p.93) are good examples, with highly stylized temple facades.

CHULTÚN Man-made cistern lined with plaster, common in the Puuc region.

CORBEL VAULT "False arch" where each stone slightly overlaps the one below. A relatively primitive technique which severely limits the width of doorways and interiors. The Labná arch (see p.76) is particularly beautiful.

GLYPH Element in Maya writing, roughly the equivalent of a letter or phrase; used to record historical events. Some glyphs are phonetic, while others represent an entire description or concept as in Chinese characters. Dominant Classic and Postclassic sites had unique emblem glyphs; some like Copán used several.

LINTEL Top block of stone or wood above a doorway or window, often carved to record important events and dates. Those from Yaxchilán (see p.138) are especially well executed.

MURAL Painted scene used to illustrate aspects of Maya life, mostly famously at Bonampak (see p.137) where there are stupendous images of processions, dances and ceremonies.

PALACE Maya palaces occupied prominant locations near the ceremonial heart of the city, usually resting on low platforms, and almost certainly housed the royal elite. There are particularly striking palaces at Palenque, Sayil, Kabáh, and Uxmal.

PUUC Architectural style of the Puuc hills 80km southeast of Mexico City. Typified by classically proportioned buildings, rich with columns and arches and decorated with mosaic friezes of geometric patterns (see p.72).

PUTÚN Style dominant at Ceibal in central Petén (see p.419), exhibiting strong Mexican characteristics.

RÍO BEC Style typified by long buildings with matching towers and narrow roof combs; found at the ruins of Becán, Chicanná and Río Bec itself (see p.94).

ROOF-COMB Decorative top crest on stone temples, possibly intended to enhance verticality. Originally painted in arresting colours and often framed by giant stucco figures.

SACBÉ Paved Maya road or raised causeway near the centre of Maya cities. Probably designed for ceremonial processions and to save rulers from sloshing through the lowland marshes. *Sacbés* were also trade routes and there are hundreds of kilometres still evident in the Yucatán and northern Petén today.

STELA Free-standing, often exquisitely carved stone monument. Decorating major Maya sites, stelae fulfilled a sacred and political role commemorating historical events. Among the largest and most impressive are the ones at Quiriguá (see p.378) and Copán (see p.438).

TEMPLE Monumental stone structure of pivotal religious significance built in the ceremonial heart of a city, usually with a pyramid-shaped base and topped with a narrow room or two used for secretive ceremonies and bloody sacrifices. Those at Tikal (see p.409) and El Mirador (see p.417) reach over 60m, while Calakmul (see p.95) is the bulkiest.

TOLTEC Style of the central Mexican tribal group who invaded parts of the Maya region from the Yucatán to El Salvador. Many of the major buildings at Chichén Itzá are typically Toltec.

ZOOMORPH Spectacular stone altar intricately carved with animal images and glyphs. Unique to Quiriguá (see p.378), though similar altars exist in Izapa.

INDEX

A

Abaj Takalik (G) 368
Acajutla (ES) 466
accommodation 31
Achi Maya 389, 391
Acul (G) 338
Agua Azul (M) 143
Agua Blanca (M) 387
Agua Clara (M) 142
Agua, Volcán de (G) 318
Aguacatán (G) 362
Aguateca (G) 419
Ahuachapán (ES) 468
air passes 29
airlines
  in Australia and New Zealand 12
  in Ireland 11
  in North America 3
  in the UK 9
Aké (M) 80
Akumal (M) 115
Alta Verapaz (G) 392–401
Altar de los Sacrificios (G) 420
Altun Ha (B) 203
Amatitlán, Lago de (G) 306
Ambergris Caye (B) 216–224
Anguiatú (ES) 477
ANTIGUA (G) 309–318
  accommodation 311
  arrival 310
  city, the 312
  eating 315
  history 310
  information 310
  semana santa 312
  Spanish schools 317
  transport 320
Apaneca (ES) 467
Arriaga (M) 164
Atitlán, Lago de (G) 339–350
Augustine (B) 249

B

Baboon Sanctuary (B) 202
Bacalar Chico National Park (B) 222
Baja Verapaz (G) 390
Balamku (M) 95
Balancanaché (M) 86
Barbareta (H) 460

Barillas (G) 364
Barton Creek Cave (B) 244
Bay Islands (H) 450–463
Becal (M) 88
Becán (M) 94
Belize Botanical Gardens 245
BELIZE CITY 190–201
  accommodation 194
  arrival 194
  city, the 196
  eating 198
  history 191
  information194
  nightlife 199
  North Side 196
  South Side 197
  transport 201
Belize Zoo 233
Belmopan (B) 235–237
Benemérito (M) 139
Benque Viejo del Carmen (B) 252
Bermudian Landing (B) 203
Bethel (G) 421
bicycle, travelling by 31
Bilbao (G) 370
Blue Creek (B) 279
Blue Hole National Park (B) 257
Bluefield Range (B) 229
boat, travelling by 30
Boca Lacantún (M) 139
Bocas de Dzilam (M) 70
Bochil (M) 156
Bolonchén de Rejon (M) 88
Bonacca (H) 461
Bonampak (M) 136
books 510–517
Bosque Montecristo (ES) 476
Branch Mouth (B) 243
Buenos Aires (H) 445
bus, travelling by 28

C

Cacahoatán (M) 167
Cahabón (G) 398
Cahal Pech (B) 243
Cakchiquel Maya 325, 328, 521
Calabash Caye (B) 229
Calakmul (M) 95
Calderitas (M) 124
Campeche (M) 88–91
camping 33
CANCÚN (M) 99–105
  accommodation 101

arrival 99
beaches 101
eating 102
entertainment 103
information 99
town, the 101
transport 99
Candelaria (M) 96
Candelaria caves (G) 400
Cañon del Sumidero (M) 155
car rental 30
Cara Sucia (ES) 465
Caracol (B) 250
Caye Bokel (B) 230
Caye Caulker (B) 225–228
Caye Chapel (B) 229
Cayo (B) 239–242
Cayos Cochinos (H) 462
Ceibal (G) 419
Celestún (M) 71
Cenote Azul (M) 122
Cenote Dzitnup (M) 86
Cerro Cahuí, Biotopo de (G) 408
Cerro Verde, Parque Nacional (ES) 473
Cerros (B) 215
Chaa Creek (B) 244
Chabihau (M) 70
Chachauate (H) 462
Chacmultún (M) 76
Chajul (G) 339
Chalchuapa (ES) 470
Champerico (G) 369
Chan Chich (B) 211
Chau Hiix (B) 206
Chemem (M) 70
Chetumal (M) 122–124
Chiapa de Corzo (M) 155
Chicanná (M) 95
Chiché (G) 335
Chichén Itzá (M) 78–84
Chichicastenango (G) 329–332
Chimaltenango (G) 328
Chinkultic (M) 162
Chinqué (G) 335
Chiquibul caves (B) 251
Chiquilá (M) 87
Chiquimula (G) 386
Chisec (G) 400
Chocón Machacas, Biotopo de (G) 383
Chontal Maya 169, 174

chronology of the Maya
481–483
Chuburná (M) 70
Chuj Maya 364
Chunyaxche (M) 120
Ciudad Cuauhtémoc (M) 163
Ciudad del Carmen (M) 92
Ciudad Hidalgo (M) 168
Ciudad Vieja (G) 319
Coatepeque (G) 367
Coatepeque, Lago de (ES) 474
Cobá (M) 118
Cobán (G) 393–396
Cocales (G) 369
Cockscomb Basin Wildlife
  Sanctuary (B) 265
Cocom (M) 78
Cofradía (H) 445
Comalcalco (M) 174
Comitán (M) 160
conservation 505–509
Copán (H) 434–439
Copán Ruinas town (H) 434–436
Corozal (B) 213
costs 23
Coxen Hole (H) 456
Cozumel (M) 112–115
crime 44
Cristo Rey (B) 248
Crooked Tree Wildlife
  Sanctuary (B) 205
Cubulco (G) 391
Cuchumatanes mountains (G)
  362–366
Cuello (B) 208, 481
cycling 31

D
dance 43
Dangriga (B) 258–261
dengue fever 19
Dos Pilas (G) 420
Douglas Silva (B) 249
drink 38
drugs 45, 449, 487
Dzibilchaltún (M) 69
Dzibilnocac (M) 93
Dzilam de Bravo (M) 70

E
eating and drinking 33–38
ecotourism 505–509
Edzná (M) 92

El Cusuco, Parque Nacional (H)
  445
El Baúl (G) 370
El Bosque Impossible (ES) 465
El Estor (G) 399
El Florido border (H & G) 433
El Mirador (G) 417
El Naranjo (G) 421
El Pilar (B) 246
El Puente (H) 439
El Rancho junction (G) 375
El Remate (G) 408
El Rubí (H) 439
El Tigre (M) 96
El Tintal (G) 418
El Trifinio reserve (ES) 477
El Zotz (G) 416
embassies 16
Emiliano Zapata (M) 178
entry requirements 14
Escuintla (G) 371
Esquipulas (G) 387
exchange rates 23

F
Felipe Carillo Puerto (M) 121
fiestas
  in Guatemala 289
  in southern Mexico 55
Finca Ixobel (G) 403
Five Blues Lake National Park
  (B) 257
flights
  from Australia and New Zealand
    12
  from North America 4
  from the UK and Ireland 8
  internal 29
Flor de Café (M) 163
Floral Park (B) 238
Flores (G) 403–407
food and drink 33–38
food glossary 35
Francisco Escárcega (M) 93
Francisco J. Mujica (M) 176
Fray Bartolomé de las Casas
  (G) 400
French Harbour (H) 459
Frontera Corozal (M) 137

G
Gales Point (B) 256
Gallon Jug (B) 211
glossary 521–523

Glover's Reef (B) 264
Golfete (G) 383
Guanacaste National Park (B)
  235
Guanaja (H) 460–462
GUATEMALA CITY 292–307
  accommodation 297
  addresses 295
  arrival 294
  eating 302
  history 293
  information 294
  Kaminaljuyú 302
  New City 300
  Old City 298
  transport 296, 306

H
Half Moon Caye Natural
  Monument (B) 230
Hattieville (B) 233
health 19
Hecelchakan (M) 88
history
  of Belize 185
  of El Salvador 430
  of the Garífuna 260
  of Guatemala 285
  of Honduras 426
  of Mexico 54
Hochob (M) 93
Hol Chan Marine Reserve (B)
  222
Hopelchén (M) 93
Hopkins (B) 263
Hormiguero (M) 95
Huehuetenango (G) 358–360
Huimanguillo (M) 175
Huistán (M) 154
Huixtla (M) 165
Hummingbird Highway (B)
  256–258

I
Indian Church (B) 209
Indian Creek (B) 272
insurance 17
internet 40
Ipala (G) 387
Ipala, Volcán de (G) 387
Isla Cozumel (M) 112–115
Isla Holbox (M) 87
Isla Mujeres (M) 105–107
Itzá Maya 404, 408, 522

Ixcán (G) 401
Ixil Maya 336, 522
Ixil Triangle (G) 336–339
Iximché (G) 328
Izabal, Lago de (G) 385
Izalco, Volcán de (ES) 474
Izamal (M) 78
Izapa (M) 167

J
Jacaltenango (G) 366
Jaguar Reserve (B) 266
Joya de Cerén (ES) 475
Joyabaj (G) 335
Juayúa (ES) 467
Junchavín (M) 161
jungle lodges 33

K
K'umarkaaj (G) 333
Kabáh (M)75
Kekchí Maya 277, 389, 522
Kinich Kakmo (M) 78
Kohunlich (M) 125

L
La Avellena (G) 372
La Ceiba (H) 445–448
La Cumbre de Santa Elena (G) 390
La Democracia (G) 370
La Entrada (H) 439
La Hachadura border (G & ES) 464
La Mesilla border (G) 366
La Milpa (B) 211
La Palma (M) 179
La Venta (M) 175
Lacandón Maya 136, 496
Lacanjá (M) 137
Lago Coatepeque (ES) 474
Lago de Amatitlán (G) 306
Lago de Atitlán (G) 339–350
Lago de Izabal (G) 385
Lago de Petexbatún (G) 419
Lago de Yaxhá (G) 422
Lagos de Montebello (M) 162
Laguna Bacalar (M) 122
Laguna Lachuá (G) 400
Laguna Milagros (M) 124
Laguna Miramar (M) 154
Laguna Verde (ES) 468
Lamanai (B) 209

landscape 498
language 518–520
Lanquín (G) 397
Las Coloradas (M) 87
Las Maravillas de Tenejapa (M) 163
Las Sepultras (H) 438
Lighthouse Reef (B) 230
Lívingston (G) 381–383
Loltún (M) 76
Los Cóbanos (ES) 467
Los Remedios (ES) 467
Los Sapos (H) 439
Lubaantun (B) 280
Lucky Strike (B) 204

M
Macal River (B) 244–246
Mahahual (M) 125
mail 39
malaria 19
Malpasito (M) 176
Mam Maya 325, 361, 522
Mani (M) 78
maps 27
Mariscos (G) 385
market days, Western Highlands (G) 326
Maskall (B) 204
Maximón (G) 320, 347, 356
Maya
   architectural terms 523
   astronomy 486
   calendar 486
   chronology 481–483
   languages 489, 520
   religious ritual 487
   society 484
   today 488
Maya Beach (B) 267
Maya Centre village (B) 266
Mayapán (M) 77
Mazatenango (G) 369
medical resources for travellers 21
Mennonites in Belize 207
MÉRIDA (M) 60–68
   accommodation 62
   arrival 60
   city, the 63
   eating 66
   entertainment 67
   information 61

markets 65
   transport 62,68
Metapán (ES) 476
Misol Há (M) 142
Mixco Viejo (G) 308
Momostenango (G) 357
money 23
Monkey Bay Wildlife Sanctuary (B) 234
Monkey River (B) 271
Monte Alto (G) 370
Montebello, Lagos de (M) 162
Monterrico (G) 372
Montes Azules (M) 139
Mopán Maya 277
Mopan River (B) 246
Motagua Valley (G) 375–381
motorbike, travelling by 30
Motúl (G) 408
Mountain Pine Ridge Reserve (B) 247–250
Moxviquil (M) 154
music 43

N
Nahuizalco (ES) 467
Nakbé (G) 418, 481
Nakúm (G) 423
Nebaj (G) 337
newspapers 40
Nohmul (B) 208
Nueva Armenia (H) 462

O
Oak Ridge (H) 460
Ocosingo (M) 143
Olmec civilization 54, 169, 172, 173, 481, 490
opening hours 42
Orange Walk (B) 206–208
Over the Top (B) 257
Oxkintok (M) 88
Oxkutzcab (M) 76
Oxolotán (M) 178

P
Pacaya, Volcán de (G) 307
Pacbitún (B) 248
Pajal junction (G) 397
Palenque (M) 130–135
Panajachel (G) 341–345
Panzós (G) 399
Pech (H) 451

Petén (G) 401–424
Petexbatún, Lago de (G) 419
phones 40
Pico Bonito, Parque Nacional (H)
Piedras Negras (G) 421
Pipil sites (G) 367, 370
Pisté (M) 81
Placencia (B) 268
Placencia peninsula (B)
   267–272
Planchon de Figuras (M) 139
Playa Barra de Santiago (ES)
   466
Playa de Metalío (ES) 466
Playa de Perú (H) 448
Playa del Carmen (M) 109–112
Playa Grande (G) 400
Pokomchí Maya 389
police 45
Polochic valley (G) 398–400
Pomaná (M) 179
Poptún (G) 403
Port Royal (H) 460
postal services 39
Progreso (M) 70
public holidays 42
Puerto Arista (M) 164
Puerto Barrios (G) 379–381
Puerto San José (G) 371
Puerto Morelos (M) 107–109
Punta Allen (M) 121
Punta Bete (M) 109
Punta Gorda (B) 273–276
Punta Gorda (H) 460
Pusilha (B) 279

Q

Quetzal, Biotopo de (G) 391
QUETZALTENANGO (G)
   350–355
   accommodation 353
   arrival 352
   city, the 353
   eating and drinking 354
   history 351
   information 352
Quiché Maya 325, 331–334,
   389, 511, 522
Quiriguá (G) 378

R

Rabinal (G) 390
radio 40

Rainforest Medicine Trail (B)
   244
Raxrujá (G) 400
Reforma Agraria (M) 139
Refugio de Vida Silvestre
   Cuero y Salado (H) 449
Reserva de Fauna U'Luum Chac
   Yuc (M) 95
resource centres 26
Retalhuleu (G) 368
Río Azul (G) 416
Río Bec (M) 95
Río Bec sites (M) 94–96
**Rio Bravo Conservation
   Area** (B) 210–212
Río Candelaria (M) 96
Río Dulce (G) 383
Río Hondo junction (G) 375
Río Lagartos (M) 86
Río Motagua (G) 375–381
Rio On (B) 249
Roatán (H) 456–460
Ruidosa junction (G) 379
Ruta Puuc (M) 71–76

S

Sabancuy (M) 91
Sacapulas (G) 335
safety 44, 327
Salamá (G) 390
Salcoatitán (ES) 467
Sambo Creek (H) 449
San Andrés (ES) 474
San Andrés (G) 407
San Andrés Itzapa (G) 319
San Andrés Xecul (G) 357
San Antonio, Cayo (B) 248
San Antonio, Toledo (B) 278
San Antonio Aguas Calientes
   (G) 319
San Antonio Palopó (G) 345
**SAN CRISTÓBAL DE LAS
   CASAS** (M) 144–151
   accommodation 146
   arrival 145
   city, the 147
   eating and drinking
   information 145
   markets 148
   transport 151
San Felipe (G) 384
San Felipe (M) 87
San Felipe Natural Park (M) 70
San Francisco el Alto (G) 357

San Ignacio (B) 239–242
San Javiér (M) 136
San José (G) 408
San José Succotz (B) 251
San Juan Atitán (G) 365
San Juan Chamelco (G) 396
San Juan Chamula (M) 153
San Juan Cotzal (G) 338
San Juan Ixcoy (G) 363
San Juan la Laguna (G) 349
San Juan Sacatepéquez (G)
   308
San Lucas Tolimán (G) 346
San Marcos la Laguna (G) 349
San Martín (G) 366
San Martín Jilotepeque (G) 328
San Mateo Ixtatán (G) 364
San Pablo (B) 208
SAN PEDRO (B) 216–224
   accommodation 219
   arrival 217
   diving 221
   eating and drinking 223
   information 217
   nightlife 224
   snorkelling 221
   transport 217
San Pedro Carchá (G) 396
San Pedro Chenalhó (M) 154
San Pedro Columbia (B) 280
San Pedro la Laguna (G) 348
San Pedro Sacatepéquez (G)
   308
San Pedro Sula (H) 440–444
San Vicente Pacaya (G) 307
Sandy Bay (H) 457
Santa Ana (ES) 470–473
Santa Ana, Volcán de (ES) 474
Santa Catarina (G) 319
Santa Catarina Palopó (G) 345
Santa Cruz del Quiché (G) 332
Santa Cruz la Laguna (G) 350
Santa Elena (B) 239
Santa Elena (G) 403–407
Santa Lucía Cotzumalguapa (G)
   369
Santa María de Jesús (G) 318
Santa María, Volcán de (G) 356
Santa Rita (B) 214
Santiago Atitlán (G) 346–348
Santiago Sacatepéquez (G) 327
Sapodilla Cayes Marine
   Reserve (B) 277
Sapodilla Lagoon (B) 267

Sarteneja (B) 212
Sayaxché (G) 418
Sayil (M) 75
Sebol (G) 400
Seine Bight (B) 267
Semuc Champey (G) 397
Senahú (G) 398
shamanism 490
Shipstern Nature Reserve (B) 212
Si'an Ka'an Biosphere Reserve (M) 119
Sierra Huimanguillo (M) 175
Simojovel (M) 156
Sisal (M) 70
Sittee River (B) 264
Sololá (G) 341
Soloma (G) 363
Sonsonate (ES) 466
South Water Caye (B) 262
Southern Highway (B) 263
Spanish language guide 518–520
Spanish schools 46
spirituality 490
St George's Caye (B) 229
St Herman's Cave (B) 256
Stann Creek valley (B) 258
study 46
Sumidero Canyon (M) 155

T

Tactic (G) 392
Talismán border (M) 168
Tamahú (G) 398
Tapachula (M) 165–167
Tapijulapa (M) 177
Tapir Nature Reserve (B) 237
taxis 30
Taxisco (G) 372
Tazumal (ES) 470
Teakettle (B) 239
Teapa (M) 177
Tecpán (G) 328
Tecún Umán border (G) 367
Telchac (M) 70
telephones 40
television 41

Tenam Puente (M) 161
Tenejapa (M) 154
Tenosique (M) 178
Ticul (M) 77
Tikal (G) 409–415
Tim Li Punit (B) 272
Tizimín (M) 86
Tobacco Caye (B) 262
Todos Santos (G) 364
Toledo Ecotourism Association (B) 276
Tonalá (M) 164
Toniná (M) 143
Totonicapán (G) 358
tour operators
   in Australia and
      New Zealand 13
   in Canada 7
   in Ireland 11
   in the UK 10
   in the US 6
travel agents
   in Australia and
      New Zealand 13
   in Ireland 11
   in the UK 9
   in the US and Canada 5
travel insurance 17
travel warnings 45
travelling through Mexico 5
Tucurú (G) 398
Tulum (M) 116–118
Turneffe Islands (B) 229
Tuxtla Gutiérrez
   M) 156–160
Tzeltal Maya 152, 154
Tziscao (M) 163
Tzotzil Maya 152, 156
Tzununá (G) 350
Tzutujil Maya 522

U

Uaxactún (G) 415
Unión Juárez (M) 167
Uspantán (G) 336
Utatlán (G) 333
Utila (H) 452–456
Utila Cays (H) 454
Uxbenka (B) 279
Uxmal (M) 71–75

V

Valladolid (M) 84
vegetarian food 37
Villa Luz, Parque Natural (M) 177
Villahermosa (M) 169–174
visas 14
Volcán de Agua (G) 318
Volcán de Ipala (G) 387
Volcán de Pacaya (G) 307
Volcán de Santa María (G) 356
Volcán Izalco (ES) 474
Volcán Santa Ana (ES) 474
voluntary work 46

W

water safety 20
web sites 25
West Bay (H) 459
West End (H) 457
wildlife 498–504
wiring money 23
work and study 46

X

Xcacel (M) 115
Xcalak (M) 124
Xcaret (M) 115
Xel-ha (M) 116
Xela (G) 350–355
Xlapak (M) 76
Xpu-ha (M) 115
Xpujil (M) 94
Xtacumbilxunan (M) 88
Xunantunich (B) 251

Y

Yaxchilán (M) 138
Yaxhá (G) 422
Yucalpetén (M) 70
Yucatec Maya 496

Z

Zacualpa (G) 335
Zaculeu (G) 361
Zapatista rebellion 140–142, 493–495, 516
Zinacantán (M) 153
Zoque, the (M) 176
Zunil (G) 356

Small

but perfectly informed

Every bit as stylish and irreverent as their full-sized counterparts, Mini Guides are everything you'd expect from a Rough Guide, but smaller – perfect for a pocket, briefcase or overnight bag.

Available 1998
Antigua, Barbados, Boston, Dublin, Edinburgh, Lisbon, Madrid, Seattle

Coming soon
Bangkok, Brussels, Florence, Honolulu, Las Vegas, Maui, Melbourne, New Orleans, Oahu, St Lucia, Sydney, Tokyo, Toronto

Everything you need to know about everything you want to do

¿Qué pasa?

WHAT'S HAPPENING?
A ROUGH GUIDES SERIES –
ROUGH GUIDES PHRASEBOOKS

Rough Guide Phrasebooks represent a complete shakeup of the phrasebook format. Handy and pocket sized, they work like a dictionary to get you straight to the point. With clear guidelines on pronunciation, dialogues for typical situations, and tips on cultural issues, they'll have you speaking the language quicker than any other phrasebook.

Czech, French, German, Greek, Hindi & Urdu, Hungarian, Indonesian, Italian, Japanese, Mandarin Chinese, Mexican Spanish, Polish, Portuguese, Russian, Spanish, Thai, Turkish, Vietnamese

Further titles coming soon...

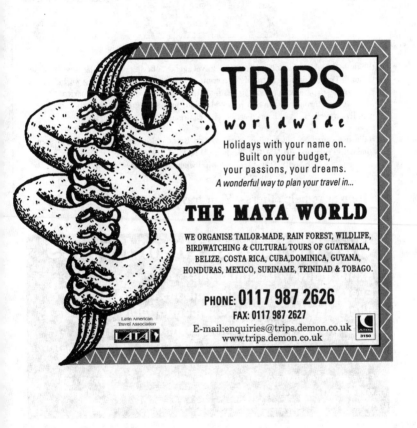

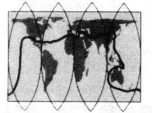

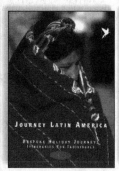